T0180303

Lecture Notes in Computer Science 12267

Founding Editors

Gerhard Goos
Karlsruhe Institute of Technology, Karlsruhe, Germany
Juris Hartmanis
Cornell University, Ithaca, NY, USA

Editorial Board Members

Elisa Bertino
Purdue University, West Lafayette, IN, USA
Wen Gao
Peking University, Beijing, China
Bernhard Steffen◉
TU Dortmund University, Dortmund, Germany
Gerhard Woeginger◉
RWTH Aachen, Aachen, Germany
Moti Yung
Columbia University, New York, NY, USA

More information about this series at http://www.springer.com/series/7412

Anne L. Martel · Purang Abolmaesumi ·
Danail Stoyanov · Diana Mateus ·
Maria A. Zuluaga · S. Kevin Zhou ·
Daniel Racoceanu · Leo Joskowicz (Eds.)

Medical Image Computing and Computer Assisted Intervention – MICCAI 2020

23rd International Conference
Lima, Peru, October 4–8, 2020
Proceedings, Part VII

 Springer

Editors
Anne L. Martel (iD)
University of Toronto
Toronto, ON, Canada

Purang Abolmaesumi (iD)
The University of British Columbia
Vancouver, BC, Canada

Danail Stoyanov (iD)
University College London
London, UK

Diana Mateus (iD)
École Centrale de Nantes
Nantes, France

Maria A. Zuluaga (iD)
EURECOM
Biot, France

S. Kevin Zhou (iD)
Chinese Academy of Sciences
Beijing, China

Daniel Racoceanu (iD)
Sorbonne University
Paris, France

Leo Joskowicz (iD)
The Hebrew University of Jerusalem
Jerusalem, Israel

ISSN 0302-9743   ISSN 1611-3349 (electronic)
Lecture Notes in Computer Science
ISBN 978-3-030-59727-6   ISBN 978-3-030-59728-3 (eBook)
https://doi.org/10.1007/978-3-030-59728-3

LNCS Sublibrary: SL6 – Image Processing, Computer Vision, Pattern Recognition, and Graphics

© Springer Nature Switzerland AG 2020
This work is subject to copyright. All rights are reserved by the Publisher, whether the whole or part of the material is concerned, specifically the rights of translation, reprinting, reuse of illustrations, recitation, broadcasting, reproduction on microfilms or in any other physical way, and transmission or information storage and retrieval, electronic adaptation, computer software, or by similar or dissimilar methodology now known or hereafter developed.
The use of general descriptive names, registered names, trademarks, service marks, etc. in this publication does not imply, even in the absence of a specific statement, that such names are exempt from the relevant protective laws and regulations and therefore free for general use.
The publisher, the authors and the editors are safe to assume that the advice and information in this book are believed to be true and accurate at the date of publication. Neither the publisher nor the authors or the editors give a warranty, expressed or implied, with respect to the material contained herein or for any errors or omissions that may have been made. The publisher remains neutral with regard to jurisdictional claims in published maps and institutional affiliations.

This Springer imprint is published by the registered company Springer Nature Switzerland AG
The registered company address is: Gewerbestrasse 11, 6330 Cham, Switzerland

Preface

The 23rd International Conference on Medical Image Computing and Computer-Assisted Intervention (MICCAI 2020) was held this year under the most unusual circumstances, due to the COVID-19 pandemic disrupting our lives in ways that were unimaginable at the start of the new decade. MICCAI 2020 was scheduled to be held in Lima, Peru, and would have been the first MICCAI meeting in Latin America. However, with the pandemic, the conference and its program had to be redesigned to deal with realities of the "new normal", where virtual presence rather than physical interactions among attendees, was necessary to comply with global transmission control measures. The conference was held through a virtual conference management platform, consisting of the main scientific program in addition to featuring 25 workshops, 8 tutorials, and 24 challenges during October 4–8, 2020. In order to keep a part of the original spirit of MICCAI 2020, SIPAIM 2020 was held as an adjacent LatAm conference dedicated to medical information management and imaging, held during October 3–4, 2020.

The proceedings of MICCAI 2020 showcase papers contributed by the authors to the main conference, which are organized in seven volumes of *Lecture Notes in Computer Science* (LNCS) books. These papers were selected after a thorough double-blind peer-review process. We followed the example set by past MICCAI meetings, using Microsoft's Conference Managing Toolkit (CMT) for paper submission and peer reviews, with support from the Toronto Paper Matching System (TPMS) to partially automate paper assignment to area chairs and reviewers.

The conference submission deadline had to be extended by two weeks to account for the disruption COVID-19 caused on the worldwide scientific community. From 2,953 original intentions to submit, 1,876 full submissions were received, which were reduced to 1,809 submissions following an initial quality check by the program chairs. Of those, 61% were self-declared by authors as Medical Image Computing (MIC), 6% as Computer Assisted Intervention (CAI), and 32% as both MIC and CAI. Following a broad call to the community for self-nomination of volunteers and a thorough review by the program chairs, considering criteria such as balance across research areas, geographical distribution, and gender, the MICCAI 2020 Program Committee comprised 82 area chairs, with 46% from North America, 28% from Europe, 19% from Asia/Pacific/Middle East, 4% from Latin America, and 1% from Australia. We invested significant effort in recruiting more women to the Program Committee, following the conference's emphasis on equity, inclusion, and diversity. This resulted in 26% female area chairs. Each area chair was assigned about 23 manuscripts, with suggested potential reviewers using TPMS scoring and self-declared research areas, while domain conflicts were automatically considered by CMT. Following a final revision and prioritization of reviewers by area chairs in terms of their expertise related to each paper, over 1,426 invited reviewers were asked to bid for the papers for which they had been suggested. Final reviewer allocations via CMT took account of reviewer bidding, prioritization of area chairs, and TPMS scores, leading to allocating about 4 papers per reviewer. Following an initial double-blind review phase by reviewers, area chairs provided a meta-review summarizing key points of reviews and a recommendation for each paper. The program chairs then evaluated the reviews and their scores, along with the recommendation from the area chairs, to directly accept 241 papers (13%) and reject 828 papers (46%); the remainder of the papers were sent for rebuttal by the authors. During the rebuttal phase, two additional area chairs were assigned to each paper using the CMT and TPMS scores while accounting for domain conflicts. The three area chairs then independently scored each paper to accept or reject, based on the reviews, rebuttal, and manuscript, resulting in clear paper decisions using majority voting. This process resulted in the acceptance of a further 301 papers for an overall acceptance rate of 30%. A virtual Program Committee meeting was held on July 10, 2020, to confirm the final results and collect feedback of the peer-review process.

For the MICCAI 2020 proceedings, 542 accepted papers have been organized into seven volumes as follows:

- Part I, LNCS Volume 12261: Machine Learning Methodologies
- Part II, LNCS Volume 12262: Image Reconstruction and Machine Learning
- Part III, LNCS Volume 12263: Computer Aided Intervention, Ultrasound and Image Registration
- Part IV, LNCS Volume 12264: Segmentation and Shape Analysis
- Part V, LNCS Volume 12265: Biological, Optical and Microscopic Image Analysis
- Part VI, LNCS Volume 12266: Clinical Applications
- Part VII, LNCS Volume 12267: Neurological Imaging and PET

For the main conference, the traditional emphasis on poster presentations was maintained; each author uploaded a brief pre-recorded presentation and a graphical abstract onto a web platform and was allocated a personal virtual live session in which they talked directly to the attendees. It was also possible to post questions online allowing asynchronous conversations – essential to overcome the challenges of a global conference spanning many time zones. The traditional oral sessions, which typically included a small proportion of the papers, were replaced with 90 "mini" sessions where all of the authors were clustered into groups of 5 to 7 related papers; a live virtual session allowed the authors and attendees to discuss the papers in a panel format.

We would like to sincerely thank everyone who contributed to the success of MICCAI 2020 and the quality of its proceedings under the most unusual circumstances of a global pandemic. First and foremost, we thank all authors for submitting and presenting their high-quality work that made MICCAI 2020 a greatly enjoyable and successful scientific meeting. We are also especially grateful to all members of the Program Committee and reviewers for their dedicated effort and insightful feedback throughout the entire paper selection process. We would like to particularly thank the MICCAI society for support, insightful comments, and continuous engagement with organizing the conference. Special thanks go to Kitty Wong, who oversaw the entire process of paper submission, reviews, and preparation of conference proceedings. Without her, we would have not functioned effectively. Given the "new normal", none of the workshops, tutorials, and challenges would have been feasible without the true leadership of the satellite events organizing team led by Mauricio Reyes: Erik Meijering (workshops), Carlos Alberola-López (tutorials), and Lena Maier-Hein (challenges). Behind the scenes, MICCAI secretarial personnel, Janette Wallace and Johanne Langford, kept a close eye on logistics and budgets, while Mehmet Eldegez and his team at Dekon Congress and Tourism led the professional conference organization, working tightly with the virtual platform team. We also thank our sponsors for financial support and engagement with conference attendees through the virtual platform. Special thanks goes to Veronika Cheplygina for continuous engagement with various social media platforms before and throughout the conference to publicize the conference. We would also like to express our gratitude to Shelley Wallace for helping us in Marketing MICCAI 2020, especially during the last phase of the virtual conference organization.

The selection process for Young Investigator Awards was managed by a team of senior MICCAI investigators, led by Julia Schnabel. In addition, MICCAI 2020 offered free registration to the top 50 ranked papers at the conference whose primary authors were students. Priority was given to low-income regions and Latin American students. Further support was provided by the National Institutes of Health (support granted for MICCAI 2020) and the National Science Foundation (support granted to MICCAI 2019 and continued for MICCAI 2020) which sponsored another 52 awards for USA-based students to attend the conference. We would like to thank Marius Linguraru and Antonion Porras, for their leadership in regards to the NIH sponsorship for 2020, and Dinggang Shen and Tianming Liu, MICCAI 2019 general chairs, for keeping an active bridge and engagement with MICCAI 2020.

Marius Linguraru and Antonion Porras were also leading the young investigators early career development program, including a very active mentorship which we do hope, will significantly catalyze young and briliant careers of future leaders of our scientific community. In link with SIPAIM (thanks to Jorge Brieva, Marius Linguraru, and Natasha Lepore for their support), we also initiated a Startup Village initiative, which, we hope, will be able to bring in promising private initiatives in the areas of MICCAI. As a part of SIPAIM 2020, we note also the presence of a workshop for Peruvian clinicians. We would like to thank Benjaming Castañeda and Renato Gandolfi for this initiative.

MICCAI 2020 invested significant efforts to tightly engage the industry stakeholders in our field throughout its planning and organization. These efforts were led by Parvin Mousavi, and ensured that all sponsoring industry partners could connect with the conference attendees through the conference's virtual platform before and during the meeting. We would like to thank the sponsorship team and the contributions of Gustavo Carneiro, Benjamín Castañeda, Ignacio Larrabide, Marius Linguraru, Yanwu Xu, and Kevin Zhou.

We look forward to seeing you at MICCAI 2021.

October 2020

Anne L. Martel
Purang Abolmaesumi
Danail Stoyanov
Diana Mateus
Maria A. Zuluaga
S. Kevin Zhou
Daniel Racoceanu
Leo Joskowicz

Organization

General Chairs

Daniel Racoceanu   Sorbonne Université, Brain Institute, France
Leo Joskowicz   The Hebrew University of Jerusalem, Israel

Program Committee Chairs

Anne L. Martel   University of Toronto, Canada
Purang Abolmaesumi   The University of British Columbia, Canada
Danail Stoyanov   University College London, UK
Diana Mateus   Ecole Centrale de Nantes, LS2N, France
Maria A. Zuluaga   Eurecom, France
S. Kevin Zhou   Chinese Academy of Sciences, China

Keynote Speaker Chair

Rene Vidal   The John Hopkins University, USA

Satellite Events Chair

Mauricio Reyes   University of Bern, Switzerland

Workshop Team

Erik Meijering (Chair)   The University of New South Wales, Australia
Li Cheng   University of Alberta, Canada
Pamela Guevara   University of Concepción, Chile
Bennett Landman   Vanderbilt University, USA
Tammy Riklin Raviv   Ben-Gurion University of the Negev, Israel
Virginie Uhlmann   EMBL, European Bioinformatics Institute, UK

Tutorial Team

Carlos Alberola-López (Chair)   Universidad de Valladolid, Spain

Clarisa Sánchez   Radboud University Medical Center, The Netherlands
Demian Wassermann   Inria Saclay Île-de-France, France

Challenges Team

Lena Maier-Hein (Chair)	German Cancer Research Center, Germany
Annette Kopp-Schneider	German Cancer Research Center, Germany
Michal Kozubek	Masaryk University, Czech Republic
Annika Reinke	German Cancer Research Center, Germany

Sponsorship Team

Parvin Mousavi (Chair)	Queen's University, Canada
Marius Linguraru	Children's National Institute, USA
Gustavo Carneiro	The University of Adelaide, Australia
Yanwu Xu	Baidu Inc., China
Ignacio Larrabide	National Scientific and Technical Research Council, Argentina
S. Kevin Zhou	Chinese Academy of Sciences, China
Benjamín Castañeda	Pontifical Catholic University of Peru, Peru

Local and Regional Chairs

Benjamín Castañeda	Pontifical Catholic University of Peru, Peru
Natasha Lepore	University of Southern California, USA

Social Media Chair

Veronika Cheplygina	Eindhoven University of Technology, The Netherlands

Young Investigators Early Career Development Program Chairs

Marius Linguraru	Children's National Institute, USA
Antonio Porras	Children's National Institute, USA

Student Board Liaison Chair

Gabriel Jimenez	Pontifical Catholic University of Peru, Peru

Submission Platform Manager

Kitty Wong	The MICCAI Society, Canada

Conference Management

DEKON Group
Pathable Inc.

Program Committee

Ehsan Adeli	Stanford University, USA
Shadi Albarqouni	ETH Zurich, Switzerland
Pablo Arbelaez	Universidad de los Andes, Colombia
Ulas Bagci	University of Central Florida, USA
Adrien Bartoli	Université Clermont Auvergne, France
Hrvoje Bogunovic	Medical University of Vienna, Austria
Weidong Cai	The University of Sydney, Australia
Chao Chen	Stony Brook University, USA
Elvis Chen	Robarts Research Institute, Canada
Stanley Durrleman	Inria, France
Boris Escalante-Ramírez	National Autonomous University of Mexico, Mexico
Pascal Fallavollita	University of Ottawa, Canada
Enzo Ferrante	CONICET, Universidad Nacional del Litoral, Argentina
Stamatia Giannarou	Imperial College London, UK
Orcun Goksel	ETH Zurich, Switzerland
Alberto Gomez	King's College London, UK
Miguel Angel González Ballester	Universitat Pompeu Fabra, Spain
Ilker Hacihaliloglu	Rutgers University, USA
Yi Hong	University of Georgia, USA
Yipeng Hu	University College London, UK
Heng Huang	University of Pittsburgh and JD Finance America Corporation, USA
Juan Eugenio Iglesias	University College London, UK
Madhura Ingalhalikar	Symbiosis Center for Medical Image Analysis, India
Pierre Jannin	Université de Rennes, France
Samuel Kadoury	Ecole Polytechnique de Montreal, Canada
Bernhard Kainz	Imperial College London, UK
Marta Kersten-Oertel	Concordia University, Canada
Andrew King	King's College London, UK
Ignacio Larrabide	CONICET, Argentina
Gang Li	University of North Carolina at Chapel Hill, USA
Jianming Liang	Arizona State University, USA
Hongen Liao	Tsinghua University, China
Rui Liao	Siemens Healthineers, USA
Feng Lin	Nanyang Technological University, China
Mingxia Liu	University of North Carolina at Chapel Hill, USA
Jiebo Luo	University of Rochester, USA
Xiongbiao Luo	Xiamen University, China
Andreas Maier	FAU Erlangen-Nuremberg, Germany
Stephen McKenna	University of Dundee, UK
Bjoern Menze	Technische Universität München, Germany
Mehdi Moradi	IBM Research, USA

Dong Ni	Shenzhen University, China
Marc Niethammer	University of North Carolina at Chapel Hill, USA
Jack Noble	Vanderbilt University, USA
Ipek Oguz	Vanderbilt University, USA
Gemma Piella	Pompeu Fabra University, Spain
Hedyeh Rafii-Tari	Auris Health Inc., USA
Islem Rekik	Istanbul Technical University, Turkey
Nicola Rieke	NVIDIA Corporation, USA
Tammy Riklin Raviv	Ben-Gurion University of the Negev, Israel
Hassan Rivaz	Concordia University, Canada
Holger Roth	NVIDIA Corporation, USA
Sharmishtaa Seshamani	Allen Institute, USA
Li Shen	University of Pennsylvania, USA
Feng Shi	Shanghai United Imaging Intelligence Co., China
Yonggang Shi	University of Southern California, USA
Michal Sofka	Hyperfine Research, USA
Stefanie Speidel	National Center for Tumor Diseases (NCT), Germany
Marius Staring	Leiden University Medical Center, The Netherlands
Heung-Il Suk	Korea University, South Korea
Kenji Suzuki	Tokyo Institute of Technology, Japan
Tanveer Syeda-Mahmood	IBM Research, USA
Amir Tahmasebi	CodaMetrix, USA
Xiaoying Tang	Southern University of Science and Technology, China
Tolga Tasdizen	The University of Utah, USA
Pallavi Tiwari	Case Western Reserve University, USA
Sotirios Tsaftaris	The University of Edinburgh, UK
Archana Venkataraman	Johns Hopkins University, USA
Satish Viswanath	Case Western Reserve University, USA
Hongzhi Wang	IBM Almaden Research Center, USA
Linwei Wang	Rochester Institute of Technology, USA
Qian Wang	Shanghai Jiao Tong University, China
Guorong Wu	University of North Carolina at Chapel Hill, USA
Daguang Xu	NVIDIA Corporation, USA
Ziyue Xu	NVIDIA Corporation, USA
Pingkun Yan	Rensselaer Polytechnic Institute, USA
Xin Yang	Huazhong University of Science and Technology, China
Zhaozheng Yin	Stony Brook University, USA
Tuo Zhang	Northwestern Polytechnical University, China
Guoyan Zheng	Shanghai Jiao Tong University, China
Yefeng Zheng	Tencent, China
Luping Zhou	The University of Sydney, Australia

Mentorship Program (Mentors)

Ehsan Adeli	Stanford University, USA
Stephen Aylward	Kitware, USA
Hrvoje Bogunovic	Medical University of Vienna, Austria
Li Cheng	University of Alberta, Canada
Marleen de Bruijne	University of Copenhagen, Denmark
Caroline Essert	University of Strasbourg, France
Gabor Fichtinger	Queen's University, Canada
Stamatia Giannarou	Imperial College London, UK
Juan Eugenio Iglesias Gonzalez	University College London, UK
Bernhard Kainz	Imperial College London, UK
Shuo Li	Western University, Canada
Jianming Liang	Arizona State University, USA
Rui Liao	Siemens Healthineers, USA
Feng Lin	Nanyang Technological University, China
Marius George Linguraru	Children's National Hospital, George Washington University, USA
Tianming Liu	University of Georgia, USA
Xiongbiao Luo	Xiamen University, China
Dong Ni	Shenzhen University, China
Wiro Niessen	Erasmus MC - University Medical Center Rotterdam, The Netherlands
Terry Peters	Western University, Canada
Antonio R. Porras	University of Colorado, USA
Daniel Racoceanu	Sorbonne University, France
Islem Rekik	Istanbul Technical University, Turkey
Nicola Rieke	NVIDIA, USA
Julia Schnabel	King's College London, UK
Ruby Shamir	Novocure, Switzerland
Stefanie Speidel	National Center for Tumor Diseases Dresden, Germany
Martin Styner	University of North Carolina at Chapel Hill, USA
Xiaoying Tang	Southern University of Science and Technology, China
Pallavi Tiwari	Case Western Reserve University, USA
Jocelyne Troccaz	CNRS, Grenoble Alpes University, France
Pierre Jannin	INSERM, Université de Rennes, France
Archana Venkataraman	Johns Hopkins University, USA
Linwei Wang	Rochester Institute of Technology, USA
Guorong Wu	University of North Carolina at Chapel Hill, USA
Li Xiao	Chinese Academy of Science, China
Ziyue Xu	NVIDIA, USA
Bochuan Zheng	China West Normal University, China
Guoyan Zheng	Shanghai Jiao Tong University, China
S. Kevin Zhou	Chinese Academy of Sciences, China
Maria A. Zuluaga	EURECOM, France

Additional Reviewers

Alaa Eldin Abdelaal
Ahmed Abdulkadir
Clement Abi Nader
Mazdak Abulnaga
Ganesh Adluru
Iman Aganj
Priya Aggarwal
Sahar Ahmad
Seyed-Ahmad Ahmadi
Euijoon Ahn
Alireza Akhondi-asl
Mohamed Akrout
Dawood Al Chanti
Ibraheem Al-Dhamari
Navid Alemi Koohbanani
Hanan Alghamdi
Hassan Alhajj
Hazrat Ali
Sharib Ali
Omar Al-Kadi
Maximilian Allan
Felix Ambellan
Mina Amiri
Sameer Antani
Luigi Antelmi
Michela Antonelli
Jacob Antunes
Saeed Anwar
Fernando Arambula
Ignacio Arganda-Carreras
Mohammad Ali Armin
John Ashburner
Md Ashikuzzaman
Shahab Aslani
Mehdi Astaraki
Angélica Atehortúa
Gowtham Atluri
Kamran Avanaki
Angelica Aviles-Rivero
Suyash Awate
Dogu Baran Aydogan
Qinle Ba
Morteza Babaie

Hyeon-Min Bae
Woong Bae
Wenjia Bai
Ujjwal Baid
Spyridon Bakas
Yaël Balbastre
Marcin Balicki
Fabian Balsiger
Abhirup Banerjee
Sreya Banerjee
Sophia Bano
Shunxing Bao
Adrian Barbu
Cher Bass
John S. H. Baxter
Amirhossein Bayat
Sharareh Bayat
Neslihan Bayramoglu
Bahareh Behboodi
Delaram Behnami
Mikhail Belyaev
Oualid Benkarim
Aicha BenTaieb
Camilo Bermudez
Giulia Bertò
Hadrien Bertrand
Julián Betancur
Michael Beyeler
Parmeet Bhatia
Chetan Bhole
Suvrat Bhooshan
Chitresh Bhushan
Lei Bi
Cheng Bian
Gui-Bin Bian
Sangeeta Biswas
Stefano B. Blumberg
Janusz Bobulski
Sebastian Bodenstedt
Ester Bonmati
Bhushan Borotikar
Jiri Borovec
Ilaria Boscolo Galazzo

Alexandre Bousse
Nicolas Boutry
Behzad Bozorgtabar
Nadia Brancati
Christopher Bridge
Esther Bron
Rupert Brooks
Qirong Bu
Tim-Oliver Buchholz
Duc Toan Bui
Qasim Bukhari
Ninon Burgos
Nikolay Burlutskiy
Russell Butler
Michał Byra
Hongmin Cai
Yunliang Cai
Sema Candemir
Bing Cao
Qing Cao
Shilei Cao
Tian Cao
Weiguo Cao
Yankun Cao
Aaron Carass
Heike Carolus
Adrià Casamitjana
Suheyla Cetin Karayumak
Ahmad Chaddad
Krishna Chaitanya
Jayasree Chakraborty
Tapabrata Chakraborty
Sylvie Chambon
Ming-Ching Chang
Violeta Chang
Simon Chatelin
Sudhanya Chatterjee
Christos Chatzichristos
Rizwan Chaudhry
Antong Chen
Cameron Po-Hsuan Chen
Chang Chen
Chao Chen
Chen Chen
Cheng Chen
Dongdong Chen

Fang Chen
Geng Chen
Hao Chen
Jianan Chen
Jianxu Chen
Jia-Wei Chen
Jie Chen
Junxiang Chen
Li Chen
Liang Chen
Pingjun Chen
Qiang Chen
Shuai Chen
Tianhua Chen
Tingting Chen
Xi Chen
Xiaoran Chen
Xin Chen
Yuanyuan Chen
Yuhua Chen
Yukun Chen
Zhineng Chen
Zhixiang Chen
Erkang Cheng
Jun Cheng
Li Cheng
Xuelian Cheng
Yuan Cheng
Veronika Cheplygina
Hyungjoo Cho
Jaegul Choo
Aritra Chowdhury
Stergios Christodoulidis
Ai Wern Chung
Pietro Antonio Cicalese
Özgün Çiçek
Robert Cierniak
Matthew Clarkson
Dana Cobzas
Jaume Coll-Font
Alessia Colonna
Marc Combalia
Olivier Commowick
Sonia Contreras Ortiz
Pierre-Henri Conze
Timothy Cootes

Luca Corinzia
Teresa Correia
Pierrick Coupé
Jeffrey Craley
Arun C. S. Kumar
Hui Cui
Jianan Cui
Zhiming Cui
Kathleen Curran
Haixing Dai
Xiaoliang Dai
Ker Dai Fei Elmer
Adrian Dalca
Abhijit Das
Neda Davoudi
Laura Daza
Sandro De Zanet
Charles Delahunt
Herve Delingette
Beatrice Demiray
Yang Deng
Hrishikesh Deshpande
Christian Desrosiers
Neel Dey
Xinghao Ding
Zhipeng Ding
Konstantin Dmitriev
Jose Dolz
Ines Domingues
Juan Pedro Dominguez-Morales
Hao Dong
Mengjin Dong
Nanqing Dong
Qinglin Dong
Suyu Dong
Sven Dorkenwald
Qi Dou
P. K. Douglas
Simon Drouin
Karen Drukker
Niharika D'Souza
Lei Du
Shaoyi Du
Xuefeng Du
Dingna Duan
Nicolas Duchateau

James Duncan
Jared Dunnmon
Luc Duong
Nicha Dvornek
Dmitry V. Dylov
Oleh Dzyubachyk
Mehran Ebrahimi
Philip Edwards
Alexander Effland
Jan Egger
Alma Eguizabal
Gudmundur Einarsson
Ahmed Elazab
Mohammed S. M. Elbaz
Shireen Elhabian
Ahmed Eltanboly
Sandy Engelhardt
Ertunc Erdil
Marius Erdt
Floris Ernst
Mohammad Eslami
Nazila Esmaeili
Marco Esposito
Oscar Esteban
Jingfan Fan
Xin Fan
Yonghui Fan
Chaowei Fang
Xi Fang
Mohsen Farzi
Johannes Fauser
Andrey Fedorov
Hamid Fehri
Lina Felsner
Jun Feng
Ruibin Feng
Xinyang Feng
Yifan Feng
Yuan Feng
Henrique Fernandes
Ricardo Ferrari
Jean Feydy
Lucas Fidon
Lukas Fischer
Antonio Foncubierta-Rodríguez
Germain Forestier

Reza Forghani
Nils Daniel Forkert
Jean-Rassaire Fouefack
Tatiana Fountoukidou
Aina Frau-Pascual
Moti Freiman
Sarah Frisken
Huazhu Fu
Xueyang Fu
Wolfgang Fuhl
Isabel Funke
Philipp Fürnstahl
Pedro Furtado
Ryo Furukawa
Elies Fuster-Garcia
Youssef Gahi
Jin Kyu Gahm
Laurent Gajny
Rohan Gala
Harshala Gammulle
Yu Gan
Cong Gao
Dongxu Gao
Fei Gao
Feng Gao
Linlin Gao
Mingchen Gao
Siyuan Gao
Xin Gao
Xinpei Gao
Yixin Gao
Yue Gao
Zhifan Gao
Sara Garbarino
Alfonso Gastelum-Strozzi
Romane Gauriau
Srishti Gautam
Bao Ge
Rongjun Ge
Zongyuan Ge
Sairam Geethanath
Yasmeen George
Samuel Gerber
Guido Gerig
Nils Gessert
Olivier Gevaert

Muhammad Usman Ghani
Sandesh Ghimire
Sayan Ghosal
Gabriel Girard
Ben Glocker
Evgin Goceri
Michael Goetz
Arnold Gomez
Kuang Gong
Mingming Gong
Yuanhao Gong
German Gonzalez
Sharath Gopal
Karthik Gopinath
Pietro Gori
Maged Goubran
Sobhan Goudarzi
Baran Gözcü
Benedikt Graf
Mark Graham
Bertrand Granado
Alejandro Granados
Robert Grupp
Christina Gsaxner
Lin Gu
Shi Gu
Yun Gu
Ricardo Guerrero
Houssem-Eddine Gueziri
Dazhou Guo
Hengtao Guo
Jixiang Guo
Pengfei Guo
Yanrong Guo
Yi Guo
Yong Guo
Yulan Guo
Yuyu Guo
Krati Gupta
Vikash Gupta
Praveen Gurunath Bharathi
Prashnna Gyawali
Stathis Hadjidemetriou
Omid Haji Maghsoudi
Justin Haldar
Mohammad Hamghalam

Bing Han
Hu Han
Liang Han
Xiaoguang Han
Xu Han
Zhi Han
Zhongyi Han
Jonny Hancox
Christian Hansen
Xiaoke Hao
Rabia Haq
Michael Hardisty
Stefan Harrer
Adam Harrison
S. M. Kamrul Hasan
Hoda Sadat Hashemi
Nobuhiko Hata
Andreas Hauptmann
Mohammad Havaei
Huiguang He
Junjun He
Kelei He
Tiancheng He
Xuming He
Yuting He
Mattias Heinrich
Stefan Heldmann
Nicholas Heller
Alessa Hering
Monica Hernandez
Estefania Hernandez-Martin
Carlos Hernandez-Matas
Javier Herrera-Vega
Kilian Hett
Tsung-Ying Ho
Nico Hoffmann
Matthew Holden
Song Hong
Sungmin Hong
Yoonmi Hong
Corné Hoogendoorn
Antal Horváth
Belayat Hossain
Le Hou
Ai-Ling Hsu
Po-Ya Hsu

Tai-Chiu Hsung
Pengwei Hu
Shunbo Hu
Xiaoling Hu
Xiaowei Hu
Yan Hu
Zhenhong Hu
Jia-Hong Huang
Junzhou Huang
Kevin Huang
Qiaoying Huang
Weilin Huang
Xiaolei Huang
Yawen Huang
Yongxiang Huang
Yue Huang
Yufang Huang
Zhi Huang
Arnaud Huaulmé
Henkjan Huisman
Xing Huo
Yuankai Huo
Sarfaraz Hussein
Jana Hutter
Khoi Huynh
Seong Jae Hwang
Emmanuel Iarussi
Ilknur Icke
Kay Igwe
Alfredo Illanes
Abdullah-Al-Zubaer Imran
Ismail Irmakci
Samra Irshad
Benjamin Irving
Mobarakol Islam
Mohammad Shafkat Islam
Vamsi Ithapu
Koichi Ito
Hayato Itoh
Oleksandra Ivashchenko
Yuji Iwahori
Shruti Jadon
Mohammad Jafari
Mostafa Jahanifar
Andras Jakab
Amir Jamaludin

Won-Dong Jang
Vincent Jaouen
Uditha Jarayathne
Ronnachai Jaroensri
Golara Javadi
Rohit Jena
Todd Jensen
Won-Ki Jeong
Zexuan Ji
Haozhe Jia
Jue Jiang
Tingting Jiang
Weixiong Jiang
Xi Jiang
Xiang Jiang
Jianbo Jiao
Zhicheng Jiao
Amelia Jiménez-Sánchez
Dakai Jin
Taisong Jin
Yueming Jin
Ze Jin
Bin Jing
Yaqub Jonmohamadi
Anand Joshi
Shantanu Joshi
Christoph Jud
Florian Jug
Yohan Jun
Alain Jungo
Abdolrahim Kadkhodamohammadi
Ali Kafaei Zad Tehrani
Dagmar Kainmueller
Siva Teja Kakileti
John Kalafut
Konstantinos Kamnitsas
Michael C. Kampffmeyer
Qingbo Kang
Neerav Karani
Davood Karimi
Satyananda Kashyap
Alexander Katzmann
Prabhjot Kaur
Anees Kazi
Erwan Kerrien
Hoel Kervadec

Ashkan Khakzar
Fahmi Khalifa
Nadieh Khalili
Siavash Khallaghi
Farzad Khalvati
Hassan Khan
Bishesh Khanal
Pulkit Khandelwal
Maksym Kholiavchenko
Meenakshi Khosla
Naji Khosravan
Seyed Mostafa Kia
Ron Kikinis
Daeseung Kim
Geena Kim
Hak Gu Kim
Heejong Kim
Hosung Kim
Hyo-Eun Kim
Jinman Kim
Jinyoung Kim
Mansu Kim
Minjeong Kim
Seong Tae Kim
Won Hwa Kim
Young-Ho Kim
Atilla Kiraly
Yoshiro Kitamura
Takayuki Kitasaka
Sabrina Kletz
Tobias Klinder
Kranthi Kolli
Satoshi Kondo
Bin Kong
Jun Kong
Tomasz Konopczynski
Ender Konukoglu
Bongjin Koo
Kivanc Kose
Anna Kreshuk
AnithaPriya Krishnan
Pavitra Krishnaswamy
Frithjof Kruggel
Alexander Krull
Elizabeth Krupinski
Hulin Kuang

Serife Kucur
David Kügler
Arjan Kuijper
Jan Kukacka
Nilima Kulkarni
Abhay Kumar
Ashnil Kumar
Kuldeep Kumar
Neeraj Kumar
Nitin Kumar
Manuela Kunz
Holger Kunze
Tahsin Kurc
Thomas Kurmann
Yoshihiro Kuroda
Jin Tae Kwak
Yongchan Kwon
Aymen Laadhari
Dmitrii Lachinov
Alexander Ladikos
Alain Lalande
Rodney Lalonde
Tryphon Lambrou
Hengrong Lan
Catherine Laporte
Carole Lartizien
Bianca Lassen-Schmidt
Andras Lasso
Ngan Le
Leo Lebrat
Changhwan Lee
Eung-Joo Lee
Hyekyoung Lee
Jong-Hwan Lee
Jungbeom Lee
Matthew Lee
Sangmin Lee
Soochahn Lee
Stefan Leger
Étienne Léger
Baiying Lei
Andreas Leibetseder
Rogers Jeffrey Leo John
Juan Leon
Wee Kheng Leow
Annan Li

Bo Li
Chongyi Li
Haohan Li
Hongming Li
Hongwei Li
Huiqi Li
Jian Li
Jianning Li
Jiayun Li
Junhua Li
Lincan Li
Mengzhang Li
Ming Li
Qing Li
Quanzheng Li
Shulong Li
Shuyu Li
Weikai Li
Wenyuan Li
Xiang Li
Xiaomeng Li
Xiaoxiao Li
Xin Li
Xiuli Li
Yang Li (Beihang University)
Yang Li (Northeast Electric Power
    University)
Yi Li
Yuexiang Li
Zeju Li
Zhang Li
Zhen Li
Zhiyuan Li
Zhjin Li
Zhongyu Li
Chunfeng Lian
Gongbo Liang
Libin Liang
Shanshan Liang
Yudong Liang
Haofu Liao
Ruizhi Liao
Gilbert Lim
Baihan Lin
Hongxiang Lin
Huei-Yung Lin

Jianyu Lin
C. Lindner
Geert Litjens
Bin Liu
Chang Liu
Dongnan Liu
Feng Liu
Hangfan Liu
Jianfei Liu
Jin Liu
Jingya Liu
Jingyu Liu
Kai Liu
Kefei Liu
Lihao Liu
Luyan Liu
Mengting Liu
Na Liu
Peng Liu
Ping Liu
Quande Liu
Qun Liu
Shengfeng Liu
Shuangjun Liu
Sidong Liu
Siqi Liu
Siyuan Liu
Tianrui Liu
Xianglong Liu
Xinyang Liu
Yan Liu
Yuan Liu
Yuhang Liu
Andrea Loddo
Herve Lombaert
Marco Lorenzi
Jian Lou
Nicolas Loy Rodas
Allen Lu
Donghuan Lu
Huanxiang Lu
Jiwen Lu
Le Lu
Weijia Lu
Xiankai Lu
Yao Lu

Yongyi Lu
Yueh-Hsun Lu
Christian Lucas
Oeslle Lucena
Imanol Luengo
Ronald Lui
Gongning Luo
Jie Luo
Ma Luo
Marcel Luthi
Khoa Luu
Bin Lv
Jinglei Lv
Ilwoo Lyu
Qing Lyu
Sharath M. S.
Andy J. Ma
Chunwei Ma
Da Ma
Hua Ma
Jingting Ma
Kai Ma
Lei Ma
Wenao Ma
Yuexin Ma
Amirreza Mahbod
Sara Mahdavi
Mohammed Mahmoud
Gabriel Maicas
Klaus H. Maier-Hein
Sokratis Makrogiannis
Bilal Malik
Anand Malpani
Ilja Manakov
Matteo Mancini
Efthymios Maneas
Tommaso Mansi
Brett Marinelli
Razvan Marinescu
Pablo Márquez Neila
Carsten Marr
Yassine Marrakchi
Fabio Martinez
Antonio Martinez-Torteya
Andre Mastmeyer
Dimitrios Mavroeidis

Jamie McClelland
Verónica Medina Bañuelos
Raghav Mehta
Sachin Mehta
Liye Mei
Raphael Meier
Qier Meng
Qingjie Meng
Yu Meng
Martin Menten
Odyssée Merveille
Pablo Mesejo
Liang Mi
Shun Miao
Stijn Michielse
Mikhail Milchenko
Hyun-Seok Min
Zhe Min
Tadashi Miyamoto
Aryan Mobiny
Irina Mocanu
Sara Moccia
Omid Mohareri
Hassan Mohy-ud-Din
Muthu Rama Krishnan Mookiah
Rodrigo Moreno
Lia Morra
Agata Mosinska
Saman Motamed
Mohammad Hamed Mozaffari
Anirban Mukhopadhyay
Henning Müller
Balamurali Murugesan
Cosmas Mwikirize
Andriy Myronenko
Saad Nadeem
Ahmed Naglah
Vivek Natarajan
Vishwesh Nath
Rodrigo Nava
Fernando Navarro
Lydia Neary-Zajiczek
Peter Neher
Dominik Neumann
Gia Ngo
Hannes Nickisch

Dong Nie
Jingxin Nie
Weizhi Nie
Aditya Nigam
Xia Ning
Zhenyuan Ning
Sijie Niu
Tianye Niu
Alexey Novikov
Jorge Novo
Chinedu Nwoye
Mohammad Obeid
Masahiro Oda
Thomas O'Donnell
Benjamin Odry
Steffen Oeltze-Jafra
Ayşe Oktay
Hugo Oliveira
Marcelo Oliveira
Sara Oliveira
Arnau Oliver
Sahin Olut
Jimena Olveres
John Onofrey
Eliza Orasanu
Felipe Orihuela-Espina
José Orlando
Marcos Ortega
Sarah Ostadabbas
Yoshito Otake
Sebastian Otalora
Cheng Ouyang
Jiahong Ouyang
Cristina Oyarzun Laura
Michal Ozery-Flato
Krittin Pachtrachai
Johannes Paetzold
Jin Pan
Yongsheng Pan
Prashant Pandey
Joao Papa
Giorgos Papanastasiou
Constantin Pape
Nripesh Parajuli
Hyunjin Park
Sanghyun Park

Seyoun Park
Angshuman Paul
Christian Payer
Chengtao Peng
Jialin Peng
Liying Peng
Tingying Peng
Yifan Peng
Tobias Penzkofer
Antonio Pepe
Oscar Perdomo
Jose-Antonio Pérez-Carrasco
Fernando Pérez-García
Jorge Perez-Gonzalez
Skand Peri
Loic Peter
Jorg Peters
Jens Petersen
Caroline Petitjean
Micha Pfeiffer
Dzung Pham
Renzo Phellan
Ashish Phophalia
Mark Pickering
Kilian Pohl
Iulia Popescu
Karteek Popuri
Tiziano Portenier
Alison Pouch
Arash Pourtaherian
Prateek Prasanna
Alexander Preuhs
Raphael Prevost
Juan Prieto
Viswanath P. S.
Sergi Pujades
Kumaradevan Punithakumar
Elodie Puybareau
Haikun Qi
Huan Qi
Xin Qi
Buyue Qian
Zhen Qian
Yan Qiang
Yuchuan Qiao
Zhi Qiao

Chen Qin
Wenjian Qin
Yanguo Qin
Wu Qiu
Hui Qu
Kha Gia Quach
Prashanth R.
Pradeep Reddy Raamana
Jagath Rajapakse
Kashif Rajpoot
Jhonata Ramos
Andrik Rampun
Parnesh Raniga
Nagulan Ratnarajah
Richard Rau
Mehul Raval
Keerthi Sravan Ravi
Daniele Ravì
Harish RaviPrakash
Rohith Reddy
Markus Rempfler
Xuhua Ren
Yinhao Ren
Yudan Ren
Anne-Marie Rickmann
Brandalyn Riedel
Leticia Rittner
Robert Robinson
Jessica Rodgers
Robert Rohling
Lukasz Roszkowiak
Karsten Roth
José Rouco
Su Ruan
Daniel Rueckert
Mirabela Rusu
Erica Rutter
Jaime S. Cardoso
Mohammad Sabokrou
Monjoy Saha
Pramit Saha
Dushyant Sahoo
Pranjal Sahu
Wojciech Samek
Juan A. Sánchez-Margallo
Robin Sandkuehler

Rodrigo Santa Cruz
Gianmarco Santini
Anil Kumar Sao
Mhd Hasan Sarhan
Duygu Sarikaya
Imari Sato
Olivier Saut
Mattia Savardi
Ramasamy Savitha
Fabien Scalzo
Nico Scherf
Alexander Schlaefer
Philipp Schleer
Leopold Schmetterer
Julia Schnabel
Klaus Schoeffmann
Peter Schueffler
Andreas Schuh
Thomas Schultz
Michael Schwier
Michael Sdika
Suman Sedai
Raghavendra Selvan
Sourya Sengupta
Youngho Seo
Lama Seoud
Ana Sequeira
Saeed Seyyedi
Giorgos Sfikas
Sobhan Shafiei
Reuben Shamir
Shayan Shams
Hongming Shan
Yeqin Shao
Harshita Sharma
Gregory Sharp
Mohamed Shehata
Haocheng Shen
Mali Shen
Yiqiu Shen
Zhengyang Shen
Luyao Shi
Xiaoshuang Shi
Yemin Shi
Yonghong Shi
Saurabh Shigwan

Hoo-Chang Shin
Suprosanna Shit
Yucheng Shu
Nadya Shusharina
Alberto Signoroni
Carlos A. Silva
Wilson Silva
Praveer Singh
Ramandeep Singh
Rohit Singla
Sumedha Singla
Ayushi Sinha
Rajath Soans
Hessam Sokooti
Jaemin Son
Ming Song
Tianyu Song
Yang Song
Youyi Song
Aristeidis Sotiras
Arcot Sowmya
Rachel Sparks
Bella Specktor
William Speier
Ziga Spiclin
Dominik Spinczyk
Chetan Srinidhi
Vinkle Srivastav
Lawrence Staib
Peter Steinbach
Darko Stern
Joshua Stough
Justin Strait
Robin Strand
Martin Styner
Hai Su
Pan Su
Yun-Hsuan Su
Vaishnavi Subramanian
Gérard Subsol
Carole Sudre
Yao Sui
Avan Suinesiaputra
Jeremias Sulam
Shipra Suman
Jian Sun

Liang Sun
Tao Sun
Kyung Sung
Chiranjib Sur
Yannick Suter
Raphael Sznitman
Solale Tabarestani
Fatemeh Taheri Dezaki
Roger Tam
José Tamez-Peña
Chaowei Tan
Jiaxing Tan
Hao Tang
Sheng Tang
Thomas Tang
Xiongfeng Tang
Zhenyu Tang
Mickael Tardy
Eu Wern Teh
Antonio Tejero-de-Pablos
Paul Thienphrapa
Stephen Thompson
Felix Thomsen
Jiang Tian
Yun Tian
Aleksei Tiulpin
Hamid Tizhoosh
Matthew Toews
Oguzhan Topsakal
Jordina Torrents
Sylvie Treuillet
Jocelyne Troccaz
Emanuele Trucco
Vinh Truong Hoang
Chialing Tsai
Andru Putra Twinanda
Norimichi Ukita
Eranga Ukwatta
Mathias Unberath
Tamas Ungi
Martin Urschler
Verena Uslar
Fatmatulzehra Uslu
Régis Vaillant
Jeya Maria Jose Valanarasu
Marta Vallejo

Fons van der Sommen
Gijs van Tulder
Kimberlin van Wijnen
Yogatheesan Varatharajah
Marta Varela
Thomas Varsavsky
Francisco Vasconcelos
S. Swaroop Vedula
Sanketh Vedula
Harini Veeraraghavan
Gonzalo Vegas Sanchez-Ferrero
Anant Vemuri
Gopalkrishna Veni
Ruchika Verma
Ujjwal Verma
Pedro Vieira
Juan Pedro Vigueras Guillen
Pierre-Frederic Villard
Athanasios Vlontzos
Wolf-Dieter Vogl
Ingmar Voigt
Eugene Vorontsov
Bo Wang
Cheng Wang
Chengjia Wang
Chunliang Wang
Dadong Wang
Guotai Wang
Haifeng Wang
Hongkai Wang
Hongyu Wang
Hua Wang
Huan Wang
Jun Wang
Kuanquan Wang
Kun Wang
Lei Wang
Li Wang
Liansheng Wang
Manning Wang
Ruixuan Wang
Shanshan Wang
Shujun Wang
Shuo Wang
Tianchen Wang
Tongxin Wang

Wenzhe Wang
Xi Wang
Xiangxue Wang
Yalin Wang
Yan Wang (Sichuan University)
Yan Wang (Johns Hopkins University)
Yaping Wang
Yi Wang
Yirui Wang
Yuanjun Wang
Yun Wang
Zeyi Wang
Zhangyang Wang
Simon Warfield
Jonathan Weber
Jürgen Weese
Donglai Wei
Dongming Wei
Zhen Wei
Martin Weigert
Michael Wels
Junhao Wen
Matthias Wilms
Stefan Winzeck
Adam Wittek
Marek Wodzinski
Jelmer Wolterink
Ken C. L. Wong
Jonghye Woo
Chongruo Wu
Dijia Wu
Ji Wu
Jian Wu (Tsinghua University)
Jian Wu (Zhejiang University)
Jie Ying Wu
Junyan Wu
Minjie Wu
Pengxiang Wu
Xi Wu
Xia Wu
Xiyin Wu
Ye Wu
Yicheng Wu
Yifan Wu
Zhengwang Wu
Tobias Wuerfl

Pengcheng Xi
James Xia
Siyu Xia
Yingda Xia
Yong Xia
Lei Xiang
Deqiang Xiao
Li Xiao (Tulane University)
Li Xiao (Chinese Academy of Science)
Yuting Xiao
Hongtao Xie
Jianyang Xie
Lingxi Xie
Long Xie
Xueqian Xie
Yiting Xie
Yuan Xie
Yutong Xie
Fangxu Xing
Fuyong Xing
Tao Xiong
Chenchu Xu
Hongming Xu
Jiaofeng Xu
Kele Xu
Lisheng Xu
Min Xu
Rui Xu
Xiaowei Xu
Yanwu Xu
Yongchao Xu
Zhenghua Xu
Cheng Xue
Jie Xue
Wufeng Xue
Yuan Xue
Faridah Yahya
Chenggang Yan
Ke Yan
Weizheng Yan
Yu Yan
Yuguang Yan
Zhennan Yan
Changchun Yang
Chao-Han Huck Yang
Dong Yang

Fan Yang (IIAI)
Fan Yang (Temple University)
Feng Yang
Ge Yang
Guang Yang
Heran Yang
Hongxu Yang
Huijuan Yang
Jiancheng Yang
Jie Yang
Junlin Yang
Lin Yang
Xiao Yang
Xiaohui Yang
Xin Yang
Yan Yang
Yujiu Yang
Dongren Yao
Jianhua Yao
Jiawen Yao
Li Yao
Chuyang Ye
Huihui Ye
Menglong Ye
Xujiong Ye
Andy W. K. Yeung
Jingru Yi
Jirong Yi
Xin Yi
Yi Yin
Shihui Ying
Youngjin Yoo
Chenyu You
Sahar Yousefi
Hanchao Yu
Jinhua Yu
Kai Yu
Lequan Yu
Qi Yu
Yang Yu
Zhen Yu
Pengyu Yuan
Yixuan Yuan
Paul Yushkevich
Ghada Zamzmi
Dong Zeng

Guodong Zeng
Oliver Zettinig
Zhiwei Zhai
Kun Zhan
Baochang Zhang
Chaoyi Zhang
Daoqiang Zhang
Dongqing Zhang
Fan Zhang (Yale University)
Fan Zhang (Harvard Medical School)
Guangming Zhang
Han Zhang
Hang Zhang
Haopeng Zhang
Heye Zhang
Huahong Zhang
Jianpeng Zhang
Jinao Zhang
Jingqing Zhang
Jinwei Zhang
Jiong Zhang
Jun Zhang
Le Zhang
Lei Zhang
Lichi Zhang
Lin Zhang
Ling Zhang
Lu Zhang
Miaomiao Zhang
Ning Zhang
Pengfei Zhang
Pengyue Zhang
Qiang Zhang
Rongzhao Zhang
Ru-Yuan Zhang
Shanzhuo Zhang
Shu Zhang
Tong Zhang
Wei Zhang
Weiwei Zhang
Wenlu Zhang
Xiaoyun Zhang
Xin Zhang
Ya Zhang
Yanbo Zhang
Yanfu Zhang

Yi Zhang
Yifan Zhang
Yizhe Zhang
Yongqin Zhang
You Zhang
Youshan Zhang
Yu Zhang
Yue Zhang
Yulun Zhang
Yunyan Zhang
Yuyao Zhang
Zijing Zhang
Can Zhao
Changchen Zhao
Fenqiang Zhao
Gangming Zhao
Haifeng Zhao
He Zhao
Jun Zhao
Li Zhao
Qingyu Zhao
Rongchang Zhao
Shen Zhao
Tengda Zhao
Tianyi Zhao
Wei Zhao
Xuandong Zhao
Yitian Zhao
Yiyuan Zhao
Yu Zhao
Yuan-Xing Zhao
Yue Zhao
Zixu Zhao
Ziyuan Zhao
Xingjian Zhen
Hao Zheng
Jiannan Zheng
Kang Zheng

Yalin Zheng
Yushan Zheng
Jia-Xing Zhong
Zichun Zhong
Haoyin Zhou
Kang Zhou
Sanping Zhou
Tao Zhou
Wenjin Zhou
Xiao-Hu Zhou
Xiao-Yun Zhou
Yanning Zhou
Yi Zhou (IIAI)
Yi Zhou (University of Utah)
Yuyin Zhou
Zhen Zhou
Zongwei Zhou
Dajiang Zhu
Dongxiao Zhu
Hancan Zhu
Lei Zhu
Qikui Zhu
Weifang Zhu
Wentao Zhu
Xiaofeng Zhu
Xinliang Zhu
Yingying Zhu
Yuemin Zhu
Zhe Zhu
Zhuotun Zhu
Xiahai Zhuang
Aneeq Zia
Veronika Zimmer
David Zimmerer
Lilla Zöllei
Yukai Zou
Gerald Zwettler
Reyer Zwiggelaa

Contents – Part VII

DWI and Tractography

Functional Brain Networks

Neuroimaging

Positron Emission Tomography

Brain Development and Atlases

A New Metric for Characterizing Dynamic Redundancy of Dense Brain Chronnectome and Its Application to Early Detection of Alzheimer's Disease

Maryam Ghanbari[1], Li-Ming Hsu[1], Zhen Zhou[1], Amir Ghanbari[2],
Zhanhao Mo[1], Pew-Thian Yap[1], Han Zhang[1], and Dinggang Shen[1(✉)]

[1] Department of Radiology and BRIC, University of North Carolina at Chapel Hill,
Chapel Hill, NC 27599, USA
{hanzhang,dgshen}@med.unc.edu
[2] Department of Civil, Construction, and Environmental Engineering,
North Carolina State University, Raleigh, NC 27695, USA

Abstract. Graph theory has been used extensively to investigate information exchange efficiency among brain regions represented as graph nodes. In this work, we propose a new metric to measure how the brain network is robust or resilient to any attack on its nodes and edges. The metric measures redundancy in the sense that it calculates the minimum number of independent, not necessarily shortest, paths between every pair of nodes. We adopt this metric for characterizing (i) the redundancy of time-varying brain networks, i.e., chronnectomes, computed along the progression of Alzheimer's disease (AD), including early mild cognitive impairment (EMCI), and (ii) changes in progressive MCI compared to stable MCI by calculating the probabilities of having at least 2 (or 3) independent paths between every pair of brain regions in a short period of time. Finally, we design a learning-based early AD detection framework, coined "REdundancy Analysis of Dynamic functional connectivity for Disease Diagnosis (READ³)", and show its superiority over other AD early detection methods. With the ability to measure dynamic resilience and robustness of brain networks, the metric is complementary to the commonly used "cost-efficiency" in brain network analysis.

Keywords: Graph theory · Complex brain networks · Disease diagnosis

This work is supported by NIH grants EB022880, AG041721, AG042599 and AG049371.

Electronic supplementary material The online version of this chapter (https://doi.org/10.1007/978-3-030-59728-3_1) contains supplementary material, which is available to authorized users.

© Springer Nature Switzerland AG 2020
A. L. Martel et al. (Eds.): MICCAI 2020, LNCS 12267, pp. 3–12, 2020.
https://doi.org/10.1007/978-3-030-59728-3_1

1 Introduction

The human brain can be modeled as a complex network based on functional connectivity (FC) that reflects information exchanges or communication among different brain regions [1]. Alzheimer's disease (AD) is regarded as a disconnection disease [2] with gradual brain network topological changes over a long period with a concealed onset [3]. Many recent efforts have been put forth to understand the neural underpinning of AD in its early (preclinical) stage, known as mild cognitive impairment (MCI) [4]. Resting-state functional MRI (rs-fMRI) is a noninvasive functional imaging technique that has been widely used to investigate brain functional connectome widely used in MCI studies. Dynamic functional connectivity (dFC) was proposed to characterize the time-resolved connectome, or "chronnectome", which is regarded as essential markers for adaption, preparedness, alertness, and various high-level cognitive functions [5,6]. Among many imaging-based AD studies, graph theory has been adopted as a powerful tool to reveal the degenerating brain functional network due to AD [7]. Many of the previous studies on the alterations caused by AD and other diseases have been largely based on the characteristic (shortest) path length and its derivatives (e.g., global efficiency) [8–11]. They have found that AD is a disconnected syndrome with suboptimal and less efficient brain FC networks [12,13]. However, most of the previous complex brain network studies focused on the "cost-efficiency" measurements in a *sparse* scenario, one of the important aspects of the network topology, mainly focusing on the shortest paths and the related nodes. However, there can be another aspect, considering the number of paths that do not share any node(s), call independent paths. By using this technique, we focus on the connectedness of the network when some of the nodes or edges being attacked (or removed from the network). This metric evaluates the compensatory effect of the network for maintaining normative cognition and it is dearer in denser networks.

Here, we designed several metrics that comprehensively capture the redundancy attributes for the entire network, especially the minimal number of independent paths between every pair of nodes; two paths between nodes a and b are independent if they do not have any node(s) in common except a and b. These redundant (alternative) paths can be defined in any networks but have not been well studied in the network neuroscience. For instance, it is valuable to know if the traffic network is still well functioning when one pathway went down; other roads, as backup alternatives, can be very important to maintain the function of the entire network. We further adopt this concept in the time-varying brain functional network analysis by quantifying *dynamic redundancy*. Specifically, we use a transition probability matrix between defined states and also the probability of maintaining each specific state. We did a proof-of-concept study using the well adopted ADNI dataset and then developed a computer-aided diagnosis/prognosis framework for early AD detection and convention prediction based on a large cohort of subjects. We finally proved the reproducibility, reliability, and external validity of our method and findings.

2   Method

2.1   Theoretical Analysis

Denote a network G with a node set $V(G)$ and an edge set $E(G)$. G is connected if there is a path between any pair of nodes (Fig. 1A, B). A connected network G is called 2-connected if, for every two node $x, y \in V(G)$, there are at least two independent paths between x and y (Fig. 1C) and similarly is called 3-connected if there are at least three independent paths between x and y (Fig. 1D). The network in Fig. 1A, B is not quite robust, whereas the robustness enhanced in Fig. 1C, D. Under disease attacks, the latter two are more stable because of holding more independent paths between every pair of nodes. Of note, increasing network density will make a network gradually change from disconnected to connected and to 2- (and 3-)connected. This poses useful information to understand the network's topology. As mentioned earlier, in dense settings, redundant paths become vital, whereas the cost-efficiency is less prominent. Thus redundant metric could lead to a highly sensitive measurement for disease detection.

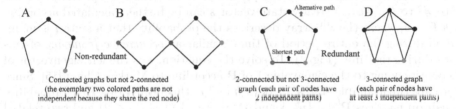

Fig. 1. Examples of connected (A, B), 2-connected (C) and 3-connected graphs (D)

2.2   Overall Procedure

The method applies to rs-fMRI data, where dynamic FC network (chronnectome) is first constructed by a sliding window correlation strategy. On each window (among all T windows), multiple binary networks are formed with N different density levels, where various dynamic redundancy features are extracted for brain disease diagnosis. Supplementary Fig. 1 shows the diagram of the overall analyses, with our method "REdundancy Analysis of Dynamic functional connectivity for Disease Diagnosis (READ³)". Next, we describe the READ³ in details.

2.3   Core Algorithm: READ³

Step 1. We apply N density levels on each t, $(1 \leq t \leq T)$ of all the T weighted dynamic FC networks to create N binary networks for calculating connectedness properties. This provides different views of the same FC network at each time slot (windows) because connectedness properties vary at different network density levels. By considering temporal variation, this creates comprehensive spatiotemporal descriptions of a weighted brain network. To sum them up, we further define various *state vectors* to quantitatively characterize such spatiotemporal changes of network redundancy. Here, we present two state vector definitions as an example. The other state vectors can be defined similarly. Let b := $\{b_t\}$ ($1 \leq t \leq T$) be the "**2-conn&conn**" **state vector** where $b_t = 1$ if the minimally connected network in t (among all N binary networks in t) is not 2-connected and $b_t = 2$, otherwise (Fig. 2). We also define more sensitive state vectors to conduct more challenging task, e.g., MCI progression prediction [14]. To this end, we further define a generalized "**3-conn&2-conn**" **state vector** c := $\{c_t\}$ ($1 \leq t \leq T$), where $c_t = 1$ if the minimally 2-connected network in t (among all N binary networks in t) is not 3-connected and $c_t = 2$, otherwise. To keep it simple, we take these two state vectors as examples to describe later steps in READ³ unless otherwise stated.

Step 2. To concisely quantify dynamic properties of the state vectors and facilitating comparisons among subjects, we define a transition probability matrix $\mathbf{P}$ from a state vector, whose array p_{ij} describes the transition probability from state #i to #j. Also, a steady state vector s can be further calculated according to $s \cdot \mathbf{P} = s$, where the ith array describes the probability that a state i is maintained during the entire period of time, similar as *occurrence frequency* of this state during the time (Fig. 2). To solve the equation, s is the left eigenvector of $\mathbf{P}$ corresponding to the eigenvalue 1 of $\mathbf{P}$ according to Markov Chain [15]. Since there are two available states for both b and c, this results two 2×2 probability transition matrices $\mathbf{P}^b := \{p_{i,j}^b\}$ and $\mathbf{P}^c := \{p_{i,j}^c\}$ ($1 \leq i,j \leq 2$) and two related steady states s^b and s^c of length 2. Therefore $p_{11}^b + p_{12}^b = p_{21}^b + p_{22}^b = s_1^b + s_2^b = 1$. This means a total dependency between p_{11} and p_{12}, p_{21} and p_{22}, and s_1 and s_2 (only 3 independent features out of the total 6 features for each of b and c.).

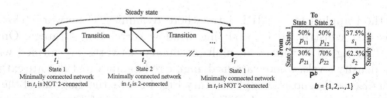

Fig. 2. Definition of the 2-conn&conn state vector

Step 3. We use comprehensively engineered dynamic redundancy features including the aforementioned ones (more of them are explained in Sect. 3.2) for machine learning-based disease diagnosis. Of note, all the features engineered in Step 2 can be fed in traditional statistical analysis, too; however, conducting mass-univariate statistical analysis on all of these features will suffer reduced statistical power and inflated false negatives (unless they are empirically selected, as we did in a proof-of-concept study in Sect. 3.1). Therefore, we treat all of them equivalently and feed them into a pattern recognition task as a machine-learning multivariate analysis (as the main algorithm of READ³).

3   Experiments and Results

We adopted ADNI dataset (http://adni.loni.usc.edu/), the world's largest publicly available multi-center AD progression data [16] as the main testbed of our method. It consists of 1351 data from 565 NCs (normal controls), 653 MCIs and 133 ADs. Sophisticated experiments were designed separately testing the validity (a proof-of-concept study), reproducibility, reliability, and external validity (based on an independent data out of ADNI samples) of our method, all described in Sect. 3.1, as well as a machine learning study on early AD detection in Sect. 3.2. We also tested the feasibility of early prediction for MCI progression, an even challenging task (Sect. 3.1). Figure 3 provides an overview and a summary of all experiments we have conducted.

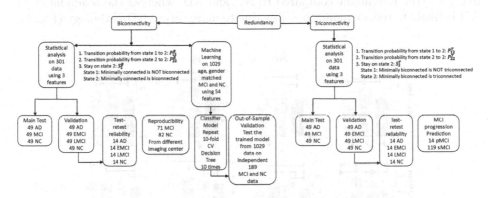

Fig. 3. Data management and experimental design

All rs-fMRI data (each contains 7-min scans) from ADNIgo and ADNI2 was processed according to the same, standard pipeline [17] based on a well adopted toolbox (AFNI [18], see details [19]). Time-varying, dynamic FC networks were built based on a 268-region brain atlas [20] by sliding window correlation with a window length of 20 volumes (60 s) and a step size of 1 volume (3 s) [21], resulting in $T = 111$ windows. We applied $N = 19$ densities to binarize each network, starting from 5% with a step size of 5%.

3.1   Proof of Concept and Validation Studies

Main Test: Characterizing AD Progression. We used baseline scans from all 49 AD subjects in ADNI and the same number of age-, gender-matched NCs and MCIs to compare their dynamic redundancy properties in the brain chronnectome as a proof of concept study, where statistical between-group comparisons were carried out to demonstrate the effectiveness of our method in detection of imaging markers for AD. We selected only 49 NCs and MCIs to make sample size matched for maximizing statistical power. For simplicity, we extracted six features (2-conn&conn and 3-conn&2-conn). All NC and MCI data will be used later with machine learning. A Kruskal-Wallis test (a non-parametric version of the one-way ANOVA) was used to detect group differences among the three groups (Family Wise Error (FWE) corrected $p < 0.05$). For results with significant group differences, Mann-Withney U-tests (a non-parametric version of the two-sample t-test) were used to conduct post hoc pairwise comparisons ($p < 0.05$, FWE corrected). As shown in Supplementary Table 4, MCI groups had a larger probability to stay in 2-conn&conn steady state (s_2^b) compared to NC and AD groups. In a more redundant setting (3-conn&2-conn), MCI shows increased transition p_{12}^c (from the state that the minimal 2-connected is not 3-connected to the state that the minimal 2-connected is 3-connected) that confirms higher chance to stay at the 3-conn&2-conn state (higher p_{22}^c and s_2^c) compared to NCs. The results indicated that the brain network in MCI is more likely to stay redundant compared to NC and AD, whereas the redundancy in AD is likely to reduce again, possibly due to more severe AD pathology (Fig. 4).

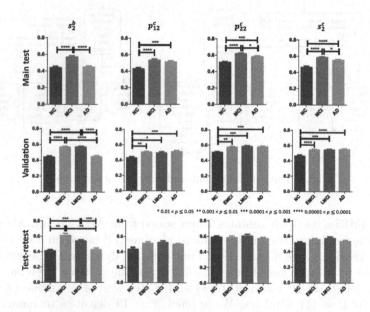

Fig. 4. Results of statistical analysis on the dynamic redundancy measures

Validation and Test-Retest Reliability: Early MCI Detection. To validate above results, we conducted a validation study by replacing the original MCI group with an independent dataset consisting of 49 age- and gender-matched early MCI (EMCI) and 49 late MCI (LMCI) subjects. We were not only able to replicate all the results from main test but also found that it is possible to detect AD-caused dynamic redundancy changes at an even earlier stage (EMCI stage instead of MCI stage). The main findings still hold in another retest dataset consisting of follow-up scans from the same 14 subjects in each group (Supplementary Table 4, Fig. 4).

External Validation with Out-of-Sample Data for Reproducibility Assessment. In addition to the ADNI data, we used an independent dataset consisting of 67 NC and 71 amnestic MCI (diagnosed according to [22], from a collaborative hospital for assessment of the external validity of our method (see Supplementary Table 3 for detailed subject information). We focused on the statistical comparison of the steady state of 2-conn&conn (s_2^b) as all the previous tests have consistently demonstrated the sensitivity of this metric in early AD detection (both in MCI vs. NC and in EMCI vs. NC). Once again, we found significant changes in s_2^b ($p = 0.015$) between amnestic MCI group and NC group, further proved that MCI may have more tendency than NC to be also 2-connected when the network is first become connected (Supplementary Fig. 2A).

Detecting Differences Between Progressive MCI and Stable MCI. While characterizing differences in MCI is important, prediction of the MCI's conversion to AD could be more clinically urgent, given the fact that the MCI group is heterogenous and only a portion of them eventually progress to AD [23]. Therefore, we identified 14 pMCI (progressive MCI who eventually progressed to AD, 5 males and 9 females, age 71.9 ± 6.8) from 119 sMCI (stable MCI who stay unchanged according to the last follow-up, 61 males and 58 females, age 75.6 ± 8) in ADNI data. Due to limited and unbalanced samples, we only found a trend to significant difference ($p = 0.071$, uncorrected) in the steady state of 3-conn&2-conn between sMCI and pMCI, indicating that sMCI's brain network has a larger tendency to be redundant compared to pMCI (Supplemenatry Fig. 2B). Such a difference cannot be detected with 2-conn&conn (a less redundant setting). It is likely that the higher redundancy earn sMCI longer time to have reserved cognitive abilities (Supplementary Fig. 2B).

3.2 Individualized Early AD Diagnosis with READ³

We expended our analysis to a full scale after the comprehensive validations with the entire framework of the READ³, including engineering more sophisticated dynamic redundancy features and a machine learning-based individual detection on a big dataset (565 NCs and 653 MCIs). First, in addition to the 2-conn&conn state vector, we further define $m := \{m_t\}$ ($1 \leq t \leq T$) as the "minimally 2-connected" state vector where m_t shows the minimum applied density level in t that leads to the 2-connected network. Four states were calculated from it as the most cases occurred with a density between 10% to 25%, which led to 16 transition features p_{ij}^m and four steady-state features s_{ij}^m ($2 \leq i, j \leq 5$). Second, we define $g := \{g_t\}$ $(1 \leq t \leq T)$ as the **"2-connected gap" state vector** where g_t denotes the gap between the density levels that leads to the minimally connected and the minimally 2-connected networks. Four states were derived (focusing on the density gap range 0%–15%), generating 16 transition features p_{ij}^g and four steady-state features s_{ij}^g $(1 \leq i, j \leq 4)$. Third, we calculate the occurence ratio of the 2-connected networks among the total temporal windows $(T = 111$ in our study) in eight major density levels $(5\%, 10\%, 15\%, \ldots 40\%)$. With all the 48 features in addition to the six features from the previously defined 2-conn&conn state vector, we built a decision tree with Weka 3 (https://www. cs.waikato.ac.nz/ml/weka, [24]), a well-adopted open source machine learning software with the training set and evaluate the performance on the testing set with 10-fold cross validation repeated for 10 times. Note that we make sure that all the scans from the same subject were either in the training or in testing set to avoid seeing the testing subject.

The early AD diagnosis model performed very well. This is comparable to one of the best performance on MCI classification reported from a recent state-of-the-art study with significantly smaller sample size based on leave-one-out cross validation [25]. To further validate our model, we applied the trained model on an independent, out-of-sample dataset from ADNI (189 data consist of 117 MCIs and 72 NCs that had never been seen by the model), see Table 1.

Table 1. Results of machine learning, %(SD), AUC, area under ROC curve, BAC, balanced accuracy, YI, Youden's Index

	SEN	SPE	ACC	AUC	F-Score	BAC	YI
Main test	90.0(2.0)	88.8(0.8)	89.4(1.1)	90.9(0.8)	89.8(1.2)	89.4(1.1)	78.8(2.2)
Validation	88.0	86.1	87.3	90.0	89.6	87.1	74.1

4   Conclusion and Future Works

This is the first study investigating the global redundancy and its fluctuations in brain dynamic functional networks. We explored various newly defined connectedness features that was proved to be highly sensitive to neuropathological alterations due to AD. Our results suggest that MCIs tend to have more redundant brain networks, possibly as a neuromechanism of cognitive reservation. Such an increase in redundancy could even be detected at an early stage of MCI (EMCI). This topological changes could make MCI's brain network more robust and resilient to widespread AD attacks, thanks to the back-up paths. This promotes a better understanding for early detection and timely intervention. The REdundancy Analysis of Dynamic functional connectivity for Disease Diagnosis (READ^3) model successfully captured subtle spatiotemporal redundancy changes and outperformed the previously reported diagnosis accuracy with other state-of-the-art methods [25]. This is due to the strictly defined redundancy metrics based on graph connectedness, instead of other loosely defined network attributes, e.g., smallwordness. Our method holds its promise in the future works on better understanding of brain diseases, even on the analysis of other brain networks (e.g., structural connectome). Importantly, with READ[3], it is for the first time that the redundant networks show comparable, if not better, diagnostic values than the well studied cost-efficiency measurements. The highly complementary nature of the brain redundancy analysis to the conventional complex brain network analysis warrants our method a bright future.

References

1. Sporns, O.: Structure and function of complex brain networks. Dialogues Clin. Neurosci. **15**(3), 247 (2013)
2. Dai, Z., et al.: Disrupted structural and functional brain networks in Alzheimer's disease. Neurobiol. Aging **75**, 71–82 (2019)
3. Adeli, H., Ghosh-Dastidar, S., Dadmehr, N.: Alzheimer's disease and models of computation: imaging, classification, and neural models. J. Alzheimers Dis. **7**(3), 187–199 (2005)
4. Gauthier, S., et al.: Mild cognitive impairment. Lancet **367**(9518), 1262–1270 (2006)
5. Calhoun, V.D., Miller, R., Pearlson, G., Adalı, T.: The chronnectome: time-varying connectivity networks as the next frontier in fMRI data discovery. Neuron **84**(2), 262–274 (2014)
6. Allen, E.A., Damaraju, E., Plis, S.M., Erhardt, E.B., Eichele, T., Calhoun, V.D.: Tracking whole-brain connectivity dynamics in the resting state. Cereb. Cortex **24**(3), 663–676 (2014)
7. Binnewijzend, M.A., et al.: Resting-state fMRI changes in Alzheimer's disease and mild cognitive impairment. Neurobiol. Aging **33**(9), 2018–2028 (2012)
8. Meier, J., Tewarie, P., Van Mieghem, P.: The union of shortest path trees of functional brain networks. Brain Connectivity **5**(9), 575–581 (2015)
9. Newman, M.E.: Modularity and community structure in networks. Proc. Natl. Acad. Sci. **103**(23), 8577–8582 (2006)
10. Ravasz, E., Barabási, A.L.: Hierarchical organization in complex networks. Phys. Rev. E **67**(2), 026112 (2003)
11. Achard, S., Salvador, R., Whitcher, B., Suckling, J., Bullmore, E.: A resilient, low-frequency, small-world human brain functional network with highly connected association cortical hubs. J. Neurosci. **26**(1), 63–72 (2006)
12. Dennis, E.L., Thompson, P.M.: Functional brain connectivity using fMRI in aging and Alzheimer's disease. Neuropsychol. Rev. **24**(1), 49–62 (2014)
13. Stam, C.J., Jones, B., Nolte, G., Breakspear, M., Scheltens, P.: Small-world networks and functional connectivity in Alzheimer's disease. Cereb. Cortex **17**(1), 92–99 (2006)
14. Jie, B., Liu, M., Zhang, D., Shen, D.: Sub-network kernels for measuring similarity of brain connectivity networks in disease diagnosis. IEEE Trans. Image Process. **27**(5), 2340–2353 (2018)
15. Williams, N.J., Daly, I., Nasuto, S.: Markov model-based method to analyse time-varying networks in EEG task-related data. Front. Comput. Neurosci. **12**, 76 (2018)
16. Jack Jr., C.R., et al.: The Alzheimer's disease neuroimaging initiative (ADNI): MRI methods. J. Magn. Reson. Imaging **27**(4), 685–691 (2008)

17. Chao-Gan, Y., Yu-Feng, Z.: DPARSF: a MATLAB toolbox for "pipeline" data analysis of resting-state fMRI. Front. Syst. Neurosci. **4** (2010)
18. Cox, R.W.: AFNI: software for analysis and visualization of functional magnetic resonance neuroimages. Comput. Biomed. Res. **29**(3), 162–173 (1996)
19. Chen, X., Zhang, H., Zhang, L., Shen, C., Lee, S.W., Shen, D.: Extraction of dynamic functional connectivity from brain grey matter and white matter for MCI classification. Hum. Brain Mapp. **38**(10), 5019–5034 (2017)
20. Shen, X., Tokoglu, F., Papademetris, X., Constable, R.T.: Groupwise whole-brain parcellation from resting-state fMRI data for network node identification. NeuroImage **82**, 403–415 (2013)
21. Leonardi, N., Van De Ville, D.: On spurious and real fluctuations of dynamic functional connectivity during rest. NeuroImage **104**, 430–436 (2015)
22. Petersen, R.C.: Mild cognitive impairment as a diagnostic entity. J. Intern. Med. **256**(3), 183–194 (2004)
23. Petersen, R.C., et al.: Current concepts in mild cognitive impairment. Arch. Neurol. **58**(12), 1985–1992 (2001)
24. Frank, E., Hall, M., Trigg, L., Holmes, G., Witten, I.H.: Data mining in bioinformatics using weka. Bioinformatics **20**(15), 2479–2481 (2004)
25. Chen, X., Zhang, H., Gao, Y., Wee, C.Y., Li, G., Shen, D.: Alzheimer's disease neuroimaging initiative: high-order resting-state functional connectivity network for MCI classification. Hum. Brain Mapp. **37**(9), 3282–3296 (2016)

A Computational Framework for Dissociating Development-Related from Individually Variable Flexibility in Regional Modularity Assignment in Early Infancy

Mayssa Soussia[1], Xuyun Wen[1], Zhen Zhou[1], Bing Jin[1], Tae-Eui Kam[1], Li-Ming Hsu[1], Zhengwang Wu[1], Gang Li[1], Li Wang[1], Islem Rekik[2], Weili Lin[1,3], Dinggang Shen[1], Han Zhang[1(✉)], and the UNC/UMN Baby Connectome Project Consortium

[1] Department of Radiology and Biomedical Research Imaging Center (BRIC),
University of North Carolina at Chapel Hill, Chapel Hill, NC, USA
hanzhang@med.unc.edu
[2] BASIRA Lab, Faculty of Computer and Informatics,
Istanbul Technical University, Istanbul, Turkey
[3] Department of Biomedical Engineering,
University of North Carolina at Chapel Hill, Chapel Hill, NC, USA

Abstract. Functional brain development in early infancy is a highly dynamic and complex process. Understanding each brain region's topological role and its development in the brain functional connectivity (FC) networks is essential for early disorder detection. A handful of previous studies have mostly focused on how FC network is changing regarding age. These approaches inevitably overlook the effect of individual variability for those at the same age that could shape unique cognitive capabilities and personalities among infants. With that in mind, we propose a novel computational framework based on across-subject across-age multilayer network analysis with a fully automatic (for parameter optimization), robust community detection algorithm. By detecting group consistent modules without losing individual information, this method allows a first-ever dissociation analysis of the two variability sources – age dependency and individual specificity – that greatly shape early brain development. This method is applied to a large cohort of 0–2 years old infants' functional MRI data during natural sleep. We not only detected the brain regions with greatest flexibility in this early developmental period but also identified five categories of brain regions with distinct development-related and individually variable flexibility changes. Our method is highly valuable for more thorough understanding of the early brain functional organizations and sheds light on early developmental abnormality detection.

Keywords: Brain network · Early development · Individual variability

Electronic supplementary material The online version of this chapter (https://doi.org/10.1007/978-3-030-59728-3_2) contains supplementary material, which is available to authorized users.

© Springer Nature Switzerland AG 2020
A. L. Martel et al. (Eds.): MICCAI 2020, LNCS 12267, pp. 13–21, 2020.
https://doi.org/10.1007/978-3-030-59728-3_2

1 Introduction

The infant brain undergoes rapid postnatal structural and functional development, shaping later behavioral and cognitive performance that largely differ among individuals. Understanding age-dependent, subject-specific alterations of each brain region's topological role and its rewiring in the entire brain connectome is a key to understand such a scientifically and clinically important question [1, 2]. Resting-state functional MRI (rs-fMRI) and its derived functional connectivity (FC) offer an excellent non-invasive tool to investigate the *in vivo* brain functional network and its evolution in the early postnatal life [1].

Most of previous rs-fMRI studies, however, focused only on how subject-consistent, group mean brain functional connectome changes across ages. For example, Yin et al. used whole-brain FC-based clustering to identify different age groups, each of which has similar FC patterns [2]. Gao et al. used a large cohort of normal pediatric subjects to reveal temporal and spatial evolution of brain network topology across different age groups [3]. However, considering age as the most important factor to shape functional wiring of the brain is very simplistic. FC is more complex since it can be altered not only by age but also, most importantly, by childhood experience (environment, nutrition, caregivers, etc.) according to CDC (Centers for Disease Control and Prevention). All these factors, concluded in individual variability, influence the emergence and development of behavior, cognition, and personality [4]. Therefore, investigating individual variability of functional connectome is highly important. On one hand, it helps to understand how FC patterns in early developmental stages are translated into individual differences in a later age [5]. On the other side, rather than focusing on generalized group-level investigations [4], using individualized imaging markers can be a tool for predicting neurodevelopmental abnormalities [5]. However, studies delineating infant brain FC variability are still scarce. For instance, by focusing on the genetic influences on the brain network formation between singletons and twins, a study reported an increasing inter-subject variability with decreasing genetic sharing magnitude [6].

On the other hand, to better understand brain segregation and integration, modular analysis has been widely used in the network neuroscience. Some studies detected network modules with a group-mean FC matrix averaged across all subjects in a certain age group [7], while others detected modules from individual-level FC networks before averaging them into group-level modules [8]. However, the averaging process not only blurs network topology but also cannot account for individual variability. One way to mitigate this limitation is to use multi-layer modularity analysis [9]. In [10], individual FC matrix constitute a multi-layer network for each of the three age groups (neonate, one and two years old) by adding inter-layer connections as an additional constraint. This analysis makes modular structure consistent across subjects while preserving individual variability in regional modular affiliations. However, due to limited sample size and large gaps between two neighboring ages, such an approach is likely to overlook fine developmental patterns that might occur continuously with development. In addition to that, parameters used for multi-layer modularity detection are usually determined in a way with more or less human interference [11], leading to biased results.

To address the aforementioned issues, we build a multi-layer FC network with a significantly improved, automatic community detection algorithm and applied it to a large-scale longitudinal infant rs-fMRI data for investigation of fine-grained age-dependent variability (development-related) and age-independent variability (individual variability). The novelty in our work is four-fold. *First,* we conduct a quantitative dissociation of the two sources of variability that shape the functional fingerprint in infant brain. *Second,* we adopt a fully automated parameter determination for detection of more robust modularity structure at different hierarchical levels [7]. *Third,* our model is tested with a large infant cohort and a model of continuous changes across age. *Finally,* we provide the first-ever data-driven brain region categorization based on their distinct attributes in both age-dependent and age-independent dimensions.

2 Materials and Methods

2.1 Modularity Analysis of Multi-layer Networks

Multi-layer Network-Based Modularity Detection. We first build a multi-layer FC network [12] where entries in each layer represent the pairwise correlation of regional rs-fMRI time series. We subsequently apply Gen-Louvain algorithm [9], a robust modularity detection algorithm that identifies modularity structure from a multi-layer network-derived supra-adjacency matrix (including all the adjacency matrices from all subjects and all inter-layer connections so the modularity can be detected for each of the subjects at the same time). The algorithm is governed by two key parameters, the resolution scaling γ and the inter-subject coupling ω. The γ allows one to find out modules of different sizes and ω controls similarity of modularity structure across subjects. Our main contribution at this level is, unlike using selected and fixed values of γ and ω that focus on a single scale [11] or less automatic heuristic parameter determination [10], we propose an automated way to optimize the parameters.

Automated Heuristic Parameters Optimization. Due to the significant effect of γ and ω on the detected modules, one should be careful when choosing the optimal values. Both parameters should be jointly optimized. We calculate the heatmaps of total module number (K) and inter-subject similarity (measured by normalized mutual information, *NMI*) (Fig. 1) by varying γ and ω. To prevent the stochastic aspect of Gen-Louvain algorithm, we repeat the calculation 50 times at each set of parameters to generate averaged heatmaps. Unlike [10] where γ and ω were selected mainly according to high modularity values Q, which could lead to unstable result, we automatically select the centroid of the most robust areas in the K heatmap (Fig. 1b). We also exclude the area comprehending very high values of $K > 12$ (Fig. 1a) and *NMI* > 0.7 (Fig. 1c). In fact, we want to select γ and ω that a slightly change does not affect the major result (i.e., robust areas) while solely relying on maximum Q value does not necessarily guarantee that. On the other hand, in [10], modularity was analyzed only for $K = 5$ because it is considered as most "reasonable". However, the brain network is known to be hierarchically organized [7], hence it may be more reasonable to examine different levels of hierarchy. Therefore, we choose multiple scales as they occupied large areas in Fig. 1b (more robust results).

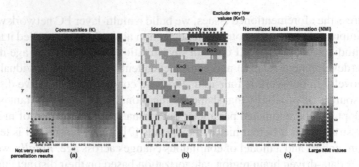

Fig. 1. Heatmaps of communities K and NMI values of all subjects.

General Modular Consistency. After obtaining subject-level modules as output from Gen-Louvain, we further detect regions with group consistent modular assignments. Instead of setting an arbitrary cutting-off threshold in [12], we generate three maps delineating general (across subjects across ages) modular consistency from different aspects without any pre-set parameters (Fig. 2). In addition to a majority voting modular structure of all subjects (Fig. 2a), we calculate a *consistency measurement* for each brain region, indicating how each region's modular affiliation is consistent across subjects and ages (Fig. 2b, for $K = 2$ and $K = 5$ only, results of other K values are shown in Fig. S1).

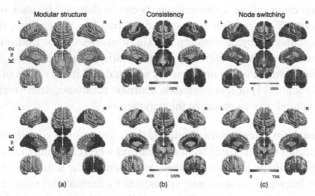

Fig. 2. Consistency and variability in modular affiliation for all brain regions across subjects and across age at two modularity levels ($K = 2$ and $K = 5$, for other Ks, see Fig. S1).

Inspired from [13], we also calculate *node switching rate* for each region (Fig. 2c). This is done by first arranging all subjects according to their ages and then calculating switch rate of modularity. This is a good indicator of the dynamicity of modular attributes across age.

2.2 Post Modularity Analysis for Dissociating Age-Dependency and Individual Variability

Adaptive Fine Age Sampling. We further qualitatively investigate region-wise variability with two sources (age and subject) considered. It is undeniable that the evolution of brain functional topology is complex and quite dynamic; minor changes, though having big impact, can occur at a fine time scale and can be easily overlooked. To this end, we apply a sliding window strategy to the spatiotemporally evolving modularity structures to investigate finer changes in the modularity variability. Each window includes a group of subjects with similar ages. The age window is adaptively defined with 1 to 4 months in length and 15 to 30 days in stride to accommodate faster development in earlier infancy [2] and to make sure that the sample sizes in different windows are largely comparable (Fig. S2).

Quantitative Dissociation of Age-Dependent and Age-Independent Variability. With sliding age windows, we are able to investigate different sources of variabilities in modularity structure. We introduce two measures based on the age windows: 1) *mode flexibility* that reflects the age dependency of the window-averaged (mode of) modularity structure, 2) *unlikability* that mirrors the individual variability in each age group.

Mode Flexibility for Assessment of Age Dependency. In each sliding window, the age effect is relatively minimized because of the short window length, so we can calculate the average (mode of) modularity for the samples in each age group and track its change along age windows. For each brain region, once the mode of modularity is calculated, mode flexibility f is computed ($f = 1$ if there is a switch in the mode from an age window to the next, otherwise 0). After normalizing by the total number of age windows, this index is bounded between 0 and 1. It summarizes age dependency patterns during the first two years after birth.

Unlikability for Assessment of Subject Variability in Each Age Group. In order to track how much individual variability is involved in brain development, we calculate how variable subjects are from each other in terms of region-wise modular assignment. To this end, at each brain region, we use the coefficient of unlikability u, defined in Eq. 1, to measure how different modular attributes are among the subjects of similar age (in the same age window) [14].

$$u = 1 - \sum_i p_i^2 \tag{1}$$

Where $p_i = k_i/n$, n is the number of subjects, and k_i the number of subjects having the same modular category i. Of note, there could still be minimal age effect captured by Eq. 1 as subject variability in each age window as their postmenstrual ages could be slightly different. However, it is less likely such since if this effect exists, we expect a gradually smaller individual variability along age windows for most of brain regions, which is not observed.

Grouping Brain Regions into Categories According to the Variability Sources. Once we calculate the mode flexibility (age effect) and the mean unlikability across age (subject variability independent of age) for each brain region, we then group the brain regions into different categories based on their variability sources. K-means clustering was conducted with the optimal number of clusters chosen based on Silhouette score. Such analysis is helpful to interpret region-wise modularity variability in a context of functional networks to discern important regions in the early brain development for future studies on charting normative and abnormal development.

3   Experiments and Results

Participants and Parameters Settings. We applied our method to a longitudinal high-quality rs-fMRI dataset of 207 infants from neonate to two years old. One subject may have multiple scans at different ages, results in a total of 435 samples. After preprocessing using an infant-dedicated pipeline, individual FC network was constructed based on a 112-regions atlas. Thus, each functional network profile represents a single layer of the used multi-layer network. Due to the hierarchical structure of the brain networks, we investigated the modularity at different scales ($K = 2, 3, 5$, and 7). For each K, an optimal (ω, γ) was determined (Table S1). Results are highly consistent across all K, so we report results at a coarse ($K = 2$) and finer ($K = 5$) scales.

General Consistency Across Subjects and Age. We found a prominent decrease in modularity consistency when the brain was decomposed into more modules (Fig. 2, Fig. S1), hence an increase in individual variability. By visiting each brain region for its modular affiliation and its variability, we identified two major patterns: 1) A high variability in the bilateral superior parietal lobule, supramarginal, and cingulate gyrus, which are all located in high-order cognition-related areas; 2) A high consistency in the amygdala and nucleus accumbens for all modularity levels, which belongs to the limbic system and is responsible for the perception of emotions and basic instinct.

Brain Regions Categories. Most of the brain regions are identified as having low mode flexibility in modular assignment across age. This is reasonable as age-related rewiring is believed to be minimal [15]. For example, when $K = 5$, 83 regions have low flexibility (mode flexibility $= 0$) and 29 have high flexibility (with non-zero mode flexibility, Fig. 3). On the other hand, as evaluated by unlikability, individual variability of modularity for different brain regions largely varied (from 0 to 0.8) but a consistent behavior is noticed. That is, regions with high individual variability remain high, while regions with low individual variability remains low at most of the ages (Fig. 4). For instance, the bilateral superior parietal lobule and supramarginal gyrus have the highest individual variability for both $K = 2$ (u is 0.4–0.5, and 0.5 is the ceiling value in $K = 2$) and $K = 5$ (0.6–0.8). On the contrary, regions with lowest individual variability involved the amygdala, pallidum, and accumbens (see details of how individual variability fluctuate along development in Fig. 4).

Subsequently, with mode flexibility (age effect) and mean unlikability (subject variability), we identified five categories of brain regions. The pattern of each category shows a tightly clustered, symmetric distribution. Each category of regions carries distinct functions from others (Figs. 5 and 6, Figs. S3 and S4).

Fig. 3. Regions with least (0, blue), medium (0.1, orange), and high (> 0.1, green) across-age mode flexibility for $K = 2, 3, 5$, and 7. (Color figure online)

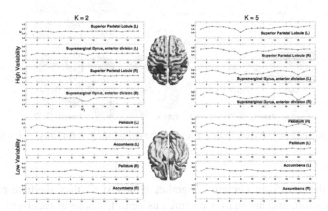

Fig. 4. Top four regions with least and highest variability at two modularity levels.

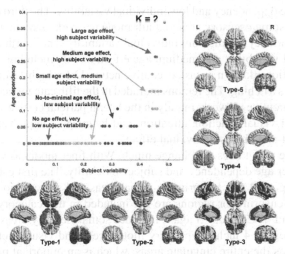

Fig. 5. Different categories/types of brain regions based on their variability characteristics for $K = 2$.

For $K = 2$, the first category of regions has no age dependency and low individual variability. They encompass the ventral visual pathway, ventral anterior cingulate cortex

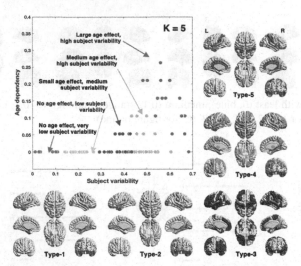

Fig. 6. Different categories/types of brain regions based on their variability characteristics for K = 5.

(vACC), and the lentiform nucleus. Together with vACC, they mediate reward, reinforcement, emotion, and are main structures as neurotransmitter receivers. The second category mainly include primary motor and visual areas. It also includes most of the limbic system and high-order motor and visual areas (or dorsal visual pathway). It again has no-to-minimal age dependency and low individual variability. The third category mainly includes primary somatosensory area, default mode network, and language network. It has low age dependency but medium individual variability. The fourth category has the highest individual variability and medium age effect, mainly including some high-level lateral frontal cortices (known as task executive network) for high-level reasoning, task maintenance, and switching. The regions included in the fifth category constitute the rest part of the task executive network, mainly in the lateral parietal cortices. Their functions include high-level visual function, attention, and language comprehension. It has the greatest age effect and highest individual effect.

For $K = 5$, the result does not change much. With finer modularity structure, more regions have larger age dependency and subject variability. The first category has a few regions left. Category 2 still has primary visual areas and some regions in the ventral visual pathway. Sensorimotor regions are not included in this category but distributed in categories 3 and 4. Category 3 again includes somatosensory areas but also lateral frontal areas. Category 4 includes primary motor areas and visual motion areas while category 5 includes the entire cingulate areas, which is an important part of the limbic system, and the lateral parietal cortices, part of the dorsal visual systems.

4 Conclusions

In this paper, we presented a novel method for investigating and dissociating two important sources of modularity variability in early brain development based on multi-scale, fine-grained multi-layer network analysis. We delineated the first-ever pictures of age dependency and subject variability in the modularity structure of the brain connectome. Our work stresses on the importance of subject variability during brain development. We advocate that future focus needs to be shifted more to neuroimaging markers that mirror individual variability in behavior, cognition, personal traits and their developmental trajectories. Our findings open a new road for detecting neurodevelopmental disorders.

Acknowledgments. This work utilizes approaches developed by NIH grants (1U01MH110274, MH116225, and MH117943) and the efforts of the UNC/UMN Baby Connectome Project (BCP) Consortium.

References

1. Grayson, D.S., Fair, D.A.: Development of large-scale functional networks from birth to adulthood: a guide to the neuroimaging literature. Neuroimage **160**, 15–31 (2017)
2. Yin, W., Chen, M.H., Hung, S.C., Baluyot, K.R., Li, T., Lin, W.: Brain functional development separates into three distinct time periods in the first two years of life. Neuroimage **189**, 715–726 (2019)
3. Gao, W., et al.: Temporal and spatial evolution of brain network topology during the first two years of life. PLoS ONE **6** (2011)
4. Sharda, M., Foster, N.E., Hyde, K.L.: Imaging brain development: benefiting from individual variability: supplementary issue: behavioral neuroscience. J. Exp. Neurosci. **9**, JEN-S32734 (2015)
5. Stoecklein, S., et al.: Variable functional connectivity architecture of the preterm human brain: impact of developmental cortical expansion and maturation. Proc. Natl. Acad. Sci. **117**, 1201–1206 (2020)
6. Gao, W., et al.: Intersubject variability of and genetic effects on the brain's functional connectivity during infancy. J. Neurosci. **34**, 11288–11296 (2014)
7. Meunier, D., Lambiotte, R., Fornito, A., Ersche, K., Bullmore, E.T.: Hierarchical modularity in human brain functional networks. Front. Neuroinform. **3**, 37 (2009)
8. Wen, X., et al.: First-year development of modules and hubs in infant brain functional networks. NeuroImage **185**, 222–235 (2018)
9. Jutla, I.S., Jeub, L.G., Mucha, P.J.: A generalized Louvain method for community detection implemented in MATLAB (2011). http://netwiki.amath.unc.edu/GenLouvain
10. Zhang, H., Stanley, N., Mucha, P.J., Yin, W., Lin, W., Shen, D.: Multi-layer large-scale functional connectome reveals infant brain developmental patterns. In: Frangi, A.F., Schnabel, J.A., Davatzikos, C., Alberola-López, C., Fichtinger, G. (eds.) MICCAI 2018. LNCS, vol. 11072, pp. 136–144. Springer, Cham (2018). https://doi.org/10.1007/978-3-030-00931-1_16
11. Bassett, D.S., Porter, M.A., Wymbs, N.F., Grafton, S.T., Carlson, J.M., Mucha, P.J.: Robust detection of dynamic community structure in networks. Chaos Interdiscipl. J. Nonlinear Sci. **23**, 013142 (2013)
12. Kivela, M., Arenas, A., Barthelemy, M., Gleeson, J.P., Moreno, Y., Porter, M.A.: Multilayer networks. J. Complex Netw. **2**, 203–271 (2014)
13. Pedersen, M., Zalesky, A., Omidvarnia, A., Jackson, G.D.: Multilayer network switching rate predicts brain performance. Proc. Natl. Acad. Sci. **115**, 13376–13381 (2018)
14. Kader, G.D., Perry, M.: Variability for categorical variables. J. Stat. Educ. **15** (2007)
15. Zhang, H., Shen, D., Lin, W.: Resting-state functional MRI studies on infant brains: a decade of gap-filling effort. NeuroImage **185**, 664–686 (2019)

Domain-Invariant Prior Knowledge Guided Attention Networks for Robust Skull Stripping of Developing Macaque Brains

Tao Zhong[1,2], Yu Zhang[1(✉)], Fenqiang Zhao[2], Yuchen Pei[2], Lufan Liao[2], Zhenyuan Ning[1,2], Li Wang[2], Dinggang Shen[2], and Gang Li[2(✉)]

[1] Guangdong Provincial Key Laboratory of Medical Image Processing, School of Biomedical Engineering, Southern Medical University, Guangzhou, China
yuzhang@smu.edu.cn
[2] Department of Radiology and BRIC, University of North Carolina at Chapel Hill, Chapel Hill, USA
gang_li@med.unc.edu

Abstract. Non-human primates, especially macaque monkeys, with close phylogenetic relationship to humans, are highly valuable and widely used animal models for human neuroscience studies. In neuroimaging analysis of macaques, brain extraction or skull stripping of magnetic resonance imaging (MRI) is a crucial step for following processing. However, the current skull stripping methods largely focus on human brains, and thus often lead to unsatisfactory results when applying to macaque brains, especially for macaque brains during early development. In fact, the macaque brain during infancy undergoes regionally-heterogeneous dynamic development, leading to poor and age-variable contrasts between different anatomical structures, posing great challenges for accurate skull stripping. In this study, we propose a novel framework to effectively combine intensity information and domain-invariant prior knowledge, which are important guidance information for accurate brain extraction of developing macaques from 0 to 36 months of age. Specifically, we introduce signed distance map (SDM) and center of gravity distance map (CGDM) based on the intermediate segmentation results and fuse their information by Dual Self-Attention Module (DSAM) instead of local convolution. To evaluate the performance, we adopt two large-scale and challenging MRI datasets from rhesus macaques and cynomolgus macaques, respectively, with totally 361 scans from two different scanners with different imaging protocols. We perform cross-validation by using one dataset for training and the other one for testing. Experimental results show the robustness of our plug-and-play method on cross-source MRI datasets without any transfer learning.

Keywords: Macaques skull stripping · Dual self-attention · Prior knowledge

© Springer Nature Switzerland AG 2020
A. L. Martel et al. (Eds.): MICCAI 2020, LNCS 12267, pp. 22–32, 2020.
https://doi.org/10.1007/978-3-030-59728-3_3

1   Introduction

In both humans and macaques, the early postnatal stage is a particularly dynamic and crucial period of the brain structural, functional and cognitive development. The study of early brain developmental changes in macaques with close phylogenetic relationship to humans is very important to better understand the potential mechanism of normal brain development, evolution and brain disorders [1–3]. The increasing availability of high-resolution MR images of macaque brains [4] enables us to study dynamic early brain development in macaques. Nevertheless, a major obstacle to fully utilize these datasets is the decisive lack of computational tools enabling reliable processing of macaque neurodevelopmental MRI data. Among necessary MRI processing steps, skull stripping, also known as brain extraction or whole-brain segmentation, is a critical step. It performs the process of removing non-brain tissues, such as skull, dura and eyes, and retaining the brain tissues. Hence, it plays an important role for following processing, such as tissue segmentation, cortical surface reconstruction and analysis [5–8]. At present, existing tools [9–11], which were mainly developed for human brains, typically perform poorly on macaque brains, due to remarkable inter-species differences in brain shape and appearances and age-variable contrasts between different anatomical structures as shown in Fig. 1(a). Moreover, during the early postnatal period, the brain and skull show extremely low contrast, making the brain surface difficult to detect. Development of automatic and robust skull stripping algorithms for macaque brains during early postnatal stages is thus of great importance.

Deep learning based methods, especially convolution neural networks (CNNs), have been rapidly developed in the field of medical image analysis in recent years. Due to the strong power in data representation, CNNs show excellent performance in many medical image tasks, including medical image segmentation [12–14]. Among these CNNs segmentation algorithms, U-Net shows robust performance and therefore becomes the current baseline network for various medical image segmentation tasks and inspires many following works [15]. For instance, its 3D form [16] as well as other similar 3D architectures [17,18] have been widely used in MRI segmentation, since it can provide more spatial contextual information and thus is more suitable for the 3D characteristics of MRI than 2D form. However, due to more parameters and higher computational requirements, most of these 3D U-Net-like methods are patch-based, thus lacking global position information. Meanwhile, many previous networks only consider intensity information in feature extraction, ignoring other general prior knowledge. Although these previous networks can automatically learn effective feature hierarchies in a data-driven manner, they are seriously challenged by new unlabeled subjects that differ from the labeled training subjects due to variations in inter-species, scanners, imaging protocols and sites, as illustrated in Fig. 1(b) and (c). A possible solution is to use transfer learning to fit the model to new data. However, in practice, a model that can be used immediately without transfer learning is more ideal and desired.

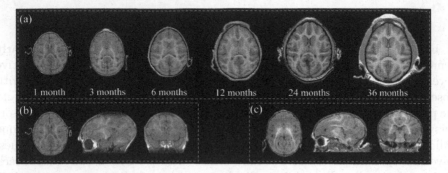

Fig. 1. (a) shows cynomolgus macaque T1w MRI at different ages. (b) and (c) are 1-month-old cynomolgus and rhesus macaque T1w MRI from different sources, respectively.

Our goal is to develop a plug-and-play algorithm for robust skull stripping of macaque brains across ages and data sources. To this end, we propose a Domain-invariant Prior Knowledge Guided Attention Networks (DiPKA-nets), which embeds domain-invariant prior knowledge about the target brain regions. Specifically, we first train a 3D U-Net to achieve an initial rough segmentation. Then, based on this intermediate segmentation, we estimate Center of Gravity (COG) of the brain and the brain boundary. Afterwards, we construct Center of Gravity Distance Map (CGDM) to compensate for global location information that patch-based methods typically miss. Meanwhile, based on this initial brain boundary, we construct Signed Distance Map (SDM), which embeds points and contours into higher-dimensional spaces, enabling it to encode rich information on structural features. These two kinds of prior knowledge will be used as guidance to train subsequent cascaded DiPKA-nets for precise estimation of the brain region. Considering that the input distance maps have a complex relationship with the intensity information, the early fusion as well as the commonly used feature fusion process of direct pixel-wise summation or channel-wise concatenation may introduce irrelevant signals and noise to the final outputs. To address this problem, we use multi-stream architecture and Dual Self-Attention Module (DSAM) to effectively fuse high-level features of intensity information and prior knowledge. In computer vision problems, many studies have demonstrated the effectiveness of attention mechanism [19–21]. Compared with regular feature fusion strategy, DSAM can integrate local features with their corresponding global dependencies and adaptively highlight interdependent channels, thus selectively fuse the useful information from different types of inputs and suppress the respective noise signals. We evaluate the proposed approach on two cross-source challenging datasets, including a cynomolgus macaque MRI dataset and a rhesus macaque MRI dataset. To validate the robustness of our method, we train the network on one dataset and test it on the other one, which is extremely challenging due to large differences in image intensity, appearance, and brain shapes between them. Cross-validation on these two datasets demonstrates the superior

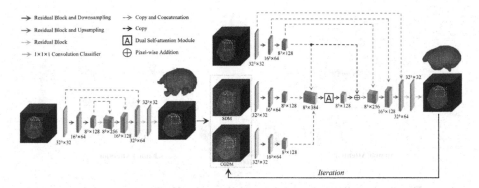

Fig. 2. Diagram of our framework for skull stripping. SDM means Signed Distance Map and CGDM means Center of Gravity Distance Map. For better inspection, the 3D surfaces of model results are also presented.

performance of the proposed method, compared to existing methods. Ablation studies show that both prior knowledge as well as the DSAM can improve the robustness of the model to cross-source data.

2 Method

2.1 Datasets

This study used 361 T1-weighted MR images in total, including N = 206 from cynomolgus macaques and N = 155 from rhesus macaques. Images were scanned by two different scanners with different imaging protocols. The cynomolgus macaque dataset with the age range from 1 to 36 months was acquired by a GE Signa HDxT 3.0T MRI scanner, with the parameters: matri = 256×256, thickness = $1.0 \, \text{mm}$, resolution = $0.4688 \times 0.4688 \times 0.5 \, \text{mm}^3$. The rhesus macaque dataset with the age range from 0.5 to 36 months was acquired by a GE MR750 3.0T MRI scanner, with the following parameters: matrix = 256×256, thickness = $0.8 \, \text{mm}$, resolution = $0.55 \times 0.55 \times 0.8 \, \text{mm}^3$ [4]. The scan age distribution during 0–12, 13–24 and 25–36 months is 60.7%, 30.1% and 9.2% in cynomolgus and 55.5%, 36.8%, and 7.7% in rhesus, respectively. Brain masks were manually-labeled in both datasets using ITK-SNAP [22]. While training the model, we used image standardization to enhance the generalization ability of the model by centralizing data via de-mean.

2.2 Generation of Domain-Invariant Prior Knowledge

To derive the prior knowledge as guidance for the following DiPKA-nets, we need to firstly generate an initial brain mask. Inspired by the recent success of the 3D U-Net in medical image segmentation, we use it as our initial network for a rough estimation [16]. This encoding-decoding architecture takes the intensity

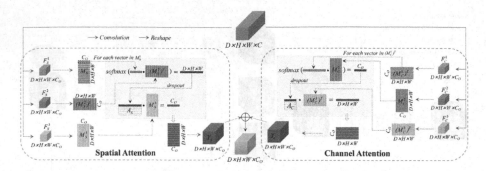

Fig. 3. Details of the spatial and channel self-attention modules.

information as input and finally outputs a prediction of the brain mask. Specially, we replace the convolution with the residual block to avoid gradient vanishing [23]. Except the last convolutional layer for classification, all convolution and deconvolution kernel sizes are set to $3 \times 3 \times 3$. We randomly extract $32 \times 32 \times 32$ 3D patches from training images. Cross-entropy is used as the loss function. Training images and their corresponding brain masks are employed to train the network.

Based on this rough initial estimation, we can directly construct a SDM (i.e., a level set function) with respect to the boundary of brain, as shown in Fig. 2. Essentially, the value at each voxel of SDM is the shortest distance to its nearest point on the boundary of brain and the sign represents whether the point is outside the boundary (negative) or inside the boundary (positive). And the zero level set corresponds to the brain surface. Moreover, the position of COG of the brain can be roughly estimated by using the initial brain extraction. Afterwards, we can construct CGDM, which presents the Euclidean distance from each point in the whole MRI volume to the COG. Such distance can provide the global spatial position of each voxel, which is lacking if only intensity information is used.

Although SDM can also provide location information to certain extent, the accuracy of the location depends on the predicted brain contour. Especially when the predicted contour has relatively larger fluctuating errors, the provided position information also fluctuates greatly. Unlike SDM, the estimated COG typically only deviates slightly from the true center, due to its robustness to the predicted brain contour, thus the overall position information provided is stable and not largely affected by contour changes. That is, SDM is an implicit shape representation that provides information about contour changes, while CGDM provides stable location information to each local patch. Compared to domain-dependent intensity information, these two kinds of prior knowledge are determined by the predicted contour. Although the initial predictions may be biased, the design of the cascaded architecture enables them to be optimized iteratively.

2.3   Domain-Invariant Prior Knowledge Guided Attention Network

Overall Network Architecture. The proposed DiPKA-nets take the intensity information as well as two types of prior knowledge as input. As mentioned earlier, single path for early fusion of features with vast differences may introduce irrelevant noise signals to the final output. To achieve late fusion, we apply a multi-stream architecture to implement separated encoding of these three inputs. The concatenation of these three types of high-level and high-abstract features are then further fed into Dual Self-Attention Module (DSAM), which are composed by a pair of spatial and channel self-attention modules. Afterwards, we apply a pixel-wise addition to combine the attention features and intensity features, which is similar to the residual connections [23]. It is worth noting that only intensity information passes low-level features to up-sampling stream by skip connection, while the two types of prior knowledge do not so that no irrelevant signals of low-level features are introduced. Moreover, we design DiPKA-nets into an iterative form, i.e., the output result can generate the corresponding prior knowledge again and serve as the input of the next DiPKA-net, thus continuously refining the result.

Dual Self-attention Module. To achieve effective fusion of different types of features, each position of the output features should depend on all positions of the input features, and each channel of the output features should depend on all channels of the input features. Local operations such as convolution and deconvolution limit the local receptive field of output features, which is difficult to meet such requirements. To address these limitations of standard CNNs, we apply the DSAM, including spatial and channel attention modules. It captures the long-range relationship of input high-level features (including intensity information and prior knowledge) and reweights the features. For spatial weights, it captures the spatial dependencies between any two positions of the feature maps. For channel weights, it captures the channel dependencies between any two channel maps. Three $1 \times 1 \times 1$ convolutions are used for linear mapping to generate features for calculating internal weights, and compress the channel number to be consistent with the DSAM output features. Figure 3 has clarified these DSAM details.

Spatial Attention Module. Let X represent the input to the attention module, Y_S represent the output of the spatial attention module and C_O is the channel numbers of Y_S. The X is passed through three $1 \times 1 \times 1$ convolutions in three branch, resulting in three features F_S^1, F_S^2 and F_S^3. Then all three features would be unfolded and reshaped into $D \times H \times W \times C_O$ matrices M_S^1, M_S^2 and M_S^3, respectively. The spatial attention mechanism is applied on these three matrices, defined as

$$A_S = softmax(M_S^1 (M_S^2)^T / \sqrt{C_O}), \quad and \quad Y_S = A_S M_S^3, \tag{1}$$

where the dimension of the spatial attention matrix A_S is $(D \times H \times W) \times (D \times H \times W)$ and the dimension of the output Y_S is $(D \times H \times W) \times C_O$. To better

Table 1. Skull stripping results on 155 scans of rhesus macaque dataset. Model is trained by 206 scans of cynomolgus macaque dataset. 'Unet' and 'Unet*' refer to 3D-Unet and its DSAM-version with only intensity information as input, respectively. 'C-Unet' refers to two 3D-Unet as cascade structure, with the first one for rough segmentation and the second one using prior knowledge as additional input. 'C-M-Unet' is similar to 'C-Unet', except that the second network adopts a multi-stream structure to encode intensity information and two prior knowledge respectively. 'DiPKA' replaces the bottom block of the second network in 'C-M-Unet' with Dual Self-Attention Module, so that its second network becomes the proposed DiPKA-net. 'DiPKA2' executes one more DiPKA-net as a iterative refinement to further improve the extraction results.

Method	Unet	Unet*	C-Unet	C-M-Unet
Dice (%)	95.08 ± 2.32	95.27 ± 3.72	77.47 ± 6.35	95.20 ± 1.51
95th HD (mm)	6.17 ± 4.98	2.85 ± 1.99	8.48 ± 1.76	2.16 ± 1.07
ASD (mm)	0.81 ± 0.66	0.72 ± 0.64	3.05 ± 0.90	0.61 ± 0.21
Method	DiPKA	DiPKA2	BET	BSE
Dice (%)	96.27 ± 1.02	$\mathbf{96.45 \pm 0.92}$	74.31 ± 4.48	89.10 ± 9.46
95th HD (mm)	1.70 ± 1.20	$\mathbf{1.47 \pm 0.55}$	13.04 ± 0.99	5.75 ± 4.50
ASD (mm)	0.46 ± 0.15	$\mathbf{0.42 \pm 0.13}$	3.82 ± 2.00	1.78 ± 2.17

describe the details, we take one vector from M_S^1 as an example. In the spatial attention module, this vector will take interaction with all vectors in $(M_S^2)^T$ in sequence, where the dot-production between every two vectors produces a scalar weight for the corresponding M_S^1 vectors. This scalar weight is a weighted sum indicating the relation between one spatial point to all other points, where the weights are normalized through softmax. This process is repeated for all vectors in M_S^1 and finally generates Y_S.

Channel Attention Module. Similarly, three features F_C^1, F_C^2 and F_C^3 are generated from input X and subsequently unfolded and reshaped to $D \times H \times W \times C_O$ matrices M_C^1, M_C^2 and M_C^3. The channel attention mechanism is applied on these three matrices, defined as

$$A_C = softmax((M_C^1)^T M_C^2 / \sqrt{D \times H \times W}), \quad and \quad Y_C = A_C(M_C^3)^T, \quad (2)$$

where the dimension of the channel attention matrix A_C is $C_O \times C_O$ and the dimension of the output Y_C is $C_O \times (D \times H \times W)$. Different from spatial attention modules, each scalar weight generated by $(M_C^1)^T$ and M_C^2 indicates the relation between one channel to all other channels. Finally, both attention matrices Y_S and Y_C are folded to $D \times H \times W \times C_O$ features patches, which are then fused into dual self-attention features by pixel-wise addition.

3   Experiments

We use two popular skull stripping tools BET [9] and BSE [10] for comparison. Besides, we perform ablation studies to show the effectiveness of each part of

Table 2. Skull stripping results on 206 scans of cynomolgus macaque dataset. Model is trained by 155 scans of rhesus macaque dataset. M12 means scans with the age range from 0–12 months, M24 means scans with the age range from 12–24 months, and M36 means scans with the age range from 24–36 months.

Method		Unet	The Proposed	BET	BSE
M12	Dice (%)	87.57 ± 13.12	$\mathbf{96.70 \pm 0.87}$	92.13 ± 4.70	90.34 ± 10.57
	95th HD (mm)	7.01 ± 4.25	$\mathbf{1.42 \pm 0.53}$	4.99 ± 2.75	4.11 ± 4.63
	ASD (mm)	1.36 ± 0.88	$\mathbf{0.36 \pm 0.10}$	1.00 ± 0.70	1.28 ± 1.63
M24	Dice (%)	92.42 ± 2.40	$\mathbf{96.30 \pm 1.10}$	94.23 ± 3.03	92.67 ± 6.10
	95th HD (mm)	6.76 ± 4.12	$\mathbf{1.82 \pm 0.97}$	4.63 ± 3.01	3.26 ± 3.09
	ASD (mm)	1.14 ± 0.50	$\mathbf{0.44 \pm 0.16}$	0.75 ± 0.44	0.99 ± 1.17
M36	Dice (%)	90.39 ± 2.35	$\mathbf{95.75 \pm 1.18}$	91.75 ± 1.73	91.39 ± 10.81
	95th HD (mm)	10.30 ± 3.63	$\mathbf{2.21 \pm 1.12}$	7.74 ± 1.44	3.58 ± 4.63
	ASD (mm)	1.59 ± 0.51	$\mathbf{0.52 \pm 0.17}$	1.15 ± 0.25	1.27 ± 2.23

the proposed DiPKA-nets. Specially, we investigate the following parts: multi-stream architecture, Dual Self-Attention Module, prior knowledge. To demonstrate the cross-source performance of the model, we use 206 scans from cynomolgus macaque dataset for training and 155 scans from rhesus macaque dataset for testing. We quantitatively evaluate the results by using the Dice ratio, 95th percentile Hausdorff distance (95th HD) and average surface distance (ASD). As shown in Table 1, early fusion of low-level features from intensity information and prior knowledge leads to even worse results than only using intensity information, likely due to the introduction of irrelevant signals and noise signals caused by the low-level features of prior knowledge. Adopting the multi-stream architecture can effectively avoid this situation. Compared to commonly-used local convolutions, DSAM can better realize the fusion of the concatenation of features. For the proposed DiPKA-nets, the iteration design, which cannot be realized using only intensity information, can further refine the results, especially in terms of Hausdorff distance and average surface distance.

For cross-validation, we also use 155 scans from rhesus macaque dataset for training and 206 scans from cynomolgus macaque dataset for testing. We divide this testing dataset into three age groups for comparison, as shown in Table 2. Cross-validation results on both datasets demonstrate that, compared with other methods, our method performs more robustly and accurately on cross-source data. Representative results in both datasets are provided in Fig. 4. Brain masks are indicated using red masks and overlaid in the original with-skull images, shown in axial, sagittal, and coronal views. Moreover, the 3D surface rendering results are presented for better inspection. One scan from cynomolgus macaque dataset is shown in the left part, which was scanned at 12 months of age. The right part shows one scan with 1 month of age from rhesus macaque dataset. As can be seen, the scan at earlier age generally has little cerebrospinal fluid, and thus the space between brain and skull is narrow, posing great challenges to brain

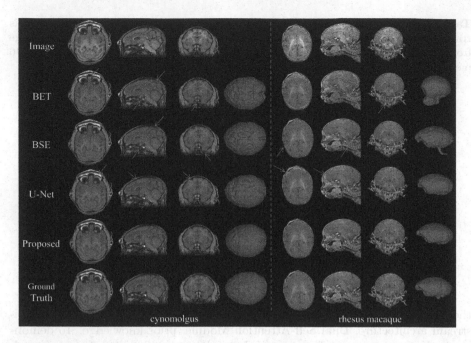

Fig. 4. Representative results in both datasets. Some inaccurate regions are indicated by arrows.

extraction. Compared with the proposed method, the comparison methods are likely to remain extra non-brain tissues near brain stem, while remove portions of the brain, especially at early age.

4   Conclusion

This paper presents the plug-and-play DiPKA-nets for skull stripping of cross-source developing macaque MR images by leveraging domain-invariant prior knowledge. For better fusion of heterogeneous features, we apply Dual Self-Attention Module to aggregate global information through both spatial and channel dimensions. The results of ablation study and cross-validation on two large macaque datasets demonstrate the contribution of each of our designed components, including two types of prior knowledge, multi-stream encoding, Dual Self-Attention Module and cascaded architecture. In future, we will perform more validations on more datasets and make our model publically available to greatly advance neuroimaging studies in macaques.

References

1. Xia, J., Wang, F., Wu, Z., et al.: Mapping hemispheric asymmetries of the macaque cerebral cortex during early brain development. Hum. Brain Mapp. **41**(1), 95–106 (2020)
2. Seidlitz, J., Sponheim, C., Glen, D., et al.: A population MRI brain template and analysis tools for the macaque. Neuroimage **170**, 121–131 (2018)
3. Wang, F., Lian, C., Xia, J., et al.: Construction of spatiotemporal infant cortical surface atlas of rhesus macaque. In: 15th International Symposium on Biomedical Imaging (ISBI 2018), pp. 704–707. IEEE (2018)
4. Young, J., Shi, Y., Niethammer, M., et al.: The UNC-Wisconsin rhesus macaque neurodevelopment database: a structural MRI and DTI database of early postnatal development. Front. Neurosci. **11**, 29–29 (2017). https://www.nitrc.org/projects/uncuw_macdevmri
5. Wang, L., Nie, D., Li, G., et al.: Benchmark on automatic six-month-old infant brain segmentation algorithms: the iSeg-2017 challenge. IEEE Trans. Med. Imaging **38**(9), 2219–2230 (2019)
6. Li, G., Wang, L., Yap, P., et al.: Computational neuroanatomy of baby brains: a review. NeuroImage **185**, 906–925 (2019)
7. Zhao, F., et al.: Harmonization of infant cortical thickness using surface-to-surface cycle-consistent adversarial networks. In: Shen, D., et al. (eds.) MICCAI 2019. LNCS, vol. 11767, pp. 475–483. Springer, Cham (2019). https://doi.org/10.1007/978-3-030-32251-9_52
8. Dubois, J., Lefèvre, J., Angleys, H., et al.: The dynamics of cortical folding waves and prematurity-related deviations revealed by spatial and spectral analysis of gyrification. Neuroimage **185**, 934–946 (2019)
9. Smith, S.: Fast robust automated brain extraction. Hum. Brain Mapp. **17**(3), 143–155 (2002)
10. Shattuck, D., Sandor-Leahy, S., Schaper, K., et al.: Magnetic resonance image tissue classification using a partial volume model. NeuroImage **13**(5), 856–876 (2001)
11. Wang, Y., Nie, J., Yap, P., et al.: Knowledge-guided robust MRI brain extraction for diverse large-scale neuroimaging studies on humans and non-human primates. PLoS ONE **9**(1), e77810 (2014)
12. Liang, S., et al.: Deep-learning-based detection and segmentation of organs at risk in nasopharyngeal carcinoma computed tomographic images for radiotherapy planning. Eur. Radiol. **29**(4), 1961–1967 (2018). https://doi.org/10.1007/s00330-018-5748-9
13. Zhong, T., Huang, X., Tang, F., et al.: Boosting-based cascaded convolutional neural networks for the segmentation of CT organs-at-risk in nasopharyngeal carcinoma. Med. Phys. **46**(12), 5602–5611 (2019)
14. Tang, F., et al.: Postoperative glioma segmentation in CT image using deep feature fusion model guided by multi-sequence MRIs. Eur. Radiol. **30**(2), 823–832 (2019). https://doi.org/10.1007/s00330-019-06441-z
15. Ronneberger, O., Fischer, P., Brox, T.: U-Net: convolutional networks for biomedical image segmentation. In: Navab, N., Hornegger, J., Wells, W.M., Frangi, A.F. (eds.) MICCAI 2015. LNCS, vol. 9351, pp. 234–241. Springer, Cham (2015). https://doi.org/10.1007/978-3-319-24574-4_28

16. Çiçek, Ö., Abdulkadir, A., Lienkamp, S.S., Brox, T., Ronneberger, O.: 3D U-Net: learning dense volumetric segmentation from sparse annotation. In: Ourselin, S., Joskowicz, L., Sabuncu, M.R., Unal, G., Wells, W. (eds.) MICCAI 2016. LNCS, vol. 9901, pp. 424–432. Springer, Cham (2016). https://doi.org/10.1007/978-3-319-46723-8_49
17. Dolz, J., Gopinath, K., Yuan, J., et al.: HyperDense-Net: a hyper-densely connected CNN for multi-modal image segmentation. Eur. Radiol. **38**(5), 1116–1126 (2018)
18. Wang, L., et al.: Volume-based analysis of 6-month-old infant brain MRI for autism biomarker identification and early diagnosis. In: Frangi, A.F., Schnabel, J.A., Davatzikos, C., Alberola-López, C., Fichtinger, G. (eds.) MICCAI 2018. LNCS, vol. 11072, pp. 411–419. Springer, Cham (2018). https://doi.org/10.1007/978-3-030-00931-1_47
19. Fu, J., Liu, J., Tian, H., et al.: Dual attention network for scene segmentation. In: Proceedings of the IEEE Conference on Computer Vision and Pattern Recognition (CVPR 2019), pp. 3146–3154. IEEE (2019)
20. Wang, X., Girshick, R., Gupta, R., et al.: Non-local neural networks. In: Proceedings of the IEEE Conference on Computer Vision and Pattern Recognition (CVPR 2018), pp. 7794–7803. IEEE (2018)
21. Zhao, H., et al.: PSANet: point-wise spatial attention network for scene parsing. In: Ferrari, V., Hebert, M., Sminchisescu, C., Weiss, Y. (eds.) ECCV 2018. LNCS, vol. 11213, pp. 270–286. Springer, Cham (2018). https://doi.org/10.1007/978-3-030-01240-3_17
22. Yushkevich, P., Piven, J., Hazlett, C., et al.: User-guided 3D active contour segmentation of anatomical structures: significantly improved efficiency and reliability. Neuroimage **31**(3), 1116–1128 (2006). www.itksnap.org
23. He, K., Zhang, X., Ren, S., et al.: Deep residual learning for image recognition. In: Proceedings of the IEEE Conference on Computer Vision and Pattern Recognition (CVPR 2016), pp. 770–778. IEEE (2016)

Parkinson's Disease Detection from fMRI-Derived Brainstem Regional Functional Connectivity Networks

Nandinee Fariah Haq[✉], Jiayue Cai, Tianze Yu, Martin J. McKeown, and Z. Jane Wang

The University of British Columbia, Vancouver, Canada
nandinee@ece.ubc.ca

Abstract. Parkinson's disease is the second most prevalent neurode-generative disorder after Alzheimer's disease. The brainstem, despite its early and crucial involvement in Parkinson's disease, is largely unexplored in the domain of functional medical imaging. Here we propose a data-driven, connectivity-pattern based framework to extract functional sub-regions within the brainstem and devise a machine learning based tool that can discriminate Parkinson's disease from healthy participants. We first propose a novel framework to generate a group model of brainstem functional sub-regions by optimizing a community quality function, and generate a brainstem regional network. We then extract graph theoretic features from this brainstem regional network and, after employing an SVM classifier, achieve a sensitivity of disease detection of 94% – comparable to approaches that normally require whole-brain analysis. To the best of our knowledge, this is the first study that employs brainstem functional sub-regions for Parkinson's disease detection.

Keywords: Parkinson's disease · Brainstem · Functional sub-regions

1 Introduction

Parkinson's disease (PD) is the second most prevalent neurodegenerative disorder after Alzheimer's disease [31]. Parkinsonism is characterized by a progressive psychomotor syndrome reflecting the multi-system nature of the disease, that may include rigidity, tremor, bradykinesia, postural instability, depression, sleep disturbances, and dementia [5,18]. Parkinson's disease is still considered largely idiopathic with the pathophysiology of the disease is not fully understood [30]. There is no cure available, and treatments are designed to reduce the symptoms once the disease has been clinically diagnosed. Due to PD's overlap with other neurological conditions, especially in its early stages, the misdiagnosis rate can be very high [1,22]. Therefore an imaging based non-invasive technique for Parkinson's disease diagnosis can help in the characterization of the disease and more accurately differentiate between similar disorders, especially during the early stages of the disease when clinical symptoms are unnoticeable.

© Springer Nature Switzerland AG 2020
A. L. Martel et al. (Eds.): MICCAI 2020, LNCS 12267, pp. 33–43, 2020.
https://doi.org/10.1007/978-3-030-59728-3_4

The motor symptoms associated with Parkinson's disease are caused mainly by a progressive loss of dopaminergic neurons in the substantia nigra in the brainstem. Hence Parkinson's disease is often associated with brainstem dysfunction and many brainstem alterations occur during early disease stages when the clinical symptoms may be unnoticeable [8,15]. Yet despite its importance in Parkinson's disease and other neurodegenerative processes, the brainstem and its sub-structures are relatively unexplored in functional medical image analysis [13]. Although functional Magnetic Resonance Imaging (fMRI) has been used widely to characterize brain functionality and connectivity alterations in PD, all studies have emphasized whole-brain cortical networks [9,14,23,30]. Only a few studies are designed to develop a data-driven diagnostic tool for Parkinson's disease classification [6,7,29], and these studies also incorporate whole-brain cortical and subcortical structures. The literature on brainstem subregions mainly consist of extraction of anatomical regions [3,4,17,19,26] whereas data-driven functional segments remained unexplored.

In this work, we propose a data-driven, connectivity-pattern based framework to extract functional sub-regions within the brainstem and devise a machine learning based tool that is sensitive to Parkinson's disease-related changes. We first propose a novel framework to extract data-driven functional segments within the brainstem on a participant-by-participant basis by optimizing a community quality function. We then combine the participant-level partitions via a consensus-based partition agglomeration approach to generate a group-model for brainstem functional sub-regions. Data-driven features are then extracted from the proposed group-model based regional network and a soft-margin Support Vector Machine (SVM) classification is employed for Parkinson's disease detection. We validate the proposed method on a balanced dataset of thirty-four participants. To the best of our knowledge, this is the first study to target the extraction and incorporation of brainstem regional functional networks in Parkinson's disease detection.

2   Materials and Methods

2.1   Data Acquisition and Preprocessing Protocols

Dataset-I. The dataset consists of fifteen healthy control (HC) participants. The participants underwent a resting-state fMRI (rsfMRI) scanning session at the University of British Columbia (UBC). The average age of the healthy participants was 69.4 ± 4.76 years and out of these fifteen, five were female and the rest of them were male participants. The study was approved by the UBC research ethics board and the participants provided their written, informed consent before the study.

Dataset-II. The dataset consists of seventeen individuals diagnosed with Parkinson's disease (PD), and seventeen age-matched elderly healthy control (HC) participants. The individuals had not gone through any prior neurosurgical procedures and did not have a history of other neurological diseases.

The participants underwent a resting-state fMRI scanning session. The average age of the patients with Parkinson's disease was 67.7 ± 4.7 years and out of these seventeen, eight were female and the rest of them were male participants. For the healthy control participants, the average age was 68.1 ± 5.2 years and out of the seventeen participants, ten were female. For the individuals diagnosed with Parkinson's disease, the severity of motor symptoms were assessed with the Hoehn and Yahr (H&Y) scale [11] and Unified Parkinson's Disease Rating Scale (UPDRS) motor examination score [12]. All individuals with Parkinson's disease had mild to moderate Parkinson's disease (H&Y stage 1–3) with a disease duration of 5.8 ± 3.7 years and UPDRS score of 26.7 ± 11.5. The study was approved by the UBC research ethics board and the participants provided their written, informed consent prior to the study.

This dataset was the rsfMRI part of a larger task-based fMRI study that involved a horizontally-oriented balance simulator based on the principle of an inverted pendulum. Since balance deficits in PD are typically dopamine 'unresponsive', we specifically tested participants on medication. PD participants were on Levodopa medication and scanned exactly one hour after the intake of their medication to coincide with their subjectively best clinical 'on' condition. Participants were debriefed afterwards. While participants were instructed to "not think of anything in particular", we note that this was followed up by a motor-task (balance) study (not reported here), and no one was asleep at the start of the motor task. Participants were excluded if any medical issues influenced their balanced (excessive levodopa-induced dyskinesia, documented proprioceptive loss, etc.). In total three participant's data were excluded from the study. Out of the seventeen PD participants two had an H&Y score of 3, three participants had an H&Y score of 1 and the rest of the participants had a score of 2.

Imaging Protocol. The resting state fMRI data were acquired using a 3T MRI scanner (Achieva, Philips Healthcare, Best, The Netherlands) equipped with a headcoil. The participants laid on their back with their eyes closed during the examination during which a whole-brain T1-weighted images were acquired with a repetition time of 7.9 ms, echo time of 3.5 ms and flip angle of 8°. The functional run spanned eight minutes during which blood oxygen level dependent (BOLD) contrast echo-planar (EPI) T2*-weighted images were acquired with a repetition time of 2000 ms, echo time of 30 ms and flip angle of 90°. The field of view (FOV) was set to 240 mm × 240 mm and the matrix size was 80 × 80. In total 240 time-points were acquired with 3 mm thickness. The pixel size was 3 mm × 3 mm. Voxels were resliced to ensure isotropic voxels of 3 mm on each size. Thirty-six axial slices were collected in each volume, with a gap thickness of 1 mm. The duration of the fMRI task was 8 min based on a single trial per participant. We have done statistics on head movement and the mean volume-to-volume framewise displacement was less than 0.34 mm. Statistical comparison found no significant main effect of group, or interaction effect between group and task, for mean framewise displacement. As part of our pipeline, FreeSurfer segmentations were visualized to ensure accuracy. The resolution for the 3D structural MRI was 1 mm × 1 mm, with a scan duration of 394 s, flip angle of 8°, matrix size of 256 × 256 and a repetition time of 7.73 ms.

Preprocessing. The fMRI datasets were processed with SPM12 software package using the framework reported in [32]. The preprocessing steps included despiking, slice time correction, 3-D isotropic reslicing, slice time correction, and a motion correction technique reported in [32]. After the preprocessing and motion correction, only minimal motion was estimated in the brainstem. Spatial normalization was carried out to all fMRI volumes to transform the data to a common MNI space. The nuisance regression was used to remove white-matter signal, and cerebro-spinal fluid signal. The fMRI signal was then detrended, filtered and iteratively smoothed with a Gaussian kernel of 6 mm. After pre-processing, the motion observed inside the brainstem was less than 0.05 mm, rotation (pitch, roll, yaw) was less than 0.4°.

2.2   Group Model Generation for Brainstem Functional Sub-regions

We first generated a group model of the brainstem functional sub-regions with the healthy control participants from Dataset-I. For each of the healthy control participants, we generated the brainstem connectivity network where voxels were represented as nodes and edges between the nodes were generated using the following equation: $e_{mn} = \delta(\rho_{mn} \geq \rho_T)$, where $\delta(\cdot)$ is an indicator function. ρ_{mn} represents the Pearson correlation coefficient between the fMRI timecourses of the brainstem voxels m and n, and ρ_T is a threshold that ensures the degree distribution of the voxel nodes in the generated connectivity network follows a power-law pattern, to comply with previous observations on real networks [2,21,24]. $e_{mn} = 1$ represents the existence of an edge between nodes m and n. The connectivity network was generated for each healthy participant separately.

The extraction of the functional sub-regions from the brainstem connectivity network was formulated as a network community detection problem. To extract the functional sub-networks, we incorporated an unsupervised community detection approach that has shown to outperform other literature-based methods in detecting small sub-networks from a parent network [16]. The method is based on maximizing a community quality function named *weighted modularity*. For a brainstem network with L edges and N nodes divided into k sub-regions, the weighted-modularity, q is defined as:

$$q = \sum_i [1 + 2l_i/(n_i^2 - n_i)][(l_i/L) - (d_i/2L)^2] = \sum_i \lambda_i m_i \qquad (1)$$

Here, n_i is the total number of nodes and l_i is the total number of edges within the brainstem sub-region-i, and d_i is the sum of degrees of nodes in the sub-region-i. The term λ_i represents how strong a brainstem sub-network is in terms of its conductance, and the term m_i represents how far the sub-network community is from that of a random network, defined as the difference between the fraction of edges that exist within the members of a sub-network i and the expected such fraction if the edges were distributed at random. The community detection method proposed in [16] targets to find such a partition of the network for which the weighted-modularity of the network, q is maximum by iteratively merging nodes until no further merging increases the quality metric.

We applied the aforementioned community detection method on each participant separately to generate participant-level partitions. The partition with the highest weighted-modularity produced the functional sub-regions at the participant-space. Then a partition agglomeration approach based on consensus clustering [28] was applied on the participant-level partitions to generate a consensus network that combines the participant-space partitions. In the consensus network, edges are drawn between two brainstem voxel nodes m and n if m and n ended up in the same sub-region in the majority of the participant-level partitions. Then we applied the weighted-modularity based community detection approach on the consensus network to find the optimal partition and divide the network into k sub-regions. The final partition with k sub-regions represented the group model of the brainstem functional sub-regions.

2.3 Brainstem Regional Connectivity Network Generation

In the second phase of the framework, we generated brainstem regional connectivity networks for all the participants in Dataset-II individually. We first map the group-model of brainstem functional sub-regions to each of the participant's fMRI space in Dataset-II. For a participant-s we then generated brainstem regional connectivity network, $\mathcal{G}$ with k nodes where nodes represent each of the k functional sub-regions derived from the group-model in Sect. 2.2. The representative regional signal, r_c of a brainstem functional sub-region c with n_c voxels is generated by taking the mean of the fMRI signals of all voxels included in the associated sub-region, i.e. $r_c = (1/n_c) \sum_{x;x \in c} v_x$; where v_x is the fMRI signal for the x-th voxel. The edges between the nodes in $\mathcal{G}$ are generated by two fMRI-based connectivity models as described below.

FDR-Controlled PC Based Connectivity Network (PC_{fdr}). To generate the edges of the brainstem regional connectivity network, $\mathcal{G}$ we first used the FDR-controlled PC algorithm (PC_{fdr}) [20] which estimates the functional connectivity between the sub-regions from their associated signals r_c, where $c \in \{1, 2, \cdots, k\}$. The PC_{fdr} algorithm is suitably adapted from the PC algorithm [27], which is a conditional independence based network structure learning approach, by incorporating a false discovery rate (FDR) control procedure. Therefore, the PC_{fdr} algorithm can control the FDR of the estimated network structure under a pre-defined level. In this study, the significance level of the FDR was set to be 0.05. By applying the PC_{fdr} algorithm, a $k \times k$ binary symmetric matrix was obtained, with functional connectivity indicated by the non-zero elements of the estimated matrix, which represent the edges for the PC_{fdr}-based brainstem regional connectivity network, $\mathcal{G}_{PC_{fdr}}$.

Sparse Inverse Covariance Based Connectivity Network ($SICov$). The inverse covariance matrix is another efficient way to estimate the edges of the network by incorporating their functional connectivity. Under the assumed sparse nature of functional connectivity between the k brainstem functional sub-regions, a regularization strategy can be applied to the inverse covariance matrix generated from the associated regional signals r_c, $c \in \{1, 2, \cdots, k\}$. Here we incorporated the connectivity modeling approach using the sparse inverse covariance matrix ($SICov$) [10], which was estimated by imposing a sparsity constraint on the inverse covariance matrix through the Least Absolute Shrinkage and Selection Operator (LASSO) method. This results in a $k \times k$ sparse weighted symmetric matrix, with functional connectivity indicated by the non-zero elements of the estimated matrix. These non-zero elements of the matrix generated the edges for the $SICov$-based network $\mathcal{G}_{SICov}$. Specifically, a sparse estimate of the inverse covariance matrix is obtained by minimizing the penalized negative log likelihood: $\hat{\Theta} = \arg\min\{tr(\mathcal{S}\Theta) - \log|\Theta| + \Lambda\|\Theta\|_1\}$; where Θ is the inverse covariance matrix, $\mathcal{S}$ is the sample covariance matrix, $\|\Theta\|_1$ is the element-wise L1-norm of Θ, and Λ is the penalty parameter controlling the sparsity of the network.

2.4   Feature Extraction and Classification

After generating the brainstem regional connectivity network, $\mathcal{G}$ for each participant separately, the following graph theoretic features were extracted using the brain functional connectivity toolbox [25] that represent the topology of the network:

Characteristic Path Length (CPL): defined as the average shortest path length between all pairs of nodes in the network.

Global Efficiency (GE): defined as the average over the inverse of the shortest path lengths in the brainstem regional network.

Clustering Coefficient (CC): for one node, defined as the fraction of the node's neighbors that are also neighbors of each other. Over a network, the clustering coefficient is defined as the average clustering coefficient of its nodes.

Modularity (MD): defined as the sum of the differences between the fraction of edges that exist within a group of nodes, or *modules* and the expected such fraction if the edges of the network were distributed at random. These differences are summed over all the modules of the network when the network is divided into non-overlapping modules such a way that maximizes the number of within-module edges while minimizing between-module edges.

Transitivity (TS): defined as the ratio of triangles (any three nodes that are connected with three edges) to triplets (any three nodes that are connected with two or more edges) in the network.

Assortativity Coefficient (AC): defined as the correlation coefficient between the degrees of all connected nodes. The degree of a node is the total number of edges attached to the node, and a positive assortativity coefficient indicates that nodes of the network tend to link to other nodes with a similar degree.

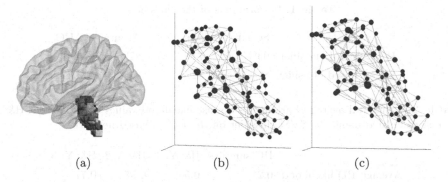

(a)   (b)   (c)

Fig. 1. Brainstem functional regions. (a) Sagittal view of the brainstem functional sub-regions. (b) Brainstem regional connectivity network for a healthy control participant. (c) Brainstem regional connectivity network for a PD patient. Both networks were generated from PC_{fdr}-based connectivity model.

Fiedler Value (FD): defined as the second smallest eigenvalue of the Laplacian matrix of the network.

Normalized Fiedler Value (nFD): defined as the second smallest eigenvalue of the normalized Laplacian matrix of the network.

Sychronizability (SYC): defined as the ratio of the maximum eigenvalue to the second smallest eigenvalue of the Laplacian matrix of the network.

We trained two different classifiers to classify patients diagnosed with Parkinson's disease and healthy control participants using the features extracted from $\mathcal{G}_{PC_{fdr}}$ and $\mathcal{G}_{SICov}$ networks separately. Soft margin Support Vector Machine (SVM) classifiers were trained on each feature set separately by tuning two parameters: the margin violation penalty weight, C, and the Radial Basis Function (RBF) kernel parameter, γ. The classifiers were tuned by cross-validation on a leave-one-participant-out basis. We investigated the possible combinations of C and γ by a grid search on $C \in \{2^{-10}, 2^{-9}, \cdots, 2^{10}\}$ and $\gamma \in \{2^{-10}, 2^{-9}, \cdots, 2^{10}\}$, and the cross-validation was targeted at maximizing the Area Under the receiver operating characteristic Curve (AUC).

3   Results

We generated the group model of brainstem functional sub-regions in healthy individuals from the Dataset-I. The framework generated 84 functional sub-regions in the brainstem from healthy individuals and all the functional sub-regions were spatially contiguous. The classification experiments were carried out on a separate dataset (Dataset-II) with an equal number of patients diagnosed with Parkinson's disease and age-matched healthy individuals. The brainstem functional sub-regions derived from Dataset-I were mapped to each of the participants in Dataset-II. For the participants in Dataset-II, we then generated the brainstem regional connectivity network with two connectivity modeling approaches- PC_{fdr} and $SICov$. Each of the brainstem regional connectivity

Table 1. Performance of the classifiers.

	Sensitivity	Specificity	Accuracy	AUC
PC_{fdr} based classifier	94%	71%	82%	0.81
$SICov$ based classifier	82%	82%	82%	0.77

Table 2. Generated average Parkinson's disease likelihood values with different H&Y scores, calculated using the SVM classifier on the PC_{fdr}-based network.

	HC samples	H& Y: 1	H& Y:2	H& Y: 3
Average PD likelihood	0.21	0.56	0.57	0.77

networks consisted of 84 nodes, where nodes represent the derived brainstem functional sub-regions. Figure 1 shows the generated group model for brainstem functional sub-regions along with the examples of the generated PC_{fdr}-based brainstem regional networks for one healthy control and one Parkinson's disease patient. The networks, as can be seen from Fig. 1, are structurally different.

The proposed nine-dimensional feature vector was extracted from each of the networks. We trained the classifiers based on the feature sets generated from PC_{fdr}-based and $SICov$-based networks separately. The classifiers were cross-validated on a leave-one-participant-out basis. Table 1 reports the classification performances with different connectivity models at optimal operating points, where cutoff is applied to the *a posteriori* class probabilities. With the $SICov$-based classifier, we were able to achieve 82% sensitivity and 82% specificity. The classifier trained on features from the PC_{fdr}-based brainstem regional network was able to achieve a better sensitivity of 94% with only one patient misclassified as healthy control. We also investigated the average Parkison's disease likelihood generated by this classifier, and the likelihood values for patient's with different H&Y scores are reported in Table 2. We observed that the mean Parkinson's disease likelihood increases with the severity of the disease. For the patients with the H&Y score of 1, the generated mean PD likelihood was 0.56, whereas, for more severe patients with H&Y score of 3, an average likelihood of 0.77 was observed.

As no prior studies incorporated brainstem regional functional connectivities for Parkinson's disease detection, we could not compare our approach with literature-based methods. However, one of the best performing classifiers based on whole-brain fMRI connectivity on a balanced dataset was reported in [7], where a sensitivity of 90.47% was achieved with 150 features, and a higher sensitivity of 95.24% was achieved when the number of features was tuned for maximizing classification performances, with 149.15 features on average. More recent work used fewer features to achieve an accuracy of 85.7% using whole-brain dynamic connectivities on a less balanced dataset (sensitivity was not reported) [6]. Although our reported classification performances are not better than [7], note that here we have only used the brainstem regional connectivities – the site of initial patholoy in PD and therefore likely to occur early – whereas in [7] whole-brain connectivity network was used. Nevertheless, we could achieve promising performance with only nine features extracted from brainstem regional network alone, as opposed to ~150 features in [7]. The performance of our classifier shows the potential of brainstem regional connectivity based features as Parkinson's disease biomarkers.

4 Conclusion

We have developed a novel data-driven framework for Parkinson's disease detection solely from brainstem regional functional connectivity networks. The method incorporates a community detection algorithm on a participant-level and a consensus-clustering based partition agglomeration approach to generate group-level brainstem functional sub-regions. Features from this group-level approach were sensitive to Parkinson's disease detection. With a soft margin support vector machine classifier, we were able to achieve 94% sensitivity with an AUC of 0.81.

To the best of our knowledge, this is the first study that targets the generation of brainstem functional sub-regions and the application of the associated network in Parkinson's disease detection. Our next target is to incorporate the connectivity alterations of the extracted brainstem sub-regions with other cortical and subcortical brain regions into the Parkinson's disease detection framework.

References

1. Bajaj, N.P., Gontu, V., Birchall, J., Patterson, J., Grosset, D.G., Lees, A.J.: Accuracy of clinical diagnosis in tremulous parkinsonian patients: a blinded video study. J. Neurol. Neurosurg. Psychiatry **81**(11), 1223–1228 (2010)
2. Barabási, A.L., Albert, R.: Emergence of scaling in random networks. Science **286**(5439), 509–512 (1999)
3. Bianciardi, M., Toschi, N., Edlow, B.L., Eichner, C., Setsompop, K., et al.: Toward an in vivo neuroimaging template of human brainstem nuclei of the ascending arousal, autonomic, and motor systems. Brain Connect. **5**(10), 597–607 (2015)
4. Bianciardi, M., et al.: In vivo functional connectome of human brainstem nuclei of the ascending arousal, autonomic, and motor systems by high spatial resolution 7-Tesla fMRI. Magn. Reson. Mater. Phys. Biol. Med. **29**(3), 451–462 (2016). https://doi.org/10.1007/s10334-016-0546-3
5. Braak, H., Del Tredici, K., Rüb, U., De Vos, R.A., Steur, E.N.J., Braak, E.: Staging of brain pathology related to sporadic Parkinson's disease. Neurobiol. Aging **24**(2), 197–211 (2003)
6. Cai, J., Liu, A., Mi, T., Garg, S., Trappe, W., et al.: Dynamic graph theoretical analysis of functional connectivity in Parkinson's disease: the importance of Fiedler Value. IEEE J. Biomed. Health Inf. **23**(4), 1720–1729 (2019)
7. Chen, Y., Yang, W., Long, J., Zhang, Y., Feng, J., et al.: Discriminative analysis of Parkinson's disease based on whole-brain functional connectivity. PLOS ONE **10**(4), e0124153 (2015)

8. Del Tredici, K., Rüb, U., De Vos, R.A., Bohl, J.R., Braak, H.: Where does Parkinson disease pathology begin in the brain? J. Neuropathol. Exp. Neurol. **61**(5), 413–426 (2002)
9. Engels, G., Vlaar, A., McCoy, B., Scherder, E., Douw, L.: Dynamic functional connectivity and symptoms of Parkinson's disease: a resting-state fMRI study. Front. Aging Neurosci. **10**, 388 (2018)
10. Friedman, J., Hastie, T., Tibshirani, R.: Sparse inverse covariance estimation with the graphical lasso. Biostatistics **9**(3), 432–441 (2008)
11. Goetz, C.G., Poewe, W., Rascol, O., Sampaio, C., Stebbins, G.T., et al.: Movement Disorder Society Task Force report on the Hoehn and Yahr staging scale: status and recommendations. Mov. Disord. **19**(9), 1020–1028 (2004)
12. Goetz, C.G., Tilley, B.C., Shaftman, S.R., Stebbins, G.T., Fahn, S., et al.: Movement Disorder Society-sponsored revision of the Unified Parkinson's Disease Rating Scale (MDS-UPDRS): scale presentation and clinimetric testing results. Mov. Disord. **23**(15), 2129–2170 (2008)
13. González-Villà, S., Oliver, A., Valverde, S., Wang, L., Zwiggelaar, R., Lladó, X.: A review on brain structures segmentation in magnetic resonance imaging. Artif. Intell. Med. **73**, 45–69 (2016)
14. Göttlich, M., Münte, T.F., Heldmann, M., Kasten, M., Hagenah, J., Krämer, U.M.: Altered resting state brain networks in Parkinson's disease. PLOS ONE **8**(10), e77336 (2013)
15. Grinberg, L.T., Rueb, U., di Lorenzo Alho, A.T., Heinsen, H.: Brainstem pathology and non-motor symptoms in PD. J. Neurol. Sci. **289**(1–2), 81–88 (2010)
16. Haq, N.F., Moradi, M., Wang, Z.J.: Community structure detection from networks with weighted modularity. Pattern Recogn. Lett. **122**, 14–22 (2019)
17. Iglesias, J.E., Van Leemput, K., Bhatt, P., Casillas, C., et al.: Bayesian segmentation of brainstem structures in MRI. NeuroImage **113**, 184–195 (2015)
18. Jankovic, J.: Parkinson's disease: clinical features and diagnosis. J. Neurol. Neurosurg. Psychiatry **79**(4), 368–376 (2008)
19. Lehéricy, S., Sharman, M.A., Santos, C.L.D., Paquin, R., Gallea, C.: Magnetic resonance imaging of the substantia nigra in Parkinson's disease. Mov. Disord. **27**(7), 822–830 (2012)
20. Li, J., Wang, Z.J.: Controlling the false discovery rate of the association/causality structure learned with the PC algorithm. J. Mach. Learn. Res. **10**, 475–514 (2009)
21. Maslov, S., Sneppen, K.: Specificity and stability in topology of protein networks. Science **296**(5569), 910–913 (2002)
22. Meara, J., Bhowmick, B.K., Hobson, P.: Accuracy of diagnosis in patients with presumed Parkinson's disease. Age Ageing **28**(2), 99–102 (1999)
23. Pyatigorskaya, N., Gallea, C., Garcia-Lorenzo, D., Vidailhet, M., Lehericy, S.: A review of the use of magnetic resonance imaging in Parkinson's disease. Ther. Adv. Neurol. Disord. **7**(4), 206–220 (2014)
24. Redner, S.: How popular is your paper? An empirical study of the citation distribution. Eur. Phys. J. B-Condens. Matter Complex Syst. **4**(2), 131–134 (1998)
25. Rubinov, M., Sporns, O.: Complex network measures of brain connectivity: uses and interpretations. NeuroImage **52**(3), 1059–1069 (2010)
26. Sander, L., Pezold, S., Andermatt, S., Amann, M., Meier, D., et al.: Accurate, rapid and reliable, fully automated MRI brainstem segmentation for application in multiple sclerosis and neurodegenerative diseases. Hum. Brain Mapp. **40**(14), 4091–4104 (2019)
27. Spirtes, P., Glymour, C.N., Scheines, R., Heckerman, D.: Causation, Prediction, and Search. MIT Press, Cambridge (2000)

28. Strehl, A., Ghosh, J.: Cluster ensembles - a knowledge reuse framework for combining multiple partitions. J. Mach. Learn. Res. **3**, 583–617 (2002)
29. Szewczyk-Krolikowski, K., Menke, R.A., Rolinski, M., Duff, E., Salimi-Khorshidi, G., et al.: Functional connectivity in the basal ganglia network differentiates PD patients from controls. Neurology **83**(3), 208–214 (2014)
30. Tahmasian, M., Bettray, L.M., van Eimeren, T., Drzezga, A., Timmermann, L., et al.: A systematic review on the applications of resting-state fMRI in Parkinson's disease: does dopamine replacement therapy play a role? Cortex **73**, 80–105 (2015)
31. Willis, A.W.: Parkinson disease in the elderly adult. Mo. Med. **110**(5), 406 (2013)
32. Yu, T.: A robust strategy for cleaning motion artifacts in resting state fMRI (2019). https://doi.org/10.14288/1.0379472

Persistent Feature Analysis of Multimodal Brain Networks Using Generalized Fused Lasso for EMCI Identification

Jin Li[1], Chenyuan Bian[1,3], Dandan Chen[1], Xianglian Meng[2], Haoran Luo[1],
Hong Liang[1(✉)] (iD), and Li Shen[3(✉)] (iD)

[1] College of Automation, Harbin Engineering University, Harbin, Heilongjiang, China
lh@hrbeu.edu.cn
[2] School of Computer Science and Information Engineering, Changzhou
Institute of Technology, Changzhou, Jiangsu, China
[3] Department of Biostatistics, Epidemiology and Informatics, Perelman School of Medicine,
University of Pennsylvania, Philadelphia, PA, USA
li.shen@pennmedicine.upenn.edu

Abstract. Early Mild Cognitive Impairment (EMCI) involves very subtle changes in brain pathological process, and thus identification of EMCI can be challenging. By jointly analyzing cross-information among different neuroimaging data, an increased interest recently emerges in multimodal fusion to better understand clinical measurements with respect to both structural and functional connectivity. In this paper, we propose a novel multimodal brain network modeling method for EMCI identification. Specifically, we employ the structural connectivity based on diffusion tensor imaging (DTI), as a constraint, to guide the regression of BOLD time series from resting state functional magnetic resonance imaging (rs-fMRI). In addition, we introduce multiscale persistent homology features to avoid the uncertainty of regularization parameter selection. An empirical study on the Alzheimer's Disease Neuroimaging Initiative (ADNI) database demonstrates that the proposed method effectively improves classification performance compared with several competing approaches, and reasonably yields connectivity patterns specific to different diagnostic groups.

Keywords: Brain connectivity · Multimodal · Persistent homology · EMCI

1 Introduction

Mild cognitive impairment (MCI) is a preclinical and presymptomatic stage of dementia and may increase the risk of developing Alzheimer's disease (AD) in the future. In particular, an accurate detection of early MCI (EMCI), commonly characterized by early clinical symptom of cognitive deficits, can be beneficial to early intervention for delaying the transition from EMCI to MCI through medications as well as non-medication approaches. In past years, neuroimaging-based techniques have revealed that brain characteristics can be measured from the perspective of connectivity, which is associated with the interactions between neuronal activation patterns of anatomically segregated

© Springer Nature Switzerland AG 2020
A. L. Martel et al. (Eds.): MICCAI 2020, LNCS 12267, pp. 44–52, 2020.
https://doi.org/10.1007/978-3-030-59728-3_5

brain regions within a complex network. Currently, most of functional brain network modeling approaches for EMCI classification are based on pairwise correlation such as Pearson's correlation (PC). This approach allows for analyzing the brain as a functionally related network of dynamically interacting pairwise brain regions. However, recent studies have demonstrated that the neurological processes involve the interactions of many co-activated brain regions (i.e., more than two regions) rather than just pairwise interactions.

The least absolute shrinkage and selection operator (Lasso) method and sparse representation (SR) have been applied to construct a sparse brain network [1] by considering more complex interactions among multiple co-activated brain regions. Nevertheless, the Lasso approaches have their own deficiencies. For example, most of them use a fixed regularization parameter λ that may not be optimal to control the model sparsity. It will lead to an uncertainty to quantify the sparse brain network using some measurements, such as local efficiency, betweenness centrality, and so on. Moreover, another problem with Lasso is that, feature extraction of sparse networks needs a constructed network with precise connection strengths. However, traditional lasso method has been shown biased [2], and may not provide reliable estimation for building brain networks. Therefore, a subsequent connectivity strength estimation process should be performed to eliminate the shrinking effect, which naturally adds the complexity of modeling. In order to address above limitations, a novel persistent homology framework [4, 5] is proposed in this study. The proposed method constructs the brain network over multiscale regularization parameter space and only focuses on the network structure (binary network) rather than connection strength (weight network) between regions.

Currently, a lot of brain network modeling methods only consider the neurological processes from a single modality [7], while compelling evidences have demonstrated the advantage of acquiring and fusing complementary information via different neuroimaging modalities for accurate classification. Especially, diffusion tensor imaging (DTI) has been applied to map white matter tractography that outputs structural connectivity (SC). On the other hand, resting state functional MRI (rs-fMRI) measures intrinsic functional connectivity (FC) through spontaneous fluctuations of brain activity. Joint investigation of SC and FC can offer a complete characterization of the brain network incorporating both structural and functional connectivity.

In this paper, we propose a novel multimodal modeling method for EMCI identification, which integrates brain connectivity information from both rs-fMRI and DTI data. Specifically, a novel generalized fused lasso framework is applied to linearly regress BOLD time series, and is guided by SC prior information. In addition, the pairwise correlation is further introduced as an additional guidance to regularize regression coefficients between ROIs. Furthermore, we develop a multiscale network quantification method using persistent homology for the proposed model. We show that after integrating the brain network information with different sparsity for each subject, persistent homology can effectively characterize the multiscale networks via graph filtration, which overcomes the uncertainty of optimal parameter selection.

To the best of our knowledge, no previous brain network modeling methods ever fuse both generalized fused lasso and persistent homology features into a sparse representation, upon which our novel framework is built. Based on the proposed method, we perform our empirical study using rs-fMRI and DTI data from the publicly available Alzheimer's Disease Neuroimaging Initiative (ADNI) database. Participants in this study include 29 EMCI subjects, and 29 healthy controls (CN). We demonstrate the promise of our method over the competing methods on both classification performance and connectivity pattern identification.

2 Materials and Methods

2.1 Dataset and Preprocessing

Data were obtained from the ADNI database (adni.loni.usc.edu). The ADNI was launched in 2003 as a public-private partnership, led by Principal Investigator Michael W. Weiner, MD. The primary goal of ADNI has been to test whether serial magnetic resonance imaging (MRI), positron emission tomography (PET), other biological markers, and clinical and neuropsychological assessment can be combined to measure the progression of MCI and early AD. In this study, the rs-fMRI, DTI, and T1 imaging data were collected from 58 subjects, and divided into two diagnostic groups: EMCI group (N = 29, 19 males and 10 females, age 63–89), cognitive normal (CN) group (N = 29, 13 males and 16 females, age 61–87). The rs-fMRI data were preprocessed by SPM8 and DPABI, and then used to extract the mean value of BOLD time series corresponding to each ROI in the AAL template. The rs-fMRI scans are co-registered to the individual T1 image after realignment. For the preprocessing of DTI data, we used a package called pipeline toolbox for analyzing brain diffusion images (PANDA) based on the FMRIB Software Library (FSL). The DTI data with significant distortion in co-registration with FA and T1 image or with T1 image and MNI template were excluded from the study. Of note, since T1 scans were used for jointly guiding both DTI and rs-fMRI registrations, the multimodal images were registered onto a same reference template.

2.2 Methods

Multimodal Brain Networks Modeling. Let us assume that we have N subjects and M ROIs. For each ROI, a regional mean fMRI time series (BOLD signal) is available. We suppose that the BOLD time series with respect to the i-th ROI can be denoted as $x_i = \{x_{1i}, x_{2i}, \ldots, x_{Ti}\} \in R^T$, where T is the number of time points. $\beta_i = \{\beta_{1i}, \beta_{2i}, \ldots, \beta_{Mi}\} \in R^M$ is the coefficient vector that represents the indices of other co-activated ROIs associated with the i-th ROI. We can estimate the whole-brain network $B = \{\beta_1, \beta_2, \ldots, \beta_M\} \in R^{M \times M}$ by solving the following l_1-norm problem:

$$\min_{\beta} \underbrace{\frac{1}{2} \left\| x_i - \sum_{j \neq i}^{M} x_j \beta_{ji} \right\|_2^2}_{Loss\ Function} + \underbrace{\lambda_1 \sum_{j \neq i}^{M} D_{ji} |\beta_{ji}|}_{Regularization} + \underbrace{\frac{\lambda_2}{2} \sum_{u}^{M} \sum_{u \neq v}^{M} P(x_u, x_v) |\beta_{(u,i)} - \beta_{(v,i)}|}_{Generalized\ Fused\ Lasso}$$

(1)

Where, λ_1 is a non-negative regularization parameter. D_{ji} represents the structural information from DTI to guide the functional network modeling. A stronger structural connectivity will lead to a larger functional connectivity, and in turn a lower penalty to $\{\boldsymbol{\beta}_i\}_{i=1}^M$. Hence, we set $D_{ji} = \exp(-\rho_{ji}^2/\sigma)$ to penalize the estimated connection between j-th and i-th ROIs, where ρ_{ji} denotes the structural connectivity coefficient, and σ is the average of standard variances of all subjects' structural network elements. In the generalized fused lasso term, $P(x_u, x_v)$ is a non-negative Pearson correlation coefficient between u-th and v-th ROIs, which controls the similarity by shrinking the differences between all pair of ROIs toward zero see (Fig. 1a).

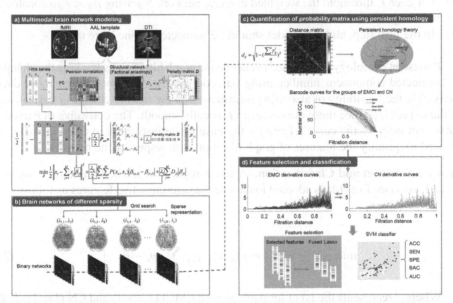

Fig. 1. a) Proposed multimodal brain network modeling framework; b) Production for a group of networks with different sparsity levels, which correspond to a sequence of regularization parameters; c) After integrating the network group using a distance matrix, a graph filtration for the distance matrix can be constructed with a visualization via barcode curves; d) The derivative curves corresponding to each barcode curve can be used to feature selection and SVM classifier.

Feature Quantification Using Persistent Homology. Because there is no definite rule to determinate the proper λ_1 and λ_2 for the proposed model in (1), it will lead to inconsistency of network structure and uncertainty of results that follow. The problem can be remedied by using persistent homology to perform statistical inference over every possible λ. More specifically, suppose that a group of brain networks $N_G = (N_{\lambda 1}, N_{\lambda 2}, \ldots, N_{\lambda n})$ corresponding to different regularization parameters ($\lambda_1 < \lambda_2 < \ldots, < \lambda_n$) rather than a fixed parameter (see Fig. 1b), we can integrate the network group into an integrated network N_{int}. The elements in N_{int} can be defined as probability-of-appearance of an edge in the network group N_G.

Assuming $\gamma = 1$ or 0 represents an edge exists or not, n is the number of networks in the group, we use distance network N_d to convert the elements of N_{int} by $d_{ij} = \sqrt{1 - (\sum_l^n \gamma_{ij}^l / n)^2} \in N_d$ (see Fig. 1c). Furthermore, a nested brain network group— also called graph filtration in persistent homology can be constructed over the distance network N_d as follow [6]:

(1)   Initial step is corresponding to the set of all brain regions;
(2)   Linearly increase the filtration distance ε (i.e., threshold) within the interval $[0, 1]$, where the maximum number of generated networks is set as 1000.
(3)   For each ε, threshold the weighted distance network N_d using $\rho_{ij} < \varepsilon$ to construct a binary network.
(4)   In the final step, all brain nodes should be connected to one large unit.

Persistent homology can be used to encode the graph filtration by tracking the change of connected component number using barcode curves. A theme in functional data analysis is the possibility of also using information on the rates of change or derivatives of the curves [3], since these curves are intrinsically smooth. The derivative of barcode curve can magnify the curve's features, the ensuing derivative curve (see Fig. 1d) can be used to quantify the features of graph filtration with respect to the network.

Feature Selection and Classification. A linear regression method based on common fused Lasso (see Fig. 1d) is adopted to choose the discriminative features as follow:

$$\min_\theta \frac{1}{2} \|l - F\Theta\|_2^2 + \omega\|\Theta\|_1 + \phi \sum_{i=2}^{T} |\theta_i - \theta_{i-1}| \tag{2}$$

Where, l represents the label for patients with EMCI ($l = -1$) and CN ($l = 1$); $F \in R^{1 \times T}$ is the sample with T features; the selected feature index is $\Theta = \{\theta_1, \theta_2, \ldots, \theta_T\} \in R^{T \times 1}$. It should be noted that the feature extraction and selection just involve the training samples. The testing sample will execute a dimensionality reduction corresponding to the selected indices. A support vector machine (SVM) is trained using the selected features for EMCI classification. We apply a two-layer leave-one-out cross validation (LOOCV) framework to evaluate classification performance. The outer layer is used to evaluate the classification performance, while the inner layer is applied for parameter optimization. A grid search is applied to search the optimal parameter combination. For obtaining the sequence of networks with different sparsity, a group of regularization parameter λ_1 are selected in the range of $[0, 0.9]$ with a uniform step size. We set the sampling number of λ_1 values as a free parameter $N_{sam}(\lambda_1)$, and the candidate values for grid search are $[100, 200, \ldots, 500]$. The candidate values for generalized fused lasso parameter λ_2 are $[0.1, 0.2, \ldots, 0.9]$. For the feature selection parameters ω and φ, the candidate values both are $[0.1, 0.2, \ldots, 0.8]$. In a word, the proposed method involves four parameters $\{N_{sam}(\lambda_1), \lambda_2, \omega, \varphi\}$ that should be optimized for receiving the best classification performance using inner LOOCV.

3 Results

3.1 Classification and Performance Evaluation

We compared our proposed method with several competing methods, such as Pearson's correlation (PC), Lasso, and group Lasso (GLasso). Moreover, we evaluated the performances of using different features for quantifying the brain network, including local efficiency (LE), upper triangular of connectivity matrix (UTCM), and persistent homology (PH). Specifically, we directly extracted the features of LE and UTCM from the PC-based dense network. For PH quantification of the network, we set a series of linearly increasing thresholds to construct a graph filtration. For networks from SR-based models (Lasso, GLasso, and proposed), we employed a grid search to determine the optimal regularization (without feature selection in Eq. 2) and extracted the features of LE and UTCM from the sparse network. Moreover, each of these SR-based methods was analyzed with our PH method following the entire framework shown in Fig. 1. From Table 1, persistent homology features show a relatively better classification performance than other quantification methods, and the proposed model with persistent homology quantification achieves the best classification performance with an accuracy of 79.31% (see Fig. 2b). GLasso method gains 5% accuracy improvement over Lasso, and the proposed method gains 3.45% further improvement over GLasso. The UTCM and PH show the significant improvement tendency for different models, whereas LE doesn't show that. ROC curves (see Fig. 2a) indicate that the proposed method yields the largest area under curves (AUC) of 0.87.

Table 1. Performance comparison on classification

Method	Features	ACC (%)	SEN (%)	SPE (%)	BAC (%)	AUC
PC	LE	60.34	60.00	60.17	60.36	0.61
	UTCM	60.34	60.00	60.17	60.36	0.61
	PH	63.79	63.33	64.29	63.81	0.67
Lasso	LE	65.52	63.64	68.00	65.82	0.68
	UTCM	68.97	68.97	68.97	68.97	0.70
	PH	70.69	71.43	70.00	70.71	0.77
GLasso	LE	67.24	67.86	66.67	67.26	0.68
	UTCM	72.41	69.70	76.00	72.85	0.74
	PH	75.86	72.73	80.00	76.36	0.83
Proposed method	LE	63.79	65.38	62.50	63.94	0.67
	UTCM	72.41	70.97	74.07	72.52	0.79
	PH	79.31	77.42	81.48	79.45	0.87

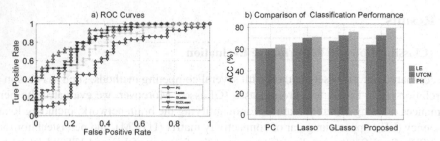

Fig. 2. The comparison of classification performance among different methods. a) The ROC curves for different methods; b) A histogram for visualizing the difference among approaches.

3.2 The Influence of Regularizations

We examine a specific set of optimal parameters $\{N_{sam}(\lambda_1), \lambda_2, \omega, \varphi\} = \{300, 0.3, 0.3, 0.6\}$ using inner LOOCV in the first case, i.e., holding out the first subject. For exploring the advantage of regularization, we fix the feature selection parameters ω and φ, and then a grid search is used to evaluate the classification performance by a sequence of regularization parameters using LOOCV with all subjects. The same process to fix $N_{sam}(\lambda_1)$ and λ_2 is also executed. The results in Fig. 3a and b show the classification accuracies with different settings of regularization parameters. The best classification performance is achieved with the accuracy of 82.76% when $\left\{\hat{N}_{sam}(\lambda_1), \hat{\lambda}_2\right\} = \{400, 0.4\}$(see Fig. 3a), which is very close to the accuracy in our results with the optimization of four parameters. The same effect for $\left\{\hat{\omega}, \hat{\phi}\right\} = \{0.3, 0.6\}$ is also produced (see Fig. 3b) receiving the accuracy of 84.48%. It should also be seen that a smaller $N_{sam}(\lambda_1)$ leads to less accuracy. That is because an inadequate sampling number in [0, 0.9] may ignore some edges with the change of sparsity level, persistent homology could not capture the information with respect to these edges. Moreover, a large $N_{sam}(\lambda_1)$ will bring biases which are defined as that some edges that drop at a certain sparsity level λ_1 may come back as λ_1 goes larger, and then quickly disappear again.

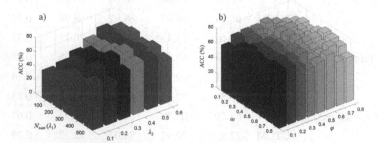

Fig. 3. The classification performance corresponding to: a) the influence of model parameters; and b) the influence of feature selection parameters.

3.3   Connectivity Pattern Identification

During the procedure of graph filtration for each subject, some edges continue to appear with the growth of filtration distance. Moreover, because of appearance of the new connections, the number of connected components tends to decrease, i.e., accelerate the downtrend of the barcode curve. Particularly, these edges can be defined as hub connections controlling the globality and locality of a brain network, which indicates an interesting neurobiological communication pattern.

We record all the hub connections during the graph filtration for individual subjects. Furthermore, a group analysis is performed to evaluate the frequency connections for different diagnostic groups, and then a network difference analysis between EMCI and CN groups is carried out, which outputs the specific connections for different groups. Furthermore, EMCI-CN (see Fig. 4a) indicates that compared with CN group, EMCI subjects exhibit the hub connections that could be decreased functional connectivity within left frontal gyrus mainly involving middle frontal gyrus, precentral gyrus, inferior frontal gyrus. The connectivity from left paracentral lobule and left gyrus rectus to right medial prefrontal cortex is revealed. Moreover, EMCI group show the specific connectivity from the right Thalamus to the whole brain. Some EMCI specific brain regions such as Lingual gyrus, precuneus, and olfactory also can be observed. CN-EMCI (see Fig. 4b) shows the CN specific connectivity mainly concentrates on left hippocampus and parahippocampus, and the brain integration involving left inferior parietal lobule to right postcentral gyrus, superior occipital gyrus, caudate nucleus and calcarine cortex. In other words, CN-EMCI can be regarded as the sub-network for the EMCI patients with disrupted connectivity compared to health subject, while EMCI-CN is used for compensating the loss of network centrality and efficiency.

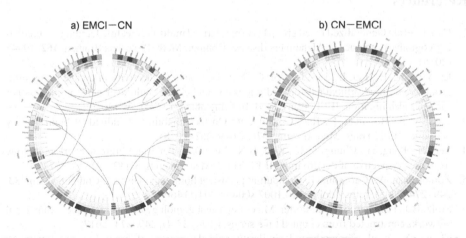

a) EMCI−CN   b) CN−EMCI

Fig. 4. The hub connections for EMCI and CN groups, where a) EMCI-CN represents the specific connectivity for EMCI; b) CN-EMCI represents the specific connectivity for CN.

4   Conclusion

We have proposed a novel multimodal brain network modeling framework coupled with a subsequent persistent homology feature analysis approach. The proposed method is different from most existing methods focusing on single modality analysis, and also different from current network evaluation methods with fixed regularization parameters. The main methodological contributions are: 1) proposing a multimodal framework for EMCI identification, which fuses the information from rs-fMRI and DTI data using sparse representation; 2) developing a multiscale network quantification method using persistent homology for characterizing the multimodal brain network. Experimental results using the ADNI data show that our method outperforms the existing methods on classification performance and can discover the specific disease-related brain connectivity for biomarkers.

Acknowledgment. The work was supported by the National Natural Science Foundation of China (61773134 and 61803117), the Natural Science Foundation of Heilongjiang Province of China (YQ2019F003), the Fundamental Research Funds for the Central Universities (3072020CF0402) at Harbin Engineering University. This work was also supported in part by the National Institutes of Health (R01 EB022574) at University of Pennsylvania. Data used in preparation of this article were obtained from the Alzheimer's disease neuroimaging initiative (ADNI) database (adni.loni.usc.edu). A complete listing of ADNI investigators and the complete ADNI Acknowledgement can be found at: https://adni.loni.usc.edu/wp-content/uploads/how_to_apply/ADNI_Acknowledgement_List.pdf.

References

1. Cao, P., et al.: Generalized fused group lasso regularized multi-task feature learning for predicting cognitive outcomes in Alzheimers disease. Comput. Meth. Programs Biomed. **162**, 19–45 (2018)
2. Li, Y., Yang, H., Lei, B., Liu, J., Wee, C.: Novel effective connectivity inference using ultra-group constrained orthogonal forward regression and elastic multilayer perceptron classifier for MCI identification. IEEE Trans. Med. Imaging **38**(5), 1227–1239 (2019)
3. Cassidy, B., Bowman, F., Rac, C., Solo, V.: On the reliability of individual brain activity networks. IEEE Trans. Med. Imaging **37**(2), 649–662 (2018)
4. Lee, H., Kang, H., Chung, M.K., Kim, B.N., Lee, D.S.: Persistent brain network homology from the perspective of dendrogram. IEEE Trans. Med. Imaging **31**(12), 2267–2277 (2012)
5. Zomorodian, A., Carlsson, G.: Computing persistent homology. Discrete Comput. Geom. **33**, 249–274 (2005). https://doi.org/10.1007/s00454-004-1146-y
6. Stolz, B.J., Harrington, H.A., Porter, M.A.: Persistent homology of time-dependent functional networks constructed from coupled time series. Chaos **27**(4), 249–274 (2017)
7. Zhang, Y., et al.: Strength and similarity guided group-level brain functional network construction for MCI diagnosis. Pattern Recogn. **88**, 421–430 (2019)

Recovering Brain Structural Connectivity from Functional Connectivity via Multi-GCN Based Generative Adversarial Network

Lu Zhang[1(✉)], Li Wang[1,2], and Dajiang Zhu[1]

[1] Department of Computer Science and Engineering,
University of Texas at Arlington, Arlington, TX, USA
lu.zhang2@mavs.uta.edu
[2] Department of Mathematics, University of Texas at Arlington, Arlington, TX, USA

Abstract. Understanding brain structure-function relationship, e.g., the relations between brain structural connectivity (SC) and functional connectivity (FC), is critical for revealing organizational principles of human brain. However, brain's many-to-one function-structure mode, i.e., diverse functional patterns may be associated with the same SC, and the complex direct/indirect interactions in both structural and functional connectivity make it challenge to infer a reliable relationship between SC and FC. Benefiting from the advances in deep neural networks, many deep learning based approaches are developed to model the complex and non-linear relations that can be overlooked by traditional shallow methods. In this work, we proposed a multi-GCN based generative adversarial network (MGCN-GAN) to infer individual SC based on corresponding FC. The generator of MGCN-GAN is composed by multiple multi-layer graph convolution networks (GCNs) which have the capability to model complex indirect connections in brain connectivity. The discriminator of MGCN-GAN is a single multi-layer GCN which aims to distinguish predicted SC from real SC. To overcome the inherent unstable behavior of GAN, we designed a new structure-preserving (SP) loss function to guide the generator to learn the intrinsic SC patterns more effectively. We tested our model on Human Connectome Project (HCP) dataset and the proposed MGCN-GAN model can generate reliable individual SC based on FC. This result implies that there may exist a common regulation between specific brain structural and functional architectures across different individuals.

Keywords: Structural connectivity · Functional connectivity · Graph convolution networks · Generative adversarial network

1 Introduction

One of the major challenges in modern neuroscience is to understand brain structure-function relationship [1], such as the relations between brain struc-

© Springer Nature Switzerland AG 2020
A. L. Martel et al. (Eds.): MICCAI 2020, LNCS 12267, pp. 53–61, 2020.
https://doi.org/10.1007/978-3-030-59728-3_6

tural connectivity (SC) [2] and functional connectivity (FC) [3]. Brain connectivity can be represented using a graph, comprising the nodes (e.g., brain regions) and the connecting edges. For SC, the edges are often represented as the count of diffusion MRI derived fibers connecting to the regions. FC can be defined via Blood-Oxygen-Level-Dependent (BOLD) signal correlations using functional MRI (fMRI). Many studies have been published to investigate the potential relationship between brain structure and function, specifically, how SC and FC influence each other. Koch et al. [4] directly compared SC and FC and found a positive correlation between them in regions along the central sulcus. Greicius et al. [5] studied the relations between SC and four default mode network (DMN) related regions and found that strong functional connectivity can exist without direct structural connections. Skudlarski et al. [6] reported a significant overall agreement between SC and FC. Other studies [7–9] also reported similar results: strong structural connections are accompanied with strong functional connections. But functional connections can be observed between regions with little or no direct structural connections, which indicates functional connection may be mediated by indirect structural connections. In general, how to jointly represent and analyze these two types of brain networks is still challenging: because of brain's many-to-one function-structure mode, traditional regression methods cannot be directly used to explore the relationship between SC and FC. Moreover, the individual variability and the non-linearity of SC and FC need to be considered simultaneously.

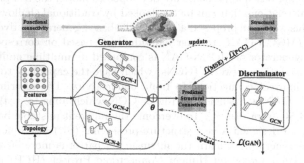

Fig. 1. An illustration of the proposed multi-GCN based generative adversarial network (MGCN-GAN). Firstly, by using Destrieux atlas [10] along with diffusion MRI and rs-fMRI data, we extracted the averaged BOLD signal of each brain region (148 regions in total). Then we created FC by Pearson's correlation coefficient and constructed SC by ratio of number of fibers connecting two regions to the total number of fibers. SC was used as real samples to train the discriminator. FC was used as: 1) features associated with the nodes and 2) initialization of the GCN topology. The features and topology were fed into generator to predict SC. The predicted SC were used to 1) iteratively update the GCN topology and 2) train discriminator as fake samples. The generator is updated based on structure preserving (SP) loss function composed of MSE loss, PCC loss and GAN loss.

To tackle the above mentioned difficulties and motivated by the recent development of deep neural network based methods, we proposed a multi-GCN based generative adversarial network (MGCN-GAN) (Fig. 1) to generate individual SC based on corresponding individual FC. Specifically, we adopted generative adversarial network [11,12] to handle brain's many-to-one function-structure mode. Moreover, in order to capture the complex relationship buried in both direct and indirect brain connections, we designed the generator and discriminator of MGCN-GAN using graph convolution networks (GCN) [13,14]. Compared to traditional CNN-based GAN that can only operate on regular, Euclidean data, our model can handle interrelated and hidden structures that beyond the grid neighbors, such as brain connectivity. In addition, to overcome the inherent unstable behavior of GAN, we proposed a novel structure-preserving (SP) loss function to guide the generator to learn the intrinsic SC patterns more effectively. We tested our method on Human Connectome Project (HCP) [15] dataset and the proposed MGCN-GAN can generate reliable individual SC based on FC. More importantly, our results imply that there may exist a common regulation between specific brain structural and functional architectures across individuals.

2 Methods

2.1 Data Collection and Preprocessing

In this work, we used diffusion magnetic resonance imaging (diffusion MRI) and resting state functional magnetic resonance imaging (rs-fMRI) of 300 subjects in Human Connectome Project (HCP) [15] dataset. The diffusion MRI data has 111 slices and FOV = 210×180 with 1.25 mm isotropic voxels, TE = 89.5 ms, TR = 5.52 s, flip angle = 78°. The rs-fMRI data has 72 slices and FOV = 208×180 with 2.0 mm isotropic voxels, TE = 33.1 ms, TR = 0.72 s, flip angle = 52° and there are 1200 volumes for each subject.

We applied standard preprocessing procedures including skull removal for both modalities, spatial smoothing, slice time correction, temporal pre-whitening, global drift removal and band pass filtering (0.01–0.1 Hz) for rs-fMRI, eddy current correction and fiber tracking via MedINRIA for diffusion MRI, registering rsfMRI to diffusion MRI space using FLIRT and adopt the Destrieux Atlas [10] for ROI labeling. The brain cortex was partitioned into 148 regions after removing two unknown areas and two empty areas.

2.2 Problem Description

In this work, we proposed a MGCN-GAN model to generate individual SC based on corresponding FC. Specifically, the whole brain is represented as a network with $N = 148$ nodes (brain regions). We used the ratio of the number of fibers connecting two ROIs to the total number of fibers to create SC, denoted as $A \in R^{N \times N}$. As for FC, we used Pearson's correlation coefficient between two average fMRI signals of two ROIs to create FC, denoted as $P \in R^{N \times N}$. The proposed MGCN-GAN model is built on two components: Multi-GCN based generator and single-GCN based discriminator. The generator takes the following steps to generate an SC for a given FC: (i) FC is used as both features associated with nodes and the initialization of topology of brain network; (ii) based on current topology, FC is mapped to different feature spaces by each multi-layer GCN component of generator in order to explore the latent relationship between SC and FC, so that multiple output feature matrices can be obtained; (iii) all the output feature matrices are combined by learnable coefficients to generate predicted SC; (iv) the topology is updated by the predicted SC. The discriminator is a classifier to label the input SC as real SC samples or fake samples. Given the training data consisting of FC samples and their corresponding real SC samples, the generator is trained based on SP loss function (Sect. 2.4) and the discriminator is trained by standard cross-entropy loss [11,12].

2.3   Multi-GCN Based GAN (MGCN-GAN)

Similar to vanilla GAN [11,12], MGCN-GAN is composed of two components, i.e., generator and discriminator. The generator is trained to generate real-like individual SC by competing with the discriminator based on an adversarial training scheme. Inspired by the great success of CNN that uses multiple filters to learn features from different feature spaces, the proposed generator consists of multiple multi-layer GCNs. Different GCN components are designed for different feature space and each of them will learn a latent mapping from individual FC to its corresponding SC. Through paralleling multiple GCNs, generator has the capacity to model complex relationship between FC and SC, which will be demonstrated by our experimental results in Sect. 3. The discriminator is composed by a single multi-layer GCN and two fully-connect layers, which aims to distinguish the predicted SC from real SC.

Generator. The generator is composed by k multi-layer GCNs. It is formulated as:

$$g(T, P, \theta) = \theta \oplus (G_1 \| G_2 \| G_3 \| \dots \| G_k), \tag{1}$$

$$SC^p(P, \theta) = g(g(T, P, \theta), P, \theta), \tag{2}$$

where G_i, $i = 1, 2, \dots, k$ represents i^{th} GCN and $\|$ denotes parallel operation. Each GCN takes the individual FC samples as input and outputs a predicted SC of the same individual. Then, we used the learnable coefficient θ to fuse ($\oplus$) these k predictions to form $g(T, P, \theta)$, and obtained the final prediction, denoted as SC^p, by updating current topology T with the updated $T = g(T, P, \theta)$. Each n-layer GCN G_i is defined as:

$$G_i(T, P) = f(T H_i^{n-1} W_i^n), \tag{3}$$

$$H_i^n = \begin{cases} f(T H_i^{n-1} W_i^n), & n \geq 1, \\ P, & n = 0. \end{cases} \tag{4}$$

As shown in Eq. (3) and Eq. (4), each GCN has two inputs that represent the features and topology of the graph data. In our work, we used FC matrix P as features. The topology T was initialized by P and iteratively updated by SC^p. f is the nonlinear activation function and we used $Relu$ in our experiments. H_i^n is the output of nth graph convolution layer of G_i. $W_i^n \in R^{D_i \times D_o}$ is the weight matrix of nth graph convolution layer of G_i, D_i is the dimension of input features and D_o is the dimension of output features. Each graph convolution layer selects and combines features from its neighbors based on topology and maps this combination to output feature space based on W_i^n. By stacking multiple layers, information from high-order neighbors (the nodes that are connected via other nodes) are integrated along the topology SC^p, which enables the generator to capture complex indirect relationship. After training, each multi-layer GCN defines a mapping from FC to SC, which reflects a latent relationship between FC and SC. In order to enhance the capability of generator, we parallel multiple GCNs to capture the complex interrelated relationships between SC and FC.

Discriminator. In order to distinguish the two sets of graph data (predicted SC and real SC), the discriminator consists of a multi-layer GCN, $G_d(SC, I)$, and two fully-connect layers. The input SC represents the real SC matrix – A, derived from diffusion MRI and predicted SC matrix – SC^p, from generator. They are treated as real and fake samples for the discriminator training. Different from generator, we used identity matrix as input feature matrix for discriminator. This is because discriminator aims to learn the rules that can be used to decide whether the input connectivity matrix is a valid SC matrix or not, any external knowledge should be excluded.

2.4 Structure-Preserving (SP) Loss Function

The generator is optimized according to the feedback of discriminator. However, in the SC prediction task, the discriminator is much easier to train than the generator. The discriminator may easily classify real SC from predicted SC after a few training iterations and the generative adversarial loss would be close to 0, resulting in zero back-propagated gradients in generator. In such case, the generator cannot be optimized and will keep generating invalid SC. To break this dilemma, maintaining the balance between generator and discriminator regarding the optimization capability during the entire training process is important. We designed a new structure-preserving (SP) loss function to train discriminator and generator, which is a combination of three loss functions: mean squared error (MSE) loss, Pearson's correlation coefficient (PCC) loss and GAN loss. SP loss function is formulated by Eq. (5).

$$SPLoss = GAN + \alpha MSE + \beta PCC, \tag{5}$$

where the regularization parameters α and β are initialized by 1 and will keep decreasing during the training process. MSE loss aims to force the predicted SC to be the same scale with real SC at element-wise level. PCC loss try to maximize the similarity of overall pattern between predicted SC and real SC. It consists of two components: 1) brain-level PCC loss and 2) region-level PCC loss. Brain-level PCC loss calculates the PCC between predicted SC matrix and real SC matrix, which measures the overall correlation between the predicted SC and real SC. Region-level PCC loss calculates the correlation between predicted SC and real SC of each brain region (each row/column of the connectivity matrix).

3   Results

3.1   Predicted Structural Connectivity

In our experiment, we used 180 subjects as training dataset and 120 subjects as testing dataset. All results showed in this section are from testing dataset. For detailed network architecture, three two-layer GCNs are paralleled in generator and the discriminator is composed of one three-layer GCN followed by two fully-connect layers. The feature dimensions of GCNs in generator are: $G_1 = (74, 148)$, $G_2 = (148, 148)$, $G_3 = (296, 148)$. $G_i = (F_1, F_2, \ldots, F_n)$ represents an n-layer GCN and output feature dimension of layer i is F_i. Similarly, feature dimensions of discriminator are : $G_d = (148, 296, 148)$, which is followed by two fully connected layers with output feature dimensions 1024 and 2, respectively.

Figure 2(a) shows the predicted SC and real SC of 5 randomly selected subjects. As shown in Fig. 2(a), the overall similarity between the real SC and the corresponding predicted SC is very high. To better demonstrate the details of the prediction result, we extracted two patches at the same location of predicted SC and real SC for all 5 subjects. These patches are enlarged and showed in the middle of Fig. 2(a). From the enlarged patches, we can see that different individuals possess different SC though their overall patterns are similar. Our model can not only generate the similar patterns across individuals, but also predict the subtle individual differences. All these predictions are based on individual FC.

Figure 2(b) shows the top 15 strongest connectivity of real SC and predicted SC for the same 5 subjects in the brain space. Because of individual variability, the top 15 connectivity of different subjects are different. But our model can accurately predict these differences as well as individual patterns based on individual FC only. This result further confirms that our method can effectively generate accurate individual SC instead of generating common SC patterns at population level. Note that we used individual SC and FC as a pair-input for training and testing, which means the learned model represents a common mapping between individual SC and FC. This result suggests that there may exist a common regulation between specific brain structural and functional architectures across individuals.

3.2   Model Comparison

As mentioned before, the generator of MGCN-GAN is composed by multiple GCNs. In order to verify the necessity of multi-GCN architecture, we conducted

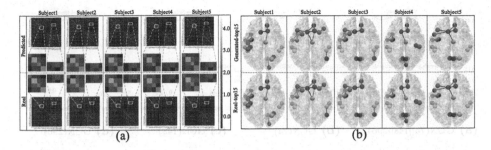

Fig. 2. Illustration of predicted SC and real SC of 5 randomly selected subjects. **(a)** shows the predicted SC matrices (the first row) and real SC matrices (the second row) derived from diffusion MRI. Each column belongs to different individuals. Two patches of the matrices are extracted from the same location and their enlarged patches are showed in the middle. **(b)** shows the top 15 strongest connectivity of real SC and predicted SC in the brain space. The colorful bubbles and links represent different brain regions and structural connectivity, respectively. The colors used in this figure are the same in Destrieux atlas in FreeSurfer. The five subjects showed in **(b)** are the same ones in **(a)**. (Color figure online)

comparison experiments with different generator architectures and evaluated our results by three measures: 1) MSE (real, gen), 2) MSE (other-reals, gen) and 3) MSE (other-reals, gen)-MSE (real, gen). MSE (real, gen) is the average MSE between real SC and predicted SC from the same subject, which measures the similarity between the real SC and the corresponding predicted SC. Smaller MSE (real, gen) indicates higher similarity. Thus, to generate reliable SC, the MSE (real, gen) should keep decreasing before converged. MSE (other-reals, gen) is the average MSE between predicted SC and real SC of other subjects. A reliable predicted SC should avoid to be "trapped" in common SC patterns at population level. Therefore, we expect MSE (other-reals, gen) to keep increasing during training process. MSE (other-reals, gen)-MSE (real, gen) is the difference of MSE (real, gen) and MSE (other-reals, gen) and an increasing value is expected. Figure 3 shows the results of different architectures, which are evaluated by the three measures. It is obvious that the predicted SCs generated from multi-GCN generator can maintain the individual differences in SCs, while single-GCN generator shows obvious worse performance.

The multiple GCNs in the generator are combined with learnable coefficients. In our experiments, we initialized the coefficients with different values and found that the coefficients with different initializations will converge to a consistent ratio that all the GCN components seem to contribute equally to the results and each of them is indispensable. One explanation is that similar to the filters in CNN, multiple GCNs with different size of output features may be more flexible and efficient for characterizing the complex SC-FC mapping.

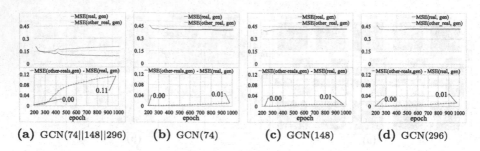

(a) GCN(74||148||296)   **(b)** GCN(74)   **(c)** GCN(148)   **(d)** GCN(296)

Fig. 3. Results of different generator architectures. The GCN($D_1||D_2||\ldots||D_k$) represents the architecture of generator, the generator is composed of k two-layer GCNs, and the output feature dimension of the first layer of ith GCN is D_i. The results of different generator architectures are evaluated by MSE (real, gen), MSE (other-reals, gen) and MSE (other-reals, gen)-MSE (real, gen).

3.3 Loss Function Comparison

To demonstrate the superiority of the proposed SP loss function, we trained our network with different loss function and the results of comparison are showed in Fig. 4. From the results, we can see that our SP loss function outperforms other loss function. The reason is that MSE only focuses on the element-wise similarity within the connectivity and ignores the overall patterns. Though PCC have better performance to describe the overall connectivity patterns, it may also overlook the connection magnitude across different connectivity. However, both of them are important in our designed SP loss to capture the subtle differences between real and predicted SC.

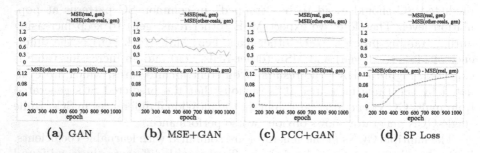

(a) GAN   **(b)** MSE+GAN   **(c)** PCC+GAN   **(d)** SP Loss

Fig. 4. Results of MGCN-GAN with different loss functions. We used single GAN loss, the combination of GAN loss and MSE loss, the combination of GAN loss and PCC loss and the proposed SP loss to conduct experiments and the results are evaluated based on the three measures discussed in Sect. 3.2.

4 Conclusion and Discussion

In this work, we proposed a novel multi-GCN based generative adversarial network (MGCN-GAN) to generate individual SC based on corresponding FC. We adopted GCN based generator and discriminator to model the interrelated hidden structures of brain network and used multi-GCN architecture to capture the complex relationship between SC and FC. Moreover, we designed a new structure-preserving loss function to make generator more effective when differentiating real and predicted SCs. Using HCP dataset as a testbed, our MGCN-GAN can not only predict reliable individual SC, but also capture the subtle difference across individuals.

References

1. Park, H.J., Friston, K.: Structural and functional brain networks: from connections to cognition. Science **342**(6158), 1238411 (2013)
2. Yeh, F.C., et al.: Quantifying differences and similarities in whole-brain white matter architecture using local connectome fingerprints. PLOS Comput. Biol. **12**(11), e1005203 (2016)
3. Gratton, C.: Functional brain networks are dominated by stable group and individual factors, not cognitive or daily variation. Neuron **98**(2), 439–452 (2018)
4. Koch, M.A., Norris, D.G., Hund-Georgiadis, M.: An investigation of functional and anatomical connectivity using magnetic resonance imaging. Neuroimage **16**(1), 241–250 (2002)
5. Greicius, M.D., Supekar, K., Menon, V., Dougherty, R.F.: Resting-state functional connectivity reflects structural connectivity in the default mode network. Cereb. Cortex **19**(1), 72–78 (2009)
6. Skudlarski, P., Jagannathan, K., Calhoun, V.D., Hampson, M., Skudlarska, B.A., Pearlson, G.: Measuring brain connectivity: diffusion tensor imaging validates resting state temporal correlations. Neuroimage **43**(3), 554–561 (2008)
7. Hagmann, P., et al.: Mapping the structural core of human cerebral cortex. PLOS Biol. **6**(7), e159 (2008)
8. Honey, C.: Predicting human resting-state functional connectivity from structural connectivity. Proc. Natl. Acad. Sci. **106**(6), 2035–2040 (2009)
9. Teipel, S.J.: Regional networks underlying interhemispheric connectivity: an EEG and DTI study in healthy ageing and amnestic mild cognitive impairment. Hum. Brain Mapp. **30**(7), 2098–2119 (2009)
10. Destrieux, C., Fischl, B., Dale, A., Halgren, E.: Automatic parcellation of human cortical gyri and sulci using standard anatomical nomenclature. Neuroimage **53**(1), 1–15 (2010)
11. Goodfellow, I.: Nips 2016 tutorial: Generative adversarial networks. arXiv preprint arXiv:1701.00160 (2016)
12. Hong, Y., Hwang, U., Yoo, J., Yoon, S.: How generative adversarial networks and its variants work: an overview of GAN. arXiv preprint arXiv:1711.05914 (2017)
13. Wu, Z., Pan, S., Chen, F., Long, G., Zhang, C., Yu, P.S.: A comprehensive survey on graph neural networks. arXiv preprint arXiv:1901.00596 (2019)
14. Zhou, J., et al.: Graph neural networks: A review of methods and applications. arXiv preprint arXiv:1812.08434 (2018)
15. Van Essen, D.C., et al.: The human connectome project: a data acquisition perspective. Neuroimage **62**(4), 2222–2231 (2012)

From Connectomic to Task-Evoked Fingerprints: Individualized Prediction of Task Contrasts from Resting-State Functional Connectivity

Gia H. Ngo[1]($\boxtimes$), Meenakshi Khosla[1], Keith Jamison[2], Amy Kuceyeski[2,3], and Mert R. Sabuncu[1,2,4]

[1] School of Electrical and Computer Engineering, Cornell University, Ithaca, USA
ghn8@cornell.edu
[2] Radiology, Weill Cornell Medicine, New York, USA
[3] Brain and Mind Research Institute, Weill Cornell Medicine, New York, USA
[4] Nancy E. and Peter C. Meinig School of Biomedical Engineering,
Cornell University, Ithaca, USA

Abstract. Resting-state functional MRI (rsfMRI) yields functional connectomes that can serve as cognitive fingerprints of individuals. Connectomic fingerprints have proven useful in many machine learning tasks, such as predicting subject-specific behavioral traits or task-evoked activity. In this work, we propose a surface-based convolutional neural network (BrainSurfCNN) model to predict individual task contrasts from their resting-state fingerprints. We introduce a reconstructive-contrastive loss that enforces subject-specificity of model outputs while minimizing predictive error. The proposed approach significantly improves the accuracy of predicted contrasts over a well-established baseline. Furthermore, BrainSurfCNN's prediction also surpasses test-retest benchmark in a subject identification task. (Source code is available at https://github.com/ngohgia/brain-surf-cnn)

Keywords: Functional connectivity · Task-induced fingerprint · Surface-based convolutional neural network

1 Introduction

Functional connectomes derived from resting-state functional MRI (rsfMRI) carry the promise of being inherent "fingerprints" of individual cognitive functions [1,2]. Such cognitive fingerprints have been used in many machine-learning applications [3], such as predicting individual developmental trajectories [4],

---

Electronic supplementary material The online version of this chapter (https://doi.org/10.1007/978-3-030-59728-3_7) contains supplementary material, which is available to authorized users.

© Springer Nature Switzerland AG 2020
A. L. Martel et al. (Eds.): MICCAI 2020, LNCS 12267, pp. 62–71, 2020.
https://doi.org/10.1007/978-3-030-59728-3_7

behavioral traits [5], or task-induced brain activities [6,7]. In this work, we propose BrainSurfCNN, a surface-based convolutional neural network for predicting individual task fMRI (tfMRI) contrasts from their corresponding resting-state connectomes. Figure 1 gives an overview of our approach: BrainSurfCNN minimizes prediction's error with respect to the subject's true contrast map, while maximizing subject identifiability of the predicted contrast.

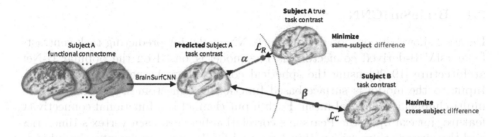

Fig. 1. BrainSurfCNN learns to predict an individual task contrast from their surface-based functional connectome by optimizing two objectives - minimizing the predictive error L_R while maximizing the average difference L_C with other subjects.

Prediction of individual task contrasts from rsfMRI and structural MRI features was previously explored in [6,7] using linear regression. In this work, we approached the same task using deep learning techniques. This was made possible by the increased availability of rsfMRI and tfMRI imaging data from initiatives like the Human Connectome Project (HCP) [8]. Furthermore, several projects (HCP included) also repeat collection of imaging data for the same subjects on separate test and retest sessions. Such test-retest data offer an empirical upper-bound on the reliability and replicability of neuroimaging results, including individual task contrasts.

Convolutional neural networks (CNNs) were previously used for prediction of disease status from functional connectomes [9], albeit in volumetric space. Instead, we used a new convolutional operator [10] suited for icosahedral meshes, which are commonly used to represent the brain cortex [11,12]. Working directly on the surface mesh circumvents resampling to volumetric space with unavoidable mapping errors [13]. Graph CNN [14,15] is also closely related to mesh-based CNN, but there is no consensus on how pooling operates in unconstrained graphs. In contrast, an icosahedral mesh is generated by regular subdivision of faces from a mesh of a lower resolution [16], making pooling straightforward [10]. We also introduced a reconstructive-contrastive (R-C) loss that optimizes a dual objective of making accurate prediction while maximizing the subject's identifiability in relation to other individuals. This objective is related to metric learning techniques [17,18]. Yet, to our knowledge, we are the first to examine their utility in medical image computing.

Overall, our experiments showed that the proposed BrainSurfCNN in conjunction with R-C loss yielded markedly improvement in accuracy of predicting individual task contrasts compared to an established baseline. The proposed approach also outperforms retest contrasts in the subject identification task, suggesting that the model predictions might be useful task-evoked fingerprints for individual subjects.

2   Materials and Methods

2.1   BrainSurfCNN

Figure 2 shows the proposed BrainSurfCNN model for predicting task contrasts from rsfMRI-derived connectomes. The model is based on the popular U-Net architecture [19,20] using the spherical convolutional kernel proposed in [10]. Input to the model is surface-based functional connectomes, represented as a multi-channel icosahedral mesh. Each input channel is a functional connectivity feature, for example, the Pearson's correlation between each vertex's timeseries and the average timeseries within a target ROI. In our experiments, the subject-specific target ROIs were derived from dual-regression of group-level independent component analysis (ICA) [21]. The input and output surface meshes are fs_LR meshes [11] with 32,492 vertices (fs_LR 32k surface) per brain hemisphere. The fs_LR atlases are symmetric between the left and right hemispheres, e.g., the same vertex index in the both hemi-spheres correspond to cotra-lateral analogues. Thus, each subject's connectomes from the two hemispheres can be concatenated, resulting in a single input icosahedral mesh with the number of channels equals twice the number of ROIs. BrainSurfCNN's output is also a multi-channel icosahedral mesh, in which each channel corresponds to one fMRI task contrast. This multi-task prediction setting promotes weight sharing across contrast predictions.

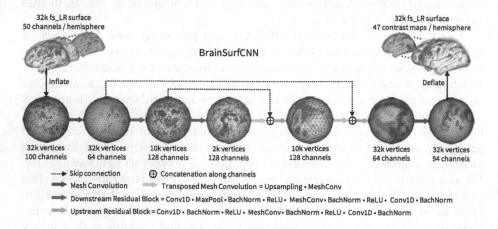

Fig. 2. BrainSurfCNN architecture

2.2 Reconstructive-Contrastive Loss

Given a mini batch of N samples $B = \{\mathbf{x}_i\}$, in which $\mathbf{x}_i$ is the target multi-contrast image of subject i, let $\hat{\mathbf{x}}_i$ denote the corresponding predicted contrast image. The reconstructive-contrastive loss (R-C loss) is given by:

$$\mathcal{L}_R = \frac{1}{N} \sum_{i=1}^{N} d(\hat{\mathbf{x}}_i, \mathbf{x}_i) \quad ; \quad \mathcal{L}_C = \frac{1}{(N^2 - N)/2} \sum_{\substack{\mathbf{x}_j \in B_i \\ j \neq i}} d(\hat{\mathbf{x}}_i, \mathbf{x}_j) \quad (1)$$

$$\mathcal{L}_{RC} = [\mathcal{L}_R - \alpha]_+ + [\mathcal{L}_R - \mathcal{L}_C + \beta]_+ \quad (2)$$

where $d(.)$ is a loss function (e.g. l^2-norm). $\mathcal{L}_R$, α are the same-subject (reconstructive) loss and margin, respectively. $\mathcal{L}_C$, β are the across-subject (contrastive) loss and margin, respectively. The combined objective enforces the same-subject error $\mathcal{L}_R$ to be within α margin, while encouraging the average across-subject difference $\mathcal{L}_C$ to be large such that $(\mathcal{L}_C - \mathcal{L}_R) > \beta$.

3 Experiments

3.1 Data

We used the minimally pre-processed, FIX-cleaned 3-Tesla resting-state fMRI (rsfMRI) and task fMRI (tfMRI) data from the Human Connectome Project (HCP), with the acquisition and processing pipelines described in [8,21,22]. rsfMRI data was acquired in four 15-min runs, with 1,200 time-points per run per subject. HCP also released the average timeseries of independent components derived from group-level ICA for individual subjects. We used the 50-component ICA timeseries data for computing the functional connectomes. HCP's tfMRI data comprises of 86 contrasts from 7 task domains [22], namely: WM (working memory), GAMBLING, MOTOR, LANGUAGE, SOCIAL RELATIONAL, and EMOTION. Similar to [6], redundant negative contrasts were excluded, resulting in 47 unique contrasts.

HCP released 3T imaging data of 1200 subjects, out of which 46 subjects also have retest (second visit) data. By considering only subjects with all 4 rsfMRI runs and 47 tfMRI contrasts, our experiments included 919 subjects for training/validation and held out 39 test-retest subjects for evaluation.

4 Baseline

4.1 Linear Regression

We implemented the linear regression model of [6], given by $\mathbf{y}_i^k = \mathbf{X}_i^k \beta_i^k$, in which $\mathbf{y}_i^k$, $\mathbf{X}_i^k$, β_i^k are the vectorized activation pattern, input features, and regressor of the k-th parcel in the i-th subject. The parcellation was derived from group-level ICA and provided by HCP. $\mathbf{y}_i^k$ is a vector of length n_k - the number of vertices in the k'th parcel in both hemispheres. $\mathbf{X}_i^k$ is a $n_k \times M$ functional connectivity matrix, with each element computed as the Pearson's correlation between a vertex and each of the M subject-specific independent components' average timeseres (same timeseries used to compute BrainSurfCNN's input). As in [6], a linear regressor was fitted for every parcel and every task of each training/validation sample. For prediction, all fitted regressors corresponding to every parcel and task contrast were averaged as one average regressor per parcel.

4.2   Lower Bound: Group-Average Contrast

Different tasks could exhibit different degrees of inter-individual variability and we want to assess this variability in prediction. Thus, we computed the correlation of individual contrasts with the group average as a naive baseline. This lower bound would be low/high for tasks with high/low inter-subject variability.

4.3   Upper Bound: Retest Contrast

We used the retest (repeat) tfMRI scans to quantify the reliability of the contrast maps and assess the prediction performance of our model and the baseline. The retest contrasts were compared to the test (first) contrasts both in terms of overall correlation and in the subject identification task. We consider the test-retest results as an effective upper-bound on performance.

5   Experimental Setup

5.1   Ensemble Learning:

Each subject in our experiments has 4 rsfMRI runs with 1200 time-points each. All 4800 rsfMRI time-points are often used to compute the functional connectome, resulting in one connectome per subject [6,7]. On the other hand, there is evidence that stable functional connectome estimates can be computed from fewer than 1200 time-points [5]. We exploited this observation for data augmentation when training the models. Specifically, each of the 4 rsfMRI runs was split into two contiguous segments of 600 time-points. One functional connectome was computed on each segment, resulting in 8 input samples per subject. During BrainSurfCNN training, one connectome was randomly sampled for each subject, essentially presenting a slightly different sample per subject in every batch. For the baseline model, all 8 samples per subjects were used for training. At test time, 8 predictions were made for each subject and then averaged for a final prediction.

5.2   Training Schedule

BrainSurfCNN was first trained for 100 epochs with a batch size of 2 with l^2 reconstruction loss (L_R in Eq. 2) using Adam optimizer. Upon convergence, the average reconstructive loss L_R and L_C were computed from all training subjects, and used as initial values for the margins α and β in Eq. 2 respectively. This initialization encourages the model to not diverge from the existing reconstructive loss while improving on the contrastive loss. We then continued training for another 100 epochs, with the same-subject margin α halved and across-subject margin β doubled every 20 epochs, thus applying continuously increased pressure on the model to refine.

5.3   Evaluation

Pearsons' correlation coefficients were computed between the models' predicted individual task contrast maps and the tfMRI contrast maps of all subjects. This yields a 39 by 39 correlation matrix for each contrast, where each entry is the correlation between a subject's predicted contrast (column) and an observed tfMRI contrast map (row), of same or another subject. The diagonal values (correlation with self) thus quantify the (within subject) predictive accuracy for a given task contrast. The difference between diagonal and average off-diagonal values (correlation of self vs others) captures how much better one subject's prediction correlates with the corresponding subject's own tfMRI contrast compared to other subject contrasts. From another perspective, the i-th subject can be identified among all test subjects by the predicted contrast if the i-th element of the i-th row has the highest value. For a given contrast and prediction model, we compute subject identification accuracy as the fraction of subjects with a maximum at the diagonal.

6   Results

6.1   Contrasts Prediction Quality

Figure 3A shows the correlation of models' prediction with the same subject's observed contrast maps. Only reliably predictable task contrasts, defined as those whose average test-retest correlation across all test subjects is greater than the average across all subjects and contrasts, are shown in subsequent figures. We include results for all contrasts in the Supplementary Materials. Figure 3B shows the surface visualization of 2 task contrasts for 2 subjects. While the group-average match individual contrasts' coarse pattern, subject-specific contrasts exhibit fine details that are replicated in the retest session but washed out in the group averages (circled in Fig. 3B). On the other hand, predictions by the linear regression model missed out the gross topology of activation specific to some contrasts (e.g. second row of Fig. 3B). Overall, BrainSurfCNN's prediction consistently yielded the highest correlation with the individual tfMRI contrasts, approaching the upper bound of the subjects' retest reference.

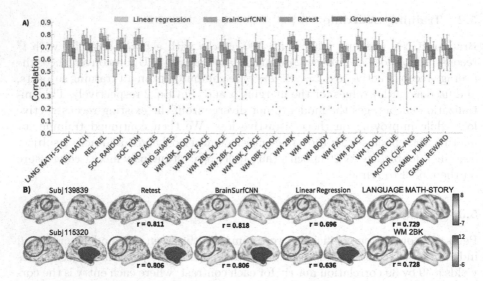

Fig. 3. (A) Correlation of predicted with true individual task contrasts (only reliable contrasts are shown). LANG, REL, SOC, EMO, WM, and GAMBL are short for LANGUAGE, RELATIONAL, SOCIAL, EMOTION, WORKING MEMORY and GAMBLING respectively. (B) Surface visualization for 2 task contrasts of 2 subjects. The right-most column shows the group-average contrasts for comparison.

6.2　Subject Identification

Figure 4A shows the correlation matrices between the individual tfMRI task contrasts (rows) and the predicted task contrasts (columns) for two contrasts across all test subjects. Similar to [6], the matrices were normalized for visualization to account for higher variability in true versus predicted contrasts. All matrices have dominant diagonals, indicating that the individual predictions are generally closest to same subjects' contrasts. Across all reliable task contrasts, the task contrasts predicted by BrainSurfCNN have consistently better subject identification accuracy as compared to the linear regression model, shown in Fig. 4B and the clearer diagonals in Fig. 4A.

6.3　Ablation Analysis

Table 1 shows the effects of ensemble learning and reconstructive-contrastive (R-C) loss on BrainSurfCNN performance. Ensemble learning (Sect. 5.1) improves upon training with one sample per subject in predictive accuracy (diagonals of correlation matrices in Fig. 4), but results in smaller difference between predictions of one subject versus other subjects' contrasts (off-diagonal values). However, the introduction of the R-C loss made the model prediction more specific to the subjects of interest. Scheduled tuning of the loss margins (Sect. 5.2) further improved the specificity of the predictions.

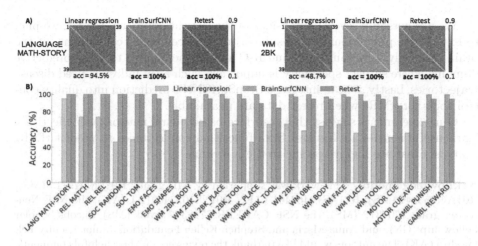

Fig. 4. (A) Correlation matrices (normalized) of prediction versus true subject contrasts for 2 task contrasts across 39 test subjects (B) Subject identification accuracy of predictions for 23 reliably predictable task contrasts.

Table 1. Effects of design choices on BrainSurfCNN predictions.

Model	Correlation with self	Correlation of self minus other
1 sample/subject	0.64 ± 0.11	0.060 ± 0.036
Ensemble (8 samples/subject)	0.66 ± 0.11	0.046 ± 0.026
Ensemble + 100 more epochs with l^2 loss	0.66 ± 0.11	0.048 ± 0.026
Ensemble + R-C Loss	0.66 ± 0.11	0.081 ± 0.045
Ensemble + scheduled R-C Loss	0.66 ± 0.11	0.087 ± 0.047
Retest	0.61 ± 0.13	0.181 ± 0.089

7   Discussion and Conclusion

Cognitive fingerprints derived from rsfMRI have been of great research interest [5,23]. The focus of tfMRI, on the other hand, has been mostly on seeking consensus of task contrasts across individuals. Recent work exploring individuality in task fMRI mostly utilized sparse activation coordinates reported in the literature [24,25] and/or simple modeling methods [6,7,23]. In this paper, we presented a novel approach for individualized prediction of task contrasts from functional connectomes using surface-based CNN. In our experiments, the previously published baseline model [6] achieved lower correlation values than the group-averages, which might be due to the ROI-level modeling that misses relevant signal from the rest of the brain. The proposed BrainSurfCNN yielded predictions that were overall highly correlated with and highly specific to the individuals' tfMRI constrasts . We also introduced a reconstructive-contrastive (R-C) loss that significantly improved subject identifiability, which are on par with the test-retest upper bound.

We are pursuing several extensions of the current approach. Firstly, we plan to extend the predictions to the sub-cortical and cerebellar components of the brain. Secondly, BrainSurfCNN and R-C loss can be applied to other predictive domains where subject specificity is important, such as in individualized disease trajectories. Lastly, we can integrate BranSurfCNN's prediction into quality control tools for tfMRI when retest data are unavailable.

Our experiments suggest that a surface-based neural network can effectively learn useful multi-scale features from functional connectomes to predict tfMRI contrasts that are highly specific to the individual.

Acknowledgements. This work was supported by NIH grants R01LM012719 (MS), R01AG053949 (MS), R21NS10463401 (AK), R01NS10264601A1 (AK), the NSF NeuroNex grant 1707312 (MS), the NSF CAREER 1748377 grant (MS), Jacobs Scholar Fellowship (GN), and Anna-Maria and Stephen Kellen Foundation Junior Faculty Fellowship (AK). The authors would like to thank the reviewers for their helpful comments, Ms. Hao-Ting Wang for her pointers on preprocessing HCP data and Mr. Minh Nguyen for his comments on the early drafts.

References

1. Biswal, B.B., et al.: Toward discovery science of human brain function. Proc. Natl. Acad. Sci. **107**(10), 4734–4739 (2010)
2. Kelly, C., Biswal, B.B., Cameron Craddock, R., Xavier Castellanos, F., Milham, M.P.: Characterizing variation in the functional connectome: promise and pitfalls. Trends Cogn. Sci. **16**(3), 181–188 (2012)
3. Khosla, M., Jamison, K., Ngo, G.H., Kuceyeski, A., Sabuncu, M.R.: Machine learning in resting-state fMRI analysis. Magn. Reson. Imaging **64**, 101–121 (2019)
4. Dosenbach, N.U.F., et al.: Prediction of individual brain maturity using fMRI. Science **329**(5997), 1358–1361 (2010)
5. Finn, E.S., et al.: Functional connectome fingerprinting: identifying individuals using patterns of brain connectivity. Nat. Neurosci. **18**(11), 1664 (2015)
6. Tavor, I., Jones, O.P., Mars, R.B., Smith, S.M., Behrens, T.E., Jbabdi, S.: Task-free MRI predicts individual differences in brain activity during task performance. Science **352**(6282), 216–220 (2016)
7. Cole, M.W., Ito, T., Bassett, D.S., Schultz, D.H.: Activity flow over resting-state networks shapes cognitive task activations. Nat. Neurosci. **19**(12), 1718 (2016)
8. Glasser, M.F., et al.: The minimal preprocessing pipelines for the human connectome project. Neuroimage **80**, 105–124 (2013)
9. Khosla, M., Jamison, K., Kuceyeski, A., Sabuncu, M.R.: Ensemble learning with 3d convolutional neural networks for functional connectome-based prediction. Neuroimage **199**, 651–662 (2019)
10. Chiyu, M.J., Huang, J., Kashinath, K., Prabhat, P.M., Niessner, M.: Spherical CNNs on unstructured grids. In: International Conference on Learning Representations (2019)
11. Van Essen, D.C., Glasser, M.F., Dierker, D.L., Harwell, J., Coalson, T.: Parcellations and hemispheric asymmetries of human cerebral cortex analyzed on surface-based atlases. Cereb. Cortex **22**(10), 2241–2262 (2012)

12. Fischl, B., Sereno, M.I., Tootell, R.B.H., Dale, A.M.: High-resolution intersubject averaging and a coordinate system for the cortical surface. Hum. Brain Mapp. **8**(4), 272–284 (1999)
13. Wu, J., et al.: Accurate nonlinear mapping between MNI volumetric and freesurfer surface coordinate systems. Hum. Brain Mapp. **39**(9), 3793–3808 (2018)
14. Kawahara, J., et al.: BrainNetCNN: convolutional neural networks for brain networks; towards predicting neurodevelopment. NeuroImage **146**, 1038–1049 (2017)
15. Niepert, M., Ahmed, M., Kutzkov, K.: Learning convolutional neural networks for graphs. In: International Conference on Machine Learning, pp. 2014–2023 (2016)
16. Baumgardner, J.R., Frederickson, P.O.: Icosahedral discretization of the two-sphere. SIAM J. Numer. Anal. **22**(6), 1107–1115 (1985)
17. Koch, G., Zemel, R., Salakhutdinov, R.: Siamese neural networks for one-shot image recognition. In: ICML Deep Learning Workshop (2015)
18. Schroff, F., Kalenichenko, D., Philbin, J.: Facenet: a unified embedding for face recognition and clustering. In: Proceedings of the IEEE Conference on Computer Vision and Pattern Recognition, pp. 815–823 (2015)
19. Ronneberger, O., Fischer, P., Brox, T.: U-net: convolutional networks for biomedical image segmentation. In: International Conference on Medical Image Computing and Computer-assisted Intervention, pp. 234–241 (2015)
20. Milletari, F., Navab, N., Ahmadi, S.-A.: V-net: fully convolutional neural networks for volumetric medical image segmentation. In: 2016 Fourth International Conference on 3D Vision (3DV), pp. 565–571. IEEE (2016)
21. Smith, S.M., et al.: Resting-state fMRI in the human connectome project. Neuroimage **80**, 144–168 (2013)
22. Barch, D.M., et al.: Function in the human connectome: task-fMRI and individual differences in behavior. Neuroimage **80**, 169–189 (2013)
23. Amico, E., Goñi, J.: The quest for identifiability in human functional connectomes. Sci. Rep. **8**(1), 1–14 (2018)
24. Yeo, B.T.T., et al.: Functional specialization and flexibility in human association cortex. Cereb. Cortex **25**(10), 3654–3672 (2015)
25. Ngo, G.H., et al.: Beyond consensus: embracing heterogeneity in curated neuroimaging meta-analysis. NeuroImage **200**, 142–158 (2019)

Disentangled Intensive Triplet Autoencoder for Infant Functional Connectome Fingerprinting

Dan Hu, Fan Wang, Han Zhang, Zhengwang Wu, Li Wang, Weili Lin, Gang Li(✉), Dinggang Shen(✉), and for UNC/UMN Baby Connectome Project Consortium

Department of Radiology and BRIC, University of North Carolina at Chapel Hill, Chapel Hill, NC 27599, USA

gang_li@med.unc.edu, dinggang.shen@gmail.com

Abstract. Functional connectome "fingerprint" is a highly characterized brain pattern that distinguishes one individual from others. Although its existence has been demonstrated in adults, an unanswered but fundamental question is whether such individualized pattern emerges since infancy. This problem is barely investigated despite its importance in identifying the origin of the intrinsic connectome patterns that mirror distinct behavioral phenotypes. However, addressing this knowledge gap is challenging because the conventional methods are only applicable to developed brains with subtle longitudinal changes and typically fail on the dramatically developing infant brains. To tackle this challenge, we invent a novel model, namely, disentangled intensive triplet autoencoder (DI-TAE). First, we introduce the triplet autoencoder to embed the original connectivity into a latent space with higher discriminative capability among infant individuals. Then, a disentanglement strategy is proposed to separate the latent variables into identity-code, age-code, and noise-code, which not only restrains the interference from age-related developmental variance, but also captures the identity-related invariance. Next, a cross-reconstruction loss and an intensive triplet loss are designed to guarantee the effectiveness of the disentanglement and enhance the inter-subject dissimilarity for better discrimination. Finally, a variance-guided bootstrap aggregating is developed for DI-TAE to further improve the performance of identification. DI-TAE is validated on three longitudinal resting-state fMRI datasets with 394 infant scans aged 16 to 874 days. Our proposed model outperforms other state-of-the-art methods by increasing the identification rate by more than 50%, and for the first time suggests the plausible existence of brain functional connectome "fingerprint" since early infancy.

Keywords: Infant functional connectome · Rs-fMRI · Triplet autoencoder

1 Introduction

Using brain functional connectivity profiles to establish individual uniqueness among a cohort is important for individualized characterization of disease and health [1], understanding intrinsic patterns of brain organization [2] and their relationship with distinct

© Springer Nature Switzerland AG 2020
A. L. Martel et al. (Eds.): MICCAI 2020, LNCS 12267, pp. 72–82, 2020.
https://doi.org/10.1007/978-3-030-59728-3_8

behavioral phenotypes [3]. To date, it has been shown that the brains of adults [1–4] and adolescents [5] exhibit highly individualized functional connectome patterns, which is unique enough to be taken as "fingerprint" for distinguishing an individual from others. Of note, most of the functional connectome fingerprinting studies focus on adults, in which the brain function is relatively stable across different scans. Only a few studies involved the developing brains from adolescent cohorts [4, 5]. To the best of our knowledge, there is no study on the brain functional connectome fingerprinting in infants, whose brains are undergoing dramatic development, although brain folding fingerprinting in infants has been investigated [22]. However, studying the fingerprinting capability of the infant functional connectivity is of great neuroscientific significance with the examination of: 1) Whether such individualized functional connectome pattern emerges early during infancy, which features the most critical and dynamic postnatal brain development [6, 7, 18, 19]; 2) Which functional connection(s) and network(s) manifest more individualized uniqueness during the early brain development. Addressing these questions is challenging because the intrinsic patterns for identifying an individual infant from their peers are overwhelmed by the rapid brain development. Conventional methods designed for adults only suite the scenario with subtle longitudinal brain change and are thus typically fail on infant data.

To fill this knowledge gap, we develop a novel model called disentangled intensive triplet autoencoder (DI-TAE). It restrains the overwhelming interference from brain development by separating the invariance of the individualized brain connectome from the variance of the dramatic brain development. Specifically, at first, triplet autoencoder [8, 9] is chosen as the basic model to enhance the discrimination capability of function connectivity for its potential on capturing high-order discriminative information from comparison within triplet sample. Then, the latent variables of the autoencoder are disentangled into identity-code, age-code, and noise-code, representing the individualized information, developmental information, and unconcerned noise, respectively. This new strategy helps to not only effectively extract the discriminative information for identification but also simultaneously model the variance and invariance in the brain connectome by unifying age prediction and individual identification in a single framework. A cross-reconstruction loss is further designed requiring the identity codes obtained from the same subjects are replaceable with each other in the reconstruction process, so as to guarantee the effectiveness of the disentanglement. Next, equipping with a new defined intensive triplet loss, the inter-subject dissimilarity is deeply emphasized to learn a more discriminative feature variable. Finally, since the high dimension of the whole brain functional connectivity features poses a significant challenge for efficient learning, a variance-guided bootstrap aggregating is designed, only including a small portion of features at each time, to boost the accuracy while preventing overfitting.

In experiments based on a longitudinal infant dataset, the high identification accuracy obtained by DI-TAE not only validates the superiority of our proposed model but also, for the first time, proves that brain functional connectome "fingerprint" emerges since infancy. With further analysis, networks that manifest more on individualized uniqueness during the early brain development were also identified for revealing the developmental trajectory of brain connectome fingerprint from infants to adults.

2 Method

2.1 Disentangled Intensive Triplet Autoencoder

Unifying disentanglement, age prediction, and individual identification into a triplet autoencoder, the disentangled intensive triplet autoencoder (DI-TAE) is trained with specifically defined losses and dedicatedly designed for infant functional connectome fingerprinting. The framework of DI-TAE is depicted in Fig. 1 and detailed below.

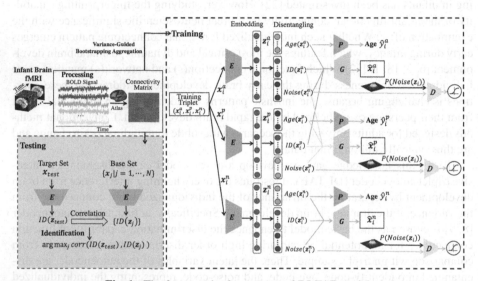

Fig. 1. The framework of our proposed DI-TAE model.

The individual infant identification test is performed across paired of scans consisting of one "target" and one "base" data, with the requirement that the target and base sessions are acquired from different ages. That is, each subject has two longitudinal fMRI scans from two different sessions. In the process of identification, one scan will be selected from the target set iteratively with the goal of determining the corresponding scan obtained from the same subject in the base set. The proposed model uses triplet examples to train the network. Denoted by $\left(x_i^a, x_i^p, x_i^n\right)$, the three input functional connectomes form the i-th triplet, where x_i^a (anchor) and x_i^p (positive) are of the same subject and from the target set and the base set, respectively, while x_i^n (negative) belongs to a different subject and is from the base set. Herein, $i = 1, \cdots, M$ and M is the total number of the triplets.

Encoding. The three inputs x_i^a, x_i^p, and x_i^n employ a neural network, denoted as E, as their shared encoder. The outputs of the encoder are called the latent variables, which denoted as z_i^a, z_i^p, and z_i^n. Indices a, p, and n will be omitted unless otherwise specified when we are referring to a common process for x_i^a, x_i^p, and x_i^n.

Latent variable disentanglement Since the age-related dramatic developmental variance highly interfere identifying the same subject's functional connectome from the base set, we should separate the age-related variance and identity-related invariance in functional connectome. Here, z_i is disentangled into three parts: $Age(z_i)$, $ID(z_i)$, and $Noise(z_i)$. They are called age-code, identity-code, and noise-code, which represent the developmental information, individualized information, and unconcerned noise, respectively. The basic requirements of the disentanglement are:

(1) The concatenation of $Age(z_i)$, $ID(z_i)$, and $Noise(z_i)$ equals z_i;
(2) $ID(z_i^a)$ and $ID(z_i^p)$ should be as similar as possible, while $ID(z_i^a)$ differs from $ID(z_i^n)$ and also $ID(z_i^p)$ differs from $ID(z_i^n)$ as much as possible.
(3) $Age(z_i)$ is capable of age prediction;
(4) $Noise(z_i)$ obeys a Gaussian distribution.

Cross reconstruction requirements. The elements in the triplet employ a neural network, denoted as G, as their shared decoder. Conventionally, since $z_i = [Age(z_i), ID(z_i), Noise(z_i)]$ is the latent variable encoded from x_i, a direct requirement is the reconstruction of x_i from z_i, which signifies the similarity between x_i and $\hat{x}_i = G(z_i)$. On the other side, since $ID(z_i)$ represents the identity-related invariance, $ID(z_i^a)$ and $ID(z_i^p)$ should be capable of replacing each other in reconstructing x_i^a and x_i^p. Therefore, to further ensure the effectiveness of the disentanglement, we introduce the cross reconstruction requirements: the similarity between x_i^a and $G([Age(z_i^a), ID(z_i^p), Noise(z_i^a)])$, and the similarity between x_i^p and $G([Age(z_i^p), ID(z_i^a), Noise(z_i^p)])$.

Age predictor and adversarial discriminator. To ensure that the $Age(z_i)$ learns the age-related information, a neural network is designed as the regressor P to predict age from $Age(z_i)$. Furthermore, a discriminator D is designed to impose the adversarial regularization on $Noise(z_i)$, which tries to ensure $Noise(z_i)$ follows a Gaussian distribution through adversarial learning [16].

E, G, P, and D are all parameterized and learned together with the following losses.

Intensive triplet loss. Ordinary triplet loss merely focuses on the relative distance between the (Anchor, Positive) and (Anchor, Negative) pairs. Considering that (Positive, Negative) is also a pair of different labels, as shown in Fig. 2, the inter-subject dissimilarity can be deeply enhanced if the relative distance between (Anchor, Positive) and (Positive, Negative) is also measured as a new constraint. Thus, a new intensive triplet loss $\mathcal{L}_{I-tri}$ is defined as follows, where *corr* is the Pearson correlation:

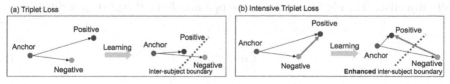

Fig. 2. Compared with the triplet loss (a), intensive triplet loss (b) maximizes not only the distance between anchor and negative but also the distance between positive and negative.

$$\mathcal{L}_{I-tri} = \mathcal{L}_{tri} + \mathcal{L}_I \tag{1}$$

$$\mathcal{L}_{tri} = \sum_{i=1}^{M} corr\big(ID\big(E\big(x_i^a\big)\big), ID\big(E\big(x_i^p\big)\big)\big) - corr\big(ID\big(E\big(x_i^a\big)\big), ID\big(E\big(x_i^n\big)\big)\big) \tag{2}$$

$$\mathcal{L}_I = \sum_{i=1}^{M} corr\big(ID\big(E\big(x_i^a\big)\big), ID\big(E\big(x_i^p\big)\big)\big) - corr\big(ID\big(E\big(x_i^p\big)\big), ID\big(E\big(x_i^n\big)\big)\big) \tag{3}$$

Reconstruction loss. The reconstruction loss is defined based on the cross-reconstruction requirements described above. It consists of ordinary reconstruction and cross reconstruction from the triplet samples. $\mathbb{E}$ is the expectation operator.

$$\mathcal{L}_{recon} = \mathcal{L}_{recon\_ordi} + \mathcal{L}_{recon\_cross} \tag{4}$$

$$\mathcal{L}_{recon\_ordi} = \sum_{j=a,p,n} \mathbb{E}_{x_i^j}\big(x_i^j - G\big(\big[Age\big(E\big(x_i^j\big)\big), ID\big(E\big(x_i^j\big)\big), Noise\big(E\big(x_i^j\big)\big)\big]\big)\big) \tag{5}$$

$$\mathcal{L}_{recon\_cross} = \sum_{j\in B=\{a,p\}} \mathbb{E}_{x_i^j}\big(x_i^j - G\big(\big[Age\big(E\big(x_i^j\big)\big), ID\big(E\big(x_i^{B\backslash\{j\}}\big)\big), Noise\big(E\big(x_i^j\big)\big)\big]\big)\big) \tag{6}$$

Age prediction loss L2 norm is adopted as our regression loss for age prediction:

$$\mathcal{L}_{age} = \sum_{j=a,p,n} \mathbb{E}_{x_i^j}\big(y_i^j - P\big(Age\big(E\big(x_i^j\big)\big)\big)\big) \tag{7}$$

Where y_i^j is the real age corresponding to x_i^j.

Adversarial loss. Let $Prob(Noise(z_i)) = \mathcal{N}(Noise(z_i)|\mu(x_i), \sigma(x_i))$ be the prior distribution of $Noise(z_i)$, $Prob(x_i)$ be the distribution of the data, and $q(Noise(z_i)|x_i)$ be the encoding distribution. The distribution requirement on $Noise(z_i)$, defined by the disentanglement, requires the aggregated posterior distribution $q(Noise(z_i)) = \int_{x_i} q(Noise(z_i)|x_i)Prob(x_i)dx_i$ matches the predefined prior $Prob(Noise(z_i))$. This regularization on $Noise(z_i)$ is realized by an adversarial procedure with the discriminator D, which leads to a $\min_E \max_D \mathcal{L}_{adv}$ problem, where

$$\mathcal{L}_{adv} = \sum_{j=a,p,n} \mathbb{E}_{x_i^j} \log D\big(Noise\big(E\big(x_i^j\big)\big)\big) + \mathbb{E}_{z_i^j} \log\big(1 - D\big(Noise\big(z_i^j\big)\big)\big) \tag{8}$$

Full Objective. The objective functions to optimize E, G, P, and D are written as:

$$\mathcal{L}_D = \mathcal{L}_{adv} \tag{9}$$

$$\mathcal{L}_{E,G,P} = \lambda_1 \mathcal{L}_{I\_tri} + \lambda_2 \mathcal{L}_{recon} + \mathcal{L}_{adv\_E} + \lambda_3 \mathcal{L}_{age} \tag{10}$$

where $\mathcal{L}_{adv\_E} = \sum_{j=a,p,n} \mathbb{E}_{x_i^j} \log D\big(Noise\big(E\big(x_i^j\big)\big)\big)$, λ_1, λ_2, and λ_3 are trade off parameters. The model alternatively updates E, G, P, and D with $\mathcal{L}_{E,G,P}$ and $\mathcal{L}_D$.

2.2   Variance-Guided Bootstrap Aggregating

Brain functional connectome can be represented by the upper triangle of the functional connectivity matrix. However, the whole-brain functional connectivity matrix is a high dimensional vector that is inefficient for training or trends to overfit. It has been proved that the "thin slice" of the functional connectome may still lead to comparable accuracy for individual identification [12]; therefore, bootstrap aggregating with randomly chosen partial connectivity links from the full connectome is introduced to promote the learning efficiency and effectiveness. Specifically, 1) the discriminative capability (DC) of a connection e is measured by $\mathrm{DC}(e) = \sigma\{C_i(e)|i = 1, \cdots, N\}$, where C_i is the functional connectome of the i-th scan, σ is the standard deviation operator, and N is the number of scans in the base set; 2) K connectivity links with a dimensionality far smaller than that of the original connectome are randomly chosen out of the full connectome with the probability of $\{P\_e = \mathrm{DC}(e)/\sum_e \mathrm{DC}(e)\}$. By applying the chosen indices to all connectomes repetitively, we generate bootstrap samples; 3) T models are fitted by T bootstrap samples before the final identification result can be obtained by majority voting. We set $K = 5000$ and $T = 50$ in our experiment after several empirical tests.

3   Experiments

3.1   Data Description

We verified the effectiveness of the proposed DI-TAE model and study the infant brain connectome fingerprinting on a high-resolution resting-state fMRI (rs-fMRI) data including 104 subjects (53 females/51 males) with 394 longitudinal scans acquired at different ages ranging from 16 to 874 days in the UNC/UMN Baby Connectome Project [23]. All infant MR images were acquired during natural sleeping on a 3T Siemens Prisma MRI scanner using a Siemens 32 channel head coil. T1-weighted and T2-weighted MR images were obtained with the resolution = $0.8 \times 0.8 \times 0.8$ mm^3. The rs-fMRIs scans were acquired with TR/TE = 800/37 ms, FA = $80°$, FOV = 220 mm, resolution = $2 \times 2 \times 2$ mm^3, and total volume = 421 (5 min 47 s). All structural and functional MR images were preprocessed following a state-of-the-art infant-tailored pipeline [21, 24–27]. Cortical surfaces were reconstructed and aligned onto a public 4D infant surface atlases [20, 28, 29]. At each cortical vertex on the middle cortical surface, its representative fMRI time-series were extracted [17]. An infant-specific functional parcellation template with 420 cortical ROIs were then constructed and warped onto each individual cortical surface. The time series within each ROI were averaged and further correlated with those from all others. The functional connectivity matrix was derived by calculating the Pearson correlation coefficient between time series of each pair of ROIs. Fishers r-to-z transformation was conducted to improve the normality of the functional connectivity. To validate our model based on data sets with different distributions of age and inter-session time gap, three datasets (i.e., Dataset 1, Dataset 2, and Dataset 3) were generated from the 394 longitudinal rs-fMRI scans. Figure 3. illustrates how the datasets were generated and the distribution of each dataset.

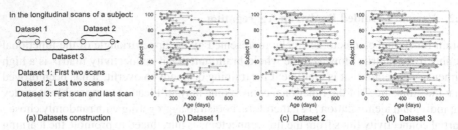

Fig. 3. Experimental datasets description. (a) The way that the three datasets constructed from the longitudinal scans; (b-d) The age distributions of the three datasets. Each line indicates a subject and each circle indicates a scan.

3.2 Validation of DI-TAE

We compare the proposed DI-TAE model with following seven methods: four state-of-the-art methods in brain connectome fingerprinting study including (1) Euclidean distance based 1-nearest neighbors algorithm (1-NN) [10]; (2) the Pearson correlation-based identification (P-Corr) [3, 4]; (3) PCA-reconstruction based identification (PCA-based) [11]; and (4) dynamic functional connectivity strength-based identification (DFC-Str) [1]. Three models derived from our DI-TAE for validating each of our proposed strategies, including: (5) taking differential power measure (DP) [3] as the contribution index to replace the discriminative capability measure, DC, defined in our model; (6) applying random selection [12] to replace the variance-guidance in the bootstrap aggregating in our model; and (7) taking the ordinary triplet loss to replace the intensive triplet loss in our model.

The encoder E and decoder G in DI-TAE were all designed as a two-layer perceptron neural networks. The predictor P constitutes of 6 densely connected layers of dimension (300, 500, 100,100, 20, 1) with ReLU as the activation function. The discriminator D constitutes of 5 densely connected layers of dimension (300, 30, 30, 10, 1) with ReLU as the activation function of the first 4 layers and Sigmoid as the activation function of the last layer. DI-TAE was implemented with Pytorch and optimized with Adam by a fixed learning rate as 0.001. The batch size was set as 200. The dimension of the latent variable was 2000, while the dimensions of age code, identity code, and noise code were set as 300, 1400, and 300, respectively. $\lambda_1 = 0.1$, $\lambda_2 = 0.8$, and $\lambda_3 = 0.1$. Except the dedicated different parts for comparison, methods (5)–(7) share the same architecture with DI-TAE for the fairness of the comparison. For DFC-Str based identification, the sliding window has a width of 125 TR (i.e., 100 s) and slide on time with a time step of 1 TR (i.e., 800 ms). The PCA components number was set to 80 in PCA-based identification.

The identification rate was measured as the percentage of subjects whose identity was correctly predicted out of the total number of subjects. The predicted identity of the scan is correct means the corresponding scan obtained from the same subject in the base set is determined. The comparison results are shown in Table 1. Without training required, the identification tests of methods (1)–(4) were implemented directly. With training and testing required, our model and methods (5)–(7) were assessed by 10 times of 10-fold cross validation. The means and standard deviations of the 10 identification accuracies are reported. Our DI-TAE model outperformed the four state-of-the-art methods by increasing their identification accuracy by more than 50%. On Dataset 2, although the age gap between the two sessions are in average 191 days, the identification accuracy still reaches 81.7%. When changing the DC in our model to DP (or random selection) or changing the intensive triplet loss proposed by us to the ordinary triplet loss, the accuracy of the model was significantly reduced, further validating the effectiveness of the proposed strategies.

Table 1. The comparison of DI-TAE with other seven methods with identification rate (%). The scans in Session 2 were acquired later than those in Session 1.

Target set-Base set	Session 2- Session 1			Session 1- Session 2		
	Dataset1	Dataset 2	Dataset 3	Dataset 1	Dataset 2	Dataset 3
1-NN [10]	21.12	33.64	20.19	23.08	34.62	16.35
P-Corr [3]	39.42	50.96	32.69	42.31	58.65	33.65
PCA-based [11]	38.46	52.88	28.85	37.50	55.77	29.81
DFC-Str [1]	39.42	53.85	31.73	38.46	56.73	31.73
DP [1] + ours	49.1 ± 1.3	62.5 ± 0.9	42.6 ± 1.1	47.5 ± 0.7	61.4 ± 1.5	42.6 ± 1.4
Random [12] + ours	50.2 ± 3.8	65.2 ± 2.6	42.3 ± 3.5	46.2 ± 3.6	59.7 ± 2.8	38.9 ± 2.7
Triplet loss [8] + ours	59.2 ± 1.3	77.6 ± 1.7	57.3 ± 1.3	58.8 ± 1.4	75.3 ± 1.8	57.1 ± 1.5
DI-TAE (proposed)	**65.6 ± 1.3**	**81.7 ± 1.5**	**63.5 ± 1.3**	**66.5 ± 1.5**	**80.1 ± 1.7**	**62.7 ± 1.3**

3.3 Infant Functional Connectome Fingerprinting

Based on our proposed model DI-TAE, the identification rate of infants on the three data sets are over 70% on average, suggesting the plausible existence of brain functional "fingerprint" during early infancy. The most contributive connections for infant finger-printing were further analyzed by the weights of the learned encoder in DI-TAE and shown in Fig. 4. It seems that the visual and somatomotor networks manifest more individualized uniqueness during the early brain development. Compared to our findings, the connections in the frontoparietal network are more important in adult functional fingerprinting [3, 14, 15], which shows that there may be difference between the developing infant brains and the stably developed adult brains. Moreover, since better identification performance were always obtained on Dataset 2 with all the methods, we can see that it is easier to identify the identity of the scan with more developed brains and smaller age difference between the two scan sessions.

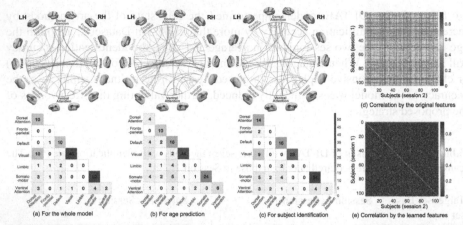

(a) For the whole model   (b) For age prediction   (c) For subject identification   (d) Correlation by the original features   (e) Correlation by the learned features

Fig. 4. The most contributive connections for the whole identification model (a), for age prediction (b), and for subject identification (c). The most contributive connections were obtained by thresholding the whole connectome at the 99.9 percentile of weights. In the circle plots, the ROIs are organized into 7 networks [13] and lines represent connections. The numbers in the colored matrices are the number of contributive connections within and between each pair of networks. The correlation matrix between the scans of two sessions based on the original features and that based on the learned features by DI-TAE are shown in (d) and (e), respectively. Figure (e) shows that the correlation between the scans of the same subject is much larger than that of different subjects, indicating the significantly increased discriminative capability of the learned features. (Color figure online)

4   Conclusion

In this paper, we proposed a disentangled intensive triplet autoencoder to address the absence of effective methods in studying functional connectome fingerprinting of infant brains. Disentangling the age-related variance from subject identity-related invariance, our model successfully captures individualized patterns of infant brain functional connectivity out of the overwhelming dramatic brain development. With a high identification rate for infants, for the first time, our results suggest that the brain functional "fingerprint" may exist from early infancy. Our proposed DI-TAE model serves as a potentially powerful method for studying individualized brain connectome pattern and its development, even such connectome is undergoing dramatic changes.

Acknowledgments. This work was partially supported by NIH grants (MH116225, MH117943, MH104324, MH109773). This work also utilizes approaches developed by an NIH grant (1U01MH110274) and the efforts of the UNC/UMN Baby Connectome Project Consortium.

References

1. Liu, J., Liao, X., Xia, M., et. al.: Chronnectome fingerprinting: Identifying individuals and predicting higher cognitive functions using dynamic brain connectivity patterns. Hum. Brain Mapp. **39**(2), 902–915 (2018)

2. Miranda-Dominguez, O., Feczko, E., Grayson, D.S., et. al.: Heritability of the human connectome: a connectotyping study. Netw. Neurosci. **2**(02), 175–199 (2018)
3. Finn, E.S., Shen, X., Scheinost, D., et. al.: Functional connectome fingerprinting: identifying individuals using patterns of brain connectivity. Nat. Neurosci. **18**(11), 1664–1674 (2015)
4. Horien, C., Shen, X., Scheinost, D., et. al.: The individual functional connectome is unique and stable over months to years. Neuroimage **189**, 676–687 (2019)
5. Kaufmann, T., Alnæs, D., Doan, N.T., et. al.: Delayed stabilization and individualization in connectome development are related to psychiatric disorders. Nat. Neurosci. **20**(4), 513–515 (2017)
6. Gilmore, J.H., Knickmeyer, R.C., Gao, W.: Imaging structural and functional brain development in early childhood. Nat. Rev. Neurosci. **19**(3), 123 (2018)
7. Zhang, H., Shen, D., Lin, W.: Resting-state functional MRI studies on infant brains: a decade of gap-filling efforts. NeuroImage **185**, 664–684 (2019)
8. Hoffer, E., Ailon, N.: Deep metric learning using triplet network. In: Feragen, A., Pelillo, M., Loog, M. (eds.) SIMBAD 2015. LNCS, vol. 9370, pp. 84–92. Springer, Cham (2015). https://doi.org/10.1007/978-3-319-24261-3_7
9. Yang, Y., Chen, H., Shao, J.: Triplet enhanced autoencoder: model-free discriminative network embedding. In: Proceedings of the 28th International Joint Conference on Artificial Intelligence, pp. 5363–5369. AAAI Press (2019)
10. Bishop, C.M.: Pattern Recognition and Machine Learning (Information Science and Statistics). Springer-Verlag, New York Inc, Secaucus, NJ, USA (2006)
11. Amico, E., Goñi, J.: The quest for identifiability in human functional connectomes. Sci. Rep. **8**(1), 1–14 (2018)
12. Byrge, L., Kennedy, D.P.: High-accuracy individual identification using a "thin slice" of the functional connectome. Netw. Neurosci. **3**(2), 363–383 (2019)
13. Thomas Yeo, B.T., Krienen, F.M., Sepulcre, J., et. al.: The organization of the human cerebral cortex estimated by intrinsic functional connectivity. J. Neurophysiol. **106**(3), 1125–1165 (2011)
14. Demeter, D.V., Engelhardt, L.E., Mallett, R., et. al.: Functional connectivity fingerprints at rest are similar across youths and adults and vary with genetic similarity. iScience **23**(1), 100801 (2020)
15. Vanderwal, T., Eilbott, J., Finn, E.S., et. al.: Individual differences in functional connectivity during naturalistic viewing conditions. Neuroimage **157**, 521–530 (2017)
16. Makhzani, A., Shlens, J., Jaitly, N., Goodfellow, I., Frey, B.: Adversarial autoencoders (2015). arXiv preprint arXiv:1511.05644
17. Glasser, M.F., Sotiropoulos, S.N., Wilson, J.A., et. al.: The minimal preprocessing pipelines for the Human Connectome Project. Neuroimage **80**, 105–124 (2013)
18. Zhang, H., Stanley, N., Mucha, Peter J., Yin, W., Lin, W., Shen, D.: Multi-layer large-scale functional connectome reveals infant brain developmental patterns. In: Frangi, Alejandro F., Schnabel, Julia A., Davatzikos, C., Alberola-López, C., Fichtinger, G. (eds.) MICCAI 2018. LNCS, vol. 11072, pp. 136–144. Springer, Cham (2018). https://doi.org/10.1007/978-3-030-00931-1_16
19. Stoecklein, S., Hilgendorff, A., Li, M., et. al.: Variable functional connectivity architecture of the preterm human brain: Impact of developmental cortical expansion and maturation. Proc. Natl. Acad. Sci. **117**(2), 1201–1206 (2020)
20. https://www.nitrc.org/projects/infantsurfatlas
21. Li, G., Wang, L., Yap, P.-T., et al.: Computational neuroanatomy of baby brains: a review. Neuroimage **185**, 906–925 (2019)
22. Duan D., Xia S., Rekik I., et al.: Individual identification and individual variability analysis based on cortical folding features in developing infant singletons and twins. Hum. Brain Mapp. **41**(8), 1985–2003 (2020)

23. Howell, B.R., Styner, M.A., Gao, W., et al.: The UNC/UMN baby connectome project (BCP): an overview of the study design and protocol development. NeuroImage **185**, 891–905 (2019)

24. Wang, L., et al.: Volume-based analysis of 6-month-old infant brain MRI for autism biomarker identification and early diagnosis. In: Frangi, A., Schnabel, J., Davatzikos, C., Alberola-López, C., Fichtinger, G. (eds.) MICCAI 2018. LNCS, vol. 11072, pp. 411–419. Springer, Cham (2018). https://doi.org/10.1007/978-3-030-00931-1_47

25. Li, G., Nie, J., Wang, L., Shi, F., et al.: Measuring the dynamic longitudinal cortex development in infants by reconstruction of temporally consistent cortical surfaces. NeuroImage **90**, 266–279 (2014)

26. Li, G., Wang, L., Shi, F., Lin, W., Shen, D.: Simultaneous and consistent labeling of longitudinal dynamic developing cortical surfaces in infants. Med. Image Anal. **18**(8), 1274–1289 (2014)

27. Sun L., Zhang D., Lian C., Wang L., et al.: Topological correction of infant white matter surfaces using anatomically constrained convolutional neural network. NeuroImage **198**, 114–124 (2019)

28. Li, G., Wang, L., Shi, F., Gilmore, J.H., Lin, W., Shen, D.: Construction of 4D high-definition cortical surface atlases of infants: methods and applications. Med. Image Anal. **25**(1), 22–36 (2015)

29. Wu, Z., Wang, L., Lin, W., Gilmore, J.H., Li, G., Shen, D.: Construction of 4D infant cortical surface atlases with sharp folding patterns via spherical patch-based group-wise sparse representation. Hum. Brain Mapp. **40**(13), 3860–3880 (2019)

COVLET: Covariance-Based Wavelet-Like Transform for Statistical Analysis of Brain Characteristics in Children

Fan Yang[1]([envelope]), Amal Isaiah[2], and Won Hwa Kim[1]

[1] University of Texas at Arlington, Arlington, USA
fan.yang3@mavs.uta.edu
[2] University of Maryland School of Medicine, Baltimore, USA

Abstract. Adolescence is a period of substantial experience-dependent brain development. A major goal of the Adolescent Brain Cognitive Development (ABCD) study is to understand how brain development is associated with various environmental factors such as socioeconomic characteristics. While ABCD study offers a large sample size, it still requires a sensitive method to detect subtle associations when studying typically developing children. Therefore, we propose a novel transform, i.e. covariance-based multi-scale transform (COVLET), which derives a multi-scale representation from a structured data (i.e., P features from N samples) that increases performance of downstream analyses. The theory driving our work stems from wavelet transform in signal processing and orthonormality of the principal components of a covariance matrix. Given the microstructural properties of brain regions from children enrolled in the ABCD study, we demonstrate a multi-variate statistical group analysis on family income using the multi-scale feature derived from brain structure and validate improvement in the statistical outcomes. Furthermore, our multi-scale descriptor reliably identifies specific regions of the brain that are susceptible to socioeconomic disparity.

1 Introduction

Adolescence is a period of rapid brain development shaped by genetic, physiologic and socioeconomic variables [1,8]. While previous studies have utilized techniques largely focusing on macrostructural properties of the cerebral cortex such as its thickness, surface area and volume [14], the microstructural characteristics such as diffusion of water along the tracts of the neuronal fibers may provide insights into the functional properties of the brain [13]. These properties, measured with high-resolution Diffusion Tensor Imaging (DTI), have previously been used to study the association of socioeconomic disadvantage with brain

Electronic supplementary material The online version of this chapter (https://doi.org/10.1007/978-3-030-59728-3_9) contains supplementary material, which is available to authorized users.

© Springer Nature Switzerland AG 2020
A. L. Martel et al. (Eds.): MICCAI 2020, LNCS 12267, pp. 83–93, 2020.
https://doi.org/10.1007/978-3-030-59728-3_9

structure and function in children. Fractional anisotropy (FA) from DTI, representing the diffusion of water perpendicular to the orientation of the neuronal fibers, has significant potential to identify association of the brain characteristics with neurobehavioral outcomes such as cognitive development [5,19,20].

The Adolescent Brain and Cognitive Development (ABCD) study [28], a longitudinal assessment of nearly 12,000 children commencing at the age of 9–11 years through adulthood, provides an unprecedented opportunity to explore development of the brain in adolescence with novel statistical tools. Therefore, we used the baseline dataset from the ABCD study (version 2.0.1) to examine the association between major socioeconomic characteristics, household income and microstructural characteristics (i.e., FA) of cortical regions. While ABCD provides a large sample size, the subtle variations in FA between closely-spaced groups within the spectrum of socioeconomic strata are still difficult to capture, requiring a more sensitive method that transforms the data into a new domain where the differences between the groups can be ascertained better.

Here, we have developed a novel transform that derives a multi-scale feature from structured data $X \in \mathbb{R}^{N \times P}$ with N samples and P features, which can improve its downstream analyses. The technical core of our method is inspired from wavelet transform in traditional signal processing. Wavelet transform transforms a signal $f(x)$ in x (in the Euclidean space) to the frequency space and its wavelet representation yields "multi-scale" representation of the original signal $f(x)$ [23]. Such a multi-scale representation of signals has provided successful results in Computer Vision for providing efficient features for robust comparisons of images [3,18,22], and shown benefits for statistical group analysis [15,17]. Wavelets behave as band-pass filters in the frequency space where the scales are defined by the bandwidth covered by the filters [11]. Therefore, if such a filter can be designed in a dual space (e.g., frequency space) defined by orthogonal bases (e.g., Fourier bases), we can design a novel transform that derives multi-scale representation of signals even in a complex domain [4,12].

The main barrier in our setting is that we are given with a structured data (e.g., FA of regions of interest (ROIs) from N subjects) instead of images, where the underlying space of the data is unknown. In this scenario, we utilize a precision matrix, i.e., inverse covariance matrix, which is symmetric and positive definite and thus has a set of "orthonormal" eigenvectors. The orthonormality lets us define an orthogonal transform, and together with filter functions on the spectrum of eigenvalues, we can design a novel multi-scale representation of the original measurement X. With a premise that multi-scale comparison of data can enhance downstream inference [2], we define a multi-scale descriptor based on the developed transform to increase sensitivity of a statistical analysis.

In summary, we propose a framework which utilizes a precision matrix to provide a multi-scale descriptor on the original features. Our main contributions are: 1) We develop a novel **cov**ariance-based wave**let**-like transform (**COVLET**) which delivers a multi-scale representation of the original feature measures; 2) We conduct extensive experiments on ABCD dataset, which demonstrates significant performance improvements over raw measurements; 3) We identify clinically meaningful cortical ROIs, which are susceptible to socioeconomic inequality.

2   Continuous Wavelets Transform in the $L^2(\mathbb{R})$ Space

Conventional wavelets transform is well understood in the $L^2(\mathbb{R})$ space and is fundamental to our proposed framework. To make this paper self-contained, we provide a brief review of wavelets transform in this section.

Wavelets transform transforms a signal $f(x)$ to the frequency space by decomposing the signal $f(x)$ as a linear combination of oscillating basis functions and their coefficients [23]. Although similar to Fourier transform, however, wavelet transform make use of a localized basis function, i.e., providing a compact finite support that is centered at a specific position. This contrasts wavelet transform from Fourier transform which uses $sin()$ as a basis with infinite duration.

Wavelet transforms require a mother wavelet $\psi_{s,a}$ as the basis. The scale parameter s and translation parameter a control the dilation and location of the mother wavelet respectively. A set of mother wavelets is formalized as

$$\psi_{s,a} = \frac{1}{s}\psi(\frac{t-a}{s}). \tag{1}$$

The forward wavelet transform of a signal $f(x)$ is defined as an inner product of these wavelets with the signal $f(x)$, which yields wavelet coefficients $W_f(s, a)$ as

$$W_f(s, a) = \langle f, \psi_{s,a}\rangle = \frac{1}{s}\int_{-\infty}^{\infty} f(x)\psi^*(\frac{x-a}{s})dx, \tag{2}$$

where ψ^* is complex conjugate of ψ. Moreover, defining the scaling in the Fourier domain let us further express the wavelet coefficients as

$$W_f(s, a) = \frac{1}{2\pi}\int_{-\infty}^{\infty} e^{i\omega a}\hat{\psi}^*(s\omega)\hat{f}(\omega)d\omega, \tag{3}$$

where $\hat{f}(\omega)$ denotes the Fourier representation of the $f(x)$ in the frequency space ω [11]. Briefly, (3) suggests that filtering $\hat{f}$ at multiple scales at s with the mother wavelet $\hat{\psi}$ offers a multi-scale view of the original signal $f(x)$.

3   Multi-scale Analysis via Covariance: COVLET

Let $X \in \mathbb{R}^{P \times N}$ be a standardized (zero-mean) feature matrix with N samples, each of which has P features. Computing a covariance matrix from X yields $\Sigma_{P \times P} = \frac{1}{N}XX^T$, and a precision matrix is defined as the inverse convariance matrix, $\Omega = \Sigma^{-1}$. In the multivariate normal distribution setting, the precision matrix reveals conditional independence relations across different variables, i.e., pair-wise features, as a graphical model [16]. Specifically, $\Omega_{ij} = 0$ implies that features x_i and x_j are conditionally independent given other features $\{x_k\}_{k \neq i,j}$.

The precision matrix $\Omega_{P \times P}$ is symmetric and positive definite (p.d.), and thus has a set of positive eigenvalues $0 < \lambda_1 \leq \lambda_2 \leq \ldots \leq \lambda_P$ with corresponding orthonormal eigenvectors $\nu_1, \nu_2, \ldots, \nu_P$ as bases. Then we define a Hilbert space H on $\mathbb{R}^P$ with inner product such that $\langle f, h\rangle = \sum_{i=1}^{P} f_i h_i \in \mathbb{R}$ for any $f, h \in H$.

With the background above, we can define an orthogonal transform for any signal/measurement $f \in H$, where the transformed signal $\hat{f}$ is given by

$$\hat{f}(\ell) = \langle \nu_\ell, f \rangle = \sum_{p=1}^{P} \nu_\ell(p) f(p), \tag{4}$$

and its inverse transform expresses the original f as an expansion using the $\hat{f}$ as

$$f(p) = \sum_{\ell=1}^{P} \hat{f}(\ell) \nu_\ell(p). \tag{5}$$

Due to the orthonormality of the bases ν_ℓ, a Parseval relation exists such that $\langle f, h \rangle = \langle \hat{f}, \hat{h} \rangle$. Based on the precision matrix Ω, we define a linear bounded operator $T_g^s \in B(H, H)$ at scale s such that

$$T_g^s \nu_\ell = g(s\lambda_\ell) \nu_\ell, \tag{6}$$

for any eigenvector ν_ℓ, where g is a bounded operator from $\mathbb{R}$ to $\mathbb{R}$ (i.e., a kernel function as a band-pass filter). We term it as Covariance-wavelet (Covlet) operator. Based on the definition of the Covlet on eigenvectors, it can be naturally extended on the whole eigenspace. Since eigenvector bases are complete on $\mathbb{R}^P$, T_g^s is well defined on $\mathbb{R}^P$.

Lemma 1. T_g^s is a self-adjoint operator, i.e., $\langle T_g^s f, h \rangle = \langle f, T_g^s h \rangle$.

The self-adjoint property from Lemma 1, whose proof is given in supplement, together with (4) consequently implies that

$$\widehat{T_g^s f}(\ell) = \langle \nu_\ell, T_g^s f \rangle = \langle T_g^s \nu_\ell, f \rangle = g(s\lambda_\ell) \hat{f}(\ell), \tag{7}$$

which means that the operator is equivalent to applying a filter function $g(\cdot)$ on top of coefficients $\hat{f}$. According to Eq. (7) and the orthonormal property, applying the inverse transform in (5) then shows

$$T_g^s f(p) = \sum_{\ell=1}^{P} g(s\lambda_\ell) \hat{f}(\ell) \nu_\ell(p), \tag{8}$$

where the operator T_g^s is applied on the p-th feature. This operation in (8) is defined as the Covlet transform of an original signal $f(p)$ (i.e. feature) as

$$C_f(s, p) = \langle T_g^s \delta_p, f \rangle, \tag{9}$$

which yields Covlet coefficients $C_f(s, p)$ where δ_p denotes a Dirac delta function at p. As claimed by Lemma 1, the self-adjoint property implies that

$$C_f(s, p) = \langle \delta_p, T_g^s f \rangle = T_g^s f(p). \tag{10}$$

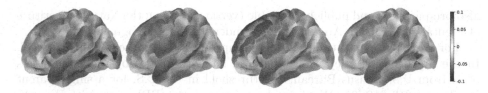

Fig. 1. Multi-scale FA. First: FA measures, Second: CMD at scale $s_1 = 2.11e - 05$, Third: CMD at scale $s_2 = 4.27e - 06$, Fourth: CMD at scale $s_3 = 8.67e - 07$.

We observe a close analogy between our Covlet operator and the conventional wavelets operator as they both define the mapping through bases. However, as indicated by Eqs. (3) and (8), they utilize different sets of bases according to eigenvectors of the precision matrix and Fourier bases, respectively. Furthermore, such a transform delivers a multi-scale view of signals defined on each features by repeating this procedure for multiple scales. Therefore, we define the Covlet Multi-scale Descriptor (CMD) as a set of Covlet coefficients on each feature p for each scale in $\mathcal{S} = \{s_1, s_2, \cdots, s_{|S|}\}$,

$$\text{CMD}_f(p) = \{C_f(s,p) | s \in \mathcal{S}\}. \tag{11}$$

This CMD is a multi-scale feature that is derived from the original univariate measurement/signal by performing multi-scale filtering in a dual space spanned by the eigenvectors ν, i.e., PCA. An example of (standardized) CMD from FA measure is shown in Fig. 1. It captures local context along the geometry of the manifold where the data X are defined. When the geometry is given as a graph, the Ω in our framework can be replaced by graph Laplacian and will be formulated as Spectral Graph Wavelet Transform (SGWT) in [11].

4   Identifying Changes in Microstructure of Neuron Tracts with Family Income

4.1   Experimental Design

Dataset. The ABCD study is the largest long-term study on brain development [28] and child health in the U.S. supported by the National Institutes of Health (NIH). The dataset included 11,873 children enrolled by October 2018, which is

Table 1. Demographics of the ABCD study.

Demographics	BP	NP	H	M	L
# of Subjects	954	8883	4208	2794	2835
Gender (M/F)	488/466	4610/4273	2000/2208	1345/1449	1394/1441
Age (mean, std)	118.5 ± 7.3	119.1 ± 7.5	119.4 ± 7.5	118.8 ± 7.5	118.7 ± 7.5

BP: below-poverty, NP: non-poverty, H: high, M: middle, L: low; Age is measured in months also pre-packaged and publicly available (version 2.0.1) on the National Institute of Mental Health Data Archive (NDA) under the data use agreement.

For our experiments, children were grouped based on household income level. In the first analysis, they were separated into two groups by the poverty criteria from U.S. Census Bureau; the threshold in the U.S. for a single parent family was $16,910 [21]. We defined a below-poverty (BP) group with the subjects with the family income level below level 4 in the dataset (i.e., <$16,000), and a non-poverty (NP) group with the remaining subjects. For the second analysis, subjects were divided into three groups based on the following household income bracket [25]: we regarded household income below $50,000 as Low, between $50,000 and $100,000 as Middle, and above $100,000 as High income groups. 9,837 children were included following exclusion of missing data. The demographic characteristics of the children are presented in Table 1.

For brain structural characteristics, we specifically analyzed the mean FA at each ROI from the diffusion tensor imaging (DTI), which represents a fundamental microstructural property of the brain. FA values were obtained from 148 distinct regions of interest (ROIs) based on the Destrieux atlas [6].

Group Comparison/Parameters. We performed group analyses to demonstrate that CMD enhances downstream statistical analysis and identify income-related ROIs. For the baseline, we used a general linear model (GLM) on the original univariate FA measure to correct for covariates (i.e., age, biological sex at birth, and scanner serial number), and obtained p-values at each ROI. We then applied a multivariate general linear model (MGLM) on CMD, which is a multi-variate feature derived using the Covlet, and resultant p-values were adjusted for the covariates. For both analyses, multiple comparisons were corrected with Bonferroni correction at $\alpha = 0.01$, and the final p-values and ROIs that met the defined threshold were compared.

For the kernel function $g(\cdot)$ for CMD, we used a spline function defined in [11]. We used total of 4 scales for the BP vs. NP analysis and 5 scales for Low/Middle/High income comparisons. The scales were defined in the spectrum of the precision matrix, i.e., $[0, \lambda_P]$.

4.2   Group Analysis Results

Table 2 summaries the number of significant ROIs whose p-values met the multiple comparisons correction. A larger number of significant ROIs were obtained

Table 2. Number of ROIs showing variation based on family income level.

Feature	BP vs NP	H vs L	H vs M	M vs L
Original FA	6	7	0	1
CMD (COVLET)	22	48	2	7

BP: below-poverty, NP: non-poverty, H: high, M: middle, L: low.

utilizing CMD compared to the results obtained utilizing the raw FA values, also demonstrating an improvement in statistical sensitivity in every category.

Below-poverty vs. Non-poverty. Comparing the BP and NP groups, we detected only 6 ROIs that met the Bonferroni correction at $\alpha = 0.01$ using the raw FA values. However, using CMD, we identified 22 different ROIs that met the same Bonferroni correction with improved p-values. Interestingly, the 6 ROIs that were discovered by the baseline were subsumed by the ROIs found with CMD. The list of surviving ROIs from BP vs. NP analysis and corresponding p-values are given in Table 3, and these ROIs and their p-values are further demonstrated in Fig. 2 on a cortical surface of the brain. Looking at the top 11 ROIs in the left column of Table 3, we observed that many top ROIs with the lowest p-values are located within the frontal region in the brain, and detailed interpretation of this observation will be given in Sect. 4.4.

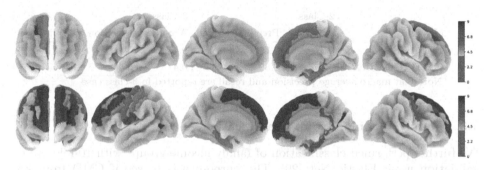

Fig. 2. Group analysis results from Below-poverty vs. Non-poverty family income groups. p-value maps in $-\log_{10}$ scale are shown on a brain surface. Top: using original FA values, Bottom: using CMD. Notice much stronger signal in the bottom.

High vs. Middle vs. Low Income Groups. While the group differences between High and Low income groups were discernible (Table 2), the number of significant ROIs for the comparisons between High and Middle, and Middle and Low groups were small. However, using CMD, we found two ROIs for High vs. Middle group analysis, and 7 ROIs from the Middle vs. Low group comparisons. In Table 3, we present the list of significant ROIs when comparing Middle income versus Low income groups. Again, we identified only one region using the raw FA values, but seven ROIs using CMD with subsequent improvement in statistical outcomes. From these comparisons, we concluded that CMD enables the underlying signal to become more detectable, even with subtle differences.

Table 3. Identified ROIs and p-values from BP vs. NP (Left) and Mid vs. Low income (Right) analyses.

(a) BP vs. NP

Idx	ROI	p-value	Idx	ROI	p-value
1	s.front.middle.lh	6.9e-09	12	g.precentral.rh	5.7e-06
2	g.front.sup.rh	2.1e-08	13	g.precentral.lh	1.1e-05
3	g.front.sup.lh	7.1e-08	14	g.cing.post.dorsal.rh	1.1e-05
4	g.and.s.subcentral.lh	4.6e-07	15	g.cing.post.ventral.rh	1.2e-05
5	g.front.middle.lh	6.7e-07	16	s.front.sup.rh	1.4e-05
6	s.front.middle.rh	7.6e-07	17	s.temp.transverse.lh	1.7e-05
7	s.parieto.occipital.rh	7.7e-07	18	g.temp.sup.plan.polar.lh	1.9e-05
8	g.and.s.transv.frontopol.rh	1.4e-06	19	g.temp.sup.plan.polar.rh	2.2e-05
9	g.oc.temp.med.parahip.rh	3.2e-06	20	g.postcentral.lh	2.3e-05
10	s.occipital.ant.lh	4.2e-06	21	g.oc.temp.med.parahip.lh	2.3e-05
11	g.and.s.cingul.ant.rh	5.6e-06	22	s.interm.prim.jensen.lh	4.2e-05

(b) Mid vs. Low income

Idx	ROI	p-value
1	g.front.sup.lh	6.0e-07
2	s.front.sup.rh	6.6e-07
3	s.occipital.ant.lh	1.0e-06
4	s.front.middle.rh	2.0e-06
5	g.front.sup.rh	1.3e-05
6	s.parieto.occipital.rh	4.2e-05
7	s.interm.prim.jensen.lh	5.5e-05

Table 4. Classification performance measurements.

Measures	2-Class			3-Class		
	Accuracy	Precision	Recall	Accuracy	Precision	Recall
Original FA	0.77	0.76	0.89	0.41	0.40	0.42
CMD (COVLET)	0.85	0.82	0.91	0.47	0.46	0.46

*Note that macro average precision and recall are reported in 3-class case.

4.3 Family Income Group Classification

We further performed classification of family income groups with 10-fold cross-validation using Elastic Net [29]. The purpose was to see if CMD from FA improves prediction performance over the raw FA measures, especially when it has shown improved statistical outcomes in Sect. 4.2. Due to class imbalance, we used NearMiss under-sampling [24]. Classification performances were evaluated by accuracy, precision and recall metrics which are summarized in Table 4. Using CMD, the accuracy improves by 8% and precision gets increased by 6% in binary case, and similarly for 3-class case, both accuracy and precision improved by 6%. These results show that CMD improves the prediction ability over the raw measurements, controlling for Type-1 error with increased precision.

4.4 Neuroscientific Interpretation

The use of a covariance-based wavelet-like (COVLET) transform facilitated more sensitive inference on household income compared to raw FA alone. The finding that majority of the brain ROIs identified in the current study as being within or close to the frontal lobe of the brain is consistent with previous literature that examined the association between socioeconomic characteristics and brain structure. In the largest previous study that included 1,100 children, household income accounted for significant variation in regions within the bilateral frontal, temporal and parietal lobes [26]. In smaller studies that assessed the relationship between white matter integrity and socioeconomic characteristics, individuals earning higher incomes demonstrated higher FA as well as cognitive ability [10].

Despite the dominance of ROIs within the frontal lobe as identified in the current study, previous studies do not appear to consistently demarcate ROIs in a standardized fashion, in part due to the varied impact of developmental processes on cortical columns, synaptic formation and pruning [7]. Indeed, the frontal lobe is central to executive functioning–a domain that spans cognition and behavior–and therefore remains vulnerable to stressors during childhood development [9,27]. Previous studies have generally focused on macrostructural characteristics of the brain such as cortical thickness, surface area and volume, which could be susceptible to overlapping developmental influences. Importantly, the current study provides the first ever large scale evidence that the associations between brain and socioeconomic status extend to their microstructural properties.

5   Conclusion

To increase sensitivity in statistical inference/prediction methods for structured data, we proposed a novel transform that utilizes its covariance structure, i.e., Covlet. The Covlet captures local context information along the geometry of precision matrix and provide a multi-scale feature, which lets us compare samples with different labels more robustly. We performed statistical analysis and classification of children based on family income using large-scale ABCD dataset and demonstrated quantitative improvements in their outcomes. As qualitative results, we identified several ROIs whose microstructure is susceptible to socioeconomic inequality, which were not identifiable with conventional approaches.

Acknowledgement. This research was supported by GAANN Doctoral Fellowships in Computer Science and Engineering at UTA sponsored by the U.S. Department of Education, NIH R01 AG059312 and IITP-2020-2015-0-00742. Numerous funding agencies have continued to support the ABCD study. A full list is provided at https://abcdstudy.org. We also would like to thank Dr. Rui Meng for insightful discussions and comments that greatly improved the manuscript.

References

1. Blakemore, S.J.: Imaging brain development: the adolescent brain. Neuroimage **61**(2), 397–406 (2012)
2. Bullmore, E., Fadili, J., Breakspear, M., Salvador, R., Suckling, J., Brammer, M.: Wavelets and statistical analysis of functional magnetic resonance images of the human brain. Stat. Methods Med. Res. **12**(5), 375–399 (2003)
3. Cai, Z., et al.: A unified multi-scale deep convolutional neural network for fast object detection. In: Leibe, B., Matas, J., Sebe, N., Welling, M. (eds.) ECCV 2016. LNCS, vol. 9908, pp. 354–370. Springer, Cham (2016). https://doi.org/10.1007/978-3-319-46493-0_22
4. Coifman, R.R., Maggioni, M.: Diffusion wavelets. Appl. Comp. Harmonic Anal. **21**(1), 53–94 (2006)

5. DeRosse, P., Ikuta, T., Karlsgodt, K.H., et al.: History of childhood maltreatment is associated with reduced fractional anisotropy of the accumbofrontal 'reward' tract in healthy adults. Brain Imaging Behav. **14**, 1–9 (2020)
6. Destrieux, C., et al.: Automatic parcellation of human cortical gyri and sulci using standard anatomical nomenclature. Neuroimage **53**(1), 1–15 (2010)
7. Farah, M.J.: The neuroscience of socioeconomic status: correlates, causes, and consequences. Neuron **96**(1), 56–71 (2017)
8. Fuhrmann, D., Knoll, L.J., Blakemore, S.J.: Adolescence as a sensitive period of brain development. Trends Cogn. Sci. **19**(10), 558–566 (2015)
9. Fuster, J.M.: Frontal lobe and cognitive development. J. Neurocytol. **31**(3–5), 373–385 (2002)
10. Gianaros, P.J., Marsland, A.L., Sheu, L.K., Erickson, K.I., Verstynen, T.D.: Inflammatory pathways link socioeconomic inequalities to white matter architecture. Cereb. Cortex **23**(9), 2058–2071 (2013)
11. Hammond, D.K., Vandergheynst, P., Gribonval, R.: Wavelets on graphs via spectral graph theory. Appl. Comp. Harmonic Anal. **30**(2), 129–150 (2011)
12. Hammond, D.K., Vandergheynst, P., Gribonval, R.: The Spectral graph wavelet transform: fundamental theory and fast computation. In: Stanković, L., Sejdić, E. (eds.) Vertex-Frequency Analysis of Graph Signals. SCT, pp. 141–175. Springer, Cham (2019). https://doi.org/10.1007/978-3-030-03574-7_3
13. Jednoróg, K., et al.: The influence of socioeconomic status on children's brain structure. PloS One **7**(8), e42486 (2012)
14. Jernigan, T.L., Brown, T.T., Hagler Jr., D.J., et al.: The pediatric imaging, neurocognition, and genetics (ping) data repository. Neuroimage **124**, 1149–1154 (2016)
15. Kim, W.H., et al.: Wavelet based multi-scale shape features on arbitrary surfaces for cortical thickness discrimination. In: NeurIPS, pp. 1241–1249 (2012)
16. Kim, W.H., Kim, H.J., Adluru, N., Singh, V.: Latent variable graphical model selection using harmonic analysis: applications to the human connectome project (HCP). In: CVPR, pp. 2443–2451 (2016)
17. Kim, W.H., et al.: Multi-resolutional shape features via non-euclidean wavelets: applications to statistical analysis of cortical thickness. NeuroImage **93**, 107–123 (2014)
18. Lai, W.S., Huang, J.B., Ahuja, N., Yang, M.H.: Deep laplacian pyramid networks for fast and accurate super-resolution. In: CVPR, pp. 624–632 (2017)
19. Lebel, C., Deoni, S.: The development of brain white matter microstructure. Neuroimage **182**, 207–218 (2018)
20. Lebel, C., et al.: Microstructural maturation of the human brain from childhood to adulthood. Neuroimage **40**(3), 1044–1055 (2008)
21. Lee, A.: Us poverty thresholds and poverty guidelines: What's the difference. Population Reference Bureau (2019) (2018)
22. Lowe, D.G.: Object recognition from local scale-invariant features. In: ICCV, vol. 2, pp. 1150–1157. IEEE (1999)
23. Mallat, S.G.: A theory for multiresolution signal decomposition: the wavelet representation. TPAMI **11**(7), 674–693 (1989)
24. Mani, I., Zhang, I.: k-NN approach to unbalanced data distributions: a case study involving information extraction. In: Proceedings of Workshop on Learning from Imbalanced Datasets, vol. 126 (2003)
25. Marshall, A.T., et al.: Association of lead-exposure risk and family income with childhood brain outcomes. Nat. Med. **26**(1), 91–97 (2020)

26. Noble, K.G., et al.: Family income, parental education and brain structure in children and adolescents. Nat. Neurosci. **18**(5), 773 (2015)
27. Sowell, E.R., Delis, D., Stiles, J., Jernigan, T.L.: Improved memory functioning and frontal lobe maturation between childhood and adolescence: a structural mri study. J. Int. Neuropsychol. Soc. **7**(3), 312–322 (2001)
28. Volkow, N.D., et al.: The conception of the abcd study: from substance use to a broad nih collaboration. Dev. Cogn. Neurosci. **32**, 4–7 (2018)
29. Zou, H., Hastie, T.: Regularization and variable selection via the elastic net. J. Roy. Stat. Soc. **67**(2), 301–320 (2005)

Species-Shared and -Specific Structural Connections Revealed by Dirty Multi-task Regression

Tuo Zhang[1], Zhibin He[1], Xi Jiang[2], Lei Guo[1], Xiaoping Hu[3], Tianming Liu[4], and Lei Du[1($\boxtimes$)]

[1] School of Automation, Northwestern Polytechnical University, Xi'an, China
dulei@nwpu.edu.cn
[2] School of Life Science and Technology, MOE Key Lab for Neuroinformation, University of Electronic Science and Technology of China, Chengdu, China
[3] Department of Bioengineering, UC Riverside, Riverside, CA, USA
[4] Cortical Architecture Imaging and Discovery Lab, Department of Computer Science and Bioimaging Research Center, The University of Georgia, Athens, GA, USA

Abstract. Comparative studies across species, such as primates in this work, reveal the shared structural or functional patterns that might be inherited from the common ancestors and the specific ones that might be related to individualized evolution strategies. Both the shared or specific patterns could help promote the understanding of mechanisms of brain structural and functional architectures and brain dynamics. Many previous studies can be found to report the comparative results on species pairs. However, very few studies were found to perform a comparison of large-scale connectomes across multiple species *via* a data-driven method. To this end, we construct brain connectomes for three primates, macaque, chimpanzee and human, by using Brodmann areas as graphic nodes and diffusion MRI derived white matter fibers to define edges and edge weights. On these connectomes, a novel dirty multi-task regression method is developed in the attempt to automatically identified the species-shared and -specific connections. The concordance of the findings *via* our method and previous reports demonstrate the effectiveness and the promise of this framework.

Keywords: Species comparison · Diffusion MRI · Large-scale connectome

1 Introduction

Comparative studies of brain connectomes across species have provided a unique and valuable avenue to study the development and the evolution of brain structural and functional architectures [1–6]. In this work, we focus on comparisons among three primates, including macaque, chimpanzee and human, which have close phylogenetic relationship [1]. Usually, comparative studies can not only highlight the common structural substrate that is shared across species and may be inherited from the common ancestor, but also

© Springer Nature Switzerland AG 2020
A. L. Martel et al. (Eds.): MICCAI 2020, LNCS 12267, pp. 94–103, 2020.
https://doi.org/10.1007/978-3-030-59728-3_10

infer the brain specialization making each species unique, such as the vital capability of language of human [1].

However, establishing the relation for the brain anatomy and function among different species is not straightforward. For example, the expansion of cerebral cortex is disproportionally faster than that of cranial volume due to the more pronounced convolution on higher primates' brains, making their differences are not just a simple matter of scale [7], but the complexity of the underlying wiring diagrams [1–3]. It has been found in many previous studies that some organizations of white matter pathways have been preserved across primate brains while tremendous differences have also been quantified [1, 2, 8]. However, most of these works focused on either comparisons between species pairs [7] or regions of interest, such as language pathways [1] or connections of higher-order cognitive cortex [4]. A brain-wide data-driven investigation across multiple species is rarely studied. This lacking could be attributed to the limitations of *ex vivo* imaging techniques [2].

This work attempts to use diffusion MRI (dMRI) and develop a novel data-driven method to estimate and compare whole-brain-scale connectomes of three primates, including human, chimpanzee and macaque. The widely used BA atlas (Brodmann areas) and BB atlas (von Bonin and Bailey) [17] are used as common graphic nodes to construct connectomes across species and individuals. The dMRI derived white matter fibers are used to define graphic edges. To conduct a data-driven investigation, we borrow the ideas of multi-task in [9] and propose a novel regression algorithm to simultaneously identify the species-shared and -specific connections. The effectiveness and promise of the framework are demonstrated by reproducibility studies and the identified connections and fibers which are consistent with previous reports.

2 Materials and Methods

2.1 Datasets

Human Brain Imaging: Sixty human subjects from the Q1 release of WU-Minn Human Connectome Project (HCP) consortium[1] were included in this study. T1 weighted structural MRI parameters are as follows: TR = 2400 ms; TE = 2.14 ms; flip angle = 8°; image matrix = 260 × 311 × 260; and spatial resolution = 0.7 × 0.7 × 0.7 mm^3. The dMRI used in spin-echo EPI sequence, TR = 5520 ms; TE = 89.5 ms; flip angle = 78°; refocusing flip angle = 160°; matrix = 168 × 144; spatial resolution = 1.25 × 1.25 × 1.25 mm^3; echo spacing = 0.78 ms. Diffusion-weighting gradients applied in 90 directions on 3 shells of b = 1000, 2000, 3000 s/mm^2, respectively.

Chimpanzee Brain Imaging: Twenty-eight chimpanzee subjects are from the National Primate Research Center. T1-weighted MRI data are optimized at 3T and the parameters are: TR = 2400 ms; TE = 4.13 ms; flip angle = 8°; an image matrix = 256 × 256 × 192; and spatial resolution = 1.0 × 1.0 × 0.8 mm^3. For dMRI data, TR = 5900 ms; TE = 84 ms; Fov = 130 × 130 mm^2; the spatial resolution is 1.8 × 1.8 × 1.8 mm^3; diffusion-weighting gradients applied in 60 directions and b value of 1000 s/mm^2.

---

[1] https://www.humanconnectome.org/.

Macaque Brain Imaging: Fifteen macaque subjects are from a publicly available resource at University of California Davis[2]. The dataset includes diffusion MRI and T1 weighted MRI data from 19 macaques. The T1-weighted structural MRI parameters are: TR = 2500 ms; TE = 3.65 ms; flip angle = 7°, image matrix = 480 × 512 × 512; spatial resolution = 0.3 × 0.3 × 0.3 mm³. The basic parameters for dMRI data acquisition are: voxel resolution of 1.4 × 1.4 × 1.4 mm³, TE = 115 ms, TR = 6400 ms, slice gap = 1.4 mm. Diffusion weighted data consisted of 2 shells of b = 800, 1600 s/mm² interspersed with an approximately equal number of acquisitions on each shell.

2.2 Data Preprocessing

For T1-weighted MRI of human and chimpanzee, skull removal is performed automatically *via* FSL [6]. For macaque, skull removal is manually conducted. FSL-FAST is used to perform tissue segmentation (white matters, gray matters and cerebral spinal fluid) [10]. White matter cortical surfaces were then reconstructed *via* FreeSurfer [11]. For dMRI data, skull removal and eddy currents correction are performed *via* FSL-FDT [6]. The model-free generalized Q-sampling imaging (GQI) method [12] in DSI Studio is adopted to estimate the density of diffusing water at different orientations. The deterministic streamline tracking algorithm [13] in DSI Studio is used to reconstruct 4 × 10⁴ fiber tracts for each subject using the default parameters (max turning angle = 60°, step length = 1 mm, quantitative anisotropy threshold = 0.2). DMRI data is defined as the intra-subject standard space. To align the T1-weighted-MRI-derived surface to the dMRI space, T1-weighted MRI volumes are linearly and nonlinearly warped to FA map of dMRI *via* FSL-FLIRT [14] and FSL-FNIRT [15] in sequence. The linear transformation matrix and the nonlinear warp field are then applied to the surface *via* Connectome workbench[3].

2.3 Estimation of Structural Connective Networks and Matrices

A graph, $G = (V, E, W)$ is defined for each subject, where V is the set of N cortical patches/nodes, E is the set of edges and W is the weight matrix. Usually a common brain atlas is used to define graphic nodes. However, there are no such common atlases available for all three species. In previous studies, the BA (Brodmann areas) atlas [16] and the BB (von Bonin and Bailey) atlas [19] were both available for macaque brains and have been integrated to the "F99" macaque surface atlas [20]. A similar BB38 atlas [17] was used to compare connectomes between human and chimpanzee brains [18]. However, this BB38 atlas for chimpanzee is not digitalized and the cortical parcellation in [18] was performed *via* manual labeling. Fortunately, cortical areas in BB atlas were characterized by distinct cytoarchitectural signatures in a similar way to Brodmann areas (BAs) and there is a close relation and a great deal of overlapping between the two atlases [18]. Therefore, we use the BA parcellation scheme for the three species to define the graphic nodes in V (the first column in the green panel of Fig. 1). the template surface in

---

[2] http://fcon_on_1000.projects.nitrc.org/indi/indiPRIME.html.
[3] https://www.humanconnectome.org/software/connectome-workbench.

"F99" macaque atlas is warped to each macaque subject' white matter surface to obtain the BAs *via* the surface registration method [21]. Acquisition of BAs on human and chimpanzee brains follows the suggestions in [18]. For human, the standard MNI152 template T1-weighted MRI is nonlinearly warped to individual spaces *via* FSL-fnirt [7], such that BA atlas in this standard space is warped to surfaces in individual spaces. For chimpanzee, we nonlinearly warped the human BAs on cortical surfaces to the surface of a randomly selected chimpanzee template *via* the surface registration method [21]. We manually checked and modify the parcellations by comparing them with those in the [18]. Then, the improved parcellation on the template was nonlinearly warped to surfaces of other chimpanzee subjects *via* [21].

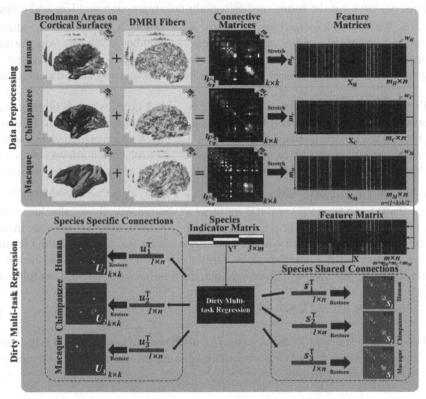

Fig. 1. Flow chart of data preprocessing steps and the dirty multi-task regression algorithm.. (Color figure online)

Because the fibers and the surface with BA atlas are in same space for each subject, an edge e_{ij} is present if dMRI streamline fibers between BAs i and j are found. The fiber counts are defined as the connective strength w_{ij} to weigh the corresponding edge e_{ij}. We use $\mathbf{W}_H$s, $\mathbf{W}_C$s and $\mathbf{W}_M$s to denote the weight matrices for the three species (the third column in upper panel of Fig. 1). The upper triangular part of $\mathbf{W}$ was stretched to a feature vector $\vec{w}$, because $\mathbf{W}$ is symmetric. Within each species, these vectors $\vec{w}$s comprise a feature matrix, denoted by $\mathbf{X}_H$, $\mathbf{X}_c$ and $\mathbf{X}_M$ (the last column).

2.4 The Dirty Multi-task Regression

Our objective is to simultaneously identify the connections that are preserved across the three species and the connections that are specific to one species. This is equivalent to identify the columns which are similar across $\mathbf{X}_H$, $\mathbf{X}_c$ and $\mathbf{X}_M$, while identifying the columns that are unique to one of the matrices (the peach-color panel in Fig. 1). The presence of a column in all $\mathbf{X}_H$, $\mathbf{X}_c$ and $\mathbf{X}_M$ does not necessarily indicate that this connection was preserved across species, because its strength could be different.

This objective can be formulated as a multi-task regression problem with feature selection. We defined a merged feature matrix $\mathbf{X}_{m \times n} = \left[\mathbf{X}_H^T \mathbf{X}_C^T \mathbf{X}_M^T \right]^T$ and an indicator matrix $\mathbf{Y}_{m \times 3}$, where $m = m_H + m_C + m_M$ is the total number of subjects from the three species and n is the feature dimension. Each row of $\mathbf{Y}$ corresponds to a subject, and "1" indicates which species it belongs to. There are no overlaps among the three columns of $\mathbf{Y}$.

Two types of weight matrices are defined, $\mathbf{S}_{n \times 3}$ and $\mathbf{U}_{n \times 3}$, where $\mathbf{S}$ highlights the patterns shared by all species and $\mathbf{U}$ highlights those specie-specific patterns. Effects of weights in $\mathbf{S}$ and $\mathbf{U}$ were imposed to $\mathbf{X}$ by $\mathbf{X}(\mathbf{S} + \mathbf{U})$, which is expected to yield a species indicator matrix $\mathbf{Y}'$ close to $\mathbf{Y}$ as much as possible. The Frobenius norm was introduced to achieve the multi-task, $\|\mathbf{X}(\mathbf{S} + \mathbf{U}) - \mathbf{Y}_F^2\|$ [9]. Columns of $\mathbf{S}$ are expected to be close to each other. The $l_{2,1}$-norm $\|\mathbf{S}\|_{2,1} = \sum_{j=1}^{n} \sqrt{s_{j1}^2 + s_{j2}^2 + s_{j3}^2}$ is thus introduced. We do not use the $l_{\infty,1}$-norm in [9] since it is too strict to yield identically equal values within each row in $\mathbf{S}$. This is impractical because the shared patterns across species are usually similar but not the same. Each column of $\mathbf{U}$, $i.e.$ $\mathbf{u}_i$, is set free to highlight the features that are relevant to the ith species alone. Only the l_1-norm is introduced to each $\mathbf{u}_i$ to control the individual sparsity. Taken together, the loss function is defined as follows:

$$\mathcal{L}_0(\mathbf{S}, \mathbf{U}) = \|\mathbf{X}(\mathbf{S} + \mathbf{U}) - \mathbf{Y}\|_F^2 + \lambda_s \|\mathbf{S}\|_{2,1} + \sum_{i-1}^{3} \lambda_{u_i} \|\mathbf{u}_i\|_1 \qquad (1)$$

This problem is non-smooth due to the $l_{2,1}$-norm and the l_1-norm, but it is bi-convex (it is convex $\mathbf{S}$ if we fix $\mathbf{U}$, and $vice\ versa$). To enable an efficient algorithm, we minimize the following problem instead

$$\mathcal{L}(\mathbf{S}, \mathbf{U}) = \|\mathbf{X}\mathbf{S} - \mathbf{Y}\|_F^2 + \|\mathbf{X}\mathbf{U} - \mathbf{Y}\|_F^2 + tr\left(\|\mathbf{X}\mathbf{S}\|_2^2\right) + tr\left(\|\mathbf{X}\mathbf{U}\|_2^2\right) + \lambda_s \|\mathbf{S}\|_{2,1} + \sum_{i=1}^{3} \lambda_{u_i} \|\mathbf{u}_i\|_1 \quad (2)$$

which is an upper bound of the Eq. (1) (proof is omitted due to space limitation). Now, we first have the objective with respect to $\mathbf{S}$ with $\mathbf{U}$ fixed

$$\mathcal{L}(\mathbf{S}) = \|\mathbf{X}\mathbf{S} - \mathbf{Y}\|_F^2 + tr\left(\|\mathbf{X}\mathbf{S}\|_2^2\right) + \lambda_s \|\mathbf{S}\|_{2,1} \qquad (3)$$

Taking the derivate and setting it to zero, we have

$$\left(2\mathbf{X}^T\mathbf{X} + \lambda_s \mathbf{D}_s\right)\mathbf{S} = \mathbf{X}^T\mathbf{Y} \qquad (4)$$

where $\mathbf{D}_s$ is a diagonal matrix with the jth element as $\frac{1}{2\|s^j\|_2} (j = 1, \ldots, n)$, and s^j is the jth row of $\mathbf{S}$. It is easier to derive the closed-form updating rule

$$\mathbf{S} = \left(2\mathbf{X}^T\mathbf{X} + \lambda_s\mathbf{D}_s\right)^{-1}\mathbf{X}^T\mathbf{Y} \tag{5}$$

After the $\mathbf{S}$ is attained, we solve each $\mathbf{u}_i$ in a similar way. The updating rule of $\mathbf{u}_i$ is

$$\mathbf{u}_i = \left(2\mathbf{X}^T\mathbf{X} + \lambda_u\mathbf{D}_u\right)^{-1}\mathbf{X}^T\mathbf{y}_i \tag{6}$$

where $\mathbf{D}_s$ is a diagonal matrix where the jth element is $\frac{1}{2\|u_{ij}\|_2}(i = 1, 2, 3; j = 1, \ldots, n)$.

The solutions to $\mathbf{S}$ and $\mathbf{U}$ are attained by alternatively updating them. The algorithm terminates when either the predefined iterations or tolerance error is satisfied. We run the algorithm for 50 times and average their results to enable a stable result.

3 Results

3.1 Parameter Settings and Reproducibility

It is noteworthy that only BA1–BA28 that are easily identified across the three species are included in the current work. The identified connections are only limited between these regions. Also, asymmetry between hemispheres are not of the interest of this work. We report the results that are averaged over both hemispheres.

Because we only have 15 macaque subjects, we randomly select 15 human subjects (out of 60) and 15 chimpanzee subjects (out of 28) to match the sample sizes. These subjects are combined to give a 45 subjects' dataset, to which the algorithm is applied. On this dataset, we use a five-fold training-testing scheme to estimate $\mathbf{U}$ and $\mathbf{S}$. There are four parameters (λ_s and $\{\lambda_{u_i}\}$) that control the sparsity of the identified connections in $\mathbf{S}$ and $\mathbf{U}_i$, respectively. The three λ_{u_i}s are set as the same to give no preference to any species. Different λ_s and $\{\lambda_{u_i}\}$ are applied to the 45 subjects' dataset. All parameters are selected from a pool ranging from 1×10^{-3} to 1000 with 10^t as the interval. The 45 subjects' dataset selections are repeated for 100 times. The combinations of λ_s and $\{\lambda_{u_i}\}$ that yield the average minimal residual $\|\mathbf{XS} - \mathbf{Y}\|_F^2$ on all testing experiments is used in the following experiments ($\lambda_s = 0.01$, $\lambda_{u_i} = 200$).

The reproducibility is evaluated by examining if the identified species-shared and -specific connective patterns are consistent across different selections of the 45 subjects' datasets. We use the Pearson correlation coefficient (reported in Table 1) to measure the similarity of $\mathbf{S}$s or $\mathbf{U}$s from two different random trials. High values (>0.95) demonstrate the robustness of the algorithm. The results in the following sections are based on the averaged $\mathbf{S}$s or $\mathbf{U}$s over these datasets selections.

3.2 The Identified Species-Shared and -Specific Connections

Weight matrices $\mathbf{S}$s highlight the connections that are shared by the three species. The similarity among $\mathbf{S}$s from three species is observable in Fig. 2(a). These shared connections could constitute the common backbone of the three species. In general, 9 clusters are

Table 1. The mean Pearson correlation coefficient ($\times 10^{-2}$, $\pm$std.) for the weight matrices between the 100 times of random selections.

S_H	S_C	S_M	U_H	U_C	U_M
99.75 ± 0.14	99.84 ± 0.11	99.85 ± 0.11	97.54 ± 0.92	96.12 ± 2.14	99.15 ± 0.47

identified by overlapping the upper triangular part of three Ss because of the symmetry (Fig. 2(b)). The 9 clusters are #1: connections within primary motor and somatosensory regions (BA2–BA4); #2: connections between BA7–8 and BA4–8, which relate to visuo-motor coordination; #3: connections between BA7–8 (visuo-motor regions) and BA10–11 (anterior frontal regions); #4: connections between BA9 (dorsal frontal cortex) and anterior frontal regions (BA9, 10, 12 and 13); #5: connections between BA6–7 (visuo-motor) and BA18–19 (V2–V5)/BA20–22 (temporal lobe); #6: connections between BA9–11 (anterior frontal cortex), BA18–19 (V2–V5), and BA20–22 (temporal cortex); #7: connections within the visual cortex (BA17–19); #8: connections between the visual cortex (BA17–19) and the temporal cortex (BA20–22); #9: connections within the temporal cortex. Many of these shared connections have been reported in previous species comparative studies [22, 23].

Weight matrices Us highlight the connections that are specific to each species regarding their strength (bottom row of Fig. 2(a)). For example, the BA4–BA4 (within primary motor cortex) connections and BA9–BA9 (within prefrontal cortex) connections are specific to macaque brains. Connections between middle and inferior temporal gyrus (BA20–21) and anterior frontal cortex (BA11) as well as connections between visual cortex (BA18–19) and temporal lobe (BA20–21) are specific to chimpanzee. Connections within BA11, BA19 and BA20, as well as connections between inferior temporal gyrus (BA20) and anterior frontal cortex (BA11) are specific to human. Connections with lower weights are not discussed due to the limited space.

It is noteworthy that there are overlapping connections which are specific to both chimpanzee and human. For example, the connections between visual cortex (BA18/19) and temporal lobe (BA20/21) highlight the importance and uniqueness of the ventral stream of the visual system [24], also known as the "what pathway" that is involved with object identification and recognition. The specificity of the ventral stream in higher primate contrasts with the dorsal stream, known as "where pathway", which leads to the parietal lobe and is identified as "shared" connections among species in cluster #6 in this work. The dorsal stream was suggested to be involved in spatial awareness and guidance of actions, a relatively lower brain function than the ventral stream [24]. Also, specific connections between BA11 and BA20 could be a part of arcuate fasciculus that is involved in human language [1]. The specificity of these connections to human and chimpanzee other than macaque suggests a gradient in this functional change from macaque to human [1].

By further grouping those BAs to lobes and summing up the weight in Us for each lobe (left panel of Fig. 2(c)), we find that heavily weighted connections specific to species are mostly found for frontal lobes and temporal lobes. By grouping BAs into primary cortex, unimodal cortex and multimodal cortex (right panel of Fig. 2(c)), we find that

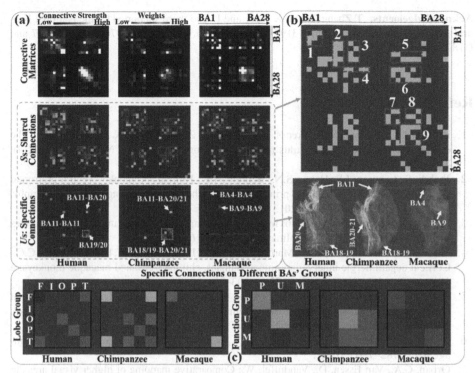

Fig. 2. (a) Top row: Mean connective strength matrices averaged over all subjects within each species; Middle row: species-shared connections Ss; Bottom row: species-specific connections Us; Ss and Us are averaged over all 45-subjects' dataset selections. (b) Top: clusters of the species-shared connections; Bottom: species-specific cortical regions and fibers. The fibers connecting the same pairs of BAs on different species have the same color; (c) Left: species-specific connection matrices Us in (a) with BAs in rows and columns grouped into lobes: frontal (F), insular (I), occipital (O), parietal (P) and temporal (T); Right: Us in (a) with BAs grouped into functionally distinct regions: primary (P), unimodal (U) and multimodal (M). (Color figure online)

connections within the primary cortex are specific to macaque brains, while unimodal and multimodal connections are specific to human and chimpanzee brains. These results are in line with previous reports that higher intelligence of chimpanzees and humans are more related to their elaborated connections of the higher-order cortex [1, 2, 5, 25, 26].

4 Conclusions

In this work, comparative studies of the dMRI derived connectomes among three primate species are performed based on a novel data-driven dirty multi-task regression algorithm. By this way, connections that are shared by species and those that are specific to one of them are identified and find supporting interpretations from previous reports. Our results provide new clues to organizational architectures of primate brains and how they evolve along the phylogenic tree.

Acknowledgements. T Zhang, L Du, X Jiang and L Guo were supported by the National Natural Science Foundation of China (31971288, 61973255, 61703073, 61976045, 61936007 and U1801265).

References

1. Rilling, J.K., Glasser, M.F., Preuss, T.M., Ma, X., Zhao, T., Hu, X., Behrens, T.E.: The evolution of the arcuate fasciculus revealed with comparative DTI. Nat. Neurosci. **11**(4), 426–428 (2008)
2. Jbabdi, S., Lehman, J.F., Haber, S.N., Behrens, T.E.: Human and monkey ventral prefrontal fibers use the same organizational principles to reach their targets: tracing versus tractography. J. Neurosci. **33**(7), 3190–3201 (2013)
3. Li, L., et al.: Mapping putative hubs in human, chimpanzee and rhesus macaque connectomes via diffusion tractography. NeuroImage **80**, 462–474 (2013)
4. Raghanti, M.A., Stimpson, C.D., Marcinkiewicz, J.L., Erwin, J.M., Hof, P.R., Sherwood, C.C.: Cortical dopaminergic innervation among humans, chimpanzees, and macaque monkeys: a comparative study. Neuroscience **155**(1), 203–220 (2008)
5. Smaers, J.B., Steele, J., Case, C.R., Cowper, A., Amunts, K., Zilles, K.: Primate prefrontal cortex evolution: human brains are the extreme of a lateralized ape trend. Brain Behav. Evol. **77**(2), 67–78 (2011)
6. Jenkinson, M., Beckmann, C., Behrens, T.E.J., Woolrich, M.W., Smith, S.M.: FSL. NeuroImage **62**(2), 782–790 (2012)
7. Orban, G.A., Van Essen, D., Vanduffel, W.: Comparative mapping of higher visual areas in monkeys and humans. Trends Cogn. Sci. **8**(7), 315–324 (2004)
8. De Schotten, M.T., Dellacqua, F., Valabregue, R., Catani, M.: Monkey to human comparative anatomy of the frontal lobe association tracts. Cortex **48**(1), 82–96 (2012)
9. Jalali, A., Sanghavi, S., Ruan, C., Ravikumar, P.K.: A dirty model for multi-task learning. In: Advances in neural information processing systems. USA, pp. 964–972 (2010)
10. Zhang, Y., Brady, M., Smith, S.: Segmentation of brain MR images through a hidden Markov random field model and the expectation-maximization algorithm. IEEE Trans. Med. Imag. **20**(1), 45–57 (2001)
11. Fischl, B., Liu, A., Dale, A.M.: Automated manifold surgery: constructing geometrically accurate and topologically correct models of the human cerebral cortex. IEEE Trans. Med. Imaging **20**(1), 70–80 (2001)
12. Yeh, F.C., Wedeen, V.J., Tseng, W.I.: Generalized q-sampling imaging. IEEE Trans. Med. Imaging **29**(9), 1626–1635 (2010)
13. Yeh, F.C., Verstynen, T.D., Wang, Y., Fernández-Miranda, J.C., Tseng, W.Y.I.: Deterministic diffusion fiber tracking improved by quantitative anisotropy. PLoS ONE **8**(11), e80713 (2013)
14. Jenkinson, M., Bannister, P., Brady, M., Smith, S.: Improved optimization for the robust and accurate linear registration and motion correction of brain images. Neuroimage **17**(2), 825–841 (2002)
15. Andersson, J.L.R., Jenkinson, M., Smith, S.: Non-linear registration, aka spatial normalisation. FMRIB technical report TR07JA2. FMRIB Analysis Group of the University of Oxford (2010)
16. Brodmann, K.: Vergleichende Lokalisationslehre der Grosshirnrinde (in German). Johann Ambrosius Barth, Leipzig (1909)
17. Bailey, P., von Bonin, G., McCulloch, W.S.: The Isocortex of the Chimpanzee. University of Illinois Press, Urbana (1950)

18. Ardesch, D.J., Scholtens, L.H., Li, L., Preuss, T.M., Rilling, J.K., van den Heuvel, M.P.: Evolutionary expansion of connectivity between multimodal association areas in the human brain compared with chimpanzees. Proc. Natl. Acad. Sci. **116**(14), 7101–7106 (2019)
19. von Bonin, G., Bailey, P.: The Neocortex of Macaca Mulatta. The University of Illinois Press, Urbana (1947)
20. Van Essen, D.C.: Surface-based approaches to spatial localization and registration in primate cerebral cortex. Neuroimage **23**(Suppl 1), S97–S107 (2004)
21. Yeo, B.T.T., Sabuncu, M.R., Vercauteren, T., Ayache, N., Fischl, B., Golland, P.: Spherical demons: fast diffeomorphic landmark-free surface registration. IEEE Trans. Med. Imaging **29**(3), 650–668 (2010)
22. Kötter, R.: Online retrieval, processing, and visualization of primate connectivity data from the CoCoMac database. Neuroinformatics **2**(2), 127–144 (2004)
23. Orban, G.A., Van Essen, D., Vanduffel, W.: Comparative mapping of higher visual areas in monkeys and humans. Trends Cogn. Sci. **8**(7), 315–324 (2004)
24. Goodale, M.A., Milner, A.D.: Separate visual pathways for perception and action. Trends Neurosci. **15**(1), 20–25 (1992)
25. Kaas, J.H.: Evolution of the neocortex. Curr. Biol. **16**(21), R910–R914 (2006)
26. Goldman-Rakic, P.S.: Topography of cognition: parallel distributed networks in primate association cortex. Ann. Rev. Neurosci. **11**(1), 137–156 (1988)

Self-weighted Multi-task Learning
for Subjective Cognitive Decline Diagnosis

Nina Cheng[1], Alejandro Frangi[2], Zhi-Guo Zhang[1], Denao Deng[3], Lihua Zhao[4],
Tianfu Wang[1], Yichen Wei[4], Bihan Yu[4], Wei Mai[4], Gaoxiong Duan[4],
Xiucheng Nong[4], Chong Li[4], Jiahui Su[4], and Baiying Lei[1(✉)]

[1] National-Regional Key Technology Engineering Laboratory for Medical Ultrasound,
Guangdong Key Laboratory for Biomedical Measurements and Ultrasound Imaging, School of
Biomedical Engineering, Health Science Center, Shenzhen University, Shenzhen 518055, China
leiby@szu.edu.cn
[2] CISTIB Centre for Computational Imaging and Simulation Technologies in Biomedicine,
School of Computing and the School of Medicine, University of Leeds, Leeds LS2 9JT, UK
[3] Department of Radiology, The People's Hospital of Guangxi Zhuang Autonomous Region,
Nanning 530021, Guangxi, China
[4] First Affiliated Hospital, Guangxi University of Chinese Medicine, Nanning 530021, China

Abstract. Subjective cognitive decline (SCD) is an early stage of mild cognitive impairment (MCI) and may represent the first symptom manifestation of Alzheimer's disease (AD). Early diagnosis of MCI is important because early identification and intervention can delay or even reverse the progression of this disease. This paper proposes an automatic diagnostic framework for SCD and MCI. Specifically, we design a new multi-task learning model to integrate neuroimaging functional and structural connectivity in a predictive framework. We construct a functional brain network by sparse low-rank brain network estimation methods, and a structural brain network is constructed using fiber bundle tracking. Subsequently, we use multi-task learning methods to select features for integrated functional and structural connections, the importance of each task and the balance between both modalities are automatically learned. By integrating both functional and structural information, the most discriminative features of the disease are obtained for diagnosis. The experiments on the dataset show that our proposed method achieves good performance and is superior to the traditional algorithms. In addition, the proposed method can identify the most discriminative brain regions and connections. These results follow current clinical findings and add new findings for disease detection and future medical analysis.

Keywords: Subjective cognitive decline · Feature selection · Multi-task learning

1 Introduction

Subjective cognitive decline (SCD) is an important risk factor for Alzheimer's disease (AD) and can be expressed before cognitive impairment begins. From preclinical SCD to

© Springer Nature Switzerland AG 2020
A. L. Martel et al. (Eds.): MICCAI 2020, LNCS 12267, pp. 104–113, 2020.
https://doi.org/10.1007/978-3-030-59728-3_11

mild cognitive impairment (MCI) to AD, it comes with abnormal changes in brain structure and function. SCD refers to the decline in the self-reported memory of the patient compared to his or her normal memory, but it is normal on traditional neuropsychological tests. At this time, AD-related positive biomarkers can be found. Many studies have shown that the ratio of SCD to MCI and AD is much higher than normal aging, and it is very important to use SCD as an early intervention target to delay disease progression [1, 2]. In this work, we hope to find SCD subjects at an earlier stage for early intervention and treatment.

In recent years, neuroimaging-based techniques (e.g., magnetic resonance imaging (MRI), diffusion tensor imaging (DTI)), and resting state functional magnetic resonance imaging (rs-fMRI)) have proven to be a powerful tool for the classification of neurodegenerative diseases, especially for SCD. Therefore, many studies aim to infer the potential characteristics of brain-connected networks through neuroimaging data, and to fuse multi-modal imaging information (e.g., DTI and rs-fMRI) using brain network estimation and feature extraction via machine learning techniques [3–5]. However, most previous studies usually directly link or merge feature information of different modalities, and rarely explore the intrinsic common information from multi-modal neuroimaging data.

We model the connection between structural DTI image and functional rs-fMRI image. Specifically, after constructing a functional brain network using a sparse low-rank brain network estimation method and a fiber bundle tracking to construct a structural brain network, the feature selection is performed using the self-weighted multi-task learning (SWMT) method. The selected most disease relevant features are sent to the support vector machine (SVM) classifier for the automatic diagnosis of SCD and MCI. Each modality is modeled as a separate task to contribute to the final prediction. The importance of each task and the balance of these modalities are automatically learned separately, so that the multi-task learning automatically obtains weights. The classification is performed by the weights obtained in each task. In addition, our approach enables these modalities to work together to improve the predictive performance of each task, which can reveal more interesting patterns not found in the model built by a single task. The joint learning of multi-modal information is very useful for identifying individuals with SCD and MCI from NC subjects. We use the leave one out (LOO) strategy to evaluate SCD diagnosis performance. Experimental results show that the model has higher classification accuracy. Compared with the existing methods, the proposed model achieves good performance. In addition, it can detect brain abnormalities more accurately to better explain the pathological abnormalities of SCD and MCI patients.

2 Method

The overall process of the method is shown in Fig. 1. First, the multi-modal image data (rs-fMRI and DTI) are preprocessed. Second, we construct the brain function network using sparse low rank learning. Third, the functional and structural networks are extracted as inputs, and the self-weight centralized multi-task learning model is used for feature selection. Finally, the selected features are entered into the SVM for classification.

2.1 Data Acquisition and Feature Extraction

In this study, our data is from the local hospital with two modalities: fMRI and DTI. 58 SCD patients (39F/19M), 89 MCI patients (63F/26M) and 67 healthy group controls (43F/24M) are obtained. The ages (mean ± SD) of the SCD, MCI, and HC groups are 65.24 ± 5.56, 65.31 ± 6.70, and 64.48 ± 5.73, respectively.

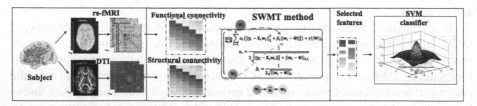

Fig. 1. General framework of the proposed method for classification.

Preprocessing of DTI images uses the PANDA toolbox [6] based on the FMRIB software library (FSL, https://fsl.fmrib.ox.ac.uk/fsl/), which generates global brain determinism fiber bundle imaging by using the FACT algorithm with default parameters. After brain tissue extraction and correction of eddy current distortion, we calculate the mean diffusivity (MD) and fractional anisotropy (FA) coefficients. The FA and MD volumes are then registered with the corresponding T1 anatomical images to obtain high resolution FA and MD maps. The brain space is divided into 116 regions of interest (ROI)s by aligning the automatic anatomical landmarks (AAL) [7] to each image.

For rs-fMRI data preprocessing, we use the widely used rs-fMRI data analysis software: statistical parameter mapping (SPM12) [8] software package. rs-fMRI data processing assistant (DPARSF) toolbox [9] and analysis toolkit (REST). Pre-processing includes time registration, head motion correction, spatial normalization, smoothing, removal of baseline drift, and filtering of high frequency signal interference. Finally, by aligning the AAL map with the rs-fMRI image, the brain space is divided into 90 ROI (excluding 26 ROIs from the cerebellum).

2.2 Functional Brain Network (FBN) Estimation

After data preprocessing, the brain has been divided into n ROIs, each is corresponding to the observed time series $t_i \in \mathbb{R}^m$, $i = 1, 2, ..., n$. $\{t_i\}_{i=1}^n$ denotes network node set in an m-dimensional space, $\mathbf{T} = [t_1, t_2, ..., t_n] \in \mathbb{R}^m \times n$. $\mathbf{U} \in \mathbb{R}^{n \times n}$ denotes the weight matrix.

Regarding functional brain networks analysis for rs-fMRI data, we use the matrix regularization network-learning framework to encode the modular priors. After constructing the network, we further describe the problem of sparse low rank graph learning, and then solve it using an efficient optimization algorithm [10].

This functional brain network model is described as:

$$\min_{\mathbf{U}} ||\mathbf{T} - \mathbf{TU}||_F^2 + \lambda_1 ||\mathbf{U}||_0 + \lambda_2 \text{rank}(\mathbf{U}), \tag{1}$$

where $||\mathbf{T} - \mathbf{TU}||_F^2$ is a data fitting term that can obtain the inverse covariance structure in the data, $||\mathbf{U}||_0$ indicates the number of non-zero elements in $\mathbf{U}$, which can measure the sparsity of the network, and rank($\mathbf{U}$) is the rank of matrix $\mathbf{U}$, which integrates with $||\mathbf{U}||_0$ for modeling the modularity of the network. We relax the l_1-norm $||\mathbf{U}||_1$ and trace norm $||\mathbf{U}||_*$, and obtain the following objective function:

$$\min_{\mathbf{U}} ||\mathbf{T} - \mathbf{TU}||_F^2 + \lambda_1 ||\mathbf{U}||_1 + \lambda_2 ||\mathbf{U}||_*, \tag{2}$$

where λ_1 and λ_2 are regularization parameters used to control the balance among the three terms of Eq. (2).

The algorithm for solving Eq. (2) is summarized in Algorithm 1.

In this paper, we solve Eq. (2) based on the proximal method, where $\mathbf{U}\text{diag}(\sigma_1, \ldots, \sigma_n)\mathbf{V}^T$ is the singular value decomposition (SVD) of matrix $\mathbf{U}$, and σ_k is the step size in gradient descent.

For constructing the DTI structural brain network, the AAL template aligned to each subject's DTI is converted to a common space as a node. The PANDA is used to calculate the ROI and the structural connection between them as the total number of standardized connected fibers between the ROI pairs i and j to construct a DTI network:

$$w_{ij}^s = \sum_{i,j \in N, i \neq j} \frac{n(f)}{(\frac{a_i + a_j}{2})}, \tag{3}$$

where $i, j \in N = \{1, 2, \ldots, 90\}$ and $i \neq j$, $n(f)$ is the total number of fibers linking ROIs i and j, a_i is the surface area of ROI i between gray matter and white matter. $\frac{a_i + a_j}{2}$ is used to correct deviations in structural connection strength estimates caused by different ROI sizes.

Algorithm 1 FBN estimation via sparse low rank regularization

---

Initialize: U
Update:
1. $\mathbf{U} \leftarrow \mathbf{U} - \alpha(-2\mathbf{T}^T\mathbf{T} + 2\mathbf{T}^t\mathbf{TU})$
2. $\mathbf{U} \leftarrow \text{prox}_{\lambda_1||\cdot||_1}(\mathbf{U}) = [sgn(U_{ij}) \cdot \max\{|U_{ij}| - \lambda_1, 0\}]_{n \times n}$
3. $\mathbf{U} \leftarrow \text{prox}_{\lambda_2||\cdot||_1}(\mathbf{U}) = \mathbf{U}\text{diag}(\max\{\sigma_1 - \lambda_2, 0\}, \ldots, \max\{\sigma_n - \lambda_2, 0\})\mathbf{V}^T$

2.3 Self-weight Multi-task Learning (SWMT)

For a matrix $\mathbf{X} = [x_{ij}]$, $\mathbf{x}^i$ and $\mathbf{x}_j$ represent the i-th row and j-th column, respectively. We also denote the Frobenius norm and the l_1-norm of a matrix $\mathbf{X}$ as $||\mathbf{X}_F|| = \sqrt{\sum_j ||\mathbf{X}_j||_2^2}$ and $||\mathbf{X}_1|| = \sum_{ij} |x_{ij}|$, respectively. $\mathbf{X}^T$, tr($\mathbf{X}$), and $\mathbf{X}^{-1}$ indicate the transpose operator, the trace operator, and the inverse of a matrix $\mathbf{X}$, respectively.

Let $\mathbf{X} \in \mathbb{R}^{n \times d}$ and $\mathbf{y} \in \mathbb{R}^n$ denote the feature matrix and its associated label vector of n subjects, d dimensionality of features. We then use the least square loss function to measure their relationship [11–13], which is defined as

$$\min_{\mathbf{w}} ||\mathbf{y} - \mathbf{Xw}||_2^2, \tag{4}$$

where the coefficient vector $\mathbf{w} \in \mathbb{R}^d$ maps $\mathbf{X}$ to $\mathbf{y}$ to achieve the minimal prediction residual $\|\mathbf{y} - \mathbf{X}\mathbf{w}\|_2^2$, and $\mathbf{X}\mathbf{w}$ is the prediction of $\mathbf{y}$.

The least square regression in Eq. (4) has a closed form solution, *i.e.*, $(\mathbf{X}^T\mathbf{X})^{-1}\mathbf{X}^T\mathbf{y}$. However, to the best of our knowledge, Eq. (4) is often over-fitted to the dataset with small subjects and high-dimensional features, *e.g.*, the large number of d ($d > n$) in our case. Here, a regularization is always recommended [14] to address the over-fitting problem. We thus reformulate Eq. (4) as:

$$\min_{\mathbf{w}} \|\mathbf{y} - \mathbf{X}\mathbf{w}\|_2^2 + \lambda \|\mathbf{w}\|_1, \tag{5}$$

where λ is a nonnegative tuning parameter, and a large value of λ encourages the sparsity of the model.

After solving Eq. (5), the features with zero coefficients in $\mathbf{w}$ are regarded as unimportant features, while the remaining features with nonzero coefficients are regarded as important features. In this way, we can use Eq. (5) to conduct feature selection in the individual groups. It is noteworthy that our method can deal with cases where the number of the subjects and the dimensions of the features are different in these tasks. We further use the least square loss function to achieve the minimal prediction error of all tasks and to select the most informative features with the following multi-task learning formulation: $\widehat{\mathbf{X}}^m$

$$\min_{\mathbf{W}^m} \sum_{m=1}^{k} \|\mathbf{y}^m - \mathbf{X}^m\mathbf{w}^m\|_2^2 + \gamma \|\mathbf{W}\|_1, \tag{6}$$

where $\mathbf{W} = [w^1, \ldots, w^m] \in \mathbb{R}^{d \times k}$ and γ is a nonnegative tuning parameter to control the sparsity ratio of $\mathbf{W}$.

In this study, to achieve the goal of collaborative assistance for different modalities, we use a centralized regularization to penalize the variance of the coefficient vectors (i.e., $\mathbf{w}^m$, $m = 1, \ldots, k$) by optimizing the following objective function:

$$\min_{\mathbf{w}^m, \bar{\mathbf{w}}} \sum_{m=1}^{k} \sqrt{\|\mathbf{y}^m - \mathbf{X}^m\mathbf{w}^m\|_2^2 + \|\mathbf{w}^m - \bar{\mathbf{w}}\|_{2,1}} + \gamma \|\mathbf{W}\|_1 \tag{7}$$

To solve the optimization problem of Eq. (7), *i.e.*, optimizing the variables $\mathbf{w}^m$ ($m = 1, \ldots, k$) and $\bar{\mathbf{w}}$, we compute the derivatives of the square root in Eq. (7) and alternatively solving these formulas iteratively. Then, we define the objective function as:

$$\begin{cases} \min_{\mathbf{W}^m, \bar{\mathbf{w}}} \sum_{m=1}^{k} \alpha^m \left(\|\mathbf{y}^m - \mathbf{X}^m\mathbf{w}^m\|_2^2 + \beta^m \|\mathbf{w}^m - \bar{\mathbf{w}}\|_2^2 \right) + \gamma \|\mathbf{W}\|_1 \\ \alpha^m = \dfrac{1}{2\sqrt{\|\mathbf{y}^m - \mathbf{X}^m\mathbf{w}^m\|_2^2 + \|\mathbf{w}^m - \bar{\mathbf{w}}\|_{2,1}}} \\ \beta^m = \dfrac{1}{2\sqrt{\|\mathbf{w}^m - \bar{\mathbf{w}}\|_2}} \end{cases} \tag{8}$$

We reformulate Eq. (7) as:

$$\min_{\mathbf{w}^m, \bar{\mathbf{w}}} \sum_{m=1}^{k} \left\| \widehat{\mathbf{y}}^m - \widehat{\mathbf{X}}^m \mathbf{w}^m \right\|_2^2 + \gamma \|\mathbf{W}\|_1 \tag{9}$$

The algorithm for solving Eq. (7) is summarized in Algorithm 2.

Algorithm 2 The optimization algorithm for Eq.(7)

Input: γ, $\mathbf{X}^m$, $\mathbf{y}^m (m = 1, ..., k)$;

Output: α^m, $\mathbf{w}^m$, $\bar{\mathbf{w}}$;

Initialize $\alpha^m = \frac{1}{k}$;

repeat

$$\mathbf{W} \leftarrow \min_{\mathbf{w}^m, \bar{\mathbf{w}}} \sum_{m=1}^{k} \alpha^m (\|\mathbf{y}^m - \mathbf{X}^m \mathbf{w}^m\|_2^2 + \beta^m \|\mathbf{w}^m - \bar{\mathbf{w}}\|_2^2) + \gamma \|\mathbf{W}\|_1;$$

$$\alpha^m \leftarrow \frac{1}{2\sqrt{\|\mathbf{y}^m - \mathbf{X}^m \mathbf{w}^m\|_2^2 + \|\mathbf{w}^m - \bar{\mathbf{w}}\|_{2,1}}};$$

Until Eq.(7) converges

---

3 Experimental Results

3.1 Experimental Setup

In our study, we perform three binary classification experiments on a dataset collected from a local hospital: NC vs. SCD, SCD vs. MCI, and NC vs. MCI. We compare different network estimation methods and multi-task feature selection methods. Specifically, network estimation methods include Pearson's correlation (PC), low rank (LR), sparse representation (SR) [10]. Comparative feature selection methods include Lasso [15], clustered multi-task learning (CMTL) [16], robust multi-task feature learning (rMTFL) [11] and sparse low-rank feature learning (SLFL) [17]. We use a leave one out (LOO) algorithm to fairly evaluate the classification performance. Although LOO cross-validation algorithm is computationally expensive, the sample utilization rate is the highest and suitable for small samples in our tasks. For the classification performance evaluation, we use classification accuracy (the disease state of the subject is correctly classified as the actual disease state of each category of subjects) (ACC), sensitivity (SEN), specificity (SPE) and Area Under Curve (AUC).

3.2 Results and Discussions

Table 1 shows the performance of different network estimation methods and different multi-task feature selection methods on the same dataset, including the classification results of NC vs. SCD, SCD vs. MCI, NC vs. MCI. It can be seen that our method performs best in terms of all the four evaluation metrics. 1, 2, 3, 4, 5 represent Lasso, CMTL, rMTFL, SLFL and our method.

Among the three classification problems, the proposed method is superior to the most commonly used comparison methods. Our model has classification accuracies of 84.80%, 89.12% and 87.82% on the classification of NC vs. SCD, SCD vs. MCI and NC vs. MCI, respectively. This suggests that our proposed method can accurately classify MCI and SCD patients from normal controls. The AUC reaches 93.95%, 95.39% and 93.86%, respectively, in the three classification problems. The larger the AUC, the better the classification effect of the classifier.

Figure 2 shows the functional connectivity networks of NC, SCD, and MCI, respectively. Several functionally connected networks exhibit relatively different modes in terms of network topology and strength. In several subcategories of MCI, the three

Table 1. Comparisons of classification performances of different methods. 1, 2, 3, 4, 5 represent Lasso, CMTL, rMTFL, SLFL and our method.

FCN	FS	NC vs. SCD				SCD vs. MCI				NC vs. MCI			
		ACC	SEN	SPE	AUC	ACC	SEN	SPE	AUC	ACC	SEN	SPE	AUC
PC	1	60.00	65.52	55.22	56.72	56.46	53.93	60.34	84.11	61.54	59.55	64.18	70.07
	2	73.60	70.69	76.12	72.72	70.07	70.79	68.97	77.49	63.46	58.43	70.15	68.20
	3	69.60	70.69	68.66	74.99	75.51	78.65	70.69	84.91	68.59	66.29	71.64	79.27
	4	69.60	**74.14**	65.67	**80.75**	78.23	78.65	77.59	89.95	78.95	75.28	**83.58**	85.51
	5	**74.40**	72.41	**76.12**	79.95	**79.59**	78.65	81.03	92.21	79.49	**77.53**	82.09	**88.29**
SR	1	68.00	75.86	61.19	77.69	63.95	68.54	56.90	72.14	74.36	79.78	67.16	86.21
	2	68.80	70.69	67.16	84.43	78.91	80.90	75.86	90.49	76.28	78.65	73.13	85.53
	3	73.60	79.31	68.66	89.19	78.91	79.78	77.59	87.16	78.85	78.65	79.10	89.37
	4	77.60	79.31	76.12	89.99	63.27	64.04	62.07	70.96	81.41	82.02	80.60	88.88
	5	**80.80**	**84.48**	**77.61**	**90.48**	**80.95**	**82.02**	**79.31**	**92.85**	**83.33**	**85.39**	80.60	**93.61**
LR	1	63.30	68.97	58.21	83.48	63.95	66.29	60.34	67.15	74.36	75.28	73.13	83.00
	2	73.60	77.59	70.15	87.93	79.59	76.40	84.48	92.48	79.49	77.53	82.09	87.74
	3	71.20	67.24	**74.63**	81.34	68.71	68.54	68.97	79.17	83.97	83.15	85.07	92.65
	4	77.60	82.76	73.13	83.40	74.83	75.28	74.14	80.74	81.41	80.90	82.09	89.94
	5	**80.80**	**89.66**	73.13	**90.48**	**89.12**	**89.89**	**87.93**	**95.39**	**85.90**	83.15	**89.55**	**93.22**
Ours	1	70.40	60.34	79.10	86.49	78.91	77.52	81.03	87.16	80.13	80.90	79.10	88.56
	2	73.60	74.14	73.13	87.93	74.83	70.79	81.03	84.79	82.05	85.39	77.61	90.32
	3	76.00	79.31	73.13	80.91	83.67	82.02	86.21	93.24	84.62	83.15	86.57	92.40
	4	81.60	79.31	83.58	89.45	86.39	84.27	89.66	94.01	85.26	82.02	**89.55**	92.03
	5	**84.80**	**84.48**	**85.07**	**93.95**	**89.12**	88.76	**89.66**	**95.39**	**87.82**	**88.76**	86.57	**93.86**

types are progressively distributed, and the degree of cognitive impairment is gradually increased. We noted some connections are destroyed and the number of connections is gradually reduced compared with NC subjects. For all classification tasks, we also

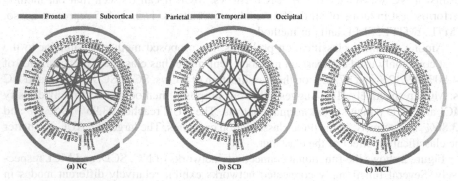

Fig. 2. The structure of four aforementioned networks for NC (a), SCD (b) and MCI (c).

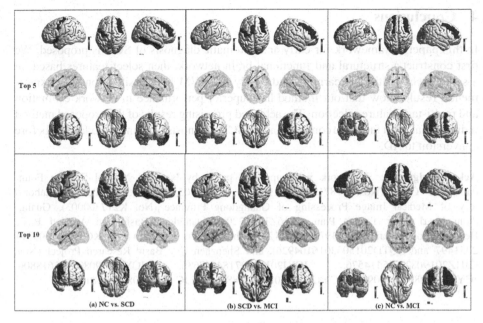

Fig. 3. Top 5 and 10 identified brain regions of various classification tasks.

extract the top five and ten weights of the selected features in each classification task, and the corresponding brain regions are shown in Fig. 3.

The brain regions are associated with the top ten connections selected by the NC vs. SCD classifications using our proposed method are precentral gyrus (PreCG.L), middle frontal gyrus (MFG.R), olfactory cortex (OLF.L), insula (INS.L and INS.R), anterior cingulate and paracingulate gyri (ACG.L and ACG.R), median cingulate and paracingulate gyri (DCG.R), posterior cingulate gyrus (PCG.R), hippocampus (HIP.L), cuneus (CUN.L), postcentral gyrus (PoCG.L), angular gyrus (ANG.R), precuneus (PCUN.L), thalamus (THA.L), and temporal pole: superior temporal gyrus (TPOsup.L). The top ten connections related to ROIs selected from NC vs. MCI classification using our proposed method are superior frontal gyrus, dorsolateral (SFGdor.L), MFG.R, olfactory cortex (OLF.R), amygdala (AMYG.L), CUN.L, superior occipital gyrus (SOG.L), middle occipital gyrus (MOG.R), superior parietal gyrus (SPG.R), angular gyrus (ANG.L), lenticular nucleus, pallidum (PAL.L), thalamus (THA.R), heschl gyrus (HES.R), middle frontal gyrus (MFG.L), inferior frontal gyrus, triangular part (IFGtriang.L), posterior cingulate gyrus (PCG.L), hippocampus (HIP.R), and superior occipital gyrus (SOG.R). For SCD vs. MCI classification, the most informative connections related ROIs are PCG.L, parahippocampal gyrus (PHG.L), HIP.L, cuneus (CUN.R), PreCG.L, superior frontal gyrus, orbital part (ORBsup.L and ORBsup.R), MFG.R, supplementary motor area (SMA.L), INS.L, parahippocampal gyrus (PHG.R), AMYG.L, CUN.L, ANG.L, precuneus (PCUN.R), THA.L and inferior temporal gyrus (ITG.R).

4 Conclusions

In this paper, a framework for early and automatic diagnosis of SCD is proposed. We first construct a structural and functional brain network, then select features based on a self-weight multi-task learning, and finally use SVM for classification. The experimental results show that our method has superior performance in network estimation and multi-task feature selection. The achieved promising results of the proposed method indicate that it can facilitate computer-aided SCD diagnosis from multimodal data before conversion to AD.

Acknowledgments. This work was supported partly by National Natural Science Foundation of China (Nos. 61871274, U1909209, 61801305 and 81571758), Key Laboratory of Medical Image Processing of Guangdong Province (No. K217300003). Guangdong Pearl River Talents Plan (2016ZT06S220), Guangdong Basic and Applied Basic Research Foundation (No. 2019A1515111205), Shenzhen Peacock Plan (Nos. KQTD201605311 2051497 and KQTD2015033016104926), and Shenzhen Key Basic Research Project (Nos. GJHZ20190822095414576, JCYJ20180507184647636, JCYJ20190808155618806, JCYJ20170818094109846, JCYJ20190808155618806, and JCYJ20190808145011259).

References

1. Jessen, F., et al.: AD dementia risk in late MCI, in early MCI, and in subjective memory impairment. Alzheimers Dement **10**, 76–83 (2014)
2. Morris, J.C., et al.: Mild cognitive impairment represents early-stage Alzheimer disease. Arch. Neurol.-Chicago **58**, 397–405 (2001)
3. Guo, H., Zhang, F., Chen, J., Xu, Y., Xiang, J.: Machine learning classification combining multiple features of a hyper-network of fMRI data in Alzheimer's disease. Front. Neurosci. **11**, 1–22 (2017)
4. Qian, L., Zheng, L., Shang, Y., Zhang, Y., Zhang, Y.: Alzheimer's disease Neuroimaging Initiative: Intrinsic frequency specific brain networks for identification of MCI individuals using resting-state fMRI. Neurosci. Lett. **664**, 7–14 (2018)
5. Tong, T., Gray, K., Gao, Q., Chen, L., Rueckert, D.: Multi-modal classification of Alzheimer's disease using nonlinear graph fusion. Pattern Recogn. **63**, 171–181 (2017)
6. Cui, Z., Zhong, S., Xu, P., Gong, G., He, Y.: PANDA: a pipeline toolbox for analyzing brain diffusion images. Front. Hum. Neurosci. **7**, 42 (2013)
7. Craddock, R.C., James, G.A., Holtzheimer III, P.E., Hu, X.P., Mayberg, H.S.: A whole brain fMRI atlas generated via spatially constrained spectral clustering. Hum. Brain Mapp. **33**, 1914–1928 (2012)
8. Ashburner, J., et al.: SPM12 Manual. Wellcome Trust Centre for Neuroimaging, London (2014)
9. Yan, C., Zang, Y.: DPARSF: a MATLAB toolbox for "pipeline" data analysis of resting-state fMRI. Front. Syst. Neurosci. **4**, 13 (2010)
10. Qiao, L., Zhang, H., Kim, M., Teng, S., Zhang, L., Shen, D.: Estimating functional brain networks by incorporating a modularity prior. NeuroImage **141**, 399–407 (2016)
11. Argyriou, A., Evgeniou, T., Pontil, M.: Multi-task feature learning. In: Advances in Neural Information Processing Systems, pp. 41–48 (2007)

12. Liu, J., Ji, S., Ye, J.: Multi-task feature learning via efficient l 2, 1-norm minimization. In: Proceedings of the Twenty-Fifth Conference on Uncertainty in Artificial Intelligence, pp. 339–348. AUAI Press (2012)
13. Zhu, X., Suk, H.-I., Wang, L., Lee, S.-W., Shen, D., Alzheimer's disease Neuroimaging Initiative: A novel relational regularization feature selection method for joint regression and classification in AD diagnosis. Med. Image Anal. **38**, 205–214 (2017)
14. Peng, H., Fan, Y.: Direct sparsity optimization based feature selection for multi-class classification. In: IJCAI, pp. 1918–1924 (2016)
15. Vorlíčková, J.: Least absolute shrinkage and selection operator method (2017)
16. Jacob, L., Vert, J.-p., Bach, F.R.: Clustered multi-task learning: a convex formulation. In: Advances in Neural Information Processing Systems, pp. 745–752 (2012)
17. Chen, J., Liu, J., Ye, J.: Learning incoherent sparse and low-rank patterns from multiple tasks. ACM Trans. Knowl. Discov. Data **5**, 1–31 (2012)

Unified Brain Network with Functional and Structural Data

Jing Yang, Qi Zhu$^{(\boxtimes)}$, Rui Zhang, Jiashuang Huang, and Daoqiang Zhang

College of Computer Science and Technology,
Nanjing University of Aeronautics and Astronautics, Nanjing, China
zhuqinuaa@163.com

Abstract. Brain network analysis has been proved as an effective technology for brain disease diagnosis. For improving diagnosis performance, some efforts have been made to merge functional network and structural network. Whether using single modal or multi-modal data, the construction of brain network plays an important role in the whole diagnosis system. However, the existing multi-modal brain network analysis methods usually construct functional network and structural network separately, in which the complementary information of different modalities is difficult to embed. In this paper, a unified brain network construction algorithm that is jointly learned from both functional and structural data is proposed, and it is applied to epilepsy diagnosis. First, we built a correlation model among all brain regions with functional data by low-rank representation, and simultaneously embed the local manifold with structural data into this model. The constructed network then captures the global brain region correlation by the low-rank constraint and preserves the local structural information by manifold learning. Second, we adaptively estimate the importance of different brain regions by PageRank algorithm. Finally, we utilize a multi-kernel method to fuse the connectivity and node information from the constructed unified network for classification. The proposed method (UBNfs) is evaluated on multi-modal epilepsy dataset, and the experimental results show that our method is effective and can achieve a promising performance in diagnosis of epilepsy.

Keywords: Multi-modal brain network · PageRank algorithm · Node importance

1 Introduction

Brain network analysis has been widely utilized to analysis and diagnosis of brain diseases [1]. To the best of our knowledge, a brain network can be abstracted as a collection of edges and nodes, in which nodes represent regions of interest (ROIs) and edges represent the connection of different brain regions, respectively [2]. Functional MRI (fMRI) can reflect functional connectivity patterns of the brain, while diffusion tensor imaging (DTI) can reveal the physical connectivity between the functionally relevant gray matter regions [1]. Therefore, we

© Springer Nature Switzerland AG 2020
A. L. Martel et al. (Eds.): MICCAI 2020, LNCS 12267, pp. 114–123, 2020.
https://doi.org/10.1007/978-3-030-59728-3_12

can extract functional connectivity (FC) from fMRI and structural connectivity (SC) from DTI in brain network analysis. Traditionally, brain network construction methods always focus on either FC or SC. However, recent researches have proved that combining FC and SC to construct brain networks is an efficient and promising technique in diagnosing brain diseases.

Most of the existing multi-modal brain network analysis methods can be divided into two categories [3,20]. In the first category, effective machine learning technologies were adopted, such as principal component analysis (PCA) and multi-kernel learning (MKL) [3]. In the second category, utilizing one modality to assist the other modality is a common strategy. However, they neither consider the information of global brain regions nor the information of nodes. Even though some papers have considered the information of nodes, they only used simple attributes such as clustering coefficient and connectivity, which can not be enough to obtain high-order information of nodes.

To address this issue, we propose a unified brain network with functional and structural data (UBNfs) algorithm. The major contributions are as follows: First, we utilize a unified framework to construct brain network by using both FC and SC. Second, the relationship between multiple brain regions can be comprehensively considered instead of only considering two brain regions by adding a low-rank constraint. Third, we extracted significant node information from brain network and DTI network by PageRank algorithm. Fourth, in order to fuse connectivity and node information from the unified brain network, an effective multi-kernel technology is utilized for classification. The experimental results show that our method achieved a promising performance in the diagnosis of epilepsy. In summary, Fig. 1 gives a schematic illustration of our proposed method.

2   Proposed Method

2.1   Construction of Unified Brain Network

Our goal is to construct a unified brain network which is represented by a matrix $W \in R^{N \times N}$ and its entry W_{ij} not only contains the information of FC but also reflects the information of SC between brain region i and brain region j. Suppose $X = [x_1, x_2, ..., x_N]$ is a feature matrix of brain connection, where $x_i \in R^{K \times 1}$ is a feature vector of fMRI time series for brain region i. N is the number of brain regions and K is the number of time points of time series. The matrix $G \in R^{N \times N}$ is defined to reflect the physical connections whose entry $G_{ij} \geq 0$ represents the fiber number between the i-th brain region and the j-th brain region. Besides, the degree matrix of $G \in R^{N \times N}$ is defined as D, which is a diagonal matrix, whose entries are column sums of G, $D_{ii} = \sum_j G_{ij}$. Then the Laplacian matrix is defined as $L = D - G$. The algorithm for constructing the unified brain network with functional and structural data proposed in our paper is as follows.

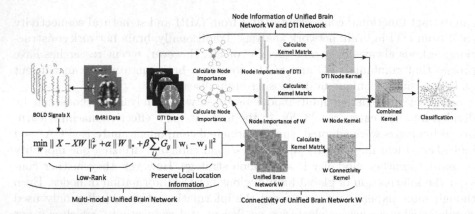

Fig. 1. A schematic illustration of our proposed method for constructing multi-modal unified brain network with significant information of nodes.

Unified Brain Network. First we suppose the feature matrix of brain activities can be linearly represented by the weight matrix W. It can be formulated as $X = XW$ and further written as $\min_{W} \parallel X - XW \parallel_F^2$ (The Frobenius norm designates $\|A\|_F^2 = \sum_{ij} a_{ij}^2$). Then we introduce the low-rank constraint to consider the global brain region information. Assume that each brain region can be approximately represented by a combination of only a few other brain regions, rank of the matrix W is a small number. So objective function is reformulated as $\min_{W} \parallel X - XW \parallel_F^2 + rank(W)$. Since the rank minimization problem is non-convex and NP-hard [4,22]. According to [4,22], $\min_{W} \parallel X - XW \parallel_F^2 + rank(W)$ is equivalent to

$$\min_{W} \parallel X - XW \parallel_F^2 + \parallel W \parallel_* \tag{1}$$

where $\parallel \cdot \parallel_*$ is the trace or nuclear norm of a matrix, i.e. $\|W\|_* = \sum_i |\sigma_i|$, where σ_i is the i-th singular value of matrix W. In addition, we introduce the physical connection matrix G into Eq. (1) to enrich the information of the weight matrix W, because DTI can reveal the physical connectivity between the functionally relevant gray matter regions. The matrix G is extracted from DTI to reflect the physical connections. It is well known SC is the foundation of FC [5,21]. A reasonable assumption is that the more fibers between brain region i and brain region j, the closer W_i and W_j are. Thus, the following objective function is constructed inspired by [19]

$$\min \sum_{i,j} G_{ij} \parallel w_i - w_j \parallel^2 \tag{2}$$

In summary, the final objective function is defined by jointly minimizing the above two problems

$$\min_{W} \parallel X - XW \parallel_F^2 + \alpha \parallel W \parallel_* + \beta \sum_{i,j} G_{ij} \parallel w_i - w_j \parallel^2 \tag{3}$$

where α and β are two positive scalars weight the corresponding terms in Eq. (3). It is easy to prove that the $\sum\limits_{i,j} G_{ij} \parallel w_i - w_j \parallel^2$ can be rewritten as $tr(WLW^T)$, where $L = D - G$ [6,17]. Therefore the above objective function can be transformed as

$$\min_W \parallel X - XW \parallel_F^2 + \alpha \parallel W \parallel_* + \beta tr(WLW^T)$$

$$s.t. \quad L = D - G \tag{4}$$

It is worth noting that the matrix W is the solution to Eq. (4), and the unified brain network represented by it not only reflects the information of FC, but also the information of SC.

Optimization Algorithm. Although it is difficult to directly optimize all variables in Eq. (4), some alternative optimization methods can be adopted to solve it. Here, we optimize our proposed objective function by the alternating direction method of multipliers (ADMM) algorithm [6]. First, we make an equivalent transformation by introducing two auxiliary variables to make the problem separable, and then Eq. (4) can be rewritten as

$$\min_{W,P,Q} \parallel X - XW \parallel_F^2 + \alpha \parallel P \parallel_* + \beta tr(QLQ^T)$$

$$s.t. \quad L = D - G, P = W, Q = W \tag{5}$$

We solve Eq. (5) by minimizing the following augmented Lagrange multiplier (ALM) function L

$$L(W,P,Q,Y_1,Y_2) = \parallel X - XW \parallel_F^2 + \alpha \parallel P \parallel_* + \beta tr(QLQ^T) + \langle Y_1, P - W \rangle$$

$$+ \langle Y_2, Q - W \rangle + \frac{\mu}{2}(\parallel P - W \parallel_F^2 + \parallel Q - W \parallel_F^2) \tag{6}$$

where Y_1 and Y_2 are Lagrange multipliers and $\mu > 0$ is a penalty parameter. Then, the variables W, Q, P, the Lagrangian multipliers Y_1 and Y_2, and iteration step-size $\rho(\rho > 1)$ can be updated by the following equations, respectively.

$$W^* = (2XX^T + 2\mu I)^{-1}(Y_1 + Y_2 + 2XX^T + \mu(P + Q)) \tag{7}$$

$$Q^* = (\mu W - Y_2)(\beta(L + L^T) + \mu I)^{-1} \tag{8}$$

$$P^* = \vartheta_{1/\mu}(W - \frac{Y_1}{\mu}) \tag{9}$$

$$\begin{cases} Y_1 = Y_1 + \mu(P - W) \\ Y_2 = Y_2 + \mu(Q - W) \\ \mu = \min(\rho\mu, \mu_{max}) \end{cases} \tag{10}$$

where $\vartheta_\lambda(X) = US_\lambda(\Sigma)V^T$ is a thresholding operator with respect to a singular value λ; $S_\lambda(\Sigma_{ij}) = sign(\Sigma_{ij}) \max(0, |\Sigma_{ij} - \lambda|)$ is the soft-thresholding operator; $X = U\Sigma V^T$ is the singular value decomposition of X. In summary, the process of solving (5) is summarized in Algorithm 1. Noting that those balanced parameters α, β are tuned in experiment, while other parameters ρ, ϵ, μ, and μ_{max} are set empirically.

Algorithm 1. Solving Problem (5) by ADMM

Input: X, G, α and β;
Initialization: $Y_1 = Y_2 = 0$; $\mu = 0.1$; $\mu_{max} = 10^{-7}$; $\rho = 1.01$; $\epsilon = 10^{-7}$;
While not converged **do**
1.Fix the other variables and update W by using (7);
2.Fix the other variables and update Q by using (8);
3.Fix the other variables and update P by using (9);
4.Update the multipliers and parameters by (10);
5.Check the convergence conditions
    $\| P - W \|_\infty < \epsilon$; $\| Q - W \|_\infty < \epsilon$
End While
Output: W

2.2 Fuse Connectivity and Node Information

After the unified brain network is constructed, we utilize PageRank algorithm to estimate the importance of different brain regions. The PageRank algorithm, one of the most widely used methods in Web page analysis, indicates that if a node has important links to it, its links to other nodes are also significant [7]. [18] proposes that PageRank algorithm can be applied to brain networks because brain networks have similar properties. So we compare brain regions to web pages, and the connections between brain regions to links between web pages. Then we use PageRank to estimate the importance of brain regions. According to [8], a simplified version of PageRank is defined as: $s_u = \sum\limits_{v \in P(u)} \frac{s_v}{N_v}$. Where u represents a node, $P(u)$ is the set of nodes that connect to node u, N_v denotes the number of links of node v and s_u is defined as score of node u. A significant properties of PageRank: The bigger is s_u, the more significant is u-th node [8]. The algorithm and the calculation steps are illustrated in Fig. 2. For example, in Fig. 2, $P(u) = \{a, b\}$ and $s_u = s_a/2 + s_b/2$. In our experiment, we calculate the node importance vectors of brain network W and DTI networks, respectively. Then the two node importance vectors are fused to make use of the complementary information of functional and structural data for classification.

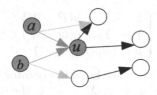

Fig. 2. A sample diagram illustrating the calculation formula of PageRank algorithm.

After obtaining the connectivity and node importance information from the constructed unified network and DTI network, we use a multi-kernel SVM algorithm to fuse these important information. We make the unified brain network as the first modality, the node importance of unified brain network as the second modality, and the node importance of DTI data as the third modality. To deal with this three-modality problem, a multi-kernel SVM method [9] is utilized for classification. We interpret $k(x_i, x_j) = \sum_m c_m k^{(m)}(x_i^{(m)}, x_j^{(m)})$ as a mixed kernel between the multi-modal training sample x_i and x_j. And $k(x_i, x) = \sum_m c_m k^{(m)}($ $x_i^{(m)}, x^{(m)})$ indicates the mixed kernel between the multi-modal training sample x_i and the test sample x. It is important that we constrain $\sum_m c_m = 1$ and employ a coarse-grid search to determine the optimal c_m. After obtaining the optimal c_m, we use c_m to combine three kernels into a mixed kernel, and then a standard SVM is performed for classification.

3 Results

3.1 Materials and Preprocessing

Before our experiment, raw rs-fMRI data and DTI data are collected from 306 individuals, including 114 normal controls (NC), 103 frontal lobe epilepsy (FLE) patients and 89 temporal lobe epilepsy (TLE) patients. Those data are obtained by Siemens Trio 3T scanner. We utilize the SPM8 in the DPARSF toolbox version 2.0 to pre-process all rs-fMRI images before the experiments. By using the AAL atlas, the resulting volumes consist of 240 time points and are partitioned into 90 brain regions of interest (ROIs). Thus, the information about brain activity are reflected by time series. Besides we use the PANDA suite to process the DTI data so that the number of fiber can be regarded as strength of physical connections in the brain network.

3.2 Experimental Results

In order to evaluate the performance of our proposed method, we apply it to four different classification experiments, including NC vs FLE, NC vs TLE, FLE vs TLE, and NC vs (FLE and TLE). We also compared our method with some related works which can be divided into three categories: fMRI based methods, DTI based methods, fMRI and DTI based methods. More specifically, fMRI based methods are Pearson coefficient (PC) [10], Sparse representation (SR) [11], Topology connectivity (tHOFC) [12], Graph-CNN (GCNN) [13], Siamese-GCN (SGCN) [14]. DTI based methods include Graph kernel (GK) [15], Graph-CNN (GCNN) [13]. fMRI and DTI based methods are Multi-kernel (MK) [16], our method without node importance information, our proposed methods (UBNfs). What's more, Canonical analysis (CCA), Kernel-canonical analysis (KCCA) and Manifold regularized (M2TFS) algorithms are all used to fuse multi-modal data.

For all our experiments, a 5-fold cross validation and a unified feature extraction method (LASSO) are adopted to ensure the fairness of the experimental results. Experiment results are showed in Table 1.

Table 1. Performance of proposed method and comparative methods.

	Methods	NC: FLE	NC: TLE	FLE: TLE	NC: (FLE and TLE)
fMRI based methods	PC [10]	62.1	63.9	51.7	65.6
	SR [11]	61.7	70.9	44.9	63.9
	tHOFC [12]	61.3	62.7	55.4	62.9
	GCNN [13]	55.8	67.5	61.4	67.0
	SGCN [14]	67.3	74.5	**70.5**	69.3
DTI based methods	GK [15]	56.3	53.0	54.1	61.3
	GCNN [13]	51.6	54.5	56.4	62.6
fMRI and DTI based methods	MK [16]	61.8	70.2	59.9	68.1
	CCA	62.6	67.3	59.2	68.6
	KCCA	64.6	68.5	60.7	66.7
	M2TFS	60.8	64.5	60.2	66.5
	Our method*	68.9	70.9	65.6	66.7
	Our method	**71.3**	**75.1**	69.0	**71.9**

Note that: * indicates that our proposed method without node importance information.

From the Table 1, we can see that the accuracies of the proposed method in the four classification tasks are 71.3%, 75.1%, 69.0%, 71.9%, respectively. Compared with other methods, the proposed method has the highest accuracies in the classification tasks of NC vs FLE, NC vs TLE, NC vs (FLE and TLE). In the FLE vs TLE task, although SGCN algorithm has achieved the highest classification accuracy, the discrepancy between our accuracy and that of theirs is acceptable. Many other conclusions can be drawn from the table. First, the methods based on fMRI are more effective than those based on DTI, which shows that fMRI contains more significant information than DTI data. Second, those methods that combined fMRI and DTI generally achieved better results, which shows that fusing fMRI and DTI data is indeed a potential disease diagnosis technology. Third, we utilize our proposed method without node importance information for classification, but the accuracies are only 68.9%, 70.9%, 65.6%, 66.7%. In contrast to adding node importance information, the results are relatively poor. It suggests that the node importance information measured by PageRank algorithm does contain significant information.

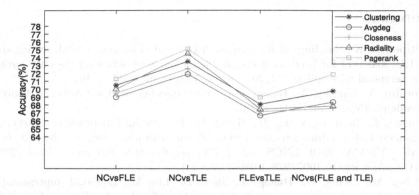

Fig. 3. Comparison of experimental results of five different topological attribute measurement methods (Clustering, Avgdeg, Closeness, Radiality and PageRank algorithm) under four different classification tasks (NC vs FLE, NC vs TLE, FLE vs TLE, NC vs (FLE and TLE)).

3.3   Comparison of Other Topological Attributes

In order to prove the rationality of selecting PageRank algorithm to estimate the importance of different brain regions. We compared PageRank algorithm with some other common topological attribute measurement methods, such as Clustering coefficient (Clustering), Average degree (Avgdeg), Closeness centrality (Closeness) and Radiality. For all our experiments, we guarantee that the other experimental settings are consistent. As can be seen from Fig. 3, compared with other measurement methods, introducing PageRank algorithm can achieve the highest accuracies in four different classification tasks. It can prove that compared with other measurement methods, PageRank algorithm is more effective in evaluating the node importance of unified brain network.

4   Conclusion

In this paper, a unified brain network construction algorithm that is jointly learned from both functional and structural data is proposed. In our unified brain network, the relationship between multiple brain regions can be comprehensively considered instead of only considering two brain regions. And the local manifold with structural data is embedded into this model simultaneously. Besides, we take into account not only the connectivity of brain network, but also the information about the importance of different brain regions which is extracted by PageRank algorithm. In addition, we utilize a multi-kernel method to fuse the connectivity and node information for classification. The proposed method is evaluated on multi-modal epilepsy dataset. Experimental results show that our method is effective and can achieve a promising performance in diagnosis of epilepsy.

References

1. Osipowicz, K., Sperling, M.R., Sharan, A.D., et al.: Functional MRI, resting state fMRI, and DTI for predicting verbal fluency outcome following resective surgery for temporal lobe epilepsy. J. Neurosurg. **124**(4), 929–937 (2016)
2. Fornito, A., Zalesky, A., Bullmore, E.: Fundamentals of Brain Network Analysis. Academic Press, Cambridge (2016)
3. Huang, J., Zhou, L., Wang, L., Zhang, D.: Integrating functional and structural connectivities via diffusion-convolution-bilinear neural network. In: Shen, D., et al. (eds.) MICCAI 2019. LNCS, vol. 11766, pp. 691–699. Springer, Cham (2019). https://doi.org/10.1007/978-3-030-32248-9_77
4. Wang, M., Zhang, D., Huang, J., Shen, D., Liu, M.: Low-rank representation for multi-center autism spectrum disorder identification. In: Frangi, A.F., Schnabel, J.A., Davatzikos, C., Alberola-López, C., Fichtinger, G. (eds.) MICCAI 2018. LNCS, vol. 11070, pp. 647–654. Springer, Cham (2018). https://doi.org/10.1007/978-3-030-00928-1_73
5. Honey, C., Sporns, O., Cammoun, L., et al.: Predicting human resting-state functional connectivity from structural connectivity. Proc. Natl. Acad. Sci. U.S.A. **106**(6), 2035–2040 (2009)
6. Xu, Y., Fang, X., Wu, J., et al.: Discriminative transfer subspace learning via low-rank and sparse representation. IEEE Trans. Image Process. **25**(2), 850–863 (2015)
7. Florescu, C., Caragea, C.: A position-biased PageRank algorithm for keyphrase extraction. In: Thirty-First AAAI Conference on Artificial Intelligence (2017)
8. Yan, E., Ding, Y.: Discovering author impact: a PageRank perspective. Inf. Process. Manag. **47**(1), 125–134 (2011)
9. Zhang, D., Wang, Y., Zhou, L., et al.: Multimodal classification of Alzheimer's disease and mild cognitive impairment. Neuroimage **55**(3), 856–867 (2011)
10. Betzel, R.F., Fukushima, M., He, Y., et al.: Dynamic fluctuations coincide with periods of high and low modularity in resting-state functional brain networks. NeuroImage **127**, 287–297 (2016)
11. Yu, R., Zhang, H., An, L., Chen, X., Wei, Z., Shen, D.: Connectivity strength-weighted sparse group representation-based brain network construction for MCI classification. Hum. Brain Mapp. **38**(5), 2370–2383 (2017)
12. Zhang, H., et al.: Topographic information based high-order functional connectivity and its application in abnormality detection for mild cognitive impairment. J. Alzheimers Dis. **54**(3), 1095–1112 (2016)
13. Mao, B., Huang, J., Zhang, D.: Node based row-filter convolutional neural network for brain network classification. In: Geng, X., Kang, B.-H. (eds.) PRICAI 2018. LNCS (LNAI), vol. 11012, pp. 1069–1080. Springer, Cham (2018). https://doi.org/10.1007/978-3-319-97304-3_82
14. Ktena, S.I., et al.: Distance metric learning using graph convolutional networks: application to functional brain networks. In: Descoteaux, M., Maier-Hein, L., Franz, A., Jannin, P., Collins, D.L., Duchesne, S. (eds.) MICCAI 2017. LNCS, vol. 10433, pp. 469–477. Springer, Cham (2017). https://doi.org/10.1007/978-3-319-66182-7_54
15. Kang, U., Tong, H., Sun, J.: Fast random walk graph kernel. In: Proceedings of the 2012 SIAM International Conference on Data Mining, pp. 828–838. Society for Industrial and Applied Mathematics (2012)

16. Dyrba, M., Grothe, M., Kirste, T., et al.: Multimodal analysis of functional and structural disconnection in Alzheimer's disease using multiple kernel SVM. Hum. Brain Mapp. **36**(6), 2118–2131 (2015)
17. Yu, R., Qiao, L., Chen, M., et al.: Weighted graph regularized sparse brain network construction for MCI identification. Pattern Recogn. **90**, 220–231 (2019)
18. Gleich, D.F.: PageRank beyond the web. SIAM Rev. **57**(3), 321–363 (2015)
19. He, X., Niyogi, P.: Locality preserving projections. In: Advances in Neural Information Processing Systems, pp. 153–160 (2004)
20. Huang, J., Zhou, L., Wang, L., et al.: Attention-diffusion-bilinear neural network for brain network analysis. IEEE Trans. Med. Imaging **39**, 2541–2552 (2020)
21. Stam, C.J., Van Straaten, E.C., Van Dellen, E., et al.: The relation between structural and functional connectivity patterns in complex brain networks. In. J. Psychophysiol. **103**, 149–160 (2016)
22. Wang, M., Zhang, D., Huang, J., et al.: Identifying autism spectrum disorder with multi-site fMRI via low-rank domain adaptation. IEEE Trans. Med. Imaging **39**(3), 644–655 (2019)

Integrating Similarity Awareness and Adaptive Calibration in Graph Convolution Network to Predict Disease

Xuegang Song[1], Alejandro Frangi[2], Xiaohua Xiao[3], Jiuwen Cao[4], Tianfu Wang[1], and Baiying Lei[1(✉)]

[1] Shenzhen University, Shenzhen, China
leiby@szu.edu.cn
[2] University of Leeds, Leeds, UK
[3] Affiliated Hospital of Shenzhen University, Shenzhen, China
[4] Hangzhou Dianzi University, Hangzhou, China

Abstract. Significant memory concern (SMC) is the earlier stage of mild cognitive impairment (MCI), and its early treatment is quite vital to delay further disease-induced deterioration. To predict the deterioration, graph convolution network (GCN) with current adjacency matrix still suffers from limited prediction performance due to their subtle difference and obscure features. For this reason, we propose a *similarity-aware adaptive calibrated* GCN (SAC-GCN), which can combine functional and structural information to predict SMC and MCI. We utilize an adaptive calibration mechanism to construct a *data-driven* adjacency matrix. Specifically, we first design a similarity-aware graph using different receptive fields to consider the disease statuses. Namely, the labeled subjects are only connected with those subjects who have the same status in the convolution operation. Then we compute more *accurate* weights in graph edges from functional and structural scores. Current edge weights are used to construct an initial graph and *pre-train* the GCN. Based on the pre-trained GCN, the differences between scores replace the traditional correlation distances to evaluate edge weights. Lastly, we devise a *calibration* technique to *fuse* functional and structural information for edge weighting. The proposed method is tested on the Alzheimer's Disease Neuroimaging Initiative (ADNI) dataset. The experimental results demonstrate that our proposed method is effective to predict disease-induced deterioration and superior over other related algorithm.

Keywords: Disease-induced deterioration prediction · Similarity- aware calibrated graph convolution network · Dual-modal information

1 Introduction

Alzheimer's disease (AD) is yet incurable and no effective medicines exist, while the deterioration process of its early stages (*e.g.*, mild cognitive impairment (MCI) and significant memory concern (SMC)) stages can be delayed with certain cognitive training and pharmacological treatment [1]. To improve the treatment effect, early prediction can

© Springer Nature Switzerland AG 2020
A. L. Martel et al. (Eds.): MICCAI 2020, LNCS 12267, pp. 124–133, 2020.
https://doi.org/10.1007/978-3-030-59728-3_13

better retain cognitive functions [2, 3]. However, the accurate disease prediction of SMC and MCI is still a challenging task due to their subtle differences in neuroimaging features during deterioration and insufficient samples.

There are two popular kinds of methods to solve the limitations above: one is using multi-modal data to describe/strengthen features from multiple information sources [4–7], while the other uses graph theory and convolution filters to suppress noise in features [8–12]. For disease deterioration prediction using multi-modal neuroimaging, integrating functional magnetic resonance imaging (fMRI) and diffusion tensor imaging (DTI) is shown to achieve good performance by integrating their complementary cues [6, 7]. For example, Lei et al. [6] developed a multi-task learning method to select features from fMRI functional and DTI structural brain networks, and then the selected features were sent into a support vector machine (SVM) for final prediction. Li et al. [7] used the DTI tractography as penalty parameters in a ultra-weighted-lasso algorithm to construct more accurate functional brain networks. These works show that the performance of using multi-modal neuroimaging is better than using single modal neuroimaging for disease prediction. Since graph convolution networks (GCN) in deep learning have shown their effectiveness due to their powerful representation ability, graph theory has received ample attention in disease prediction [8–12]. For example, Sarah et al. [8] integrated phenotypic information (e.g., gender, acquisition site, and ages) into edges for autism and AD prediction. Zhang et al. [10] proposed an adaptive pooling scheme for brain disease prediction. Kazi et al. [11] designed different kernel sizes in spectral convolution to predict brain disease. These studies show that edges and spectral convolution are keys for improving prediction performance. The integration of multi-modal neuroimaging in GCN via graph theory can boost performance [10].

Even though multi-modal fusion and GCN can achieve good performance for AD/MCI identification [6–12], there are still remaining limitations. First, using multi-modal GCN for feature learning and then concatenating features [10] increases the dimension of feature vector, which may increase system burden. Second, existing GCN methods for disease prediction [6–12] fail to consider the difference between disease statuses. Ignoring disease staging in graph construction may affect prediction performance since there are only subtle differences in neuroimaging features between different statuses (e.g., SMC vs. EMCI). Third, the current edge weights [8–10, 12] are estimated roughly by calculating the correlation distance between extracted feature vectors, which is inaccurate and eventually affects convolution performance especially for SMC and MCI prediction due to their subtle difference.

To overcome these limitations, we design a *similarity-aware* adaptive calibrated GCN structure, which uses two GCN classifiers to correspond to fMRI and DTI data, and balances their outputs via a voting strategy. Particularly, three techniques are proposed in our method. Firstly, similarity-aware receptive fields are designed on graphs to consider the differences of disease statuses. Specifically, every labeled node in training samples is only connected with those labeled nodes that have the same disease status, whereas every unlabeled node in validation samples is allowed to connect with every node. Secondly, we propose an *adaptive* mechanism by using the difference between pre-scores, which can replace correlation distance to get more accurate edge weights. Specifically, we use the initial edge weights calculated from the correlation distance to construct initial graph and pre-train GCN using training samples. And then, we use the pre-trained GCN to score subjects. The difference between these pre-scores is used to form the updated edge weights. This is motivated by the fact that *pre-trained* GCN can evaluate similarities better than correlation distance. Thirdly, based on the relevant and complementary relationship between fMRI functional network and DTI structural network, we propose a *calibration* technique to *fuse* functional and structural information into edge weights. Overall, the main contributions of our work are as follows:

1) Similarity-aware receptive fields are designed on graph to consider the difference between disease statuses by similarity constraints.
2) An adaptive method is introduced to construct more accurate edge weights by pre-training GCN.
3) A calibration mechanism is devised to fuse functional and structural information.

We validate our method by using the Alzheimer's Disease Neuroimaging Initiative (ADNI) (https://ida.loni.usc.edu) public database. Experimental results show that our method achieves quite promising performance for disease deterioration prediction.

2 Method

Figure 1 shows the overview of our proposed prediction framework. To utilize fMRI and DTI information, we develop two GCN models and each is trained and utilized independently. For a total of n subjects, each subject is denoted as a node represented by fMRI, DTI and phenotypic information (*e.g.*, gender and equipment type), where each node is assigned as a label $l \in \{0, 1\}$. We construct functional connection (FC) brain network and structural connection (SC) brain network for every subject. The functional graph and structural graph are constructed from FCs and SCs. Both graphs are input into GCN and softmax layer outputs scores of all subjects. Finally, we employ a voting strategy to balance outputs of the two GCN models for the final disease deterioration prediction.

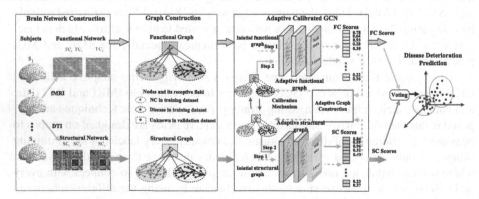

Fig. 1. General framework of our proposed disease deterioration prediction algorithm.

2.1 Data

A total of 170 subjects from the ADNI database is used as dataset. Our data contains 17 male SMC patients and 27 female SMC patients, 22 male early MCI (EMCI) patients and 22 female EMCI patients, 19 male late MCI (LMCI) patients and 19 female LMCI patients, and 22 male normal control (NC) and 22 female NC. The equipment style of SMC contains 21 GE, 21 SIEMENS and 2 PHILIPS, EMCI contains 9 GE, 30 SIEMENS and 5 PHILIPS, LMCI contains 26 GE, 9 SIEMENS and 3 PHILIPS, and NC contains 14 GE, 25 SIEMENS and 5 PHILIPS.

For fMRI data preprocessing, we apply the standard procedures, including the removal of the first 10 volumes of each subject, head motion correction, registration, resampling, spatial normalization, and Gaussian smoothing. By aligning the fMRI image using automatic anatomical landmarks (AAL) [13], we get the brain space with 90 regions of interests (ROIs). DTI is preprocessed using the PANDA Toolbox [14] to get the global brain determinism fiber bundle. We obtain the fractional anisotropy (FA) as feature vectors. By aligning AAL to each image, we get the brain space of 90 ROIs. For FC network construction from rs-fMRI data, we use simple Pearson's correlation (PC) and finally get a 90×90 FC network for every subject. For SC network construction from DTI data, the average FA of links between network nodes is defined as the connection weight in the DTI network. We finally get a 90×90 SC network for every subject.

2.2 Graph Construction

We establish a functional graph and a structural graph, respectively. Nodes on the two graphs represent corresponding subjects and their brain networks. To reduce the dimension of the two 90×90 brain networks, we use recursive feature elimination (RFE) to extract features. Then every node on graph is represented by a low-dimensional feature vector. Edge weights between nodes represent their similarities. Let an initial graph denoted as AX, $A \in \mathbb{R}^{n \times n}$ represent the adjacency matrix, and $X \in \mathbb{R}^{n \times m}$ represent the feature matrix. n represents the number of subjects and m is the number of extracted features for every subject.

Similarity-Aware Receptive Fields: We use three receptive fields, where two receptive fields are for labeled subjects and one receptive field is for un-labeled subjects based on the similarity of subject's characteristics. Namely, for a labeled patient, all labeled patients are used as its receptive field. For a labeled NC, all labeled NCs are used as its receptive field. For every unlabeled subject, all subjects are used as its receptive field.

Initial Adjacency Matrix: Every established value in the adjacency matrix A is calculated using the correlation coefficient [8]. Let ρ be the correlation distance, σ be the width of the kernel, $Sim(F_v, F_w) = \exp\left(-\frac{[\rho(x(v), x(w))]^2}{2\sigma^2}\right)$ is the similarity between a subject v and subject w, F_v and F_w denote their corresponding feature vectors, the adjacency matrix A between them is defined as

$$A(v, w) = Sim(F_v, F_w) \times (r_G(M_h(v), M_h(w)) + r_E(M_h(v), M_h(w))), \qquad (1)$$

where M_h represents non-image phenotypic information, r_G represents distance of gender, and r_E represents distance of acquisition equipment, r is defined as:

$$r(M_h(v), M_h(w)) = \begin{cases} 1, & M_h(v) = M_h(w), \\ 0, & otherwise. \end{cases} \qquad (2)$$

2.3 Adaptive Calibrated GCN

Estimating edges weights by using correlation distance is limited and causes unsatisfactory performance. For this reason, we devise an adaptive adjacency matrix based on the pre-trained GCN model. Specifically, we exploit an adaptive similarity metric to replace correlation distance. To fuse fMRI and DTI data in a better way, we further develop a calibration mechanism to integrate them into an adjacency matrix.

Adaptive Adjacency Matrix: Firstly, we pre-train every single modal GCN using training samples. The initial graph is constructed by initial adjacency matrix. Second, we input subjects to the pre-trained GCN, and get their scores. Lastly, based on these scores, we construct an adaptive adjacency matrix to achieve better prediction performance. The adaptive similarities based on scores are calculated as follows:

$$Sim(F_v, F_w) = \exp\left(-\frac{[Score(v) - Score(w)]^2}{2\sigma^2}\right). \qquad (3)$$

By Eqs. (1), (2) and(3), we finally get a more accurate adjacency matrix A adaptively during experiments.

Calibration Mechanism: As adjacency matrix determines the performance of GCN, we propose a calibration mechanism to integrate fMRI functional and DTI structural information into the adjacency matrix. The calibrated matrix is defined as:

$$A_{calibrated} = A_{fMRI} \circ A_{DTI}, \qquad (4)$$

where A_{fMRI} represents the adjacency matrix calculated from fMRI data, while A_{DTI} is calculated from DTI data, and $\circ$ represents Hadamard product.

3   Experiments and Results

GCN parameters in experiments are set as below: dropout rate is 0.1, l_2 regularization is 5×10^{-4}, learning rate is 0.005, the number of epochs is 200, the number of neurons per layer is 32 and the number of extracted features is 30. We use a nested leave-one-out cross-validation strategy to evaluate the proposed method. Prediction accuracy (ACC), sensitivity (SEN), specificity (SPE) are used as evaluation metrics. Six binary classification experiments including NC vs. SMC, NC vs. EMCI, NC vs. LMCI, SMC vs. EMCI, SMC vs. LMCI and EMCI vs. LMCI are designed to validate the prediction performance.

Table 1. Disease prediction performance in NC vs. SMC, NC vs. EMCI and NC vs. LMCI.

Modal	Method	NC vs. SMC				NC vs. EMCI				NC vs. LMCI			
		ACC	SEN	SPE	AUC	ACC	SEN	SPE	AUC	ACC	SEN	SPE	AUC
fMRI	MLP	56.81	68.18	45.45	57.13	56.27	59.09	45.45	52.79	62.19	63.15	79.54	54.04
	RF	62.5	68.18	56.81	65.39	58.81	63.63	50	56.61	69.51	76.31	63.63	78.29
	SVM	61.36	68.18	54.54	60.28	57.95	63.63	52.27	60.02	69.75	84.21	77.72	75.84
	GCN	70.45	72.72	68.18	76.50	69.31	65.90	72.72	64.82	75.60	52.63	95.45	65.60
	S-GCN	74.13	76.13	77.27	85.38	70.45	70.45	70.45	78.67	79.26	73.68	93.18	85.71
	SA-GCN	76.13	77.27	75.00	85.64	77.27	72.72	81.81	86.05	71.83	40.74	90.90	87.29
	SAC-GCN	78.41	81.81	75.00	86.26	77.27	72.72	81.81	86.83	86.58	86.84	86.36	94.26
DTI	MLP	61.36	61.36	61.36	58.68	59.09	54.54	63.63	62.60	71.83	48.14	86.36	48.14
	RF	61.36	65.90	56.81	63.27	65.90	61.36	70.45	75.31	73.17	89.47	59.09	73.17
	SVM	65.63	70.45	56.81	69.32	62.41	47.72	70.45	71.18	74.39	94.73	56.81	90.90
	GCN	72.72	77.27	68.18	76.39	75.00	68.18	81.81	78.67	80.28	62.96	90.90	88.47
	S-GCN	76.13	79.54	72.72	78.41	78.41	81.81	75	86.26	80.48	78.94	90.90	85.83
	SA-GCN	80.22	86.36	84.09	91.84	80.68	77.27	87.40	93.18	87.80	84.21	90.90	93.84
	SAC-GCN	81.36	86.36	86.36	92.36	84.09	79.54	88.63	94.20	90.14	81.48	95.45	94.53
Dual	MLP	62.50	56.81	68.18	65.34	59.09	52.27	65.90	60.74	71.95	68.42	93.18	65.44
	RF	64.77	68.18	61.36	66.53	61.36	50	72.72	63.43	68.29	63.15	90.90	77.99
	SVM	67.04	72.72	61.36	71.95	64.77	54.54	75.00	66.06	69.51	68.42	88.63	78.83
	GCN	76.13	79.54	72.72	78.41	76.13	70.45	81.81	77.84	80.48	73.68	86.36	87.50
	S-GCN	78.41	93.18	63.63	93.44	77.27	79.54	84.09	87.55	81.70	73.68	88.63	86.42
	SA-GCN	81.81	88.63	75	93.65	85.50	88.63	86.36	89.36	87.80	89.47	96.23	86.36
	SAC-GCN	84.09	81.81	86.36	92.30	85.50	88.63	86.36	89.36	90.14	77.77	97.72	88.80

Table 2. Disease prediction performance in SMC vs. EMCI, SMC vs. LMCI and EMCI vs. LMCI.

Modal method		SMC vs. EMCI				SMC vs. LMCI				EMCI vs. LMCI			
		ACC	SEN	SPE	AUC	ACC	SEN	SPE	AUC	ACC	SEN	SPE	AUC
fMRI	MLP	60.22	56.63	56.81	61.88	61.97	37.07	77.27	60.19	59.15	45.92	79.54	51.09
	RF	65.90	59.09	90.90	72.68	65.85	50	79.54	71.05	64.78	47.03	81.81	59.43
	SVM	64.77	56.81	72.72	67.98	64.63	47.36	79.54	67.58	60.56	43.33	77.27	54.12
	GCN	71.59	75.00	68.18	70.51	71.95	65.78	77.27	81.34	72.46	51.85	93.18	72.47
	S-GCN	75.00	79.54	70.45	81.35	75.60	65.78	84.09	87.68	78.04	66.31	98.42	88.55
	SA-GCN	77.27	72.72	81.81	86.05	76.82	68.42	84.09	91.10	81.91	62.96	98.42	86.28
	SAC-GCN	80.09	84.09	84.09	87.55	78.04	68.42	86.36	92.00	81.91	62.96	98.42	86.28
DTI	MLP	64.72	54.54	75.00	70.92	64.78	40.74	79.54	70.12	62.33	44.81	81.81	41.67
	RF	71.59	61.36	81.81	77.89	69.51	73.68	65.90	75.36	67.60	37.03	86.36	65.74
	SVM	70.45	65.90	75.00	75.26	65.85	50	79.54	71.05	63.38	37.03	79.54	52.95
	GCN	77.27	70.45	84.09	84.40	80.48	81.21	77.27	80.46	74.39	86.63	63.63	70.08
	S-GCN	79.54	72.72	86.36	89.29	82.92	86.84	79.54	91.27	76.82	89.47	65.90	88.88
	SA-GCN	82.95	81.81	84.09	89.31	86.58	86.84	86.36	93.60	82.92	94.73	72.72	91.75
	SAC-GCN	84.09	81.81	86.36	89.57	87.32	70.37	97.72	95.71	84.14	94.73	75	92.88

(*continued*)

Table 2. (*continued*)

Modal method		SMC vs. EMCI				SMC vs. LMCI				EMCI vs. LMCI			
		ACC	SEN	SPE	AUC	ACC	SEN	SPE	AUC	ACC	SEN	SPE	AUC
Dual	MLP	65.90	56.81	75.00	67.15	64.78	53.33	74.09	63.80	64.53	44.73	70.45	47.12
	RF	70.45	65.90	75.00	71.28	70.73	65.78	75	76.08	67.07	63.15	70.45	71.77
	SVM	65.90	70.90	70.27	72.68	71.95	65.78	77.27	81.34	68.85	60.52	70.45	68.72
	GCN	77.27	72.72	81.81	77.27	79.26	84.21	75	81.42	78.04	73.68	81.81	79.25
	S-GCN	80.68	75.00	86.36	79.60	85.91	72.96	85.45	85.44	79.26	94.73	65.90	90.43
	SA-GCN	83.50	81.81	88.18	89.15	86.58	86.84	86.36	87.32	84.14	94.73	75	92.88
	SAC-GCN	87.50	84.09	93.18	91.17	86.58	86.84	86.36	87.88	85.36	94.73	77.27	93.72

Tables 1 and 2 summarize our disease deterioration prediction results and other classifiers including GCN [8], multiple layer perception (MLP) [15], random forest (RF) [16] and SVM [17]. Table 3 shows the comparison of the proposed method with related algorithms [4, 6, 7, 18–20]. The key parameters of MLP are as: two layers with every layer 32 neurons, the activation function is 'logistic', the learning rate is 0.001, and the maximum number of iterations is 500. The parameters of RF are: The number of trees is 500, and the maximum depth is 3. The parameters of SVM are: The kernel is 'sigmoid', the kernel coefficient is 0.1, the regularization parameter is 0.1, and the maximum number of iterations is 500. The top 10 most discriminative connections and associated ROI brain regions are shown in Fig. 2. In this subsection, we describe the GCN with our similarity-aware receptive fields as S-GCN, SA-GCN represents the GCN using our similarity-aware receptive fields and adaptive adjacency matrix. SAC-GCN represents the GCN using the similarity-aware receptive fields and adaptive calibration mechanism.

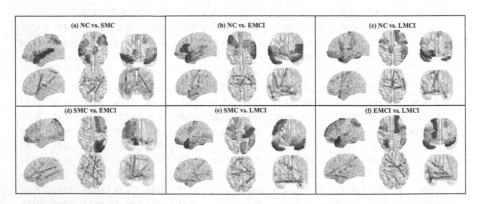

Fig. 2. The top 10 most discriminative connections and ROI brain regions in six tasks.

We can see that our SAC-GCN has achieved quite good performance compared to traditional GCN methods and other popular used classifiers (MLP, RF and SVM). In the proposed three techniques, our similarity-aware receptive fields and adaptive adjacency matrix are used to construct a more accurate single modal adjacency matrix. These two

Table 3. Algorithm comparison with related works.

Algorithm	Subject	Methods, # ROIs, # Modality	Task	ACC	SEN	SPE
Wee et al. [18]	29 EMCI, 30 NC	Fused multiple graphical lasso, 90, fMRI	EMCI vs. NC	79.6	75.8	70.0
Yu et al. [19]	50 MCI, 49 NC	Weighted Sparse Group Representation, 90, fMRI	MCI vs. NC	84.8	91.2	78.5
Guo et al. [20]	33 EMCI, 32 LMCI, 28 NC	Multiple Features of Hyper-Network, 90, fMRI	EMCI vs. NC	72.8	78.2	67.1
			LMCI vs.NC	78.6	82.5	72.1
Li et al. [7]	36 MCI, 37 NC	Adaptive dynamic functional connectivity, 90 fMRI + DTI	MCI vs. NC	87.7	88.9	86.5
Zhu et al. [4]	99 MCI, 53 NC	SPMRM model, 93, MRI + PET + CSF	MCI vs. NC	83.5	95.0	62.8
Ni et al. [6]	40 LMCI, 77 EMCI, 67 NC	Low-Rank Self-calibrated Brain Network, Joint Non-Convex Multi-Task Learning, 90, fMRI + DTI	NC vs. SMC	82.95	88.64	77.27
			NC vs. EMCI	85.23	86.36	84.09
			NC vs. LMCI	87.80	84.21	90.91
			SMC vs. EMCI	84.09	81.82	86.36
			SMC vs. LMCI	90.24	89.47	90.91
			EMCI vs. LMCI	81.71	78.95	84.09
Ours	40 LMCI, 77 EMCI, 67 NC	Similarity-aware adaptive calibrated GCN, 90, fMRI + DTI	NC vs. SMC	84.09	81.81	86.36
			NC vs. EMCI	85.50	88.63	86.36
			NC vs. LMCI	90.14	77.77	97.72
			SMC vs. EMCI	87.50	84.09	93.18
			SMC vs. LMCI	86.58	86.84	86.36
			EMCI vs. LMCI	85.36	94.73	77.27

extensions can significantly improve the prediction results, which means that distinguishing patient disease status has impact on convolutions and our adaptive adjacency matrix in GCN has better ability to estimate edge weights than correlation distance in traditional GCN. The calibration mechanism is proposed to combine functional and structural information into a new adjacency matrix. Experimental results show that this technique can improve the prediction performance.

Overall, comparing our method with GCN, average ACC based on dual-modal information for six tasks increases by 8.64%, average SEN increases by 9.93%, and average SPE increases by 7.91%. Table 3 shows the comparison of the proposed method with other related methods in the literature. Our proposed method has achieved promising performance. Our three techniques aim to improve adjacency matrix and the achieved good performance validates their effectiveness. The significant improvement by using our method also demonstrates that the construction of adjacency matrix plays a vital role in GCN structure. The proposed three techniques can also combine with current pooling [10] and kernel [11] design techniques.

4 Conclusion

In this paper, we proposed an improved GCN structure, which combines functional and structural information for disease-induced deterioration prediction. We developed three strategies to construct a more accurate adjacency matrix to identify the obscure features in disease-induced deterioration. The similarity-aware receptive fields and adaptive adjacency matrix can be used in single-modal tasks independently. The calibration mechanism is explored to fuse the functional and structural information. Experimental results validated that our method can significantly improve prediction performance in the public ADNI data.

Acknowledgement. This work was supported partly by National Natural Science Foundation of China (Nos. 61871274, U1909209, 61801305 and 81571758), China Postdoctoral Science Foundation (Nos. 2019M653014), Key Laboratory of Medical Image Processing of Guangdong Province (No. K217300003). Guangdong Pearl River Talents Plan (2016ZT06S220), Guangdong Basic and Applied Basic Research Foundation (No. 2019A1515111205), Shenzhen Peacock Plan (Nos. KQTD2016053112051497 and KQTD2015033016104926), and Shenzhen Key Basic Research Project (Nos. GJHZ20190822095414576, JCYJ20180507184647636, JCYJ20190808155618806, JCYJ20170818094109846, JCYJ20190808155618806, and JCYJ20190808145011259).

References

1. Zhang, Y., et al.: Strength and similarity guided group-level brain functional network construction for MCI diagnosis. Pattern Recognit. **88**, 421–430 (2019)
2. Wee, C.Y., Yap, P.T., Zhang, D., Wang, L., Shen, D.: Group-Constrained Sparse fMRI Connectivity Modeling for Mild Cognitive Impairment Identification. Brain Struct. Funct. **219**(2), 641–656 (2014)
3. Li, Y., Yang, H., Lei, B., Liu, Y., Wee, C.Y.: Novel effective connectivity inference using ultra-group constrained orthogonal forward regression and elastic multilayer perceptron classifier for MCI identification. IEEE Trans. Med. Imaging **38**(5), 1227–1239 (2019)
4. Zhu, Q., Yuan, N., Huang, J., Hao, X., Zhang, D.: Multi-modal AD classification via self-paced latent correlation analysis. Neurocomputing **355**, 143–154 (2019)
5. Li, Y., Liu, J., Gao, X., Jie, B., Kim, M., Yap, P.T., et al.: Multimodal hyper-connectivity of functional networks using functionally-weighted LASSO for MCI classification. Med. Image Anal. **52**, 80–96 (2019)
6. Lei, B., Cheng, N., Frangi, A.F., Tan, E.L., Cao, J., Yang, P., et al.: Self-calibrated brain network estimation and joint non-convex multi-task learning for identification of early Alzheimer's disease. Med. Image Anal. **61**, 101652 (2020)
7. Li, Y., Liu, J., Tang, Z., Lei, B.: Deep spatial-temporal features fusion from adaptive dynamic functional connectivity for MCI diagnosis. IEEE Trans. Med. Imaging, 1–10 (2019)
8. Sarah, P., et al.: Disease prediction using graph convolutional networks: application to autism spectrum disorder and Alzheimer's disease. Med. Image Anal. **48**, 117–130 (2018). S1361841518303554
9. Ktena, S.I., et al.: Metric learning with spectral graph convolutions on brain connectivity networks. Neuroimage **169**, 431–442 (2018)
10. Zhang, Yanfu., Zhan, Liang., Cai, Weidong., Thompson, Paul, Huang, Heng: Integrating heterogeneous brain networks for predicting brain disease conditions. In: Shen, Dinggang, et al. (eds.) MICCAI 2019. LNCS, vol. 11767, pp. 214–222. Springer, Cham (2019). https://doi.org/10.1007/978-3-030-32251-9_24

11. Kazi, Anees., et al.: InceptionGCN: receptive field aware graph convolutional network for disease prediction. In: Chung, Albert C.S., Gee, James C., Yushkevich, Paul A., Bao, Siqi (eds.) IPMI 2019. LNCS, vol. 11492, pp. 73–85. Springer, Cham (2019). https://doi.org/10.1007/978-3-030-20351-1_6

12. Kipf, T.N., Welling, M.: Semi-supervised classification with graph convolutional networks. arXiv preprint arXiv:1609.02907 (2016)

13. Tzouriomazoyer, N., et al.: Automated anatomical labeling of activations in SPM using a macroscopic anatomical parcellation of the MNI MRI single-subject brain. NeuroImage **15**, 273–289 (2002)

14. Goto, M., Abe, O., Aoki, S., et al.: Diffeomorphic anatomical registration through exponentiated lie algebra provides reduced effect of scanner for cortex volumetry with atlas-based method in healthy subjects. Neuroradiology **55**, 869–875 (2013)

15. Babu, G.S., Suresh, S., Mahanand, B.S.: Meta-cognitive Q-Gaussian RBF network for binary classification: application to mild cognitive impairment (MCI). In: International Joint Conference on Neural Networks (2013). https://doi.org/10.1109/IJCNN.2013.6706731

16. Gray, K.R., Aljabar, P., Heckemann, R.A., Hammers, A., Rueckert, D.: Random forest-based similarity measures for multi-modal classification of Alzheimer's disease. NeuroImage **65**, 167–175 (2013)

17. Haller, S., Nguyen, D., Rodriguez, C., Emch, J.S., Gold, G., Bartsch, A., et al.: Individual prediction of cognitive decline in mild cognitive impairment using support vector machine-based analysis of diffusion tensor imaging data. J. Alzheimers Dis. **22**(1), 315–327 (2010)

18. Wee, C.Y., Yang, S., Yap, P.T., Shen, D.: Sparse temporally dynamic resting-state functional connectivity networks for early MCI identification. Brain Imaging Behav. **10**(2), 342–356 (2016)

19. Yu, R., Zhang, H., An, L., Chen, X., Wei, Z., Shen, D.: Connectivity strength-weighted sparse group representation-based brain network construction for MCI classification. Hum. Brain Mapp. **38**(5), 2370–2383 (2017)

20. Guo, H., Zhang, F., Chen, J., Xu, Y., Xiang, J.: Machine learning classification combining multiple features of a hyper-network of fMRI data in Alzheimer's disease. Front. Neurosci. **11**, 615 (2017)

Infant Cognitive Scores Prediction with Multi-stream Attention-Based Temporal Path Signature Features

Xin Zhang[1], Jiale Cheng[1], Hao Ni[2], Chenyang Li[1], Xiangmin Xu[1], Zhengwang Wu[3], Li Wang[3], Weili Lin[3], Dinggang Shen[3], and Gang Li[3(✉)]

[1] School of Electronic and Information Engineering, South China University of Technology, Guangzhou, China
[2] Department of Mathematics, University College London, London, UK
[3] Department of Radiology and BRIC, University of North Carolina at Chapel Hill, Chapel Hill, USA
gang_li@med.unc.edu

Abstract. There is stunning rapid development of human brains in the first year of life. Some studies have revealed the tight connection between cognition skills and cortical morphology in this period. Nonetheless, it is still a great challenge to predict cognitive scores using brain morphological features, given issues like small sample size and missing data in longitudinal studies. In this work, for the first time, we introduce the path signature method to explore hidden analytical and geometric properties of longitudinal cortical morphology features. A novel BrainPSNet is proposed with a differentiable temporal path signature layer to produce informative representations of different time points and various temporal granules. Further, a two-stream neural network is included to combine groups of raw features and path signature features for predicting the cognitive score. More importantly, considering different influences of each brain region on the cognitive function, we design a learning-based attention mask generator to automatically weight regions correspondingly. Experiments are conducted on an in-house longitudinal dataset. By comparing with several recent algorithms, the proposed method achieves the state-of-the-art performance. The relationship between morphological features and cognitive abilities is also analyzed.

Keywords: Path signature feature · Infant brain · Cognitive ability

1 Introduction

With the advancement of magnetic resonance imaging (MRI) and image processing techniques, early structural development of the human brain is attracting more and more attention [11,13,27,30]. However, only few works related the infant brain cognitive scores to the cortical morphology. In fact, in the first

---

X. Zhang and J. Cheng—Equal contribution.

© Springer Nature Switzerland AG 2020
A. L. Martel et al. (Eds.): MICCAI 2020, LNCS 12267, pp. 134–144, 2020.
https://doi.org/10.1007/978-3-030-59728-3_14

year of life, the cortical structure is tightly connected to the acquisition and refinement of information processing as well as visual and language skills [9,16]. Thus, understanding the quantitative relationship between cognitive skills and morphological features of the infant cerebral cortex is of immense importance .

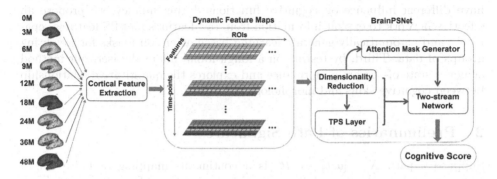

Fig. 1. Illustration of BrainPSNet. Inputs are longitudinal MRI data (grey brains indicating missing data) and output is the predicted cognitive scores.

To this end, in this paper, we aim to learn a representation for each infant by using longitudinal brain MRI data to predict cognitive development. Specifically, given longitudinal brain MRI scans from infants, we can compute multiple biologically meaningful cortical measurements [20]. Meanwhile, we have five Mullen Scales of Early Learning (MSEL) [5] at 48 months of age to measure the cognition skills of each infant comprehensively. Hence, our goal is to build a machine learning method to predict these cognition scales using longitudinal morphological cortical features. However, there are three major challenges, including the small sample size, high dimensionality of data and missing scans. Recently, several methods are proposed to address these problems. The Bag-of-Words (BoW) based method was employed to slash the overlarge dimensionality of neuroimaging data [1]. In [33], authors generated a latent representation for each subject leveraging the complementary information among different time-points and introduced a set of indicator variant to eliminate the loss brought by incomplete data. They both achieved encouraging performance, but their optimization strategy is too complicated. Also, they can not analyze the correspondence between cerebral regions and cognitive scores since their representations for each subject did not preserve brain structural information. More importantly, the simple linear formulation they used cannot explore the temporal relationship sufficiently.

In this work, we introduce the path signature (PS) method for the first time as descriptors of dynamic dependencies in longitudinal infant cortical structure. The path signature originated from Chen's study [7] as an essential characteristic of piece-wise smooth paths in rough path theory. Lyons used it to make sense of the solution to differential equations driven by very rough signals [10]. Recently, there is an emerging research area, which combines path signature feature with machine learning and achieves state-of-the-art results [4,17,19,24,26,32].

Based on above discussions, we conclude our contributions as follow. First, we propose BrainPSNet with a temporal path signature (TPS) layer. To the best of our knowledge, this is the first work to apply the path signature method into longitudinal brain analysis and generate informative representations of multiple time points and temporal granules. Second, considering different brain regions have different influence on cognitive functions during infancy, we propose an effective network to exploit information from raw features and PS features separately and automatically generate learning-based attention masks for weighting groups of data. Third, by testing on a longitudinal infant dataset, our method achieves state-of-the-art performance and explores the quantitative relationship between cognitive skills and morphological features.

2   Preliminaries of Path Signature

Suppose a path $X : [a, b] \rightarrow R^d$ is a continuous mapping of finite length from interval $[a, b]$ to a d-dimensional vector space. For any $t \in [a, b]$, $X_t = (X_t^1, X_t^2, \cdots, X_t^d)$, where X_t^i denotes the ith coordinate of X_t and $i \in \{1, 2, \cdots, d\}$. Before introducing the signature, let us introduce the kth fold iterated integral of a path X, denoted by $S_k(X)_{a,b}$

The 1st iterated integral of X along the ith coordinate, denoted by $Sig(X)_{a,b}^i$, is $Sig(X)_{a,b}^i = \int_{a<t_1<b} dX_{t_1}^i$, which equals the increment of X at i^{th} coordinates, i.e. $X_b^i - X_a^i$. The 1st fold iterated integral is the collection of $Sig(X)_{a,b}^i$ for $i \in \{1, 2 \cdots, d\}$, i.e.

$$S_1(X)_{a,b} = \int_{a<t_1<b} dX_{t_1}. \tag{1}$$

Notably, $t \mapsto Sig(X)_{a,t}^i$ is still a real-valued path defined within $t \in [a, b]$. Then, the 2nd iterated integral indexed by (i_1, i_2) is denoted by $Sig(X)_{a,b}^{i_1,i_2}$ and defined as integral of $Sig(X)_{a,\cdot}^{i_1}$ against $X.^{i_2}$:

$$Sig(X)_{a,b}^{i_1,i_2} = \int_{a<t<b} Sig(X)_{a,t}^{i_1} dX_t^{i_2} = \int_{a<t_1<t_2<b} dX_{t_1}^{i_1} dX_{t_2}^{i_2}. \tag{2}$$

Similarly, the 2nd fold iterated integral of X is the collection of all 2nd iterated integrals of X with possible index (i_1, i_2), i.e. $\left(Sig(X)_{a,b}^{i_1,i_2} \right)_{i_1,i_2 \in \{1,\cdots,d\}}$, which can be written as the tensor form as follows:

$$S_2(X)_{a,b} = \int_{a<t_1<t_2<b} dX_{t_1} \otimes dX_{t_2}. \tag{3}$$

Generally, the k-th fold iterated integral of X, $S_k(X)_{a,b}$, is defined to be as follows:

$$S_k(X)_{a,b} = \int_{a<t_1<\cdots<t_k<b} dX_{t_1} \otimes dX_{t_2} \cdots \otimes dX_{t_k}. \tag{4}$$

Here the dimension of the k-th fold iterated integrals of the path X is d^k. The signature of a path is a graded infinite series, which contains all the k fold iterated integrals. In practice, we may truncated the signature up to the finite degree. Let $Sig^k(X)$ denoted the truncated signature of X up to degree k as follows:

$$Sig_k(X)_{a,b} = (1, \ S_1(X)_{a,b}, \ S_2(X)_{a,b}, \cdots, \ S_k(X)_{a,b}). \tag{5}$$

By convention, the 0th iterated integral is equal to 1. The dimension of the truncated signature in Eq. (5) is $(d^{k+1} - 1)/(d - 1)$.

If a path $X : [a, b] \to \mathbb{R}^d$ is linear, then the signature of $X_{[a,b]}$ can be computed explicitly as follows:

$$Sig(X)_{a,b}^{i_1,i_2,\cdots,i_k} = \frac{1}{k!} \prod_{j=1}^{k} (X_b^{i_j} - X_a^{i_j}). \tag{6}$$

The signature of a piecewise path can be computed by Chen's identity [7]. In practice, we often observe the discrete time series, which can be embedded in the path space by the linear interpolation. The corresponding signature of the embedded path can be used as a non-linear feature of the time series data.

In this application, we interpret that path X are time series on cerebral regions and that d stands for the dimension of cortical representation. The time interval $[a, b]$ are discretized into 9 different time points of MRI acquisitions on the infants, which will be further introduced in the next section.

The signature of a path has many algebraic and analytic proprieties, which make it an effective feature set of the streamed data. For example, the signature of path uniquely determines the path up to time re-parameterization [3,10]. Secondly, the signature feature is an universal, which implies that any continuous functions on the unparamertized path can be well approximated by the linear functional on the signature [18]. It is a global descriptor of the sequential data in terms of its effect, which can be often useful for dimension reduction. Interested readers can refer to [18] and [8] for more details.

3   Dataset and Feature Extraction

In this study, 23 normal infants with their T1w and T2w MR images were collected at 9 different time points (i.e., 0, 3, 6, 9, 12, 18, 24, 36 and 48 months after birth). Since not all participants are able to show up at all scheduled time points, there are missing scans, as illustrated in Fig. 1. For feature extraction, we processed MR images by following an infant MRI computational pipeline [20, 21] and computed 7 different morphological cortical measurements at each vertex of the reconstructed cortical surfaces, including cortical thickness (THI), local gyrification index (LGI), mean curvature (CUR), vertex area (ARE), vertex volume (VOL), sulcal depth in Euclidean distance (SDE) and sulcal depth in string distance (SDS) [22,25]. These cortical features are the most commonly used measurements to quantify brain development [23]. Afterwards, we parcellated the cerebral cortex into 70 anatomically meaningful regions of interest (ROIs) with an infant cortical surface atlas [31] for reducing the feature dimensionality. In each ROI, feature values of the same type of all vertices are averaged (for THI, LGI, CUR, SDE, SDS) or summarized (for ARE, VOL), thus forming a 7-dimension feature. Finally, for each available scan at a timepoint, we can extract a feature map whose width and depth equal to the number of ROIs ($N = 70$) and cortical measurements ($d = 7$) respectively. By concatenating these feature maps along the time axis, we can get a cohort of dynamic feature maps as shown in Fig. 1. Five Mullen cognitive scores are estimated at 48 months age for each participant, i.e., Visual Receptive Scale (VRS), Fine Motor Scale (FMS), Receptive Language Scale (RLS), Expressive Language Scale (ELS) and Early Learning Composite (ELC), which are firmly correlated to the morphological attributes mentioned above [5].

4 Network Architecture

To accurately predict the cognitive scores according to the cortical measurements, we propose a novel BrainPSNet consisting of three components: a temporal path signature layer, a two-stream network and an attention mask generator, shown in Fig. 2. At first, considering limited sample size, a 1×1 convolutional layer is introduced to further decrease the feature dimension of each ROI.

Temporal Path Signature Layer. A temporal path signature layer is then proposed to extract dynamic information and generate discriminative representations, shown in Fig. 2(b) in detail. For the first step, 70 paths are defined along the time axis and split by the overlapping sliding window with the size W and a sliding stride $s = 1$. Consequently, for each path, $\widetilde{T} = 9 - (W - 1)$ sub-paths are obtained to further explore local temporal properties. For every sub-path, we employ Eqs. (5) and (6) to compute its corresponding path signature features with a receptive field of W and denote the output dimension as $n_{PS} = (d^{k+1} - 1)/(k - 1)$. Afterwards, an 1×1 convolutional layer is introduced to conduct a feature transformation from n_{PS} to $d' = 8$.

Two-Stream Network. Inspired by [19], a two-stream network is proposed to process raw data and PS separately believing that each of them represents a kind of temporal information aggregated to a certain level. Considering ROIs influence cognition abilities differently along time, we introduce group fully connected layers in both two streams (surrounded by blue and pink in Fig. 2(a)) regarding features from each time point as a group. Then, group-specific fully connected layers are applied to encode cortical structures at corresponding stages of brain development. At the bottom of BrainPSNet, we concatenate the informative vectors produced by two streams and output a final cognitive score y.

Attention Mask Generator. With the aim of emphasizing the most influential region in each stage, an attention mask generator is constructed in the middle of Fig. 2(a). Group fully connected layers are applied sequentially to output an intermediate cognitive score $y_i, i \in \{1, 2, \cdots, 9\}$ for each group of input data.

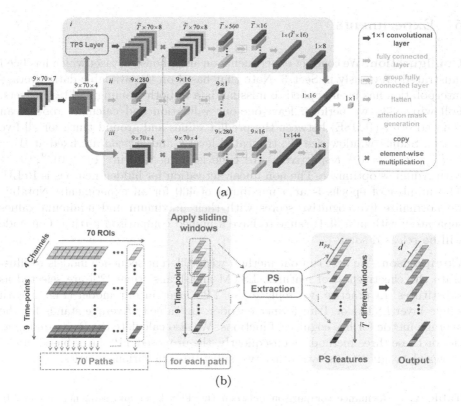

Fig. 2. The illustration of TPS layer and network structure of BrainPSNet. (a) presents a two-stream network with an attention mask generator surrounded by blue, pink and green areas separately; (b) shows the procedure of TPS layer implemented in (a). (Color figure online)

Afterwards, we sum over parameters of fully connected layers which generate nine 1×70 vectors corresponding to nine developmental stages and 70 ROIs. Element-wise multiplications are conducted between groups of features and corresponding attention masks to weight ROIs differently along time. Notably, we calculate moving average on attention masks to fit in $\widetilde{T}$ groups of features in PS stream. In this work, the intermediate output $\hat{y} = (y_1, y_2, \cdots, y_9)$ is just used to assist generating attention masks with the loss function defined as:

$$Loss = \lambda ||\hat{Y} - \hat{y}||_{l_1} + |Y - y| \tag{7}$$

We denote the ground truth corresponds to y and $\hat{y}$ as Y and $\hat{Y} = (Y_1, Y_2, \cdots, Y_9)$ respectively. It is noteworthy that $\hat{Y}$ is a duplication of Y at nine time points. λ is introduced to balance these two different losses.

5 Experiments

Configuration. We conduct experiments on an in-house dataset which has been illustrated previously in Sect. 3. Note that based on the available data, average interpolation has been applied to missing data in both training and testing sets. Following [33], we perform leave-one-out validation and calculate root mean squared error (RMSE) between the predict values and ground truth for all five scores. Sliding window size W, truncated level k and *lambda* are fixed at $W = 4$, $k = 2$, $\lambda = 0.1$ respectively. We tune learning rate in $\{10^{-3}, 10^{-4}, 10^{-5}\}$ with Adam as optimizer. The non-linear activation for hidden neurons is ReLU. The number of epochs is at a maximum of 400 for all experiments. Notably, we normalize five cognitive scores with their maximum and minimum values separately with in a $[0, 1]$ range to have a unified comparison setting. Our code will be released soon.

Comparison. We first run out method with different sequence models to illustrate the effectiveness of features. LSTM and Transformer [29] are selected as substitutes. In practice, we replace the TPS layer in our model (Fig. 1) with single layer LSTM or Transformer encoder. In Table 1, Average stands for the average metric for five cognitive functions. We also calculate the R-squared metric for these three methods. Consequently, the proposed TPS layer-based model shows clear advantages over other two substitutes in various metrics.

Table 1. Performance comparison between the TPS layer and sequence models. In the last column, we calculate the total time cost for 1200 epochs of our method with different substitutes.

Methods	Metrics	VRS	FMS	RLS	ELS	ELC	Average	Time
Transformer	RMSE	0.076	0.090	0.134	0.066	0.075	0.088	578 s
	R^2	0.637	0.719	0.556	0.527	0.732	0.634	
LSTM	RMSE	0.084	0.084	0.120	**0.037**	0.081	0.081	2147 s
	R^2	0.738	0.773	0.689	**0.928**	0.795	0.785	
TPS layer	RMSE	**0.046**	**0.075**	**0.095**	0.063	**0.057**	**0.067**	405 s
	R^2	**0.893**	**0.801**	**0.714**	0.714	**0.892**	**0.803**	

To validate the performance of our method, several recent algorithms are selected as baselines, including: 1) NN (nearest neighbour); 2) MtJFS (Multi-Task Learning with Joint Feature Selection) [2]; 3) RMTL (Robust Multi-Task Feature Learning) [6]; 4) TrMTL (Trace-Norm Regularized Multi-Task Learning) [14] and 5) LPMvRL (Latent Partial Multi-view Representation Learning) [33]. To make these methods comparable, we applied the same preprocessing method including normalization and interpolation. From Table 2, we find that **BrainPSNet** outperforms the other algorithms under the same settings. Additionally, an ablation study is conducted to explore the ability of path signature features and attention vectors respectively. It is observed that both of them bring improvements to the final result, which proves the effectiveness of our method.

Result Analysis. In this section, we try to investigate which morphological features and ROIs are more important in early postnatal period utilizing testing data and the trained models. Motivated by [28], we compute the gradient of testing data w.r.t. the loss by backpropagation and regard features with higher gradient are paid more attention by the network. First, we compare the importance of seven anatomical measurements w.r.t. five cognitive scores. As Fig. 3(a) illustrates, curvature collects more attentions for most tasks. In rest

Table 2. Performance comparison of BrainPSNet (in terms of RMSE)

Methods	VRS	FMS	RLS	ELS	ELC	Average
NN	0.219	0.259	0.165	0.196	0.182	0.204
MtJFS [2]	0.276	0.273	0.189	0.214	0.134	0.217
RMTL [6]	0.146	0.200	0.178	0.188	0.137	0.170
TrMTL [14]	0.279	0.276	0.192	0.217	0.136	0.220
LPMvRL [33]	0.162	0.189	0.139	0.165	0.138	0.158
BrainPSNet(*w/o attention*)	0.092	0.108	0.162	0.077	0.103	0.108
BrainPSNet(*w/o PS*)	0.059	0.100	0.103	0.066	0.089	0.084
BrainPSNet	**0.046**	**0.075**	**0.095**	**0.063**	**0.057**	**0.067**

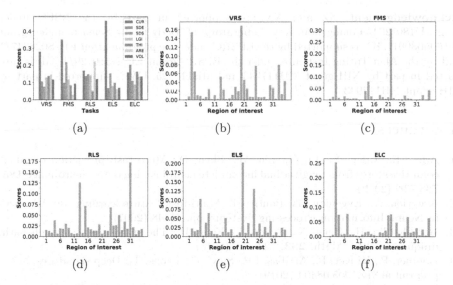

Fig. 3. The illustration of influence of anatomical features and ROIs w.r.t. five Mullen scores. (a) depicts the importance of seven anatomical features, while the rest show the importance distribution among different regions w.r.t. five cognitive scores respectively.

subfigures, the x-axis denotes indices of different ROIs, which can be found in surfer.nmr.mgh.harvard.edu/fswiki/CorticalParcellation. In practice, we sum up the importance coefficient of corresponding ROIs in left or right hemispheres. It can be seen that the RLS is more concentrated on the linguistic region, e.g. the supramarginal gyrus (ROI 31) [15], while FMS is more correlated to postcentral gyrus (22), one of the supplementary motor areas [12]. An interesting observation is that the pars triangularis (ROI 20) and medial orbitofrontal cortex (ROI 3) are more important for ELS and ELC separately, which is consistent with [9].

6   Conclusion

In this paper, we propose a novel model, BrainPSNet, to predict cognitive scores using longitudinal cortical features during infancy. For the first time, the path signature feature is introduced to explore hidden anatomical and geometric properties of the cortical developmental trajectories by a TPS layer. Based on path signature features and raw features, a multi-stream model is constructed to combine information of various granules and generate informative representation for each participant. Furthermore, considering different ROIs' influence on cognition abilities along time, we propose an attention generator to produce learning-based attention masks to weight ROIs at different developmental stages. Experiments and ablation study show that our method outperforms all baselines and achieves the state-of-the-art performance. Both path signature features and attention masks contribute to the final result.

Acknowledgement. XZ and XX are supported in part by the NSFC under grant U1801262; Guangzhou Key Laboratory of Body Data Science under grant 201605030011. HN is supported by the EPSRC under the program grant EP/S026347/1 and by the Alan Turing Institute under the EPSRC grant EP/N510129/1. GL is supported in part by NIH grant MH117943 and MH116225. LW is supported in part by NIH grant MH117943.

References

1. Adeli, E., Meng, Y., Li, G., Lin, W., Shen, D.: Multi-task prediction of infant cognitive scores from longitudinal incomplete neuroimaging data. NeuroImage **185**, 783–792 (2019)
2. Argyriou, A., Evgeniou, T., Pontil, M.: Multi-task feature learning. In: Advances in Neural Information Processing Systems, pp. 41–48 (2007)
3. Boedihardjo, H., Geng, X., Lyons, T., Yang, D.: The signature of a rough path: uniqueness. Adv. Math. **293**, 720–737 (2016)
4. Bonnier, P., Kidger, P., Arribas, I.P., Salvi, C., Lyons, T.: Deep signatures. arXiv preprint arXiv:1905.08494 (2019)
5. Braaten, E.B.: Mullen scales of early learning. In: The SAGE Encyclopedia of Intellectual and Developmental Disorders, vol. 34, no. 4, pp. 379–382 (2018)
6. Chen, J., Zhou, J., Ye, J.: Integrating low-rank and group-sparse structures for robust multi-task learning. In: Proceedings of the ACM SIGKDD International Conference on Knowledge Discovery and Data Mining, pp. 42–50 (2011)

7. Chen, K.T.: Integration of paths-a faithful representation of paths by noncommutative formal power Series. Trans. Am. Math. Soc. **89**(2), 395 (1958)
8. Chevyrev, I., Kormilitzin, A.: A primer on the signature method in machine learning. arXiv preprint arXiv:1603.03788 (2016)
9. Girault, J.B., et al.: Cortical structure and cognition in infants and toddlers. Cereb. Cortex **30**(2), 786–800 (2020)
10. Hambly, B., Lyons, T.: Uniqueness for the signature of a path of bounded variation and the reduced path group. Ann. Math. **171**(1), 109–167 (2010)
11. Hazlett, H.C., et al.: Early brain development in infants at high risk for autism spectrum disorder. Nature **542**(7641), 348–351 (2017)
12. Hopfinger, J.B., Buonocore, M.H., Mangun, G.R.: The neural mechanisms of top-down attentional control. Nat. Neurosci. **3**(3), 284–291 (2000)
13. Jha, S.C., et al.: Environmental influences on infant cortical thickness and surface area. Cereb. Cortex **29**(3), 1139–1149 (2018)
14. Ji, S., Ye, J.: An accelerated gradient method for trace norm minimization. In: Proceedings of the 26th International Conference On Machine Learning (ICML), pp. 457–464 (2009)
15. Jung, R.E., Haier, R.J.: The parieto-frontal integration theory (P-FIT) of intelligence: converging neuroimaging evidence. Behav. Brain Sci. **30**(2), 135–154 (2007)
16. Kagan, J., Herschkowitz, N., Herschkowitz, E.: A Young Mind in a Growing Brain. Psychology Press, New York (2006)
17. Lai, S., Jin, L., Yang, W.: Toward high-performance online HCCR: a CNN approach with dropdistortion, path signature and spatial stochastic max-pooling. Pattern Recogn. Lett. **89**, 60–66 (2017)
18. Levin, D., Lyons, T., Ni, H.: Learning from the past, predicting the statistics for the future, learning an evolving system. arXiv preprint arXiv:1309.0260 (2013)
19. Li, C., Zhang, X., Liao, L., Jin, L., Yang, W.: Skeleton-based gesture recognition using several fully connected layers with path signature features and temporal transformer module. In: Proceedings of the AAAI Conference on Artificial Intelligence, vol. 33, pp. 8585–8593 (2019)
20. Li, G., Wang, L., Shi, F., Gilmore, J.H., Lin, W., Shen, D.: Construction of 4D high-definition cortical surface atlases of infants: methods and applications. Med. Image Anal. **25**(1), 22–36 (2015)
21. Li, G., Wang, L., Shi, F., Lin, W., Shen, D.: Simultaneous and consistent labeling of longitudinal dynamic developing cortical surfaces in infants. Med. Image Anal. **18**(8), 1274–1289 (2014)
22. Li, G., et al.: Mapping longitudinal development of local cortical gyrification in infants from birth to 2 years of age. Eur. J. Neurosci. **34**(12), 4228–4238 (2014)
23. Li, G., et al.: Computational neuroanatomy of baby brains: a review. NeuroImage **185**, 906–925 (2019)
24. Liu, M., Jin, L., Xie, Z.: PS-LSTM: capturing essential sequential online information with path signature and LSTM for writer identification. In: Proceedings of the International Conference on Document Analysis and Recognition (ICDAR), vol. 1, pp. 664–669 (2017)
25. Lyall, A.E., et al.: Dynamic development of regional cortical thickness and surface area in early childhood. Cereb. Cortex **25**(8), 2204–2212 (2015)
26. Lyons, T., Ni, H., Oberhauser, H.: A feature set for streams and an application to high-frequency financial tick data. In: ACM International Conference Proceeding Series, pp. 1–8 (2014)

27. Rekik, I., Li, G., Yap, P.T., Chen, G., Lin, W., Shen, D.: Joint prediction of longitudinal development of cortical surfaces and white matter fibers from neonatal MRI. NeuroImage **152**, 411–424 (2017)
28. Selvaraju, R.R., Cogswell, M., Das, A., Vedantam, R., Parikh, D., Batra, D.: Grad-CAM: visual explanations from deep networks via gradient-based localization. In: International Conference on Computer Vision, pp. 618–626 (2017)
29. Vaswani, A., et al.: Attention is all you need. In: Advances in Neural Information Processing Systems (NIPS), pp. 5999–6009 (2017)
30. Wang, L., et al.: Volume-based analysis of 6-month-old infant brain MRI for autism biomarker identification and early diagnosis. In: Frangi, A.F., Schnabel, J.A., Davatzikos, C., Alberola-López, C., Fichtinger, G. (eds.) MICCAI 2018. LNCS, vol. 11072, pp. 411–419. Springer, Cham (2018). https://doi.org/10.1007/978-3-030-00931-1_47
31. Wu, Z., Wang, L., Lin, W., Gilmore, J.H., Li, G., Shen, D.: Construction of 4D infant cortical surface atlases with sharp folding patterns via spherical patch-based group-wise sparse representation. Hum. Brain Mapp. **40**(13), 3860–3880 (2019)
32. Yang, W., Lyons, T., Ni, H., Schmid, C., Jin, L., Chang, J.: Leveraging the path signature for skeleton-based human action recognition. arXiv preprint arXiv: 1707.03993 (2017)
33. Zhang, C., Adeli, E., Wu, Z., Li, G., Lin, W., Shen, D.: Infant brain development prediction with latent partial multi-view representation learning. IEEE Trans. Med. Imaging **38**(4), 909–918 (2019)

Masked Multi-Task Network for Case-Level Intracranial Hemorrhage Classification in Brain CT Volumes

Dongang Wang[1,2](✉) ⓘ, Chenyu Wang[1,2] ⓘ, Lynette Masters[3], and Michael Barnett[1,2] ⓘ

[1] Brain and Mind Centre, The University of Sydney, Sydney, Australia
dongang.wang@sydney.edu.au
[2] Sydney Neuroimaging Analysis Centre, Sydney, Australia
[3] I-Med Radiology Network, Sydney, Australia

Abstract. We propose a novel Masked Multi-Task Network (MMT-Net) to detect brain CT volumes with intracranial hemorrhage and distinguish hemorrhage type(s) using only case-level labels. Different types of intracranial hemorrhage (The five types of intracranial hemorrhage (ICH) are intraparenchymal hemorrhage (IPH), intraventricular hemorrhage (IVH), subarachnoid hemorrhage (SAH), subdural hemorrhage (SDH) and epidural hemorrhage (EDH).) are defined by their anatomical locations. To utilize the brain structural information that is relevant to types of intracranial hemorrhage, brain masks were extracted during image preprocessing using a pre-trained brain CT segmentation network. Regional brain masks were then constructed for the central (cBrain) and the peripheral (pBrain) parts of the brain. These masks were later used as the input and the ground-truth brain masks to train the neural network. We designed a new two-branch network that encoded region-related features. The features were then fed into multi-task classifiers, which predicted both the regional brain masks and the region-related hemorrhage types. We also used the message passing module based on the conditional random field (CRF) model to refine features. We trained and tested our MMT-Net with a large in-house clinical dataset, and demonstrated superior performance of MMT-Net compared with the baseline ResNeXt50 network with the squeeze-and-excitation module. When tested using the 2019 RSNA intracranial hemorrhage challenge dataset, our MMT-Net trained with case-level labels more accurately detected hemorrhage cases and classified hemorrhage types than the challenge winner.

Keywords: Intracranial hemorrhage · Multi-label classification · Multi-branch neural network

Electronic supplementary material The online version of this chapter (https://doi.org/10.1007/978-3-030-59728-3_15) contains supplementary material, which is available to authorized users.

© Springer Nature Switzerland AG 2020

A. L. Martel et al. (Eds.): MICCAI 2020, LNCS 12267, pp. 145–154, 2020.
https://doi.org/10.1007/978-3-030-59728-3_15

1   Introduction

Computerized Tomography (CT) scan is a critical imaging modality for the diagnosis of life-threatening brain disease. CT can rapidly detect abnormalities including brain tumor, intracranial hemorrhage, midline shift and skull fracture; and provides critical diagnostic information that informs time-sensitive patient management. However, in clinical settings, CT volumes are sequentially interpreted by radiologists in the order of their acquisition. Cases with high-risk abnormalities, such as intracranial hemorrhage (ICH), can therefore be subsumed by a large volume of non-critical cases, potentially delaying diagnosis and the initiation of treatment. An automated CT triage system that detects critical abnormalities based on machine learning techniques could potentially address this challenge by rapidly bringing such cases to the attention of expert radiologists.

Recently, there have been significant improvements in automated detection of ICH in brain CT scans, particularly with deep learning approaches [2,3,11]. Most of the methods use detailed labels in each slice of a 3D CT volume, and the validation results are also performed at the slice level [3,12,20]. Some methods even rely on detailed segmentation annotations that outline the regions of pathology to reach a final decision [10]. Although model performance in these methods reaches a satisfactory level, the whole training procedure is both labor-intensive and high-cost as it requires expert radiologists for detailed annotation and/or segmentation labels for each slice of a 3D CT scan. In many scenarios these labels are not available, significantly limiting the applicability of models that require detailed annotations.

Using *case-level* labels, *i.e.* labels assigned to the whole 3D volume, in deep neural networks reduces the effort required for labelling, and thereby simplifies training and validation with a larger dataset [14]. However, hemorrhage is usually only present in a subset of the slices within a 3D CT scan and is heterogeneously distributed through 'affected' slices. *Case-level* labels therefore compromise the performance of neural networks in a weakly supervised setting. For example, in the work of Jnawali *et al.* [8], the AUC of the proposed 3D neural network based on case-level labels was 0.87, which may be insufficient in clinical settings.

Here we utilize the location information related to hemorrhage types to improve the neural network performance for intracranial hemorrhage classification using only case-level labels. All brain scans have similar structure/topography, and intracranial hemorrhages are typically categorized by their anatomical location. For example, subdural hemorrhage (SDH) and epidural hemorrhage (EDH) are mostly located in the peripheral part of the brain, whereas intraparenchymal hemorrhage (IPH) and intraventricular hemorrhage (IVH) are generally located towards the central part of the brain. Previous work [15] utilized the self-built brain masks to reduce extracranial noise, but the structural information of different regions of the brain was not explored.

Therefore, we propose a new **Masked Multi-Task Network** (MMT-Net) by using the location information of each category to improve the performance of neural networks using only the case-level labels. In our MMT-Net, we designed a two-branch neural network with branches encoding the features of the central brain area (marked as cBrain) and peripheral brain areas (marked as pBrain) accordingly. The output of the cBrain branch is the central brain mask (*i.e.* cBrain mask) and the multi-label classification result for IPH and IVH. Similarly, the output of the pBrain branch is the peripheral brain mask (*i.e.* pBrain mask) and the multi-label classification result for SDH and EDH.

Furthermore, some hemorrhage are not strictly constrained by the cBrain or pBrain masks as most of the cases of that type. For example, IPH (designated to occur within the cBrain mask) may be more superficial, or even restricted to the cortex (*i.e.* within the pBrain mask). Besides, to distinguish subarachnoid hemorrhage (SAH) and to predict the general hemorrhage status of the whole brain (marked as ICH, including all the five types), which should involve the cBrain and the pBrain regions, the classifiers should consider features from both cBrain and pBrain. To tackle these issues, we also added a message passing module based on conditional random field (CRF) to refine the features from branches and combine the features to predict subarachnoid hemorrhage (SAH) and general intracranial hemorrhage status (ICH).

To summarize, our contributions are three-fold:

1) To the best of our knowledge, we are the first to utilize brain structural information for intracranial hemorrhage classification. Different brain masks can focus the network on the cBrain areas and the pBrain areas and suppress noise.

2) We propose a new multi-branch neural network with multi-task classifiers. The network takes masked non-contrast brain CT scans as the input and encodes features through the cBrain branch and the pBrain branch. The cBrain masks and the pBrain masks also serve as the ground-truth for the segmentation task in the training stage. The message passing module contributes to refining features from the branches and combining the features for the prediction of SAH and ICH.

3) We constructed a large IntraCranial Hemorrhage Analysis dataset (ICIIA) with 6,660 non-contrast brain CT cases to develop and evaluate our method. Gold labelling of intracranial hemorrhages (*i.e.*, IPH, IVH, SDH, EDH and SAH) was performed by retrospectively screening radiological reports, followed by careful review of CT scans by an expert clinical reviewer. All post-operative cases were excluded in this study.

2   Data Preprocessing

We sought to identify CT scans containing ICH among a dataset that included both normal scans and those with pathologies; and to predict the type(s) of hemorrhage for each case. This is a multi-label classification task as each scan may contain none hemorrhage, one type or many different types of hemorrhages.

Note the dataset $\mathbf{X} = \{\mathbf{x}^{(i)}\}_{i=1}^{N}$, where N is the number of 3D brain CT volumes. For brain CT volumes, each case $\mathbf{x}^{(i)}$ consists of several axial slices of the same size. The label of the i-th case is $\mathbf{y}^{(i)}$, where $\mathbf{y}^{(i)}$ is a six-dimensional vector of independent binary label 0's and 1's for all the five types of hemorrhage

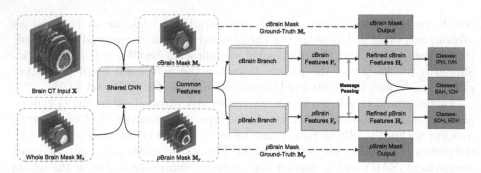

Fig. 1. The proposed structure of our **Masked Multi-Task Network** (MMT-Net). The original brain CT volumes and three types of brain masks are fed into the network. The network is divided into two branches by the separation of the central and the peripheral brain masks. With the help of message passing module, the features from either branch are refined and output to multi-task classifiers. The brain masks are also used as the ground truth for the segmentation output.

plus ICH. If the case $\mathbf{x}^{(i)}$ contains no hemorrhage, the corresponding $\mathbf{y}^{(i)}$ contains only zeros. Otherwise, the label $\mathbf{y}^{(i)}$ should contain at least two 1's, *i.e.* ICH and the specific type(s) of hemorrhage.

Preprocessing was initiated by extracting whole brain masks $\mathbf{M}_b = \{\mathbf{m}_b^{(i)}\}_{i=1}^N$ from original cases $\mathbf{X}$ with a pre-trained brain extraction tool [1]. Each output mask $\mathbf{m}_b^{(i)}$ has the same shape as the original $\mathbf{x}^{(i)}$, with each voxel marked as 1 for the brain areas and 0 for the background and other non-brain parts.

Whole brain masks $\mathbf{M}_b$ were further eroded into masks $\mathbf{M}_c$ for the cBrain area, with the difference between dilated $\mathbf{M}_b$ and $\mathbf{M}_c$ forming the masks $\mathbf{M}_p$ for the pBrain area. We assumed that most IPH and IVH regions should be included in $\mathbf{M}_c$ areas, and most EDH and SDH regions should be included in $\mathbf{M}_p$ areas.

We employed two Hounsfield Unit (HU) windows and the above three masks to form three channels for each slice. An original input $\mathbf{x}^{(i)}$ was first normalized within the HU window for acute blood (window level = 50, window width = 80) and then formed channel one through $\mathbf{x}^{(i)} \odot \mathbf{m}_b^{(i)}$, where $\odot$ denotes element-wise multiplication. Similarly, the input $\mathbf{x}^{(i)}$ was normalized within the HU window for tissue (window level = 60, window width = 360) and then was computed through $\mathbf{x}^{(i)} \odot \mathbf{m}_c^{(i)}$ and $\mathbf{x}^{(i)} \odot \mathbf{m}_p^{(i)}$ for channel two and three accordingly.

With the assistance of different brain masks in the input, the filters of the neural network are forced to focus on different brain areas. This modification also helps to suppress the extracranial imaging noise.

3 Masked Multi-Task Network

The overall structure of our proposed Masked Multi-Task Network (MMT-Net) is shown in Fig. 1, which includes a multi-branch module with the masked CT volumes as input and a message passing module between branches to refine features.

3.1   Multi-branch Module

We introduced a multi-branch module in the top neural network layers to better utilize the masks $\mathbf{M}_b$, $\mathbf{M}_c$ and $\mathbf{M}_p$ (Fig. 1). Following the shared CNN, we defined two branches based on the cBrain masks and the pBrain masks, named as 'cBrain branch' and 'pBrain branch' accordingly. For either branch, the features were fed into a multi-task classifier and output both the predicted brain masks for the cBrain (or pBrain) area and the classification results for the region-related types of hemorrhage, $i.e.$ IPH and IVH for cBrain branch and SDH and EDH for pBrain. During the training process, we used the summation of one classification loss and two segmentation losses as

$$\mathcal{L} = \lambda \mathcal{L}_{classification} + \mu_c \mathcal{L}_c + \mu_p \mathcal{L}_p, \tag{1}$$

where $\mathcal{L}_{classification}$ is the summation of the binary cross entropy of each type of hemorrhage and ICH. The $\mathcal{L}_c$ and $\mathcal{L}_p$ are the dice loss of the output cBrain/pBrain masks and the corresponding ground truth masks. We set the parameters λ, μ_c and μ_p to be all 1's to balance the influences of different losses.

Specifically, our MMT-Net is built with ResNeXt-50 model [18] and squeeze-and-excitation (SE) module [7]. The output from $layer3$ of ResNeXt-50 was treated as the shared features and the structure and initial weights of $layer4$ were duplicated to build the branches. To train the 2D network with 3D input, we adopted a similar strategy proposed in the Temporal Segmentation Network [17], whereby one whole CT volume was split into 30 parts along the axial axis and one random slice from each part was extracted to form one training case (in total 30 slices). The output $case$-$level$ classification results were the average results of these slices.

3.2   Message Passing Module

We denote the multi-branch features for one training sample as $\mathbf{F}^{(i)} = \{\mathbf{f}_c^{(i)}, \mathbf{f}_p^{(i)}\}$ representing cBrain feature and pBrain feature respectively. Our objective is to estimate the refined feature $\mathbf{H}^{(i)} = \{\mathbf{h}_c^{(i)}, \mathbf{h}_p^{(i)}\}$ in the neural network structure. Here we present an energy function for the CRF from the pBrain branch to the cBrain branch as a simpler form:

$$E_c^{(i)}(\mathbf{H}^{(i)}, \mathbf{F}^{(i)}, \Theta_c) = \phi(\mathbf{h}_c^{(i)}, \mathbf{f}_c^{(i)}) + \psi(\mathbf{h}_p^{(i)}, \mathbf{h}_c^{(i)}), \tag{2}$$

in which ϕ is the unary potential and ψ is the pairwise potential.

For unary potential, we consider the $\mathbf{h}_c^{(i)}$ should be similar to $\mathbf{f}_c^{(i)}$ to retain most information from the original branch, and for pairwise potential, we model the relationships between the refined features $\mathbf{h}_c^{(i)}$ and $\mathbf{h}_p^{(i)}$ by a bilinear potential function as previously proposed in [16, 19]. The potentials can be written as:

$$\phi(\mathbf{h}_c^{(i)}, \mathbf{f}_c^{(i)}) = -\frac{\alpha_c^{(i)}}{2}\|\mathbf{h}_c^{(i)} - \mathbf{f}_c^{(i)}\|^2, \quad \psi(\mathbf{h}_p^{(i)}, \mathbf{h}_c^{(i)}) = \mathbf{h}_c^{(i)\top}\mathbf{W}_{p,c}\mathbf{h}_p^{(i)}. \tag{3}$$

Following [16, 19], the refined features $\mathbf{h}_c^{(i)}$ can be obtained by iteratively applying

$$\mathbf{h}_c^{(i)} = \frac{1}{\alpha_c^{(i)}}(\alpha_c^{(i)}\mathbf{f}_c^{(i)} + \mathbf{W}_{p,c}\mathbf{h}_p^{(i)}), \tag{4}$$

where the $\alpha_c^{(i)}$ and $\mathbf{W}_{p,c}$ can be learnt from the training process. The process is similar for $\mathbf{h}_p^{(i)}$. We implemented the message passing by adding convolutional layers between feature maps of the two branches according to [5].

Moreover, features generated from the two branches are high-level and abstract, so the summation of the refined features may not represent the features of SAH and ICH correctly. Therefore, we concatenated the refined features from the two branches, and passed the newly combined feature to another convolutional layer to predict SAH and ICH (as shown in Fig. 1).

In summary, our Masked Multi-Task Network (MMT-Net) consists of a multi-branch module with message passing, which takes the masked CT volumes as input and the multi-task classifier outputs both brain masks and different types of intracranial hemorrhage. In the training phase, we used the pre-trained weights on ImageNet as the initialization and updated our network weights by utilizing the Adam optimizer [9] with learning rate as 0.0001, which decays 10 times after every 5 epochs for 15 epochs.

4   Datasets and Experiments

4.1   IntraCranial Hemorrhage Analysis (ICHA) Dataset

In order to evaluate our MMT-Net, we built a new ICHA dataset. By referring to the method proposed by Titano *et al.* [14], we retrospectively collected more than 10,000 non-contrast brain CT scan volumes and associated radiologist reports. For each case, trained clinicians extracted and annotated five types of hemorrhage labels, if any, from descriptive clinical reports. For each hemorrhage case identified, the images were further reviewed to confirm the decision. Considering that the primary utility of a CT triage system is likely to be in an outpatient setting, we excluded post-operative cases. While often containing hemorrhage in the acute phase, such post-operative cases are highly complex and would potentially compromise the applicability of our model in the desired clinical setting. The final refined ICHA dataset with 6,660 brain CT scans included 394 hemorrhage cases and 6,266 non-hemorrhage cases (2,172 normal cases and 4,094 cases with non-hemorrhage abnormalities). Detailed statistics are summarized in Table 1.

Table 1. Summary of the numbers of cases in each dataset.

Dataset	Total	ICH	IPH	IVH	SAH	SDH	EDH
ICHA	6,660	394	93	33	59	220	11
RSNA [6]	21,784	8,889	5,324	3,692	3,936	3,814	354
Refined RSNA	15,273	4,968	2,785	1,464	2,054	2,203	165

4.2 Results

We evaluated our MMT-Net under a five-fold cross-validation setting, ensuring that patients in training and validation sets within each fold did not overlap. We conducted experiments for the baseline network (*i.e.* ResNeXt-50 with SE module) and MMT-Net. The results shown in Table 2 demonstrate the effectiveness of MMT-Net. According to the F1-measure of the binary classification, MMT-Net is able to select cases that contain hemorrhage more accurately than the baseline network. The mean average precision and AUC scores suggest that MMT-Net also better discriminates among specific hemorrhage types.

We also tested the baseline network using the same input as MMT-Net (noted as *baseline with masked input*) and the MMT-Net without message passing (noted as *MMT-Net w/o message passing* in Table 2). Even with the same input, MMT-Net exhibited superior performance, demonstrating that MMT-Net is able to learn more specific features for *c*Brain and *p*Brain through the multi-branch network with message passing and the multi-task classifiers.

Table 2. Performance of models with ICHA dataset. All figures are the average of five-fold cross-validation. F1-Measure is based on the performance of detecting ICH cases. Mean AP is the mean of the average precision for all five hemorrhage types plus ICH. The AUC is the average AUC of all five types plus ICH. Best figures are highlighted.

Method	F1-Measure	Mean AP	AUC
Baseline (ResNeXt50[18] with SE [7])	0.7167	0.5001	0.8760
Baseline with masked input	0.7140	0.5129	0.8928
MMT-Net w/o message passing	0.7397	0.5473	0.9013
MMT-Net	**0.7482**	**0.5590**	**0.9023**

4.3 Comparison on RSNA Dataset

The original RSNA dataset was developed for the Kaggle challenge for intracranial hemorrhage detection [6]. The training and validation data of stage one were released with detailed annotations for the five hemorrhage types for each slice, including 19530 cases (674,258 slices) for training and 2,214 cases (78,545 slices) for validation.

We cleaned the dataset by: 1) removing post-operative cases; 2) removing duplicated slices within one case; and 3) removing slices that failed to reconstruct into 3D volumes because of ambiguous DICOM header information. We retained the original split for the refined dataset, resulting in 13,979 cases as training and 1,294 cases as validation (as shown in Table 1).

We implemented the method from Shen *et al.* [13], the winner of this challenge. This model included three CNNs to extract features and logits, followed by a GRU-based [4] network. For the purpose of comparison we modified the input/output of Shen *et al.*'s method while retaining all other aspects of the network structure as the default. Briefly, the *case-level* labels were derived from the maximum score from all *slice-level* labels per individual cases for each hemorrhage category.

As illustrated in Table 3, our proposed MMT-Net outperformed both the baseline model and Shen *et al.*'s method trained using only case-level labels, which suggests that the superiority of MMT-Net in selecting semantic features from 3D CT volumes results from our modification to the baseline model.

Although trained with *case-level* labels, MMT-Net yielded a mean average precision and AUC performance that was comparable with the Shen *et al.*'s method (trained with slice-level labels); and performed the best in detecting hemorrhage cases among all CT scans (F1 Measure). MMT-Net is therefore able to encode sufficient features, even with case-level labels, to achieve comparable performance achieved with the CNN+GRU method trained with slice-level labels. With significantly reduced workload in labelling, MMT-Net may be a preferable solution for similar 3D classification tasks in clinical imaging settings.

Table 3. Results on RSNA dataset compared with the top-ranked model in the challenge. All metrics are computed at the case-level. Best figures are highlighted.

Method	Labels	F1-Measure	Mean AP	AUC
Shen *et al.* [13]	slice-level	0.8814	**0.8201**	0.9622
Shen *et al.* [13]	case-level	0.8740	0.7804	0.9508
Our baseline	case-level	0.9228	0.7694	0.9435
MMT-Net	case-level	**0.9456**	0.8142	**0.9664**

5   Conclusion

In this paper, we propose a new Masked Multi-Task Network (MMT-Net) for case-level intracranial hemorrhage multi-label classification in brain CT volumes. In our method, brain masks are extracted from original non-contrast CT volumes, and further processed into cBrain masks and pBrain masks, which together with the original CT volumes, form the model input. Two region-related features are encoded through a multi-branch module with message passing, and multi-task classifiers generate localized brain masks and also predict location-related hemorrhage types. With the proposed MMT-Net, our experimental results demonstrates that the model can achieve satisfactory results by training only on case-level labels, significantly lowering the barrier to develop abnormality detection models from existing clinical data.

MMT-Net could be deployed as an automatic brain CT triage system to rapidly identify potential critical cases with brain hemorrhage, and alert the reporting radiologist in near real-time. Future work includes clinical validation of the proposed method and its application to other location-related brain abnormalities.

Acknowledgement. This work is supported by an Australian Federal government CRC-P grant and the Nerve Research Foundation (University of Sydney).

References

1. Akkus, Z., Kostandy, P., Philbrick, K.A., Erickson, B.J.: Robust brain extraction tool for CT head images. Neurocomputing (2019)
2. Chang, P.D., et al.: Hybrid 3D/2D convolutional neural network for hemorrhage evaluation on head CT. Am. J. Neuroradiol. **39**(9), 1609–1616 (2018)
3. Chilamkurthy, S., et al.: Deep learning algorithms for detection of critical findings in head CT scans: a retrospective study. Lancet **392**(10162), 2388–2396 (2018)
4. Cho, K., et al.: Learning phrase representations using RNN encoder-decoder for statistical machine translation. arXiv preprint arXiv:1406.1078 (2014)
5. Chu, X., Ouyang, W., Wang, X., et al.: CRF-CNN: modeling structured information in human pose estimation. In: Advances in Neural Information Processing Systems, pp. 316–324 (2016)
6. Flanders, A.E., et al.: Construction of a machine learning dataset through collaboration: the RSNA 2019 brain CT hemorrhage challenge. Radiol.: Artif. Intell. **2**(3), e190211 (2020)
7. Hu, J., Shen, L., Sun, G.: Squeeze-and-excitation networks. In: Proceedings of the IEEE Conference on Computer Vision and Pattern Recognition, pp. 7132–7141 (2018)
8. Jnawali, K., Arbabshirani, M.R., Rao, N., Patel, A.A.: Deep 3D convolution neural network for CT brain hemorrhage classification. In: Medical Imaging 2018: Computer-Aided Diagnosis, vol. 10575, p. 105751C. International Society for Optics and Photonics (2018)
9. Kingma, D.P., Ba, J.: Adam: a method for stochastic optimization. In: Bengio, Y., LeCun, Y. (eds.) 3rd International Conference on Learning Representations (2015)
10. Kuo, W., Häne, C., Yuh, E., Mukherjee, P., Malik, J.: PatchFCN for intracranial hemorrhage detection. arXiv preprint arXiv:1806.03265 (2018)
11. Lee, H., et al.: An explainable deep-learning algorithm for the detection of acute intracranial haemorrhage from small datasets. Nat. Biomed. Eng. **3**(3), 173 (2019)
12. Nguyen, N.T., Tran, D.Q., Nguyen, N.T., Nguyen, H.Q.: A CNN-LSTM architecture for detection of intracranial hemorrhage on CT scans. In: Medical Imaging with Deep Learning (2020)
13. Shen, T.: Top-1 Algorithm in RSNA Intracranial Hemorrhage Detection Challenge (2019). https://github.com/SeuTao/RSNA2019_Intracranial-Hemorrhage-Detection

14. Titano, J.J., et al.: Automated deep-neural-network surveillance of cranial images for acute neurologic events. Nat. Med. **24**(9), 1337–1341 (2018)
15. Vidya, M.S., Mallya, Y., Shastry, A., Vijayananda, J.: Recurrent sub-volume analysis of head CT scans for the detection of intracranial hemorrhage. In: Shen, D., et al. (eds.) MICCAI 2019. LNCS, vol. 11766, pp. 864–872. Springer, Cham (2019). https://doi.org/10.1007/978-3-030-32248-9_96
16. Wang, D., Ouyang, W., Li, W., Xu, D.: Dividing and aggregating network for multi-view action recognition. In: Ferrari, V., Hebert, M., Sminchisescu, C., Weiss, Y. (eds.) ECCV 2018. LNCS, vol. 11213, pp. 457–473. Springer, Cham (2018). https://doi.org/10.1007/978-3-030-01240-3_28
17. Wang, L., et al.: Temporal segment networks: towards good practices for deep action recognition. In: Leibe, B., Matas, J., Sebe, N., Welling, M. (eds.) ECCV 2016. LNCS, vol. 9912, pp. 20–36. Springer, Cham (2016). https://doi.org/10.1007/978-3-319-46484-8_2
18. Xie, S., Girshick, R., Dollár, P., Tu, Z., He, K.: Aggregated residual transformations for deep neural networks. In: Proceedings of the IEEE Conference on Computer Vision and Pattern Recognition, pp. 1492–1500 (2017)
19. Xu, D., Ouyang, W., Alameda-Pineda, X., Ricci, E., Wang, X., Sebe, N.: Learning deep structured multi-scale features using attention-gated CRFs for contour prediction (2017)
20. Ye, H., et al.: Precise diagnosis of intracranial hemorrhage and subtypes using a three-dimensional joint convolutional and recurrent neural network. Eur. Radiol. **29**(11), 6191–6201 (2019). https://doi.org/10.1007/s00330-019-06163-2

Deep Graph Normalizer: A Geometric Deep Learning Approach for Estimating Connectional Brain Templates

Mustafa Burak Gurbuz and Islem Rekik[✉] [ID]

BASIRA Lab, Faculty of Computer and Informatics,
Istanbul Technical University, Istanbul, Turkey
irekik@itu.edu.tr
http://basira-lab.com

Abstract. A connectional brain template (CBT) is a normalized graph-based representation of a population of brain networks —also regarded as an 'average' connectome. CBTs are powerful tools for creating representative maps of brain connectivity in typical and atypical populations. Particularly, estimating a well-centered and representative CBT for populations of *multi-view* brain networks (MVBN) is more challenging since these networks sit on complex manifolds and there is no easy way to fuse different heterogeneous network views. This problem remains unexplored with the exception of a few recent works rooted in the assumption that the relationship between connectomes are mostly linear. However, such an assumption fails to capture complex patterns and non-linear variation across individuals. Besides, existing methods are simply composed of sequential MVBN processing blocks without any feedback mechanism, leading to error accumulation. To address these issues, we propose Deep Graph Normalizer (DGN), *the first geometric deep learning (GDL) architecture* for normalizing a population of MVBNs by integrating them into a single connectional brain template. Our end-to-end DGN learns how to fuse multi-view brain networks while capturing non-linear patterns across subjects and preserving brain graph topological properties by capitalizing on graph convolutional neural networks. We also introduce a randomized weighted loss function which also acts as a regularizer to minimize the distance between the population of MVBNs and the estimated CBT, thereby enforcing its *centeredness*. We demonstrate that DGN significantly outperforms existing state-of-the-art methods on estimating CBTs on both small-scale and large-scale connectomic datasets in terms of both representativeness and discriminability (i.e., identifying distinctive connectivities fingerprinting each brain network population). Our DGN code is available at https://github.com/basiralab/DGN.

Keywords: Connectional brain templates · Deep Graph Normalizer · Population multiview brain network integration

© Springer Nature Switzerland AG 2020
A. L. Martel et al. (Eds.): MICCAI 2020, LNCS 12267, pp. 155–165, 2020.
https://doi.org/10.1007/978-3-030-59728-3_16

1   Introduction

The field of network neuroscience has made substantial advances in characterizing the human brain network (or connectome modeling the pairwise relationship between brain regions of interest (ROIs)) by means of large-scale connectomic datasets collected through various projects such as Human Connectome Project (HCP) [1] and Connectome Related to Human Disease (CRHD) [2]. These rich and multimodal brain datasets allow us to map brain connectivity and efficiently detect atypical deviations from the healthy brain connectome. Particularly, learning how to *normalize* a population of brain networks by estimating a *well-centered* and *representative* connectional brain template (CBT) is an essential step for group comparison studies as well as discovering the integral signature of neurological disorders [3]. Intuitively, a CBT can be defined as a 'normalized connectome' of a population of brain networks, which can be simply produced by linear averaging. However, such a normalization technique is very sensitive to outliers and overlooks non-linear relationships between subjects. This normalization process can be regarded as an 'integration' or 'standardization' of brain networks.

More broadly, estimating a CBT of a population of heterogeneous multi-view brain networks, where each view captures particular traits of the brain construct (e.g., cortical thickness, function, cognition), is even a more challenging task since such connectomic data might lie on complex high-dimensional manifolds. To address this challenge, [3] proposed a clustering-based approach based on similarity network fusion (SNF) [4] to fuse multi-view brain networks in each cluster. Fused networks are then linearly averaged to produce a CBT for a population of multi-view brain networks (MVBN). Despite its promising results, [3] heavily depends on the selection of the number of clusters. In order to overcome this problem, [5] introduced the netNorm framework, which instead of clustering, constructs a high-order graph using cross-view connectional features as nodes and their Euclidean distance as dissimilarity measure to select the most centered brain connections in a population of MVBN. Next, the selected connections are integrated into a single network using SNF [4]. Currently, netNorm presents the state-of-the-art method by outperforming SCA [3] and other baseline methods in the CBT estimation task. However, netNorm [5] has several limitations. *First*, it uses Euclidean distance as a *pre-defined metric* for selecting the most representative brain connection which might fail to capture complex non-linear patterns in the brain connectome across subjects. *Second*, netNorm also uses SNF for fusing different views. Even though SNF is a powerful tool since it is a generic unsupervised technique, it comes with assumptions such as emphasizing top k local connections for each node (i.e., brain region) and equally averaging the global topology of complementary networks for each iterative update to ultimately merge them. Instead of relying on such general assumptions, this MVBN normalization process can instead be *learned* to decide which information provided by the networks is important for the target CBT estimation. *Third*, netNorm consists of *independent* feature extraction, feature selection, and fusion steps. These fully independent steps cannot provide feedback to each other in order to globally optimize the CBT estimation process. Therefore errors might accumulate throughout the estimation pipeline.

To address all these limitations, we propose **Deep Graph Normalizer (DGN)**: an unprecedented approach capitalizing on geometric deep learning (GDL) to learn how to normalize a population of heterogeneous MVBNs and generate a well-representative and centered CBT in an *end-to-end* fashion. Although GDL achieved remarkable results in several recent biomedical data analysis works such as disease classification [6] and protein interface prediction [7], to the best of our knowledge, no previous works used GDL to address the problem of integrating a population of multi-view networks [8,9]. To fill this gap, we present several major contributions to the state-of-the-art as follows. *First*, we design a GDL architecture that takes multi-view brain networks and maps them into a normalized CBT. Specifically, we propose a GDL architecture that maps MVBN of a training subject to a population-representative CBT. Brain networks of each training subject passes through several layers of graph convolutional neural networks that are consecutively applied to learn hidden embeddings for each node (i.e., brain ROI) by locally integrating connectivities offered by different heterogeneous views and blending the previous layer's embeddings using integrated connectivities. Next, we compute the pairwise absolute difference of the final layer's node embeddings to derive connectivity weights of the generated CBT. *Second*, we introduce the Subject Normalization Loss (SNL) which is a randomized weighted loss function that evaluates the representativeness of a generated *subject-biased* CBT (i.e. obtained by feeding a particular subject to the model) against a random subset of brain networks in the training set to achieve *subject-to-population mapping*. Besides forcing the model to learn how to generate population-based representative CBTs by fusing complementary information supplied by MVBNs, SNL also acts as a regularization due to randomization and different weights assigned to each view according to their connectivity weight distributions. *Third*, finalized CBT can be obtained by feeding an arbitrary subject of the training population to the trained model since the model learns how to map any subject to a population-representative CBT thanks to SNL optimization. However, the choice of the subject biases the output CBT and leads to non-optimal performance. We introduce a post-training step to overcome this bias and further refine the finalized CBT.

2   Proposed Method

In this section, we detail the components of our DGN architecture for estimating CBTs (Fig. 1). First, each subject in a population of multi-view brain networks is represented by an undirected fully-connected graph where each node (i.e., brain ROI) is initialized with identity features (trivially set to 1) and each edge has n_v attributes that correspond to connectivity weights in different network views. We generate CBTs using a training set of MVBNs $T = \{\mathbf{T}_1^1, \mathbf{T}_2^1, \ldots, \mathbf{T}_i^v, \ldots, \mathbf{T}_N^{n_v}\}$, where $\mathbf{T}_i^v$ denotes the vth brain view of subject i, and evaluate the representativeness on a testing set using 5-fold cross-validation. These training subjects

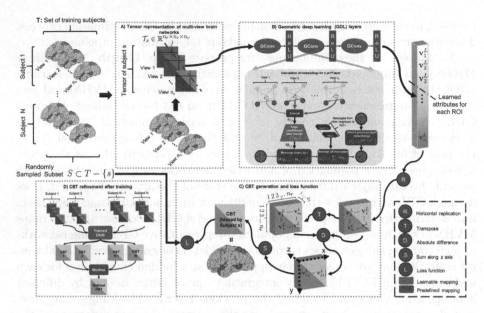

Fig. 1. *Proposed Deep Graph Normalizer (DGN) architecture for estimating connectional brain templates for a given population of multi-view brain networks.* **(A) Tensor representation of multi-view brain networks.** Each subject s is represented by $\mathcal{T}_s \in \mathbb{R}^{n_r \times n_r \times n_v}$, composed of a set of undirected, fully connected graphs, each capturing single connectional feature. **(B) Geometric deep learning layers.** Our model includes a sequence of edge conditioned [10] graph convolutional neural network layers which are separated by ReLU non-linearity. Each layer learns deeper embeddings for ROIs by utilizing activation of the previous layer and topological structure of the brain network. **(C) CBT generation and loss function.** ROI embeddings that are output by the final layer are passed through a series of tensor operations to calculate the pairwise absolute difference of each pair of nodes for CBT construction. Next, the representativeness of the estimated CBT is evaluated against a random subset of training views for loss calculation. **(D) CBT refinement after training.** To select the most centered connections for final CBT generation, we first pass each training subject through the trained model to generate its corresponding CBT. Finally, we produce the final CBT by selecting the element-wise median of all training CBTs.

pass through 3 layers of GDL layers that includes edge conditioned filter learner (a shallow neural network). From layer to layer, deeper embeddings are learned for each ROI using edge-conditioned graph convolution [10] which aggregates the information passed by its neighbours while taking into consideration the multi-view attributes of its neighboring edges. We then use ROI embeddings output by the final layer to produce the connectivity matrix of the generated CBT by calculating the between the final embeddings of each ROI pair. This generated CBT is evaluated against a random subset of the training MVBNs for loss optimization. Once the DGN architecture is fully trained using this randomized training sample selection strategy, each training subject is then fed to the trained model to produce a population representative CBTs that are *biased by the given input subject*. Finally, we eliminate outlier connectivities due to subject bias by taking the element-wise median of all possible CBTs. We detail all these steps in what follows.

A - Tensor Representation of Multi-view Brain Networks. Given a population of subjects, we represent each subject s by a tensor $\mathcal{T}_s \in \mathbb{R}^{n_r \times n_r \times n_v}$ (Fig. 1–A) that is composed by stacking connectivity matrices of n_v brain networks where each network has n_r nodes (i.e., ROI). Note that using this subject-specific brain tensor representation, an $\mathbf{e}_{ij} \in \mathbb{R}^{n_v \times 1}$ connecting ROIs i and j encapsulates n_v attributes. We set diagonal entries in the tensor to zero to eliminate self-loops (i.e., ROI self-connectivity). In addition to inputting edge multi-view attributes, our DGN architecture also takes a node attributes matrix $\mathbf{V}^0 \in \mathbb{R}^{n_r \times d_0}$ as an input, where d_0 denotes the number of initial attributes for each ROI. As for each brain ROI, we do not have predefined attributes, we set each entry of the $\mathbf{V}^0$ matrix to '1' (i.e., identity), and through our deep model training for optimizing the SNL function, we learn these node-specific implicit attribute representations by simply using the input edge attributes. In each graph convolution layer and for each multi-view brain connection $\mathbf{e}_{ij}$ linking nodes i and j, we generate an edge-specific weight matrix utilizing an *edge-conditioned filter learner* [10]. Then these weight matrices multiplied by ROIs attributes to compute the next layer's ROI attributes therefore after the first convolution each ROI will have a different set of attributes even though they were identical in the beginning.

B - Geometric Deep Learning Layers. In this section, we detail the graph convolutional layers of our architecture that maps ROIs with identical attributes to a high dimensional distinctive representations by utilizing edge features $\mathbf{e}_{ij}$ between ROIs. This is achieved through 3 graph convolutional network layers (**Fig. 1–B**) with edge-conditioned convolution operation [10] that are separated by ReLU non-linearity. Each layer $l \in \{1, 2, ..., L\}$ includes edge-conditioned filter learner neural network $F^l : \mathbb{R}^{n_v} \mapsto \mathbb{R}^{d_l \times d_{l-1}}$ that dynamically generates edge specific weights for filtering message passing between ROIs i and j given the features of $\mathbf{e}_{ij}$. This operation is defined as follows:

$$\mathbf{v}_i^l = \frac{1}{|N(i)| + 1} \left(\Theta^l . \mathbf{v}_i^{l-1} + \sum_{j \in N(i)} F^l(\mathbf{e}_{ij}; \mathbf{W}^l) \mathbf{v}_j^{l-1} + \mathbf{b}^l \right) ; F^l(\mathbf{e}_{ij}; \mathbf{W}^l) = \Theta_{ij}$$

where $\mathbf{v}_i^l$ is the embedding of ROI i at layer l, Θ^l is a learnable parameter, and $N(i)$ denotes the neighbours of ROI i. $\mathbf{b}^l \in \mathbb{R}^{d_l}$ denotes a network bias and F^l is a neural network that maps $\mathbb{R}^{n_v}$ to $\mathbb{R}^{d_l \times d_{l-1}}$ with weights $\mathbf{W}^l$. Θ_{ij} represents the dynamically generated edge specific weights by F^l. Note that F^l can be any type of neural network and vary in each layer depending on the characteristics and complexity of edge weights.

C - CBT Construction Layer and Subject Normalization Loss Function. After obtaining the output $\mathbf{V}^L = \left[\mathbf{v}_1^L, \mathbf{v}_2^L, ..., \mathbf{v}_{n_r-1}^L, \mathbf{v}_{n_r}^L\right]^T$ of the final DGN layer, which consists of embeddings for each ROI, we compose the output CBT by computing the pair-wise absolute difference of the learned embeddings. We formulate this process using several tensor operations (**Fig.** 1–C) for easy and efficient backpropagation. First, $\mathbf{V}^L$ is replicated horizontally n_r times to obtain $\mathcal{R} \in \mathbb{R}^{n_r \times n_r \times d_L}$. Next, $\mathcal{R}$ is transposed (replacing all elements $\mathcal{R}_{xyz}$ with $\mathcal{R}_{yxz}$) to get $\mathcal{R}^T$. Last, we compute the element-wise absolute difference of $\mathcal{R}$ and $\mathcal{R}^T$. The resulting tensor is summed along z-axis (i.e. size of node embeddings) to estimate the final CBT $\mathbf{C} \in \mathbb{R}^{n_r \times n_r}$.

Subject Normalization Loss (SNL) Optimization. We propose to evaluate the representativeness of the generated CBT using a random subset of the training subject views. This random selection procedure has two main advantages compared to evaluating against all training subjects. First, randomization has a regularization effect since it is much easier for the model to overfit if the loss is calculated against the same set of subjects in each iteration. Secondary, the sample size can be fixed to a constant number so that the magnitude of the loss and the computation time will be independent of the size of the training set. Note that since SNL compares generated CBT with a subset of training subject views, model weights updated in a way so that the generated CBT represents a population of MVBNs even though it is rooted in a single subject input. Given the generated CBT $\mathbf{C}_s$ for subject s and a random subset S of training subject indices, we define our SNL for training subject s and the optimization loss as follows:

$$SNL_s = \sum_{v=1}^{n_v} \sum_{i \in S} \|\mathbf{C}_s - \mathbf{T}_i^v\|_F \times \lambda_v; \quad \min_{\mathbf{W}_1, \mathbf{b}_1 ... \mathbf{W}_L, \mathbf{b}_L} \frac{1}{|T|} \sum_{s=1}^{|T|} SNL_s$$

The λ_v is a view specific normalization term that is defined as $\lambda_v = \frac{\max\{\mu_j\}_{j=1}^{n_v}}{\mu_v}$, where μ_v is the mean of brain graph connectivity weights of view v and $\max\{\mu_j\}_{j=1}^{n_v}$ is the maximum of means μ_1 to μ_{n_v}. We use this view-specific normalization weight since brain network connectivity distribution and value range might largely vary across views. This will help avoid view-biased CBT estimation where the trained model might overfit some views and overlook others. Related problems in the literature are addressed by normalizing the connectivity matrix. For example, SNF [4] divides connectivities in each row by the sum of the entries in that row to normalize measurements; however, this breaks the symmetry in the views, therefore, it is not applicable in our case. Another simple normalization approach such as using min-max scaling can saturate our inputs at 0 and 1 while standard z-score scaling generates negative connectivities in the graph that is not suitable for representing a fully positive brain connectomes (such as structural or morphological). Therefore, we introduce λ_v to ensure that the model gives equal attention to each brain view regardless of their value range.

D - CBT Refinement After the Training. Our model learns to map multi-view brain networks of a particular subject s to a population-based representative CBT C_s. Although all of the CBTs generated by the model are representative of the randomly sampled training population, they are biased towards the given input subject s. To eliminate this bias, we propose an additional step (Fig. 1–D) to obtain a more refined and representative CBT for the whole training set. First, each subject is fed through the trained model to obtain corresponding CBTs. Next, most centered connections are selected from these CBTs by calculating the element-wise median. The median operation produces a valid view with a non-negative symmetrical adjacency matrix. This operation could also be replaced with other measures of central tendency; however, we used the representativeness score to verify that the median is the most suitable for our case.

3   Results and Discussion

Connectomic Datasets and Model Hyperparameter Setting. We benchmarked our DGN against state-of-the-art method netNorm for CBT estimation [5] on two small-scale and large-scale connectomic datasets using 5-fold cross-validation. The first dataset (AD/LMCI dataset) consists of 77 subjects (41 subjects diagnosed with Alzheimer's diseases (AD) and 36 with Late Mild Cognitive Impairment (LMCI)) from the Alzheimer's Disease Neuroimaging Initiative (ADNI) database GO public dataset [11]. Each subject is represented by 4 cortical morphological brain networks derived from maximum principal curvature, the mean cortical thickness, the mean sulcal depth, and the average curvature as in [12–14]. The second dataset (NC/ASD dataset) is collected from the Autism Brain Imaging Data Exchange ABIDE I public dataset [15] and includes 310 subjects (155 normal control (NC) and 155 subjects with autism spectral disorder (ASD)) with 6 cortical morphological brain networks extracted from the 4 aforementioned cortical measures in addition to cortical surface area and minimum principle area. For each hemisphere, the cortical surface is reconstructed from T1-weighted MRI using FreeSurfer pipeline [16] and parcellated into 35 ROIs using Desikan-Killiany atlas [17] and its corresponding brain network is derived by computing the pairwise absolute difference in cortical measurements between pairs of ROIs.

We trained 8 different models to generate CBTs for both hemispheres of 4 populations namely; AD, LMCI, NC, and ASD. We empirically set all hyperparameters for the DGN models using grid search. Each model includes 3 edge-conditioned convolutional neural network layers with an edge-conditioned filter learner neural network that maps 4 (for AD/LMCI dataset) or 6 (for NC/ASD dataset) attributes obtained from heterogeneous views to $\mathbb{R}^{d_l \times d_{l-1}}$. These layers are separated by ReLU activation function and output embeddings with 36, 24 and 5 (for AD/LMCI dataset) or 8 (for NC/ASD dataset) dimensions for each ROI in the MVBN, respectively. We trained all models using gradient descent with Adam optimizer with a learning rate of 0.0005. We fixed the number of random samples in our SNL function to 10.

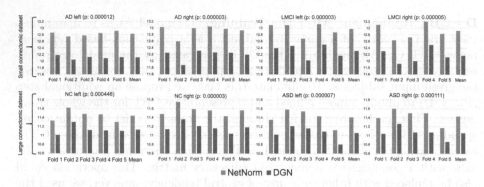

Fig. 2. *Representativeness comparison between CBTs generated by the proposed model and netNorm* [5]. Charts illustrate the average Frobenius distance between the CBTs generated using the training set and the network views in the testing set. Also, p-values obtained by two-tailed t-test are reported for each population. LH: left hemisphere. RH: right hemisphere.

CBT Representativeness Test. To evaluate the representativeness of generated CBT, we computed mean Frobenius distance which is calculated as $d_F(A, B) = \sqrt{\sum_i \sum_j |A_{ij} - B_{ij}|^2}$ between the estimated CBT and the different views in the testing set. We split both datasets into training and testing sets using 5-fold cross-validation for reproducibility and generalizability. Figure 2 depicts the average Frobenius distance between CBTs generated by DGN and netNorm [5] using the training set and the views in the left out test population. We note that our proposed model significantly ($p < 0.001$) outperforms netNorm in terms of representativeness across all left-out folds and evaluation datasets.

CBT Discriminativeness Reproducibility Test. We hypothesize that a well-representative CBT can capture the most discriminative traits of a population of MVBNs, acting as a connectional brain fingerprint. To test this hypothesis, we first spot the top k most discriminative brain connectivities where a class-A CBT largely differs from a class-B CBT. To do so, we compute the absolute difference between both estimated CBTs using respectively A and B populations. Next, we sum the columns of this difference matrix to obtain discriminability score for each brain ROI. We then pick the top k most discriminative ROIs with the highest score. To evaluate the reproducibility of CBT-based discriminative ROIs, for each brain view v, we independently train a support vector machine (SVM) and with a supervised feature selection method. Specifically, we extract connectional features from each brain network view by vectorizing the upper triangle entries. Next, for each network view, we use 5-fold randomized partitioning to divide each population p^A and p^B into 5 subpopulations. For each brain view v and a combination of p_i^A and p_j^B a SVM is trained and a weight vector $\mathbf{w}_{ij}^v$ that scores the discriminativeness of each feature (i.e., ROI) is learned using Multiple Kernel Learning (MKL), which is a wrapper method assigning weights to features according to their distinctiveness for the given classification task. The final feature weight vector is computed by summing up the weight vectors for all views and all possible A-B combinations of their 5 subpopulations as follows: $\omega = \sum_{\mathbf{w}=1}^{n_v} \sum_{i,j=1}^{5} \mathbf{w}_{i,j}^{v}$. Next, we anti-vectorize ω vector and obtain matrix $\mathbf{M} \in \mathbb{R}^{n_r \times n_r}$. By summing the columns of the resulting matrix we get ROIs discriminability scores. Finally, we picked the top k ROIs with the highest score. Table 1 reports the overlap between the top $k = 15$ ROIs identified using CBT-based method (netNorm and DGN) and MKL-based SVM method. Remarkably, our proposed model not only generates more representative and centered CBTs but is significantly more reproducible in discriminability than netNorm [5].

Discovery of Most Discriminative Brain ROIs for Each Disordered Population. DGN also revealed left insula cortex, left superior temporal sulcus (STS) and right frontal pole as most discriminative regions of ASD population, which resonates with existing findings on autism. [18] reports that the alteration of the left insula in the ASD population might be the cause of abnormalities in emotional and affective functions. Next, by comparing activation of STS in different social scenarios, [19] shows that the dysfunction of STS is the essential factor of social perception impairment in autism. For instance, in contrast to NC subjects, individuals with autism show hypoactivation in the STS when exposed to matched visual and auditory information. Furthermore, [19] demonstrates that healthy children had greater response in STS triggered by biological (e.g. human movement) than by non-biological motions (e.g. clock). However, STS activation's of children with autism do not differ significantly depending on the nature of the motion. Lastly, [20] shows that the faces of boys with ASD have atypical right dominant asymmetry and suggests that the asymmetric growth of the right frontal pole can explain this facial anomaly. As for the AD-LMCI dataset, DGN picked the left temporal pole (TP) and right entorhinal cortex (EC) as the most discriminative regions of the brain. [21] highlights that the pathological changes in TP are a common trait among all AD patients. Moreover, [22] confirms that the alteration of the EC is a good biomarker of AD and LMCI and indicates that the AD patients show greater atrophy in the right EC which supports DGN's choice.

Table 1. Overlap rate between ROIs selected by MKL and CBT-based methods.

Overlap rate	netNorm [5]	DGN	Overlap rate	netNorm [5]	DGN
AD-LMCI Left Hem.	0.60	**0.73**	NC-ASD Left Hem.	0.53	**0.53**
AD-LMCI Right Hem.	0.33	**0.40**	NC-ASD Right Hem.	0.33	**0.40**

4   Conclusion

In this paper, we introduced Deep Graph Normalizer for estimating connectional brain templates for a given population of multi-view brain networks. Beside capturing non-linear patterns across subjects, the proposed method also learns how to fuse complementary information offered by MVBNs in an end-to-end fashion. We showed that the proposed DGN outperformed state-of-the-art method for estimating CBTs in terms of both representativeness and discriminability. In our future work, we will evaluate our architecture on multi-modal brain networks such as functional and structural brain networks while capitalizing on geometric deep learning for estimating *holistic* CBTs. Also, we will introduce topological loss constraints such as Kullback-Leibler divergence of node degree distributions of generated CBTs and population brain networks to further ensure that the generated CBTs are topologically sound.

Acknowledgments. I. Rekik is supported by the European Union's Horizon 2020 research and innovation programme under the Marie Sklodowska-Curie Individual Fellowship grant agreement No. 101003403 (http://basira-lab.com/normnets/).

References

1. Essen, D., et al.: The human connectome project: a data acquisition perspective. NeuroImage **62**, 2222–2231 (2012)
2. Van Essen, D.C., Glasser, M.F.: The human connectome project: progress and prospects. In: Cerebrum: the Dana Forum on Brain Science, vol. 2016. Dana Foundation (2016)
3. Dhifallah, S., Rekik, I., Initiative, A.D.N., et al.: Clustering-based multi-view network fusion for estimating brain network atlases of healthy and disordered populations. J. Neurosci. Methods **311**, 426–435 (2019)
4. Wang, B., et al.: Similarity network fusion for aggregating data types on a genomic scale. Nat. Methods **11**, 333 (2014)
5. Dhifallah, S., Rekik, I.: Estimation of connectional brain templates using selective multi-view network normalization. Med. Image Anal. **59**, 101567 (2019)
6. Rhee, S., Seo, S., Kim, S.: Hybrid approach of relation network and localized graph convolutional filtering for breast cancer subtype classification, pp. 3527–3534 (2018)
7. Fout, A., Byrd, J., Shariat, B., Ben-Hur, A.: Protein interface prediction using graph convolutional networks. In: Guyon, I., Luxburg, U.V., Bengio, S., Wallach, H., Fergus, R., Vishwanathan, S., Garnett, R. (eds.) Advances in Neural Information Processing Systems 30, pp. 6530–6539. Curran Associates, Inc. (2017)
8. Wu, Z., Pan, S., Chen, F., Long, G., Zhang, C., Yu, P.: A comprehensive survey on graph neural networks (2019)
9. Zhou, J., Cui, G., Zhang, Z., Liu, Z., Sun, M.: Graph neural networks: a review of methods and applications (2018)
10. Simonovsky, M., Komodakis, N.: Dynamic edge-conditioned filters in convolutional neural networks on graphs, pp. 29–38 (2017)
11. Mueller, S., et al.: The Alzheimer's disease neuroimaging initiative. Neuroimaging Clin. North Am. **15**, 869–77, xi (2005)
12. Raeper, R., Lisowska, A., Rekik, I.: Cooperative correlational and discriminative ensemble classifier learning for early dementia diagnosis using morphological brain multiplexes. IEEE Access **6**, 43830–43839 (2018)
13. Lisowska, A., Rekik, I., for the ADNI: Joint pairing and structured mapping of convolutional brain morphological multiplexes for early dementia diagnosis. Brain Connect. **9**, 22–36 (2019)

14. Nebli, A., Rekik, I.: Gender differences in cortical morphological networks. Brain Imaging Behav., 1–9 (2019). https://doi.org/10.1007/s11682-019-00123-6
15. Martino, D., et al.: The autism brain imaging data exchange: towards a large-scale evaluation of the intrinsic brain architecture in autism. Mol. Psychiatry **19**, 659–667 (2014)
16. Fischl, B.: Freesurfer. NeuroImage **62**, 774–781 (2012)
17. Fischl, B., et al.: Automatically parcellating the human cerebral cortex. Cerebral Cortex **14**, 11–22 (2004). (New York, N.Y.: 1991)
18. Yamada, T., et al.: Altered functional organization within the insular cortex in adult males with high - functioning autism spectrum disorder: evidence from connectivity-based parcellation. Mol. Autism **7**, 1–15 (2016)
19. Pelphrey, K., Carter, E.: Brain mechanisms for social perception lessons from autism and typical development. Ann. New York Acad. Sci. **1145**, 283–299 (2009)
20. Hammond, P., et al.: Face-brain asymmetry in autism spectrum disorders. Mol. Psychiatry **13**, 614–623 (2008)
21. Arnold, S.E., Hyman, B.T., Van Hoesen, G.W.: Neuropathologic changes of the temporal pole in Alzheimer's disease and pick's disease. Arch. Neurol. **51**, 145–150 (1994)
22. Zhou, M., Zhang, F., Zhao, L., Qian, J., Dong, C.: Entorhinal cortex: a good biomarker of mild cognitive impairment and mild Alzheimer's disease. Rev. Neurosci. **27**(2), 185–195 (2016)

Supervised Multi-topology Network Cross-Diffusion for Population-Driven Brain Network Atlas Estimation

Islem Mhiri[1,2], Mohamed Ali Mahjoub[2], and Islem Rekik[1(✉)]

[1] BASIRA Lab, Faculty of Computer and Informatics,
Istanbul Technical University, Istanbul, Turkey
irekik@itu.edu.tr
[2] Ecole Nationale d'Ingénieurs de Sousse, LATIS - Laboratory of Advanced
Technology and Intelligent Systems, Université de Sousse, 4023 Sousse, Tunisie
http://basira-lab.com

Abstract. Estimating a representative and discriminative brain network atlas (BNA) is a nascent research field with untapped potentials in mapping a population of brain networks in health and disease. Although limited, existing BNA estimation methods have several limitations. *First*, they primarily rely on a similarity network diffusion and fusion technique, which only considers node degree as a topological measure in the cross-network diffusion process, thereby overlooking rich topological measures of the brain network (e.g., centrality). *Second*, both diffusion and fusion techniques are implemented in fully unsupervised manner, which might decrease the discriminative power of the estimated BNAs. To fill these gaps, we propose a supervised multi-topology network cross-diffusion (SM-netFusion) framework for estimating a BNA satisfying : (i) well-representativeness (captures shared traits across subjects), (ii) well-centeredness (optimally close to all subjects), and (iii) high discriminativeness (can easily and efficiently identify discriminative brain connections that distinguish between two populations). For a specific class, given the cluster labels of the training data, we *learn* a weighted combination of the topological diffusion kernels derived from degree, closeness and eigenvector centrality measures *in a supervised manner*. Specifically, we learn the cross-diffusion process by normalizing the training brain networks using the learned diffusion kernels. This normalization well captures shared networks between individuals at different topological scales, improving the representativeness and centeredness of the estimated multi-topology BNA. Our SM-netFusion produces the most centered and representative template in comparison with its variants and state-of-the-art methods and further boosted the classification of autistic subjects by 5 to 15%. SM-netFusion presents the first work for supervised network cross-diffusion based on graph topological measures, which can be further leveraged to design an efficient graph feature selection method for training predictive learners in network neuroscience. Our SM-netFusion code is available at https://github.com/basiralab/SM-netFusion.

© Springer Nature Switzerland AG 2020
A. L. Martel et al. (Eds.): MICCAI 2020, LNCS 12267, pp. 166–176, 2020.
https://doi.org/10.1007/978-3-030-59728-3_17

Keywords: Brain network atlas learning · Supervised network cross-diffusion and fusion · Heterogeneous manifold learning

1   Introduction

Estimating a representative and discriminative *brain network atlas* (BNA) marked a new era for mapping a population of brain networks in health and disease. A few recent landmark studies have relied on developing the concept of a network atlas estimated from a population of brain networks. One pioneering work includes [1] on estimating a brain network atlas from a population of both morphological and functional brain networks using diffusive-shrinking graph technique [2]. Later, [3] introduced brain the morpho-kinectome (i.e., population-based brain network atlas) to investigate the relationship between brain morphology and connectivity kinetics in developing infants. Another work [4] proposed the concept of population-driven connectional brain template for multi-view brain networks using a cluster-based diffusion and fusion technique. More recently, [5] designed a sample selection technique followed up by a graph diffusion and fusion step. [6] estimated also a brain network atlas-guided feature selection (NAGFS) method to differentiate the healthy from the disordered connectome.

Although they presented compelling results, these works have several limitations. *First*, all these promising works [1,3–6] have relied on the similarity network fusion (SNF) and diffusion technique introduced in [2]. Although compelling, [?] non-linearly diffuses and fuses brain networks without considering their heterogeneous distributions or the possibility of them lying on different subspaces. This might not preserve the pairwise associations between different networks in complex manifold they sit on. *Second*, [2] *solely* uses node degree as a topological measure in the cross-network diffusion process. However, measures of the degree or strength provide only partial information of the role (significance) of a node in a network. So, one cannot capture the full structure of a network because node degree only considers the immediate and local neighborhood of a given node (i.e., anatomical region of interest (ROI) in a brain network). Also, it treats all node connections equally [7]. Hence, it captures the quantitative aspect of node (how many neighbors it has) but not the qualitative aspect of a node (the quality of its neighbors). *Third*, both diffusion and fusion techniques were implemented in a fully *unsupervised* manner without considering the heterogeneous distribution of the brain network population (e.g., typical or autistic), which would eventually affect the representativeness of the estimated BNAs.

To address all these limitations, we propose a supervised multi-topology network cross-diffusion (SM-netFusion) framework for *learning* a BNA which satisfies the following constraints: (i) it is *well-representative* that consistently captures the unique and distinctive traits of a population of functional networks, (ii) it is *well-centered* that occupies a center position optimally near to all individuals, and (iii) it reliably identifies the most *discriminative* disordered brain connections by comparing templates estimated using disordered and healthy brains, respectively. *First*, to handle data heterogeneity within each specific class, we learn the pairwise similarities between connectomes and map them into different subspaces where we assign to each brain network living in the same subspace the same label. This clustering step allows to explore the underlying data distribution prior to the diffusion process for BNA estimation. *Second*, for each training sample in the given class, we define a tensor stacking as frontal views the degree, closeness and eigenvector centrality matrices. By fusing the tensor frontal views, we generate an average topological matrix which nicely characterize both local and global relationships between brain ROIs. *Third*, to preserve the heterogeneous distribution of the data in a specific class, we supervisedly learn a *subject-specific weight* to map each average topological matrix to its cluster label. Next, for each subject, we multiply each weight with its training average topological matrix to generate *the normalization kernel*, whose inverse normalizes the original brain network. *Fourth*, in a specific class, we nonlinearly cross-diffuse the normalized brain networks so that all diffused networks lie close to each other for the final fusion step to generate the target of a specific class. The proposed cross-diffusion process well captures shared connections across individuals at different topological scales, improving the representativeness and centeredness of the estimated multi-topology BNA. More importantly, by *comparing* the learned healthy and disordered BNAs, we also investigate the discriminative potential of our estimated brain network atlases in reliably differentiating between typical and disordered brains which can be eventually used to train a predictive learner for accurate and fast diagnosis. The main contributions of our method are three-fold:

1. *On a methodological level.* SM-netFusion presents the first work on *supervised* and *class-specific* network cross-diffusion based on graph topological measures, which can be also leveraged to design an efficient feature selection method for training predictive learners in network neuroscience.
2. *On a clinical level.* By comparing BNAs produced by SM-netFusion in healthy and disordered groups, one can easily spot a connectional fingerprint of a disorder (i.e., a set of altered brain connectivities).
3. *On a generic level.* Our framework is a generic method as it can be applied to brain networks derived from any neuroimaging modality (e.g., morphological and structural connectomes) given that they are isomorphic.

2 Proposed Method

In the following, we present the main steps of the proposed SM-netFusion framework for estimating a representative, centered and discriminative BNA (Fig. 1).

A - Class-specific Feature Extraction and Clustering. Given a population of N^c brain networks in class c, each network i is encoded in a symmetric matrix $\mathbf{X}_i^c \in \mathbb{R}^{r \times r}$, where r denotes the number of anatomical regions of interest (ROIs). Since each matrix $\mathbf{X}_i^c$ is symmetric, we extract a feature vector for subject i in class c by simply vectorizing its upper off-diagonal triangular part. Next, we horizontally stack feature vectors of all subjects to define a data feature matrix of size $N^c \times \frac{r \times (r-1)}{2}$ (Fig. 1-A). Next, we disentangle the heterogeneous

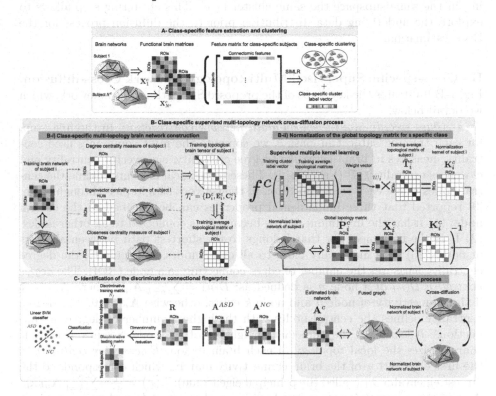

Fig. 1. *Illustration of the proposed supervised multi-topology network cross-diffusion (SM-netFusion) framework with application to brain connectomes.* **(A) Class-specific feature extraction and clustering**. For each subject i in class c, we vectorize the upper triangular part of its connectivity matrix $\mathbf{X}_i^c$. Next, we concatenate all feature vectors into a data feature matrix which we cluster similar functional brain networks into non-overlapping subspaces using SIMLR framework [8] where we assign to each brain network living in the same subspace the same label. **(B) Class-specific supervised multi-topology network cross-diffusion.** For each training sample i in class c, we define a tensor $\mathcal{T}_i^c$ stacking as frontal views the degree, closeness and eigenvector centrality matrices. By fusing the tensor views, we generate an average topological matrix $\bar{\mathbf{T}}_i^c$. Next, to preserve the heterogeneous distribution of the data in class c, we supervisedly learn a subject-specific weight to map each $\bar{\mathbf{T}}_i^c$ to its cluster label. Then, for each subject, we multiply its learned weight with its $\bar{\mathbf{T}}_i^c$ to generate the normalization kernel $\mathbf{K}_i^c$, whose inverse normalizes the original brain network. Later, we nonlinearly cross-diffuse the normalized brain networks so that all diffused networks lie close to each other for the final fusion step to generate the target BNA. **(C) Identification of the discriminative connectional biomarker.** By computing the absolute difference matrix $\mathbf{R}$ between $\mathbf{A}_{ASD}$ and $\mathbf{A}_{NC}$ network atlases, we select the top N_f features with the highest discrepancy and use those to train a linear support vector machine (SVM) classifier within a five-fold cross-validation scheme.

distribution of the brain networks by clustering similar functional brain networks into non-overlapping subspaces using Single Cell Interpretation via Multikernel Learning (SIMLR) framework [8] where we assign to each brain network living in the same subspace the same cluster label. This clustering step allows to explore the underlying data distribution prior to the diffusion process for the BNA estimation.

B - Class-specific Supervised Multi-topology Network Cross-diffusion.
Fig. 1-B illustrates the key steps of the proposed SM-netFusion framework, which we detail below.

i- Class-specific multi-topology brain network construction. In the first step, for each training subject in class c, we compute the most commonly used centrality measures in brain networks (degree centrality, eigenvector centrality and closeness centrality) [7] (Fig. 1-B- i). These topological measures define the central nodes where each communication in the network should pass through them. [9] reported that three fundamental properties can be ascribed to the central node: (1) It has the maximum degree because it is connected to all other nodes. (2) It is the best mediator that belongs to the shortest path between all pairs of nodes. (3) It is maximally close to all other nodes. Particularly, the degree centrality measures the number of edges connecting to a node (ROI). The *degree centrality* $D(n)$ of a node n is defined as: $D(n) = \sum_{n \neq k} \mathbf{A}_{nk}$, where $\mathbf{A}_{nk} = 1$ if the connectivity of node n and node k exists; otherwise $\mathbf{A}_{nk} = 0$. The degree centrality defines the central nodes with the highest number of degree or connections. It examines the immediate neighbors of the node. So, in our case, it characterizes the local topology of each brain region. *Eigenvector centrality* is the first eigenvector of the brain connectivity matrix, which corresponds to the largest eigenvalue λ_1 (called the principal eigenvalue): $E(n) = \frac{1}{\lambda_1} \times \sum_{k=1}^{r} \mathbf{A}_{nk} \mathbf{x}_k$, $\mathbf{A}_{nk}$ is the connectivity strengths between nodes n and k, and $\mathbf{x}$ is a nonzero vector that, when multiplied by $\mathbf{A}$, satisfies the condition $\mathbf{A}\mathbf{x} = \lambda \mathbf{x}$. The *closeness centrality* $C(n)$ reflects the closeness between a node n and other nodes in a brain network: $C(n) = \frac{r-1}{\sum_{n \neq k} l_{nk}}$, where l_{nk} is the shortest path length between nodes n and k. This centrality measure defines the mean distance between the central node and all other nodes in a network. It captures the effective outreach via closest path. Specifically, the node with the highest closeness will affect all other nodes in a short period of time (shortest path). These topological measures have been extensively examined in the literature of network neuroscience, where brain function integration and segregation was shown to work through brain hubs (i.e., central nodes) [10]. In fact, these centrality measures define the most significant ROIs (central nodes) nesting function and cognitive neural flow. Hence, we adopt these metrics in order to characterize both local and global relationships between brain ROIs. Once the topological matrices are defined for each subject, we stack them into a tensor $\mathcal{T}_i^c = \{\mathbf{D}_i^c, \mathbf{E}_i^c, \mathbf{C}_i^c\}$, which is fused into an average topological matrix $\bar{\mathbf{T}}_i^c$ in class c (Fig. 1-B-i).

ii- Supervised multiple kernel normalization. To preserve the heterogeneous distribution of the data in class c, we supervisedly learn a subject-specific weight to map each average topological matrix to its cluster label. Hence, we apply a supervised machine learning method based on multiple kernel learning (MKL) called EasyMKL [11] in order to find the optimal mixture of kernels over the different training average topological matrices (Fig. 1-B-ii). EasyMKL achieves higher scalability with respect to the number of kernels to be combined at a low computational cost in comparison with other MKL methods. Given a class c, we learn a mapping f^c (i.e., a weight vector $\mathbf{w} \in \mathbb{R}^{n_{tr} \times 1}$) transforming the training average topological matrices (i.e., a set of kernels) onto their corresponding cluster labels by solving a simple quadratic optimization loss:

$$f^c = \min_{\mathbf{w}:||\mathbf{w}||_2=1} \min_{\gamma \in \Gamma} \gamma^T \mathbf{Y}(\sum_{i=0}^{n_{tr}} w_i \bar{\mathbf{T}}_i^c)\mathbf{Y}\gamma + \lambda||\gamma||^2, \tag{1}$$

where $\mathbf{Y}$ is a diagonal matrix with training cluster labels on the diagonal, λ is a regularization hyper-parameter, $\mathbf{w}$ is the weight vector that maximizes the pairwise margin between different subspaces. The domain Γ represents the domain of probability distributions $\gamma \in \mathbb{R}_+^{n_{tr}}$ defined over the sets of subspaces (clusters), that is $\Gamma = \left\{\gamma \in \mathbb{R}_+^{n_{tr}} \mid \sum_{i \in subspace_j} \gamma_i = 1, j = 1, \ldots, n_c\right\}$. It turns out this quadratic functional has a closed form solution where each learned weight coefficient for subject i is defined as $w_i = \gamma^T \mathbf{Y}(\frac{\bar{\mathbf{T}}_i^c}{Tr(\bar{\mathbf{T}}_i^c)})\mathbf{Y}\gamma$, where $Tr(\bar{\mathbf{T}}_i^c)$ is the trace of a basic kernel (i.e., average topological matrix of subject i). Next, we multiply each weight with its training average topological matrix to generate the normalization kernel $\mathbf{K}_i^c$ of each subject in class c.

iii- Class-specific cross-diffusion process for BNA estimation. Previously, to learn the cross-diffusion process in the SNF [2] technique, one needs to first define a status matrix, also referred to as the global topology matrix $\mathbf{P}_i$, capturing the global structure of each individual i and carrying the full information about the similarity of each ROI to all other ROIs. This status matrix is iteratively updated by diffusing its structure across the average global structure of other brain networks. Conventionally, $\mathbf{P}_i$ is a normalized weight matrix $\mathbf{P}_i(k,l) = \begin{cases} \frac{1}{2}\mathbf{D}_i^{-1}\mathbf{X}_i(k,l) & l \neq k \\ 1/2, & l = k \end{cases}$, where $\mathbf{D}_i$ is the diagonal degree (strength) matrix of subject i [2–6]. However, this normalization overlooks rich topological measures of the brain network (e.g., centrality) since the degree measure only focuses on the immediate and local neighborhood of a node. One way of casting a more *topology-perserving normalization* of a brain network i in class c is by using the learned normalization kernel $\mathbf{K}_i^c$ to define a *multi-topology aware* status matrix as: $\mathbf{P}_i^c(k,l) = \begin{cases} \frac{1}{2}(\mathbf{K}_i^c)^{-1}\mathbf{X}_i^c(k,l) & l \neq k \\ 1/2, & l = k \end{cases}$, where $\mathbf{X}_i^c(k,l)$ denotes the connectivity between ROIs k and l (Fig. 1–B-ii). Next, for class c, we define a kernel similarity matrix $\mathbf{Q}_i^c$ for each individual i, which encodes its local structure by computing the similarity between each of its elements ROI k and its nearest ROIs l as follows: $\mathbf{Q}_i^c(k,l) = \begin{cases} \frac{\mathbf{X}_i^c(k,l)}{\sum_{p \in n_k} \mathbf{X}_i^c(k,p)} & l \in n_k \\ 0, & otherwise \end{cases}$, where n_k represents the set of

q neighbors of ROI k identified using KNN algorithm. In order to integrate the different networks into a single network, each multi-topology matrices $\mathbf{P}_i^c$ is iteratively updated for each individual by diffusing the topological structure of $\mathbf{P}_j^c$ of $N^c - 1$ networks $(j \neq i)$ along the local structure $\mathbf{Q}_i^c$ of subject i as follows: $\mathbf{P}_i^c = \mathbf{Q}_i^c \times \left(\frac{\sum_{j \neq i} \mathbf{P}_j^c}{N^c - 1} \right) \times (\mathbf{Q}_i^c)^T$, $j \in \{1, \ldots, N^c\}$, where $\frac{\sum_{j \neq i} \mathbf{P}_j^c}{N^c - 1}$ denotes the average diffused networks in class c excluding subject i. This step is iterated $n^\star$ times and generates N^c parallel interchanging diffusion processes on N^c networks. If two connectivities are similar in all data types, their similarity will be enhanced through the diffusion process and vice versa. By fusing the cross-diffused networks within class c, we estimate the target BNA: $\mathbf{A}^c = \frac{\sum_{i=1}^{N^c} (\mathbf{P}_i^c)^{n^\star}}{N^c}$ (Fig. 1-B-iii).

C - Identification of the Discriminative Connectional Fingerprint. To investigate the discriminative power of our estimated brain network atlas, we select the most relevant features distinguishing between two populations by computing the absolute difference between both estimated training network atlas matrices $\mathbf{A}^{ASD}$ and $\mathbf{A}^{NC}$ as follows: $\mathbf{R}(NC, ASD) = |\mathbf{A}^{ASD} - \mathbf{A}^{NC}|$ (Fig. 1-C). By taking all elements in the upper off-diagonal part of the residual matrix $\mathbf{R}$, we select the top N_f features with the largest non-zero values as these identify the brain connectivities where both BNAs largely differ. Next, using the top N_f selected connectivities derived from the training set, we train a linear support vector machine (SVM) classifier. In the testing stage, we extract the same features from the testing functional networks, then pass the selected features to the trained classifier for predicting the labels of the testing subjects.

3   Results and Discussion

Evaluation Dataset and Parameters. We used five-fold cross-validation to evaluate the proposed SM-netFusion framework on 505 subjects (266 ASD and 239 NC) from Autism Brain Imaging Data Exchange (ABIDE) preprocessed public dataset[1]. Several preprocessing steps were implemented by the data processing assistant for resting-state fMRI (DPARSF) pipeline. Each brain rfMRI was partitioned into 116 ROIs. For SIMLR parameters [8], we tested SM-netFusion using $n_c = \{1, 2, \ldots, 6\}$ clusters and we found that the best result was $n_c = 3$. For the cross-diffusion process parameters, we also set the number of iterations $n^\star = 20$ as recommended in [2] for convergence. We fixed the number of closest neighbors $K = 25$ across comparison methods.

Evaluation and Comparison Methods. *Representativeness.* To evaluate the centeredness and representativeness of our brain network atlas estimation, we benchmarked our method against five network fusion strategies: (1) D-SNF

---

[1] http://preprocessed-connectomes-project.org/abide/.

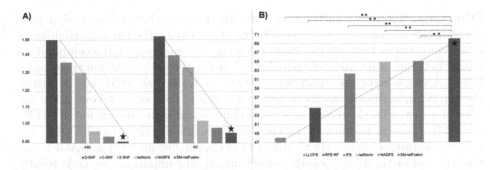

Fig. 2. *Evaluation.* **A) Evaluation of the estimated network atlas for NC and ASD populations using different fusion strategies.** We display the mean Frobenius distance between estimated brain network atlas and all individual networks in the population using D-SNF [2], C-SNF, E-SNF, netNorm [5], NAGFS [6] and SM-netFusion. Clearly, SM-netFusion achieves the minimum distance in both ASD and NC groups. **B) ASD/NC classification using different brain networks.** Average classification accuracies for our method (SM-netFusion+SVM), (IFS+SVM) [12], (net-Norm+SVM) [5], (RF-RFE) [13] and (LLCFS+SVM) [14]. The best performance was achieved by our method. ⋆: Our method and (∗∗) for p-value < 0.05 using two-tailed paired t-test.

method [2] which considers only node degree as a topological measure in the cross-network diffusion process, (2) C-SNF method which considers only close ness centrality as a topological measure, (3) E-SNF method which considers only eigenvector centrality as a topological measure, (4) netNorm² method [5] which uses a high-order sample selection technique to build a connectional template, and (5) NAGFS³ method which uses SNF diffusion and fusion techniques along with clustering.

As illustrated in Fig. 2-A, we computed the mean Frobenius distance defined as as $d_F(\mathbf{A}, \mathbf{B}) = \sqrt{\sum_i \sum_j |a_{ij} - b_{ij}|^2}$ between the estimated network atlas and individual networks in the population. A smaller distance indicates a more centered network atlas with respect to all individuals in the population. We observe that our proposed multi-topology BNA remarkably outperforms conventional techniques by achieving the minimum distance for both ASD and NC populations.

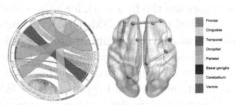

Fig. 3. *The strongest connections present the 5 most discriminative network connections between ASD and NC groups. The circular graphs were generated using Circos table viewer [15]. We used BrainNet Viewer Software [16] to display the regions of interest involving the most discriminative connectivities.*

---

² https://github.com/basiralab/netNorm-PY.
³ https://github.com/basiralab/NAGFS-PY.

Discriminativeness. Furthermore, we demonstrate that SM-netFusion produces highly discriminative BNAs in terms of identifying the most discriminative brain connections between two classes. Specifically, we conducted a comparative study between ASD and NC populations using the estimated multi-topology BNAs. Using 5-fold cross-validation strategy, we trained an SVM classifier using the top N_f most discriminative features identified by each of the following feature selection methods: (1) recursive feature elimination with random forest (RFE-RF) [17], (2) local learning-based clustering feature selection (LLCFS) [14], (3) infinite feature selection (IFS) [12], (4) netNorm [5], and (5) a NAGFS [6]. Clearly, our method significantly outperformed all comparison methods results as shown in Fig. 2-B in terms of classification accuracy ($p - value < 0.05$ using two-tailed paired t-test). Our results also demonstrate that our SM-netFusion for BNA estimation outperforms state-of-the-art methods along with its ablated versions in terms of both representativeness and discriminativeness.

Neuro-biomarkers. Fig. 3 displays the top 5 discriminative ROIs distinguishing between healthy and autistic subjects by computing the absolute difference between the estimated BNAs and pinning down regions with highest differences. We notice that most of the discriminative functional brain connectivities involved the frontal lobe. Indeed, previous studies reported that the frontal lobe has a major role in speech and language production, understanding and reacting to others, forming memories and making decisions which might explain the prevalence of altered brain connectivities in this brain lobar region [18]. Our SM-netFusion is a generic framework for supervised graph integration, which can be further leveraged to design an efficient graph feature selection method for training predictive learners for examining graph-based data representations.

4   Conclusion

We proposed the first work for supervised network cross-diffusion based on graph topological measures (SM-netFusion) by enhancing the non-linear fusion process using a weighted mixture of multi-topological measures. Our framework can be also leveraged to design an efficient feature selection method for training predictive learners in network neuroscience. The proposed SM-netFusion produces the most centered and representative BNAs in comparison with its variants as well as state-of-the-art methods and further boosted the classification of autistic subjects by $5-15\%$. In our future work, we will evaluate our framework on larger connectomic datasets covering a diverse range of neurological disorders such as brain dementia. Furthermore, we aim to explore the discriminative power of brain network atlases derived from other brain modalities such as structural [19] and morphological brain networks [20,21].

Acknowledgments. I. Rekik is supported by the European Union's Horizon 2020 research and innovation programme under the Marie Sklodowska-Curie Individual Fellowship grant agreement No. 101003403 (http://basira-lab.com/normnets/).

References

1. Rekik, I., Li, G., Lin, W., Shen, D.: Estimation of brain network atlases using diffusive-shrinking graphs: application to developing brains. In: International Conference on Information Processing in Medical Imaging, pp. 385–397 (2017)
2. Wang, B., et al.: Similarity network fusion for aggregating data types on a genomic scale. Nat. Methods **11**, 333 (2014)
3. Rekik, I., Li, G., Lin, W., Shen, D.: Do baby brain cortices that look alike at birth grow alike during the first year of postnatal development?, pp. 566–574 (2018)
4. Dhifallah, S., Rekik, I., Alzheimer's Disease Neuroimaging Initiative: Clustering-based multi-view network fusion for estimating brain network atlases of healthy and disordered populations. J. Neurosci. Methods **311**, 426–435 (2018)
5. Dhifallah, S., Rekik, I., Initiative, A.D.N., et al.: Estimation of connectional brain templates using selective multi-view network normalization. Med. Image Anal. **59**, 101567 (2020)
6. Mhiri, I., Rekik, I.: Joint functional brain network atlas estimation and feature selection for neurological disorder diagnosis with application to autism. Med. Image Anal. **60**, 101596 (2020)
7. Fornito, A., Zalesky, A., Bullmore, E.: Fundamentals of Brain Network Analysis. Academic Press, Cambridge (2016)
8. Wang, B., Ramazzotti, D., De Sano, L., Zhu, J., Pierson, E., Batzoglou, S.: SIMLR: a tool for large-scale genomic analyses by Multi-Kernel learning. Proteomics **18**, 1700232 (2018)
9. Freeman, L.C., Roeder, D., Mulholland, R.R.: Centrality in social networks: II. experimental results. Soc. Netw. **2**, 119–141 (1979)
10. Bassett, D.S., Sporns, O.: Network neuroscience. Nat. Neurosci. **20**, 353 (2017)
11. Aiolli, F., Donini, M.: EasyMKL: a scalable multiple kernel learning algorithm. Neurocomputing **169**, 215–224 (2015)
12. Roffo, G., Melzi, S., Cristani, M.: Infinite feature selection. In: Proceedings of the IEEE International Conference on Computer Vision, pp. 4202–4210 (2015)
13. Nembrini, S.: Machine learning methods for feature selection and rule extraction in genome-wide association studies (GWASs) (2013)
14. Zeng, H., Cheung, Y.M.: Feature selection and kernel learning for local learning-based clustering. IEEE Trans. Pattern Anal. Mach. Intell. **33**, 1532–1547 (2010)
15. Krzywinski, M.I., et al.: CIRCOS: an information aesthetic for comparative genomics. Genome Res. **19**(9), 1639–1645 (2009)
16. Xia, M., Wang, J., He, Y.: BrainNet viewer: a network visualization tool for human brain connectomics. PLoS ONE **8**, e68910 (2013)
17. Granitto, P.M., Furlanello, C., Biasioli, F., Gasperi, F.: Recursive feature elimination with random forest for PTR-MS analysis of agroindustrial products. Chemometr. Intell. Lab. Syst. **83**, 83–90 (2006)
18. Kumar, A., Sundaram, S.K., Sivaswamy, L., Behen, M.E., Makki, M.I., Ager, J., Janisse, J., Chugani, H.T., Chugani, D.C.: Alterations in frontal lobe tracts and corpus callosum in young children with autism spectrum disorder. Cereb. Cortex **20**, 2103–2113 (2010)

19. Park, H.J., Friston, K.: Structural and functional brain networks: from connections to cognition. Science **342**(6158) (2013)
20. Nebli, A., Rekik, I.: Gender differences in cortical morphological networks. Brain Imaging Behav. 1–9 (2019). https://doi.org/10.1007/s11682-019-00123-6
21. Bilgen, I., Guvercin, G., Rekik, I.: Machine learning methods for brain network classification: application to autism diagnosis using cortical morphological networks. arXiv preprint arXiv:2004.13321 (2020)

Partial Volume Segmentation of Brain MRI Scans of Any Resolution and Contrast

Benjamin Billot[1]([✉]), Eleanor Robinson[1], Adrian V. Dalca[2,3], and Juan Eugenio Iglesias[1,2,3]

[1] Centre for Medical Image Computing, University College London, London, UK
benjamin.billot.18@ucl.ac.uk
[2] Martinos Center for Biomedical Imaging, Massachusetts General Hospital and Harvard Medical School, Boston, USA
[3] Computer Science and Artificial Intelligence Laboratory, Massachusetts Institute of Technology, Cambridge, USA

Abstract. Partial voluming (PV) is arguably the last crucial unsolved problem in Bayesian segmentation of brain MRI with probabilistic atlases. PV occurs when voxels contain multiple tissue classes, giving rise to image intensities that may not be representative of any one of the underlying classes. PV is particularly problematic for segmentation when there is a large resolution gap between the atlas and the test scan, e.g., when segmenting clinical scans with thick slices, or when using a high-resolution atlas. Forward models of PV are realistic and simple, as they amount to blurring and subsampling a high resolution (HR) volume into a lower resolution (LR) scan. Unfortunately, segmentation as Bayesian inference quickly becomes intractable when "inverting" this forward PV model, as it requires marginalizing over all possible anatomical configurations of the HR volume. In this work, we present PV-SynthSeg, a convolutional neural network (CNN) that tackles this problem by directly learning a mapping between (possibly multi-modal) LR scans and underlying HR segmentations. PV-SynthSeg simulates LR images from HR label maps with a generative model of PV, and can be trained to segment scans of any desired target contrast and resolution, even for previously unseen modalities where neither images nor segmentations are available at training. PV-SynthSeg does not require any preprocessing, and runs in seconds. We demonstrate the accuracy and flexibility of our method with extensive experiments on three datasets and 2,680 scans. The code is available at https://github.com/BBillot/SynthSeg.

Keywords: Partial volume segmentation · Brain MRI

Electronic supplementary material The online version of this chapter (https://doi.org/10.1007/978-3-030-59728-3_18) contains supplementary material, which is available to authorized users.

© Springer Nature Switzerland AG 2020
A. L. Martel et al. (Eds.): MICCAI 2020, LNCS 12267, pp. 177–187, 2020.
https://doi.org/10.1007/978-3-030-59728-3_18

1   Introduction

Segmentation of brain MRI scans is a key step in neuroimaging studies, as it is a prerequisite for an array of subsequent analyses, e.g., volumetry or connectivity studies. Although manual segmentation remains the gold standard, this expensive procedure can be replaced by automated tools, which enable reproducible segmentation of large datasets. However, a well-known problem of automated segmentation is the partial volume (PV) effect [8,24]. PV arises when different tissues are mixed within the same voxel during acquisition, resulting in averaged intensities that may not be representative of any of the underlying tissues. For instance, in a T1 scan, the edge between white matter and cerebrospinal fluid (CSF) will often appear the same color as gray matter, even though no gray matter is present. This problem particularly affects scans with low resolution in any orientation (e.g., clinical quality images with thick slices), and fine-detailed brain regions like the hippocampus in research quality scans.

Modern supervised segmentation approaches based on convolutional neural networks (CNN) [18,22,29] can learn to segment with PV, given appropriate training data. However, they do not generalize well to test scans with significantly different resolution or intensity distribution [3,17,19], despite recent advances in transfer learning and data augmentation [7,11,17,21,31,37]. In contrast, Bayesian segmentation methods stand out for their generalization ability, which is why they are used by all major neuroimaging packages (e.g., FreeSurfer [12], SPM [5], and FSL [27]). Bayesian segmentation with probabilistic atlases builds on generative models that combine a prior describing neuroanatomy (an atlas) and a likelihood distribution that models the image formation process (often a Gaussian mixture model, or GMM, combined with a model of bias field). Bayesian inference is used to "invert" this generative model and compute the most likely segmentation given the observed intensities and the atlas. Unfortunately, these models can be greatly affected by PV.

A popular class of Bayesian methods uses an unsupervised likelihood term and estimates the GMM parameters from the test scan, which makes them adaptive to MRI contrast [5,28,32,36]. This is a highly desirable feature in neuroimaging, since differences in hardware and pulse sequences can have a large impact on the accuracy of supervised approaches, which are not robust to such variability. Unsupervised likelihood models also enable the segmentation of *in vivo* MRI with high resolution atlases built with *ex vivo* modalities (e.g., histology [15]).

PV can easily be incorporated into the generative model of Bayesian segmentation by considering a high resolution (HR) image generated with the conventional non-PV model, and by appending smoothing and subsampling operations to yield the observed low resolution (LR) image. However, inferring the most likely HR segmentation from the LR voxels quickly becomes intractable, as estimating the model parameters requires to marginalize over the HR label configurations. Early methods attempted to circumvent this limitation by approximating the posterior of the HR label [20,25], or by explicitly modeling the most common PV classes (e.g., white matter with CSF) with dedicated Gaussian intensity distributions [26,30]. Van Leemput et al. [33] formalized the problem and proposed a principled statistical framework for PV segmentation. They were able to simplify the marginalization and solve it for simple cases, given specific assumptions on the number of mixing classes and blurring kernel. Even with these simplifications, their method remains impractical for most real world scans, particularly when multiple MRI contrasts with different resolutions are involved.

In this paper, we present PV-SynthSeg, a novel and fast method for PV-aware segmentation of (possibly multi-modal) brain MRI scans. Specifically, we propose to synthesize training scans based on the forward model of Bayesian segmentation, with a focus on PV effects. We train a CNN with these scans, which are generated on the fly with random model parameters [6]. The CNN can be trained to segment scans of any desired target resolution and contrast by adjusting the probability distribution of these parameters. As with classical Bayesian segmentation, the method only needs segmentations (no images) as training data. PV-SynthSeg leverages machine learning to achieve, for the first time, PV segmentation of MRI scans of unseen, arbitrary resolution and contrast without any limiting simplifying assumptions. PV-SynthSeg is very flexible and can readily segment multi-modal and clinical images, which would be unfeasible with exact Bayesian inference.

2 Methods

2.1 Generative Model of MRI Scans with PV: Intractable Inference

Let A be a probabilistic atlas that provides, at each spatial location, a vector with the occurrence probabilities for K neuroanatomical classes. The atlas is spatially warped by a deformation field ϕ parametrized by θ_ϕ, which follows a distribution $p(\theta_\phi)$. Further, let $L = \{L_j\}_{1 \le j \le J}$ be a 3D label map (segmentation) of J voxels defined on a HR grid, where $L_j \in \{1, ..., K\}$. We assume that each L_j is independently drawn from the categorical distribution given by the deformed atlas at each location: $p(L, \theta_\phi | A) = p(\theta_\phi) p(L | \theta_\phi, A) = p(\theta_\phi) \prod_{j=1}^{J} p(L_j | \theta_\phi, A)$.

Given a segmentation L, image intensities $I = \{I_j\}_{1 \le j \le J}$ at HR are assumed to be independent samples of a (possibly multivariate) GMM conditioned on the anatomical labels: $p(I, \theta_G, \theta_B | L) = p(\theta_G) p(\theta_B) \prod_{j=1}^{J} \mathcal{N}\left(I_j - B_j(\theta_B); \mu_{L_j}, \Sigma_{L_j}\right)$, where θ_G is a vector grouping the means and covariances associated with each of the K classes, and $B_j(\theta_B)$ is the bias field at voxel j in logarithmic domain, parameterized by θ_B. Both θ_G and θ_B have associated prior distributions $p(\theta_G)$ and $p(\theta_B)$, which complete the classical non-PV model.

We model PV by assuming that, instead of the HR image I, we observe $\mathcal{D}(I) = \{\mathcal{D}(I)_{j'}\}_{1 \le j' \le J'}$, defined over a coarser LR grid with $J' < J$ voxels, where $\mathcal{D}$ is a blurring and subsampling operator. If the blurring is linear, the likelihood $p(\mathcal{D}(I) | L, \theta_B, \theta_G)$ is still Gaussian (since every LR voxel is a linear combination of Gaussian HR voxels) but, in general, does not factorize over j'.

Bayesian segmentation often uses point estimates for the model parameters to avoid intractable integrals. This requires finding the most likely model parameters given the atlas and observed image, by maximizing $p(\theta_\phi, \theta_B, \theta_G | \mathcal{D}(I), A)$.

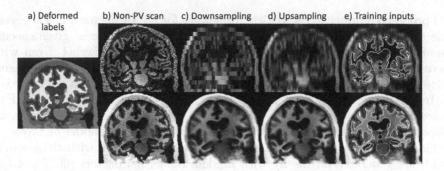

a) Deformed   b) Non-PV scan   c) Downsampling   d) Upsampling   e) Training inputs
labels

Fig. 1. Generation of a synthetic multi-modal MRI scan ($1 \times 9 \times 1$ mm axial FLAIR and a $1 \times 1 \times 9$ mm coronal T1). We sample a HR image (b) from a deformed label map (a). We then simulate PV scans at LR with blurring and subsampling steps (c). The LR scans are upscaled to the isotropic HR voxel grid (d) to generate training pairs (e).

Applying Bayes' rule and marginalizing over the unknown segmentation, the optimization problem is:

$$\arg\max_{\theta_\phi, \theta_B, \theta_G} p(\theta_\phi) p(\theta_B) p(\theta_G) \sum_L p(\mathcal{D}(I)|L, \theta_B, \theta_G) p(L|\theta_\phi, A).$$

Without PV (i.e., $\mathcal{D}(I) = I$), the sum over segmentations L is tractable because both the prior $p(L|\theta_\phi, A)$ and the likelihood $p(I|L, \theta_B, \theta_G)$ factorize over voxels. However, in the PV case, blurring introduces dependencies between the underlying HR voxels, and the sum is intractable, as it requires evaluating K^J terms. Even with simplifying assumptions, such as limiting the maximum number of classes mixing in a LR voxel to two, using a rectangular blurring kernel, and exploiting redundancy in likelihood computations [33], computing the sum is prohibitively expensive: it requires $K(K-1)2^{(M-1)}$ evaluations of the prior and $K(K-1)(1+M)/2$ evaluations of the likelihood (where M is the voxel size ratio between LR and HR), and only remains tractable for very low values of M.

2.2   PV-aware Segmentation with Synthesis and Supervised CNNs

Rather than explicitly inverting the PV model of Bayesian segmentation, we employ a CNN that directly learns the mapping between LR intensities $\mathcal{D}(I)$ and HR labels L. We train this network with synthetic images sampled from the generative model (see example in Fig. 1). Specifically, every minibatch consists of a synthetic MRI scan and a corresponding segmentation, generated as follows.

(a) Starting from a training dataset $\{S_t\}$ with T segmentations, we first use a public GPU implementation [6] to sample the non-PV joint distribution:

$$p(I, L, \theta_\phi, \theta_G, \theta_B | \{S_t\}) = p(I|L, \theta_G, \theta_B) p(L|\theta_\phi, \{S_t\}) p(\theta_\phi) p(\theta_G) p(\theta_B), \quad (1)$$

where the standard probabilistic atlas prior is replaced by a model where a label map is randomly drawn from $\{S_t\}$ and deformed with ϕ, i.e., $p(L|\theta_\phi, \{S_t\}) = (1/T)\sum_t \delta[L = (S_t \circ \phi)]$, where δ is the Kronecker delta. This model yields label maps that are more spatially regular than atlas samples (Fig. 1a). The deformation field ϕ is obtained by sampling a stationary velocity field as a $10 \times 10 \times 10 \times 3$ zero-mean Gaussian field with diagonal covariance, integrating it with a scaling-and-squaring approach [4] to obtain a diffeomorphic field, and composing it with a random linear transform, with translation, rotation, scaling and shearing parameters sampled from uniform distributions. The intensity parameters $p(\theta_G)$ are sampled independently for each MRI contrast, using Gaussian distributions for the means and the logarithm of the variances. The bias field is obtained by sampling a $4 \times 4 \times 4$ zero-mean Gaussian field with diagonal covariance, upscaling it to the input volume size, and taking the element-wise exponential. This process yields a multi-modal HR image I from a HR label map L (Fig. 1b).

(b) We simulate voxel thickness independently for each channel of I, by blurring them with anisotropic Gaussian kernels to simulate the target resolution of the LR images. Specifically, we design the standard deviation of the kernel such that the power of the HR signal is divided by 10 at the cut-off frequency. As the standard deviations in the spatial and discrete frequency domain are related by $\sigma_f \sigma_s = (2\pi)^{-1}$, the standard deviation of the blurring kernel is:

$$\sigma_s = 2\log(10)/(2\pi)r_n/r_a \approx (3/4)r_n/r_a,$$

where r_n is the (possibly anisotropic) voxel size of the test scan in channel n, and r_a is the isotropic voxel size of the atlas. We further multiply σ_s by a factor α ($\sigma_s = 0.75\alpha r_n/r_a$), sampled from a uniform distribution of predefined range, to introduce small resolution variations and increase robustness in the method.

(c) Because in real data slice thickness and spacing are not necessarily equal, we simulate slice spacing by subsampling the blurred version of I (still defined in the HR grid) to obtain $\mathcal{D}(I)$, defined on the LR grid (Fig. 1c).

(d) Finally, we upsample $\mathcal{D}(I)$ back into the original HR space with linear interpolation (Fig. 1d). This step mimics the processing at test time, when we upscale the input to the target isotropic HR, so that the CNN can obtain a label map on the HR grid that represents anatomy within the LR voxels.

2.3 Learning

We train a 3D U-net [29] with synthetic pairs generated on the fly with the PV model. The U-net has 5 levels with 2 layers each ($3 \times 3 \times 3$ kernel size and ELU activation [10]). The first layer has 24 kernels, this number being doubled after each max-pooling, and halved after each upsampling. The last layer uses a softmax activation. The optimization loss is defined as the average soft Dice coefficient over all predicted labels [22]. Our method (generative model and CNN) is entirely implemented on the GPU, using Keras [9] with a Tensorflow backend [2].

The hyperparameters governing the distributions of θ_ϕ and θ_B are drawn from uniform distributions with relatively wide ranges (Table S1 in the supplementary material), which increases the robustness of the CNN [6]. The hyperparameters of θ_G are modality specific. In practice, we estimate them from unlabeled scans as follows. First, we run a publicly available Bayesian segmentation method (SAMSEG [28]). Second, we compute estimates of the means and variances of each class using robust statistics (median and median absolute deviation). Importantly, the estimated variances are multiplied by the ratio of the voxel size volumes at HR and LR, such that the blurring decreases the variances to the expected levels at LR. And third, we fit a Gaussian distribution to these parameters. Finally, we artificially increase the estimated standard deviations by a factor of 5, with two purposes: making the CNN resilient to changes in acquisition parameters, and mitigating segmentation errors made by SAMSEG.

3   Experiments and Results

3.1   Datasets

T1-39: 39 1 mm isotropic T1 brain scans with segmentation for 39 regions of interest (ROIs) [12]: 36 cerebral (manual) and 3 extra-cerebral (semi-automated).

FLAIR: 2413 T2-FLAIR scans from ADNI [1] at $1 \times 1 \times 5$ mm resolution (axial).

CobraLab: 5 multimodal (T1/T2) .6 mm isotropic scans [34] with manual labels for 5 hippocampal subregions (CA1, CA23, CA4, subiculum, molecular layer). We segmented the rest of brain ROIs with FreeSurfer to obtain dense label maps.

ADNI-HP: 134 Alzheimer's disease (AD) cases and 134 controls from ADNI [1], with T1 (1 mm) and T2 ($.4 \times .4 \times 2$ mm coronal, covering only the hippocampus).

3.2   Experimental Setup

We evaluate PV-SynthSeg with three sets of experiments:

T1-spacing: We assess performance at different PV levels with the T1-39 dataset. We simulate sparse clinical scans in coronal, sagittal and axial orientation, at 3, 6 and 9 mm slice spacing, with 3 mm slice thickness. We use our method to train a network to provide segmentations on the 1 mm isotropic grid. We use segmentations from 20 cases for training, and the rest of the subjects for testing.

FLAIR: To evaluate our method on scans representative of clinical quality data, with real thick-slice images and a contrast other than T1, we use the same 20 label maps from the T1-39 dataset to train our method to segment the FLAIR scans, on a 1 mm isotropic grid. The Gaussian hyperparameters are estimated from a subset of 20 FLAIR scans, and the remaining 2393 are used for testing. We use FreeSurfer [12] segmentations of corresponding T1 ADNI scans as ground truth. We emphasize that such T1 scans are often not available in clinical protocols, but here we can use these for evaluation purposes only.

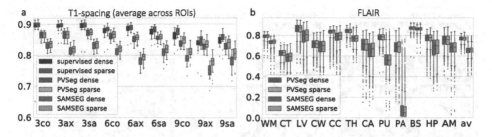

Fig. 2. (a) Box plot of Dice scores in T1-spacing experiment with 3, 6 and 9 mm spacing in coronal (co), axial (ax), and sagittal (sa) orientations, averaged over 12 representative ROIs: cerebral white matter (WM) and cortex (CT); lateral ventricle (LV); cerebellar white matter (CW) and cortex (CC); thalamus (TH); caudate (CA); putamen (PU); pallidum (PA); brainstem (BS); hippocampus (HP); and amygdala (AM). (b) Box plot of Dice scores for the 12 ROIs in the FLAIR experiment and their average (av).

Hippocampus: We also evaluate our method on a multi-modal MRI dataset with different resolutions for each channel, in the context of a neuroimaging group study. We use the segmentations from the CobraLab dataset to train our model to segment the hippocampal subregions on the ADNI-HP dataset, on the 0.6 mm isotropic grid. Since no ground truth is available for the target dataset, we use the ability to separate groups and detect known atrophy patterns in AD [13,16,23,35] as a proxy for segmentation accuracy.

We compare the proposed approach with two other competing methods. First, Bayesian segmentation without PV; this is a natural alternative to our approach, as it only requires label maps for supervision, and adapts to MRI contrast (including multi-modal). In the first two experiments, we use SAM-SEG [28] (trained on the same 20 scans from T1-39) to segment the upsampled HR inputs (we also tried segmenting the LR scans directly, with inferior results). In the third experiment, we use a publicly available hippocampal segmentation algorithm [14], with a probabilistic atlas created from the CobraLab data.

The second competing approach is a supervised CNN trained on LR images from the target modality, which requires paired imaging and segmentation data. We test this approach on the first and third experiments, which represent the settings in which manual labels may be available. Specifically, we train the same 3D U-net architecture with real scans blurred to the target resolution, and using the same augmentation strategy as for our method. We emphasize that such methods are only applicable in more rare supervised settings, but the performance of these networks provides an informative upper bound for the accuracy of PV-SynthSeg. We evaluate all methods on both the HR ("dense") and the LR grid ("sparse"), obtained by downsampling the HR labels.

3.3 Results

Figure 2a shows the mean Dice scores for the T1-spacing experiment. PV-SynthSeg consistently outperforms SAMSEG by up to 6 Dice points, and is

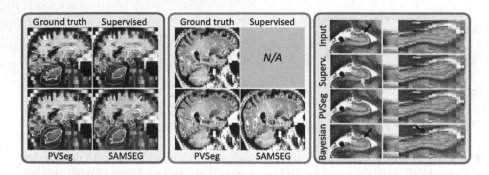

Fig. 3. Examples of dense segmentations. Red box: $1 \times 1 \times 9$ mm volume from T1-spacing experiment. Green box: sample from FLAIR experiment. Blue box: Hippocampus (T2 with partial coverage overlaid on T1). See main text for a description of the arrows. More sample segmentations are shown in Figs. S2–S4 in the supplement. (Color figure online)

Table 1. Effect sizes (Cohen's d) and p values of non-parametric Wilcoxon tests, comparing the volumes of the hippocampal substructures in AD subjects vs. controls.

Method	CA1	CA23	CA4	Subiculum	Molec. layer	Whole
Supervised: d	1.94	1.66	1.87	1.84	2.15	2.10
Supervised: p	$<10^{-29}$	$<10^{-23}$	$<10^{-28}$	$<10^{-27}$	$<10^{-34}$	$<10^{-33}$
PV-SynthSeg: d	2.06	1.62	1.73	1.33	1.48	1.92
PV-SynthSeg: p	$<10^{-32}$	$<10^{-25}$	$<10^{-25}$	$<10^{-15}$	$<10^{-19}$	$<10^{-29}$
Bayesian: d	1.93	1.42	1.73	1.96	0.48	1.79
Bayesian: p	$<10^{-29}$	$<10^{-18}$	$<10^{-24}$	$<10^{-29}$	$<10^{-4}$	$<10^{-26}$

robust to large slice spacings: even at 9 mm, it yields competitive Dice scores (0.83 mean), both when evaluated densely and on the sparse slices. Comprehensive structure-wise results are shown in Fig. S1 in the supplement; they reveal that, with increasing slice spacing, accuracy decreases the most for the thin and convoluted cerebral cortex. This is also apparent from the example in Fig. 3 (red box, $1 \times 1 \times 9$ mm resolution), where the cortex is inaccurate for all methods. Due to PV effects, SAMSEG almost completely fails to segment the caudate (yellow arrow), which our method successfully recovers. Having access to the exact intensity distributions, the supervised approach outperforms PV-SynthSeg (only marginally at higher slice spacing), but is only an option in the rare scenario where one has access to manually labeled HR scans of the target contrast.

On FLAIR scans, PV-SynthSeg achieves a mean Dice score of 0.77 (Fig. 2b). This is a remarkable result, considering the low contrast of these scans and their large slice thickness (5 mm). In contrast, SAMSEG only yields 0.65 Dice (12 points below), and consistently labels the pallidum as putamen. This is shown in Fig. 3 (green box), where the pallidum is pointed by the yellow arrow.

Although PV-SynthSeg uses hyperparameters computed with SAMSEG, it successfully recovers the pallidum (Dice $\approx$ 0.75), which highlights its robustness against inaccurate hyperparameter estimation. PV-SynthSeg is also noticeably more accurate in other structures in this example, like the hippocampus (in yellow). As in T1-spacing, neither method is accurate for the cortex at this resolution (Dice $\approx$ 0.60) – again, partly due to the low gray-white matter contrast.

In the hippocampus experiment, PV effects in the T2 scan cause the interface between white matter and the lateral ventricle to appear as gray matter, leading to segmentation errors in the Bayesian algorithm (red arrows in blue box of Fig. 3). Despite having been trained on only five cases, the supervised method does not have this problem, but follows the internal structure of the hippocampus (revealed by the molecular layer: the dark band pointed by the yellow arrow) much less accurately than PV-SynthSeg. While all three methods detect large effect sizes in the AD experiment (Table 1), PV-SynthSeg replicates well-known differential atrophy patterns (derived from manual [23] and semi-automated segmentations [35]) much better than the other two approaches, with CA1 showing stronger atrophy than CA4, and the subiculum remaining relatively spared.

4   Conclusion

We have presented PV-SynthSeg, a novel learning-based segmentation method for brain MRI scans with PV effects. PV-SynthSeg can accurately segment most brain ROIs in scans with very large slice thickness, regardless of their contrast (even when previously unseen), and replicates differential atrophy patterns in the hippocampus in an AD study. A general limitation of PV segmentation is the low accuracy for the cortex at larger spacing, which precludes application to cortical thickness and parcellation analyses. We will tackle this problem by combining our approach with image imputation. PV-SynthSeg enables morphology studies of large clinical datasets of any modality, which has enormous potential in the discovery of imaging biomarkers in a wide array of neurodegenerative disorders.

Acknowledgement. Work supported by the ERC (Starting Grant 677697), EPSRC (UCL CDT in Medical Imaging, EP/L016478/1), Alzheimer's Research UK (Interdisciplinary Grant ARUK-IRG2019A-003), NIH (1R01AG064027-01A1, 5R01NS105820-02), the Department of Health's NIHR-funded Biomedical Research Centre at UCLH.

References

1. Alzheimer's Disease Neuroimaging Initiative. http://adni.loni.usc.edu/
2. Abadi, M., Barham, P., Chen, J., Chen, Z., Davis, A., et al.: TensorFlow: a system for large-scale machine learning. OSDI **16**, 265–283 (2016)
3. Akkus, Z., Galimzianova, A., Hoogi, A., Rubin, D.L., Erickson, B.J.: Deep learning for brain MRI segmentation: state of the art and future directions. J. Digit. Imaging **30**(4), 449–459 (2017). https://doi.org/10.1007/s10278-017-9983-4

4. Arsigny, V., Commowick, O., Pennec, X., Ayache, N.: A log-Euclidean framework for statistics on diffeomorphisms. In: Larsen, R., Nielsen, M., Sporring, J. (eds.) MICCAI 2006. LNCS, vol. 4190, pp. 924–931. Springer, Heidelberg (2006). https://doi.org/10.1007/11866565_113
5. Ashburner, J., Friston, K.: Unified segmentation. NeuroImage **26**, 839–851 (2005)
6. Billot, B., Greve, D., Van Leemput, K., Fischl, B., Iglesias, J., Dalca, A.: A Learning Strategy for Contrast-agnostic MRI Segmentation. arXiv:2003.01995 (2020)
7. Chaitanya, K., Karani, N., Baumgartner, C.F., Becker, A., Donati, O., Konukoglu, E.: Semi-supervised and task-driven data augmentation. In: Chung, A.C.S., Gee, J.C., Yushkevich, P.A., Bao, S. (eds.) IPMI 2019. LNCS, vol. 11492, pp. 29–41. Springer, Cham (2019). https://doi.org/10.1007/978-3-030-20351-1_3
8. Choi, H., Haynor, D., Kim, Y.: Partial volume tissue classification of multichannel magnetic resonance images - a mixel model. IEEE Trans. Med. Imaging **10**(3), 395–407 (1991)
9. Chollet, F.: Keras
10. Clevert, D.A., Unterthiner, T., Hochreiter, S.: Fast and Accurate Deep Network Learning by Exponential Linear Units (ELUs). arXiv:1511.07289 [cs] (2016)
11. Eaton-Rosen, Z., Bragman, F., Ourselin, S., Cardoso, M.J.: Improving data augmentation for medical image segmentation. In: International Conference on Medical Imaging with Deep Learning (2018)
12. Fischl, B.: FreeSurfer. NeuroImage **62**(2), 774–781 (2012)
13. Fox, N., et al.: Presymptomatic hippocampal atrophy in Alzheimer's disease. A longitudinal MRI study. Brain J. Neurol. **119**, 2001–2007 (1996)
14. Iglesias, J.E.: A computational atlas of the hippocampal formation using ex vivo, ultra-high resolution MRI: application to adaptive segmentation of in vivo MRI. Neuroimage **115**, 117–137 (2015)
15. Iglesias, J.E.: A probabilistic atlas of the human thalamic nuclei combining ex vivo MRI and histology. NeuroImage **183**, 314–326 (2018)
16. Jack, C.: Prediction of AD with MRI-based hippocampal volume in mild cognitive impairment. Neurology **52**(7), 1397–1403 (1999)
17. Jog, A., Hoopes, A., Greve, D., Van Leemput, K., Fischl, B.: PSACNN: pulse sequence adaptive fast whole brain segmentation. NeuroImage **199**, 553–569 (2019)
18. Kamnitsas, K.: Efficient multi-scale 3D CNN with fully connected CRF for accurate brain lesion segmentation. Med. Image Anal. **36**, 61–78 (2017)
19. Karani, N., Chaitanya, K., Baumgartner, C., Konukoglu, E.: A lifelong learning approach to brain MR segmentation across scanners and protocols. In: Frangi, A.F., Schnabel, J.A., Davatzikos, C., Alberola-López, C., Fichtinger, G. (eds.) MICCAI 2018. LNCS, vol. 11070, pp. 476–484. Springer, Cham (2018). https://doi.org/10.1007/978-3-030-00928-1_54
20. Laidlaw, D., Fleischer, K., Barr, A.: Partial-volume Bayesian classification of material mixtures in MR volume data using voxel histograms. IEEE Trans. Med. Imaging **17**(1), 74–86 (1998)
21. Long, M., Zhu, H., Wang, J., Jordan, M.: Deep transfer learning with joint adaptation networks. In: International Conference on Machine Learning, pp. 2208–2217 (2017)
22. Milletari, F., Navab, N., Ahmadi, S.A.: V-Net: fully convolutional neural networks for volumetric medical image segmentation. In: 2016 4th International Conference on 3D Vision (3DV), pp. 565–571 (2016)
23. Mueller, S.G., et al.: Systematic comparison of different techniques to measure hippocampal subfield volumes in ADNI2. NeuroImage Clin. **17**, 1006–1018 (2018)

24. Niessen, W., Vincken, K., Weickert, J., Romeny, B., Viergever, M.: Multiscale segmentation of three-dimensional MR brain images. Int. J. Comput. Vis. **31**(2), 185–202 (1999)
25. Nocera, L., Gee, J.: Robust partial-volume tissue classification of cerebral MRI scans, pp. 312–322. International Society for Optics and Photonics (1997)
26. Noe, A., Gee, J.C.: Partial volume segmentation of cerebral MRI scans with mixture model clustering. In: Insana, M.F., Leahy, R.M. (eds.) IPMI 2001. LNCS, vol. 2082, pp. 423–430. Springer, Heidelberg (2001). https://doi.org/10.1007/3-540-45729-1_44
27. Patenaude, B., Smith, S., Kennedy, D., Jenkinson, M.: A Bayesian model of shape and appearance for subcortical brain segmentation. NeuroImage **56**, 907–22 (2011)
28. Puonti, O., Iglesias, J.E., Van Leemput, K.: Fast and sequence-adaptive whole-brain segmentation using parametric Bayesian modeling. NeuroImage **143**, 235–249 (2016)
29. Ronneberger, O., Fischer, P., Brox, T.: U-Net: convolutional networks for biomedical image segmentation. In: Navab, N., Hornegger, J., Wells, W.M., Frangi, A.F. (eds.) MICCAI 2015. LNCS, vol. 9351, pp. 234–241. Springer, Cham (2015). https://doi.org/10.1007/978-3-319-24574-4_28
30. Shattuck, D., Sandor-Leahy, S., Schaper, K., Rottenberg, D., Leahy, R.M.: Magnetic resonance image tissue classification using a partial volume model. NeuroImage **13**(5), 856–876 (2001)
31. Shin, H., Roth, H., Gao, M., Lu, L., et al.: Deep convolutional neural networks for computer-aided detection: CNN architectures, dataset characteristics and transfer learning. IEEE Trans. Med. Imaging **35**(5), 1285–1298 (2016)
32. Van Leemput, K., Maes, F., Vandermeulen, D., Suetens, P.: Automated model-based tissue classification of MR images of the brain. IEEE Trans. Med. Imaging **18**(10), 897–908 (1999)
33. Van Leemput, K., Maes, F., Vandermeulen, D., Suetens, P.: A unifying framework for partial volume segmentation of brain MR images. IEEE Trans. Med. Imaging **22**(1), 105–119 (2003)
34. Winterburn, J.: A novel in vivo atlas of human hippocampal subfields using high-resolution 3T magnetic resonance imaging. NeuroImage **74**, 254–265 (2013)
35. Yushkevich, P.A.: Nearly automatic segmentation of hippocampal subfields in in vivo focal T2-weighted MRI. Neuroimage **53**(4), 1208–1224 (2010)
36. Zhang, Y., Brady, M., Smith, S.: Segmentation of brain MR images through a hidden Markov random field model and the expectation-maximization algorithm. IEEE Trans. Med. Imaging **20**(1), 45–57 (2001)
37. Zhao, A., Balakrishnan, G., Durand, F., Guttag, J., Dalca, A.V.: Data augmentation using learned transformations for one-shot medical image segmentation. In: Proceedings of the IEEE CVPR, pp. 8543–8553 (2019)

BDB-Net: Boundary-Enhanced Dual Branch Network for Whole Brain Segmentation

Yu Zhang[1], Bo Liu[1,2(✉)], Yinuo Wang[1], Zhengzhou Gao[1], Xiangzhi Bai[1,2(✉)], and Fugen Zhou[1,2]

[1] Image Processing Center, Beihang University, Beijing 100191, China
{bo.liu,jackybxz}@buaa.edu.cn
[2] Beijing Advanced Innovation Center for Biomedical Engineering,
Beihang University, Beijing 100083, China

Abstract. Whole brain segmentation is of large value for scientific research and clinical practice. Because of the long processing time of multi-atlas based segmentation methods, deep learning based methods have been extensively studied in recent years. Under the framework of the state-of-the-art method spatially localized atlas network tiles (SLANT), we proposed a novel Boundary-enhanced Dual Branch Network (BDB-Net) for whole brain segmentation. It contains a semantic segmentation branch and a boundary detection branch. Through delicate coupling of these branches, both the texture and shape information could be better utilized. Besides, we also designed a dual-heads architecture for the segmentation branch to incorporate more context information and reduce the information truncation. Furthermore, in view of the symmetricity of the brain, we proposed a new splitting pattern of the volumes and reduce the number of networks. The utility of these improvements was validated through experiments conducted on two dataset. The experimental results shown the proposed method could obtain better results using less training time (97% less) and testing time (50% less) compared with the SLANT.

Keywords: Whole brain segmentation · MR image · Convolutional neural network

1 Introduction

The segmentation of whole brain into more than 100 fine-grained regions plays a significant role in many brain analysis tasks, such as the research of neuroanatomy and the diagnose of brain disorders. Considering the large number of labels, manual segmentation is a challenging task involving tremendous manual labor. Accurate and automatic segmentation of whole brain is a long-standing desire but is not satisfactorily met yet. Before the era of deep learning, multi-atlas segmentation (MAS) was considered to be

Electronic supplementary material The online version of this chapter (https://doi.org/10.1007/978-3-030-59728-3_19) contains supplementary material, which is available to authorized users.

© Springer Nature Switzerland AG 2020
A. L. Martel et al. (Eds.): MICCAI 2020, LNCS 12267, pp. 188–197, 2020.
https://doi.org/10.1007/978-3-030-59728-3_19

the standard method due to its superior performance [1], but suffers from high computing complexity and could take more than 30 h to segment one image [2].

Recently, deep convolutional neural networks (DCNN) have been applied to this task. The scarcity of manually-traced training data and the limited GPU memory are two challenges for DCNN based methods. Initially, patch-based DCNN approaches were adopted to address the problem [3–6]. Then, 2D fully convolutional neural network (FCNN) were proposed to take advantage of global context information [7, 8]. In recent two years, 3D FCNNs methods were also proposed [2, 9, 10]. To cater for the limited GPU memory, the whole volume was usually split into overlapped subvolumes to process. Semi-supervised training on large number of auxiliary data was utilized to relieve the problem of limited training data [2, 9].

Among all methods, the spatially localized atlas network tiles (SLANT) method [2] is the most extensively validated method with state-of-the-art performance. In its best-performing form, SLANT split the image into 27 overlapped subvolumes on each of which a 3D U-Net was separately trained. Each 3D U-Nets was firstly pre-trained on 5111 auxiliary images segmented using MAS and then fine-tuned. The strategy of separately trained spatially localized networks and the utilization of auxiliary images largely improved the segmentation performance, however, they also lengthen the training and testing time. Let along the tremendous time required to prepare the auxiliary data, the training of SLANT already takes 27 days [2].

In this paper, we investigated a new method under the framework of spatially localized atlas network tiles. A novel Boundary-enhanced Dual Branch Network (BDB-Net) was proposed to segment each subvolume which contains two branches. One is a dual-heads encoder-decoder network for semantic segmentation and the other is a convolutional network for boundary detection. By delicately controlling the information interaction between these branches and using a multi-tasks loss function, the boundary branch helps to disentangle texture and shape representations, and improves segmentation accuracy. Besides, we designed a dual-heads architecture for the segmentation network which contains one encoding path and two decoding paths. Furthermore, in view of the symmetricity of the brain, we propose a new splitting pattern of the volumes and only use six subvolumes to cover all brain regions. The symmetrically distributed regions could be segmented with one network and the number of networks was largely reduced. In comparison of SLANT, our method could achieve better performance using much less training and testing time.

2 Method

2.1 The Proposed Method

Boundary-Enhanced Dual Branch Network (BDB-Net). Although CNNs have achieved promising result for image segmentation, it has been recently argued that current architectures may be suboptimal as it processes the shape and texture features simultaneously but is biased towards texture features [11]. Separate processing of shape and other features would increase weights of shape bias and improve the accuracy [12]. For this reason, we developed a boundary-enhanced dual branch network for the task of whole brain segmentation where there is rich shape information among more than

100 labels. Figure 1 shows the architecture of our BDB-Net, which consists of two main branches called dual-heads segmentation branch (B_{seg}) and boundary detection branch (B_{bd}). B_{seg} is an extension of U-Net [13] with one encoder path and dual decoder paths. The basic convolutional blocks of the encoder in each level of spatial resolution were replaced by a residual block [14] to diminish the influence of gradient vanishing problem. B_{bd} has a simpler structure with several residual blocks and boundary-gated blocks [12]. Feature maps in B_{bd} were with the full image resolution accounting for the thin trait of boundaries.

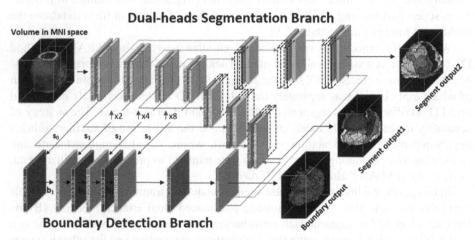

Fig. 1. BDB-Net with a dual-heads segmentation branch (B_{seg}) and a boundary detection branch (B_{bd})

At the front part of BDB-Net, features from the B_{seg} are infused into the B_{bd} continually in a multi-scale way after being upsampled into the full image resolution. The boundary-gated blocks were utilized to couple the features from B_{seg} and B_{bd} and to make the B_{bd} focus on the boundary of brain tissues. The boundary-gated blocks acted like feature filters which help the B_{bd} to focus on boundary-relevant information and de-emphasize the rest, which can be written as:

$$G(s_t, b_t) = \left[g(cat(s_t, b_t)) \otimes b_t \right] \oplus b_t \tag{1}$$

where s_t are the upsampled features from B_{seg} and b_t are the output of the previous residual block of the B_{bd}. $t \in \{0, 1, ..., m\}$ is the index for the t_{th} boundary-gated block, with m the number of boundary-gated blocks in the network. Given the inputs s_t and b_t, a function $g(\cdot)$ composed of two slightly different convolutional blocks is applied on their concatenation to compute an attention map A. A is applied on the feature b_t through Hadamard product $\otimes$ to obtain the boundary-related information needed to be focused on. Finally, an element-wise addition $\oplus$ is utilized to increase the weight of relevant regions. There are three intermediate layers in our BDB-Net. At the end part of BDB-Net, the highlighted boundary information is appended back to B_{seg} to refine the boundary of brain tissues.

In order to cope with the limitation of GPU memory, the whole brain MRI is split into subvolumes, which cuts off many brain tissues located at the edge and causes feature truncation. To mitigate this issue, we integrated a dual-heads strategy into B_{seg} which took two neighboring subvolumes as input and had two output decoding branches. Therefore, the overlapped regions between two neighboring subvolumes are kept for unbroken feature extraction of those "middle" tissues. And the number of localized networks were also reduced.

A New Splitting Pattern. The brain has a good symmetricity with many paired regions with similar shape and texture. Therefore, we can use less subvolumes to cover all brain regions after flipping the right hemisphere to the left (or vice versa). In this way, not only the number of training data is doubled, but the number of networks is also greatly reduced. In view of this, we proposed a new splitting pattern of the volumes by using eight subvolumes to cover all brain regions, as shown in Fig. 2. Though only six subvolumes are minimally required, the pieces 7 and 8 located at the middle of the anterior-posterior axis are also included to enable the majority voting for center part of the brain. With the BDB-Net which takes two subvolumes as input, only four BDB-Nets are needed to segment the whole brain.

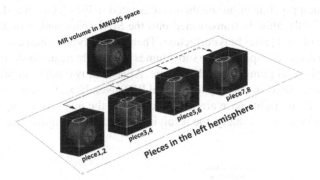

Fig. 2. The proposed new splitting pattern of subvolumes

It needs to be noted that the number of subvolumes trades off the accuracy and efficiency. As the final result is the majority voting of subvolumes, using more subvolumes usually could improve the accuracy, just as shown by the AssemblyNet which contained an assembly of 125 U-nets [10]. However, more subvolumes mean more training and testing time. Unlike AssemblyNet, we took a different path by using less networks and resorting to the high capacity of the BDB-Net to ensure the accuracy.

2.2 Training Loss Function

There are three outputs in BDB-Net, two for B_{seg} and one for B_{bd}. Three loss functions are optimized together to find the optimum solution. Our multi-tasks loss function was defined as

$$Loss = \lambda_1 Loss_{bound} + \lambda_2 \left(Loss_{seg1} + Loss_{seg2} \right) \tag{2}$$

in which $Loss_{bound}$ denotes a weighted cross entropy loss function to compare the predicted against the ground truth boundary voxel-by-voxel:

$$Loss_{bound} = -\sum_{j=1}^{m} \left[\beta \cdot y_j \log y_j + (1 - \beta)(1 - y_j) \log(1 - \hat{y}_j) \right] \quad (3)$$

where $\hat{y}_j \in [0, 1]$ stands for the probability that belong to boundary for the j_{th} voxel and $y_j \in \{0, 1\}$ means the truth label of the current voxel. In view of the severe imbalance between boundary and non-boundary voxels, we follow [15, 16] to make use of β as a coefficient to weight boundary voxels. β equals the ratio of non-boundary voxels to the whole input volume.

We use the negative mean Dice similarity coefficient (DSC) loss function to make the outputs of segmentation branch be closer to the manual delineations. Two hyper-parameters λ_1 and λ_2 are configured to weight the boundary loss and the segmentation loss.

2.3   The Segmentation Pipeline

The segmentation pipeline of our method is illustrated in Fig. 3. Given a 3D brain image as input, it is firstly affinely transformed into the MNI space and normalized into the intensity range of [0, 1] after bias correction. Then, the 3D brain volume is divided into 8 subvolumes in each hemisphere. The subvolumes in the right hemisphere are flipped into the left hemisphere aligning the middle plane. After that, two adjacent pieces from the left or right space are segmented by the trained BDB-Net. Next, the segmentation results of subvolumes in the right space are flipped back and the majority voting is performed to fuse these subvolumes. Finally, the result is restored to its original space.

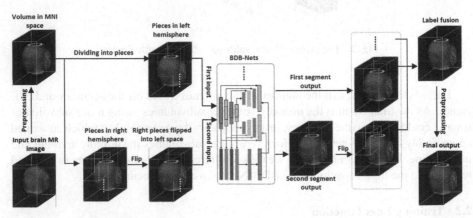

Fig. 3. The segmentation pipeline of our method.

3   Experiments

3.1   Datasets

Two datasets were used in this work.

MICCAI dataset: the dataset provided by the MICCAI 2012 Challenge on Multi-Atlas Labeling, which contains 35 T1w MR scans with manual labels delineated according to BrainCOLOR protocol.

OASIS dataset: contains 40 MR scans of 20 subjects from the OASIS data [17]. Each subject was scanned twice with different parameters and the two scans were separately labeled.

We selected 30 scans from MICCAI dataset for training and test on the remaining 5 scans and the 40 scans of the OASIS dataset. The results were obtained via two-folded cross-validation.

3.2   Implement Details

Our method is implemented in PyTorch framework under Linux Ubuntu 16.4 (64 Bit) operating system on a powerful workstation equipped with two Intel® Xeom™ E5 2630V4 CPUs (2.20 GHz) and four NVIDIA GTX 1080 Ti graphic cards with the memory of 11G RAM. The networks were optimized by Adam optimizer with a fixed learning rate of 10^{-4}. The λ_1 and λ_2 were chosen experimentally to 1 and 0.5.

We also utilized a neighbor transfer learning strategy to share knowledge between neighboring networks and facilitate the training. At beginning, the first network was trained from scratch for 100 epochs with all the layers initialized using the Xavier algorithm. Afterwards, the subsequent networks were initialized using parameters of the best model of its neighboring trained network. In this way, compared with the first network, it takes 70% less time for each network to sufficiently converge, which saves a lot of training time.

3.3   Experimental Design

We conducted a series of experiments to analyze the utility of different parts of our BDB-Net, which are listed in Table 1. Under the proposed splitting pattern, we first investigated the segmentation branch with only one output, i.e. the residual U-net (R-U-net). Then the dual-heads segmentation branch without boundary enhancement was tested (R-U-net$_{dh}$). These variants were compared with the whole BDB-net.

Three quantitative metrics were employed to evaluate the performance. The first is the widely used Dice similarity coefficient (DSC). The second is the Volume Overlap Error (VOE) which measures the overlay error between the predicted segmentation and the ground truth. Furthermore, we include mean Average Symmetric Surface Distance (mASD) to measure the symmetric surface distance.

Table 1. Experimental design

Conditions	With dual heads	With B_{bd}
R-U-net	×	×
R-U-net$_{dh}$	✓	×
BDB-Net	✓	✓

4 Results

Table 2 shows the results for various experiments. After changing the backbone network from single head to dual heads with larger input region, there was a gain for all metrics. With the enhancement of boundary information, the results were further improved and compared favorably with SLANT, the results of which were computed use the Docker provided by Huo et al. [2]. These results validated the utility of the dual-heads architecture and the boundary enhancement strategy. The results for the OASIS dataset were consistent. The proposed BDB-Net achieved a better result with a large improvement of VOE and ASD. The improvement of our method over R-U-net$_{dh}$ and SLANT was statistically significant with $p < 0.05$ on OASIS dataset. ROI-wise DICE scores were provided in the supplementary material.

Table 2. Quantitative results of different methods.

Methods	MICCAI (5 test images)			OASIS (40 test images)		
	DSC [%]	VOE [%]	mASD [mm]	DSC [%]	VOE [%]	mASD [mm]
R-U-net	76.83	36.36	0.448	73.03	41.01	0.485
R-U-net$_{dh}$	77.81	35.08	0.412	76.44	37.25	0.396
BDB-Net	**78.87**	**33.40**	**0.393**	**78.92**	**33.97**	**0.381**
SLANT [2]	78.15	34.64	0.410	77.60	39.09	0.461

Figure 4 shows an example of the segmentation on a coronal slice and an enlarged ROI, in which the SLANT failed to segment the right SMC supplementary motor cortex while BDB-net did well.

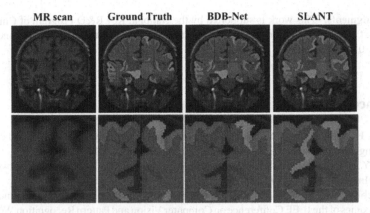

Fig. 4. Visualization of the segmentation on a coronary slice for one test image from the MICCAI dataset.

Table 3 compares the training and testing time for different methods. The training of SLANT takes more than 27 days because of the pre-training on a large cohort of auxiliary data. And the testing time is about 15 min. The proposed method did not use pre-training and only involved four networks. Therefore, the training and testing time were greatly reduced. The training time is approximate 50 times less than SLANT and it is two times faster to segment an image.

Table 3. Summary of computational time

Methods	Number of networks	Number of training images	Training time	Testing time
R-U-net	8	30	13.57 h	8.88 min
R-U-net$_{dh}$	4	30	9.28 h	7.02 min
BDB-Net	4	30	14.57 h	7.05 min
SLANT [2]	27	5111 + 45	678 h	15 min

5 Conclusion

In this paper, we proposed a novel Boundary-enhanced Dual Branch Network (BDB-Net) and a new splitting pattern of the brain under the framework of spatially localized atlas network tiles [2]. As shown in the experiments, the proposed boundary detection branch and the dual-heads architecture helped to improve the segmentation accuracy. Compared with the state-of-the-art method SLANT, our method could achieve a higher accuracy using much less training and testing time.

Acknowledgments. This work is supported by the National Key R&D Program of China under Grant No. 2018YFA0704101 and the National Natural Science Foundation of China under Grant Nos. 61601012.

References

1. Wang, H., Yushkevich, P.A.: Multi-atlas segmentation with joint label fusion and corrective learning—an open source implementation. Front. Neuroinf. **7**, 27 (2013)
2. Huo, Y., et al.: 3D whole brain segmentation using spatially localized atlas network tiles. NeuroImage **194**, 105–119 (2019)
3. de Brebisson, A., Montana, G.: Deep neural networks for anatomical brain segmentation. In: Proceedings of the IEEE Conference on Computer Vision and Pattern Recognition Workshops, pp. 20–28 (2015)
4. Mehta, R., Majumdar, A., Sivaswamy, J.: BrainSegNet: a convolutional neural network architecture for automated segmentation of human brain structures. J. Med. Imaging (Bellingham) **4**, 024003 (2017)
5. Wachinger, C., Reuter, M., Klein, T.: DeepNAT: deep convolutional neural network for segmenting neuroanatomy. NeuroImage **170**, 434–445 (2018)
6. Nguyen, D.M., Vu, H.T., Ung, H.Q., Nguyen, B.T.: 3D-brain segmentation using deep neural network and Gaussian mixture model. In: 2017 IEEE Winter Conference on Applications of Computer Vision (WACV), Santa Rosa, pp. 815–824. IEEE (2017)
7. Roy, A.G., Conjeti, S., Sheet, D., Katouzian, A., Navab, N., Wachinger, C.: Error corrective boosting for learning fully convolutional networks with limited data. In: Descoteaux, M., Maier-Hein, L., Franz, A., Jannin, P., Collins, D., Duchesne, S. (eds.) International Conference on Medical Image Computing and Computer-Assisted Intervention. LNCS, vol. 10435, pp. 231–239. Springer, Cham (2017). https://doi.org/10.1007/978-3-319-66179-7_27
8. Ganaye, P.-A., Sdika, M., Benoit-Cattin, H.: Semi-supervised learning for segmentation under semantic constraint. In: Frangi, A., Schnabel, J., Davatzikos, C., Alberola-López, C., Fichtinger, G. (eds.) Medical Image Computing and Computer Assisted Intervention – MICCAI 2018. LNCS, vol. 11072, pp. 595–602. Springer, Cham (2018). https://doi.org/10.1007/978-3-030-00931-1_68
9. Zhao, Y.-X., Zhang, Y.-M., Song, M., Liu, C.-L.: Multi-view semi-supervised 3D whole brain segmentation with a self-ensemble network. In: Shen, D., et al. (eds.) MICCAI 2019. LNCS, vol. 11766, pp. 256–265. Springer, Cham (2019). https://doi.org/10.1007/978-3-030-32248-9_29
10. Coupé, P., et al.: AssemblyNet: a novel deep decision-making process for whole brain MRI segmentation. In: Shen, D., et al. (eds.) MICCAI 2019. LNCS, vol. 11766, pp. 466–474. Springer, Cham (2019). https://doi.org/10.1007/978-3-030-32248-9_52
11. Geirhos, R., Rubisch, P., Michaelis, C., Bethge, M., Wichmann, F.A., Brendel, W.: ImageNet-trained CNNs are biased towards texture; increasing shape bias improves accuracy and robustness. arXiv preprint arXiv:1811.12231 (2018)
12. Takikawa, T., Acuna, D., Jampani, V., Fidler, S.: Gated-SCNN: gated shape CNNs for semantic segmentation. In: Proceedings of the IEEE International Conference on Computer Vision, pp. 5229–5238 (2019)
13. Ronneberger, O., Fischer, P., Brox, T.: U-net: convolutional networks for biomedical image segmentation. In: Navab, N., Hornegger, J., Wells, W., Frangi, A. (eds.) International Conference on Medical Image Computing and Computer-Assisted Intervention. LNCS, vol. 9351, pp. 234–241. Springer, Cham (2015). https://doi.org/10.1007/978-3-319-24574-4_28

14. He, K., Zhang, X., Ren, S., Sun, J.: Deep residual learning for image recognition. In: Proceedings of the IEEE Conference on Computer Vision and Pattern Recognition, pp. 770–778 (2016)

15. Yu, Z., Feng, C., Liu, M.-Y., Ramalingam, S.: CASENet: deep category-aware semantic edge detection. In: Proceedings of the IEEE Conference on Computer Vision and Pattern Recognition, pp. 5964–5973 (2017)

16. Xie, S., Tu, Z.: Holistically-nested edge detection. Int. J. Comput. Vision **125**, 3–18 (2017)

17. Marcus, D.S., Wang, T.H., Parker, J., Csernansky, J.G., Morris, J.C., Buckner, R.L.: Open Access Series of Imaging Studies (OASIS): cross-sectional MRI data in young, middle aged, nondemented, and demented older adults. J. Cogn. Neurosci. **19**, 1498–1507 (2007)

Brain Age Estimation from MRI Using a Two-Stage Cascade Network with Ranking Loss

Ziyang Liu[1], Jian Cheng[2,3], Haogang Zhu[2,3], Jicong Zhang[1,2], and Tao Liu[1,2(✉)]

[1] Beijing Advanced Innovation Center for Biomedical Engineering, The School of Biological Science and Medical Engineering, Beihang University, Beijing, China
{liuziyang1106,jian_cheng,tao.liu}@buaa.edu.cn
[2] Beijing Advanced Innovation Center for Big Data-Based Precision Medicine, Beijing, China
[3] School of Computer Science and Engineering, Beihang University, Beijing, China

Abstract. As age increases, human brains will be aged, and people tend to experience cognitive decline with a higher risk of neuro-degenerative disease and dementia. Recently, it was reported that deep neural networks, e.g., 3D convolutional neural networks (CNN), are able to predict chronological age accurately in healthy people from their T1-weighted magnetic resonance images (MRI). The predicted age, called as "brain age" or "brain predicted age", could be a biomarker of the brain ageing process. In this paper, we propose a novel 3D convolutional network, called as two-stage-age-net (TSAN), for brain age estimation from T1-weighted MRI data. Compared with the state-of-the-art CNN by Cole et al., TSAN has several improvements: 1) TSAN uses a two-stage cascade architecture, where the first network is to estimate a discretized age range, then the second network is to further estimate the brain age more accurately; 2) Besides using the traditional mean square error (MSE) loss between chronological and estimated ages, TSAN considers two additional novel ranking losses, based on paired samples and a batch of samples, for regularizing the training process; 3) TSAN uses densely connected paths to combine feature maps with different scales; 4) TSAN considers gender labels as input features for the network, considering brains of male and female age differently. The proposed TSAN was validated in three public datasets. The experiments showed that TSAN could provide accurate brain age estimation in healthy subjects, yielding a mean absolute error (MAE) of 2.428, and a Pearson's correlation coefficient (PCC) of 0.985, between the estimated and the chronological ages.

Keywords: Brain age · Two-stage cascade network · Ranking loss

---

Co-first authors—Z. Liu and J. Cheng contributed equally.

© Springer Nature Switzerland AG 2020
A. L. Martel et al. (Eds.): MICCAI 2020, LNCS 12267, pp. 198–207, 2020.
https://doi.org/10.1007/978-3-030-59728-3_20

1   Introduction

With the world population ageing, the burden of age-related cognitive functional decline and disease is increasing [1]. However, the aging process is biologically complex [2], and despite the widespread negative effects of ageing, there are significant differences in the timing of aging effects. Ageing causes significant changes in brain structure and function. Brain morphometric pattern analysis has been increasingly investigated to identify age-related imaging biomarkers from structural magnetic resonance imaging (MRI) [3].

Using structural or functional neuroimaging data, it is now possible to estimate chronological age accurately in healthy people [4–6]. The estimated age is called as *"brain age"* or *"brain-predicted age"* which has potential to be used as a biomarker to investigate the brain ageing process, neuro-degeneration and age-associated brain diseases [4–6]. Recently, deep neural networks offer a new way of statistical modelling in neuroimaging and brain age estimation [7,8] which can formulate a massively high-dimensional regression model, fitting large 3D T1 images as inputs to predict chronological ages as scalar outputs. A recent work by Cole et al. [7] trained a 3D convolutional neural network (CNN) on T1 images with 2001 subjects, and provided a state-of-the-art [6] result for this task, where the Mean Absolute Error (MAE) of the brain age estimation was 4.65 years. However, CNN in [7] has several limitations: 1) It dose not take full advantage of the features from different scales. 2) CNN in [7] just minimizes the MAE loss between the chronological age and the brain-predicted age, without considering any ranking loss between a set of chronological and predicted ages. 3) It ignores gender labels of MR images, while brain ages differently between males and females.

In this paper, we propose a novel deep neural network architecture with MSE and ranking losses for brain age estimation. The main contributions of this paper are:

- We propose a two-stage cascade network architecture, called as two-stage-age-net (TSAN), where the first network is to roughly estimate the correct discretized age, and the second refine network is to further predict more accurate age by using the discretized predicted age from the first stage.
- Besides traditional mean square error (MSE), we consider two ranking losses to regularize the training of TSAN. For two samples, the first loss is defined as the MSE between the chronological age difference and estimated age difference of the two samples. For a set of samples, the second loss is defined based on Spearman's rank correlation coefficient (SRCC) of the true rank of ages and the estimated rank of ages.
- In the first and second stages, inspired by DenseNet [9], TSAN uses a novel scaled dense (ScaledDense) net architecture, which contains densely connected paths to combine feature maps with different scales.
- TSAN considers gender labels as input features for the network, considering gender is a known factor for MRI data.

2   Proposed Method

Two-Stage-Age-Net (TSAN): A sketch map of the proposed TSAN is shown in Fig. 1. The first-stage network is trained to roughly estimate the brain age from an input MR image and a known gender label. Then, the second-stage refine network is trained to further estimate more accurate brain age based on the input MR image, gender label and discretized predicted age from the first-stage network. The idea of cascade network regression has been widely used in computer vision [10].

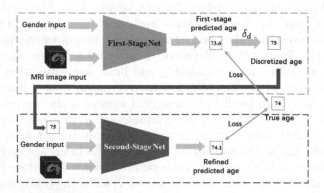

Fig. 1. Two-Stage-Age-Net (TSAN). The first-stage network is to roughly estimate a discretized age, and the second-stage refine network is to further predict more accurate age by using the discretized predicted age from the first stage.

Our contribution in TSAN is to use the *discretized* predicted age from the first-stage network as an input of the second-stage network, not the original predicted age. In this way, the first-stage network aims to estimate discretized number of age values, which is easier than estimating continuous age values in $\mathbb{R}^1$. As shown in Fig. 1, δ_d is used to discretize the age range in $\mathbb{R}^1$. Let y be the true chronological age, and $\hat{y}$ be the predicted brain age by the first-stage network. Then the discretized predicted age $D(\hat{y})$ is

$$D(\hat{y}) = \begin{cases} \text{Round}(\frac{\hat{y}}{\delta_d}) \cdot \delta_d, & \text{if } \delta_d > 0 \\ \hat{y}, & \text{if } \delta_d = 0 \end{cases} \tag{1}$$

where $\text{Round}(\hat{y})$ is to round $\hat{y}$ to the nearest integer multiple of δ_d. Thus, if $\delta_d = 5$, then $D(73.6) = 75$. See Fig. 1. If $\delta_d = 0$, then the discretized predicted age equals the predicted age itself, i.e., $D(\hat{y}) = \hat{y}$. Thus, the discretization process with δ_d is introduced as a hyper-parameter to tune the degree of discretization.

Theorem 1 shows that the discretized predicted age $D(\hat{y})$ is a good approximation of the chronological age y and also the true discretized age $D(y)$, if we set $\delta_d > |y - \hat{y}|$. The proof of this theorem is trivial, considering discretization the discretization in Eq. (1) is performed in $\mathbb{R}^1$.

Theorem 1 (Discretization Approximation). *Let y be the true chronological age, and $\hat{y}$ be the predicted brain age. Let $\epsilon = |y - \hat{y}|$ denote the absolute error (AE), and δ_d denote the discretization parameter shown in Eq. (1). If we set $\delta_d \geq \epsilon$, then we have: 1) $|D(y) - D(\hat{y})| = 0$, or δ_d; 2) $|D(\hat{y}) - y| \leq \frac{1}{2}\delta_d + \epsilon$.*

Fig. 2 (B) and (C) show the detailed first- and second-stage networks. In both networks, the input gender label is coded as a 2 dimensional one-hot vector, and is concatenated with feature maps after global average pooling by using Fully Connected (FC) layers. In the second-stage network, the discretized predicted age is used as an input by using FC layers. Based on Theorem 1, the second-stage network only needs to estimate a residual age between chronological age y and discretized predicted age $D(\hat{y})$, which results in the final predicted age by summing the discretized predicted age from the first-stage network.

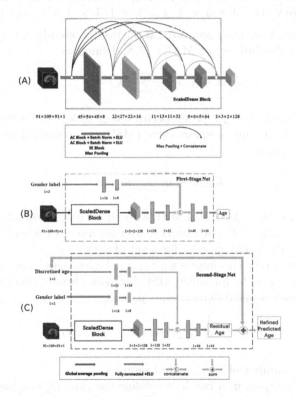

Fig. 2. Detailed architectures of TSAN. (**A**): ScaledDense block, which concatenates feature maps from different scales by using pooling and concatenation. (**B**): The first-stage network, with an MR image and a gender label as its inputs. (**C**): The second-stage network, with an MR image, a gender label, and the discretized predicted age by the first-stage network as its inputs.

ScaledDense Block: The first- and second-stage networks in Fig. 2 (B) and (C) use a novel CNN block, called ScaledDense block, to obtain feature maps from input MR images. The ScaledDense block is described in Fig. 2 (A), which is inspired with DenseNet [9]. The densely connected paths in dense block in DenseNet [9] connects feature maps from preceding layers with the same scale size. While in ScaledDense block, the densely connected paths are used to concatenate feature maps from preceding layers with different scales by using pooling plus concatenation. Each layer in ScaledDense block has direct access to the gradients from the loss function and the original input image, leading to an implicit deep supervision and better parameter efficiency.

Note that different non-linear transformations could be used for layers in ScaledDense block, just like DenseNet. Here we design the transform in each later as two Asymmetric Convolution (AC) blocks [11] with batch norm [12] and the Exponential Linear Unit (Elu) activation function, followed by Squeeze-and-Excitation (SE) block [13] and max pooling. We revise AC block for MR images with four 3D Conv (i.e., $3 \times 3 \times 3, 3 \times 1 \times 1, 1 \times 3 \times 1$, and $1 \times 1 \times 3$).

Loss Functions: For brain age estimation task, a standard loss function for training is mean absolute error (MAE) [7,8] defined as

$$\mathcal{L}_{\text{MAE}} = \frac{1}{N} \sum_i |y_i - \hat{y}_i| \tag{2}$$

where N is the batch size, y represents chronological age and $\hat{y}$ stands predicted brain age. Considering mean square error (MSE) loss penalizes more than MAE when MAE > 1, we use

$$\mathcal{L}_{\text{MSE}} = \frac{1}{N} \sum_i (y_i - \hat{y}_i)^2 \tag{3}$$

for training TSAN. Both MSE and MAE are defined on individual samples. However, when comparing different samples, we may also care about the difference between ages, or the ranking order for a set of ages.

Therefore, for two given samples with chronological ages y_i and y_j, we propose the age difference loss to minimize MSE between chronological age difference $y_i - y_j$ and predicted age difference $\hat{y}_i - \hat{y}_j$, i.e.,

$$\mathcal{L}_{\text{AD}} = \frac{1}{N_p} \sum_{(i,j)} ((y_i - y_j) - (\hat{y}_i - \hat{y}_j))^2 \tag{4}$$

where N_p is the number of (i, j) paired samples.

For a set of samples in a batch, we define the ranking loss based on Spearman's rank correlation coefficient (SRCC)[1], i.e.,

$$\mathcal{L}_{\text{r}} = 1 - r_s = \frac{6 \sum_i (\text{Rank}(y_i) - \text{Rank}(\hat{y}_i))^2}{N(N^2 - 1)}, \tag{5}$$

where r_s is SRCC, and $\text{Rank}(y_i)$ is the rank order of y_i. The rank operator in Eq. (5) is not differentiable, which results in problems to optimize TSAN via gradient descent based optimizer.

---

[1] https://en.wikipedia.org/wiki/Spearman's-rank-correlation-coefficient.

Table 1. Population characteristics of dataset.

Data set	N_{img}	Age range	Mean age $\pm$ SD	Gender proportion (male/female)
ADNI	1020	60–93	77.4 $\pm$ 5.08	531/489
OASIS	2926	18–98	63.9 $\pm$ 22.72	1157/1769
PAC-2019	2640	17–90	35.9 $\pm$ 16.21	1237/1403
Combined data	6586	17–98	54.7 $\pm$ 24.44	2925/3661

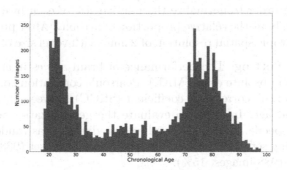

Fig. 3. Histogram of the chronological age of the combined dataset.

Here we use SoDeep [14] to pre-train a differentiable network S to approximate the rank operator function by using supervised learning on simulated ranking data. Then, after replacing $\text{Rank}(\hat{y}_i)$ with $S(\hat{y}_i)$, $\mathcal{L}_r$ is differentiable with respect to $\hat{y}$, and TSAN can be trained using this differentiable proxy of $\mathcal{L}_r$. Note that $\mathcal{L}_r$ is the ranking loss based on SRCC, and the age difference loss $\mathcal{L}_{AD}$ could be also seen a ranking loss, which optimizes both the sign and the magnitude of the age difference.

Thus, the total loss for training two networks is

$$\mathcal{L} = \mathcal{L}_{\text{MSE}} + \lambda_1 \mathcal{L}_{\text{AD}} + \lambda_2 \mathcal{L}_r \tag{6}$$

where λ_1 and λ_2 are regularization parameters. Note that if the network is trained to be optimal with $\mathcal{L}_{\text{MSE}} = 0$, then the other two losses $\mathcal{L}_{\text{AD}}$ and $\mathcal{L}_r$ also equal zero. The proposed two ranking losses are used to regularize the MSE loss.

3   Experiments

Datasets and Data Preprocessing: Three public datasets were used in experiments, including the Alzheimer's Disease Neuroimaging Initiative (ADNI) [15], the Open Access Series of Imaging Studies (OASIS) [16], and Predictive Analytics Competition 2019 (PAC-2019)[2]. We selected the healthy elders among them

---

[2] https://www.photon-ai.com/pac2019.

to form our cohort. Note that ADNI dataset only has elders, PAC-2019 dataset has much more young people than elders. In order to make the age distribution in the data set as even as possible, we combined the three data sets for experiments. This cohort consists total 6586 T1-weighted MRI images. The detailed demographic information of each dataset is shown in Table 1, and the histogram of the age of the combined dataset is shown in Fig. 3.

All data were acquired at either 1.5T or 3T T1-weighed MRI. We processed all MR images via a standard pipeline by FSL 5.10^3 [17–19], including nonlinear registration into the standard MNI space, brain extraction and voxel value normalization in order to normalize the relative size of each brain, without losing information about the relative proportion of atrophy. After preprocessing, all images have isotropic spatial resolution of $2\,\mathrm{mm}^3$ with voxel size of $91 \times 109 \times 91$.

Experimental Setting: The performance of brain age estimation was evaluated by the mean absolute error (MAE), Pearson's correlation coefficient (PCC) and Spearman's rank correlation coefficient (SRCC) between the brain age and the chronological age. In order to evaluate the generalization ability and the robustness of a specific model, the combination dataset was randomly split into 3 sets: the training set (4610 images, 70%), the validation set (988 images, 15%), and the test set (988 images, 15%).

In order to compare our proposed TSAN model with the state-of-the-art method, we first implemented and trained the CNN model in [7,8]. For the first-stage network in TSAN, ADAM optimizer [20] was used to minimize the loss, with the initial learning rate = 0.001, and the batch size of 32. The He initialization strategy [21] was used to initialize the trainable parameters, and we also considered L_2 weight regularization of 5×10^{-4}. To train the proposed TSAN with two stage networks, first, we trained the first-stage network to achieve its best performance. And we chose $\delta_d = 5$ based on Theorem 1, considering that the MAE of the first-stage network is less than 5. Then, we fixed the first-stage network, and only train the second-stage refine network.

Considering the predicted age of the first-stage network is already very closed to the chronological age, we set a small initial learning rate of 10^{-5}. Moreover, in order to compare results of TSAN with different loss functions, we trained TSAN with $\mathcal{L}_{\mathrm{MSE}}$, and with the total loss $\mathcal{L}$ in Eq. (6). We set the regularization weight $\lambda_1 = \lambda_2 = 10$ and the number of paired samples $N_p = 40$. At last, we trained TSAN with the total loss $\mathcal{L}$ three times with three different random initialization, and then ensembled these three models by averaging their predicted ages.

All models were implemented using Pytorch 1.3.0 and were trained on four GPUs (Nvidia TITAN Xp). The learning rate was reduced to a half if the training loss function no longer decreased within 5 consecutive epochs. Furthermore, to reduce the risk of overfitting, data augmentation was performed by applying a spatial transformation to training data.

Results: Figure 4 shows scatter plots of predicted brain ages by different models against chronological ages in the test data. The detailed evaluation criteria

---

^{3} https://fsl.fmrib.ox.ac.uk/fsl/fslwiki/FSL.

(MAE, STD of AE, PCC, SRCC) for the predicted age by different models are summarized in Table 2. Table 2 demonstrates that compared with CNN model in [7], all proposed models generally yield better results in brain age prediction task. The first-stage network with AC and SE blocks in Fig. 2 and the total loss $\mathcal{L}$ in (6) has better results, compared with the network using Conv block and the traditional MSE loss. The proposed ranking loss and age difference loss were playing an important role in model optimization. TSAN with two stage networks performs better than just using the first-stage network. The ensemble TSAN yields the best result with the lowest MAE (2.428), STD of AE (3.470),

Table 2. Brain age estimation criteria by different models in test data.

Model	Loss function	MAE $\pm$ STD	PCC	SRCC
CNN in [7]	$\mathcal{L}_{MSE}$	4.060 $\pm$ 4.625	0.967	0.959
First-stage net with Conv	$\mathcal{L}_{MSE}$	3.666 $\pm$ 4.661	0.970	0.964
First-stage net with AC + SE	$\mathcal{L}_{MSE}$	3.237 $\pm$ 3.930	0.978	0.970
First-stage net with AC + SE	Total loss $\mathcal{L}$	3.052 $\pm$ 3.614	0.981	0.972
TSAN	Total loss $\mathcal{L}$	2.629 $\pm$ 3.569	0.983	0.975
Ensemble TSAN	**Total loss $\mathcal{L}$**	**2.428 $\pm$ 3.470**	**0.985**	**0.977**

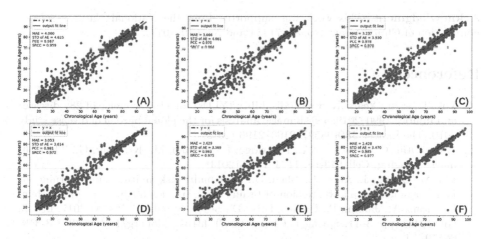

Fig. 4. Scatter plots of predicted brain ages by different models against chronological ages in the test data. (**A**): CNN in [7] with MSE loss function. (**B**): The first-stage network with Conv block and MSE loss function. (**C**): The first-stage network with AC block + SE block, and the MSE loss $\mathcal{L}_{MSE}$. (**D**): The first-stage network with AC block + SE block, and the total loss $\mathcal{L}$ in Eq. (6). (**E**): TSAN with the total loss $\mathcal{L}$ in Eq. (6). (**F**): Ensemble TSAN with the total loss $\mathcal{L}$ in Eq. (6). In all subfigures, the blue dashed lines indicate the ideal estimation model $y = x$, and the red lines are the linearly fitted line of the predicted brain age against with chronological age. MAE: mean absolute error, STD of AE: the standard deviation of absolute error, PCC: pearson's correlation coefficient, SRCC: Spearman's rank correlation coefficient.

the largest PCC and SRCC. Note that the MAE by ensemble TSAN is lower than the winner of PAC-2019 (MAE = 2.90), although we did not use the test data of PAC-2019, since the chronological age label was not released. In addition, due to the unbalanced age distribution in the dataset, as shown in Fig. 3, the number of people in the dataset in the range of 40–60 years is relatively small, which results in a larger prediction error in this range.

4   Conclusion

In this paper, we propose a novel neural network architecture, called as two-stage-age-net (TSAN), for brain age estimation from T1-weighted MRI data. Compared with the state-of-the-art CNN method by Cole et al. [7], TSAN uses a two-stage cascade architecture, where the second-stage network is to refine the estimated age based on the discretized output of the first-stage network. In both stages, TSAN uses a ScaledDense block to concatenate feature maps from different scales, and considers both MR images and gender labels as inputs of the networks. Two ranking losses are introduced to regularize the training of the network. The proposed method was validated using three datasets, yielding an MAE of 2.428, and a Pearson's correlation coefficient (PCC) of 0.985, between the estimated and the chronological ages.

Acknowledgment. This work was supported from the National Natural Science Foundation of China (Grant No. 81871434 and No. 61971017).

References

1. Vos, T., et al.: Years lived with disability (YLDs) for 1160 sequelae of 289 diseases and injuries 1990–2010: a systematic analysis for the global burden of disease study 2010. The Lancet **380**(9859), 2163–2196 (2012)
2. López-Otín, C., Blasco, M.A., Partridge, L., Serrano, M., Kroemer, G.: The hallmarks of aging. Cell **153**(6), 1194–1217 (2013)
3. Liu, M., Zhang, J., Adeli, E., Shen, D.: Deep multi-task multi-channel learning for joint classification and regression of brain status. In: Descoteaux, M., Maier-Hein, L., Franz, A., Jannin, P., Collins, D.L., Duchesne, S. (eds.) MICCAI 2017. LNCS, vol. 10435, pp. 3–11. Springer, Cham (2017). https://doi.org/10.1007/978-3-319-66179-7_1
4. Franke, K., Ziegler, G., Klöppel, S., Gaser, C., Initiative, A.D.N., et al.: Estimating the age of healthy subjects from T1-weighted MRI scans using kernel methods: exploring the influence of various parameters. Neuroimage **50**(3), 883–892 (2010)
5. Dosenbach, N.U.F., et al.: Prediction of individual brain maturity using fMRI. Science **329**(5997), 1358–1361 (2010)
6. Cole, J.H., Franke, K.: Predicting age using neuroimaging: innovative brain ageing biomarkers. Trends Neurosci. **40**(12), 681–690 (2017)
7. Cole, J.H., et al.: Predicting brain age with deep learning from raw imaging data results in a reliable and heritable biomarker. NeuroImage **163**, 115–124 (2017)
8. Cole, J.H., et al.: Brain age predicts mortality. Mol. Psychiatry **23**(5), 1385 (2018)

9. Huang, G., Liu, Z., Van Der Maaten, L., Weinberger, K.Q.: Densely connected convolutional networks. In: Proceedings of the IEEE Conference on Computer Vision and Pattern Recognition, pp. 4700–4708 (2017)
10. Sun, Y., Wang, X., Tang, X.: Deep convolutional network cascade for facial point detection. In: Proceedings of the IEEE Conference on Computer Vision and Pattern Recognition, pp. 3476–3483 (2013)
11. Ding, X., Guo, Y., Ding, G., Han, J.: ACNet: strengthening the kernel skeletons for powerful CNN via asymmetric convolution blocks. In: Proceedings of the IEEE International Conference on Computer Vision, pp. 1911–1920 (2019)
12. Ioffe, S., Szegedy, C.: Batch normalization: accelerating deep network training by reducing internal covariate shift. arXiv preprint arXiv:1502.03167 (2015)
13. Hu, J., Shen, L., Sun, G.: Squeeze-and-excitation networks. In: Proceedings of the IEEE Conference on Computer Vision and Pattern Recognition, pp. 7132–7141 (2018)
14. Engilberge, M., Chevallier, L., Pérez, P., Cord, M.: SoDeep: a sorting deep net to learn ranking loss surrogates. In: Proceedings of the IEEE Conference on Computer Vision and Pattern Recognition, pp. 10792–10801 (2019)
15. Jack Jr., C.R., et al.: The Alzheimer's disease neuroimaging initiative (ADNI): MRI methods. J. Magn. Reson. Imaging 27(4), 685–691 (2008). An Official Journal of the International Society for Magnetic Resonance in Medicine
16. Marcus, D.S., Fotenos, A.F., Csernansky, J.G., Morris, J.C., Buckner, R.L.: Open access series of imaging studies: longitudinal MRI data in nondemented and demented older adults. J. Cogn. Neurosci. 22(12), 2677–2684 (2010)
17. Smith, S.M., et al.: Advances in functional and structural MR image analysis and implementation as FSL. Neuroimage 23, S208–S219 (2004)
18. Woolrich, M.W., et al.: Bayesian analysis of neuroimaging data in FSL. Neuroimage 45(1), S173–S186 (2009)
19. Jenkinson, M., Beckmann, C.F., Behrens, T.E.J., Woolrich, M.W., Smith, S.M.: FSL. Neuroimage 62(2), 782–790 (2012)
20. Kingma, D., Ba, J.: Adam: A method for stochastic optimization. arXiv preprint arXiv:1412.6980 (2014)
21. He, K., Zhang, X., Ren, S., Sun, J.: Delving deep into rectifiers: surpassing human-level performance on imagenet classification. In: The IEEE International Conference on Computer Vision (ICCV) (December 2015)

Context-Aware Refinement Network Incorporating Structural Connectivity Prior for Brain Midline Delineation

Shen Wang[1,2], Kongming Liang[3]([✉]), Yiming Li[4], Yizhou Yu[4], and Yizhou Wang[2,3,5]

[1] Center for Data Science, Peking University, Beijing, China
[2] Advanced Institute of Information Technology, Peking University, Hangzhou, China
[3] Department of Computer Science, Peking University, Beijing, China
kongming.liang@pku.edu.cn
[4] Deepwise AI Lab, Beijing, China
[5] Center on Frontiers of Computing Studies, Peking University, Beijing, China

Abstract. Brain midline delineation can facilitate the clinical evaluation of brain midline shift, which plays an important role in the diagnosis and prognosis of various brain pathology. Nevertheless, there are still great challenges with brain midline delineation, such as the largely deformed midline caused by the mass effect and the possible morphological failure that the predicted midline is not a connected curve. To address these challenges, we propose a context-aware refinement network (CAR-Net) to refine and integrate the feature pyramid representation generated by the UNet. Consequently, the proposed CAR-Net explores more discriminative contextual features and larger receptive field, which is of great importance to predict largely deformed midline. For keeping the structural connectivity of the brain midline, we introduce a novel connectivity regular loss (CRL) to punish the disconnectivity between adjacent coordinates. Moreover, we address the ignored prerequisite of previous regression-based methods that the brain CT image must be in the standard pose. A simple pose rectification network is presented to align the source input image to the standard pose image. Extensive experimental results on the CQ dataset and one inhouse dataset show that the proposed method requires fewer parameters and outperforms three state-of-the-art methods in terms of four evaluation metrics. Code is available at https://github.com/ShawnBIT/Brain-Midline-Detection.

Keywords: Brain midline delineation · Computer aided diagnosis · Context-aware refinement network · Connectivity regular loss

---

This work was done when Shen Wang was an intern at Deepwise AI Lab.

Electronic supplementary material The online version of this chapter (https://doi.org/10.1007/978-3-030-59728-3_21) contains supplementary material, which is available to authorized users.

© Springer Nature Switzerland AG 2020
A. L. Martel et al. (Eds.): MICCAI 2020, LNCS 12267, pp. 208–217, 2020.
https://doi.org/10.1007/978-3-030-59728-3_21

1   Introduction

The human brain in healthy subjects is approximately bilateral symmetrical and divided into two cerebral hemispheres that are separated by the ideal midline on the axial plane of CT images. However, various pathological conditions, such as traumatic brain injuries, strokes, and tumors, could break the symmetry by distorting the ideal midline (IML) to deformed midline (DML) and lead to brain midline shift (MLS). As a sign of increased intracranial pressure, the degree of MLS can serve as a quantitative indicator for physicians to make diagnosis and outcome prediction more accurate. For example, the guideline of Brain Trauma Foundation recommended emergency surgery for any traumatic epidural, subdural, or intracerebral hematoma causing an MLS larger than 5 mm [5]. Since the complex and quantitative analysis of MLS is challenging and time-consuming for neurologists, computer-aided brain midline delineation could not only improve the accuracy and efficiency of MLS estimation [11] but also reduce the interrater variability among neurologists [8].

Traditional methods for brain midline delineation are classified into two types: symmetry-based [1,6] and landmark-based ones [2,7]. For example, Liao et al. [6] decomposed the deformed midline into three segments and formulated the central curved segment as a quadratic Bezier curve, which is fit by using local symmetry. Liu et al. [7] proposed to build the deformed midline by localizing the anatomical points. However, these traditional methods may fail in the cases with largely deformed brain due to the following two reasons: (1) The midline is relatively difficult to be identified given low soft-tissue contrast; (2) The predefined anatomical points or parts may not be visible due to large deformation [11].

Recently, approaches based on deeplearning [8,10,11] have served in brain midline delineation, which can overcome the above issues to some extent. Hao et al. [11] formulated the brain midline delineation as a regression task and proposed a regression-based line detection network. Pisov et al. [8] introduced a two-head convolutional neural network with shared input layers to predict the midline limits and regress the midline coordinates. However, the performance of such regression-based methods is limited due to the following aspects: (1) They ignore the structural connectivity prior that the midline is a connected and smooth curve. (2) The feature extraction network is not well designed for a largely deformed midline, or harder to train due to the high complexity. (3) They all share a common assumption that for each vertical coordinate y there is at most one horizontal coordinate x of midline pixel, which may fail in some extreme poses of the brain. For taking the structural connectivity prior into account, Wang et al. [10] proposed a post-processing stage called pathfinding based on the segmentation probability map to build the midline. Their method can not be trained end-to-end which is sub-optimal.

To address such issues, this paper proposes a context-aware refinement network (CAR-Net) to enhance the feature extraction ability and introduce a novel connectivity regular loss (CRL) to incorporate prior knowledge of midline structural connectivity. Specifically, the main contributions are summarized as follows: (1) We propose a context-aware refinement network (CAR-Net) to refine

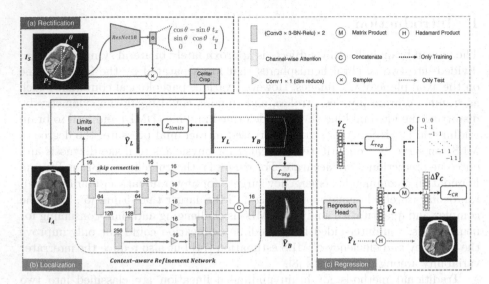

Fig. 1. The illustration of the pipeline of our proposed method for brain midline delineation, which consists of three parts, (a) rectification, (b) localization and (c) regression.

and integrate the base feature pyramid for exploring more discriminative contextual features and larger receptive field. (2) We introduce a novel connectivity regular loss (CRL) to model the connectivity prior explicitly and guarantee the connectivity of the predicted midline. (3) We address the prerequisite ignored by the previous regression-based method and present a simple pose rectification module to satisfy the above prerequisite. The proposed method is evaluated on the CQ dataset and one inhouse dataset with the results showing that our method outperforms three state-of-the-art methods with fewer parameters.

2 Method

Figure 1 shows the pipeline of our proposed method for brain midline delineation, which consists of three parts, (a) rectification, (b) localization and (c) regression. First, we present a pose rectification network to align the source CT image I_S to a canonical pose image I_A. Second, the proposed context-aware refinement network (CAR-Net) takes the aligned CT image $I_A \in R^{H \times W}$ as input and generate the midline limits $\hat{Y}_L \in R^H$ (the vertical range of midline coordinates) through the limits head [8] and the segmentation probability map $\hat{Y}_B \in R^{H \times W}$ of the midline band(the width expanded midline). Finally, the regression head [11] takes the segmentation probability map $\hat{Y}_B$ as input and outputs the midline coordinates $\hat{Y}_C \in R^H$. In addition, the midline coordinates $\hat{Y}_C$ is multiplied by the transformation matrix Φ and obtain the adjacent coordinate difference vector $\Delta \hat{Y}_C \in R^H$, which can be utilized to compute the connectivity regular loss L_{CR}. We adopt the same structure of the limits head [8] and the regression head [11].

2.1 Pose Rectification Module

Previous methods share a common assumption that for each vertical axis coordinate y, there is at most one horizontal coordinate x of midline pixel, which may fail in some extreme poses of the brain, due to improper distance, angle or displacement between the camera and patients, especially in real clinical application. Thus, we present a pose rectification network to align the images to the standard pose, which can guarantee the above assumption.

As shown in Fig. 1(a), the anterior flax point P_1 and posterior flax point P_2 of the ground truth midline are used to calculate the rotational angle and the brain center, which can form as a rigid transformation. Then, we can align the source CT image I_S to form the target image pair I_T. Given I_S, the pose rectification network ϕ transforms I_S to $\phi(I_S)$. Specifically, we use a light-weighted ResNet-18 [3] as the backbone of ϕ and minimize the loss $L_2(\phi(I_S), I_T)$. The output of the pose rectification network is a group of parameters (t_x, t_y, θ) of rigid transformation. t_x and t_y stand for horizontal and vertical displacements and θ stands for the rotational angle. To this end, I_S is transformed to I_A following:

$$I_A = \phi(I_S) = B\left(\begin{pmatrix} \cos\theta & -\sin\theta & t_x \\ \sin\theta & \cos\theta & t_y \end{pmatrix} G(I_S), \quad I_S\right) \tag{1}$$

where B stands for a bilinear interpolating function, and G represents a regular grid function. Furthermore, the aligned images are center cropped to a uniform size for the midline delineation.

2.2 Context-Aware Refinement Network

For the midline delineation task, the normal parts of the midline are easy to process. However, it is difficult to locate the shifted parts of the largely deformed midline accurately, which requires a larger receptive field and more discriminative contextual information. As shown in [12], low-level and high-level features are complementary by nature, where low-level features are rich in spatial details and high-level features are rich in semantic concepts. Therefore, based on the feature pyramid representation $\{f_i \mid i = 1, 2, 3, 4, 5\}$ generated by U-Net [9], we attach a context-aware feature refinement module, which can refine each scale features and integrate them adaptively to explore more discriminative contextual features and achieve larger receptive field for the harder shifted parts of the deformed midline.

Specifically, as shown in Fig. 1(b), we first refine each scale feature map f_i to obtain local refined feature representation f_i^l by applying several basic convolution blocks. Given the trade-off between effectiveness and efficiency, more basic convolution blocks are stacked into deeper layers. Then we adopt the SE block [4] as the channel-wise attention, which can recalibrate the local refined representation f_i^l to extract more discriminative features f_i^a for a specific scale. Finally, the representative features f_i^a of different levels are integrated via bilinear interpolation upsampling, concatenating and one basic convolution block to form the context-aware refinement representation f^R. Compared to the feature representation f_1 of original UNet, the context-aware refinement representation f^R have larger receptive field and more discriminative contextual information.

2.3   Connectivity Regular Loss

For the supervision of the midline coordinates, the previous regression-based methods only used mean square error loss (MSE) [8,11]. They ignored the structural connectivity prior that the brain midline is a continuous curve, which may lead to the possible discontinuity of the midline. The segmentation-based method [10] proposed post-processing, which relies heavily on the segmentation probability map of the midline and cannot be optimized in an end-to-end way. Based on the above observations, we propose a novel continuity regular loss (CRL) to incorporate structural connectivity prior, which can keep the morphology consistency between the predicted midline and the ground truth midline.

Specifically, we first give the definition of the midline connectivity. For the midline coordinates $X = (x_1, x_2, ..., x_n)^T$, if $|x_i - x_{i-1}| \leq \delta$ holds for every $i = 2, 3, ..., n$, we call the the midline coordinates X satisfy δ-*connectivity*. Then we denote $\Delta X = (0, \Delta x_1, \Delta x_2, ..., \Delta x_n)^T$, where $\Delta x_i = x_i - x_{i-1}$ for every $i = 2, 3, ..., n$. The derivation between X and ΔX are as follows:

$$\Delta X = \begin{bmatrix} 0 \\ x_1 - x_0 \\ x_2 - x_1 \\ \vdots \\ x_{n-1} - x_{n-2} \\ x_n - x_{n-1} \end{bmatrix} = \begin{bmatrix} 0 & 0 \\ -1 & 1 \\ & -1 & 1 \\ & & \ddots & \ddots & \ddots \\ & & & -1 & 1 \\ & & & & -1 & 1 \end{bmatrix} \begin{bmatrix} x_0 \\ x_1 \\ x_2 \\ \vdots \\ x_{n-2} \\ x_{n-1} \\ x_n \end{bmatrix} = \Phi X \quad (2)$$

where Φ is the transformation matrix. Thus, we define the CRL as follows, which can effectively punish the disconnectivity between adjacent coordinates with the margin δ to guarantee the predicted midline coordinates $\hat{Y}_C$ satisfy δ-*connectivity*.

$$L_{CR}(\hat{Y}_C) = f(\Delta \hat{Y}_C) = f(\Phi \cdot \hat{Y}_C), \text{ where } f(x) = \sum_{i=1}^{n} \max(0, |x_i| - \delta)) \quad (3)$$

2.4   Loss Function and Optimization

The whole framework is trained in an end-to-end way except the pose rectification network. The loss function $\mathcal{L}_{\text{limits}}$ of midline limits $\hat{Y}_L$ is the binary cross entropy loss and the loss function $\mathcal{L}_{\text{seg}}$ of segmentation probability map $\hat{Y}_B$ is the weight cross entropy loss. For the supervision of midline coordinates $\hat{Y}_C$, we take L_1 loss as the regression loss $\mathcal{L}_{\text{reg}}$ and connectivity regular loss L_{CR} as the regular term. The total loss function of the midline delineation is defined as:

$$\mathcal{L}_{total} = \lambda \mathcal{L}_{\text{limits}} + \gamma \mathcal{L}_{\text{seg}} + \xi \mathcal{L}_{reg} + \mu \mathcal{L}_{CR} \quad (4)$$

where λ, γ, ξ and μ denote the balanced weights of different parts.

In the inference phase, the source input CT image I_S is first aligned to the standard pose image I_A by the pose rectification network. Then the aligned image I_A is sent to the CAR-Net and regression head successively to obtain the midline limits $\hat{Y}_L$ and the midline coordinates $\hat{Y}_C$. The midline limits $\hat{Y}_L$ are converted to binary one by a suitable threshold. Then the midline coordinates $\hat{Y}_C$ is multiplied by the midline limits $\hat{Y}_L$ with Hadamard product to form the real midline coordinates. Finally, we draw the real midline coordinates into the aligned image I_A, as shown in Fig. 1(c).

3   Experiments

Dataset and Evaluation Metric. We evaluate our method on the CQ dataset and one inhouse dataset. The CQ dataset is a subset of CQ500 dataset[1], which consists of 63 midline shift subjects and the same number of healthy subjects. 59% of the subjects have a significant midline shift (≥ 5 mm) and the mean MLS is 7.59 ± 5.16 mm. Our inhouse dataset consists of 203 CT series which have different degrees of MLS caused by cerebral hemorrhage. 78% of the subjects have a significant midline shift (≥ 5 mm) and the mean MLS is 9.04 ± 5.54 mm. For both datasets, a total of 10 CT slices with the largest brain area in each subject were selected to be manually delineated by doctors for the midline golden standard. For the CQ dataset and our inhouse dataset, we randomly split the dataset into 76/20/30 and 120/30/53 as train/validation/test set respectively. We employ four metrics to measure the midline delineated by different methods, including line distance error (LDE) [11], max shift distance error (MSDE) [11], hausdorff distance (HD) [10] and average symmetric surface distance (ASD) [10].

Implementation Details. For data pre-processing, each CT slice is resampled to uniform resolution (0.5×0.5 mm^2), aligned by the pose rectification network and then center cropped into a patch with the size of 400×304 and 400×336 for the CQ dataset and our inhouse dataset respectively. Random horizontal flipping is applied as cheap data augmentation. The proposed model is implemented in Pytorch. We use Adam to train the model by setting $\beta_1 = 0.9$, $\beta_2 = 0.99$ with an initial learning rate of $1e^{-3}$. The poly learning rate policy is employed. The batch size for training is set to 24, and the maximum number of epochs is set to 200. In Eq. (4), we set $\lambda = \gamma = \xi = 1$ and $\mu = 0.5$. And the margin δ in Eq. (3) is set to 1. Moreover, the results and training details of the pose rectification network are presented in the supplementary material.

Effect of Context-Aware Refinement Network. We replace the CAR-Net with plain U-Net in our pipeline as the baseline model. In order to obtain more contextual features, we attach a context-aware refine module based on the feature pyramid generated by the U-Net. For verifying the effectiveness of the

---

[1] http://headctstudy.qure.ai/dataset.

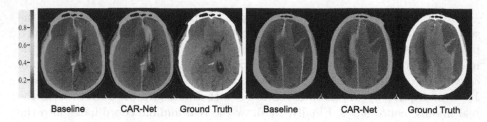

Fig. 2. Qualitative comparison results of segmentation probability maps between the baseline model and the proposed CAR-Net.

CAR-Net, we perform ablation study on proposed CAR-Net under two loss conditions, one is training with CRL and the other is training without CRL. As shown in the last four rows of Table 2, under both loss conditions, we observe that CAR-Net yields better performance consistently in four evaluation metrics on both datasets, compared to the baseline model. As shown in Fig. 2, the segmentation probability map of midline generated by the CAR-Net is more accurate, especially in shifted parts of largely deformed midline. The quantitative and qualitative results demonstrate that our proposed CAR-Net can obtain more contextual features, which can predict the largely deformed midline better.

Effect of Connectivity Regular Loss. To verify the effectiveness of the proposed CRL, we conduct experiments with the baseline model and CAR-Net. It could be observed from the last four rows of Table 2 that employing CRL achieves better performance compared to the model without CRL supervision, especially in the MSDE and HD metric, which indicates the proposed CRL can reduce the error of maximum shift significantly. Furthermore, in the inference stage, the CRL of the predicted midline can also serve as a connectivity indicator to verify the performance gain of the structural connectivity. As shown in Table 1, the connectivity indicator of the model with CRL is far smaller than counterpart without CRL. In summary, the proposed CRL can improve not only the distance performance of the midline delineation but also the midline structural connectivity effectively. Some qualitative comparisons are shown in Fig. 3, which further demonstrated the effectiveness of the CRL.

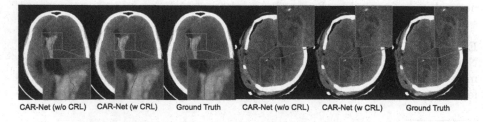

Fig. 3. Qualitative comparison between the CAR-Net with or without CRL.

Table 1. Quantitative results of the connectivity indicator in terms of mean (std) on the inhouse dataset and the CQ500 dataset.

Method	In-house dataset		CQ dataset	
	w/o CRL	w CRL	w/o CRL	w CRL
Baseline	0.10(1.20)	0.02(0.16)	1.12(3.72)	0.08(1.06)
CAR-Net	0.41(1.86)	0.00(0.00)	0.34(1.92)	**0.01(0.12)**

Comparisons to State-of-the-Art. We provide qualitative and quantitative comparisons to three state-of-the-art algorithms of brain midline delineation: RLDN [11], Pisov et al. [8] and MD-Net [10] on our inhouse dataset and the CQ dataset. All the experiments take the aligned image I_A as input for fair comparison. As shown in Table 2, our proposed model performs better than all the three methods in four evaluation metrics on both datasets, only except the comparable ASD on the inhouse dataset with the MD-Net. The experiment shows the good generalization capability and promising effectiveness of our proposed method. Figure 4 shows some delineation results of the challenging deformed brain midline. It can be inferred that our proposed method can delineate a more accurate and smoother midline, compared to the other methods, which can provide more accurate clinical judgement of pathological deformation of brain. Furthermore, the parameters of our proposed model are 3.90 M, fewer than the ones of the other three methods, which can meet the needs of practical application better.

Table 2. Quantitative results on the inhouse dataset and CQ dataset. "*" means that MD-Net is combined with a post-processing stage, which is not an end-to-end method.

Method	# Params	Inhouse dataset				CQ dataset			
		LDE	MSDE	HD	ASD	LDE	MSDE	HD	ASD
RLDN [11]	7.95 M	1.60	4.35	3.62	1.51	1.58	4.36	3.65	1.53
Pisov et al. [8]	11.57 M	1.43	3.77	3.40	1.41	0.98	3.02	2.60	0.96
MD-Net* [10]	4.31 M	1.10	3.49	2.94	**1.06**	1.02	3.50	2.90	0.99
Baseline(w/o CRL)	3.84 M	1.63	4.27	3.90	1.59	1.15	3.74	3.07	1.10
Baseline(w CRL)	3.84 M	1.45	4.02	3.56	1.42	1.05	3.33	2.83	1.03
CAR-Net(w/o CRL)	3.90 M	**1.08**	3.24	2.84	**1.06**	0.90	3.14	2.54	0.87
CAR-Net(w CRL)	3.90 M	**1.08**	**3.07**	**2.70**	1.07	**0.85**	**2.78**	**2.33**	**0.84**

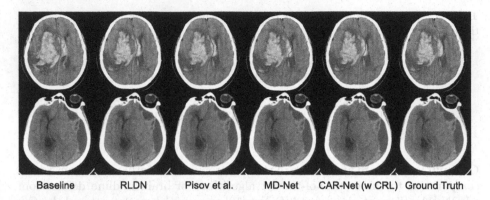

Baseline   RLDN   Pisov et al.   MD-Net   CAR-Net (w CRL) Ground Truth

Fig. 4. Qualitative comparison between baseline, RLDN, Pisov et al., MD-Net and CAR-Net with CRL, showing two examples of the midline delineation.

4   Conclusions

We propose a context-aware refinement network (CAR-Net) to explore more discriminative contextual features and larger receptive field, which is crucial for the shifted parts of largely deformed midline. Besides, a novel connectivity regular loss (CRL) is introduced to guarantee the structural connectivity. Moreover, we address the prerequisite that the brain CT image must be in the standard pose, which is ignored by previous regression-based methods. A simple pose rectification network is presented to align the source input image to the standard pose image. The proposed method is evaluated on the CQ dataset and one inhouse dataset with the results showing that our method outperforms three state-of-the-art methods with fewer parameters.

Acknowledgments. This work was supported in part by following grants, MOST-2018AAA0102004, NSFC-61625201, Key Program of Beijing Municipal Natural Science Foundation (7191003), and following institutes, Center on Frontiers of Computing Studies, Adv. Inst. of Info. Tech and Dept. of Computer Science, Peking University.

References

1. Chen, M., et al.: Automatic estimation of midline shift in patients with cerebral glioma based on enhanced voigt model and local symmetry. Australas. Phys. Eng. Sci. Med. **38**(4), 627–641 (2015). https://doi.org/10.1007/s13246-015-0372-3
2. Chen, W., Najarian, K., Ward, K.: Actual midline estimation from brain CT scan using multiple regions shape matching. In: 2010 20th International Conference on Pattern Recognition, pp. 2552–2555. IEEE (2010)
3. He, K., Zhang, X., Ren, S., Sun, J.: Deep residual learning for image recognition. In: Proceedings of the IEEE Conference on Computer Vision and Pattern Recognition, pp. 770–778 (2016)

4. Hu, J., Shen, L., Sun, G.: Squeeze-and-excitation networks. In: Proceedings of the IEEE Conference on Computer Vision and Pattern Recognition, pp. 7132–7141 (2018)
5. Liao, C.C., Chen, Y.F., Xiao, F.: Brain midline shift measurement and itsautomation: a review of techniques and algorithms. Int. J. Biomed. Imaging **2018**, 1–13 (2018)
6. Liao, C.C., Chiang, I.J., Xiao, F., Wong, J.M.: Tracing the deformed midline on brain CT. Biomed. Eng. Appl. Basis Commun. **18**(06), 305–311 (2006)
7. Liu, R., et al.: Automatic detection and quantification of brain midline shift using anatomical marker model. Comput. Med. Imaging Graph. **38**(1), 1–14 (2014)
8. Pisov, M., et al.: Incorporating task-specific structural knowledge into cnns for brain midline shift detection. In: Suzuki, K., et al. (eds.) ML-CDS 2019, IMIMIC 2019. LNCS, vol. 11797, pp. 30–38. Springer, Cham (2019). https://doi.org/10.1007/978-3-030-33850-3_4
9. Ronneberger, O., Fischer, P., Brox, T.: U-net: convolutional networks for biomedical image segmentation. In: Navab, N., Hornegger, J., Wells, W.M., Frangi, A.F. (eds.) MICCAI 2015. LNCS, vol. 9351, pp. 234–241. Springer, Cham (2015). https://doi.org/10.1007/978-3-319-24574-4_28
10. Wang, S., et al.: Segmentation-based method combined with dynamic programming for brain midline delineation. In: 2020 IEEE 17th International Symposium on Biomedical Imaging (ISBI), pp. 772–776. IEEE (2020)
11. Wei, H., et al.: Regression-based line detection network for delineation of largely deformed brain midline. In: Shen, D., et al. (eds.) MICCAI 2015. LNCS, vol. 9351, pp. 839–847. Springer, Cham (2019). https://doi.org/10.1007/978-3-319-24574-4_28
12. Zhang, Z., Zhang, X., Peng, C., Xue, X., Sun, J.: Exfuse: enhancing feature fusion for semantic segmentation. In: Ferrari, V., Hebert, M., Sminchisescu, C., Weiss, Y. (eds.) ECCV 2018. LNCS, vol. 11214, pp. 273–288. Springer, Cham (2018). https://doi.org/10.1007/978-3-030-01249-6_17

Optimizing Visual Cortex Parameterization with Error-Tolerant Teichmüller Map in Retinotopic Mapping

Yanshuai Tu[1] ⓘ, Duyan Ta[1], Zhong-Lin Lu[2,3] ⓘ, and Yalin Wang[1](✉)

[1] Arizona State University, Tempe, AZ 85201, USA
{yanshuai,ylwang}@asu.edu
[2] New York University, New York, NY, USA
[3] NYU Shanghai, Shanghai, China

Abstract. The mapping between the visual input on the retina to the cortical surface, i.e., retinotopic mapping, is an important topic in vision science and neuroscience. Human retinotopic mapping can be revealed by analyzing cortex functional magnetic resonance imaging (fMRI) signals when the subject is under specific visual stimuli. Conventional methods process, smooth, and analyze the retinotopic mapping based on the parametrization of the (partial) cortical surface. However, the retinotopic maps generated by this approach frequently contradict neuropsychology results. To address this problem, we propose an integrated approach that parameterizes the cortical surface, such that the parametric coordinates linearly relates the visual coordinate. The proposed method helps the smoothing of noisy retinotopic maps and obtains neurophysiological insights in human vision systems. One key element of the approach is the Error-Tolerant Teichmüller Map, which uniforms the angle distortion and maximizes the alignments to self-contradicting landmarks. We validated our overall approach with synthetic and real retinotopic mapping datasets. The experimental results show the proposed approach is superior in accuracy and compatibility. Although we focus on retinotopic mapping, the proposed framework is general and can be applied to process other human sensory maps.

Keywords: Retinotopic maps · Surface parametrization · Smoothing

1 Introduction

There is a great interest to understand, quantify, and simulate the human retinotopic mapping, i.e. the mapping between the visual field on the retina to the cortical surface. Since the first time functional magnetic resonance imaging (fMRI) was introduced to measure human retinotopic maps in vivo [1, 2], many improvements have been made: New experimental protocol were carried out, especially the traveling wave experiment

The work was supported in part by NIH (RF1AG051710 and R01EB025032) and Arizona Alzheimer Consortium.

© Springer Nature Switzerland AG 2020
A. L. Martel et al. (Eds.): MICCAI 2020, LNCS 12267, pp. 218–227, 2020.
https://doi.org/10.1007/978-3-030-59728-3_22

[3]; The population receptive field model (pRF) was proposed to better interpret fMRI data [4]. Those researches bring inspiring insights to understand human vision systems.

Besides the great scientific interest, human retinotopic maps are also applied in several fields. In ophthalmology, there is a great need to evaluate the visual organization of amblyopia, which affects ~2% of all children [5] and may cause significant visual impairment if untreated. The retinotopic map is a better detection method and guides a proper treatment for amblyopia patients even for adults, which is usually believed incurable [6–8]. In neurology, fMRI signal and retinotopic maps have been adopted to help register cortical surfaces and discover more brain visual-related areas [9]. The retinotopic maps are also adopted in computer vision, e.g. a retinotopic Spiking Neural Network is inspired to recognize moving objects [10].

Although great progress has been made, there are several key characteristics, e.g. cortical magnification, have not been quantified precisely for human retinotopic maps due to several challenges. The fundamental challenge is the fMRI signal is of low signal-noise ratio and low spatial resolution, which makes the retinotopic maps noisy and blurry. Meanwhile, the cortical surface is complicated and convoluted, which makes the spatial smoothing extremely difficult for the noisy retinotopic maps.

Previous works tackle these challenges in separated steps [11–13]: the cortical surface is parametrized to a 2D domain, then smoothing methods are applied to the noisy retino-topic data, based on fitting smooth function on the parametrization domain. Although intuitive, the smoothed results by this approach are not compatible with the neuroscientific results: the retinotopic maps are topological/diffeomorphic (preserve the neighboring relationship) within each visual area in neuroscientific results [12, 14], yet smoothed result does not preserve the neighboring relationship.

We address the parametrization and smoothing simultaneously and propose a novel cortical parametrization approach. The reason one shall combine them is that the parametrization influences the smoothing complexity, and vice versa. The smoothing is processed on the parametrized coordinates, where a small change of the coordinates may significantly reduce the complexity of smoothing in the 2D domain; On the other hand, high-quality visual coordinates can be used to guide the desired parametrization. Therefore, the combined approach has the potential to balance the difficulties of surface parametrization and smoothing. In specific, we first formulate the problem as a parameterization optimization problem. Then we solve the problem iteratively with Laplacian smoothing [15] and the proposed Error-Tolerant Teichmüller Map (ETTM). The ETTM can handle self-contradicting landmarks, so one can set landmarks for the parametrization with errors. This is the first approach that aligns the retinotopic parameters to the stimulus visual field and provides canonical space for retinotopic maps. The ETTM is proposed in general so it can be adapted to other sensory cortex like auditory maps [16].

2 Method

2.1 Background on Retinotopic Maps

We briefly explain the retinotopic mapping and introduce the notations. Suppose the visual stimulation at position $v = \left(v^{(1)}, v^{(2)}\right)$ is $s(t, v)$. **Note** we take the polar angle system for the visual position, i.e. $v^{(1)}$ is the radical distance to the origin (i.e. eccentricity), and $v^{(2)}$ is the polar angle in the visual field (i.e. polar angle). The visual system will perception the stimulation and eventually activate a population of neurons, illustrated in Fig. 1. The main purpose of retinotopic mapping is to find the center v and the extent $\sigma \in R^+$ of its receptive field for each point $P = (X, Y, Z) \in \mathbb{R}^3$ on the visual cortex. fMRI provides a noninvasive way to determine v and σ for P, based on the following procedure: (1) Design a stimulus $s(t; v)$, such that it is unique respect to location, i.e., $s(t; v_1) \neq s(t; v_2), \forall v_1 \neq v_2$; (2) Present the stimulus sequence to an individual and record the fMRI signals during the stimulation; (3) For each point P on cortical, collect the fMRI signal along the time, $y(t; P)$; (4) Determine the parameters, including its central location v and its size σ, that most-likely generated the fMRI signals. Specifically, one assumes the neurons' spatial response $r(v'; v, \sigma)$ model, and the hemodynamic function $h(t)$, to predict the fMRI signal by, $\hat{y}(v, \sigma) = \beta(\int r(v'; v, \sigma)s(t, v')dv') * h(t)$, where β is a coefficient that converts the units of response to the unit of fMRI activation. The parameters v and σ are estimated by minimizing the prediction error, i.e. $(v, \sigma) = \arg\min|\hat{y}(v, \sigma) - y(t; P)|^2$. The retinotopic maps are obtained when (v, σ) is solved for every point on the cortical surface. Figure 1(b) shows a typical retinotopic mapping decoded and rendered on the inflated cortical surface. Besides the retinotopic maps, one can further evaluate the goodness of retinotopic parameters for each location by computing the variance explained, $R^2 = \int|\hat{y} - \bar{y}|^2 dt / \int|y - \bar{y}|^2 dt$.

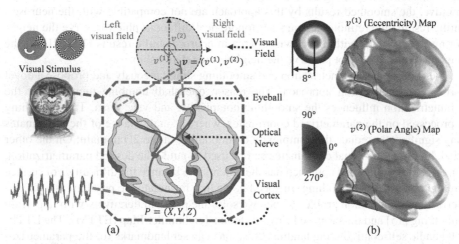

Fig. 1. (a) Illustration of the human visual system and retinotopic mapping procedure: The Visual Stimulus is presented in front of the subject's visual field, and then recording the fMRI signal during the process; (b) The retinotopic coordinates $v = \left(v^{(1)}, v^{(2)}\right)$ are decoded, and rendered on the inflated cortical surface by population receptive field (pRF) analysis: The top and bottom are the visual eccentricities $v^{(1)}$ and visual polar angles $v^{(2)}$ on the cortical surface, respectively.

2.2 Problem Statement

We wish to parametrize the visual cortex such that the parametric coordinates, $\hat{u} = \left(\hat{u}^{(1)}, \hat{u}^{(2)}\right)$ in polar coordinates linearly relate the retinotopic coordinates $v =$

$(v^{(1)}, v^{(2)})$. Namely, $\hat{\rho} = k_1 v^{(1)} + b_1$, $\hat{\theta} = k_2 v^{(2)} + b_2$, where $\hat{\rho} = |\hat{u}^{(1)} + i\hat{u}^{(2)}|$, $\hat{\theta} = \arg(\hat{u}^{(1)} + i\hat{u}^{(2)})$, $k = (k^{(1)}, k^{(2)})$, and $b = (b^{(1)}, b^{(2)})$ are constants. However, the raw retinotopic coordinates v is noisy. It will violate the topological condition by simply enforcing the coordinate $\hat{u}$ to the noisy coordinates. We propose a method to generate a smooth and topological parametrization. Mathematically, the problem is to find the minimum of energy,

$$(\hat{u}, \hat{v}) = \arg \min E = \int \left(\hat{\rho} - k_1 \hat{v}^{(1)} - b_1 \right)^2 + \left(\hat{\theta} - k_2 \hat{v}^{(2)} - b_2 \right)^2$$
$$+ \lambda_1 |\nabla_{\hat{u}} \hat{v}|^2 + \lambda_2 w |\hat{v} - v|^2 ds, \; s.t. |\mu_{u \to \hat{u}}| < 1, \tag{1}$$

where $\hat{u} = (\hat{u}^{(1)}, \hat{u}^{(2)})$ is the desired parametrization coordinates, $\hat{v} = (\hat{v}^{(1)}, \hat{v}^{(2)})$ is the desired smoothing retinotopic coordinates, $\nabla_{\hat{u}}$ is the gradient operator defined on the parametric domain $\hat{u}$, i.e. $\nabla_{\hat{u}} = (\partial/\partial \hat{u}^{(1)}, \partial/\partial \hat{u}^{(2)})$, λ_1, λ_2 are constants, w is a weight coefficient with the purpose of emphasis high-quality points, and $\mu_{u \to \hat{u}}$ is the Beltrami coefficient [17] associated with the mapping from the initial parametrization u to the desired $\hat{u}$. The first two terms in Eq. (1) are introduced to linearly align the parametric coordinates to the smoothed retinotopic coordinates. Likewise, the last two terms are introduced with the purpose of smooth the noisy v. Lastly, the constraint, $|\mu_{u \to \hat{u}}| < 1$, is introduced to ensure the new parametric coordinates is topological respect to the cortical surface [18].

2.3 The Iterative Parametrization

The optimization of energy in Eq. (3) is difficult as the $\hat{u}$ and $\hat{v}$ have influences on each other. We adopt the ADMM [19] to separate the problem into two sub-problems, namely the smoothing problem and the parametrization problem, then solve the sub-problems iteratively. In practice, the cortical surface is discretized as triangular mesh consists of triangular faces and vertices, denoted by $S = (F, V)$. The retinotopic parameters (v, σ, R) are solved by the pRF method [4, 20] for each vertex. We denote the surface with retinotopic parameters by (F, V, v, R), which is the input of the method.

The overall pipeline of the parametrization is illustrated in Fig. 2. (1) Given the surface with retinotopic parameters, as illustrated in Fig. 2(a), we first find the region of interest (ROI). In this paper, we select the region of interest as the V1/V2/V3 complex; (2) Then we find a geodesic patch that contains the ROI. Specifically, pick a point as the center, find geodesic distances from the center point to all vertices, and keep the portion of the surface whose geodesic distance is within certain value r. We call this patch as the geodesic patch, $P = (F_P, V_P, v_P, R_P)$. The purpose to bound the patch by geodesic distance is to reduce distance distortion; (3) Later, we parametrize the patch to unit disk by conformal [21] mapping c, denoted by $u = c(P)$. This is the initial coordinates for our method, as illustrated in Fig. 2 (b); (4) The retinotopic coordinates are smoothed on the domain of u. Specifically, with the initial parametrization u and the raw retinotopic coordinates v, fitting a smooth function $\hat{v}(u)$ to approach the raw coordinates. Figure 2(d) shows the smoothed result from the raw result Fig. 2(c) in the ROI; (5) Adjust the parametric coordinate from u to $\hat{u}$ such that $\hat{u}'s$ polar coordinates linearly relate to the visual coordinates v, illustrated in Fig. 2(e). During the adjusting, we will ensure the adjusted coordinates still have one-to-one mapping to the cortical surface, namely keeping the topological condition by enforcing $|\mu_{u \to \hat{u}}| < 1$; (6) The adjusting step (5) will break the ideal linearity, so procedure (4)(5) are repeated until the error is within tolerance. The key part of the pipeline is the Error-Tolerant Teichmüller Map (ETTM) in Step (5). The idea to move coordinates from u to the desired location $\hat{u}$ is by setting landmarks and move accordingly.

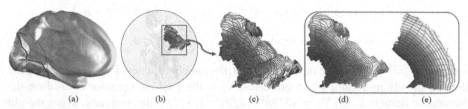

(a)   (b)   (c)   (d)   (e)

Fig. 2. The pipeline of the iterative parametrization: (a) Select the ROI, i.e. V1/V2/V3 complex and compute a geodesic disk patch contains the ROI; (b) Map the patch (enclosed by the blue curve in the occipital lobe) to the 2D unit disk; (c) A zoomed view of the ROI; (d) Apply Laplacian smoothing on the retinotopic data; (e) Adjust the parametric coordinates by ETTM according to the smoothed data. The ellipse which encloses (d)(e) means the steps are repeated. (Color figure online)

Error Tolerant Teichmüller Map

To move coordinates toward the target, we set some landmarks. Specifically, all the points within the ROI are selected as landmarks. The landmark target is set by $\hat{u}^{(1)} = k_1 \hat{v}^{(1)} + b_1$ (similar for $u^{(2)}$). Although $\hat{v}$ is smoothed, the landmarks may still have errors. Previous work, e.g. Teichmüller map (T-map) [22] cannot handle this situation. The Error Tolerant Teichmüller Map (ETTM) is proposed to enhance the T-map to tackle landmarks with errors. The key idea of ETTM is to check the topology condition, $|\mu_{u \to \hat{u}}| < 1$, and seek the most similar alternative parametrization that is topological. $\mu_{u \to \hat{u}}$ is defined as $\mu_{u \to \hat{u}} = \left(\frac{\partial \hat{u}}{\partial u^{(1)}} + i \frac{\partial \hat{u}}{\partial u^{(2)}} \right) / \left(\frac{\partial \hat{u}}{\partial u^{(1)}} - i \frac{\partial \hat{u}}{\partial u^{(2)}} \right), i = \sqrt{-1}$. The partial derivatives are approximated by piecewise linear interpretation of the discrete values. If the topology is violated, i.e. $|\mu_{u \to \hat{u}}| > 1$, we will shrink the magnitude, $\mu'_{u \to \hat{u}} = \alpha \mu_{u \to \hat{u}}$ to ensure $|\mu'_{u \to \hat{u}}|$ close but less than 1. $\mu'_{u \to \hat{u}}$ corresponds to the topological map that is closest to the previous non-topological map. Once the proper $\mu'_{u \to \hat{u}}$ is given, we recovery from $\mu'_{u \to \hat{u}}$ to $\hat{u}$ by Linear Beltrami Solver (LBS). We explain the LBS in brief and refer readers to [22] for the details. Denote $\mu'_{u \to \hat{u}} = \rho + i\tau$, according to the definition, we have $-\frac{\partial \hat{u}^{(1)}}{\partial u^{(2)}} = \alpha_1 \frac{\partial \hat{u}^{(2)}}{\partial u^{(1)}} + \alpha_2 \frac{\partial \hat{u}^{(2)}}{\partial u^{(2)}}$ and $\frac{\partial \hat{u}^{(1)}}{\partial u^{(1)}} = \alpha_1 \frac{\partial \hat{u}^{(2)}}{\partial u^{(1)}} + \alpha_2 \frac{\partial \hat{u}^{(2)}}{\partial u^{(2)}}$, where $\alpha_1 = \frac{(\rho-1)^2 + \tau^2}{1 - \rho^2 - \tau^2}$, $\alpha_2 = -\frac{2\tau}{1 - \rho^2 - \tau^2}$ and $\alpha_3 = \frac{1 + 2\rho + \rho^2 + \tau^2}{1 - \rho^2 - \tau^2}$. Apply $\frac{\partial}{\partial u^{(1)}}$ on the first equation, and plus $\frac{\partial}{\partial u^{(2)}}$ on the second one, one can write, $\nabla \cdot A \nabla \hat{u}^{(1)} = 0$, where $A = \begin{pmatrix} \alpha_1 & \alpha_2 \\ \alpha_2 & \alpha_3 \end{pmatrix}$. Then one can solve $\hat{u}^{(1)}$ with boundary conditions. Similarly, $\hat{u}^{(2)}$ can be solved. We summarize ETTM in Algorithm 1, and the overall procedure in Algorithm 2.

Algorithm 1. Error Tolerant Teichmüller Map

Input: Surface (F, V), initial coordinates u, and non-topological landmarks $\{l_i, \hat{T}_i\}$.
Result: $\hat{u}$ with uniform distortion and minimal landmark misalignment.
Initialize: $\hat{u}_i \leftarrow \hat{T}_i$, if i is a landmark point, else $\hat{u}_i = u_i$.
    repeat
        1. Compute $\mu_{u \to \hat{u}}$, and chop $\mu'_{u \to \hat{u}} = \alpha\mu_{u \to \hat{u}}$ for those $|\mu'_{u \to \hat{u}}| < 1$.
        2. Uniform $\mu''_{u \to \hat{u}} = \beta\mu'_{u \to \hat{u}}$, with $\beta = mean(|\mu'_{u \to \hat{u}}|)$.
        3. Recovery $\hat{u}$ the with $\mu''_{u \to \hat{u}}$ and landmarks $\{l_i, \hat{T}_i\}$ by LBS.
    until $|\mu_{u \to \hat{u}}| < 1$ and $||\mu_{u \to \hat{u}}| - \beta| < \epsilon$
return $\hat{u}$.

Algorithm 2. Iterative Parametrization

Input: Retinotopic coordinates on the surface $(F, V, v^{(1)}, v^{(2)}, R)$, and radius r.
Result: Parametrized coordinates $\hat{u}$, that linearly aligns to visual coordinates.
    1. Pick a point as center and compute the geodesic distance to this point.
    2. Keep the portion of surface within r, denote as $P = (F_p, V_p, v_p^{(1)}, v_p^{(2)})$
    3. Compute initial $u = c(P)$, and initialize $\hat{u} = u$, and $\hat{v} = v$.
    repeat
        4. Smoothing the eccentricity $\hat{v}^{(1)}$ to get new $\hat{v}^{(1)}$.
        5. Determine k_1, b_1 and adjust $\hat{\rho}$ to enforce $\hat{\rho} = k_1\hat{v}^{(1)} + b_1$.
        6. Set landmarks and apply the ETTM to get new $(u^{(1)}, \hat{u}^{(2)})$.
        7. Smoothing the polar angle $\hat{v}^{(2)}$ to get new $\hat{v}^{(2)}$.
        8. Determine k_2, b_2 and adjust $\hat{\theta}$ to enforce $\hat{\theta} = k_2\hat{v}^{(2)} + b_2$.
        9. Set landmarks and apply the ETTM to get new $(u^{(1)}, \hat{u}^{(2)})$.
    until $\max|\hat{\rho} - k_1\hat{v}^{(1)} - b_1| < \epsilon$ and $\max|\hat{\theta} - k_2\hat{v}^{(2)} - b_2| < \epsilon$
return $\hat{u}, \hat{v}$.

---

3 Dataset and Evaluation Method

3.1 Synthetic Data

The problem of the real dataset is there is no ground truth. We generate a synthetic dataset to compare the performance. Specifically, we take the average of cortical surface (with cortical registration) in the Human Connectome Project (HCP) [20] dataset (only use the anatomical surface), map it to the 2D by orthographical projection. Then we generate the ground truth retinotopic coordinates by the complex-log-model with the formula, $u = k \ln\left(\hat{v}^{(1)}e^{i\hat{v}^{(2)}} + a\right)$, with $k = 1, a = 1$. The complex-log-model is a good approximation of the retinotopic mapping introduced by Schwartz [23]. Finally, add noise to $\hat{v}$, i.e. $v = \hat{v} + noise$.

3.2 Evaluation Metric

The evaluation is, given noisy v, which algorithm can recovery best visual coordinates respect to the ground truth $\hat{v}$, cortical magnification, and the compatibility to neuroscientific results. (1) The visual coordinates error is computed with Euclidean distance;

(2) The cortical magnification factor M is defined as the area of corresponding cortical surface $A(P)$ divided by the area of visual field $A(\hat{v})$ for a small patch σ around the center $\hat{v}$, namely $M = \lim_{\sigma \to 0} \frac{A(P)}{A(\hat{v})}$. In the discrete triangular mesh (F, V), for each point $P \in V$, we select the dual cell for P as the patch σ. Then compute the dual cell area $A(P)$, and its corresponding area in visual field $A(\hat{v})$. (3) We use the number of non-topological points $\tilde{T}$, i.e. the point moves out of the polygon consisted of neighbors' points, to quantify the compatibility. The ideal result is no such non-topological points exist, i.e. $\tilde{T} = 0$.

3.3 HCP Dataset

The Human Connectome Project (HCP) is a high-quality retinotopy dataset [20]. The data is collected on a modern MRI machine of 7T magnetitic field with care-fully designed visual stimuli. Even so, the result is still noisy. We also applied our method and compare it with harmonic parametrization [24], orthographic projection [12], angle-preserving parametrization [21], area-preserving parametrization [25], and nearly isometric parametrization [26], based on same smoothing setting.

4 Result

4.1 Synthetic Data

We first show the method on synthetic data. The proposed method is compared with other parametrization methods with the same smoothing setting. Methods and their performances are listed in Table 1. We find: (1) the proposed method can recover the best visual coordinates, evaluate the best cortical magnification factor, and most compatible with neuroscientific results; (2) Angle-preserving and the nearly isometric methods are in the second rank. However, the nearly isometric method is more time consuming; (3) Area-preserving map, harmonic map, and orthographic projection are in the third rank with similar performance.

4.2 HCP Data

We apply the proposed algorithm to the HCP data. The raw retinotopic maps of the first subject (in the left hemisphere) is shown in Fig. 3(a). Figure 3(b)–(c) are for angle-preserving and area-preserving respectively. The proposed method is in Fig. 3(d). The same data are overlaid on the inflated cortical surface in Fig. 3(e)–(h), respectively. Visually, the proposed result is smoother and closer to neuroscientific results.

Although no ground-truth is available, we try to evaluate the results indirectly by two aspects: (1) whether the smoothed result is compatible with the neuropsychology result; and (2) whether the cortical magnification factor (CMF), agrees to public records. For the first subject, we report the violation numbers are: $\tilde{T} = 189$ (raw), $\tilde{T} = 90$ (harmonic), $\tilde{T} = 101$ (orthographic), $\tilde{T} = 85$ (angle-preserving), $\tilde{T} = 120$ (area-preserving), $\tilde{T} = 83$ (nearly-isometric), and $\tilde{T} = 20$ (proposed). We see the method generated the least number of topology violations, which means the proposed method generates more reasonable results than other methods.

Table 1. Compare different methods by three metrics, visual coordinate $\hat{v}$ difference, the cortical magnification factor M difference relative to the ground truth, and the number of topology violations. The metrics are evaluated for a small noise level (PSNR = 20) and a big noise level (PSNR = 10) (with the separation symbol '/'). "Avg." is the average difference, and "SD" is the standard deviation of the difference.

Method	$\hat{v}$ error		M error		$\tilde{T}$	Time/s
	Avg.	SD	Avg.	SD		
Raw Data	0.385/0.694	0.225/0.392	27179/27628	13602/13788	645/680	**0.0/0.0**
Harmonic	0.343/0.616	0.205/0.362	26992/27567	13518/13759	646/685	1.9/1.8
Orthographic	0.346/0.620	0.201/0.355	27022/27580	13550/13770	645/686	2.0/2.0
Angle-Preserving	0.341/0.614	0.205/0.359	26985/27567	13514/13761	650/689	2.3/2.2
Area-Preserving	0.342/0.618	0.198/0.351	27019/27576	13560/13776	649/683	16.2/16.2
Nearly-Isometric	0.339/0.613	0.197/0.353	27010/27576	13567/13774	649/683	32.1/33.5
Proposed	**0.142/0.216**	**0.119/0.136**	**18728/21422**	**12291/12629**	**564/677**	7.1/6.4

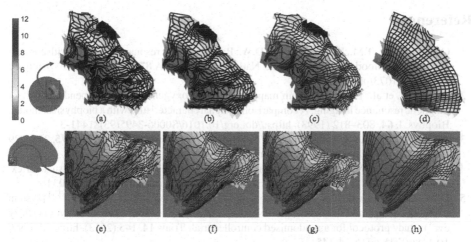

Fig. 3. First subject's visual coordinates contour: (a) The conformal parameterization with the raw retinotopic coordinates; (c) Smoothed on the conformal parameterization; (d) Smoothed based on area-preserving parametrization; (d) Our method; (e)–(h) Results on the inflated surface by same data of (a)–(h)'s, respectively. Adjacent blue lines are drawn with an 0.5° eccentricity interval, and the black lines are drawn with a 10° polar angle interval. (Color figure online)

We further estimate CMF by our method. Figure 4(a)–(c) shows the first three CMF overlaid on the parametric space. The extra benefit of the proposed method is the parametric coordinates have been aligned if the constants k, b are the same for all subjects. To take the constants k, b from the first subject, our method can directly take an average of the parametric domain across the subjects, which is shown in Fig. 4(d). Previous methods [12, 14] can only estimate CMF as a function of eccentricity in the periphery. Contrast to previous work where the CMF is assumed to be symmetric along the polar angle [12], we provide the first quantification of CMF along with different polar angles near the fovea. It shows the CMF is not symmetric, which is compatible to the overall observation that the visual field is compressed vertically [27].

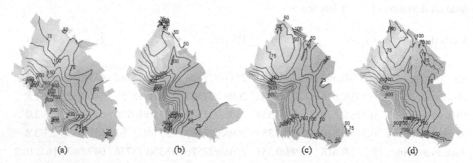

(a)   (b)   (c)   (d)

Fig. 4. (a)–(c): the first three CMF; (d) The average CMF for the first three subjects.

References

1. Ogawa, S., Lee, T.M., Kay, A.R., Tank, D.W.: Brain magnetic resonance imaging with contrast dependent on blood oxygenation. Proc. Natl. Acad. Sci. U S A **87**, 9868–9872 (1990). https://doi.org/10.1073/pnas.87.24.9868

2. Ogawa, S., et al.: Functional brain mapping by blood oxygenation level-dependent contrast magnetic resonance imaging. A comparison of signal characteristics with a biophysical model. Biophys. J. **64**, 803–812 (1993). https://doi.org/10.1016/S0006-3495(93)81441-3

3. Sato, T.K., Nauhaus, I., Carandini, M.: Traveling waves in visual cortex. Neuron **75**, 218–229 (2012). https://doi.org/10.1016/j.neuron.2012.06.029

4. Dumoulin, S.O., Wandell, B.A.: Population receptive field estimates in human visual cortex. Neuroimage **39**, 647–660 (2008). https://doi.org/10.1016/j.neuroimage.2007.09.034

5. Foss, A.J., et al.: Evaluation and development of a novel binocular treatment (I-BiT^{TM}) system using video clips and interactive games to improve vision in children with amblyopia ('lazy eye'): study protocol for a randomised controlled trial. Trials **14**, 145 (2013). https://doi.org/10.1186/1745-6215-14-145

6. Li, X., Dumoulin, S.O., Mansouri, B., Hess, R.F.: The fidelity of the cortical retinotopic map in human amblyopia. Eur. J. Neurosci. **25**, 1265–1277 (2007). https://doi.org/10.1111/j.1460-9568.2007.05356.x

7. Conner, I.P., Schwartz, T.L., Odom, J. V, Mendola, J.D.: Monocular retinotopic mapping in amblyopic adults. J. Vis. **3**, 112–112 (2010). https://doi.org/10.1167/3.9.112

8. Quinlan, E.M., Lukasiewicz, P.D.: Amblyopia: challenges and opportunities the Lasker/IRRF initiative for innovation in vision science. Vis. Neurosci. **35** (2018). https://doi.org/10.1017/s0952523817000384

9. Glasser, M.F., et al.: A multi-modal parcellation of human cerebral cortex. Nature **536**, 171–178 (2016). https://doi.org/10.1038/nature18933

10. Paulun, L., Wendt, A., Kasabov, N.: A retinotopic spiking neural network system for accurate recognition of moving objects using neucube and dynamic vision sensors. Front. Comput. Neurosci. **12**, 42 (2018). https://doi.org/10.3389/fncom.2018.00042

11. Qiu, A., Rosenau, B.J., Greenberg, A.S., Hurdal, M.K., Barta, P., Yantis, S., Miller, M.I.: Estimating linear cortical magnification in human primary visual cortex via dynamic programming. Neuroimage **31**, 125–138 (2006). https://doi.org/10.1016/j.neuroimage.2005. 11.049

12. Benson, N.C., Winawer, J.: Bayesian analysis of retinotopic maps. Elife **7** (2018). https://doi. org/10.7554/eLife.40224

13. Warnking, J., et al.: fMRI retinotopic mapping—step by Step. Neuroimage **17**, 1665–1683 (2002). https://doi.org/10.1006/NIMG.2002.1304

14. Schira, M.M., Tyler, C.W., Spehar, B., Breakspear, M.: Modeling magnification and anisotropy in the primate foveal confluence. PLoS Comput. Biol. **6**, e1000651 (2010). https://doi.org/10. 1371/journal.pcbi.1000651

15. Eilers, P.H.C.: A perfect smoother. Anal. Chem. **75**, 3631–3636 (2003). https://doi.org/10. 1021/ac034173t

16. Barton, B., Venezia, J.H., Saberi, K., Hickok, G., Brewer, A.A.: Orthogonal acoustic dimensions define auditory field maps in human cortex. Proc. Natl. Acad. Sci. U S A **109**, 20738–20743 (2012). https://doi.org/10.1073/pnas.1213381109

17. Gardiner, F.P.: Quasiconformal Teichmüller theory. American Mathematical Society, Providence (2000)

18. Lam, K.C., Lui, L.M.: Landmark and intensity-based registration with large deformations via quasi-conformal maps. SIAM J. Imaging Sci. **7**, 2364–2392 (2014). https://doi.org/10.1137/ 130943406

19. Boyd, S., Parikh, N., Chu, E., Peleato, B., Eckstein, J.: Distributed optimization and statistical learning via the alternating direction method of multipliers. Found. Trends Mach. Learn. **3**, 1–122 (2010). https://doi.org/10.1561/2200000016

20. Benson, N.C., et al.: The HCP 7T retinotopy dataset: description and pRF analysis. bioRxiv 308247 (2018). https://doi.org/10.1101/308247

21. Zeng, W., Gu, X.D.: Ricci Flow for Shape Analysis and Surface Registration. Theories, Algorithms and Applications. Springer, New York (2013). https://doi.org/10.1007/978-1-4614-8781-4

22. Lui, L.M., Lam, K.C., Wong, T.W., Gu, X.: Texture map and video compression using Beltrami representation. SIAM J. Imaging Sci. **6**, 1880–1902 (2013). https://doi.org/10.1137/120 866129

23. Schwartz, E.L.: Computational anatomy and functional architecture of striate cortex: a spatial mapping approach to perceptual coding. Vis. Res. **20**, 645–669 (1980). https://doi.org/10. 1016/0042-6989(80)90090-5

24. Shi, R., et al.: Hyperbolic harmonic mapping for surface registration. IEEE Trans. Pattern Anal. Mach. Intell. **39**, 965–980 (2017)

25. Su, Z., Zeng, W., Shi, R., Wang, Y., Sun, J., Gu, X.: Area preserving brain mapping. In: Proceedings of the IEEE Computer Society Conference on Computer Vision and Pattern Recognition, pp. 2235–2242 (2013)

26. Balasubramanian, M., Polimeni, J.R., Schwartz, E.L.: Near-isometric flattening of brain surfaces. Neuroimage **51**, 694–703 (2010). https://doi.org/10.1016/j.neuroimage.2010.02.008

27. Mamassian, P., de Montalembert, M.: A simple model of the vertical-horizontal illusion. Vis. Res. **50**, 956–962 (2010). https://doi.org/10.1016/j.visres.2010.03.005

Multi-scale Enhanced Graph Convolutional Network for Early Mild Cognitive Impairment Detection

Shuangzhi Yu[1], Shuqiang Wang[2], Xiaohua Xiao[3], Jiuwen Cao[4], Guanghui Yue[1],
Dongdong Liu[1], Tianfu Wang[1], Yanwu Xu[5], and Baiying Lei[1(✉)]

[1] National-Regional Key Technology Engineering Laboratory for Medical Ultrasound,
Guangdong Key Laboratory for Biomedical Measurements and Ultrasound Imaging, School of
Biomedical Engineering, Shenzhen University, Shenzhen 518060, China
leiby@szu.edu.cn
[2] Shenzhen Institutes of Advanced Technology, Chinese Academy of Sciences, Shenzhen
518000, China
[3] Affiliated Hospital of Shenzhen University, Health Science Center, Shenzhen University
Shenzhen, Second People's Hospital, Shenzhen, China
[4] Artificial Intelligence Institute, Hangzhou Dianzi University, Zhejiang 310010, China
[5] Ningbo Institute of Industrial Technology, Chinese Academy of Sciences, Ningbo, China

Abstract. Early mild cognitive impairment (EMCI) is an early stage of MCI,
which can be detected by brain connectivity networks. To detect EMCI, we design
a novel framework based on multi-scale enhanced GCN (MSE-GCN) in this paper,
which fuses the functional and structural information from the resting-state functional magnetic resonance imaging and diffusion tensor imaging, respectively.
Then both functional and structural information in connectivity networks are integrated via the local weighted clustering coefficients (LWCC), which are concatenated as the feature vectors to represent the vertices of population graph. Simultaneously, the subject's gender and age in-formation is combined with the multi-
modal neuroimaging feature to build a sparse graph. Then, we design multiple parallel GCN layers with different inputs by random walk embedding, which can identify the intrinsic MCI graph information from the embedding in GCN. Finally, we
concatenate the output of all the GCN layers in the full connection layer for detection. The proposed method is capable of simultaneously representing the individual
features and information associations among subjects from potential patients. The
experimental results on the public Alzheimer's Disease Neuroimaging Initiative
(ADNI) dataset demonstrate that our proposed method achieves impressive EMCI
identification performance compared with all competing methods.

Keywords: Early mild cognitive impairment · Multi-scale enhanced graph
convolutional network · Functional and structural information

1 Introduction

Alzheimer's disease (AD) is a prevalent neurodegenerative disease among the old population and it is characterized by decreased cognitive functions in memory, language, and

© Springer Nature Switzerland AG 2020
A. L. Martel et al. (Eds.): MICCAI 2020, LNCS 12267, pp. 228–237, 2020.
https://doi.org/10.1007/978-3-030-59728-3_23

attention [1]. Mild cognitive impairment (MCI) is an early stage of AD with a conversion rate as high as 10%–15% per year in 5 years. Therefore, effective predictive model construction for early MCI (EMCI) detection has become a hot topic [2]. The resting-state functional magnetic resonance imaging (R-fMRI) [3] is a non-radioactive process, possessing high spatial and temporal resolution, which can provide effective functional connectivity (FC) information for detecting EMCI. On the other hand, diffusion tensor imaging (DTI) [4] can provide structural information of the white matter fiber bundles by detecting the opposite values in the brain. DTI reveals the changes in fiber bundle connection number, fiber bundle length, and anisotropy values, which can provide effective structural information for EMCI detection. The previous studies have shown that multimodal fusion can discover complementary information, which is beneficial to improve the feature representation and model detection performance [5–7]. The white matter is the channel of information transmission in the brain, and fiber tracking in the white matter through DTI can construct the brain structure connectivity (SC) network. Many studies [8, 9] indicate that both FC and SC are complementary, and hence fusion of SC and FC to supplement each other for feature representation via the local weighted clustering coefficients (LWCC) is highly desirable. Therefore, we extract both FCs and SCs from one subject and concatenate them via LWCC to achieve multimodal fusion for feature representation.

Apart from the image information, integration of non-image information such as subject's gender and age information can boost the EMCI detection. To fuse the non-image information, the graph convolutional network (GCN) provides an effective way, which can directly perform detection by graph representations in an end-to-end training model. In fact, traditional GCNs may lead to sub optimal detection accuracy due to the limitation of receptive field. Therefore, many researchers explore different ways to enhance GCNs receptive field to improve detection performance [10]. The multi-scale GCN (MS-GCN) model not only enhances the receptive field of the network, but also makes better use of the high-order information of the brain [11]. It is found that random walk has powerful performance in graph embedding for performance boosting [12]. Therefore, Sami et al. [13] proposed a model to merge two lines of GCNs and random walk for semi-supervised detection. Motivated by this, we devise a multi-scale enhanced GCN (MSE-GCN) to improve the receptive field of traditional GCNs based on the random walks theory for EMCI detection.

In this paper, we propose a MSE-GCN to explore individual differences and information association among subjects to improve the EMCI detection. The complementarity of FC and SC is explored via data fusion to improve the performance of a single model. We design the multiple parallel GCN layers with different inputs by random walk embedding for the MCI graph analysis. Our proposed MSE-GCN model is able to learn rich features by leveraging image and population phenotypic information. We verify the validity of the model on the Alzheimer's Disease Neuroimaging Initiative (ADNI) dataset. Our proposed model achieves quite promising EMCI detection performance and outperforms the related algorithms.

2 Method

Figure 1 shows the proposed framework for EMCI detection. Specifically, we first use a non-overlapping slide window to divide R-fMRI into several subseries, and obtain dynamic FCs by calculating Pearson correlation (PC) coefficient of the pair-subseries. Simultaneously, the connection of white matter fiber bundles be-tween each pair of brain regions is regarded as a structural network. Then, we extract the LWCC of both FC and SC, and concatenate it as a feature vector to represent the vertices of population graph. The edges of the graph represent the similarity between subjects and incorporate the non-image information. Finally, MSE-GCN is used for MCI detection.

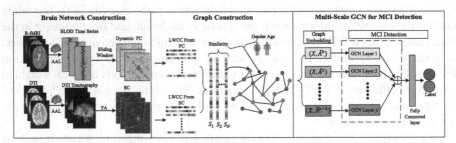

Fig. 1. The framework of our proposed method.

2.1 Data and Pre-processing

We use a total of 184 subjects obtained from the ADNI dataset including 25 late MCI (LMCI) male patients and 15 LMCI female patients, 39 EMCI male patients and 38 EMCI female patients, and 28 normal control (NC) male and 39 female NC. The mean age of LMCI, EMCI and NC is 74.5,74.8 and 75.4, respectively, and the standard deviation of LMCI, EMCI and NC is 6.9, 6.1, 6.5, respectively.

The R-fMRI data preprocessing procedure is performed using GRETNA. To keep magnetization equilibrium, we discard the first 20 acquired R-fMRI volumes of each subject. Afterward, the head-motion artifacts in the R-fMRI time-series are removed by registering all the following volumes in comparison with the first volume. After registration, we use DARTEL to spatially smooth the dataset for spatial normalization. Each regional mean time series is regressed against the average cerebrospinal fluid and white-matter signals as well as the six parameters from motion correction. A parcellation of the brain space into 90 ROIs is then performed by warping the automated anatomical labeling (AAL) atlas to R-fMRI images. Finally, we obtain the time series of each individual ROI of each subject over all voxels in that particular ROIs.

The DTI data preprocessing procedure is performed using PANDA. We convert the DICOM format into the NIFTI format, which generates three files, *i.e.*, bvals text files, bvecs text files, and 4D data files. Then, we resample the skull stripping data since DTI has a high resolution of $0.9 \times 0.9 \times 1 \text{ mm}^3$. The image is cut with a parameter of 3 mm and head movements and eddy currents are corrected to reduce the influence of peripheral noise. Finally, we define the tracking conditions and network nodes, generate the structural network matrix based on the deterministic fiber tracking, and set the tracking stopping conditions. The average number of fraction anisotropy (FA) coefficients between different nodes is regarded as the weight of SC.

2.2 LWCC Extraction and Data Fusion

Most of the existing research gets the upper half matrix of FC or SC of the subject as the feature vector. However, such an operation will bring the high feature dimension and destroy the original structure of the network. To address this problem, for a connectivity matrix $W^{ij} \in \mathbb{R}^{r \times r}$, we first extract the LWCC $F = \{f_i | (i = 1, 2, \ldots, r)\}$ from both FC and SC to compose a feature vector. If one subject has λ FCs and one SC, we can get $\lambda + 1$ feature vector F. Then, we concatenate the LWCC extracted from one subject as a feature vector $S_N = \{f_1, f_2, \ldots, f_{(\lambda+1)r)}\}$, where N is subject's number. Compared with traditional methods, our method not only reduces the feature dimension, but also quantifies the clustering of each node in the weighted network. Specifically, the weight of the edge connecting vertex i and vertex j for each network (i.e., the i-th node) is denoted as:

$$f_i = \frac{2 \sum_{j:j \in \varepsilon_i} (w_{ij})^{\frac{1}{3}}}{|\varepsilon_i|(|\varepsilon_i| - 1)} \tag{1}$$

where ε_i denotes the set of vertices directly connected to vertex i, and $|\varepsilon_i|$ is the number of elements in ε_i. w_{ij} is the weight of FC or SC.

2.3 Graph Construction

In this study, we construct a spare graph to combine information on the image data (including R-fMRI and DTI) and demographic information (*e.g.* gender and age). The incorporation of both information in our model can reveal the similarity between each subject's features and help to predict labels. Supposing the proposed undirected graph is defined as $G(V, E, A)$, where V is the feature vector set extracted from subjects. Edges E models the similarity between the corresponding subjects and incorporates the phenotypic information. The adjacency matrix A describes the vertex connectivity and can be obtained by calculating the similarity matrix S of the sample point distance metric, which is denoted as

$$A_{nm} = S(S_n, S_m) \sum\nolimits_{p=1}^{P} \mathcal{P}(M_p(S_n), M_p(S_m)), \tag{2}$$

where p is denoted as non-image measures $M = \{M_p\}$, and $S(S_n, S_m)$ is denoted as the feature similarity between subjects n and m ($m, n = 1, 2, \ldots, N$). $\mathcal{P}(\ )$ is denoted as the distance among measures M. $\mathcal{P}(\ )$ is defined as

$$\begin{aligned}
& \mathcal{P}(M_p(S_n), M_p(S_m)) \\
& = \begin{cases} 1 & if \left| M_{age}(S_n) - M_{age}(S_m) \right| < \beta \ \& \left| M_{sex}(S_n) - M_{sex}(S_m) \right| = 0 \\ 0 & otherwise \end{cases}
\end{aligned} \tag{3}$$

where β is the standard deviation of the subject's age. We use the distance correlation method to compute the distance between vectors S_n and S_m, which is defined as

$$S(S_n, S_m) = \frac{(S_n - \bar{S}_n) \odot (S_m - \bar{S}_m)}{\left\| (S_n - \bar{S}_n) \right\|_2 \left\| (S_m - \bar{S}_m) \right\|_2}, \tag{4}$$

where $\bar{S}_n$ is the mean of vector S_n, and $\odot$ is the dot product.

2.4 Spectral Convolution

GCN effectively implements convolution operations on non-Euclidean spatial data. For the convolution operation of graph data, it can be regarded as the multiplication of both the filter and the signal into the Fourier domain. The Fourier transform of the signal is realized by multiplying with the eigenvectors vector of the Laplacian. Specifically, the normalized graph Laplacian matrix is computed as

$$L = D - A = D^{-\frac{1}{2}}(D - A)D^{-\frac{1}{2}} = U\Lambda U^T \tag{5}$$

where D is a diagonal matrix $D_{ii} = \sum_j A_{ij}$ and Λ is a diagonal matrix. The convolution filter parameters are shared across all locations in the network layers. The feature map is implemented to calculate the spatial feature by the weighted sum of the central pixel and the adjacent pixel. For the normalized adjacency matrix $\hat{A} = D^{-\frac{1}{2}}AD^{-\frac{1}{2}}$, the network layer is denoted as

$$H^{(l+1)} = f\left(H^{(l)}, \hat{A}\right), \tag{6}$$

$$f\left(H^{(l)}\hat{A}\right) = \sigma\left(\hat{A}H^{(l)}W^{(l)}\right), \tag{7}$$

where $W^{(l)}$ is the weight matrix of the l-th layer neural networks, and $H^{(l)}$ is the input of l-th layer. In addition, $\sigma(\cdot)$ is the non-linear activation function. Therefore, the two-layer GCN model is calculated as

$$Z = f\left(X; \hat{A}\right) = \sigma_1\left(\hat{A}\sigma_0\left(\hat{A}XW^{(0)}\right)W^{(1)}\right) \tag{8}$$

2.5 Multi-scale GCN

Recent study shows that traditional GCNs may lead to suboptimal detection accuracy due to the limitation of receptive field [10, 13]. To address this problem, we use random walks embedding techniques on graphs to obtain node representations.

Random walk is a special form of Markov chain, which represents the probability of the information from one vertices going to another vertices of the graph. This probability matrix is statistically known as a co-occurrence matrix Y. Therefore, random walk essentially transforms the vertices of a graph into a continuous vector space. The expectation on Y is written as

$$\mathcal{E}|Y| = \mathcal{E}_{q \sim Q}\left[\left(D^{-1}A\right)^q\right] = \mathcal{E}_{q \sim Q}\left[(\mathcal{L})^q\right] \tag{9}$$

where q is step of the random walk, and $\mathcal{L}$ is row normalized transition matrix. In addition, Q is abide by the super-parameters of the random walk. Where $\mathcal{L}$ is a row normalization transition matrix.

In fact, in one particular case, the GCN can simulate the principle of a random walk. For example, assuming the activation function σ_0 is identical as $\sigma_0(z) = z$, and $W^{(0)}$ is an identity matrix, then Eq. (8) is reformulated as

$$Z = f\left(X; \hat{A}\right) = \sigma_1\left(\hat{A}\hat{A}XW^{(1)}\right) = \sigma_1\left(\hat{A}^2 XW^{(1)}\right) \tag{10}$$

As can be seen from Eq. (10), Z can be regarded as a GCN layer with input $(X, \hat{A}^2)$, where $\hat{A}^2$ is denoted as:

$$\hat{A}^2 = \left(D^{-\frac{1}{2}}AD^{-\frac{1}{2}}\right)\left(D^{-\frac{1}{2}}AD^{-\frac{1}{2}}\right) = D^{-\frac{1}{2}}A(D^{-1}A)D^{-\frac{1}{2}} = D^{-\frac{1}{2}}A\mathcal{L}D^{-\frac{1}{2}}. \tag{11}$$

In this way, the GCN model is effectively doing a one-step random walk. Next, we expand the above formula to the p-degree polynomial as

$$\hat{A}^p = D^{-\frac{1}{2}}A\mathcal{L}^{p-1}D^{-\frac{1}{2}} \tag{12}$$

The p-th power contains statistics from the p-th step of a random walk on the graph. Therefore, our MSE-GCN model is able to combine information from various graph scales. Using the p power of the normalized adjacency matrix $\hat{A}$ as input can explore the higher order similarity of features, which is beneficial to understanding of diseases. Motivated by this, we further design p parallel GCN layers, and the input of the p-th GCN layer is $(X, \hat{A}^{p-1})$, the output of each layer of GCN is a matrix $\mathbb{R}^{N \times C_p}$, C_p is the latent dimensionality. Finally, we concatenate the output of all the GCN layers into the full connection layer for MCI detection.

3   Experiments

In this study, three kinds of binary detection tasks are performed, *i.e.*, (1) LMCI vs. NC; (2) EMCI vs. NC; (3) LMCI vs. EMCI. We use a leave one-out (LOO) cross-validation strategy in all methods. For all the GCN-based competing methods, we use the same model parameters: 20% dropout rate, 10^{-5} weight of the regularization term, 0.002 learning rate, and 200 epochs. We tested our models at different scales and selected the best scale p from the average cross-validation results.

In order to demonstrate the superiority of our proposed method over traditional methods, we compare our proposed method with the following methods: (1) Support Vector Machine (SVM) [14]; (2) Two layers of GCNs for detection [15]; (3) MS-GCN with same normalized adjacency matrix [10]. Table 1 shows that the detection performance of our method and other competing methods. For convenient viewing, we use Ours (R), Ours (D), and Ours (F) to represent the proposed method with the R-fMRI, DTI and fused data as input, respectively. It is found that GCN has the advantages in analyzing EMCI compared with traditional machine learning methods. In addition, experiments show that increasing the receptive field of GCN is beneficial for EMCI detection. Moreover, the experiments also demonstrate that the EMCI detection is significantly improved after random walk graph embedding. Our analysis suggests that a random walk graph embedding may be an efficient way to extract the brain's high-order information. The ROC curves of different models and tasks are given in Fig. 2. In general, our proposed method has the best average accuracy of 84.72%, 89.72%, and 92.31% in the tasks of EMCI vs. NC, LMCI vs. EMCI and LMCI vs. NC, respectively. The fused data achieves better detection results than the single modality in the detection tasks of LMCI vs. NC and LMCI vs. EMCI.

Table 1. Detection performance of different methods in three tasks (%).

Method	EMCI vs. NC				LMCI vs. NC				LMCI vs. EMCI			
	Acc	Sen	Spec	F1	Acc	Sen	Spec	F1	Acc	Sen	Spec	F1
SVM(R)	63.19	67.53	58.21	66.24	69.16	62.50	73.13	60.24	68.38	47.50	79.22	50.69
SVM(D)	63.19	75.32	49.25	68.43	75.70	72.50	77.61	69.05	72.65	67.50	75.32	62.79
SVM(F)	68.75	61.19	75.32	64.57	78.50	67.50	85.07	70.13	76.07	72.50	77.92	67.44
GCN(R)	60.42	77.92	40.30	67.80	70.09	83.58	47.50	77.78	57.26	66.23	40.00	67.11
GCN(D)	68.50	59.35	77.61	58.46	71.03	85.07	47.05	78.62	64.10	76.92	56.41	59.82
GCN(F)	71.53	67.53	76.12	71.72	73.83	86.57	52.50	80.56	75.21	84.42	57.50	81.76
MS-GCN(R)	75.69	76.12	75.32	74.45	78.63	77.50	79.22	71.25	80.34	85.71	70.00	85.16
MS-GCN(D)	70.14	65.67	74.03	67.18	74.77	74.63	75.00	78.74	79.49	87.01	65.00	84.81
MS-GCN(F)	81.25	72.73	91.04	80.58	85.05	89.55	77.50	88.24	84.62	90.91	72.50	88.61
Ours(R)	77.08	85.71	67.16	80.00	86.92	89.55	82.50	89.55	89.74	93.51	82.50	92.31
Ours(D)	81.94	89.61	73.13	84.15	89.72	92.54	85.00	91.85	90.60	94.81	82.50	92.99
Ours(F)	85.42	86.57	84.42	84.67	93.46	94.03	92.50	94.74	92.31	93.51	90.00	94.12

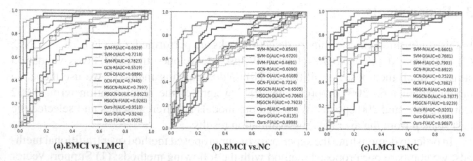

Fig. 2. The ROC curves of different models in different tasks.

Different parts of the brain are responsible for different tasks and not all regions are closely related to EMCI. Hence, we attempt to utilize our proposed method to search for these relevant ROIs for understanding brain abnormalities. We shield one brain regions in turn and then get 90 detection results. According to the corresponding detection performance, we analyze the impact of the corresponding ROI on the disease. Figure 3 shows that top 10 brain regions and functional connectivity of different tasks using our proposed method. In addition, we visualize connections between brain regions in patients at different stages. Figure 4 shows the structural connectivity of our method, which shows the structural connections of brain regions are different in patients at different stages. Table 2 shows the algorithm comparisons of the related algorithms. We can see that our proposed method has achieved quite impressive performance for EMCI detection.

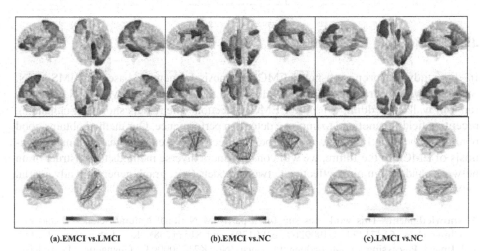

| (a).EMCI vs.LMCI | (b).EMCI vs.NC | (c).LMCI vs.NC |

Fig. 3. Top 10 brain regions and functional connectivity of 3 tasks using our proposed method.

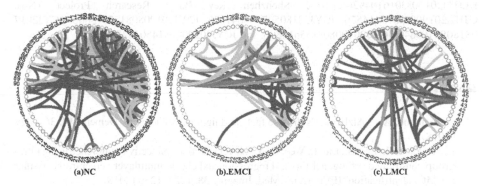

| (a).NC | (b).EMCI | (c).LMCI |

Fig. 4. The structural connectivity of our method.

Table 2. Algorithm comparison results in the literature (Null means no information available).

Method	Modality	Subject	ACC	SEN	SPEC	AUC
Zhao et al. [16]	R-fMRI+DTI	184	78.4	84.7	Null	0.81
Kipf et al. [15]	MRI	540	78.8	Null	Null	0.86
Xing et al. [11]	R-fMRI+MRI	368	79.73	86.49	72.97	Null
Proposed	R-fMRI+DTI	184	85.42	86.57	84.42	0.8998

4 Conclusion

In this study, we propose a novel EMCI diagnosis framework based on EMS-GCN. Specifically, we extract the LWCC from FC and SC. An enhanced MS-GCN model by random walk embedding is used for EMCI detection. The results show that enhancing receptive field is beneficial to improve detection performance. Our method obtains good results on the ADNI dataset, and can be an effective reference for early clinical diagnosis of EMCI. In the future, we will consider more diverse methods to construct brain networks and design more effective network models (e.g., graph generation adversarial network).

Acknowledgment. This work was supported partly by National Natural Science Foundation of China (Nos. 61871274, U1909209, 61801305 and 81571758), Key Laboratory of Medical Image Processing of Guangdong Province (No. K217300003). Guangdong Pearl River Talents Plan (2016ZT06S220), Guangdong Basic and Applied Basic Research Foundation (No. 2019A1515111205), Shenzhen Peacock Plan (Nos. KQTD2016053112051497 and KQTD2015033016104926), and Shenzhen Key Basic Research Project (Nos. GJHZ20190822095414576, JCYJ20180507184647636, JCYJ20190808155618806, JCYJ2017 0818094109846, JCYJ20190808155618806, and JCYJ20190808145011259).

References

1. Association, A.s.: Alzheimer's disease facts and figures. Alzheimer's Dement. **14**, 367–429 (2018)
2. Li, Y., Yang, H., Lei, B., Liu, J., Wee, C.-Y.: Novel effective connectivity inference using ultra-group constrained orthogonal forward regression and elastic multilayer perceptron classifier for MCI identification. IEEE Trans. Med. Imaging **38**, 1227–1239 (2018)
3. Huettel, S.A., Song, A.W., McCarthy, G.: Functional Magnetic Resonance Imaging. Sinauer Associates, Sunderland, MA (2004)
4. Mori, S., Zhang, J.: Principles of diffusion tensor imaging and its applications to basic neuroscience research. Neuron **51**, 527–539 (2006)
5. Chen, X., Zhang, H., Zhang, L., Shen, C., Lee, S.-W., Shen, D.: Extraction of dynamic functional connectivity from brain grey matter and white matter for MCI classification. Hum. Brain Mapp. **38**, 5019–5034 (2017)
6. Zhu, D., Zhang, T., Jiang, X., Hu, X., Chen, H., Yang, N., et al.: Fusing DTI and fMRI data: a survey of methods and applications. Neuroimage **102**, 184–191 (2014)

7. Zhang, D., Shen, D.: Multi-modal multi-task learning for joint prediction of multiple regression and classification variables in Alzheimer's disease. NeuroImage **59**, 895–907 (2012)
8. Skudlarski, P., Jagannathan, K., Calhoun, V.D., Hampson, M., Skudlarska, B.A., Pearlson, G.: Measuring brain connectivity: diffusion tensor imaging validates resting state temporal correlations. NeuroImage **43**, 554–561 (2008)
9. Lei, B., Cheng, N., Frangi, A.F., Tan, E.-L., Cao, J., Yang, P., et al.: Self-calibrated brain network estimation and joint non-convex multi-task learning for identification of early Alzheimer's disease. Med. Image Anal. **61**, 101652 (2020)
10. Kazi, A., et al.: InceptionGCN: receptive field aware graph convolutional network for disease prediction. In: Chung, Albert C.S., Gee, James C., Yushkevich, Paul A., Bao, S. (eds.) IPMI 2019. LNCS, vol. 11492, pp. 73–85. Springer, Cham (2019). https://doi.org/10.1007/978-3-030-20351-1_6
11. Xing, X., et al.: Dynamic spectral graph convolution networks with assistant task training for early MCI diagnosis. In: Shen, D., Liu, T., Peters, Terry M., Staib, Lawrence H., Essert, C., Zhou, S., Yap, P.-T., Khan, A. (eds.) MICCAI 2019. LNCS, vol. 11767, pp. 639–646. Springer, Cham (2019). https://doi.org/10.1007/978-3-030-32251-9_70
12. Abu-El-Haija, S., Kapoor, A., Perozzi, B., Lee, J.: N-gcn: multi-scale graph convolution for semi-supervised node classification (2018). arXiv preprint arXiv:1802.08888
13. Azran, A.: The rendezvous algorithm: multiclass semi-supervised learning with markov random walks. In: Proceedings of the 24th International Conference on Machine Learning, pp. 49–56 (2007)
14. Suykens, J.A., Vandewalle, J.: Least squares support vector machine classifiers. Neural Process. Lett. **9**, 293–300 (1999)
15. Kipf, T.N., Welling, M.: Semi-supervised classification with graph convolutional networks (2016). arXiv preprint arXiv:1609.02907
16. Zhao, X., Zhou, F., Ou-Yang, L., Wang, T., Lei, B.: Graph convolutional network analysis for mild cognitive impairment prediction. In: 2019 IEEE 16th International Symposium on Biomedical Imaging (ISBI 2019), pp. 1598–1601 (2018)

Construction of Spatiotemporal Infant Cortical Surface Functional Templates

Ying Huang[1,2], Fan Wang[1], Zhengwang Wu[1], Zengsi Chen[3], Han Zhang[1], Li Wang[1], Weili Lin[1], Dinggang Shen[1], Gang Li[1(✉)], and the UNC/UMN Baby Connectome Project Consortium

[1] Department of Radiology and BRIC, University of North Carolina at Chapel Hill, Chapel Hill, NC, USA
gang_li@med.unc.edu
[2] School of Automation, Northwestern Polytechnical University, Xi'an, China
[3] College of Sciences, China Jiliang University, Hangzhou, China

Abstract. Infant cortical surface templates play an essential role in spatial normalization of cortical surfaces across individuals in pediatric neuroimaging analysis. However, existing infant surface templates have two major limitations in functional MRI analysis. First, they are constructed by co-registration of cortical surfaces based on structural attributes, which cannot lead to accurate functional alignment, due to the highly variable relationship between cortical folds and functions. Second, they are constructed by simply averaging co-registered cortical attributes, which is sensitive to registration errors and lead to blurred attribute patterns on templates, thus deteriorating the accuracy in spatial normalization. Therefore, construction of infant cortical functional templates encoding sharp functional architectures is critical for infant fMRI analysis. To this end, we construct the first set of spatiotemporal infant cortical surface functional templates using Wasserstein barycenter and a state-of-the-art functional feature, namely the gradient density of functional connectivity. To address the first issue, we leverage functional gradient density to drive surface registration to improve inter-individual functional correspondences. To address the second issue, we compute templates based on the Wasserstein barycenter of functional gradient density maps across individuals. The motivation is that Wasserstein barycenter represents a meaningful mean under the Wasserstein distance metric, which takes into account the alignment of local spatial distribution of cortical attributes and thus is robust to registration errors, leading to sharp and detailed patterns on templates. Experiments on a dataset with 207 fMRI scans between 0 and 2 years of age show the validity and accuracy of our constructed infant cortical functional templates.

Keywords: Infant · Functional templates · Wasserstein barycenter

1 Introduction

In neuroimaging studies of early brain development, infant cortical surface templates or atlases play a fundamental role for spatial normalization, analysis, visualization, and

© Springer Nature Switzerland AG 2020
A. L. Martel et al. (Eds.): MICCAI 2020, LNCS 12267, pp. 238–248, 2020.
https://doi.org/10.1007/978-3-030-59728-3_24

comparison of results across individuals and different studies [1]. Many infant cortical surface templates have been constructed and are widely used in pediatric neuroimaging community [2, 3]. However, when applying to infant functional MRI analysis, these available infant surface templates have two fundamental limitations. First, they are constructed by co-registration of a population of cortical surfaces based on cortical attributes derived from structural images [4–9], e.g., curvature, sulcal depth and myelin content, which cannot establish accurate functional alignment, especially in high-order association regions. Therefore, functionally corresponding areas across the population are not well represented on these templates. In fact, increasing evidences show that cortical functional alignment is as important as conventionally adopted cortical structural alignment in analyzing fMRI data [10–13]. Second, existing infant surface templates are typically constructed by simply averaging the cortical attributes across individuals after co-registration, which is sensitive to co-registration errors and usually leads to blurred cortical attribute patterns on these templates. When aligning new individual cortical surfaces onto these templates, the blurred cortical attribute patterns without detailed and informative architecture typically bring ambiguities and deteriorate the registration accuracy, thereby hampering the quality of the subsequent analyses. Therefore, to advance infant functional MRI analysis, it is crucial to construct infant cortical surface functional templates, which should encode sharp, detailed, age-specific, population-representative functional architectures to enable establishing functionally meaningful and accurate inter-individual cortical correspondences. However, this is a challenging task due to difficulties in both acquisition and accurate processing of multimodal infant MR images, which typically exhibit low contrast, dynamic image appearance, brain structure and function.

To densely cover the early postnatal stages, we construct infant cortical functional templates at 6 representative ages, i.e., 3, 6, 9, 12, 18 and 24 months of age. Specifically, to address the first issue, we leverage gradient density of functional connectivity to drive surface registration to greatly improve inter-individual functional correspondences. The functional gradient density is a reliable, meaningful functional attribute to indicate the boundary of functional connectivity [14] and has been widely used in adult fMRI studies [15, 16], thus can be leveraged to boost the functional alignment across individuals. To address the second issue and create sharp patterns of cortical functional attributes on the surface templates, we compute cortical functional templates based on the unbalanced Wasserstein barycenter of functional gradient density maps of individuals. The motivation is that the unbalanced Wasserstein barycenter represents a physically meaningful mean under the Wasserstein distance metric, which takes into account the alignment of local spatial distribution of cortical attributes and thus is more robust to co-registration errors than Euclidean average, leading to more accurate and sharper patterns of functional architecture on constructed surface templates. Of note, the unbalanced Wasserstein metric not only inherits the advantage of the classic Wasserstein metric, but also overcomes the issue raised by the assumption of the same mass of distribution in the classic Wasserstein barycenter [17–19]. Moreover, to further improve our surface templates, we further refine them gradually and iteratively by: 1) aligning all individual surfaces in the same age group to the current age-specific cortical surface functional template;

and 2) based on the improved inter-individual cortical correspondences, updating cortical surface functional templates by computing the unbalanced Wasserstein barycenter of functional gradient density maps across individuals. Both qualitative and quantitative experiments demonstrate the advantage of our constructed infant cortical surface functional templates based on the Wasserstein barycenter of functional gradient density maps.

2   Materials and Methods

2.1   Datasets and Image Processing

207 longitudinal multimodal MRI scans from 119 healthy infants from the UNC/UMN Baby Connectome Project [20] are used to construct our spatiotemporal cortical surface functional templates. The acquisition parameters of T1-weighted images (208 sagittal slices) are as follows: TR/TE $= 2400/2.24$ ms, flip angle $= 8$, acquisition matrix $= 320 \times 320$, and resolution $= 0.8 \times 0.8 \times 0.8$ mm^3. The acquisition parameters of T2-weighted images (208 sagittal slices) are: TR/TE $= 3200/564$ ms, flip angle $=$ VAR and resolution $= 0.8 \times 0.8 \times 0.8$ mm^3. All resting state-fMRI images (72 axial slices) during natural sleep are acquired with the parameters: TR/TE $= 800/37$ ms, flip angle $= 52$, acquisition matrix $= 104 \times 91$, and resolution $= 2 \times 2 \times 2$ mm^3. All scans are grouped as 6 age groups, i.e., 3, 6, 9, 12, 18 and 24 months of age. The numbers of subjects in the 6 age groups are 30, 37, 35, 36, 37, and 32, respectively.

All structural images are processed using an infant structural image computation pipeline [21–23]. After surface reconstruction and spherical mapping, we use a longitudinally-consistent infant cortical surface registration strategy to align all cortical surfaces into the HCP 32k_LR space [24] based on cortical folding attributes, including average convexity and mean curvature. Specifically, 1) for each subject, we co-register [14] the longitudinal cortical surfaces and average the their cortical attribute maps to obtain the intra-subject mean surface maps; 2) We co-register all the intra-subject mean surface maps and then average them to get the group mean surface map; 3) We align the group mean surface to the HCP 32k_LR atlas as in [24]. All registrations are carried out by Spherical Demons [25]. By concatenating the three deformation fields from the abovementioned three step registrations, we can align each individual cortical surface into the HCP 32k_LR space. In this space, we resample each warped individual surface with a surface with 32,492 vertices for establishing vertex-to-vertex cortical correspondences across all scans. All fMRI scans are processed following the HCP fMRI processing pipeline [26]. The functional time series are then extracted for each cortical vertex and slightly smoothed on the cortical surface.

2.2   Computing Functional Gradient Density

The functional gradient density [27] is a reliable, meaningful and state-of-the-art functional feature derived from fMRI data, and is widely used in adult fMRI studies [15, 16]. Essentially, the functional gradient density reflects the likelihood of each vertex sitting on the functional boundary. Conventionally, the functional gradient density is generated based on the population-mean connectivity matrix, which only captures coarse patterns of functional architecture on the cortical surface. Herein, we aim to generate a functional gradient density map for each fMRI scan to reveal finer patterns of functional architecture. The computation of this functional gradient density map of each scan is summarized as following steps: 1) for each hemisphere, the connectivity profile of each vertex is computed by correlating its time series with that of all other cortical vertices of both hemispheres; 2) each connectivity profile is transformed through Fisher's r-to-z transformation; 3) for each hemisphere, an individual's similarity matrix of connectivity profile is computed as the pairwise spatial correlations between all vertices' connectivity profiles, thus forming a 32k × 32k correlation matrix; 4) the gradient on each column of the correlation matrix is computed, thus forming a 32k × 32k gradient matrix; 5) the watershed-based segmentation is applied on each column of the gradient matrix to generate a binarized boundary map, and 6) the functional gradient density map is obtained by averaging all boundary maps [27].

2.3 Constructing Cortical Surface Functional Templates

To build cortical surface templates, conventional methods simply calculate the Euclidean average of cortical attributes across individuals after co-registration. However, this strategy is sensitive to registration errors and typically results in blurred cortical attribute patterns on the surface templates, thus deteriorating the reliability and accuracy when registering new subjects onto the blurred templates. To preserve the sharpness and details of attribute patterns on surface templates, we propose to utilize the unbalanced Wasserstein barycenter, which represents a geometrically and physically meaningful population mean under the unbalanced Wasserstein distance metric. It is particularly suitable for building cortical surface templates, especially in the presence of the potential co-registration errors. Specifically, the inherited ability of Wasserstein distance is to quantify the distance of two normalized distributions with same mass as the least cost to reshape one into the other. Rooted on the advantage of Wasserstein distance, the unbalanced Wasserstein distance additionally takes into account a prior geometric knowledge on the arbitrary "unbalanced" data, so as to free the requirement of the same mass distribution or normalization [18].

Considered N co-registered cortical surfaces with functional gradient density maps, the unbalanced Wasserstein barycenter of these functional gradient density maps are computed in a patch-wise manner on the spherical surface. Supposing $\mathcal{N}^v$ is a spherical patch centered at the vertex v with totally d vertices, the spatial position of all vertices within $\mathcal{N}^v$ is encoded in a vector $x^v \in R^{d \times 3}$. For each of the N co-registered surfaces, the corresponding functional attributes at x^v can be described as $a_1^v, \cdots, a_n^v, \cdots, a_N^v$, where $a_n^v \in R_+^d$ denotes the functional attributes distribution within the patch $\mathcal{N}^v$ from n-th subject. Denoting $q^v \in R_+^d$ is the barycenter under unbalanced Wasserstein metric, which minimizes the sum of the unbalanced transport cost toward every vector of all N patches under the unbalanced Wasserstein distance formula $W_U(\cdot, \cdot)$ [17]:

$$q^v \in \underset{q^v \in R_+^d}{\arg\min} \frac{1}{N} \sum_{n=1}^{N} W_U\left(q^v, a_n^v\right), \tag{1}$$

In general, the unbalanced Wasserstein distance $W_U(\cdot, \cdot)$ under the theory of optimal transport measures the distance between any two vectors q^v and a_n^v, which can be obtained by seeking the transport plan $T \in R_+^{d \times d}$. The transport plan should 1) fulfill low transport cost $\langle T, M \rangle$, where $\langle T, M \rangle = tr\left((T)^T M\right)$ stands for the trace of the product of two matrices T and M, with symbol $\mathcal{T}$ representing the matrix transposition, $M \in R_+^{d \times d}$ is the cost matrix to measure the pairwise distances between any two vertices i and j and defined as $M_{i,j}^v = x^v(i) - x^v(j)_1$; 2) possess marginals $T1$ and $T^T 1$ that are as close as possible to q^v and a_n^v, respectively, in the definition of Kullback-Leibler (KL) divergence: $KL(x, y) = x, log(x/y) + y - x, 1$ and 1 represents the vector of ones in R^d; and 3) has high entropy. To achieve these three requirements, $W_U(\cdot, \cdot)$ can be defined as:

$$W_U\left(q^v, a_n^v\right) = \min_{T \in R_+^{d \times d}} G\left(T, q^v, a_n^v\right), \tag{2}$$

$$G\left(T, q^v, a_n^v\right) = \langle T, M \rangle - \varepsilon E(T) + \gamma KL\left(T1 | q^v\right) + \gamma KL\left(T^T 1 | a_n^v\right), \tag{3}$$

and $\varepsilon, \gamma > 0$ are parameters, which represent weight of entropy and weight of marginal constraints, respectively. $E(T)$ is the entropy of T and the unbalanced transports will be strongly penalized by the large value of γ. The entropy regularization [28] makes the problem strictly convex and computationally faster to solve. Furthermore, we utilized Fenchel-Rockafellar duality, which allows to minimize over dual variables $\mu, v \in R^d$ instead of considering plans $T \in R_+^{d \times d}$ as pointed out in [19]. Thus, the Eq. (2) can be replaced as the Fenchel-Rockafellar dual problem:

$$W_U\left(q^v, a_n^v\right) = \max_{\mu, \tau \in R_+^d} \left[-\varepsilon \langle \mu \otimes v - 1, K \rangle - \gamma \left\langle -\frac{\varepsilon}{\gamma} \mu^{-\frac{\varepsilon}{\gamma}} - 1, q^v \right\rangle - \gamma \left\langle v^{-\frac{\varepsilon}{\gamma}} - 1, a_n^v \right\rangle \right]. \tag{4}$$

Based on Eq. (4), the unbalanced Wasserstein distance can be computed through a generalized Sinkhorn algorithm [19], therefore obtaining the unbalanced Wasserstein barycenter of cortical functional gradient density maps in each spherical patch. Due to patch overlapping, each vertex is covered by multiple spherical patches. Therefore, the final cortical functional gradient density at each vertex is computed as the average of its estimated values on all associated patches. In this manner, the resulted unbalanced Wasserstein barycenter is not very sensitive to surface registration errors, thus leading to cortical surface templates with sharp and detailed functional architecture.

2.4 Refining Cortical Surface Functional Templates

By computing the unbalanced Wasserstein barycenter of the functional gradient density maps across individuals, we can construct meaningful infant cortical surface function templates, which have sharper patterns than those based on Euclidean-based averaging. However, the inter-individual cortical correspondences are established by cortical folding features, e.g., average convexity and mean curvature, which does not necessarily lead to accurate functional alignment across individuals. This is because there are highly-variable relationships between cortical folds and functions, especially in high-order association regions. Therefore, we leverage functional gradient density as a functional feature for co-registration of cortical surfaces across individuals, by incorporating functional gradient density as a feature in Spherical Demons [25].

To this end, we perform the following procedures iteratively. 1) Based on the established inter-individual cortical correspondences, we compute the cortical surface functional templates using the unbalanced Wasserstein barycenter of functional gradient density maps across individuals in each age group. 2) To improve inter-individual cortical functional correspondences, we align all individual surfaces in the same age group to the current age-specific cortical surface template by using Spherical Demons by incorporating functional gradient density as a feature. 3) We go back to Step 1 if not converged. These steps are iteratively repeated several times until convergence, which can be evaluated by measuring the difference of the surface template constructed before and after a round of registration.

3   Results

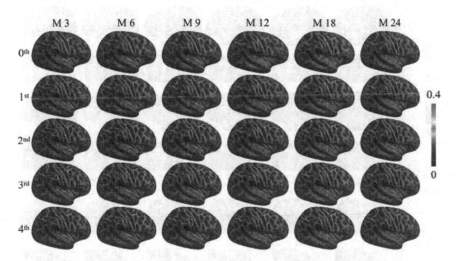

Fig. 1. Illustration of iteratively refined spatiotemporal infant cortical surface functional templates based on the gradient density of functional connectivity. The first row (0th iteration) represents the constructed surface functional templates based on the registration of cortical folding features only, without using functional gradient density for inter-individual cortical registration. The second row to fifth row represent the constructed surface functional templates after 1st to 4th rounds of surface registration based on functional gradient density.

In all experiments, we empirically set the parameters ε and γ in Eq. (4) as 0.01 and 0.1, respectively. We use the 2-ring neighbor patch for each vertex on the spherical surface mesh with 32,492 vertices. We repeat the procedure in Sect. 2.4 for 4 iterations to obtain the final cortical surface functional templates at 6 ages, i.e., 3, 6, 9,

12, 18 and 24 months of age. Figure 1 illustrates the iteratively refined spatiotemporal infant cortical surface functional templates at 6 age groups, by using the gradient density of functional connectivity as a functional feature for improving inter-individual functional correspondences. It can be seen that initially the functional gradient density maps are relatively blurry, and lacking detailed functional architecture due to the poor alignment of functional boundaries, when purely using cortical folding features for driving inter-individual surface co-registration. After leveraging functional gradient density for improving inter-individual cortical functional correspondences, the clarity and sharpness of the cortical functional gradient density maps on all constructed surface templates are gradually improved with the increase of iterations of functional feature-based registration. Importantly, many detailed patterns of functional architecture can be clearly revealed. Meanwhile, we can observe regionally variable changes of functional gradient density patterns across ages during infancy.

To show the advantage of the proposed method using unbalanced Wasserstein barycenter, we visually compare the constructed cortical surface functional templates by our method and those by the conventional Euclidean average in Fig. 2. As can be seen,

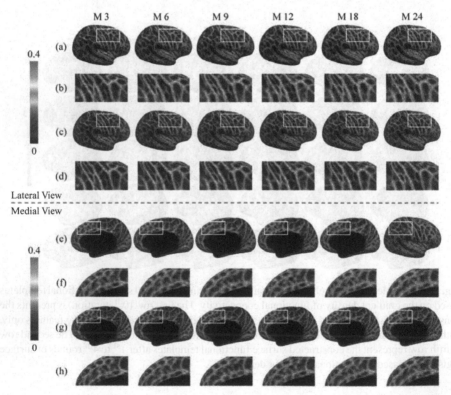

Fig. 2. Comparison of the functional gradient density maps on the constructed infant cortical surface functional templates by the proposed unbalanced Wasserstein barycenter method (a, e) and the Euclidean average method (c, g). For better inspection, surface regions in the white rectangles in (a, e) and (c, g) are zoomed in (b, f) and (d, h), respectively.

the surface templates constructed by our proposed method preserve more informative, detailed, sharp patterns, outperforming those based on Euclidean average.

Table 1. Average and standard deviation of correlation coefficient of cortical gradient density maps after aligning the testing subjects onto constructed surface templates by the proposed unbalanced Wasserstein barycenter and the Euclidean average at each iteration. (EA: templates built with Euclidean average; UWB: templates built with unbalanced Wasserstein barycenter).

Age (Month)	1st Iteration		2nd Iteration		3rd Iteration		4th Iteration	
	EA	UWB	EA	UWB	EA	UWB	EA	UWB
3	0.410 ± 0.037	0.415 ± 0.036	0.461 ± 0.035	0.466 ± 0.034	0.485 ± 0.044	0.494 ± 0.043	0.517 ± 0.041	0.525 ± 0.041
6	0.371 ± 0.075	0.374 ± 0.071	0.420 ± 0.071	0.424 ± 0.071	0.455 ± 0.080	0.462 ± 0.079	0.488 ± 0.078	0.494 ± 0.076
9	0.380 ± 0.058	0.384 ± 0.059	0.430 ± 0.056	0.434 ± 0.057	0.459 ± 0.071	0.468 ± 0.070	0.493 ± 0.069	0.501 ± 0.070
12	0.392 ± 0.057	0.396 ± 0.056	0.441 ± 0.057	0.446 ± 0.055	0.470 ± 0.048	0.472 ± 0.049	0.502 ± 0.047	0.505 ± 0.049
18	0.380 ± 0.041	0.400 ± 0.041	0.446 ± 0.041	0.452 ± 0.042	0.470 ± 0.035	0.475 ± 0.035	0.504 ± 0.034	0.508 ± 0.035
24	0.365 ± 0.053	0.367 ± 0.053	0.415 ± 0.052	0.419 ± 0.051	0.465 ± 0.042	0.470 ± 0.041	0.498 ± 0.040	0.503 ± 0.040

We also quantitatively evaluate our constructed cortical surface functional templates. Intuitively, surface templates with sharper functional attribute patterns would lead to better registration results. Therefore, we can compare the functional pattern similarity across individual surfaces when aligning them onto the templates constructed by different methods. Therefore, for each age group, we randomly divide the subjects into a training set (2/3 subjects) and a testing set (1/3 subjects). Then, the subjects in the testing set are aligned onto the corresponding age-matched surface template constructed by the training set by using Spherical Demons with functional gradient density as the functional feature for driving the registration.

For any two subjects after functional alignment, we compute the Pearson's correlation of their functional gradient density maps. Ideally, the sharper the templates are, the larger the correlation coefficients will be. Therefore, we can obtain the average and standard deviation of correlation coefficient for all possible pairs of subjects at each age group, where larger correlation coefficients indicate better alignment of the functional gradient density. Table 1 shows the quantitative performance of the constructed templates at different age groups using the proposed unbalanced Wasserstein barycenter (UWB) and the conventional Euclidean average, respectively. To better evaluate the effectiveness of the refinement, we also report the comparison of performance of constructed templates by the two methods in each iteration. As indicated by the larger correlation coefficients in Table 1, surface templates constructed by our method lead to better alignment of individual surfaces in each age group and at each iteration. Clearly, the iterative refinement substantially improves the alignment quality, suggesting the necessity of iteratively refining the templates as proposed in our work.

To further test if our proposed method brought significant improvement, we conducted paired t-test on the mean correlation coefficient of any pairs of subjects (4th iteration) between the proposed method and the Euclidean average. The results show that our method has statistically significant better performance in majority of groups (3 M (p = 0.006), 6 M (p = 0.029), 9 M (p = 0.014), 18 M (p = 0.014), and 24 M (p = 0.009)), suggesting the superiority of our method compared to Euclidean average.

4   Conclusion

This paper has three major contributions. First, we constructed the first set of spatiotemporal infant cortical surface functional templates based on functional gradient density, densely covering multiple time points, i.e., 3, 6, 9, 12, 18 and 24 monthes. Second, we proposed to compute the unbalanced Wasserstein barycenter, which leads to more accurate and detailed patterns of functional architecture on surface templates than the conventional Euclidean average. Third, to improve the cortical functional correspondeces across individuals, we firstly leveaged the functional gradient density as a functional feature and incoporated it into Spherical Demons to drive the surface registration. Moreover, we used an iterative strategy to graudally and greatly improve inter-indivdual cortical functional correspondences. Of note, the proposed framwork is generic to incoprate other functional features for improving functional aligment and building high-quality surface functional templates. Our constructed infant cortical surface functional templates will be released to the public to serve as a reference for infant functional MRI studies.

Acknowledgments. This work was partially supported by NIH grants (MH116225 and MH117943). This work also utilizes approaches developed by an NIH grant (1U01MH110274) and the efforts of the UNC/UMN Baby Connectome Project Consortium.

References

1. Li, G., Wang, L., Yap, P.-T., Wang, F., Wu, Z., Meng, Y., Dong, P., Kim, J., Shi, F., Rekik, I.: Computational neuroanatomy of baby brains: a review. NeuroImage **185**, 906–925 (2019)
2. Oishi, K., Chang, L., Huang, H.: Baby brain atlases. NeuroImage **185**, 865–880 (2019)
3. Wu, Z., Wang, L., Lin, W., Gilmore, J.H., Li, G., Shen, D.: Construction of 4D infant cortical surface atlases with sharp folding patterns via spherical patch-based group-wise sparse representation. Hum. Brain Mapp. **40**(13), 3860–3880 (2019)
4. Bozek, J., Makropoulos, A., Schuh, A., Fitzgibbon, S., Wright, R., Glasser, M.F., Coalson, T.S., O'Muircheartaigh, J., Hutter, J., Price, A.N.: Construction of a neonatal cortical surface atlas using multimodal surface matching in the developing Human Connectome Project. NeuroImage **179**, 11–29 (2018)
5. Li, G., Wang, L., Shi, F., Lin, W., Shen, D.: Constructing 4D infant cortical surface atlases based on dynamic developmental trajectories of the cortex. In: International Conference on Medical Image Computing and Computer-Assisted Intervention, pp. 89–96 (2014)

6. Wang, F., Lian, C., Xia, J., Wu, Z., Duan, D., Wang, L., Shen, D., Li, G.: Construction of spatiotemporal infant cortical surface atlas of rhesus macaque. In: 2018 IEEE 15th International Symposium on Biomedical Imaging, pp. 704–707 (2018)
7. Wright, R., Makropoulos, A., Kyriakopoulou, V., Patkee, P.A., Koch, L.M., Rutherford, M.A., Hajnal, J.V., Rueckert, D., Aljabar, P.: Construction of a fetal spatio-temporal cortical surface atlas from in utero MRI: application of spectral surface matching. NeuroImage **120**, 467–480 (2015)
8. Wu, Z., Li, G., Wang, L., Lin, W., Gilmore, J.H., Shen, D.: Construction of spatiotemporal neonatal cortical surface atlases using a large-scale dataset. In: 2018 IEEE 15th International Symposium on Biomedical Imaging, pp. 1056–1059 (2018)
9. Xia, J., Wang, F., Benkarim, O.M., Sanroma, G., Piella, G., González Ballester, M.A., Hahner, N., Eixarch, E., Zhang, C., Shen, D.: Fetal cortical surface atlas parcellation based on growth patterns. Hum. Brain Mapp. **40**(13), 3881–3899 (2019)
10. Conroy, B., Singer, B., Haxby, J., Ramadge, P.J.: fMRI-based inter-subject cortical alignment using functional connectivity. In: Advances in Neural Information Processing Systems, pp. 378–386 (2009)
11. Jiang, D., Du, Y., Cheng, H., Jiang, T., Fan, Y.: Groupwise spatial normalization of fMRI data based on multi-range functional connectivity patterns. Neuroimage **82**, 355–372 (2013)
12. Sabuncu, M.R., Singer, B.D., Conroy, B., Bryan, R.E., Ramadge, P.J., Haxby, J.V.: Function-based intersubject alignment of human cortical anatomy. Cereb. Cortex **20**(1), 130–140 (2010)
13. Yeo, B.T., Krienen, F.M., Sepulcre, J., Sabuncu, M.R., Lashkari, D., Hollinshead, M., Roffman, J.L., Smoller, J.W., Zöllei, L., Polimeni, J.R.: The organization of the human cerebral cortex estimated by intrinsic functional connectivity. J. Neurophysiol. (2011)
14. Wig, G.S., Laumann, T.O., Cohen, A.L., Power, J.D., Nelson, S.M., Glasser, M.F., Miezin, F.M., Snyder, A.Z., Schlaggar, B.L., Petersen, S.E.: Parcellating an individual subject's cortical and subcortical brain structures using snowball sampling of resting-state correlations. Cereb. Cortex **24**(8), 2036–2054 (2014)
15. Glasser, M.F., Coalson, T.S., Robinson, E.C., Hacker, C.D., Harwell, J., Yacoub, E., Ugurbil, K., Andersson, J., Beckmann, C.F., Jenkinson, M.: A multi-modal parcellation of human cerebral cortex. Nature **536**(7615), 171–178 (2016)
16. Laumann, T.O., Gordon, E.M., Adeyemo, B., Snyder, A.Z., Joo, S.J., Chen, M.-Y., Gilmore, A.W., McDermott, K.B., Nelson, S.M., Dosenbach, N.U.: Functional system and areal organization of a highly sampled individual human brain. Neuron **87**(3), 657–670 (2015)
17. Chizat, L., Peyré, G., Schmitzer, B., Vialard, F.-X.: Unbalanced optimal transport: Dynamic and Kantorovich formulations. J. Funct. Anal. **274**(11), 3090–3123 (2018)
18. Chizat, L., Peyré, G., Schmitzer, B., Vialard, F.-X.: Scaling algorithms for unbalanced optimal transport problems. Math. Comput. **87**(314), 2563–2609 (2018)
19. Janati, H., Cuturi, M., Gramfort, A.: Wasserstein regularization for sparse multi-task regression. In: The 22nd International Conference on Artificial Intelligence and Statistics, pp. 1407–1416 (2018)
20. Howell, B.R., Styner, M.A., Gao, W., Yap, P.-T., Wang, L., Baluyot, K., Yacoub, E., Chen, G., Potts, T., Salzwedel, A.: The UNC/UMN baby connectome project (BCP): an overview of the study design and protocol development. NeuroImage **185**, 891–905 (2019)
21. Li, G., Nie, J., Wang, L., Shi, F., Gilmore, J.H., Lin, W., Shen, D.: Measuring the dynamic longitudinal cortex development in infants by reconstruction of temporally consistent cortical surfaces. Neuroimage **90**, 266–279 (2014)
22. Li, G., Wang, L., Shi, F., Gilmore, J.H., Lin, W., Shen, D.: Construction of 4D high-definition cortical surface atlases of infants: methods and applications. Med. Image Anal. **25**(1), 22–36 (2015)

23. Wang, F., Lian, C., Wu, Z., Zhang, H., Li, T., Meng, Y., Wang, L., Lin, W., Shen, D., Li, G.: Developmental topography of cortical thickness during infancy. Proc. Natl. Acad. Sci. **116**(32), 15855–15860 (2019)
24. Van Essen, D.C., Glasser, M.F., Dierker, D.L., Harwell, J., Coalson, T.: Parcellations and hemispheric asymmetries of human cerebral cortex analyzed on surface-based atlases. Cereb. Cortex **22**(10), 2241–2262 (2012)
25. Yeo, B.T., Sabuncu, M.R., Vercauteren, T., Ayache, N., Fischl, B., Golland, P.: Spherical demons: fast diffeomorphic landmark-free surface registration. IEEE Trans. Med. Imaging **29**(3), 650–668 (2009)
26. Glasser, M.F., Sotiropoulos, S.N., Wilson, J.A., Coalson, T.S., Fischl, B., Andersson, J.L., Xu, J., Jbabdi, S., Webster, M., Polimeni, J.R.: The minimal preprocessing pipelines for the Human Connectome Project. Neuroimage **80**, 105–124 (2013)
27. Gordon, E.M., Laumann, T.O., Adeyemo, B., Huckins, J.F., Kelley, W.M., Petersen, S.E.: Generation and evaluation of a cortical area parcellation from resting-state correlations. Cereb. Cortex **26**(1), 288–303 (2016)
28. Cuturi, M.: Sinkhorn distances: lightspeed computation of optimal transport. In: Advances in neural information processing systems, pp. 2292–2300 (2013)

DWI and Tractography

Tract Dictionary Learning for Fast and Robust Recognition of Fiber Bundles

Ye Wu, Yoonmi Hong, Sahar Ahmad, Weili Lin, Dinggang Shen,
Pew-Thian Yap$^{(\boxtimes)}$, and the UNC/UMN Baby Connectome Project Consortium

Department of Radiology and Biomedical Research Imaging Center (BRIC),
University of North Carolina, Chapel Hill, USA
ptyap@med.unc.edu

Abstract. In this paper, we propose an efficient framework for parcellation of white matter tractograms using discriminative dictionary learning. Key to our framework is the learning of a compact dictionary for each fiber bundle so that the streamlines within the bundle can be sufficiently represented. Dictionaries for multiple bundles are combined for whole-brain tractogram representation. These dictionaries are learned jointly to encourage inter-bundle incoherence for discriminative power. The proposed method allows tractograms to be assigned to more than one bundle, catering to scenarios where tractograms cannot be clearly separated. Experiments on a bundle-labeled HCP dataset and an infant dataset highlight the ability of our framework in grouping streamlines into anatomically plausible bundles.

Keywords: Diffusion MRI · Tractography · Fiber bundle · Dictionary learning

1 Introduction

Diffusion magnetic resonance imaging (DMRI) [1] allows analysis of white matter (WM) axonal trajectories via streamlines (i.e., tractogram) generated by a process called tractography. Automatically grouping several millions of streamlines into anatomically meaningful bundles is an important yet challenging task [2–4], since streamlines within a bundle can have different shapes, lengths, and endpoints.

A fiber tract is a collection of axons having common origin and destination sites. Automatic tract identification strategies can be based on regions of interest (ROIs) [5], clustering [2,3], atlases [2,6], and segmentation [7,8]. Many existing methods rely on point correspondences between streamlines [9]. However, even within the same bundle, streamlines can have different lengths and endpoints. Therefore, standard geometric distance measures often lead to poor results. Moreover, the streamlines are often first aligned to a common space

---

This work was supported in part by NIH grants (NS093842, EB006733, and MH110274) and the efforts of the UNC/UMN Baby Connectome Project Consortium.

© Springer Nature Switzerland AG 2020
A. L. Martel et al. (Eds.): MICCAI 2020, LNCS 12267, pp. 251–259, 2020.
https://doi.org/10.1007/978-3-030-59728-3_25

defined for example by a tract atlas and then resampled with the same number of points to facilitate computation of distances between streamlines [3,10]. If the underlying anatomy is altered due to pathology or development, meaningful information might be lost in the process of resampling [11].

In this paper, we propose a method to efficiently parcellate the whole-brain tractogram, catering especially to scenarios where streamline separation is challenging. This is achieved via tract dictionary learning (TractDL) to learn tractogram exemplars for fast and automated analysis of large datasets. Unlike existing dictionary-based approaches [12,13], our method adopts a natural means of enforcing consistency across hemispheres and is unconfounded by the lengths of streamlines. Instead of learning the dictionary in the native point space, we map the tractograms to a Hilbert space via cosine series representation. Parcellation is performed in the cosine representation space via a sparse framework with a set of learned dictionaries, each for a bundle. We exploit structured incoherence and shared features across bundles so that within-bundle variability is small but between-bundle variability is large. Using the dictionaries, whole-brain bilateral clustering is applied for simultaneous bundle parcellation in both hemispheres. We evaluated TractDL based on HCP data and infant data in comparison with existing bundle parcellation methods.

2 Methods

2.1 Modeling Fiber Streamlines

We represent the streamlines in Hilbert space [11]. Let $l \in \mathbb{R}^{n \times 3}$ denote a streamline of a fiber bundle, consisting of n points $\{p^{(j)}\}_{j=1}^{n}$. Note that n can be different for each streamline. We consider a function f^{-1} that maps these points onto the unit interval $[0, 1]$ as

$$f^{-1} : p^{(j)} \to \frac{\sum_{i=2}^{j} \|p^{(i)} - p^{(i-1)}\|}{\sum_{i=2}^{n} \|p^{(i)} - p^{(i-1)}\|} = \gamma^{(j)}, \quad f^{-1}(p^{(1)}) = 0. \tag{1}$$

That is, $\gamma^{(j)}$ indicates the ratio between the arc-length from the point $p^{(1)}$ to $p^{(j)}$, and the total arc-length from $p^{(1)}$ to $p^{(n)}$. We can parameterize the smooth inverse map $f : [0, 1] \to l$ as a linear combination of smooth basis function.

Let the coordinates of f be (f_1, f_2, f_3). Then, each coordinate can be approximated using K degree cosine series expansion [11]:

$$f_i(t) \simeq \sum_{k=0}^{K} c_{ki} \psi_k(t), \tag{2}$$

where $\{\psi_k\}$ is a cosine basis. Then, for $\{\gamma^{(j)}\}_{j=1}^{n}$ corresponding to n sampling points $\{p^{(j)}\}_{j=1}^{n}$, we have

$$f_i(\gamma^{(j)}) \simeq \sum_{k=0}^{K} c_{ki} \psi_k(\gamma^{(j)}). \tag{3}$$

The matrix of cosine coefficients $C = \{c_{ki}\} \in \mathbb{R}^{(K+1)\times 3}$ can be estimated from $\mathbf{f} = \{f_i(\gamma^{(j)})\} \in \mathbb{R}^{n\times 3}$ in the least-squares manner as

$$C = \left(\Psi_K^T \Psi_K\right)^{-1} \Psi_K^T \mathbf{f}, \tag{4}$$

where $\Psi_K = \{\psi_k(\gamma^{(j)})\} \in \mathbb{R}^{n\times(K+1)}$. We note that the dimension of the coefficients $C \in \mathbb{R}^{(K+1)\times 3}$ only depends on the degree K of cosine series ($K = 19$ in this paper), but not on the number of sampling points along the streamline.

2.2   Tract Dictionary Learning

Let $\mathbf{X}_t$ represent the set of cosine coefficients of the streamlines of t-th bundle. We learn a dictionary $\mathbf{D}_t$ for the t-th bundle using sparse dictionary learning (DL) by minimizing the following objective function:

$$\min_{\mathbf{A}_t,\mathbf{D}_t} \frac{1}{2}\|\mathbf{X}_t - \mathbf{D}_t\mathbf{A}_t\|_F^2 + \lambda\|\mathbf{A}_t\|_1. \tag{5}$$

Each column of $\mathbf{X}_t$ can be represented as a linear combination of a set of vectors in an over-complete dictionary $\mathbf{D}_t$ with sparse coefficients in the corresponding column of $\mathbf{A}_t$. Based on the coefficients, the streamlines can be classified into different bundles.

We train the dictionaries of multiple fiber bundles jointly. Note that if the dictionaries of the individual bundles are trained separately, they are not necessarily discriminative enough to help distinguish the streamlines from the different bundles. To obtain incoherent discriminative dictionaries, we let $\mathbf{X} = [\mathbf{X}_1, \mathbf{X}_2, \ldots]$, $\mathbf{D} = [\mathbf{D}_1, \mathbf{D}_2, \ldots]$, and $\mathbf{A} = \left[\mathbf{A}_1^T, \mathbf{A}_2^T, \ldots\right]^T$, and solve the following problem:

$$\min_{\mathbf{A},\mathbf{D}} \frac{1}{2}\|\mathbf{X} - \mathbf{D}\mathbf{A}\|_F^2 + \lambda\|\mathbf{A}\|_1 + \eta \sum_{t_1 \neq t_2} \left\|\mathbf{D}_{t_1}^T \mathbf{D}_{t_2}\right\|_F^2, \quad \text{s.t.} \quad \mathbf{A} \succeq 0, \tag{6}$$

where $\sum_{t_1 \neq t_2} \left\|\mathbf{D}_{t_1}^T \mathbf{D}_{t_2}\right\|_F^2$ encourages orthogonality between each dictionary pair [14]. λ and η are scalar tuning parameters. The size of each bundle dictionary is fixed as m. Each row of $\mathbf{X}$ is normalized to have zero mean and unit variance to remove the effects of distribution location and scale. In this paper, we solved (6) using an open source dictionary learning toolbox (DICTOL)[1].

2.3   Streamline Classification

The sparse code $\mathbf{a}_t$ of the cosine representation $\mathbf{x}$ of a streamline with respect to the dictionary of bundle t can be used for streamline classification. This is achieved by solving

---

[1] https://github.com/tiepvupsu/DICTOL.

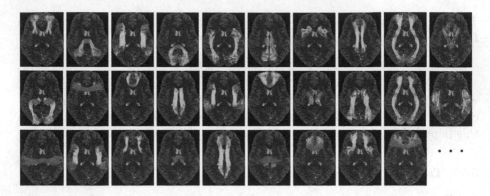

Fig. 1. Inter-hemispheric bilateral clustering of the whole-brain tractogram.

$$t^* = \arg\min_t \frac{1}{2} \|\mathbf{x} - \mathbf{D}_t \mathbf{a}_t\|_2^2 + \lambda \|\mathbf{a}_t\|_1 + (1 - \lambda) \|\mathbf{a}_t\|_2, \text{ s.t. } \mathbf{a}_t \succeq 0, \qquad (7)$$

where t^* is the label of streamline $\mathbf{x}$, and λ is a regularization parameter.

To rapidly classify whole-brain streamlines into bundles, we first perform unsupervised clustering to cluster the streamlines into a number of clusters. We employ a fast k-medoids clustering algorithm on the cosine representation coefficients of the streamlines. To improve clustering robustness, bilateral clustering is applied for simultaneous bundle parcellation in both cerebral hemispheres. A total of 2000 of fiber clusters are generated for good anatomical separation of the streamlines while maintaining good clustering consistency across subjects [3]. Figure 1 shows the clustering results, color-coded by local streamline orientations. We then randomly select 50 streamlines from each cluster and label each streamline via solving (7). The final bundle label assigned to each cluster is the label with count fraction (out of 50) greater than a threshold v.

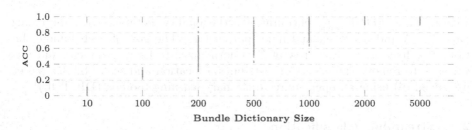

Fig. 2. ACC as a function of the dictionary size m.

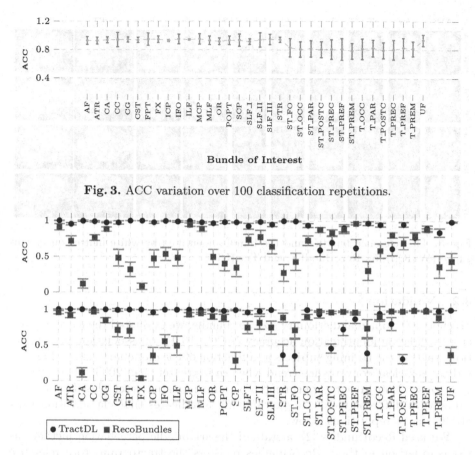

Fig. 3. ACC variation over 100 classification repetitions.

Fig. 4. The identification ACC of each tract across subjects measured in two ways; $ACC(\mathcal{X}_{GT}, \mathcal{X}_{RES})$ (top) and $ACC(\mathcal{X}_{RES}, \mathcal{X}_{GT})$ (bottom).

3   Experimental Results

3.1   Dataset

The dataset used for evaluation consisted of 72 WM tract bundles for each of 105 young adults from the Human Connectome Project (HCP) [15]. The ground-truth tracts were extracted semi-automatically from whole-brain tractograms [16]. 70 subjects were used for training and the remaining 35 subjects were used for testing. The fiber streamlines of each subject were transformed to a common space via affine transformation determined by volumetric registration. For each subject, 1000 streamlines were randomly selected from each bundle for training. For bundles with less than 1000 streamlines, all streamlines were selected. The abbreviations of the fiber bundles are defined in [16].

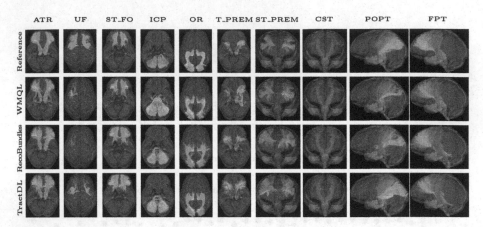

Fig. 5. The reference bundles and the bundles identified by white matter query language (WMQL) [5], RecoBundles, and TractDL.

3.2 Validation

To choose the optimal dictionary size per bundle, we evaluated the leave-one-out cross-validation identification accuracy (ACC) [16,17] of association and projection tracts of the training subjects as a function of the dictionary size m. Figure 2 indicates a clear convergence trend when m is greater than 2000. Therefore, we used $m = 2000$ in our experiments. We also repeated tract classification 100 times with different tract samples and Fig. 3 indicates that classification variability across repetitions is low.

We used RecoBundles [2], a state-of-the-art bundle parcellation method, as the comparison method. RecoBundles registers the tractograms to a reference subject and uses clustering to detect streamlines that are similar to reference tracts. We used the default parameters while running RecoBundles on the 35 test subjects. For evaluation, we combined the 72 fiber bundles for each test subject to form whole-brain tractograms. To compare the accuracy of the methods, we let $\mathcal{X}_{\text{GT}}$ and $\mathcal{X}_{\text{RES}}$ be the ground-truth streamlines and the identified streamlines, respectively, and define the ACC of the tract identification in two ways:

$$\text{ACC}(\mathcal{X}_{\text{GT}}, \mathcal{X}_{\text{RES}}) = \frac{|\mathcal{X}_{\text{GT}} \cap \mathcal{X}_{\text{RES}}|}{|\mathcal{X}_{\text{GT}}|}, \ \text{ACC}(\mathcal{X}_{\text{RES}}, \mathcal{X}_{\text{GT}}) = \frac{|\mathcal{X}_{\text{GT}} \cap \mathcal{X}_{\text{RES}}|}{|\mathcal{X}_{\text{RES}}|}. \quad (8)$$

Figure 4 indicates that TractDL yields higher classification accuracy in general, especially in identifying association and projection tracts.

To evaluate the robustness of TractDL, we regenerated the whole-brain tractogram of one subject randomly chosen from the testing dataset. We used MRtrix to compute the fiber orientation distribution functions with multi-shell multi-tissue constrained spherical deconvolution and generated two million fibers with anatomically constrained probabilistic tractography. By employing TractDL, we were able to identify difficult bundles such as UF, OR, CST, FPT, and POPT (Fig. 5).

To study hemispheric asymmetry of the bundles, we computed the laterality index: $LI = (L - R)/(L + R)$, where R and L are the streamline counts in the right and left hemispheres, respectively. Table 1 shows the absolute values of LI [18,19], which ranges from 0 (not lateralized) to 1 (completely lateralized). This confirms that fiber bundles identified by TractDL are more symmetric for most of the bundles, which is in line with previous studies [19,20].

To evaluate the generalizability of TractDL, we applied it to a 54-days-old infant subject image acquired as part of Baby Connectome Project (BCP) [21], with a protocol that is different from the training subjects. Tractography was conducted with asymmetry spectrum imaging (ASI) as described in [22,23]. ASI fits a mixture of asymmetric fiber orientation distribution function (AFODF) to the diffusion signal. Fiber streamlines were then generated by successively

Table 1. Laterality index.

Laterality	ATR	UF	ST_FO	ICP	OR	T_PREM	ST_PREM	CST	POPT	FPT
Reference	0.2640	0.5539	0.2796	0.3311	0.3339	0.1066	0.2019	0.3669	0.0058	0.0887
WMQL	0.5236	0.5870	0.0470	0.0877	0.4539	0.5322	0.1483	0.0178	0.0714	0.3850
RecoBundles	0.5459	0.9872	0.0292	0.0178	0.2288	0.1581	0.1044	0.1706	0.4079	0.4501
TractDL	0.3071	0.2172	0.0844	0.0494	0.1143	0.2206	0.2188	0.0023	0.0896	0.0905

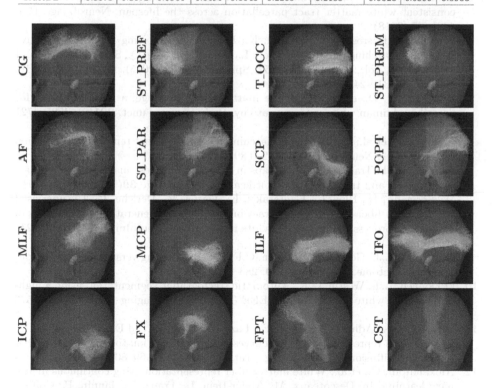

Fig. 6. Fiber bundles identified by TractDL in an infant subject.

following local directions determined from the AFODF [23]. Figure 6 indicates that the bundles are correctly identified by TractDL.

4   Conclusion

We presented a method for fast and robust identification of fiber bundles of interest from a large number of streamlines. The coordinates of each streamline were parameterized as coefficients of cosine series expansions. Based on this representation, we constructed dictionaries for multiple bundles of the whole-brain tractogram. The dictionaries were learned jointly to encourage incoherence for tractogram classifications. The effectiveness, robustness, generalizability, and bilaterality of our method were validated by the experimental results.

References

1. Johansen-Berg, H., Behrens, T.E.: Diffusion MRI: From Quantitative Measurement to In Vivo Neuroanatomy. Academic Press, London (2013)
2. Garyfallidis, E., et al.: Recognition of white matter bundles using local and global streamline-based registration and clustering. NeuroImage **170**, 283–295 (2018)
3. Zhang, F., et al.: An anatomically curated fiber clustering white matter atlas for consistent white matter tract parcellation across the lifespan. NeuroImage **179**, 429–447 (2018)
4. Kumar, K., Desrosiers, C., Siddiqi, K.: Brain fiber clustering using non-negative kernelized matching pursuit. In: Zhou, L., Wang, L., Wang, Q., Shi, Y. (eds.) MLMI 2015. LNCS, vol. 9352, pp. 144–152. Springer, Cham (2015). https://doi.org/10.1007/978-3-319-24888-2_18
5. Wassermann, D., et al.: The white matter query language: a novel approach for describing human white matter anatomy. Brain Struct. Funct. **221**(9), 4705–4721 (2016)
6. Eckstein, I., et al.: Active fibers: matching deformable tract templates to diffusion tensor images. Neuroimage **47**, T82–T89 (2009)
7. Hua, K., et al.: Tract probability maps in stereotaxic spaces: analyses of white matter anatomy and tract-specific quantification. NeuroImage **39**(1), 336–347 (2008)
8. Wassermann, D., Bloy, L., Kanterakis, E., Verma, R., Deriche, R.: Unsupervised white matter fiber clustering and tract probability map generation: applications of a Gaussian process framework for white matter fibers. NeuroImage **51**(1), 228–241 (2010)
9. O'Donnell, L.J., Golby, A.J., Westin, C.F.: Fiber clustering versus the parcellation-based connectome. NeuroImage **80**, 283–289 (2013)
10. O'Donnell, L.J., Westin, C.F.: Automatic tractography segmentation using a high-dimensional white matter atlas. IEEE Trans. Med. Imaging **26**(11), 1562–1575 (2007)
11. Chung, M.K., Adluru, N., Lee, J.E., Lazar, M., Lainhart, J.E., Alexander, A.L.: Cosine series representation of 3D curves and its application to white matter fiber bundles in diffusion tensor imaging. Stat. Interface **3**(1), 69–80 (2010)
12. Alexandroni, G., et al.: White matter fiber representation using continuous dictionary learning. In: Descoteaux, M., Maier-Hein, L., Franz, A., Jannin, P., Collins, D.L., Duchesne, S. (eds.) MICCAI 2017. LNCS, vol. 10433, pp. 566–574. Springer, Cham (2017). https://doi.org/10.1007/978-3-319-66182-7_65

13. Kumar, K., Siddiqi, K., Desrosiers, C.: White matter fiber analysis using kernel dictionary learning and sparsity priors. Pattern Recogn. **95**, 83–95 (2019)
14. Ramirez, I., Sprechmann, P., Sapiro, G.: Classification and clustering via dictionary learning with structured incoherence and shared features. In: IEEE Computer Society Conference on Computer Vision and Pattern Recognition, pp. 3501–3508. IEEE (2010)
15. Van Essen, D.C., et al.: The WU-Minn human connectome project: an overview. NeuroImage **80**, 62–79 (2013)
16. Wasserthal, J., Neher, P., Maier-Hein, K.H.: TractSeg - fast and accurate white matter tract segmentation. NeuroImage **183**, 239–253 (2018)
17. Taha, A.A., Hanbury, A.: Metrics for evaluating 3D medical image segmentation: analysis, selection, and tool. BMC Med. Imaging **15**(1), 29 (2015)
18. O'Donnell, L.J., et al.: The fiber laterality histogram: a new way to measure white matter asymmetry. In: Jiang, T., Navab, N., Pluim, J.P.W., Viergever, M.A. (eds.) MICCAI 2010. LNCS, vol. 6362, pp. 225–232. Springer, Heidelberg (2010). https://doi.org/10.1007/978-3-642-15745-5_28
19. Propper, R.E., et al.: A combined fMRI and DTI examination of functional language lateralization and arcuate fasciculus structure: effects of degree versus direction of hand preference. Brain Cogn. **73**(2), 85–92 (2010)
20. de SchottenSchotten, M.T., et al.: Atlasing location, asymmetry and inter-subject variability of white matter tracts in the human brain with MR diffusion tractography. NeuroImage **54**(1), 49–59 (2011)
21. Howell, B.R., et al.: The UNC/UMN baby connectome project (BCP): an overview of the study design and protocol development. NeuroImage **185**, 891–905 (2019)
22. Wu, Y., Lin, W., Shen, D., Yap, P.-T.: Asymmetry spectrum imaging for baby diffusion tractography. In: Chung, A.C.S., Gee, J.C., Yushkevich, P.A., Bao, S. (eds.) IPMI 2019. LNCS, vol. 11492, pp. 319–331. Springer, Cham (2019). https://doi.org/10.1007/978-3-030-20351-1_24
23. Wu, Y., Hong, Y., Feng, Y., Shen, D., Yap, P.T.: Mitigating gyral bias in cortical tractography via asymmetric fiber orientation distributions. Med. Image Anal. **59**, 101543 (2020)

Globally Optimized Super-Resolution of Diffusion MRI Data via Fiber Continuity

Ye Wu, Yoonmi Hong, Sahar Ahmad, Wei-Tang Chang, Weili Lin,
Dinggang Shen, and Pew-Thian Yap[✉]

Department of Radiology and Biomedical Research Imaging Center (BRIC),
University of North Carolina, Chapel Hill, USA
ptyap@med.unc.edu

Abstract. In this paper, we introduce a technique for super-resolution reconstruction of diffusion MRI, harnessing fiber-continuity (FC) as a constraint in a global whole-brain optimization framework. FC is a biologically-motivated constraint that relates orientation information between neighboring voxels. We show that it can be used to effectively constrain the inverse problem of recovering high-resolution data from low-resolution data. Since voxels are inter-related by FC, we devise a global optimization framework that allows solutions pertaining to all voxels to be solved simultaneously. We demonstrate that the proposed super-resolution framework is effective for diffusion MRI data of a glioma patient, a healthy subject, and a macaque.

Keywords: Diffusion MRI · Super-resolution · Fiber continuity

1 Introduction

Diffusion magnetic resonance imaging (DMRI) with high angular and spatial resolution is plagued by low signal-to-noise ratio (SNR) and long acquisition time [1]. These are inevitable consequences of the smaller voxel size and the large number of diffusion-weighted (DW) volumes that need to be acquired for multiple diffusion directions and scales. Instead of relying on expensive scanner upgrades and sophisticated MRI sequences, super-resolution (SR) techniques can be used to infer high-resolution (HR) images from low-resolution (LR) images.

Regularization-based SR methods harness constraints such as smoothness, sparsity, and low-rank [2–7] to infer HR information. These methods leverage inter-voxel spatial redundancy that is typical in images for data recovery. For example, in [8], spatial regularization is used to improve estimation of orientation distribution functions. Ning et al. [6] coupled compressed sensing with SR for accelerated HR DMRI reconstruction and demonstrated that spatial regularization reduces sensitivity to noise.

This work was supported in part by NIH grants (NS093842 and EB006733).

© Springer Nature Switzerland AG 2020

A. L. Martel et al. (Eds.): MICCAI 2020, LNCS 12267, pp. 260–269, 2020.
https://doi.org/10.1007/978-3-030-59728-3_26

Another form of regularization that is more specific to DMRI is fiber continuity (FC). FC is a biologically-motivated constraint that arises from the spatially-continuous nature of fiber tracts. The orientation information at each voxel location captures localized information about white matter pathways. Based on this observation, the FC constraint requires that orientations transit smoothly across voxels and is therefore a means of linking information within and across voxels. Recent studies have shown that FC [9–12] can be harnessed for enhancing image resolution and improving the estimation of fiber orientation distributions.

In this paper, we propose a technique for SR reconstruction of DMRI data by harnessing FC constraint based on intra-voxel orientation information. Note that our method does not rely explicitly on tractography. The term "fiber continuity" comes from the fact that at each voxel DMRI captures the local orientation of a fiber bundle. Since fibers are continuous spatially, the orientations are expected to vary smoothly across space. We show that FC in tandem with signal representation based on asymmetric fiber orientation distributions [12,13] can be used to regularize the ill-posed inverse problem associated with the recovery of the HR DMRI data from its LR counterpart. We (i) formulate a novel SR technique that uses intra-voxel orientation information; (ii) use a global optimization framework for the spatio-angular recovery of multi-shell DMRI data, reducing sensitivity to noise; (iii) demonstrate the efficacy of the technique in tumorous and healthy human brains and a macaque brain; and (iv) demonstrate the utility of the technique in recovering HR data from highly incomplete or under-sampled LR DMRI data [14]. Experimental results indicate that our technique enables the recovery of rich structural details.

2 Methods

2.1 Forward Model

The LR DW volumes are considered as down-sampled versions of HR DW volumes that need to be estimated. For this purpose, we let $\mathbf{Y} \in \mathbb{R}^{N_v \times M_g}$ denote a set of LR DW volumes with N_v voxels per volume and M_g gradient directions across different shells. The LR volumes $\mathbf{Y}$ are related to the HR volumes $\mathbf{S} \in \mathbb{R}^{M_v \times M_g}$ by

$$\mathbf{Y} = \mathbf{DS} + \boldsymbol{\mu}, \tag{1}$$

where $\mathbf{D}$ is a down-sampling matrix that averages neighboring voxels and $\boldsymbol{\mu}$ denotes noise. The sampling of $\mathbf{Y}$ can be encoded by a binary matrix $\mathbf{B}$ such that

$$\mathbf{B} \odot \mathbf{Y} = \mathbf{B} \odot (\mathbf{DS} + \boldsymbol{\mu}), \tag{2}$$

where $\odot$ is the element-wise multiplication operator. The model is general and can account for different spatio-angular subsampling schemes determined by $\mathbf{B}$ and $\mathbf{D}$.

2.2 Fiber Continuity (FC)

Our method uses FC across voxels to regularize the inverse problem of recovering the HR volumes. FC [12] is a natural constraint supporting the fact that orientations should be consistent along fiber tracts. A model based on asymmetric fiber orientation distribution functions (AFODFs) [12] is used to represent the sub-voxel configurations. In DMRI, the signal profile is typically assumed to be antipodal symmetric, implying that orientation in a positive hemisphere is always identical to its counterpart in the negative hemisphere. Symmetric FODFs are not sufficient in regions with, for example, fanning and bending fiber trajectories. To improve sub-voxel fiber continuity, we estimate AFODFs by incorporating information from neighboring voxels, allowing FODF asymmetry to better represent complex configurations [10,13,15]. The discontinuity of AFODFs, $\mathcal{F}_{\text{aniso}}$, over all voxels and directions ($\mathbf{u} \in \mathbb{S}^2$) is measured as

$$\Phi(\mathcal{F}_{\text{aniso}}) = \int_{\mathbf{u} \in \mathbb{S}^2} \|\mathcal{F}_{\text{aniso}}(\mathbf{u}) \otimes \mathbf{W}(\mathbf{u}) - \mathcal{F}_{\text{aniso}}(\mathbf{u})\|_{\text{F}}^2 \, d\mathbf{u}, \tag{3}$$

where $\mathbf{W}$ is a normalized directional probability distribution function as defined in [12] and $\otimes$ is a column-wise multiplication operator.

2.3 Spherical Convolution

We use a multi-tissue spherical convolution model to represent the diffusion signal at each voxel of $\mathbf{S}$. Specifically, $\mathbf{S}$ can be decomposed as $\mathbf{S} = \mathcal{R}\mathcal{X}$, with $\mathcal{R} = [\mathbf{R}_{\text{aniso}}, \mathbf{R}_{\text{aniso}}, \mathbf{R}_{\text{iso},1}, \cdots, \mathbf{R}_{\text{iso},n}]$ being the multi-tissue axially symmetric response function (RF) consisting of an anisotropic component $\mathbf{R}_{\text{aniso}}$ and n isotropic compartments $\{\mathbf{R}_{\text{iso},i}\}_{i=1}^{n}$ as defined in [16]. Each column of

$$\mathcal{X} = \left[\mathbf{X}_{\text{aniso}}^{+}, \mathbf{X}_{\text{aniso}}^{-}, \mathbf{X}_{\text{iso},1}, \cdots, \mathbf{X}_{\text{iso},n}\right]^{\top}$$

is the spherical harmonics (SH) coefficients of AFODF at each voxel location. The AFODF is represented by two sets of even-order spherical harmonics [12], capturing potentially asymmetric sub-voxel fiber configurations. That is,

$$\mathcal{F}_{\text{aniso}}(\mathbf{u}) = \begin{cases} \mathbf{A}(\mathbf{u}) \cdot \mathbf{X}_{\text{aniso}}^{+}, & \mathbf{u} \in \mathbb{S}_{+}^2, \\ \mathbf{A}(\mathbf{u}) \cdot \mathbf{X}_{\text{aniso}}^{-}, & \mathbf{u} \in \mathbb{S}_{-}^2, \end{cases} \tag{4}$$

where $\mathbf{A}(\mathbf{u})$ is the real even-order SH basis function sampled in direction $\mathbf{u}$, and the column vectors of $\mathbf{X}_{\text{aniso}}^{+}$ and $\mathbf{X}_{\text{aniso}}^{-}$ are the corresponding SH coefficients for the positive and negative hemispheres ($\mathbb{S}_{+}^2$ and $\mathbb{S}_{-}^2$).

2.4 Super-Resolution Reconstruction

Based on Eq. (2), we estimate $\mathbf{S}$ and $\mathcal{X}$ by solving

$$\min_{\mathbf{S}, \mathcal{X}} \frac{1}{2} \|\mathbf{B} \odot (\mathbf{Y} - \mathbf{DS})\|^2 + \lambda \|\mathcal{L}\mathcal{X}\|^2, \text{ s.t. } \begin{cases} \mathbf{S} = \mathcal{R}\mathcal{X}, \\ \mathbf{A}\mathcal{X} \succeq 0, \\ \Phi(\mathcal{F}_{\text{aniso}}) \leq \epsilon, \\ \mathbf{S} \succeq 0, \end{cases} \tag{5}$$

where the Laplace-Beltrami regularization [17] is realized via $\mathcal{L}$ = diag $[\mathbf{L}, \mathbf{L}, 0, \cdots, 0]$ where $\mathbf{L}_{jj} = \ell_j(\ell_j + 1)$ with ℓ_j being the order associated with the j-th coefficient. λ is the regularization parameter and the matrix $\mathcal{A} = \mathrm{diag}\,[\mathbf{A}, \mathbf{A}, a_0, \cdots, a_0]$ maps the SH coefficients $\mathcal{X}$ to the AFODF amplitudes for imposing AFODF non-negativity. $a_0 = \sqrt{\frac{1}{4\pi}}$ is the 0-th order SH basis function.

Problem (5) is solved using alternating direction method of multipliers (ADMM) [18]. Specifically, the problem can be cast as a strictly convex quadratic programming (QP) problem, which can be solved by an operator splitting solver for quadratic programs (OSQP) [19]. Following common SR frameworks [5–7], we used linearly interpolated data to initialize ADMM.

2.5   Implementation Details

A white matter (WM) RF is estimated for each b-shell from the average of the reoriented diffusion signal profiles of voxels with high anisotropy in WM. Also isotropic RFs are set with diffusivity values ranging from $0.1 \times 10^{-3}\,\mathrm{mm}^2/\mathrm{s}$ to $3 \times 10^{-3}\,\mathrm{mm}^2/\mathrm{s}$ and step size $0.2 \times 10^{-3}\,\mathrm{mm}^2/\mathrm{s}$. This will allow better characterization of tissue microstructure in healthy and tumorous brains.

We used k-fold cross-validation to determine the optimal regularization parameter λ in (5). Two thousand random WM voxels from an HCP DMRI dataset and 61 candidate values for λ, logarithmically spanning the interval between 0.01 and 10, were considered [12,13]. We found that the optimal value was 0.01. This value was applied to all experiments.

3   Experimental Results

We compared our method, fiber-continuity super-resolution (FCSR), with four existing methods, including bicubic interpolation, Lanczos-3 resampling, TV-L1 reconstruction [20], and TV-L2 reconstruction [21]. We assumed that LR DW volumes $\mathbf{Y}$ are spatially downsampled from HR DW volumes $\mathbf{S}$ by a factor of 2 for each dimension. Objective evaluation was performed using Blind/Referenceless Image Spatial Quality Evaluator (BRISQUE) [22] and Naturalness Image Quality Evaluator (NIQE) [23]. Both BRISQUE and NIQE are no-reference image quality scores, with lower values indicating better image quality. Three datasets, summarized in Table 1, were used for validation, involving (i) a pre-surgical glioma patient [24]; (ii) a healthy subject with data acquired using slice-interleaved diffusion encoding (SIDE) [14]; and (iii) a macaque with histological data [25];

3.1   Glioma Dataset

Representative results for fractional anisotropy (FA), isotropic volume fraction (IVF), apparent diffusion coefficient (ADC), intra-cellular volume fraction

Table 1. Datasets

| | Glioma [24] | SIDE [14] | Macaque [25] | |
			LR	HR
Dimensions	96 × 96 × 60	128 × 128 × 100	48 × 96 × 64	96 × 192 × 128
Resolution	2.5 mm³	1.5 mm³	0.8 mm³	0.4 mm³
Acceleration	N/A	Multiband = 5	N/A	
b-value (s/mm²)	700,1200,2800	500,1000,2000,3000	3000,6000,9000,120000	
# Gradient directions	100	160	404	
# Non-DW volumes	2	1	16	

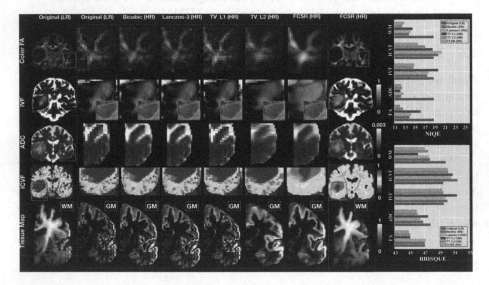

Fig. 1. Color FA, IVF, ADC, ICVF, and WM tissue maps of a patient with glioma. NIQE and BRISQUE scores are shown on the right. The T1-weighted reference image is shown in the insets of the IVF results.

(ICVF)[1], and tissue maps are shown in Fig. 1. Among the methods, FCSR recovers more structural details, especially in the zoomed-in regions. Moreover, FCSR retains the shape of the tumor, similar to the T1-weighted image that is shown in the insets. FCSR results in lower BRISQUE and NIQE scores, indicating better image quality. Figure 2 shows that FCSR improves the tractography of fiber bundles connecting cortical or sub-cortical regions.

3.2 SIDE Dataset

We also evaluated FCSR with SIDE [14] data acquired with acceleration factors $R = 2, 4$, and 10. Collecting the full data ($R = 1$) took a total acquisition time of

---

[1] Computed using AMICO [26].

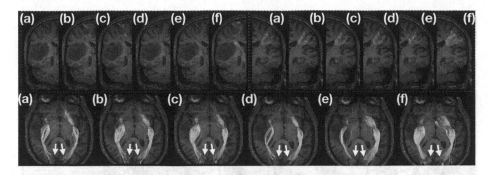

Fig. 2. Fiber bundles given by (a) the original LR data, (b) bicubic interpolation, (c) Lanczos-3 resampling, (d) TV-L1 reconstruction, (e) TV-L2 reconstruction, and (f) FCSR.

8.32 min. Therefore, the acquisition time is $8.32/R$ minutes for acceleration factor R. The results are summarized in Fig. 3, demonstrating that FCSR recovers more structural details especially in the cortical regions. The effectiveness of FCSR is further confirmed by the lower NIQE and BRISQUE scores. Note that $R = 10$ corresponds to less than one minute of acquisition time. Coupling SIDE with FCSR allows rich information on tissue microstructure to be collected in a very short amount of time.

We also evaluated FCSR by ICVF values along tractography streamlines. Figure 4(d, e) show that FCSR improves the tractography of u-fibers connecting small cortical or subcortical regions, with high consistency between full acquisition (i.e., FCSR (HR)) and acquisitions with different acceleration factors.

Figure 5 compares the FODFs generated by (a) spatially upsampled SH coefficients [17] of the full LR data ($R = 1$) and (b) FCSR. It can be seen that details near the cortex cannot be sufficiently recovered by upsampling via interpolation. On the other hand, FCSR yields superior orientation details in the cortical region, critical for mitigating gyral bias and improving the estimation of cortico-cortical connections [12].

3.3 Macaque Dataset

Figure 6 summarizes the results for the macaque dataset, including color FA, axon diameter index, and tissue maps. Note that HR and SR DMRI data are reconstructed from original LR and HR DMRI data, respectively. The results again indicate that FCSR is superior in preserving details and consistent across HR and SR reconstruction. The efficacy of FCSR is confirmed by the mean squared error (MSE) and structural similarity index (SSIM), which are computed between the reconstructed HR data and the original HR data, averaged across volumes.

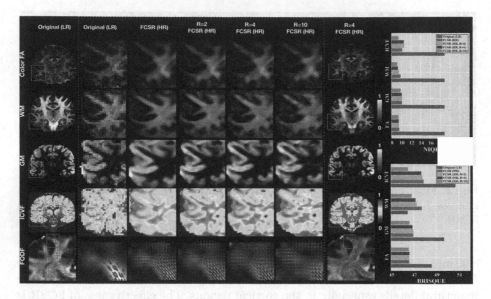

Fig. 3. Color FA map, WM tissue map, GM tissue map, ICVF map, and FODF glyphs of the SIDE data acquired from a healthy subject. NIQE and BRISQUE scores are shown on the right.

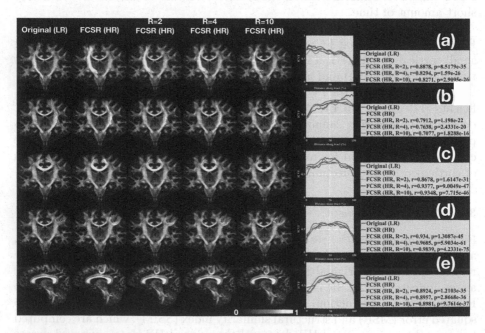

Fig. 4. The tract streamlines and along-tract ICVF values for five major white matter bundles. On the right, the ICVF values averaged across streamlines in a bundle are plotted along-tract locations. The Pearson correlation coefficients (r) and the p-values of mean ICVF values between the full and accelerated acquisitions are shown.

(a)   (b)

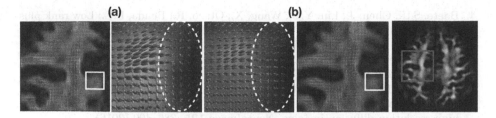

Fig. 5. Comparison of HR FODFs computed by (a) upsampling the SH coefficients and (b) FCSR of the full LR data ($R = 1$). Close-up views are shown for the cortical region marked by the red rectangle. (Color figure online)

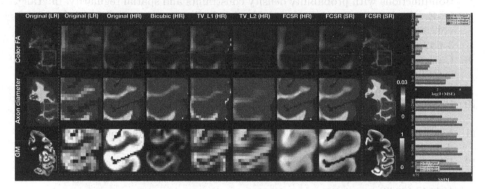

Fig. 6. Color FA, axon diameter, and GM tissue maps of the macaque brain. MSE and SSIM values are shown on the right. FCSR (HR) and FCSR (SR) are reconstructed from original LR and HR DMRI, respectively.

4 Conclusion

We demonstrated that spatial resolution can be improved using the fiber-continuity constraint in a global whole-brain optimization framework. Our evaluation with datasets acquired with different resolutions, imaging sequences, and scanners for humans and non-human primates indicate that our method is effective in resolution enhancement.

References

1. Johansen-Berg, H., Behrens, T.E.: Diffusion MRI: from quantitative measurement to in vivoneuroanatomy. Academic Press (2013)
2. Shi, F., Cheng, J., Wang, L., Yap, P.-T., Shen, D.: Super-resolution reconstruction of diffusion-weighted images using 4D low-rank and total variation. In: Fuster, A., Ghosh, A., Kaden, E., Rathi, Y., Reisert, M. (eds.) Computational Diffusion MRI. MV, pp. 15–25. Springer, Cham (2016). https://doi.org/10.1007/978-3-319-28588-7_2
3. Haldar, J.P., et al.: Improved diffusion imaging through SNR-enhancing joint reconstruction. Magn. Reson. Med. **69**(1), 277–289 (2013)

4. Baete, S.H., Chen, J., Lin, Y.C., Wang, X., Otazo, R., Boada, F.E.: Low rank plus sparse decomposition of ODFs for improved detection of group-level differences and variable correlations in white matter. NeuroImage **174**, 138–152 (2018)
5. Shi, F., Cheng, J., Wang, L., Yap, P.T., Shen, D.: LRTV: MR image super-resolution with low-rank and total variation regularizations. IEEE Trans. Med. Imaging **34**(12), 2459–2466 (2015)
6. Ning, L., et al.: A joint compressed-sensing and super-resolution approach for very high-resolution diffusion imaging. NeuroImage **125**, 386–400 (2016)
7. Lum, E.: Super resolution of HARDI images using compressed sensing techniques. Master's thesis, University of Waterloo (2015)
8. Goh, A., Lenglet, C., Thompson, P.M., Vidal, R.: Estimating orientation distribution functions with probability density constraints and spatial regularity. In: Yang, G.-Z., Hawkes, D., Rueckert, D., Noble, A., Taylor, C. (eds.) MICCAI 2009. LNCS, vol. 5761, pp. 877–885. Springer, Heidelberg (2009). https://doi.org/10.1007/978-3-642-04268-3_108
9. Calamante, F., Tournier, J.D., Jackson, G.D., Connelly, A.: Track-density imaging (TDI): super-resolution white matter imaging using whole-brain track-density mapping. Neuroimage **53**(4), 1233–1243 (2010)
10. Reisert, M., Kellner, E., Kiselev, V.G.: About the geometry of asymmetric fiber orientation distributions. IEEE Trans. Med. Imaging **31**(6), 1240–1249 (2012)
11. Yap, P.T., An, H., Chen, Y., Shen, D.: Fiber-driven resolution enhancement of diffusion-weighted images. NeuroImage **84**, 939–950 (2014)
12. Wu, Y., Hong, Y., Feng, Y., Shen, D., Yap, P.T.: Mitigating gyral bias in cortical tractography via asymmetric fiber orientation distributions. Med. Image Anal. **59**, 101543 (2020)
13. Bastiani, M., et al.: Improved tractography using asymmetric fibre orientation distributions. Neuroimage **158**, 205–218 (2017)
14. Hong, Y., et al.: Multifold acceleration of diffusion MRI via slice-interleaved diffusion encoding (SIDE). arXiv (2020)
15. Karayumak, S.C., Özarslan, E., Unal, G.: Asymmetric orientation distribution functions (AODFs) revealing intravoxel geometry in diffusion MRI. Magn. Reson. Imaging **49**, 145–158 (2018)
16. Wu, Y., Lin, W., Shen, D., Yap, P.-T.: Asymmetry spectrum imaging for baby diffusion tractography. In: Chung, A.C.S., Gee, J.C., Yushkevich, P.A., Bao, S. (eds.) IPMI 2019. LNCS, vol. 11492, pp. 319–331. Springer, Cham (2019). https://doi.org/10.1007/978-3-030-20351-1_24
17. Tournier, J.D., Calamante, F., Connelly, A.: Robust determination of the fibre orientation distribution in diffusion MRI: non-negativity constrained super-resolved spherical deconvolution. Neuroimage **35**(4), 1459–1472 (2007)
18. Boyd, S., Parikh, N., Chu, E., Peleato, B., Eckstein, J.: Distributed optimization and statistical learning via the alternating direction method of multipliers. Found. Trends Mach. Learn. **3**(1), 1–122 (2011)
19. Stellato, B., Banjac, G., Goulart, P., Bemporad, A., Boyd, S.: OSQP: an operator splitting solver for quadratic programs. In: 2018 UKACC 12th International Conference on Control (CONTROL), p. 339. IEEE (2018)
20. Mani, M., Jacob, M., Guidon, A., Magnotta, V., Zhong, J.: Acceleration of high angular and spatial resolution diffusion imaging using compressed sensing with multichannel spiral data. Magn. Reson. Med. **73**(1), 126–138 (2015)
21. Marquina, A., Osher, S.J.: Image super-resolution by TV-regularization and bregman iteration. J. Sci. Comput. **37**(3), 367–382 (2008)

22. Mittal, A., Moorthy, A.K., Bovik, A.C.: No-reference image quality assessment in the spatial domain. IEEE Trans. Image Process. **21**(12), 4695–4708 (2012)
23. Mittal, A., Soundararajan, R., Bovik, A.C.: Making a "completely blind" image quality analyzer. IEEE Signal Process. Lett. **20**(3), 209–212 (2012)
24. Aerts, H., et al.: Modeling brain dynamics in brain tumor patients using the virtual brain. eNeuro **5**(3) (2018)
25. Schilling, K., Gao, Y., Janve, V., Stepniewska, I., Landman, B.A., Anderson, A.W.: Confirmation of a gyral bias in diffusion MRI fiber tractography. Hum. Brain Mapp. **39**(3), 1449–1466 (2018)
26. Daducci, A., Canales-Rodríguez, E.J., Zhang, H., Dyrby, T.B., Alexander, D.C., Thiran, J.P.: Accelerated microstructure imaging via convex optimization (AMICO) from diffusion MRI data. NeuroImage **105**, 32–44 (2015)

White Matter Tract Segmentation with Self-supervised Learning

Qi Lu, Yuxing Li, and Chuyang Ye[✉]

School of Information and Electronics, Beijing Institute of Technology, Beijing, China
Chuyang.Ye@bit.edu.cn

Abstract. White matter tract segmentation based on *diffusion magnetic resonance imaging* (dMRI) plays an important role in brain analysis. Deep learning based methods of white matter tract segmentation have been proposed to improve the segmentation accuracy. However, manual delineations of white matter tracts for network training are especially difficult to obtain. Therefore, in this paper, we explore how to improve the performance of deep learning based white matter tract segmentation when the number of manual tract delineations is limited. Specifically, we propose to exploit the abundant unannotated data using a self-supervised learning approach, where knowledge about image context can be learned in a well designed pretext task that does not require manual annotations. The knowledge can then be transferred to the white matter tract segmentation task, so that when manual tract delineations for training are scarce, the performance of the network can be improved. To allow the image context knowledge to be relevant to white matter tracts, the pretext task in this work is designed to predict the density map of fiber streamlines, where training data can be obtained using tractography without manual efforts. The model pretrained for the pretext task is then fine-tuned by the small number of tract annotations for the target segmentation task. In addition, we explore the possibility of combining self-supervised learning with a complementary pseudo-labeling strategy of using unannotated data. We validated the proposed approach using dMRI scans from the Human Connectome Project dataset, where the benefit of the proposed method is shown when tract annotations are scarce.

Keywords: White matter tract segmentation · Self-supervised learning · Deep network

1 Introduction

White matter tract segmentation based on *diffusion magnetic resonance imaging* (dMRI) provides a quantitative tool for the analysis of brain connections [20]. In particular, volumetric segmentation strategies have been developed, where each voxel in a dMRI scan is labeled according to the fiber tract to which it belongs, and no tractography needs to be performed. For example, in [3] the voxels are labeled based on an atlas and the directional information in dMRI using a Markov

© Springer Nature Switzerland AG 2020
A. L. Martel et al. (Eds.): MICCAI 2020, LNCS 12267, pp. 270–279, 2020.
https://doi.org/10.1007/978-3-030-59728-3_27

random field. In [19] and [12], random forests and k-nearest neighbor classification are used to classify the voxels based on diffusion features, respectively. More recently, *convolutional neural networks* (CNNs) have been used for white matter tract segmentation, where segmentation results are computed from fiber orientation maps and the segmentation accuracy is greatly improved [18].

For CNNs to achieve decent segmentation performance, a large number of training scans with manual annotations are required in general. However, manual annotations are time-consuming and expensive, especially for the delineations of white matter tracts, which are much more difficult than the delineations of other brain anatomical structures. Therefore, it is desirable to improve the performance of CNN-based white matter tract segmentation when only a few annotated training images are available.

Because usually a large amount of unannotated data is available, methods have been developed to improve the model performance for CNNs when annotated data is scarce by combining annotated and unannotated data. In particular, self-supervised learning [11] has been proposed, which aims at learning high-level image features using a pretext task that does not require annotations. In the pretext task, the unannotated image is mapped to a different image according to a designed rule, and CNNs can be trained to learn the mapping using these generated image pairs [4, 11]. The knowledge learned from the pretext task can then be transferred to the target task via fine-tuning, so that even with a small amount of annotated data, CNNs can still perform with adequate accuracy. Since unannotated dMRI scans are also abundant, it is possible to explore self-supervised learning for white matter tract segmentation, which, to the best of our knowledge, has not been explored.

In this paper, we propose a self-supervised learning approach to CNN-based white matter tract segmentation. The TractSeg architecture [18] is used as the backbone network due to its state-of-the-art performance. We design a pretext task that is related to white matter tracts, so that knowledge about generic characteristics of tracts can be learned from unannotated images. Specifically, the pretext task aims to predict a density map of fiber streamlines, which are representations of white matter pathways and can be computed automatically. The pretext model is then fine-tuned with a small number of tract annotations for white matter tract segmentation. In addition, we have explored the possibility of combining self-supervised learning with another complementary strategy of using unannotated data, where pseudo-labeling [1] is integrated in the fine-tuning process. We validated our approach using the publicly available *Human Connectome Project* (HCP) dataset [17]. Experimental results show that the proposed method remarkably improves the performance of white matter tract segmentation when only a small number of scans are annotated for training.

2 Methods

2.1 CNN-Based White Matter Tract Segmentation

CNNs have been used for improving the accuracy of white matter tract segmentation. In particular, the TractSeg architecture is developed in [18] and has achieved state-of-the-art performance. Thus, TractSeg is used as our backbone network. The core of TractSeg is an encoder-decoder CNN, which performs 2D processing for the input data and generates the probability map of each tract for each orientation (coronal/axial/sagittal). The outputs of the CNN that correspond to the three orientations are then merged (by averaging). The encoder-decoder CNN in TractSeg is inspired by the U-net architecture proposed in [13]. In addition, according to the publicly available code provided by [18], deep supervision is further introduced for improved segmentation.[1] A second 2D CNN could be also used for segmentation refinement. However, since the second CNN is optional [18] and its training is time-consuming with very minor improvements, it is not used in this work.

To allow the network to be applied to dMRI data acquired with various protocols, TractSeg uses the map of fiber orientations as input. These fiber orientations are computed with the *multi-shell multi-tissue constrained spherical deconvolution* (MSMT-CSD) method [7] in MRtrix [16]. A maximum number of three fiber orientations is used at each voxel, and thus the input has nine channels. Note that if a voxel has fewer than three fiber orientations, the values in the corresponding empty channels are set to zero.

2.2 Self-supervised Learning for White Matter Tract Segmentation

Although TractSeg has achieved state-of-the-art segmentation performance, its success relies on sufficient training scans with annotated white matter tracts. However, manual annotations can be difficult to acquire for white matter tracts and only scarce annotated training data may be available. To address this problem, it is possible to explore the massive amount of unannotated data for network training. Self-supervised learning provides an effective method for exploiting unannotated data and has been successfully applied to various tasks [4,11]. Therefore, we develop a self-supervised learning strategy for improving CNN-based white matter tract segmentation given scarce annotated training scans.

In self-supervised learning, a pretext task is designed, which does not require manual annotations to generate training data. By learning to perform the pretext task, the network can learn useful features for image understanding using the large amount of unannotated data. This knowledge can then be transferred to the target task of interest. We seek to design a pretext task that is associated with the characteristics of white matter tracts. Specifically, in the pretext task, the network is trained to predict the density map of fiber streamlines. The fiber streamlines are connected line segments with directions that represent white matter pathways, and thus the density map is related to the characteristics of white matter tracts in general. The fiber streamlines can be automatically computed with fiber tracking, which is also known as tractography [2]. In this way, no annotations are needed to train the network for the pretext task.

In this work, we track the fiber streamlines with the deterministic tractography method in Dipy [5], and brain masks are used to constrain the fiber tracking

---

[1] The TractSeg code is available at https://github.com/MIC-DKFZ/TractSeg/.

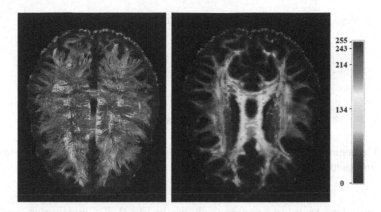

Fig. 1. An example of the fiber streamlines (left) and density map (right) overlaid on the fractional anisotropy map that represents the degree of diffusion anisotropy.

result. The step size is 0.5 mm and the maximum turning angle is 30°. One seed is placed in each voxel, and the density map is derived by counting the number of streamlines that intersect with each voxel. An example of the fiber streamlines and the derived density map is shown in Fig. 1.

In the training for the pretext task, the network structure is slightly modified from TractSeg, because the segmentation problem becomes a regression problem. Specifically, the activation of the last layer is switched to a *rectified linear unit* (ReLU) [9] function because the density is always nonnegative. The weights learned for the pretext task are then used to initialize the TractSeg architecture, except for the last layer, which is randomly initialized. The TractSeg network is then fine-tuned with the annotated training scans for white matter tract segmentation. Note that for the pretext task, both annotated and unannotated images can be used for training, although the annotations are not needed, whereas during fine-tuning for segmentation, only annotated images are used.

2.3   Integration with Pseudo-Labeling

Another common strategy to exploit unannotated data is pseudo-labeling [1], where pseudo-labels are generated for unannotated data to retrain the deep network. While self-supervised learning can provide richer information than pseudo-labeling, the two approaches are complementary. Thus, we further explore the integration of self-supervised learning with pseudo-labeling. Suppose the model pretrained for the pretext task is $\mathcal{M}_0$ and the model fine-tuned from $\mathcal{M}_0$ for tract segmentation is $\mathcal{M}_1$. We first produce pseudo-annotations by applying $\mathcal{M}_1$ to the unannotated images. The pseudo-annotations—i.e., the prediction given by $\mathcal{M}_1$ for the unannotated images—are then used together with the true annotations to retrain the segmentation model, which gives $\mathcal{M}_2$. Finally, $\mathcal{M}_2$ is used to segment test images.

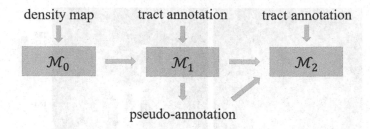

Fig. 2. A schematic of the complete training process that integrates self-supervised learning and pseudo-labeling.

The complete training process is shown in Fig. 2. To summarize, we use all annotated and unannotated training scans to train $\mathcal{M}_0$, but the annotations are not needed for the pretext task. We only use annotated training scans to train $\mathcal{M}_1$. Both annotated and unannotated training scans are used for training $\mathcal{M}_2$, where true annotations and pseudo-annotations are used, respectively.

2.4   Implementation Details

We implemented the proposed method using PyTorch [10]. For the pretext task, the network is trained by minimizing the mean squared error of the estimated density map; for the segmentation task, we follow the settings in [18], where the cross-entropy loss is minimized for each tract using a multi-label strategy. In all cases, Adamax [8] is selected as the optimizer, and dropout [14] with a probability of 0.4 is used [18]. Like in [18], 72 major white matter tracts are segmented. For the complete list of tracts, we refer readers to [18].

3   Results

We used 155 subjects from the HCP dataset [17] for evaluation. The corresponding dMRI scans were acquired with 270 diffusion gradients and 18 $b0$ images. The image resolution is 1.25 mm isotropic. These images have been processed by the minimal preprocessing pipeline, including distortion correction, motion correction, and brain extraction [6]. The 155 dMRI scans included 37 annotated and 118 unannotated scans. The annotations were obtained from [18].[2] Five annotated scans and 95 unannotated scans were included in the training set and used for network training as described in Sect. 2.3. Two other annotated scans and the other 23 unannotated scans were used as a validation set during the training of the segmentation network and the pretext model, respectively. The remaining 30 annotated scans were used for testing.

The proposed method was first evaluated qualitatively. Cross-sectional views of the segmentation results are shown in Fig. 3 for representative test subjects

---

[2] The annotations are available at https://doi.org/10.5281/zenodo.1088277.

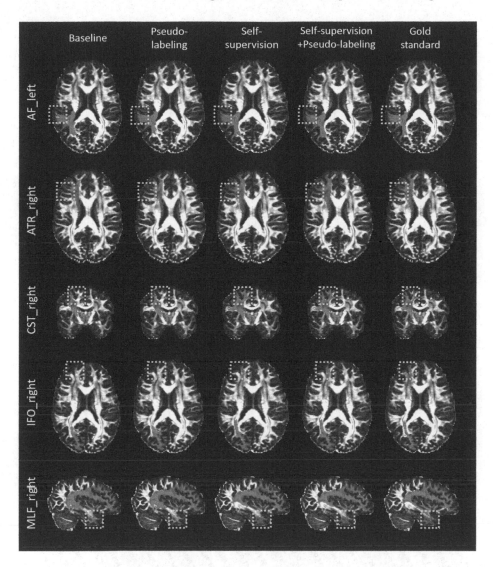

Fig. 3. Cross-sectional views of the segmentation results (red) overlaid on the fractional anisotropy maps for representative test subjects and white matter tracts. The manual delineation is also shown for reference. Note the highlighted regions for comparison. (Color figure online)

and white matter tracts, where the manual delineations (gold standard) are also displayed for reference.[3] The proposed method was compared with the baseline TractSeg method that only uses annotated training images. In addition, we compared the proposed method with the pseudo-labeling strategy that exploits

---

[3] For the meaning of the abbreviations for tract names, refer to [18].

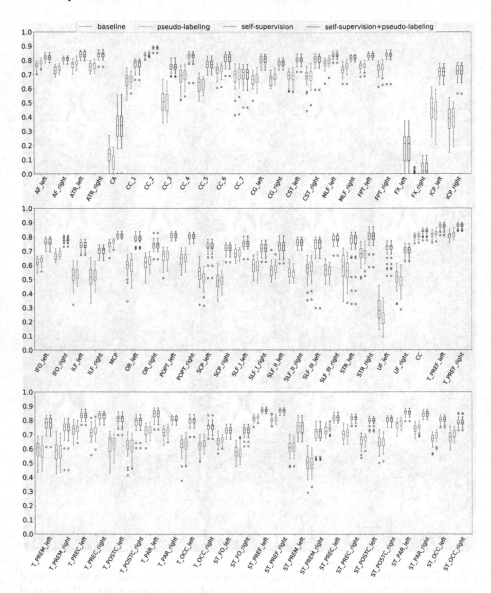

Fig. 4. Boxplots of the Dice coefficients for all 72 tracts.

unannotated data. Also, to demonstrate the benefit of the proposed self-supervised learning strategy alone, the results obtained without the integration of pseudo-labeling are shown. It can be seen that with self-supervision (both with and without the integration of pseudo-labeling), the results are more similar to the manual delineations than those of the competing methods are.

Next, the proposed method was quantitatively evaluated. We computed the Dice coefficient [15] between the segmentation result and manual delineation

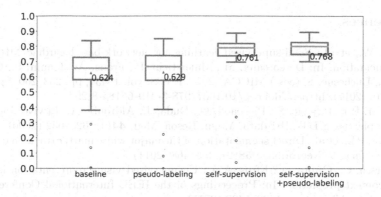

Fig. 5. Boxplots of the average Dice coefficient for each tract. The means of the average Dice coefficients are also indicated.

for the test scans, and the results are summarized in the boxplots in Fig. 4 for all 72 tracts. Our method, with or without pseudo-labeling integration, remarkably outperforms the competing methods for each tract. Here, the result of the baseline method is much worse than that reported in [18], because far fewer labeled scans were used for training. Although compared with self-supervision alone, the improvement using pseudo-labeling integration is not obvious, quantitatively the average Dice coefficient is higher with the integration for 70 out of the 72 tracts. The average Dice coefficient for each tract is then summarized in Fig. 5, where the means of these average Dice coefficients are also indicated. Consistent with Fig. 4, self-supervision improves the segmentation performance, and its integration with pseudo-labeling slightly increases the segmentation accuracy. These results together show that the self-supervised learning strategy can substantially improve the performance of white matter tract segmentation when the number of annotated training images is limited. In addition, the integration of pseudo-labeling with self-supervision can introduce marginal improvements.

4   Conclusion

We have developed a self-supervised learning method for CNN-based white matter tract segmentation with scarce annotated training data. A pretext task is designed to predict the density map of fiber streamlines. The network pretrained for the pretext task is then fine-tuned for segmentation. We have also explored the integration of the proposed self-supervised learning strategy with pseudo-labeling. Experimental results on the HCP dataset indicate the benefit of the proposed method when tract annotations are scarce.

Acknowledgements. This work is supported by Beijing Natural Science Foundation (L192058 & 7192108) and Beijing Institute of Technology Research Fund Program for Young Scholars. The HCP dataset was provided by the Human Connectome Project, WU-Minn Consortium and the McDonnell Center for Systems Neuroscience at Washington University.

References

1. Bai, W., et al.: Semi-supervised learning for network-based cardiac MR image segmentation. In: Descoteaux, M., Maier-Hein, L., Franz, A., Jannin, P., Collins, D.L., Duchesne, S. (eds.) MICCAI 2017. LNCS, vol. 10434, pp. 253–260. Springer, Cham (2017). https://doi.org/10.1007/978-3-319-66185-8_29
2. Basser, P.J., Pajevic, S., Pierpaoli, C., Duda, J., Aldroubi, A.: In vivo fiber tractography using DT-MRI data. Magn. Reson. Med. **44**(4), 625–632 (2000)
3. Bazin, P.L., et al.: Direct segmentation of the major white matter tracts in diffusion tensor images. NeuroImage **58**(2), 458–468 (2011)
4. Doersch, C., Gupta, A., Efros, A.A.: Unsupervised visual representation learning by context prediction. In: Proceedings of the IEEE International Conference on Computer Vision, pp. 1422–1430 (2015)
5. Garyfallidis, E., et al.: Dipy, a library for the analysis of diffusion MRI data. Front. Neuroinform. **8**(8), 1–17 (2014)
6. Glasser, M.F., et al.: The minimal preprocessing pipelines for the human connectome project. NeuroImage **80**, 105–124 (2013)
7. Jeurissen, B., Tournier, J.D., Dhollander, T., Connelly, A., Sijbers, J.: Multi-tissue constrained spherical deconvolution for improved analysis of multi-shell diffusion MRI data. NeuroImage **103**, 411–426 (2014)
8. Kingma, D.P., Ba, J.: Adam: a method for stochastic optimization. arXiv preprint arXiv:1412.6980 (2014)
9. Nair, V., Hinton, G.E.: Rectified linear units improve restricted Boltzmann machines. In: Proceedings of the 27th International Conference on Machine Learning, pp. 807–814 (2010)
10. Paszke, A., et al.: PyTorch: an imperative style, high-performance deep learning library. In: Advances in Neural Information Processing Systems, pp. 8024–8035 (2019)
11. Pathak, D., Krahenbuhl, P., Donahue, J., Darrell, T., Efros, A.A.: Context encoders: feature learning by inpainting. In: Proceedings of the IEEE Conference on Computer Vision and Pattern Recognition, pp. 2536–2544 (2016)
12. Ratnarajah, N., Qiu, A.: Multi-label segmentation of white matter structures: application to neonatal brains. NeuroImage **102**, 913–922 (2014)
13. Ronneberger, O., Fischer, P., Brox, T.: U-Net: convolutional networks for biomedical image segmentation. In: Navab, N., Hornegger, J., Wells, W.M., Frangi, A.F. (eds.) MICCAI 2015. LNCS, vol. 9351, pp. 234–241. Springer, Cham (2015). https://doi.org/10.1007/978-3-319-24574-4_28
14. Srivastava, N., Hinton, G., Krizhevsky, A., Sutskever, I., Salakhutdinov, R.: Dropout: a simple way to prevent neural networks from overfitting. J. Mach. Learn. Res. **15**(1), 1929–1958 (2014)
15. Taha, A.A., Hanbury, A.: Metrics for evaluating 3D medical image segmentation: analysis, selection, and tool. BMC Med. Imaging **15**(1), 29 (2015)
16. Tournier, J.D., Calamante, F., Connelly, A.: Robust determination of the fibre orientation distribution in diffusion MRI: non-negativity constrained super-resolved spherical deconvolution. NeuroImage **35**(4), 1459–1472 (2007)
17. Van Essen, D.C., Smith, S.M., Barch, D.M., Behrens, T.E., Yacoub, E., Ugurbil, K.: Wu-Minn HCP Consortium: the WU-Minn human connectome project: an overview. NeuroImage **80**, 62–79 (2013)
18. Wasserthal, J., Neher, P., Maier-Hein, K.H.: TractSeg - fast and accurate white matter tract segmentation. NeuroImage **183**, 239–253 (2018)

19. Ye, C., Yang, Z., Ying, S.H., Prince, J.L.: Segmentation of the cerebellar peduncles using a random forest classifier and a multi-object geometric deformable model: application to spinocerebellar ataxia type 6. Neuroinformatics **13**(3), 367–381 (2015)
20. Zhang, F., Hoffmann, N., Karayumak, S.C., Rathi, Y., Golby, A.J., O'Donnell, L.J.: Deep white matter analysis: fast, consistent tractography segmentation across populations and dMRI acquisitions. In: Shen, D., et al. (eds.) MICCAI 2019. LNCS, vol. 11766, pp. 599–608. Springer, Cham (2019). https://doi.org/10.1007/978-3-030-32248-9_67

Estimating Tissue Microstructure with Undersampled Diffusion Data via Graph Convolutional Neural Networks

Geng Chen[1], Yoonmi Hong[1], Yongqin Zhang[2], Jaeil Kim[3], Khoi Minh Huynh[1], Jiquan Ma[4], Weili Lin[1], Dinggang Shen[1], Pew-Thian Yap[1(✉)], and the UNC/UMN Baby Connectome Project Consortium

[1] Department of Radiology and BRIC, University of North Carolina, Chapel Hill, USA
ptyap@med.unc.edu
[2] School of Information Science and Technology, Northwest University, Xi'an, China
[3] School of Computer Science and Engineering, Kyungpook National University, Daegu, South Korea
[4] Department of Computer Science and Technology, Heilongjiang University, Harbin, China

Abstract. Advanced diffusion models for tissue microstructure are widely employed to study brain disorders. However, these models usually require diffusion MRI (DMRI) data with densely sampled q-space, which is prohibitive in clinical settings. This problem can be resolved by using deep learning techniques, which learn the mapping between sparsely sampled q-space data and the high-quality diffusion microstructural indices estimated from densely sampled data. However, most existing methods simply view the input DMRI data as a vector without considering data structure in the q-space. In this paper, we propose to overcome this limitation by representing DMRI data using graphs and utilizing graph convolutional neural networks to estimate tissue microstructure. Our method makes full use of the q-space angular neighboring information to improve estimation accuracy. Experimental results based on data from the Baby Connectome Project demonstrate that our method outperforms state-of-the-art methods both qualitatively and quantitatively.

Keywords: Diffusion MRI · Graph CNN · Microstructure imaging

1 Introduction

Diffusion MRI (DMRI) is capable of measuring the signal attenuation caused by the anisotropic motion of water molecules in the human nervous system [1–3]. This makes DMRI a unique non-invasive imaging technique for in vivo examination of brain tissue microstructure and white matter pathways. With advanced

This work was supported in part by NIH grants (NS093842, EB006733, MH104324, and MH110274) and the efforts of the UNC/UMN Baby Connectome Project Consortium.

© Springer Nature Switzerland AG 2020
A. L. Martel et al. (Eds.): MICCAI 2020, LNCS 12267, pp. 280–290, 2020.
https://doi.org/10.1007/978-3-030-59728-3_28

diffusion models [4–8], DMRI affords rich characterizations of the brain, providing biomarkers useful for diagnosis of brain disorders. However, many microstructure models, e.g., diffusion kurtosis imaging (DKI) [4] and neurite orientation dispersion and density imaging (NODDI) [5], require DMRI data densely sampled in q-space, i.e., multi-shell data with a sufficient angular resolution. The q-space sampling density is determined by the number of acquired diffusion-weighted images (DWIs). Increasing the number of DWIs will inevitably prolong the acquisition time, which can be prohibitive in real-world applications.

Deep learning (DL) techniques have been employed to improve microstructural estimation without requiring dense q-space sampling [9–15]. A typical example is q-DL [9], which utilizes a multilayer perceptron to learn the relationship between sparsely sampled q-space data and high-quality microstructure indices estimated from densely sampled q-space data, thus reducing the acquisition time. Moreover, time-consuming model fitting is replaced by an efficient network. However, this method simply views the DMRI signals in a voxel as a vector without considering q-space data structure. Signal correlation between angular neighbors is overlooked in the process of microstructural estimation.

To overcome this limitation, we represent DMRI data using graphs and then utilize graph convolutional neural networks (GCNNs) to estimate tissue microstructure. Specifically, we first represent q-space signal measurements using a graph that encodes the geometric structure of q-space sampling points. We then utilize residual GCNNs to learn the mapping between sparsely sampled q-space data and high-quality estimates of microstructure indices. Our method is capable of not only reducing the data acquisition time but also accelerating the estimation procedure. Thanks to the graph representation, our method explicitly takes into account the q-space data structure and harnesses information from angular neighbors to improve the estimation accuracy of tissue microstructure. We evaluate our method using data from the Baby Connectome Project [16,17]. The results indicate that our method yields microstructural estimates with remarkably improved accuracy.

2   Methods

In this section, we will first show how to represent DMRI data using graphs. We will then introduce graph Fourier analysis and its application to fast and localized spectral filtering [18], which is the basis of GCNNs and has been applied in a number of DMRI data prediction tasks [19–22]. Finally, we will describe our network architecture in detail.

2.1   Graph Representation of DMRI Data

A graph can be denoted as $\mathcal{G} = \{\mathcal{E}, \mathcal{V}, W\}$, where $\mathcal{V} = \{v_i \in \mathcal{M} : i = 1, \ldots, N\}$ is a set of points on a manifold $\mathcal{M}$, $\mathcal{E} \subset \mathcal{V} \times \mathcal{V}$ is a set of edges connecting the vertices, and $W = (w_{i,j}) \in \mathbb{R}^{N \times N}$ is an adjacency matrix, which is symmetric with weight $w_{i,j} > 0$ when nodes i and j are connected.

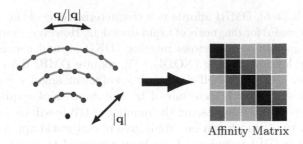

Fig. 1. Graph representation of q-space.

Figure 1 illustrates the graph representation of q-space. Similar to [23–25], to represent DMRI data using graphs, we define the adjacency weight between two nodes (i.e., sampling points) i and j in q-space using two Gaussian kernels, accounting for differences in gradient directions and diffusion weightings, i.e.,

$$w_{i,j} = \exp\left\{-\frac{1-(\hat{\mathbf{q}}_i^\top \hat{\mathbf{q}}_j)^2}{2\sigma_a^2}\right\}\exp\left\{-\frac{(\sqrt{b_i}-\sqrt{b_j})^2}{2\sigma_b^2}\right\}, \tag{1}$$

where $\hat{\mathbf{q}}_i = \mathbf{q}_i/\|\mathbf{q}_i\|$ is a normalized wavevector with $\mathbf{q}_i \in \mathbb{R}^3$, $b_i = t|\mathbf{q}_i|^2$ is the corresponding b-value with diffusion time t, σ_a and σ_b are two parameters controlling the bandwidths of two Gaussian kernels. Our formulation of the adjacency weight encourages a large weight to be assigned to two nodes sharing similar gradient directions and diffusion weightings. In this way, the q-space is represented as a graph $\mathcal{G}$ that encodes the geometric structure of q-space sampling points, and the DMRI signals in one voxel can be viewed as a function f defined on $\mathcal{G}$.

2.2   Graph Fourier Analysis

The graph Laplacian, L, is the key operator in graph Fourier analysis. Following [18], we define $L = D - W$, where $D = \text{diag}\{d_1, d_2 \ldots, d_N\}$ is a degree matrix with $d_i = \sum_j w_{i,j}$. The graph Laplacian can be further normalized using

$$L = I - D^{-1/2}WD^{-1/2}, \tag{2}$$

where I is an identity matrix. We perform eigen decomposition for L to obtain $L = U\Lambda U^\top$, where U and Λ are matrices containing the eigenvectors and eigenvalues, respectively.

As discussed in [18], U can be viewed as the basis for graph Fourier transform (GFT). Therefore, we define the forward and inverse GFTs as $\hat{f} = U^\top f$ and $f = U\hat{f}$, respectively, where $\hat{f}$ is the Fourier coefficients. The convolution theorem states that convolution is equivalent to point-wise multiplication in the transform domain. This serves as the basis for spectral graph convolution. Given a convolution kernel function h, we have

$$h*f = U(U^\top h \odot U^\top f) = U(\widehat{h} \odot \widehat{f}) = U(\text{diag}(\widehat{h})U^\top f), \tag{3}$$

where $\odot$ represents a point-wise product and $\text{diag}(\widehat{h})$ is a diagonal matrix with diagonal elements specified by $\widehat{h}$. However, this framework suffers from two limitations: (i) The eigen decomposition and forward/inverse GFT are computationally expensive; and (ii) The convolution is expected to be localized, but is not guaranteed to be so.

2.3   Fast and Localized Spectral Filtering

To address these two limitations, a fast and localized spectral filtering technique was proposed in [18]. Specifically, replacing $\text{diag}(\widehat{h})$ with another diagonal matrix, $g_\theta(\Lambda)$, parametrized by θ, we then have

$$h*f = U(g_\theta(\Lambda)U^\top f) = g_\theta(U\Lambda U^\top)f = g_\theta(L)f. \tag{4}$$

The filter is now a function of the graph Laplacian, avoiding eigen decomposition and forward/inverse GFT. Computational complexity is therefore significantly reduced.

Direct learning of θ involves a complexity of $\mathcal{O}(N)$ and does not guarantee localized filters. These problems can be resolved by using a polynomial filter defined as

$$g_\theta(L) = \sum_{k=0}^{K} \theta_k L^k, \tag{5}$$

where $\theta = [\theta_0, \theta_1, \ldots, \theta_K] \in \mathbb{R}^{K+1}$ is a vector of polynomial coefficients. This reduces the learning complexity to $\mathcal{O}(K)$. Based on Parseval's theorem [18], smoothness in the spectral domain corresponds to the localization in the spatial domain. More specifically, the spectral filter approximated by the K-th order polynomials of the Laplacian is exactly K-localized. Following [18], we utilize Chebyshev polynomials $T_k(\cdot)$ to design the filter, i.e.,

$$g_\theta(L)f = \sum_{k=0}^{K} \theta_k T_k(\tilde{L})f, \tag{6}$$

where $\tilde{L}$ is the scaled Laplacian, defined as $\tilde{L} = 2L/\lambda_{\max} - I$ with $\lambda_{\max}$ being the maximal eigenvalue of L. Chebyshev polynomials have a recurrence relation, i.e., $T_k(\lambda) = 2\lambda T_K(\lambda) - T_{k-2}(\lambda)$ with $T_1(\lambda) = \lambda$ and $T_0(\lambda) = 1$. Finally, a feature map $f^{(l)}$ at the l-th graph convolutional layer is given by

$$f^{(l)} = \xi\left(\sum_{c=1}^{C} g_{\theta_c^{(l)}}(L)f_c^{(l-1)} + b^{(l)}\right), \tag{7}$$

where $\xi(\cdot)$ is a non-linear activation function, $f_c^{(l-1)}$ is the c-th channel feature map at the $(l-1)$-th layer, $\theta_c^{(l)}$ is the corresponding learning parameters, and $b^{(l)}$ is the bias.

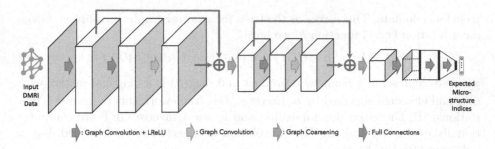

Fig. 2. An overview of the proposed GCNN.

2.4 Network Architecture

An overview of our network architecture is shown in Fig. 2. The input is sparsely sampled q-space data and the output is a vector of microstructural estimates. The input data is first fed to a graph convolutional layer followed by a leaky ReLU (LReLU) activation function. This is followed by two residual blocks, each with a graph coarsening layer. Each residual block consists of two graph convolutional layers, a LReLU activation function, and a residual skip connection to improve training [26]. We utilize the method described in [18] for graph coarsening to increase the receptive field, similar to the pooling operation in conventional CNNs for 2D/3D images [27]. After the second graph coarsening, a final graph convolution layer is employed to integrate the feature maps into a single map. The features from the map are fed into two fully-connected (FC) layers to predict the microstructure indices. The number of nodes in the first FC layer is identical to the number of elements in the input to the layer. The number of nodes in the second FC layer is determined by the number of microstructure indices that need to be estimated. As commonly done in regression tasks, we train the model using ℓ_1 loss:

$$\mathcal{L} = \frac{1}{N} \sum_{i=1}^{N} |M_i - \hat{M}_i|, \tag{8}$$

where M_i is the i-th ground truth microstructural index, $\hat{M}_i$ is the corresponding estimate, and N is the number of microstructural indices.

3 Experiments

3.1 Dataset

Our dataset consisted of 13 subjects randomly selected from the Baby Connectome Project (BCP) [16,17]. We utilized 5 of them for training and the rest for testing. All data were acquired using a Siemens 3T Magnetom Prisma MR scanner with the following imaging protocol: 140 × 105 imaging matrix, 1.5 × 1.5 × 1.5 mm³ resolution, TE = 88 ms, TR = 2,365 ms,

$b = 500, 1000, 1500, 2000, 2500, 3000 \, \text{s/mm}^2$, and a total of 144 non-collinear gradient directions. All enrolled subjects had written informed consent provided by parents/guardians. The experimental protocols were approved by the Institutional Review Board of the University of North Carolina (UNC) School of Medicine.

3.2 Implementation Details

We trained our network to predict NODDI [28] indices, including intra-cellular volume fraction (ICVF), isotropic volume fraction (ISOVF), and orientation dispersion index (ODI). To construct the training data, we computed NODDI indices from the complete DMRI data (144 DWIs) of all training subjects using AMICO [29] as prediction targets. The DMRI data was subsampled uniformly in q-space with factors 2 (72 DWIs), 3 (48 DWIs), and 4 (36 DWIs). Finally, we randomly selected 20,000 voxels from the brain region of each training subject to form our training dataset with a total of 100,000 samples. The testing dataset was created in a similar way, but using the DMRI data of testing subjects. Note that the network was trained separately for the different subsampling rates.

The proposed network was implemented using TensorFlow 1.2 [30]. In all experiments, we trained the network using the ADAM optimizer [31] with an initial learning rate of 0.01 and an exponential decay rate of 0.95. Other hyper-parameters were set as follows: (1) The polynomial order K was set to 10. (2) The number of feature maps for each residual block was set to 8. (3) We set $\sigma_a = \sqrt{1 - \cos^2(30°)} \approx 0.5$, where the angular degree 30° was determined by grid search from 10° to 50°. (4) Since our data is shell-sampled, we set σ_b to a small value, 0.1. An early stopping strategy was adopted to prevent over-fitting. The network was trained using a computer equipped with an NVIDIA GeForce GTX 1080 Ti GPU with 11 GB RAM. We utilized AMICO and MLP as our comparison baselines. Multilayer perceptron (MLP) was implemented based on [9] with the same network architecture and hyper-parameters.

3.3 Results

We first performed quantitative evaluations using the peak signal-to-noise ratio (PSNR) as the metric. The results, shown in Fig. 3, indicate that GCNN outperforms two baseline methods in all cases. Particularly, the overall PSNR values for all indices, shown in the right of Fig. 3, indicate that GCNN improves estimation accuracy for all three subsampling rates. In contrast, AMICO fails to provide satisfactory results when the subsampling rate is larger than 2. MLP gives poor performance, in comparison with the other two methods, when the subsampling rate is 2.

The ICVF maps, shown in Fig. 4, further confirm our conclusions based on Fig. 3. For all subsampling factors, GCNN gives high-quality ICVF maps that are close to the gold standard. For better visualization, we computed the ICVF error maps for different methods and subsampling factors. The results, shown in Fig. 4, indicate that GCNN reduces estimation errors.

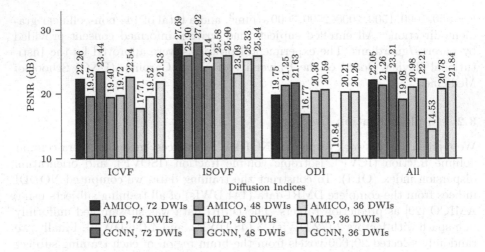

Fig. 3. Average PSNR values computed across the eight testing subjects.

Table 1. Computation time based on totally 395,515 voxels in the brain region of a randomly selected testing subject.

	AMICO	MLP	GCNN
Time (s)	2,252.3	19.2	32.1

Finally, we compared the computation times of different methods. All the methods were tested using a computer equipped with a four-core 2.9 GHz Intel Core i7 CPU. For fair comparison, MLP and GCNN were set to operate in CPU mode. The results, shown in Table 1, indicate that both MLP and GCNN reduce the computation time significantly. Specifically, the two DL methods are at least 70 times faster than AMICO, facilitating microstructural estimation in large-scale studies.

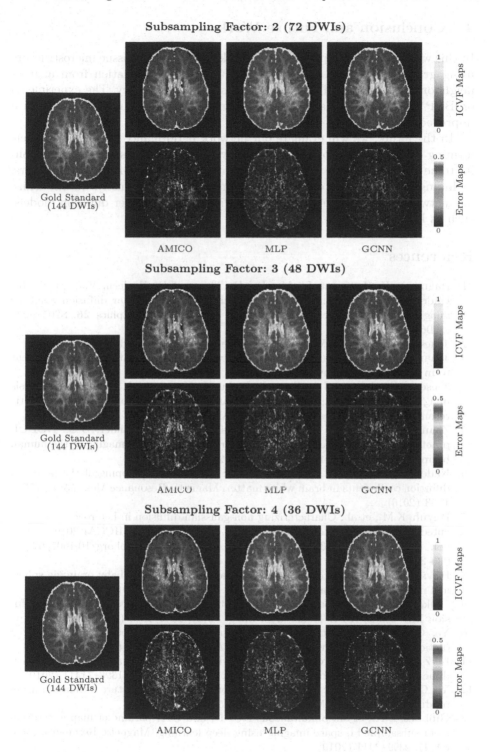

Fig. 4. Visual comparison of ICVF maps and associated error maps.

4   Conclusion and Future Work

In this work, we have proposed a framework for estimating tissue microstructure using graph CNNs. Our method makes full use of information from angular neighbors in q-space, and thus improves estimation accuracy. The experiments on BCP data indicate that our method yields microstructure index maps with improved quality.

In the future, we will evaluate our network performance thoroughly by performing cross-validation on some well-known DMRI datasets, e.g., Human Connectome Project [32]. We will also investigate the influence of hyper-parameters, including the polynomial order and the number of filters. Finally, we will utilize our network to predict microstructure indices given by other diffusion models, such as DKI [4].

References

1. Hagmann, P., Jonasson, L., Maeder, P., Thiran, J.P., Wedeen, V.J., Meuli, R.: Understanding diffusion MR imaging techniques: from scalar diffusion-weighted imaging to diffusion tensor imaging and beyond. Radiographics **26**, S205–S223 (2006)
2. Jones, D.K.: Diffusion MRI. Oxford University Press, Oxford (2010)
3. Johansen-Berg, H., Behrens, T.E.: Diffusion MRI: from quantitative measurement to in vivo neuroanatomy. Academic Press (2013)
4. Jensen, J.H., Helpern, J.A., Ramani, A., Lu, H., Kaczynski, K.: Diffusional kurtosis imaging: the quantification of non-gaussian water diffusion by means of magnetic resonance imaging. Magnetic Resonance Med. **53**(6), 1432–1440 (2005)
5. Zhang, H., Schneider, T., Wheeler-Kingshott, C.A., Alexander, D.C.: NODDI: practical in vivo neurite orientation dispersion and density imaging of the human brain. NeuroImage **61**(4), 1000–1016 (2012)
6. Kaden, E., Kruggel, F., Alexander, D.C.: Quantitative mapping of the per-axon diffusion coefficients in brain white matter. Magnetic Resonance Med. **75**(4), 1752–1763 (2016)
7. Huynh, K.M., et al.: Characterizing non-gaussian diffusion in heterogeneously oriented tissue microenvironments. In: Shen, D., et al. (eds.) MICCAI 2019. LNCS, vol. 11766, pp. 556–563. Springer, Cham (2019). https://doi.org/10.1007/978-3-030-32248-9_62
8. Huynh, K.M., et al.: Probing tissue microarchitecture of the baby brain via spherical mean spectrum imaging. IEEE Trans. Med. Imag. (2020)
9. Golkov, V., et al.: Q-space deep learning: twelve-fold shorter and model-free diffusion MRI scans. IEEE Trans. Med. Imag. **35**(5), 1344–1351 (2016)
10. Ye, C.: Tissue microstructure estimation using a deep network inspired by a dictionary-based framework. Med. Image Anal. **42**, 288–299 (2017)
11. Li, Z., et al.: Fast and robust diffusion kurtosis parametric mapping using a three-dimensional convolutional neural network. IEEE Access **7**, 71398–71411 (2019)
12. Ye, C., Li, X., Chen, J.: A deep network for tissue microstructure estimation using modified LSTM units. Med. Image Anal. **55**, 49–64 (2019)
13. Gibbons, E.K., et al.: Simultaneous NODDI and GFA parameter map generation from subsampled q-space imaging using deep learning. Magnetic Resonance Med. **81**(4), 2399–2411 (2019)

14. Ye, C., et al.: Super-resolved q-space deep learning. In: Shen, D., et al. (eds.) MICCAI 2019. LNCS, vol. 11766, pp. 582–589. Springer, Cham (2019). https://doi.org/10.1007/978-3-030-32248-9_65

15. Ye, C., Li, Y., Zeng, X.: An improved deep network for tissue microstructure estimation with uncertainty quantification. Med. Image Anal. **61**, 101650 (2020)

16. Fallik, D.: The human connectome project turns to mapping brain development, from birth through early childhood. Neurol. Today **16**(19), 7–8 (2016)

17. Howell, B.R., et al.: The UNC/UMN baby connectome project (BCP): an overview of the study design and protocol development. NeuroImage **185**, 891–905 (2019)

18. Defferrard, M., Bresson, X., Vandergheynst, P.: Convolutional neural networks on graphs with fast localized spectral filtering. In: Advances in Neural Information Processing Systems, pp. 3844–3852 (2016)

19. Kim, J., Hong, Y., Chen, G., Lin, W., Yap, P.-T., Shen, D.: Graph-based deep learning for prediction of longitudinal infant diffusion MRI Data. In: Bonet-Carne, E., Grussu, F., Ning, L., Sepehrband, F., Tax, C.M.W. (eds.) MICCAI 2019. MV, pp. 133–141. Springer, Cham (2019). https://doi.org/10.1007/978-3-030-05831-9_11

20. Hong, Y., Chen, G., Yap, P.-T., Shen, D.: Multifold acceleration of diffusion MRI via deep learning reconstruction from slice-undersampled data. In: Chung, A.C.S., Gee, J.C., Yushkevich, P.A., Bao, S. (eds.) IPMI 2019. LNCS, vol. 11492, pp. 530–541. Springer, Cham (2019). https://doi.org/10.1007/978-3-030-20351-1_41

21. Hong, Y., Kim, J., Chen, G., Lin, W., Yap, P.T., Shen, D.: Longitudinal prediction of infant diffusion MRI data via graph convolutional adversarial networks. IEEE Transactions on Medical Imaging (2019)

22. Hong, Y., Chen, G., Yap, P.T., Shen, D.: Reconstructing high-quality diffusion MRI data from orthogonal slice-undersampled data using graph convolutional neural networks. In: International Conference on Medical Image Computing and Computer-Assisted Intervention, pp. 529–537 (2019)

23. Chen, G., Dong, B., Zhang, Y., Lin, W., Shen, D., Yap, P.T.: Denoising of infant diffusion MRI data via graph framelet matching in x-q space. IEEE Transactions on Medical Imaging (2019)

24. Chen, G., Wu, Y., Shen, D., Yap, P.T.: Noise reduction in diffusion MRI using non-local self-similar information in joint x-q space. Med. Image Anal. **53**, 79–94 (2019)

25. Chen, G., Dong, B., Zhang, Y., Lin, W., Shen, D., Yap, P.T.: XQ-SR: joint x-q space super-resolution with application to infant diffusion MRI. Med. Image Anal. **57**, 44–55 (2019)

26. He, K., Zhang, X., Ren, S., Sun, J.: Deep residual learning for image recognition. In: Proceedings of the IEEE Conference on Computer Vision and Pattern Recognition, pp. 770–778 (2016)

27. LeCun, Y., Bottou, L., Bengio, Y., Haffner, P., et al.: Gradient-based learning applied to document recognition. Proc. IEEE **86**(11), 2278–2324 (1998)

28. Sone, D.: Neurite orientation and dispersion density imaging: clinical utility, efficacy, and role in therapy. Reports Med. Imag. **12**, 17 (2019)

29. Daducci, A., Canales-Rodríguez, E.J., Zhang, H., Dyrby, T.B., Alexander, D.C., Thiran, J.P.: Accelerated microstructure imaging via convex optimization (AMICO) from diffusion MRI data. NeuroImage **105**, 32–44 (2015)

30. Abadi, M., et al.: Tensorflow: a system for large-scale machine learning. In: 12th USENIX Symposium on Operating Systems Design and Implementation (OSDI 16). pp. 265–283 (2016)
31. Kingma, D.P., Ba, J.: Adam: a method for stochastic optimization. arXiv preprint arXiv:1412.6980 (2014)
32. Van Essen, D.C., et al.: The WU-Minn human connectome project: an overview. NeuroImage, **80** 62–79 (2013)

Tractogram Filtering of Anatomically Non-plausible Fibers with Geometric Deep Learning

Pietro Astolfi[1,2,3]($\boxtimes$), Ruben Verhagen[2], Laurent Petit[4], Emanuele Olivetti[1,2], Jonathan Masci[6], Davide Boscaini[5], and Paolo Avesani[1,2]

[1] NeuroInformatics Laboratory (NILab), Bruno Kessler Foundation, Trento, Italy
{pastolfi,avesani}@fbk.eu
[2] Center for Mind and Brain Sciences (CIMeC), University of Trento, Trento, Italy
[3] PAVIS, Italian Institute of Technology, Genova, Italy
[4] GIN, IMN, CNRS, CEA, Université de Bordeaux, Bordeaux, France
[5] Technologies of Vision (TeV), Bruno Kessler Foundation, Trento, Italy
[6] NNAISENSE, Lugano, Switzerland

Abstract. Tractograms are virtual representations of the white matter fibers of the brain. They are of primary interest for tasks like presurgical planning, and investigation of neuroplasticity or brain disorders. Each tractogram is composed of millions of fibers encoded as 3D polylines. Unfortunately, a large portion of those fibers are not anatomically plausible and can be considered artifacts of the tracking algorithms. Common methods for tractogram filtering are based on signal reconstruction, a principled approach, but unable to consider the knowledge of brain anatomy. In this work, we address the problem of tractogram filtering as a supervised learning problem by exploiting the ground truth annotations obtained with a recent heuristic method, which labels fibers as either anatomically plausible or non-plausible according to well-established anatomical properties. The intuitive idea is to model a fiber as a point cloud and the goal is to investigate whether and how a geometric deep learning model might capture its anatomical properties. Our contribution is an extension of the Dynamic Edge Convolution model that exploits the sequential relations of points in a fiber and discriminates with high accuracy plausible/non-plausible fibers.

1 Introduction

Tractography represents a powerful method to reconstruct the white matter fibers from diffusion magnetic resonance (MR) recordings [2]. While this method provides a good approximation of the brain connectivity structure, there is an open issue of artifactual fibers [11,12], i.e. anatomically non-plausible pathways. We address the task of filtering out such artifactual fibers using a deep learning model.

P. Astolfi—We gratefully acknowledge the support of NVIDIA Corporation with the donation of the Titan Xp GPU used for this research.

© Springer Nature Switzerland AG 2020
A. L. Martel et al. (Eds.): MICCAI 2020, LNCS 12267, pp. 291–301, 2020.
https://doi.org/10.1007/978-3-030-59728-3_29

The structural connectivity of the brain can be reconstructed from diffusion MR signal by a step of local estimation of the diffusivity model [22] and a subsequent step of fiber tracking [7]. The outcome is a tractogram, a virtual representation of the axonal pathways in the white matter, where each fiber is encoded as 3D polylines, commonly referred to as *streamlines*. Typically, a whole brain tractogram is composed of millions of streamlines.

Tractograms are providing valuable contributions to critical tasks like presurgical intervention planning, the detection of biomarkers for brain disorders and the investigation of neuroplasticity. For these purposes, the accuracy of fiber tracking is of paramount importance. While in the preprocessing of diffusion data it is common practice to denoise the signal before estimating the diffusivity model [8,26], there is no similar step after fiber tracking to filter out noisy streamlines.

The assessment of the accuracy of fiber tracking has been approached a few years ago with an open contest[1] involving many (20) research groups. The contest was designed as a task of bundle detection on a dataset composed of simulated diffusion MRI data. The joint effort allowed the evaluation of the quality and limits of the most common tracking methods [12]. The positive outcome has been the lack of false negative streamlines, the critical issue has concerned the many false positive errors, e.g. artifactual streamlines.

The occurrence of false positive streamlines is not surprising. The general strategy of tracking methods is to oversample the possible pathways to preserve the property of coverage of all true positive fibers [20]. The tacit assumption is to postpone the task of filtering false positive streamlines to a subsequent post-processing step. The reason for this strategy is the difficulty of encoding anatomical priors into tracking algorithms.

The most common approach to reduce artifactual streamlines are methods based on the inverse problem of signal reconstruction, e.g. Life [16], SIFT [21], Commit [4]. The intuitive idea is to estimate how much the orientation of a streamline explains the diffusion signal. Despite the principled criterion, these methods do not take into account the knowledge of brain anatomy, like another method based on the topological properties of streamlines [25].

A recent rule-based method, namely ExTractor [17], has been proposed to filter out artifactual streamlines from tractograms by following anatomical principles. The rules that it proposes encode the geometrical and spatial properties of the streamlines with respect to the basics of white matter neuroanatomy in terms of association, projection, and commissural fibers. As output, ExTractor labels streamlines as *anatomically plausible* or *anatomically non-plausible*.

In this work, we address for the first time the problem of tractogram filtering as a supervised learning problem. We need to train a binary classifier to discriminate between two classes: anatomically plausible (P) and non-plausible (nP) fibers. The intuitive idea is to exploit the labeling of fibers provided by the rule-based method [17] and to adopt deep learning models to learn the features of streamlines underlying the rules. The ultimate goal is to have a fast run-time

---

[1] www.tractometer.org/ismrm_2015_challenge.

solution to filter large tractograms and a flexible method to transpose new expert annotations.

Given the sequential structure of a streamline, we have chosen as reference learning model a bidirectional LSTM (bLSTM) neural network [10]. Although this model can exploit the sequential information, it requires forcing the streamline representation to a fixed number of points. For this reason, we consider Geometric Deep Learning (GDL) models [13] that support more flexible and appropriate data representations. We investigate a PointNet (PN) model [19], where a streamline can be represented as a point cloud i.e. set of 3D points, and a Dynamic Edge Convolution (DEC) model [24], which in addition to PN considers the relations between points belonging to the same spherical local context. Our experiments shows that both GDL models provide an improvement with respect to bLSTM.

Despite the better results provided by PN and DEC, these models are invariant to permutations of points in the input point cloud. It means that if we permute the points in a streamline classified as plausible, the model will continue to classify it as plausible albeit the altered sequence of points. To overcome this issue we propose a Sequence Dynamic Edge Convolution (sDEC) model, an extension of the DEC model that introduces the property of being sequence sensitive.

While the sDEC model provides only a modest increase in accuracy with respect to PN in classifying P and nP fibers, the analysis of error distribution shows different behaviours. sDEC is more robust when fibers are long and curved: those are the type of fibers where PN performs worst and produces significantly more false positive errors. In addition, visual inspection of the false negatives errors made by sDEC shows that these fibers look truly anatomically non-plausible. We may argue that this apparent mismatch might be related to the noise of the labelling process.

2   Materials

Dataset. Our reference dataset is composed of a collection of tractograms of 20 subjects randomly selected from the HCP dataset [23], which is a publicly available curated MRI dataset. The tractograms were obtained computing (i) the constrained spherical deconvolution (CSD) model [22] on the 3T DWI (1.25 mm, 270 multishell gradients), and the (ii) Particle Filtering Anatomically Constrained Tractography (PF-ACT) algorithm [7]. Specifically, the tracking generated around ∼ 1M fibers for each tractogram by seeding 16 points for each voxel with step size 0.5 mm. The tractogram of each subject has been non linearly coregistered to the MNI standard space, and, for computational purposes, all the fibers have been compressed to the most significant points [18].

ExTractor Labelling. According to the premise of a supervised learning approach, we created a dataset where for each tractogram we labeled the fiber as either plausible (P) or non-plausible (nP). The procedure of labelling followed

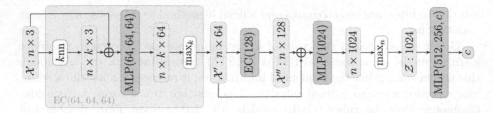

Fig. 1. The DEC architecture adopted. Green, gray, and red blocks represent input, intermediate, and output tensors, respectively. Parametric layers are colored in blue, while fixed layers in white. (Color figure online)

the heuristic rules defined by ExTractor [17], a tool that encodes the current knowledge on the anatomical pathways of white matter structures. In particular, ExTractor carries out a 2-step procedure. First, fibers are marked as nP when they are either (i) shorter than 20 mm, (ii) contain a loop, or (iii) are truncated, i.e., they terminate in the deep white matter. The second step is concerned with the labeling of fibers marked as P, by splitting the main pathways into the three macro classes: association, projection, and commissural. This selection of fibers is further refined to filter out non-plausible pathways using a clustering method [3]. The outcome of the ExTractor procedure is a balanced partition between P and nP fibers, irrespective of the different tracking algorithms and data sources [17]. On our dataset, Extractor resulted in $49.7 \pm 1.5\%$ of P streamlines on average on the 20 subjects, but more significantly it showed the presence of a massive percentage, $31.8 \pm 1.2\%$, of nP streamlines shorter than 20 mm.

3 Methods

The intuition underlying our work is to treat a streamline as an undirected sequence of 3D points, aiming to learn geometric and spatial features relevant for the tractography filtering task. Currently, the best way to achieve such a goal is by employing GDL models [13], which are designed to learn geometric features of graphs and point clouds. Among the existing GDL approaches, PointNet [19] is the most adopted method both for its simplicity and effectiveness. Nevertheless, such an approach does not consider relations between points. It learns global properties of a point cloud just by encoding all the points separately and then aggregating them in a single descriptor through global pooling. Conversely, Dynamic Edge Convolution (DEC) [24] considers the points relations, by encoding them as edges of a graph dynamically induced by the point cloud.

Dynamic Edge Convolution. Considering a point cloud $\mathcal{X} = \{\mathbf{x}_1, \mathbf{x}_2, \dots, \mathbf{x}_n\}$, $\mathbf{x}_i \in \mathbb{R}^3$, the DEC model first guesses an initial graph structure for the point cloud by retrieving for each point $\mathbf{x}_i$ the set of k nearest neighbors, $\mathrm{knn}(\mathbf{x}_i) = \{\mathbf{x}_{j_{i_1}}, \dots, \mathbf{x}_{j_{i_k}}\}$, in terms of Euclidean distance (see Fig. 2a). Hence, DEC builds

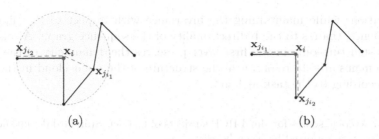

(a)   (b)

Fig. 2. Comparison between Euclidean k-nn (a), and k-nn based on the sequence graph (b).

a k-nn graph, $\mathcal{G}(\mathcal{V}, \mathcal{E})$, where $\mathcal{V} = \mathcal{X}$ is the set of nodes, and an edge $(i, j) \in \mathcal{E}$ exists iff $\mathbf{x}_j \in \mathrm{knn}(\mathbf{x}_i)$. Then, each point representation, $\mathbf{x}_i$, is enriched with the representation of each of its neighbors $\mathbf{x}_{j_i}$, creating edges features $\mathbf{e}_{ij}$, which are learnt through a neural network h_Θ, i.e. $\mathbf{e}_{ij} = h_\Theta(\mathbf{x}_i \oplus (\mathbf{x}_j - \mathbf{x}_i))$, where $\oplus$ denotes the concatenation operator. Finally, a new representation of a point, $\mathbf{x}_i'$, is obtained by aggregating all the learned edge features with a pooling operator, i.e. $\mathbf{x}_i' = \mathrm{pool}(\mathbf{e}_{ij})$, $j \colon (i, j) \in \mathcal{E}$, where pool is either max or mean. The sequence of operations that from $\mathcal{X}$ produce $\mathcal{X}'$ define an Edge Convolution (EC) layer, which in the DEC model is repeated multiple times. Referring to our architecture, see Fig. 1, two EC layers are stacked in depth to produce new representations $\mathcal{X}'$ and $\mathcal{X}''$ with 64 and 128 features respectively. Each of the two EC layers computes its own k-nn graph in order to adjust the local neighborhood of points to its input representation, i.e, $\mathcal{X}$ and $\mathcal{X}'$. The re-computation of knn is what defines the DEC model as *dynamic*. Finally, the different learned representations are concatenated, encoded with a learning layer, g_Φ, to 1024 features, and pooled to obtain a single descriptor of the point cloud, $\mathcal{Z} = \mathrm{pool}(g_\Phi(\mathcal{X}' \oplus \mathcal{X}''))$, which is classified using a fully connected (FC) network.

Dynamic Edge Convolution of a Sequence. A remarkable property of the DEC model (also shared by PN) is the invariance to the permutation of the points in the input point cloud. Indeed, such models make use only of operators invariant to the order e.g., FC layers, max/mean pooling layers. Although this property is fundamental in the point cloud domain, it becomes undesired if the input is a sequence as in our case. To solve this issue, we propose a simple but well-motivated modification of the DEC model, in which we impose the input point cloud to have a graph structure, without needing a Euclidean k-nn to induce it. According to the streamline structure, we impose the input to be a bidirectional sequence graph where each non-terminal point, $\mathbf{x}_{i \neq 0, n}$, has two neighbors: the previous and the next point in the sequence, while the terminal points, $\mathbf{x}_0, \mathbf{x}_n$, have just one neighbor (see Fig. 2b):

$$\mathcal{G}(\mathcal{V}, \mathcal{E}'), \, e_{ij}' \in \mathcal{E}' \colon \mathbf{x}_i \to \mathbf{x}_j, \, j = i + 1 \vee j = i - 1.$$

It is important to remark that we impose this structure only in the first sDEC layer, which is enough to lose the invariance with respect to the input permutations while maintaining the invariance with respect to the flipping of the sequence, thanks to the bidirectionality of the sequence graph. Also, imposing this structure only in the first layer preserves the dynamicity of the model, which remains able to re-organize the structure of the point cloud in the latent space according to the task at hand.

Table 1. Average scores for the 4 HCP subjects of test set. Standard deviation among the 4 subjects is reported between brackets.

Method	Accuracy	Precision	Recall	DSC
bLSTM	92.8 (±0.3)	93.7 (±0.5)	96.1 (±0.2)	94.9 (±0.3)
PN	94.5 (±0.1)	95.4 (±0.2)	96.8 (±0.2)	96.1 (±0.2)
DEC	94.3 (±0.1)	95.4 (±0.3)	96.5 (±0.2)	95.9 (±0.2)
sDEC	**95.2** (±0.1)	**96.2** (±0.3)	**96.9** (±0.1)	**96.6** (±0.2)

4   Experiments and Results

The main purpose of the experiments is to perform an empirical assessment of the behaviour of different models for the task of tractogram filtering. In our comparison, we consider a reference model, bLSTM, and three competing models based on geometric deep learning: PN, DEC, and sDEC.

Before setting the training of learning models, we carried out a few preprocessing steps. The first step was the pruning of fibers. An analysis of the distribution of fibers between P and nP according to the ExTractor's rules, highlighted a massive percentage of very short streamlines, i.e. length below 20 mm. All of them were labeled as nP. To reduce this potential bias for the learning models we removed such streamlines from the tractograms. After the pruning, the average distribution of P and nP classes was 68% and 32% respectively. The second preprocessing step concerned the resampling of the points of streamlines. Traditional learning models, e.g. bLSTM, require input to be represented as fixed vectorial representations. Therefore, despite GDL models can deal with a varying number of points, we have to resample all streamlines to have the same number of points [6,9,14]. We computed the resampling using a cubic B-spline interpolation and empirically compared different representations based on 12, 16 and 20 points. No meaningful performance differences were noticed. In Table 1 we report the results for streamlines resampled to 16 points.

To perform a fair comparison of the four models, we have configured all of them to have a similar number of parameters, approximately around 900K. While the architecture of DEC and sDEC models is reported in Fig. 1, the configuration of the remaining models is:

bLSTM: `MLP(128)` → `LSTM(256)` ⊕ `LSTM⁻¹(256)` → `MLP(256, 128)` → `FC(2)`;
PN: `MLP(64,64,64,128,1024)` → `MAX` → `MLP(512,256,40)` → `FC(2)`,

where FC is a Fully Connected layer, and MLP contains sequences of (FC, BatchNorm, ReLU). For the implementation of the models, we adopted the PyTorch library [15] with the PyTorch Geometric extension [5].

For all the experiments we considered a dataset of 20 tractograms from 20 different subjects. We partitioned the data into three sets: 12 tractograms for training the models, 4 tractograms for hyperparameters tuning and model selection, and 4 tractograms for testing. The training was designed as follows: 1000 epochs with evaluation step every 20 epochs; cross-entropy loss; Adam optimizer with default alfa and beta momentum $(0.9, 0.99)$; initial learning rate of 10^{-3} multiplied by a factor of 0.7 every 90 epochs until a minimum value of $5 \cdot 10^{-5}$ is reached. In the training procedure, we used mini-batches composed of 16K streamlines randomly sampled from two subjects, 8K from each of them. A subject is sampled only once for each epoch. On the test set, we computed the following evaluation measures: accuracy, precision, recall, and DSC. In Table 1 the values refer to the average for each subject. Notice that the classification task is single-streamline, therefore the size of our test set is composed of ~3 million streamlines.

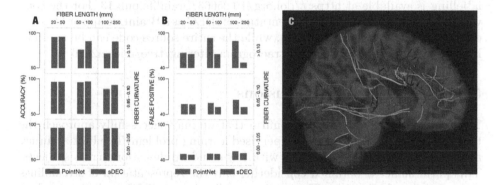

Fig. 3. Analysis of the error distribution for PN and sDEC models with respect to streamlines length and curvature: (A) accuracy, (B) false positive rate. (C) Sample of false negative streamlines, mistakenly classified as anatomically non-plausible.

An additional experiment was designed to test the invariance of DEC and sensitivity of sDEC with respect to the order of points in a streamline. To this end, we tested the two models on a version of the test set where the the sequence of points of streamlines were randomly permuted. In agreement with the working hypothesis, the accuracy for DEC remained the same, 94.3%, while there was a drop for sDEC to 30.0%.

A further analysis concerned the examination of the error distribution. We restricted the analysis to PN and sDEC only. Our interest was to characterize whether and how the error differs between the two models. We considered a couple of features in the analysis: length and curvature of streamlines. All streamlines were partitioned into three categories with respect to length (short $[0, 50]$ mm, medium $[50, 100]$ mm, long $[100, 300]$ mm) and curvature (straight $[0.0, 0.05]$, curved $[0.05, 0.10]$, very curved $[0.10, 0.20]$), where each of them contained at least a portion of 15% of streamlines. Combining the partitions we obtained 9 categories. In Fig. 3A we depict how the accuracy score varies across the categories. The task becomes more difficult when both length and curvature are greater. A similar analysis was carried out focusing on the distribution of false positive error, i.e. streamlines mistakenly classified as anatomically plausible. The results are reported in Fig. 3B. In this case, we observe a major difference between the two models in the most critical categories, namely long and curved streamlines. In Fig. 3C we illustrate a qualitative example of false negative errors, when streamlines should be recognized as anatomically plausible while they are classified as anatomically non-plausible. Visual inspection by an expert anatomist confirms that the classifier was indeed correct in those cases and that the labelling process was noisy.

Code and Data. For the sake of reproducibility, we provide both the code and the dataset used in our experiments. We adopt the BrainLife[2] [1] platform to distribute them. The dataset containing the 20 tractograms with the respective labelling is available at https://doi.org/10.25663/brainlife.pub.13. For the code we distribute a pre-trained implementation of sDEC as a BrainLife app at https://doi.org/10.25663/brainlife.app.390, while the entire source code can be found at https://github.com/FBK-NILab/tractogram_filtering/tree/miccai2020.

5   Discussion and Conclusions

The results reported in Table 1 confirm that we may successfully approach the task of tractogram filtering as a supervised learning problem. The best accuracy achieved by sDEC is beyond 95% with low standard deviation across subjects. This performance is obtained considering only the representation of streamlines as a sequence of 3D points. The runtime application of sDEC model is very fast. We may filter a whole tractogram with $\sim 1M$ streamlines in less than one minute (46.2 s using a gpu NVIDIA Titan Xp 12 Gb).

We argue that the accuracy is underestimated and the true score may be even higher. If we look at the portion of false negative error, as reported in Fig. 3C, we may agree that some of those streamline trajectories can be considered anatomically non-plausible, even though the true label states the contrary. Therefore, the computation of accuracy is biased by this apparent mismatch, which we can consider as part of the noise in the labelling process. Moreover, we may claim that the sDEC model has a good generalization capability and behaves accurately even in the presence of misleading labels.

The geometric deep learning models seem to provide only a small, even though meaningful (t-test with p-value < 0.001), improvement in terms of accuracy compared to bLSTM. Nevertheless PN and sDEC support higher flexibility in the streamlines representation, both as points clouds or graphs. The sDEC

---

[2] https://brainlife.io/.

model seems the most appropriate for tractogram filtering because it is robust with respect to the order of points in the streamlines while preserving the highest accuracy in the discrimination of anatomical plausibility.

The analysis of error distribution allows a better understanding of the difference between PN and sDEC models. Around 40% of the misclassification error concerns different streamlines, indicating that the two models behave differently: in Fig. 3A the most critical streamlines are those longer and more curved. Nevertheless, sDEC is more robust and the drop in accuracy is lower than PN. We may explain this difference with the property of sDEC to capture the relations among the points because it is considering also the edges of streamlines. When streamlines are long and curved, edges become more informative and provide a competitive advantage. As illustrated in Fig. 3B, PN has the bias to classify long and curved streamlines as anatomically plausible doing more false positive error.

We believe that a fast and accurate filtering of tractograms, like the one supported by the sDEC model, is the premise for further investigations on how tasks like bundle segmentation may take advantage of the removal of artifactual streamlines.

References

1. Avesani, P., et al.: The open diffusion data derivatives, brain data upcycling via integrated publishing of derivatives and reproducible open cloud services. Sci Data 6(1), 1–13 (2019). https://doi.org/10.1038/s41597-019-0073-y
2. Basser, P.J., Pajevic, S., Pierpaoli, C., Duda, J., Aldroubi, A.: In vivo fiber tractography using DT-MRI data. Magnetic Resonance Med. 44(4), 625–632 (2000). https://doi.org/10.1002/1522-2594(200010)44:4%3C625::AID-MRM17%3E3.0.CO;2-O
3. Côté, M.A., Garyfallidis, E., Larochelle, H., Descoteaux, M.: Cleaning up the mess: tractography outlier removal using hierarchical QuickBundles clustering. In: Proceedings of the International Society of Magnetic Resonance in Medicine (ISMRM) (2015). http://archive.ismrm.org/2015/2844.html
4. Daducci, A., Dal Palù, A., Lemkaddem, A., Thiran, J.P.: COMMIT: convex optimization modeling for microstructure informed tractography. IEEE Trans Med. Imag. 34(1), 246–257 (2015). https://doi.org/10.1109/TMI.2014.2352414
5. Fey, M., Lenssen, J.E.: Fast graph representation learning with PyTorch geometric. In: ICLR Workshop on Representation Learning on Graphs and Manifolds (2019). https://arxiv.org/abs/1903.02428
6. Garyfallidis, E., Brett, M., Correia, M.M., Williams, G.B., Nimmo-Smith, I.: QuickBundles, a method for tractography simplification. Front. Neurosci. 6 (2012). http://dx.doi.org/10.3389/fnins.2012.00175
7. Girard, G., Whittingstall, K., Deriche, R., Descoteaux, M.: Towards quantitative connectivity analysis: reducing tractography biases. NeuroImage 98, 266–278 (2014). https://doi.org/10.1016/j.neuroimage.2014.04.074
8. Glasser, M.F., et al.: The minimal preprocessing pipelines for the Human Connectome Project. NeuroImage 80, 105–124 (2013). http://dx.doi.org/10.1016/j.neuroimage.2013.04.127

9. Gupta, V., Thomopoulos, S.I., Rashid, F.M., Thompson, P.M.: FiberNET: an ensemble deep learning framework for clustering white matter fibers. In: Descoteaux, M., Maier-Hein, L., Franz, A., Jannin, P., Collins, D.L., Duchesne, S. (eds.) MICCAI 2017. LNCS, vol. 10433, pp. 548–555. Springer, Cham (2017). https://doi.org/10.1007/978-3-319-66182-7_63

10. Huang, Z., Xu, W., Yu, K.: Bidirectional LSTM-CRF models for sequence tagging. arXiv preprint arXiv:1508.01991 (2015). https://arxiv.org/abs/1508.01991

11. Maier-Hein, K., et al.: Tractography-based connectomes are dominated by false-positive connections. bioRxiv, pp. 084137+ (2016). http://dx.doi.org/10.1101/084137

12. Maier-Hein, K.H., et al.: The challenge of mapping the human connectome based on diffusion tractography. Nat. Commun. **8**(1) (2017). https://doi.org/10.1038/s41467-017-01285-x

13. Masci, J., Rodolà, E., Boscaini, D., Bronstein, M.M., Li, H.: Geometric deep learning. In: SIGGRAPH ASIA 2016 Courses, pp. 1–50. SA 2016, Association for Computing Machinery, Macau, November 2016. https://doi.org/10.1145/2988458.2988485

14. O'Donnell, L.J., Westin, C.F.F.: Automatic tractography segmentation using a highdimensional white matter atlas. IEEE Trans. Med. Imag. 1562–1575 (2007). https://doi.org/10.1109/TMI.2007.906785

15. Paszke, A., et al.: PyTorch: An imperative style, high-performance deep learning library. In: Advances in Neural Information Processing Systems, pp. 8024–8035 (2019)

16. Pestilli, F., Yeatman, J.D., Rokem, A., Kay, K.N., Wandell, B.A.: Evaluation and statistical inference for human connectomes. Nat. Methods **11**(10), 1058–1063 (2014). http://dx.doi.org/10.1038/nmeth.3098

17. Petit, L., Rheault, F., Descoteaux, M., Tzourio-Mazoyer, N.: Half of the streamlines built in a whole human brain tractogram is anatomically uninterpretable (2019). https://ww5.aievolution.com/hbm1901/index.cfm?do=abs.viewAbs&abs=3220

18. Presseau, C., Jodoin, P.M., Houde, J.C., Descoteaux, M.: A new compression format for fiber tracking datasets. NeuroImage **109**, 73–83 (2015). https://doi.org/10.1016/j.neuroimage.2014.12.058

19. Qi, C.R., Su, H., Mo, K., Guibas, L.J.: PointNet: deep learning on point sets for 3D classification and segmentation. In: Proceedings of the IEEE Conference on Computer Vision and Pattern Recognition, pp. 652–660 (2017). https://doi.org/10.1109/CVPR.2017.16

20. Rheault, F., et al.: Bundle-specific tractography with incorporated anatomical and orientational priors. NeuroImage **186**, 382–398 (2019). https://doi.org/10.1016/j.neuroimage.2018.11.018

21. Smith, R.E., Tournier, J.D.D., Calamante, F., Connelly, A.: SIFT: spherical-deconvolution informed filtering of tractograms. NeuroImage **67**, 298–312 (2013). https://doi.org/10.1016/j.neuroimage.2012.11.049

22. Tournier, J.D., Calamante, F., Connelly, A.: Robust determination of the fibre orientation distribution in diffusion MRI: non-negativity constrained super-resolved spherical deconvolution. NeuroImage **35**(4), 1459–1472 (2007). http://dx.doi.org/10.1016/j.neuroimage.2007.02.016

23. Van Essen, D.C., Smith, S.M., Barch, D.M., Behrens, T.E.J., Yacoub, E., Ugurbil, K.: The WU-Minn human connectome project: an overview. NeuroImage **80**, 62–79 (2013). http://dx.doi.org/10.1016/j.neuroimage.2013.05.041

24. Wang, Y., Sun, Y., Liu, Z., Sarma, S.E., Bronstein, M.M., Solomon, J.M.: Dynamic graph CNN for learning on point clouds. ACM Trans. Graph. (TOG) **38**(5), 146 (2019). https://doi.org/10.1145/3326362
25. Yeh, F.C., et al.: Automatic removal of false connections in diffusion MRI tractography using topology-informed pruning (TIP). Neurotherapeutics **16**(1), 52–58 (2018). https://doi.org/10.1007/s13311-018-0663-y
26. Zhuang, J., et al.: Correction of eddy-current distortions in diffusion tensor images using the known directions and strengths of diffusion gradients. J. Magnetic Resonance Imag. JMRI **24**(5), 1188–1193 (2006). https://doi.org/10.1002/jmri.20727

Unsupervised Deep Learning
for Susceptibility Distortion Correction
in Connectome Imaging

Yuchuan Qiao and Yonggang Shi[✉]

USC Stevens Neuroimaging and Informatics Institute, Keck School of Medicine
of USC, University of Southern California, Los Angeles, USA
Yonggang.Shi@loni.usc.edu

Abstract. To reduce the residual distortion in high resolution diffusion
MRI (dMRI) data preprocessed by the HCP-Pipeline, we propose an
unsupervised deep learning based method to correct the residual susceptibility induced distortion. Instead of using B0 images from two phase
encoding (PE), fiber orientation distribution (FOD) images computed
from dMRI data, which provide more reliable contrast information, are
used in our method. Our deep learning framework named DistoRtion
Correction Net (DrC-Net) uses an U-Net to capture the latent features
from FOD images and estimates a deformation field along the phase
encoding direction. With the help of a transformer network, we can propagate the deformation feature to the FOD images and back propagate
the losses between the deformed images and true undistorted images.
The proposed DrC-Net is trained on 60 subjects randomly selected from
100 subjects in the Human Connectome Project (HCP) dataset. We evaluated the DrC-Net on the rest 40 subjects and the results show a similar
performance compared to the training dataset. Our evaluation method
used mean squared difference (MSD) of fractional anisotropy (FA) and
minimum angular difference between two PEs. We compared the DrC-
Net to *topup* method used in the HCP-Pipeline, and the results show a
significant improvement to correct the susceptibility induced distortions
in both evaluation methods.

1 Introduction

HCP-Pipeline [1] is widely used to process the multi-shell diffusion MRI (dMRI)
data acquired by the connectome imaging protocols developed by the Human
Connectome Project (HCP) [2]. Although they already used two phase encodings (PEs) to correct the susceptibility-induced distortions in dMRI [1,3], there
are still significant distortions remaining in regions such as the brainstem [4]
shown in Fig. 1, which would result in false analyses of the brain pathways. As

Y. Shi—This work was supported by the National Institute of Health (NIH) under
grants RF1AG056573, R01EB022744, R21AG064776, R01AG062007, P41EB015922,
P50AG05142.

© Springer Nature Switzerland AG 2020
A. L. Martel et al. (Eds.): MICCAI 2020, LNCS 12267, pp. 302–310, 2020.
https://doi.org/10.1007/978-3-030-59728-3_30

the distortion of the dMRI data is mainly along the PE direction due to the susceptibility of the magnetic field to the tissue/air boundary [5], we can model it using a one dimensional deformation constraint [3,6,7]. In the HCP-Pipeline, B0 images from both PEs were used under the *topup* tool from FSL to estimate the deformation field. Lacking of contrast in B0 image results in the misalignment in the distortion correction, especially in the brainstem area. The fiber orientation distributions (FODs) images [8] computed from the dMRI data can provide more detailed contrast to guide the deformation field estimation. Previous studies had shown usefulness of the FOD images to correct the distortion [9], which we will also use in a deep learning framework.

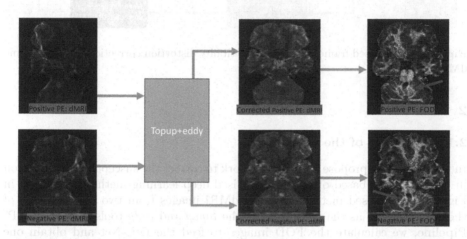

Fig. 1. An illustration of residual distortion in dMRI after susceptibility distortion correction using the *topup* tool in HCP-Pipeline. The red arrows indicate the remaining distortion in the brainstem area. (Color figure online)

Deep learning shows an impressive strength to estimate the deformation field between two images in a supervised or unsupervised manner [10–12]. They can not, however, directly be used in our application because the true undistorted image is unknown initially. To develop a network suitable for our situation, we propose a new unsupervised deep learning framework to estimate the deformation field from FOD images of both PEs and then apply it to the dMRI data. The proposed unsupervised deep learning network is named DistoRtion Correction Net (DrC-Net), using an U-Net to capture the latent features from FODs of two PEs and a transformer network to propagate the deformation field. With the iteratively updating the true undistorted FOD image, we can minimize the mean squared difference between the deformed FOD images of two PEs and the true undistorted image. In our experiments, we compared our method with *topup* method in the HCP-Pipeline on 100 subjects from HCP.

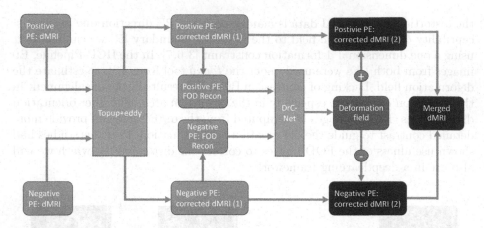

Fig. 2. The proposed framework for susceptibility distortion correction for connectome dMRI data.

2   Methods

2.1   Overview of the Framework

In this paper, we propose a new framework to correct the susceptibility distortion in dMRI images based on an unsupervised deep learning method. As shown in Fig. 2, the proposed method uses the dMRI images from two opposite PEs of the same subject as the inputs. After the *topup* and *eddy* tools from the HCP-Pipeline, we calculate the FOD images to feed the DrC-Net and obtain one predicted deformation field. Using the obtained deformation field, we apply it to both PEs of dMRI data with the opposite directions and finally merge them together to obtain the undistorted dMRI data.

FOD images were calculated from the multi-shell dMRI data with the multi-compartment model in [8]. It is represented as the coefficients to the spherical harmonics (SPHARMs) at each voxel. Although the FOD representation is 4D volume, we focus on the first coefficient component of FOD image for simplicity in the following. To be clear, our proposed framework also works for the whole 4D volume.

2.2   Unsupervised DrC-Net

The proposed unsupervised DrC-Net is briefly illustrated in Fig. 3. To simplify the description of PEs, we treat right-to-left (R/L) or posterior-to-anterior (P/A) phase encoding direction as positive PE (I_+) and left-to-right (L/R) or anterior-to-posterior (A/P) as negative PE (I_-). As the FOD images share the same voxel location as dMRI images and have more discriminative contrasts, we use them instead of the B0 images as inputs to train the DrC-Net and predict the deformation field between the distorted data and the undistorted data. The underlying assumption of DrC-Net is that the deformation field is along the phase encoding direction with opposite sign for both PE images [3,5]. This deformation field ϕ can be predicted by minimizing the difference between positive/negative PE image and the mean undistorted image I_M. The mean image I_M is iteratively updated by averaging the deformed positive PE and the deformed negative PE. The iterative optimization scheme can be formulated as follows:

$$\widehat{\phi} = \arg\min_{\phi}\{L_{sim}(I_+ \circ \phi, I_M) + L_{sim}(I_- \circ \phi^{-1}, I_M) + \lambda L_{smooth}(\phi)\} \qquad (1)$$

where $\widehat{\phi}$ is the optimal deformation field, $I_+ \circ \phi$ is the deformed image, $L_{sim}(\cdot, \cdot)$ is the similarity measurement function and $L_{smooth}(\cdot)$ is the regularization term on deformation field with the regularization parameter λ.

The commonly used similarity measurement function L_{sim} are mutual information, cross-correlation and mean squared difference. As we have the same modality and same acquisition parameter for both PEs, we use mean squared difference (MSD) as the metric in our method. The regularization term L_{smooth} ensures the smoothness of the deformation field and here we use the linear operation on the spatial gradient: $L_{smooth} = \sum_{p \in \Omega} \| \nabla \phi(p)\|^2$, where p is image voxel position and Ω is the whole domain of the image.

The deformation field ϕ is modeled by a conventional neural network named U-Net [10,13], and with this deformation field we apply it to both PEs with opposite directions using a spatial transformer [14] in DrC-Net. From the deformed PEs we obtain the mean image as the reference image and the whole DrC-Net evaluates the loss function in Eq. (1). With the help of stochastic gradient descent, we can learn the optimal deformation field from the training dataset within a reasonable time. There is no need of anatomical landmarkers to instruct the learning procedure. Given a new dMRI data with two PEs, we can predict a new deformation field for this data.

The architecture of U-Net contains encoder-decoder with skip connections to link shallow layers with deeper ones. The inputs of U-Net is formed by concatenating positive and negative PEs to a 2-channel 3D image, which is of size $144 \times 168 \times 110 \times 2$ in our experiment. For each stage of encoder and decoder, a 3D conventional layer with a kernel size of $3 \times 3 \times 3$ is applied and followed with a Leaky ReLu activation layer. The encoding stage is with 4 downsampling steps using 32 convolutional filters to reduce the input volume by two and result in a volume size of $(1/16)^3$ at the fourth downsampling layer. In the decoding stage, we have 4 upsampling layers alternatively with 4 convolution layers (filter size is 32) and followed by 2 refining convolution layers with filter size of 16 to enable the spatial alignment accuracy. Skip connections are used between the encoding and decoding stage for the same filter size to propagate the learned features. The output of U-Net is a deformation representation of size $144 \times 168 \times 110 \times 3$. Although there are 3 deformation components in the fourth dimension of the deformation field, only 1 deformation component is nonzero and the rest two are constrained to zero. In our experiment, the x-direction component is nonzero as HCP data is acquired along RL-LR phase encoding direction.

To apply the learned deformation field to positive and negative PEs during training, we use a differentiable module named spatial transformer [14]. To be

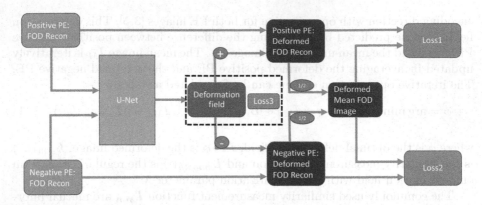

Fig. 3. The proposed unsupervised deep learning network to predict the deformation for connectome dMRI data. Loss1 and loss2 are the similarity measurement term L_{sim} and loss3 is the regularization term L_{smooth}.

clear, there is only one deformation field learned during training and only the direction of the deformation field is changed for two PEs at the spatial transform stage. With the deformed positive and negative PEs, we can obtain the mean undistorted image using an averaging layer. After that, we can back propagate the losses during the optimization.

The proposed DrC-Net was implemented using Keras [15] with a Tensorflow backend [16] and with some modules from Neuron [17]. The source code will be distributed online.

3   Experimental Results

3.1   Experiment Setup

To evaluate the performance of our proposed method, we used 100 subjects from the 900-subject release of HCP. Each subject has two raw dMRI scans in the R/L and L/R PEs acquired from 97 gradient directions distributed on three shells with b-values 1000, 2000, and 3000 s/mm^2 at an isotropic spatial resolution of 1.25 mm. The data was first processed by *topup* and *eddy* from HCP-Pipeline with their default parameter settings, which is the baseline method for our comparison. For the step of calculating FODs, the maximum SPHARM order of 8 is chosen.

For DrC-Net, ADAM optimizer was used during the optimization with a learning rate of $1e^{-3}$. The regularization parameter was chosen as 0.001. 2000 epochs and 100 steps for each epoch were used during training. The training dataset consists of 60 subjects randomly selected from the whole 100 subjects. The rest 40 subjects form the test dataset which were unseen for the DrC-Net. All training and testing experiments were ran on a workstation with an Intel Xeon i7-6850K CPU at 3.60 GHz and NVIDIA GTX 1080 Ti GPU. Although the training time was almost 2 days, it takes only less than 10 seconds to obtain the predicted deformation field for unseen new data. This time cost is much shorter than *topup* method, which is usually 2 or 3 h.

3.2 Evaluation Method

To quantitively measure the improvement of our proposed method in distortion correction, we evaluate the difference between two PEs after *topup* and DrC-Net. If the distortion is exactly corrected, the differences between two PEs should be zero. Two methods were used to measure this kind of difference. The first method utilizes the mean squared difference (MSD) of the fractional anisotropy (FA) generated from the tensor model on the dMRI data. The second method uses the angular difference of main fiber directions represented by the FODs, which are calculated from the deformed dMRI data of two PEs [9]. Briefly, the angular difference is computed by computing the minimum angle between the main fiber (largest magnitude) in the positive PE FOD and the top three fibers ordered in magnitude in the negative PE FOD.

The brainstem area plays a critical role in brain disorders such as the Alzheim-er's disease, where it is considered as the earliest site of tau pathology according to the Braak staging [18], but it suffers high distortion in dMRI. We thus focus on the brainstem area in our evaluation. We first segmented the brainstem region [19] in T1 image using Freesurfer 6.0 (https://surfer.nmr.mgh. harvard.edu/). The brainstem segmentation is then linearly mapped back to dMRI using the transformation between T1 and dMRI image. In particular, we considered the pons region in the brainstem as the region of interest (ROI).

3.3 Results

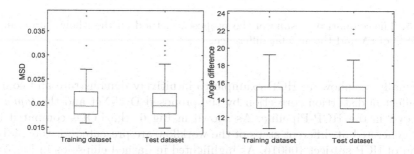

Fig. 4. The results of the proposed method on training dataset and test dataset evaluated on MSD of FA and the angular difference of the main fibers.

For deep learning based distortion correction we first evaluated the performance of DrC-Net on test dataset which were unseen during the training step. As shown in Fig. 4, each boxplot in training contains the results from 60 subjects while 40 subjects for testing. It shows that the DrC-Net have a similar performance on both training and test dataset based on the two evaluation methods. There is no group difference between the training and test data as the p-value of the t-test are 0.85 and 0.98, respectively, for the MSD of FA and the angular difference of the main fibers. This means that the proposed DrC-Net can be directly used for new HCP data with a similar distortion correction performance for training data. As the proposed method is general, it can also be trained for data with other phase encoding direction data like PA-AP direction.

From the previous results on training and test dataset, we included the whole 100 subjects to compare the performance of two methods. Compared to *topup* method in the HCP-Pipeline, the proposed DrC-Net dramatically improved the distortion correction effects as shown in Fig. 5. The median value of MSD for *topup* method is 0.036, while 0.02 for the proposed DrC-Net. The median angular difference for DrC-Net is 14.3 which is smaller than the value 17.5 of *topup* method. The Wilcoxon signed-rank test on two methods gave a statistically significant difference result for two evaluation methods, as both p-values are smaller than 0.05. It means that the DrC-Net can significantly reduce the distortion between two PEs and obtain an improved dMRI with much reduced distortion in fiber pathways.

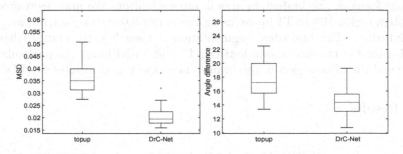

Fig. 5. The comparison results of the proposed method on the whole data evaluated on MSD of FA and the angular difference.

Finally, we show an HCP example to intuitively demonstrate and compare the effect of distortion correction by the proposed DrC-Net and the *topup* tool included in the HCP-Pipeline. As shown in Fig. 6, the FODs computed from data generated at different steps of the workflow are presented for the midbrain region of HCP subject 106016. As highlighted in dashed ellipsoids in Fig. 6 (B), (C) and (D), the preprocessed data by *topup* contains critical false fiber trajectories. What we found is that the trajectories of the fiber tracts of the cerebellar peduncles were distorted toward the left and right side for the two PEs, and this is the reason why the merged data showed two possible fiber trajectories in each hemisphere. This would lead to errors in anatomical analyses of fiber trajectories in this region. As shown in Fig. 6 (E), (F) and (G), the distortion between both PEs were recovered and those two fiber pathways were well kept after the merging step in the proposed using DrC-Net framework.

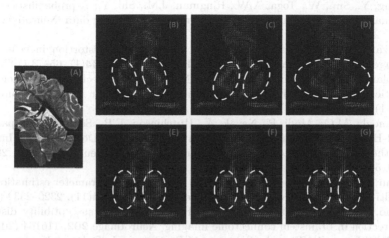

Fig. 6. An illustrative example with results from HCP subject 106016 in the brainstem ROI. (A) Yellow bar indicates the location of the ROI on the mid-sagittal slice. (B) and (C) show the FODs computed with data from the R/L and L/R PE after preprocessed by HCP-Pipeline, respectively. (D) show the FODs computed with the corrected data from HCP-Pipeline after merging data from R/L and L/R PEs. (E) and (F) show the FODs computed with the deformed PEs using DrC-Net from the R/L and L/R PEs, respectively. (G) show the FODs computed with the merged data from our method. (Color figure online)

4   Conclusions and Discussion

In this paper, we proposed a new method for distortion correction in dMRI data using an unsupervised deep learning network. The proposed method can reduce susceptibility induced distortion in dMRI data within 10 s on a GPU. As the residual distortions in connectome imaging data can be minimized by our proposed DrC-Net, we can greatly improve the modeling of the connectivity for brain pathways. In the future, we would like to extend our work on other phase encodings such as PA-AP and more extensive evaluations on the whole brain regions.

References

1. Glasser, M.F., et al.: The minimal preprocessing pipelines for the Human Connectome Project. NeuroImage **80**, 105–124 (2013)
2. Essen, D.V., Ugurbil, K., et al.: The human connectome project: a data acquisition perspective. NeuroImage **62**(4), 2222–2231 (2012)

3. Andersson, J.L., Skare, S., Ashburner, J.: How to correct susceptibility distortions in spin-echo echo-planar images: application to diffusion tensor imaging. NeuroImage **20**(2), 870–888 (2003)
4. Tang, Y., Sun, W., Toga, A.W., Ringman, J.M., Shi, Y.: A probabilistic atlas of human brainstem pathways based on connectome imaging data. NeuroImage **169**, 227–239 (2018)
5. Jezzard, P., Balaban, R.S.: Correction for geometric distortion in echo planar images from B0 field variations. Magn. Resonance Med. **34**(1), 65–73 (1995)
6. Holland, D., Kuperman, J.M., Dale, A.M.: Efficient correction of inhomogeneous static magnetic field-induced distortion in Echo Planar Imaging. NeuroImage **50**(1), 175–183 (2010)
7. Irfanoglu, M.O., Modi, P., Nayak, A., Hutchinson, E.B., Sarlls, J., Pierpaoli, C.: DR-BUDDI (Diffeomorphic Registration for Blip-Up blip-Down Diffusion Imaging) method for correcting echo planar imaging distortions. NeuroImage **106**, 284–299 (2015)
8. Tran, G., Shi, Y.: Fiber orientation and compartment parameter estimation from multi-shell diffusion imaging. IEEE Trans. Med. Imag. **34**(11), 2320–2332 (2015)
9. Qiao, Y., Sun, W., Shi, Y.: Fod-based registration for susceptibility distortion correction in brainstem connectome imaging. NeuroImage **202**, 116164 (2019)
10. Balakrishnan, G., Zhao, A., Sabuncu, M.R., Guttag, J., Dalca, A.V.: An unsupervised learning model for deformable medical image registration. In: Proceedings of the IEEE Conference on Computer Vision and Pattern Recognition, pp. 9252–9260 (2018)
11. de Vos, B.D., Berendsen, F.F., Viergever, M.A., Staring, M., Išgum, I.: End-to-End unsupervised deformable image registration with a convolutional neural network. In: Cardoso, M.J., et al. (eds.) DLMIA/ML-CDS -2017. LNCS, vol. 10553, pp. 204–212. Springer, Cham (2017). https://doi.org/10.1007/978-3-319-67558-9_24
12. Li, H., Fan, Y.: Non-rigid image registration using fully convolutional networks with deep self-supervision. arXiv preprint arXiv:1709.00799 (2017)
13. Ronneberger, O., Fischer, P., Brox, T.: U-Net: convolutional networks for biomedical image segmentation. In: Navab, N., Hornegger, J., Wells, W.M., Frangi, A.F. (eds.) MICCAI 2015. LNCS, vol. 9351, pp. 234–241. Springer, Cham (2015). https://doi.org/10.1007/978-3-319-24574-4_28
14. Jaderberg, M., Simonyan, K., Zisserman, A., et al.: Spatial transformer networks. In: Advances in Neural Information Processing Systems, pp. 2017–2025 (2015)
15. Chollet, F., et al.: Keras. https://github.com/fchollet/keras (2015)
16. Abadi, M., Agarwal, A., et al.: TensorFlow: Large-scale machine learning on heterogeneous systems, Software available from tensorflow.org (2015)
17. Dalca, A.V., Guttag, J., Sabuncu, M.R.: Anatomical priors in convolutional networks for unsupervised biomedical segmentation. In: Proceedings of the IEEE Conference on Computer Vision and Pattern Recognition, pp. 9290–9299 (2018)
18. Braak, H., Thal, D.R., Ghebremedhin, E., Del Tredici, K.: Stages of the pathologic process in Alzheimer disease: age categories from 1 to 100 years. J. Neuropathol. Experimental Neurol. **70**(11), 960–969 (2011)
19. Iglesias, J.E., et al.: Bayesian segmentation of brainstem structures in MRI. Neuroimage **113**, 184–195 (2015)

Hierarchical Geodesic Modeling on the Diffusion Orientation Distribution Function for Longitudinal DW-MRI Analysis

Heejong Kim[1]([✉]), Sungmin Hong[2], Martin Styner[3,4], Joseph Piven[3], Kelly Botteron[5], and Guido Gerig[1]

[1] Department of Computer Science and Engineering, New York University, New York, NY, USA
heejong.kim@nyu.edu
[2] Department of Neurology, MGH, Harvard Medical School, Boston, MA, USA
[3] Department of Psychiatry, University of North Carolina, Chapel Hill, NC, USA
[4] Department of Computer Science, University of North Carolina, Chapel Hill, NC, USA
[5] Department of Psychiatry, Washington University, St. Louis, MO, USA

Abstract. The analysis of anatomy that undergoes rapid changes, such as neuroimaging of the early developing brain, greatly benefits from spatio-temporal statistical analysis methods to represent population variations but also subject-wise characteristics over time. Methods for spatio-temporal modeling and for analysis of longitudinal shape and image data have been presented before, but, to our knowledge, not for diffusion weighted MR images (DW-MRI) fitted with higher-order diffusion models. To bridge the gap between rapidly evolving DW-MRI methods in longitudinal studies and the existing frameworks, which are often limited to the analysis of derived measures like fractional anisotropy (FA), we propose a new framework to estimate a population trajectory of longitudinal diffusion orientation distribution functions (dODFs) along with subject-specific changes by using hierarchical geodesic modeling. The dODF is an angular profile of the diffusion probability density function derived from high angular resolution diffusion imaging (HARDI) and we consider the dODF with the square-root representation to lie on the unit sphere in a Hilbert space, which is a well-known Riemannian manifold, to respect the nonlinear characteristics of dODFs. The proposed method is validated on synthetic longitudinal dODF data and tested on a longitudinal set of 60 HARDI images from 25 healthy infants to characterize dODF changes associated with early brain development.

Keywords: Diffusion weighted imaging · Longitudinal analysis · Hierarchical geodesic modeling

Electronic supplementary material The online version of this chapter (https://doi.org/10.1007/978-3-030-59728-3_31) contains supplementary material, which is available to authorized users.

© Springer Nature Switzerland AG 2020
A. L. Martel et al. (Eds.): MICCAI 2020, LNCS 12267, pp. 311–321, 2020.
https://doi.org/10.1007/978-3-030-59728-3_31

1   Introduction

The understanding of subject-wise anatomical change driven by a biological process is important for diagnosis of neurological disorders or planning of therapeutic intervention. The need is even more significant when the timing of diagnosis and therapeutic planning is critical due to the rapid rate of anatomical change, e.g. in the early developing brain of an infant at risk of autism. The longitudinal analysis of anatomical change has recently gained more attention because of its ability to provide analysis of subject-wise anatomical changes while also estimating of a population trend, in addition to accounting for the inherent correlation of longitudinal data [12,15–17,22].

Most recent clinical studies involve longitudinal data acquisition where multiple repeated scans of individual subjects are acquired. Because repeated scans of an individual subject are inherently correlated, conventional cross-sectional analysis assuming independence of given data is not suitable to be applied to longitudinal data. So far, spatio-temporal statistical analysis methods were suggested and broadly used for longitudinal data derived from medical images to study a representative anatomical change of a population of medical images [8,14,24,29]. However, spatio-temporal analysis of higher-order diffusion models of high angular resolution diffusion imaging (HARDI) images has not been extensively studied until recently.

In [19], authors presented a framework for longitudinal multi-shell HARDI image analysis which includes time and orientation resolved multi-tissue average template building. A consistent atlas building of longitudinal HARDI images was suggested in [18]. These studies mainly focused on reflecting temporal differences of images of different age groups rather than constructing a fully continuous longitudinal atlas. There was an attempt to create a continuous longitudinal atlas using spherical harmonics (SPHARM) coefficients of diffusion orientation distribution function (dODF) [16] which showed the continuous change of dODFs in the corpus callosum. However, the method is limited by the fact that an estimated atlas might include invalid dODFs due to the application of linear mixed effects modeling to individual SPHARM coefficients without considering the characteristics of a dODF as a probability density function (PDF).

In this paper, we present a novel application of a hierarchical geodesic modeling method [15,17,25] to estimate a representative change of longitudinal dODFs. A dODF, a diffusion PDF on a sphere, is expressed on a Riemannian manifold as suggested in [6,13]. A subject-specific spatio-temporal trajectory of dODFs is estimated by geodesic modeling with a series of dODFs from repeatedly observed HARDI images of an individual subject. The population-level longitudinal change is then estimated from the set of subject-specific trajectories via hierarchical modeling to account for repeated data. We validate the feasibility of the proposed method with a synthetic example of longitudinal dODFs. The proposed method was applied to a longitudinal set of 60 HARDI images from 25 healthy infants from a real-world clinical study in order to estimate a normative longitudinal trajectory of healthy infant brain development as expressed with diffusion imaging.

2   Method

2.1   Square-Root dODF on the Sphere Manifold

The dODF, $f(s)$, $\mathbf{s} \in \mathbb{S}^2$, is an angular profile of the diffusion probability density function (PDF), which is a non-negative and normalized function of water molecule motion on the unit sphere. The square-root representation of dODF results in manifold valued data lying on the unit sphere in a Hilbert space with L^2 metric [26]. In this paper, the manifold-valued dODF is defined as $y = \sqrt{f(s)}$ and determined in the space $Y = \{y : \mathbb{S}^2 \to \mathbb{R}^+ | y(s) \geq 0, \int_{s \in \mathbb{S}^2} y^2(s)ds = 1\}$. In practice, a dODF is discretely sampled from the unit 2-sphere [11] with approximately equal area. We assume that the samples are d evenly distributed points from the domain unit 2-sphere of a dODF. A discretized dODF is then represented as a d-dimensional point y, which satisfies $\frac{1}{a} \sum_{i=1}^{d} y^2(i) \approx 1$, where a is the area that each sampled point of dODF represents on the 2-sphere. Since the area a is constant, we can simply normalize all dODFs y to be on the surface of the unit $(d - 1)$-sphere that satisfies $\sum_{i=1}^{d} y^2(i) = 1$. Then a square-root dODF can be expressed on the $d - 1$-sphere manifold, $y \in \mathbb{S}^{d-1}$. We used a symmetric sphere with 724 vertices.

A sphere manifold is a well-known Riemannian manifold with constant curvature of 1.0. A geodesic is a zero acceleration curve on a Riemannian manifold M. Each point p on M is associated with a tangent vector space T_pM. Let v be a tangent vector on T_pM, $v \in T_pM$. An exponential map $Exp(p, v) = q$ is a mapping function that maps p along a geodesic that starts from p in the direction and magnitude of v for a unit time. The exponential map of the $\mathbb{S}^{d-1}$ sphere manifold is given by rotation of p by the norm of v, $Exp(p, v) = p \cos\theta + \frac{\sin\theta}{\theta}v$, where $\theta = ||v||$. A Riemannian log map between two points $Log(p, q) = v$ is the inverse of the exponential map that returns a tangent vector $v \in T_pM$ of a geodesic that connects p and q. The log map of $\mathbb{S}^{d-1}$ is the initial velocity of the rotation between the two points, $Log(p, q) = \frac{\theta(q - \pi_p(q))}{||q - \pi_p(q)||}$, where $\theta = \arccos(\langle p, q \rangle)$ and $\pi_p(q) = p\langle p, q \rangle$ [10]. A Riemannian distance between two points $d(p, q)$ measures the length of the geodesic between p and q, which is the norm of v, $d(p, q) = ||v|| = ||Log(p, q)||$. Parallel transport $\psi_{p \to q}(v)$ transports a tangent vector $v \in T_pM$ from one point $p \in M$ to another point $q \in M$ along a geodesic between p and q while preserving the angle and the scale of v.

2.2   Hierarchical Geodesic Model

A linear mixed effect model is a statistical model reflecting both fixed effects and random effects that are variables randomly distributed across individual subjects in a longitudinal study or groups from a hierarchical structure in Euclidean space [9]. In our case, given longitudinal observations of a non-linear response variable on the sphere manifold, we estimate subject-specific and population-level changes by hierarchical geodesic modeling (HG) [1,15,17,25]. The HG model estimates subject-specific longitudinal trajectories from repeatedly observed dODFs of individual subjects, and in turn, estimates a population-level spatio-temporal change from the collection of subject-wise trajectories.

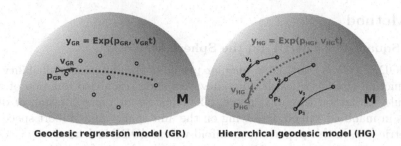

Geodesic regression model (GR)   Hierarchical geodesic model (HG)

Fig. 1. Illustration of geodesic regression model (Left) and hierarchical geodesic model (Right) with random effects from the correlation of longitudinal data. Each subject has a different intercept and slope (Black lines, Right).

Subject-Wise Trajectory. A subject-wise trajectory and the corresponding least squares criterion are written as

$$y_i = Exp(\hat{p}_i, \hat{v}_i t), \quad (\hat{p}_i, \hat{v}_i) = \arg\min_{p_i, v_i} \sum_{j=1}^{N_{obs,i}} d^2(y_{ij}, Exp(p_i, v_i t_{ij})), \qquad (1)$$

where $y_{ij} \in M$ is the ith subject's j^{th} observation, $N_{obs,i}$ the number of observations of the subject i, $p_i \in M$ the intercept, $v_i \in T_{p_i}M$ the slope tangent vector, and $t_{ij} \in \mathbb{R}$ the observation time. Equation 1 is solved by the alternating naive tangent space approximation method [15].

Hierarchical Geodesic Model. A population trajectory is given as

$$y = Exp(\hat{P}, \hat{V}t), \qquad (2)$$

$$\hat{P} = \arg\min_{P} \sum_{i=1}^{N_{subj}} d^2(P, \hat{p}_i), \quad \hat{V} = \arg\min_{V} \sum_{i=1}^{N_{subj}} d_{\mathbb{R}}^2(V, \psi_{\hat{p}_i \to P}(\hat{v}_i)), \qquad (3)$$

where the ith subject's optimized intercept and slope are denoted $\hat{p}_i$ and $\hat{v}_i$, and N_{subj} is the number of subjects. The least squares formulation on the left of Eq. 3 assumes that the subject-wise intercept $\hat{p}_i$ is distributed around $\hat{P}$ following the Riemannian normal distribution of the intercept's random effects: $\hat{p}_i = Exp(\hat{P}, \epsilon_p)$, where $\epsilon_p \sim N_M(0, \sigma_p^2)$ [28]. The least squares formulation of the right of Eq. 3 represents the random effects of slope. As we need to bring the subject-wise tangent vectors to the same tangent space before estimating the slope $\hat{V}$, the tangent vector $\hat{v}_i \in T_{\hat{p}_i}M$ is parallel transported to $T_{\hat{P}}M$, denoted as $\psi_{p_i \to P}(\hat{v}_i)$. The distance function $d_{\mathbb{R}}$ is the standard L^2 norm on $T_{\hat{P}}M$.

3   Experimental Validations and Results

The difference between a geodesic regression (GR) model and a hierarchical geodesic (HG) model for a series of longitudinal data on a sphere manifold M is illustrated in Fig. 1. Due to the inherent correlation of longitudinal data, the random effects of subjects should be reflected in estimating a population trajectory. A GR model assumes data independence thus the model cannot capture longitudinal changes correctly while an HG model contains the random effects of slope and intercept. In the following, we validate our method with synthetic longitudinal dODF, and demonstrate clinical application using longitudinal HARDI images of the developing infant brain.

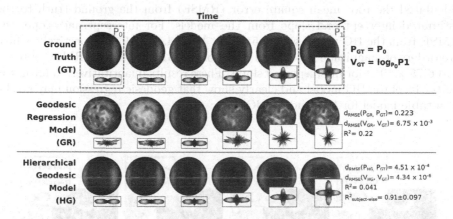

Fig. 2. Synthetic example of longitudinal dODF. Color mapped spheres represent dODF values and the glyphs next to the spheres are radially scaled shapes. (Row 1) Ground truth. The red dashed boxes show P_0 with a single direction and P_1 with crossing fibers. The ground truth geodesic follows the tangent vector $V = log_{P_0}P_1$. (Row 2) Estimated geodesic regression model. (Row 3) Estimated hierarchical geodesic model. (Color figure online)

Synthetic longitudinal dODFs. We construct a series of synthetic longitudinal dODF data to evaluate the performance of the HG model and compare with the result from GR. We establish a ground truth geodesic by the logarithm map from a dODF with a single peak P_0 to a dODF with perpendicular crossing peaks P_1, $V = Log(P_0, P_1)$ (First row, Fig. 2) [6]. The two dODFs P_0 and P_1 were generated by the multi-tensor method with 6th order real spherical harmonics [5]. A total of 2470 dODFs of 1000 subjects with two or three observations associated with time points ranged between 0 and 15 were generated by Eq. 2 with the random effects on intercepts $\epsilon_P \sim N(0, 0.005^2)$ and slopes $\epsilon_V \sim N(0, 0.001^2)$, and the data observation error $\epsilon \sim N(0, 0.005^2)$. In addition to the random effects on the intercepts, we injected additional variation to perturb subject-wise intercept points along a tangent vector perpendicular to the tangent vector V. This is intended to demonstrate feasibility of the proposed method to handle subject-specific variations which mimick the scenario of Fig. 1.

Figure 2 shows the estimated geodesic of the GR model (Second row, Fig. 2) and the HG model (Third row, Fig. 2). The HG model successfully estimated the ground truth population trajectory by accounting for the longitudinal effect while the estimated GR model did not provide a suitable result. The R^2 of HR and GR with respect to the ground truth geodesic were 0.041 and 0.22 respectively. The relatively low R^2 value of the estimated HG model is not surprising because R^2 does not take into account the longitudinal effect, it just measures the ratio of the explained variance to the total variance of an entire population. The average R^2 value of the subject-wise trajectories of the HG model was 0.91 ± 0.097 (a comparable value cannot be measured by GR). We calculated the root mean square error (RMSE) from the ground truth to the estimated intercept and slope from the models. For intercept and slope, the RMSE from the HG model were 4.51×10^{-4} and 4.34×10^{-6} respectively, which are orders of magnitude lower than those of the GR model with RMSE of 0.223 and 6.75×10^{-3} for intercept and slope. These results quantitatively confirm the better fit of the HG model and clearly show that geodesic regression may not be a suitable model for longitudinal dODFs.

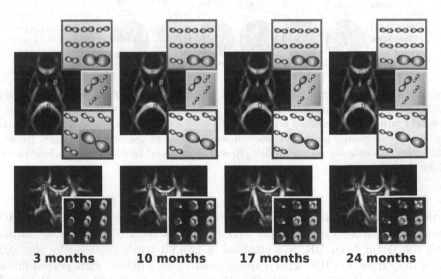

3 months   10 months   17 months   24 months

Fig. 3. Population geodesic trajectory of longitudinal dODFs superimposed on generalized fractional anisotropy (GFA) in early developing infants sampled at different ages. Red, green, blue and yellow boxes show changes in the genu of corpus callosum (GCC), the anterior limb of the internal capsule (ALIC), the splenium of corpus callosum (SCC) and the region with crossing fibers where corticospinal tracts and corpus callosum (CC) pass, respectively. Larger glyphs are used for enhanced visualization. (Color figure online)

Longitudinal DW Images of Developing Infant Brain. The brain undergoes rapid structural changes due to axonal maturation, which is also expressed by developing cortical folding, presenting asymptotic growth at an early age [7,21]. Several longitudinal studies have investigated early maturation of white matter (WM) measured by fractional anisotropy (FA) and mean diffusivity (MD) [3,22], but less is known about how the dODF changes with age. We apply our new method to a longitudinal set of 60 HARDI brain images from 25 healthy developing infants with an age range from 3 to 25 months, scanned on 3-T Siemens TIM Trio, with 64 directional DWI volumes sampled on the half sphere, b-value at $2000\,s/mm^2$, and $2 \times 2 \times 2\,mm^3$ voxel resolution, followed by preprocessing and multivariate atlas building similarly to [16]. Manifold-valued dODFs are obtained voxel-wise from all HARDI images aligned in the common atlas space. We re-parametrize subject age by taking the natural log to model the asymptotic development of the infant brain [7].

One benefit of the analysis of dODF is that it provides information on brain maturation by derived measurements, such as generalized fractional anisotropy (GFA) or peaks of the ODFs [4,27] rather than modeling derived measures independently. We analyze the estimated trajectories of dODFs and derived measures in selected anatomical regions of white matter including genu (GCC) and splenium (SCC) of the corpus callosum, anterior limb of the internal capsule (ALIC), posterior limb of the internal capsule (PLIC), and brain regions with crossing fibers where corpus callosum (CC) and corticospinal tracts (CST) pass. Myelination of the selected regions is known to occur during early development [7,21].

Figure 3 illustrates the voxel-wise population geodesic trend of the estimated dODF changes over age in the selected WM regions. The dODF shapes become sharper in the GCC, SCC, and ALIC as age increases. The change is even more pronounced in the crossing fiber region (Fig. 3, Bottom row). The map of the derived GFA indices is shown in the background of dODFs displaying that GFA indices are lower in the crossing fiber regions (bottom row) than those in regions where dODFs had one peak (top row). The overall R^2 values of GR and HG are 0.27 and 0.26 respectively and the overall subject-wise R^2 of HG was 0.92.

The results of the changes of dODF peaks, also known as maxima, from the estimated HG model are illustrated in Fig. 4. The peak values of GCC and ALIC are slightly increased while the SCC and PLIC did not show any change as shown in Fig. 4(a). The flat slope may indicate that the maturation of the SCC and PLIC begins earlier compared to the GCC and ALIC. The slight increase in the slope of the single peaks may be induced from large individual variability which is an observation also reported in another recent longitudinal study [20]. This variability may be a combination of factors related to brain development and scanner variability not captured by our model. Figure 4(b) shows the peak value of ROIs with crossing fibers. The second peak value increases in both left and right hemispheres while the first peak stays similar over time. This result suggests that the dODF trajectory is reflecting crossing fiber development in much more detail than the derived measures, as is also illustrated in Fig. 4(c).

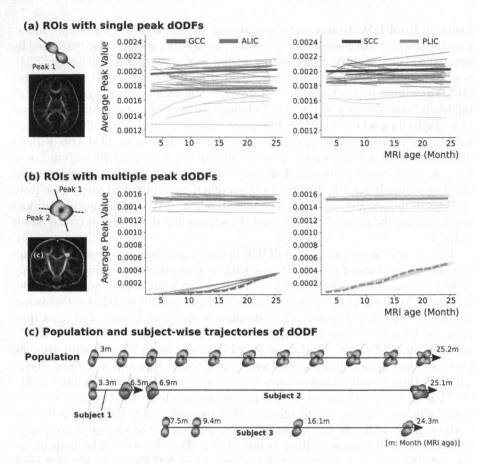

Fig. 4. Changes of peak diffusion of dODFs estimated from geodesic trajectories. (a) Results from ROIs with the dODF having a single peak with genu of corpus callosum (GCC), splenium of corpus callosum (SCC), anterior limb of the internal capsule (ALIC), and posterior limb of the internal capsule (PLIC). (b) Results of the crossing fiber regions having multiple peaks. (c) Example of the dODF trajectories of the population and three selected subjects was taken at one voxel marked in yellow from the crossing fiber ROI. Primary (red) and secondary (green) peaks from the population-level trajectory are illustrated with the dODFs. (Color figure online)

4   Conclusion

We propose a new hierarchical geodesic modeling (HG) of diffusion orientation distribution function (dODF) for longitudinal analysis of diffusion weighted MR images (DW-MRI). The proposed method estimates a population trajectory and also subject-specific trajectories of the age-related change of dODFs, which are represented as square root manifold-valued data to respect the nonlinear characteristics of dODFs. We showed via synthetic data that the geodesic regression model is not suitable for the analysis of longitudinal dODFs, demonstrating the importance of properly modeling intra-subject correlation. The application to a real-world data offered promising results that supported clinical findings of early brain growth from a population trajectory of dODFs. The method is generic and applicable to any longitudinal set of dODF data for the analysis of a temporal change of dODFs related to early development, degeneration, or disease progression. The HG model on dODFs enables analysis of derived information, such as generalized fractional anisotropy (GFA) or tractography-based analysis, which has been broadly used for longitudinal analysis of DW-MRI. As this method provides a basis for creating a normative model, there are several directions for future works such as hypothesis testing for longitudinal group differences between a disease group and controls or prediction of physiological age. Future perspective for the methodology will be to develop a better longitudinal model for dODF, for example, a REML-like-mixed-effect model [1,2,23].

Acknowledgements. This work was supported by the NIH grants R01-HD055741-12, 1R01HD089390-01A1, 1R01DA038215-01A1 and 1R01HD088125-01A1.

Conflict of Interest Statement. The authors declare that there are no conflicts or commercial interest related to this article.

References

1. Allassonnière, S., Chevallier, J., Oudard, S.: Learning spatiotemporal piecewise-geodesic trajectories from longitudinal manifold-valued data. In: Advances in Neural Information Processing Systems, pp. 1152–1160 (2017)
2. Bône, A., Colliot, O., Durrleman, S.: Learning distributions of shape trajectories from longitudinal datasets: a hierarchical model on a manifold of diffeomorphisms. In: IEEE Conference on Computer Vision and Pattern Recognition, pp. 9271–9280 (2018)
3. Chen, Y., et al.: Longitudinal regression analysis of spatial-temporal growth patterns of geometrical diffusion measures in early postnatal brain development with diffusion tensor imaging. Neuroimage 58(4), 993–1005 (2011)
4. Cohen-Adad, J., Descoteaux, M., Wald, L.L.: Quality assessment of high angular resolution diffusion imaging data using bootstrap on q-ball reconstruction. J. Magnetic Resonance Imag. 33(5), 1194–1208 (2011)
5. Descoteaux, M., Angelino, E., Fitzgibbons, S., Deriche, R.: Regularized, fast, and robust analytical q-ball imaging. Magnetic Resonance Med. Official J. Int. Soc. Magnetic Resonance Med. 58(3), 497–510 (2007)
6. Du, J., Goh, A., Kushnarev, S., Qiu, A.: Geodesic regression on orientation distribution functions with its application to an aging study. NeuroImage 87, 416–426 (2014)
7. Dubois, J., Dehaene-Lambertz, G., Kulikova, S., Poupon, C., Hüppi, P.S., Hertz-Pannier, L.: The early development of brain white matter: a review of imaging studies in fetuses, newborns and infants. Neuroscience 276, 48–71 (2014)
8. Durrleman, S., Pennec, X., Trouvé, A., Braga, J., Gerig, G., Ayache, N.: Toward a comprehensive framework for the spatiotemporal statistical analysis of longitudinal shape data. Int. J. Comput. Vis. 103(1), 22–59 (2013)

9. Fitzmaurice, G.M., Laird, N.M., Ware, J.H.: Applied longitudinal analysis, vol. 998. John Wiley & Sons (2012)
10. Fletcher, P.T.: Geodesic regression and its application to shape analysis. In: Innovations for Shape Analysis, pp. 35–52. Springer, Heidelberg (2013). https://doi.org/10.1007/978-3-642-34141-0_2
11. Garyfallidis, E., et al.: Dipy, a library for the analysis of diffusion MRI data. Front. Neuroinform. **8**, 8 (2014)
12. Gerig, G., Fishbaugh, J., Sadeghi, N.: Longitudinal modeling of appearance and shape and its potential for clinical use. Med. Image Anal. **33**, 114–121 (2016)
13. Goh, A., Lenglet, C., Thompson, P.M., Vidal, R.: A nonparametric riemannian framework for processing high angular resolution diffusion images (hardi). In: IEEE Conference on Computer Vision and Pattern Recognition, pp. 2496–2503. IEEE (2009)
14. Guizard, N., Fonov, V.S., García-Lorenzo, D., Nakamura, K., Aubert-Broche, B., Collins, D.L.: Spatio-temporal regularization for longitudinal registration to subject-specific 3d template. PLoS ONE **10**(8), 10 (2015)
15. Hong, S., Fishbaugh, J., Wolff, J.J., Styner, M.A., Gerig, G.: Hierarchical multi-geodesic model for longitudinal analysis of temporal trajectories of anatomical shape and covariates. In: Shen, D., et al. (eds.) MICCAI 2019. LNCS, vol. 11767, pp. 57–65. Springer, Cham (2019). https://doi.org/10.1007/978-3-030-32251-9_7
16. Kim, H., Styner, M., Piven, J., Gerig, G.: A framework to construct a longitudinal dw-mri infant atlas based on mixed effects modeling of dodf coefficients. In: International Conference on Medical Image Computing and Computer-Assisted Intervention. Springer (2019)
17. Kim, H.J., Adluru, N., Suri, H., Vemuri, B.C., Johnson, S.C., Singh, V.: Riemannian nonlinear mixed effects models: analyzing longitudinal deformations in neuroimaging. In: IEEE Conference on Computer Vision and Pattern Recognition, pp. 2540–2549 (2017)
18. Kim, J., Chen, G., Lin, W., Yap, P.-T., Shen, D.: Graph-constrained sparse construction of longitudinal diffusion-weighted infant atlases. In: Descoteaux, M., Maier-Hein, L., Franz, A., Jannin, P., Collins, D.L., Duchesne, S. (eds.) MICCAI 2017. LNCS, vol. 10433, pp. 49–56. Springer, Cham (2017). https://doi.org/10.1007/978-3-319-66182-7_6
19. Pietsch, M., et al.: A framework for multi-component analysis of diffusion mri data over the neonatal period. NeuroImage **186**, 321–337 (2019)
20. Reynolds, J.E., Grohs, M.N., Dewey, D., Lebel, C.: Global and regional white matter development in early childhood. Neuroimage **196**, 49–58 (2019)
21. Rutherford, M.A.: MRI of the Neonatal Brain. Elsevier Health Sciences (2002)
22. Sadeghi, N., Prastawa, M., Fletcher, P.T., Wolff, J., Gilmore, J.H., Gerig, G.: Regional characterization of longitudinal dt-mri to study white matter maturation of the early developing brain. Neuroimage **68**, 236–247 (2013)
23. Schiratti, J.B., Allassonniere, S., Colliot, O., Durrleman, S.: A bayesian mixed-effects model to learn trajectories of changes from repeated manifold-valued observations. J. Mach. Learn. Res. **18**(1), 4840–4872 (2017)
24. Serag, A., et al.: Construction of a consistent high-definition spatio-temporal atlas of the developing brain using adaptive kernel regression. NeuroImage **59**(3), 2255–2265 (2012)
25. Singh, N., Hinkle, J., Joshi, S., Fletcher, P.T.: Hierarchical geodesic models in diffeomorphisms. Int. J. Comput. Vis. **117**(1), 70–92 (2016)

26. Srivastava, A., Jermyn, I., Joshi, S.: Riemannian analysis of probability density functions with applications in vision. In: IEEE Conference on Computer Vision and Pattern Recognition, pp. 1–8. IEEE (2007)

27. Van Hecke, W., Emsell, L., Sunaert, S.: Diffusion Tensor Imaging: A Practical Handbook, Springer, New York (2015). https://doi.org/10.1007/978-1-4939-3118-7

28. Zhang, M., Fletcher, T.: Probabilistic principal geodesic analysis. In: Advances in Neural Information Processing Systems, pp. 1178–1186 (2013)

29. Zhang, Y., Shi, F., Wu, G., Wang, L., Yap, P.T., Shen, D.: Consistent spatial-temporal longitudinal atlas construction for developing infant brains. IEEE Trans. Med. Imag. **35**(12), 2568–2577 (2016)

TRAKO: Efficient Transmission of Tractography Data for Visualization

Daniel Haehn[1]($\boxtimes$)(iD), Loraine Franke[1](iD), Fan Zhang[3](iD),
Suheyla Cetin-Karayumak[3](iD), Steve Pieper[2](iD), Lauren J. O'Donnell[3](iD),
and Yogesh Rathi[3](iD)

[1] University of Massachusetts Boston, Boston, USA
{haehn,franke}@mpsych.org
[2] Isomics, Inc., Cambridge, USA
pieper@isomics.com
[3] Harvard Medical School, Boston, USA
{fzhang,skarayumak,odonnell,yogesh}@bwh.harvard.edu

Abstract. Fiber tracking produces large tractography datasets that are tens of gigabytes in size consisting of millions of streamlines. Such vast amounts of data require formats that allow for efficient storage, transfer, and visualization. We present TRAKO, a new data format based on the Graphics Layer Transmission Format (glTF) that enables immediate graphical and hardware-accelerated processing. We integrate a state-of-the-art compression technique for vertices, streamlines, and attached scalar and property data. We then compare TRAKO to existing tractography storage methods and provide a detailed evaluation on eight datasets. TRAKO can achieve data reductions of over 28x without loss of statistical significance when used to replicate analysis from previously published studies.

Keywords: Compression · Diffusion imaging · Tractography

1 Introduction

Diffusion-weighted magnetic resonance imaging (MRI) allows estimation of the brain's white matter properties [2]. Fiber tracking methods [3] then produce clusters of streamlines corresponding to 3D fiber bundles (Fig. 1). Each fiber in these bundles is a line with a collection of x, y, z coordinates, typically represented using 32-bit floating point numbers. Researchers may attach scalars to these coordinates (per-vertex) to record values such as estimates of local tissue integrity. These values can be of arbitrary dimension, size, and data type. Researchers may also attach many different property values to individual streamlines (per-fiber). Modern tractography studies with scalars and properties can result in datasets that are tens of gigabytes in size per subject [26]. Storing such data can be expensive while transferring and processing the data for visualization can be inefficient. To optimize the costs and minimize overall delays, we

© Springer Nature Switzerland AG 2020
A. L. Martel et al. (Eds.): MICCAI 2020, LNCS 12267, pp. 322–332, 2020.
https://doi.org/10.1007/978-3-030-59728-3_32

Fig. 1. Examples of diffusion tractography fiber tracts. (left) separate fiber clusters, (right) wholebrain tractography. Individual tracts are colored by anatomical orientation. (Color figure online)

need to explore compression techniques and their effect on tractography based neuroanalysis.

Currently existing compression methods are using two approaches by either reducing the number of fiber tracts in a dataset by downsampling [1,11–13, 16,19,23,30,32] or compressing the data of individual fibers [5,7,14,15,21,24]. However, none of the existing methods approaches the problem from the perspective of optimizing storage for graphical processing, nor do they leverage recent developments in data representation and compression standards for spatial computing. In this paper, we present TRAKO, a new tractography data format for efficient transmission and visualization. TRAKO is based on the fully extendable glTF [27] container, which among other things is designed to minimize runtime processing when uploading data to a graphical processing unit (GPU). Furthermore, TRAKO applies state-of-the-art 3D geometry compression techniques which allow to explicitly control the data reduction (lossiness). In addition, TRAKO compresses vertices of each fiber tract and attached scalars and properties, an advantage over existing tractography compression methods.

We compare TRAKO against two compression schemes that are specifically designed for fiber tracts: *zfib* [24] and *qfib* [20]. Zfib, which is now part of the Dipy [10] library, reduces the number of vertices in each fiber tract but does not change the vertices itself (downsampling). Qfib is a recently presented algorithm that compresses individual vertices and allows to choose between a 8 bit and 16 bit precision. Neither zfib nor qfib support the compression of attached per-vertex scalars or per-fiber properties. In contrast, TRAKO encodes vertices and all attached values with the Draco algorithm [4] that combines quantization, prediction schemes, and attribute encoding.[1]

Most tractography compression schemes are configurable to trade-off information loss and data size. Therefore, we explore different settings of TRAKO to encode data points with the goal of sufficiently preserving accuracy for quantitative analysis. We test and evaluate the methods TRAKO, zfib, and qfib on multiple datasets to measure the loss of vertices, scalars, and properties after encoding. TRAKO reduces data sizes by a factor of 10–28 with an average error that is lower than the voxel size of the original diffusion MRI. We further perform

---

[1] https://github.com/google/draco.

a sensitivity analysis and replicate two previously published tractography studies with compressed versions of the original data. We find that compressed fiber tracts are very suitable for real-world processing. Finally, we publicly release all our data, code, experiments, and results[2].

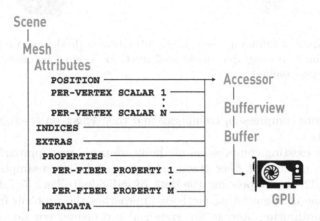

Fig. 2. The TRAKO data format stores fiber tracts in a standardized glTF [27] container. This way, we can use existing mechanisms such as position attributes and indices to store the streamlines as buffers. These buffers are accessible and configurable through accessors and bufferviews and are immediately ready for transmission to the GPU. glTF containers are fully extendable and allow TRAKO to support the storage of per-vertex scalars, per-fiber properties, and metadata in any format.

2   Data Format

2.1   Structure

The TRAKO data format with file extension .tko, is built off the Graphics Library Transmission Format (glTF) [27], a JSON-based royalty-free format for efficient transmission and loading of 3D scenes (i.e. to be the "JPEG of 3D"). glTF containers include mechanisms to store computer graphics scenes but the specification is fully extendable and flexible.

For TRAKO, we define a set of fiber tracts using the glTF mesh data structure (Fig. 2). This structure is defined with arrays of primitives corresponding directly to data required for draw calls of a GPU. Specifically, we use the POSITION attributes (Vec3 floats) to store the vertices of the fiber tracts and then map them to individual streamlines using the INDICES property. Since TRAKO files are valid glTF files as well, we can leverage the whole glTF ecosystem that includes validators, viewers, optimizers, and converters. For examples, we can

---

[2] https://github.com/bostongfx/trako, current version: 0.3.4.dev9.

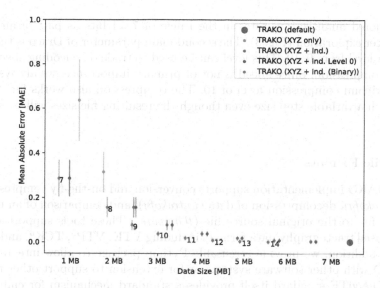

Fig. 3. Parameter exploration of TRAKO on the ISMRM 2015 dataset with an original size of 34.1 Megabytes. We test the default parameters of TRAKO (blue, quantization bits (q_bit) 14, compression level (cl) 1), a variation that only compresses the vertices (XYZ, orange), one that compresses XYZ and indices (Ind., green), the same but with compression level 0 for faster speed (red), and finally, TRAKO converted to binary using the glTF Pipeline (purple). The lower left corner indicated low errors and high compression rates. The numbers in the plot indicate the quantization bits. (Color figure online)

convert ASCII JSON .tko-files to binary versions with existing converter tools such as the Cesium glTF Pipeline[3] or gltf-pack[4].

2.2 Compression

Internally, TRAKO leverages the Draco compression scheme that enables the compression of meshes and point cloud data by combining multiple techniques. For meshes, Draco uses the Edgebreaker algorithm [28]. For point clouds, Draco offers a kd-tree based encoding that re-arranges all points, or a sequential encoding that preserves their order. Preserving the order is important for tractography data since we need to keep track of all vertices and any mapped values along the streamlines. We integrated Draco's sequential encoding method to TRAKO. This method combines entropy reduction using a configurable quantization rate of 1–31 bits with prediction schemes that compute differences between stored values (similar to delta encoding) [8,9,29].

There are two main parameters to control the compression. The quantization rate controls how many bits are used to encode individual values (default: 14). Higher rates allow for greater data precision but yield larger data sizes.

---

[3] https://github.com/CesiumGS/gltf-pipeline.

[4] https://github.com/zeux/meshoptimizer.

We explored quantization rates in the range of 7–14 bits as part of an initial parameter exploration (Fig. 3). The second main parameter of Draco is the compression level from 0–10. This level can be used to trade off encoding speed with better compression. Since speed is not of primary importance, we always select the maximum compression level of 10. The compression also works for streamlines with a variable step size even though the resulting file sizes will be slightly larger.

2.3   File Formats

Our TRAKO implementation supports conversion and on-the-fly compression of data (*trakofy*), decompression of data (*untrakofy*), and comparison of an uncompressed file to the original source file (*tkompare*). These tools support various widely used tractography data formats including VTK, VTP[5], TCK[6], and TRK[7] files. In addition, we provide a reusable Python package to allow integration of TRAKO with other software systems or for extension to support other file formats. The glTF standard itself provides a standard mechanism for embedding domain-specific data within glTF JSON structures, and there exists a wide range of extensions to support features such as advanced graphical rendering, animation, and multiple levels-of-detail[8]. The same approach can be used with TRAKO to embed custom experimental metadata without breaking compatibility with the core standard. By default, our encoding matches the coordinate system of the underlying image data but it also fully supports adding transformation matrices or image space information.

3   Evaluation and Results

3.1   Performance

We consider the TRAKO, zfib, and qfib data formats for efficient tractography storage. We test these formats with eight different datasets and compute the following metrics to measure compression and data loss. Five datasets only include fiber tracts (Table 1, top) while three datasets include mapped per-vertex scalars and per-fiber properties (Table 1, bottom).

Following the qfib paper [20], we use the compression ratio C_r. This ratio yields the percentage in reduction of compressed to original size.

$$C_r = 100 \times (1 - \frac{\text{compressed size}}{\text{original size}}) \tag{1}$$

---

[5] https://vtk.org/wp-content/uploads/2015/04/file-formats.pdf.

[6] https://mrtrix.readthedocs.io/en/latest/getting_started/image_data.html.

[7] http://www.trackvis.org/dtk/?subsect=format.

[8] https://github.com/KhronosGroup/glTF/blob/master/extensions/README.md.

Table 1. We evaluate TRAKO on eight different datasets. The top five datasets only contain streamlines and vertices (TCK format). The bottom three datasets include attached per-vertex scalars and per-fiber properties, resulting in large data sizes (VTK and VTP formats). Abbreviations: UKF - unscented Kalman Filter tractography; iFOD1: 1st order integration over fiber orientation distributions tractography; HCP - Human Connectome Project (one example young healthy adult); dHCP - Developing Human Connectome Project (one example neonate); ADHD - Attention deficit hyperactivity disorder dataset (including 30 ADHD patients and 29 healthy control subjects)

Dataset	Streamlines	Vertices	Tracking	Scalars	Properties	Format	Size
qfib-data [20]	480,000	171,666,931	iFOD1	–	–	TCK	734.21M
ISMRM2015 [17]	200,433	19,584,878	synth etic	–	–	TCK	16.55M
HCP (anatomical tracts) [31,32]	7,410	364,002	UKF	–	–	TCK	0.15M
ADHD (whole brain tract) [33]	199,240	30,897,382	UKF	–	–	TCK	1.23M
dHCP (whole brain tract) [18]	153,537	5,650,084	UKF	–	–	TCK	187.08M
HCP [31]	7,410	364,002	UKF	5	5	VTP	33.00M
ADHD [33]	19,898,754	2,971,986,861	UKF	9	5	VTP	149,678.00M
dHCP [18]	153,537	5,650,084	UKF	4	-	VTK	530.00M

Further, to facilitate comparison with other published results, we compute the compression factor C_f to compare the size of original and compressed data.

$$C_f = \frac{\text{original size}}{\text{compressed size}} \tag{2}$$

TRAKO and qfib do not change the number of points and we calculate individual data loss by measuring point-wise errors as L^2-norm.

$$E = \sqrt{\sum_i |f_i - g_i|^2}, \tag{3}$$

for two fiber tracts, f before and g after compression, with the same number of vertices ($i \in N$). We also calculate the endpoint errors by only considering the start and end points of each fiber. This allows to compare with zfib, a method that changes the numbers of fiber points.

3.2 Sensitivity Analysis

Suprathreshold Fiber Cluster Whole Brain Tractography Statistics. In this experiment, we assessed if group-wise tractography differences can be preserved using restored data after applying TRAKO (compress and restore). To do so, we performed a suprathreshold fiber cluster (STFC) statistical analysis [33] on the ADHD dataset to identify group differences in the whole brain tactography between the ADHD and healthy population. The STFC method first performs a data-driven tractography parcellation to obtain white matter

Table 2. Detailed comparison of qfib (8bit and 16 bit), zfib/Dipy, and TRAKO (JSON and Binary). The first five datasets only contain fiber tracts. TRAKO yields a lower mean error in 4 out of 5 datasets with compression rates of up to 28 ×. The bottom three datasets include per-vertex scalars and per-fiber properties. Lowest errors are **bold**, and second-to-lowest are *italic*. zfib/Dipy yields the lowest endpoint error but changes the number of fiber points. For 4 out of 5 datasets, TRAKO offers the lowest error and second-to-lowest endpoint error.

	Size	Ratio Factor C_r	C_f	Error min	max	mean	Endpoints Error min	max	mean	Timings [min.] enc.	dec.
qfib-data	734.21M										
qfib (8bit) [20]	22.9M	96.881%	32.064×	0.0	0.758	0.058±0.023	0.0	0.74	0.038±0.038	476.644	65.973
qfib (16bit) [20]	44.24M	93.975%	16.597×	0.0	0.019	**0.002±0.001**	0.0	0.017	*0.001±0.001*	476.738	66.711
zfib/Dipy [24]	118.65M	83.839%	6.188×	-	-	-	0.0	0	**0.0±0.000**	95.14	2997.115
TRAKO	46.18M	93.71%	15.899×	0.0	0.018	0.01±0.003	0.0	0.018	0.01±0.002	273.328	190.095
TRAKO (Binary)	34.63M	95.283%	21.199×	0.0	0.018	0.01±0.003	0.0	0.018	0.01±0.002	272.421	188.598
ISMRM2015	16.55M										
qfib (8bit) [20]	0.98M	94.103%	16.957×	0.0	59.541	11.686±6.327	0.0	59.522	10.501±10.501	269.627	45.37
qfib (16bit) [20]	1.74M	89.465%	9.492×	0.0	59.316	11.61±6.293	0.0	59.296	10.443±10.443	272.044	48.281
zfib/Dipy [24]	8.69M	47.512%	1.905×	-	-	-	0.0	0.0	**0.0±0.000**	46.237	354.191
TRAKO	1.46M	91.2%	11.364×	0.0	0.233	**0.092±0.027**	0.001	0.229	*0.092±0.015*	32.803	48.85
TRAKO (Binary)	1.09M	93.401%	15.154×	0.0	0.233	**0.092±0.027**	0.001	0.229	*0.092±0.015*	16.708	26.481
HCP (tracts only)	0.15M										
qfib (8bit) [20]	0.01M	94.442%	17.992×	0.0	18.687	0.418±0.251	0.0	18.687	0.351±0.351	9.432	2.847
qfib (16bit) [20]	0.01M	91.362%	11.576×	0.0	116.186	0.456±0.321	0.0	116.186	0.451±0.451	9.571	3.137
zfib/Dipy [24]	0.08M	48.524%	1.943×	-	-	-	0.0	0.0	**0.0±0.000**	1.498	0.305
TRAKO	0.01M	91.385%	11.608×	0.001	0.27	**0.097±0.028**	0.005	0.247	*0.097±0.016*	0.923	0.949
TRAKO (Binary)	0.01M	91.731%	12.093×	0.001	0.27	**0.097±0.028**	0.005	0.247	*0.097±0.016*	1.314	1.206
ADHD Single (tracts only)	1.23M										
qfib (8bit) [20]	0.04M	96.38%	27.624×	0.0	72.832	1.762±1.391	0.0	71.284	1.496±1.496	165.298	40.044
qfib (16bit) [20]	0.08M	93.286%	14.895×	0.0	120.936	4.123±3.119	0.0	120.936	3.331±3.331	165.486	40.681
zfib/Dipy [24]	0.25M	80.058%	5.014×	-	-	-	0.0	0.0	**0.0±0.000**	36.811	12.235
TRAKO	0.06M	95.349%	21.501×	0.0	0.276	**0.08±0.023**	0.001	0.264	*0.079±0.013*	61.298	40.806
TRAKO (Binary)	0.04M	96.523%	28.76×	0.0	0.276	**0.08±0.023**	0.001	0.264	*0.079±0.013*	66.261	42.501
dHCP (tracts only)	187.08M										
qfib (8bit) [20]	9.33M	95.01%	20.041×	0.0	53.695	0.452±0.235	0.0	53.695	0.282±0.282	14.954	2.027
qfib (16bit) [20]	14.68M	92.154%	12.746×	0.0	53.381	0.475±0.375	0.0	53.381	0.442±0.442	15.647	2.408
zfib/Dipy [24]	73.68M	60.616%	2.539×	-	-	-	0.0	0.0	**0.0±0.000**	23.993	2532.927
TRAKO	12.7M	93.213%	14.734×	0.001	0.273	**0.152±0.043**	0.005	0.271	*0.152±0.025*	9.575	5.963
TRAKO (Binary)	9.52M	94.91%	19.645×	0.001	0.273	**0.152±0.043**	0.005	0.271	*0.152±0.025*	9.091	5.921

	Mean Error		Mean Error

HCP [31], 13.43M, C_r: 59.162%, C_f: 2.449×

Scalars		Properties	
EstimatedUncertainty (N, range: 0.032-15233.791)	0.135±0.081	EmbeddingCoordinate (N, range: -4.543-3.047)	0.00026±3.72188e-05
tensor1 ($N \times 9$, range: -0.00095-0.0024)	1.121e-07±2.27e-08	ClusterNumber (N, range: 8-665)	0.4237±0.4763
tensor2 ($N \times 9$, range: -0.00087-0.0021)	8.73e-08±1.78e-08	EmbeddingColor (N, range: 0-180)	0.8776±0.4748
HemisphereLocataion (N, range: 1.0-3.0)	0.0±0.0	TotalFiberSimilarity (N, range: 199220.9-920767.25)	8.0194±4.7547
cluster_idx (N, range: 0-39)	0.246±0.361	MeasuredFiberSimilarity (N, range: 0.00179-0.00266)	7.4e-09±4.5e-09

ADHD [33], 50,462.34M, C_r: 66.286%, C_f: 2.966×

Scalars		Properties	
NormalizedSignalEstimationError (N, range: 0.0-0.05)	0.0±0.0	EmbeddingCoordinate ($N \times 10$, range: -3.18-4.93)	0.0±0.0
EstimatedUncertainty (N, range: 0.04-31041.65)	0.3±0.176	ClusterNumber (N, range: 12-768)	0.0±0.0
RTOP1 (N, range: 1.13-23901.94)	0.04±0.023	EmbeddingColor ($N \times 3$, range: 2-180)	0.869±0.511
RTOP2 (N, range: 1.32-8651.45)	0.014±0.008	TotalFiberSimilarity (N, range: 149876.58-696306.3)	5.599±3.341
RTAP1 (N, range: -13541.7-7914.96)	0.031±0.018	MeasuredFiberSimilarity (N, range: 0.0-0.0)	0.0±0.0
RTAP2 (N, range: 1.11-6820.54)	0.01±0.006		
RTPP1 (N, range: 0.71-9.88)	0.0±0.0		
RTPP2 (N, range: 0.71-15.96)	0.0±0.0		
SignalMean (N, range: 0.0-0.04)	0.0±0.0		

dHCP [18], 256.31M, C_r: 52.799%, C_f: 2.119×

Scalars		Properties	
FreeWater (N, range: 0.0-1.0)	1.42e-05±9.34e-06	-	
tensor1 ($N \times 9$, range: -0.00132-0.0031)	2.27e-07±4.63e-08		
tensor2 ($N \times 9$, range: -0.00132-0.0043)	2.895e-07±5.9e-08		
EstimatedUncertainty (N, range: 0.0332-196.16)	0.291±0.177		

fiber parcels (a total of 1416 tract parcels). Diffusion measure of interest, i.e., return-to-the-origin probability (RTOP) [22], was extracted from each fiber parcel and tested between the two populations using a student t-test. Then, a non-parametric permutation test was performed to correct for multiple comparisons

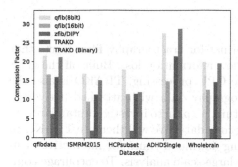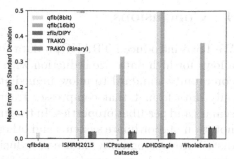

Fig. 4. On the five datasets that include only streamlines and vertices, TRAKO produces a comparable compression factor to qfib (and superior to zfib), and in average, a lower mean error (4 out of 5 cases). TRAKO is the only method that supports the three datasets with attached per-vertex scalars and per-fiber properties.

across all fiber parcels. Overall, the output of the analysis includes STFCs, i.e. a fiber cluster of multiple fiber parcels that are significantly different when comparing the RTOP diffusion measure (p < 0.05) (Fig. 4).

We performed the STFC analysis on the original tractography data, as well as the restored data. Each individual fiber parcel was compressed and decompressed using TRAKO using the default options, yielding the compression factors and error rates as reported in Table 2. In the original data, there were two sets of STFCs (corrected p values 0.015 and 0.035, respectively). In the restored data, the same sets of STFCs were identified (corrected p values 0.009 and 0.028, respectively), suggesting good performance of TRAKO on preserving group-wise tractography differences.

Bhattacharyya Overlap Distance. To ensure TRAKO does not alter the fiber tract points, we have additionally implemented the Bhattacharyya analysis and computed the overlap score (B) to quantify the agreement between the original and restored tract points [6,25]:

$$B = \tfrac{1}{3}\left(\int \sqrt{P_o(x)P_r(x)}dx + \int \sqrt{P_o(y)P_r(y)}dy + \int \sqrt{P_o(z)P_r(z)}dz\right),$$ with the ground truth probability distribution $P_o(.)$ of the original fiber tract, $P_r(.)$ the probability distribution from the restored fiber tract, and the fiber coordinates $\mathbf{x} = (x, y, z) \in \mathbb{R}^3$. B becomes 1 for a perfect match between two fiber bundles from original and restored data and 0 for no overlap at all.

We performed the Bhattacharyya overlap distance analysis on the corpus callosum (CC) tract, which was parcellated using [33] for both original and restored fiber tracts. We then computed the overlap score between the original and restored CC in all subjects ($0.99 \pm 1.6231e\text{-}04$). The very high overlap between original and restored tract points indicates that TRAKO can successfully preserve this information during compression.

4   Conclusions

We have introduced TRAKO, a data format for tractography fiber tracts that allows for high data size reduction with low information loss. Built-off the glTF community standard to allow immediate GPU processing, TRAKO is also the only data format that compresses tractography data with attached per-vertex scalars and per-fiber properties. In the future, we plan to investigate standardized notation of coordinate systems and other metadata. We will then use TRAKO to distribute tractography datasets, reducing download times for interactive visualization and data transmission costs for large-scale analysis. To encourage community adoption, we release TRAKO and our results as free and open research at https://github.com/bostongfx/trako.

Acknowledgements. This research was supported by NIH R01MH119222 and NIH P41EB015902.

References

1. Alexandroni, G., et al.: The fiber-density-coreset for redundancy reduction in huge fiber-sets. NeuroImage **146**, 246–256 (2017)
2. Basser, P.J., Mattiello, J., LeBihan, D.: MR diffusion tensor spectroscopy and imaging. Biophys. J. **66**(1), 259–267 (1994)
3. Basser, P.J., et al.: In vivo fiber tractography using DT-MRI data. Magn. Reson. Med. **44**(4), 625–632 (2000)
4. Brettle, J., Galligan, F.: Introducing Draco: compression for 3D graphics (2017)
5. Caiafa, C.F., Pestilli, F.: Multidimensional encoding of brain connectomes. Sci. Rep. **7**(1), 1–13 (2017)
6. Cetin Karayumak, S., Kubicki, M., Rathi, Y.: Harmonizing diffusion MRI data across magnetic field strengths. In: Frangi, A.F., Schnabel, J.A., Davatzikos, C., Alberola-López, C., Fichtinger, G. (eds.) MICCAI 2018. LNCS, vol. 11072, pp. 116–124. Springer, Cham (2018). https://doi.org/10.1007/978-3-030-00931-1_14
7. Chung, M.K., et al.: Efficient parametric encoding scheme for white matter fiber bundles. In: 2009 Annual International Conference of the IEEE Engineering in Medicine and Biology Society, pp. 6644–6647. IEEE (2009)
8. Deering, M.F.: Compression of three-dimensional graphics data including quantization, delta-encoding, and variable-length encoding. US Patent 5,867,167, February 1999
9. Devillers, O., Gandoin, P.-M.: Geometric compression for interactive transmission. In: Proceedings Visualization 2000. VIS 2000 (Cat. No.00CH37145), pp. 319–326 (2000)
10. Garyfallidis, E., et al.: Dipy, a library for the analysis of diffusion MRI data. Front. Neuroinform. **8**, 8 (2014)
11. Garyfallidis, E., et al.: Quickbundles, a method for tractography simplification. Front. Neurosci. **6**, 175 (2012)
12. Gori, P., et al.: Parsimonious approximation of streamline trajectories in white matter fiber bundles. IEEE Trans. Med. Imaging **35**(12), 2609–2619 (2016)
13. Guevara, P., et al.: Robust clustering of massive tractography datasets. Neuroimage **54**(3), 1975–1993 (2011)

14. Kumar, K., Desrosiers, C.: A sparse coding approach for the efficient representation and segmentation of white matter fibers. In: 2016 IEEE 13th International Symposium on Biomedical Imaging (ISBI), pp. 915–919. IEEE (2016)
15. Lindstrom, P.: Fixed-rate compressed floating-point arrays. IEEE Trans. Visual Comput. Graphics **20**(12), 2674–2683 (2014)
16. Liu, M., Vemuri, B.C., Deriche, R.: Unsupervised automatic white matter fiber clustering using a Gaussian mixture model. In: 2012 9th IEEE International Symposium on Biomedical Imaging (ISBI), pp. 522–525. IEEE (2012)
17. Maier-Hein, K., et al.: Tractography challenge ISMRM 2015 high-resolution data, May 2017. https://doi.org/10.5281/zenodo.579933
18. Makropoulos, A., et al.: The developing human connectome project: a minimal processing pipeline for neonatal cortical surface reconstruction. Neuroimage **173**, 88–112 (2018)
19. Mercier, C., et al.: Progressive and efficient multi-resolution representations for brain tractograms (2018)
20. Mercier, C., Rousseau, S., Gori, P., Bloch, I., Boubekeur, T.: QFib: fast and efficient brain tractogram compression. Neuroinformatics **18**, 627–640 (2020). https://doi.org/10.1007/s12021-020-09452-0
21. Moreno, G.Z., Alexandroni, G., Sochen, N., Greenspan, H.: Sparse representation for white matter fiber compression and calculation of inter-fiber similarity. In: Fuster, A., Ghosh, A., Kaden, E., Rathi, Y., Reisert, M. (eds.) MICCAI 2016. MV, pp. 133–143. Springer, Cham (2017). https://doi.org/10.1007/978-3-319-54130-3_11
22. Ning, L., Westin, C.-F., Rathi, Y.: Estimating diffusion propagator and its moments using directional radial basis functions. IEEE Trans. Med. Imaging **34**(10), 2058–2078 (2015)
23. Olivetti, E., et al.: Comparison of distances for supervised segmentation of white matter tractography. In: 2017 International Workshop on Pattern Recognition in Neuroimaging (PRNI), pp. 1–4. IEEE (2017)
24. Presseau, C., et al.: A new compression format for fiber tracking datasets. NeuroImage **109**, 73–83 (2015)
25. Rathi, Y., Gagoski, B., Setsompop, K., Michailovich, O., Grant, P.E., Westin, C.-F.: Diffusion propagator estimation from sparse measurements in a tractography framework. In: Mori, K., Sakuma, I., Sato, Y., Barillot, C., Navab, N. (eds.) MICCAI 2013. LNCS, vol. 8151, pp. 510–517. Springer, Heidelberg (2013). https://doi.org/10.1007/978-3-642-40760-4_64
26. Rheault, F., Houde, J.-C., Descoteaux, M.: Visualization, interaction and tractometry: dealing with millions of streamlines from diffusion MRI tractography. Front. Neuroinform. **11**, 42 (2017)
27. Robinet, F., et al.: gLTF: designing an open-standard runtime asset format. GPU Pro **5**, 375–392 (2014)
28. Rossignac, J.: Edgebreaker: connectivity compression for triangle meshes. IEEE Trans. Visual Comput. Graphics **5**(1), 47–61 (1999)
29. Schnabel, R., Klein, R.: Octree-based point-cloud compression. In: Botsch, M., Chen, B. (eds.) Symposium on Point-Based Graphics 2006. Eurographics, July 2006
30. Siless, V., et al.: Anatomicuts: hierarchical clustering of tractography streamlines based on anatomical similarity. NeuroImage **166**, 32–45 (2018)
31. Van Essen, D.C., et al.: The WU-Minn human connectome project: an overview. Neuroimage **80**, 62–79 (2013)

32. Zhang, F., et al.: An anatomically curated fiber clustering white matter atlas for consistent white matter tract parcellation across the lifespan. NeuroImage **179**, 429–447 (2018)
33. Zhang, F., et al.: Suprathreshold fiber cluster statistics: leveraging white matter geometry to enhance tractography statistical analysis. NeuroImage **171**, 341–354 (2018)

Spatial Semantic-Preserving Latent Space Learning for Accelerated DWI Diagnostic Report Generation

Aydan Gasimova[1(✉)], Gavin Seegoolam[1], Liang Chen[1], Paul Bentley[2], and Daniel Rueckert[1]

[1] BioMedIA, Department of Computing, Imperial College London,
London SW7 2AZ, UK
{ag6516,kgs13,lc12,dr}@ic.ac.uk
[2] Department of Brain Sciences, Faculty of Medicine, Imperial College London,
London SW7 2AZ, UK
p.bentley@imperial.ac.uk

Abstract. In light of recent works exploring automated pathological diagnosis, studies have also shown that medical text reports can be generated with varying levels of efficacy. Brain diffusion-weighted MRI (DWI) has been used for the diagnosis of ischaemia in which brain death can follow in immediate hours. It is therefore of the utmost importance to obtain ischaemic brain diagnosis as soon as possible in a clinical setting. Previous studies have shown that MRI acquisition can be accelerated using variable-density Cartesian undersampling methods. In this study, we propose an accelerated DWI acquisition pipeline for the purpose of generating text reports containing diagnostic information. We demonstrate that we can learn a semantic-preserving latent space for minor as well as extremely undersampled MR images capable of achieving promising results on a diagnostic report generation task.

1 Introduction

Patients that have suffered the symptoms of a stroke have a very short time frame in which to be effectively treated; therefore, it is imperative that radiologists determine the cause of the symptoms in order to provide the appropriate treatment. The majority of strokes are caused by cerebral ischaemia, which can be characterised as reduced blood flow to the brain, causing poor oxygenation that can lead to permanent brain cell death. Both computed tomography (CT) and multi-modal magnetic resonance imaging (MRI) are effective in assessing brain ischaemia, but diffusion-weighted MRI (DWI) is particularly advantageous as it provides highest sensitivity to early ischaemic lesions. In comparison to CT, typical DWI has a much longer acquisition time which additionally makes the scans more susceptible to patient motion and subsequent unwanted imaging

---

A. Gasimova and G. Seegoolam—Both authors contributed equally to this study.

© Springer Nature Switzerland AG 2020
A. L. Martel et al. (Eds.): MICCAI 2020, LNCS 12267, pp. 333–342, 2020.
https://doi.org/10.1007/978-3-030-59728-3_33

artefacts. Furthermore, requiring patients to lay dormant without any motion for long periods of time may lead to discomfort. A well-explored approach for accelerating scan-time is through *undersampling* whereby fewer scanner measurements are taken, violating the Nyquist-Shannon sampling theorem and thus introducing aliasing artefacts into the reconstruction of the image. Several studies are focused on the dealiasing of such images, validating undersampled MRI as an accepted acceleration technique [4,5,13–15,17,27,27].

Assessing the quality of the MR image reconstruction is typically focused on calculating similarity metrics such as peak signal-to-noise ratio (PSNR) and structural similarity (SSIM) index between the dealiased reconstruction and the fully-sampled image [20]. This does not, however, guarantee the retention of pathological features necessary for a diagnosis, especially at more aggressive acceleration rates. Therefore, a complimentary way of reviewing extremely accelerated images is through the use of real-time diagnostic tasks such as segmentation and classification [16]. In our study, we explore the automated generation of radiological text reports containing relevant diagnostic and contextual information. The logging of diagnostic reports generated by qualified radiologists is standard hospital protocol. As a result, datasets for studies involving automated text report generation can be acquired directly from hospital archives. In contrast, segmentation and classification tasks require non-standard time-consuming manual annotations. In addition, DWI diagnostic reports typically detail contextual information as well as the presence/absence of an acute lesion, such as anatomical location and severity of the lesion, and being able to auto-generate them will additionally expedite the process of identifying and documenting acute ischaemia.

To this end we have developed a pipeline that 1) learns an implicit context-preserving manifold of brain DWIs that captures both spatial and pathological information, 2) enforces a latent code for the accelerated DWIs that performs in a similar fashion to the fully-sampled images 3) utilises these accelerated brain DWI image representations to learn to automatically generate reports using a recurrent neural network. To our knowledge, this is the first demonstration of deep latent space learning for the retention of semantic feature information required for accelerated report generation, and the first demonstration of learning to auto-generate reports from brain DWI images.

2   Previous Work

Latent Space Learning of Accelerated MRI. Previous work has shown the use of deep latent space learning for performing tasks such as segmentation and reconstruction in the context accelerated MRI [16,27]. Accelerated MRI data acquisition is centred around the ability to reconstruct image data in a typically ill-conditioned inverse regression problem. However, certain tasks will only require certain parts of information from the sensor space, called 'k-space'. For example, approximate motion estimation from cardiac cine MRI can be performed with acceleration rates of 51.2 [17]. [16] shows that cardiac segmentation can be performed by a single line acquisition in k-space. Inspired by this we explore the use of deep latent space learning for learning diagnostically-relevant contextual image embeddings. Whilst [16] shows that deep latent space learning provides a manifold that can be robust to different undersampling patterns, they also show that at extreme acceleration rates, deep latent space learning can outperform conventional approaches.

Radiology Report Generation. Learning to automate report generation for radiological images has thus far been heavily influenced by image captioning models formulated as an encoder-decoder machine translation problem. In image captioning, image representations are extracted from a pre-trained convolutional neural network (the encoder) and passed as inputs alongside captions to a sequence-learning decoder by, for instance, mapping the word and image representations to the same feature space [10,19]. Such a framework was used by [18] to predict structured medical subject heading (MeSH®) annotations for chest X-ray images.

More recently, learning to attend to spatial visual features has been shown to be effective in image captioning [23] and medical report generation [7,24–26]. Using structured reports in a dual-attention framework, Zhang et al. [26] were able to improve features used for classifying histopathology images. The co-attention network of Jing et al. [7] is fed visual as well as semantic features in order to provide high-level semantic information to the text-generation task. Xue et al. [24] break down the task of report generation into subtasks of generating one sentence at a time where each succeeding sentence is conditioned on image features and previous sentences. Yuan et al. [25] also demonstrate the benefit of learning radiology-related features from an initial classification task and go a step further by learning features from multi-view 2-D images (chest X-rays) by introducing a cross-view consistency loss.

The accelerated acquisition of brain DWI has been previously studied in the context of image reconstruction [2,11,21,22]. However, in our study, we explore its use for automated text report generation. We demonstrate how the latent space learned by the accelerated reconstruction network captures both spatial semantic and pathology information required in order to learn to generate reports.

3   Method

Our study accelerates DWI acquisition through aggressive variable-density Cartesian undersampling as has been studied in several previous works such as [16,17]. In our study, we start with attempting a zero-fill reconstruction whereby the lines in k-spaces that are not acquired are filled with zeros. An example of a fully sampled image and a corresponding undersampled, zero-filled image reconstruction is shown in Fig. 2. For all acceleration rates, we always sample the two most central lines in k-space whilst the other lines are acquired following a Gaussian distribution centred at the point of highest energy in k-space. During training, undersampling masks are generated on the fly and images are also augmented with additional rotations and translations.

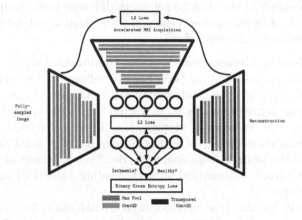

Fig. 1. An autoencoder is trained to reconstruct the fully-sampled image through an L2 loss. The latent space is conditioned to encode pathological information by performing a classification of ischaemia, trained with a binary cross-entropy loss. The latent space encoding learned at the bottleneck is used as a training target for the encoding branch which only sees the accelerated image.

3.1 Latent Space Learning

In our approach, we use an autoencoder network that takes as input the original fully-sampled DWI brain MRI. The purpose of this is to learn a latent space at the bottleneck that contains spatial and contextual information that may be useful for a text report generator. In particular, we manipulate the embedding manifold toward one more suitable for text report generation by introducing an ischaemia-classification loss as a regulariser. This loss can be summarised by Eq. (1) where an Adam optimiser with learning rate 1.0×10^{-5}, $\beta_1 = 0.9$ and $\beta_2 = 0.999$ was used.

$$L(x, y) = ||D(E(x)) - x||_2^2 - \gamma(y \log C(E(x)) + (1 - y) \log(1 - C(E(x)))), \quad (1)$$

where E, D and C are the encoder, decoder and classifier networks (from Fig. 1) respectively, x is our fully-sampled image, y is a binary classification label for ischaemia and $\gamma = 8000$. We can measure the performance of the latent space learnt as a combination of reconstruction error (in particular of the ischaemia) and of the classification error.

Along side this, we use a structurally-identical encoding branch to learn a latent space for the accelerated MRI acquisition. We use the approach of performing a zero-fill reconstruction whereby after convolutional layers can be used to identify aliasing artefacts as directly relevant image features themselves. The latent space is trained against the bottleneck of the autoencoder using an L2 loss and another Adam optimizer with the same optimizer parameters. This is summarised in Fig. 1 and in Eq. (2). Note, for each acceleration rate used in our study, a unique encoder is learned to generate the required latent space. An advantage of deep latent space learning is that we can train the specific encoder associated with different acceleration rates towards the same manifold which avoids the need for retraining of the text report generator model.

$$L(x, x_{\mathrm{acc}}) = ||E(x) - x_{\mathrm{acc}}||_2^2, \tag{2}$$

where x_{acc} is our accelerated, aliased image and E_{acc} is our encoding branch for the accelerated images.

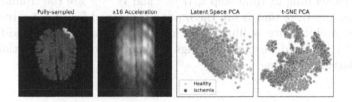

Fig. 2. Left to right: (1) An example of a brain with ischaemia (2) The corresponding x16 accelerated image is zero-fill reconstructed from k-space using a 2D Fourier Transform. Note that this image is infected with heavy aliasing artefacts. (3) A projection of the first two principle components in a PCA analysis of the latent space. Some clustering can be seen (4) a t-SNE projection of the latent space showing clear clustering.

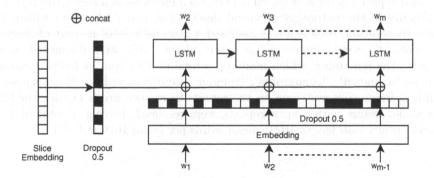

Fig. 3. Clinical report generation model from accelerated image latent space embeddings.

3.2 Report Generation Model

We use a report generation model based on [3] where the report word sequence is modelled using the Long Short-Term Memory (LSTM) [6], and conditioned on image embeddings at each time step through concatenation at the input to the LSTM. At each time step, the input, output and forget gates control how much of the previous time steps is propagated through to the output. For an input embedding sequence $\{x_1, \ldots, x_n\}$ where $x_i \in \mathbb{R}^D$, the internal hidden state $h_t \in \mathbb{R}^h$ and memory state $m_t \in \mathbb{R}^m$ are updated as follows:

$$h_t = f_t \odot h_{t-1} + i_t \odot \tanh(W^{(hx)} x_t + W^{(hm)} m_{t-1})$$
$$m_t = o_t \odot \tanh(h_t) \tag{3}$$

where $x_t \in \mathbb{R}^D$ is the concatenation of the latent space image embedding and word embedding at time step t, $W^{(hx)}$ and $W^{(hm)}$ are the trainable weight parameters, and i_t, o_t and f_t are the input, output and forget gates respectively. The model architecture is illustrated in Fig. 3. We additionally add Dropout layers after image and word embeddings to force the model to condition on both thus regularising training.

4 Experiments

The Data. The dataset consists of 1226 DWI scans and corresponding radiological reports of acute stroke patients. All the images and reports were fully anonymised and ethical approval was granted by Imperial College Joint Regulatory Office. The scans were pre-processed according to the steps outlined in [1]: images were resampled into uniform pixel size of 1.6×1.6 mm, and pixel intensities were normalised to zero mean and unit variance. The number of slices per image varies between 7 and 52, and the slice dimensions are 128×128.

Each report contains between 1 and 2 sentences summarising the presence or absence of the pathology, a visual description, and its location within the brain. In addition, each exam is assigned a diagnostic label as part of hospital protocol: 54% were diagnosed 'no acute infarct', 46% were diagnosed 'acute infarct'. The remaining, which made up a total of <1% and included diagnoses such as 'unknown', 'haematoma', 'tumour', were removed for the purpose of training. Processing was done on the reports to remove words outside the 99th percentile, exams with empty reports were removed, leaving a total of 1104 exams, total vocab length 1021, mean words per exam 10.8, std. 6.3.

In order to simplify the problem, we created a 2D dataset of acute and non-acute (normal) slices from these images. For the acute set, we used the brain ischemia segmentation network developed by Chen et al. [1] to segment the images labelled with acute ischemia, thresholded at 0.8, and selected slices where the total area of ischemia was >10 pixels. For the normal set, we sampled slices from the non-acute labelled images according to the same axial plane distribution as the acute set.

Experimental Settings. Reports were padded with 'start' and 'end' tokens to length 19 (mean + 1 std. + 'start' + 'end'). The word embedding layer maps one-hot encoded word embeddings into a 256 dimensional space. The LSTM hidden state is also set to dim 256, and the LSTM units are unrolled up to 19 time steps. We train the model on non-accelerated latent embeddings and their associated reports by minimising the categorical cross-entropy loss over the generated words. All models are trained with batch size 128, using Adam optimisation [8], learning rate = 0.0001 for 300 epochs.

Results. Inference was performed by first sampling from the LSTM using a 'start' token concatenated with the accelerated embeddings, and consequently appending the output word embedding to the input and sampling until an 'end' token was reached. The quality of the generated reports was evaluated by measuring BLUE [12] and ROUGE [9] scores averaged over all the reports, which are a form of n-gram precision commonly used for evaluating image captioning as they maintain high correlation with human judgement. We observe that the both the BLEU and ROUGE scores decrease with increasingly accelerated images, as expected. We note that there is a significant reduction in performance between the ×4 and ×8 accelerated images possibly due to some contextual information not being captured by the latent space.

We also assess the sampled reports qualitatively in Fig. 4. We observe no major grammatical errors for all accelerations, an no major content errors for lower accelerations with ×2 and ×4 correctly identifying the presence/absence of ischemia as well as the location. Note: the last example shows a text report that was ischemic but was classified as healthy. This is likely to have confused the latent code for this example resulting in poor text report generations (Table 1).

Table 1. BLEU1,2,3,4-gram and ROUGE1 f1, precision (P) and recall (R) metric comparisons on increasingly accelerated image embeddings.

	BLEU-1	BLEU-2	BLEU-3	BLEU-4	ROUGE-1 F1	ROUGE-1 P	ROUGE-1 R
Acc.× 1	38.12	27.26	20.28	15.59	47.10	52.89	44.96
Acc.× 2	34.07	23.31	15.55	11.57	44.00	51.86	40.68
Acc.× 4	31.36	19.42	12.29	8.31	41.17	48.09	38.80
Acc.× 8	21.32	10.37	5.06	2.55	29.53	32.92	29.52
Acc.× 64	21.58	11.11	4.97	2.35	30.39	35.10	29.07

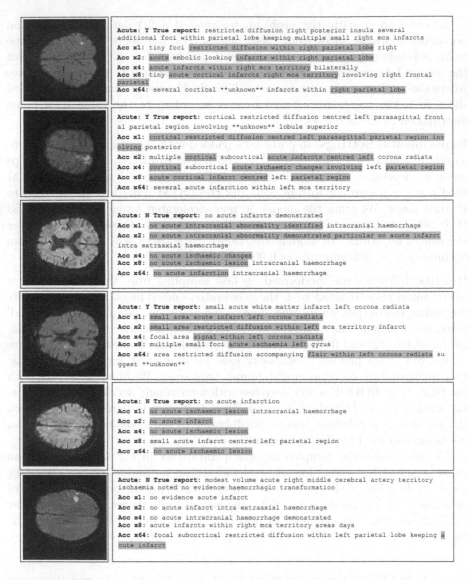

Fig. 4. Sample brain slices and associated reports generated from non-accelerated and increasingly accelerated image embeddings. Correctly identified pathology (acute/non-acute) and spatial contexts are highlighted in blue. (Color figure online)

5   Conclusion and Future Work

We demonstrate how a latent space capturing pathalogical and spatial information can be learned from accelerated brain DWI images and subsequently used to train a diagnostic report generation network with promising results.

In future works, we wish to explore radial undersampling trajectories for DWI brain imaging which are expected to provide improved diagnostic embeddings.

References

1. Chen, L., Bentley, P., Rueckert, D.: Fully automatic acute ischemic lesion segmentation in dwi using convolutional neural networks. NeuroImage: Clinical **15**, 633–643 (2017)
2. Ciritsis, A., Rossi, C., Marcon, M., Van, V.D.P., Boss, A.: Accelerated diffusion-weighted imaging for lymph node assessment in the pelvis applying simultaneous multislice acquisition: a healthy volunteer study. Medicine **97**(32), e11745 (2018)
3. Gasimova, A.: Automated enriched medical concept generation for chest X-ray images. In: Suzuki, K., et al. (eds.) ML-CDS/IMIMIC -2019. LNCS, vol. 11797, pp. 83–92. Springer, Cham (2019). https://doi.org/10.1007/978-3-030-33850-3_10
4. Griswold, M.A., et al.: Generalized autocalibrating partially parallel acquisitions (grappa). Magnetic Resonance Med. Official J. Int. Soc. Magnetic Resonance Med. **47**(6), 1202–1210 (2002)
5. Hammernik, K., et al.: Learning a variational network for reconstruction of accelerated MRI data. Magnetic Resonance Med. **79**(6), 3055–3071 (2018)
6. Hochreiter, S., Schmidhuber, J.: Long short-term memory. Neural Comput. **9**(8), 1735–1780 (1997)
7. Jing, B., Xie, P., Xing, E.: On the automatic generation of medical imaging reports. In: Proceedings of the 56th Annual Meeting of the Association for Computational Linguistics (Volume 1: Long Papers), pp. 2577–2586 (2018)
8. Kingma, D.P., Ba, J.: Adam: A method for stochastic optimization. arXiv preprint arXiv:1412.6980 (2014)
9. Lin, C.Y., Hovy, E.: Automatic evaluation of summaries using n-gram co-occurrence statistics. In: Proceedings of the 2003 Human Language Technology Conference of the North American Chapter of the Association for Computational Linguistics, pp. 150–157 (2003)
10. Mao, J., Xu, W., Yang, Y., Wang, J., Huang, Z., Yuille, A.: Deep captioning with multimodal recurrent neural networks (M-RNN). In: ICLR (2015)
11. Merrem, A., et al.: Rapid diffusion-weighted magnetic resonance imaging of the brain without susceptibility artifacts: single-shot steam with radial undersampling and iterative reconstruction. Investigative Radiol. **52**(7), 428–433 (2017)
12. Papineni, K., Roukos, S., Ward, T., Zhu, W.J.: Bleu: a method for automatic evaluation of machine translation. In: Proceedings of the 40th Annual Meeting on Association for Computational Linguistics. pp. 311–318. Association for Computational Linguistics (2002)
13. Pruessmann, K.P., Weiger, M., Scheidegger, M.B., Boesiger, P.: Sense: sensitivity encoding for fast MRI. Magnetic Resonance Med. Official J. Int. Soc. Magnetic Resonance Med. **42**(5), 952–962 (1999)
14. Qin, C., Schlemper, J., Caballero, J., Price, A.N., Hajnal, J.V., Rueckert, D.: Convolutional recurrent neural networks for dynamic MR image reconstruction. IEEE Trans. Med. Imag. **38**(1), 280–290 (2018)
15. Schlemper, J., Caballero, J., Hajnal, J.V., Price, A.N., Rueckert, D.: A deep cascade of convolutional neural networks for dynamic MR image reconstruction. IEEE Trans. Med. Imag. **37**(2), 491–503 (2017)

16. Schlemper, J., et al.: Cardiac MR segmentation from undersampled k-space using deep latent representation learning. In: Frangi, A.F., Schnabel, J.A., Davatzikos, C., Alberola-López, C., Fichtinger, G. (eds.) MICCAI 2018. LNCS, vol. 11070, pp. 259–267. Springer, Cham (2018). https://doi.org/10.1007/978-3-030-00928-1_30
17. Seegoolam, G., Schlemper, J., Qin, C., Price, A., Hajnal, J., Rueckert, D.: Exploiting motion for deep learning reconstruction of extremely-undersampled dynamic MRI. In: Shen, D., et al. (eds.) MICCAI 2019. LNCS, vol. 11767, pp. 704–712. Springer, Cham (2019). https://doi.org/10.1007/978-3-030-32251-9_77
18. Shin, H.C., Roberts, K., Lu, L., Demner-Fushman, D., Yao, J., Summers, R.M.: Learning to read chest x-rays: Recurrent neural cascade model for automated image annotation. In: Proceedings of the IEEE Conference on Computer Vision and Pattern Recognition, pp. 2497–2506 (2016)
19. Vinyals, O., Toshev, A., Bengio, S., Erhan, D.: Show and tell: a neural image caption generator. In: 2015 IEEE Conference on Computer Vision and Pattern Recognition (CVPR), pp. 3156–3164. IEEE (2015)
20. Wang, Z., Bovik, A.C., Sheikh, H.R., Simoncelli, E.P.: Image quality assessment: from error visibility to structural similarity. IEEE Trans. Image Process. **13**(4), 600–612 (2004)
21. Weiss, J., et al.: Feasibility of accelerated simultaneous multislice diffusion-weighted MRI of the prostate. J. Magnetic Resonance Imag. **46**(5), 1507–1515 (2017)
22. Wu, W., Miller, K.L.: Image formation in diffusion MRI: a review of recent technical developments. J. Magnetic Resonance Imag. **46**(3), 646–662 (2017)
23. Xu, K., et al.: Show, attend and tell: neural image caption generation with visual attention. In: International Conference on Machine Learning, pp. 2048–2057 (2015)
24. Xue, Y., et al.: Multimodal recurrent model with attention for automated radiology report generation. In: Frangi, A.F., Schnabel, J.A., Davatzikos, C., Alberola-López, C., Fichtinger, G. (eds.) MICCAI 2018. LNCS, vol. 11070, pp. 457–466. Springer, Cham (2018). https://doi.org/10.1007/978-3-030-00928-1_52
25. Yuan, J., Liao, H., Luo, R., Luo, J.: Automatic radiology report generation based on multi-view image fusion and medical concept enrichment. In: Shen, D., et al. (eds.) MICCAI 2019. LNCS, vol. 11769, pp. 721–729. Springer, Cham (2019). https://doi.org/10.1007/978-3-030-32226-7_80
26. Zhang, Z., Xie, Y., Xing, F., McGough, M., Yang, L.: Mdnet: a semantically and visually interpretable medical image diagnosis network. In: Proceedings of the IEEE Conference on Computer Vision and Pattern Recognition, pp. 6428–6436 (2017)
27. Zhu, B., Liu, J.Z., Cauley, S.F., Rosen, B.R., Rosen, M.S.: Image reconstruction by domain-transform manifold learning. Nature **555**(7697), 487–492 (2018)

Trajectories from Distribution-Valued Functional Curves: A Unified Wasserstein Framework

Anuja Sharma[1](✉)[iD] and Guido Gerig[2][iD]

[1] School of Computing, SCI Institute, University of Utah, Salt Lake City, UT, USA
anuja.sharma.phd@gmail.com
[2] Department of Computer Science and Engineering, Tandon School of Engineering,
New York University, Brooklyn, NY, USA
gerig@nyu.edu

Abstract. Temporal changes in medical images are often evaluated along a parametrized function that represents a structure of interest (e.g. white matter tracts). By attributing samples along these functions with distributions of image properties in the local neighborhood, we create distribution-valued signatures for these functions. We propose a novel, comprehensive framework which models their temporal evolution trajectories. This is achieved under the unifying scheme of Wasserstein distance metric. The regression problem is formulated as a constrained optimization problem and solved using an alternating projection algorithm. The solution simultaneously preserves the functional characteristics of the curve, models the temporal change in distribution profiles and forces the estimated distributions to be valid. Hypothesis testing is applied in two ways using Wasserstein based test statistics. Validation is presented on synthetic data. Estimation of a population trajectory is shown using diffusion properties along DTI tracts from a healthy population of infants. Detection of delayed growth is shown using a case study.

Keywords: Spatiotemporal regression · Diffusion-MRI · Neurodevelopment.

1 Introduction

Regression analysis is a crucial tool to understand the effects of covariates like age, gender and cognitive scores on the human anatomy and physiology. It is valuable in building smooth growth trajectories for individuals and populations from medical images acquired at limited, discrete time points. In this context,

Supported by NIH grants U54 EB005149 (NA-MIC), R01-HD055741-12 (ACE-IBIS), MH064065 (Conte Center), 1R01HD088125-01A1 (Infant DS), 1R01DA038215-01A1 (Infant Drug exposure). We thank Dr. John Gilmore, Dr. Martin Styner and team (University of North Carolina, Chapel Hill, USA) and Dr. Maria L. Escolar (University of Pittsburgh, USA) for providing the Diffusion-MRI data.

© Springer Nature Switzerland AG 2020
A. L. Martel et al. (Eds.): MICCAI 2020, LNCS 12267, pp. 343–353, 2020.
https://doi.org/10.1007/978-3-030-59728-3_34

functional data representations are often employed for tasks like biological shape regression [12,23,24] and statistical analysis of white matter tracts [9,19,27,28]. However, most such methods associate a single, real-valued measurement of the image properties with each parametrized location along these functions. This creates scalar-valued functional curves [18,24]. In this paper, we instead associate these functions with univariate distributions arising from proximal voxels, creating distribution-valued functional curves. This probabilistic interpretation of the function's attributes can be used to encode various types of uncertainties, e.g. uncertain segmentation boundaries, fuzzy streamline estimations or physiological changes reflected in image properties [15,20,21].

Quantile regression methods that simultaneously model several quantiles of interest (while avoiding the implicit problem of crossing quantiles) can be used to quantify the localized evolutions of these distributions [1,8,13,26]. However, most are computationally intensive when considering application at a sufficiently large number of function locations to ensure functional smoothness, specially for larger datasets. Moreover, the covariate relationships described for the individual quantiles are harder to interpret in the larger context of the change in the entire distribution. To remedy this, we leverage optimal transport theory and the special case of Wasserstein distance for $\mathbb{R}^1$ as our distance metric which provides an intuitive notion of transforming one distribution into another [14,17]. It has a closed form solution where the optimal transport coupling is given via the inverted CDF (quantile) functions Q for probability measures ρ_0 and ρ_1 (Eq. 1). It also has strong theoretical properties as it is a Hilbertian metric between probability measures [17,22]. We denote the distance as dW_1 for $p = 1$ and dW_2 for $p = 2$.

$$dW_p^p(\rho_0, \rho_1) = \int_0^1 |Q_{\rho_0}(u) - Q_{\rho_1}(u)|^p du. \tag{1}$$

Related methods using the Wasserstein distance for regression of distributions rely heavily on histogram representations which add discretization errors [11,20] and do not apply to functionally correlated distributions [2,11,16]. Some either use parametric assumptions like Gaussian Processes or do not use the functional relationship to drive the optimization framework [15,21].

Our driving application is the analysis of diffusion in white matter tracts for modeling neurodevelopment. The 3D tract geometries are converted to functional curves along with correspondence between parametrized tract locations across subjects [25]. The DTI properties in the tract cross sections provide us the probabilistic signatures for these functions (Fig. 1). Our goal is to estimate the temporal trajectories of these uncertain functional curves to characterize population-level changes. We propose a novel, comprehensive framework which finds the global solution of the regression problem by jointly minimizing a squared loss function based on the Wasserstein metric, over a set of constraints. To fully exploit the estimated trajectories, we also propose an inference framework to establish null distributions of Wasserstein-based test statistics that can serve as a benchmark of normative growth trends. Individual subjects can then be assessed against this benchmark via single images or individual trajectories. Our

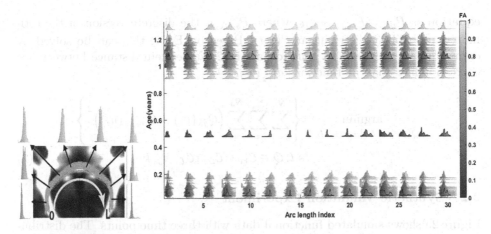

Fig. 1. Left:Selected Fractional Anisotropy (FA) distributions from cross sections along the Splenium tract's arc-length [0,L]. Right:Original FA distributions along splenium for 100 subjects (H-healthy). Distributions from delayed subject D are overlaid (marked with black edges). D has 3 longitudinal scans (age:14 days, 6 months, 1 year).

strength is in borrowing inspiration from both fields- functional data analysis and optimal transport- for a unified statistical analysis framework.

2   Methodology

2.1   Formulating the Regression Problem

We frame the task as a constrained minimization problem of estimating a distribution valued spatiotemporal trajectory under the following constraints.

$\mathcal{C}_{\mathcal{W}}$: Preserve the functional nature of the curves and enforce a smooth transition in the shapes of the distributions spatially.

$\mathcal{C}_{\mathcal{L}}$: The temporal changes in the distribution profiles are 'linear' with respect to the Wasserstein metric. Moreover, spatially localized differences in temporal trends are permitted.

$\mathcal{C}_{\mathcal{I}}$: At any point in space and time, the estimates should be meaningful distribution shapes, i.e. in the space of valid quantile functions.

Let, continuous variables u,s and t represent probability values, space and time, which are indexed by $i = [1, \ldots, N_q]$, $j = [1, \ldots, N_s]$ and $k = [1, \ldots, N_t]$ respectively. N_q is the number of uniformly spaced quadrature points (quantiles) where quantile functions are numerically approximated ($u \in [0, 1], u_i = i/N_q$). N_s and N_t are the discrete number of parametrized spatial locations and time points respectively. Using this, we define a probability distribution P_{jk} (with its associated inverse CDF function $Q \in \mathbb{R}^{N_q}$) at function location j and discrete-time k. Our regression problem can be formulated in terms of the classic regression equation as $P_{jk} = \tilde{P}_{s_j,t_k} + \varepsilon_{jk}$, where $\tilde{P}_{s_j,t_k}$ is the discrete version of the estimated probability distribution $\tilde{P}(s,t)$. Based on Eq. 1, this can be solved by expressing the related cost function as the 2-Wasserstein distance between the corresponding quantile functions $d_{W_2}^2(Q_{jk}, \tilde{Q}_{s_j,t_k})$.

$$\underset{\tilde{Q}(j=[1...N_s],k=[1...N_t])}{\text{argmin}} \left\{ \sum_{k=1}^{N_t} \sum_{j=1}^{N_s} \sum_{i=1}^{N_q} \left(Q_{jk}(u_i) - \tilde{Q}_{s_j,t_k}(u_i) \right)^2 \right\}$$

$$s.t. \tilde{Q} \in \mathcal{C_W} \cap \mathcal{C_L} \cap \mathcal{C_I}, \ \forall j,k \tag{2}$$

2.2 Synthetic Validation Experiment

Figure 2a shows simulated functional data with three time points. The distributions are generated as a sum of two beta distributions. The shape parameters of the beta distributions are chosen to create a cumulative effect from the following: 1) From left to right, shift the symmetry to create distributions with heavy right tails. 2) From bottom to top, unimodal to bimodal to simulate shifting peaks. The simulated effects have been chosen to exhibit a spectrum of variations in the distribution shapes. They also conform to the assumptions of smooth and gradual changes, analogous to normal along-tract diffusion. The result in Fig. 2b shows the smooth estimated trajectory $\tilde{P}(s,t)$ where the simulated effects have been captured as intended.

2.3 Computational Algorithm

The constrained least square optimization problem in Eq. 2 is solved using the iterative projection algorithm by [5,7]. The idea is that if the convex region created by multiple constraints on the parameters can be represented as a finite intersection of simpler convex regions, then the solution can be obtained by sequentially projecting onto these simpler convex regions. The projections onto these sub-regions are usually easier (even, analytical) to compute. For an infinite-dimensional Hilbert space with projections onto arbitrary, closed convex sets, convergence guarantee was provided by [5]. We define a closed, convex set $\mathcal{C} \subseteq \mathbb{R}^{N_q}$ such that the projection of a point $z \in \mathbb{R}^{N_q}$ onto $\mathcal{C}$ is defined as $P_{\mathcal{C}}(z) = \underset{\tilde{z}}{\text{argmin}} \{\|z - \tilde{z}\| | \tilde{z} \in \mathcal{C}\}$. This is a convex optimization problem where the optimal value provides the minimum distance between $\mathcal{C}$ and z [3]. To solve Eq. 2, the solution region $\mathcal{C}$ can be expressed as $\mathcal{C_W} \cap \mathcal{C_L} \cap \mathcal{C_I}$. Then, instead of solving for $P_{\mathcal{C}}(Q)$, the problem can be reformulated as a sequence $\{Q^{(m)}\}$ of projections: $Q^{(m+1)} = P_{\mathcal{C_I}}(P_{\mathcal{C_L}}(P_{\mathcal{C_W}}(Q^{(m)})))$, where $Q^{(0)} = Q$. The sequence $\{Q^{(m)}\}$ converges to the optimal minimizing estimate $\tilde{Q}$ as $n \to \infty$ [5]. In practice, a reasonable estimate is achieved within a few hundred iterations.

Projection 1. $(P_{\mathcal{C_W}}$, Fig. 2a,c): Assuming that a known parametric form for the functional correlation is unknown, we implement this restriction by replacing each distribution by a kernel-smoothed barycenter distribution of its local

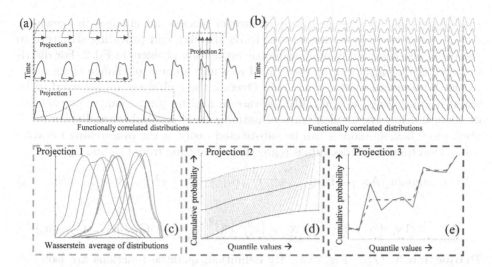

Fig. 2. a) Distribution-valued functional curves with three timepoints (black, blue, green). Color-coded box overlays depict the projections for the 3 constraints. b) Estimated spatiotemporal distribution-valued trajectory. c) C_W(cyan): Kernel weighted barycenter distribution (solid-cyan) with a spatially moving kernel window (dashed-cyan in (a)). d) C_L(red): Individual linear models along time (red lines) for every quantile. CDFs correspond to the 3 distributions inside the dashed-red box in (a)). e) C_I(magenta): Isotonic regression applied to each distribution in (a) (dashed-magenta box drawn only over selected distributions for simplicity). Magenta arrows point to increasing quantile values achieved by the fitted magenta curve in (e). (Color figure online)

spatial neighbors during each projection cycle. The barycenter minimizes a weighted sum of squared Wasserstein distance between itself and the neighbors. The Wasserstein barycenter is equivalent to the Fréchet mean in the space of quantile functions under the L_2 norm [17]. A Nadarya-Watson kernel $K_\lambda(s, s_j)$ is used to assign normalized weights w_j within a moving kernel window (the optimal kernel bandwidth λ is decided using cross-validation). This makes the barycenter a convex combination of the local neighbors ($\sum w_j = 1$, $w_j \geq 0$) [4].

$$\forall k \ \underset{\tilde{Q}_{s_j,t_k} \in C_W}{\operatorname{argmin}} \sum_{j=1}^{N_s} \sum_{i=1}^{N_q} w_j \left(\tilde{Q}_{s_j,t_k}(u_i) - Q_{jk}(u_i) \right)^2 \tag{3}$$

Projection 2. (P_{C_L}, Fig. 2a,d): To encode the temporal dynamics, each individual quantile is fitted with a linear growth model with time as the covariate. The estimated $N_s * N_q * 2$ regression parameters allow to completely characterize and reconstruct the spatiotemporal trajectory of the distributions. The values between two adjacent quantiles represent a smaller segment of the underlying population [16]. Requiring independent fits to each of this sub-population allows the distributions to exhibit a wide range of temporal changes like translation, scaling, gradual emergence-disappearance of modes and changes in skewness. Also, a parametric linear model aids in regularizing and providing structure to the otherwise completely nonparametric estimation problem in Eq. 2. For distributions, the linearity can be thought of as a unit amount of change along a line in the Wasserstein metric space [16]. Overall, these changes are assumed to be smooth along time, as is usually the case in healthy brain changes or patterns of general delay. For sudden transformations, trend reversals or multiple covariates, more flexible models can be substituted easily as the overarching iterative projection framework decouples regression along time from $\mathcal{C}_\mathcal{W}$ and $\mathcal{C}_\mathcal{I}$.

$$\forall i,j, \quad \underset{x_{ij}^0, x_{ij}^1}{\mathrm{argmin}} \|\mathbf{A}\mathbf{x}_{ij} - \mathbf{b}_{ij}\|^2, \quad s.t. \quad \tilde{Q}_{jk}(u_i) = x_{ij}^0 + x_{ij}^1 t_k \ , k = [1 \ldots N_t]. \quad (4)$$

$$\underset{\in \mathbb{R}^{N_t \times 2}}{\mathbf{A}} = \left[\mathbf{1}_{N_t} \ [t_1 \ldots t_{N_t}]^T \right], \underset{\in \mathbb{R}^2}{\mathbf{x}} = \left[x_{ij}^0 \ x_{ij}^1 \right]^T, \underset{\in \mathbb{R}^{N_t}}{\mathbf{b}} = [Q_{j1}(u_i) \ldots Q_{jN_t}(u_i)]^T$$

Projection 3. ($P_{\mathcal{C}_\mathcal{I}}$, Fig. 2a,e): By definition, quantile functions are isotonic. The projection step $P_{\mathcal{C}_\mathcal{L}}$ can violate this condition as the parametric fit is estimated independently for each quantile, potentially leading to crossing quantiles along time. To restore the validity of the estimated quantile functions, this projection uses the *Pool Adjacent Violators algorithm* to solve the quadratic problem in Eq. 5 [6]. The algorithm estimates an order preserving sequence which minimizes the squared error loss by using back-averaging to reinstate the monotonicity.

$$\forall j,k, \quad \underset{\tilde{Q}_{s_j,t_k} \in \mathcal{C}_\mathcal{I}}{\mathrm{argmin}} \sum_{i=1}^{N_q} \left(Q_{jk}(u_i) - \tilde{Q}_{s_j,t_k}(u_i) \right)^2, s.t. \ \tilde{Q}_{s_j,t_k}(u_i) \leq \tilde{Q}_{s_j,t_k}(u_{i+1}) \quad (5)$$

3   Statistical Inference Framework

We present two ways to utilize the above framework for subsequent statistical inference. We leverage the availability of complete distribution profiles along the spatiotemporal trajectory to evaluate two test statistics- **1-Wasserstein slope:** ϕ_j^{W1}, Eq. 6 and **2-Wasserstein residuals:** η_j^{W2}, Eq. 7, as a function of the spatial variable s. Since a parametric distribution form is not known for both, we use nonparametric methods to generate sampling distributions for them (under the general null hypothesis that all subjects are healthy) to create normative benchmarks. We only need to resample from the healthy population to estimate these null distributions and the associated critical threshold values required to reject the null hypothesis at a given significance level. Next, to compare a new, single subject with the normative trajectory as in a typical radiological task, we only require the respective test-statistic value for the subject and the estimated critical values to accept or reject the 'healthy' hypothesis. It is important to note that in our setting, any resampling strategy to build a sampling distribution should operate on the entire function as a random variable. When randomizing the order or group membership, the entire functional curve

$Q_{jk}(u_i), i = [1, \ldots, N_q], j = [1, \ldots, N_s]$ has to be moved around to avoid destroying the functional structure. Additionally, both the test statistics are estimated at discrete locations $s_j, j = [1, \ldots, N_s]$. Therefore, with each resampled dataset, N_s values for the statistics are generated, contributing to a separate sampling distribution at each s_j. Even though the interpretation of ϕ_j^{W1} and η_j^{W2} stays the same across s_j, we choose not to pool these values together across s_j. This allows us to capture local effects of interest at different spatial locations.

$$\forall\, j,\ \phi_j^{W1} = \frac{1}{N_t - 1} \cdot \sum_{k=1}^{N_t - 1} dW_1\left(\tilde{Q}_{s_j, t_k}, \tilde{Q}_{s_j, t_{k+1}}\right), \tag{6}$$

Equation 6 gives the slope value derived from the 1-Wasserstein distance. The idea is analogous to the linear slope and quantifies the effect size as the change in dW1 corresponding to a unit change in time [16]. A non-zero value for ϕ_j^{W1} indicates a smooth transformation in the distribution along time. The linear trends of individual quantiles ensure that the distances between distributions in Eq. 6 are not from spurious noise or natural variability between subjects. To generate a sampling distribution, we draw 500 bootstrap data sets with replacement from the available data and re-estimate the trajectory and ϕ_j^{W1}. Using the percentiles, we build point-wise 95% confidence bands at each spatial location [10].

$$\forall\, j,\ \eta_j^{W2} = dW_2\left(\tilde{Q}_{s_j, t_k}, G_{s_j, t_k}\right) \tag{7}$$

Equation 7 gives the residuals calculated as the 2-Wasserstein distance between distributions from the estimated trajectory and distribution-valued function G sourced from an independent test data set. When G is a healthy subject from the population, η_j^{W2} can be interpreted as a normative deviation from the healthy progression. Therefore, a sampling distribution of η_j^{W2} at each s_j represents the normal range of variability within the population. To avoid training data bias, we apply a 10-fold cross validation scheme with 50 repetitions to create random data partitions. The average prediction error over the k-th fold (used as independent test data), contributes to the sampling distribution of η_j^{W2}. To assess the significance of hypothesis tests at each location s_j, we apply FDR (false discovery rate) corrections to address the issue of multiple testing.

4   Application to DTI White Matter Tracts

We apply the framework to DTI images from 100 healthy infants (H) with ages clustered around 1 month and 1 year (50 per group). The raw distribution-valued functions generated from the splenium tract are shown in Fig. 1. We also show 3 longitudinal scans from an infant with clinically diagnosed developmental delay (D). Figure 3a shows results for the estimated population-level trajectory which shows an overall increase in FA stemming from neurodevelopment, reflected as change in skew and color along time. Additionally, different tract locations have notably distinctive patterns of along-time changes. Further, subject D is used as a case study where a single subject is compared to the norm to show the feasibility of our method in a clinical setting. The trajectory estimate for D in Fig. 3a shows a notably delayed growth when compared to H. For solidifying this general conclusion, we compare D with H under two clinically relevant scenarios and show results on two different tracts- genu and splenium. 1) The comparison with H is done via 1-Wasserstein slopes (ϕ_j^{W1}, Eq. 6) for the complete trajectories. Figure 3c shows the result which clearly differentiates D as delayed. 2) We assume that only a single D scan is available at a time. Note that the trajectory for H can be estimated smoothly along time (Eq. 4). This permits a direct comparison of a single distribution-valued tract profile for D, with H's trajectory estimate evaluated at D's age. For this case, we use 2-Wasserstein residuals (η_j^{W2}, Eq. 7) to discover significantly different tract locations between each individual D scan when compared with the H population, one at a time (Fig. 3b). Most tract locations confirm the delay for D.

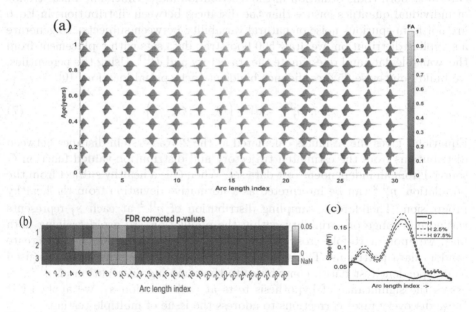

Fig. 3. a) Splenium: Estimated spatiotemporal population trajectory for H (top half of the violin plots) and individualized trajectory for D (bottom half of the violin plots). Both trajectories evaluated at same arclength locations and times to allow visual comparison. b) Splenium: FDR corrected p-values (test-statistic:2-Wasserstein residuals) for comparison of H's trajectory with 3 DTI images from D, one at a time: 14 days(row 1),6 mo(row 2),1 yr(row 3). NaN:non-significant tract locations. c) Genu:1-Wasserstein slope shown with 95% confidence bands for H along with the slope estimated for D.

5   Discussion and Conclusion

Our framework is able to detect the differences very early in time (when D is 14 days old). We know that these detected differences are not a product of noise since they match the expected findings. We note that there are visual similarities in the distributions in Fig. 1 between D and the 1 month group making it hard to notice any delayed growth. However, our method is able to distinguish at a very early time point indicating a promising improvement in discriminatory power. Moreover, the distribution-based slopes (ϕ_j^{W1}) can also potentially increase the separability between trajectories as it encapsulates differences arising out of variability as well. In comparison, other methods like averaging tract profiles to scalar-valued functional curves or further reducing large regions-of-interest to a scalar summary statistic may not detect these early differences. This is because the distinguishing differences may reflect as a change in the distribution profile rather than local statistical summaries of image neighborhoods. Similarly, early differences may be too subtle and spatially diffused to be identified by voxel-based methods. In this regard, the proposed framework borrows from the best of the two worlds. It summarizes local information as distributions, thereby creating a rich 'summary' statistic while also retaining and employing the knowledge of the variability for improved statistical power. The strength of the framework also lies in its flexibility to manage aspects of the optimization problem independently. For e.g., applications to non-functional data or more flexible temporal trends can be implemented by adjusting the respective projections. The overall modular design essentially creates an extensible and broadly applicable framework while also splitting the problem into simpler sub-problems. Among the proposed inference strategies, ϕ_j^{W1} compactly characterizes the entire trajectory with only a few, descriptive parameters which can be used to compare progression of individuals with populations or different populations. In comparison, η_j^{W2} facilitates inference at a finer granularity by allowing comparisons for single scans from individual subjects.

References

1. Bondell, H.D., Reich, B.J., Wang, H.: Noncrossing quantile regression curve estimation. Biometrika **97**(4), 825–838 (2010)
2. Bonneel, N., Peyré, G., Cuturi, M.: Wasserstein barycentric coordinates: histogram regression using optimal transport. ACM Trans. Graph. **35**(4), 71–1 (2016)
3. Boyd, S., Dattorro, J., et al.: Alternating projections. EE392o, Stanford University (2003)
4. Boyd, S., Vandenberghe, L.: Convex Optimization. Cambridge University Press, Cambridge (2004)
5. Boyle, J.P., Dykstra, R.L.: A method for finding projections onto the intersection of convex sets in hilbert spaces. In: Dykstra, R., Robertson, T., Wright, F.T. (eds.) Advances in Order Restricted Statistical Inference, pp. 28–47. Springer, New York (1986). https://doi.org/10.1007/978-1-4613-9940-7_3

6. De Leeuw, J.: Correctness of kruskal's algorithms for monotone regression with ties. Psychometrika **42**(1), 141–144 (1977)
7. Dykstra, R.L.: An algorithm for restricted least squares regression. J. Am. Stat. Assoc. **78**(384), 837–842 (1983)
8. Fan, J., Yao, Q., Tong, H.: Estimation of conditional densities and sensitivity measures in nonlinear dynamical systems. Biometrika **83**(1), 189–206 (1996)
9. Goldsmith, J., Crainiceanu, C.M., Caffo, B., Reich, D.: Longitudinal penalized functional regression for cognitive outcomes on neuronal tract measurements. J. Royal Stat. Soc.: Ser. C (Applied Statistics) **61**(3), 453–469 (2012)
10. Hastie, T., Tibshirani, R., Friedman, J.: The Elements of Statistical Learning: Data Mining, Inference, and Prediction. Springer, New York (2009). https://doi.org/10.1007/978-0-387-84858-7
11. Irpino, A., Verde, R.: Linear regression for numeric symbolic variables: a least squares approach based on wasserstein distance. Adv. Data Anal. Classification **9**(1), 81–106 (2015)
12. Joshi, S.H., Klassen, E., Srivastava, A., Jermyn, I.: A novel representation for riemannian analysis of elastic curves in RN. In: 2007 IEEE Conference on Computer Vision and Pattern Recognition, pp. 1–7. IEEE (2007)
13. Koenker, R., Hallock, K.F.: Quantile regression. J. Econ. Perspectives **15**(4), 143–156 (2001)
14. Kundu, S., Kolouri, S., Erickson, K.I., Kramer, A.F., McAuley, E., Rohde, G.K.: Discovery and visualization of structural biomarkers from mri using transport-based morphometry. NeuroImage **167**, 256–275 (2018)
15. Mallasto, A., Feragen, A.: Learning from uncertain curves: the 2-wasserstein metric for gaussian processes. In: Advances in Neural Information Processing Systems, pp. 5660–5670 (2017)
16. Mueller, J., Jaakkola, T., Gifford, D.: Modeling persistent trends in distributions. J. Am. Stat. Assoc. **113**(523), 1296–1310 (2018)
17. Peyré, G., Cuturi, M., et al.: Computational optimal transport. Found. Trends® Machine Learn. **11**(5–6), 355–607 (2019)
18. Ramsay, J.O., Silverman, B.W.: Functional Data Analysis. Springer Series in Statistics. Springer, New York (2005). https://doi.org/10.1007/b98888
19. Sharma, A., Durrleman, S., Gilmore, J.H., Gerig, G.: Longitudinal growth modeling of discrete-time functions with application to DTI tract evolution in early neurodevelopment. In: 2012 9th IEEE International Symposium on Biomedical Imaging (ISBI), pp. 1397–1400. IEEE (2012)
20. Sharma, A., et al.: Parametric regression scheme for distributions: analysis of DTI fiber tract diffusion changes in early brain development. In: 2014 IEEE 11th International Symposium on Biomedical Imaging (ISBI), pp. 559–562. IEEE (2014)
21. Sharma, A., et al.: Spatiotemporal modeling of distribution-valued data applied to DTI tract evolution in infant neurodevelopment. In: 2013 IEEE 10th International Symposium on Biomedical Imaging, pp. 684–687. IEEE (2013)
22. Solomon, J.: Transportation Techniques for Geometric Data Processing. Ph.D. thesis, University of British Columbia (2015)
23. Srivastava, A., Klassen, E., Joshi, S.H., Jermyn, I.H.: Shape analysis of elastic curves in euclidean spaces. IEEE Trans. Pattern Anal. Mach. Intell. **33**(7), 1415–1428 (2011). https://doi.org/10.1109/TPAMI.2010.184
24. Srivastava, A., Klassen, E.P.: Functional and Shape Data Analysis, vol. 475. Springer, New York (2016). https://doi.org/10.1007/978-1-4939-4020-2
25. Verde, A.R., et al.: UNC-UTAH na-mic framework for DTI fiber tract analysis. Front. Neuroinform. **7**, 51 (2014)

26. Yu, K., Jones, M.: Local linear quantile regression. J. Am. Stat. Assoc. **93**(441), 228–237 (1998)
27. Zhang, Z., et al.: Mapping population-based structural connectomes. NeuroImage **172**, 130–145 (2018)
28. Zhu, H., et al.: Fadtts: functional analysis of diffusion tensor tract statistics. NeuroImage **56**(3), 1412–1425 (2011)

Characterizing Intra-soma Diffusion
with Spherical Mean Spectrum Imaging

Khoi Minh Huynh[1,2], Ye Wu[2], Kim-Han Thung[2], Sahar Ahmad[2],
Hoyt Patrick Taylor IV[2], Dinggang Shen[1,2], and Pew-Thian Yap[1,2(✉)]

[1] Department of Biomedical Engineering, University of North Carolina,
Chapel Hill, USA
ptyap@med.unc.edu
[2] Department of Radiology and Biomedical Research Imaging Center,
University of North Carolina, Chapel Hill, USA

Abstract. Most brain microstructure models are dedicated to the quantification of white matter microstructure, using for example sticks, cylinders, and zeppelins to model intra- and extra-axonal environments. Gray matter presents unique micro-architecture with cell bodies (somas) exhibiting diffusion characteristics that differ from axons in white matter. In this paper, we introduce a method to quantify soma microstructure, giving measures such as volume fraction, diffusivity, and kurtosis. Our method captures a spectrum of diffusion patterns and scales and does not rely on restrictive model assumptions. We show that our method yields unique and meaningful contrasts that are in agreement with histological data. We demonstrate its application in the mapping of the distinct spatial patterns of soma density in the cortex.

1 Introduction

Biophysical models utilizing diffusion magnetic resonance imaging (dMRI) are powerful tools for mapping brain microstructure, affording insights into tissue architecture [1–5] and revealing pathological and developmental patterns [6]. The focus of most microstructure models is white matter, where water molecules diffuse directionally. In gray matter, the microstructure is more heterogeneous, involving somas (cell bodies), dendrites, glial cells, unmyelinated axons, etc. Models dichotomizing gray matter signal as either extra-neurite or intra-neurite suffer from model simplification and are bound to bias microstructure estimates.

It has been shown for the first time in [7] that intra-soma diffusion can be modeled as a separate compartment distinct from intra-neurite and extra-neurite compartments. The soma and neurite density imaging (SANDI) [7] model relies on the assumptions that extra-neurite diffusion is isotropic and that intra-soma diffusivity is similar to that of free water. These assumptions do not hold in practice as extra-neurite diffusion are shown to be anisotropic [2,4,5] and intra-soma diffusion is isotropic and restricted [8]. In this paper, we demonstrate that

This work was supported in part by NIH grants (NS093842 and EB022880).

© Springer Nature Switzerland AG 2020
A. L. Martel et al. (Eds.): MICCAI 2020, LNCS 12267, pp. 354–363, 2020.
https://doi.org/10.1007/978-3-030-59728-3_35

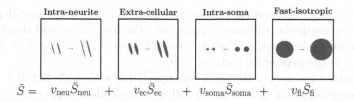

$$\bar{S} = \quad v_{\text{neu}}\bar{S}_{\text{neu}} \quad + \quad v_{\text{ec}}\bar{S}_{\text{ec}} \quad + \quad v_{\text{soma}}\bar{S}_{\text{soma}} \quad + \quad v_{\text{fi}}\bar{S}_{\text{fi}}$$

Fig. 1. Model. The spherical mean signal is contributed by the intra-neurite (neu), extra-cellular (ec), intra-soma (soma), and fast-isotropic (fi) diffusion compartments. SMSI represents each compartment with atoms of multiple diffusivity values.

spherical mean spectrum imaging (SMSI) [1,2] can be extended to quantify intra-soma diffusion. SMSI captures a spectrum of diffusion patterns from coarse to fine scales. We extended SMSI for quantification of soma microstructure, giving measures such as volume fraction, diffusivity, and kurtosis. Our method captures a spectrum of diffusion patterns and scales and does not rely on restrictive assumptions, such as fixed compartment number and diffusivity. We show that our method yields unique and meaningful contrasts that are in agreement with histological data. We demonstrate its application in mapping the distinct spatial patterns of soma density in the cortex.

2 Method

2.1 Soma Compartment Model

As observed in the spherical mean technique (SMT) [3], the spherical mean of the dMRI signal $\bar{S}_b$ only depends on b-value and diffusivity but not the fiber orientation distribution. For a micro-environment with diffusion that can be represented using a tensor model, the spherical mean is defined as

$$\frac{\bar{S}_b}{S_0} = \int_0^1 \exp\left(-b\lambda_\perp\right) \exp\left(-b(\lambda_\parallel - \lambda_\perp)x^2\right) dx \tag{1}$$

$$= \int_0^1 h_b(\lambda_\parallel, \lambda_\perp, x)dx = \bar{h}_b(\lambda_\parallel, \lambda_\perp), \tag{2}$$

where $\lambda_\parallel$ is the parallel diffusivity and $\lambda_\perp$ is the perpendicular diffusivity [3]. SMSI [1] views the spherical mean as a linear combination of contributions from multiple micro-environments, i.e.,

$$\bar{S}_b = S_0 \sum_i \nu[i]\bar{h}_b(\lambda_\parallel[i], \lambda_\perp[i]). \tag{3}$$

The i-th micro-environment is associated with parallel diffusivity $\lambda_\parallel[i]$, perpendicular diffusivity $\lambda_\perp[i]$, and volume fraction $\nu[i]$. Different sub-spectra can be derived from the spherical mean spectrum as follows:

- The intra-neurite (neu) diffusion sub-spectrum with high parallel and low to no perpendicular diffusion, typical in neurites (axons and dendrites) and commonly represented as "sticks" or cylinders with $\tau^{-2}\lambda_\parallel[i] \geq \lambda_\perp[i] \geq 0$ where τ is the geometric tortuosity [9].
- The extra-cellular (ec) diffusion sub-spectrum with high parallel and moderate perpendicular diffusion, typical in extra-cellular space and commonly represented as zeppelins with $\lambda_\parallel[i] > \lambda_\perp[i] > \tau^{-2}\lambda_\parallel[i]$. Unlike SANDI [7], this condition allows the extra-cellular compartment to be anisotropic, as widely shown in [1,4,5].
- The intra-soma (is) diffusion sub-spectrum with slow isotropic diffusion, represented as spheres with diffusion that is more restricted than free water [7], i.e., $\lambda_\parallel[i] = \lambda_\perp[i] \leq 1\,\mu m^2/ms$. This range covers typical diffusivity within cell bodies [8].
- The fast-isotropic (fi) diffusion sub-spectrum including free-water diffusion, represented by spheres with $2\,\mu m^2/ms \leq \lambda_\parallel[i] = \lambda_\perp[i] \leq 3\,\mu m^2/ms$.

Figure 1 illustrates the model.

2.2 Implementation Details

SMSI solves for the volume fraction $\nu[i]$ via elastic net

$$\nu = \underset{\nu \succeq 0}{arg\,min}\left\| \begin{pmatrix} A \\ \sqrt{\gamma_2}I \end{pmatrix}\nu - \begin{pmatrix} \bar{S} \\ 0 \end{pmatrix} \right\|_2^2 + \gamma_1 \|diag(w)\nu\|_1, \qquad (4)$$

where $A = [\bar{h}_b(\lambda_\parallel[1],\lambda_\perp[1]), \bar{h}_b(\lambda_\parallel[2],\lambda_\perp[2]),\ldots] \in \mathbb{R}^{n \times p}$ is a dictionary with atoms representing spherical mean signals of micro-environments covering the different sub-spectra as described above. n is the number of b-shells and p is the number of atoms. w is a weight vector and γ_1 and γ_2 are tuning parameters that control the contributions of the $\ell 1$ and $\ell 2$ regularization terms, respectively.

It has been reported that the spherical mean signal from linear encoding dMRI can be ambiguous [10]. That is, within the typical range of b-values ($b \leq 3000\,s/mm^2$), the spherical mean signal of an anisotropic tensor can be indistinguishable from the spherical mean signal of a combination of multiple isotropic tensors with different diffusivity values. We address this problem by using the full direction-sensitized diffusion signal to disambiguate between anisotropic and isotropic diffusion.

Weighting with Full Signal Spectrum (FSS): The full diffusion signal S can be represented as the spherical convolution between the fiber orientation distribution function (fODF) and the kernel h. Using spherical harmonics (SHs), S can be expressed as the product of rotational SHs, H, the SH of even order up to order L, $\mathcal{Y}_L$, and the SH coefficients of the fODF, φ. In line with [9] and the spirit of SMSI, let $\mathcal{H}(\lambda_\parallel[i], \lambda_\perp[i])$ be the matrix of rotational SHs of

$h(g|\omega, \lambda_\parallel[i], \lambda_\perp[i])$, and φ_i be the SH coefficients of the fODF corresponding to $h(g|\omega, \lambda_\parallel[i], \lambda_\perp[i])$, the full signal can be discretized as [11]

$$S \approx \sum_i \mathcal{H}(\lambda_\parallel[i], \lambda_\perp[i])\mathcal{Y}_L\varphi_i = \mathcal{B}\Phi. \tag{5}$$

$\mathcal{B}$ can be seen as a dictionary matrix and Φ, a matrix containing φ_i, $\forall i$, can be solved with Tikhonov regularization [9]

$$\min_\Phi \left\| \begin{pmatrix} \mathcal{B} \\ \sqrt{\gamma_3}\mathrm{diag}(w') \end{pmatrix} \Phi - \begin{pmatrix} S \\ 0 \end{pmatrix} \right\|_2^2. \tag{6}$$

To ensure that the fODF of anisotropic atoms does not degenerate to become isotropic, we first solve (6) with weight vector w' set to one for all atoms and reapply (6) with w' set to a higher value for any atom with GFA < 0.3. This approach penalizes low GFA anisotropic fODF and disambiguates anisotropic and isotropic diffusion in case of degeneracy [1]. From the final solution, a set of weights, ν_{FSS}, is calculated as the 0-th order SH coefficient from Φ.

Weighting with Spherical Mean Spectrum (SMS): Similar to [1], we first use the spherical mean signals of shells with $b \leq 1000\,\mathrm{s/mm}^2$ in solving (4) with w set to one for all atoms. This will help improve the estimates of the volume fractions of fast isotropic diffusion atoms as the associated signals decay rapidly and become trivial at higher b value. The solution to this step results in a set of weights, ν_{SMS}.

Iterative Estimation: We then solve for the volume fractions using all b-shells via iterative re-weighted elastic net, where in the j-th iteration we have

$$\nu_j = \underset{\nu_j \succeq 0}{\arg\min} \left\| \begin{pmatrix} A \\ \sqrt{\gamma_2}I \end{pmatrix} \nu_j - \begin{pmatrix} \bar{S} \\ 0 \end{pmatrix} \right\|_2^2 + \gamma_1\|\mathrm{diag}(w_j)\nu_j\|_1, \tag{7}$$

where $w_j[i] = \frac{1}{\xi + \nu_{j-1}[i]}$ with ξ being a constant and ν_0 is computed as the element-wise geometric mean of ν_{FSS} and ν_{SMS}. Regularization parameters γs are determined via grid search as in [1].

2.3   Intra-soma Diffusion Properties

From ν, the volume fraction of the intra-soma compartment can be determined. Note that intra-soma diffusion can be characterized by multiple slow isotropic diffusion atoms with different diffusivity values and hence deviates from Gaussianity. To characterize diffusional non-Gaussianity, we derive a soma kurtosis model from [12]

$$\ln \bar{S}_{\mathrm{soma}}(b) = -b\lambda_{\mathrm{soma}} + \frac{b^2}{6}K_{\mathrm{soma}}\lambda_{\mathrm{soma}}^2, \tag{8}$$

where $\bar{S}_{\mathrm{soma}}$ is the normalized spherical mean signal contribution from the soma compartment, λ_{soma} is the soma diffusivity, and K_{soma} is the soma kurtosis.

3   Experiments

For evaluation, we used the dMRI data of 4 healthy adults, each with 12, 24, and 48 diffusion-weighted images respectively for $b = 1000, 2000, 3000 \, \text{s/mm}^2$ and 6 B0 images. Each diffusion-weighted image has an isotropic resolution of 1.5 mm. The images were corrected for motion and off-resonance artifacts [13]. SMSI parameters were set according to [1].

3.1   Microstructure

Figure 2 presents the parametric maps for a representative subject. In white matter, the intra-neurite volume fraction (v_{neu}) is high, in line with previous observations that these regions contain mostly myelinated axons [2,4,14], giving a clear contrast for major fiber bundles such as forceps major, forceps minor, cortical spinal tract. The extra-cellular volume fraction (v_{ec}) is higher in superficial white matter and some gray matter regions. The fast-isotropic diffusion volume fraction (v_{fi}) is high in the ventricles and peripheral regions where there is little to no microscopic barriers to water diffusion.

The intra-soma volume fraction (v_{soma}) is higher in the cortical ribbon. The typical value is between 0.1–0.2, which are in line with observations in [7,15]. The soma diffusivity (λ_{soma}) is mostly around $0.6 \, \mu\text{m}^2/\text{ms}$ in the cortex and is slightly lower in the cerebellum. The soma kurtosis (K_{soma}), although small, is non-zero and is highest in the cerebellar gray matter. This could be due to the unique structure of the cerebellar cortex with a dense layer of granule cells and Purkinje cells with complex dendritic spines [8].

3.2   Histology

Figure 3 illustrates the similarity between our results and ex-vivo histological images. The intra-neurite volume fraction map is strikingly similar to myelin stain. The intra-soma volume fraction map is similar to cell nuclei stain, with higher values in the cerebral and cerebellar gray matter. These results demonstrate that our method provides biologically meaningful contrasts resembling ex-vivo stains. This also underscores the importance of dMRI as an *in vivo* histology tool that can avoid the limitations of ex-vivo staining, such as distortions caused by the slicing and staining processes.

3.3   Cortical Patterns

We constructed the cortical surfaces from the T1- and T2-weighted images as described in [16,17] and mapped the parametric maps onto the cortical surface as described in [18]. Figure 4 shows the average maps of 4 healthy adults. The intra-neurite volume fraction is higher in the motor and somatosensory areas, confirming the pattern observed in [19]. On the other hand, the soma maps reveal distinct patterns, with relatively low values in the motor area, but higher values in the occipital and temporal lobes.

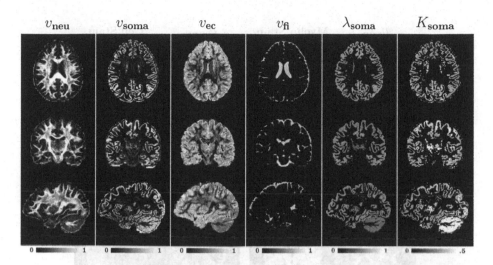

Fig. 2. Tissue Microstructure. Microstructural properties of a representative subject: Intra-neurite volume fraction (v_{neu}), intra-soma volume fraction (v_{soma}), extracellular volume fraction (v_{ec}), fast-isotropic diffusion volume fraction (v_{fi}), soma diffusivity (λ_{soma}), and soma kurtosis (K_{soma}).

3.4   Number of Shells

To evaluate the effect of the number of b-shells on microstructure estimation using our model, we acquired a 21-shell data of a healthy adult with b-values ranging from $500\,\mathrm{s/mm^2}$ to $3000\,\mathrm{s/mm^2}$ with step size $125\,\mathrm{s/mm^2}$. There are 4 to 24 diffusion-weighted (DW) images in each shell, and 13 non-DW images, resulting in a total of 307 volumes. We fitted our model to 4 different sampling schemes:

1. The 21-shell dataset consisting of all volumes;
2. The 11-shell dataset with b-values from $500\,\mathrm{s/mm^2}$ to $3000\,\mathrm{s/mm^2}$ with step size $250\,\mathrm{s/mm^2}$;
3. The 6-shell dataset with b-values from $500\,\mathrm{s/mm^2}$ to $3000\,\mathrm{s/mm^2}$ with step size $500\,\mathrm{s/mm^2}$;
4. The 3-shell-1000 with b-values from $1000\,\mathrm{s/mm^2}$ to $3000\,\mathrm{s/mm^2}$ with step size $1000\,\mathrm{s/mm^2}$; and
5. The 3-shell-500 dataset with b-values from $500\,\mathrm{s/mm^2}$ to $2500\,\mathrm{s/mm^2}$ with step size $1000\,\mathrm{s/mm^2}$.

In Fig. 5, indices from different schemes were compared with those from the reference (21-shell). The higher number of shells, the closer the results to the reference. However, even at only 3 b-shells, almost all indices are comparable to the reference with correlation coefficient (R) greater than 0.95. The only exception is v_{fi} from the 3-shell-1000 scheme, showing slightly lower R due to the lack of a lower b-shell for effective estimation of the fast isotropic diffusion compartment. Nevertheless, the correlation coefficient $R > 0.89$ is still sufficiently high

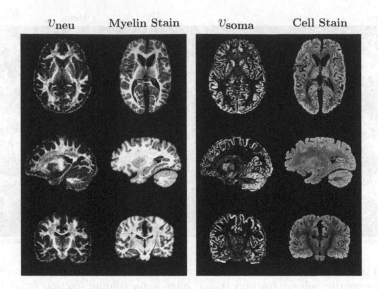

Fig. 3. Resemblance to Stained Sections. Intra-neurite volume fraction (v_{neu}), which provides contrast related to neurite density, poses striking similarity with myelin stain. Intra-soma volume fraction (v_{soma}), which provides information related to soma density, shows remarkable resemblance with cell stain. Stained sections were obtained from https://msu.edu/~brains/brains/human/index.html.

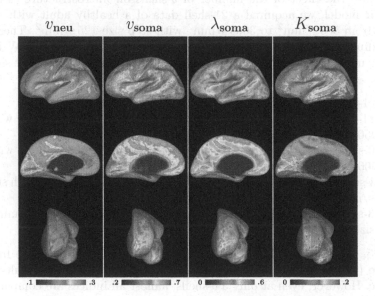

Fig. 4. Cortical Patterns. Average cortical maps of intra-neurite volume fraction (v_{neu}), intra-soma volume fraction (v_{soma}), soma diffusivity (λ_{soma}), and soma kurtosis (K_{soma}) of 4 healthy adults.

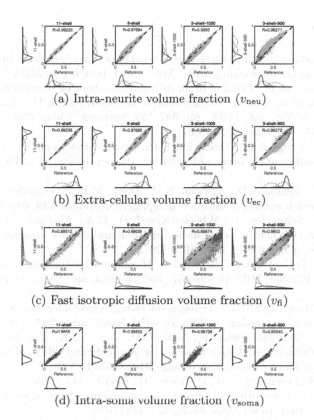

(a) Intra-neurite volume fraction (v_{neu})

(b) Extra-cellular volume fraction (v_{ec})

(c) Fast isotropic diffusion volume fraction (v_{fi})

(d) Intra-soma volume fraction (v_{soma})

Fig. 5. Number of b-Shells. Scatter plots and histograms of representative indices given by sampling schemes 11-shell, 6-shell, 3-shell-1000, and 3-shell-500 with 21-shell as the reference. Voxels are classified as CSF (red), gray matter (blue), or white matter (yellow). For better visibility, only one in every six voxels is shown. Since intra-soma volume fraction is negligible in white matter and CSF, only gray matter voxels are shown in (d). (Color figure online)

for most practical situations. The results demonstrate that our method is suitable for datasets with at least 3 b-shell, such as the Human Connectome Project (HCP) [20] and the Baby Connectome Project (BCP) [21].

4   Conclusions

We have presented a method to characterize soma diffusion properties and have shown that biologically meaningful contrasts resembling histological data can be produced. Future work entails applying our method to investigating changes in the cerebral cortex in relation to development, aging, and diseases.

References

1. Huynh, K.M., et al.: Probing tissue microarchitecture of the baby brain via spherical mean spectrum imaging. IEEE Trans. Med. Imaging 1 (2020)
2. Huynh, K.M., et al.: Probing brain micro-architecture by orientation distribution invariant identification of diffusion compartments. In: Shen, D., et al. (eds.) MICCAI 2019. LNCS, vol. 11766, pp. 547–555. Springer, Cham (2019). https://doi.org/10.1007/978-3-030-32248-9_61
3. Kaden, E., Kruggel, F., Alexander, D.C.: Quantitative mapping of the per-axon diffusion coefficients in brain white matter. Magnet. Reson. Med. **75**(4), 1752–1763 (2016)
4. Kaden, E., Kelm, N.D., Carson, R.P., Does, M.D., Alexander, D.C.: Multi-compartment microscopic diffusion imaging. NeuroImage **139**, 346–359 (2016)
5. Zhang, H., Schneider, T., Wheeler-Kingshott, C.A., Alexander, D.C.: NODDI: practical in vivo neurite orientation dispersion and density imaging of the human brain. Neuroimage **61**(4), 1000–1016 (2012)
6. Alexander, D.C., Dyrby, T.B., Nilsson, M., Zhang, H.: Imaging brain microstructure with diffusion MRI: practicality and applications. NMR Biomed. **32**, e3841 (2017)
7. Palombo, M., et al.: SANDI: a compartment-based model for non-invasive apparent soma and neurite imaging by diffusion MRI. NeuroImage **245**, 116835 (2020)
8. Tax, C.M., Szczepankiewicz, F., Nilsson, M., Jones, D.K.: The dot-compartment revealed? Diffusion MRI with ultra-strong gradients and spherical tensor encoding in the living human brain. NeuroImage **210**, 116534 (2020)
9. White, N.S., Leergaard, T.B., D'Arceuil, H., Bjaalie, J.G., Dale, A.M.: Probing tissue microstructure with restriction spectrum imaging: histological and theoretical validation. Hum. Brain Map. **34**(2), 327–346 (2013)
10. Szczepankiewicz, F.: Imaging diffusional variance by MRI: the role of tensor-valued diffusion encoding and tissue heterogeneity. Ph.D. thesis, Lund University (2016)
11. Tournier, J.D., Calamante, F., Gadian, D.G., Connelly, A.: Direct estimation of the fiber orientation density function from diffusion-weighted MRI data using spherical deconvolution. NeuroImage **23**(3), 1176–1185 (2004)
12. Huynh, K.M., et al.: Characterizing non-gaussian diffusion in heterogeneously oriented tissue microenvironments. In: Shen, D., et al. (eds.) MICCAI 2019. LNCS, vol. 11766, pp. 556–563. Springer, Cham (2019). https://doi.org/10.1007/978-3-030-32248-9_62
13. Andersson, J.L., Sotiropoulos, S.N.: An integrated approach to correction for off-resonance effects and subject movement in diffusion MR imaging. Neuroimage **125**, 1063–1078 (2016)
14. Mori, S., Oishi, K., Faria, A.V.: White matter atlases based on diffusion tensor imaging. Curr. Opin. Neurol. **22**(4), 362 (2009)
15. Lampinen, B., et al.: Searching for the neurite density with diffusion MRI: Challenges for biophysical modeling. Hum. Brain Mapp. **40**(8), 2529–2545 (2019)
16. Ahmad, S., et al.: Surface-volume consistent construction of longitudinal atlases for the early developing brain. In: Shen, D., et al. (eds.) MICCAI 2019. LNCS, vol. 11765, pp. 815–822. Springer, Cham (2019). https://doi.org/10.1007/978-3-030-32245-8_90
17. Li, G., Wang, L., Shi, F., Gilmore, J.H., Lin, W., Shen, D.: Construction of 4D high-definition cortical surface atlases of infants: Methods and applications. Med. Image Anal. **25**(1), 22–36 (2015)

18. Glasser, M.F., Van Essen, D.C.: Mapping human cortical areas in vivo based on myelin content as revealed by T1-and T2-weighted MRI. J. Neurosci. **31**(32), 11597–11616 (2011)
19. Fukutomi, H., et al.: Neurite imaging reveals microstructural variations in human cerebral cortical gray matter. Neuroimage **182**, 488–499 (2018)
20. Van Essen, D.C., et al.: The WU-Minn human connectome project: an overview. Neuroimage **80**, 62–79 (2013)
21. Howell, B.R., et al.: The UNC/UMN baby connectome project (BCP): an overview of the study design and protocol development. NeuroImage **185**, 891–905 (2018)

Functional Brain Networks

Estimating Common Harmonic Waves of Brain Networks on Stiefel Manifold

Jiazhou Chen[1,2], Guoqiang Han[1], Hongmin Cai[1], Junbo Ma[2], Minjeong Kim[3], Paul Laurienti[4], and Guorong Wu[2(✉)]

[1] School of Computer Science and Engineering, South China University of Technology, Guangzhou, China
[2] Department of Psychiatry, University of North Carolina at Chapel Hill, Chapel Hill, USA
grwu@med.unc.edu
[3] Department of Computer Science,
University of North Carolina at Greensboro, Greensboro, USA
[4] Department of Radiology, Wake Forest School of Medicine, Winston Salem, USA

Abstract. Network neuroscience has been widely studied in understanding brain functions as well as the neurobiological underpinnings of cognition and behavior that are related to the development of neuro-disorders. Since the network organization is inherently governed by the harmonic waves (Eigensystem) of the underlying Laplacian matrix, discovering the harmonic-like alterations emerges as a new research interest in understanding the factors behind brain developmental and neurodegenerative diseases, where an unbiased reference space of harmonic waves is often required to quantify the difference across individuals with standard measurement. However, simple arithmetic averaging over the individual harmonic waves is commonly used in current studies, despite that such Euclidean operation might break down the intrinsic data geometry of harmonic waves. To overcome this limitation, we propose a novel manifold optimization framework to find the group mean (aka. common harmonic waves), where each set of harmonic waves from the individual subject is treated as a data sample residing on the Stiefel manifold. To further improve the robustness of learned common harmonic waves to possible outliers, we promote the common harmonic waves to the setting of a geometric median on Stiefel manifold, instead of Fréchet mean, by optimizing towards the ℓ_1-norm shortest overall geodesic distance on the manifold. We have compared our proposed method with the existing methods on both synthetic and real network data. The experimental results indicate that our proposed approach shows improvements in accuracy and statistical power.

Keywords: Brain network · Manifold optimization · Harmonics · Fréchet mean · Geometric median

1 Introduction

Recent advances in neuroimaging techniques allow us to explore the connections between two anatomical regions *in-vivo* [1–3]. A comprehensive description of the structural connectivity can be represented by a complex network – the 'connectome', which

© Springer Nature Switzerland AG 2020
A. L. Martel et al. (Eds.): MICCAI 2020, LNCS 12267, pp. 367–376, 2020.
https://doi.org/10.1007/978-3-030-59728-3_36

is often encoded in a graph data structure [4]. Since mounting evidence shows many neuro-disorders manifest network alterations before the onset of clinical symptoms, various computational and statistical inference methods have been proposed to quantify the topological properties in the aspect of nodes, links, and motifs [5, 6].

As the role of volumetric image atlas in neuroimaging studies, an unbiased reference is also of high demand in network neuroscience to provide the standardized measurement for the downstream analyses of group comparison. In light of this, several computational methods have been proposed to estimate the common network by the naïve arithmetic average [7] or network diffusion [8]. However, Euclidean operations such as link-wise averaging are applied under the assumption that the brain network is a regular data structure in the Euclidean space. On the contrary, the brain network is indeed an irregular data representation with a very random pattern of neighborhood occurring at different nodes. Hence, it is highly possible that such Euclidean operation may break down the intrinsic topology of brain network. Also, since there are substantial dependencies among network links, it is computationally prohibitive to jointly estimate the connectivity degrees in the common network.

In control theory, the property of brain network can be summarized by its own Eigensystem which is a set of harmonic waves derived from the underlying Laplacian matrix [7, 9, 10]. The orthogonality in harmonic waves sheds the new light to identify harmonic-like alterations between two clinic cohorts by examining each harmonic wave separately. To do so, common harmonic waves are required to unify individual Eigensystems. Since each harmonic wave is associated with specific Eigenvalue, it is not reasonable to find the latent common harmonic waves by simple averaging for each base separately in the classic Euclidean space.

To address this challenge, we propose a first-ever manifold optimization scheme to discover the common harmonic waves by estimating the group mean from the observed individual harmonic waves. Due to the orthogonality, we consider each set of harmonic waves as a data instance sampled from the Stiefel manifold. Then, we propose to estimate the group mean of harmonic waves which is expected to have the shortest geodesic distance to all individual instances on the manifold. As demonstrated in [11], the geometric median is more robust to outliers in constructing group mean, and hence we adopt the ℓ_1-norm geodesic distance in our manifold optimization. The outcome of our manifold optimization is a set of orthonormal vectors located at the geometric median location of the Stiefel manifold, which is considered as the common harmonic waves learned from the brain network population. Since each harmonic wave exhibits the unique self-organized oscillation patterns across the brain network, the learned common harmonic waves provide a new window to explore the propagation of neuropathological burdens across brain networks in the progression of Alzheimer's disease (AD). We evaluate the effectiveness and robustness of our manifold learning method on synthetic data and neuroimaging data from ADNI database. Compared to the conventional approach [12] using network averaging method on Euclidian space, we have achieved enhanced statistical power and replicability in test/retest experiments using the learned common harmonic waves.

2 Method

Suppose we have m individual networks. Each brain network is encoded in a graph $\mathcal{G} = (V, \mathcal{E}, W)$, where $V = \{v_i | i \in 1, \cdots, n\}$ represents the node set with n nodes associated with anatomic regions and $\mathcal{E} = \{e_{ij} | (v_i, v_i) \in V \times V\}$ is the set of all possible links. Let $W \in \mathbb{R}^{n \times n}$ be a weighted adjacency matrix, where each element w_{ij} in W measures the strength of connectivity between two regions. As shown in the top of Fig. 1, conventional methods usually average all the adjacency matrices $\{W_s | s = 1, 2, \cdots, m\}$ of the individual brain networks on the Euclidean space to estimate the common network. As we will explain in Fig. 3, applying Euclidean operation to the adjacency matrix directly will break down the intrinsic data geometry since graph is not a regular data structure in the Euclidean space. Since each brain network is governed by its own harmonic waves, learning the common harmonic waves from individual harmonic waves in an irregular data structure requires special manifold algebra as demonstrated in the bottom of Fig. 1.

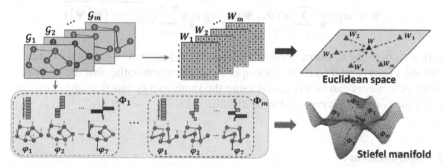

Fig. 1. Conventional methods (top) often consider each brain network as an adjacency matrix and then apply the matrix averaging method on Euclidian space. Our manifold learning method (bottom) represents each brain network as individual harmonic waves, which fully respects the irregular graph data structure, then discovers common harmonic waves on the Stiefel manifold. (Color figure online)

2.1 Find Common Harmonic Waves by Learning on Stiefel Manifold

Calculation of Individual Harmonic Waves. Given the adjacency matrix W of an individual network, its symmetric graph Laplacian matrix L can be calculated by $L = D - W$, where D is a diagonal matrix with $D_{ii} = \sum_{j=1}^{n} w_{ij}$ denoted the degree matrix of the graph. Since L is symmetric, we calculate the individual harmonic waves Φ by solving the eigenvalue problem $L\Phi = \Lambda\Phi$ with $\Lambda = diag(\lambda_1, \lambda_2, \cdots, \lambda_n)$ being the corresponding eigenvalues of L. Without loss of generality, each eigenvector in Φ can be sorted column by column, in increasing order of eigenvalues. As the eigenvalue increases, the corresponding eigenvector exhibits higher frequency patterns (fast and localized oscillation patterns) across the brain network (grey box at the bottom of Fig. 1). However, since the harmonic waves associated with high frequency (larger eigenvalues) are more sensitive to the possible noise, we only consider the first $p(p \leq n)$ harmonic waves in each Φ. At last, the individual harmonic waves of all subjects are represented as $\Phi_s \in \mathbb{R}^{n \times p}, s = 1, 2, \cdots, m$.

Estimation of Common Harmonic Waves. Given m individual harmonic waves $\{\Phi_1, \Phi_2, \cdots, \Phi_m\}$, since each individual harmonic waves $\Phi_s \in \mathcal{V}(n, p)$ is a $n \times p$ orthonormal matrix, it can be regarded as a point sitting on Stiefel manifold $\mathcal{V}(n, p)$, one of well-studied space, which is generally defined as a set of ordered orthonormal p-frames of vectors in $\mathbb{R}^n$. It is reasonable to reckon that the latent common harmonic waves located at the manifold mean which has the shortest geodesic distances to all individual harmonic waves $\{\Phi_s\}$. In this regard, we adopt a common robust estimator of centrality on Stiefel manifold, geometric median, to estimate common harmonic waves from all individual harmonic waves (red arrow at the bottom of Fig. 1). Specifically, we extend the notion of the geometric median in Euclidean space to Stiefel manifold space by minimizing:

$$\Psi = \arg\min_{\Psi} \sum_{s=1}^{m} d(\Phi_s, \Psi) = \arg\min_{\Psi} \sum_{s=1}^{m} \sqrt{\left(p - tr(\Phi_s^T \Psi)\right)} \tag{1}$$

where $d(\cdot, \cdot)$ is the ℓ_1-norm geodesic distance [13] between two points on the Stiefel manifold $\mathcal{V}(n, p)$ and $tr(\cdot)$ is the trace operation. It is worth noting that the Fréchet mean of harmonic waves can be estimated using the same energy function above except that the distance metric d is replaced with $d^2(\cdot, \cdot)$.

2.2 Optimization

In general, our optimization falls into the classic problem of solving geometric median on the Stiefel manifold which can be efficiently solved using the Weiszfeld algorithm [14]. Specifically, we alternately perform the following two steps until converge:

(1) From manifold to the tangent plane. Suppose $\Psi^{(k)}$ is the current (k^{th} iteration) estimation of the geometric median. We calculate the gradient $\nabla_{\Psi^{(k)}} F \in \mathcal{T}_{\Psi^{(k)}}$ of energy function $F = d(\Phi_s, \Psi^{(k)}) = \sqrt{p - tr(\Phi_s^T \Psi^{(k)})}$ at point $\Psi^{(k)}$ on Stiefel manifold, where $\mathcal{T}_{\Psi^{(k)}}$ is the tangent space at $\Psi^{(k)}$ (the grey flat plane in Fig. 2(a)), which consists of a set of tangents $\{\Delta\}$ such that $(\Psi^{(k)})^T \Delta = 0$. Thus, the gradient can be obtained by [15] $\nabla_{\Psi^{(k)}} F = (\Psi^{(k)} \Phi_s^T \Psi^{(k)} - \Phi_s) / \sqrt{p - tr(\Phi_s^T \Psi^{(k)})}$, which are denoted by the black arrows in Fig. 2(a). Finally, the mean tangent $\Delta \Psi^{(k+1)} \in \mathcal{T}_{\Psi^{(k)}}$ (purple triangle on the tangent plane $\mathcal{T}_{\Psi^{(k)}}$ in Fig. 2(a)) can be calculated by:

$$\Delta \Psi^{(k+1)} = -\sum_{s=1}^{m} \nabla_{\Psi^{(k)}} F = -\sum_{s=1}^{m} \frac{\Psi^{(k)} \Phi_s^T \Psi^{(k)} - \Phi_s}{\sqrt{p - tr(\Phi_s^T \Psi^{(k)})}} \tag{2}$$

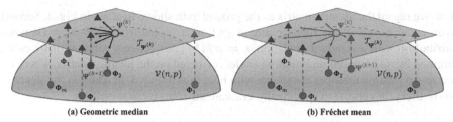

(a) Geometric median   (b) Fréchet mean

Fig. 2. Illustration for the optimization of common harmonic waves Ψ on Stiefel manifold by using geometric median (a) and Fréchet mean (b). Individual harmonics (blue circle) and an outlier (green circle) are located on the Stiefel manifold $\mathcal{V}(n, p)$ (blue hemisphere). Each individual harmonics is projected to a corresponding point (grey triangle) in the tangent space $\mathcal{T}_{\Psi^{(k)}}$ (grey flat plane) at k^{th} estimated geometric median $\Psi^{(k)}$ (purple hollow circle). The mean tangent of geometric median $\Delta\Psi^{(k+1)}$ (purple triangle) is calculated based on all gradient direction $\nabla_{\Psi^{(k)}}F$ (black arrow). Finally, the new geometric median $\Psi^{(k+1)}$ (purple circle) is estimated by mapping the mean tangent back to the Stiefel manifold. The geometric median is more robust to outliers than Fréchet mean since it penalizes the tangent vector based on the geodesic distance to the current estimation of mean location on the manifold. (Color figure online)

As demonstrated in [14], $\Delta\Psi^{(k+1)}$ specifies the direction from the current $\Psi^{(k)}$ to the latent mean on the manifold. It is worth noting that the estimation of a mean tangent for Fréchet mean is the same expect without the denominator in Eq. (2). As compared in Fig. 2(a) and (b), our geometric median penalizes the outlier tangent vectors from the outliers since they usually have a larger distance to the current mean location on the manifold. As a result, our geometric median (purple triangles and circles in Fig. 2(a)) is more robust to outliers than Fréchet mean (red triangles and circles in Fig. 2(b)).

(2) From tangent plane back to the manifold. We map the mean tangent $\Delta\Psi^{(k+1)}$ back to the Stiefel manifold to obtain the new estimation of the geometric median as $\Psi^{(k+1)} = exp_{\Psi^{(k)}}(\Delta\Psi^{(k+1)})$ (purple circle in Fig. 2(a)) by an exponential mapping operation [16].

By iteratively estimating the optimal descent direction and mapping it back to the manifold, we can obtain the optimal geometric median Ψ (common harmonic waves).

3   Experiments

In the following experiments, we evaluate the performance of the common harmonic waves associated with the geometric median Ψ_g optimized by our Stiefel manifold learning method, Fréchet mean Ψ_f optimized by minimizing the sum-of-squared distances on Stiefel manifold [17], and the pseudo manifold mean Ψ_p calculated by first averaging the adjacency matrices and then applying SVD on the Laplacian matrix derived from the average adjacency matrix [12].

3.1   Evaluate the Accuracy and Robustness on Synthetic Dataset

Here, we test the performance of our method by a set of 3D orthonormal rotation matrices (individual harmonic waves). We generate a set of random rotation matrices as follows.

First, we regard the identity matrix as the ground truth shown in green in Fig. 3. Second, given rotation axis u, the rotation angles $\{\theta_i\}$ are sampled from zero-mean Gaussian distribution with a standard deviation $\sigma = \pi/15$. Third, twenty rotation matrices are obtained by rotation axis and rotation angles, centered on the identity matrix, where the first seven rotation matrices are shown with blue axes in Fig. 3. In addition, we generate two outliers (in yellow) to specifically evaluate the robustness to outliers.

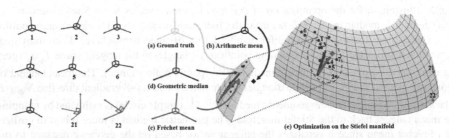

Fig. 3. Comparison of arithmetic mean, Fréchet mean, and geometric median across individual orthonormal matrices. Left three columns: 7 rotation matrices (blue) generated by the different rotation of identity matrix (a) and 2 outliers (yellow). Middle: the ground truth (a), arithmetic mean (b), Fréchet mean (c), and geometric median (d). Right: all rotation matrices and optimization process on the Stiefel manifold (e). (Color figure online)

Since we do not have the adjacency matrices, we apply arithmetic mean Ψ_a which uses simple averaging operation defined in the Euclidean space, geometric median Ψ_g and Fréchet mean Ψ_f to estimate the common rotation matrix (common harmonic waves) from in total 22 random rotation matrices, as shown in Fig. 3(b), (c) and (d), respectively. It is clear that (1) the arithmetic mean is out of manifold (non-orthogonal matrix), as three axes are not perpendicular to each other; (2) our iterative manifold optimization can quickly converge to the latent manifold mean; (3) manifold means (Fréchet mean Ψ_f and geometric median Ψ_g) by Stiefel manifold learning method are more accurate than the arithmetic mean Ψ_a; and (4) our geometric median is more robust to outlier issue than the Fréchet mean, where the convergence trajectory of Ψ_g and Ψ_f are displayed in purple and red, respectively in Fig. 3(e).

3.2 Evaluate the Statistic Power on ADNI Database

We select in total of 94 subjects from the ADNI database to learn the common harmonic waves. Each subject has T1-weighted MRI and DWI (diffusion-weighted imaging) images. The demographic information is shown in Table 1. We first parcellate the cortical surface into 148 cortical regions and then apply fiber tractography [18] to construct a 148 × 148 structural brain network. Furthermore, we estimate the pseudo manifold mean Ψ_p, Fréchet mean Ψ_f and geometric median Ψ_g based on these 94 brain networks. In addition, we select another 47 Alzheimer's Disease (AD) subjects and 50 Cognitive Normal (CN) subjects from ADNI data. For each subject, we also parcellate its T1-weighted image into 148 regions and then calculate the mean cortical thickness and SUVR (standard uptake value ratio) of amyloid burden for each region, respectively. In our experiments, we adopt the following calculation procedure to obtain harmonic-specific energy and total harmonic energy. For each common harmonic wave ψ_h (h^{th} column vector in Ψ), the harmonic power coefficient of ψ_h is estimated by $\alpha_h = f, \psi_h$, where f is the column vector of observed regional AD biomarker values (cortical thickness or amyloid) of the individual subject. Then, the corresponding harmonic-specific energy of ψ_h and the total harmonic energy are obtained by $E_h = |\alpha_h|^2$ and $E_{total} = \sum_{h=1}^{p} E_h$, respectively.

Table 1. Demographic information of training data in ADNI database.

Gender	Number	Range of age	Average age	CN	SMC	EMCI	LMCI	AD
Male	47	55.0–90.3	74.3	7	5	16	8	11
Female	47	55.6–87.8	73.0	10	13	8	8	8
Total	94	55.0–90.3	73.7	17	18	24	16	19

Evaluation of the Replicability. We evaluate the replicability of common harmonic waves by the resample test. For each common harmonic wave estimation method, we apply the following resample procedure for 100 times: (1) randomly sample 70 networks from 94 brain networks; (2) continue to sample another two sets of networks from the remaining subjects separately, each with 5 networks. (3) form two paired cohorts by combining the networks sampled in step 1 and 2. Then, we run all methods on two databases independently. Since two paired cohorts only have 6.7% differences, the replicability can be evaluated by examining the significant difference at each element in the harmonic waves via the paired t-test ($p < 0.05$). Less number of significant elements means better replicability. We find that Stiefel manifold mean, regardless of Fréchet mean (86% fewer elements showing difference than Ψ_p) or geometric median (87% fewer than Ψ_p), achieves more stable results than pseudo manifold mean Ψ_p.

Association between the Oscillation Patterns in Harmonic Waves and Neurodegenerative process. In this experiment, we are interested to investigate whether the common harmonic waves underline the neurodegenerative process. Given the common harmonic waves, we repeat the following steps for 50 times: (1) randomly select 30 out of 47 AD subjects and 30 out of 50 CN subjects as training data and form the amyloid vector f; (2) identify the harmonic power difference α_h between CN and AD for each harmonic wave ψ_h; (3) calculate positive power $\alpha_h^+ = f, \psi_h^+$ and negative power $\alpha_h^- = |f, \psi_h^-|$ of the remaining 37 subjects (testing data), where ψ_h^+ and ψ_h^- present the positive and negative segments in each ψ_h; (4) apply the t-test to detect the statistical CN vs AD difference of $|\alpha_h^+ - \alpha_h^-|$ on each identified significant harmonic wave.

As shown in Fig. 4(a), pseudo mean Ψ_p, Fréchet mean Ψ_f, and geometric median Ψ_g find average 10.88, 9.76, and 9.40 harmonic waves showing significant power difference on amyloid in step (2). Next, we hypothesize that the difference (kinetic potentials due to the oscillations in harmonic waves) between a_h^+ and a_h^- is the factor leading to such significance. As shown in the last column in Fig. 4(a), 70% of the significances identified on the geometric median Ψ_g follow such hypothesis as average 6.52 harmonic waves exhibit statistical significance $(p < 10^{-3})$ in step (4). The results in Fig. 4(b) and (c) further support our hypothesis of kinetic potential. Specifically, we display the oscillation mapping of one significant harmonic wave on the cortical surface in the left of Fig. 4(b), besides the underlying cortical mapping of the elementwise multiplication $\psi. * f$. It is apparent that two cortical mappings have a strong resemblance, which is also supported by the statistical significance between α^+ and a^- $(p < 10^{-5})$. Vice versa, such resemblance is not presented in the non-significant harmonic wave (Fig. 4(c)), where no significance has been detected between α^+ and a^- $(p = 0.27)$.

(a) Statistics	Har. Power	+/- Power
Pseudo mean Ψ_p	10.88 ± 3.12	3.52 ± 1.80
Fréchet mean Ψ_f	9.76 ± 2.25	5.50 ± 1.42
Geo. median Ψ_g	9.40 ± 2.65	6.52 ± 1.57

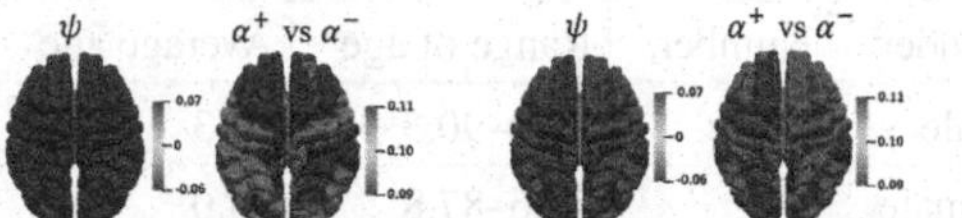

(b) Oscillation pattern vs kinetic potential pattern on significant harmonic wave   (c) Oscillation pattern vs kinetic potential pattern on non-significant harmonic wave

Fig. 4. Statistics results of the association between the oscillation patterns in harmonic waves and the neurodegeneration process. Please see the above text for more information.

Statistical Analyses on Activated Harmonic Energy in Neurodegeneration. Here, we explore the frequency-wise alterations on the cortical thickness between AD and CN through using the learned common harmonic waves estimated by geometric median Ψ_g. First, we measure the total harmonic energy of cortical thickness for each subject and plot the statistics (mean and standard deviation) for AD and CN groups separately in Fig. 5(a), where the AD group (13.13 ± 3.39) holds significantly lower $(p < 10^{-4})$ total harmonic energy than the CN group (16.23 ± 3.39). Furthermore, we plot the distribution of total harmonic energy of cortical thickness in Fig. 5(b). These results demonstrate that neurodegenerations occurred in AD subjects might result in a reduced metabolism level and brain activity. Second, we examine the energy difference for each harmonic wave, where the mean harmonic-specific energy of cortical thickness for AD and CN are showed in the outer and inner rings in Fig. 5(c). The harmonic waves exhibiting significant energy difference $(p < 0.01)$ are tagged with red '*'. The magnitude of the difference at each common harmonic wave is displayed in Fig. 5(d).

Statistical Analyses on Activated Harmonic Energy in Neuropathology. Similarly, we calculate the total harmonic energy of amyloid level for each subject and plot the results in Fig. 5(e) and (f), where the AD group (3.95 ± 1.61) holds significantly higher $(p < 10^{-4})$ total energy than the CN group (2.77 ± 1.13). Then, we show the energy difference of each harmonic wave in Fig. 5(g) and (h), where there are a total of nine harmonic waves exhibiting significant difference $(p < 0.01)$ between CN and AD, in terms of harmonic energy of amyloid burden. These results support the evidence that aggregation of amyloid peptides plays an important role in the AD progression.

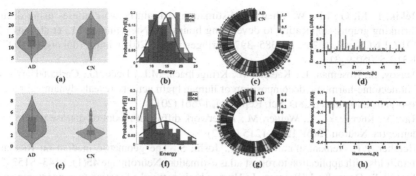

Fig. 5. Harmonic energy alterations between AD and CN identified using the learned common harmonic waves Ψ_g. Top: Result of statistical testing for cortical thickness. (a)–(b): Significant difference of total harmonic energy between AD and CN. (c): Harmonic waves exhibiting significant energy differences between AD and CN cohorts. (d): The plot of groupwise energy difference of each harmonic wave. Bottom: Result of statistical testing on amyloid burden (e–h). (Color figure online)

4   Conclusions

We present a novel Stiefel manifold optimization method to estimate common harmonic waves, which resides on the geometric median location on the manifold with the shortest geodesic distance to all individual harmonic waves. Enhanced statistical power and replicability have been observed in analyzing the propagation of AD-related pathological burdens using our common harmonic waves, compared to existing approaches that simply use arithmetic averaging. In the future, we will apply our learning-based method of common harmonic waves to other neuro-diseases such as frontotemporal dementia which also shows network dysfunction symptoms.

References

1. Brier, M.R., Thomas, J.B., Ances, B.M.: Network dysfunction in Alzheimer's disease: refining the disconnection hypothesis. Brain Connect. **4**(5), 299–311 (2014)
2. Palop, J.J., Chin, J., Mucke, L.: A network dysfunction perspective on neurodegenerative diseases. Nature **443**(7113), 768–773 (2006)
3. Dickerson, B.C., Sperling, R.A.: Large-scale functional brain network abnormalities in Alzheimer's disease: insights from functional neuroimaging. Behav. Neurol. **21**(1–2), 63–75 (2009)
4. Sporns, O.: Structure and function of complex brain networks. Dial. Clin. Neurosci. **15**(3), 247 (2013)
5. Seeley, W.W., Crawford, R.K., Zhou, J., Miller, B.L., Greicius, M.D.: Neurodegenerative diseases target large-scale human brain networks. Neuron **62**(1), 42 (2009)
6. Rubinov, M., Sporns, O.: Complex network measures of brain connectivity: uses and interpretations. NeuroImage **52**(3), 1059–1069 (2010)
7. Atasoy, S., Donnelly, I., Pearson, J.: Human brain networks function in connectome-specific harmonic waves. Nat. Commun. **7**(1), 10340 (2016)

8. Rekik, I., Li, G., Lin, W., Shen, D.: Estimation of brain network atlases using diffusive-shrinking graphs: application to developing brains. In: Niethammer, M., et al. (eds.) IPMI 2017. LNCS, vol. 10265, pp. 385–397. Springer, Cham (2017). https://doi.org/10.1007/978-3-319-59050-9_31

9. Atasoy, S., Roseman, L., Kaelen, M., Kringelbach, M.L., Deco, G., Carhart-Harris, R.L.: Connectome-harmonic decomposition of human brain activity reveals dynamical repertoire re-organization under LSD. Sci. Rep. **7**(1), 17661 (2017)

10. Raj, A., Kuceyeski, A., Weiner, M.: A network diffusion model of disease progression in dementia. Neuron **73**(6), 1204–1215 (2012)

11. Fletcher, P.T., Venkatasubramanian, S., Joshi, S.: The geometric median on Riemannian manifolds with application to robust atlas estimation. NeuroImage **45**(1), S143–S152 (2009)

12. Atasoy, S., Donnelly, I., Pearson, J.: Human brain networks function in connectome-specific harmonic waves. Nat. Commun. **7**, 10340 (2016)

13. Chikuse, Y.: Statistics on Special Manifolds. Springer, New York (2012). https://doi.org/10.1007/978-0-387-21540-2

14. Aftab, K., Hartley, R., Trumpf, J.: Generalized weiszfeld algorithms for lq optimization. IEEE Trans. Pattern Anal. Mach. Intell. **37**(4), 728–745 (2014)

15. Edelman, A., Arias, T.A., Smith, S.T.: The geometry of algorithms with orthogonality constraints. SIAM J. Matrix Anal. Appl. **20**(2), 303–353 (1998)

16. Cetingul, H.E., Vidal, R.: Intrinsic mean shift for clustering on Stiefel and Grassmann manifolds. In: 2009 IEEE Conference on Computer Vision and Pattern Recognition, pp. 1896–1902. IEEE (2009)

17. Fletcher, P.T., Lu, C., Joshi, S.: Statistics of shape via principal geodesic analysis on Lie groups. In: 2003 IEEE Computer Society Conference on Computer Vision and Pattern Recognition, 2003. Proceedings, p. I. IEEE (2003)

18. Destrieux, C., Fischl, B., Dale, A., Halgren, E.: Automatic parcellation of human cortical gyri and sulci using standard anatomical nomenclature. Neuroimage **53**(1), 1–15 (2010)

Neural Architecture Search for Optimization of Spatial-Temporal Brain Network Decomposition

Qing Li[1,2] ⓘ, Wei Zhang[3], Jinglei Lv[4], Xia Wu[1,2(✉)], and Tianming Liu[3]

[1] School of Artificial Intelligence, Beijing Normal University, Beijing, China
wuxia@bnu.edu.cn
[2] Engineering Research Center of Intelligent Technology and Educational Application, Ministry of Education, Beijing, China
[3] Department of Computer Science and Bioimaging Research Center,
The University of Georgia, Athens, GA, USA
[4] Department of Biomedical Engineering, University of Melbourne, Parkville, VIC, Australia

Abstract. Using neural networks to explore spatial patterns and temporal dynamics of human brain activities has been an important yet challenging problem because it is hard to manually design the most optimal neural networks. There have been several promising deep learning methods that can decompose neuro-scientifically meaningful spatial-temporal patterns from 4D fMRI data, e.g., the deep sparse recurrent auto-encoder (DSRAE). However, those previous studies still depend on hand-crafted neural network structures and hyperparameters, which are not optimal in various senses. In this paper, we employ evolutionary algorithms to optimize such DSRAE neural networks by minimizing the expected loss of the generated architectures on data reconstruction via the neural architecture search (NAS) framework, named NAS-DSRAE. The optimized NAS-DSRAE is evaluated by the publicly available human connectome project (HCP) fMRI datasets and our promising results showed that NAS-DSRAE has sufficient generalizability to model the spatial-temporal features and is better than the hand-crafted model. To our best knowledge, the proposed NAS-DSRAE is among the earliest NAS models that can extract connectome-scale meaningful spatial-temporal brain networks from 4D fMRI data.

Keywords: Neural architecture search · Recurrent neural network · Auto-encoder

1 Introduction

The brain function is comprised with complex neural processes that are spatially distributed and temporally dynamic. Therefore, it is desirable to model spatial and temporal

---

Electronic supplementary material The online version of this chapter (https://doi.org/10.1007/978-3-030-59728-3_37) contains supplementary material, which is available to authorized users.

© Springer Nature Switzerland AG 2020
A. L. Martel et al. (Eds.): MICCAI 2020, LNCS 12267, pp. 377–386, 2020.
https://doi.org/10.1007/978-3-030-59728-3_37

information at the same time when analyzing 4D functional Magnetic Resonance Imaging (fMRI) data to explore and understand brain functions [1]. For this purpose, a variety of deep learning methods have been recently proposed on fMRI data, such as deep belief network (DBN) [2], convolutional neural network (CNN) [3], and recurrent neural network (RNN) [4]. However, these previous studies focus on either spatial or temporal modeling of fMRI data separately and they rarely model both spatial and temporal domains simultaneously, thus significantly limiting the scope and ability of modeling the spatial-temporal variation patterns of functional brain networks. More recently, to characterize and analyze the unified complex spatial-temporal functional states of human brain with 4D fMRI data, a deep sparse recurrent auto-encoder (DSRAE) has been proposed in the literature to apply on fMRI data, and promising results were reported [9].

However, existing current deep learning models for fMRI data, including the above-mentioned DSRAE, are limited as their neural network architectures are hand-crafted, and they heavily rely on the human expertise in neural network and prior knowledge of specific tasks, which are not optimal in various senses such as structures and hyperparameters. For instance, despite the fact that these methods, such as DSRAE, can achieve meaningful results, they are still limited in only searching possible models from some empirically designed structures or hyperparameters. Essentially, the lack of optimal neural network architecture will fundamentally limit the potential of using deep learning for fMRI data representation, e.g., mapping spatial-temporal brain networks, given that the dimensions and characteristics of those meaningful spatial-temporal network patterns are unknown in advance. Therefore, it is much desirable to optimize the neural network architectures with the hyperparameter optimization so that they can potentially match the true spatial-temporal structures embedded in 4D fMRI data with artificial neural networks. Along this direction, neural architecture search (NAS) [5], the process of automating neural network architecture engineering, offers a promising framework for deep learning model optimization over the hand-crafted models and thus it is adopted in this paper to optimize DSRAE for spatial-temporal decomposition of functional brain networks from 4D fMRI data.

NAS is attracting increasing attention in automating machine learning and models derived by NAS have shown promising performance on image classification, keyword spotting, and facial recognition [6]. For example, the authors in [5] used reinforce policy gradient algorithm to optimize RNN to sequentially sample a string of images and outperformed peer methods. Inspired by pervious NAS frameworks [6, 7] and aiming to better map the spatial-temporal features of 4D fMRI and understand brain networks, we adopted the light-weighted evolutionary algorithm [7, 8] as the optimization engine and designed a novel NAS framework based on the DSRAE model [9], named NAS-DSRAE. The proposed framework was applied on the joint representation and decomposition of spatial-temporal brain networks from 4D fMRI data. To our best knowledge, the proposed NAS-DSRAE framework is among the earliest efforts in adopting NAS strategy for a unified spatial-temporal representation of 4D fMRI data in the literature. To evaluate the performance of our framework, both spatial and temporal validation experiments were performed on tfMRI datasets from human connectome project (HCP). Our experiment results showed that the NAS-DSRAE framework can learn connectome-scale meaningful spatial-temporal brain networks and exhibit substantial improvements over the original DSRAE.

2   Materials and Methods

2.1   Overview

Figure 1 illustrates an overview of the NAS-DSRAE framework. In general, the aim of the work is to optimize neural network architecture of the original DSRAE model for spatial-temporal decomposition of brain networks from fMRI data. In Sect. 2.2, data processing was performed on individual brain space. With the pre-processed fMRI data, the NAS (Sect. 2.3) framework was designed and applied on the DSRAE model.

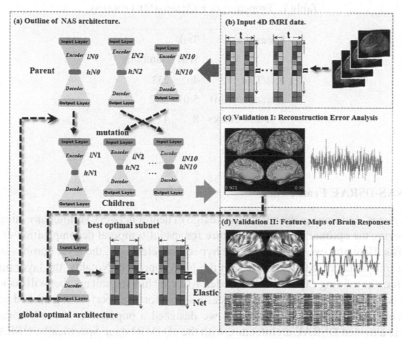

Fig. 1. Illustration of NAS-DSRAE framework and the two validation experiments. (a) The outline of NAS- DSRAE framework, in which the best model is optimized by the global optimal architecture based on the mutation and search procedure. (b) The input of NAS-DSRAE is the 4D fMRI data, which is a series of 3D brain volumes acquired in each task session. (c) Validation I: the NAS optimized objective, which is the signal reconstruction error based on Pearson correlation between reconstructed output and original input. (d) Validation II: spatial maps, derived from latent layer time series via Elastic Net, the time series, and the correlation matrix between the obtained networks and original volumes.

2.2 Experimental Data and Preprocessing

In this paper, the publicly available HCP (https://db.humanconnectome.org) grayordinate tfMRI data [10] were used for algorithmic development and validation. In total, 200 healthy adult participants out of 791 subjects that participated in all seven HCP tasks were randomly selected and used in this study. The HCP grayordinate data models the gray matter as combined cortical surface vertices and subcortical voxels across subjects in the standard MNI space. The preprocessing steps of the fMRI dataset include spatial smoothing, temporal filtering, nuisance regression, and motion censoring. The task design information is shown in Table 1. In working memory (WM) task, a version of the N-back task was used to assess WM capability; in gambling task, participants were required to play card guessing games in which they needed to guess the number on a card, and won money if hit, or lost money if missed.

Table 1. Properties of HCP task-fMRI datasets.

Parameters	Task	
	WM	Gambling
# of TRs	405	253
Duration (Min)	5:01	3:12
# of task blocks	8	4

2.3 NAS-DSRAE Framework

In this paper, we focus on the automatic design of neural network architecture, aiming at discovering the optimal neural architecture for spatial-temporal decomposition of brain networks. Here, the two most important hyperparameters, i.e., the layer number and the hidden unit number, are optimized with the NAS approach. Notably, the layer number will affect the training expense of the model, while the hidden unit number will decide the model is over-fitting or not. To automatically search for high-performing unified spatial-temporal neural network architectures, we designed a population of models, each of which is a trained DSRAE architecture with the 4D fMRI data. Specifically, DSRAE, as a novel LSTM-based deep unsupervised sequential neural network framework [9], possessed remarkable capability of modeling connectome-scale functional brain networks based on fMRI data. The DSRAE is composed of an encoder and a decoder: the encoder part encodes the input into high-level features and is comprised of an input layer, a fully connected layer (which could retain the most spatial information), and recurrent layers (which could capture the temporal information across the time series); the decoder part reconstructs the input and is comprised of recurrent layers, a fully connected layer, and an output layer.

Here, the NAS-DSRAE framework is designed based on the particle swarm optimization (PSO) [8, 11] to optimize the layer number and hidden unit number of encoder part; and the decoder part is correspondingly trained with the encoder part. Firstly, for the initialization step, ten DSRAE models are generated with random depth and width, and then the best initialized model, evaluated by the mean square error (MSE) loss, is recorded as the best model. Secondly, during each evolutionary iteration, we take the mutation of the initialized parent to modify copy as the child with the different layer numbers and hidden unit numbers. After the child model has been created, it is trained and evaluated on the validation dataset with MSE and compared with the parent model regarding MSE loss. The better one then becomes alive, i.e., free to act as a parent and undergo reproduction.

Mathematically, the optimization objective of NAS-DSRAE framework during the training process is made up of three components, shown as follows:

$$J(W, b) = MSE(x\|\hat{x}) + \Omega_1 \|O_{Full}\| + \Omega_2 \|W_{Full}\|^2 \tag{1}$$

where x and $\hat{x}$ are the input and output of the DSRAE model. The first term is the overall error cost based on the MSE loss function. The last two terms in Eq. (1) are the sparsity penalties on the output O_{Full} and the weight matrix W_{Full} of each layer.

Based on the procedures above, the NAS-DSRAE framework based on the evolutionary algorithm [7] is summarized as follows:

Algorithm1. Neural Architecture Search

Input: μ, iterations // μ is the number of candidate solutions (models)
Output: S_{best} // the best solution (model)
Population ⟵ InitializeParent(μ) // initialize the original models
Parent. loss ⟵ EvaluatePopulation(*Parent. strategy*) // evaluate the models with MSE
S_{best}, S_{best_iter} ⟵ GetBest(*Population*, μ) // record the best initialized model
While the maximum number of iterations unreached
　For $i = 0$ to μ
　　Parent ⟵ GetParent(*Population*, i) // choose the i-th model as the Parent
　　Child.strategy ⟵ Mutate(*Parent. strategy*) // mutate Parent for new Child model based
on S_{best} and S_{best_iter}
　　Child.loss ⟵ EvaluatePopulation(*Child. strategy*)//evaluated Child model with MSE
　　S_{best} ⟵ GetBest(*Population*, 2) // find the better DSRAE model compared with Parent
and replace the pervious Parent
　End
　S_{best_iter} ⟵ GetBest(*Population*, μ) // obtain the best iteration model
End
S_{best} ⟵ GetBest(*Population*, μ) // obtain the best DSRAE model out of iterations
Return(S_{best})

With the NAS-DSRAE framework, we can obtain the optimal DSRAE model. Then based on the encoding time series (output of encoder), the corresponding spatial feature maps are derived by the Elastic Net [12] based on such encoding time series:

$$\hat{\beta} = \arg\min_{\beta} \|y - X\beta\|^2 + \lambda_2 \|\beta\|^2 + \lambda_1 \|\beta\|_1 \tag{2}$$

where X is the predictor matrix, y is the response vector, λ_1 and λ_2 are the parameters for L1- regularization and L2- regularization, respectively. Here, the L1 ratio is empirically set as 0.005.

The NAS-DSRAE framework was trained on 200 HCP subjects' tfMRI dataset with WM task and gambling task. For both tasks, all the parameters are the same: the number of learning subnets (models) is set as 10, the layer number of encoder procedure (including the dense layer and recurrent layers) is between 2 to 7, the first hidden unit number is between 100 to 200, the learning rate is set as 0.01, the epoch is set as 5, the batch size is set as 1 due to the memory limitation. Notably, during the training of NAS-DSRAE, we use the L1 - regularization (10e−7) and L2 - regularization (10e−4) empirically at the same time to be consistent with the parameters used in [9]. In this paper, we implemented the NAS-DSRAE model with Keras, and ran on a GPU of Quadro K600.

3   Results

We used 200 randomly selected subjects of two datasets, including WM and gambling tfMRI data from HCP, for training the NAS-DSRAE models. Testing results showed good performance with NAS optimized DSRAE model for stimulus-evoked brain networks identification, demonstrating that our NAS-DSRAE framework is generic and not limited to specific cognitive tasks.

3.1   NAS-DSRAE Reconstruction Error Analysis

The goal of the NAS-DSRAE framework is to minimize the MSE loss between the reconstruction fMRI signals and the original fMRI signals, that is, the reconstruction error could be a good validation measure. To quantitatively evaluate and validate the signal reconstruction by NAS-DSRAE, here we used one randomly selected subject in WM task as an example to calculate the Pearson correlation coefficients (PCCs) between original fMRI signals and reconstructed signals. The reconstruction results in both spatial and temporal dimension are illustrated in Fig. 2, which shows good reconstruction accuracy. That is, all the correlations are larger than 0.92. We achieved similar results and conclusion in the gambling task, which is summarized in supplemental Fig. 1. These high correlations between the original signals and reconstructed signals indicate that our NAS-DSRAE can truly optimize the deep learning model and encode good spatial-temporal representations of brain networks.

3.2   Interpreting Feature Maps of Brain Responses via NAS-DSRAE

To further evaluate the effectiveness of our NAS-DSRAE framework, we compared the derived task-related feature maps (chosen by PCC) via NAS-DSRAE with the benchmark maps (derived via Elastic Net based on the temporal task design). For WM task, we obtained 81 networks (derived from the width of recurrent layer of the most optimal model). For gambling task, we obtained 126 networks (for the specific architectures of 10 learned models, please see Table 2 and supplemental Table 1). Here, we take WM task as an example. Three stimuli were embedded in WM task, including 0-back memory, 2-back memory, and cue period. As shown in Fig. 3a, the maps of the cue period related benchmark network and NAS-DSRAE-derived result have a high PCC of 0.742. The highest PCC between network #30 (the most cue-related network chosen by PCC)

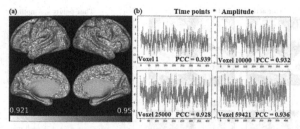

Fig. 2. Performance of NAS-DSRAE in reconstructing the WM task fMRI signals. (a) The PCCs between the reconstructed signals by NAS-DSRAE and the original signals in spatial dimension. (b) Temporal fluctuation comparison of the reconstructed voxels and original voxels. Blue curves are the reconstruction time series. Orange curves are the time series of original fMRI data. (Color figure online)

and the cue-period ground truth is 0.627, which is much higher than that in the original DSRAE with 0.538 [9]. This result shows the effectiveness of NAS-DSRAE framework, i.e., the NAS can truly optimize the corresponding deep learning model to derive more meaningful brain networks. Though the 0-back and 2-back stimuli have very similar activation maps and they are hard to be classified [10], we still obtain the 0-back and 2-back task-specific spatial maps, as shown in Figs. 3b and 3c. Here, the 2-back related spatial map via NAS-DSRAE (network #45) is similar to that benchmark, with the PCC of 0.826. And the time series of network #77 is positively correlated with that of 2-back stimulus ground truth (PCC is 0.503). While the 0-back related map via NAS-DSRAE has the PCC of 0.811 with the benchmark in spatial, and the correlation is 0.433 in temporal dimension. That are both better than in [9], which shows the temporal PCCs with 0.426 for 2-back and 0.367 for 0-back stimuli.

Table 2. Learned architectures by NAS of WM task.

Encoder dense layer	Encoder recurrent layer	Decoder recurrent layer	Decoder dense layer
59421 → 142	142 → 69	69 → 142	142 → 59421
59421 → 176	176 → 92 → 48 → 24	24 → 48 → 92 → 176	176 → 59421
59421 → 183	183 → 154 → 130	130 → 154 → 183	183 → 59421
59421 → 191	191 → 39	39 → 191	191 → 59421
59421 → 111	111 → 81	81 → 111	111 → 59421
59421 → 166	166 → 125	125 → 166	166 → 59421
59421 → 253	253 → 96 → 36 → 13 → 12 → 12	12 → 12 → 13 → 36 → 96 → 253	253 → 59421
59421 → 135	135 → 12 → 12	12 → 12 → 135	135 → 59421
59421 → 289	289 → 18	18 → 289	289 → 59421
59421 → 111	111 → 32	32 → 111	111 → 59421

To evaluate the robustness of the NAS-DSRAE framework, we also validated it on the gambling task dataset and obtained promising accuracy in detecting corresponding

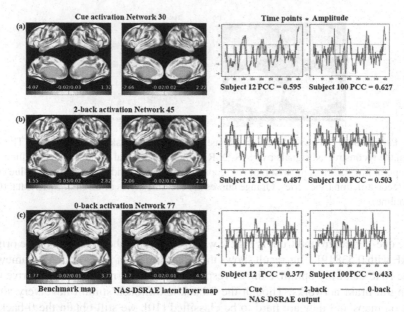

Fig. 3. Comparison between NAS-DSRAE and benchmark outputs of WM task. (a) The spatial benchmark activation map, the spatial activation map predicted by NAS-DSRAE, and corresponding temporal fluctuations and ground truth of cue stimulus. Here, we showed the comparison results of two randomly selected subjects. (b) The spatial activation maps and corresponding temporal fluctuations of 2-back stimulus. (c) The spatial activation maps and corresponding temporal fluctuations of 0-back stimulus.

networks (as shown in supplemental Fig. 2). Again, all of these results demonstrated the robustness of the NAS-DSRAE framework, since the optimized model can not only detect the subtle difference between the stimuli, but also worked well across tasks.

3.3   Decoding Brain States During Task Periods via NAS-DSRAE

To examine the efficiency of NAS-DSRAE in decoding brain states during task performance periods, we investigated the Pearson correlation of the input fMRI volumetric data and the learned feature networks via NAS optimized DSRAE to measure how well the NAS framework represents the original fMRI data. In the correlation matrix, each row represents a network, and each column represents the original volume. In Fig. 4, the learned networks of WM task are highly correlated with the stimulus with the high correlation value of 0.44, which is much higher than that in DSRAE [9] (with the PCC of 0.37, which was got based on the same hyperparameters in [9]). For results of gambling task, please see supplemental Fig. 3. This result, again, demonstrated that our NAS-DSRAE framework achieved true optimization over DSRAE model, which can reveal interesting patterns of spatial-temporal brain networks and their temporal dynamics better than state-of-the-art methods.

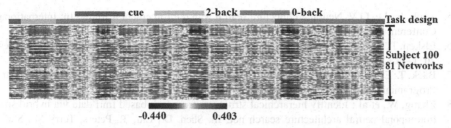

Fig. 4. The correlation matrix of the networks derived by NAS-DSRAE and the fMRI volumes for WM task.

4 Discussion and Conclusion

In this work, we designed a novel and effective NAS framework to optimize the hyperparameters of DSRAE model, i.e., the layer number and the hidden unit number, in order to identify and characterize connectome-scale spatial-temporal functional networks from 4D fMRI. We used the HCP WM and gambling tasks as our experiment testbed in this study and obtained promising results. To our best knowledge, the proposed NAS-DSRAE is among the earliest NAS-based unified spatial-temporal deep learning models that can search the optimal architecture to decompose large-scale brain networks from 4D fMRI data. By analyzing the feature maps of the brain responses, we validated that the NAS-DSRAE framework is efficient and robust across different cognitive tasks, which can not only decompose better networks and the corresponding temporal fluctuations, but also decode the original volumes with higher PCCs, by optimizing the layer number and the hidden unit number. In our future work, we will explore other kinds of NAS methods [6] and try to gain more neuroscientific insights of these models, e.g., how the optimized neural network architectures better match and represent real human brain networks. We will also test NAS-DSRAE framework on fMRI from disordered brains for its possibility of characterizing the spatial-temporal patterns of potentially disrupted brain networks.

Acknowledgment. This work was supported by the General Program of National Natural Science Foundation of China (Grant No. 61876021), and the program of China Scholarships Council (No. 201806040083). We thank the HCP projects for sharing their valuable fMRI datasets.

References

1. Logothetis, N.K.: What We Can Do and What We Cannot Do with fMRI. Nature **453**, 869–878 (2008)
2. Hu, X., et al.: Latent source mining in fMRI via restricted boltzmann machine. Hum. Brain Mapp. **39**, 2368–2380 (2018). https://doi.org/10.1002/hbm.24005
3. Zhao, Y., et al.: 4D Modeling of fMRI data via Spatio-Temporal Convolutional Neural Networks (ST-CNN). IEEE Trans. Cogn. Dev. Syst. 1–11 (2019). https://doi.org/10.1109/tcds.2019.2916916
4. Wang, H., et al.: Recognizing brain states using deep sparse recurrent neural network. IEEE Trans. Med. Imaging **38**, 1058–1068 (2018). https://doi.org/10.1109/TMI.2018.2877576

5. Zoph, B., Le, Q.V: Neural architecture search with reinforcement learning. In: International Conference on Learning Representations - ICLR2017, pp. 1–16 (2017)
6. Elsken, T., Metzen, J.H., Hutter, F.: Neural architecture search: a survey. J. Mach. Learn. Res. **20**, 1–21 (2019)
7. Bäck, T.: Evolutionary Algorithms in Theory and Practice: Evolution Strategies, Evolutionary Programming. Genetic Algorithms. Oxford University Press Inc., New York (1996)
8. Zhang, W., et al.: Identify hierarchical structures from task-based fmri data via hybrid spatiotemporal neural architecture search net. In: Shen, D., Liu, T., Peters, Terry M., Staib, Lawrence H., Essert, C., Zhou, S., Yap, P.-T., Khan, A. (eds.) MICCAI 2019. LNCS, vol. 11766, pp. 745–753. Springer, Cham (2019). https://doi.org/10.1007/978-3-030-32248-9_83
9. Li, Q., et al.: Simultaneous spatial-temporal decomposition of connectome-scale brain networks by deep sparse recurrent auto-encoders. In: Chung, A.C.S., Gee, J.C., Yushkevich, P.A., Bao, S. (eds.) IPMI 2019. LNCS, vol. 11492, pp. 579–591. Springer, Cham (2019). https://doi.org/10.1007/978-3-030-20351-1_45
10. Barch, D.M., et al.: Function in the human connectome: Task-fMRI and individual differences in behavior. Neuroimage **80**, 169–189 (2013). https://doi.org/10.1016/j.neuroimage.2013.05.033
11. Fernandes Junior, F.E., Yen, G.G.: Particle swarm optimization of deep neural networks architectures for image classification. Swarm Evol. Comput. **49**, 62–74 (2019). https://doi.org/10.1016/j.swevo.2019.05.010
12. Zou, H., Hastie, T.: Regularization and variable selection via the elastic net. J. R. Stat. Soc. Ser. B. **67**, 301–320 (2005). https://doi.org/10.1037/h0100860

Attention-Guided Deep Graph Neural Network for Longitudinal Alzheimer's Disease Analysis

Junbo Ma[1], Xiaofeng Zhu[2], Defu Yang[1], Jiazhou Chen[1], and Guorong Wu[1](✉)

[1] Department of Psychiatry, University of North Carolina at Chapel Hill, Chapel Hill, NC, USA
{junboma,defu,jiazhou,grwu}@email.unc.edu
[2] School of Natural and Computational Sciences, Massey University, Auckland, New Zealand
S.Zhu@massey.ac.nz

Abstract. Alzheimer's disease (AD) is the main reason for dementia among aged people. Since AD is less likely reversible and has no cure yet, monitoring its progress is essential for adjusting the therapy plan of the patients to delay its deterioration. The computer-aided longitudinal AD data analysis is helpful to this kind of task, which can be used to evaluate the disease status, identify discriminative brain regions, and reveal the progression of the disease. However, most of the existing methods exist two main issues: i) the graph features are extracted globally from the entire graph, which is very sensitive to the noises; ii) they have difficulties in processing dynamic graphs, whereas the brain networks are highly variable, as they vary from individuals or changes along time or by disease. To address these issues, a novel Attention-Guided Deep Graph Neural (AGDGN) network is proposed in this paper, which utilizes an Attention-Guided Random Walk (AGRW) module to extract the structural graph features from the brain network. Since AGRW only needs the local information around the neighborhood nodes at each step of random walk, it is robust to the graph noise and flexible in dealing with dynamic graphs. Moreover, the global attention mechanism is integrated into the sequence processing module. The two attention mechanisms are jointly trained to reveal the most informative brain regions from both structural and temporal domain for AD analysis. Experimental results and analysis on the Alzheimer's Disease Neuroimaging Initiative (ADNI) dataset demonstrate the effectiveness and efficiency of the proposed method.

Keywords: Graph neural network · Attention mechanism · Random walk · Alzheimer's disease · Longitudinal analysis

1 Introduction

Alzheimer's disease (AD) is an irreversible, progressive neurodegenerative disease that results in a slow loss of cognitive functioning, such as thinking, remembering, and reasoning, eventually, lose the ability to perform daily activates [10]. According to a

Electronic supplementary material The online version of this chapter (https://doi.org/10.1007/978-3-030-59728-3_38) contains supplementary material, which is available to authorized users.

© Springer Nature Switzerland AG 2020
A. L. Martel et al. (Eds.): MICCAI 2020, LNCS 12267, pp. 387–396, 2020.
https://doi.org/10.1007/978-3-030-59728-3_38

recent survey report, about 5.8 million Americans are suffering from AD, which costs $290 billion for health care each year [1]. As pre-symptom interventions may ultimately constitute the best long-term therapeutic strategy [18], monitoring AD progression is essential for adjusting the therapy plan of the patients to moderate the cognitive decline. Thus, the computer-aided AD data analysis is in high demand, which can help to evaluate the disease status [25], identify discriminative brain regions [23], and reveal the progression of the disease [5]. During the past few decades, Magnetic Resonance Imaging (MRI) is one of the dominant tools for AD diagnoses and treatments [26], and the brain network is derived from it.

Brain network is a representation of the structural or functional connectivity between brain regions. It provided an efficient way to reveal the complex organizations of the brain and help to understand brain functions constrained by its anatomy structure [6]. Graph theory can be applied to neuroscientific data to analyze the brain's structure and function. However, the graph itself is an irregular data type, which is relatively hard to exploit the structural information among it [5]. The conventional way to extract structural features is by calculating the graph statistics [3], such as the node degree, clustering coefficient, and closeness centrality. Since these features are usually extracted from the entire graph, they may be efficient in summarizing the network properties but do not robust to noise and lack specifically emphasizing the key structures inside the graph.

In recent years, with the rapid development of machine learning techniques, the focus has shifted towards learning data-driven graph features [25], which aims to automatically learn the task-relevant features from the given dataset. Since the graphs belonging to a specific class may have some common patterns that are not typically observed among other classes, the learned graph features can then be used to analyze certain characteristics of the class [16, 20]. Deep graph neural network is one of the most efficient ways to learn data-driven graph features, which extends the success of deep learning techniques from the regular Euclidean data (e.g., images (2D grid), text (1D sequence) to the irregular graph data [2, 31]. There are roughly two main categories of deep graph neural networks, the spectral methods, and the spatial methods [28, 31]. The spectral methods utilize spectral graph theory to explore the graph features [17, 27], which has achieved great success in solving node classification tasks in the citation networks, social networks, and recommendation networks [8, 29]. However, since it usually needs to calculate the Laplacian matrix of the graph, the graph structure has to be fixed across the population [7, 30]. The spatial methods are usually relying on the random walk process to sample the graph structure [4, 22], which has advantages in solving the tasks that the graph structure changes from individuals or along time. However, these methods usually lack the mechanism to optimize the objective of the target task.

To address the issues mentioned above, an Attention-Guided Deep Graph Neural network is proposed in this paper. Our main contributions are highlighted as follows.

1. A novel AGDGN model is proposed for longitudinal Alzheimer's disease analysis, which utilizes two attention mechanisms to reveal the most relevant brain regions at the graph level and the essential time points at the sequence level. The proposed AGDGN is designed to respect both the individual variance across the population, and the network changes along time. Also, it is flexible to variant sequence lengths.

2. A novel attention-guided random walk (AGRW) process is proposed to extract the structural information among the input graph.

   – The attention mechanism in this process can actively highlight the most informative region of the brain network [13, 14], which will then guide the random node selection process. Additionally, the random walk process is guided not only by the attention mechanism but also by the edge weights extracted from the MRI data. In this way, the structural information from edge weights is delicately included and avoid using the exponential number of graph edges.
   – It is worth noting that this process is iteratively running on the local neighborhood of a selected node and does not require the global information of the entire graph. Thus, the proposed AGRW introduces the flexibility of dealing with variant graph structures into the proposed model.
   – To ensure AGRW can achieve an optimal solution for the target task, a reward mechanism inspired by reinforcement learning is introduced.
   – Furthermore, since the proposed process is a random sampling process, it can partially relieve the high data requirement for training such a complex model.

3. A global attention mechanism is integrated into the proposed model, which can highlight the essential time points related to the diagnosis labels of graph sequences.
4. The experimental results on the ADNI dataset demonstrate the effectiveness of the proposed model.

2 Proposed Method

As illustrated in Fig. 1, the proposed Attention-Guided Deep Graph Neural (AGDGN) network has two main modules. One is the attention-guided random walk module; the other one is the sequence processing module. In the following sections, we will first formally formulate the longitudinal AD analysis problem, and then introduce these two modules one by one in details.

2.1 Problem Formulation

The longitudinal AD analysis can be formulated into a graph sequence classification problem. The input is a sequence of graphs, which represents a series of MRI scans from the same person along the time. The output is the clinical diagnosis labels. After the model is trained to converge, the two attentions in AGDNG will be analyzed to reveal the most relevant part of the brain region and essential time points. Formally, the problem can be defined as below:

Definition 1. Graph Sequence Classification: Given a set of graph sequences $G = \{(G_1, l_1), (G_2, l_2), \ldots, (G_n, l_n)\}$, the goal is to learn a function $f : G \to L$, where G is the inputs, and L is the corresponding labels. Each graph sequence $G_i = \{g_{i1}, g_{i2}, \ldots, g_{im_i}\}$ contains a set of graphs, where m_i is the total number of graphs in graph sequence i. Please note that the sequence length of each graph sequence may not necessarily be the

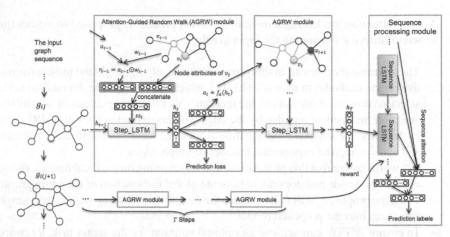

Fig. 1. The proposed model framework. On the left is the input graph sequence, which represents the diagnoses of the same subject across time. g_{ij} is the j-th graph in the i-th sequence, which represents the diagnosis of the i-th subject at the j-th timepoint. The AGRW module will process through the given graph node by node until reaching the maximum random walk length T. Thus, there are T instances of the AGRW module for each graph g_{ij}. The history vector h_T at the last step of the AGRW module is considered as the extracted representation of the entire graph g_{ij} and will be fed into the sequence processing module to make the final prediction. The length of the sequence processing module is corresponding to the length of the graph sequence, which means the proposed model is flexible to the various length of diagnoses across subjects.

same. Each graph g_{ij} has an attribute matrix $D_{g_{ij}} \in R^{d_{ij} \times A}$, where d_{ij} is the number of nodes in the i-th sequence and j-th graph, A is the number of attributes. The label $l_i \in L$ can be either a single label of the whole sequence or a sequence of labels.

Because we currently lack the subjects' data that go through different AD stages across time (which means the graphs in the graph sequence have different diagnosis labels across the sequence), the rest of this paper will focus on the single label of the whole sequence setting. Nevertheless, please note that the proposed AGDGN can be easily extended to the sequence to sequence setting, in which the model will be trained to produce a sequence of diagnosis labels corresponding to the graph sequence. The graph sequence classification accuracy can be used to evaluate how good the model has learned from the dataset. A higher accuracy indicates the more relevant of the learned attention to the diagnosis label.

2.2 Attention-Guided Random Walk Module

The attention-guided random walk (AGRW) module aims to actively highlight the most informative regions in the brain and guide the node selection process for the random walk process to extract the structural information from the graph.

The random walk process can be considered as an agent traveling through the given graph. At each step, the agent will randomly select a node to walk on from the one-hop neighborhood. This random selection is based on a rank vector that represents the probabilities of the nodes to choose. On a weighted graph, this rank vector is usually derived from the edge weights that are connecting to the current node. The higher edge weight, the more probable the agent walks through this edge to the neighbor node. However, this node selection process may not be the same as the function of the brain network, as the brain may select the most relevant regions instead of the most weighted edges. Thus, the attention mechanism is introduced to guide this node selection process, which can assign a higher probability to the brain region that is most relevant to the AD diagnosis labels for the graph sequence classification task. The detailed AGRW process is described below.

At the initializing stage, the starting node v_0 is randomly chosen from the uniform distribution, and the attention vector a_0 is also initialized to the uniform distribution across all the nodes. The current rank vector r_0 is then calculated by $r_0 = a_0 \odot w_0$, where $\odot$ represents the elementwise production and w_0 is the edge weights vector. If a node is connecting to v_0, the corresponding value is set to the edge weight, otherwise zero. Then, the rank vector is normalized as a probability distribution, where all the non-zero elements are in the range $[0, 1]$, and the sum of them is 1. Based on this rank vector, the next node to walk on is selected randomly.

After a new node is selected at time step t, the current attention vector a_t and the features of the selected node are projected to a hidden space by linear layers with parameter θ_a^1 and θ_a^2. Then, the output hidden embeddings are concatenated into a long vector and processed by a linear layer with parameter θ_a^3 to produce the current step state ss_t. In this way, the information from both the graph structure and the node features are delicately extracted and combined with the current attention information.

The step state ss_t will then be fed into a Long Short Term Memory (LSTM) network to memorize this step state. The history vector of LSTM from the hidden layer can be considered as a summary of all the nodes that the agent has walked so far. The history vector is updated by $h_t = f_{steplstm}(ss_t, h_{t-1}; \theta_{steplstm})$, where h_{t-1} is the history vector summarized at the previous step, $\theta_{steplstm}$ represents the parameters in Step-LSTM. h_t is then used to predict the graph label by a fully connected *softmax* layer. The loss score of this prediction, together with the attention score of the selected new node, will be used to tune the network parameters later. At the same time, the new attention vector is produced by $a_{t+1} = f_a(h_t)$, which will be used to guide the next node selection.

The walking path cannot be optimal if the agent chooses the nodes in a greedy manner. Sometimes, the agent has to go through some 'bad' node to reach the most task-relevant area. This is the so-called delayed reward in reinforcement learning. To include this delay reward feature, a reward is given to the agent when the random walk ends at maximum length. At the last step T, the $reward_T = 1$ if the step LSTM correctly predict the graph label and $reward_T = 0$ otherwise. Since the agent does not have the global information of the entire graph, this is a typical Partially Observable Markov Decision Process (POMDP) [19], in which the agent only observed partial information of the graph through the node selection process. The goal of AGRW is to learn a random walk policy π so that the selected walk path can maximize the rewards.

AGRW module produces two outputs: the step state ss_T of the last step and the total loss score of the AGRW module. ss_T will then be used as the graph embedding of the entire graph to input into the sequence process module. Since the first several steps cannot be good in most cases, a score fading feature is introduced into the attention score calculation. Each attention score is penalized by a coefficient $\mu \in [0, 1]$ that is slowing growing to 1 according to the number of steps. The loss score is calculated by:

$$loss_{AGRW} = \sum_{steps} loss_{steplstmprediction} + reward_T * \sum_{steps} \mu Score_{attention}$$

2.3 Sequence Processing Module

The sequence processing module is following the latest sequence processing model with a global attention mechanism, as shown in Fig. 1. This module aims to process the longitudinal AD data collected from the same subject and reveal the essential time points in the diagnosis sequence. The inputs of this module are the outputs of the (AGRW) module, which are considered as the graph representation learned from both the graph structure and the node attributes. The LSTM is also used to summarize the longitudinal data that has seen from the sequence. The attention mechanism is following the global attention settings from Thang Luong's paper [15].

After the whole sequence is processed, two vectors are concatenated together to produce the final prediction. One vector is the longitudinal summary vector from the LSTM history state at the last time point. The other one is the attention vector calculated from the outputs of the LSTM at each time point. The prediction loss of the sequence processing module is combined with the AGRW loss by $loss = \sum_{seq} (l_{seq} + l_{AGRW})$.

Since the two modules are jointly optimized, the extracted graph embeddings will respect both the structural and temporal relevance of the diagnosis labels. It is worth noting that AGRW only needs the local information of the graph. Thus, it has the flexibility of dealing with various structures of the brain networks. Furthermore, since it is a random sampling process and the step state only contains the selected node and edge information, AGRW can iteratively generate "new" training samples to train the complex LSTM network, which may partially relieve its high training data requirements.

3 Experimental Setup

The proposed model is tested on the Alzheimer's Disease Neuroimaging Initiative (ADNI) dataset [11]. It is the largest public AD dataset, which is continuously collecting AD data since 2004. A subset of 94 subjects is collected from the ADNI dataset. The MRI images are firstly parcellated into 148 cortical regions. Then the fiber tractography is applied to construct the 148×148 connection matrixes, which represents the brain networks. The details of the 148 cortical regions can be found in the supplementary material. Then, the disparity filtering is applied to sparse the brain networks [24]. There are 325 brain networks in total from 94 subjects. The sequence lengths of the subjects are varying from 1 to 6, with an average of 3.45. The first scan of each subject is called the baseline scan. Then, the follow-up scans are at the 6-th month, 12-th month, the 24-th month, and so on, after the baseline scan.

There are 3 attributes for each brain region, the cortical thickness derived from T1-weighted MRI images, the FDG level derived from ^{18}F-FDG PET images, and the amyloid β level [9]. All the attributes are rescaled to [0, 1]. The dataset contains 4 diagnosis labels: Cognitively Normal (CN), Significant Memory Concern (SMC), Mild Cognitive Impairment (MCI) and AD. To relieve the data shortage, we merged the CN and SMC as the CN group; and merged MCI and AD as the AD group, which results in a two-class classification problem.

The baseline model we are comparing with only uses the baseline scan as input and a Support Vector Machine (SVM) as the classifier. The graph features are extracted in the traditional way. We use the node degree, local efficiency, and cluster coefficient as the graph features combined with the 3 node attributes to train the SVM.

To compare with the baseline model and demonstrate the effectiveness of the proposed attention-guided random walk (AGRW), we train our proposed model only on the baseline scan and only with the AGRW module called AGRW-baseline. Then, we train our proposed AGDGN model on the full sequence to demonstrate its ability to process longitudinal data. The proposed AGDGN model is written in PyTorch [21] and trained on a deep learning server equipped with 4 RTX-TITAN GPUs. The random walk length is set to 150. The hidden units' number of step-LSTM is set to 128, and the sequence-LSTM is set to 256. The network is trained by the Adam optimizer [12] until 500 iterations or the loss value stop decreasing for 50 iterations.

4 Results and Discussion

The dataset is randomly split into 70 subjects for training and 24 subjects for testing. All the models are randomly initialized for 5 times, and the average classification accuracy is reported in Table 1. From Table 1, we can see that the AGRW-baseline achieves significantly higher classification accuracy than the SVM baseline, which means the proposed AGRW is able to extract more diagnosis label relevant graph features and produce more noise-robust graph embeddings. The classification accuracy is further improved by the proposed AGDNG model, which means the temporal information is successfully extracted from the sequence.

Table 1. Classification accuracy

Model	SVM-baseline	AGRW-baseline	AGDNG
Accuracy	83.33%	91.42%	93.67%

We further analyze the attention vectors learned by the best AGDNG model. Figure 2 shows the attention vector of the last step for Subject ID: 016_S_4591, Graph ID: S144582. We can clearly see that the attention vector highlighted several nodes that have significantly higher probabilities than others. We also observe that the attention vector may change while the graph still correctly classified, which indicates that there may be multiple optimal solutions. Thus, we put all the top 10 nodes of the last 30 steps into a large list and summarize the frequencies of each unique node. There are 22 unique nodes in this large list. The frequencies of these 22 unique nodes in this list are shown in Fig. 3. Several nodes almost always in the top10 list across the steps, such as the Node ID 10, 21, and 95 have 30, 29, 29 frequencies, respectively. Then, we project these 22 nodes back to the brain. As shown in Fig. 4, the bigger node size indicates the higher frequency. We can see that these top nodes and edges are mainly selected on the reasoning and memory areas, which are highly related to the AD according to the clinical reports [25, 26].

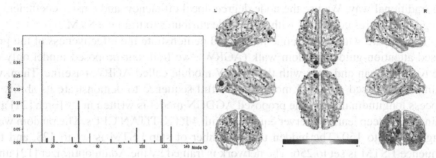

Fig. 2. The last step attention vector. The left figure shows the actual values of the attention on each node. The right figure shows the attention to the brain. The node size represents the attention value. The node color represents the node ID. (Color figure online)

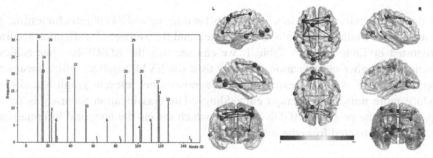

Fig. 3. The node frequency of the top 10 nodes in each of the last 30 steps. The left figure shows the actual frequency values. The right figure shows the positions of these nodes on the brain. The node size represents the frequency values. The node color represents the node ID. (Color figure online)

The subject ID 016_S_4591 has taken 4 scans so far, with the Graph ID: S144582, S154152, S170150, S185716. The same analysis also has been done on these graphs. We summarize the nodes that appeared in the top 10 of the last 30 steps across all 4 scans, which results in a set of 20 unique nodes. Since the number of unique nodes for all 4 scans is 22, 20, 21, and 21 respectively, this indicates that the most informative brain areas extracted by the proposed model are stable along time.

For the longitudinal analysis, the sequential attention of this subject is [0.23823874, 0.2448868, 0.25634217, 0.26053232] corresponding to the 4 scans. The sequential attentions are roughly even, which correctly reflects the fact that all 4 graphs have the same diagnose labels as AD, while the slowly increasing number of attention value reflects the irreversible and progressive characteristics of AD. This pattern can be seen in all AD subjects, whereas the sequential attention of CN subjects are more even and do not have a clear pattern.

5   Conclusion

In this paper, a novel Attention-Guided Deep Graph Neural (AGDGN) network model is proposed for longitudinal Alzheimer's disease analysis. Two attention mechanisms are integrated and jointly trained to extract both structural and temporal graph features. By utilizing the proposed attention-guided random walk (AGRW) process, the proposed model can deal with the individual variances of the brain networks across the population, reveal the most informative regions to the diagnosis labels, and extract more noise-robust graph embeddings. The analyses of the experimental results demonstrated that the proposed model successfully identifies the AD's characteristics reported by the clinical studies. Although this paper only focuses on the 'sequence to one label' problem, it is worth mention that the proposed model can be easily extended to the 'sequence to sequence' setting. We will test the proposed model in this setting when the corresponding data is ready in the future.

References

1. Alzheimer's Association: 2019 Alzheimer's disease facts and figures. Alzheimer's & Dementia **15**(3), 321–387 (2019)
2. Bai, Y., Ding, H., Bian, S., Chen, T., Sun, Y., Wang, W.: Simgnn: a neural network approach to fast graph similarity computation. In: Proceedings of the Twelfth ACM International Conference on Web Search and Data Mining, pp. 384–392 (2019)
3. Ellens, W., Kooij, R.E.: Graph measures and network robustness. arXiv preprint arXiv:1311. 5064 (2013)
4. Fey, M., Lenssen, J.E.: Fast graph representation learning with pytorch geometric. arXiv preprint arXiv:1903.02428 (2019)
5. Fisher, C.K., Smith, A.M., Walsh, J.R.: Machine learning for comprehensive forecasting of alzheimer's disease progression. Sci. Rep. **9**(1), 1–14 (2019)
6. Fleischer, V., et al.: Graph theoretical framework of brain networks in multiple sclerosis: a review of concepts. Neuroscience **403**, 35–53 (2019)
7. Gama, F., Marques, A.G., Leus, G., Ribeiro, A.: Convolutional neural network architectures for signals supported on graphs. IEEE Trans. Signal Process. **67**(4), 1034–1049 (2018)
8. Garcia, V., Estrach, J.B.: Few-shot learning with graph neural networks. In: 6th International Conference on Learning Representations, ICLR 2018 (2018)
9. Hansson, O., et al.: Csf biomarkers of alzheimer's disease concord with amyloid-β pet and predict clinical progression: a study of fully automated immunoassays in biofinder and adni cohorts. Alzheimer's Dementia **14**(11), 1470–1481 (2018)
10. Heneka, M.T., et al.: Neuroinflammation in alzheimer's disease. Lancet Neurol. **14**(4), 388–405 (2015)
11. Jack Jr., C.R., et al.: The Alzheimer's disease neuroimaging initiative (ADNI): MRI methods. J. Magnet. Reson. **27**(4), 685–691 (2008). Imaging: An Official Journal of the International Society for Magnetic Resonance in Medicine

12. Kingma, D.P., Ba, J.: Adam: a method for stochastic optimization. arXiv preprint arXiv:1412. 6980 (2014)
13. Lee, J.B., Rossi, R., Kong, X.: Graph classification using structural attention. In: Proceedings of the 24th ACM SIGKDD International Conference on Knowledge Discovery & Data Mining. pp. 1666–1674 (2018)
14. Lee, J., Lee, I., Kang, J.: Self-attention graph pooling. In: International Conference on Machine Learning, pp. 3734–3743 (2019)
15. Luong, M.T., Pham, H., Manning, C.D.: Effective approaches to attention-basedneural machine translation. In: Proceedings of the 2015 Conference on EmpiricalMethods in Natural Language Processing, pp. 1412–1421 (2015)
16. Ma, G., et al.: Deep graph similarity learning for brain data analysis. In: Proceedings of the 28th ACM International Conference on Information and Knowledge Management, pp. 2743–2751 (2019)
17. Ma, Y., Wang, S., Aggarwal, C.C., Tang, J.: Graph convolutional networks with eigenpooling. In: Proceedings of the 25th ACM SIGKDD International Conference on Knowledge Discovery & Data Mining, pp. 723–731 (2019)
18. Mathys, H., et al.: Single-cell transcriptomic analysis of Alzheimer's disease. Nature 570(7761), 332–337 (2019)
19. Mnih, V., Heess, N., Graves, A., et al.: Recurrent models of visual attention. In: Advances in Neural Information Processing Systems, pp. 2204–2212 (2014)
20. Park, H.J., Friston, K.: Structural and functional brain networks: from connections to cognition. Science 342(6158), 1238411 (2013)
21. Paszke, A., et al.: Automatic differentiation in pytorch (2017)
22. Perozzi, B., Al-Rfou, R., Skiena, S.: Deepwalk: online learning of social representations. In: Proceedings of the 20th ACM SIGKDD International Conference on Knowledge Discovery and Data Mining, pp. 701–710 (2014)
23. Selkoe, D.J.: Early network dysfunction in Alzheimer's disease. Science 365(6453), 540–541 (2019)
24. Serrano, M.A., Boguna, M., Vespignani, A.: Extracting the multiscale backbone of complex weighted networks. Proc. Natl. Acad. Sci. 106(16), 6483–6488 (2009)
25. Tanveer, M., et al.: Machine learning techniques for the diagnosis of Alzheimer's disease: a review. In: ACM Transactions on Multimedia Computing, Communications, and Applications (TOMM) (2019)
26. Veitch, D.P., et al.: Understanding disease progression and improving alzheimer's disease clinical trials: Recent highlights from the alzheimer's disease neuroimaging initiative. Alzheimer's Dementia 15(1), 106–152 (2019)
27. Wu, F., Souza, A., Zhang, T., Fifty, C., Yu, T., Weinberger, K.: Simplifying graph convolutional networks. In: International Conference on Machine Learning, pp. 6861–6871 (2019)
28. Wu, Z., Pan, S., Chen, F., Long, G., Zhang, C., Yu, P.S.: A comprehensive survey on graph neural networks. arXiv preprint arXiv:1901.00596 (2019)
29. Ying, R., He, R., Chen, K., Eksombatchai, P., Hamilton, W.L., Leskovec, J.: Graph convolutional neural networks for web-scale recommender systems. In: Proceedings of the 24th ACM SIGKDD International Conference on Knowledge Discovery & Data Mining, pp. 974–983 (2018)
30. Zeng, J., Pang, J., Sun, W., Cheung, G.: Deep graph laplacian regularization for robust denoising of real images. In: Proceedings of the IEEE Conference on Computer Vision and Pattern Recognition Workshops (2019)
31. Zhou, J., et al.: Graph neural networks: a review of methods and applications. arXiv preprint arXiv:1812.08434 (2018)

Enriched Representation Learning in Resting-State fMRI for Early MCI Diagnosis

Eunjin Jeon[1], Eunsong Kang[1], Jiyeon Lee[1], Jaein Lee[1], Tae-Eui Kam[2], and Heung-Il Suk[1,2(✉)]

[1] Department of Brain and Cognitive Engineering, Korea University, Seoul, Republic of Korea
[2] Department of Artificial Intelligence, Korea University, Seoul, Republic of Korea
hisuk@korea.ac.kr

Abstract. In recent studies, we have witnessed the applicability of deep learning methods on resting-state functional Magnetic Resonance Image (rs-fMRI) analysis and on its use for brain disease diagnosis, *e.g.*, early Mild Cognitive Impairment (eMCI) identification. However, to our best knowledge, many of the existing methods are generally limited from improving the performance in a target task, *e.g.*, eMCI diagnosis, by the unexpected information loss in transforming an input into hierarchical or compressed representations. In this paper, we propose a novel network architecture that discovers enriched representations of the spatio-temporal patterns in rs-fMRI such that the most compressed or latent representations include the maximal amount of information to recover the original input, but are decomposed into diagnosis-relevant and diagnosis-irrelevant features. In order to learn those favourable representations, we utilize a self-attention mechanism to explore spatially more informative patterns over time and information-oriented techniques to maintain the enriched but decomposed representations. In our experiments over the ADNI dataset, we validated the effectiveness of the proposed network architecture by comparing its performance with that of the counterpart methods as well as the competing methods in the literature.

Keywords: Early Mild Cognitive Impairment · Brain disease diagnosis · Resting-state functional magnetic resonance imaging · Deep learning · Self-attention · Mutual information

1 Introduction

Alzheimer's Disease (AD) progresses slowly, typically accompanying memory loss and impaired cognitive functions, from the preclinical stage of dementia, Mild Cognitive Impairment (MCI), within a few years. Since there has been

E. Jeon and E. Kang—Equally contributed.

© Springer Nature Switzerland AG 2020
A. L. Martel et al. (Eds.): MICCAI 2020, LNCS 12267, pp. 397–406, 2020.
https://doi.org/10.1007/978-3-030-59728-3_39

no effective and appropriate treatment for AD yet, MCI identification, particularly at its early stage, is of great importance to possibly delay the development to AD. When considering the early stage, it is more likely that the functional changes precede the structural changes. In this regard, in order to capture functional abnormalities that can cause cognitive impairments, resting-state functional Magnetic Resonance Image (rs-fMRI) that measures Blood-Oxygenation-Level-Dependent (BOLD) signals of a subject in the absence of any explicit task has been considered as one of the major tools.

Recently, deep learning methods have been actively applied to neuroimaging from the perspectives of representation learning and classification. In order to get insights on neuroscientific findings and to understand the structural and functional characteristics of a human brain, some studies focused on spatio-temporal representation learning of fMRI with unsupervised deep models (*i.e.*, stacked auto-encoder [17] or restricted Boltzmann machines [8,11]). Meanwhile, with its advantages of automatically extracting discriminative features for a target task, many studies [14,15] exploited deep models to get high-level disease-related features from BOLD signals or functional connectivity for diagnosis.

While many deep-learning models presented the reasonable performance in their own work, it is common for deep models to lose information in the original input due to hierarchical compression as progressing to the upper layers of a network. According to the Information Bottleneck (IB) theory [18] that explains a trade-off between an efficient representation and good predictive power, the supervised deep models mostly focus on finding class-discriminative features without ensuring how rich the features reflect the original data. In this paper, we propose a novel framework for eMCI diagnosis using rs-fMRI by lessening the IB concern in a deep neural network. Recently, Mutual Information (MI) based deep models [6,9,13] have been proposed to obtain the concise representation that is maximally expressive about the output, while being maximally compressive about the input. Inspired by [6,9,13], we hypothesize that it is possible to obtain rich-descriptive feature representations by maximizing MI between features of different layers and also take more eMCI diagnosis-relevant factors out from features entangled with unidentified factors by minimizing the MI between class-relevant factors and class-irrelevant factors [13,22]. Furthermore, as a way of strengthening the representational power, we utilize an attention mechanism [19] to selectively emphasize the spatial patterns, which could be contextually informative for the downstream task, *i.e.*, eMCI identification.

The main contributions are as follows: (i) Our model learns spatial and temporal patterns simultaneously, but has high interdependence between them to get meaningful spatio-temporal pattern with the use of neural estimator of MI. (ii) Based on the neurological view of functional dynamics, we impose the temporal emphasis via attention mechanism. Time-varying characteristics have been supposed to be more informative than static characteristics that analyze the entire sequences all together [2]. (iii) Furthermore, we separate diagnostic factors out for classification from the spatio-temporal feature that might also include the potential noises or sources that have low relations to disease. We demonstrate that our proposed method has a great potential to learn informative spatio-temporal patterns and identify eMCI by testing over the public ADNI dataset.

2 Data and Preprocessing

We utilized 38 eMCI and 26 Cognitively Normal (CN) subjects from a baseline dataset of the Alzheimer's Disease Neuroimaging Initiative (ADNI) cohort[1] (ADNI 2 and ADNI Go). The mean age of each class, *i.e.*, eMCI and CN, is 74.2 ± 5.8 and 71.6 ± 7.5, respectively. The images were scanned using 3.0T Philips Achieva scanners in multi-center with following protocol and parameters: Repetition Time (TR) = $3,000$ ms, Echo Time (TE) = 30 ms, flip angle = $80°$, acquisition image size = 64×64, 48 slices, 140 timepoints, and a voxel thickness = 3.3 mm.

The images were preprocessed using the Data Processing Assistant for rs-fMRI (DRARSF) [20] based on SPM12[2] and REST[3]. We discarded the first 10 timepoints for each sample for magnetization equilibrium. Subsequently, the remaining volumes were spatially normalized to the MNI space and resliced to a voxel size of $2 \times 2 \times 2$ mm^3. Then, to reduce spatial noise, we smoothed the images by 4 mm FWHM using a Gaussian kernel. We bandpass-filtered the temporal BOLD signals from 0.01 to 0.1 Hz to retain low-frequency fluctuations in rs-fMRI. The brain space was then parcellated into 114 regions of interest (ROIs) based on the 17 networks from the functional atlas [21]. For each of the parcellated regions, we obtained the regional mean BOLD signal by taking the average of the signals of voxels within the ROI.

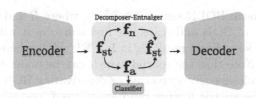

Fig. 1. An overall framework. Our network is composed of an encoder, a decomposer-entangler, and a decoder. Details of each component are illustrated in Fig. 2 and 3.

3 Proposed Method

Our proposed method is comprised of three modules: an encoder, a decomposer-entangler, and a decoder, as illustrated in Fig. 1. Similar to a typical auto-encoder, the role of the encoder and the decoder is to transform an input

---

[1] http://adni.loni.usc.edu.
[2] https://www.fil.ion.ucl.ac.uk/spm/software/spm12/.
[3] http://www.restfmri.net/forum/.

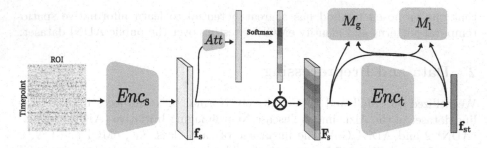

Fig. 2. Details of an encoding module. An input is embedded to the spatial feature $\mathbf{f}_s$ through a spatial encoder Enc_s. An attention layer Att emphasizes the $\mathbf{f}_s$ along with temporal axis, which results into $\mathbf{F}_s$ by multiplying $Att(\mathbf{f}_s)$ and $\mathbf{f}_s$ as represented as $\otimes$. Also, we utilize two MINEs [1], *i.e.*, M_g and M_l to improve the relations between the $\mathbf{F}_s$ and the spatio-temporal feature $\mathbf{f}_{st}$ from the temporal point of view.

$\mathbf{x}$ into a latent space and to recover back into the input space, respectively. The decomposer-entangler module, which is one of the key computational components in our network, basically conducts two functions: (i) to partition the embedded representation $\mathbf{f}_{st}$ into $\mathbf{f}_n$ and $\mathbf{f}_a$, each of which is irrelevant and relevant to the disease diagnosis, and (ii) to restore the embedded representation $\hat{\mathbf{f}}_{st}$. In regard to the eMCI diagnosis, the disease-relevant feature $\mathbf{f}_a$ is only fed into a classifier.

3.1 Embedding for Spatio-Temporal Feature Representations

Given a regional mean BOLD signal $\mathbf{x} \in \mathbb{R}^{T \times R}$, where R and T denote, respectively, the number of ROIs and scans, we first convolve it with a set of spatial kernels of $1 \times R$ in size, Enc_s, resulting in $\mathbf{f}_s \in \mathbb{R}^{T \times 1 \times d_1}$, where d_1 is the number of spatial kernels. Note that the spatial kernels can be understood as functional networks, *i.e.*, simultaneously activating or deactivating ROIs due to functional integration, and the spatial feature representations $\mathbf{f}_s$ correspond to the brainwise abstraction in terms of those functional networks across T time points. However, as the spatial convolution is conducted for each time point independently, the temporal features of $1 \times d_1$ in $\mathbf{f}_s$ is limited to carry the information of functional dynamics. Figure 2 represents an architecture of encoder.

Self-attention. In order to compensate for the lack of temporal information in the spatially convolved feature representations, we apply an interesting mechanism of self-attention [10] to Enc_s. Basically, our self-attention mechanism takes into account the temporal context of the spatially embedded representations and assigns relatively higher weights to time points at which the corresponding representations carry informative features for a target task. Here, the informativeness is determined adaptively with the learnable parameters in combination with other objectives described below.

Concisely, the self-attention layer Att takes the spatially embedded features $\mathbf{f}_s$ as input and outputs an attention map of $Att(\mathbf{f}_s) \in \mathbb{R}^{T \times 1}$. Subsequently, we calculate a temporally attended feature representations $\mathbf{F}_s$ as follows:

$$\mathbf{F}_s = \text{softmax}(Att(\mathbf{f}_s)) \otimes \mathbf{f}_s \qquad (1)$$

where softmax($\cdot$) and $\otimes$ denote a softmax function and an element-wise multiplication, respectively. The spatially embedded and temporally attended feature representations $\mathbf{F}_s$ then go through the temporal convolution Enc_t, by which we compress the input $\mathbf{x}$ into a spatio-temporal feature representation of $\mathbf{f}_{st} \in \mathbb{R}^{d_2}$ where d_2 denotes the dimension of channels. The architectural characteristic of our $Enc_s - Att - Enc_t$ that decomposes the spatial and temporal operations into two sequential steps is comparable to the previous approaches of using recurrent neural networks (RNNs) that intersperse the spatial and temporal operations over time to directly model the functional dynamics. While the typical RNNs suffer from a long-term dependency problem due to sequential encoding, our $Enc_s - Att - Enc_t$ architecture is efficiently handle it with the use of global context over the whole time points via an attention mechanism.

Maximization Mutual Information. To enhance the representational power, we further take an information-theoretic approach such that the MI between $\mathbf{F}_s$ and $\mathbf{f}_{st}$, $i.e.$, $\mathbb{I}(\mathbf{F}_s; \mathbf{f}_{st})$, to be maximized. Since it is infeasible for exact computation of MI, we leverage the neural-network based approximator, Mutual Information Neural Estimators (MINE) [1]. In brief, MINE approximates MI by taking account of the difference between the joint distribution $\mathbb{P}$ and the product of marginal distributions $\mathbb{P} \times \hat{\mathbb{P}}$ defined as follows:

$$\mathbb{I}(X; Z) = \mathbb{E}_{\mathbb{P}}[-\text{sp}(-M(x, z))] - \mathbb{E}_{\mathbb{P} \times \hat{\mathbb{P}}}[\text{sp}(M(x', z))] \qquad (2)$$

where M is a neural network and sp($\cdot$) denotes a softplus function. Specifically, inspired by [9], we consider two kinds of MI, namely, global and local MI, by regarding the whole or individual features in $\mathbf{F}_s$. First, the global MI, $\mathcal{I}_g$, is defined and maximized with a network M_g as follows:

$$\mathcal{I}_g = \sum_{i=1}^{N} \mathbb{I}(\mathbf{F}_s^{(i)}; \mathbf{f}_{st}^{(i)} | M_g) \qquad (3)$$

where N is a mini-batch size. Second, the local MI, $\mathcal{I}_l$, estimated via another network M_l is defined in a similar manner but for each time point t in $\mathbf{F}_s$ as follows:

$$\mathcal{I}_l = \sum_{i=1}^{N} \sum_{t=1}^{T} \mathbb{I}(\mathbf{F}_s^{(i,t)}; \mathbf{f}_{st}^{(i)} | M_l). \qquad (4)$$

According to [9], the maximization of the element-wise MI with respect to the higher layer feature representations helps to improve the quality of representations for a downstream task.

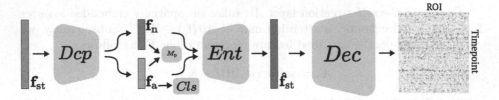

Fig. 3. An architecture of our decoding module. The spatio-temporal feature $\mathbf{f}_{st}$ is separated into the diagnostic feature $\mathbf{f}_a$ and the non-diagnostic feature $\mathbf{f}_n$ through a decomposer Dcp and a MINE M_p depending on a classifier Cls. Both features are entangled to the reconstructed spatio-temporal feature $\hat{\mathbf{f}}_{st}$ in an entangler Ent. Then, a decoder Dec reconstructs the raw input from $\hat{\mathbf{f}}_{st}$.

3.2   Decomposition into Diagnostic and Non-diagnostic Feature

Note that the feature representation $\mathbf{f}_{st}$ is encoded to compress the spatio-temporal information in the input, but not necessarily to be discriminative for a target task of eMCI identification. In this regard, we decompose it into diagnosis-related and diagnosis-unrelated factors as shown in Fig. 3, which still can be trained jointly with other modules in our network.

Decomposer-Entangler. A decomposer Dcp decomposes the spatio-temporal feature $\mathbf{f}_{st}$ into a diagnostic feature $\mathbf{f}_a$ and a non-diagnostic feature $\mathbf{f}_n$. Here, we again utilize the MI-based approach with a network M_p for good decomposition:

$$\mathcal{I}_p = \sum_{i=1}^{N} \mathbb{I}(\mathbf{f}_a^{(i)}, \mathbf{f}_n^{(i)} | M_p). \tag{5}$$

Unlike the previous two MIs in Eq. (3) and Eq. (4), the MI between decomposed feature representations $\mathbf{f}_a$ and $\mathbf{f}_n$ should be minimized. Once decomposed, the diagnostic feature representation $\mathbf{f}_a$ is fed into a classifier Cls, which is trained by minimizing the cross-entropy loss $\mathcal{L}_{cls}$ defined as follows:

$$\mathcal{L}_{cls} = -\sum_{i=1}^{N} \mathbf{y}^{(i)} \log(Cls(\mathbf{f}_a^{(i)})) \tag{6}$$

where $\mathbf{y}^{(i)}$ is a label vector of the input $\mathbf{x}^{(i)}$. Further, in order to guarantee that the decomposed feature representations still hold the spatio-temporal information in $\mathbf{f}_{st}$, we make use of an internal auto-encoder, called an entangler Ent, i.e., $\mathbf{f}_{st}^{(i)} \simeq \hat{\mathbf{f}}_{st}^{(i)}$.

By taking the re-entangled representation $\hat{\mathbf{f}}_{st}^{(i)}$ as input, the decoder Dec reconstructs the original input $\mathbf{x}^{(i)}$ with a series of temporal and spatial deconvolution layers by minimizing the following mean squared error loss:

$$\mathcal{L}_{recon} = \sum_{i=1}^{N} ||\mathbf{x}^{(i)} - Dec(\hat{\mathbf{f}}_{st}^{(i)})||_2^2. \tag{7}$$

3.3   Objective Function

Our proposed method is trained in an end-to-end manner by minimizing the composite objective functions:

$$\max_{Enc,M_g} \mathcal{I}_g + \max_{Enc,M_l} \mathcal{I}_l + \min_{\substack{Enc, \\ Att,Dcp}} \max_{M_p} \mathcal{I}_p + \min_{\substack{Enc,Att, \\ Dcp,Cls}} \mathcal{L}_{cls} + \min_{\substack{Enc,Dcp, \\ Ent,Dec}} \mathcal{L}_{recon} \tag{8}$$

where Enc denotes $\{Enc_s, Enc_t\}$. Note that MINE [1] should be trained by gradient ascent method due to the supremum of the Donsker-Varadhan representation [4]. For the decomposer in Eq. (5), since it is required to minimize the MI between $\mathbf{f}_a$ and $\mathbf{f}_n$, we actually add a gradient reversal layer [7] that plays no role in forward propagation, but reverses the gradient direction during backpropagation in a training phase.

4   Experiments

4.1   Experimental Settings

We basically took a 10-fold cross validation technique for evaluation and repeated it 10 times for reliability in results. The reported performance is the average of the results in terms of four metrics: Area Under the receiver operating characteristic Curve (AUC), accuracy, sensitivity, and specificity.

Proposed Network. The spatial convolutional layer with a kernel size of 1×114 took raw rs-fMRI as an input and then outputed the spatial feature $\mathbf{f}_s \in \mathbb{R}^{130 \times 1 \times 40}$. Then, the $\mathbf{f}_s$ was fed into the temporal convolutional layer with a kernel size of 130×1, which resulted in the spatio-temporal feature $\mathbf{f}_{st} \in \mathbb{R}^{40}$. In the M_g, the other spatial convolutional layer embedded the temporal attended feature $\mathbf{F}_s$ to $\mathbb{R}^{40}$. We concatenated it with $\mathbf{f}_{st}$ and then fed the concatenated feature to two Fully-Connected Layers (FCLs) with the units of $\{20, 1\}$. The latter unit was used to calculate Eq. (3). Meanwhile, our M_l was made of the encode-and-dot architecture according to [9]. While the $\mathbf{F}_s$ was taken into a 1×1 convolutional layer with 50 units, the $\mathbf{f}_{st}$ was fed into a FCL with the same size of units. Each scan of the $\mathbf{F}_s$ was performed the dot-product with $\mathbf{f}_{st}$ and then the results were averaged to calculate Eq. (4). In the Dcp, two FCLs transformed $\mathbf{f}_{st}$ into the diagnostic feature $\mathbf{f}_a \in \mathbb{R}^{20}$ and the non-diagnostic feature $\mathbf{f}_n \in \mathbb{R}^{20}$, respectively. Then, the Cls composed of two FCLs with $\{40, 2\}$ units was trained with $\mathbf{f}_a$. Another MINE M_p consisted of two FCLs and each layer received $\mathbf{f}_a$ or $\mathbf{f}_n$, where the number of hidden units was set 40. Subsequently, we integrated both outputs of two layers into one unit and fed it to two FCLs with $\{20, 1\}$. The Ent consisted of a FCL embedded the concatenated feature with $\mathbf{f}_a$ and $\mathbf{f}_n$ to $\hat{\mathbf{f}}_{st} \in \mathbb{R}^{40}$. Finally, our Dec consisted of a temporal deconvolutional layer with a kernel size of 130×1 with 40 units and a 1×114 spatial deconvolutional layer with a unit.

Table 1. Performance on the classification between CN and eMCI. (BA: Balanced Accuracy)

	SVM [3]	LSTM [5]	Model I	Model II	**Ours**
AUC	$0.497 \pm 0.015^*$	$0.534 \pm 0.030^*$	$0.658 \pm 0.032^*$	$0.622 \pm 0.027^*$	**0.705 ± 0.021**
Accuracy	$0.528 \pm 0.017^*$	$0.589 \pm 0.029^*$	$0.673 \pm 0.030^*$	$0.647 \pm 0.024^*$	**0.709 ± 0.021**
Sensitivity	$0.690 \pm 0.014^*$	**$0.826 \pm 0.053^*$**	0.742 ± 0.049	0.753 ± 0.091	0.729 ± 0.037
Specificity	$0.292 \pm 0.025^*$	$0.242 \pm 0.068^*$	$0.573 \pm 0.069^*$	$0.492 \pm 0.120^*$	**0.681 ± 0.045**
BA	$0.491 \pm 0.018^*$	$0.534 \pm 0.030^*$	$0.658 \pm 0.032^*$	$0.622 \pm 0.027^*$	**0.705 ± 0.021**

(*: $p < 0.05$)

We used a dropout with 0.5 rate and a weight decay with the corresponding coefficient to 0.05 to avoid overfitting. Except for three MINEs, we also applied a batch normalization [12] to all layers. We set a mini-batch size as 5 and utilized leaky ReLU as an activation function. All modules were trained using an Adam optimizer [16] with a learning rate of 0.001.

Baseline Methods. To validate the effectiveness of our method, we compared our results with the following methods: (i) functional connectivity features estimated by Pearson's correlation coefficients and a linear Support Vector Machine (SVM)[4] classifier [3][5], (ii) a joint learning of the disease-discriminative and generative features via Long Short-Term Memory network (LSTM) from regional mean BOLD signals [5], and (iii) our methods without each component: (Model I) no use of MI-guided learning in Eqs. (3)–(4) and (Model II) no use of the self-attention in Eq. (1).

4.2 Experimental Results

Table 1 shows the averaged performance of the comparative methods. It is noteworthy that our proposed method achieved the best accuracy of 0.709 and the best AUC of 0.705 with a statistical significance of $p < 0.05$ to all the competing methods. Regarding the results of the model I and II that corresponded to the ablation study of our method, we demonstrated the significance of both self-attention and MI maximization in discovering feature representations. Especially, we observed that the balanced accuracy, defined as the average of sensitivity and specificity, in our proposed method was the highest by balancing the performance on both sensitivity and specificity. From those results, we believed that the MI maximization as well as the global attention mechanism helped to enrich the representational power and to separate disease-related features.

5   Conclusion

In this paper, we proposed a novel framework that learns spatio-temporal representations of regional mean BOLD signals for eMCI identification by systematically

---

[4] The hyperparameter was determined in $\{10^{-5}, 10^{-2}, \dots, 10^4\}$.

[5] It is the most typical pipeline in brain disease diagnosis with rs-fMRI [3].

combining computational mechanisms of self-attention and mutual-information maximization. Notably, our architecture was devised to resolve the information bottleneck problem in a hierarchical compression of the input. In our experiments on the ADNI dataset, the proposed method showed a superiority to the competing methods considered in this work on various metrics, denoting its applicability of identifying a subject with MCI at his/her early stage.

Acknowledgement. This work was supported by National Research Foundation of Korea (NRF) grant funded by the Korea government (MSIT) (No. 2019R1A2C1006543) and partially by Institute of Information & communications Technology Planning & Evaluation (IITP) grant funded by the Korea government (MSIT) (No. 2019-0-00079, Artificial Intelligence Graduate School Program (Korea University)).

References

1. Belghazi, M.I., et al.: Mutual information neural estimation. In: International Conference on Machine Learning, pp. 531–540 (2018)
2. Calhoun, V.D., Miller, R., Pearlson, G., Adalı, T.: The chronnectome: time-varying connectivity networks as the next frontier in fMRI data discovery. Neuron **84**(2), 262–274 (2014)
3. Dadi, K., et al.: Benchmarking functional connectome-based predictive models for resting-state fMRI. NeuroImage **192**, 115–134 (2019)
4. Donsker, M.D., Varadhan, S.S.: Asymptotic evaluation of certain Markov process expectations for large time. IV. Commun. Pure Appl. Math. **36**(2), 183–212 (1983)
5. Dvornek, N.C., Li, X., Zhuang, J., Duncan, J.S.: Jointly discriminative and generative recurrent neural networks for learning from fMRI. In: Suk, H.-I., Liu, M., Yan, P., Lian, C. (eds.) MLMI 2019. LNCS, vol. 11861, pp. 382–390. Springer, Cham (2019). https://doi.org/10.1007/978-3-030-32692-0_44
6. Fedorov, A., et al.: Prediction of progression to Alzheimer's disease with deep infoMax. In: 2019 IEEE EMBS International Conference on Biomedical & Health Informatics (BHI), pp. 1–5. IEEE (2019)
7. Ganin, Y., et al.: Domain-adversarial training of neural networks. J. Mach. Learn. Res. **17**(1), 2030–2096 (2016)
8. Hjelm, R.D., Calhoun, V.D., Salakhutdinov, R., Allen, E.A., Adali, T., Plis, S.M.: Restricted Boltzmann machines for neuroimaging: an application in identifying intrinsic networks. NeuroImage **96**, 245–260 (2014)
9. Hjelm, R.D., et al.: Learning deep representations by mutual information estimation and maximization. In: International Conference on Learning Representations (2019)
10. Hu, J., Shen, L., Sun, G.: Squeeze-and-excitation networks. In: Proceedings of the IEEE Conference on Computer Vision and Pattern Recognition, pp. 7132–7141 (2018)
11. Hu, X., et al.: Latent source mining in fMRI via restricted Boltzmann machine. Hum. Brain Mapp. **39**(6), 2368–2380 (2018)
12. Ioffe, S., Szegedy, C.: Batch normalization: accelerating deep network training by reducing internal covariate shift. arXiv preprint arXiv:1502.03167 (2015)
13. Jeon, E., Ko, W., Yoon, J.S., Suk, H.I.: Mutual information-driven subject-invariant and class-relevant deep representation learning in BCI. arXiv preprint arXiv:1910.07747 (2019)

14. Kam, T.E., Suk, H.I., Lee, S.W.: Multiple functional networks modeling for autism spectrum disorder diagnosis. Hum. Brain Mapp. **38**(11), 5804–5821 (2017)
15. Kang, E., Suk, H.-I.: Probabilistic source separation on resting-state fMRI and its use for early MCI identification. In: Frangi, A.F., Schnabel, J.A., Davatzikos, C., Alberola-López, C., Fichtinger, G. (eds.) MICCAI 2018. LNCS, vol. 11072, pp. 275–283. Springer, Cham (2018). https://doi.org/10.1007/978-3-030-00931-1_32
16. Kingma, D.P., Ba, J.: Adam: a method for stochastic optimization. arXiv preprint arXiv:1412.6980 (2014)
17. Suk, H.I., Wee, C.Y., Lee, S.W., Shen, D.: State-space model with deep learning for functional dynamics estimation in resting-state fMRI. NeuroImage **129**, 292–307 (2016)
18. Tishby, N., Zaslavsky, N.: Deep learning and the information bottleneck principle. In: 2015 IEEE Information Theory Workshop (ITW), pp. 1–5. IEEE (2015)
19. Vaswani, A., et al.: Attention is all you need. In: Advances in Neural Information Processing Systems, pp. 5998–6008 (2017)
20. Yan, C.G., Wang, X.D., Zuo, X.N., Zang, Y.F.: DPABI: data processing & analysis for (resting-state) brain imaging. Neuroinformatics **14**(3), 339–351 (2016)
21. Yeo, B.T., et al.: The organization of the human cerebral cortex estimated by intrinsic functional connectivity. J. Neurophysiol. **106**(3), 1125 (2011)
22. Yoon, J.S., Ko, W., Suk, H.I.: A plug-in method for representation factorization. arXiv preprint arXiv:1905.11088 (2019)

Whole MILC: Generalizing Learned Dynamics Across Tasks, Datasets, and Populations

Usman Mahmood[1](✉), Md Mahfuzur Rahman[1], Alex Fedorov[2], Noah Lewis[2], Zening Fu[1], Vince D. Calhoun[1,2,3], and Sergey M. Plis[1]

[1] Georgia State University, Atlanta, Georgia
{umahmood1,mrahman21}@student.gsu.edu, {zfu,vcalhoun,splis}@gsu.edu
[2] Georgia Institute of Technology, Atlanta, Georgia
afedorov@gatech.edu, lhd231@gmail.com
[3] Emory University, Atlanta, GA, USA

Abstract. Behavioral changes are the earliest signs of a mental disorder, but arguably, the dynamics of brain function gets affected even earlier. Subsequently, spatio-temporal structure of disorder-specific dynamics is crucial for early diagnosis and understanding the disorder mechanism. A common way of learning discriminatory features relies on training a classifier and evaluating feature importance. Classical classifiers, based on handcrafted features are quite powerful, but suffer the curse of dimensionality when applied to large input dimensions of spatio-temporal data. Deep learning algorithms could handle the problem and a model introspection could highlight discriminatory spatio-temporal regions but need way more samples to train. In this paper we present a novel self supervised training schema which reinforces whole sequence mutual information local to context (whole MILC). We pre-train the whole MILC model on unlabeled and unrelated healthy control data. We test our model on three different disorders (i) Schizophrenia (ii) Autism and (iii) Alzheimers and four different studies. Our algorithm outperforms existing self-supervised pre-training methods and provides competitive classification results to classical machine learning algorithms. Importantly, whole MILC enables attribution of subject diagnosis to specific spatio-temporal regions in the fMRI signal.

Keywords: Transfer learning · Self-supervised · Deep learning · Resting state fMRI.

1 Introduction

Mental disorders manifest in behavior that is driven by disruptions in brain dynamics [4,12]. Functional MRI captures the nuances of spatio-temporal dynamics that could potentially provide clues to the causes of mental disorders and enable early diagnosis. However, the obtained data for a single subject is of

© Springer Nature Switzerland AG 2020
A. L. Martel et al. (Eds.): MICCAI 2020, LNCS 12267, pp. 407–417, 2020.
https://doi.org/10.1007/978-3-030-59728-3_40

high dimensionality m and to be useful for learning, and statistical analysis, one needs to collect datasets with a large number of subjects n. Yet, for any kind of a disorder, demographics or other types of conditions, a single study is rarely able to amass datasets large enough to go out of the $m \gg n$ mode. Traditionally small data problem is approached by handcrafting features [18] of much smaller dimension, effectively reducing m via dimensionality reduction. Often, the dynamics of brain function in these representations vanishes into proxy features such as correlation matrices of functional network connectivity (FNC) [33].

Our goal is to enable the direct study of brain dynamics in the $m \gg n$ situation. In the case of brain data it, in turn, can enable an analysis of brain function via model introspection. In this paper, we show how one can achieve significant improvement in classification directly from dynamical data on small datasets by taking advantage of publicly available large but unrelated datasets. We demonstrate that it is possible to train a model in a self-supervised manner on dynamics of healthy control subjects from the Human Connectome Project (HCP) [32] and apply the pre-trained model to a completely different data collected across multiple sites from healthy controls and patients. We show that pre-training on dynamics allows the encoder to generalize across a number of datasets and a wide range of disorders: schizophrenia, autism, and Alzheimer's disease. Importantly, we show that learnt dynamics generalizes across different data distributions, as our model pre-trained on healthy adults shows improvements in children and elderly.

2   Related Work

Unsupervised pre-training is a well-known technique to get a head start for the deep neural network [9]. It finds wide use across a number of fields such as computer vision [13], natural language processing (NLP) [6] and automatic speech recognition (ASR) [22]. However, outside NLP unsupervised pre-training is not as popular as supervised.

Recent advances in self-supervised methods with mutual information objectives are approaching performance of supervised training [2,16,26] and can scale pre-training to very deep convolutional networks (e.g., 50-layer ResNet). They were shown to benefit structural MRI analysis [10], learn useful representations from the frames in Atari games [1] and for speaker identification [28]. Pre-trained models can outperform supervised methods by a large margin in case of small data [13].

Earlier work in brain imaging [20,27] have been based on unsupervised methods to learn the dynamics and structure of the brain using approaches such as ICA [3] and HMM [8]. Deep learning for capturing the brain dynamics has also been previously proposed [14,15,19]. In some very small datasets, transfer learning was proposed for use in neuroimaging applications [21,25,30]. Yet another idea is the data generating approach [31]. ST-DIM [1] has been used for pre-training on unrelated data with subsequent use for classification [24].

3   MILC

We present MILC as an unsupervised pre-training method. We use MILC to pre-train on large unrelated and unlabelled data to better learn data representation. The learnt representations are then used for classification on downstream tasks adding a simple linear network on top of the pre-training architecture. The fundamental idea of MILC is to establish relationship between windows (a time slice from the entire sequence) and their respective sequences through learning useful signal dynamics. In all of our experiments we use encoded rsfMRI ICA time courses as our sequences and a consecutive chunk of time points as windows. The model uses the idea to distinguish among sequences (subjects) which proves to be extremely useful in downstream tasks e.g. classification of HC or SZ subjects. To realize the concept, we maximize the mutual information of the latent space of a window and the corresponding sequence as a whole.

Let $D = \{(u_t^i, v^j) : 1 \leq t \leq T, 1 \leq i, j \leq N\}$ be a dataset of pairs computed from ICA time courses. u_t^i is the local embedding of t-th window taken from sequence i, v^j is the global embedding for the entire sequence j. T is the number of windows in a sequence, and N is the total number of sequences. Then $D^+ = \{(u_t^i, v^j) : 1 \leq t \leq T, i = j\}$ is called a dataset of positive pairs and $D^- = \{(u_t^i, v^j) : 1 \leq t \leq T, i \neq j\}$—of negative pairs. The dataset D^+ refers to a joint distribution and D^-—a marginal distribution of the whole sequence and the window in the latent space. Eventually, the lower bound with InfoNCE estimator [26] $\mathcal{I}_f(D^+)$ is defined as:

$$\mathcal{I}(D^+) \geq \mathcal{I}_f(D^+) \triangleq \sum_{i=1}^{N} \sum_{t=1}^{T} \log \frac{\exp f((u_t^i, v^i))}{\sum_{k=1}^{N} \exp f((u_t^i, v^k))}, \tag{1}$$

where f is a critic function. Specifically, we are using separable critic $f(u_t, v_s) = \phi(u_t^i)^\mathsf{T}(v^j)$, where ϕ is some embedding function parameterized by neural networks. Such embedding function is used to calculate value of a critic function in same dimensional space from two dimensional inputs. Critic learns an embedding function such that critic assigns higher values for positive pairs compared to negative pairs: $f(D^+) \gg f(D^-)$.

Our critic function takes the latent representation of a window and sequence as input. We define latent state of window as an output z_t^i produced by the CNN part of MILC, given input from t-th window x_t^i of sequence i. The latent state of sequence as c^j is the global embedding obtained from MILC architecture. Thus the critic function for input pair (x_t^i, x^j)—a window and a sequence—is $f = \phi(z_t^i)^\mathsf{T}(c^j)$. The loss is InfoNCE with f as $L = I_f$. The scheme of the MILC is shown in Fig. 1.

3.1   Transfer and Supervised Learning

In the downstream task, we use the representation (output) of the attention model pre-trained using MILC as input to a simple binary classifier on top. Refer to Sect. 4.1 for further details.

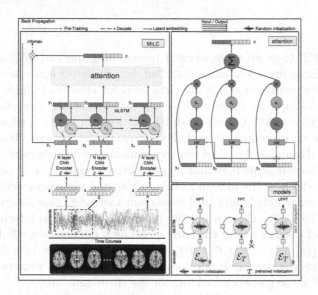

Fig. 1. Left: MILC architecture used in pre-training. ICA time courses are computed from the rsfMRI data. Results contain statistically independent spatial maps (top) and their corresponding time courses. **Right Up:** Detail of attention model used in MILC. **Right Down:** Three different models are used for downstream tasks.

4   Experiments

In this section we study the performance of our model on both, synthetic and real data. To compare and show the advantage of pre-training on large unrelated dataset we use three different kind of models—1) FPT (Frozen Pre-Trained): The pre-trained model is not further trained on the dataset of downstream task, 2) UFPT (Unfrozen Pre-Trained): The pre-trained model is further trained on the dataset of downstream task and 3) NPT (Not Pre-trained): The model is not pre-trained at all and only trained on the dataset of downstream task. The models are shown in Fig. 1. In each experiment, we compare all three models to demonstrate the effectiveness of unsupervised pre-training.

4.1   Setup

The CNN Encoder of MILC for simulation experiment consists of 4 1D convolutional layers with output features $(32, 64, 128, 64)$, kernel sizes $(4, 4, 3, 2)$ respectively, followed by ReLU after each layer followed by a linear layer with 256 units. For real data experiments, we use 3 1D convolutional layers with output features $(64, 128, 200)$, kernel sizes $(4, 4, 3)$ respectively, followed by ReLU after each layer followed by a linear layer with 256 units. We use stride 1 for all of the convolution layers. We also test against autoencoder based pre-training for simulation experiment, for which we use the same CNN encoder as for MILC in the reduction phase. For the decoder, we use the reverse architecture of the encoder that result in 10×20 windows at the output.

In MILC based pre-training, for all possible pairs in the batch, we take feature z from the output layer of CNN encoder. The latent representation of the entire time series is then passed through biLSTM. The output of biLSTM is used as input to the attention model to get a single vector c, which represents the entire time series. Scores are calculated using z and c as explained in Sect. 3. Using these scores, we compute the loss. The neural networks are trained using Adam optimizer.

In downstream tasks we are more interested in subjects for classification task, for each subject the output of attention model (c) is used as input to a feed forward network of two linear layers with 200 and 2 units to perform binary classification. For experiments, a hold out is selected for testing and is never used through the training/validation phase. For each experiment, 10 trials are performed to ensure random selection of training subjects and, in each case, the performance is evaluated on the hold out (test data). The code is available at: https://github.com/UsmanMahmood27/MILC.

4.2   Simulation

To generate synthetic data, we generate multiple 10-node graphs with 10×10 stable transition matrices. Using these we generate multivariate time series with autoregressive (VAR) and structural vector autoregressive (SVAR) models [23].

50 VAR times series with size 10×20000 are split into three time slices respectively for training, validation and testing. Using these samples, We pre-train MILC to assign windows to respective time series.

In the final downstream task, we classify the whole time-series into VAR or SVAR (obtained by randomly dropping 20% VAR samples) groups. We generate 2000 samples and split as 1600 for training, 200 for validation and 200 for hold-out test. For both pre-training and downstream task, we follow the same set up as described in Sect. 4.1.

We compare the effectiveness of MILC with the model used in [24] and two variations of autoencoder based pre-training. The two variations of autoencoder are acquired by replacing the CNN encoder of [24] and MILC by the pre-trained or randomly initialized autoencoder during downstream classification, depending on the model as explained in Sect. 4. We refer to these two variations as *AE_STDIM* and *AE_STDIM+attention*. Note that difference between the two is the added attention layer in the later during downstream classification.

It is observed that the MILC based pre-trained models can easily be fine-tuned only with small amount of downstream data. Note, with very few samples, models based on the pre-trained MILC (FPT and UFPT) outperform the un-pre-trained models (NPT), ST-DIM models, autoencoder based models. ST-DIM based pre-training model [24] performs reasonably well compared to autoencoder and NPT models, however, MILC steadily outperforms ST-DIM. Results show that autoencoder based self-supervised pre-training does not assist in VAR vs. SVAR classification. Refer to Fig. 2 **Left** for the results of simulation experiments.

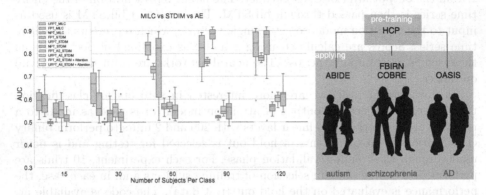

Fig. 2. Left: Area Under Curve (AUC) scores for VAR vs. SVAR time-series classification using MILC, ST-DIM and autoencoder based pre-training methods. MILC based pre-training greatly improves the performance of downstream task with small datasets. On the other side, ST-DIM works better than autoencoder based pre-training which completely fails to learn dynamics and thus exhibits poor performance. **Right:** Datasets used for pre-training and classification tasks. Healthy controls from the HCP [32] are used for pre-training guided by data dynamics alone (See footnote 1). The pre-trained model is then used in downstream classification tasks of 3 different diseases, 4 independently collected datasets, many of which contain data from a number of sites, and consist of populations with significant age difference. The age distributions in the datasets have the following mean and standard deviation: **HCP:** 29.31±3.67; **ABIDE:** 17.04 ± 7.29; **COBRE:** 37.96 ± 12.90; **FBIRN:** 37.87 ± 11.25; **OASIS:** 67.67 ± 8.92.

4.3   Brain Imaging

Datasets. Next, we apply MILC to brain imagining data. We use rsfMRI data for all brain data experiments. Refer to Fig. 2 for the details of the datasets used. We compare MILC with ST-DIM based pre-training shown in [24].

Four datasets used in this study are collected from[1] FBIRN (Function Biomedical Informatics Research Network[2]) [17] project, from COBRE (Center of Biomedical Research Excellence) [5] project, from release 1.0 of ABIDE (Autism Brain Imaging Data Exchange[3]) [7] and from release 3.0 of OASIS (Open Access Series of Imaging Studies[4]) [29].

---

[1] Human silhouettes are by Natasha Sinegina for Creazilla.com without modifications, https://creativecommons.org/licenses/by/4.0/.

[2] These data were downloaded from Function BIRN Data Repository, Project Accession Number 2007-BDR-6UHZ1.

[3] http://fcon_1000.projects.nitrc.org/indi/abide/.

[4] https://www.oasis-brains.org/.

Preprocessing. We preprocess the fMRI data using statistical parametric mapping (SPM12, http://www.fil.ion.ucl.ac.uk/spm/) under MATLAB 2016 environment. After the preprocessing, subjects were included in the analysis if the subjects have head motion $\leq 3°$ and ≤ 3 mm, and with functional data providing near full brain successful normalization [11].

For each dataset, 100 ICA components are acquired using the same procedure described in [11]. However, only 53 non-noise components as determined per slice (time point) are used in all experiments. For all experiments, the fMRI sequence is divided into overlapping windows of 20 time points with 50% overlap along time dimension.

Schizophrenia. For schizophrenia classification, we conduct experiments on two different datasets, FBIRN [17] and COBRE [5]. The datasets contain labeled Schizophrenia (SZ) and Healthy Control (HC) subjects.

FBIRN. The dataset has total 311 subjects. We use two hold-out sets with sizes 32 and 64 for validation and test respectively, remaining are used for supervised training. The details of the results are shown in Fig. 3. We see, the pre-trained MILC models outperform NPT and also ST-DIM based pre-trained models.

COBRE. The dataset has total 157 subjects—a collection of 68 HC and 89 affected with SZ. We use two hold-out sets of size 32 each for validation and test respectively. The remaining data is used for supervised training. The results in Fig. 3 strengthen the efficiency of MILC. That is, with only 15 training subjects, FPT and UFPT perform significantly better than NPT having $\simeq 0.20$ difference in their median AUC scores.

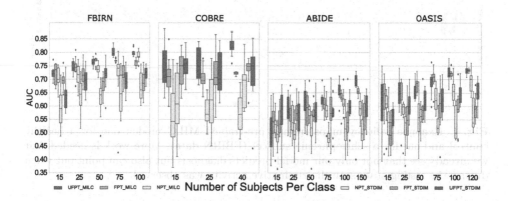

Fig. 3. AUC scores for all the three models (Refer to Fig. 1) on real dataset. With every dataset, models pre-trained with MILC (FPT, UFPT) perform noticeably better than not pre-trained model (NPT). Results also show that the learnability of MILC model dramatically increases with small increase in training data (x-axis). As we can see across the datasets, MILC outperforms ST-DIM with a large margin offering ~10% higher AUC when maximum achievable AUC scores are compared.

Autism. With 569 total subjects, 255 are HC and 314 are affected with autism. We use 100 subjects each for validation and test purpose. The remaining data is used for downstream training i.e., autism vs. HC classification. Figure 3 shows, MILC pre-trained models perform reasonably better than NPT and thus reinforces our hypothesis that unsupervised pre-training learns signal dynamics useful for downstream tasks. We suspect that the reason why pre-trained models do not work well for 15 subjects is that the dataset is much different than HCP. The big age gap between subjects of HCP and ABIDE is a major difference and 15 subjects are not enough even for pre-trained models. Refer to Fig. 2 for the demographic information of all the datasets.

Alzheimer's Disease. The dataset OASIS [29] has total 372 subjects with equal number (186) of HC and AZ patients. We use two hold-out sets each of size 64 respectively for validation and test purpose. The remaining are used for supervised training. Refer to Fig. 3 for results. The AUC scores of pre-trained models is higher than NPT starting from 15 subjects, even with 120 subjects NPTdoes not perform equally well.

4.4 Saliency

Our experiments demonstrate that with the whole MILC pre-training we're able to achieve reasonable prediction performance from complete dynamics even on small data. Importantly, we're now able to investigate what in the dynamics was the most discriminative (see Fig. 4).

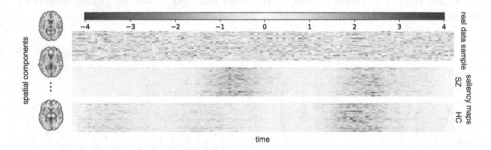

Fig. 4. Example saliency maps from a pre-trained MILC model: one for a healthy control and one for a schizophrenia subject (FBIRN data). More work is needed, but we already see that not only our model predicts diagnosis but also can point out when during the resting state scan discriminative activity was observed.

5 Conclusions and Future Work

As we have demonstrated, self-supervised pre-training of a spatio-temporal encoder gives significant improvement on the downstream tasks in brain imaging datasets. Learning dynamics of fMRI helps to improve classification results for all three dieseases and speed up the convergence of the algorithm on small datasets, that otherwise do not provide reliable generalizations. Although the utility of these results is highly promising by itself, we conjecture that direct application to spatio-temporal data will warrant benefits beyond improved classification accuracy in the future work. Working with ICA components is a smaller and thus easier to handle space that exhibits all dynamics of the signal, in future we will move beyond ICA pre-processing and work with fMRI data directly. We expect further model introspection to yield insight into the spatio-temporal biomarkers of schizophrenia. It may indeed be learning crucial information about dynamics that might contain important clues into the nature of mental disorders.

Acknowledgement. This study was in part supported by NIH grants 1R01AG063153 and 2R01EB006841. We'd like to thank and acknowledge the open access data platforms and data sources that were used for this work, including: Human Connectome Project (HCP), Open Access Series of Imaging Studies (OASIS), Autism Brain Imaging Data Exchange (ABIDE I), Function Biomedical Informatics Research Network (FBIRN) and Centers of Biomedical Research Excellence (COBRE).

References

1. Anand, A., Racah, E., Ozair, S., Bengio, Y., Côté, M.A., Hjelm, R.D.: Unsupervised state representation learning in Atari. arXiv preprint arXiv:1906.08226 (2019)
2. Bachman, P., Hjelm, R.D., Buchwalter, W.: Learning representations by maximizing mutual information across views. arXiv preprint arXiv:1906.00910 (2019)
3. Calhoun, V.D., Adali, T., Pearlson, G.D., Pekar, J.: A method for making group inferences from functional MRI data using independent component analysis. Hum. Brain Mapp. **14**(3), 140–151 (2001)
4. Calhoun, V.D., Miller, R., Pearlson, G., Adalı, T.: The chronnectome: time-varying connectivity networks as the next frontier in fMRI data discovery. Neuron **84**(2), 262–274 (2014)
5. Çetin, M.S., et al.: Thalamus and posterior temporal lobe show greater internetwork connectivity at rest and across sensory paradigms in schizophrenia. Neuroimage **97**, 117–126 (2014)
6. Devlin, J., Chang, M.W., Lee, K., Toutanova, K.: Bert: Pre-training of deep bidirectional transformers for language understanding. arXiv preprint arXiv:1810.04805 (2018)
7. Di Martino, A., et al.: The autism brain imaging data exchange: towards a large-scale evaluation of the intrinsic brain architecture in autism. Mol. Psychiatry **19**(6), 659 (2014)
8. Eavani, H., Satterthwaite, T.D., Gur, R.E., Gur, R.C., Davatzikos, C.: Unsupervised learning of functional network dynamics in resting state fMRI. In: Gee, J.C., Joshi, S., Pohl, K.M., Wells, W.M., Zöllei, L. (eds.) IPMI 2013. LNCS, vol. 7917, pp. 426–437. Springer, Heidelberg (2013). https://doi.org/10.1007/978-3-642-38868-2_36
9. Erhan, D., Bengio, Y., Courville, A., Manzagol, P.A., Vincent, P., Bengio, S.: Why does unsupervised pre-training help deep learning? J. Mach. Learn. Res. **11**, 625–660 (2010)
10. Fedorov, A., et al.: Prediction of progression to Alzheimers disease with deep Info-Max. arXiv preprint arXiv:1904.10931 (2019)

11. Fu, Z., et al.: Altered static and dynamic functional network connectivity in Alzheimer's disease and subcortical ischemic vascular disease: shared and specific brain connectivity abnormalities. Hum. Brain Mapp. (2019)
12. Goldberg, D.P., Huxley, P.: Common Mental Disorders: A Bio-social Model. Tavistock/Routledge, London (1992)
13. Hénaff, O.J., Razavi, A., Doersch, C., Eslami, S., Oord, A.V.D.: Data-efficient image recognition with contrastive predictive coding. arXiv preprint arXiv:1905.09272 (2019)
14. Hjelm, R.D., Calhoun, V.D., Salakhutdinov, R., Allen, E.A., Adali, T., Plis, S.M.: Restricted Boltzmann machines for neuroimaging: an application in identifying intrinsic networks. NeuroImage **96**, 245–260 (2014)
15. Hjelm, R.D., Damaraju, E., Cho, K., Laufs, H., Plis, S.M., Calhoun, V.D.: Spatio-temporal dynamics of intrinsic networks in functional magnetic imaging data using recurrent neural networks. Front. Neurosci. **12**, 600 (2018)
16. Hjelm, R.D., et al.: Learning deep representations by mutual information estimation and maximization. arXiv preprint arXiv:1808.06670 (2018)
17. Keator, D.B., et al.: The function biomedical informatics research network data repository. Neuroimage **124**, 1074–1079 (2016)
18. Khazaee, A., Ebrahimzadeh, A., Babajani-Feremi, A.: Application of advanced machine learning methods on resting-state fMRI network for identification of mild cognitive impairment and Alzheimer's disease. Brain Imaging and Behavior **10**(3), 799–817 (2016). https://doi.org/10.1007/s11682-015-9448-7
19. Khosla, M., Jamison, K., Kuceyeski, A., Sabuncu, M.R.: Detecting abnormalities in resting-state dynamics: an unsupervised learning approach. In: Suk, H.-I., Liu, M., Yan, P., Lian, C. (eds.) MLMI 2019. LNCS, vol. 11861, pp. 301–309. Springer, Cham (2019). https://doi.org/10.1007/978-3-030-32692-0_35
20. Khosla, M., Jamison, K., Ngo, G.H., Kuceyeski, A., Sabuncu, M.R.: Machine learning in resting-state fMRI analysis. Magnet. Reson. Imaging (2019)
21. Li, H., Parikh, N.A., He, L.: A novel transfer learning approach to enhance deep neural network classification of brain functional connectomes. Front. Neurosci. **12**, 491 (2018). https://doi.org/10.3389/fnins.2018.00491, https://www.frontiersin.org/article/10.3389/fnins.2018.00491
22. Lugosch, L., Ravanelli, M., Ignoto, P., Tomar, V.S., Bengio, Y.: Speech model pre-training for end-to-end spoken language understanding. arXiv preprint arXiv:1904.03670 (2019)
23. Lütkepohl, H.: New Introduction to Multiple Time Series analysis. Springer, Heidelberg (2005). https://doi.org/10.1007/978-3-540-27752-1
24. Mahmood, U., Rahman, M.M., Fedorov, A., Fu, Z., Plis, S.: Transfer learning of fMRI dynamics. arXiv preprint arXiv:1911.06813 (2019)
25. Mensch, A., Mairal, J., Bzdok, D., Thirion, B., Varoquaux, G.: Learning neural representations of human cognition across many fMRI studies. In: Advances in Neural Information Processing Systems, pp. 5883–5893 (2017)
26. Oord, A.V.D., Li, Y., Vinyals, O.: Representation learning with contrastive predictive coding. arXiv preprint arXiv:1807.03748 (2018)
27. Plis, S.M., et al.: Deep learning for neuroimaging: a validation study. Front. Neurosci. **8**, 229 (2014)
28. Ravanelli, M., Bengio, Y.: Learning speaker representations with mutual information. arXiv preprint arXiv:1812.00271 (2018)
29. Rubin, E.H., et al.: A prospective study of cognitive function and onset of dementia in cognitively healthy elders. Arch. Neurol. **55**(3), 395–401 (1998)

30. Thomas, A.W., Müller, K.R., Samek, W.: Deep transfer learning for whole-brain fMRI analyses. arXiv preprint arXiv:1907.01953 (2019)
31. Ulloa, A., Plis, S., Calhoun, V.: Improving classification rate of schizophrenia using a multimodal multi-layer perceptron model with structural and functional MR. arXiv preprint arXiv:1804.04591 (2018)
32. Van Essen, D.C., et al.: The WU-Minn human connectome project: an overview. Neuroimage **80**, 62–79 (2013)
33. Yan, W., et al.: Discriminating schizophrenia from normal controls using resting state functional network connectivity: a deep neural network and layer-wise relevance propagation method. In: 2017 IEEE 27th International Workshop on Machine Learning for Signal Processing (MLSP), pp. 1–6. IEEE (2017)

A Physics-Informed Geometric Learning Model for Pathological Tau Spread in Alzheimer's Disease

Tzu-An Song[1,2], Samadrita Roy Chowdhury[1,2], Fan Yang[1,2],
Heidi I. L. Jacobs[2], Jorge Sepulcre[2], Van J. Wedeen[2], Keith A. Johnson[2],
and Joyita Dutta[1,2](✉) [iD]

[1] University of Massachusetts Lowell, Lowell, MA, USA
dutta.joyita@mgh.harvard.edu
[2] Massachusetts General Hospital and Harvard Medical School, Boston, MA, USA

Abstract. Tau tangles are a pathophysiological hallmark of Alzheimer's disease (AD) and exhibit a stereotypical pattern of spatiotemporal spread which has strong links to disease progression and cognitive decline. Preclinical evidence suggests that tau spread depends on neuronal connectivity rather than physical proximity between different brain regions. Here, we present a novel physics-informed geometric learning model for predicting tau buildup and spread that learns patterns directly from longitudinal tau imaging data while receiving guidance from governing physical principles. Implemented as a graph neural network with physics-based regularization in latent space, the model enables effective training with smaller data sizes. For training and validation of the model, we used longitudinal tau measures from positron emission tomography (PET) and structural connectivity graphs from diffusion tensor imaging (DTI) from the Harvard Aging Brain Study. The model led to higher peak signal-to-noise ratio and lower mean squared error levels than both an unregularized graph neural network and a differential equation solver. The method was validated using both two-timepoint and three-timepoint tau PET measures. The effectiveness of the approach was further confirmed by a cross-validation study.

Keywords: Alzheimer's disease · Tau spread · Graph neural networks · PET · DTI

1 Introduction

Alzheimer's disease (AD) is a debilitating neurodegenerative disorder and a looming public health challenge. Extracellular amyloid-β (Aβ) plaques and intracellular tau tangles, the two hallmark pathologies of AD, are believed to play

Supported by the National Institute on Aging grant K01AG050711.
T.-A. Song and S. R. Chowdhury—These authors contributed equally.

© Springer Nature Switzerland AG 2020
A. L. Martel et al. (Eds.): MICCAI 2020, LNCS 12267, pp. 418–427, 2020.
https://doi.org/10.1007/978-3-030-59728-3_41

key mechanistic roles in AD [1]. Studies show that tau pathology in the medial temporal lobe (MTL) is a key driver of memory impairment in AD and is an important marker for neurodegeneration [6,14,16]. It is known that the spatiotemporal spread of tau tangles follows a stereotypical trajectory starting in the locus coeruleus and the transentorhinal cortex and then extending to the entorhinal cortex, the hippocampus, and finally the neocortex [3,5]. A growing body of evidence indicates that tau spreads through the brain in a prion-like fashion with neurons carrying pathological tau species transmitting them to their connected neighboring neurons via anatomical or synaptic connections [8,18]. Comprehension of neurodegenerative pathogenesis requires the understanding of the mechanisms of proliferation and accumulation of tau. Network diffusion [19] and epidemic spread [22] models have had reasonable success at explaining the relationship between structural and functional variables in the human brain. These methods have enabled group-level inference of the sources of atrophy [10,21,23]. Yet quantitative, patient-tailored, predictive methods based on these models that use learned population-level information remain unexplored.

In recent years, deep neural networks have been successfully used to solve real-world problems relating to physics-based natural phenomena [9,17]. A novel subcategory of this research uses physics-informed neural networks to explain naturally occurring dynamic processes [15,20]. While the principles of physics may correctly model some facets of real-life datasets, data-driven learning can fill the gaps between the known physics and real observations. For tau propagation, source modeling is an open problem, and there tends to be a high degree of subject-to-subject variability when group-level fitting of physics-based models is performed. Here, we present a novel physics-informed geometric learning model for predicting tau spread that (i) is capable of learning patterns of tau buildup not explained by passive diffusion alone, (ii) allows us to incorporate additional variables (e.g. scalar connectivity and diffusivity measures and potentially Aβ) which may influence the complex seeding processes for tau, and (iii) could offer robustness against local inaccuracies in the structural connectivity measures (e.g. imperfections of tractography) and local departures from physics guidance. Regularization would also help prevent overfitting, reduce generalization error, and thus ensure effective training with smaller datasets compared to a purely data-driven approach.

In this work, we use longitudinal ^{18}F-flortaucipir tau positron emission tomography (PET) scans for obtaining regional tau measures [12]. White matter fiber bundles generated via diffusion tensor imaging (DTI) are used to map the structural connectome for each subject. In Sect. 2, we describe the geometric learning and physics models. Details on data processing and experiments are provided in Sect. 3. Our main findings are reported in Sect. 4. In Sect. 5, we summarize this work and present our envisioned future directions.

2   Theory

2.1   Fisher-KPP Model for Tau Propagation and Generation

The structural network of the brain can be represented as a graph, $\mathcal{G} = (\mathcal{V}, \mathcal{E}, \boldsymbol{W})$, where $\nu_i \in \mathcal{V}$ is the ith node representing a gray-matter parcellation or anatomical region of interest (ROI), $|\mathcal{V}| = N$ is the number of nodes, $\epsilon_{ij} \in \mathcal{E}$ is the edge connecting the ith and jth nodes, and $\boldsymbol{W} \in \mathbb{R}^{N \times N}$ is the weighted adjacency matrix. Tau aggregation at a given timepoint can be represented as a graph signal $\boldsymbol{x}(t) \in \mathbb{R}^N$, the spatiotemporal evolution of which can be modeled as a diffusion process by the inhomogeneous partial differential equation (PDE):

$$\frac{\partial \boldsymbol{x}(t)}{\partial t} = -\beta \boldsymbol{L} \boldsymbol{x}(t) + \boldsymbol{s}(t, \boldsymbol{x}(t)). \tag{1}$$

Here $\boldsymbol{s}(t, \boldsymbol{x}(t)) \in \mathbb{R}^N$ is a source term modeling tau generation or clearance processes not explained by node-to-node diffusion, and $\boldsymbol{L} = \boldsymbol{I} - \boldsymbol{D}^{-\frac{1}{2}} \boldsymbol{W} \boldsymbol{D}^{-\frac{1}{2}}$ is the normalized graph Laplacian matrix ($\boldsymbol{I} \in \mathbb{R}^{N \times N}$ is the identity matrix and $\boldsymbol{D} \in \mathbb{R}^{N \times N}$ is the weighted degree matrix computed from $\boldsymbol{W}$).

As part of our prior work, we have used impulse-based representations for $\boldsymbol{s}(t, \boldsymbol{x}(t))$ which led to simple, closed-form, analytic solutions [23]. Such source models do not account for the dependence of tau seeding on the current concentration of tau. In this work, we model tau seeding and spread using the Fisher-Kolmogorov-Petrovski-Puskinovand (Fisher-KPP) equation [7,13], which is a *reaction-diffusion equation* and has the following source term:

$$\boldsymbol{s}(\boldsymbol{x}(t)) = \boldsymbol{x}(t) \odot (1 - \boldsymbol{x}(t) \oslash \boldsymbol{\kappa}). \tag{2}$$

Here the $\boldsymbol{\kappa}$ is the carrying capacity, $\odot$ represents the entrywise Hadamard multiplication, and $\oslash$ represents Hadamard division. Unlike source terms that only rely on time t, the semilinear Fisher-KPP source depends on the tau burden $\boldsymbol{x}(t)$. Although usually not solvable in closed form, such a model is physiologically meaningful since pathological tau species act as seeds or templates promoting further aggregation and spread from cell to cell in a prion-like fashion. Here, we will use the Fisher-KPP model to incorporate physics knowledge into a geometric learning framework. A numerical solution of the Fisher-KPP equation will serve as one of the reference approaches, the other being a standalone geometric learning framework without physics-based guidance.

2.2   Graph Neural Network

Graph Neural Network Architecture. The geometric learning model underlying this study is a graph neural network (GNN) based on combinatorial generalization among nodes, edges, and the entire graph [2]. Such models have been previously utilized to learn complex physical interactions and infer trajectories of dynamical systems from the system's current state. As shown in Fig. 1, the GNN comprises three blocks: an encoder, a core recurrent neural network (RNN), and a decoder. The encoder maps the input graph signal to a latent space, where the physics-based constraints are enforced. The RNN block is a rendition of a non-local neural network with update and aggregation functions. The decoder maps the latent space representation back to the observation domain to generate the final output. The GNN is set up to learn residuals in the form of mean annualized differential standardized uptake value ratios (ADSUVRs) for each ROI.

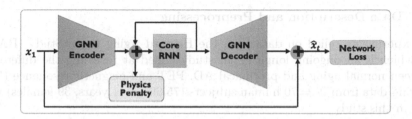

Fig. 1. Physics-regularized GNN architecture

Physics-Informed Loss Function. A complex phenomenon such as tau spread is not governed by single-variable dynamics. Instead, it is involves multivariable interactions that are not easily explained by known physical models and need to be learned from the data. A latent space representation could lead to a learned composite variable dependent not only on the tau burden but also on a variety of other inputs, e.g., scalar connectivity and diffusivity measures and potentially Aβ. We, therefore, apply the physics-based constraint in the latent space instead of the observation space. This form of physics guidance is effectively a regularizer that stabilizes the underlying inverse problem. The physics-informed loss function uses the Fisher-KPP model in (1) discretized in time and formulated as a difference equation:

$$\frac{\lambda_{n,i} - \lambda_{n-1,i}}{t_n - t_{n-1}} = \sum_j -\beta L_{ij}\lambda_{n,j} + r\lambda_{n-1,i}(1 - \lambda_{n-1,i}/\kappa_i). \tag{3}$$

Here $\lambda_{n,i}$ is a latent space variable, i and j are node indices, n is a time index, t_n is the nth timepoint, L_{ij} is (i,j)th element of the Laplacian, and β and r are hyperparameters. The net loss function, J, comprises an observation-domain L_2-norm data-fit term and a latent space L_2-norm penalty term:

$$J = \sum_{n=1}^{T} \|x_n - \hat{x}_n\|^2 + \alpha \sum_{n=1}^{T-(M-1)} \|\lambda_n - \lambda_{n-1} + \beta L\lambda_{n-1} - r\lambda_{n-1} \odot (1 - \lambda_{n-1} \oslash \kappa))\|^2. \tag{4}$$

Here x_n and $\hat{x}_n$ are the observed and predicted graph signal vectors representing tau burden in the observation domain, λ_n is the latent space vector, and α is a regularization parameter. The data-fit loss is updated T times with T at least as large as the order of temporal derivative. The physics-based loss is updated $T - (M - 1)$ times, where $M - 1$ is the number of required predictive steps.

3   Methods

3.1   Data Description and Preprocessing

All experiments relied on data from the Harvard Aging Brain Study (HABS) [4], which is an ongoing longitudinal study aimed at revealing the differences between normal aging and preclinical AD. PET and magnetic resonance (MR) imaging data from $N = 70$ human subjects (75.66 ± 6.11 years, 39 females) were used in this study.

Tau PET. Serial tau PET images at 0.6–3.6 years gap between consecutive scans were used to compute regional tau burden. Following the injection of 10 mCi ^{18}F-flortaucipir, PET data were acquired for 30 min using a 3D list-mode dynamic protocol on a Siemens ECAT HR+ scanner. One subset of the data comprised serial tau PET scans at only two timepoints ($N = 60$), henceforth referred to as the two-timepoint or 2TP cohort. A second subset comprised PET scans at three timepoints ($N = 10$), henceforth referred to as the three-timepoint or 3TP cohort. From the PET images, we calculate mean standardized uptake value ratios (SUVRs) for 85 anatomical ROIs based on the FreeSurfer Desikan-Killiany atlas with cerebellar gray matter as the reference.

Diffusion MR. The diffusion-weighted scans were acquired using a spin-echo echo-planar imaging sequence: echo time (TE) 84 ms, repetition time (TR) 8,040 ms, field-of-view $256 \times 256 \times 128$, and voxel size 2 mm isotropic with 30 isotropically distributed orientations for the diffusion-sensitizing gradients at a b-value of $700 \, s/mm^2$. Diffusion data were preprocessed using FSL to perform corrections relating to subject motion, eddy current distortion, and susceptibility. Diffusion tensors were reconstructed using DSI Studio. Fractional anisotropy (FA) and median diffusivity (MD) measures were computed from the reconstructed tensors. Deterministic fiber tracking via DSI Studio was performed to obtain the number of streamlines between various brain regions. For streamline tracking, we used an angular threshold of 45° and retained default values for all other parameters. The tracts were normalized by length, and only tracts ending in 85 gray-matter ROIs from the Desikan-Killiany atlas were used. The reconstructed streamlines were counted for each pair of ROIs to compute pairwise inter-ROI connection strengths. This led to a series of 85×85 adjacency matrices capturing individualized structural connectivity profiles for each human subject.

3.2 Experiments

Performance Comparison and Evaluation Metrics. The physics-informed GNN (GNN-P) was compared with an unregularized GNN and a numerical ordinary differential equation (ODE) solver. As quantitative figures-of-merit, we compute the mean squared error (MSE) and peak signal-to-noise ratio (PSNR).

Network Training. GNN and GNN-P implementation was done on the TensorFlow suite using the DeepMind Graph Nets library [2]. Without loss of generality, the carrying capacity of the governing Fisher-KPP equation was set to 1 in the latent space of the graph. The GNN and GNN-P networks were provided the following inputs as graph signal vectors: baseline tau signal vector (x_1) and FA and MD values computed from diffusion MR. The graph adjacency matrices (represented as a list of edge weights) were provided as additional inputs to the networks. GNN and GNN-P training was performed using the 2TP cohort: $N_{train} = 54$. A batch size of 6 and 1000 epochs were used for network training. The regularization parameter was set to $\alpha = 0.00002$. The hyperparameter values were based on Fisher-KPP literature: $\beta = 0.035$ and $r = 0.0005$.

Network Validation. For the 2TP cohort, the goal was to compute the tau signal vector at follow-up (x_2) from the baseline tau (x_1), FA values, and MD values given the individual structural connectivity profiles. The trained GNN and GNN-P models ($N_{train} = 54$, 2TP cohort) was independently validated using $N_{test\text{-}2TP} = 6$ distinct samples from the same cohort. This was followed by 10-fold cross-validation. The 3TP cohort was used for validation alone: $N_{test\text{-}3TP} = 10$. To ensure longer-term prediction capability of downstream tau aggregation from a baseline scan, the core module of the GNN was implemented as an RNN. Currently, our data is limited to a maximum of three timepoints. As more data points become available in the HABS cohort, the RNN capabilities can be fully exploited. For the 3TP cohort, the model was iterated over three timepoints to predict tau at t_2 and t_3 from tau at t_1.

4 Results

A comparison of prediction results in two subjects based on the three methods (ODE, GNN, and GNN-P) is shown in Fig. 2. The figure shows coronal slices in MNI152 space with observed and predicted mean ROI tau SUVRs and ADSUVRs overlaid on an anatomical template. The ROIs displayed in this slice are the entorhinal cortex, fusiform gyrus, inferior temporal cortex, middle temporal cortex, superior temporal cortex, amygdala, and posterior cingulate cortex, all of which are considered critical for the assessment of tau burden in early AD [11]. Tau accumulation is a slow process. Typically the regional tau profiles at consecutive timepoints of serial tau PET scans exhibit a high degree of correlation. For both visual and quantitative assessment, we, therefore, rely on the accuracy of predicted ADSUVRs computed from $\hat{x}_2 - x_1$, instead of $\hat{x}_2$. Rows 2 and 4

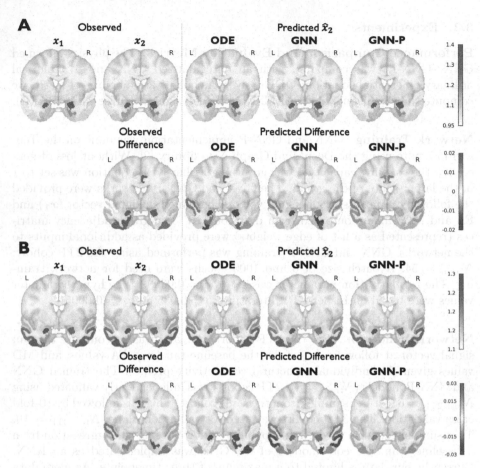

Fig. 2. Prediction results from the 2TP cohort using ODE, GNN, and GNN-P for two archetypal subjects with (A) increasing and (B) non-increasing global tau burden. Mean SUVRs and ADSUVRs in several tau-critical ROIs are plotted on coronal slices in MNI152 space and overlaid on an anatomical MR template. Rows 2 and 4 show a comparison of the ADSUVRs between t_1 and t_2.

of Fig. 2 suggest a higher degree of agreement between the observed ADSUVR and the GNN-P prediction relative to both reference approaches. This was true for both subjects with globally increasing (Fig. 2A) and non-increasing (Fig. 2B) cortical tau. Table 1 shows the predictive accuracy as captured by the mean and standard deviation of the PSNR and MSE values in the validation group of the 2TP cohort for all three methods. To assess the robustness and reproducibility of the results, a 10-fold cross-validation study was performed. The mean, standard deviation, maximum, and minimum values for the PSNR are provided in Table 2.

Table 1. Performance comparison in the 2TP cohort

Metric	ODE	GNN	GNN-P
PSNR (standard deviation)	15.6222 (1.6367)	18.8797 (3.1953)	19.0485 (2.2301)
MSE (standard deviation)	0.0687 (0.0200)	0.0348 (0.0153)	0.0314 (0.0086)

A comparison of predicted and observed ADSUVRs in one subject from the 3TP cohort is depicted in Fig. 3. Validation in the 3TP cohort was based on the model trained using the 2TP cohort data. GNN-P clearly outperforms both GNN and ODE in this even more challenging scenario thereby demonstrating its strength at making longer-term predictions.

Table 2. Cross-validation results

Method	Mean PSNR	PSNR standard deviation	Maximum PSNR	Minimum PSNR
GNN	17.2074	0.9646	19.5943	16.2967
GNN-P	18.7978	0.9571	20.3015	17.3277

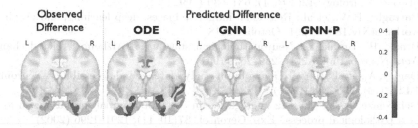

Fig. 3. Prediction results in one subject from the 3TP cohort using ODE, GNN, and GNN-P. Mean ADSUVRs in several tau-critical ROIs are plotted on coronal slices in MNI152 space and overlaid on an anatomical MR template. The model trained on the 2TP cohort was used to predict tau burden in the 3TP cohort at timepoint t_3 from the baseline scan at t_1. The MSEs of the residual for this subject are as follows: ODE 0.8174, GNN 0.8758, and GNN-P 0.6216. These prediction results are demonstrative of the longer-term prediction capabilities of GNN-P.

5   Conclusion

In this work, we developed and validated a physics-informed geometric learning framework for predicting the spatiotemporal trajectory of misfolded tau protein along the structural network of the brain. We used the Fisher-KPP reaction-diffusion equation as the governing physics model and incorporated physics guidance through a regularization penalty in the latent space generated by an encoder-decoder GNN architecture. To demonstrate proof of concept, we evaluated predictive accuracy of the physics-informed GNN-P network using 2TP and 3TP cohorts. We used MSE and PSNR as figures-of-merit and a numerical ODE solver and an unregularized GNN as benchmarks. We demonstrated that GNN-P is both qualitatively and quantitatively superior to both reference approaches. The improved prediction accuracy with GNN-P extended to both subjects with increasing and decreasing global tau burden. GNN-P was especially robust at the longer-term prediction task of computing the tau signal vector at timepoint t_3 from baseline data at t_1. Such longitudinal tracking of tau differentials is of great significance in AD prognosis. As part of our future work, we will incorporate regional Aβ profiles as additional GNN inputs. As more longitudinal data become available, we will increase the training sample size so as to boost the robustness of the GNN and GNN-P models. With the availability of tau PET scans at more timepoints, we will be able to test the prediction capability of the models over even longer observation windows.

References

1. Arriagada, P.V., Growdon, J.H., Hedley-Whyte, E.T., Hyman, B.T.: Neurofibrillary tangles but not senile plaques parallel duration and severity of Alzheimer's disease. Neurology **42**(3 Pt 1), 631–639 (1992)
2. Battaglia, P.W., et al.: Relational inductive biases, deep learning, and graph networks. arXiv:1806.01261, October 2018
3. Braak, H., Braak, E.: Neuropathological stageing of Alzheimer-related changes. Acta Neuropathol. **82**(4), 239–259 (1991)
4. Dagley, A., et al.: Harvard aging brain study: dataset and accessibility. Neuroimage **144**(Pt B), 255–258 (2017)
5. Delacourte, A., et al.: Tau aggregation in the hippocampal formation: an ageing or a pathological process? Exp. Gerontol. **37**(10–11), 1291–1296 (2002)
6. Dickson, D.W., et al.: Identification of normal and pathological aging in prospectively studied nondemented elderly humans. Neurobiol. Aging **13**(1), 179–189 (1992)
7. Fisher, R.A.: The wave of advantageous genes. Ann. Eugenics **7**(4), 355–369 (1937)
8. Frost, B., Diamond, M.I.: Prion-like mechanisms in neurodegenerative diseases. Nat. Rev. Neurosci. **11**(3), 155–159 (2010)
9. Hashemi, S.M.H., Psaltis, D.: Deep-learning PDEs with unlabeled data and hardwiring physics laws. arXiv:1904.06578, April 2019
10. Hu, C., Hua, X., Ying, J., Thompson, P.M., Fakhri, G.E., Li, Q.: Localizing sources of brain disease progression with network diffusion model. IEEE J. Sel. Top. Sig. Process. **10**(7), 1214–1225 (2016)
11. Jack, C.R., et al.: Longitudinal tau PET in ageing and Alzheimer's disease. Brain **141**(5), 1517–1528 (2018)
12. Johnson, K.A., et al.: Tau positron emission tomographic imaging in aging and early Alzheimer disease. Ann. Neurol. **79**(1), 110–119 (2016)

13. Kolmogorov, A.N., Tikhomirov, V.M., Kolmogorov, A.N.: Mathematics and mechanics. No. v. 1 in Selected works of A.N. Kolmogorov, Kluwer Academic Publishers, Dordrecht; Boston (1991)
14. McKee, A.C., Kosik, K.S., Kowall, N.W.: Neuritic pathology and dementia in Alzheimer's disease. Ann. Neurol. **30**(2), 156–165 (1991)
15. Nabian, M.A., Meidani, H.: Physics-driven regularization of deep neural networks for enhanced engineering design and analysis. J. Comput. Inf. Sci. Eng. **20**(1), 011006 (2020)
16. Neve, R.L., Robakis, N.K.: Alzheimer's disease: a re-examination of the amyloid hypothesis. Trends Neurosci. **21**(1), 15–19 (1998)
17. Noé, F., Olsson, S., Köhler, J., Wu, H.: Boltzmann generators - sampling equilibrium states of many-body systems with deep learning. arXiv:1812.01729, July 2019
18. Nussbaum, J.M., Seward, M.E., Bloom, G.S.: Alzheimer disease: a tale of two prions. Prion **7**(1), 14–19 (2013)
19. Raj, A., Kuceyeski, A., Weiner, M.: A network diffusion model of disease progression in dementia. Neuron **73**(6), 1204–1215 (2012)
20. Seo, S., Liu, Y.: Differentiable physics-informed graph networks. arXiv:1902.02950, February 2019
21. Torok, J., Maia, P.D., Powell, F., Pandya, S., Raj, A.: A method for inferring regional origins of neurodegeneration. Brain **141**(3), 863–876 (2018)
22. Vogel, J.W., et al.: Alzheimer's disease neuroimaging initiative, Swedish BioFinder study: spread of pathological tau proteins through communicating neurons in human Alzheimer's disease. Nat. Commun. **11**(1), 1–15 (2020)
23. Yang, F., Roy Chowdhury, S., Jacobs, H.I.L., Johnson, K.A., Dutta, J.: A longitudinal model for tau aggregation in Alzheimer's disease based on structural connectivity. Inf. Process. Med. Imaging 11492, 384–393 (2019)

A Deep Pattern Recognition Approach for Inferring Respiratory Volume Fluctuations from fMRI Data

Roza G. Bayrak[1]($\boxtimes$) ⓘD, Jorge A. Salas[1] ⓘD, Yuankai Huo[1] ⓘD, and Catie Chang[1,2,3] ⓘD

[1] Department of Electrical Engineering and Computer Science, Vanderbilt University, Nashville, TN 37215, USA
roza.g.bayrak@vanderbilt.edu
[2] Department of Biomedical Engineering, Vanderbilt University, Nashville, TN 37215, USA
[3] Vanderbilt University, Institute of Imaging Science, Nashville, TN 37215, USA

Abstract. Functional magnetic resonance imaging (fMRI) is one of the most widely used non-invasive techniques for investigating human brain activity. Yet, in addition to local neural activity, fMRI signals can be substantially influenced by non-local physiological effects stemming from processes such as slow changes in respiratory volume (RV) over time. While external monitoring of respiration is currently relied upon for quantifying RV and reducing its effects during fMRI scans, these measurements are not always available or of sufficient quality. Here, we propose an end-to-end procedure for modeling fMRI effects linked with RV, in the common scenario of missing respiration data. We compare the performance of multiple deep learning models in reconstructing missing RV data based on fMRI spatiotemporal patterns. Finally, we demonstrate how the inference of missing RV data may improve the quality of resting-state fMRI analysis by directly accounting for signal variations associated with slow changes in the depth of breathing over time.

Keywords: Respiration data · fMRI · Pattern recognition · Physiological artifact removal

1 Introduction

Functional magnetic resonance imaging (fMRI) is a valuable technique for studying cognition at the individual and population level. However, the reliability of the blood oxygen level dependent (BOLD) fMRI signal as an indicator of neural activity can be compromised due to head motion as well as physiological variation that arises from respiration and cardiac activity [1]. One major source of physiological variation arises from natural, slowly varying (<0.15 Hz) changes in the depth and rate of breathing over time [2–4]. Variations in respiratory volume (RV) affect fMRI by altering blood

---

Electronic supplementary material The online version of this chapter (https://doi.org/10.1007/978-3-030-59728-3_42) contains supplementary material, which is available to authorized users.

© Springer Nature Switzerland AG 2020
A. L. Martel et al. (Eds.): MICCAI 2020, LNCS 12267, pp. 428–436, 2020.
https://doi.org/10.1007/978-3-030-59728-3_42

oxygen concentrations, and are shown to widely correlate with fMRI signals across the brain and to greatly impact the interpretation of fMRI results [5, 6]. Low-frequency RV modulation is distinct from (and produces effects in fMRI beyond) the cyclic respiration artifacts that are synchronized with the breathing cycle itself [7].

Respiration data can be acquired with a pneumatic belt placed around a subject's abdomen during fMRI data acquisition, providing valuable information for determining respiration-related confounds (or effects of interest) in fMRI signals. Using such recordings, several studies have investigated the temporal dynamics of fMRI responses to changes in RV [3, 8–11]. Notably, low-frequency RV effects are not handled by methods designed to reduce the aliased cyclic effects of breathing (such as RETROICOR [7]). Further, popular data-driven approaches, such as global signal regression and ICA, do not unambiguously separate RV from neurally driven BOLD signals without using a recorded respiratory waveform for reference [5, 12–14]. Currently, respiratory and cardiac recordings are necessary for specifically modeling and/or removing RV effects.

Yet, acquisition of external respiration measures during fMRI is not always possible in practice, or the quality of respiratory recordings is not always sufficient. Thus, it is important to have automated methods for extracting key peripheral physiological signals using other means, such as the fMRI data itself. While data-driven estimation methods have been proposed for identifying cyclic effects of respiration (e.g. [15]), we are not aware of existing methods that can infer the RV signal directly from fMRI data.

In this paper, we propose a novel approach for reconstructing low-frequency RV signals directly from fMRI data using state-of-the-art deep neural networks. We construct and evaluate our models using resting-state fMRI data from the Human Connectome Project [16]. As input to the networks, we engineer input features by dividing voxels into regions of interest by clustering voxels that share coherent respiration responses, here examining divisions (parcellations) of the brain into 10, 42, and 90 regions of interest. We train and compare state-of-the-art deep learning models, including those that are capable of combining low- and high-level features (U-Net), or which learn from past and future temporal patterns (bidirectional LSTM). Furthermore, we evaluate the amount of temporal variance explained by the estimated RV signal in fMRI data across the brain, to gauge its effectiveness in capturing respiratory-driven fMRI signal changes.

The remainder of the paper is organized as follows. Section 2 briefly explains the pre-processing, ROI extraction and deep learning models that are used in this work. In Sect. 3, the experimental results are demonstrated and the models are compared. In Sect. 4, we discuss the model performance and the implications of this contribution to the analysis of brain activity.

2   Methods

2.1   Data Preprocessing

Data consisted of 200 resting-state fMRI scans from the Human Connectome Project (HCP) 1200 Subject Release. Resting-state fMRI data were acquired with the following parameters: TR = 0.72 s, duration of 864 s (14.4 min), and spatial resolution of 2 mm isotropic. During these scans, participants were instructed to keep their eyes open and fixate on a cross-hair. Respiration was monitored using a belt placed around the abdomen, sampled at 400 Hz.

The scans used in this study were selected based on the quality of respiration data. Automated criteria were first used to reject scans whose respiration signals had more than 500 samples of clipping (values equal to 0 or 4095), and the list was then refined after manual inspection to remove those with additional artifacts. We used fMRI data that had been pre-processed with the "FIX" de-noising pipeline [17]. From the respiration data of each scan, a time series of respiration volume (RV) was extracted by calculating the temporal standard deviation of the raw respiration waveform in a window of 6 s centered at each TR (every 0.72 s) of the fMRI data [8]. All fMRI data were band-pass filtered in a range of 0.01–0.15 Hz and downsampled by a factor of 2, yielding a new effective temporal sampling of 1.44 s/volume (600 time points). The same filtering and downsampling procedures were applied to the RV signals. This procedure was performed in order to make the input data comparable to more typical fMRI acquisitions, in which the temporal sampling rate is slower that 1 s.

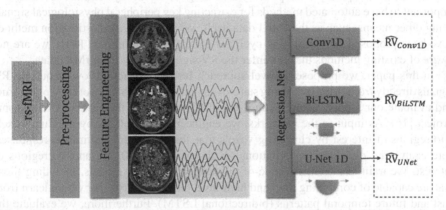

Fig. 1. Workflow of the analysis conducted in this study. Region of Interests (ROIs) were formed using k-means clustering of voxels that share coherent respiration responses, using a set of scans that was held out from subsequent neural network model training and evaluation. Three sets of ROIs, corresponding to divisions into k = 10, 42, and 90 regions, were considered. Using the time courses extracted from these ROIs, three candidate network architectures were trained to predict the RV signal. The predicted RV was compared against the measured ("ground-truth") RV signal using Pearson correlation.

2.2 Regions of Interest and Time Series Extraction

We employed a domain-knowledge guided approach to designing input features for the neural network. Here, rather than using fMRI data at the voxel-wise level as input to the networks, time courses were extracted from voxels averaged within selected regions of interest (ROIs) whose constituent voxels have similar respiration response dynamics. The motivation behind this approach is to cluster voxels based on their shared temporal responses to RV. We performed the clustering in a completely unbiased way, with a held-out dataset. Specifically, ~30% of the data, a held-out set of 62 scans, was first reserved for deriving these ROIs. For each of the 62 scans in this set, we calculated the temporal cross-correlation between each voxel's fMRI time course and the RV signal. These cross-correlation functions were then averaged across all 62 scans, and k-means clustering (with k = 10, 42, 90) was applied to identify k groups of voxels having shared respiration response dynamics. In this way, the partitioning ("parcellation") of fMRI data into ROIs is guided by the presence of shared information about RV, which may not directly align with established parcellations that were derived from clustering of resting-state signals (e.g. [18]). To obtain more homogeneous groupings of voxels, only the voxels with the top 40% closest distance to its respective cluster centroid were retained. Example slices for each parcellation scheme are shown in Fig. 1. Importantly, all subsequent model training and testing did not utilize the 62 scans reserved for ROI derivation, but rather was performed entirely on the remaining 138 scans.

For each parcellation, the average fMRI time series was extracted from all voxels within each ROI. Importantly, since the units of BOLD and RV signals are both arbitrary, we temporally normalized all signals to zero mean and unit variance before passing them into the neural network models.

2.3   Implementation Details

We explored three candidate network models: a single-neuron 1D convolutional network without a nonlinearity (hereafter referred to as the "Conv1D" model), a bidirectional LSTM, and a 1D U-Net. All of the models, which will be further described below, were trained in a 5-fold cross-validation paradigm. Input to the networks consisted of ROI time series, each of which was $T = 600$ time points long. For a given parcellation scheme, the constituent ROIs are provided to the network as different channels. The output of each network is an estimated RV time series of the same length as the input (i.e., was $T = 600$ time points). All networks were trained with learning rates ranging from 1.0e−2 to 1.0e−6, and the optimal learning rate was determined separately for each model. For all networks, a batch size of 32 was used. The models were all trained using the ADAM optimizer with default parameters and were allowed to train up to 3000 epochs. The best model was saved based on the validation loss and an early stopping criterion was imposed when the validation loss did not improve for 50 epochs. For each of the three models, parameters are shown in Table 1. The experiments were performed on an NVIDIA RTX 2080Ti GPU. Programs were implemented with Python using the Pytorch deep learning library.

2.4   Deep Regression Models

Conv1D. We trained a simple, single-neuron regression network that is comprised of a single 1D convolution. Specifications of this network are kernel size 1, stride 1 and padding 0, and this single neuron did not contain a nonlinear activation function. The learning rate for this model was 1.0e−2.

U-Net. U-Net is a state-of-the-art network whose success comes from its ability to combine low and high-level feature representations. This quality is particularly important for the problem at hand, since fMRI time series are complex signals that contain a mixture of neural activity and systemic physiological processes. We adapt the original 2D U-Net to 1D version, wherein the contracting path consists of four 1D convolutional layers, each followed by a max-pooling operation. We fixed the learning rate to $1.0e-6$ with a decay rate of 0.05 at every 400 epochs.

Bidirectional LSTM. LSTM-based models are capable of sequential learning, which makes them a good candidate for modeling temporal patterns in neural and physiological signals. Bidirectional LSTM (Bi-LSTM), in addition to memorizing samples it has seen in the past, is capable of utilizing future information. This strengthens the model by learning the patterns in forward and backward directions. We trained Bi-LSTM model with 600 hidden units. Similarly, for this model, we fixed the learning rate to $1.0e-5$ with a decay rate 0.05 at every 30 epochs.

2.5 Evaluation

We performed 5-fold cross-validation (CV) over the set of 138 scans that was not used to build the parcellations. In order to avoid overfitting, we used train-validation-test splits during training. Each fold consisted of 82 training scans, 28 validation scans, and 28 testing (withheld) scans. The best models were saved based on validation accuracy, while keeping the testing split untouched. This allowed an unbiased stopping criteria. Pearson's correlation coefficient was used to measure the correspondence between the predicted and actual RV time series. We used Pearson correlation both for loss function and when evaluating our model. In addition, to gauge the impact of the estimated RV on reducing respiration-related fMRI signal fluctuations, we examined the percent variance explained in each fMRI voxel time course by the predicted RV time course. Here, the predicted RV time course was first convolved with a previously determined transfer function ("respiration response function") that captures the forward mapping between RV and fMRI fluctuations [3], along with its time and dispersion derivatives [19] to allow for small deviations in latency and shape. The percent variance reduced was defined as the fraction by which a voxel's original temporal variance is reduced after projecting out (with ordinary least squares) a linear combination of the aforementioned RV regressors, and multiplying by 100. For the voxelwise analysis, moderate spatial smoothing (4 mm FWHM) was performed.

3 Results

The 5-fold cross validation performance for each of the three model classes is shown in Fig. 2. It can be seen that the U-Net has the best RV prediction performance compared with the Conv1D and Bi-LSTM models across all parcellation schemes, with a median Pearson correlation (r) score of 0.490. For the Conv1D model, the median is $r = 0.312$, followed by the Bi-LSTM model with median $r = 0.473$. Table 1 shows, for each model, the Pearson correlation along with the corresponding number of model parameters. Highlighted entries indicate the parcellation schemes ($k = 10$, 42, or 90) giving rise to the highest median correlation between the estimated and ground-truth RV.

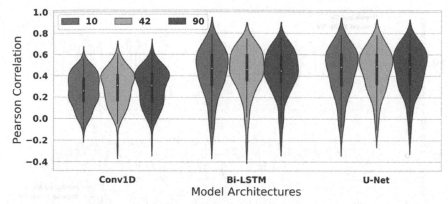

Fig. 2. Model predictions are evaluated using Pearson correlation between the actual and predicted RV signals. Each violin represents results over the unseen test data in 5-fold cross-validation, and are color-coded according to parcellation scheme.

Figure 3 demonstrates examples of the estimated and ground-truth RV signals in two different scans, where the estimate was produced from the U-Net model trained using 90 ROIs. The Pearson correlation between the predicted and ground-truth RV signals were $r = 0.78$ (top row) and $r = 0.45$ (bottom row). We then quantified how much temporal variance the predicted RV explains in fMRI data. For the scans in Fig. 3, maps of the percent variance explained at each voxel are shown in Fig. 4. As can be seen, the RV signals predicted by the model explains fMRI variance almost as strongly, and in nearly the same spatial distribution, as the ground truth RV.

Table 1. Comparison of models from each network architecture.

Models	Median Pearson Corr.	Parcellation Mode	Model Parameters
	0.262	10	11
Conv1D	**0.312**	**42**	**43**
	0.311	90	91
	0.473	**10**	**2938801**
Bi-LSTM	0.461	42	3092901
	0.448	90	3322801
	0.483	10	2599890
U-Net	**0.490**	**42**	**2602962**
	0.488	90	2607570

4   Discussion and Conclusion

In this paper, we present a novel approach for estimating RV signals directly from fMRI data, in the absence of respiration recordings. Therefore, this work sets a baseline for

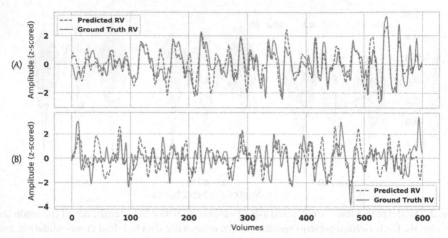

Fig. 3. Direct comparison of predicted and "ground-truth" (measured) RV. Examples are shown for two different scans: (A) one with high performance, r = 0.78, and (B) one with moderate performance, r = 0.45.

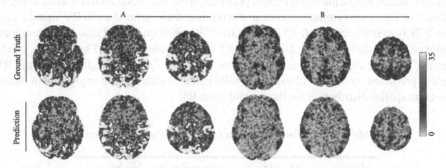

Fig. 4. Percentage of temporal variance explained by ground truth RV (above) and predicted RV (below) at each fMRI voxel, for the same scans shown in Fig. 3(A, B)

predicting RV signals using deep learning approaches that have been successful in other biomedical image analysis domains. While much work has been done on physiological correction techniques, existing methods for low-frequency RV correction require a recorded respiration signal as an input. The present work proposes a technique for decoding RV time series based on fMRI data alone, for scans where concurrent respiratory monitoring is absent or corrupted.

Our experimental results demonstrate that the U-Net and Bi-LSTM models were able to learn RV time series directly from fMRI data, and even from a relatively small number of scans. Furthermore, as shown in Fig. 4, the measured and estimated RV signals demonstrated similar magnitudes and spatial patterns of variance in fMRI fluctuations across the brain. We also note that although we are using the measured RV signal as "ground truth", respiratory signals are known to be noisy; therefore, in some scans, the accuracy may be under-estimated.

Another interesting observation was that the different parcellation schemes did not make much difference in the model performance. The results shown in Fig. 2 indicate that partitioning the brain into 10 large clusters (producing 10 input channels) yielded performance that was similar to that of a potentially richer set of 90 smaller clusters. One possible explanation is that the networks are drawing upon information provided by a small number of highly informative regions; another possibility arises from the spatial smoothness in the relationship between RV and fMRI data. These questions will be further investigated in future work. Using regions of interests (ROIs) also enabled modeling RV in a computationally efficient way, and renders the approach less sensitive to the precise spatial resolution of the acquired fMRI data. We note that parcellation was performed only for the purpose of deriving the RV signal. Once the RV signal (one-dimensional time series) has been extracted, it can be used for voxel-wise fMRI analysis, and existing RV-correction methods (such as RVHRcor [8]) can be applied for denoising.

Here, parcellations were obtained by clustering voxels based on their temporal responses to RV in a held-out dataset. We also ran experiments with two established parcellation schemes [18, 20] that were obtained by grouping voxels by their resting-state fMRI time series similarity. The resulting performance was comparable to that of our custom parcellations (median r ~ 0.45 for the U-Net model). The comparisons to these published parcellation schemes are shown in Supplementary Fig. 1.

Figure 4 implies that there can be considerable scan-to-scan variability in terms of how much variance even the measured RV explains in fMRI data, an observation that has been pointed out in the past [21]. This may depend on factors such as the manner in which the subject breathes, or how tightly respiration belt was strapped to the subject.

As this study used only resting-state data from healthy young adult subjects, future work will examine the generalizability and impact of this approach on task fMRI data. Future work will also extend this approach to subject cohorts that exhibit greater variability in brain anatomy and physiology, such as in development or aging.

Notes
The source code is available at https://github.com/neurdylab/deep-physio-recon.

Acknowledgements. This work was supported by NIH grant K22 ES028048 (C.C.).

References

1. Murphy, K., Birn, R.M., Bandettini, P.A.: Resting-state fMRI confounds and cleanup. Neuroimage **80**, 349–359 (2013)
2. Birn, R.M., et al.: Separating respiratory-variation-related fluctuations from neuronal-activity-related fluctuations in fMRI. Neuroimage **31**(4), 1536–1548 (2006)
3. Birn, R.M., et al.: The respiration response function: the temporal dynamics of fMRI signal fluctuations related to changes in respiration. Neuroimage **40**(2), 644–654 (2008)
4. Wise, R.G., et al.: Resting fluctuations in arterial carbon dioxide induce significant low frequency variations in BOLD signal. Neuroimage **21**(4), 1652–1664 (2004)
5. Glasser, M.F., et al.: Using temporal ICA to selectively remove global noise while preserving global signal in functional MRI data. NeuroImage **181**, 692–717 (2018)

6. Power, J.D., et al.: Sources and implications of whole-brain fMRI signals in humans. Neuroimage **146**, 609–625 (2017)
7. Glover, G.H., Li, T.Q., Ress, D.: Image-based method for retrospective correction of physiological motion effects in fMRI: RETROICOR. Magnet. Reson. Med. **44**(1), 162–167 (2000)
8. Chang, C., Cunningham, J.P., Glover, G.H.: Influence of heart rate on the BOLD signal: the cardiac response function. Neuroimage **44**(3), 857–869 (2009)
9. Falahpour, M., Refai, H., Bodurka, J.: Subject specific BOLD fMRI respiratory and cardiac response functions obtained from global signal. Neuroimage **72**, 252–264 (2013)
10. Golestani, A.M., et al.: Mapping the end-tidal CO2 response function in the resting-state BOLD fMRI signal: Spatial specificity, test–retest reliability and effect of fMRI sampling rate. Neuroimage **104**, 266–277 (2015)
11. Kassinopoulos, M., Mitsis, G.D.: Identification of physiological response functions to correct for fluctuations in resting-state fMRI related to heart rate and respiration. Neuroimage **202**, 116150 (2019)
12. Kundu, P., et al.: Differentiating BOLD and non-BOLD signals in fMRI time series using multi-echo EPI. Neuroimage **60**(3), 1759–1770 (2012)
13. Bright, M.G., et al., Vascular physiology drives functional brain networks. NeuroImage 116907 (2020)
14. Caballero-Gaudes, C., Reynolds, R.C.: Methods for cleaning the BOLD fMRI signal. Neuroimage **154**, 128–149 (2017)
15. Beall, E.B., Lowe, M.J.: Isolating physiologic noise sources with independently determined spatial measures. Neuroimage **37**(4), 1286–1300 (2007)
16. Van Essen, D.C., et al.: The Human Connectome Project: a data acquisition perspective. Neuroimage **62**(4), 2222–2231 (2012)
17. Griffanti, L., et al.: ICA-based artefact removal and accelerated fMRI acquisition for improved resting state network imaging. Neuroimage **95**, 232–247 (2014)
18. Shen, X., et al.: Groupwise whole-brain parcellation from resting-state fMRI data for network node identification. Neuroimage **82**, 403–415 (2013)
19. Henson, R.N., et al.: Detecting latency differences in event-related BOLD responses: application to words versus nonwords and initial versus repeated face presentations. Neuroimage **15**(1), 83–97 (2002)
20. Shirer, W.R., et al.: Decoding subject-driven cognitive states with whole-brain connectivity patterns. Cereb. Cortex **22**(1), 158–165 (2012)
21. Chang, C., Glover, G.H.: Relationship between respiration, end-tidal CO2, and BOLD signals in resting-state fMRI. Neuroimage **47**(4), 1381–1393 (2009)

A Deep-Generative Hybrid Model to Integrate Multimodal and Dynamic Connectivity for Predicting Spectrum-Level Deficits in Autism

Niharika Shimona D'Souza[1]([✉]), Mary Beth Nebel[2,3], Deana Crocetti[2], Nicholas Wymbs[2,3], Joshua Robinson[2], Stewart Mostofsky[2,3,4], and Archana Venkataraman[1]

[1] Department of Electrical and Computer Engineering, Johns Hopkins University, Baltimore, USA
Shimona.Niharika.Dsouza@jhu.edu
[2] Center for Neurodevelopmental and Imaging Research, Kennedy Krieger Institute, Baltimore, USA
[3] Department of Neurology, Johns Hopkins School of Medicine, Baltimore, USA
[4] Department of Psychiatry and Behavioral Science, Johns Hopkins School of Medicine, Baltimore, USA

Abstract. We propose an integrated deep-generative framework, that jointly models complementary information from resting-state functional MRI (rs-fMRI) connectivity and diffusion tensor imaging (DTI) tractography to extract predictive biomarkers of a disease. The generative part of our framework is a structurally-regularized Dynamic Dictionary Learning (sr-DDL) model that decomposes the dynamic rs-fMRI correlation matrices into a collection of shared basis networks and time varying patient-specific loadings. This matrix factorization is guided by the DTI tractography matrices to learn anatomically informed connectivity profiles. The deep part of our framework is an LSTM-ANN block, which models the temporal evolution of the patient sr-DDL loadings to predict multidimensional clinical severity. Our coupled optimization procedure collectively estimates the basis networks, the patient-specific dynamic loadings, and the neural network weights. We validate our framework on a multi-score prediction task in 57 patients diagnosed with Autism Spectrum Disorder (ASD). Our hybrid model outperforms state-of-the-art baselines in a five-fold cross validated setting and extracts interpretable multimodal neural signatures of brain dysfunction in ASD.

1 Introduction

Autism Spectrum Disorder (ASD) is a complex neurodevelopmental disorder characterized by impaired social communicative skills and awareness, coupled

Electronic supplementary material The online version of this chapter (https://doi.org/10.1007/978-3-030-59728-3_43) contains supplementary material, which is available to authorized users.

© Springer Nature Switzerland AG 2020
A. L. Martel et al. (Eds.): MICCAI 2020, LNCS 12267, pp. 437–447, 2020.
https://doi.org/10.1007/978-3-030-59728-3_43

with restricted/repetitive behaviors. These symptoms and levels of disability vary widely across the ASD spectrum. Neuroimaging techniques such as rs-fMRI and DTI are gaining popularity for studying aberrant brain connectivity in ASD [7]. Rs-fMRI allows us to assess the functional organization of the brain by tracking changes in steady-state co-activation [19], while DTI measures structural connectivity via the diffusion of water molecules in the brain [3]. However, the high data dimensionality, coupled with noise and patient variability, have limited our ability to integrate these modalities to understand behavioral deficits.

Techniques integrating structural and functional connectivity focus heavily on groupwise discrimination from the static connectomes. Methods include statistical tests on the node or edge biomarkers [29], data-driven representations [31], and neural networks [2] for classification. However, none of these methods tackle continuous-valued prediction, e.g., quantifying level of deficit. Deep learning is becoming increasingly popular for continuous prediction. The work of [17] proposes a specialized end-to-end convolutional network that predicts clinical outcomes from DTI connectomes. The authors of [14] combine a dictionary learning on the rs-fMRI correlations with an ANN to predict clinical severity in ASD patients. However, these methods focus on a single neuroimaging modality and do not leverage complementary information between structure and function.

There is now growing evidence that functional connectivity between regions is a dynamically evolving process [8], and that modeling this evolution is crucial to understanding disorders like ASD [25,27]. Hence, recent methods have been proposed that use either a sparse decomposition of the rs-fMRI connectomes [9], or a temporal clustering for ASD/control discrimination [26]. While promising, these approaches focus exclusively on rs-fMRI and ignore structural information.

We propose a hybrid deep-generative model that integrates structural and dynamic functional connectivity with behavior into a unified optimization framework. Our generative component is a structurally-regularized Dynamic Dictionary Learning (sr-DDL) model, which uses anatomical priors from DTI to regularize a time-varying decomposition of the rs-fMRI correlation matrices. Here, the connectivity profiles are explained by shared basis networks and time-varying patient-specific loadings. Simultaneously, these loadings are input to a deep network which uses an LSTM (Long Short Term Memory Network) to model temporal trends and an ANN (Artificial Neural Network) to predict clinical severity. Our optimization procedure learns the bases, loadings, and neural network weights most predictive of behavioral deficits in ASD. We obtain a representation which is both interpretable and generalizes to unseen patients, thus providing a comprehensive characterization of the disorder.

2   A Deep-Generative Hybrid Model for Connectomics

Figure 1 illustrates the generative (sr-DDL) and deep (LSTM-ANN) components of our framework. Let P be the number of ROIs in our brain parcellation and N be the number of patients. The rs-fMRI dynamic correlation matrices for patient n are denoted by $\{\boldsymbol{\Gamma}_n^t\}_{t=1}^{T_n} \in \mathcal{R}^{P \times P}$, with T_n being the number of time steps. $\mathbf{L}_n \in \mathcal{R}^{P \times P}$ is the corresponding DTI connectivity information, and $\mathbf{y}_n \in \mathcal{R}^{M \times 1}$ is a vector of M concatenated severity measures. Given the inputs $\mathcal{P} = \{\{\Gamma_n^t\}, \mathbf{L}_n, \mathbf{y}_n\}_{n=1}^N$, our framework optimizes the following joint objective:

$$\mathcal{J}(\mathbf{B}, \{\mathbf{c}_n^t\}, \Theta; \mathcal{P}) = \underbrace{\sum_n \mathcal{D}(\mathbf{B}, \{\mathbf{c}_n^t\}; \{\Gamma_n^t\}, \mathbf{L}_n)}_{\text{sr-DDL loss}} + \lambda \underbrace{\sum_n \mathcal{L}(\Theta, \{\mathbf{c}_n^t\}; \mathbf{y}_n)}_{\text{deep network loss}} \quad (1)$$

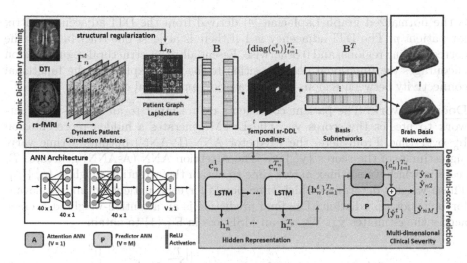

Fig. 1. Framework to integrate structural & dynamic functional connectivity for multi-task prediction **Gray Box:** sr-DDL module for rs-fMRI dynamic correlation matrices and DTI connectivity matrices. **Blue Box:** LSTM-ANN for multi-score prediction. (Color figure online)

sr-DDL Factorization: We represent the correlation matrices Γ_n^t by a shared basis $\mathbf{B} \in \mathcal{R}^{P \times K}$ that captures template patterns of co-activity and temporal loadings $\mathbf{c}_n^t \in \mathcal{R}^{K \times 1}$ that indicate their time-varying strength:

$$\mathcal{D}(\mathbf{B}, \{\mathbf{c}_n^t\}; \{\Gamma_n^t\}, \mathbf{L}_n) = \sum_t \frac{1}{T_n} ||\Gamma_n^t - \mathbf{B}\mathrm{diag}(\mathbf{c}_n^t)\mathbf{B}^T||_{\mathbf{L}_n} \quad s.t. \ \mathbf{B}^T\mathbf{B} = \mathcal{I}_K \quad (2)$$

Here, K is the size of our basis, and $\mathbf{diag}(\mathbf{c}_n^t)$ is a diagonal matrix based on the elements of $\mathbf{c}_n^t$, and $\mathcal{I}_K$ is the identity matrix of size K. The positive semi-definiteness of $\{\Gamma_n^t\}$ further implies that $\mathbf{c}_n^t$ is non-negative. The orthonormality constraint on $\mathbf{B}$ helps us learn uncorrelated sub-networks that explain the rs-fMRI data well and implicitly regularize the optimization.

Notice that Eq. (2) uses a weighted Frobenius norm, rather than the standard ℓ_2 penalty. Mathematically, this norm is computed as $||\mathbf{X}||_{\mathbf{L}_n} = \mathrm{Tr}(\mathbf{X}^T\mathbf{L}_n\mathbf{X})$ [20,28], with $\mathbf{X} = \Gamma_n^t - \mathbf{B}\mathrm{diag}(\mathbf{c}_n^t)\mathbf{B}^T$. The matrix $\mathbf{L}_n \in \mathcal{R}^{P \times P}$ in our case

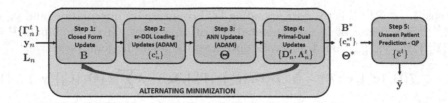

Fig. 2. Alternating minimization strategy for joint optimization of Eq. (4)

is the normalized graph Laplacian [4] derived from the DTI adjacency matrix for patient n. The DTI adjacency is 1 if there is at least one tract between the corresponding regions, and 0 otherwise. Essentially, this structural-regularization encourages the functional decomposition to focus on explaining the functional connectivity between regions with an a-priori anatomical connection.

Deep Network: The patient coefficients c_n^t are input to an LSTM-ANN network to predict the scores y_n. The LSTM generates a hidden representation h_n^t over time. From here, the Predictor ANN (P-ANN) outputs a time varying estimate of the scores $\{\hat{y}_n^t\}_{t=1}^{T_n}$. The Attention ANN (A-ANN) generates T_n scalars, which we softmax across time to obtain the attention weights: $\{a_n^t\}_{t=1}^{T_n}$. These weights determine which time points for each patient are most relevant for behavioral prediction. The final prediction is an attention-weighted average across the estimates $\hat{y}_n^t$. We use an MSE loss in Eq. (1) to obtain:

$$\mathcal{L}(\{c_n^t\}, y_n; \Theta) = \|\hat{y}_n - y_n\|_F^2 = \left\|\sum_t^{T_n} \hat{y}_n^t a_n^t - y_n\right\|_F^2 \tag{3}$$

We employ a two layered LSTM with hidden layer width 40. As seen in Fig. 1, both the P-ANN and the A-ANN have two hidden layers with width 40 with ReLU activations, with output size (V) as M and 1 respectively. We observed that these modeling choices are robust to issues with saturation and vanishing gradients that can hinder the training of deep neural networks. Finally, we fix the trade-off between the losses in Eq. (1) at $\lambda = 3$, and the number of networks to $K = 15$ based on a grid search.

2.1 Coupled Optimization Strategy

We use alternating minimization to optimize Eq. (1) with respect to $\{B, \{c_n^t\}, \Theta\}$. Here, we iteratively cycle through the updates for the dictionary B, loadings $\{c_n^t\}$, and the LSTM-ANN weights Θ to obtain a *joint solution*.

We note that there is a closed-form Procrustes solution for quadratic objectives [15]. However, Eq. (1) is bi-quadratic in B, so it cannot be directly applied. Therefore, we adopt the strategy in [12–14], by which we introduce the constraints of the form $D_n^t = B\mathbf{diag}(c_n^t)$, with corresponding augmented

Lagrangian variables $\{\Lambda_n^t\}$. Thus, our objective from Eq. (1) now becomes:

$$\mathcal{J}_c = \sum_{n,t} \frac{1}{T_n}\|\Gamma_n^t - \mathbf{D}_n^t\mathbf{B}^T\|_{\mathbf{L}_n} + \lambda\sum_n \mathcal{L}(\Theta,\{\mathbf{c}_n^t\};\mathbf{y}_n) \quad s.t. \quad \mathbf{B}^T\mathbf{B} = \mathcal{I}_K$$

$$+ \sum_{n,t} \frac{\gamma}{T_n}\left[\mathrm{Tr}\left[(\Lambda_n^t)^T(\mathbf{D}_n^t - \mathbf{Bdiag}(\mathbf{c}_n^t))\right] + \frac{1}{2}\|\mathbf{D}_n^t - \mathbf{Bdiag}(\mathbf{c}_n^t)\|_F^2\right] \quad (4)$$

Figure 2 outlines our coupled optimization strategy, with steps detailed as follows:

Step 1: Closed form Solution for B. Notice that Eq. (4) reduces to a Procrustes objective $\mathbf{B}^* = \arg\min_{\mathbf{B}:\ \mathbf{B}^T\mathbf{B}=\mathcal{I}_K} \|\mathbf{M} - \mathbf{B}\|_F^2$ where:

$$\mathbf{M} = \sum_n \frac{1}{T_n}\sum_t (\Gamma_n^t\mathbf{L}_n + \mathbf{L}_n\Gamma_n^t)\mathbf{D}_n^t + \gamma\mathbf{D}_n^t\mathbf{diag}(\mathbf{c}_n^t) + \gamma\Lambda_n^t\mathbf{diag}(\mathbf{c}_n^t)$$

Given the singular value decomposition $\mathbf{M} = \mathbf{USV}^T$, then $\mathbf{B}^* = \mathbf{UV}^T$. Thus, $\mathbf{B}$ spans the anatomically weighted space of patient correlation matrices.

Step 2: Updating the sr-DDL Loadings $\{\mathbf{c}_n^t\}$. The objective $\mathcal{J}_c$ in Eq. (4) decouples across patients. We can also incorporate the non-negativity constraint $\mathbf{c}_{nk}^t \geq 0$ by passing an intermediate vector $\hat{\mathbf{c}}_n^t$ through a ReLU. The ReLU pre-filtering allows us to optimize an unconstrained version of Eq. (4), which can be done via the stochastic ADAM algorithm [18]. In essence, this optimization couples the parametric gradient from the augmented Lagrangians with the backpropagated gradient from the deep network (defined by fixed Θ). After convergence, the thresholded loadings $\mathbf{c}_n^t = ReLU(\hat{\mathbf{c}}_n^t)$ are used in subsequent steps.

Step 3: Updating the Deep Network Weights Θ. We use backpropagation on the loss $\mathcal{L}(\cdot)$ to solve for Θ. Notice that we can handle missing clinical data by dropping the contributions of the unknown value of $\mathbf{y}_{nm}$ to the network during backpropagation. We use the ADAM [18] optimizer with random initialization, a learning rate of 10^{-4}, scaled by 0.95 every 5 epochs, and batch-size 1.

Step 4: Updating the Constraint Variables $\{\mathbf{D}_n^t,\Lambda_n^t\}$. We perform parallel primal-dual updates for the constraint pairs $\{\mathbf{D}_n^t,\Lambda_n^t\}$ [1]. Here, we cycle through the closed form update for $\mathbf{D}_n^t$ and gradient ascent for Λ_n^t until convergence.

Step 5: Prediction on Unseen Data. In our cross-validated setting, we need to compute the sr-DDL loadings $\{\bar{\mathbf{c}}^t\}_{t=1}^{\bar{T}}$ for a new patient based on the training $\mathbf{B}^*$. Since we do not know the score $\bar{\mathbf{y}}$ for this patient, we remove the contribution $\mathcal{L}(\cdot)$ from Eq. (4) and assume the constraints $\bar{\mathbf{D}}^t = \mathbf{B}^*\mathbf{diag}(\bar{\mathbf{c}}^t)$ hold with equality, thus removing the Lagrangian terms. Essentially, the optimization for $\{\bar{\mathbf{c}}^t\}$ reduces to decoupled quadratic programming (QP) objectives $\mathcal{Q}_t$ across time:

$$\bar{\mathbf{c}}^{*t} = \arg\min_{\bar{\mathbf{c}}^t} \frac{1}{2}(\bar{\mathbf{c}}^t)^T\bar{\mathbf{H}}\bar{\mathbf{c}}^t + \bar{\mathbf{f}}^T\bar{\mathbf{c}}^t \quad s.t. \quad \bar{\mathbf{A}}\bar{\mathbf{c}}^t \leq \bar{\mathbf{b}}$$

$$\bar{\mathbf{H}} = 2(\mathbf{B}^{*T}\bar{\mathbf{L}}\mathbf{B}^*); \quad \bar{\mathbf{f}} = -[(\mathbf{B}^{*T}(\bar{\Gamma}\bar{\mathbf{L}} + \bar{\mathbf{L}}\bar{\Gamma})\mathbf{B}^*)\circ\mathcal{I}_K]\mathbf{1}; \quad \bar{\mathbf{A}} = -\mathcal{I}_K \ \bar{\mathbf{b}} = \mathbf{0}$$

where, ∘ denotes the Hadamard product. Finally, we estimate $\bar{y}$ via a forward pass through the LSTM-ANN.

2.2 Baseline Comparisons

We compare the predictive performance of our framework against three baselines:

1. Two channel BrainNet CNN [17] on static rs-fMRI and DTI connectomes
2. PCA on DTI weighted dynamic rs-fMRI correlation features + LSTM-ANN
3. Decoupled sr-DDL factorization followed by the LSTM-ANN

The first baseline integrates multi-modal DTI connectivity with static rs-fMRI connectivity via the BrainNet CNN introduced in [17]. The original architecture is designed to predict cognitive scores from DTI. Here, we modify the BrainNet CNN to have two branches, one for rs-fMRI patient correlation matrices $\Gamma_n \in \mathcal{R}^{P \times P}$ and the other for the DTI Laplacians $\mathbf{L}_n \in \mathcal{R}^{P \times P}$. We also modify the ANN in [17] to pool the learned representations and predict M clinical severity measures. The hyperparameters are fixed according to [17].

For the second baseline, we weight the dynamic $P \times (P - 1)/2$ rs-fMRI correlation features by the respective DTI Laplacian features. We then use Principal Component Analysis (PCA) to reduce the data dimensionality to $K = 15$, followed by a similar LSTM-ANN framework to map onto behavior.

Finally, we examine the score prediction upon excluding the DTI regularization from our deep-generative hybrid. This helps us evaluate the advantage of our multi-modal data integration, as opposed to analyzing rs-fMRI data alone.

3 Experimental Evaluation and Results

Data and Preprocessing. We validate our framework on a cohort of 57 children with high-functioning ASD. Rs-fMRI and DTI scans are acquired on a Philips $3T$ Achieva scanner (**rs-fMRI:** EPI, TR/TE $= 2500/30$ ms, flip angle $= 70$, res $= 3.05 \times 3.15 \times 3$ mm, duration $= 128$ or 156 time samples; **DTI:** EPI, SENSE factor $= 2.5$, TR/TE $= 6356/75$ ms, res $= 0.8 \times 0.8 \times 2.2$ mm, b-value $= 700$ s/mm^2, 32 gradient directions). Rs-fMRI data was preprocessed through a standard pipeline that included motion correction, normalization to the MNI template, spatial and temporal filtering, and nuisance regression with CompCorr [6]. DTI data was preprocessed using the FDT pipeline in FSL [16]. We perform tractography using the BEDPOSTx and PROBTRACKx functions in FSL [5].

We use the Automatic Anatomical Labeling (AAL) atlas [32] to define 116 brain ROIs. A sliding window protocol (length $= 45$, stride $= 5$) was used to extract dynamic rs-fMRI correlations matrices. We subtract the first eigenvector, which is a roughly constant bias, and use the residual matrices as the inputs $\{\Gamma_n^t\}$ for all methods. The DTI connectivity matrix is binary, where 1 corresponds to at least one tract between the two regions. We impute the DTI connectivity for the 11 patients, who do not have DTI based on the training data.

We rely on three clinical measures to characterize various impairments associated with ASD. The Autism Diagnostic Observation Schedule (ADOS) [23] captures socio-communicative deficits and restricted/repetitive behaviors via clinician evaluation (dynamic range: 0−30). The Social Responsiveness Scale (SRS) [23] quantifies impaired social functioning via a parent/teacher questionnaire (dynamic range: 70−200). Finally, Praxis [11,21] measures the ability to perform skilled motor gestures on command. A videotaped performance of the child is scored by two research-reliable raters (dynamic range: 0−100).

Multi-dimensional Severity Prediction. Table 1 reports the *multi-score regression performance* of all methods. Figure 3 contrasts the performance of the deep-generative hybrid against the best performing baseline. We have included performance comparisons against the remaining baselines in Fig. 1 of the Supplementary Document. Here, we plot the severity score as given by the clinician on the **x**-axis, and the score predicted by the algorithm on the **y**-axis. The training and testing performance is illustrated by the red and blue points, respectively. The bold **x** = **y** diagonal line indicates ideal performance. Notice that all methods have a good training fit for all the scores. However, in case of testing performance, our method outperforms the baselines in almost all cases. Empirically, we are able to tune the baseline hyperparameters to obtain good testing performance on a single score (e.g. ADOS for Baseline 2), but the prediction of the remaining scores suffer. In contrast, the testing predictions from our framework follow the diagonal line more closely for all the scores. We believe that the representational flexibility of our deep network along with the joint optimization helps us generalize well.

Table 1. Performance based on **Median Absolute Error (MAE)** and **Mutual Information (MI)**. Lower MAE and higher MI indicate better performance.

Score	Method	MAE train	MAE test	MI train	MI test
ADOS	BrainNetCNN	1.90	3.50	0.96	0.25
	PCA & LSTM-ANN	0.34	**2.47**	0.96	**0.35**
	Without DTI reg	0.13	3.27	0.99	0.26
	Our framework	**0.08**	<u>2.84</u>	**0.99**	<u>0.34</u>
SRS	BrainNetCNN	5.25	18.96	0.83	0.75
	PCA & LSTM-ANN	4.73	19.05	0.95	0.68
	Without DTI reg	**0.49**	18.70	0.97	0.77
	Our framework	<u>0.51</u>	**17.81**	**0.98**	**0.88**
Praxis	BrainNetCNN	3.78	15.15	0.95	0.19
	PCA & LSTM-ANN	2.21	20.71	0.90	0.47
	Without DTI reg	1.09	17.34	0.99	0.49
	Our framework	**0.13**	**13.50**	**0.99**	**0.85**

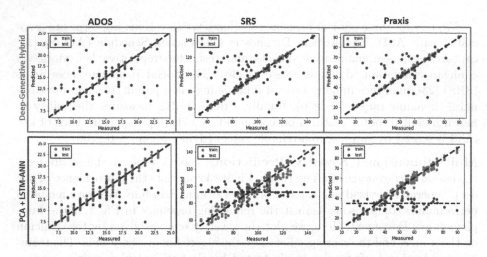

Fig. 3. Multi-score prediction by **Left:** ADOS **Middle:** SRS **Right:** Praxis by **Yellow Box:** deep-generative hybrid. **Green Box:** PCA+LSTM-ANN (Color online figure)

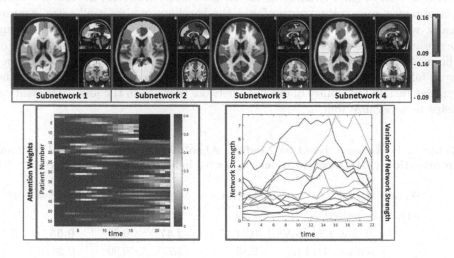

Fig. 4. Top: Subnetworks identified by the deep-generative hybrid. The red and orange regions are anti-correlated with the blue and green regions **Bottom: (Left)** Learned attention weights **(Right)** Variation of network strength over time (Color figure online)

Clinical Interpretability. Figure 4 (top) illustrates four representative subnetworks learned in **B**. (We have included the complete set of sub-network characterizations in Fig. 2 in the Supplementary Document.) Regions storing positive values are anticorrelated with negative regions. Subnetwork 1 includes regions from the default mode network (DMN), which has been widely reported in ASD [22]. Subnetwork 2 exhibits contributions from higher order visual processing and sensorimotor areas, concurring with behavioral reports of reduced visual-motor integration in ASD [22]. Subnetworks 3 exhibits contributions from the central executive control network and insula, believed to be essential for switching between goal-directed and self-referential behavior [30]. Subnetwork 4 includes prefrontal and DMN regions, along with subcortical areas: associated with social-emotional regulation [24].

Figure 4 (bottom left) illustrates the learned attentions output by the A-ANN for all 57 patients during testing. We group patients with shorter scans in the first few rows of the plot. We have blackened the rest of the time points for these patients. The colorbar indicates the strength of the attention weights. The flagged non-zero weights denote intervals of the scan considered especially relevant for prediction. We observe that the network highlights the start of the scan for several patients, while it prefers focusing on the end of the scan for some others. This is indicative of the underlying patient heterogeneity.

Lastly, we illustrate the variation of the network strength for a patient in the cohort over the scan duration in Fig. 4 (bottom right). Each solid colored line corresponds to one of the 15 sub-networks. Over the scan duration, each network cycles through phases of activity and relative inactivity. Thus, only a few networks at each time step contribute to the patient's dynamic connectivity profile. This parallels the transient brain-states hypothesis in dynamic rs-fMRI connectivity [10], with active states as corresponding sub-networks in **B**.

4 Conclusion

We have introduced a novel deep-generative framework to integrate complementary information from the functional and structural neuroimaging domains, and simultaneously explain behavioral deficits in ASD. Our unique structural regularization elegantly injects anatomical information into the rs-fMRI functional decomposition, thus providing us with an interpretable brain basis. Our LSTM-ANN term not only models the temporal variation, but also helps isolate key dynamic resting-state signatures, indicative of clinical impairments. Our coupled optimization procedure ensures that we learn effectively from limited training data and generalize well to unseen patients. Finally, our framework makes very few assumptions and can potentially be applied to study other neuro-psychiatric disorders (e.g. ADHD, Schizophrenia) as an effective diagnostic tool.

References

1. Afonso, M.V., Bioucas-Dias, J.M., Figueiredo, M.A.: An augmented Lagrangian approach to the constrained optimization formulation of imaging inverse problems. IEEE Trans. Image Process **20**(3), 681–695 (2010)
2. Aghdam, M.A., Sharifi, A., Pedram, M.M.: Combination of rs-fMRI and sMRI data to discriminate autism spectrum disorders in young children using deep belief network. J. Digit. Imaging **31**(6), 895–903 (2018)
3. Assaf, Y., Pasternak, O.: Diffusion tensor imaging (DTI)-based white matter mapping in brain research: a review. J. Mol. Neurosci. **34**(1), 51–61 (2008). https://doi.org/10.1007/s12031-007-0029-0

4. Banerjee, A., Jost, J.: On the spectrum of the normalized graph Laplacian. Linear Algebra Appl. **428**(11–12), 3015–3022 (2008)
5. Behrens, T.E., Berg, H.J., Jbabdi, S., Rushworth, M.F., Woolrich, M.W.: Probabilistic diffusion tractography with multiple fibre orientations: what can we gain? Neuroimage **34**(1), 144–155 (2007)
6. Behzadi, Y., et al.: A component based noise correction method (CompCor) for BOLD and perfusion based fMRI. Neuroimage **37**(1), 90–101 (2007)
7. Bennett, I.J., Rypma, B.: Advances in functional neuroanatomy: a review of combined DTI and fMRI studies in healthy younger and older adults. Neurosci. Biobehav. Rev. **37**(7), 1201–1210 (2013)
8. Cabral, J., Kringelbach, M.L., Deco, G.: Functional connectivity dynamically evolves on multiple time-scales over a static structural connectome: models and mechanisms. NeuroImage **160**, 84–96 (2017)
9. Cai, B., Zille, P., Stephen, J.M., Wilson, T.W., Calhoun, V.D., Wang, Y.P.: Estimation of dynamic sparse connectivity patterns from resting state fMRI. IEEE Trans. Med. Imaging **37**(5), 1224–1234 (2017)
10. Damaraju, E., et al.: Dynamic functional connectivity analysis reveals transient states of dysconnectivity in schizophrenia. NeuroImage: Clin. **5**, 298–308 (2014)
11. Dziuk, M., Larson, J.G., Apostu, A., Mahone, E.M., Denckla, M.B., Mostofsky, S.H.: Dyspraxia in autism: association with motor, social, and communicative deficits. Dev. Med. Child Neurol. **49**(10), 734–739 (2007)
12. D'Souza, N.S., Nebel, M.B., Wymbs, N., Mostofsky, S., Venkataraman, A.: A generative-discriminative basis learning framework to predict clinical severity from resting state functional MRI data. In: Frangi, A.F., Schnabel, J.A., Davatzikos, C., Alberola-López, C., Fichtinger, G. (eds.) MICCAI 2018. LNCS, vol. 11072, pp. 163–171. Springer, Cham (2018). https://doi.org/10.1007/978-3-030-00931-1_19
13. D'Souza, N.S., Nebel, M.B., Wymbs, N., Mostofsky, S., Venkataraman, A.: A coupled manifold optimization framework to jointly model the functional connectomics and behavioral data spaces. In: Chung, A.C.S., Gee, J.C., Yushkevich, P.A., Bao, S. (eds.) IPMI 2019. LNCS, vol. 11492, pp. 605–616. Springer, Cham (2019). https://doi.org/10.1007/978-3-030-20351-1_47
14. D'Souza, N.S., Nebel, M.B., Wymbs, N., Mostofsky, S., Venkataraman, A.: Integrating neural networks and dictionary learning for multidimensional clinical characterizations from functional connectomics data. In: Shen, D. (ed.) MICCAI 2019. LNCS, vol. 11766, pp. 709–717. Springer, Cham (2019). https://doi.org/10.1007/978-3-030-32248-9_79
15. Everson, R.: Orthogonal, but not orthonormal, procrustes problems. Adv. Comput. Math. **3**(4), 782–790 (1998)
16. Jenkinson, M., Beckmann, C.F., Behrens, T.E., Woolrich, M.W., Smith, S.M.: FSL. Neuroimage **62**(2), 782–790 (2012)
17. Kawahara, J., et al.: BrainNetCNN: convolutional neural networks for brain networks; towards predicting neurodevelopment. NeuroImage **146**, 1038–1049 (2017)
18. Kingma, D.P., Ba, J.L.: Adam: a method for stochastic optimization (2015)
19. Lee, M.H., Smyser, C.D., Shimony, J.S.: Resting-state fMRI: a review of methods and clinical applications. Am. J. Neuroradiol. **34**(10), 1866–1872 (2013)
20. Manton, J.H., Mahony, R., Hua, Y.: The geometry of weighted low-rank approximations. IEEE Trans. Sig. Process **51**(2), 500–514 (2003)
21. Mostofsky, S.H., Dubey, P., Jerath, V.K., Jansiewicz, E.M., Goldberg, M.C., Denckla, M.B.: Developmental dyspraxia is not limited to imitation in children with autism spectrum disorders. J. Int. Neuropsychol. Soc. **12**(3), 314–326 (2006)

22. Nebel, M.B., et al.: Intrinsic visual-motor synchrony correlates with social deficits in autism. Biol. Psychiatry **79**(8), 633–641 (2016)
23. Payakachat, N., et al.: Autism spectrum disorders: a review of measures for clinical, health services and cost-effectiveness applications. Expert Rev. Pharmacoeconomics Outcomes Res. **12**(4), 485–503 (2012)
24. Pouw, L.B., Rieffe, C., Stockmann, L., Gadow, K.D.: The link between emotion regulation, social functioning, and depression in boys with ASD. Res. Autism Spectrum Disord. **7**(4), 549–556 (2013)
25. Price, T., Wee, C.-Y., Gao, W., Shen, D.: Multiple-network classification of childhood autism using functional connectivity dynamics. In: Golland, P., Hata, N., Barillot, C., Hornegger, J., Howe, R. (eds.) MICCAI 2014. LNCS, vol. 8675, pp. 177–184. Springer, Cham (2014). https://doi.org/10.1007/978-3-319-10443-0_23
26. Rabany, L., et al.: Dynamic functional connectivity in schizophrenia and autism spectrum disorder: convergence, divergence and classification. NeuroImage Clin. **24**, 101966 (2019)
27. Rashid, B., Damaraju, E., Pearlson, G.D., Calhoun, V.D.: Dynamic connectivity states estimated from resting fMRI identify differences among schizophrenia, bipolar disorder, and healthy control subjects. Front. Hum. Neurosci. **8**, 897 (2014)
28. Schnabel, R.B., Toint, P.L.: Forcing sparsity by projecting with respect to a non-diagonally weighted Frobenius norm. Math. Program. **25**(1), 125–129 (1983). https://doi.org/10.1007/BF02591723
29. Skudlarski, P., Jagannathan, K., Calhoun, V.D., Hampson, M., Skudlarska, B.A., Pearlson, G.: Measuring brain connectivity: diffusion tensor imaging validates resting state temporal correlations. Neuroimage **43**(3), 554–561 (2008)
30. Sridharan, D., et al.: A critical role for the right fronto-insular cortex in switching between central-executive and default-mode networks. Proc. Nat. Acad. Sci. **105**(34), 12569–12574 (2008)
31. Sui, J., et al.: Combination of resting state fMRI, DTI, and sMRI data to discriminate schizophrenia by n-way MCCA+ JICA. Front. Hum. Neurosci. **7**, 235 (2013)
32. Tzourio-Mazoyer, N., et al.: Automated anatomical labeling of activations in SPM using a macroscopic anatomical parcellation of the MNI MRI single-subject brain. Neuroimage **15**(1), 273–289 (2002)

Poincaré Embedding Reveals Edge-Based Functional Networks of the Brain

Siyuan Gao[1](✉), Gal Mishne[2], and Dustin Scheinost[3]

[1] Department of Biomedical Engineering, Yale University, New Haven, CT, USA
siyuan.gao@yale.edu
[2] Halıcıoğlu Data Science Institute, University of California, San Diego, CA, USA
[3] Department of Radiology and Biomedical Imaging, Yale School of Medicine,
New Haven, CT, USA

Abstract. Many approaches have been applied to fMRI data in order
to understand the network organization of the brain. While the majority
of these works defines networks as a collection of regions (*i.e.*, nodes),
there is ample evidence that defining networks as a collection of connections between regions (*i.e.*, edges) offers numerous advantages, including
a natural way of grouping regions into multiple networks. Here, we proposed a framework for creating edge-based networks from resting-state
functional connectivity data. This framework relies on a novel embedding
approach—based on the Poincaré embedding—to handle the large number of edges found in fMRI data (*e.g.*, $O(N^2)$). We applied this framework to resting-state fMRI data from the Human Connectome Project
and compared the resultant networks to networks derived from clustering
nodes and from previously proposed methods for clustering edges. While
previous methods for clustering edges failed to discover a valuable network representation of the human brain, the edge-based networks derived
from clustering the Poincaré embedding showed clear and interpretable
functional networks. Overall, our framework provides a novel tool for
characterizing the functional network organization of the brain.

Keywords: Brain networks · Poincaré embedding · Clustering

1 Introduction

Elucidating the functional organization of the human brain by grouping distinct
brain regions into functional networks is a major goal of current fMRI research
[5]. Using measures of functional connectivity or spatiotemporal patterns of brain
activity [10], many approaches have been used to form ∼10 functional networks
(*e.g.*, motor and default mode networks) [4,12,14,16].

Electronic supplementary material The online version of this chapter (https://
doi.org/10.1007/978-3-030-59728-3_44) contains supplementary material, which is
available to authorized users.

© Springer Nature Switzerland AG 2020
A. L. Martel et al. (Eds.): MICCAI 2020, LNCS 12267, pp. 448–457, 2020.
https://doi.org/10.1007/978-3-030-59728-3_44

An important problem with these approaches is the so-called "resolution limit" [9]. As a system becomes larger, the expected number of connections between regions decreases, eventually leading to situations where merging two distinct networks is better than keeping them separated. Additionally, a region's membership to a particular network is likely fuzzy, such that two networks can overlap in a particular region [13,18].

An alternative method for creating networks within a large system is the "link community" paradigm, where the networks are redefined as sets of links (*i.e.*, edges or connections) rather than regions [1,7]. This framework provides a natural way to allow regions to belong to multiple networks as edges originating from a particular node can belong to many networks [1,6,7].

However, the large number of edges in fMRI data (*e.g.*, $O(N^2)$) poses challenges in terms of computation and representation when finding link communities [1,6,7]. Here, we show that, while traditional approaches for finding link communities fail to discover a valuable network representation of the human brain, a novel embedding approach—based on the Poincaré embedding [11]–offers a naturalistic approach to find link communities in high-dimensional fMRI space. An overview of our approach and how it differs from region clustering and previous link community detection approaches is shown in Fig. 1.

2   Methods

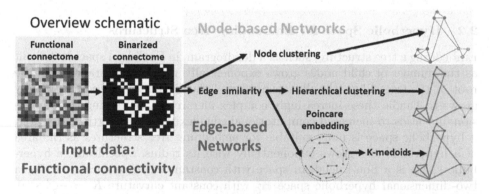

Fig. 1. Overview of using the Poincaré embedding to form edge-based networks. Starting with functional connectivity matrices, or connectomes (*blue box*), functional brain networks can be formed based on clustering nodes or edges. Previous approaches using fMRI data have focused only on creating node-based networks (*yellow box*). Yet, approaches to create edge-based networks exist. Here, we show that the link community detection methods proposed by Ahn *et al.* [1] do not reveal interpretable functional networks (*top row in red box*) and that our novel Poincaré embedding approach does (*bottom row in red box*). (Color figure online)

2.1   Link Community Detection

Let $G = (V, E)$ be a graph with vertex set V and edge set E. Traditional community detection methods define a community as a set of nodes that have more internal than external connections. Link community detection methods work in a similar way, but define a set of interrelated edges as the community. Each node then inherits all memberships of its edges and, thus, can belong to multiple, overlapping communities. As edges—rather than nodes—are assigned to different communities, similarities between edges need to be determined. One of the first methods, proposed in Ahn *et al.* [1], calculates the similarity between edges e_{ik} and e_{jk} that share a common node k. The similarity is calculated as the Jaccard index between the sets of node neighbors from the outer node i and j: $S(e_{ik}, e_{jk}) = |n(i) \cap n(j)| / |n(i) \cup n(j)|$, where $n(i)$ is the set of neighboring nodes of node i. With the similarity defined, standard hierarchical clustering is applied to group edges into link communities as it also allows to reveal hierarchy. This relies on applying a threshold to the hierarchical clustering dendrogram to create distinct communities. Partition density is a measure to determine the quality of the partitions and to find the optimal threshold to cut the dendrogram. For a network with M links, the partition density is defined as $D = \frac{2}{M} \sum_c m_c \frac{m_c - n_c - 1}{(n_c - 2)(n_c - 1)}$, where the candidate partition creates c subsets with each subset having m_c links and n_c nodes. Yet, even when determined through a systematic way (*e.g.*, partition density), this thresholding may lose information between different tree levels, leading to an uninterpretable number of communities.

2.2   Hyperbolic Space for Embedding Tree Structures

Embedding a tree structure, such as a dendrogram, in Euclidean space is difficult as the number of child nodes grows exponentially with their distance from the root of the tree. Thus, the dimensionality of the Euclidean embedding rapidly grows to handle these increasingly complex hierarchies. Increasing this dimensionality leads to increased computational complexity and overfitting. However, a hyperbolic space is more suitable for embedding tree structures as the area of a hyperbolic disc grows exponentially with its radius. Specifically, a hyperbolic space is a non-Euclidean space with constant negative curvature. For a two-dimensional hyperbolic space $\mathbb{H}^2_\zeta$ with constant curvature $K = -\zeta^2 < 0$, the length of a circle and the area of a disk with hyperbolic radius r, are $L(r) = 2\pi \sinh \zeta r, A(r) = 2\pi (\cosh \zeta r - 1)$, both growing exponentially as $e^{\zeta r}$ with r (Fig. 2). With this property, hyperbolic spaces can be constructed as continuous versions of trees. This is not possible in $\mathbb{R}^2$.

2.3   Poincaré Ball Model and Embedding

To take advantage of a hyperbolic space for embedding edge similarities, we use the Poincaré embedding, an approach based on the Poincaré ball model [11]. Let $\mathcal{B}^d = \{x \in \mathbb{R}^d \mid ||x|| < 1\}$ be the open d-dimensional unit ball where $||x||$

is the Euclidean norm. Then, the Poincaré ball model corresponds to a Riemannian manifold $(\mathcal{B}^d, g_x)$. The Riemannian metric tensor is $g_x = (\frac{2}{1-||x||^2})^2 g^E$, where $x \in \mathcal{B}^d$ and g^E represents the Euclidean metric tensor. From the Riemannian metric tensor, the Poincaré distance between points $u, v \in \mathcal{B}^d$ is given as $d(u, v) = \text{arcosh}(1 + 2\frac{||u-v||^2}{(1-||u||^2)(1-||v||^2)})$. Geodesics in $\mathcal{B}^d$ are circles perpendicular to the boundary $\delta\mathcal{B}$. Moreover, the model excludes the boundary $\delta\mathcal{B}$.

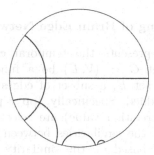

Fig. 2. Geodesics of Poincaré disk model.

The goal of the Poincaré embedding is to find a representation $\Theta = \{\theta_i\}_{i=1}^n$, where $\theta_i \in \mathcal{B}^d$, that minimizes the loss function $\mathcal{L}(\Theta)$. Specifically, a soft ranking loss function is used:

$$\mathcal{L}(\Theta) = \sum_{(u,v)\in\mathcal{D}} \log \frac{e^{-d(\theta_u,\theta_v)}}{\sum_{v'\in\mathcal{N}(u)} e^{-d(\theta_u,\theta_{v'})}},$$

where the set $\mathcal{D} = \{(u, v)\}$ is the set containing input pairs that are similar, $\mathcal{N}(u) = \{v|(u, v) \notin \mathcal{D})\}\cup\{u\}$ is the set of negative examples for u. Ten negative examples are chosen during training. This loss function encourages similar points (*i.e.*, edges) to be close in the hyperbolic space with regard to their Poincaré distance.

Since the Poincaré ball model has a Riemannian manifold structure, manifold optimization methods such as Riemannian stochastic gradient descent (RSGD) [2] can be used to minimize the loss function, which requires to calculate the Riemannian gradient and apply the retraction operator to map the gradient from the tangent space onto the manifold. The Riemannian gradient can be obtained by scaling the Euclidean gradient ∇_E by the inverse of the Poincaré ball metric tensor $g_\theta^{-1} = \frac{(1-||\theta_t||^2)^2}{4}$. The retraction operation we use is $\Re_\theta(v) = \theta + v$. The embedding is further restricted within the Poincaré ball via the projection.

$$\text{proj}(\theta) = \begin{cases} \theta/||\theta|| - \epsilon, & \text{if } ||\theta|| \geq 1 \\ \theta, & \text{otherwise} \end{cases}.$$

One full update of a single embedding is thus given by

$$\boldsymbol{\theta}_{t+1} \leftarrow \text{proj}(\boldsymbol{\theta}_t - \eta_t \frac{(1 - \|\boldsymbol{\theta}_t\|^2)^2}{4} \nabla_E),$$

where η_t is the learning rate. It is also worth mentioning that this combination of Riemannian gradient with the simple retraction operation corresponds to the natural gradient method.

2.4   Poincaré Embedding of Brain Edge Network

Functional connectivity represents the temporal correlation of time series between brain regions. Let $G = (V, E)$ be a functional connectivity with brain regions V and edge set E, a subset of edges $e_{ij} \in E$ is first selected as the objects to be embedded. Specifically, top x percent of edges with the strongest edge weight (correlation value) are selected, resulting in a binary connectivity matrix. Next, the similarities between edges that share a common node were calculated based on the similarity measure described above $S(e_{ik}, e_{jk}) = |n(i) \cap n(j)|/|n(i) \cup n(j)|$. Edges with no common nodes will have similarity of 0. The Poincaré embedding of those edges is then calculated based on this measure of similarities. As a result, in the embedding space, an edge will be closer to edges for which they have higher similarity values than other unrelated edges.

3   Experiments and Results

3.1   Datasets and Processing

We applied our algorithm to the resting-state data from the Human Connectome Project dataset [17]. After excluding subjects for mean frame-to-frame displacement > 0.15 mm, 514 (240 males) healthy subjects were used for analysis. This conservative threshold for exclusion due to motion was used to mitigate the substantial effects of motion on functional connectivity. fMRI data were processed with standard methods and parcellated into 268 nodes using a whole-brain functional atlas defined previously in a separate sample [15]. Next, the mean time-courses of each node pair were correlated and Fisher transformed, generating a 268×268 functional connectivity matrix (also called a commectome) per individual. Connectomes were averaged over all individuals and binarized by taking the top 5% ($\sim$1800) edges based on previous work [12]. For the proposed method based on the Poincaré embedding, half of the subjects (257 subjects) were used to generate the embedding; while, the other half were used for replication of the embedding.

3.2 Traditional Link Community Detection Fails

The traditional link community detection framework, proposed by Ahn *et al.* [1] and described in Sect. 2.1, did not lead to meaningful results (Fig. 3a). Specifically, 84 networks were found by cutting the dendrogram based on maximizing the partition density. This number of clusters was significantly greater than the ~10 networks from using node-based methods [4, 12, 14, 16]. Additionally, these clusters identified disjoint functional networks that putatively should belong to the same network. For example, the green and red clusters in Fig. 3a are both part of the visual network and should be combined into a single network. An additional post-hoc analysis is needed to merge these and other clusters (*i.e.*, the cyan cluster) to from a proper functional network.

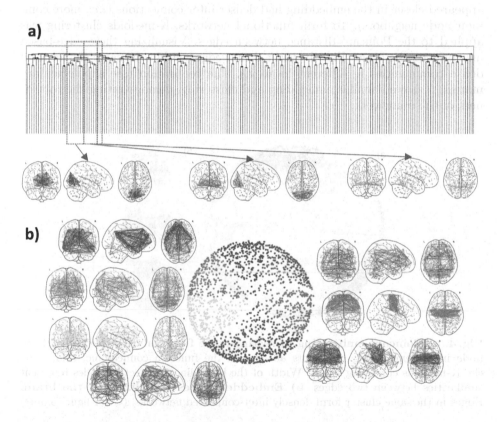

Fig. 3. a) Dendrogram from linkage clustering method. Colors of adjacent links represent the same cluster under the optimal cut threshold. In total, 84 clusters were found. Edges from three disjoint clusters that together compromise the visual network are shown. **b) Multidimensional scaling embedding and K-means clustering result.** Edges are densely located within the embedding space (*center*); but, most networks—shown on the periphery—remain mostly uninterpretable (Color figure online)

Finally, as hierarchical clustering produced too many clusters, we attempted to generate functional networks using K-means, which groups data into a specified number of clusters. In order to perform K-means, first, we generated a 2-dimensional Multidimensional scaling (MDS) embedding based on the same edge similarity as above. Edges are densely located within the embedding space, but most networks remain uninterpretable (Fig. 3b). For example, while the orange network represents the motor network, the blue and green clusters consists of edges from all over the brain and are difficult to interpret.

3.3   Poincaré Embedding of Edges

The Poincaré Embedding of the resting-state data is shown in Fig. 4a. Edges that appeared closer in the embedding had denser inter-connections (*i.e.*, more common node neighbors). To form functional networks, K-medoids clustering was applied to the Poincaré distance between edges. Visualizing these edge-based networks on the brain (Fig. 4b) verified that edges within the same cluster form dense communities in different locations. The replication (see supplementary material) showed similar embedding and clustering, demonstrating the robustness of the framework.

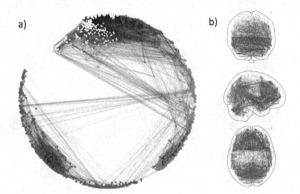

Fig. 4. a) Poincaré embedding of resting-state functional connectivity. Each node in the embedding represents an edge in the function connectome, colored by the K-medoids clustering result. Width of the black lines connecting nodes represent similarities between two edges. **b) Embedded edges visualized on the brain.** Edges in the same cluster form densely inter-connected networks. (Color figure online)

3.4   Functional Edges Show a Canonical Network Structure

Compared with the edge-based networks in Sect. 3.2, the edge-based networks derived from clustering the Poincaré embedding showed a more interpretable structure. For example, in addition to the clear motor network observed in

Sect. 3.2, the visual, default mode, auditory, language, and medial frontal networks were easily identified (Fig. 5a). Next, we compared the nodes covered by edges in each network to previously defined canonical node-based networks [8] (Fig. 5b). Visually the edge-based and the node-based networks were comprised of similar nodes. Finally, each edge's Poincaré distance from the origin $(0,0)$ represents its hierarchy in the network structure. The closer an edge is with the origin; the higher in hierarchy that edge is (see arrow in Fig. 5a). Although networks formed with higher hierarchy edges were sparser, the overall topological structure was preserved, suggesting the supporting role those edges had in the overall network topology (see supplementary material).

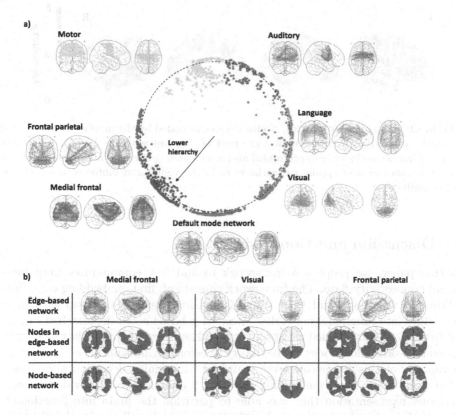

Fig. 5. a) **Edge-based networks using Poincaré embedding.** Network labels were determined by matching the nodes in the edge-based network with predefined canonical networks. Dashed circle in the embedding represents the average distance to the center. The arrow points towards lower in the hierarchy of edges within a network. b) **Comparison with node-based networks** Nodes belonging to the edge-based networks were similar to the nodes belonging to canonical networks using node community detection approaches. (Color figure online)

3.5   Overlapping Edge-Based Networks for a Node Are Meaningful

A major advantage of our edge-based networks is that each region of the brain can be associated with multiple canonical networks. For each region, we summed the number of edge-based networks associated with that node. As shown in Fig. 6, regions associated with cognitive processing (posterior cingulate cortex, prefrontal cortex, and parietal lobe) showed the highest number of overlapping networks. In contrast, regions in the motor cortex or visual lobe showed membership to the least number of networks. Overall, these results align with previous research, suggesting functional specialization in those areas [3,13].

Fig. 6. Overlapping networks. Nodes were color coded by the number of edge-based networks that edges from the node were part of. Regions with the highest number of overlapping networks were in prefrontal and association cortices, while regions with the lowest number of overlapping networks were in the visual and motor cortices. (Color figure online)

4   Discussion and Conclusion

In this paper, we propose a framework to find link communities from functional connectivity data. The framework consists of: first, embedding edges into a Poincaré disk model and, then, using K-medoids clustering to group the embedded edges into functional networks. These edge-based networks matched canonical brain networks, defined using conventional node-based approaches. Yet, edge-based networks allow nodes the flexibility to belong to multiple networks, a major advantage of this framework over standard community detection approaches. Although the Poincaré embedding has only 2 dimensions, it provided a parsimonious representation that was able to partition the brain into functionally meaningful networks. Future work includes using higher dimensional embedding to test if more information can be preserved to improve network detection. Overall, our framework provides a novel tool for characterizing the functional network organization of the brain.

Acknowledgement. Data were provided in part by the Human Connectome Project, WU-Minn Consortium (Principal Investigators: David Van Essen and Kamil Ugurbil; U54 MH091657) funded by the 16 NIH Institutes and Centers that support the NIH Blueprint for Neuroscience Research; and by the McDonnell Center for Systems Neuroscience at Washington University.

References

1. Ahn, Y.Y., Bagrow, J.P., Lehmann, S.: Link communities reveal multiscale complexity in networks. Nature **466**(7307), 761–764 (2010)
2. Bonnabel, S.: Stochastic gradient descent on Riemannian manifolds. IEEE Trans. Autom. Control **58**(9), 2217–2229 (2013)
3. Cole, M.W., Reynolds, J.R., Power, J.D., Repovs, G., Anticevic, A., Braver, T.S.: Multi-task connectivity reveals flexible hubs for adaptive task control. Nat. Neurosci. **16**(9), 1348–1355 (2013). https://doi.org/10.1038/nn.3470
4. Damoiseaux, J.S., et al.: Consistent resting-state networks across healthy subjects. Proc. Nat. Acad. Sci. **103**(37), 13848–13853 (2006). https://www.pnas.org/content/103/37/13848
5. Eickhoff, S.B., Constable, R.T., Yeo, B.T.: Topographic organization of the cerebral cortex and brain cartography. NeuroImage **170**, 332–347 (2018). http://www.sciencedirect.com/science/article/pii/S1053811917301222. Segmenting the Brain
6. Evans, T.S., Lambiotte, R.: Line graphs link partitions and overlapping communities. Phys. Rev. E **80**, 016105 (2009). https://doi.org/10.1103/PhysRevE.80.016105
7. Evans, T.S., Lambiotte, R.: Line graphs of weighted networks for overlapping communities. Eur. Phys. J. B **77**(2), 265–272 (2010). https://doi.org/10.1140/epjb/e2010-00261-8
8. Finn, E.S., et al.: Functional connectome fingerprinting: identifying individuals using patterns of brain connectivity. Nat. Neurosci. **18**(11), 1664 (2015)
9. Fortunato, S., Barthélemy, M.: Resolution limit in community detection. Proc. Natl Acad. Sci. **104**(1), 36–41 (2007). https://www.pnas.org/content/104/1/36
10. Friston, K.J.: Functional and effective connectivity: a review. Brain Connectivity **1**(1), 13–36 (2011). https://doi.org/10.1089/brain.2011.0008. PMID: 22432952
11. Nickel, M., Kiela, D.: Poincaré embeddings for learning hierarchical representations. In: Advances in Neural Information Processing Systems, pp. 6338–6347 (2017)
12. Power, J., et al.: Functional network organization of the human brain. Neuron **72**(4), 665–678 (2011). https://doi.org/10.1016/j.neuron.2011.09.006
13. Salehi, M., Karbasi, A., Barron, D.S., Scheinost, D., Constable, R.T.: Individualized functional networks reconfigure with cognitive state. NeuroImage **206**, 116233 (2020). http://www.sciencedirect.com/science/article/pii/S1053811919308249
14. Salehi, M., Karbasi, A., Shen, X., Scheinost, D., Constable, R.T.: An exemplar-based approach to individualized parcellation reveals the need for sex specific functional networks. NeuroImage **170**, 54–67 (2018). http://www.sciencedirect.com/science/article/pii/S1053811917307139. Segmenting the Brain
15. Shen, X., Tokoglu, F., Papademetris, X., Constable, R.T.: Groupwise whole-brain parcellation from resting-state fMRI data for network node identification. Neuroimage **82**, 403–415 (2013)
16. Thomas Yeo, B.T., et al.: The organization of the human cerebral cortex estimated by intrinsic functional connectivity. J. Neurophysiol. **106**(3), 1125–1165 (2011). https://doi.org/10.1152/jn.00338.2011. PMID: 21653723
17. Van Essen, D.C., et al.: The WU-Minn human connectome project: an overview. Neuroimage **80**, 62–79 (2013)
18. Wu, K., et al.: The overlapping community structure of structural brain network in young healthy individuals. PLoS ONE **6**(5), 1–14 (2011). https://doi.org/10.1371/journal.pone.0019608

The Constrained Network-Based Statistic: A New Level of Inference for Neuroimaging

Stephanie Noble[1](✉) and Dustin Scheinost[1,2,3,4,5]

[1] Department of Radiology and Biomedical Imaging, Yale University, New Haven, CT, USA
stephanie.noble@yale.edu
[2] Department of Biomedical Engineering, Yale University, New Haven, CT, USA
[3] Department of Statistics and Data Science, Yale University, New Haven, CT, USA
[4] Interdepartmental Neuroscience Program, Yale University, New Haven, CT, USA
[5] Child Study Center, Yale University, New Haven, CT, USA

Abstract. Neuroimaging research aimed at dissecting the network organization of the brain is poised to flourish under major initiatives, but converging evidence suggests more accurate inferential procedures are needed to promote discovery. Inference is typically performed at the cluster level with a network-based statistic (NBS) that boosts power by leveraging known dependence within the local neighborhood. However, existing NBS methods overlook another important form of dependence—shared membership in large-scale brain networks.

Here, we propose a new level of inference that pools information within predefined large-scale networks: the Constrained Network-Based Statistic (cNBS). We evaluated sensitivity and specificity of cNBS against existing standard NBS and threshold-free NBS by resampling task data from the largest openly available fMRI database: the Human Connectome Project. cNBS was most sensitive to effect sizes below medium, which accounts for the majority of ground truth effects. In contrast, threshold-free NBS was most sensitive to higher effect sizes. Ground truth maps showed grouping of effects within large-scale networks, supporting the relevance of cNBS. All methods controlled FWER as intended. In summary, cNBS is a promising new level of inference for promoting more valid inference, a critical step towards more reproducible discovery in neuroscience.

Keywords: fMRI · Network-based statistic · Benchmarking

1 Introduction

Functional connectivity analysis of neuroimaging data often involves tests at many thousands of individual connections (*i.e.*, edges). Multiple testing corrections are thus needed to achieve desired levels of specificity (*i.e.*, 1-false positive

© Springer Nature Switzerland AG 2020
A. L. Martel et al. (Eds.): MICCAI 2020, LNCS 12267, pp. 458–468, 2020.
https://doi.org/10.1007/978-3-030-59728-3_45

rate), but simple corrections that assume independence between tests can have markedly low sensitivity (*i.e.*, true positive rate) with so many tests. To address this issue, the activation-mapping community developed tailored corrections that improve sensitivity by pooling information across the local neighborhood, or cluster [4,11]. These strategies have been adapted for functional connectivity inference with demonstrated improvements in sensitivity [1,20,24].

However, existing strategies for cluster-level inference share two major limitations. First, they rely on the assumption that the relevant level of inference is the local neighborhood. This can miss shared membership of edges within larger-scale networks. Second, they treat statistics as identically distributed, although different networks have distinct properties. A correction that leverages known information about the structure of the connectome is needed to address both issues and thus improve sensitivity. Here, we introduce the Constrained Network-Based Statistic (cNBS), a new statistic designed to address these limitations, and we establish its empirical utility in the context of existing methods. This evaluation is intended to support the move towards more accurate tools for reproducible inference [12,15].

2 Algorithms for Network-Based Inference

The following describes three network-based statistics evaluated here and the algorithm used for nonparametric multiple comparison correction. For clarity, we will use "network-based statistic" to denote any statistic operating on a set of edges, although it was originally used for a particular statistic and technique [24].

I. Standard Network-Based Statistic (stdNBS): stdNBS represents the size of a component (*i.e.*, cluster of contiguous edges) obtained from the thresholded t-statistic graph [24]. Let the univariate test statistic $\mathbf{t}$ be the weights of the graph $\mathbf{U}(\mathbf{V}, \mathbf{E}, \mathbf{t})$ (all graphs $\mathbf{U}$ represent simple undirected graphs of $\mathbf{V}$ nodes and $\mathbf{E}$ edges without loops). Given a user-defined threshold τ, let $\mathbf{E}' \subseteq \mathbf{E}$ be the edges of the graph $\mathbf{U}'(\mathbf{V}', \mathbf{E}')$ defined as $\mathbf{E}' = \{\{i, j\}$ if $\mathbf{t}(i, j) > \tau\}$. Components $\mathbf{U}''_c \subseteq \mathbf{U}'$ are the C maximally connected subgraphs of $\mathbf{U}'$. Then the stdNBS statistic is the number of edges (*i.e.*, size) in component c:

$$\mathbf{s}_c = |\mathbf{E}''_c|. \tag{1}$$

stdNBS is threshold-dependent since it relies on the choice of τ, which is referred to as the "cluster-defining threshold" in the activation-mapping literature and will be referred to here as the "component-defining threshold". This threshold is typically defined by the user *a priori* to a value between $t = (2 - 3.5)$—here, $\tau = 3.1$. The component-defining threshold influences the size of the connected components: a large edge-level threshold is more likely to result in a smaller component than a large component-defining threshold.

II. Threshold-Free Network-Based Statistic (tfNBS): The threshold-free cluster enhancement (TFCE) statistic was originally defined for the activation-mapping literature [18] and translated to the network context by [1,20]. tfNBS roughly represents the weighted size of a component obtained from the zero-thresholded t-statistic graph.

Let $\mathbf{t}$ be the weights of $\mathbf{U}(\mathbf{V}, \mathbf{E}, \mathbf{t})$. Let $\mathbf{E}' \subseteq \mathbf{E}$ be the edges of the subgraph $\mathbf{U}'(\mathbf{V}', \mathbf{E}', \mathbf{t}')$ defined as $\mathbf{E}' = \{\{i, j\}$ if $\mathbf{t}(i, j) > 0\}$. Then for each edge e in $\mathbf{E}'$, the tfNBS statistic is defined as:

$$\mathbf{s}_e = \int_{t=t_0}^{\mathbf{t}'_e} z_e(t)^Z t^T \, dt \tag{2}$$

where t_0 is typically set to 0, $\mathbf{t}'_e$ is the t-statistic at edge $\mathbf{E}'_e$, z is the component size for the component containing $\mathbf{E}_e$ when the graph is thresholded at t, and $Z = 0.4$ and $T = 3.0$ are constants that have been chosen empirically (these were selected to match E and H in MRtrix3; see [1, 20] for a discussion about parameter choice).

Unlike stdNBS, tfNBS does not rely on a user-defined threshold and inherently includes all thresholds. Thus, the same magnitude statistic can occur for a strong localized component as for a weak but widely distributed component.

III. Constrained Network-Based Statistic (cNBS): cNBS represents the mean univariate statistic of a predefined large-scale subnetwork. In detail, the cNBS statistic is calculated as follows: let $\mathbf{t}$ be the weights of $\mathbf{U}(\mathbf{V}, \mathbf{E}, \mathbf{t})$. Given an edge-level partition $(\mathbf{N}'_1, \mathbf{N}'_2, \ldots \mathbf{N}'_C)$ of the fully connected network $\mathbf{N}$ such that $\mathbf{N} = \mathbf{N}'_1 \cup \mathbf{N}'_2 \cup \ldots \mathbf{N}'_C$, let $(\mathbf{U}'_1, \mathbf{U}'_2, \ldots \mathbf{U}'_C)$ be the partition of $\mathbf{U}$ based on $\mathbf{N}'$. Each $\mathbf{U}'_c$ in the partition will be called a "subnetwork". Then, the cNBS statistic is the mean t-statistic for a subnetwork:

$$\mathbf{s}_c = \frac{\sum_{e=1}^{E'} \mathbf{t}'_{c,e}}{|\mathbf{E}'_c|}. \tag{3}$$

cNBS also includes an additional correction step, detailed below.

2.1 Nonparametric Inference with Network-Based Statistics

Current methods for network-based inference rely on the Freedman-Lane procedure to nonparametrically estimate null hypothesis testing thresholds that provide weak control of the familywise error rate (FWER; rate of at least one false positive in a family of tests) [11, 22]. A simplified description is given in Algorithm 1 (single contrast, no exchangeability blocks), including a modification that demonstrates a special correction for cNBS for the present study. Here, the expected FWER = 5%. Nonparametric corrections are often preferred to parametric corrections in fMRI since recent work in activation-mapping has demonstrated that the latter can result in invalid cluster-based FWER control [3]. $K = 1000$ permutations, used here, are expected to yield a 95% confidence interval of FWER = 0.0500 ± 0.0138, estimated by the Wilson method [21, 22].

cNBS Correction: As shown in Algorithm 1, the cNBS correction is unique in nonparametrically estimating p-values for each network separately before FWER correction to ensure uniform false positive rates across networks. Note that simulations suggest that cNBS-based inference as described is practically equivalent to a variant that averages observations first. That is, let $\mathbf{Y}_n$ be the weights of $U(\mathbf{V}, \mathbf{E}, \mathbf{Y}_n)$ for subject n and let $\mathbf{Y}'_n$ be its partition based on N. Let

$$\bar{\mathbf{Y}}'_{n,c} \in \mathbb{R}^{N \times C} = \frac{\sum_{e=1}^{E'} \mathbf{Y}'_{c,e}}{|\mathbf{E}'_c|}. \qquad (4)$$

Then the cNBS statistic $\mathbf{s}_c$ can be defined as the t-statistic $\mathbf{t}_c$ calculated for $\bar{\mathbf{Y}}'_c$ according to the formula in Algorithm 1 and corrected as above. The Pearson's correlation between FWER-corrected p-values obtained from the original cNBS and the cNBS variation is $r > 0.99$ (practically equivalent though not identical) across 10,000 simulations using identical permutations of K = 100 and K = 1,000.

Note the two major conceptual deviations from stdNBS/tfNBS that address the two main limitations noted in the Introduction: (1) data is pooled within each predefined partition, and (2) the multiple comparison correction is adapted to nonparametrically estimate p-values for each network separately, resulting in an equivalent rate of false positives across each subnetwork allowing them to be treated more equally in the subsequent correction.

Implementation: The Matlab toolbox NBS v1.2 [10] was modified for command line use and to perform tfNBS and cNBS in the present study. The procedure for tfNBS was adapted from the toolbox MatlabTFCE [7] with parameters from the toolbox MRtrix3 [8]. All code was implemented in Matlab and adapted for Octave and is available at [9]. Run time was 24 s for stdNBS, 44 s for tfNBS, and 24 s for cNBS.

3   Benchmarking Methods

Empirically benchmarking validity (*i.e.*, sensitivity and specificity) [16] enables an understanding of the practical differences between network-based statistics. Here, we introduce a benchmarking framework based on state-of-the-art resampling methods employed in the activation-mapping community [3,13] using one of the largest openly available fMRI datasets. Although empirical measures of ground truth have limitations, the use of one of the largest available datasets and repetition of the experiment across multiple tasks promotes generalizability.

3.1   Data for Benchmarking

Minimally preprocessed data was obtained from the Human Connectome Project S1200 release [5,19]. Subjects performed two resting runs and seven tasks: Emotion (n = 1022), Gambling (n = 1057), Language (n = 1021), Motor (n = 1058), Relational (n = 1016), Working Memory (WM; n = 1058), and Social (n = 1027). BioImage Suite was used to regress confounds (24 motion parameters, white matter, cerebrospinal fluid, and global signal time courses), remove the linear trend, apply a low-pass filter, and calculate the mean timecourse within each of 268 regions in the Shen268 atlas, a parcellation of the brain based on voxel timeseries

---

Algorithm 1. Nonparametric network-based inference

input   : $\mathbf{Y} \in \mathbb{R}^{N \times E}$: N observations for E edges in a simple undirected graph;
           $\mathbf{X} \in \mathbb{R}^{N \times M}$: design matrix for M parameters of interest;
           $\mathbf{Z} \in \mathbb{R}^{N \times W}$: design matrix for W nuisance regressors (optional);
           $\mathbf{c} \in \mathbb{R}^{M}$: contrast vector;
           $\alpha \in \mathbb{R}$: target familywise error rate (FWER) threshold;
           $K \in \mathbb{Z}$: number of permutations for FWER estimation;
           $f_s \colon \mathbb{R}^E \longmapsto \mathbb{R}^E$: NBS estimator (see NBS methods I-III in section 2).
output : $\mathbf{s} \in \mathbb{R}^{C}$: NBS (stdNBS, tfNBS, or cNBS) for C components;
           $\hat{\mathbf{h}}_1 \in \mathbb{R}^{C}$: positives (rejection of the null hypothesis after correction).
init   : $\mathbf{P} \in \mathbb{R}^{N \times N \times K}$: $\{0,1\}$ permutation matrix, where each $\mathbf{P}_k$ is a $N \times N$
           matrix with a single 1 per row and column.

for $e \leq E$; do // fit unpermuted model

$\quad \{\hat{\beta}_e, \hat{\gamma}_e, \hat{\epsilon}_e\} = \underset{\beta,\gamma}{\mathrm{argmin}} \|\epsilon = \mathbf{Y}_e - \mathbf{X}\beta - \mathbf{Z}\gamma\|^2$; // Least Squares

$\quad \{\hat{\gamma}_{\mathbf{z},e}, \hat{\epsilon}_{\mathbf{z},e}\} = \underset{\gamma \mathbf{z}}{\mathrm{argmin}} \|\epsilon = \mathbf{Y}_e - \mathbf{Z}\gamma\|^2$;

$\quad t_e \in \mathbb{R} = \dfrac{\mathbf{c}^\mathsf{T}\hat{\beta}_e}{\sqrt{\hat{\epsilon}_e^\mathsf{T}\hat{\epsilon}_e \mathbf{c}^\mathsf{T}(\mathbf{X}^\mathsf{T}\mathbf{X})^{-1}\mathbf{c}/(N-M)}}$; // t-statistic for contrast

end
$\mathbf{s} = f_s(\mathbf{t})$;
$s_{max} \in \mathbb{R} = \max(\mathbf{s})$;
for $p \leq K$; do // fit permuted models

$\quad$ for $e \leq E$; do

$\qquad \mathbf{Y}_e^* = \mathbf{P}_p \hat{\epsilon}_{\mathbf{z},e} + \mathbf{Z}\hat{\gamma}_{\mathbf{z},e}$;

$\qquad \{\hat{\beta}_e^*, \hat{\gamma}_e^*, \hat{\epsilon}_e^*\} = \underset{\beta,\gamma}{\mathrm{argmin}} \|\epsilon = \mathbf{Y}_e^* - \mathbf{X}\beta - \mathbf{Z}\gamma\|^2$;

$\qquad t_e^* = \dfrac{\mathbf{c}^\mathsf{T}\hat{\beta}_e^*}{\sqrt{\hat{\epsilon}_e^{*\mathsf{T}}\hat{\epsilon}_e^* \mathbf{c}^\mathsf{T}(\mathbf{X}^\mathsf{T}\mathbf{X})^{-1}\mathbf{c}/(N-M)}}$;

$\quad$ end
$\quad \mathbf{s}_p^* = f_s(\mathbf{t}^*)$;
$\quad s_{max,p}^* \in \mathbb{R} = \max(\mathbf{s}_p^*)$;
end
if f_s is cNBS then

$\quad \mathbf{p}_c = \dfrac{\sum_{k=1}^K \mathbf{s}_c \leq \mathbf{s}_{c,k}^*}{K}$; // uncorrected p-value

$\quad \mathbf{p}_c' = \mathbf{p}_c * C$; // FWER-corrected p-value (Bonferroni)
else

$\quad \mathbf{p}_c' = \dfrac{\sum_{k=1}^K \mathbf{s}_c \leq \mathbf{s}_{max,k}^*}{K}$; // FWER-corrected p-value

end
$\hat{\mathbf{h}}_{1,c} = [\mathbf{p}_c' \leq \alpha]$. // where $[...]$ is the Iverson bracket

---

similarity [17]. The Pearson's correlation between each pair of regions was converted to a z-score using a Fisher transformation, thus providing the observations $\mathbf{Y}$. The Shen268 atlas has been partitioned into 10 node groups based on node timeseries similarity: medial frontal (MF), frontoparietal (FP), default mode network (DMN), motor (Mot), visual I (VI), visual II (VII), visual association (VAs), salience (Sal), subcortex (SC), and cerebellum (CBL) (cf. [14]). From this node-based partition follows an edge-based partition, where the edges of a 268×268 graph are assigned to $10 * 11/2 = 55$ subgraphs, or subnetworks (10 within node group and 45 between node group). This edge-based partition was used to define the network partition $\mathbf{N}$ for cNBS.

3.2 Procedure for Benchmarking Validity

Sensitivity: The sensitivity procedure for each task was informed by previous work in the activation-mapping literature [13]. All code was implemented in Matlab and adapted for Octave. The following is a brief summary; see Algorithm 2 for details. All subjects who performed both that task and REST1 were considered the full dataset for that task. **Ground truth effect size maps** were obtained by estimating the effect size (Cohen's d) of the difference between task and rest in the full dataset, for each edge. The procedure for estimating

---

Algorithm 2. Benchmarking procedure

input : $\mathbf{Y}, \mathbf{X}, \mathbf{Z}, \mathbf{c}, \alpha, K$ (see Algorithm 1)
  f : set of functions f_s for S network-based statistics;
  $N' \in \mathbb{Z}$: number of observations to subsample for resampling;
  $R \in \mathbb{Z}$: number of repetitions for resampling.
output : $\mathbb{E}(\mathbf{h}_{1|1}) \in \mathbb{R}^{E \times S}$: true positive rate (cf. [11]);
  $\mathbf{d} \in \mathbb{R}^{E}$: ground truth Cohen's d coefficients (for reference, effect size is
    classified as small $d=0.2$, medium $d=0.5$, large $d=0.8$) [2].
init   : $\mathbf{P} \in \mathbb{R}^{S \times R \times N}$: $\{0,1\}$ resampling matrix, where each $\mathbf{P}_{s,r}$ has nonzero
    elements corresponding to N' randomly selected observations.
for $e \leq E$; do
$\quad \{\hat{\beta}_e, \hat{\gamma}_e\} = \underset{\beta, \gamma}{\operatorname{argmin}} \|\mathbf{Y}_e - \mathbf{X}\beta - \mathbf{Z}\gamma\|^2;$
$\quad t_e = \dfrac{\mathbf{c}^\mathsf{T}\hat{\beta}_e}{\sqrt{\hat{\epsilon}_e^\mathsf{T}\hat{\epsilon}_e \mathbf{c}^\mathsf{T}(\mathbf{X}^\mathsf{T}\mathbf{X})^{-1}\mathbf{c}/(N-M)}};$
$\quad d_e = \dfrac{t_e}{\sqrt{N}};$
end
for $z = -1$ to 1; do // Both positive and negative effects
$\quad \mathbf{c}^\dagger = z\mathbf{c};\quad \mathbf{d}^\dagger = z\mathbf{d};$
$\quad$ for $s \leq S$; do
$\quad\quad$ for $r \leq R$; do
$\quad\quad\quad \mathbf{Y}_e^* = \mathbf{P}_{s,r}\mathbf{Y}_e;\quad \mathbf{X}_e^* = \mathbf{P}_{s,r}\mathbf{X}_e;\quad \mathbf{Z}_e^* = \mathbf{P}_{s,r}\mathbf{Z}_e;$
$\quad\quad\quad \{\mathbf{S}_{s,r}^*, \hat{\mathbf{h}}_{1,s,r}^*\} = $ Algorithm 1 : $(\mathbf{Y}^*, \mathbf{X}^*, \mathbf{Z}^*, \mathbf{c}^\dagger, \alpha, K, f_s);$
$\quad\quad$ end
$\quad\quad \forall e$ if $\mathbf{d}_e^\dagger > 0$, then $\mathbb{E}(\mathbf{h}_{1|1,s,e}) = \sum_{r=0}^{R} \dfrac{\hat{\mathbf{h}}_{1,s,r,e}^*}{R};$
$\quad$ end
end

---

task-based connectomes using HCP data is fairly straightforward, common, and associated with out-of-scanner behavior [6]. Although HCP studies do not often perform task versus rest contrasts in this way, this is a common practice in the field to isolate task-specific effects.

Sensitivity was then estimated by comparing results from repeatedly subsampled data ($N' = 40$, $R = 1000$) to ground truth effects, for both positive and negative contrasts. All surviving results showing effects in the same direction as the ground truth were labelled true positives, as in prior studies [13,18,23]. Sensitivity is then given by the true positive rate over all repetitions.

Specificity: The same procedure was used for assessing specificity with the following changes that follow the activation-mapping literature [3]. To emulate a null effect, for each subsampled subject, REST1 was randomly assigned to task or rest and REST2 to the other condition. Accordingly, all surviving positives were labelled false positives. Since the inference procedure is designed for a desired FWER, the relevant measure of specificity is 1-FWER. Based on the expected confidence interval above, the minimum permissible specificity is 93.62%.

4   Results

4.1   Ground Truth Effects are Grouped by Subnetworks

The distribution of ground truth effects used to estimate sensitivity can also be used to illustrate the relevance of cNBS. Effect sizes tended to be similar within the Shen subnetworks, supporting the relevance of large scale network-level inference (Fig. 1). This pattern was consistent across tasks, although task-specific effects also grouped within the Shen subnetworks. Furthermore, effect sizes were generally negative within subnetworks and positive between subnetworks. Consistent with activation-mapping results obtained from the same dataset [13], the majority of effect sizes (>70%) were found to be below medium.

4.2   cNBS is Most Sensitive to Edge-Level Effects, But Highly Variable

cNBS showed the highest sensitivity to edge-level effects below medium, which covers the majority of effects (Fig. 2a and Table 1). For a small effect size, the sensitivity (expected TPR) for cNBS was $\sim$6 times greater than tfNBS and stdNBS. In contrast, tfNBS was most sensitive to effects above medium. For a large effect size, nearly perfect sensitivity was attained with stdNBS and tfNBS, with cNBS $\sim$2/3 as sensitive. At a medium effect size, all methods performed about the same. stdNBS was consistently least sensitive. Much greater variability was observed for cNBS than other methods, reflecting its lack of tailoring to edge-level effects. Expected levels of specificity were attained for all methods (1-FWER$_{stdNBS}$ = 95.3%, 1-FWER$_{tfNBS}$ = 96.0%, 1-FWER$_{cNBS}$ = 94.5%). The better sensitivity of network-level inference to small but not medium-to-large effects lends insight into the effects themselves: namely, many effects may be shared across a network with the exception of relatively few strong effects occurring at isolated edges.

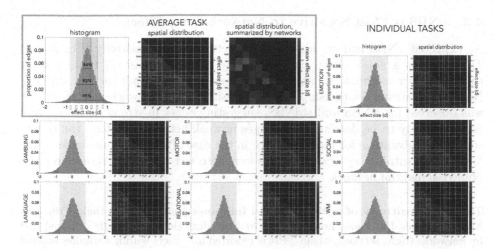

Fig. 1. Distribution of ground truth effects. Effect size histograms and spatial maps for average across tasks (top left) and individual tasks. For the average task, a map of mean within-network effect size is given and the histogram notes the number of edges below small, medium, and large effect sizes. In the spatial maps, brighter colors denote greater magnitude positive (red) and negative (blue) effect sizes. (Color figure online)

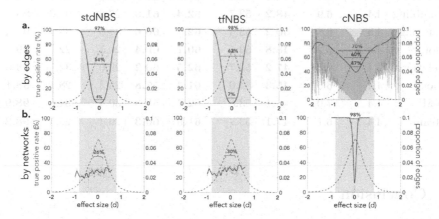

Fig. 2. Sensitivity of methods for network-based inference, summarized across tasks. True positive rates depicted as a function of effect size summarized by **a**) edges and **b**) networks. Columns show NBS methods. Each blue curve represents the spline fit to all observations from all tasks (*i.e.*, not the mean across tasks). The histogram trace for all effect size observations is underlaid in orange. Blue shaded areas depict standard deviation for edges; individual observations are shown for networks. Mean true positive rates are given for small, medium, and large effect sizes. (Color figure online)

4.3   cNBS is Most Sensitive to Network-Level Effects

As expected, cNBS had an advantage for network-level sensitivity (Fig. 2b and Table 1). For a small effect size, sensitivity for cNBS was ~3 times greater than the other methods. As above, tfNBS had a small advantage over stdNBS. Notably, no strong relationship between sensitivity and network-level effect size was observed for tfNBS and stdNBS, suggesting edges in strong networks were no more likely to be detected than edges in weak networks. In fact, the results suggest an advantage for local inference in the case of very weak networks, since local effects within very weak networks were detected at a higher rate than when pooled across the network.

Table 1. Sensitivity of network-based inference methods, by task. True positive rates from Fig. 2 are shown summarized by edges (left and middle sections) and by networks (right section). Mean TPR is reported for effects within a window around the specified effect size. Sensitivity to network-level effects is only given for $d = 0.2$ since network-level effects were less than $d = 0.5$ in many tasks. Values that are greater than the mean across statistics are in bold.

	$d_{edge} = 0.2$			$d_{edge} = 0.5$			$d_{network} = 0.2$		
	stdNBS	tfNBS	cNBS	stdNBS	tfNBS	cNBS	stdNBS	tfNBS	cNBS
Emotion	4.4	6.4	**44.1**	53.6	**61.0**	56.4	20.4	23.2	**96.3**
Gambling	4.4	6.9	**48.2**	53.7	**62.4**	61.9	27.6	31.0	**98.3**
Language	4.3	6.8	**50.2**	53.4	**62.7**	66.6	31.8	35.4	**97.2**
Motor	4.4	6.3	**48.8**	53.5	**60.7**	60.4	20.1	22.6	**99.2**
Relational	4.4	6.8	**47.2**	53.7	**62.5**	60.2	29.0	32.5	**99.5**
Social	4.4	6.5	**45.3**	54.0	**61.4**	57.8	25.3	28.1	**98.1**
WM	4.4	7.0	**46.1**	53.8	**62.7**	58.8	30.4	34.0	**98.9**
Mean	4.4	6.7	**47.1**	53.7	**61.9**	60.3	26.4	29.5	**98.2**

5   Conclusion

In summary, we introduced a new statistic for inference at the level of large-scale brain networks, cNBS, and highlighted its advantages and disadvantages relative to existing component-level inference. cNBS was typically more sensitive than component-level inference to task-related changes in connectivity. Accordingly, we observed that underlying ground truth effects were organized into the large-scale networks externally defined for cNBS. This does not preclude the possibility of interesting fine-grained effects less suited for cNBS; in fact, robust edge-level effects were sometimes observed within very weak networks. Yet overall, cNBS represents a promising starting point for promoting more valid network-based inference, needed to support flourishing research to understand the human brain.

Acknowledgements. Data were provided by the HCP, WU-Minn Consortium (PIs: David Van Essen and Kamil Ugurbil; U54 MH091657). This work was supported by the National Institutes of Mental Health under award K00MH122372.

References

1. Baggio, H., et al.: Statistical inference in brain graphs using threshold-free network-based statistics. Hum. Brain Mapp. **39**(6), 2289–2302 (2018)
2. Cohen, J.: Statistical Power Analysis for the Behavioral Sciences. Academic Press, New York (2013)
3. Eklund, A., Nichols, T.E., Knutsson, H.: Cluster failure: why fMRI inferences for spatial extent have inflated false-positive rates. Proc. Nat. Acad. Sci. **113**(28), 7900–7905 (2016)
4. Friston, K.J., Holmes, A., Poline, J.B., Price, C.J., Frith, C.D., et al.: Detecting activations in PET and fMRI: levels of inference and power. Neuroimage **4**(3), 223–235 (1996)
5. Glasser, M.F., et al.: The minimal preprocessing pipelines for the human connectome project. Neuroimage **80**, 105–124 (2013)
6. Greene, A.S., Gao, S., Scheinost, D., Constable, R.T.: Task-induced brain state manipulation improves prediction of individual traits. Nat. Commun. **9**(1), 2807 (2018)
7. MatlabTFCE: GitHub. https://github.com/markallenthornton/MatlabTFCE
8. MRtrix3: NITRC. www.nitrc.org/projects/nbs/
9. NBS Benchmarking: GitHub. https://github.com/SNeuroble/NBS_benchmarking/tree/TPR
10. Network Based Statistic (NBS): NITRC. www.nitrc.org/projects/nbs/
11. Nichols, T., Hayasaka, S.: Controlling the familywise error rate in functional neuroimaging: a comparative review. Stat. Methods Med. Res. **12**(5), 419–446 (2003)
12. Nichols, T.E., et al.: Best practices in data analysis and sharing in neuroimaging using MRI. Nat. Neurosci. **20**(3), 299–303 (2017)
13. Noble, S., Scheinost, D., Constable, R.T.: Cluster failure or power failure? Evaluating sensitivity in cluster-level inference. Neuroimage **209**, 116468 (2020)
14. Noble, S., Spann, M.N., Tokoglu, F., Shen, X., Constable, R.T., Scheinost, D.: Influences on the test-retest reliability of functional connectivity MRI and its relationship with behavioral utility. Cereb. Cortex **27**(11), 5415–5429 (2017)
15. Poldrack, R.A., et al.: Scanning the horizon: towards transparent and reproducible neuroimaging research. Nat. Rev. Neurosci. **18**(2), 115–126 (2017)
16. Shapiro, D.E.: The interpretation of diagnostic tests. Stat. Methods Med. Res. **8**(2), 113–134 (1999)
17. Shen, X., Tokoglu, F., Papademetris, X., Constable, R.T.: Groupwise whole-brain parcellation from resting-state fMRI data for network node identification. Neuroimage **82**, 403–415 (2013)
18. Smith, S.M., Nichols, T.E.: Threshold-free cluster enhancement: addressing problems of smoothing, threshold dependence and localisation in cluster inference. Neuroimage **44**(1), 83–98 (2009)
19. Van Essen, D.C., et al.: The WU-Minn human connectome project: an overview. Neuroimage **80**, 62–79 (2013)
20. Vinokur, L., Zalesky, A., Raffelt, D., Smith, R., Connelly, A.: A novel threshold-free network-based statistics method demonstration using simulated pathology. In: ISMRM (2015)

21. Wilson, E.B.: Probable inference, the law of succession, and statistical inference. J. Am. Stat. Assoc. **22**(158), 209–212 (1927)
22. Winkler, A.M., Ridgway, G.R., Webster, M.A., Smith, S.M., Nichols, T.E.: Permutation inference for the general linear model. Neuroimage **92**, 381–397 (2014)
23. Woo, C.W., Krishnan, A., Wager, T.D.: Cluster-extent based thresholding in fMRI analyses: pitfalls and recommendations. Neuroimage **91**, 412–419 (2014)
24. Zalesky, A., Fornito, A., Bullmore, E.T.: Network-based statistic: identifying differences in brain networks. Neuroimage **53**(4), 1197–1207 (2010)

Learning Personal Representations from fMRI by Predicting Neurofeedback Performance

Jhonathan Osin[1], Lior Wolf[1(✉)], Guy Gurevitch[2,3],
Jackob Nimrod Keynan[2,3,6], Tom Fruchtman-Steinbok[2,3],
Ayelet Or-Borichev[2,4], and Talma Hendler[2,3,4,5]

[1] School of Computer Science, Tel Aviv University, Tel Aviv-Yafo, Israel
liorwolf@gmail.com
[2] Sagol Brain Institute, Tel-Aviv Sourasky Medical Center, Tel Aviv-Yafo, Israel
[3] School of Psychological Sciences, Tel Aviv University, Tel Aviv-Yafo, Israel
[4] Sackler Faculty of Medicine, Tel Aviv University, Tel Aviv-Yafo, Israel
[5] Sagol School of Neuroscience, Tel Aviv University, Tel Aviv-Yafo, Israel
[6] Department of Psychiatry and Behavioral Sciences, Stanford University School of
Medicine, Stanford, US

Abstract. We present a deep neural network method that enables learning of a personal representation from samples acquired while subjects are performing a self neuro-feedback task, guided by functional MRI (fMRI). The neurofeedback task (watch vs. regulate) provides the subjects with continuous feedback, contingent on the down-regulation of their Amygdala signal. The representation is learned by a self-supervised recurrent neural network that predicts the Amygdala activity in the next fMRI frame given recent fMRI frames and is conditioned on the learned individual representation. We show that our personal representation, learned solely using fMRI images, improves the next-frame prediction considerably and, more importantly, yields superior performance in linear prediction of psychiatric traits, compared to performing such predictions based on clinical data and personality tests. Our code is attached as supplementary and the data would be shared subject to ethical approvals.

Keywords: fMRI · Amygdala-neurofeedback · Imaging based diagnosis · Psychiatry · Recurrent neural networks

1 Introduction

In this work, we propose to employ self-supervision in order to learn an individual, per-subject representation from fMRI-based neurofeedback sessions.

Electronic supplementary material The online version of this chapter (https://doi.org/10.1007/978-3-030-59728-3_46) contains supplementary material, which is available to authorized users.

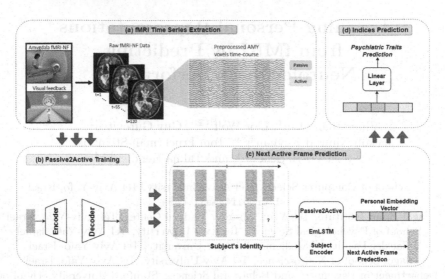

Fig. 1. Holistic overview of our method. (a) The time series are extracted from raw data. (b) The Passive2Active Translator is trained, without knowledge of subject's identity. (c) subject-conditioned LSTM and a look-up-table (LUT) are trained via the next active frame prediction task. (d) A linear classifier is trained to predict psychiatric and demographic traits based on learned per-subject representations.

Neurofeedback (NF) is a Brain Computer Interface approach for non-invasive self-neuromodulation using reinforcement learning. NF has been widely used in the last decade in research and clinical settings for training people to alter their own brain functionality; activity or connectivity.

Our learned representation is shown to be highly predictive of multiple psychiatric conditions in three different datasets: (i) individuals suffering from PTSD, (ii) individuals suffering from fibromyalgia and (iii) a control dataset of healthy individuals.

The self-supervised method predicts the activity of the Amygdala region at the next fMRI frame, based on the previous frames, conditioned on the individual's representation. For this purpose, we employ a variant of the LSTM algorithm [6], in which the personal embedding is used to condition all four LSTM gates.

The learned personal embedding is a static vector, which encodes information about the individual that is meaningful in predicting the future state of the Amygdala. Remarkably, this vector is more predictive of the subject's psychiatric traits, age and previous experience in neurofeedback, than the individual's clinical data, when predicting one trait from all other traits.

The comparison is done using linear classifiers, in order to verify that the relevant information is encoded in a relatively explicit way and to alleviate the risk of over-fitting by attempting multiple hyper-parameters.

A complete overview of our approach is illustrated in Fig. 1. The first step after extracting fMRI frames, is to train an auto-encoder which maps between the two stages of the neurofeedback session; one in which the subject is viewing passively ("Watch"), and one in which the subject is requested to control their Amygdala activity ("Regulate"). A new variant of LSTM is then trained to predict the activity in the next fMRI frame. Finally, the representation learned as part of the LSTM training is employed to predict psychiatric traits.

2   Related Work

Functional magnetic resonance imaging (fMRI), as a non-invasive imaging technique, has been extensively applied to study psychiatric disorders [3,9]. Deep learning methods have been applied to this field, mostly focusing on binary classification of subjects suffering from a specific psychopathology versus healthy subjects under resting state [4,15], i.e., using fully supervised learning. Our work is focused on self-supervised learning while participants suffering from various psychopathologies and healthy controls are performing a neurofeedback training task.

During an NF session, the trainee is given the task of regulating their brain state in a target region using some mental strategy. Brain activity modulation in the determined direction (up or down), resulting in contingent change in a rewarding perceived interface, thus reflecting level of task success [7]. Recent technological advancements in online real-time data analysis have made fMRI a popular tool for employing NF in research settings, providing brain targeting with high spatial resolution [12]. However, due to the relatively high cost of using this imaging modality and the burden of multiple sessions, fMRI-based NF could benefit from on-line personalization of the procedure, which would make the training more efficient and advance this tool into translational and clinical trials.

3   Problem Formulation

A real-time fMRI-NF task targeting down-regulation of the right Amygdala region was given to subjects. This was done using an interactive game-like feedback interface, where subjects control the speed of a skateboard rider. Similar to other studies in the field, local fMRI activation changes were measured using a two-phase NF paradigm repeated over several runs [10], where each training run was comprised of a passive and an active phase. During the passive phase, a skateboard rider and a speedometer were displayed on the screen and Amygdala activation was passively measured. Subjects were instructed to passively view the skateboard, which was moving at a constant speed. During the following active phase, the speed of the rider and the speedometer represented the on-going Amygdala signal change compared to the passive phase, which was calculated on-line and updated continuously every three seconds.

During this phase, subjects were instructed to decrease the speed of the skateboard as much as possible, by practicing mental strategies of their choosing. Down-regulation of the Amygdala, which reflects a more relaxed state, led to a lower skateboard speed and fewer objects on the screen [7]. Instructions given were not specific to the target brain functionality, in order to allow individuals to efficiently adopt different strategies [8]. At the end of each active phase, a bar indicating the average speed during the current run was presented for six seconds. Each subject performed $M = 3$ runs of Passive/Active phases, where each passive phase lasted one minute. Each active phase lasted one minute (Healthy controls and PTSD patients) or two minutes (Fibromyalgia patients).

Both the passive and the active phases gave rise to $T = 14$ temporal samples of the subject's Amygdala. We denote the spatial resolution of the relevant part of the fMRI images acquired every 3 s as $H \times W \times D$ and our dataset is, therefore, comprised of per-subject tensors in $\mathbb{R}^{2 \times H \times W \times D \times T \times M}$. In our setting, $M = 3, T = 14$. We used three datasets in our experiments: (i) **PTSD-** comprised of 53 subjects, ($H = 6, W = 5, D = 6$), (ii) **Fibromyalgia-** comprised of 24 subjects, ($H = 6, W = 5, D = 6$), and (iii) **Healthy Control-** comprised of 87 subjects, ($H = 10, W = 8, D = 10$).

In addition to the fMRI sequences, we received clinical information about each subject, which we denote as $y_n \in \mathbb{R}^3$, n being the index of the patient, and is comprised of the following: (1) **Toronto Alexithymia Scale (TAS-20)** – a self-report questionnaire measuring difficulties in expressing and identifying emotions [1], (2) **State-Trait Anxiety Inventory (STAI)** – State anxiety was measured using a validated 20-item inventory [11], and (3) **Clinician Administered PTSD Scale (CAPS-5) 1** – Patients underwent clinical assessment by a trained psychologist based on this widely-used scale for PTSD diagnosis [13]. For the control patients, we also receive the following demographic information: (1) **Age** and (2) **Past Experience in Neuro-Feedback Tasks**, quantized to three levels: no experience, two previous sessions, or six previous sessions.

fMRI Data Acquisition and Pre-processing. Structural and functional scans were performed in a 3.0T Siemens MRI system (MAGNETOM Prisma) using a 20-channel head coil. To allow high-resolution structural images, a T1-weighted three-dimensional (3D) sagittal MPRAGE pulse sequence (repetition time/echo time = 1,860/2.74 ms, flip angle = 8°, pixel size = 1 × 1 mm, field of view = 256 × 256 mm) was used. Functional whole-brain scans were performed in an interleaved top-to-bottom order, using a T2*-weighted gradient echo planar imaging pulse sequence (repetition time/echo time = 3,000/35 ms, flip angle = 90°, pixel size = 1.56 mm, field of view = 200 × 200 mm, slice thickness = 3 mm, 44 slices per volume).

Preprocessing of the fMRI data was done with the MATLAB based CONN toolbox [14] and included realignment of the functional volumes, motion correction using rigid-body transformations in six axes, normalization to MNI space and spatial smoothing with an isotropic 6-mm full width at half-maximum Gaussian kernel. The processed volumes were then run through de-noising and de-trending regression algorithms, followed by band-pass filtering in the range of 0.008–0.09 Hz. Amygdala voxels were defined as a functional cluster centered at (x = 21, y = −2, z = −24) and exported for further analysis as a 4-D matrix.

4 Method

Our neural network models were trained to predict the subjects' clinical and demographic information, given the raw fMRI sequences. This was done using two sub-networks, denoted as f, ρ respectively: (1) Learning a personalized representation for each subject, and (2) predicting the subjects' clinical and demographic information, given the representation learned by f.

4.1 Overview

The task performed by sub-network f is predicting the current active frame, given all previous passive and active frames and the current passive frame.

Next Active Frame Prediction. For each subject n, active and passive frames from the M sessions are concatenated (separately) to receive the entire passive and active fMRI *sequences*, denoted as $p^n, a^n \in \mathbb{R}^{(H,W,D,M \cdot T)}$, respectively. Thus $p^n[t], a^n[t]$ are the passive and active fMRI *frames* captured at time step t.

Capital letters $P^n[t] = (p^n[0], p^n[1], \ldots, p^n[t])$, and $A^n[t] = (a^n[0], a^n[1], \ldots, a^n[t])$ are used to denote a sequence from its beginning, and until time step t. The model f predicts the active-phase tensor at time point t of subject n:

$$\hat{a}^n[t] = f(A^n[t-1], P^n[t], n) \tag{1}$$

Predicting Subjects' Traits. A by-product of the training process of f, is a learned per-subject personal embedding vector, denoted as e_n. The prediction of ρ for subject n can be denoted as:

$$\hat{y}_n = \rho(e_n) = G^\top e_n + b \tag{2}$$

where G is a matrix and b is a vector.

4.2 Learning a Personalized Representation

The f model is composed of two deep networks. The first network, φ, maps, one by one, passive frames to the corresponding active frames. The second sub-network, ψ, is an LSTM that predicts the current active frame, given the output of the first sub-network, the previous active frame and the subject's identifier.

Passive2Active Translator. This model, φ, is trained in a supervised way to map an input frame from the passive phase, $p^n[t]$, to its coupled frame from the active phase, $a^n[t]$, with the subject's identity unknown to the model. Training is done by minimizing the following loss function:

$$\mathcal{L}_{Recon} = \sum_n \sum_{t=0}^{M \cdot T} ||a^n[t] - \varphi(p^n[t])||_2 \tag{3}$$

The architecture follows that of de-noising autoencoders, which are widely used in medical image analysis [5]. The network φ is comprised of four linear layers with expanding output sizes, followed by four shrinking linear layers, separated by DropOut and ReLU activation functions, alternately.

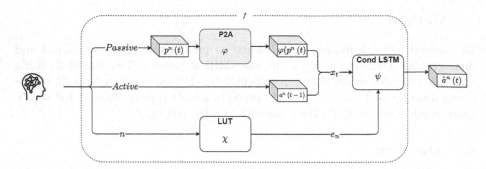

Fig. 2. In our model's second phase of training, the Passive2Active translator, φ, is frozen. The conditional LSTM, ψ, and the LUT, χ, are trained to predict $a^n(t)$, the current active frame, given $x_t = \big(\varphi(p^n[t]), a^n[t-1]\big)$, and the subject identifier, n. The conditioning is based on a LUT, which provides the embedding vector of each subject, $\chi(n) = e_n$.

The Conditioned LSTM Network. In the conventional LSTM [6], given an input $x_t = \big(\varphi(p^n[t]), a^n[t-1]\big)$, the previous hidden state h_{t-1}, and the previous cell state c_{t-1}, the LSTM's outputs c_t and h_t are calculated using four learned gates, dubbed *forget gate, input gate, update gate, output gate*. The information flow is as depicted in Eq. 4–9.

In the conditioned LSTM we employ, a representation is learned for every subject n, marked e_n. This user-embedding is used as a conditioning input to the LSTM sub-networks, by concatenating it to the input at every time step. In this setting, the information flow is as depicted by equations Eq. 4*–7*, Eq. 8–9.

VANILLA LSTM EQUATIONS

$$f_t^n = \sigma(W^f \cdot (x_t, h_{t-1})) \tag{4}$$
$$i_t^n = \sigma(W^i \cdot (x_t, h_{t-1})) \tag{5}$$
$$u_t^n = \tanh(W^u \cdot (x_t, h_{t-1})) \tag{6}$$
$$o_t^n = \sigma(W^o \cdot (x_t, h_{t-1})) \tag{7}$$

CONDITIONED LSTM EQUATIONS

$$f_t^n = \sigma(W^f \cdot (x_t, h_{t-1}, e_n)) \tag{4*}$$
$$i_t^n = \sigma(W^i \cdot (x_t, h_{t-1}, e_n)) \tag{5*}$$
$$u_t^n = \tanh(W^u \cdot (x_t, h_{t-1}, e_n)) \tag{6*}$$
$$o_t^n = \sigma(W^o \cdot (x_t, h_{t-1}, e_n)) \tag{7*}$$

$$c_t^n = c_{t-1}^n \odot f_t^n + u_t^n \odot i_t^n \tag{8}$$
$$h_t^n = o_t^n \odot \tanh(c_t^n) \tag{9}$$

Where $W^{(\cdot)}$ are learned weights for each one of the gates, $\sigma(\cdot)$ is the Sigmoid function, $\odot$ is the element-wise multiplication operator and $(\cdot, \cdot)$ is the concatenation operator.

Once the first sub-network, φ, is trained, it is frozen and we train, concurrently, the second sub-network, ψ, and the subjects' encoding vectors, which are stored in a look-up-table (LUT) χ.

With all sub-networks defined, we can write Eq. 1 more explicitly:

$$\hat{a}^n[t] = f\big(A^n[t-1], P^n[t], n\big) = \psi\big(A^n[t-1], \varphi(P^n[t]), \chi(n)\big), \tag{10}$$

where φ is applied separately for every frame of $P^n[t]$.

When training the conditioned LSTM, the input, x_t^n, is a concatenation of $\big(\varphi(p^n[t]), a^n[t-1]\big)$. The model also receives $e_n = \chi(n)$, as a conditioning input.

As illustrated in Fig. 2, the subject's LUT, χ, and conditioned LSTM, ψ, are tasked to predict the subject's current active frame, by minimizing the following loss function:

$$\mathcal{L}_{Recon} = \sum_n \sum_{t=0}^{M \cdot T} ||a^n[t] - \psi(x_t^n, e_n)||_2 \tag{11}$$

In order to demonstrate that the user embedding is beneficial, we also train a baseline model, in which a vanilla LSTM is used, without the embedding.

4.3 Predicting Psychiatric Traits Using the Subject's Representation

In the final training phase, after learning an embedding per subject, we freeze the LUT, and evaluate its utility in predicting psychiatric traits. For this purpose, we employ a linear classifier, denoted as ρ (Eq. 2), which is trained to minimize the Cross Entropy loss function, i.e, predicting the subject's psychiatric and demographic information, y_n, according to the subject's embedding, e_n.

The formulation as a classification problem and not as a regression problem is done in order to have the results of all prediction problems on the same human-interpretable scale. The quantization of the three scores (TAS-20, STAI, CAPS-5) and age is done by calculating the mean and variance for every score, and creating five labels by the following ranges: $(-\infty, \mu - 2 \cdot \sigma]$, $(\mu - 2 \cdot \sigma, \mu - \sigma]$, $(\mu - \sigma, \mu + \sigma]$, $(\mu + \sigma, \mu + 2\sigma]$, $(\mu + 2\sigma, \infty)$. Results for the regression scheme, presenting rMSE of the model trained with the L2 loss, are provided in the supplementary material.

4.4 Inference

When presenting our model with a new subject, m, we first use the already trained (and frozen) f neural network to learn an embedding vector e_m. This is done using only the raw fMRI signals, by fitting e_m in a next active frame prediction task. After e_m is learned, it is passed through the linear classifier (ρ), to receive the model's prediction, $\hat{y}_m$.

5 Experiments

Data partitioning distinguishes between train, evaluation, and test set, each composed of different subjects, with a 60-20-20 split. Each experiment was repeated 10 times on random splits, and our plots report mean and SD. In all of the below-mentioned experiments, the personal embedding vector size was set to 12 ($\mathbb{R}^{12}$).

Next Active Frame Prediction. To evaluate the performance of our conditioned LSTM method, we compared its performance in predicting the next active frame given the P2A output to (i) a vanilla LSTM model with the same hidden-state size, and (ii) our trained Passive2Active Translator. Figure 3 compares the three models. Evidently, the vanilla LSTM, which receives the data as a sequence of frames, significantly improves the performance of the memory-less Passive2Active Translator. Our conditioned LSTM, which incorporates the per-subject representation, outperforms the vanilla LSTM.

Predicting Subject's Psychiatric and Demographic Criteria. We test whether our learned representation, trained only with raw fMRI images, has the ability to predict a series of psychiatric and demographic criteria, not directly related to the neurofeedback task.

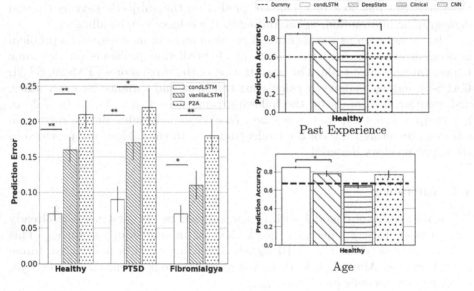

Fig. 3. Next frame prediction error. corrected re-sampled t-test [2]: *$P < 0.05$, **$P < 0.01$.

Fig. 4. Demographic accuracy

We used our method to predict (i) STAI and (ii) TAS-20 for PTSD, Fibromyalgia and control subjects, (iii) CAPS-5 for PTSD subjects. Demographic information, (iv) age, and (v) past NeuroFeedback experience were predicted for control subjects.

Our linear classification scheme, applied to the learned embedding vectors, is compared to the following baselines, which all receive the raw fMRI sequence as input, denoted as x: (1) **fMRI CNN-** Convolutional layer with $k = 10$ filters, followed by a mean pooling operation to receive $z(x) \in \mathbb{R}^{(2 \cdot M, k, T)}$, which is the input to an MLP with $l = 3$ layers, which predicts the label; (2) **fMRI Statistical Data-** This method performs two spacial pooling operations on the fMRI sequence: (i) mean and (ii) standard deviation to create the statistics tensor, $z(x) \in \mathbb{R}^{(2 \cdot M, 2, T)}$, which is fed to a linear layer, which predicts the label; (3) **Clinical Prediction-** SVM regression of every trait, according to the other traits (leave-one-trait-out, where the data contains all psychiatric traits and the two demographic traits); and (4) **Dummy Prediction-** Predicts the most common label.

The results are shown in Fig. 4, 5. It is evident that our method significantly outperforms the baseline methods in predicting the correct range of both the demographic and the psychiatric traits.

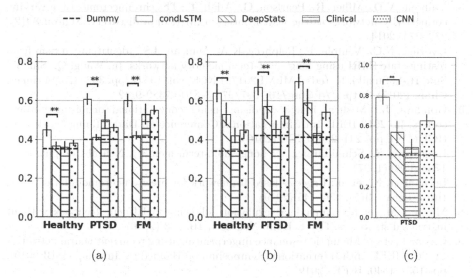

Fig. 5. Psychiatric trait predictions. (a) STAI, (b) TAS-20, (c) CAPS-5.

6   Conclusions

We present a method for learning a static, meaningful representation of a subject performing a neurofeedback task. This subject embedding is trained on a self supervised task and is shown to be highly predictive of psychiatric traits, for which no physical examinations or biological markers exist, as well as for age, and NF experience. We, therefore, open a new avenue for psychiatric diagnosis that is not based on an interview or a questionnaire.

Acknowledgments. This project has received funding from the European Research Council (ERC) under the European Unions Horizon 2020 research and innovation programme (grant ERC CoG 725974), the BRAINTRAIN consortium, 7th Framework Programme, under Grant Agreement no. 602186, and US Department of Defense grant agreement no. W81XWH-11-2-0008.

We thank Shira Reznik-Balter for insightful discussions on the analytic approach and helpful comments on the manuscript.

References

1. Bagby, R.M., Parker, J.D., Taylor, G.J.: The twenty-item Toronto Alexithymia Scale-I. Item selection and cross-validation of the factor structure. J. Psychosom. Res. **38**(1), 23–32 (1994)
2. Bouckaert, R.R., Frank, E.: Evaluating the replicability of significance tests for comparing learning algorithms. In: Dai, H., Srikant, R., Zhang, C. (eds.) PAKDD 2004. LNCS (LNAI), vol. 3056, pp. 3–12. Springer, Heidelberg (2004). https://doi.org/10.1007/978-3-540-24775-3_3
3. Calhoun, V.D., Miller, R., Pearlson, G., Adalı, T.: The chronnectome: time-varying connectivity networks as the next frontier in fMRI data discovery. Neuron **84**(2), 262–274 (2014)
4. Dvornek, N.C., Ventola, P., Pelphrey, K.A., Duncan, J.S.: Identifying autism from resting-state fMRI using long short-term memory networks. In: Wang, Q., Shi, Y., Suk, H.-I., Suzuki, K. (eds.) MLMI 2017. LNCS, vol. 10541, pp. 362–370. Springer, Cham (2017). https://doi.org/10.1007/978-3-319-67389-9_42
5. Gondara, L.: Medical image denoising using convolutional denoising autoencoders. In: 2016 IEEE 16th International Conference on Data Mining Workshops (ICDMW), pp. 241–246. IEEE (2016)
6. Hochreiter, S., Schmidhuber, J.: Long short-term memory. Neural Comput. **9**(8), 1735–1780 (1997)
7. Lubianiker, N., et al.: Process-based framework for precise neuromodulation. Nat. Hum. Behav. **3**(5), 436–445 (2019)
8. Marxen, M., et al.: Amygdala regulation following fMRI-neurofeedback without instructed strategies. Front. Hum. Neurosci. **10**, 183 (2016)
9. Oksuz, I., et al.: Magnetic resonance fingerprinting using recurrent neural networks. In: 2019 IEEE 16th International Symposium on Biomedical Imaging (ISBI 2019), pp. 1537–1540. IEEE (2019)
10. Paret, C., et al.: Current progress in real-time functional magnetic resonance-based neurofeedback: methodological challenges and achievements. NeuroImage **202**, 116107 (2019)
11. Spielberger, C.D., Gorsuch, R.L.: State-Trait Anxiety Inventory for Adults: Manual and Sample: Manual, Instrument and Scoring Guide. Consulting Psychologists Press, Palo Alto (1983)
12. Sulzer, J., et al.: Real-time fMRI neurofeedback: progress and challenges. Neuroimage **76**, 386–399 (2013)
13. Weathers, F., Blake, D., Schnurr, P., Kaloupek, D., Marx, B., Keane, T.: The clinician-administered PTSD scale for DSM-5 (CAPS-5). Interview Available from the National Center for PTSD (2013)
14. Whitfield-Gabrieli, S., Nieto-Castanon, A.: Conn: a functional connectivity toolbox for correlated and anticorrelated brain networks. Brain Connect. **2**(3), 125–141 (2012)
15. Yan, W., et al.: Discriminating schizophrenia using recurrent neural network applied on time courses of multi-site fMRI data. EBioMedicine **47**, 543–552 (2019)

A 3D Convolutional Encapsulated Long Short-Term Memory (3DConv-LSTM) Model for Denoising fMRI Data

Chongyue Zhao, Hongming Li, Zhicheng Jiao, Tianming Du, and Yong Fan[(✉)]

Center for Biomedical Image Computing and Analysis, Department of Radiology, Perelman School of Medicine, University of Pennsylvania, Philadelphia, PA 19104, USA
yong.fan@pennmedicine.upenn.edu

Abstract. Function magnetic resonance imaging (fMRI) data are typically contaminated by noise introduced by head motion, physiological noise, and thermal noise. To mitigate noise artifact in fMRI data, a variety of denoising methods have been developed by removing noise factors derived from the whole time series of fMRI data and therefore are not applicable to real-time fMRI data analysis. In the present study, we develop a generally applicable, deep learning based fMRI denoising method to generate noise-free realistic individual fMRI volumes (time points). Particularly, we develop a fully data-driven 3D convolutional encapsulated Long Short-Term Memory (3DConv-LSTM) approach to generate noise-free fMRI volumes regularized by an adversarial network that makes the generated fMRI volumes more realistic by fooling a critic network. The 3DConv-LSTM model also integrates a gate-controlled self-attention model to memorize short-term dependency and historical information within a memory pool. We have evaluated our method based on both task and resting state fMRI data. Both qualitative and quantitative results have demonstrated that the proposed method outperformed state-of-the-art alternative deep learning methods.

Keywords: Adversarial regularizer · fMRI denoising · 3D convolutional LSTM · Gate-controlled self-attention

1 Introduction

Head motion, physiological noise, and thermal noise are main sources of noise in functional magnetic resonance imaging (fMRI) data [1, 2]. To mitigate noise artifact in fMRI data analysis, a variety of methods have been developed. Particularly, the combination of global signal regression (GSR) and motion censoring [3] has achieved promising performance to reduce head motion related noise [3–5]. However, such an approach reduces motion artifact in fMRI data analysis at a risk of losing fMRI volumes and even entire participants from analyses because of insufficient data remain after scrubbing. Filtering based methods are widely used to remove cardiac and respiratory noise fluctuations with the record of the spectrum or physiological wave functions [6, 7]. However, such methods may also affect the BOLD signal at the same frequency.

© Springer Nature Switzerland AG 2020
A. L. Martel et al. (Eds.): MICCAI 2020, LNCS 12267, pp. 479–488, 2020.
https://doi.org/10.1007/978-3-030-59728-3_47

Data driven methods built upon principal component analysis (PCA) [8, 9] or independent component analysis (ICA) [10, 11] have achieved promising performance in fMRI data denoising. Deep learning methods have also been developed for denoising fMRI data [12–14], including a convolutional neural network (CNN) method for noise component identification after ICA decomposition [12], a Long Short-Term Memory (LSTM) method for denoising task-based fMRI data [13], and a deep convolutional generative adversarial network to reconstruct lost BOLD signal in resting state fMRI (rsfMRI) data [14]. However, these methods are not generally applicable in that they could only work on ICA component data, task fMRI data, or one-dimension BOLD signals.

In order to overcome limitation of the existing fMRI denoising methods, we develop a 3D convolutional LSTM method to generate noise-free fMRI volumes. Particularly, our method consists of an encoder network, a decoder network, and a critic network. The encoder network is built upon 3D convolutional encapsulated LSTM (3DConv-LSTM) structures to generate spatiotemporal data, in conjunction with the decoder network. The critic network together with an adversarial regularizer encourages the generated spatiotemporal data to be realistic by fooling the critic network which is trained to predict a mixing factor of different time points, similar to Generative Adversarial Networks (GANs) [15, 16]. We have evaluated our method in two different experiments. The first experiment with task fMRI data of the Human Connectome Project (HCP) [17] has demonstrated that our method could accurately generate fMRI volumes without altering brain activation patterns. The second experiment with rsfMRI data from ABIDE data [18] has demonstrated that our method could directly generate noise-free fMRI data by learning from supervision information generated by ICA-AROMA [11]. Different from ICA-AROMA method that identifies and removes noisy independent components, our method directly predicts noise-free individual time points. All these experimental results have demonstrated that our method is generally applicable to both task and resting state fMRI data and could achieve promising fMRI denoising performance.

2 Methods

In order to generate realistic fMRI data by learning from spatiotemporal fMRI data, an adversarial regularization together with 3D convolutional LSTM module is implemented. Assuming we have a 4D fMRI data $X \in R^{M \times N \times V \times T}$ with $M \times N \times V$ voxels and T time points, we learn a data reconstruction model by adopting a 3D convolutional LSTM encoder to obtain latent factors $h_t^k = f_\theta(X_t)$ for individual time point $X_t \in R^{M \times N \times V}$ at time t, where θ denotes parameters of the encoder. The latent factor h_t^k is then passed through a decoder $\hat{X}_t = g_\emptyset(h_t^k)$ to generate a time point $\hat{X}_t \in R^{M \times N \times V}$. A critic network together with an adversarial regularizer is adopted to encourage the generated fMRI data to be realistic by fooling the critic network which is trained to predict a mixing factor of different time points. The overall algorithm and the 3D Convolutional LSTM encoder/decoder are illustrated in Fig. 1.

The encoder network and decoder network are trained simultaneously to minimize the cost function:

$$L_p = \left\| X_t - \hat{X}_t \right\|^2,$$ (1)

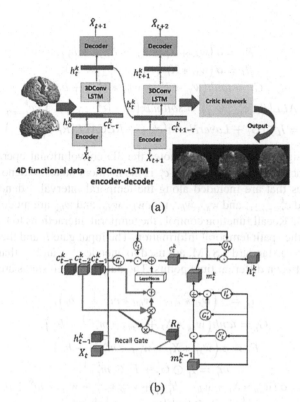

(a)

(b)

Fig. 1. Flowchart of the proposed method, including a 3DConv-LSTM encapsulated encoder-decoder and a critic network with adversarial regularizer. (a) the overall framework; (b) the 3DConv-LSTM encoder. (Color figure online)

where $\hat{X}_t$ and X_t are predicted frame point and ground truth at time t. We will give more details about critic network in Sect. 2.2.

2.1 3D Convolutional LSTM Structure (3DConv-LSTM)

The proposed 3D convolutional LSTM encoder is illustrated in Fig. 1(b), where the red arrow shows the flow of short-term memory and the blue arrow shows the flow of long-term information. The input to the 3DConv-LSTM encoder is denoted by X_t, the hidden state from the previous time stamp h_{t-1}^k, the memory state from previous time stamp c_{t-1}^k, and previous layer spatio-temporal memory m_t^{k-1}. In order to capture the long-term time point relationship, we adopt a new memory RECALL mechanism [19], defined as:

$$R_t = \sigma\left(w_{xr} * X_t + w_{hr} * h^k_{t-1} + b_r\right),$$
$$I_t = \sigma\left(w_{xi} * X_t + w_{hi} * h^k_{t-1} + b_i\right),$$
$$G_t = tanh\left(w_{xg} * X_t + w_{hg} * h^k_{t-1} + b_g\right),$$
$$RECALL\left(R_t, c^k_{t-\tau:t-1}\right) = softmax\left(R_t \cdot \left(c^k_{t-\tau:t-1}\right)^T\right) \cdot c^k_{t-\tau:t-1},$$
$$c^k_t = I_t \odot G_t + LayerNorm\left(c^k_{t-1} + RECALL\left(R_t, c^k_{t-\tau:t-1}\right)\right),$$

(2)

where σ is the sigmoid function, $*$ denotes the 3D convolutional operation, $\odot$ is the Hadamard product, R_t is the recall gate, c^k_t is the memory states, τ denotes the number of memory states that are included along the temporal interval, $\cdot$ denotes the matrix product of R_t and $c^k_{t-\tau:t-1}$, and $w_{xr}, w_{hr}, w_{xi}, w_{hi}, w_{xg}$, and w_{hg} are model parameters to be optimized. The Recall function controls the temporal interactions to learn temporally distant states of the spatiotemporal information. The input gate I_t and the input modulation G_t, similar to a standard LSTM, are used to encode c^k_{t-1} and c^k_t that connect short term changes between different time points. The output hidden states are defined as:

$$I'_t = \sigma\left(w_{xi} * X_t + w_{mi} * m^{k-1}_t + b_i\right),$$
$$G'_t = tanh\left(w_{xg} * X_t + w_{mg} * m^{k-1}_t + b_g\right),$$
$$F'_t = \sigma\left(w_{xf} * X_t + w_{mf} * m^{k-1}_t + b_f\right),$$
$$m^k_t = I'_t \odot G'_t + F'_t \odot m^{k-1}_t,$$
$$O_t = \sigma\left(w_{xo} * X_t + w_{ho} * h^k_{t-1} + w_{co} * c^k_t + w_{mo} * m^k_t + b_o\right),$$
$$h^k_t = O_t \odot tanh\left(w_{1\times1\times1} * \left[c^k_t, m^k_t\right]\right),$$

(3)

where $w_{1\times1\times1}$ is the $1 \times 1 \times 1$ convolutions. I'_t, G'_t and F'_t are gate structures of the spatiotemporal memory. O_t is the output gate.

2.2 Adversarial Regularizer for Critic Network

In order to generate fMRI time points that are realistic, indistinguishable from the real data, and semantically smooth across time points, we adopted a critic network $d_w\left(\hat{X}_{t\alpha}\right)$, similar to Generative Adversarial Networks (GANs) [15, 16], to regularize a mixture of two data points, i.e. $\hat{X}_{t\alpha} = g_\emptyset\left(\alpha h^k_{t_1} + (1 - \alpha)h^k_{t_2}\right)$, where $h^k_{t_1} = f_\theta\left(X_{t_1}\right)$ and $h^k_{t_2} = f_\theta\left(X_{t_2}\right)$ are two latent factors at t_1 and t_2 ($t_1 < t_2$) respectively, and $\alpha \in [0, 1]$ is a mixing coefficient.

The critic network is trained to predict the mixing coefficient α of $\hat{X}_{t\alpha}$. We constrain $\alpha \in [0, 0.5]$ to resolve the ambiguity between α and $1 - \alpha$. Taken together, the 3DConv-LSTM is behaving like the generative process with the control of α to generate a realistic time point from $h^k_{t_1}$ and $h^k_{t_2}$. The critic network works as a discriminator to distinguish the mixture coefficient α of latent factors $h^k_{t_1} = f_\theta\left(X_{t_1}\right)$ and $h^k_{t_2} = f_\theta\left(X_{t_2}\right)$. Particularly, the critic network $d_w\left(\hat{X}_{t\alpha}\right)$ is trained to minimize:

$$L_d = \left\|d_w\left(\hat{X}_{t\alpha}\right) - \alpha\right\|^2 + \|d_w(\gamma X_t + (1 - \gamma)g_\emptyset(f_\theta(X_t)))\|^2,$$

(4)

where $d_w\left(\hat{X}_{t\alpha}\right)$ denotes the critic network, $\hat{X}_{t\alpha} = g_{\emptyset}(\alpha f_\theta(X_{t_1}) + (1 - \alpha)f_\theta(X_{t_2}))$, and γ is a scalar hyperparameter. The second term constrains the critic network to yield an output of 0 if the input is X_t. By generating an interpolation between X_t and $g_{\emptyset}(f_\theta(X_t))$, the second term also encourages the critic network to generate realistic data even if the decoder output is poor.

The encoder-decoder network loss is finally defined as

$$L_{f,g} = \|X_t - g_{\emptyset}(f_\theta(X_t))\|^2 + \lambda\left\|d_w\left(\hat{X}_{t\alpha}\right)\right\|^2, \tag{5}$$

where the scalar parameter λ controls the weight of regularization term. Similar to train a GAN, θ and $\emptyset$ are optimized by minimizing $L_{f,g}$ and $d_w\left(\hat{X}_{t\alpha}\right)$ is optimized by minimizing L_d.

3 Experimental Results

We evaluated our method on both task and resting state fMRI data and compared it with state-of-the-art alternatives, including a 3DConv-LSTM and an implementation of GANs. Particularly, the 3DConv-LSTM method was the encoder and decoder part of the proposed method without the critic network and adversarial regularizer, and the GAN was a combination of the critic network and a 3D autoencoder without the LSTM structure. The encoder consisted of two $3 \times 3 \times 3$ convolutional layers followed by $2 \times 2 \times 2$ max pooling layer. The convolution layer was zero-padded so that the input and output of the convolutional layer are of the same size. The decoder after the 3DConv-LSTM layer consisted of two $3 \times 3 \times 3$ deconvolutional layers, followed by $2 \times 2 \times 2$ nearest neighbor upsampling. Models are trained with batch size 1 on a NVIDIA tesla P100 GPU with 12 GB memory. All the methods were implemented using TensorFlow and trained with ADAM optimizer based on the same training and validation data and tested on the same testing data.

3.1 Generation of Task fMRI Data

The proposed method was evaluated on task fMRI data of the HCP to generate realistic fMRI volumes so that they could replace noisy time points of fMRI scans instead of censoring. Particularly, 490 subjects of motor task fMRI were used in this experiment. The motor task consists of 6 events, left foot (LF), left hand (LH), right foot (RF), right hand (RH), tongue (T) and additionally 1 cue event (CUE) prior to each movement event. Each subject's motor task fMRI scan consists of 284 time points. We randomly selected 350 subjects as training data, 50 subjects for validation, and the remaining 90 subjects for testing. For each testing subject, we split the whole time series into clips of 40 time points without overlapping and the trained deep learning models were used to generate fMRI data at 20 randomly selected time points based on the other time points within each clip.

We used structural similarity index measure (SSIM), peak signal-to-noise ratio (PSNR) and mean squared error (MSE) [19] to quantitatively measure difference between the real fMRI data and those generated by the deep learning models under comparison on the testing data. As summarized in Table 1, the average measures of all testing time points have demonstrated that our method obtained substantially better performance than both the GAN and 3DConv-LSTM methods.

Table 1. Quantitative performance measures obtained on the motor task fMRI data by the deep learning models under comparison (mean ± standard deviation).

Model	PSNR	SSIM	MSE
GAN	36.722 ± 0.5744	0.970 ± 0.0031	25.796 ± 1.3058
3DConv-LSTM	39.084 ± 0.3957	0.989 ± 0.0014	11.036 ± 0.7625
Proposed method	42.545 ± 0.1136	0.992 ± 0.0003	5.818 ± 0.3243

Representative fMRI data generated by the deep learning models under comparison along with the real fMRI data are show in Fig. 2. Representative real motor task fMRI data (a) and those generated by the deep learning methods under comparison, including GANs (b), 3DConv-LSTM (c), and our method (d), demonstrating that our method could generate fMRI time points visually more similar to the real data than the alternative methods under comparison. Figure 3 shows brain activation results obtained from real fMRI data and fMRI data generated by the deep learning methods under comparison. The activation results were thresholded at a p value 0.05 (uncorrected, two tailed). These results further demonstrated that the fMRI data generated by our method did not alter the brain activation patterns in that the activation map of fMRI data generated by our method was almost identical to that of the real fMRI data.

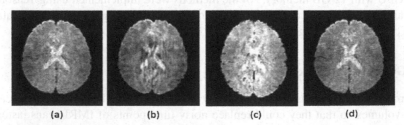

(a)   (b)   (c)   (d)

Fig. 2. Representative real motor task fMRI data (a) and those generated by the deep learning methods under comparison, including GANs (b), 3DConv-LSTM (c), and our method (d).

3.2   Generation of Resting State fMRI Data

The proposed method was evaluated on resting state fMRI data of the ABIDE study to generate noise-free fMRI data from raw fMRI scans. Particularly, we used rsfMRI data of 55 subjects from KKI site as training (80%) and validation (20%) data and rsfMRI of 38 subjects from Caltech site as testing data. All the training and testing

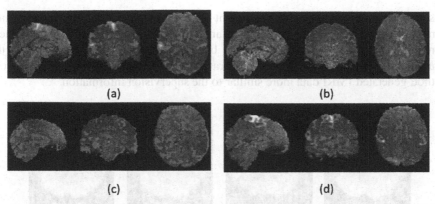

Fig. 3. Representative Activation maps for motor task fMRI. (a) and those generated by the deep learning methods under comparison, including GANs (b), 3DConv-LSTM (c), and our method (d).

data were preprocessed using fMRIPrep pipelines [20], and noise of the preprocessed rsfMRI data were removed using ICA-AROMA to generate noise-free data [11]. Based on the training data, the deep learning methods under comparison were used to train deep learning models to generate noise-free data from the preprocessed rsfMRI data with the noise-free data as supervision information. The deep learning models were finally applied to the preprocessed data of the testing dataset to generate noise-free data that were compared with those generated using ICA-AROMA.

The differences between noise-free data generated by ICA-AROMA and the deep learning models were quantitatively measured using SSIM, PSNR and MSE [19]. As summarized in Table 2, the average performance measures of all testing time points have demonstrated that our method obtained substantially better performance than both the GAN and 3DConv-LSTM methods. Consistent with the results summarized in Table 1, the 3DConv-LSTM method obtained better performance than the GAN method, and our method obtained the overall best performance.

Table 2. Quantitative performance measures obtained on the rsfMRI data by the deep learning models under comparison (mean ± standard deviation).

Model	PSNR	SSIM	MSE
GANs	28.162 ± 0.8161	0.927 ± 0.0067	68.323 ± 7.5052
3DConv-LSTM	32.382 ± 0.1789	0.950 ± 0.0026	59.735 ± 6.8117
Proposed method	33.697 ± 0.0097	0.958 ± 0.0001	55.746 ± 3.8986

We further evaluated the noise-free rsfMRI data generated by ICA-AROMA and the deep learning models using ICA. Particularly, MELODIC of FSL with its default parameters was used to compute independent components of different sets of the noise-free rsfMRI data. Figure 4 shows representative independent components computed from noise-free fMRI data generated by different methods. Compared with those computed from noise-free data generated by the GAN and 3DCOv-LSTM methods, the component computed from noise-free data generated by our method was visually closer to the component computed from the data generated by ICA-AROMA, indicating that our method generated fMRI data more similar to the supervision information.

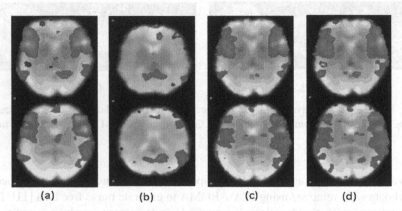

Fig. 4. Representative independent components computed from noise-free data generated by ICA-AROMA (a), GAN (b), 3DConv-LSTM (c), and our method (d), respectively.

4　Discussion and Conclusions

We develop a deep learning method to generate realistic fMRI data for denoising fMRI data in this study. Our method is built upon encapsulated 3D convolutional LSTM networks and an adversarial regularizing procedure implemented by a critic network. Particularly, the encapsulated 3D convolutional LSTM networks facilitate effective learning of spatiotemporal relation of fMRI data across different time points, and the critic network enhances generation of realistic fMRI data. Moreover, our method is generally applicable to both task and resting-state fMRI data. Experimental results have demonstrated that our method obtained better performance in terms of data generation/reconstruction than state-of-the-art alternative deep learning methods on both task and resting state fMRI data from different datasets, including HCP and ABIDE. Different from existing fMRI denoising methods that typically remove noise based on whole time series of individual subjects, our method could be used to remove noise of individual time points of fMRI data and therefore could be used to carry out real-time fMRI data analysis in conjunction deep brain decoding methods [21–23].

Acknowledgement. Research reported in this study was partially supported by the National Institutes of Health under award number [R01MH120811 and R01EB022573]. The content is solely the responsibility of the authors and does not necessarily represent the official views of the National Institutes of Health.

References

1. Caballero-Gaudes, C., Reynolds, R.C.: Methods for cleaning the BOLD fMRI signal. Neuroimage **154**, 128–149 (2017)
2. Murphy, K., Birn, R.M., Bandettini, P.A.: Resting-state fMRI confounds and cleanup. Neuroimage **80**, 349–359 (2013)
3. Power, J.D., Mitra, A., Laumann, T.O., Snyder, A.Z., Schlaggar, B.L., Petersen, S.E.: Methods to detect, characterize, and remove motion artifact in resting state fMRI. Neuroimage **84**, 320–341 (2014)
4. Ciric, R., et al.: Benchmarking of participant-level confound regression strategies for the control of motion artifact in studies of functional connectivity. Neuroimage **154**, 174–187 (2017)
5. Raut, R.V., Mitra, A., Snyder, A.Z., Raichle, M.E.: On time delay estimation and sampling error in resting-state fMRI. Neuroimage **194**, 211–227 (2019)
6. Birn, R.M., Smith, M.A., Jones, T.B., Bandettini, P.A.: The respiration response function: the temporal dynamics of fMRI signal fluctuations related to changes in respiration. Neuroimage **40**, 644–654 (2008)
7. Tijssen, R.H., Jenkinson, M., Brooks, J.C., Jezzard, P., Miller, K.L.: Optimizing RetroICor and RetroKCor corrections for multi-shot 3D FMRI acquisitions. NeuroImage **84**, 394–405 (2014)
8. Behzadi, Y., Restom, K., Liau, J., Liu, T.T.: A component based noise correction method (CompCor) for BOLD and perfusion based fMRI. Neuroimage **37**, 90–101 (2007)
9. Kay, K., Rokem, A., Winawer, J., Dougherty, R., Wandell, B.: GLMdenoise: a fast, automated technique for denoising task-based fMRI data. Front. Neurosci. **7**, 247 (2013)
10. Salimi-Khorshidi, G., Douaud, G., Beckmann, C.F., Glasser, M.F., Griffanti, L., Smith, S.M.: Automatic denoising of functional MRI data: combining independent component analysis and hierarchical fusion of classifiers. Neuroimage **90**, 449–468 (2014)
11. Pruim, R.H., Mennes, M., van Rooij, D., Llera, A., Buitelaar, J.K., Beckmann, C.F.: ICA-AROMA: a robust ICA-based strategy for removing motion artifacts from fMRI data. Neuroimage **112**, 267–277 (2015)
12. Kam, T.-E., et al.: A deep learning framework for noise component detection from resting-state functional MRI. In: Shen, D., Liu, T., Peters, Terry M., Staib, Lawrence H, Essert, C., Zhou, S., Yap, P.-T., Khan, A. (eds.) MICCAI 2019. LNCS, vol. 11766, pp. 754–762. Springer, Cham (2019). https://doi.org/10.1007/978-3-030-32248-9_84
13. Yang, Z., Zhuang, X., Sreenivasan, K., Mishra, V., Curran, T., Cordes, D.: A robust deep neural network for denoising task-based fMRI data: An application to working memory and episodic memory. Med. Image Anal. **60**, 101622 (2020)
14. Yan, Y., et al.: Reconstructing lost BOLD signal in individual participants using deep machine learning. bioRxiv 808089 (2019)
15. Goodfellow, I., et al.: Generative adversarial nets. In: Advances in Neural Information Processing Systems, pp. 2672–2680 (2014)
16. Berthelot, D., Raffel, C., Roy, A., Goodfellow, I.: Understanding and improving interpolation in autoencoders via an adversarial regularizer. arXiv preprint arXiv:1807.07543 (2018)
17. Glasser, M.F., et al.: The minimal preprocessing pipelines for the Human Connectome Project. Neuroimage **80**, 105–124 (2013)
18. Di Martino, A., Yan, C.-G., Li, Q., Denio, E., Castellanos, F.X., Alaerts, K., Anderson, J.S., Assaf, M., Bookheimer, S.Y., Dapretto, M.: The autism brain imaging data exchange: towards a large-scale evaluation of the intrinsic brain architecture in autism. Molecular Psychiatry **19**, 659–667 (2014)

19. Wang, Y., Jiang, L., Yang, M.-H., Li, L.-J., Long, M., Fei-Fei, L.: Eidetic 3D LSTM: a model for video prediction and beyond. In: International Conference on Learning Representations (2018)
20. Esteban, O., et al.: fMRIPrep: a robust preprocessing pipeline for functional MRI. Nat. Methods **16**, 111–116 (2019)
21. Li, H., Fan, Y.: Interpretable, highly accurate brain decoding of subtly distinct brain states from functional MRI using intrinsic functional networks and long short-term memory recurrent neural networks. NeuroImage **202**, 116059 (2019)
22. Li, H., Fan, Y.: Identification of temporal transition of functional states using recurrent neural networks from functional MRI. In: Frangi, Alejandro F., Schnabel, Julia A., Davatzikos, C., Alberola-López, C., Fichtinger, G. (eds.) MICCAI 2018. LNCS, vol. 11072, pp. 232–239. Springer, Cham (2018). https://doi.org/10.1007/978-3-030-00931-1_27
23. Li, H., Fan, Y.: Brain decoding from functional MRI using long short-term memory recurrent neural networks. In: Frangi, A.F., Schnabel, J.A., Davatzikos, C., Alberola-López, C., Fichtinger, G. (eds.) MICCAI 2018. LNCS, vol. 11072, pp. 320–328. Springer, Cham (2018). https://doi.org/10.1007/978-3-030-00931-1_37

Detecting Changes of Functional Connectivity by Dynamic Graph Embedding Learning

Yi Lin[1], Jia Hou[2], Paul J. Laurienti[3], and Guorong Wu[1(✉)]

[1] Department of Psychiatry, University of North Carolina at Chapel Hill,
Chapel Hill, NC, USA
grwu@med.unc.edu
[2] School of Automation, Hangzhou Dianzi University, Hangzhou, Zhejiang, China
[3] Department of Radiology, Wake Forest School of Medicine,
Winston Salem, NC, USA

Abstract. Our current understandings reach the unanimous consensus that the brain functions and cognitive states are dynamically changing even in the resting state rather than remaining at a single constant state. Due to the low signal-to-noise ratio and high vertex-time dependency in BOLD (blood oxygen level dependent) signals, however, it is challenging to detect the dynamic behavior in connectivity without requiring prior knowledge of the experimental design. Like the Fourier bases in signal processing, each brain network can be summarized by a set of harmonic bases (Eigensystem) which are derived from its latent Laplacian matrix. In this regard, we propose to establish a subject-specific spectrum domain, where the learned orthogonal harmonic-Fourier bases allow us to detect the changes of functional connectivity more accurately than using the BOLD signals in an arbitrary sliding window. To do so, we first present a novel dynamic graph learning method to simultaneously estimate the intrinsic BOLD signals and learn the joint harmonic-Fourier bases for the underlying functional connectivity network. Then, we project the BOLD signals to the spectrum domain spanned by learned network harmonic and Fourier bases, forming the new system-level fluctuation patterns, called *dynamic graph embeddings*. We employ the classic clustering approach to identify the changes of functional connectivity using the novel dynamic graph embedding vectors. Our method has been evaluated on working memory task-based fMRI dataset and comparisons with state-of-the-art methods, where our joint harmonic-Fourier bases achieves higher accuracy in detecting multiple cognitive states.

Keywords: Brain state decoding · Graph learning · Functional dynamics

1 Introduction

Empirical studies and emerging evidences suggest that human brain is a complex network with very unique topological properties [16]. Different to the definition

© Springer Nature Switzerland AG 2020
A. L. Martel et al. (Eds.): MICCAI 2020, LNCS 12267, pp. 489–497, 2020.
https://doi.org/10.1007/978-3-030-59728-3_48

of structural network [3], functional connectivity (FC) is an essential statistical concept to characterize the topological relationship between spatially separated anatomical brain regions, which is usually estimated from the BOLD signals in a series of functional MRI images [8,17]. Although plenty of efforts focus on static functional brain networks by assuming FC remain stationary during a period of data collection (aka static FC), the interest is shifting to study the dynamic changes of FC (aka dynamic FC), which might provide more insight into the fundamental properties of brain networks [10,11,19].

In the past decade, there are mainly two branches of approaches for the characterization of function dynamic: (1) temporal change points model [6,18] and (2) sliding window technique [1,5,7]. Dynamic connectivity regression (DCR) method [6] is a typical example of temporal change points model, which first partitions the time course into intervals and then estimates connectivity networks within each interval using statistical inference. Dynamic connectivity detection method [18] further improved the DCR method by utilizing a sparse matrix estimation approach and a hypothesis testing procedure to detect change points. Although change points models provide a potentially powerful method for tracking dynamic FC, they are highly dependent on a greedy partitioning scheme for determining change points and the corresponding FC states. Compared to these statistical models, sliding window approach (SW) is computationally more efficient which essentially identify changes of FC based on the clustering result of FC matrices across sliding windows. However, SW is sensitive to the window size and external noise in BOLD signals, resulting in less replicable results [9,13].

Most of current state-of-the-art change detection methods use the attributes derived from BOLD signals. Due to the technical difficulty in imaging resolution and signal acquisition, the low signal-to-noise ratio in BOLD signals is the major difficulty in detecting FC changes [13]. Since brain functions are supported by the collaboration of multiple regions, functional network exhibits more connectivities than structural network. Such high node-to-node dependency in the network also challenges the accuracy of change detection. In this regard, we propose to find a new putative attribute descriptor to alleviate the noise and redundancy issue of directing using the observed BOLD signals by projecting the BOLD signals to a learned spectrum domain. As show in Fig. 1, we first propose a dynamic graph learning method to jointly (1) estimate a graph Laplacian matrix based on the intrinsic BOLD signals, and (2) smooth the BOLD signals more effectively in the context of the latent functional connectivities. Since the topology of functional network is largely governed by the harmonic bases derived from the underlying Laplacian matrix, we present a novel dynamic graph embedding (displayed in the middle of Fig. 1) to capture the fluctuation pattern at each time point using a set of orthogonal harmonic-Fourier bases for the individual network. We further integrate our dynamic graph embedding into a classic time series clustering method and automatically detect the changes of functional connectivity without knowing the experimental setup of fMRI studies. Experiments and comparison with state-of-the-art methods show that the proposed method can achieve significant performance improvement in identify changes of FC on task-based fMRI data involving working memory.

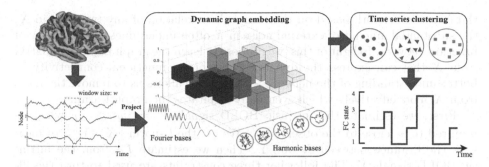

Fig. 1. The novel dynamic graph embedding (middle) is formed by projecting the BOLD signals in each sliding window into a spectrum domain which is spanned by learned joint Harmonic-Fourier bases. The new dynamic graph embeddings are used to replace BOLD signals in detecting the changes of functional network by time series clustering.

2 Methods

2.1 Estimating the Joint Harmonic-Fourier Bases

A brain network can be represented as a graph structure $G = (V, W)$, where V denotes the set of N nodes and $W = [w_{ij}]_{i,j=1}^{N}$ is the corresponding $N \times N$ weighted adjacency matrix of the functional network. Here, we use $L_G = D - W$ denotes the graph Laplacian matrix, where D is a diagonal matrix defined as $D_{ii} = \sum_{j=1}^{N} w_{ij}$. Supposing we have T acquisition time points, we can regard $x_t \in R^N$ as a signal on the graph G at acquisition time t. Then a $N \times T$ data matrix $X = [x_t]_{t=1,...,T}$ is used to denote the whole-brain BOLD time course by concatenating each x_t along the time T.

Given the data matrix X, we opt to establish a subject-specific spectrum domain to capture dynamic functional fluctuation hidden behind BOLD signals X, which is spanned by the Fourier bases Φ_T in the temporal domain and network harmonic bases Φ_G in the graph spectrum domain. Although there are numerous solutions of Φ_T and Φ_G, we reckon the bases are governed by the joint Eigensystem that emerges dynamic fluctuation of self-organized FCs. Specifically, the time Laplacian matrix $L_T \in R^{T \times T}$ characterizes Eigensystem of temporal domain, where XL_T describes the second order temporal derivative of X, i.e., $XL_T|_t = 2x_t - x_{t-1} - x_{t+1}$ (change between forward difference $x_{t+1} - x_t$ and backward difference $x_t - x_{t-1}$). Since L_T is fixed and circulant $(x_{T+1} = x_1)$, Eigen decomposition of $L_T = \Phi_T \Lambda_T \Phi_T^\top$ has the closed-form solution as the orthogonal Eigenvectors $\Phi_T(t, k) = [e^{-j(2\pi(k-1)/T)t}/\sqrt{T}]_{t,k=1,...,T}$ and the diagonal Eigenvalue matrix $\Lambda_T(t, t) = \lambda_T(t) = 2(1 - cos(2\pi(t-1)/T))$. It is clear that the Fourier bases Φ_T of the temporal domain are exactly the classic Fourier waves. Similarly, the network harmonic bases Φ_G is the Eigenvectors after applying SVD (singular vector decomposition) on the latent L_G.

Thus, the good estimation of latent graph Laplacian matrix L_G becomes the backbone of our method. Although it is efficient to obtain L_G by constructing the function network based on the Pearson's correlation of any two rows in X, the substantial amount of external noise in X often undermines the reliability of function network. In light of this, we propose to learn the graph Laplacian matrix from X that can express the dynamic behaviors of functional connectivity. A better understanding of the network topology also allows us to remove the noise from X more effectively which eventually facilitates the graph learning.

First, we estimate the intrinsic BOLD signals $Y = [y_t]_{t=1,...,T}$ which is required to be close to the observed X. We use the l_2-norm $\|X - Y\|_F^2$ to measure the distance between X and Y. Then we estimate L_G from the intrinsic BOLD signals Y. The following three constraints are used to turn the ill-posed optimization problem into a well-posed objective function. **(1) Temporal smoothness on Y.** Since human cognition is not supposed to change rapidly in a short time period, it is reasonable to assume each BOLD time course is smooth along time by penalizing the large change between y_t^i and y_{t+1}^i, which can be quantified as $\|Y\|_{L_T} = tr(Y L_T Y^\top) = \sum_{i=1}^N \sum_{t=1}^T (y_{t+1}^i - y_t^i)^2$. **(2) Graph smoothness on Y.** Instead of treating each y_t as a data array, we underline y_t in the context of the latent functional network. Thus, the ith node and j^{th} node should have similar signal y_t^i and y_t^j if there is a strong FC w_G^{ij} between these two nodes. Such graph smoothness can be quantified as $\|Y\|_{L_G} = tr(Y^\top L_G Y) = \sum_{t=1}^T \sum_{ij} w_{ij}(y_t^i - y_t^j)^2$. **(3) Regularization term on L_G.** To avoid trivial estimation of L_G, we require l_2-norm on L_G and the trace norm of L_G equals to the number of nodes in the network, which prevents L_G degenerate to all zeros. By integrating above terms, the overall energy function for estimating graph Laplacian matrix L_G becomes:

$$\arg \min_{Y, L_G} \|X - Y\|_F^2 + \mu_1 \|Y\|_{L_G} + \mu_2 \|Y\|_{L_T} + \eta \|L_G\|_F^2, \ s.t. \ tr(L_G) = N \quad (1)$$

where μ_1, μ_2 control the strength of temporal and graph smoothness, and η controls the L_2-norm constraint on the graph Laplacian matrix L_G.

To solve above optimization problem, an alternating optimization approach with two steps is employed.

Smooth Signals by Joint Filter. In this step, We optimize Y by fixing L_G and L_T. The objective function of Y becomes:

$$\arg \min_Y \|X - Y\|_F^2 + \mu_1 \cdot tr(Y^\top L_G Y) + \mu_2 \cdot tr(Y L_T Y^\top) \quad (2)$$

Since all three terms in Eq. (2) are quadratic, $\widehat{Y}$ has the following closed-form solutions:

$$vec(\widehat{Y}) = (\mu_1 I_T \otimes L_G + \mu_2 L_T \otimes I_G + I)^{-1} vec(X) \quad (3)$$

where $\otimes$ is the Kronecker product operator to unify L_T and L_G. Since L_G is symmetric, we decompose the graph Laplacian L_G into $L_G = \Phi_G \Lambda_G \Phi_G^\top$, where Φ_G and $\Lambda_G(n,n) = \lambda_G(n)$ are the eigenvectors and the corresponding eigenvalues of Laplacian L_G. In graph signal processing [15], graph Fourier transform of BOLD signals is defined as $GFT(X) = \Phi_G^\top X$, and the inverse transform is

$GFT^{-1}(X) = \Phi_G X$. Thus, Eq. (3) can be understood as filtering BOLD signals X on the temporal domain and graph spectrum domain as:

$$vec(\widehat{Y}) = h(L_G, L_T)vec(X) = \sum_{n=1, t=1}^{N,T} \Phi_J h(\lambda_G(n), \lambda_T(t))\Phi_J^\top vec(X) \quad (4)$$

where $\Phi_J = \Phi_T \otimes \Phi_G$ describes the joint harmonic-Fourier bases of the smoothing kernel. $h(\lambda_G(n), \lambda_T(t)) = 1/(1 + \mu_1\lambda_G(n) + \mu_2\lambda_T(t))$ is the parameters to further characterize the shape of low-pass filter, where the inverse of Eigenvalues in Eq. (5) indicates the preference of suppressing the high frequency part of X.

Optimize the Graph Laplacian. By fixing Y, the optimization of L_G becomes minimizing $\mu_1 \|Y\|_{L_G} + \eta \|L_G\|_F^2$. This optimization task is convex and can be solved via Alternating Direction Method of Multipliers framework [4].

Given the learned graph Laplacian L_G, the orthogonal column vectors in Φ_G form the bases of the network harmonic domain. Therefore, the joint harmonic-Fourier bases Φ_J can be formed to capture the dynamic functional changes by combining the learned harmonic bases Φ_G and the Fourier bases Φ_T, as follows.

2.2 Dynamic Graph Embedding

First, we encode a set of functional networks along sliding windows into the dynamic graph J, as a multi-layer graph shown in the right of Fig. 2. It is clear that the dynamic graph J is essentially the periodically duplicated copy of graph G at each time t, where each node is connected to itself at time $t - 1$ and $t + 1$. Thus, the spectrum of dynamic graph L_J is defined as a Cartesian product of the time Laplacian L_T and graph Laplacian L_G, denoted as $L_J = L_T \otimes I_G + I_T \otimes L_G$. The Eigenvector of L_J can be derived by applying Eigen decomposition to L_J as: $\Phi_J = \Phi_T \otimes \Phi_G$, which is the Kronecker product of learned Φ_T and Φ_G in Sect. 2.1. Since Φ_J is orthogonal, it is straightforward to project the intrinsic BOLD signals data Y into the joint spectrum domain as:

$$F_Y = \Phi_J^\top vec(Y) = (\Phi_T \otimes \Phi_G)^\top Y = \Phi_G^\top Y \Phi_T \quad (5)$$

Since F_Y characterizes the dynamics of functional network under the guidance of joint harmonic-Fourier bases, we further present the dynamic graph embedding vectors for the observed BOLD signals X in three steps. **(1)** Estimate the latent graph Laplacian matrix L_G and obtain the intrinsic BOLD signals Y by optimizing Eq. (1). **(2)** Construct joint harmonic-Fourier bases Φ_J. **(3)** For each time t, we construct a sliding window centered at t. Then we yield the dynamic graph embedding vector $F_Y(t)$ for the intrinsic BOLD signals $Y(t)$ within the sliding window by $F_Y(t) = \Phi_J^\top vec(Y(t))$ by Eq. (5).

Next, we consider these dynamic graph embedding vectors $\{F_Y(t)\}_{t=1}^T$ as the input to the classic spectral clustering method and cluster them into the predefined K clusters, where each cluster consists of very similar dynamic embedding vectors. Based on the clustering result, we automatically detect the changes of functional networks by examining the transition of cluster indexes along time.

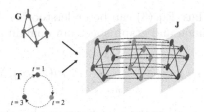

Fig. 2. The dynamic graph J is constructed by the Cartesian product of the graph G and the temporal domain denoted as a cycle graph T.

3   Experiments

In our experiment, we first evaluate the accuracy and robustness of detecting changes of functional networks using our proposed dynamic graph embeddings (dGE) in Sect. 3.1. We compare our method with two counterpart methods: (1) a recent dynamic brain state tracking method, i.e., sliding window correlation-based (SWC) method [1] which uses original BOLD signals as the input, and (2) our simplified method that only uses the learned harmonic bases Φ_G, denoted by (GE). The optimal parameters of μ and η are selected using cross validation strategy. The number of clusters K is determined by utilizing silhouette criteria for the task-based fMRI dataset [12]. In addition to change detection, we also evaluate the discriminative power of our dynamic graph embeddings in recognize different functional tasks in Sect. 3.2.

Data Description. In total 60 block-design working memory task-based fMRI data are selected from the HCP (Human Connectome Project) database [2]. The working memory task-based fMRI data consists of 2-back and 0-back task blocks of body, place, face and tools, as well as a fixation period. Each working memory data contains 393 scans, and are parcellated into 268 regions by the Shen 268 region atlas [14]. We specifically focus on 58 out of 268 brain regions that make up the attention and default mode network (DMN) areas of the brain since these regions are highly related to the working memory task.

3.1   Detection of Functional Connectivity Changes

Here, the performance of functional connectivity change detection on different methods is compared by using the same change detection method (classic clustering analysis method) but different embeddings (attributes). Since the SWC method slides rectangle window with 22 TRs across the fMRI data to extract functional connectivity embedding, in order to fairly compare the three methods, we use the same sliding rectangle window with 22 TRs to obtain corresponding embedding, then we perform the spectral clustering method on the obtained embedding to identify the changes of functional connectivity. Figure 3 (a) shows the detection results of functional connectivity changes on two randomly selected working memory task-based fMRI data obtained by feeding our dynamic graph embedding vectors into the clustering method, the change points (red triangle) we obtained are highly matched with the task event, that is, we are able to detect the beginning and end of each task. Figure 3 (b) shows the clustering accuracy results of all compared methods, our proposed method outperforms all other compared methods with an average accuracy of 0.771, compared to 0.734 by SWC and 0.663 by GE method. Meanwhile, in order to examine the sensitivity of sliding window size affects the performance of functional connectivity changes detection, we perform tests by varying the window size from 10 to 60 TRs. As shown in Fig. 3 (c), our proposed method (red curve) is more robustness to the selection of window size. Better performance of our method is attributed to the following two aspects. First, different from existing change detection methods that directly employ the attributes derived from noisy BOLD signals, the proposed method estimates the intrinsic BOLD signals in the context of the underlying functional connectivities, which alleviates the issue of detecting spurious changes caused by noise. Second, the joint harmonic-Fourier bases can better express the dynamic characteristics of functional connectivity than using the raw BOLD signals. As shown in the detection result in Fig. 3 (b), dGE achieves an improvement of 10.8% of clustering accuracy compared with the GE.

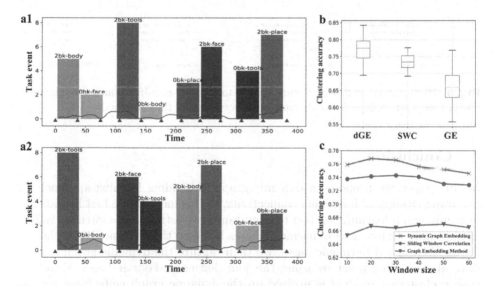

Fig. 3. Performance of detection of functional connectivity changes compared between the sliding window correlation (SWC) method, graph embedding method (GE) and our proposed method (dGE). (a) The detection performance of our proposed method on two random selected test data: the bar plots with different color represent different task events and the red triangles represent detected changes of functional connectivity. The green curve denotes the total energy of dynamic graph embedding. (b) Comparison of clustering accuracy using different embedding representation obtained from different methods. Each box shows a summary statistics of accuracy computed on 60 testing subjects. (c) Effect of the length of window size on the performance of detection of functional connectivity changes. (Color figure online)

3.2   The Performance of Classification on Different Task Events

We further investigate the classification ability of our graph embedding vectors for classifying 2-back task event versus 0-back task event in working memory task-based fMRI data. Since the ground truth of each task event are known in advance, we can obtain dynamic graph embedding of each task event by utilizing our proposed method on the subsequence of each task event in the time series of fMRI data, and utilize these embeddings to train the SVM for classifying 2-back task event and 0-back task event. In 10-fold cross validation strategy, the ROC curves of classifying 2-back task event versus 0-back task event involving body, place, face and tools are shown in Fig. 4. We can observe from the results that our classification results outperform the counterpart methods on classifying 2-back task event versus 0-back task event. The better classification ability shows that we get more discriminated embedding to distinguish changes between different back task events.

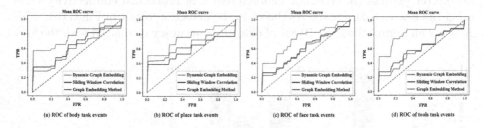

Fig. 4. ROC curves of 2-back versus 0-back task event classification involving body, place, face, and tools task events compared between the three methods.

4   Conclusion

In this paper, we proposed a dynamic graph embedding learning approach for detecting changes of functional connectivity. In this method, we first introduce a dynamic graph learning method to simultaneously estimate the intrinsic BOLD signals and estimate a set of harmonic bases based on the intrinsic BOLD signals. Given the learned harmonic bases, we then capture the dynamic graph embedding at each time point by using the joint harmonic-Fourier bases. Finally, a classic clustering method is utilized on the dynamic graph embedding vectors to detect changes of functional connectivity. We have evaluated our proposed method on working memory task-based fMRI dataset. The results show that the proposed method is effective to detect changes of functional connectivity.

References

1. Allen, E.A., Damaraju, E., Plis, S.M., Erhardt, E.B., Eichele, T., Calhoun, V.D.: Tracking whole-brain connectivity dynamics in the resting state. Cereb. Cortex **24**(3), 663–676 (2014)

2. Barch, D.M., et al.: Function in the human connectome: task-FMRI and individual differences in behavior. Neuroimage **80**, 169–189 (2013)
3. Benard, G., et al.: Mitochondrial bioenergetics and structural network organization. J. Cell Sci. **120**(5), 838–848 (2007)
4. Boyd, S., Parikh, N., Chu, E., Peleato, B., Eckstein, J., et al.: Distributed optimization and statistical learning via the alternating direction method of multipliers. Found. Trends® Mach. Learn. **3**(1), 1–122 (2011)
5. Calhoun, V.D., Miller, R., Pearlson, G., Adalı, T.: The chronnectome: time-varying connectivity networks as the next frontier in FMRI data discovery. Neuron **84**(2), 262–274 (2014)
6. Cribben, I., Haraldsdottir, R., Atlas, L.Y., Wager, T.D., Lindquist, M.A.: Dynamic connectivity regression: determining state-related changes in brain connectivity. Neuroimage **61**(4), 907–920 (2012)
7. Damaraju, E., et al.: Dynamic functional connectivity analysis reveals transient states of dysconnectivity in schizophrenia. NeuroImage: Clin. **5**, 298–308 (2014)
8. Friston, K.J.: Functional and effective connectivity: a review. Brain Connect. **1**(1), 13–36 (2011)
9. Hindriks, R., et al.: Can sliding-window correlations reveal dynamic functional connectivity in resting-state FMRI? Neuroimage **127**, 242–256 (2016)
10. Hutchison, R.M., et al.: Dynamic functional connectivity: promise, issues, and interpretations. Neuroimage **80**, 360–378 (2013)
11. Hutchison, R.M., Womelsdorf, T., Gati, J.S., Everling, S., Menon, R.S.: Resting-state networks show dynamic functional connectivity in awake humans and anesthetized macaques. Hum. Brain Mapp. **34**(9), 2154–2177 (2013)
12. Rousseeuw, P.J.: Silhouettes: a graphical aid to the interpretation and validation of cluster analysis. J. Comput. Appl. Math. **20**, 53–65 (1987)
13. Shakil, S., Lee, C.H., Keilholz, S.D.: Evaluation of sliding window correlation performance for characterizing dynamic functional connectivity and brain states. Neuroimage **133**, 111–128 (2016)
14. Shen, X., Tokoglu, F., Papademetris, X., Constable, R.T.: Groupwise whole-brain parcellation from resting-state FMRI data for network node identification. Neuroimage **82**, 403–415 (2013)
15. Shuman, D.I., Narang, S.K., Frossard, P., Ortega, A., Vandergheynst, P.: The emerging field of signal processing on graphs: extending high-dimensional data analysis to networks and other irregular domains. IEEE Signal Process. Mag. **30**(3), 83–98 (2013)
16. Sporns, O., Chialvo, D.R., Kaiser, M., Hilgetag, C.C.: Organization, development and function of complex brain networks. Trends Cogn. Sci. **8**(9), 418–425 (2004)
17. Van Den Heuvel, M.P., Pol, H.E.H.: Exploring the brain network: a review on resting-state FMRI functional connectivity. Eur. Neuropsychopharmacol. **20**(8), 519–534 (2010)
18. Xu, Y., Lindquist, M.A.: Dynamic connectivity detection: an algorithm for determining functional connectivity change points in FMRI data. Front. Neurosci. **9**, 285 (2015)
19. Zalesky, A., Fornito, A., Cocchi, L., Gollo, L.L., Breakspear, M.: Time-resolved resting-state brain networks. Proc. Natl. Acad. Sci. **111**(28), 10341–10346 (2014)

Discovering Functional Brain Networks with 3D Residual Autoencoder (ResAE)

Qinglin Dong[1], Ning Qiang[2], Jinglei Lv[3], Xiang Li[1,5], Tianming Liu[4],
and Quanzheng Li[1,5(✉)]

[1] Center for Advanced Medical Computing and Analysis, Department of Radiology,
Massachusetts General Hospital and Harvard Medical School, Boston, MA, USA
li.quanzheng@mgh.harvard.edu
[2] School of Physics and Information Technology, Shaanxi Normal University, Xi'an, China
[3] School of Biomedical Engineering and Sydney Imaging, Brain and Mind Centre,
The University of Sydney, Camperdown, Australia
[4] Cortical Architecture Imaging and Discovery Lab, Department of Computer Science and
Bioimaging Research Center, The University of Georgia, Athens, GA, USA
[5] MGH & BWH Center for Clinical Data Science, Boston, MA, USA

Abstract. Functional MRI has attracted increasing attention in cognitive neuroscience and clinical mental health research. Towards understanding how brain give rises to mental phenomena, deep learning has been applied to functional MRI (fMRI) dataset to discover the physiological basis of cognitive process. Considering the unsupervised nature of fMRI due to the complex intrinsic brain activities, an encoder-decoder structure is promising to model hidden structure of latent signal sources. Inspired by the success of deep residual learning, we propose a 68-layer 3D residual autoencoder (3D ResAE) to model deep representations of fMRI in this paper. The proposed model is evaluated on the fMRI data under 3 cognitive tasks in Human Connectome Project (HCP). The experimental results have shown that the temporal representations learned by the encoder matches the task design and the spatial representations can be interpreted to be meaningful functional brain networks (FBNs), which not only include tasks based FBNs, but also intrinsic FBNs. The proposed model also outperforms a 3-layer autoencoder, showing the key factor for the performance improvement is depth. Our work demonstrates the feasibility and success of adopting 2D advanced deep residual networks in computer vision into 3D fMRI volume modeling.

Keywords: Deep learning · fMRI · Brain networks · 3D spatiotemporal model

1 Introduction

It has been decades since the neuroscience community started to research the neural connections that are involved in cognition process, aiming for a comprehensive understanding of brain functions. Functional MRI (fMRI) provides a powerful non-invasive

---

Q. Dong and N. Qiang—Equally contribution to this work.

© Springer Nature Switzerland AG 2020
A. L. Martel et al. (Eds.): MICCAI 2020, LNCS 12267, pp. 498–507, 2020.
https://doi.org/10.1007/978-3-030-59728-3_49

tool to model cognitive behaviors of the whole brain and offers a useful information source to understand the intrinsic functional networks and the architecture of the human brain function [1–4]. In respect of modeling task-related brain function, growing evidence from fMRI (tfMRI) data [5–8] has revealed that these cognitive functions can be represented as a set of functional brain networks (FBNs), which are a collection of regions showing functional connectivity committed to different tasks [3, 4, 9]. Various computational algorithms/methods have been successfully exploited for tfMRI, such as independent component analysis (ICA) [10–13], general linear model (GLM) [9, 14] and sparse dictionary learning (SDL) [15–17]. Yet limited by their shallow nature, these existing machine learning models cannot extract fMRI intrinsic features in a hierarchical way. What's more, GLM relies on prior knowledge of task designs, ICA has independence assumption and SDL has sparsity assumption.

Deep learning has attracted much attention in the fields of machine learning and data mining. It has been proven with great performance in multiple tasks that deep learning approach is superb at learning high-level and mid-level features from low-level raw data. [18–21] Considering the complexity of fMRI data and its intrinsic weak supervised nature, unsupervised deep models have gained great popularity in fMRI data modeling due to its superior representation power in learning latent features and association representations in a hierarchical way. Among those unsupervised deep models that have been applied to fMRI data analysis, the Deep Belief Nets (DBN) [22–24], Convolutional Autoencoder (CAE) [25–27] and Recurrent Autoencoder (RAE) [28, 29] have shown great promise in yielding a compact representation of brain activity. Recently, deep residual network has achieved significant performance improvement on natural image classification datasets with a substantially deeper structure than previous deep models [30, 31]. Despite that deeper neural networks are more difficult to train the gradient vanishing issue, they have greater representation powers, and the deep residual networks solve the issue using shortcuts between layers. Inspired by the success of deep residual networks, this paper exploited the possibility of learning representations of fMRI data with a very deep model. More specifically, a 68-layer residual autoencoder (ResAE) was designed to model the task-based fMRI in an unsupervised way.

In this paper, a group-wise scheme that aggregated multiple subjects' fMRI data was designed for the effective training of ResAE models. The contribution of this work is three-fold. First, it presented an new approach to utilizing very deep models for learning meaningful FBNs from fMRI volumes. In addition, a comparison study with GLM showed that out proposed ResAE generates meaningful functional networks. Second, the enormous feature dimension challenge is tackled with convolution and pooling filters in the proposed method. Despite these recent investigations of the feature extraction and classification of MRI/fMRI data using deep networks, no study has explicitly employed whole-brain fMRI volume as an input and blindly extracted hidden features from the fMRI data. The curse of dimensionality is evident when the deep neural networks with tens of thousands of input nodes. Third, to address the inherent unsupervised nature of fMRI data, which comes with only coarse-grained labels or no labels at all, an autoencoder scheme is designed for fMRI analysis. Due to the unsupervised framework, many intrinsic FBNs were also found besides the task related FBNs, which implies the complexity of human brain activity.

2   Methods

The proposed computational framework is summarized in Fig. 1. In Sect. 2.1, fMRI data of all subjects are registered to a standard space and concatenated after preprocessing. In Sect. 2.2, the ResAE model consists of a pair of encoder and decoder which takes 3D fMRI volumes as input. The model is trained on a large-scale task fMRI dataset by reconstructing the input volumes. In Sect. 2.3, the feature representations of fMRI data were generated from the trained encoder with the latent nodes and were further visualized into interpretable FBNs.

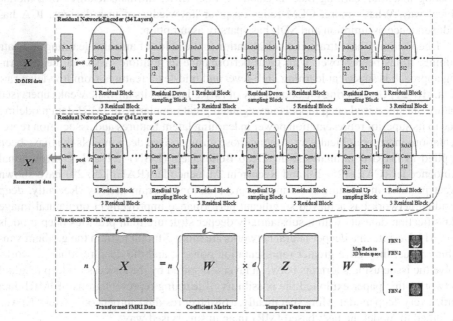

Fig. 1. Illustration of ResAE learning representations of fMRI data. The preprocessed 3D fMRI volumes are temporally concatenated as input. The proposed ResAE consists of a 34-layer encoder and a 34-layer decoder. Each residual block consists of two 3D convolution layers and an up/down pooling layer. With linear regression, the learned temporal features are used to build FBNs, which are further illustrated in Sect. 3.

2.1   Dataset and Preprocessing

The HCP task fMRI dataset is a systematic and comprehensive brain mapping collection of connectome-scale over a large population [6]. The primary goals of the HCP datasets were to identify as many core functional nodes in the brain as possible that can be correlated to structural and functional connectomes and behavior measurements. In the HCP Q3 public release, 900 subjects' fMRI datasets are available. In this paper, our experiments are based on three tasks: Emotion, Gambling and Social. Among these 900 subjects, 35 are excluded from our experiment for consistency of all tasks. The acquisition parameters of tfMRI data are as follows: 90 × 104 matrix, 220 mm FOV, 72 slices, TR = 0.72 s, TE = 33.1 ms, flip angle = 52°, BW = 2290 Hz/Px, in-plane FOV = 208 × 180 mm, 2.0 mm isotropic voxels. For tfMRI images, the preprocessing pipelines are implemented by FSL FEAT including skull removal, motion correction, slice time correction, spatial smoothing, global drift removal (high-pass filtering). All of these steps are implemented by FSL FEAT. [32, 33].

To perform group-wise ResAE training, all subjects' data were registered to the MNI152 4 × 4 × 4 mm³ standard template space, making sure that data from all subjects are in one same template space. The MNI152 template image is with 2 × 2 × 2 mm³ spatial resolution originally and was down-sampled to 4 × 4 × 4 mm³ before the registration. All volumes were variance normalized, concatenated along time dimension and shuffled. The size of the dataset is shown in Table 1. The dimension of the volumes is 49 × 58 × 47 and was padded to 64 × 64 × 64 for the convenience of the multiple down-sampling and up-sampling operations.

Table 1. Size of tfMRI data in HCP Q3

Task	Volumes	Duration (min)	Subjects	Samples
Emotion	176	2:16	865	152,240
Gambling	253	3:12	865	218,845
Social	274	3:27	865	237,010

2.2 Residual Module and ResAE

In this work, the deep residual module is adopted to address the notorious vanishing gradients problem in the training of deep neural networks. As shown in Fig. 2, given the input x of a layer, instead of fitting the regular mapping H(x) of a layer, the residual module fits a residual mapping of F(x) = H(x) − x. Thus, the original mapping is transformed into an identity mapping F(x) + x and is realized by shortcut connections of feedforward neural networks.

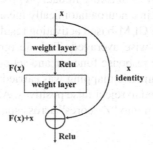

Fig. 2. Illustration of a residual block consisting of two weight layers.

Inspired by the success of deep residual nets on natural images, we propose an extension of deep residual networks for 3D neuroimage reconstruction. As illustrated in Fig. 1, the residual autoencoder network architecture creates a feature representation with its encoder. The encoder consists of 17 down-residual blocks and the decoder consists of 17 up-residual blocks. The down-residual block is composed of residual down sampling block following two 3D residual blocks, whereas the down-residual block is composed of residual down sampling block followed two 3D residual blocks. The solid side arrow in the standard residual block is a shortcut connection performing identity mapping. The dotted arrows in the up and down residual blocks are projection connections done using upsampling and max pooling, respectively. The up and the down residual blocks increase and decrease the output size, respectively.

To improve the gradient flow, the batch normalization (BN) [34] was applied to convolutional layer output before activation, which explicitly forces the activations to be unit gaussian distributed. All convolution filters are of size $3 \times 3 \times 3$. All rectified linear units (ReLU) in up-residual blocks had leak 0.3. We use Adam optimizer with a mini-batch size of 20 [35]. Mini batches take the advantage of GPU boards better and accelerate training with a proper size. However, if the batch size is too large, it may end up with less efficiency or even not converging, unless learning rate is decreased even larger. With a learning rate of 0.001, full cohort of data is trained with 100 epochs from scratch for full convergence in 20 h with a NVIDIA GTX 1080 GPU. The implementation can be found at https://github.com/QinglinDong/ResAE.

2.3 FBN Estimation

To explore the representation on the task fMRI data, we apply Lasso regression to estimate the coefficient matrix which is further used to build spatial maps. As shown in Fig. 1, the group-wise fMRI data X is fed into the trained encoder, yielding the latent variables Z from the output of encoder. Next, the FBNs W are derived from latent variables and group-wise input via Lasso regression as follow:

$$W = min\|Z - XW\|_2^2 + \lambda\|W\|_1 \tag{1}$$

After Lasso regression, W is regularized and transposed to a coefficient matrix, then each row of coefficient matrix is mapped back to the original 3D brain image space, which is the inverse operation of masking in data preprocessing. [36] Thus, the FBNs are generated and interpreted in a neuroanatomically meaningful context.

For comparison study, the GLM-based activation result was performed individually using FSL FEAT and group-wise averaged. Task designs were convoluted with the double gamma hemodynamic response function and set as the repressors of GLM. The contrast-based statistical parametric mapping was carried out with T-test and $p < 0.05$ (with cluster correction) is used to reject false positives. All the FBNs were thresholded at $Z > 2.3$ after transformation into "Z-scores" across spatial volumes.

3 Results

3.1 Temporal Features from ResAE

To further investigate the temporal feature corresponds to the FBNs, the ResAE-derived temporal features of a random subject are illustrated. As shown in Fig. 3, the ground truth is the Hemodynamic Response Function (HRF) Response to the task stimulus, indicating the brain activity corresponds the task design. The temporal features resulted from ResAE are compared with the HRF Response using Pearson correlation and it is shown that ResAE matches the task design well. To illustrate the effect of depth and residual model, a fully connected, 3-layer Autoencoder is adopted as comparison. The temporal features resulted from the 3-layer AE are also compared with the HRF Response and it shows an inferior match with task design compared to ResAE. For temporal features, the correlation between ResAE and HRF Response (average of 0.758) is greater than the correlation between AE and HRF Response (average of 0.404) at a significance level of 0.006%. It can be implied that ResAE has better capability to model the temporal information than the 3-layer AE.

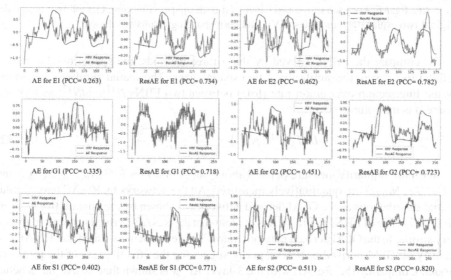

Fig. 3. Pearson correlation of temporal features based on AE and ResAE. The blue lines are the HRF responses, which are ground truth. (Color figure online)

3.2 Task-Related FBNs from ResAE

After the ResAE training, the temporal features are regressed and mapped back to the MNI152 space and superimposed onto the T1-weighted MRI image, so that the functional spatial maps are visualized and interpreted. For each node in the hidden layer, there is one functional network learned by ResAE. Due to space limit, some representative networks that are task related are selected and visualized in Fig. 4. By visual inspection, these FBNs can be well interpreted, and they agree with domain knowledge of functional network atlases in the literature. To quantitively evaluate the performance of ResAE in modeling tfMRI data, a comparison study between the proposed ResAE, a 3-layer AE and GLM (considered as benchmark) is also provided.

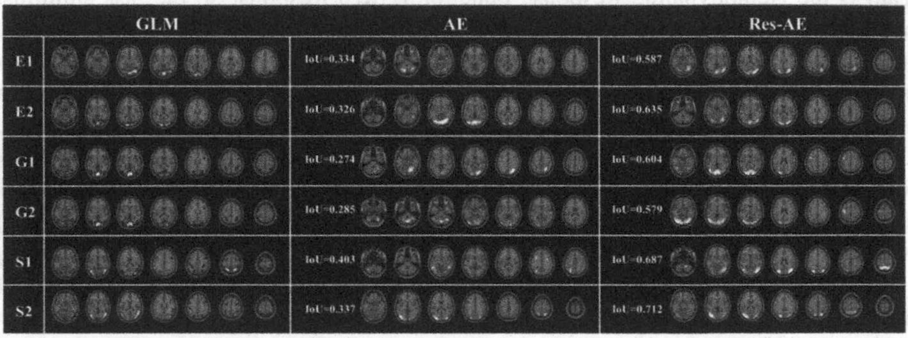

Fig. 4. Illustration of task-related FBNs showing the FBNs derived from GLM (benchmark), 3-layer AE, ResAE. For each of the tasks involved in this paper (Emotion, Gambling, Social), the original two explanatory variables (EVs) and corresponding results are shown.

To compare the FBNs derived by these three methods, the spatial overlap rate is defined to measure the similarity of two spatial maps. The spatial similarity is defined by the intersection over union rate (IoU) between two FBNs $N^{(1)} and N^{(2)}$ as follows, where n is the volume size:

$$IoU\left(N^{(1)}, N^{(2)}\right) = \frac{\sum_{i=1}^{n}\left|N_i^{(1)} \cap N_i^{(2)}\right|}{\sum_{i=1}^{n}\left|N_i^{(1)} \cup N_i^{(2)}\right|} \tag{2}$$

With the similarity measure defined above, the similarities $IoU\left(N_{ResAE}, N_{GLM}\right)$ and $IoU\left(N_{AE}, N_{GLM}\right)$ are quantitatively measured. All the networks by ResAE have similar spatial distributions as the GLM derived networks, as shown by the quantitative similarities by the side of FBNs in Fig. 4. It is evident that the ResAE-derived network maps are very similar to the GLM derived network maps. This result demonstrated that ResAE can identify all GLM-derived networks, partly suggesting the effectiveness of the proposed model. Comparing this ResAE with the 3-layer AE, it is shown that ResAE has a better match with GLM than the 3-layer AE. For task related FBNs, the IoU between ResAE and GLM (average of 0.634) is greater than the IoU between AE and GLM (average of 0.326) at a significance level of 0.0001%. It is shown that with a deeper network, the proposed ResAE can model FBNs better than the 3-layer AE, suggesting the importance of the depth effect.

3.3   Intrinsic FBNs from ResAE

In our experiment results, it was also observed that the intrinsic FBNs, or resting state networks (RSNs), were continuously dynamically active even when subjects are doing task, which provides evidence supporting the conclusion in [2].

With the similarity measure defined above, the similarities $IoU(N_{ResAE}, N_{ICA})$ and $IoU(N_{AE}, N_{ICA})$ are quantitatively measured, where ICA is considered as benchmark for the intrinsic FBNs. Comparisons of pairs by these two methods are shown in Fig. 5, and the quantitative comparison are shown with the FBNs. RSN1, RSN2 and RSN3 correspond to visual network, RSN4 correspond to default mode network (DMN), RSN5 correspond to cerebellum, RSN6 correspond to sensorimotor network, RSN7 correspond to auditory network, RSN8 correspond to executive control network, RSN9 and RSN10 correspond to frontoparietal network. For intrinsic FBNs, the IoU between ResAE and ICA (average of 0.607) is greater than the IoU between AE and ICA (average of 0.365) at a significance level of 0.002%. It is shown that with a deeper network, the proposed ResAE can model FBNs better than the 3-layer AE, suggesting the importance of the depth effect, again. Major RSNs are all covered in the ResAE derived FBNs, which shows ResAE can discover intrinsic RSNs besides task related FBNs.

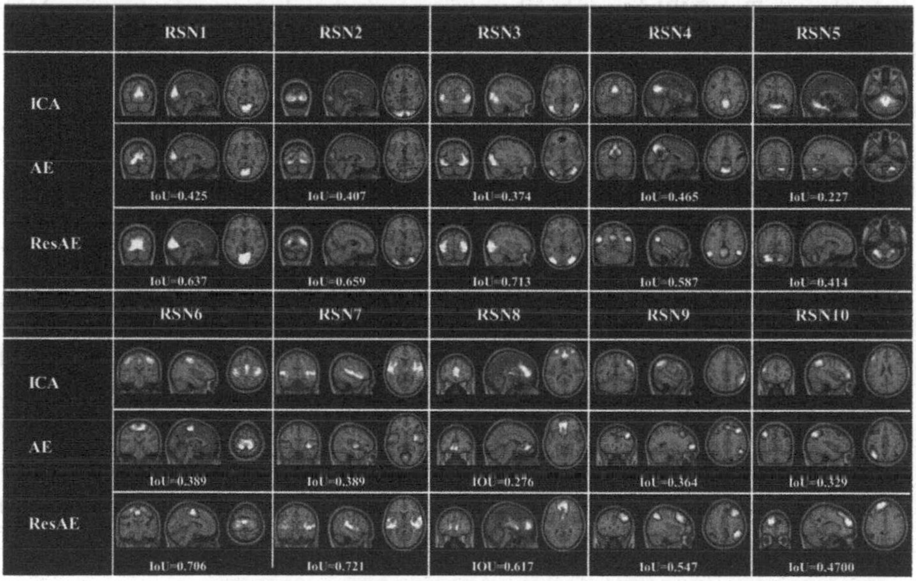

Fig. 5. Illustration of intrinsic FBNs showing the RSNs derived from ICA (benchmark), FBNs from 3-layer AE and ResAE.

4 Discussions

This paper is the first study that model fMRI networks with deep residual network to our best knowledge. In this paper, we proposed to adopt the encoder-decoder structure to exploit the deep residual network for this unsupervised task. With a group-wise experiment on massive tfMRI data, the ResAE model quantitatively and qualitatively showed its capability to learn FBNs. A comparison study with GLM, AE and ResAE shows that the FBNs learned by ResAE are meaningful and can be well interpreted.

One limitation of our current approach is that the effects of hyperparameters is not fully shown, including the model depth, which we plan to illustrate the model depth effects in further study. One promising future study is to apply the encoder representation and corresponding functional connectivity as biomarkers to brain disorder characterization such as Alzheimer's disease, ADHD, Autism, etc.

References

1. Huettel, S.A., et al.: Functional Magnetic Resonance Imaging, vol. 1. Sinauer Associates, Sunderland (2004)
2. Smith, S.M., et al.: Correspondence of the brain's functional architecture during activation and rest. Proc. Natl. Acad. Sci. **106**(31), 13040–13045 (2009)
3. Pessoa, L.: Understanding brain networks and brain organization. Phys. Life Rev. **11**(3), 400–435 (2014)
4. Lv, J., et al.: Task fMRI data analysis based on supervised stochastic coordinate coding. Med. Image Anal. **38**, 1–16 (2017)
5. Archbold, K.H., et al.: Neural activation patterns during working memory tasks and OSA disease severity: preliminary findings. J. Clin. Sleep Med. **5**(01), 21–27 (2009)
6. Barch, D.M., et al.: Function in the human connectome: task-fMRI and individual differences in behavior. Neuroimage **80**, 169–189 (2013)
7. Binder, J.R., et al.: Mapping anterior temporal lobe language areas with fMRI: a multicenter normative study. Neuroimage **54**(2), 1465–1475 (2011)
8. Dosenbach, N.U., et al.: A core system for the implementation of task sets. Neuron **50**(5), 799–812 (2006)
9. Kanwisher, N.: Functional specificity in the human brain: a window into the functional architecture of the mind. Proc. Natl. Acad. Sci. **107**(25), 11163–11170 (2010)
10. McKeown, M.J.: Detection of consistently task-related activations in fMRI data with hybrid independent component analysis. NeuroImage **11**(1), 24–35 (2000)
11. Calhoun, V.D., et al.: A method for making group inferences from functional MRI data using independent component analysis. Hum. Brain Mapp. **14**(3), 140–151 (2001)
12. Beckmann, C.F., et al.: Investigations into resting-state connectivity using independent component analysis. Philos. Trans. R. Soc. Lond. B Biol. Sci. **360**(1457), 1001–1013 (2005)
13. Calhoun, V.D., et al.: Multisubject independent component analysis of fMRI: a decade of intrinsic networks, default mode, and neurodiagnostic discovery. IEEE Rev. Biomed. Eng. **5**, 60–73 (2012)
14. Beckmann, C.F., et al.: General multilevel linear modeling for group analysis in FMRI. Neuroimage **20**(2), 1052–1063 (2003)
15. Jiang, X., et al.: Sparse representation of HCP grayordinate data reveals novel functional architecture of cerebral cortex. Hum. Brain Mapp. **36**(12), 5301–5319 (2015)
16. Lv, J., et al.: Holistic atlases of functional networks and interactions reveal reciprocal organizational architecture of cortical function. IEEE Trans. Biomed. Eng. **62**(4), 1120–1131 (2015)
17. Li, X., et al.: Multple-demand system identification and characterization via sparse representations of fMRI data. In: 2016 IEEE 13th International Symposium on Biomedical Imaging (ISBI). IEEE (2016)
18. Bengio, Y.: Learning deep architectures for AI. Found. Trends® Mach. Learn. **2**(1), 1–127 (2009)
19. Bengio, Y., et al.: Deep learning. Nature **521**(7553), 436–444 (2015)

20. Schmidhuber, J.: Deep learning in neural networks: an overview. Neural Netw. **61**, 85–117 (2015)
21. Yamins, D.L., et al.: Using goal-driven deep learning models to understand sensory cortex. Nat. Neurosci. **19**(3), 356 (2016)
22. Hjelm, R.D., et al.: Restricted Boltzmann machines for neuroimaging: an application in identifying intrinsic networks. NeuroImage **96**, 245–260 (2014)
23. Jang, H., et al.: Task-specific feature extraction and classification of fMRI volumes using a deep neural network initialized with a deep belief network: evaluation using sensorimotor tasks. NeuroImage **145**, 314–328 (2017)
24. Dong, Q., et al.: Modeling hierarchical brain networks via volumetric sparse deep belief network (VS-DBN). IEEE Trans. Biomed. Eng. (2019)
25. Huang, H., et al.: Modeling task fMRI data via mixture of deep expert networks. In: 2018 IEEE 15th International Symposium on Biomedical Imaging (ISBI 2018). IEEE (2018)
26. Huang, H., et al.: Modeling task fMRI data via deep convolutional autoencoder. IEEE Trans. Med. Imaging **37**(7), 1551–1561 (2018)
27. Zhao, Y., et al.: 4D modeling of fMRI data via spatio-temporal convolutional neural networks (ST-CNN). IEEE Trans. Cogn. Dev. Syst. (2019)
28. Wang, H., et al.: Recognizing brain states using deep sparse recurrent neural network. IEEE Trans. Med. Imaging **38**, 1058–1068 (2018)
29. Li, Q., et al.: Simultaneous spatial-temporal decomposition of connectome-scale brain networks by deep sparse recurrent auto-encoders. In: Chung, A.C.S., Gee, J.C., Yushkevich, P.A., Bao, S. (eds.) IPMI 2019. LNCS, vol. 11492, pp. 579–591. Springer, Cham (2019). https://doi.org/10.1007/978-3-030-20351-1_45
30. He, K., et al.: Deep residual learning for image recognition. In: Proceedings of the IEEE Conference on Computer Vision and Pattern Recognition (2016)
31. He, K., Zhang, X., Ren, S., Sun, J.: Identity mappings in deep residual networks. In: Leibe, B., Matas, J., Sebe, N., Welling, M. (eds.) ECCV 2016. LNCS, vol. 9908, pp. 630–645. Springer, Cham (2016). https://doi.org/10.1007/978-3-319-46493-0_38
32. Glasser, M.F., et al.: The minimal preprocessing pipelines for the human Connectome project. Neuroimage **80**, 105–124 (2013)
33. Jenkinson, M., et al.: Fsl. Neuroimage **62**(2), 782–790 (2012)
34. Ioffe, S., et al.: Batch normalization: accelerating deep network training by reducing internal covariate shift (2015)
35. Kingma, D.P., et al.: Adam: a method for stochastic optimization. arXiv preprint arXiv:1412.6980 (2014)
36. Abraham, A., et al.: Machine learning for neuroimaging with scikit-learn. Front. Neuroinform. **8**, 14 (2014)

Spatiotemporal Attention Autoencoder (STAAE) for ADHD Classification

Qinglin Dong[1], Ning Qiang[2], Jinglei Lv[3], Xiang Li[1,5], Tianming Liu[4], and Quanzheng Li[1,5(✉)]

[1] Center for Advanced Medical Computing and Analysis, Department of Radiology, Massachusetts General Hospital and Harvard Medical School, Boston, MA, USA
li.quanzheng@mgh.harvard.edu
[2] School of Physics and Information Technology, Shaanxi Normal University, Xi'an, China
[3] School of Biomedical Engineering and Sydney Imaging, Brain and Mind Centre, The University of Sydney, Camperdown, Australia
[4] Cortical Architecture Imaging and Discovery Lab, Department of Computer Science and Bioimaging Research Center, The University of Georgia, Athens, GA, USA
[5] MGH & BWH Center for Clinical Data Science, Boston, MA, USA

Abstract. It has been of great interest in the neuroimaging community to model spatiotemporal brain function and disorders based on resting state functional magnetic resonance imaging (rfMRI). A variety of spatiotemporal methods have been proposed for rfMRI so far, including deep learning models such as convolution networks (CNN) and recurrent networks (RNN). However, the dominant models fail to capture the long-distance dependency (LDD) due to their sequential nature, which becomes critical at longer sequence lengths due to memory limit. Inspired by human brain's extraordinary ability of long-term memory and attention, the attention mechanism is designed for machine translation to draw global dependencies and achieved state-of-the-art. In this paper, we propose a spatiotemporal attention autoencoder (STAAE) to discover global features that address LDDs in rfMRI. STAAE encodes the information throughout the rfMRI sequence and reveals resting state networks (RSNs) that characterize spatial and temporal properties of the data. Considering that the rfMRI is measured without external tasks, an unsupervised classification framework is developed based on the connectome generated with STAAE. This framework has been evaluated on 281 children with ADHD and 266 normal control children from 4 sites of ADHD200 datasets. The proposed STAAE reveals the global functional interaction in the brain and achieves a state-of-the-art classification accuracy from 59.5% to 77.2% on multiple sites. It is evident that the proposed attention-based model provides a novel approach towards better understanding of human brain.

Keywords: Deep learning · rfMRI · Attention mechanism · Functional networks · ADHD

Q. Dong and N. Qiang—Equally contribution to this work.

© Springer Nature Switzerland AG 2020
A. L. Martel et al. (Eds.): MICCAI 2020, LNCS 12267, pp. 508–517, 2020.
https://doi.org/10.1007/978-3-030-59728-3_50

1 Introduction

The resting state networks (RSNs) from resting state functional MRI (rfMRI) provides a powerful tool to model brain functions and disorders even in the absence of an external task [1–5]. Various machine learning methods have been successful applied on rfMRI to exploit RSNs, such as independent component analysis (ICA) [6–9] and sparse dictionary learning (SDL) [10–14]. Due to the superior representation power, deep learning models have also been increasingly employed for fMRI analysis, such as Convolution Neural Network (CNN) [15–17] and Recurrent Neural Network (RNN) [18–21]. However, evidences show that the cognitive actions of multiple regions of brains is related to their earlier actions, with a potential long distance in time [22]. While modeling, the so-called long-distance dependency (LDD), is a challenging issue for CNN and RNN to address [23].

Recently, the attention mechanism has gained popularity in sequence modeling and various tasks [23]. Compared to regular CNN and RNN, the attention mechanism models every unit in the input sequence simultaneously and draws global dependencies without regard to their distance [24]. It has also been proven that pure attention mechanism has comparable representation powers than CNNs or RNNs [23]. To utilize the superior ability of attention mechanism to mining LDD, we explore the possibility to model rfMRI with attention mechanism. Considering the unsupervised nature of rfMRI data, a spatiotemporal attention autoencoder (STAAE) is proposed to model the rfMRI sequence data. With the proposed model, the relation of two volumes/frames in the sequence is captured with an attention score measuring the distance of their embeddings. We aim to improve the classification by addressing the LDD issue. To our best knowledge, this is the first study that exploits attention mechanism for fMRI modeling.

Attention Deficit Hyperactivity Disorder (ADHD) is a mental health disorder involves multiple attention related problems, but neither a comprehensive pathophysiology model nor a biomarker for clinical practice is established yet [25–30]. The proposed model has been applied on ADHD200 datasets for evaluation. First, we examined the learned representation of the input data, which encodes the global information throughout the sequence of rfMRI. Our model reveals meaningful RSNs that characterize spatial and temporal properties of the data. Secondly, based on the learned RSNs, the connectomes are generated for each subject and are used for ADHD classification with cross-validation. The experimental results indicated that the proposed framework is capable of modeling and classifying on ADHD. It's worth noting that the proposed integrated pipeline can be easily generalized for other mental disorder classification.

2 Methods

The proposed computational framework is shown in Fig. 1. In Sect. 2.1, the preprocessed rfMRI data of all subjects are registered to a standard space for group-wise learning and masked to a 2D spatiotemporal matrix. In Sect. 2.2, a STAAE model consists of a pair of encoder and decoder which takes rfMRI volumes as input. In Sect. 2.3, the intermediate representations of rfMRI data are interpreted to RSNs. The functional connectomes are built for further classification.

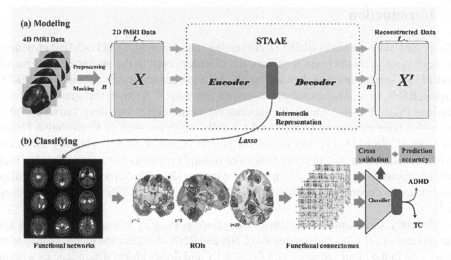

Fig. 1. Illustration of STAAE based pipeline for modeling and classifying of ADHD-200. (a) Modeling process: the outline of STAAE model, in which the input and output are raw fMRI signals and reconstructed signals respectively, and the high-level features extracted by the encoder are used to construct RSNs. (b) Classifying process: by extracting from the RSNs generated by the STAAE model, a functional connectome for each subject is calculated. A feedforward neural network is trained as classifier based on the functional connectomes and used for classification.

2.1 Dataset and Preprocessing

In this work, we used the subjects from four sites in ADHD-200 dataset: Kennedy Krieger Institute (KKI), Peking University (PU), New York University Medical Center (NYU), and NeuroImage (NI). For all our experiments, we use preprocessed data publicly available from Preprocessed Connectomes Project [27]. The Athena preprocessing pipeline was adopted, which is based on tools from the AFNI and FSL software packages, including skull striping, slice timing correction, motion correction, detrending, band filtering (0.01–0.01 Hz), normalization and masking. To perform group-wise STAAE training, all subjects' data are nonlinearly registered to the MNI152 $4 \times 4 \times 4$ mm^3 standard template space [31] (Table 1).

Table 1. Summary of fMRI dataset.

Imaging site	Total subjects	Control subjects	ADHD subjects
KKI	83	67	22
PU	194	78	116
NYU	216	98	118
NI	48	23	25

2.2   Attention Mechanism and STAAE

In respect of sequence modeling, especially high-dimension spatiotemporal sequence data like fMRI, both convolutional network and recurrent network have been used in the field. To utilize the CNN's hierarchical feature abstraction ability, a 1D temporal convolution architecture was applied on the fMRI time series [15, 16]. This approach was able to extract features from low-level to high level, however, it did not make use of the rich spatial information from fMRI. To incorporate the spatial and temporal information at the same time, recurrent network was applied on the fMRI volumes and preserving temporal features with long short-term memory (LSTM), which is a typical recurrent module [18, 20, 21, 32]. This approach established a unified spatiotemporal frame; however, it comes with three drawbacks. First, the inherently sequential nature of RNN/LSTM precludes parallelization, which causes notable time cost especially for high-dimension data like fMRI. Second, the sequential nature also leads to the notorious long-distance dependency (LDD) problem, which becomes critical at longer sequence lengths due to memory limit [24]. Third, the encoder LSTM is used to process the entire input sentence and encode it into a context vector, where the intermediate states of the encoder are ignored.

In this paper, we propose to solve the above-mentioned drawbacks by substituting the convolution and recurrent networks with the attention mechanism [22], which draws global dependencies and achieved state of the art in multiple sequence modeling tasks. The attention mechanism consists of three matrices: queries $Q \in \mathbb{R}^{n \times d_k}$, keys $K \in \mathbb{R}^{m \times d_k}$ and values $V \in \mathbb{R}^{m \times d_v}$. In the context of rfMRI, a key vector and a query vector are learned for each frame of volume, and the pairs of query-key are matched across all frame simultaneously. The output is computed as a weighted sum of the values, where the weight assigned to each value is computed by a compatibility function of the query with the corresponding key. If a pair of query-key matches, it generates a high value as output. As shown in Fig. 2, we compute the matrix of outputs as:

$$\text{Attention}(Q, K, V) = \text{softmax}\left(\frac{QK^T}{\sqrt{d_k}}\right)V \tag{1}$$

Most sequence models follow an encoder-decoder paradigm, and it also applies to our proposed STAAE. Considering the intrinsic unsupervised nature of rfMRI, i.e. no external stimulus or task is performed, an autoencoder structure is adopted, where the decoder aims to reconstruct the exact input. For STAAE, the encoder maps an input sequence of symbol representations $X = (x_1, \ldots, x_t)$ to a sequence of intermediate representations $Z = (z_1, \ldots, z_t)$. More specifically, each xi represents a volume of rfMRI and is embedded with a fully feedforward network. Given Z, the decoder tries to generate a reconstructed sequence of $X' = (x_1', \ldots, x_t')$.

Hyperbolic tangent function was chosen as the activation for the rfMRI data. To start with training, the weights and biases are initialized from a Gaussian with zero-mean and a standard deviation of 0.01. To improve the convergence, batch normalization technique was applied to each hidden layer, which explicitly forced the activations to be unit Gaussian distributed. With a learning rate of 0.0001 and batch size of 1, the models were trained for 200 epochs for convergence. All experiments were repeated 5 times to

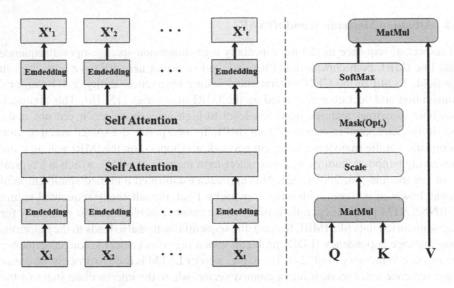

Fig. 2. Structure of STAAE and illustration of attention mechanism.

test the stability of consistency of results. The implementation of STAAE can be found at https://github.com/QinglinDong/stAAE.

2.3 Feature Interpretation and Classification

To explore the intermediate representation learned with STAAE, we apply Lasso regression to estimate the coefficient matrix which is used to build spatial maps. As shown in Fig. 1, the group-wise fMRI data X is fed into the trained encoder, yielding the intermediate representation Z from the output of encoder. Next, the RSNs W are derived from the intermediate representation and group-wise input via Lasso regression as follow:

$$W = min\|Z - XW\|_2^2 + \lambda\|W\|_1 \qquad (2)$$

After the Lasso regression, W is regularized and transposed to a coefficient matrix, then each row of coefficient matrix is mapped back to the original 3D brain image space, which is the inverse operation of masking in data preprocessing. Thus, the RSNs are generated and interpreted in a neuroanatomically meaningful context. As shown in Fig. 3, after transformation into "Z-scores" across spatial volumes, all the RSNs were thresholded at $Z > 2.3$.

To exploit the spatiotemporal features including the RSNs and the intermediate representations for further classification, we follow three steps. First, as shown in Fig. 1, with the established RSNs, a union set of regions of interests (ROIs) from all the RSNs are combined to establish a comprehensive brain atlas. Second, we extract the time series from the original training data masked by the atlas. Third, the functional connectome, which reflects the level of co-activation of brain regions, is calculated based on the Pearson correlation of the extracted time series. The upper triangle matrix values were removed for less redundancy.

For classification, the functional connectome is flattened to a one-dimensional feature vector. A deep feedforward neural network classifier is used as classifier, where cross entropy loss is used for binary classification. There are 2 hidden layers in DNN, and the numbers of nodes are 1000 and 500, respectively. A 10-fold cross validation was run 10 times to measure the prediction accuracy of whole pipeline. The results of classification accuracy on all sites through the proposed STAAE based pipeline are shown in Sect. 3.2.

3 Results

3.1 RSNs from STAAE

The RSNs derived from the STAAE is shown in Fig. 3. It is observed that the RSNs are intrinsic active even when no extra tasks the subjects are doing, which provides evidence supporting the conclusion in [2–4, 33]. By visual inspection, these RSNs can be well interpreted, and they agree with domain knowledge of functional network atlases in the literature. To quantitatively evaluate the performance of STAAE in modeling RfMRI data, a comparison study between STAEE derived RSN and templates [1] is provided in this section.

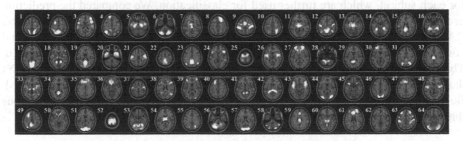

Fig. 3. Overview of the RSNs derived from STAAE.

To compare the RSNs derived by these three methods, the spatial overlap rate is defined to measure the similarity of two spatial maps. The spatial similarity is defined by the intersection over union rate (IoU) between two RSNs $N^{(1)} and N^{(2)}$ as follows, where n is the volume size:

$$IoU\left(N^{(1)}, N^{(2)}\right) = \frac{\sum_{i=1}^{n}\left|N_i^{(1)} \cap N_i^{(2)}\right|}{\sum_{i=1}^{n}\left|N_i^{(1)} \cup N_i^{(2)}\right|} \tag{3}$$

With the similarity measure defined above, the similarities $IoU(N_{ResAE}, N_{ICA})$ and $IoU(N_{AE}, N_{ICA})$ are quantitatively measured, where ICA is considered as ground truth for the intrinsic RSNs. Comparisons of pairs by these two methods are shown in Fig. 4, and the quantitative comparison are shown on the sides. This result demonstrated that STAAE can identify intrinsic RSNs very well, suggesting the effectiveness and meaningfulness of our proposed model.

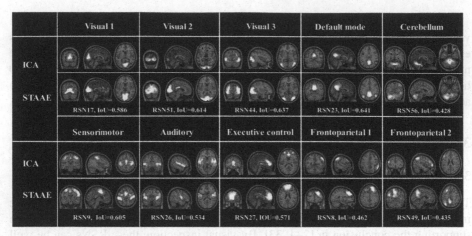

Fig. 4. Comparison of STAAE RSN with templates based on ICA [1].

3.2 Prediction Accuracy on ADHD-200

As illustrated in Sect. 2.3, we use STAAE derived RSNs to build functional connectome for each subject, which are further used for classification. We compared the prediction accuracies achieved by our STAAE based pipeline with SDL [34] based pipeline and RAE based pipeline. As shown in Fig. 5, by using the same classification framework and configurations, the STAAE based pipeline performed better than the other two method. The average prediction accuracies of STAAE based pipeline on NYU, PU, KKI and NI datasets are 59.5%, 65.2%, 77.2% and 61.0%, respectively (marked by green triangles). Besides, the variances of the STAAE based pipeline are smaller than other two methods that indicate the robust performance of our method.

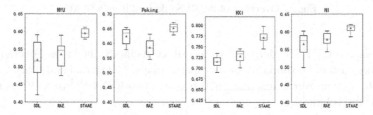

Fig. 5. Comparison of results achieved by SDL, RAE, STAAE based pipeline.

The results are also compared with other models in previous literature, including Support vector machine (SVM) and ICA. Table 2 shows the average prediction accuracies of SVM [29], ICA [30], SDL [34], RAE [18], and STAAE classification pipelines on ADHD200 dataset. It shows RAE [18] outperforms traditional shallow machine learning models such as SVM [29], ICA [30] and SDL [34] and our proposed STAAE outperforms RAE [18]. Overall, based on the RSNs derived by the STAAE model, our classification pipeline performed excellent and competitive compared to other models and methods for ADHD classification. These results also imply the effectiveness of STAAE on RSN modeling.

Table 2. The STAAE achieves better average classification accuracy than previous state-of-the-art models on the ADHD200 dataset

Name	SVM [29]	ICA [30]	SDL [34]	RAE [18]	STAAE
NYU	–	56%	52.0%	53.5%	**59.5%**
PU	58.82%	58%	62.4%	58.7%	**65.2%**
KKI	54.55%	81%	71.6%	72.8%	**77.2%**
NI	48.00%	–	56.5%	57.8%	**61.0%**

4 Discussions

This paper is among the earliest studies that explore modeling fMRI with attention mechanism, to our best knowledge. In this paper, we proposed to adopt the encoder-decoder structure to exploit the attention mechanism for the unsupervised rfMRI sequence. With a group-wise experiment on massive rfMRI data, the proposed model shows its capability to learn RSNs. A comparison study with SDL and RAE showed that the RSNs learned by STAAE are meaningful and can be well interpreted. One limitation of our current approach is that the effects of hyperparameters is not fully explored, including the model depth, number of attention head and size of attention head. By tuning the parameters, the proposed framework can even achieve higher performance in the future.

For language modeling, it is crucial to solve the issue of ambiguity, where one word can have different meanings in different context. By learning contextualized word embedding based on attention mechanism, Bidirectional Encoder Representations from Transformers (BERT) has already achieved great success and dominated the natural language processing. [35] For brain modeling, ambiguity and context issue, not only because of the incomplete supervision nature of fMRI and lack of ground truth, but also multiple RSNs are activated simultaneously and each RSN may serve more than one function. [13, 36] It is interesting and feasible to model the multiple-demand system in brain and explore RSNs in different context with extended attention network in future work.

References

1. Smith, S.M., et al.: Correspondence of the brain's functional architecture during activation and rest. Proc. Natl. Acad. Sci. **106**(31), 13040–13045 (2009)
2. Kanwisher, N.: Functional specificity in the human brain: a window into the functional architecture of the mind. Proc. Natl. Acad. Sci. **107**(25), 11163–11170 (2010)

3. Harris, K.D., et al.: Cortical connectivity and sensory coding. Nature **503**(7474), 51 (2013)
4. Pessoa, L.: Understanding brain networks and brain organization. Phys. Life Rev. **11**(3), 400–435 (2014)
5. Lv, J., et al.: Task fMRI data analysis based on supervised stochastic coordinate coding. Med. Image Anal. **38**, 1–16 (2017)
6. McKeown, M.J.: Detection of consistently task-related activations in fMRI data with hybrid independent component analysis. NeuroImage **11**(1), 24–35 (2000)
7. Calhoun, V.D., et al.: A method for making group inferences from functional MRI data using independent component analysis. Hum. Brain Mapp. **14**(3), 140–151 (2001)
8. Beckmann, C.F., et al.: Investigations into resting-state connectivity using independent component analysis. Philos. Trans. R. Soc. Lond. B Biol. Sci. **360**(1457), 1001–1013 (2005)
9. Calhoun, V.D., et al.: Multisubject independent component analysis of fMRI: a decade of intrinsic networks, default mode, and neurodiagnostic discovery. IEEE Rev. Biomed. Eng. **5**, 60–73 (2012)
10. Lv, J., et al.: Sparse representation of whole-brain fMRI signals for identification of functional networks. Med. Image Anal. **20**(1), 112–134 (2015)
11. Jiang, X., et al.: Sparse representation of HCP grayordinate data reveals novel functional architecture of cerebral cortex. Hum. Brain Mapp. **36**(12), 5301–5319 (2015)
12. Ge, F., et al.: Deriving ADHD biomarkers with sparse coding based network analysis. In: 2015 IEEE 12th International Symposium on Biomedical Imaging (ISBI). IEEE (2015)
13. Li, X., et al.: Multiple-demand system identification and characterization via sparse representations of fMRI data. In: 2016 IEEE 13th International Symposium on Biomedical Imaging (ISBI). IEEE (2016)
14. Ge, F., et al.: Exploring intrinsic networks and their interactions using group wise temporal sparse coding. In: 2018 IEEE 15th International Symposium on Biomedical Imaging (ISBI 2018). IEEE (2018)
15. Huang, H., et al.: Modeling task fMRI data via mixture of deep expert networks. In: 2018 IEEE 15th International Symposium on Biomedical Imaging (ISBI 2018). IEEE (2018)
16. Huang, H., et al.: Modeling task fMRI data via deep convolutional autoencoder. IEEE Trans. Med. Imaging **37**(7), 1551–1561 (2018)
17. Zhao, Y., et al.: Automatic recognition of fMRI-derived functional networks using 3-D convolutional neural networks. IEEE Trans. Biomed. Eng. **65**(9), 1975–1984 (2018)
18. Li, Q., et al.: Simultaneous spatial-temporal decomposition of connectome-scale brain networks by deep sparse recurrent auto-encoders. In: Chung, A.C.S., Gee, J.C., Yushkevich, P.A., Bao, S. (eds.) IPMI 2019. LNCS, vol. 11492, pp. 579–591. Springer, Cham (2019). https://doi.org/10.1007/978-3-030-20351-1_45
19. Sak, H., et al.: Long short-term memory recurrent neural network architectures for large scale acoustic modeling. In: Fifteenth Annual Conference of the International Speech Communication Association (2014)
20. Wang, L., et al.: Decoding dynamic auditory attention during naturalistic experience. In: 2017 IEEE 14th International Symposium on Biomedical Imaging (ISBI 2017). IEEE (2017)
21. Wang, H., et al.: Recognizing brain states using deep sparse recurrent neural network. IEEE Trans. Med. Imaging **38**, 1058–1068 (2018)
22. Piñango, M.M., et al.: The localization of long-distance dependency components: integrating the focal-lesion and neuroimaging record. Front. Psychol. **7**, 1434 (2016)
23. Bahdanau, D., et al.: Neural machine translation by jointly learning to align and translate (2014)
24. Vaswani, A., et al.: Attention is all you need. In: Advances in Neural Information Processing Systems (2017)
25. Riaz, A., et al.: Fusion of fMRI and non-imaging data for ADHD classification. Comput. Med. Imaging Graph. **65**, 115–128 (2018)

26. Itani, S., et al.: A multi-level classification framework for multi-site medical data: application to the ADHD-200 collection. Expert Syst. Appl. **91**, 36–45 (2018)
27. Bellec, P., et al.: The neuro bureau ADHD-200 preprocessed repository. Neuroimage **144**, 275–286 (2017)
28. dos Santos Siqueira, A., et al.: Abnormal functional resting-state networks in ADHD: graph theory and pattern recognition analysis of fMRI data. Biomed. Res. Int. **2014**, 380531 (2014)
29. Dey, S., et al.: Attributed graph distance measure for automatic detection of attention deficit hyperactive disordered subjects. Front. Neural Circuits **8**, 64 (2014)
30. Nuñez-Garcia, M., Simpraga, S., Jurado, M.A., Garolera, M., Pueyo, R., Igual, L.: FADR: functional-anatomical discriminative regions for rest fMRI characterization. In: Zhou, L., Wang, L., Wang, Q., Shi, Y. (eds.) MLMI 2015. LNCS, vol. 9352, pp. 61–68. Springer, Cham (2015). https://doi.org/10.1007/978-3-319-24888-2_8
31. Abraham, A., et al.: Machine learning for neuroimaging with scikit-learn. Front. Neuroinform. **8**, 14 (2014)
32. Cui, Y., et al.: Identifying brain networks of multiple time scales via deep recurrent neural network. In: Frangi, A.F., Schnabel, J.A., Davatzikos, C., Alberola-López, C., Fichtinger, G. (eds.) MICCAI 2018. LNCS, vol. 11072, pp. 284–292. Springer, Cham (2018). https://doi.org/10.1007/978-3-030-00931-1_33
33. Pessoa, L.: Beyond brain regions: network perspective of cognition–emotion interactions. Behav. Brain Sci. **35**(3), 158–159 (2012)
34. Lv, J., et al.: Holistic atlases of functional networks and interactions reveal reciprocal organizational architecture of cortical function. IEEE Trans. Biomed. Eng. **62**(4), 1120–1131 (2015)
35. Devlin, J., et al.: Bert: pre-training of deep bidirectional transformers for language understanding (2018)
36. Duncan, J.: The multiple-demand (MD) system of the primate brain: mental programs for intelligent behaviour. Trends Cogn. Sci. **14**(4), 172–179 (2010)

Global Diffeomorphic Phase Alignment of Time-Series from Resting-State fMRI Data

David S. Lee[1,2(✉)], Ashish Sahib[1], Katherine Narr[1,3], Elvis Nunez[1,4], and Shantanu Joshi[1,2]

[1] Ahmanson-Lovelace Brain Mapping Center, Department of Neurology, UCLA, Los Angeles, USA
dalee@mednet.ucla.edu
[2] Department of Bioengineering, UCLA, Los Angeles, USA
[3] Department of Psychiatry and Biobehavioral Sciences, UCLA, Los Angeles, USA
[4] Department of Applied Mathematics, Johns Hopkins University, Baltimore, USA

Abstract. We present a novel method for global diffeomorphic phase alignment of time-series data from resting-state functional magnetic resonance imaging (rsfMRI) signals. Additionally, we propose a multidimensional, continuous, invariant functional representation of brain time-series data and solve a general global cost function that brings both the temporal rotations and phase reparameterizations in alignment. We define a family of cost functions for spatiotemporal warping and compare time-series warps across them. This method achieves direct alignment of time-series, allows population analysis by aligning time-series activity across subjects and shows improved global correlation maps, as well as z-scores from independent component analysis (ICA), while showing new information exploited by phase alignment that was not previously recoverable.

Keywords: Resting-fMRI · Time-series · Network connectivity · ICA

1 Introduction

Over the last decade, changes in neural resting-state functional magnetic resonance imaging (rsfMRI) activity have been robustly implicated in various brain disorders as well as in healthy development. Importantly, advances in the field of acquisition, processing, and analysis have given rise to the field of functional brain connectomics [12]. Whether one performs a task-related experiment or uses a resting-state paradigm, the underlying methods that rely on correlation-based analyses assume that there is a synchronization of time-series across subjects between either the resting-state epochs or task-related activity. The problem of synchronization is less severe in task-based fMRI where there is a gated stimulus at the start and stop of each activity. Free thinking paradigms such as resting-state fMRI lack explicit timing information. Here, initiatives such as

© Springer Nature Switzerland AG 2020
A. L. Martel et al. (Eds.): MICCAI 2020, LNCS 12267, pp. 518–527, 2020.
https://doi.org/10.1007/978-3-030-59728-3_51

movie - (http://studyforrest.org) or game-watching paradigms integrated into the rsfMRI experiment have the potential to present consistent naturalistic audiovisual stimuli and potentially elicit commonalities in neural response across subjects. While these approaches aim to achieve synchronicity of stimuli, they do not model synchronicity of response. We suggest that this synchronicity of response is not only confounded by scanner noise and motion artifacts at a lower level, but also by complex inter-subject neural dynamics and brain states.

To tackle this problem, there have been several ideas that have proposed the alignment of task-based and rsfMRI activations. The hyperalignment approach solves the Procrustes problem for reduced dimensional functional activity maps, and recently connectivity patterns as well [4]. The Brainsync approach also solves the Procrustes problem, but differently, by directly aligning time-series across subjects. Another elegant idea performs diffeomorphic alignment between surfaces based on the embedded functional connectivity maps shared across subjects [9]. Lee et al. have proposed a diffeomorphic registration approach for both task-based fMRI and rsfMRI signals, however the alignment operates at the individual voxel level [6,7]. While Procrustes-based alignment methods achieve good results in terms of inter-subject resting or task-fMRI registration, they only rely on scale, translation, and rotation. Although the end result of rotational alignment achieves a good correspondence between time-series, it performs a global bending-type deformation of one time-series to the other while ignoring changes in phase. Further, what is absent in the above approaches is the idea of global time reparameterization. As a consequence, these methods exclusively detect magnitude changes and do not account for phase changes in functional activity.

Our paper presents a general solution to this problem by introducing a new idea for the global phase and magnitude alignment of fMRI signals. We propose a continuous, invariant representation of brain time-series activity from fMRI, and propose a general global cost function that can incorporate both temporal rotations and time reparameterizations, and present efficient means of optimization. In this paper, the term reparameterization refers to global temporal (amplitude+phase) reparameterization. In addition to rotational time-series transformation, our method also yields a new global, invertible, diffeomorphic, phase-synchronizing time-series transformation. The resulting global solution captures both magnitude changes and temporal shifts, and because of the diffeomorphic property, conveniently allows us to switch back and forth between the template space and the subject space. Our method enables direct warping of entire time-series data sets across subjects.

2   Global Phase Alignment of Time-Series Data

2.1   Representation

We denote the functional brain activity over n nodes by a vector valued map $\mathcal{F} \in \mathbb{L}^2(\mathbb{R}^n)$. Here n can refer to the number of vertices for surface representations, voxels for volume representations, or regions of interest from seed-based approaches. The global brain functional activity is then represented by

$$\mathcal{F} \equiv (f^1, f^2, \ldots, f^n) \mid f^i : [0, 1] \to \mathbb{R}, \tag{1}$$

where each f^i is a time-series at node i.

For the purpose of matching, we would like to ensure that this brain activity $\mathcal{F}$ is invariant to scale and translation. To achieve invariance to translation, we premultiply $\mathcal{F}$ by an idempotent matrix to achieve a centered representation,

$$\overline{\mathcal{F}} = \left(I_n - \frac{1}{n} \mathbf{1}_n \mathbf{1}_n{}^T \right) \mathcal{F}, \tag{2}$$

where I_n is the $n \times n$ identity matrix and $\mathbf{1}_n \in \{1\}^n$. To achieve invariance to scale, we divide $\overline{\mathcal{F}}$ by its norm such that $\overline{\mathcal{F}}_s = \frac{\overline{\mathcal{F}}}{\|\overline{\mathcal{F}}\|}$, where $\|\cdot\|$ is the standard $\mathbb{L}^2$ norm given by $\|\mathcal{F}\| = \sqrt{\langle \mathcal{F}, \mathcal{F} \rangle} = \sqrt{\int_0^1 \sum_{i=1}^n f^i(t) f^i(t) dt}$. With a slight abuse of notation, we refer to the scale and translation invariant functional activity $\overline{\mathcal{F}}$ as $\mathcal{F}$ throughout the paper.

2.2 Global Joint Cost Function for Alignment

Given a pair of functional brain activity data for two subjects $\mathcal{F}_1$ and $\mathcal{F}_2$, we aim to find a continuous transformation that minimizes the distance between them. This involves finding either a linear or a non-linear mapping that minimizes mismatches between the two activity patterns that manifest as rotations, temporal reparameterizations or both. The end result is that all the features (spatial or temporal) are brought into a common space of brain activity. We will first define a full cost function that includes both the rotation and the time reparameterization term and then present several variations of this cost function. Equation 3 estimates a joint rotational and phase warp

$$\widehat{\Gamma}, \widehat{\Phi} = \operatorname*{argmin}_{\Gamma, \Phi} \|\mathcal{F}_1 - \Gamma \mathcal{F}_2 \Phi\|^2, \tag{3}$$

where $\Gamma \in SO(n)$ is a rotation matrix and an element of the special orthogonal group of $n \times n$ matrices, and $\Phi \in L^2([0,1], \mathbb{R})$ is a temporal warping function. In this paper, we assume that Φ is differentiable and has a differentiable inverse and thus we aim to find a diffeomorphic temporal warping ($\dot{\Phi}(t) > 0, \forall t$) between two functional activity datasets. The problem of finding the spatial rotation matrix can be solved by using the method proposed by Goryn et al. [3] that demonstrates the estimation of rotation from noisy data. Here, one first computes the singular value decomposition (SVD) of the product of $\mathcal{F}_1$ and $\mathcal{F}_2$ as $\mathcal{F}_1 \mathcal{F}_2^T = UDV^T$, where $U, V \in SO(n)$. Then, the exact rotation matrix is given by $\widehat{\Gamma} = UV^T$. To find the optimal Γ we resort to dynamic programming. Assuming the problem of rotation is solved, then for a given $\widehat{\Gamma}$, we minimize the following additive energy function,

$$\widehat{\Phi} = \operatorname*{argmin}_{\Phi} \int_0^1 \sum_{i=1}^n \left(f_1^i(t) - f_2^i(\Phi(t)) \right) dt. \tag{4}$$

We discretize the above function by restricting to a finite sampling of the time-series denoted by T. We then define a $T \times T$ grid with samples $0 \le j, k \le T - 1$, and aim find a cumulative energy at each point (j, k) while restricting the infinitesimal derivative $\dot{\Phi} > 0$. There are several algorithms including recursion to solve this problem. In our paper, we implement this algorithm using a two pass solution, where during the first pass, a cumulative energy matrix is updated for each node (j, k), and during the second pass, the path Φ is constructed by interpolating points along local minima of this energy landscape.

In this paper, we will skip the estimation of optimal spatial rotation as defined in Eq. 3, but solve for a different rotation as described in the next section.

2.3 Family of Cost Functions for Spatiotemporal Warping

This section briefly outlines the mathematical notation for different cost functions used for spatial and temporal warping. The original approach for spatial hyperalignment proposed by Haxby et al. [4] used a cost function of the form $\|X_1 - \Gamma X_2\|^2$, where they estimate a spatial rotation Γ between the two matrices $X_1, X_2 \in \mathbb{R}^{n \times T}$. In their case, X_1, X_2 are reduced dimensional brain activity maps (not direct time-series). This solution cannot be directly used for our time-series activity representation since the solution of the rotation matrix $\Gamma \in SO(n)$ is not well-posed ($n \gg T$) for discrete time-series of T samples. The other solution is by Joshi et al. [5] who use the cost function $\|X_1 - X_2\Gamma\|^2$ to solve for an optimal temporal rotation, where X_1, X_2 are $T \times n$ matrices. However, we emphasize that the above methods do not consider the temporal reparameterization Φ in their formulation, whereas our global cost function does. This is the novelty of our approach.

2.4 Combining Warping Transforms

One can then generalize the above approaches by incorporating Φ, thus giving rise to a family of cost functions for constructing spatiotemporal warps between brain activations. In this paper, we will use the following combinations of rotations and reparameterizations.

$$\widehat{\Phi} = \operatorname*{argmin}_{\Phi} \|\mathcal{F}_1 - \mathcal{F}_2\Phi\|^2 \quad \text{temporal reparameterization} \tag{5a}$$

$$\widehat{\Gamma}, \widehat{\Phi} = \operatorname*{argmin}_{\Gamma, \Phi} \|\mathcal{F}_1 - \mathcal{F}_2\Gamma\Phi\|^2 \quad \text{temporal rotation + reparameterization} \tag{5b}$$

$$\widehat{\Gamma}, \widehat{\Phi} = \operatorname*{argmin}_{\Gamma, \Phi} \|\mathcal{F}_1 - \mathcal{F}_2\Phi\Gamma\|^2 \quad \text{temporal reparameterization + rotation} \tag{5c}$$

$$\widehat{\Gamma} = \operatorname*{argmin}_{\Gamma} \|\mathcal{F}_1^T - \Gamma\mathcal{F}_2^T\|^2 \quad \text{temporal rotation only} \tag{5d}$$

We note that Eq. 5d is the approach by Joshi et al. [5]. We solve Eqs. 5b–5c stepwise by alternating over rotations and reparameterizations or vice-versa. For example, Eq. 5b was solved by first obtaining a temporal rotation as described in [5] and then estimating the optimal temporal reparameterization obtained by solving Eq. 4, whereas Eq. 5c was solved by estimating the optimal time warp by solving dynamic programming and then obtaining the optimal temporal rotation matrix.

3   Results

3.1   Data Preprocessing

Our data was acquired from 12 healthy participants (7M/5F, ages from 20–44 years, mean age 28.5 ± 7 years) collected using the Human Connectome Project (HCP) MRI acquisition protocol. The structural scans consisted of a T1-weighed (T1w) multi-echo MPRAGE (voxel size (VS) = 0.8 mm isotropic) and a T2-weighted (T2w) acquisition (VS = 0.8 mm isotropic). Rs-fMRI data was acquired using two runs of a multiband EPI sequence (2) with opposite phase encoding directions (VS = 2 mm isotropic; TR = 800 ms; TE = 37 ms, phase enc. direction = AP/PA). Anatomical and functional data were visually inspected and minimally preprocessed using the HCP minimal pipeline [2]. MSMALL alignment was performed to achieve cortical surface alignment [11]. Following the preprocessing, all the rsfMRI scans were temporally concatenated and group-ICA [1] with dimension 8 was performed to generate a set of rsfMRI networks. Next, we chose a single subject at random from our population as a template and warped all the other subjects to it by solving different versions of Eq. 3 as given by Eqs. 5a–5d and abbreviate them as *param*, *rot-param*, *param-rot*, and *rot* respectively for comparison and visualization.

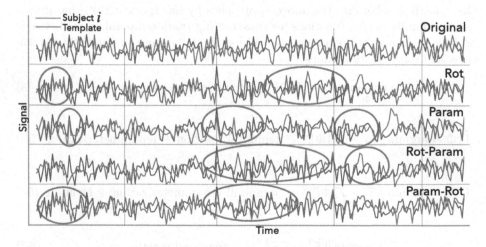

Fig. 1. Comparison of time-series alignments for cost functions for Eqs. 5a–5d. The original time-series is shown in the top row. (Color figure online)

3.2   Temporal Warping and Reparameterization

Figure 1 shows time-series plots at a random voxel for the right hemisphere for one of the subjects. The template is shown in red, whereas the warped time-series by different approaches are overlaid in blue. We observe that optimizing different cost functions yields varying alignments circled in grey, with each of the cases showing better or worse matching along the entire length of the time-series.

3.3   Global Correlations and Network Recovery

Global rotation and phase alignment can yield different results when understanding the functional connectivity derived from the rsfMRI signals. Figure 2 shows the map of average pairwise temporal correlations between the template and each subject's brain data, for original, *rot*, *param*, *rot-param*, and *param-rot*. The mean correlations for the original data do not show any patterns, whereas the global rotation (*rot*) vastly increases the correlation values, effectively recovering parts of the default mode and the ventral attention network, which suggests higher correspondence of temporal profiles following rotation. However, a global phase alignment (*param*) shows a novel finding. Although the correlation values do not increase, we see patterns in the superior frontal cortex, the inferior temporal gyrus in the left, and the visual cortex in the right hemisphere. We suggest that the temporal reparameterization has aligned the phase differences in the functional signal across subjects and therefore captures the functional connectivity patterns related to the default mode across the brain. Combining these two approaches, the result from global rotation followed by global reparameterization shows correlation patterns similar to both the separate global rotation and global reparameterization case. We expect that the algorithm enhances confidence in the inter-subject correlations in regions with higher SNR instead of increasing noise and false positives.

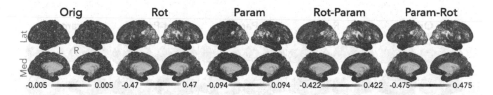

Fig. 2. Average pairwise correlations between all the 12 subjects and the template.

Figure 3 shows histograms for the above averaged pairwise correlations. Although the histogram for the *param* case has shifted only slightly to the right without increasing the magnitude of the correlations, the *param* case has changed the correlation structure of the data due to phase alignment. This suggests that the magnitude of the correlation does not always reflect the underlying connectivity in rsfMRI.

3.4 Independent Component Analysis

To better understand the effect of global rotation and global phase alignment, we further investigated resting-state functional networks derived from independent component analysis. Figure 4 shows the independent component (IC) maps of the left salience network, (left column of each panel), and right default mode network (R DMN, right column of

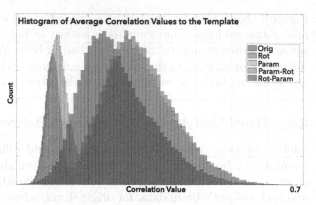

Fig. 3. Histograms of correlation maps.

each panel), for the original, *rot*, *param*, *rot-param*, and *param-rot* cases. The functional network maps demonstrate the patterns similar to the correlation maps. With *rot*, the z-scores of the IC maps are increased, whereas *param* alone does not lead to an increase in z-scores, but still preserves the spatial profile of the functional networks. The case of *param-rot* increases the z-scores even further.

Figure 4 demonstrates a novel finding (circled in orange) from the *rot-param* case in the functional map of the right somatosensory network. The original IC map demonstrates the somatosensory network lateralized to the right side. In the *rot-param* case, we see an identified activation on the left side that was not recovered in all the other cases. This splitting of the activation map for a single IC may suggest that phase alignment and rotation may further improve in localization of functional activity of the brain at rest.

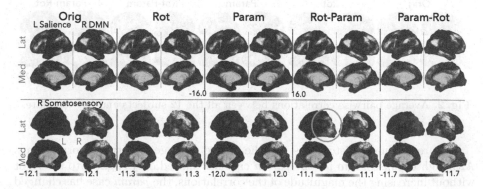

Fig. 4. IC functional network maps obtained for aligned cases using [1]. The circled region shows a bilateral finding not activated in all other cases. (Color figure online)

Figure 5 shows tabulated averages, and maxima and minima for z-scores for 8 ICs for various networks. The top mean and max z-scores are highlighted in red and blue respectively. It is observe that phase alignment caused an increase in z-scores in some form for all but one ICs.

Network	Orig	Rot	Param	Rot-Param	Param-Rot	Orig	Rot	Param	Rot-Param	Param-Rot	Orig	Rot	Param	Rot-Param	Param-Rot	Orig	Rot	Param	Rot-Param	Param-Rot
Name	L DMN					R Salience					L Visual					R DMN				
IC#	1	6	2	7	7	2	2	1	2	1	3	1	5	1	2	4	5	3	4	5
Mean	1.04	1.37	1.05	**1.44**	1.40	1.12	2.07	1.08	**2.21**	2.03	1.34	**1.76**	1.14	1.62	1.61	0.98	1.31	0.97	**1.43**	1.30
Std	3.27	3.44	3.13	3.52	3.49	3.31	3.70	3.21	3.94	3.73	2.98	3.42	2.84	3.36	3.18	3.14	3.42	3.06	3.62	3.41
Max	26.67	28.64	25.56	28.49	**29.23**	26.77	30.00	26.28	**30.35**	30.21	22.22	**22.34**	20.09	21.07	21.65	30.27	30.94	31.14	31.78	**32.05**
Min	-11.97	-11.10	-11.02	-10.15	-10.28	-14.07	-13.01	-13.06	-12.24	-13.46	-10.01	-15.02	-9.31	-14.52	-13.63	-9.20	-11.03	-9.97	-10.70	-10.95
Name	R Somatosensory					R Visual					L Salience					L Somatosensory				
IC#	5	4	4	8	4	6	8	7	6	6	7	3	6	3	3	8	7	8	5	8
Mean	1.22	1.37	1.22	1.33	**1.38**	1.05	1.30	1.04	**1.41**	1.35	0.84	1.45	0.79	1.48	**1.53**	1.11	1.20	1.17	**1.31**	1.22
Std	2.89	2.92	2.86	2.91	2.97	2.95	2.93	2.81	3.12	2.95	3.06	3.33	2.95	3.48	3.42	2.77	2.70	2.69	2.80	2.70
Max	20.19	17.87	**20.38**	18.36	18.86	**29.40**	27.25	27.50	28.49	26.77	26.07	25.26	25.49	**26.48**	25.94	**20.17**	19.16	18.82	18.59	19.32
Min	-6.95	-6.20	-7.37	-5.94	-7.04	-6.57	-6.13	-6.38	-5.60	-6.41	-9.79	-11.34	-9.52	-10.97	-11.40	-10.44	-10.52	-9.29	-11.08	-10.43

Fig. 5. Means, standard deviations, max., and min. z-scores for ICs for networks for 12 subjects. The top mean and max z-scores are highlighted in red and blue. (Color figure online)

4 Discussion and Conclusion

We introduced a novel idea for global phase alignment via temporal reparameterization of the full rsfMRI time-series signals across subjects. The non-linear global phase function is a diffeomorphism, thus allowing the mapping of the time-series back and forth from the subject to the template. Combined with either spatial rotations or temporal rotations, our approach yields new information that was not previously recoverable from pure rotations alone. We emphasize that while temporal rotations for T samples have $\frac{T(T-1)}{2}$ degrees of freedom, the temporal reparameterizations can be thought of as infinite-dimensional functions (but numerically have T degrees of freedom in the time-discretized case).

Using the 8–component ICA approach, we observed there were more clusters in the *rot* and *rot-param* case than the raw data, although we note that the group ICA procedure also includes a rotational step that aligns rsfMRI data across space and time. Thus, there are similarities between the ICA procedure and the *rot* [5] case. Performing an exclusive global phase alignment without rotation also changed the correlational structure of the data, thus giving rise to unique patterns in the inferior parietal, supramarginal, and the visual and posterior default mode network – which was not previously observed in the original correlations. Lastly, the *rot-param* case recovered a left visual component not seen either in the raw data or the *rot* case thus demonstrating that the signal strength in the visual component was boosted by phase alignment. We performed repeated data analysis with a variable number of independent components and were able to replicate this somatosensory network finding with a 9–component

ICA. In the future, we plan to use higher dimensional ICA to separate these components better and to test whether global phase alignment improves the segmentation of functional networks.

Finally, we also note that there are machine learning solutions for estimating diffeomorphic warps. The approach in Lohit et al. [8] aims to learn warping functions without templates in the context of classification whereas Weber et al. [13] use a semi-supervised approach for multi-class warping. Different from those approaches our method is completely unsupervised (for any number of classes) and allows combining with other compositional transformations such as rotations, although in the future one can also consider using deep learning strategies as given by the above approaches or more recently by Nunez et al. [10] that attempts to predict the diffeomorphic warps from a large sample of training data.

Acknowledgments. This research was partially supported by the NIH/NIAAA awards K25AA024192 and R01-AA026834. Data acquisition and processing was also supported by NIH/NIMH award U01MH11000.

References

1. Beckmann, C.F., Smith, S.M.: Probabilistic independent component analysis for functional magnetic resonance imaging. IEEE Trans. Med. Imaging **23**(2), 137–152 (2004)
2. Glasser, M.F., Sotiropoulos, S.N., Wilson, J.A., Coalson, T.S., Fischl, B., et al.: The minimal preprocessing pipelines for the human connectome project. Neuroimage **80**, 105–124 (2013)
3. Goryn, D., Hein, S.: On the estimation of rigid body rotation from noisy data. IEEE Trans. Pattern Anal. Mach. Intell. **17**(12), 1219–1220 (1995)
4. Haxby, J.V., et al.: A common, high-dimensional model of the representational space in human ventral temporal cortex. Neuron **72**(2), 404–416 (2011)
5. Joshi, A.A., Chong, M., Li, J., Choi, S., Leahy, R.M.: Are you thinking what I'm thinking? Synchronization of resting fMRI time-series across subjects. NeuroImage **172**, 740–752 (2018)
6. Lee, D.S., Leaver, A.M., Narr, K.L., Woods, R.P., Joshi, S.H.: Measuring brain connectivity via shape analysis of fMRI time courses and spectra. In: Wu, G., Laurienti, P., Bonilha, L., Munsell, B.C. (eds.) CNI 2017. LNCS, vol. 10511, pp. 125–133. Springer, Cham (2017). https://doi.org/10.1007/978-3-319-67159-8_15
7. Lee, D.S., Loureiro, J., Narr, K.L., Woods, R.P., Joshi, S.H.: Elastic registration of single subject task based fMRI signals. In: Frangi, A.F., Schnabel, J.A., Davatzikos, C., Alberola-López, C., Fichtinger, G. (eds.) MICCAI 2018. LNCS, vol. 11072, pp. 154–162. Springer, Cham (2018). https://doi.org/10.1007/978-3-030-00931-1_18
8. Lohit, S., Wang, Q., Turaga, P.: Temporal transformer networks: joint learning of invariant and discriminative time warping. In: Proceedings of the IEEE Conference on Computer Vision and Pattern Recognition, pp. 12426–12435 (2019)
9. Nenning, K.H., Liu, H., Ghosh, S.S., Sabuncu, M.R., Schwartz, E., Langs, G.: Diffeomorphic functional brain surface alignment: functional demons. NeuroImage **156**, 456–465 (2017)

10. Nunez, E., Joshi, S.H.: Deep learning of warping functions for shape analysis. In: Proceedings of the IEEE/CVF Conference on Computer Vision and Pattern Recognition Workshops, pp. 866–867 (2020)
11. Robinson, E.C., et al.: MSM: a new flexible framework for multimodal surface matching. Neuroimage **100**, 414–426 (2014)
12. Smith, S.M., et al.: Functional connectomics from resting-state fMRI. Trends Cogn. Sci. **17**(12), 666–682 (2013)
13. Weber, R.A.S., Eyal, M., Skafte, N., Shriki, O., Freifeld, O.: Diffeomorphic temporal alignment nets. In: Advances in Neural Information Processing Systems, pp. 6574–6585 (2019)

Spatio-Temporal Graph Convolution for Resting-State fMRI Analysis

Soham Gadgil[1], Qingyu Zhao[2]([✉]), Adolf Pfefferbaum[2,3], Edith V. Sullivan[2], Ehsan Adeli[1,2], and Kilian M. Pohl[2,3]

[1] Computer Science Department, Stanford University, Stanford, USA
[2] School of Medicine, Stanford University, Stanford, USA
qingyuz@stanford.edu
[3] Center of Health Sciences, SRI International, Menlo Park, USA

Abstract. The Blood-Oxygen-Level-Dependent (BOLD) signal of resting-state fMRI (rs-fMRI) records the temporal dynamics of intrinsic functional networks in the brain. However, existing deep learning methods applied to rs-fMRI either neglect the functional dependency between different brain regions in a network or discard the information in the temporal dynamics of brain activity. To overcome those shortcomings, we propose to formulate functional connectivity networks within the context of spatio-temporal graphs. We train a spatio-temporal graph convolutional network (ST-GCN) on short sub-sequences of the BOLD time series to model the non-stationary nature of functional connectivity. Simultaneously, the model learns the importance of graph edges within ST-GCN to gain insight into the functional connectivities contributing to the prediction. In analyzing the rs-fMRI of the Human Connectome Project (HCP, $N = 1,091$) and the National Consortium on Alcohol and Neurodevelopment in Adolescence (NCANDA, $N = 773$), ST-GCN is significantly more accurate than common approaches in predicting gender and age based on BOLD signals. Furthermore, the brain regions and functional connections significantly contributing to the predictions of our model are important markers according to the neuroscience literature.

1 Introduction

The BOLD signal of rs-fMRI characterizes the intrinsic functional organization of the human brain by measuring its spontaneous activity at rest [3]. One commonly used approach for identifying impact of factors, such as age and sex, on intrinsic functional networks is to predict their values by applying deep neural networks to the rs-fMRI of individual subjects [7,13,14,16]. Accurate predictors of those factors can then enhance the understanding of functional neurodevelopment across the life span [15], characterize developmental disruption caused

---

S. Gadgil and Q. Zhao—Equal contribution.

© Springer Nature Switzerland AG 2020
A. L. Martel et al. (Eds.): MICCAI 2020, LNCS 12267, pp. 528–538, 2020.
https://doi.org/10.1007/978-3-030-59728-3_52

by neurological disorders, and explain sex-specific differences in cognitive performance [22].

It is not trivial to select an appropriate network architecture for analyzing rs-fMRI as their (average) BOLD signals of each brain region are structured time series. A natural representation of such data are spatio-temporal graphs [24, 25], where the temporal graph characterizes the dynamics of brain activity at each region and the spatial graph characterizes the functional interaction between different brain regions. However, most existing deep learning works applied to rs-fMRI analysis fail to consider both aspects simultaneously. Methods that only incorporate spatial graph convolution [13, 16, 26] often transform the time series data into hand-crafted features, such as partial correlation [17], thereby potentially losing the fine temporal information of the BOLD signal. Methods based on recurrent neural networks (RNN) [6, 7, 14] can learn temporal features from the BOLD signal but neglect the functional dependency between regions-of-interests (ROIs). On the other hand, methods based on spatio-temporal networks often perform spatial convolution according to the topological arrangement among ROIs in the physical space [13, 30], which cannot model interactions among distal ROIs with similar functional properties. To address these issues, we suggest deep neural networks to incorporate spatio-temporal convolution on functional connectivity graphs, i.e., spatio-temporal Graph Convolution (ST-GC) [24, 25].

In computer vision, ST-GC Networks (ST-GCN) are popular for solving problems that base prediction on graph-structured time series [5, 24, 25]. In the context of rs-fMRI analysis, these networks have the potential to automatically extract features that jointly characterize functional connectivity patterns of the brain and their temporal dynamics within the BOLD series. To the best of our knowledge, we are the first to use ST-GCN for building predictive models based on rs-fMRI data. We train our network on short sub-sequences of BOLD time series to model the non-stationary nature of functional connectivity [20, 28]. Further, learning of an edge importance matrix associated with the ST-GC operation improves the interpretability of the model as it allows us to identify selective functional connections significantly contributing to the prediction. We apply ST-GCN to predict the age and gender of healthy individuals of two large publicly available rs-fMRI datasets: Human Connectome Project (HCP, $N = 1{,}096$) [21] and National Consortium on Alcohol and Neurodevelopment in Adolescence (NCANDA, $N = 773$) [2]. The optimal window size for the sub-sequences highly coincide between the two datasets despite their distinct imaging protocols and data processing pipelines. Furthermore, the resulting prediction accuracy is significantly higher than traditional RNN-based methods. Finally, the learned edge importance localizes meaningful brain regions and functional connections associated with aging effects and sexual differences.[1]

---

[1] The code is available at https://github.com/sgadgil6/cnslab_fmri.

2   ST-GCN for rs-fMRI Analysis

We first relate functional networks to spatio-temporal graphs and then define the ST-GC convolution on them. Next, we build the classifier ST-GCN, which uses ST-GC in each layer and models the importance of graph edges in the decision process across layers. Lastly, we train ST-GCN on short BOLD sequences.

Representing Functional Networks as Spatio-Temporal Graphs: To encode the functional networks captured by rs-fMRI, let $\mathcal{G} := (\mathcal{V}, \mathcal{E})$ (Fig. 1) be an undirected spatio-temporal graph consisting of a set of edges $\mathcal{E}$ capturing temporal and spatial connections between a set of nodes $\mathcal{V} = \{v_{t,i} | t = 1, ..., T; i = 1, ..., N\}$ defined across N ROIs and T time points. For each ROI and time point, an edge in the temporal graph connects the corresponding node to the node of the same ROI at the proceeding time point. The edges of the spatial graph connect all nodes of the same time point, where the weight of an edge is defined by the functional affinity between the corresponding regions. To define the functional affinity, we now assume that spontaneous activation for each of the N regions can be quantified by the average BOLD time series measured within that region. First, those series are concatenated across all subjects within each ROI. Then, the affinity between two regions $d(v_{tj}, v_{ti})$ is defined by the magnitude of correlation between their concatenated series. Note, this affinity is impartial to the time point.

Spatio-Temporal Graph Convolution (ST-GC): To define a convolution on such a graph structure, we denote $f_{in}(v_{ti})$ as the input feature at node v_{ti} (e.g., the average BOLD signal of ROI i at time t) and $B(v_{ti})$ as the spatio-temporal neighbourhood of v_{ti}, i.e.,

$$B(v_{ti}) := \{v_{qj} | d(v_{tj}, v_{ti}) \le K, |q - t| \le \lfloor \Gamma/2 \rfloor\}, \tag{1}$$

where K defines the size of the spatial neighborhood (i.e., spatial kernel size) and Γ the temporal neighborhood (i.e., temporal kernel size). An ST-GC operation on node v_{ti} with respect to a convolutional kernel $\mathbf{w}(\cdot)$ and a normalization factor Z_{ti} can then be defined as [24]

$$f_{out}(v_{ti}) := \frac{1}{Z_{ti}} \sum_{v_{qj} \in B(v_{ti})} f_{in}(v_{qj}) \cdot \mathbf{w}(v_{qj}). \tag{2}$$

Adopting a similar implementation as in [24], we approximate the spatio-temporal convolutional kernel $\mathbf{w}(\cdot)$ by decomposing it to a spatial graph convolutional kernel $\mathbf{W}_{SG} \in \mathbb{R}^{C \times M}$ represented in the Fourier domain and a temporal convolutional kernel $\mathbf{W}_{TG} \in \mathbb{R}^{M \times \Gamma}$. Specifically, we denote $\mathbf{f}_t \in \mathbb{R}^{N \times C}$ as the C-channel input features of the N ROIs at the tth frame, $\mathbf{f}'_t \in \mathbb{R}^{N \times M}$ as the M-channel output features, and $\mathbf{A}$ as the aforementioned affinity matrix. The spatial graph convolution at a time point t is then defined with respect to the diagonal matrix Λ (where $\Lambda^{ii} = \sum_j A^{ij} + 1$) as [11]

$$\mathbf{f}'_t := \Lambda^{-\frac{1}{2}} (\mathbf{A} + \mathbf{I}) \Lambda^{-\frac{1}{2}} \mathbf{f}_t \mathbf{W}_{SG}. \tag{3}$$

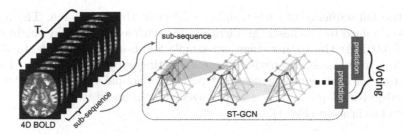

Fig. 1. Framework of classifying BOLD time series by applying a spatio-temporal graph convolutional network to sub-sequences.

Next, the temporal convolution is performed on the resulting features. Let $\mathbf{f}_i' \in \mathbb{R}^{M \times T}$ be the features of node v_i defined on the temporal graph of length T with regular grid spacing. We then perform a standard 1D convolution $\mathbf{f}_i' \circledast \mathbf{W}_{TG} \in \mathbb{R}^{\Gamma \times T}$ as the final output of ST-GC for v_i.

Classifying BOLD Time Series by ST-GCN: Our proposed ST-GCN is composed of 3 layers of ST-GC units. The input to ST-GCN are 1-channel spatio-temporal features $\mathbf{f} \in \mathbb{R}^{N \times T}$ representing the average BOLD signals of the N ROIs. Consistent with the setup in [24], each ST-GC layer produces 64-channel outputs with the temporal kernel size $\Gamma = 11$, a stride of 1, and a dropout rate of 0.5. The output of the last ST-GC layer is fed to a global average pooling and its output vector of length 64 is transformed to *class* probabilities by a fully connected layer with a sigmoid activation.

To determine the importance of spatial graph edges in defining class probabilities, we integrate a positive and symmetric "edge importance" matrix $\mathbf{M} \in \mathbb{R}^{N \times N}$ into our model. This matrix is shared across all ST-GC layers by replacing $\mathbf{A} + \mathbf{I}$ in Eq. (3) with $(\mathbf{A} + \mathbf{I}) * \mathbf{M}$ (element-wise multiplication). As such, while performing spatial graph convolution on node v_{ti}, the contribution from its neighbouring nodes $B(v_{ti})$ will be re-scaled according to the importance weights learned in the ith row of $\mathbf{M}$. Thus, the diagonal entries of $\mathbf{M}$ (self-connection) quantify importance for each ROI, while off-diagonal entries do so for each functional connection. Note, the original proposal by Yan et al. [24] learns a separate $\mathbf{M}$ for each individual ST-GC layer. Their strategy generally results in negative, asymmetric importance matrices that are difficult to interpret and vary across layers. We ease the interpretability by enforcing $\mathbf{M}$ to be consistent across layers and to be both positive and symmetric.

Training ST-GCN: Recent rs-fMRI studies have revealed that patterns of intrinsic functional connectivity are not stationary across the full rs-fMRI scan but exhibit considerable fluctuations. These dynamics are often analyzed by dividing the entire rs-fMRI sequence into sub-sequences according to a fixed window size (often chosen empirically) and then assessing the connectivity within these segments. Accordingly, we also consider training ST-GCN on sub-sequences of window size T' sampled from the full data. Specifically, at each training iteration, we sample a sub-sequence of length T' starting at a random time frame from the full sequence of each training subject in the mini-batch. The models are then trained by stochastic gradient descent with a learning and weight decay rate of 0.001. At the testing stage, we sample S sub-sequences, each starting at a random time frame, of length T' for each testing subject, derive the ST-GCN prediction for each sub-sequence, and perform a simple voting to produce the final subject-level prediction, e.g., the average of sigmoid values in the case of binary classification (Fig. 1).

3   Experiments

Understanding the dramatic neurodevelopment and the emerging sexual differences during adolescence is an important topic in neuroscience [19,22]. We investigate the age and sex difference using ST-GCN and a variety of baseline approaches on the NCANDA dataset. We further investigate sex differences in young adults of the Human Connectome Project (HCP) S1200 [21]. Note, identifying significant aging effects on HCP is unlikely due to functional organization reaching maturity after young adulthood [23].

NCANDA: The publicly released baseline data consisted of 773 rs-fMRI scans (269 frames, TR = 2 s). Among the 773 adolescents (ages 12–21 years, 388 younger than the mean age of 16 years vs. 385 older adolescents, 376 male vs. 397 females). 638 met the no-to-low alcohol drinking criteria of NIAAA (373 young vs. 265 old adolescents, 315 boys vs. 323 girls) [2]. Each rs-fMRI scan was preprocessed by the NCANDA pipeline, which registered the mean BOLD image to subject-specific T1 MRI and then non-rigidly to the standard MNI space [29]. The cortical surface was parcellated to $N = 34$ ROIs according to [12]. The average BOLD signal in each ROI was normalized to z-scores.

HCP: The data set consisted of rs-fMRI of 1096 young adults (ages 22–35 years). Excluding 5 rs-fMRIs with less than 1200 frames, we used the first session (15 min, $T = 1200$ frames, TR = 0.72 s) for each of the 498 females and 593 males. Each rs-fMRI went through the minimal processing pipeline of HCP, *fMRISurface* [9], which mapped each volume time series to the standard CIFTI grayordinates space. The cortical surface was parcellated to $N = 22$ major ROIs [8], and the average BOLD signal in each ROI was normalized to z-scores.

Experimental Setup: On NCANDA, ST-GCN first distinguished younger from older participants by performing 5-fold cross-validation on the 773 rs-fMRIs. The training and testing were repeated on sub-sequences of different window sizes, from short segments of $T' = 16$ to the full sequence. The number of sub-sequences used for voting in the testing stage was fixed at $S = 64$ ($S = 1$ for the full sequence). To ensure the prediction results were not confounded by alcohol drinking, the test accuracy was also recorded for the no-to-low drinking cohort, denoted as "ST-GCN-no-ex". Based on the optimal window size determined through cross-validation, we trained the model on the entire data set to produce an edge importance matrix summarizing the aging effects within the

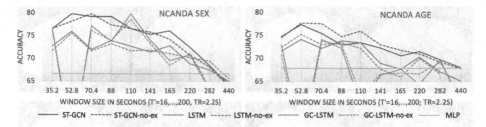

Fig. 2. Accuracy of age and sex prediction on the NCANDA dataset. "no-ex" denotes the accuracy score confined to the no-to-low drinking cohort.

entire cohort. To reduce uncertainty in the estimation caused by stochastic gradient descent, we repeated the training 20 times and derived the "average" edge importance matrix as our final outcome. Next, this experiment was repeated with respect to sex classification on NCANDA and HCP.

Baselines: The simplest approach for our comparison was a Multi-Layer Perceptron (**MLP**) applied to the upper triangular correlation matrix, which quantified the static functional connectivity between ROIs during the full scan. The MLP had 2 hidden layers, each with 64 neurons and ReLu activation. The next two baseline methods relied on end-to-end training on the BOLD time series based on Long Short-Term Memory (LSTM) model [10], a form of RNN frequently used to analyze rs-fMRI data [7,14]. Adopting a similar implementation as in [14], the first implementation of **LSTM** consisted of a recurrent cell with hidden states of dimension 256. The output of the last hidden state was fed into a fully connected layer (with a dropout of 0.5) to produce a final label. The second implementation (**GC-LSTM**) first extracted features from the BOLD signal at each time frame using spatial graph convolution. The features were then fed into an LSTM model for temporal analysis. The number of voting sequences for these two LSTM-based methods were again fixed to $S = 64$.

4   Results and Analysis

NCANDA: Figure 2 shows the prediction accuracy derived from the 5-fold cross-validation for different methods. The accuracy scores measured on all NCANDA subjects were not significantly different from results on the no-to-low drinking cohort (denoted as "no-ex", paired t-test $p > 0.5$), indicating that the predictions were not confounded by alcohol consumption in individuals. On both data sets, all three deep-learning-based methods were generally more accurate than MLP when applied to shorter sub-sequences. ST-GCN achieved significantly higher accuracy than the two LSTM-based methods across different window sizes ($p < .0001$, two-sample t-test). Performing further architecture search for the two LSTM-based methods, such as varying the hidden-state dimension and adding more LSTM layers, did not improve the results in Fig. 2. Moreover, adding more convolution layers or feature channels to GC-LSTM reduced

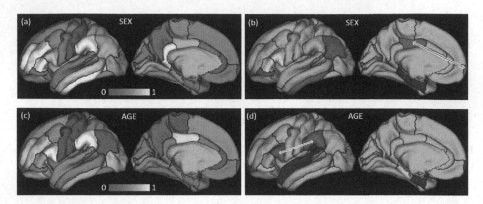

Fig. 3. Importance maps for age (a, b) and sex (c, d) prediction of the NCANDA study. (a, c): importance of functional dynamics within each ROI; (b, d): functional connections between ROIs with importance higher than 0.3 are shown by the ROIs having the same color. Highlighted by the red arrows are the default mode network for sex prediction and the inferior temporo-parieto-frontal network for age prediction. (Color figure online)

the accuracy substantially, which indicated that the strategy of training spatial graph convolution on each individual frame without incorporating temporal convolution was flawed. With respect to the no-to-low drinking participants, the highest prediction accuracy of ST-GCN with respect to age was 77.7% ($T' = 24$ or 52.8 s) and sex was 79.8% ($T' = 32$ or 70.4 s). The accuracy of sex prediction was relatively stable across $T' = [24, 40]$ (52.8–88 s). These predictions were not confounded by subject motion based on the insignificant correlation between the prediction scores and the number of outlier frames in each rs-fMRI.

We visualized the edge importance matrices associated with the optimal models in Fig. 3 with the images on the left (Fig. 3a+c) showing the importance of each ROI (diagonal entries) for prediction and the images on the right (Fig. 3b+d) showing functional connections (off-diagonal entries) with importance value higher than 0.3. For sex prediction, the most important ROI identified by ST-GCN was the inferior temporal lobe, which echoed findings from other resting-state studies [4] and from a structural MRI analysis on the NCANDA cohort [27]. We also identified a significant effect in the frontal-posterior-cingulate (PCC) connection (red in Fig. 3b), which defines the default mode network, a signature intrinsic network frequently linked to sexual differences [18]. For age prediction, the most critical ROIs were the supramarginal and par opercularis regions (Fig. 3c). Their functional connection (red in Fig. 3d) defined the inferior temporo-parieto-frontal network, which was shown to decrease in older adolescents within the NCANDA cohort by a longitudinal rs-fMRI study [29]. All the results above demonstrate that our strategy of edge importance learning can accurately localize functional properties of the brain related to significant aging and sex effects.

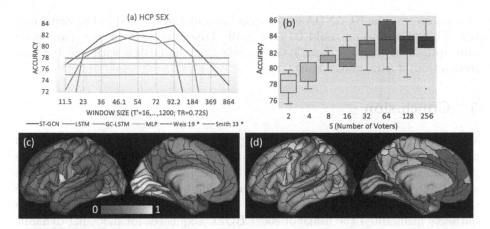

Fig. 4. Experiments on HCP: (a) sex prediction accuracy w.r.t window size. * denotes results from prior studies. (b) Distribution of prediction accuracy scores from cross-validation w.r.t. the number of sub-sequences used for voting. (c) Importance of functional dynamics within each ROI; (d) functional connections between ROIs with importance higher than 0.3 are shown by the ROIs having the same color.

HCP: Figure 4a plots the accuracy in predicting sex on the HCP dataset in relation to those of prior studies by Weis et al. [22] and Smith et al. [19]. These works applied linear classifiers and used correlation coefficients as input features respectively, which was similar to MLP. Note that their results can not be strictly compared to ours as different cohorts and data processing pipelines were used for analysis[2]. However, their accuracies were similar to the ones of MLP, which were suboptimal compared to those produced by the deep-learning-based methods applied to sub-sequences of $T' \in [32, 128]$ (23.04–92.16 s). This finding indicates that the dynamical properties of functional interactions among brain regions can not be fully captured by the static correlation coefficients and require more comprehensive spatio-temporal modeling.

An example of more comprehensive spatio-temporal modeling was ST-GCN, which achieved the highest accuracy of 83.7% at $T' = 128$ (92.16 s) and produced higher accuracies than the two LSTM-based methods across all window sizes. Increasing the number of voters did not further increase testing accuracy (Fig. 4b). Moreover, ST-GCN produced similarly optimal accuracy scores for $T' \in [64, 128]$ (46.08–92.16 s). This range was highly consistent with the one revealed in the NCANDA experiment despite the difference in imaging protocols, length of BOLD signal, brain parcellation, and data processing pipelines between the two studies. These results also converge with recent understanding in neuroscience literatures stating that dynamical functional connectivity generally have dwell times of tens of seconds [1,20]. By visualizing the edge importance matrix derived from the HCP subjects (Fig. 4c), we found that regions with significant sexual differences in young adults were spatially more concentrated compared

---

[2] The 87% accuracy in [19] on 131 HCP subjects was based on multi-modal data.

to adolescents (the NCANDA experiment) and mainly located in the visual cortex. This phenomenon could be potentially linked to the evidence that sexual dimorphism in intrinsic functional organization diminishes with age (sex-age interaction) during adolescence [18].

5   Conclusion

We introduced a framework for analyzing rs-fMRI data based on spatio-temporal graph convolution networks. By analyzing the rs-fMRI data of two large-scale neuroimaging studies, we showed that ST-GCN could accurately predict age and gender of the study participants based on short sequences of BOLD time series. The similar optimal window sizes (of the sub-sequences) between the two datasets highlighted the usage of short BOLD sequences for modeling dynamic functional connectivity. Future work will focus on defining ST-GC with respect to non-static graph structures accommodating dynamic functional states, exploring automatic determination of sliding window size, applying ST-GCN to a fine-grained brain parcellation, and identifying functional biomarkers linked to neuropsychiatric disorders. Accomplishing these goals will then show if our strategy for learning graph edge importance within the context of model interpretation is valuable for advancing knowledge in neuroscience.

Acknowledgment. This research was supported in part by NIH grants AA021697, AA005965, AA013521, and AA010723.

References

1. Allen, E., Damaraju, E., Plis, S., Erhardt, E., Eichele, T., Calhoun, V.: Tracking whole-brain connectivity dynamics in the resting state. Cereb. Cortex **24**(3), 663–676 (2014). https://doi.org/10.1093/cercor/bhs352
2. Brown, S., Brumback, T., Tomlinson, K., et al.: The national consortium on alcohol and neurodevelopment in adolescence (NCANDA): a multisite study of adolescent development and substance use. J. Stud. Alcohol Drugs. **76**(6), 895–908 (2015). https://doi.org/10.15288/jsad.2015.76.895
3. Buckner, R., Krienen, F., Yeo, B.: Opportunities and limitations of intrinsic functional connectivity MRI. Nat. Neurosci. **16**(7), 832–837 (2013)
4. Conrin, S.D., et al.: From default mode network to the basal configuration: sex differences in the resting-state brain connectivity as a function of age and their clinical correlates. Front. Psychiatry **9**, 365 (2018)
5. Covert, I., et al.: Temporal graph convolutional networks for automatic seizure detection. In: Machine Learning for HealthCare (2019)
6. Cui, Y., et al.: Identifying brain networks of multiple time scales via deep recurrent neural network. In: 21st International Conference, Granada, Spain, September 16–20, 2018, Proceedings, Part III, pp. 284–292 (September 2018)
7. Dvornek, N.C., Ventola, P., Pelphrey, K.A., Duncan, J.S.: Identifying autism from resting-state fMRI using long short-term memory networks. In: Wang, Q., Shi, Y., Suk, H.-I., Suzuki, K. (eds.) MLMI 2017. LNCS, vol. 10541, pp. 362–370. Springer, Cham (2017). https://doi.org/10.1007/978-3-319-67389-9_42

8. Glasser, M., et al.: A multi-modal parcellation of human cerebral cortex. Nature **536**, 171–178 (2016)
9. Glasser, M., et al.: The minimal preprocessing pipelines for the human connectome project. NeuroImage **80**, 105 (2013). https://doi.org/10.1016/j.neuroimage.2013.04.127
10. Hochreiter, S., Schmidhuber, J.: Long short-term memory. Neural Comput. **9**(8), 1735–1780 (1997)
11. Kipf, T.N., Welling, M.: Semi-supervised classification with graph convolutional networks. In: ICLR (2017)
12. Klein, A., Tourville, J.: 101 labeled brain images and a consistent human cortical labeling protocol. Front. Neurosci. **6**, 171 (2012). https://doi.org/10.3389/fnins.2012.00171
13. Ktena, S.I., et al.: Distance metric learning using graph convolutional networks: application to functional brain networks. In: Descoteaux, M., Maier-Hein, L., Franz, A., Jannin, P., Collins, D.L., Duchesne, S. (eds.) MICCAI 2017. LNCS, vol. 10433, pp. 469–477. Springer, Cham (2017). https://doi.org/10.1007/978-3-319-66182-7_54
14. Li, H., Fan, Y.: Brain decoding from functional MRI using long short-term memory recurrent neural networks. In: Frangi, A.F., Schnabel, J.A., Davatzikos, C., Alberola-López, C., Fichtinger, G. (eds.) MICCAI 2018. LNCS, vol. 11072, pp. 320–328. Springer, Cham (2018). https://doi.org/10.1007/978-3-030-00931-1_37
15. Li, H., Satterthwaite, T.D., Fan, Y.: Brain age prediction based on resting-state functional connectivity patterns using convolutional neural networks. In: ISBI (2018)
16. Li, X., Dvornek, N.C., Zhou, Y., Zhuang, J., Ventola, P., Duncan, J.S.: Graph neural network for interpreting Task-fMRI biomarkers. In: Shen, D., et al. (eds.) MICCAI 2019. LNCS, vol. 11768, pp. 485–493. Springer, Cham (2019). https://doi.org/10.1007/978-3-030-32254-0_54
17. Marrelec, G., et al.: Partial correlation for functional brain interactivity investigation in functional MRI. Neuroimage **32**(1), 228–237 (2006)
18. Müller-Oehring, E., et al.: Influences of age, sex, and moderate alcohol drinking on the intrinsic functional architecture of adolescent brains. Cereb. Cortex **28**, 1–15 (2017). https://doi.org/10.1093/cercor/bhx014
19. Smith, S.M., Vidaurre, D., Beckmann, C.F., et al.: Functional connectomics from resting-state fMRI. Trends Cogn. Sci. **17**(12), 666–682 (2013)
20. Taghia, J., Ryali, S., et al.: Bayesian switching factor analysis for estimating time-varying functional connectivity in fMRI. NeuroImage **155**, 271–290 (2017). https://doi.org/10.1016/j.neuroimage.2017.02.083
21. Van Essen, D.C., et al.: The WU-Minn human connectome project: an overview. Neuroimage **80**, 62–79 (2013)
22. Weis, S., Patil, K.R., Hoffstaedter, F., Nostro, A., Yeo, B.T.T., Eickhoff, S.B.: Sex classification by resting state brain connectivity. Cereb. Cortex **30**, 824 (2019). https://doi.org/10.1093/cercor/bhz129
23. Westlye, L., et al.: Life-span changes of the human brain white matter: diffusion tensor imaging (DTI) and volumetry. Cereb. Cortex **20**, 2055–68 (2010). https://doi.org/10.1093/cercor/bhp280
24. Yan, S., Xiong, Y., Lin, D.: Spatial temporal graph convolutional networks for skeleton-based action recognition. In: AAAI (2018)
25. Yu, B., Yin, H., Zhu, Z.: Spatio-temporal graph convolutional networks: a deep learning framework for traffic forecasting. In: IJCAI (2018)

26. Zhang, Y., Bellec, P.: Functional annotation of human cognitive states using graph convolution networks. In: NeurIPS 2019 Workshop Neuro AI (2019)
27. Zhao, Q., Adeli, E., Pfefferbaum, A., Sullivan, E.V., Pohl, K.M.: Confounder-aware visualization of ConvNets. In: Suk, H.-I., Liu, M., Yan, P., Lian, C. (eds.) MLMI 2019. LNCS, vol. 11861, pp. 328–336. Springer, Cham (2019). https://doi.org/10.1007/978-3-030-32692-0_38
28. Zhao, Q., Honnorat, N., Adeli, E., Pfefferbaum, A., Sullivan, E.V., Pohl, K.M.: Variational autoencoder with truncated mixture of Gaussians for functional connectivity analysis. In: Chung, A.C.S., Gee, J.C., Yushkevich, P.A., Bao, S. (eds.) IPMI 2019. LNCS, vol. 11492, pp. 867–879. Springer, Cham (2019). https://doi.org/10.1007/978-3-030-20351-1_68
29. Zhao, Q., et al.: Longitudinally consistent estimates of intrinsic functional networks. Hum. Brain Mapp. **40**, 2511–2528 (2019). https://doi.org/10.1002/hbm.24541
30. Zhao, Y., et al.: Modeling 4D fMRI data via spatio-temporal convolutional neural networks (ST-CNN). In: Frangi, A.F., Schnabel, J.A., Davatzikos, C., Alberola-López, C., Fichtinger, G. (eds.) MICCAI 2018. LNCS, vol. 11072, pp. 181–189. Springer, Cham (2018). https://doi.org/10.1007/978-3-030-00931-1_21

A Shared Neural Encoding Model for the Prediction of Subject-Specific fMRI Response

Meenakshi Khosla[1](✉), Gia H. Ngo[1], Keith Jamison[2], Amy Kuceyeski[2,3], and Mert R. Sabuncu[1,2,4]

[1] School of Electrical and Computer Engineering, Cornell University, Ithaca, USA
mk2299@cornell.edu
[2] Radiology, Weill Cornell Medical College, New York, USA
[3] Brain and Mind Research Institute, Weill Cornell Medical College, New York, USA
[4] Nancy E. and Peter C. Meinig School of Biomedical Engineering,
Cornell University, Ithaca, USA

Abstract. The increasing popularity of naturalistic paradigms in fMRI (such as movie watching) demands novel strategies for multi-subject data analysis, such as use of neural encoding models. In the present study, we propose a shared convolutional neural encoding method that accounts for individual-level differences. Our method leverages multi-subject data to improve the prediction of subject-specific responses evoked by visual or auditory stimuli. We showcase our approach on high-resolution 7T fMRI data from the Human Connectome Project movie-watching protocol and demonstrate significant improvement over single-subject encoding models. We further demonstrate the ability of the shared encoding model to successfully capture meaningful individual differences in response to traditional task-based facial and scenes stimuli. Taken together, our findings suggest that inter-subject knowledge transfer can be beneficial to subject-specific predictive models. (Our code is available at https://github.com/mk2299/SharedEncoding_MICCAI.)

1 Introduction

Naturalistic imaging paradigms, such as movies and stories, emulate the diversity and complexity of real-life sensory experiences, thereby opening a novel window into the brain. The last decade has seen an increased foothold of naturalistic paradigms in cognitive neuroimaging, fueled by the remarkable discovery of inter-subject synchrony during naturalistic viewing [1]. Naturalistic stimuli also demonstrate increased test-retest reliability and more active subject engagement in comparison to alternate paradigms such as resting-state fMRI [2]. Furthermore, experiments have shown that naturalistic stimuli can induce stronger neural response than task-based stimuli [3], suggesting that the brain is intrinsically more attuned to the former. Taken together, these benefits suggest an exciting future for naturalistic stimulation protocols in fMRI.

© Springer Nature Switzerland AG 2020
A. L. Martel et al. (Eds.): MICCAI 2020, LNCS 12267, pp. 539–548, 2020.
https://doi.org/10.1007/978-3-030-59728-3_53

With large-scale compilation of multi-subject neural data through open-source initiatives such as the Human Connectome Project (HCP) [4], the development of approaches that can handle this enormous data is becoming imperative. Two approaches, namely inter-subject correlation (ISC) analysis [1,5] and shared response model (SRM) [6], have dominated the analysis of multi-subject fMRI data under naturalistic conditions. The former approach exploits similarity in activation patterns across subjects to isolate stimulus-induced processing. The latter technique, SRM, decomposes neural activity into a shared response component and subject-specific spatial bases, and has been used for inter-subject knowledge transfer through functional alignment. While simple and efficient, both these approaches rely on a common time-locked stimulus across subjects and cannot, by design, model responses to completely unseen stimuli. On the other hand, predictive modelling of neural activity through encoding models is based upon generalization to arbitrary stimuli and can thus offer more holistic descriptions of sensory processing in an individual [7].

Neural encoding models map stimuli to fine-grained voxel-level response patterns via complex feature transformations. Previously, neural encoding models have yielded several novel insights into the functional organization of auditory and visual cortices [8–11]. Encoding models encapsulating different hypothesis about neural information processing can be pitted against each other to shed new light on how information is represented in the brain. In this manner, neural encoding models have been largely used for making group-level inferences. The potential to extract meaningful individual differences from naturalistic paradigms remains largely untapped. Understanding inter-subject variability in behavior-to-brain representations is of key interest to neuroscience and can potentially even help identify atypical response patterns [12]. Modelling individual brain function in response to naturalistic stimuli is one step in this direction; however, building accurate individual-level models of brain function often requires large amounts of data per subject for good generalization. The problem is further exacerbated by the variability in anatomy and functional topographies across individuals, making inter-subject knowledge transfer difficult. There is limited work in leveraging multi-subject data for more robust and accurate individualized neural encoding. To our knowledge, this problem has been studied only in the context of natural vision with a handful subjects using a Bayesian framework [13]. Further, the proposed method in [13] transfers knowledge from one subject's encoding model into another through a two-stage procedure and does not allow simultaneous optimization of encoding models across multiple subjects.

In this paper, we attempt to fill this gap; to this effect, we propose a deep-learning based framework to build more powerful individual-level encoding models by leveraging multi-subject data. Recent studies have revealed that coarse-grained response topographies are highly similar across subjects, suggesting that individual idiosyncrasies manifest in more fine-grained response patterns [6,14]. This hints to the idea that encoding models could share representational spaces across subjects to overcome the challenges imposed by a limited quantity of per-

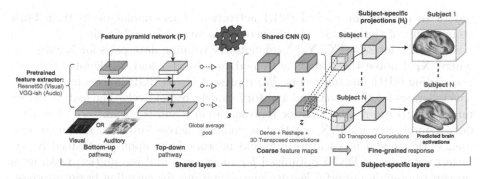

Fig. 1. Proposed approach: Feature pyramid networks are used to extract hierarchical features from pre-trained image/sound recognition networks. Dense features are reshaped into coarse 3D feature maps, which are mapped into increasingly fine-grained maps using convolutions. Coarse feature transformation layers are shared across subjects while deeper convolutional layers close to predicted response are subject-specific.

subject data. We exploit this intuition to develop a neural encoding model with a common backbone architecture for capturing shared response and subject-specific projections that account for individual response biases, as demonstrated in Fig. 1. Our proposed approach has several merits: (i) It allows us to combine data from multiple subjects watching same or different movies to build a global model of the brain. At the same time, it can capture meaningful individual-level deviations from the global model which can potentially be related to individual-specific traits. (ii) It is amenable to incremental learning with diverse, varying stimuli across seen or novel subjects with less constraints on data collection from single subjects. (iii) It poses minimal memory overhead with additional subjects and can thus handle fMRI datasets with a large number of subjects.

2   Methodology

Our proposed methodology is illustrated in Fig. 1. Neural encoding models comprise two components: (a) a feature extractor, which pulls out relevant features from raw images or audio waveforms and (b) a response model, which maps these stimuli features into brain responses. In contrast to existing works that employ a linear response model [9,11], we propose a CNN-based response model where the coarse 3D feature maps are shared across subjects and fine-grained feature maps are individual-specific. Previous studies have reported a cortical processing hierarchy where low-level features from early layers of a CNN-based feature extractor best predict responses in early sensory areas while semantically-rich deeper layers best predict higher sensory regions [8,9]. To account for this effect, we employ a hierarchical feature extractor based on feature pyramid networks [15] that combines features from early, intermediate and later layers simultaneously. The output of the feature extractor is fed into the convolutional response model to predict the evoked fMRI activation. This enables us to train both components of the network simultaneously in an end-to-end fashion.

Formally, let $\mathcal{D} = \{\mathbf{X}_i, \mathbf{Y}_i\}_{i=1}^N$ denote the training data pairs for N subjects, where $\mathbf{X}_i$ denotes the stimuli presented to subject i and $\mathbf{Y}_i$ denotes the corresponding fMRI measurements. We represent $\mathbf{X}_i$ as RGB images or grayscale spectrograms for the visual and auditory models, respectively. The feature model maps the 2D input into a vector representation $\mathbf{s}$ and is parameterized using a deep neural network $\mathbf{F}(\mathbf{X}_i; \phi)$ that is common across subjects. In our experiments, this model is a feature pyramid network built upon pre-trained recognition networks as DNNs optimized for image or sound recognition tasks have proven to provide powerful feature representations for encoding brain response. We define a differentiable function $\mathbf{G}(\mathbf{s}; \theta)$ that maps the features into a shared latent volumetric space $\mathbf{z}$, whose first 3 axes represent the 3D voxel space and the last axis captures the latent dimensionality. The predicted response for each subject is then defined using subject-specific differentiable functions $\mathbf{H}_i(\mathbf{z}; \psi_i)$ that project the coarse feature maps $\mathbf{z}$ into an individualized brain response. We represent $\mathbf{G}$ and $\mathbf{H}_i$'s using convolutional neural networks to have a sufficiently expressive model. Thus, θ and $\{\psi_i\}$ represent a mix of convolutional kernels or dense weight matrices. The number of shared parameters, $|\theta| + |\phi|$ is kept much greater than the cardinality of subject-specific parameters $|\psi_i|$ to accurately estimate the shared latent space. All parameters $\{\phi, \theta, \psi_i\}$ are trained jointly to minimize the *mean squared error* between the predicted and true response. The proposed method allows us to propagate errors through the shared network even if the subjects are not exposed to common stimuli since we can always backpropagate errors for subjects independently within each batch. Furthermore, using individualized layers to account for subject-specific biases enables the model to weigh gradients coming from losses of each subject differently according to their signal-to-noise ratio. This makes the model less susceptible to noisy measurements when responses for the same stimuli are available from multiple subjects.

2.1   Implementation Details

We employ pre-trained Resnet-50 [16] and VGG-ish [17] architectures in the bottom-up path of Fig. 1 to extract multi-scale features from images and audio spectrograms, respectively. The base architectures were selected because pre-trained weights of these networks optimized for classification on large datasets, namely Imagenet [18] and Youtube-8M [19], were publically available. For Resnet-50, we use activations of the last residual block of each stage, namely, res2, res3, res4 and res5 (notation from [20]) to construct our stimulus descriptions $\mathbf{s}$. From the VGG network, we use the activations of each convolutional block, namely, conv2, conv3, conv4 and the penultimate dense layer fc2 [21]. The first three set of activations are refined through a top-down path to enhance their semantic content, while the last activation is concatenated into $\mathbf{s}$ directly (res4 activations are vectorized using global average pool). The top-down path comprises three feature maps at different resolutions with an up-sampling factor of 2 successively from the deepest layer of the bottom-up path. Each such feature map comprising 256 channels is merged with the corresponding feature map in the bottom-up path (reduced to 256 channels by 1 × 1 convolutions) by element-wise addition. Subsequently, the feature map at each resolution is collapsed into a 256 dimensional feature vector through a global average pool operation and concatenated into s. The aggregated features are then passed onto a shared CNN (denoted **G** above) comprising the following feedforward computation: a fully connected layer to map the features into a vector space which is reshaped into a 1024-channel cuboid of size 6x7x6 followed by two 3x3x3 transposed convolutions (conv.T) with a stride of 2 to up-sample the latter and obtain z. Each convolution reduces the channel count by half, thereby, resulting in a shared latent z that is a 256 channel cuboid of size 27x31x27x256. Subject-specific functions H_i's are parameterized as a cascade of two 3x3x3 conv.T operations (stride 2) with output dimensions 128 and 1 respectively. It is important to emphasize that these operations constitute much fewer parameters, thereby favoring the estimation of a shared truth. As we demonstrate empirically, a shared space allows much better generalization. At the same time, we find that even the limited subject-specific parameters can adequately capture meaningful individual differences. All parameters were optimized using Adam [22] with a learning rate of 1e−4. Auditory and visual models were trained for 25 and 50 epochs respectively with unit batch size. Validation curves were monitored to ensure convergence.

2.2 Data and Preprocessing

We study 7T fMRI data (TR = 1 s) from a randomly selected sample of N = 10 subjects from HCP movie-watching protocol [4,23]. The dataset comprises 4 audiovisual movies, each ∼15 min long. Preprocessing protocols are described in detail in [23,24]. For our experiments, we utilize the 1.6 mm MNI-registered volumetric images of size 113x136x113 per TR. We compute log-mel spectrograms using same parameters as [17] over every 1 s of audio waveform to obtain a 2D image-like input for the VGG audio feature extractor. We extract the last frame of every second of the video to present to the image recognition network for visual features. We estimate a hemodynamic delay of 4 s using regression based encoding models, as the response latency that yields highest encoding performance. Thus, all proposed and baseline models are trained to use the above stimuli to predict the fMRI response 4 s *after* the corresponding stimulus presentation. We train and validate our models on three movies using a 9:1 train-val split and leave the fourth movie for independent testing. This yields 2000 training, 265 validation and 699 test stimulus-response pairs per subject.

2.3 Baselines

- Linear response model (individual subject): Here, we train independent models for each subject using linear response models. We note that, thus far, this is the dominant approach to neural encoding. To enable a fair comparison, we extract hierarchical features of the same dimensionality as the proposed model to present to the linear regressor. The only difference here is the lack of a top-down pathway (since it is not pre-trained), which prevents the refinement of coarse feature maps before aggregation. We apply l_2 regularization on the regression coefficients and adjust the optimal strength of this penalty through cross-validation using log-spaced values in $\{1e-10, 1e10\}$. We report the performance of the best model as 'Individual (Linear)'.

- CNN response model (individual subject): Here, we employ the same architecture as the proposed model but with only one branch of subject-specific layers. We train this network independently for each subject without weight sharing and denote its performance as 'Individual model (CNN)'.
- Shared model (mean): Here, we employ the proposed model after training but instead of computing predictions using the same subject's learned weights, we compute N predictions from all subject-specific branches. We compute the mean performance obtained by correlating each of these predictions with the ground truth response of a subject and denote this as 'Shared (mean)'.

2.4   Performance Evaluation

We measure performance on the test movie by computing the *Pearson's correlation coefficient* between the predicted and measured fMRI response at each voxel. Since different subjects have a different signal-to-noise ratio, we normalize each voxel's correlation by the subject's noise ceiling for that voxel. We compute the subject-specific noise ceiling by correlating their repeated measurements on a validation clip. Further, since we are only interested in the stimulus-driven response, we measure performance in voxels that exhibit high inter-subject correlations. We randomly split the 10 subjects into groups of 5, and correlate the mean activity of the two groups. We repeat this process 5 times and voxels that exhibit a mean correlation greater than 0.1 are identified as *synchronous* voxels. We compute the mean normalized correlations across all synchronous voxels to achieve a single metric per subject, denoted as 'Prediction accuracy'. We also correlate the predicted response of each subject against the predicted and true response of every other subject to obtain an $N \times N$ correlation matrix for shared models. To account for higher variability in measured versus predicted response, we normalize the rows and columns of this correlation matrix following [25].

2.5   Demonstration of Application: Personalized Brain Mapping

To investigate if the proposed model is indeed capturing meaningful individual differences, we use the trained encoding model to predict fMRI activations for distinct visual object categories from the HCP task battery. Specifically, we predict brain response to visual stimuli (comprising faces, places, tools and body parts) from the HCP Working Memory (WM) task and use the *predicted* response to synthesize face and scene contrasts (FACES-AVG and PLACES-AVG respectively) for each individual. The predicted and true contrasts are thresholded to keep top 5% of the voxels. We compute the Dice overlap between the predicted contrast for each subject against the true contrast of every subject (including self) to produce an $N \times N$ matrix for each contrast.

3 Results

Figure 2 shows prediction accuracy of the proposed ('Shared') and baseline methods for each subject. The performance improvement is striking between proposed and individual subject models, suggesting that a shared backbone architecture can significantly boost generalization. Comparative boxplots further show that the proposed method predicts a much higher percentage of the synchronous cortex than individual subject models. Further, the difference between 'Shared' and 'Shared (mean)' as well as the dominant diagonal structure in correlation matrices suggest that the proposed method is indeed capturing subject idiosyncrasies rather than predicting a group-averaged response. Further, while the CNN response model performs slightly better in visual encoding, it incurs a performance drop compared to linear regression in auditory encoding. This perhaps suggests that the boost in accuracy seen for shared models is largely due to inter-subject knowledge transfer rather than the convolutional response model itself.

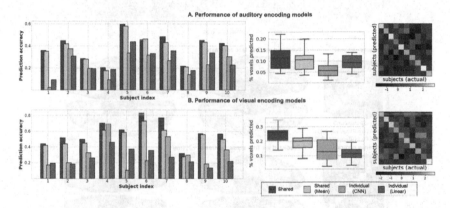

Fig. 2. Quantitative evaluation: Bar charts illustrate subject-wise prediction accuracy of all models, box plots depict the distribution over subjects for % of synchronous voxels significantly predicted ($p < 0.05$, FDR corrected). $N \times N$ correlation matrices depict the (normalized) correlation coefficient between predicted and measured responses.

In Fig. 3(A) and 3(B), we visualize the un-normalized correlations between the predicted and measured fMRI response for the proposed models, averaged across subjects. For the auditory model, we see significant correlations in the parabelt auditory cortex, extending into the superior temporal sulcus and some other language areas (55b) as well. For the visual model, while we see significant correlations across the entire visual cortex (V1–V8), the performance is much better in higher-order visual regions, presumably because of the semantically rich features. The lower performance in early visual regions could also result from the dynamic nature of visual stimulation in movies.

Figure 3(C) and 3(D) illustrate the ability of our proposed model to characterize individual differences even beyond the experimental paradigm it was trained on. The diagonal dominance in the dice matrix for both contrasts suggests that predicted contrasts are most similar to the same subject's true contrast. No prominent diagonal structure was observed for individual subject models, presumably because of their poor generalization to out-of-domain stimuli from the HCP task battery. Further, predicted contrasts consistently highlight known areas for face and scene processing, namely the fusiform face area [26] and parahippocampal areas [27] respectively.

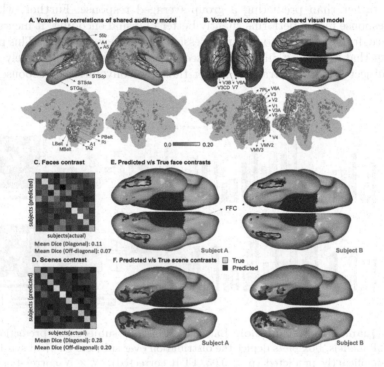

Fig. 3. (A), (B) Correlations between predicted response of the *proposed* model and true time series of each voxel averaged across subjects. Only significantly predicted voxels are shown (p < 0.05, FDR corrected). Dice matrices of predicted *versus* true contrasts for (C) faces and (D) scenes stimuli. (E) and (F) depict contrasts of two randomly selected subjects. ROIs are labelled from the HCP MMP parcellation [28].

4   Discussion

In this paper, we presented a framework for utilizing multi-subject fMRI data to improve individual-level neural encoding. We showcased our approach on both auditory and visual stimuli and demonstrated consistent improvement over competing approaches. Our experiments further suggest that a single experiment (free-viewing of movies) can characterize a multitude of brain processes at once. This has important implications for brain mapping which traditionally relies on a battery of carefully-constructed stimuli administered within block-designs. Intersubject variability in response patterns induced by the complexity of naturalistic viewing can facilitate the development of novel imaging-based biomarkers. Neural encoding models are not constrained to modeling the response to a limited set of experimental stimuli; their good generalization performance suggests that they can capture broad theories of cognitive processing. Accurate, individualized neural encoding models can thus bring us one step closer to achieving the goal of biomarker discovery.

Acknowledgements. This work was supported by NIH grants R01LM012719 (MS), R01AG053949 (MS), R21NS10463401 (AK), R01NS10264601A1 (AK), the NSF NeuroNex grant 1707312 (MS), the NSF CAREER 1748377 grant (MS) and Anna-Maria and Stephen Kellen Foundation Junior Faculty Fellowship (AK).

References

1. Hasson, U., Nir, Y., Levy, I., Fuhrmann, G., Malach, R.: Intersubject synchronization of cortical activity during natural vision. Science **303**(5664), 1634–1640 (2004)
2. Sonkusare, S., Breakspear, M., Guo, C.: Naturalistic stimuli in neuroscience: critically acclaimed. Trends Cogn. Sci. (Regul. Ed.) **23**(8), 699–714 (2019)
3. Schultz, J., Pilz, K.S.: Natural facial motion enhances cortical responses to faces. Exp. Brain Res. **194**(3), 465–475 (2009)
4. Glasser, M.F., et al.: The minimal preprocessing pipelines for the human connectome project. Neuroimage **80**, 105–124 (2013)
5. Hasson, U., Malach, R., Heeger, D.J.: Reliability of cortical activity during natural stimulation. Trends Cogn. Sci. (Regul. Ed.) **14**(1), 40–48 (2010)
6. Chen, P.-H.C., Chen, J., Yeshurun, Y., Hasson, U., Haxby, J.V., Ramadge, P. J.: A reduced-dimension fMRI shared response model. In: NIPS (2015)
7. Varoquaux, G., Poldrack, R.A.: Predictive models avoid excessive reductionism in cognitive neuroimaging. Curr. Opin. Neurobiol. **55**, 1–6 (2019)
8. Kell, A.J.E., Yamins, D.L., Shook, E.N., Norman-Haignere, S.V., McDermott, J.H.: A task-optimized neural network replicates human auditory behavior, predicts brain responses, and reveals a cortical processing hierarchy. Neuron **98**(3), 630–644 (2018)
9. Guclu, U., van Gerven, M.A.: Deep neural networks reveal a gradient in the complexity of neural representations across the ventral stream. J. Neurosci. **35**(27), 10005–10014 (2015)
10. Yamins, D.L., Hong, H., Cadieu, C.F., Solomon, E.A., Seibert, D., DiCarlo, J.J.: Performance-optimized hierarchical models predict neural responses in higher visual cortex. Proc. Natl. Acad. Sci. U.S.A. **111**(23), 8619–8624 (2014)
11. Wen, H., Shi, J., Zhang, Y., Lu, K.H., Cao, J., Liu, Z.: Neural encoding and decoding with deep learning for dynamic natural vision. Cereb. Cortex **28**(12), 4136–4160 (2018)

12. Dubois, J., Adolphs, R.: Building a science of individual differences from fMRI. Trends Cogn. Sci. (Regul. Ed.) **20**(6), 425–443 (2016)
13. Wen, H., Shi, J., Chen, W., Liu, Z.: Transferring and generalizing deep-learning-based neural encoding models across subjects. NeuroImage **176**, 152–163 (2018)
14. Güçlü, U., van Gerven, M.A.J.: Increasingly complex representations of natural movies across the dorsal stream are shared between subjects. NeuroImage **145**, 329–336 (2017)
15. Lin, T.-Y., Dollár, P., Girshick, R.B., He, K., Hariharan, B., Belongie, S.J.: Feature pyramid networks for object detection. In: 2017 IEEE Conference on Computer Vision and Pattern Recognition (CVPR), pp. 936–944 (2016)
16. He, K., Zhang, X., Ren, S., Sun, J.: Deep residual learning for image recognition. In: 2016 IEEE Conference on Computer Vision and Pattern Recognition (CVPR), pp. 770–778 (2015)
17. Hershey, S., et al.: CNN architectures for large-scale audio classification. In: 2017 IEEE International Conference on Acoustics, Speech and Signal Processing (ICASSP), pp. 131–135 (2016)
18. Deng, J., Dong, W., Socher, R., Li, L.-J., Li, K., Fei-Fei, L.: Imagenet: a large-scale hierarchical image database. In: 2009 IEEE Conference on Computer Vision and Pattern Recognition, pp. 248–255 (2009)
19. Abu-El-Haija, S., et al.: Youtube-8m: a large-scale video classification benchmark. ArXiv arxiv:1609.08675 (2016)
20. Girshick, R., Radosavovic, I., Gkioxari, G., Dollár, P., He, K.: Detectron (2018). https://github.com/facebookresearch/detectron
21. Hershley, S., et al.: Models for audioset: a large scale dataset of audio events (2016). https://github.com/tensorflow/models/tree/master/research/audioset/vggish
22. Kingma, D.P., Ba, J.: Adam: a method for stochastic optimization. CoRR arxiv:1412.6980 (2014)
23. Van Essen, D.C., et al.: The human connectome project: a data acquisition perspective. Neuroimage **62**(4), 2222–2231 (2012)
24. Vu, A.T., et al.: Tradeoffs in pushing the spatial resolution of fMRI for the 7T human connectome project. Neuroimage **154**, 23–32 (2017)
25. Tavor, I., Jones, O.P., Mars, R.B., Smith, S.M., Behrens, T.E., Jbabdi, S.: Task-free MRI predicts individual differences in brain activity during task performance. Science **352**(6282), 216–220 (2016)
26. Kanwisher, N., McDermott, J., Chun, M.M.: The fusiform face area: a module in human extrastriate cortex specialized for face perception. J. Neurosci. **17**(11), 4302–4311 (1997)
27. Nasr, S., et al.: Scene-selective cortical regions in human and nonhuman primates. J. Neurosci. **31**(39), 13771–13785 (2011)
28. Glasser, M.F., et al.: A multi-modal parcellation of human cerebral cortex. Nature **536**(7615), 171–178 (2016)

Neuroimaging

Topology-Aware Generative Adversarial Network for Joint Prediction of Multiple Brain Graphs from a Single Brain Graph

Alaa Bessadok[1,2], Mohamed Ali Mahjoub[2], and Islem Rekik[1(✉)] ⓘ

[1] BASIRA Lab, Faculty of Computer and Informatics,
Istanbul Technical University, Istanbul, Turkey
irekik@itu.edu.tr

[2] Higher Institute of Informatics and Communication Technologies,
Université de Sousse, Sousse, Tunisia
http://basira-lab.com

Abstract. Multimodal medical datasets with incomplete observations present a barrier to large-scale neuroscience studies. Several works based on Generative Adversarial Networks (GAN) have been recently proposed to predict a set of medical images from a single modality (e.g., FLAIR MRI from T1 MRI). However, such frameworks are primarily designed to operate on *images*, limiting their generalizability to non-Euclidean geometric data such as brain graphs. While a growing number of connectomic studies has demonstrated the promise of including brain graphs for diagnosing neurological disorders, no geometric deep learning work was designed for *multiple target brain graphs prediction from a source brain graph*. Despite the momentum the field of graph generation has gained in the last two years, existing works have two critical drawbacks. *First*, the bulk of such works aims to learn one model for each target domain to generate from a source domain. Thus, they have a limited scalability in *jointly* predicting multiple target domains. *Second*, they merely consider the global topological scale of a graph (i.e., graph connectivity structure) and overlook the local topology at the node scale of a graph (e.g., how central a node is in the graph). To meet these challenges, we introduce MultiGraphGAN architecture, which not only predicts multiple brain graphs from a single brain graph but also preserves the topological structure of each target graph to predict. Its three core contributions lie in: (i) designing a graph adversarial auto-encoder for jointly predicting brain graphs from a single one, (ii) handling the mode collapse problem of GAN by clustering the encoded source graphs and proposing a *cluster-specific decoder*, (iii) introducing a *topological loss* to force the reconstruction of topologically sound target brain graphs. Our MultiGraphGAN significantly outperformed its variants thereby showing its great potential in multi-view brain graph generation from a single graph. Our code is available at https://github.com/basiralab/MultiGraphGAN.

Keywords: Adversarial brain multigraph prediction · Geometric deep learning · Multigraph GAN

ⓒ Springer Nature Switzerland AG 2020
A. L. Martel et al. (Eds.): MICCAI 2020, LNCS 12267, pp. 551–561, 2020.
https://doi.org/10.1007/978-3-030-59728-3_54

1   Introduction

Multimodal image synthesis has gained a lot of attention from researchers in the medical field as it reduces the high acquisition time and cost of medical modalities (e.g., positron emission tomography (PET)). Generative Adversarial Network (GAN) [1] is nowadays the dominant method for predicting medical images of different modalities from a given modality. For instance, [2] proposed a GAN-based framework to predict PET neuroimaging from magnetic resonance imaging (MRI) for an early Alzheimer's disease diagnosis. Inspired from ColaGAN, [3] predicted double inversion recovery (DIR) scans from three source modalities (i.e., Flair, T1 and T2). However, such *one-target prediction* frameworks are incapable of *jointly* predicting multiple target modalities using a single learning model. To alleviate this issue, several *multi-target prediction* solutions have been proposed [4,5] in the computer vision field but a few attempts have been made in the medical field. Recently, [6] proposed an adversarial autoencoder framework to predict three target MRI images (i.e., T1-weighted, T2-weighted, and FLAIR) from a single source T1 MRI scan. Although promising, such models fail to generalize to geometric data such as graphs and manifolds, especially brain graphs (i.e., connectome) which are derived from MRI scans. A brain graph consists of a set of nodes representing the anatomical regions of interest (ROIs) linked by edges encoding their biological relationship. However, multimodal medical datasets are usually incomplete so it becomes very challenging to conduct multimodal connectomic studies requiring paired samples. Consequently, predicting missing brain graphs from an existing source graph is highly desired since it provides rich and complementary information for brain mapping and disease diagnosis.

So far, we have identified only two brain graph synthesis works [7,8] which proposed a geometric deep learning-based framework for *one-target prediction* from a source brain graph. The target graph of a testing subject is predicted by first aligning the training target graphs to the source graphs, then averaging the target graphs of the training subjects that share similar local neighborhoods across source and target domains. Although pioneering, these works are neither designed in an *end-to-end learning* manner nor effective for *jointly* predicting multiple target brain graphs from a single source graph. Other works [9–12] aimed to generate different types of graphs including biological ones such as molecules. To the best of our knowledge, no existing graph synthesis works attempted to solve the problem of *joint* multiple brain graph prediction from a baseline source graph [13,14]. Another important shortcoming of existing graph synthesis works [9–14], is that they do not preserve the node-wise topological properties. Mainly, they only learn the *global graph structure* (i.e., number of nodes and edges weights). However, the brain wiring has both global and local topological properties underpinning its function, and which can get altered in neurological disorders [15,16]. Hence, by overlooking the learning of the *local graph structure* one cannot capture which ROIs would be most effective for early diagnosing the disease based on the topological properties within the brain graph. By considering local topological constraints, one can learn the node's importance in a graph which can be measured using path-length based metrics such as betweenness centrality. Such centrality metrics assign a score to each node based on the shortest path between pairs of nodes. In this way, the synthesized graph will satisfy both global and local topologies of the original target graph.

To address all these drawbacks, we propose MultiGraphGAN, the first attempt to *jointly* predict multiple brain graphs from a single graph in an end-to-end deep learning fashion. We draw inspiration from the work [5] on multi-domain image translation task. Although effective for multi-target *image* prediction, [5] fails to operate on graphs as it was primarily designed for Euclidean data. Besides, it overlooks GAN mode collapse, where the generator (i.e., decoder) produces data that mimic a few modes of the target domain. To address this issue, we first propose to learn the source graph embeddings using an encoder E defined as a Graph Convolutional Network (GCN) [17]. Second, we cluster the resulting embeddings with heterogeneous distribution into homogeneous clusters where a *cluster-specific* generator is constructed to generate a specific mode of the given target domain. In other words, we define for each target domain a set of synergetic generators, each representing a cluster-specific GCN decoder. Hence, the graph prediction is learned more synergistically using our proposed cluster-specific generators, rather than using a single generator for each target domain. This generative process is regularized using one discriminator D, which enforces the generated graphs to match the original target graphs. Lastly, we introduce a *topology-aware adversarial loss function* that seeks to preserve both global and local topological properties when predicting the target graphs. Mainly, we aim to enforce the generated graphs to retain a centrality score of each nodes in the original target brain graph.

2   Proposed MultiGraphGAN for Multiple Graphs Prediction

In the following, we present the main steps of our joint *multi-target* brain graphs prediction framework from a single source graph. Fig. 1 provides an overview of the key three steps of the proposed framework: 1) extraction of multi-view brain features and construction of a graph population for each source and target domains, 2) embedding and clustering of the source graphs, and 3) prediction of multiple target brain graphs using cluster-specific generators.

A - Graph Population Representation using Multi-view Brain Graphs. Let $\mathcal{G}_d$ be a graph encoding the pairwise relationship between subjects belonging to a specific domain d where $d \in \{\mathcal{S}, \mathcal{T}_1, \ldots, \mathcal{T}_m\}$. We define our graph population as $\mathcal{G}_d = \{(\mathcal{G}_d^n, \mathcal{F}_d), \mathcal{G}_d^e\}$ where $\mathcal{G}_d^n$ denotes a set of nodes (i.e., subjects) and $\mathcal{F}_d$ denotes a feature matrix in $\mathbb{R}^{n \times f}$ vertically stacking the brain graph features of size f for n subjects. Specifically, each subject is represented by one source brain graph and m target graphs where each graph is encoded in a symmetric matrix whose elements measure the similarity between two ROIs (i.e., nodes). We vectorize the off-diagonal upper-diagonal part of each matrix to create a

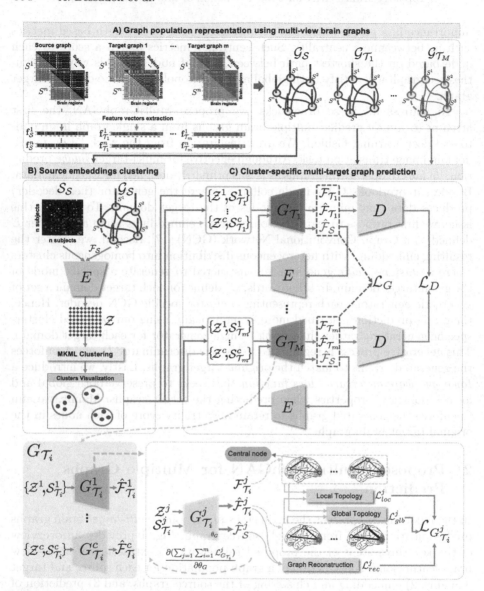

Fig. 1. *Pipeline of the proposed MultiGraphGAN framework for predicting jointly multiple target brain graphs from a single source graph.* **(A) Graph population representation using multi-view brain graphs.** Extraction of feature vectors from source and m target brain graphs for each subject. Construction of graph population denoting the similarity between subjects using the resulting features. **(B) Source embeddings clustering.** First, we learn the source graph embedding using an encoder E. Second, we use multiple kernel manifold learning to cluster the resulting source embeddings into c groups. **(C) Cluster-specific multi-target graph prediction.** For each of the m target domains, we train c *cluster-specific generators* regularized by a shared discriminator D. We introduce a *local topology loss* and a *global topology loss* to regularize the cluster-specific generators (e.g., $G_{\mathcal{T}_i}^j$), each preserving the local node topology and the global graph connectivity structure. We further propose a source *graph reconstruction loss* to map the generated target graphs back to the source domain.

feature vector $\mathbf{f}_d$ in $\mathbb{R}^{1 \times f}$ encoding the connectivity features of a subject in the domain d. Thus, $\mathcal{F}_d$ denotes the feature vectors $\{\mathbf{f}_d^1, \ldots, \mathbf{f}_d^n\}$ of n subjects. Additionally, we define $\mathcal{G}_d^e$ as a set of weighted edges encoding the similarity between each pair of subjects using their feature vectors. To do this, we propose to learn a sample similarity matrix $\mathcal{S}_d$ in $\mathbb{R}^{n \times n}$ using multi-kernel manifold learning (MKML) algorithm [18] as it efficiently fits the statistical distribution of the data by learning multiple kernels. Ultimately, for the source and m target domains we have a set of graphs $\{\mathcal{G}_\mathcal{S}, \mathcal{G}_{T_1}, \ldots, \mathcal{G}_{T_m}\}$ each represented by a set of feature matrices $\{\mathcal{F}_\mathcal{S}, \mathcal{F}_{T_1}, \ldots, \mathcal{F}_{T_m}\}$ and a set of learned adjacency matrices $\{\mathcal{S}_\mathcal{S}, \mathcal{S}_{T_1}, \ldots, \mathcal{S}_{T_m}\}$ (**Fig. 1–A**).

B - Source Graphs Embedding and Clustering. We aim in this step to learn the source graph embeddings using an encoder $E(\mathcal{F}_\mathcal{S}, \mathcal{S}_\mathcal{S})$ defined as a GCN with two layers inputing the source feature matrix $\mathcal{F}_\mathcal{S}$ and the learned sample similarity matrix $\mathcal{S}_\mathcal{S}$. We define the layers of GCN and the graph convolution function used in each layer as follows:

$$\mathcal{Z}^{(l)} = f_\phi(\mathcal{X}, \mathcal{S}_\mathcal{S} | \mathbf{W}^{(l)}); \quad f_\phi(\mathcal{X}^{(l)}, \mathcal{S}_\mathcal{S} | \mathbf{W}^{(l)}) = \phi(\widetilde{\mathbf{D}}^{-\frac{1}{2}} \widetilde{\mathcal{S}}_\mathcal{S} \widetilde{\mathbf{D}}^{-\frac{1}{2}} \mathcal{X}^{(l)} \mathbf{W}^{(l)}), \quad (1)$$

$\mathcal{Z}^{(l)}$ is the resulting source graph embeddings of the layer l. ϕ represents the *ReLU* and *linear* activation functions we used in the first and second layers, respectively. In the first layer, $\mathcal{X}$ denotes the source feature matrix $\mathcal{F}_\mathcal{S}$ while in the second layer it denotes the resulting embeddings learned from the first layer $\mathcal{Z}^{(1)}$. $\mathbf{W}^{(l)}$ is a filter used to learn the convolution in the GCN in each layer l. As in [17], we define the graph convolution function by $f_{(.)}$ where $\widetilde{\mathcal{S}}_\mathcal{S} = \mathcal{S}_\mathcal{S} + \mathbf{I}$ with $\mathbf{I}$ being an identity matrix used for self-regularization, and $\widetilde{\mathbf{D}}_{ii} = \sum_j \widetilde{\mathcal{S}}_\mathcal{S}(ij)$ is a diagonal matrix.

We aim in the following step to build a set of domain-specific decoders regularized with the discriminator D to generate the target graphs. However, in practice, the GAN generators might end up producing graphs that match a few unimodal sample of the target domain thereby overlooking its heterogeneous distribution. To handle such mode collapse of generative models, we propose to first cluster the source graph embeddings $\mathcal{Z}$ into homogeneous clusters. We further use MKML for clustering since it outperformed PCA and t-SNE clustering methods when dealing with biological datasets [18]. Specifically, it first learns the similarity between source embeddings, second it maps the learned similarity matrix into a lower dimensional space, and finally uses k-means algorithm to cluster the subjects into c clusters (Fig. 1–B).

C - Cluster-Specific Multi-target Graph Prediction. To predict the target graph of a given domain T_i where $i \in \{1, \ldots, m\}$, we propose a set of *cluster-specific generators* $G_{T_i} = \{G_{T_i}^1, \ldots, G_{T_i}^c\}$, where each generator produces a graph approximating the target data distribution of a specific cluster (Fig. 1–C). As such, we enforce the generator to learn from all examples in the cluster c thus avoiding the mode collapse issue as our learning becomes unimodal (i.e., cluster-specific). We train the generators in a sequential manner where each is defined as a GCN decoder with a similar architecture to the encoder (Eq. (1)). More specifically, for each cluster j, a generator $G_{T_i}^j$ assigned to the target domain T_i and to the cluster j takes two inputs: the source embeddings $\mathcal{Z}^j$ and the sample similarity matrix $\mathcal{S}_{T_i}^j$ learned using the target graphs in domain T_i. In that way, we enforce the generator to decode the source embeddings while approximating the real target graph structure.

The target graph prediction is optimized using the discriminator D which is a GCN with three layers. Specifically, it enforces the generated target graph to match the ground truth target distribution of a specific target domain. This is achieved in two steps. First, the discriminator measures the real-ness of the generated graphs by computing the Wasserstein distance among all domains. We formulate this using the following adversarial loss $\mathcal{L}_{adv}^j = -\mathbb{E}_{\mathcal{F}' \sim \mathbb{P}_{\mathcal{F}^j S}}[D(\mathcal{F}')] + \frac{1}{m}\sum_{i=1}^m \mathbb{E}_{\mathcal{F}'' \sim \mathbb{P}_{\hat{\mathcal{F}}_{T_i}^j}}[D(\mathcal{F}'')]$. Second, we define a binary classifier D_C on top of our discriminator D which classifies the fake graphs $\hat{\mathcal{F}}_{T_i}^j$ as 0 and the real target graphs $\mathcal{F}_{T_i}^j$ as 1. Hence, we formulate a graph domain classification loss as $\mathcal{L}_{gdc}^j = \sum_{i=1}^m \mathbb{E}_{\mathcal{F}'' \sim \mathbb{P}_{\hat{\mathcal{F}}_{T_i}^j} \cup \mathbb{P}_{\mathcal{F}_{T_i}^j}}[\ell_{MSE}(D_C(\mathcal{F}''), y(\mathcal{F}''))]$. ℓ_{MSE} is the mean squared loss and y is the ground truth label corresponding to the graph $\mathcal{F}''$. Additionally, to improve the training stability of our model we adopt the gradient penalty loss of [5] which is formulated as $\mathcal{L}_{gp}^j = (max\{0, \mathbb{E}_{\tilde{\mathcal{F}}} \sim \mathbb{P}_{\tilde{\mathcal{F}}}^{j_m} \|\nabla D(\tilde{\mathcal{F}})\| - \sigma\})^2$. $\tilde{\mathcal{F}}$ is sampled between the source graph distribution $\mathbb{P}_{\mathcal{F}_S^j}$ and the fake target graph distribution $\mathbb{P}_{\tilde{\mathcal{F}}_m^j}$ where $\tilde{\mathcal{F}}_m^j$ is a matrix stacking vertically the generated target graphs for all m domains. In particular, $\tilde{\mathcal{F}} \leftarrow \alpha \mathcal{F}_S^j + (1 - \alpha)\tilde{\mathcal{F}}_m^j$ where $\alpha \sim U[0,1]$ and U is a uniform distribution. σ is a hyper-parameter set to m as suggested in [5]. Ultimately, the discriminator guides the generators of each cluster to produce brain graphs, each associated with a specific target domain through the following loss function:

$$\mathcal{L}_D = \sum_{j=1}^c (\mathcal{L}_{adv}^j + \lambda_{gdc} \cdot \mathcal{L}_{gdc}^j + \lambda_{gp} \cdot \mathcal{L}_{gp}^j), \qquad (2)$$

λ_{gdc} and λ_{gp} are hyper-parameters to be tuned. Moreover, brain graphs have unique topological properties for functional, structural and morphological connectivities that should be preserved when predicting the target brain graphs [19,20]. To this aim, we introduce a topological loss function which constrains the generators to preserve the nodes properties while learning the global graph structure (Fig. 1–C). To do so, we compute the absolute difference between the real and predicted centralities scores of each node in the target graph. We choose three centrality measures widely used in graph theory: closeness centrality CC quantifying the closeness of a node to all other nodes [21], betweenness centrality BC measuring the number of shortest paths which pass across a node [22], and eigenvector centrality EC capturing the centralities of a node's neighbors [23]. We define their formulas in Table 1.

Given a centrality metric $\mathcal{C}$ where $\mathcal{C} \in \{CC, BC, EC\}$, a cluster j and a target domain T_i, we define $\mathcal{X}_{T_i}^j$ and $\hat{\mathcal{X}}_{T_i}^j$ as the centralities for the real graphs $\mathcal{F}_{T_i}^j$ and

Table 1. Centrality measures included in the topological loss function.

Centrality	Description
$CC(v^a) = \frac{V-1}{\sum_{v^a \neq v^b} p_{v^a v^b}}$	V is the number of nodes and $p_{v^a v^b}$ is the length of the shortestpath between nodes v^a and v^b
$BC(v^a) = \frac{2}{(V-1)(V-2)} \times \sum_{v^a \neq v^b \neq v^c} \frac{P_{(v^c, v^b)}(v^a)}{P_{(v^c, v^b)}}$	$P_{(v^c, v^b)}(v^a)$ denotes the number of shortest paths between two nodes v^c and v^b that pass through (v^a)
$EC(v^a) = x^a = \frac{1}{\lambda} \sum_{h=1}^{V} A_{ab} x^b$	A_{ab} represents all neighbors of the node a, x is the eigenvector resulted from the eigen decomposition of the adjacency matrix A and λ is the highest eigen value

the generated ones $\hat{\mathcal{F}}_{T_i}^j$, respectively. Both $\mathcal{X}$ matrices are in $\mathbb{R}^{n \times r}$ where n is the number of subjects and r is the number of brain regions. Hence, we define our proposed *local topology* loss as $\mathcal{L}_{loc}^j(\mathcal{C}) = \sum_{i=1}^{m} \ell_{MAE}(\mathcal{X}_{T_i}^j, \hat{\mathcal{X}}_{T_i}^j)$. On the other hand, we propose the *global topology* loss function to maintain the relationship between brain regions in terms of number of edges and their weights using the feature matrix $\mathcal{F}_{T_i}^j$. Hence, for a cluster j, we define it as $\mathcal{L}_{glb}^j = \sum_{i=1}^{m} \ell_{MAE}(\mathcal{F}_{T_i}^j, \hat{\mathcal{F}}_{T_i}^j)$. One of the key contributions for our proposed architecture is the topological loss function regularizing the cluster-specific generators. It is made up of local and global topology losses and defined as $\mathcal{L}_{top}^j = \mathcal{L}_{loc}^j + \mathcal{L}_{glb}^j$. Moreover, by maximizing the Eq. (2) the generators are optimally trained to produce graphs that belong to a specific target domain. However, this does not guarantee that the predicted target graphs can inversely regenerate the source graph structure in a cyclic manner. To address this problem, we propose a graph reconstruction loss function which ensures that the source brain graphs can be also generated from the predicted brain graphs (Fig. 1–C). Similar to the topological loss function $\mathcal{L}_{top}^j$, we define it as follows:

$$\mathcal{L}_{rec}^j = (\underbrace{\sum_{i=1}^{m} \ell_{MAE}(\mathcal{X}_{\mathcal{S}_i}^j, \hat{\mathcal{X}}_{\mathcal{S}_i}^j)}_{\text{reconstruction local topology loss}} + \underbrace{\sum_{i=1}^{m} \ell_{MAE}(\mathcal{F}_{\mathcal{S}_i}^j, \hat{\mathcal{F}}_{\mathcal{S}_i}^j)}_{\text{reconstruction global topology loss}}) \quad (3)$$

Furthermore, since the target domains are correlated we integrate the information maximization loss term to force the generators to correlate the predicted graphs with a specific target domain. It is defined as in [5] $\mathcal{L}_{inf}^j = \sum_{i=1}^{m} \ell_{BCE}(y = 1, D_C(\hat{\mathcal{F}}_{T_i}^j))$ where ℓ_{BCE} is the binary cross entropy. Ultimately, in our MultiGraphGAN architecture, we define the overall *topology-aware adver-*

sarial loss function of each generator as:

$$\mathcal{L}_G = \sum_{j=1}^{c}(-\frac{1}{m}\cdot\sum_{i=1}^{m}\mathbb{E}_{\mathcal{F}''\sim\hat{\mathcal{F}}_{T_i}}\left[D(\mathcal{F}'')\right] + \lambda_{top}\cdot\mathcal{L}_{top}^{j} + \lambda_{rec}\cdot\mathcal{L}_{rec}^{j} + \lambda_{inf}\cdot\mathcal{L}_{inf}^{j}), \quad (4)$$

where λ_{top}, λ_{rec} and λ_{inf} are hyper-parameters that control the relative importance of topological loss, graph reconstruction, and information maximization losses, respectively. The steps explained above are used for training our MultiGraphGAN and for a testing subject we predict its target graph by averaging the target graphs produced by the cluster-specific generators.

3   Results and Discussion

Multi-view Brain Graph Dataset and Model Architecture. A set of 310 structural T1-w MRI data extracted from Autism Brain Imaging Data Exchange (ABIDE[1]) public dataset was used. We train our model on 90% of the dataset and test it on 10%. Each subject is represented by six morphological brain graphs (MBG). For each hemisphere H (i.e., $H \in \{L, R\}$), we extract three MBGs using the following cortical measurements as introduced in [24]: MBG_H^1 maximum principal curvature, MBG_H^2 average curvature and MBG_H^3 mean sulcal depth. We consider MBG_L^1 as the source brain graphs and $\{MBG_L^2, MBG_L^3, MBG_R^1, MBG_R^2, MBG_R^3\}$ as the target graphs. We construct our encoder with a hidden layer comprising 32 neurons and an embedding layer with 16 neurons. Conversely, we define all generators with two layers each comprising 16 and 32 neurons. The discriminator comprises three layers each has 32, 16 and 1 neurons, respectively. We add to its last layer a softmax activation function representing our domain classifier. We train our model using 1000 iterations, a batch size of 70, a learning rate of 0.0001, $\beta_1 = 0.5$ and $\beta2 = 0.999$ for Adam optimizer. Using grid search we set our hyper-parameters $\lambda_{gdc} = 1$, $\lambda_{gp} = 0.1$, $\lambda_{top} = 0.1$, $\lambda_{rec} = 0.01$ and $\lambda_{inf} = 1$. We train the discriminator five times and the generators one time in an iterative manner so that their learning performances are improved. For MKML parameters [18], we fix the number of kernels to 10. After evaluating our model on different number of clusters $c \in \{2, 3, 4\}$ we choose the one which gave the best performance $c = 2$.

Evaluation and Comparison Methods. As our MultiGraphGAN is the first model aiming to jointly predict multiple target graphs from a single brain graph, we compare it with two baseline methods: **(1) Adapted MWGAN:** we use the same architecture proposed in [5] that we adapted to graph data types where we neither include the clustering step nor our proposed topology-aware loss function. **(2) Adapted MWGAN (clustering):** it is a variant of the first method where we add the MKML clustering of the source graph embeddings [18] without any topology loss. We also compare our model when using three different centrality metrics: closeness **(3) MultiGraphGAN+CC**, betweenness **(4) MultiGraphGAN+BC** and eigenvector **(5) MultiGraphGAN+EC** centralities.

---

[1] http://fcon_1000.projects.nitrc.org/indi/abide/.

Table 2. Prediction results using different evaluation metrics. PCC: pearson correlation coefficient. MAE: mean absolute error. BC: betweenness centrality. CC: closeness centrality. EC: eigenvector centrality.

Methods	Topological measures	PCC	MAE (BC)	MAE (CC)	MAE (EC)
Adapted MWGAN [5]	--	0.4869	0.0101	0.2394	0.0169
Adapted MWGAN [5] (clustering)	--	0.4272	0.0063	0.1624	0.013
MultiGraphGAN	CC	0.3428	0.0062	0.1599	0.0118
MultiGraphGAN	**BC**	**0.5037**	**0.0054**	**0.141**	**0.0113**
MultiGraphGAN	**EC**	**0.5245**	**0.0056**	**0.1449**	**0.0111**

To evaluate our framework, we compute for each target domain the Pearson Correlation Coefficient (PCC) between the ground truth and predicted graphs and the mean absolute error (MAE) between the ground truth centrality scores and the predicted ones. Then, we consider the average of all resulting PCCs, and MAEs as the final measures to evaluate our framework. Table 2 shows the outperformance of MultiGraphGAN over the baseline methods, which demonstrates the advantage of our *cluster-specific generators* in avoiding the mode collapse problem in addition to the *topological constraint* in optimally learning the target graph structure. Notably, the results also highlight the importance of using BC and EC which both ranked first best and second best using different evaluation metrics. This is explicable since considering the node neighborhoods (i.e., EC) and the frequency of being on the shortest path between nodes in the graph (i.e., BC) have much impact on identifying the most influential node rather than focusing on the average shortest path existing between a pair of nodes. As our MultiGraphGAN achieved very promising results, it can be extended in different directions such as predicting multi-target time-dependent brain graphs. This would be of high interest in foreseeing brain disorder evolution over time using brain graph representations [25–27].

4   Conclusion

We proposed MultiGraphGAN the first geometric deep learning framework for jointly predicting multiple target brain graphs from a single source graph. Our architecture has two compelling strengths: (i) clustering the learned source graph embeddings then training a set of *cluster-specific generators* which synergistically predict the target brain graphs, (ii) introducing a *topological loss function* using a centrality metric which enforces the generators to preserve local and global topology of the original target graphs. Our framework can be used for predicting other types of brain graphs such as structural and functional and extended to predict the evolution multi-target brain graphs over time from a single source brain graph.

Acknowledgement. This project has been funded by the 2232 International Fellowship for Outstanding Researchers Program of TUBITAK (Project No: 118C288, http://basira-lab.com/reprime/) supporting I. Rekik. However, all scientific contributions made in this project are owned and approved solely by the authors.

References

1. Goodfellow, I., et al.: Generative adversarial nets. In: Advances in Neural Information Processing Systems, pp. 2672–2680 (2014)
2. Pan, Y., Liu, M., Lian, C., Xia, Y., Shen, D.: Disease-image specific generative adversarial network for brain disease diagnosis with incomplete multi-modal neuroimages. In: Shen, D., et al. (eds.) MICCAI 2019. LNCS, vol. 11766, pp. 137–145. Springer, Cham (2019). https://doi.org/10.1007/978-3-030-32248-9_16
3. Kofler, F., et al.: DiamondGAN: unified multi-modal generative adversarial networks for MRI sequences synthesis. In: Shen, D., et al. (eds.) MICCAI 2019. LNCS, vol. 11767, pp. 795–803. Springer, Cham (2019). https://doi.org/10.1007/978-3-030-32251-9_87
4. Wu, P.W., Lin, Y.J., Chang, C.H., Chang, E.Y., Liao, S.W.: Relgan: multi-domain image-to-image translation via relative attributes. In: Proceedings of the IEEE International Conference on Computer Vision, pp. 5914–5922 (2019)
5. Cao, J., Mo, L., Zhang, Y., Jia, K., Shen, C., Tan, M.: Multi-marginal Wasserstein GAN. In: Advances in Neural Information Processing Systems, pp. 1774–1784 (2019)
6. Huang, P., et al.: CoCa-GAN: common-feature-learning-based context-aware generative adversarial network for glioma grading. In: Shen, D., et al. (eds.) MICCAI 2019. LNCS, vol. 11766, pp. 155–163. Springer, Cham (2019). https://doi.org/10.1007/978-3-030-32248-9_18
7. Bessadok, A., Mahjoub, M.A., Rekik, I.: Symmetric dual adversarial connectomic domain alignment for predicting isomorphic brain graph from a baseline graph. In: Shen, D., et al. (eds.) MICCAI 2019. LNCS, vol. 11767, pp. 465–474. Springer, Cham (2019). https://doi.org/10.1007/978-3-030-32251-9_51
8. Bessadok, A., Mahjoub, M.A., Rekik, I.: Hierarchical adversarial connectomic domain alignment for target brain graph prediction and classification from a source graph. In: Rekik, I., Adeli, E., Park, S.H. (eds.) PRIME 2019. LNCS, vol. 11843, pp. 105–114. Springer, Cham (2019). https://doi.org/10.1007/978-3-030-32281-6_11
9. Su, S.Y., Hajimirsadeghi, H., Mori, G.: Graph generation with variational recurrent neural network. arXiv preprint arXiv:1910.01743 (2019)
10. Liao, R., et al.: Efficient graph generation with graph recurrent attention networks. In: Advances in Neural Information Processing Systems, pp. 4257–4267 (2019)
11. Flam-Shepherd, D., Wu, T., Aspuru-Guzik, A.: Graph deconvolutional generation. arXiv preprint arXiv:2002.07087 (2020)
12. Bresson, X., Laurent, T.: A two-step graph convolutional decoder for molecule generation. arXiv preprint arXiv:1906.03412 (2019)
13. Zhang, Z., Cui, P., Zhu, W.: Deep learning on graphs: a survey. arXiv preprint arXiv:1812.04202 (2018)
14. Zhou, J., et al.: Graph neural networks: a review of methods and applications. arXiv preprint arXiv:1812.08434 (2018)
15. Fornito, A., Zalesky, A., Breakspear, M.: The connectomics of brain disorders. Nat. Rev. Neurosci. **16**, 159–172 (2015)

16. Van den Heuvel, M.P., Sporns, O.: A cross-disorder connectome landscape of brain dysconnectivity. Nat. Rev. Neurosci. **20**, 435–446 (2019)
17. Kipf, T.N., Welling, M.: Semi-supervised classification with graph convolutional networks. arXiv preprint arXiv:1609.02907 (2016)
18. Wang, B., Ramazzotti, D., De Sano, L., Zhu, J., Pierson, E., Batzoglou, S.: SIMLR: a tool for large-scale single-cell analysis by multi-kernel learning. bioRxiv 118901 (2017)
19. Liu, J., et al.: Complex brain network analysis and its applications to brain disorders: a survey. Complexity **2017** (2017)
20. Joyce, K.E., Laurienti, P.J., Burdette, J.H., Hayasaka, S.: A new measure of centrality for brain networks. PloS One **5**, e12200 (2010)
21. Freeman, L.C.: A set of measures of centrality based on betweenness. Sociometry **40**, 35–41 (1977)
22. Beauchamp, M.A.: An improved index of centrality. Behav. Sci. **10**, 161–163 (1965)
23. Bonacich, P.: Some unique properties of eigenvector centrality. Soc. Netw. **29**, 555–564 (2007)
24. Mahjoub, I., Mahjoub, M.A., Rekik, I.: Brain multiplexes reveal morphological connectional biomarkers fingerprinting late brain dementia states. Sci. Rep. **8**, 4103 (2018)
25. Ezzine, B.E., Rekik, I.: Learning-guided infinite network atlas selection for predicting longitudinal brain network evolution from a single observation. In: Shen, D., et al. (eds.) MICCAI 2019. LNCS, vol. 11765, pp. 796–805. Springer, Cham (2019). https://doi.org/10.1007/978-3-030-32245-8_88
26. Ghribi, O., Li, G., Lin, W., Shen, D., Rekik, I.: Progressive infant brain connectivity evolution prediction from neonatal MRI using bidirectionally supervised sample selection. In: Rekik, I., Adeli, E., Park, S.H. (eds.) PRIME 2019. LNCS, vol. 11843, pp. 63–72. Springer, Cham (2019). https://doi.org/10.1007/978-3-030-32281-6_7
27. Vohryzek, J., et al.: Dynamic spatiotemporal patterns of brain connectivity reorganize across development. Netw. Neurosci. **4**, 115–133 (2020)

Edge-Variational Graph Convolutional Networks for Uncertainty-Aware Disease Prediction

Yongxiang Huang[✉] and Albert C. S. Chung

Lo Kwee-Seong Medical Image Analysis Laboratory, Department of Computer Science and Engineering, The Hong Kong University of Science and Technology, Hong Kong, China
{yhuangch,achung}@cse.ust.hk

Abstract. There is a rising need for computational models that can complementarily leverage data of different modalities while investigating associations between subjects for population-based disease analysis. Despite the success of convolutional neural networks in representation learning for imaging data, it is still a very challenging task. In this paper, we propose a generalizable framework that can automatically integrate imaging data with non-imaging data in populations for uncertainty-aware disease prediction. At its core is a learnable adaptive population graph with variational edges, which we mathematically prove that it is optimizable in conjunction with graph convolutional neural networks. To estimate the predictive uncertainty related to the graph topology, we propose the novel concept of Monte-Carlo edge dropout. Experimental results on four databases show that our method can consistently and significantly improve the diagnostic accuracy for Autism spectrum disorder, Alzheimer's disease, and ocular diseases, indicating its generalizability in leveraging multimodal data for computer-aided diagnosis.

Keywords: Population-based disease prediction · Graph neural network · Deep learning

1 Introduction

Integrating imaging data with non-imaging data for disease diagnosis is an essential task in clinics. In recent years, the increasing volume of digitalized multimodal data has raised the need for computational models with the capability of exploiting different modalities automatically for improving prediction accuracy and discovering new biomarkers to study the disease mechanism (e.g., Alzheimer's disease) [23]. Despite the success of convolutional neural networks (CNNs) in medical images [8,14], exploiting both imaging and non-imaging data in populations in a unified model can be challenging. Multimodal learning-based approaches usually summarize features of all modalities with a deep neural network for disease classification [26], which ignore the interaction and association

© Springer Nature Switzerland AG 2020
A. L. Martel et al. (Eds.): MICCAI 2020, LNCS 12267, pp. 562–572, 2020.
https://doi.org/10.1007/978-3-030-59728-3_55

between subjects in a population. Graphs provide a natural way to represent the population data and enable the use of powerful tools such as clustering algorithms for disease analysis. Moreover, recent studies on graph convolutional neural networks (GCNs) [11,24] have extended the theory of signal processing on graphs [20] to complement the representation learning limitation of CNNs on irregular graph data.

In this work, we present a generalizable framework to automatically integrate multimodal data in populations for disease prediction with uncertainty estimation. Our contributions include: i) proposing a novel adaptive population graph model for representing multimodal features and associations for subjects and mathematically showing that it can be optimized in conjunction with spectral GCNs, which makes semi-supervised learning with GCNs generalizable for medical databases, ii) proposing Monte-Carlo edge dropout for estimating the predictive uncertainty with respect to the graph topology, which is new and extendable for graph neural networks, iii) designing a well-regularized spectral graph convolutional network for population-based disease prediction, alleviating the over-smoothing problem, and iv) extensively evaluating our method and recent multimodal learning methods on four challenging databases, which shows the proposed method can significantly improve the diagnostic performance for brain analysis and ocular diseases. (To the best of our knowledge, it is also the first study of GCNs on population-based ocular disease analysis.).

Related Work. Recent studies [11,13,24] have shown that a graph can serve as a regularizer on node classification tasks for semi-supervised learning with GCNs. However, these methods are evaluated on graph benchmarks where the associations between nodes are inherently defined in the data (e.g., a citation dataset [11]). Contrastively, in the medical domain, the associations between subjects (i.e., nodes) are usually uncertain and multifaceted, especially for multimodal databases. The absence of well-defined relation between two nodes leads to the uncertainty of graph topology, making it hard to adopt GCNs for population-based disease diagnosis. A few recent studies investigated the construction of affinity graphs by computing the correlation distance between subjects for brain analysis [9,17]. These methods require to manually tune distance thresholds for different modalities for the graph construction, which can heavily fluctuate the performance, leading to a lack of generalizability.

2   Methods

In this section, we present the proposed model, namely Edge-Variational GCN (EV-GCN), for incorporating multimodal data for disease prediction. The overview of the pipeline is depicted in Fig. 1. EV-GCN accepts the imaging features and non-imaging data of N subjects and constructs an adaptive population graph with partially labeled nodes and variational edges, followed by the proposed spectral graph convolutional network with edge dropout for learning to estimate the diagnostic value and the uncertainty for each testing subject.

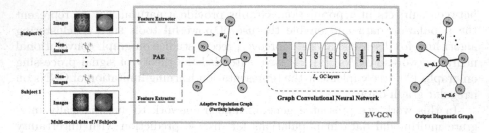

Fig. 1. Overview of the proposed method. PAE: pairwise association encoder. ED: edge dropout. GC: graph convolution. Fusion: vertex-wise concatenation. Colors in the graphs: green and orange - labeled diagnostic values (e.g., healthy or diseased), grey: unlabeled. u_i: predictive uncertainty for subject i. (Color figure online)

2.1 Edge-Variational Population Graph Modeling

Given the observation of N subjects composed of imaging and non-imaging data, let us consider constructing a population graph $G = (V, E, W)$, where V is a finite set of vertices with $|V| = N$, $E \subseteq V \times V$ is a set of edges with W being the edge weights. To associate a vertex $v \in V$ with the diagnostic features of a subject, we define the node feature $Z_i \in \mathbb{R}^C$ as a C-dimensional feature vector extracted from the imaging data of subject i, under the observation that imaging data (e.g., histology images, functional MRI) usually provide the most important evidence for diagnosis. The modeling for the graph connectivity (i.e., edge weight) is critical for the task performance as it encodes the associations between subjects. Unlike previous methods modeling the edge weight statistically [9,17], we propose to define the edge weight $w_{i,j} \in W$ between the i-th and j-th vertices as a learnable function of their non-imaging measurements $(\mathbf{x}_i, \mathbf{x}_j)$, considering non-imaging data can provide additional information (e.g., gender, age, gene) complementary to imaging features and explain potential association. The learnable function $f : (\mathbf{x}_i, \mathbf{x}_j) \mapsto \mathbb{R}$ is modeled by the proposed pairwise association encoder (PAE) with trainable parameters Ω such that $w_{i,j} = f(\mathbf{x}_i, \mathbf{x}_j; \Omega)$.

Pairwise Association Encoder. The PAE starts by normalizing the multi-modal inputs $\mathbf{x}_i$ and $\mathbf{x}_j$ to zero-mean and unit-variance element-wisely to avoid the gradient vanishing problem, which is important in our setting as data from different modalities have various statistical properties. After normalization, we use a projection network to map each normalized input to a common latent space $\mathbf{h}_i \in \mathbb{R}^{D_h}$ where cosine similarity can be better applied ($D_h = 128$). The projection network is a multi-layer perceptron (MLP) with L_p hidden layers. We set $L_p = 1$ in experiments and the latent feature for $\mathbf{x}_i$ is formulated as $\mathbf{h}_i = \Omega^{(2)}\sigma(\Omega^{(1)}\tilde{\mathbf{x}}_i + b)$, where σ is a ReLU function and $\tilde{\mathbf{x}}_i$ is the normalized input. Formally, the PAE scores the association between vertices i and j as

$$w_{i,j} = \frac{\mathbf{h}_i^\top \mathbf{h}_j}{2\|\mathbf{h}_i\|\|\mathbf{h}_j\|} + 0.5, \tag{1}$$

which gives the rescaled cosine similarity between two latent features. In training, the parameter Ω in PAE is initialized by He Initialization. Each hidden layer is equipped with batch normalization and dropout to improve convergence and avoid overfitting. Notably, we find it beneficial and robust to define the pairwise association on the latent space rather than on the input space.

2.2   Spectral Graph Convolutions on Adaptive Graphs

In this section, we first present spectral graph convolutions and prove the connectivity of the proposed adaptive population graph can be optimized in conjunction with a spectral GCN, followed by presenting our GCN architecture.

A spectral convolution of a graph signal x with a filter g_θ is defined as $g_\theta \star x = U g_\theta U^T x$, where U is the matrix of eigenvectors of the normalized graph Laplacian $L = I_N - D^{-1/2} W D^{1/2}$ with D being the diagonal degree matrix (i.e., L encodes the topological structure of graph G). The intuition behind is that spatial graph convolutions can be computed in the Fourier domain as multiplications using graph Fourier transform (GFT) [20]. To reduce the computational cost ($\mathcal{O}(N^2)$), *Chebyshev graph convolution* (ChebyGConv) [4] approximates spectral graph convolution using Chebyshev polynomials.[1] A K-order ChebyGConv is given by $g_{\theta'} \star x \approx \sum_{k=0}^{K} T_k(\tilde{L}) \theta'_k x$, where $\tilde{L}$ is the rescaled graph Laplacian, $T_k(\tilde{L}) = 2\tilde{L} T_{k-1}(\tilde{L}) - T_{k-2}(\tilde{L})$ is the Chebyshev polynomial defined recursively with $T_0(\tilde{L}) = 1$ and $T_1(\tilde{L}) = \tilde{L}$, and θ'_k are the filter parameters. As an analogy to CNNs, the polynomial term $T_k(\tilde{L})$ acts as a k-localized aggregator, i.e., it combines the neighboring nodes that are k-step away from the central node, and θ'_k acts as a node feature transformer.

Claim: *The graph connectivity modeled by PAE can be optimized in conjunction with a spectral graph convolutional model using gradient descent algorithms.*

Proof: Let us consider a convolution layer $l + 1$ in a GCN and its input graph $G^l = (V^l, E^l, W)$ with $|V^l| = N$ C^l-dimensional node feature vectors $\mathbf{H}^l \in \mathbf{R}^{N \times C^l}$. The convolution layer computes the output features as

$$\mathbf{H}^{l+1} = \sum_{k=0}^{K} T_k(\tilde{L}) \mathbf{H}^l \Theta_k^l, \tag{2}$$

where $\Theta_k^l \in \mathbf{R}^{C^l \times C^{l+1}}$ are the filter parameters. Denote $\mathcal{L}$ as the task-related loss function. To optimize the graph connectivity modeled by PAE by gradient descents, we need to guarantee that $\mathcal{L}$ is differentiable w.r.t. the parameters Ω of PAE. By chain rule, we have $\frac{\partial \mathcal{L}}{\partial \Omega} = \frac{\partial \mathcal{L}}{\partial \mathbf{H}^l} \frac{\partial \mathbf{H}^l}{\partial W} \frac{\partial W}{\partial \Omega}$. Both $\frac{\partial \mathcal{L}}{\partial \mathbf{H}^l}$ and $\frac{\partial W}{\partial \Omega}$ are derivable as they correspond to the gradients in the differentiable GCN and PAE respectively. The key is the derivative of the node feature vectors w.r.t. the

---

[1] ChebyGConv can achieve localized filtering on an irregular weighted graph with moderate computational cost, and comparatively performs well for our tasks.

input edge weights $\frac{\partial \mathbf{H}^l}{\partial W}$. For $K = 1$, based on Eq. 2, we can derive $\frac{\partial \mathbf{H}^l}{\partial W}\big|_{K=1} = \frac{\partial(I_N - D^{-1/2}WD^{1/2})}{\partial W}$, which is derivable. For $K > 1$, since the polynomial term $T_k(\tilde{L})$ in Eq. 2 is defined recursively for $k > 1$, by expanding $T_k(\tilde{L})$ and by induction we can derive that $\frac{\partial \mathbf{H}^l}{\partial W}$ is derivable and not a constant zero. Thus, the graph connectivity can be optimized to minimize the task loss.

GCN Architecture. As depicted in Fig. 1, our GCN model consists of L_G Chebyshev graph convolutional layers, each followed by ReLU activation to increase non-linearity, a fusion block, and an MLP predictor. To alleviate the over-smoothing problem [13] in deep GCNs, we propose to adopt jumping connections [25] with vertex-wise concatenation to fuse the hidden features in each depth, i.e., $\{\mathbf{H}^l\}_{l=1}^{L_G}$. We find jumping connections are more effective than residual connections [7] in avoiding a performance deterioration as L_G increases. The MLP predictor consists of two 1×1 convolutional layers (i.e., vertex-wise transformations) with 256 and C_k channels respectively, followed by a softmax function to drive a C_k-class disease probability vector for each subject. We employ cross-entropy loss on the labeled nodes to train the overall model.

2.3   Monte-Carlo Edge Dropout for Uncertainty Estimation

Motivated by Bayesian approximation for uncertainty estimation in CNNs [6,10,27], we propose *Monte-Carlo edge dropout* (MCED) to estimate the uncertainty for the constructed population graph structure.

In detail, edge dropout randomly drops a fraction of edges in the graph by placing a Bernoulli distributional mask on each $e \in E$, which can act as a graph data augmenter to reduce overfitting [19] and increase the graph sparsity in training. For inference, similar to Monte-Carlo dropout [10] for uncertainty estimation in CNNs, MCED performs T stochastic forward passes on the GCN model under random edge dropout on the population graph, and obtain T disease probability vectors for a subject i: $\{\mathbf{p}_i^{(t)}\}_{t=1}^T$ (We set $T = 128$ in our experiments). We adopt the mean predictive entropy [10] as the metric to quantize the uncertainty. Formally, the uncertainty u_i for subject i is given by $u_i = -\sum_c \mathbf{m}_{i,c} \log \mathbf{m}_{i,c}$ and $\mathbf{m}_i = \frac{1}{T}\sum_t \mathbf{p}_i^{(t)}$, where c corresponds to the c-th class. While MC dropout estimates the uncertainty on the neural network weights [6], MCED models the uncertainty on the graph topology, which is orthogonal.

3   Experiments and Results

In this section, we perform experimental evaluations of the proposed method, comparing our method with several SoTA methods for disease prediction. We consider two graph-based methods that exploit GCNs (i.e., AIG [9] and Parisot et al. [17]), a multimodal learning method (i.e., DNN-JFC [26]), and task-related unimodal methods [3,21,22].

3.1   Autism Spectrum Disorder Prediction on the ABIDE Database

Dataset and Experimental Setting. The Autism Brain Imaging Data Exchange (**ABIDE**) [5] publicly shares neuroimaging (functional magnetic resonance imaging (fMRI)) and the corresponding phenotypic data (e.g., age, gender, and acquisition site) of 1112 subjects, with binary labels indicating the presence of Autism Spectrum Disorder (ASD). For a fair comparison with the ABIDE state-of-the-art [3,9], we choose the same 871 subjects consisting of 403 normal and 468 ASD individuals, use 10-fold cross-validation, and perform the same data preprocessing steps [3] to extract a $C = 2000$ dimensional feature vector from fMRI representing a subject's functional connectivity [3]. Phenotypic data is used to compute the pairwise association.

In our experiments, we set Cheybyshev polynomial order $K = 3$ and $L_G = 4$. All models are trained using Adam optimizer with learning rate 0.01, weight decay 5×10^{-5}, and dropout rate 0.2 for 300 epochs to avoid overfitting.

Table 1. Quantitative comparisons between different methods on ABIDE. MM: multi-modality, ×: only imaging data is used, ✓: both imaging and non-imaging data are used. β is a threshold for constructing a static affinity graph used in AIG.

Methods	MM	Accuracy	AUC	F1-score	#Param. (K)
Abraham et al. [3]	×	66.80	-	-	-
DNN	×	73.25 ± 3.69	74.16 ± 4.64	74.81 ± 4.86	550
DNN-JFC [26]	✓	73.59 ± 4.15	73.48 ± 4.94	76.89 ± 4.27	635
Parisot et al. [17]	✓	75.66 ± 4.69	81.05 ± 6.13	78.85 ± 4.66	96
AIG [9]	✓	76.12 ± 6.83	80.11 ± 6.49	79.27 ± 5.27	290
AIG, $\beta = 3$ [9]	✓	72.10 ± 7.12	75.43 ± 8.85	73.55 ± 6.94	290
This work:					
EV-GCN	✓	80.83 ± 4.92	$\mathbf{84.98 \pm 5.74}$	81.24 ± 5.76	133
+ MCED	✓	$\mathbf{81.06 \pm 4.83}$	84.72 ± 6.27	$\mathbf{82.86 \pm 5.51}$	133

Table 2. Ablation study for this work. This table shows how different factors affect the performance of our method. The compared GCN architectures share the same depth. Plain: sequential GC layers. Inception: InceptionGCN [9].

Factor	Graph construction			GCN architecture			Edge dropout
Method	Random	Affinity	Adaptive	Plain	Inception	Ours	w/o ED
Accuracy	65.67	76.81	**80.83**	79.79	80.02	80.83	80.58
AUC	73.97	80.49	**84.98**	83.10	83.74	84.98	84.27

Results and Analysis. Table 1 shows the comparative results on ABIDE, where the mean and confidence interval ($p < 0.05$) are computed across ten different initialisation seeds. DNN-JFC [26] summarizes the features of all modalities by jointly fully connected layers, which marginally outperforms a DNN (i.e. MLP) on the fMRI features. Comparatively, graph-based methods (Parisot, AIG, and ours) yield larger performance gains, benefiting from exploiting associations between subjects in the population graphs. The proposed method, EV-GCN+MCED, obtains an average accuracy of 81.06%, outperforming the recent SoTA method AIG [9], which employs static affinity graphs with InceptionGCN, by a margin of 4.94% accuracy with fewer parameters. We notice that the performance of AIG is highly sensitive to the threshold β for computing age affinity, where the best $\beta = 2$ yields an average accuracy of 76.12%. To investigate the importance of learning an adaptive graph with variational edges, we train our GCN architecture on the same affinity graph used in AIG [9] and on a population graph with random connections. As depicted in Table 2, it results in a 4.02% (Affinity) and 15.16% (Random) accuracy drop respectively, indicating that the adaptive graph modeling is indeed key to achieving the best possible performance. Meanwhile, the effectiveness of the proposed GCN architecture and edge dropout regularization in training are ablatively validated in Table 2.

Table 3. Accuracy and uncertainty for models with different association (i.e. edge) inputs. We show the uncertainty as the mean value of all test subjects.

Association input	Accuracy	Uncertainty
Random noise	65.67	0.620
Gender	78.53	0.465
Gender, age	78.07	0.394
Site, gender, age	**81.06**	**0.307**

To analyze what the uncertainty estimated by MCED captures, we give the accuracy and uncertainty for models trained with different association sources (i.e. input for PAE) in Table 3. The results demonstrate that the graph uncertainty, which is approximated by averaging the predictive uncertainty of all test subjects, can be gradually eliminated with sufficient information for learning the pairwise association. The results in Table 1 and Table 3 show that MCED uncertainty estimation, on one hand, can be adopted as an ensemble approach to improve the diagnostic performance (+1.62% F1-score), and on the other hand, can be used to detect patients with highly uncertain diagnostic value, which is important for safety-critical CAD systems in reducing misdiagnosis rate.

3.2 Alzheimer's Disease Prediction on ADNI

ADNI [1] is a large-scale database and contains longitudinal brain MRI, PET data, genetic, and phenotypic information of over 1700 adults for Alzheimer's disease (AD) study. In this work, we select the same 1675 samples with Mild Cognitive Impairments (MCI) used in Parisot [17] to facilitate a fair comparison, among which 843 acquisitions will convert to AD as diagnosed during the follow-up. For the imaging feature vector, we use the volumes of $C = 138$ segmented brain structures extracted from MRI using MALP-EM [12], which are proven effective biomarkers for AD assessment [18]. We use phenotypic (age, gender) and genetic (APOE [16]) data for computing the pairwise association.

TADPOLE. [15] is a preprocessed subset of ADNI, consisting of 557 subjects each with over 350 multimodal features. Following AIG [9], the task is to classify each subject into three classes: cognitive normal, MCI, and AD. We use the segmentation features derived from MRI and PET data to obtain a 340-dimensional feature vector for each subject and use the phenotypic data, APOE and FDG-PET biomarkers for the graph construction.

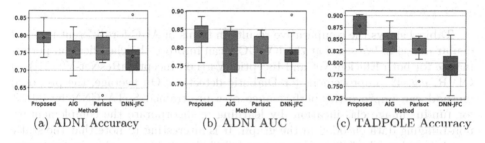

| (a) ADNI Accuracy | (b) ADNI AUC | (c) TADPOLE Accuracy |

Fig. 2. Comparative boxplots on ADNI (a, b) and TADPOLE (c) for Alzheimer's disease prediction. Results are computed from 10-fold cross-validation.

Results. Comparative boxplots for ten folds between the four methods are shown in Fig. 2. We can observe that the proposed method (EV-GCN+MCED) outperforms the competing methods on both datasets. For prediction AD conversion on ADNI, we achieve an average accuracy of 79.4%, corresponding to a 3.9% increase over the competing method Parisot [17]. For TADPOLE, our method obtains an average accuracy of 87.8%, outperforming the recent SoTA method AIG [9] (84.3%). The results also imply the generalizability of our method.

3.3 Ocular Disease Diagnosis on the ODIR Dataset

Dataset and Experimental Setting. The ODIR dataset [2] shares fundus photographs and non-imaging data including age, gender and diagnostic words of 3000 patients. Each patient has 8 binary labels for 7 types of ocular diseases including diabetes, glaucoma, etc. We compare our method with two recent SoTA CNNs [21,22] and the graph-based SoTA AIG [9], using 5-fold cross-validation. For population graph construction, we use the compared CNN without classification layers as a feature extractor to derive a C dimensional feature vector from the fundus images (for both eyes) of a patient ($C = 3072$ for InceptionV4 [21] and $C = 2048$ for EfficientNet-B0 [22]), and use the demographic data for association modeling. Diagnostic words are not used to avoid label leaking.

Table 4. Quantitative results on ODIR. (I) or (E): InceptionV4 [21] or EfficientNet [22] is used for imaging feature extraction. D: Diabetes, G: Glaucoma, C: Cataract, Overall: all 8 classes.

Methods	D	G	C	Overall
InceptionV4 [21]	64.26	69.89	95.34	84.00 ± 11.35
EV-GCN (I)	68.49	70.31	94.22	86.62 ± 11.26
EfficientNet [22]	66.90	71.91	**95.91**	84.31 ± 12.11
EV-GCN (E)	**70.78**	**73.24**	95.18	**87.63 ± 9.88**
AIG [9] (E)	58.61	68.08	87.60	78.47 ± 14.79

Table 4 shows the comparative results in terms of AUC for different types of ocular diseases. We see that the EV-GCN can improve the classification performance for both EfficientNet and InceptionV4 (i.e., InceptionResNet-V2 [21]) on ODIR, e.g. 4% improvement for Diabetic detection. On average, the proposed method can improve the performance of a pre-trained SoTA CNN by 2.97% for fundus image classification, by learning to incorporate the complementary non-imaging data encoded in the graph. It is interesting to note that the static graph-based method [9], where the required thresholds are already finetuned, degrades the performance for EfficientNet, which reassures the robustness of constructing a learnable population graph compared to a hand-crafted one.

4   Discussion and Conclusions

In this paper, we have proposed a generalizable graph-convolutional framework to tackle the challenges in learning from multi-modal data for disease prediction. Unlike previous methods, the proposed method does not hand-engineer a similarity population graph but learn to construct the graph connectivity which is mathematically proven to be optimizable with GCNs. The proposed Monte-Carlo edge dropout is the first study on graph uncertainty estimation for GCNs and is experimentally validated to be beneficial, while we admit that it requires further theoretical justification in future work. Extensive experimental results show that the proposed method can achieve superior performance on brain analysis and ocular disease prediction. Additionally, the estimated predictive uncertainty allows detecting the uncertain samples for clinical intervention, contributing to a safer deep learning-assisted diagnosis system. We believe such an extendable method can have a great impact in unlocking a better use of multi-modal data in populations for computer-aided diagnosis in clinics.

References

1. Alzheimer's Disease Neuroimaging Initiative (2019). http://adni.loni.usc.edu/
2. Ocular Disease Intelligent Recognition (2019). https://odir2019.grand-challenge. org/dataset/
3. Abraham, A., et al.: Deriving reproducible biomarkers from multi-site resting-state data: an autism-based example. NeuroImage **147**, 736–745 (2017)
4. Defferrard, M., Bresson, X., Vandergheynst, P.: Convolutional neural networks on graphs with fast localized spectral filtering. In: Advances in Neural Information Processing Systems, pp. 3844–3852 (2016)
5. Di Martino, A., et al.: The autism brain imaging data exchange: towards a large-scale evaluation of the intrinsic brain architecture in autism. Mol. Psychiatry **19**(6), 659–667 (2014)
6. Gal, Y., Ghahramani, Z.: Dropout as a Bayesian approximation: representing model uncertainty in deep learning. In: International Conference on Machine Learning, pp. 1050–1059 (2016)
7. He, K., Zhang, X., Ren, S., Sun, J.: Deep residual learning for image recognition. In: Proceedings of the IEEE Conference on Computer Vision and Pattern Recognition, pp. 770–778 (2016)
8. Huang, Y., Chung, A.C.S.: Evidence localization for pathology images using weakly supervised learning. In: Shen, D., et al. (eds.) MICCAI 2019. LNCS, vol. 11764, pp. 613–621. Springer, Cham (2019). https://doi.org/10.1007/978-3-030-32239-7_68
9. Kazi, A., et al.: InceptionGCN: receptive field aware graph convolutional network for disease prediction. In: Chung, A.C.S., Gee, J.C., Yushkevich, P.A., Bao, S. (eds.) IPMI 2019. LNCS, vol. 11492, pp. 73–85. Springer, Cham (2019). https:// doi.org/10.1007/978-3-030-20351-1_6
10. Kendall, A., Gal, Y.: What uncertainties do we need in Bayesian deep learning for computer vision? In: Advances in Neural Information Processing Systems, pp. 5574–5584 (2017)
11. Kipf, T.N., Welling, M.: Semi-supervised classification with graph convolutional networks. arXiv preprint arXiv:1609.02907 (2016)
12. Ledig, C., Heckemann, R.A., Rueckert, D., et al.: Robust whole-brain segmentation: application to traumatic brain injury. Med. Image Anal. **21**(1), 40–58 (2015)
13. Li, Q., Han, Z., Wu, X.M.: Deeper insights into graph convolutional networks for semi-supervised learning. In: Thirty-Second AAAI Conference on Artificial Intelligence (2018)
14. Litjens, G., Kooi, T., Sánchez, C.I., et al.: A survey on deep learning in medical image analysis. Med. Image Anal. **42**, 60–88 (2017)
15. Marinescu, R.V., Oxtoby, N.P., Alexander, D.C., et al.: Tadpole challenge: prediction of longitudinal evolution in Alzheimer's disease. arXiv preprint arXiv:1805.03909 (2018)
16. Mosconi, L., Perani, D., Padovani, A., et al.: MCI conversion to dementia and the APOE genotype: a prediction study with FDG-PET. Neurology **63**(12), 2332–2340 (2004)
17. Parisot, S., et al.: Spectral graph convolutions for population-based disease prediction. In: Descoteaux, M., Maier-Hein, L., Franz, A., Jannin, P., Collins, D.L., Duchesne, S. (eds.) MICCAI 2017. LNCS, vol. 10435, pp. 177–185. Springer, Cham (2017). https://doi.org/10.1007/978-3-319-66179-7_21
18. Ries, M.L., et al.: Magnetic resonance imaging characterization of brain structure and function in mild cognitive impairment: a review. J. Am. Geriatr. Soc. **56**(5), 920–934 (2008)

19. Rong, Y., Huang, W., Xu, T., Huang, J.: The truly deep graph convolutional networks for node classification. arXiv preprint arXiv:1907.10903 (2019)
20. Shuman, D.I., Narang, S.K., Vandergheynst, P., et al.: The emerging field of signal processing on graphs: extending high-dimensional data analysis to networks and other irregular domains. IEEE Signal Process. Mag. **30**(3), 83–98 (2013)
21. Szegedy, C., Ioffe, S., Vanhoucke, V., Alemi, A.A.: Inception-v4, inception-resnet and the impact of residual connections on learning. In: Thirty-First AAAI Conference on Artificial Intelligence (2017)
22. Tan, M., Le, Q.: Efficientnet: rethinking model scaling for convolutional neural networks. In: International Conference on Machine Learning, pp. 6105–6114 (2019)
23. Trojanowski, J.Q., et al.: Update on the biomarker core of the Alzheimer's disease neuroimaging initiative subjects. Alzheimer's Dement. **6**(3), 230–238 (2010)
24. Wu, Z., Pan, S., Chen, F., Long, G., Zhang, C., Yu, P.S.: A comprehensive survey on graph neural networks. arXiv preprint arXiv:1901.00596 (2019)
25. Xu, K., Li, C., Tian, Y., Sonobe, T., Kawarabayashi, K.I., Jegelka, S.: Representation learning on graphs with jumping knowledge networks. In: International Conference on Machine Learning, pp. 5453–5462 (2018)
26. Xu, T., Zhang, H., Huang, X., Zhang, S., Metaxas, D.N.: Multimodal deep learning for cervical dysplasia diagnosis. In: Ourselin, S., Joskowicz, L., Sabuncu, M.R., Unal, G., Wells, W. (eds.) MICCAI 2016. LNCS, vol. 9901, pp. 115–123. Springer, Cham (2016). https://doi.org/10.1007/978-3-319-46723-8_14
27. Yu, L., Wang, S., Li, X., Fu, C.-W., Heng, P.-A.: Uncertainty-aware self-ensembling model for semi-supervised 3D left atrium segmentation. In: Shen, D., et al. (eds.) MICCAI 2019. LNCS, vol. 11765, pp. 605–613. Springer, Cham (2019). https://doi.org/10.1007/978-3-030-32245-8_67

Fisher-Rao Regularized Transport Analysis of the Glymphatic System and Waste Drainage

Rena Elkin[1], Saad Nadeem[1(✉)], Hedok Lee[2], Helene Benveniste[2], and Allen Tannenbaum[3]

[1] Department of Medical Physics, Memorial Sloan Kettering Cancer Center, New York, NY 10065, USA
nadeems@mskcc.org
[2] Department of Anesthesiology, Yale School of Medicine, New Haven, CT 06519, USA
[3] Departments of Computer Science and Applied Mathematics and Statistics, Stony Brook University, Stony Brook, NY 11794, USA

Abstract. In this work, a unified representation of all the time-varying dynamics is accomplished with a Lagrangian framework for analyzing Fisher-Rao regularized dynamical optimal mass transport (OMT) derived flows. While formally equivalent to the Eulerian based Schrödinger bridge OMT regularization scheme, the Fisher-Rao approach allows a simple and interpretable methodology for studying the flows of interest in the present work. The advantage of the proposed Lagrangian technique is that the time-varying particle trajectories and attributes are displayed in a single visualization. This provides a natural capability to identify and distinguish flows under different conditions. The Lagrangian analysis applied to the glymphatic system (brain waste removal pathway associated with Alzheimer's Disease) successfully captures known flows and distinguishes between flow patterns under two different anesthetics, providing deeper insights into altered states of waste drainage.

Keywords: Optimal mass transport · Glymphatic system · Fisher-Rao regularization

1 Introduction

The optimal mass transport problem (OMT) entails minimizing the transportation cost associated with redistributing one probability distribution to match another. The static OMT formulation has been applied to medical image processing and registration [9,11,12]. The dynamical version of OMT [1] opened up new possibilities for numerical solutions and extensions using tools from the field of fluid dynamics [3,21]. In particular, the authors consider a regularization of the dynamical OMT formulation [1] for modeling apparent fluid flow in

© Springer Nature Switzerland AG 2020
A. L. Martel et al. (Eds.): MICCAI 2020, LNCS 12267, pp. 573–582, 2020.
https://doi.org/10.1007/978-3-030-59728-3_56

dynamic contrast enhanced MRI (DCE-MRI) images where a diffusion term has been added to the Euler equation [7,8]. Contrast transport derived using earlier models without a diffusion term were vulnerable to noise in the data [23], making the inclusion of a diffusion term advantageous from both physical and numerical standpoints. Analysis of the resulting velocity fields is typically carried out in an Eulerian framework, i.e., flow properties are considered at specific locations for each time point as compared to the Lagrangian framework, which tracks specific particles as they move over time; see Fig. 1.

The Lagrangian approach gives a useful alternative to the Eulerian scheme and has recently been presented in conjunction with the aforementioned regularized version of OMT [16]. The pipeline taken from this work has untapped practical applications for distinguishing elusive physiologically relevant flow patterns and so we adopt it in the present work to study the glymphatic system (GS) and brain waste drainage. In [16], the authors employ a regularized version of OMT by adding a diffusion term to the continuity equation in the Benamou-Brenier formulation of OMT [1]. It turns out that there are two equivalent ways to derive the Lagrangian coordinates of the optimal trajectories. The first is via a transformation of the advection-diffusion equation in the regularized problem, and the second by adding a Fisher-Rao information type term to the kinetic energy in the original dynamic formulation [4]. In the present work, we adopt the second method, i.e., Fisher-Rao regularization. We should note that employing Lagrangian coordinates derives improved visualizations of GS function in a time efficient display and also reveals new disparate dynamic waste drainage features in two different states of arousal that were previously difficult to discern.

Waste products are removed from the brain through the GS, a peri-vascular transit passage for cerebrospinal fluid (CSF) which facilitates mixing of CSF with interstitial fluid [14]. Impaired waste clearance due to glymphatic dysfunction has been associated with vascular dementia, Alzheimer's Disease (AD) [22] and sleep deprivation [24]. The GS accelerates waste clearance from the brain during slow wave sleep and with certain hypnotics when compared to other anesthetics and wakefulness [28]. A recent study showed that unconsciousness induced with dexmedetomidine and low dose isoflurane (DEXM+ISO) that mimics natural sleep enhances GS function to a greater extent when compared to deep anesthesia induced with isoflurane (ISO) [2]. These results suggest that hypnotic drugs that promote 'natural' sleep might be superior to deeper states of sleep/anesthesia regarding preservation of sleep like GS function. Novel ways to improve or maintain GS function for general brain health is urgently needed and dependent on developing robust analysis tools to quantify its function.

The main contributions of this work are as follows:

1. We directly use the Fisher-Rao regularization of the energy functional in visualizing the flows, highlighting the framework's natural treatment of small diffusion values needed for studying the GS.
2. We successfully differentiate between GS flow patterns under two different anesthetics and provide additional new insights, in particular, to the rela-

tionship between GS flow and solute clearance via pathways outside of the brain.

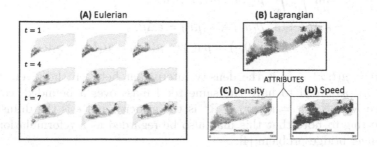

Fig. 1. Eulerian and Lagrangian visualizations of flow dynamics. (A) for each time point, streamlines are computed at a fixed set of initial locations. Color is used to distinguish streamline clusters and time-varying flow behavior is observed by comparing streamlines across time. (B) alternatively, temporal changes in particle trajectories are encompassed by pathlines and presented in a single image. Time-varying particle attributes associated with the pathlines, such as (C) density and (D) speed, exemplify the simplistic yet informative nature of our unified visualization framework.

2 Background

2.1 Regularized OMT

As alluded to above, the problem of optimal mass transport (OMT) is concerned with moving mass from one site to another so that minimal 'work' is expended, and mass is preserved, see [26,27] for a complete set of references. For our purposes with respect to medical images, we are interested in the dynamical OMT formulation due to Benamou and Brenier [1]. They proposed an alternative numerical solution by introducing time and solving a partial differential equation constrained space-time minimization problem. This formulation has the geometric interpretation of finding geodesics [20] between the given densities μ_0 and μ_1 in the space of probability densities and the trajectory of the transport is explicitly factored into the cost.

Explicit representation of the density's evolution suggests exciting capabilities for improved image registration techniques to account for dynamical aspects of physiological processes with additional aptitude for analyzing interesting time-varying phenomena. This is particularly powerful for medical applications where a complete physical model is often impractical to implement. We consider the following modified version of Benamou and Brenier's OMT formulation where a diffusion term is added in the continuity equation. The following *regularized OMT* problem over the normalized time interval $t \in [0,1]$ is used to motivate the Lagrangian framework for flow representation [16] that will be detailed in the next section:

$$\inf_{\mu,\nu} \int_0^1 \int_{\mathcal{R}} \mu(t,x) \|\nu(t,x)\|^2 \, dx \, dt \qquad (1)$$

$$\text{subject to } \partial_t \mu + \nabla \cdot (\mu\nu) = \epsilon \Delta \mu, \qquad (2)$$

$$\mu(0,\cdot) = \mu_0(\cdot), \quad \mu(1,\cdot) = \mu_1(\cdot), \ \epsilon > 0 \qquad (3)$$

where $\mu = \mu(t,x) \in \mathbb{R}$ is the density interpolant between the given densities μ_0 and μ_1, assumed to have the same total mass over a bounded, connected subspace $\mathcal{R}$ of $\mathbb{R}^d$, $\nu = \nu(t,x) \in \mathbb{R}^d$ is the velocity and ϵ is the diffusivity. It is interesting to note that this may also be regarded as a reformulation of the Schrödinger bridge problem [4].

3 Lagrangian Coordinates

Following [16], the optimal trajectory in Lagrangian coordinates for the regularized case is defined as follows. Let μ_{min} and ν_{min} denote the minimum arguments of the action (1) subject to (2). Define the augmented velocity

$$\hat{\nu}(t,x) = \nu(t,x) - \epsilon \nabla \log \mu(t,x). \qquad (4)$$

Noticing that

$$\nabla \cdot (\mu\hat{\nu}) = \nabla \cdot [(\nu - \epsilon \nabla \log \mu)\mu] = \nabla \cdot (\mu\nu) - \epsilon \Delta \mu, \qquad (5)$$

leads to the following conservation form of the constraint (2):

$$\partial_t \mu + \nabla \cdot (\mu\hat{\nu}) = 0. \qquad (6)$$

Analogous to [1], the Lagrangian coordinates of the flow $X = X(t,x)$ corresponding to the minimizing velocity ν_{min} is the solution of the differential equation

$$X(0,x) = x, \quad \partial_t X = \hat{\nu}_{min}(t, X(t,x)), \qquad (7)$$

where according to (4), $\hat{\nu}_{min} = \nu_{min} - \epsilon \nabla \log \mu_{min}$.

3.1 Fisher-Rao Regularization

It is very important to note that the regularized OMT problem is equivalent to a Fisher-Rao information theoretic regularization of OMT, which is very closely connected to the Sinkhorn approach [6], and is in fact a dynamic formulation of the Schrödinger bridge problem [4]. For small ϵ in the advection-diffusion equation above, Sinkhorn will become unstable, which is why one needs to employ a different approach in the medical imaging realm. We will therefore derive an equivalent Lagrangian formulation of regularized OMT via the Fisher-Rao regularized functional. We should note that there are a number of works demonstrating the well-known equivalence of Fisher-Rao and OMT joint interpolation functional and regularized OMT including [4,5,18,19]. We briefly sketch the proof from these works to highlight some of the key steps of going from the regularized OMT problem to the Fisher-Rao regularized one. We refer the reader to the latter works for more details and insights into the methodology.

Following the notation of the previous section and references [4,5,18,19], we claim that the problem defined by (1–3) is equivalent to

$$\inf_{\mu,\hat{\nu}} \int_0^1 \int_{\mathcal{R}} \mu(t,x)(\|\hat{\nu}(t,x)\|^2 + \epsilon^2\|\nabla \log \mu(t,x)\|^2)\, dx\, dt + 2\epsilon H(\mu_1\|\mu_0) \quad (8)$$

$$\text{subject to}: \ \partial_t\mu + \nabla \cdot (\mu\hat{\nu}) = 0, \quad \mu(0,\cdot) = \mu_0(\cdot), \quad \mu(1,\cdot) = \mu_1(\cdot), \quad (9)$$

for time-varying densities $\mu = \mu(t,x) \in \mathbb{R}$ and velocities $\nu = \nu(t,x) \in \mathbb{R}^d$ where

$$H(\mu_1\|\mu_0) := \int_{\mathcal{R}} \mu_1(x) \log \mu_1(x) - \mu_0(x) \log \mu_0(x)\, dx. \quad (10)$$

Clearly, $H(\mu_1\|\mu_0)$ is a constant. Next, noting that

$$\hat{\nu}(t,x) + \epsilon\nabla \log \mu(t,x) = \nu(x,t) \quad (11)$$

and

$$\int_0^1 \int_{\mathcal{R}} \mu\|\hat{\nu} + \epsilon\nabla \log \mu\|^2 dxdt = \int_0^1 \int_{\mathcal{R}} \mu\|\hat{\nu}\|^2 + 2\epsilon\mu\langle\hat{\nu}, \nabla \log \mu\rangle + \epsilon^2\mu\|\nabla \log \mu\|^2 dxdt, \quad (12)$$

we just need to show that

$$J := \int_0^1 \int_{\mathcal{R}} \langle\mu\hat{\nu}, \nabla \log \mu\rangle\, dx\, dt = H(\mu_1\|\mu_0) \quad (13)$$

to verify our claim. However, using integration by parts and the constraints (9) we see that

$$J = -\int_0^1 \int_{\mathcal{R}} \nabla \cdot (\mu\hat{\nu}) \log \mu\, dx\, dt = -\int_0^1 \int_{\mathcal{R}} \mu\partial_t(\log \mu)\, dx\, dt + H(\mu_1\|\mu_0). \quad (14)$$

Finally,

$$\int_0^1 \int_{\mathcal{R}} \mu\partial_t(\log \mu)\, dx\, dt = \int_0^1 \int_{\mathcal{R}} \mu\frac{\partial_t\mu}{\mu}\, dx\, dt = \int_{\mathcal{R}} (\mu_1(x) - \mu_0(x))\, dx = 0 \quad (15)$$

since the total masses of μ_1 and μ_0 are equal.

Letting $\hat{\nu}_{min}$ denote the optimal vector field for (8–9), the Lagrangian coordinate solution is then exactly that given by (7) above. As previously noted, there are very fast algorithms for solving such entropic regularized versions of OMT for sufficiently large ϵ [6]. Since we need to consider small ϵ values, we directly solve (8–9) based on the numerical scheme given in [25] where the initial and final densities μ_0, μ_1 are taken from the given DCE-MRIs.

3.2 Pathlines

In order to represent the characteristics of the flow over all time in one comprehensive figure, we use the Lagrangian framework to construct what are commonly known as **pathlines**. A pathline $X(t,x)$ with initial position $X(0,x) = x$ is given by (7) and traces the trajectory of an individual particle through-out the time interval. As detailed in [16], additional information such as %-signal from baseline is used to determine regions where flow is more likely to occur. Throughout this region of interest, p seeding points, denoted x_l, are selected uniformly. Pathlines are then computed by integrating the augmented velocity (4) with initial positions x_l. The speed $\|\nu(t, X(t, x_l))\|$ of each particle is simultaneously computed along each pathline, referred to as the **speed pathline** and denoted $X_\nu = X_\nu(t, x_l)$, by (tri)linearly interpolating the derived velocity field.

Next, in order to extract pathlines that are representative of the flow behavior in specific anatomical regions, we subsequently cluster the pathlines by proximity using the QuickBundles algorithm [10]. All computations were implemented in MATLAB and the Lagrangian analysis took approximately 1 min to run for each of the 8 datasets (5 DEXM+ISO, 3 ISO) of resolution $128 \times 128 \times 128$.

4 Discussion

While streamlines and pathlines are interchangeable for steady flows (i.e. time independent), the same cannot be said for unsteady flows (i.e. time dependent). A novel aspect of the dynamical OMT formulation [1] is its explicit description of the density's time-varying evolution, suggesting the need for Lagrangian analysis of this behavior. The Lagrangian approach provides an elegant framework to observe various attributes such as speed and density along the pathlines. Having a single representation for the history of a particle and its attributes across time lends itself to a natural means for differentiating between flows under different conditions. We show the capability of this framework as it pertains to the GS and waste drainage.

GS transport can be observed with DCE-MRI in combination with administration of para-magnetic contrast agents (e.g. DOTAREM) into the CSF [17]. However, supplementary analysis is required to extract and distinguish characteristics of the GS transport patterns and flow. Current techniques for quantifying GS transport include assessment of brain parenchymal solute uptake or clearance [14], kinetic analysis [17], and k-means cluster analysis [13,15]. Kinetic analysis strategies provide a static 'snapshot' of GS transport over 2–3 h and provide global influx and efflux parameters however, regional information at the voxel level cannot be accurately derived due to heterogeneous transport kinetics across brain regions.

Here, we present a straightforward demonstration of the equivalence between the regularized dynamical OMT problem and the Fisher-Rao regularized variant in deriving the Lagrange coordinates associated with the flow. The Fisher-Rao perspective offers an accessible alternative methodology and deeper insight into the regularized OMT formulation as previously applied [16]. We apply the

Lagrangian pipeline to measure GS function based on DCE-MRIs acquired in rats while under two different states of unconsciousness - 'light' sleep/hypnosis with DEXM+ISO versus 'deep' sleep/anesthesia with ISO based on data from [2]. Specifically, we tested the Lagrangian OMT framework's ability to differentiate GS transport and solute drainage via pathways in the brain proper as well as along cranial efflux routes between these two different states of arousal.

Clustered pathlines derived from the Lagrangian framework are shown in Fig. 2. It is evident, based on the pathlines patterns observed in the rats under the two anesthetics, that GS transport function is different. With DEXM+ISO anesthesia, GS transport is accelerated (compared to ISO) as noted by the high density of pathlines extending into the parenchyma globally and along the middle cerebral artery (MCA). In contrast, the pathlines in rats anesthetized with ISO do not align with the MCA to the same extent and parenchymal uptake is also reduced in other areas including the midbrain and hippocampus. However, paradoxically, GS transport appears vigorous in the area of the olfactory bulb including solute efflux into the nasal conchae.

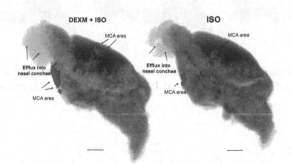

Fig. 2. Comprehensive pathline visualization of 130 min of glymphatic transport of DOTA (Gd-Dota) in a rat anesthetized with DEXM+ISO (left) and ISO (right). The pathlines in green are derived from the entire brain and nasal conchae. Both rats exhibit pathlines in the nasal conchae, signifying that Gd-DOTA exited along the olfactory nerves via the cribriform plate to lymphatic vessels in the submucosa of the nasal cavities. Pathlines that follow the middle cerebral artery (MCA) are outlined in red. More pathlines are clearly evident in the rat anesthetized with DEXM+ISO than ISO anesthesia, confirming that GS transport is more efficient during DEXM+ISO anesthesia. Scale bar = 3 mm. (Color figure online)

Figure 3 captures pathline speed (integrated over 130 min) through the GS in rats anesthetized with either DEXM+ISO or ISO. The speed pathlines associated with the whole brain are shown as a 3D volume rendered color-coded map. Higher and lower magnitudes of speed are represented by red and blue colors, respectively. More speed pathlines are apparent in the frontal part of the brain in the DEXM+ISO anesthetized rats compared to ISO. Paradoxically, in the ISO anesthetized state, pathline speed appears to be higher in the nasal conchae (arrows). In Fig. 4, we have captured the faster (red) and slower (green) moving speed lines, given in arbitrary units (a.u.) in an ISO anesthetized rat (Figs. 4A, B) compared to a DEXM+ISO anesthetized rat (Figs. 4C, D). It is obvious that the proportion of faster moving particles in the clustered pathlines is higher in ISO than DEXM+ISO anesthetized rats, as confirmed via quantitative analysis (Fig. 4E). These differences suggest that solute efflux to lymphatic vessels in the nasal conchae may be acting as an efflux 'valve' in the setting of impaired fluid flow in ISO anesthesia.

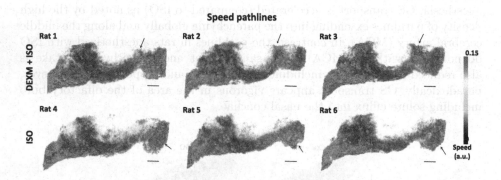

Fig. 3. Speed pathlines over 130 min of GS transport distinguishing flow behavior under two anesthetics, DEXM+ISO (top) and ISO (bottom). (Color figure online)

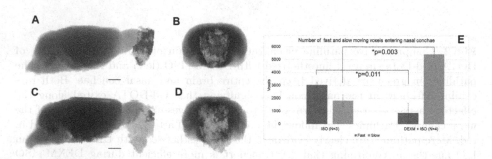

Fig. 4. Speed pathlines into the nasal conchae extracted from the GS speed 'connectome' and divided up into fast (red) speed lines with speed magnitude >0055 a.u. and slower (green) speed lines with speed magnitudes in the range of 0.001 − 0.050 a.u. (A, B) ISO anesthetized rats are characterized by rapid efflux of solute into the nasal cavity and (C, D) the vast majority of speed lines in the DEXM+ISO anesthetized rats are slower. (E) Proportion of voxels with fast moving solute. Data are mean ± SEM. (Color figure online)

5   Conclusion and Future Work

We presented a Lagrangian representation of Fisher-Rao regularized OMT to represent time-varying dynamics and various attributes in a single visualization. The resultant framework was then used to capture known GS transport flow patterns and provide additional insights in distinguishing GS function under different anesthetic conditions in addition to clearance of solutes via the olfactory nerves and into the nasal conchae. In the future, we will use the computed particle attributes as features in machine learning algorithms to differentiate and classify various transport related flow patterns for diagnostic purposes.

Acknowledgements. This study was supported by AFOSR grants (FA9550-17-1-0435, FA9550-20-1-0029), a grant from National Institutes of Health (R01-AG048769, RF1-AG053991), MSK Cancer Center Support Grant/Core Grant (P30 CA008748), and a grant from Breast Cancer Research Foundation (BCRF-17-193).

References

1. Benamou, J.D., Brenier, Y.: A computational fluid mechanics solution to the Monge-Kantorovich mass transfer problem. Numerische Math. **84**, 375–393 (2000)
2. Benveniste, H., et al.: Anesthesia with dexmedetomidine and low-dose isoflurane increases solute transport via the glymphatic pathway in rat brain when compared with high-dose isoflurane. Anesthesiol.: J. Am. Soc. Anesthesiol. **127**(6), 976–988 (2017)
3. Buttazzo, G., Jimenez, C., Oudet, E.: An optimization problem for mass transportation with congested dynamics. SIAM J. Control Optim. **48**(3), 1961–1976 (2009)
4. Chen, Y., Georgiou, T.T., Pavon, M.: On the relation between optimal transport and Schrödinger bridges: a stochastic control viewpoint. J. Optim. Theory Appl. **169**(2), 671–691 (2016)
5. Chizat, L., Peyré, G., Schmitzer, B., Vialard, F.X.: Unbalanced optimal transport: dynamic and Kantorovich formulations. J. Funct. Anal. **274**(11), 3090–3123 (2018)
6. Cuturi, M.: Sinkhorn distances: lightspeed computation of optimal transport. In: Advances in Neural Information Processing Systems, pp. 2292–2300 (2013)
7. Elkin, R., et al.: GlymphVIS: visualizing glymphatic transport pathways using regularized optimal transport. In: Frangi, A.F., Schnabel, J.A., Davatzikos, C., Alberola-López, C., Fichtinger, G. (eds.) MICCAI 2018. LNCS, vol. 11070, pp. 844–852. Springer, Cham (2018). https://doi.org/10.1007/978-3-030-00928-1_95
8. Elkin, R., et al.: Optimal mass transport kinetic modeling for head and neck DCE-MRI: initial analysis. Magn. Reson. Med. **82**(6), 2314–2325 (2019)
9. Feydy, J., Charlier, B., Vialard, F.-X., Peyré, G.: Optimal transport for diffeomorphic registration. In: Descoteaux, M., Maier-Hein, L., Franz, A., Jannin, P., Collins, D.L., Duchesne, S. (eds.) MICCAI 2017. LNCS, vol. 10433, pp. 291–299. Springer, Cham (2017). https://doi.org/10.1007/978-3-319-66182-7_34
10. Garyfallidis, E., Brett, M., Correia, M.M., Williams, G.B., Nimmo-Smith, I.: Quickbundles, a method for tractography simplification. Front. Neurosci. **6**, 175 (2012)

11. Gerber, S., Niethammer, M., Styner, M., Aylward, S.: Exploratory population analysis with unbalanced optimal transport. In: Frangi, A.F., Schnabel, J.A., Davatzikos, C., Alberola-López, C., Fichtinger, G. (eds.) MICCAI 2018. LNCS, vol. 11072, pp. 464–472. Springer, Cham (2018). https://doi.org/10.1007/978-3-030-00931-1_53

12. Haker, S., Zhu, L., Tannenbaum, A., Angenent, S.: Optimal mass transport for registration and warping. Int. J. Comput. Vis. **60**(3), 225–240 (2004)

13. Iliff, J.J., et al.: Brain-wide pathway for waste clearance captured by contrast-enhanced MRI. J. Clin. Investig. **123**(3), 1299–1309 (2013)

14. Iliff, J.J., et al.: A paravascular pathway facilitates CSF flow through the brain parenchyma and the clearance of interstitial solutes, including amyloid β. Sci. Transl. Med. **4**(147), 147ra111 (2012)

15. Jiang, Q., et al.: Impairment of the glymphatic system after diabetes. J. Cereb. Blood Flow Metab. **37**(4), 1326–1337 (2017)

16. Koundal, S., et al.: Optimal mass transport with Lagrangian workflow reveals advective and diffusion driven solute transport in the glymphatic system. Sci. Rep. **10**(1), 1–18 (2020)

17. Lee, H., et al.: The effect of body posture on brain glymphatic transport. J. Neurosci. **35**(31), 11034–11044 (2015)

18. Li, W., Yin, P., Osher, S.: Computations of optimal transport distance with fisher information regularization. J. Sci. Comput. **75**(3), 1581–1595 (2018)

19. Liero, M., Mielke, A., Savaré, G.: Optimal transport in competition with reaction: the Hellinger-Kantorovich distance and geodesic curves. SIAM J. Math. Anal. **48**(4), 2869–2911 (2016)

20. Otto, F.: The geometry of dissipative evolution equations: the porous medium equation. Communications in Partial Differential Equations (2001)

21. Papadakis, N., Peyré, G., Oudet, E.: Optimal transport with proximal splitting. SIAM J. Imaging Sci. **7**(1), 212–238 (2014)

22. Peng, W., et al.: Suppression of glymphatic fluid transport in a mouse model of Alzheimer's disease. Neurobiol. Dis. **93**, 215–225 (2016)

23. Ratner, V., et al.: Cerebrospinal and interstitial fluid transport via the glymphatic pathway modeled by optimal mass transport. Neuroimage **152**, 530–537 (2017)

24. Shokri-Kojori, E., et al.: β-amyloid accumulation in the human brain after one night of sleep deprivation. Proc. Natl. Acad. Sci. **115**(17), 4483–4488 (2018)

25. Steklova, K., Haber, E.: Joint hydrogeophysical inversion: state estimation for seawater intrusion models in 3D. Comput. Geosci. **21**(1), 75–94 (2017)

26. Villani, C.: Topics in Optimal Transportation No. 58. American Mathematical Society, Providence (2003)

27. Villani, C.: Optimal Transport: Old and New, vol. 338. Springer, Cham (2008). https://doi.org/10.1007/978-3-540-71050-9

28. Xie, L., et al.: Sleep drives metabolite clearance from the adult brain. Science **342**(6156), 373–377 (2013)

Joint Neuroimage Synthesis and Representation Learning for Conversion Prediction of Subjective Cognitive Decline

Yunbi Liu[1,2], Yongsheng Pan[1], Wei Yang[2], Zhenyuan Ning[1,2], Ling Yue[3], Mingxia Liu[1(✉)], and Dinggang Shen[1(✉)]

[1] Department of Radiology and BRIC, University of North Carolina at Chapel Hill, Chapel Hill, NC 27599, USA
mxliu@med.unc.edu, Dinggang.Shen@gmail.com
[2] School of Biomedical Engineering, Southern Medical University, Guangzhou 510515, China
[3] Department of Geriatric Psychiatry, Shanghai Mental Health Center, Shanghai Jiao Tong University School of Medicine, Shanghai 200240, China

Abstract. Predicting the progression of preclinical Alzheimer's disease (AD) such as subjective cognitive decline (SCD) is fundamental for the effective intervention of pathological cognitive decline. Even though multimodal neuroimaging has been widely used in automated AD diagnosis, there are few studies dedicated to SCD progression prediction, due to challenges of *incomplete and limited data*. To this end, we propose a Joint neuroimage Synthesis and Representation Learning (JSRL) framework with transfer learning for SCD conversion prediction using incomplete multimodal neuroimaging data. Specifically, JSRL consists of two major components: 1) a generative adversarial network for synthesizing missing neuroimaging data, and 2) a classification network for learning neuroimage representations and predicting the progression of SCD. These two subnetworks share the same feature encoding module, encouraging that the to-be-generated representations are prediction-oriented and also the underlying association among multimodal images can be effectively modeled for accurate prediction. To handle the limited data problem, we further leverage both image synthesis and prediction models learned from a large-scale ADNI database (with MRI and PET acquired from 863 subjects) to a small-scale SCD database (with only MRI acquired from 113 subjects) in a transfer learning manner. Experimental results show that the proposed JSRL can synthesize reasonable PET scans and is superior to several state-of-the-art methods in SCD conversion prediction.

1 Introduction

As a self-reported experience of cognitive impairment, subjective cognitive decline (SCD) is one of the earliest noticeable symptoms of Alzheimer's disease (AD), mild cognitive impairment (MCI), and related dementia [1–5]. Considering that individuals with SCD are at increased risk of developing MCI or

© Springer Nature Switzerland AG 2020
A. L. Martel et al. (Eds.): MICCAI 2020, LNCS 12267, pp. 583–592, 2020.
https://doi.org/10.1007/978-3-030-59728-3_57

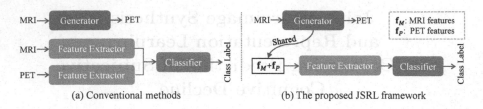

(a) Conventional methods   (b) The proposed JSRL framework

Fig. 1. Illustration of (a) conventional methods for separate neuroimage synthesis and representation learning and (b) the proposed Joint neuroimage Synthesis and Representation Learning (JSRL) framework for disease progression prediction using incomplete multimodal neuroimaging data (i.e., MRI and PET).

dementia [6], it is clinically meaningful to predict the progression of SCD for drug development and possible intervention of AD-related cognitive decline.

Existing studies have shown that structural magnetic resonance imaging (MRI) and positron emission tomography (PET) data contain complementary information to improve the performance of computer-aided brain disease diagnosis [7–9]. Unfortunately, compared with MRI, it is generally more difficult to obtain PET due to the relatively higher cost of PET scanning and other issues such as patients' concern about radioactive exposure. For instance, while all subjects in the public Alzheimer's Disease Neuroimaging Initiative (ADNI) have MRI data, only part of them have PET scans [10]. In the China Longitudinal Aging Social Survey (CLAS) dataset [11], all 113 subjects at 7 years' follow-up with definite conversion results have MRI scans but no PET data.

Previous studies usually discard subjects without PET scans, therefore significantly reducing the number of training samples and degrading the learning performance [12,13]. Recently, generative adversarial networks (GANs) have been employed to impute missing neuroimaging data [14,15], followed by multimodal representation learning and disease classification (see Fig. 1 (a)). Since image synthesis and representation learning are treated as two separate steps, these methods may lead to sub-optimal performance. Besides, existing methods often concatenate MRI and PET features for subsequent analysis, ignoring the underlying association between MRI and PET [16,17]. Intuitively, such association could be used as prior knowledge to boost the prediction performance. As shown in Fig. 1 (b), we propose to jointly perform image synthesis and representation learning for SCD conversion prediction, through which the underlying association between MRI and PET can be implicitly modeled.

In addition, we usually have very limited number of subjects for model learning. Directly training models on these limited data would degrade their robustness. To this end, we propose to leverage both image synthesis and prediction models learned from a large-scale ADNI database (with MRI and PET acquired from 863 subjects) to a small-scale SCD database (with only MRI from 113 subjects) in a transfer learning manner. The assumption is that, since SCD may be the preclinical stage of MCI and AD and AD/MCI is a progressive neurodegenerative disease, the discriminate brain changes between AD/MCI and normal controls (NCs) are potential biomarkers for SCD conversion prediction.

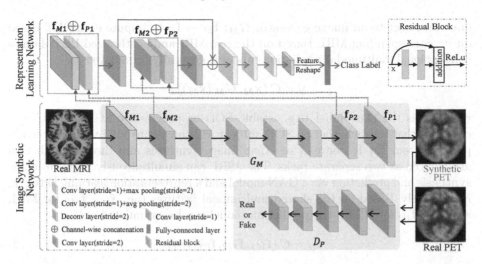

Fig. 2. Illustration of our JSRL framework for SCD conversion prediction, with a image synthesis network (bottom) and a representation learning network (top) for prediction. These two networks share the same feature maps, i.e., $[\mathbf{f}_{M1}, \mathbf{f}_{M2}]$ for MRI and $[\mathbf{f}_{P1}, \mathbf{f}_{P2}]$ for PET, encouraging that the to-be-generated representations are task-oriented for the prediction purpose. Conv: Convolution; Decov: Deconvolution.

The main contributions of this work can be summarized as follows: 1) A joint image synthesis and representation learning framework is proposed for predicting the progression of SCD subjects using incomplete multimodal neuroimaging data. This is different from previous approaches that discard data-missing subjects or treat image synthesis and feature learning as two separate tasks. 2) A transfer learning strategy is developed to handle the limited data problem, by leveraging knowledge learned from the ADNI to a small-scale SCD database.

2   Proposed Method

Our JSRL framework is illustrated in Fig. 2, containing 1) a generative adversarial network (GAN) for synthesizing missing neuroimages and generating multimodal features, and 2) a representation learning network for extracting imaging features and predicting the progression of brain disorders. These two subnetworks share the same features, i.e., $[\mathbf{f}_{M1}, \mathbf{f}_{M2}]$ for MRI and $[\mathbf{f}_{P1}, \mathbf{f}_{P2}]$ for PET, encouraging that the to-be-generated representations are prediction-oriented and the association between MRI and PET can be modeled.

Problem Formulation. In this work, we aim to utilize the domain knowledge learned from ADNI with MRI and PET scans to aid the conversion prediction of SCD with only MRI data. Let $\mathbf{I}_M$ denote the domain of MRI images and $\mathbf{I}_P$ be the domain of PET images. We denote a set of subjects (with paired MRI and PET scans) as $\mathcal{D} = \{(\mathbf{x}_M, \mathbf{x}_P) \mid \mathbf{x}_M \in \mathbf{I}_M, \mathbf{x}_P \in \mathbf{I}_P\}$. If no PET data is available, one can resort to an image generator $G_M: \mathbf{I}_M \rightarrow \mathbf{I}_P$ to impute each PET based on its corresponding MRI. Based on the real MRI and synthesized PET data, a conventional multimodal prediction model is generally formulated as

$$y = C\left(\mathbf{x}_M, G_M\left(\mathbf{x}_M\right)\right), \tag{1}$$

where y is the class label (e.g., stable SCD or progressive SCD) and C is a classifier that tells whether an SCD subject will convert to MCI within a certain period. From Eq. 1, one can see that image synthesis and disease prediction are treated as two separate tasks. The JSRL can simultaneously perform image synthesis and prediction via a GAN model and a representation learning network, respectively. Based on the shared multimodal features (i.e., $\mathbf{f}_{M1}$, $\mathbf{f}_{M2}$ for MRI, and $\mathbf{f}_{P1}$, $\mathbf{f}_{P2}$ for PET), the prediction model can be formulated as

$$y = C\left(\mathbf{f}_{M1}, \mathbf{f}_{M2}, \mathbf{f}_{P1}, \mathbf{f}_{P2}\right). \tag{2}$$

Joint Image Synthesis and Representation Learning. Our JSRL has two subnetworks for joint image synthesis and prediction, with details given as below.

1) Image Synthesis Network: We resort to a 3D GAN to synthesize missing neuroimages. Specifically, our image synthesis model contains a generator (i.e., G_M) and a discriminator (i.e., D_P). While the generator G_M is used to impute missing PET images based on MRI scans, a discriminator is used to tell whether an input PET scan is real or not. As shown in the bottom of Fig. 2, the generator contains an encoder with 3 convolutional (Conv) layers, a transfer part with 3 residual blocks, a decoder with 2 deconvolutional (Deconv) layers, and an output layer. The channels of 3 Conv layers are 16, 32 and 64, respectively. For the sake of symmetry, the channels of two Deconv layers are the same as the corresponding Conv layers. The filter size of these Conv and Deconv layers is $3 \times 3 \times 3$ except the first Conv and the last Deconv layers with the filter size of $7 \times 7 \times 7$. Two types of loss functions are used in the image synthesis network, i.e., an adversarial loss and a reconstruction loss, defined as

$$\mathcal{L}(G_M) = \sum_{\{\mathbf{x}_M \in \mathbf{I}_M, \mathbf{x}_P \in \mathbf{I}_P\}} \|G_M(\mathbf{x}_M) - \mathbf{x}_P\|_1 + \log\left(1 - D_P(G_M(\mathbf{x}_M))\right), \tag{3}$$

where the 1st term is the reconstruction loss, and the 2nd term is the adversarial loss. For D_P, we need to minimize the loss

$$\mathcal{L}(D_P) = \sum_{\{\mathbf{x}_M \in \mathbf{I}_M, \mathbf{x}_P \in \mathbf{I}_P\}} \log(1 - D_P(\mathbf{x}_P)) + \log\left(D_P\left(G_M\left(\mathbf{x}_M\right)\right)\right). \tag{4}$$

2) Representation Learning Network: To capture the association of different modalities, we develop a representation learning (RL) network to fuse multi-scale MRI and PET features for SCD conversion prediction. Since these two subnetworks share the same feature maps, one can encourage the to-be-generated representations to be prediction-oriented. Specifically, to capture multi-scale feature representations of MRI and PET, we propose to share the feature maps of the first two Conv layers from the encoder (i.e., f_{M1} and f_{M2}) in G_M with RL for MRI, and share the feature maps of the last two Deconv layers from the decoder (i.e., f_{P1} and f_{P2}) in G_M with RL for PET. Then, the channel-wise concatenation of these multi-scale and multimodal feature maps are used as input of the RL network, as shown in the top of Fig. 2. Denote the concatenation of f_{M1} and f_{P1} as $C1$ and the concatenation of f_{M2} and f_{P2} as $C2$. As shown in the top of Fig. 2, $C1$ is followed by a Conv layer with a stride of 2 and $C2$ is followed by a Conv layer with a stride of 1. Then they are concatenated, followed by four Conv layers and a fully-connected (FC) layer. The first 3 and the last Conv layers are respectively followed by the max-pooling and average-pooling with the stride of 2 and they all have 16 channels with the filter size of $3 \times 3 \times 3$. Feature maps of the last Conv layer are reshaped into a feature vector, followed by an FC layer (with $1,280$ neurons) for classification/prediction. We use the cross-entropy loss in the RL network for classification, which is defined as

$$\mathcal{L}_R = -y \log p(\mathbf{x}) - (1 - y) \log (1 - p(\mathbf{x})), \tag{5}$$

where $p(\mathbf{x})$ is the estimated probability of $\mathbf{x}$ belonging to the correct class y. For jointly training the generator and RL network, the overall loss JSRL is

$$\mathcal{L}_{total} = \mathcal{L}(G_M) + \lambda L_R, \tag{6}$$

where λ is empirically set as 1.

Transfer Learning Strategy. To deal with the problem of limited training data, we develop a transfer learning solution, by leveraging knowledge from the relatively large-scale ADNI dataset to the small-scale CLAS dataset. Specifically, we design a *label transfer* strategy to augment the sample size for model training, as well as a *model transfer* strategy for missing neuroimage imputation and computer-aided SCD conversion prediction.

The CLAS contains stable SCD (sSCD) and progressive SCD (pSCD), while subjects in ADNI were divided into four categories: 1) AD, 2) NC, 3) MCI, and 4) SCD (i.e., subjective memory complaint). According to conversion results within 36 months, NC, MCI, SCD in ADNI can be further divided into sCN and pCN, sMCI and pMCI, sSCD and pSCD, respectively, with 'p' meaning progressive and 's' denoting stable. For example, 'pSCD' means that an SCD subject will convert to MCI within 36 months. Only 16 SCD subjects have definite conversion results (i.e., 11 pSCD and 5 sSCD) in ADNI. Since pCN and pSCD subjects would convert to MCI within a period, we assume that they have similar brain changes in their neuroimages. Accordingly, we propose to use sNC, pNC and MCI to aid SCD conversion prediction due to their close relationship (i.e., preclinical or prodromal stage of AD). Denote subjects belonging to the five categories (i.e., sNC, pNC, sSCD, pSCD, and MCI) as *SCD-adjacent subjects*. We reasonably regard sNC and sSCD as positive samples, and treat pNC, pSCD and MCI as negative samples in ADNI. With such label allocation, we train JSRL for joint image synthesis and prediction on ADNI, and then apply the trained model to CLAS. Thus, the knowledge learned from ADNI can be transferred to CLAS for SCD conversion prediction.

Implementation. We first train the GAN (with G_M and D_P) for 50 epochs, and then jointly train the generator G_M and RL network for 30 epochs using 863 subjects with complete MRI and PET in ADNI. For GAN, we first train G_M by minimizing $\mathcal{L}(G_M)$ with fixed D_P, and then train D_P by minimizing $\mathcal{L}(D_P)$ with fixed G_M, iteratively. Then, we jointly train the generator G_M and RL network by minimizing $\mathcal{L}_{total}$. The Adam solver with a learning rate of 2×10^{-3} is used in the image synthesis network and a gradient descent optimizer with a learning rate of 10^{-2} is used in joint training of G_M and RL network.

3   Experiments

Datasets and Neuroimage Pre-processing. The public Alzheimer's Disease Neuroimaging Initiative (ADNI)[1] database was studied in this work. We used MRI and PET data of 863 subjects (205 sNC, 29 pNC, 629 MCI) with complete MRI and PET scans from ADNI to train our JSRL network, and a validation set (containing 79 AD subjects with complete MRI and PET scans from ADNI) was used to validate the image synthesis model in our JRSL network. To validate the image synthesis model, we use AD subjects rather than SCD-adjacent subjects to make sure that all SCD-adjacent subjects with complete MRI and PET scans from the ADNI database can be used to train our representation learning network. We also collected a total of 113 SCD subjects (with only MRI data) in the CLAS database as an independent test set, including 73 sSCD and 40 pSCD subjects. All MRI and PET scans were pre-processed using a standard pipeline, including 1) skull-stripping via FreeSurfer, 2) intensity correction, and 3) spatial normalization to the Montreal Neurological Institute (MNI) space using SPM. After pre-processing, all images will have the same size as MNI.

Experimental Setup. In the *first* group of experiments, we evaluate the quality of synthetic images generated by the image synthesis network in JSRL. Specifically, we train the image synthesis model using 863 SCD-adjacent subjects with complete MRI and PET scans in ADNI, and test this image synthesis model on 113 SCD subjects with only MRI data in CLAS. Due to the lack of ground-truth PET images in CLAS, we further test this image synthesis model on 79 subjects with complete MRI and PET scans in ADNI to validate the reliability of our model. The averaged peak signal-to-noise (PSNR) and structure similarity image index (SSIM) are used to measure the quality of those synthetic images.

---

[1] http://adni.loni.usc.edu.

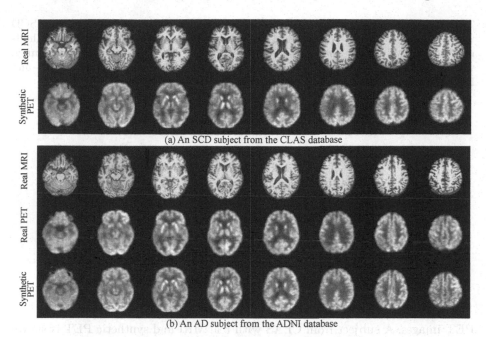

(a) An SCD subject from the CLAS database

(b) An AD subject from the ADNI database

Fig. 3. Synthetic images generated by our method and their corresponding real images for two typical subjects from the CLAS and the ADNI databases.

In the *second* group, we evaluate the performance of our JSRL in SCD conversion prediction, by comparing JSRL with three conventional methods using handcrafted features, including 1) patch-based method (PBM) [18], 2) ROI-based pattern analysis (ROI) [19], and 3) landmark-based local energy patterns (LLEP) [20]. Note that features of MRI and PET data are concatenated in these four methods, followed by a linear support vector machine for prediction. We also compare JSRL with a state-of-the-art deep learning method, called disease-image specific neural network (DSNN) [14]. DSNN contains two subnetworks to extract MRI and PET features separately. Each subnetwork in DSNN consists of 5 Conv layers with a stride of 2 to extract MRI/PET features, and the MRI and PET features are further concatenated and reshaped into an FC layer for classification. Prediction models of all methods were trained on ADNI and tested on CLAS. The performance of SCD conversion prediction is measured by the area under the receiver operating characteristic (AUC), accuracy (ACC), sensitivity (SEN), specificity (SPE), and F1-Score(F1S).

Results of Neuroimage Synthesis. We first evaluate the quality of synthetic images generated by our GAN subnetwork in JSRL. Here, the GAN model is first trained on 863 SCD-adjacent subjects with complete PET and MRI from ADNI, and then tested on 113 subjects (with MRI only) from CLAS. Due to the lack of ground-truth PET images in CLAS, we show the visual results of the synthetic

Table 1. Results achieved by four methods in SCD conversion prediction (i.e., sSCD vs. pSCD classification), with models trained on ADNI and tested on CLAS. Methods marked as "-M" denote that only subjects with MRI in ADNI are used for training, while the remaining methods employ all subjects in ADNI with complete MRI and PET for training, and the real MRI and synthetic PET in CLAS for test.

Method	AUC	ACC	SPE	SEN	F1S
ROI-M	0.597	0.611	**0.699**	0.450	0.450
PBM-M	0.500	0.443	0.397	0.525	0.400
LLEP-M	0.510	0.487	0.493	0.475	0.396
DSNN-M	0.590	0.522	0.452	0.650	0.490
ROI	0.603	0.584	0.658	0.450	0.434
PBM	0.538	0.496	0.425	0.625	0.467
LLEP	0.516	0.451	0.500	0.425	0.392
DSNN	0.557	0.558	0.589	0.500	0.444
JSRL (ours)	**0.713**	**0.655**	0.616	**0.725**	**0.598**

PET images. A subject from CLAS with real MRI and synthetic PET is shown in Fig. 3 (a). One can observe that our synthetic PET images look reasonable in appearance. We also test this model on 79 validation subjects (with paired MRI and PET) from ADNI. A subject from ADNI with real MRI, real PET, and synthetic PET is shown in Fig. 3 (b), suggesting that our synthetic PET image looks similar to its real one. The mean SSIM and PSNR values of synthetic PET on ADNI are 0.85 and 23.22, respectively. This suggests that our image synthesis model is reasonable and the synthetic PET scans have acceptable image quality.

Results of SCD Conversion Prediction. We further compare our JSRL with five competing methods in SCD conversion prediction, with results reported in Table 1. From Table 1, we can have following observations. 1) The proposed transfer learning strategy works well in SCD conversion prediction (with AUCs > 0.5 for most methods). 2) Methods with multimodal data generally outperform their single-modal counterparts in terms of AUC values. This suggests that our synthesized PET scans are helpful in boosting the prediction performance. 3) JSRL outperforms conventional handcrafted feature based methods (i.e., ROI, PBM, and LLEP) and the deep learning method (i.e., DSNN), validating the effectiveness of the proposed framework for joint image synthesis and representation learning. 4) JSRL achieves a significantly improved SEN value (i.e., 0.725), which is 7.5% higher than the second-best SEN (i.e., 0.650) achieved by DSNN-M. In real-world applications, the high sensitivity of JSRL may be very useful for accurately identifying subjects with progressive SCD.

4   Conclusion and Future Work

In this paper, we present a joint neuroimage synthesis and representation learning (JSRL) framework for SCD conversion prediction based on incomplete multimodal neuroimages. Specifically, JSRL consists of a GAN model for imputing missing neuroimages and a representation learning network for SCD conversion prediction. We also develop a transfer learning strategy to handle the limited data problem, by leveraging knowledge learned from the relatively large-scale ADNI database to the small-scale CLAS database. Experimental results suggest that JSRL can synthesize PET scans with reasonable image quality and also achieve good results in SCD conversion prediction. Our study indicates that the JSRL framework and transfer learning strategy can be potentially applied to the early detection of preclinical AD, which needs to be verified in future work. Currently, we directly apply JSRL trained on ADNI to CLAS using a label transfer and model transfer strategy. Designing advanced data adaptation methods [21] is expected to explicitly alleviate the data distribution difference between these two databases, which will be our future work.

Acknowledgements. This work was finished when Y. Pan was visiting the University of North Carolina at Chapel Hill. Y. Liu and Y. Pan contributed equally to this work.

References

1. Jessen, F., et al.: A conceptual framework for research on subjective cognitive decline in preclinical Alzheimer's disease. Alzheimer's Dement. **10**(6), 844–852 (2014)
2. Amariglio, R.E., et al.: Subjective cognitive complaints and amyloid burden in cognitively normal older individuals. Neuropsychologia **50**(12), 2880–2886 (2012)
3. Buckley, R.F., et al.: A conceptualization of the utility of subjective cognitive decline in clinical trials of preclinical Alzheimer's disease. J. Mol. Neurosci. **60**(3), 354–361 (2016). https://doi.org/10.1007/s12031-016-0810-z
4. Kryscio, R.J., et al.: Self-reported memory complaints: implications from a longitudinal cohort with autopsies. Neurology **83**(15), 1359–1365 (2014)
5. Liu, M., Zhang, J., Yap, P.T., Shen, D.: View-aligned hypergraph learning for Alzheimer's disease diagnosis with incomplete multi-modality data. Med. Image Anal. **36**, 123–134 (2017)
6. Mitchell, A., Beaumont, H., Ferguson, D., Yadegarfar, M., Stubbs, B.: Risk of dementia and mild cognitive impairment in older people with subjective memory complaints: meta-analysis. Acta Psychiatrica Scandinavica **130**(6), 439–451 (2014)
7. Kawachi, T., et al.: Comparison of the diagnostic performance of FDG-PET and VBM-MRI in very mild Alzheimer's disease. Eur. J. Nuclear Med. Mol. Imaging **33**(7), 801–809 (2006). https://doi.org/10.1007/s00259-005-0050-x
8. Zu, C., Jie, B., Liu, M., Chen, S., Shen, D., Zhang, D.: Label-aligned multi-task feature learning for multimodal classification of Alzheimer's disease and mild cognitive impairment. Brain Imaging Behav. **10**(4), 1148–1159 (2016). https://doi.org/10.1007/s11682-015-9480-7
9. Liu, M., Zhang, J., Adeli, E., Shen, D.: Landmark-based deep multi-instance learning for brain disease diagnosis. Med. Image Anal. **43**, 157–168 (2018)

10. Jack Jr, C.R., et al.: The Alzheimer's disease neuroimaging initiative (ADNI): MRI methods. J. Mag. Reson. Imaging: Off. J. Int. Soc. Magn. Reson. Med. **27**(4), 685–691 (2008)
11. Yue, L., et al.: Asymmetry of hippocampus and amygdala defect in subjective cognitive decline among the community dwelling Chinese. Front. Psychiatry **9**, 226 (2018)
12. Frisoni, G.B., Fox, N.C., Jack, C.R., Scheltens, P., Thompson, P.M.: The clinical use of structural MRI in Alzheimer disease. Nat. Rev. Neurol. **6**(2), 67–77 (2010)
13. Jie, B., Liu, M., Liu, J., Zhang, D., Shen, D.: Temporally constrained group sparse learning for longitudinal data analysis in Alzheimer's disease. IEEE Trans. Biomed. Eng. **64**(1), 238–249 (2016)
14. Pan, Y., Liu, M., Lian, C., Xia, Y., Shen, D.: Spatially-constrained Fisher representation for brain disease identification with incomplete multi-modal neuroimages. IEEE Trans. Med. Imaging **39**, 2965–2975 (2020)
15. Yi, X., Walia, E., Babyn, P.: Generative adversarial network in medical imaging: a review. Med. Image Anal. **58**, 101552 (2019)
16. Cheng, B., Liu, M., Zhang, D., Munsell, B.C., Shen, D.: Domain transfer learning for MCI conversion prediction. IEEE Trans. Biomed. Eng. **62**(7), 1805–1817 (2015)
17. Cheng, B., Liu, M., Shen, D., Li, Z., Zhang, D.: Multi-domain transfer learning for early diagnosis of Alzheimer's disease. Neuroinformatics **15**(2), 115–132 (2017). https://doi.org/10.1007/s12021-016-9318-5
18. Coupé, P., Eskildsen, S.F., Manjón, J.V., Fonov, V.S., Collins, D.L.: Simultaneous segmentation and grading of anatomical structures for patient's classification: application to Alzheimer's disease. NeuroImage **59**(4), 3736–3747 (2012)
19. Rusinek, H., et al.: Alzheimer disease: measuring loss of cerebral gray matter with MR imaging. Radiology **178**(1), 109–114 (1991)
20. Zhang, J., Liu, M., Shen, D.: Detecting anatomical landmarks from limited medical imaging data using two-stage task-oriented deep neural networks. IEEE Trans. Image Process. **26**(10), 4753–4764 (2017)
21. Wang, M., Zhang, D., Huang, J., Yap, P.T., Shen, D., Liu, M.: Identifying autism spectrum disorder with multi-site fMRI via low-rank domain adaptation. IEEE Trans. Med. Imaging **39**(3), 644–655 (2019)

Differentiable Deconvolution
for Improved Stroke Perfusion Analysis

Ezequiel de la Rosa[1,2]([✉]), David Robben[1,3,4], Diana M. Sima[1],
Jan S. Kirschke[5], and Bjoern Menze[2]

[1] icometrix, Leuven, Belgium
{ezequiel.delarosa,david.robben,diana.sima}@icometrix.com
[2] Department of Computer Science,
Technical University of Munich, Munich, Germany
bjoern.menze@tum.de
[3] Medical Imaging Research Center (MIRC), KU Leuven, Leuven, Belgium
[4] Department of Electrical Engineering, ESAT/PSI, KU Leuven, Leuven, Belgium
[5] Neuroradiology, School of Medicine,
Technical University of Munich, Munich, Germany
jan.kirschke@tum.de

Abstract. Perfusion imaging is the current gold standard for acute
ischemic stroke analysis. It allows quantification of the salvageable and
non-salvageable tissue regions (penumbra and core areas respectively). In
clinical settings, the singular value decomposition (SVD) deconvolution
is one of the most accepted and used approaches for generating interpretable and physically meaningful maps. Though this method has been
widely validated in experimental and clinical settings, it might produce
suboptimal results because the chosen inputs to the model cannot guarantee optimal performance. For the most critical input, the arterial input
function (AIF), it is still controversial how and where it should be chosen
even though the method is very sensitive to this input. In this work we
propose an AIF selection approach that is optimized for maximal core
lesion segmentation performance. The AIF is regressed by a neural network optimized through a differentiable SVD deconvolution, aiming to
maximize core lesion segmentation agreement with ground truth data. To
our knowledge, this is the first work exploiting a differentiable deconvolution model with neural networks. We show that our approach is able to
generate AIFs without any manual annotation, and hence avoiding manual rater's influences. The method achieves manual expert performance
in the ISLES18 dataset. We conclude that the methodology opens new
possibilities for improving perfusion imaging quantification with deep
neural networks.

Keywords: Perfusion imaging · SVD deconvolution · Deep learning

Electronic supplementary material The online version of this chapter (https://
doi.org/10.1007/978-3-030-59728-3_58) contains supplementary material, which is
available to authorized users.

© Springer Nature Switzerland AG 2020
A. L. Martel et al. (Eds.): MICCAI 2020, LNCS 12267, pp. 593–602, 2020.
https://doi.org/10.1007/978-3-030-59728-3_58

1   Introduction

Perfusion imaging techniques are the clinical standard for acute ischemic stroke lesion assessment. They acquire images of the passage of a contrast agent bolus through the brain tissue. Since the perfusion series are not directly clinically interpretable, they require the computation of physically meaningful parameter maps. Although different approaches may be used for their computation (e.g. compartmental models, which are mainly used over long acquisition time perfusion MRI), the preferred technique in perfusion CT analysis is the singular value decomposition (SVD) deconvolution [11,25]. The technique has been well validated in experimental [16] and clinical [1] settings and is widely implemented in perfusion CT software [7,25]. Cerebral blood flow (CBF) and time to the maximum residue function (Tmax) are typically used maps, though cerebral blood volume and time-to-peak maps are often considered as well. Parameter maps are critical for treatment decision making. They allow assessing the salvageable *penumbra* and irreversible *core* necrotic lesions, and hence determining if reperfusion techniques may reduce the disease damage severity.

The SVD deconvolution method requires as input an arterial input function (AIF), defined as the concentration time-curve inside an artery feeding the tissue under study. In practice, the AIF is mostly selected by a physician, a demanding, highly variable and poorly reproducible process. Its correct selection is the cornerstone for generating accurate maps, as has been shown that minimal changes in its location and/or shape may strongly impact the deconvolution process [13]. Although several works studied how and where the AIF should be chosen [4], the subject is still very controversial. Thus, AIF selection is suboptimal, since we do not know which function will maximize the deconvolution performance. Besides, the AIF's concept is defined based on the SVD-deconvolution theoretical model, which relies on several assumptions violated in clinical practice. For instance, limited voxel resolution, partial volume effect, time-curve delays, noise and other confounders are typically limiting the model's performance. Consequently, it is not straightforward to define which AIFs are the best to use in practice.

In this work we use neural networks to generate the AIF, aiming to find the *best* AIFs in core lesion segmentation terms. Through experiments on the ISLES18 database we show that the method is able to learn from scratch to generate AIFs that maximize the segmentation agreement with manually delineated ground truth. Thus, the AIFs are learned without any expert annotations of the AIFs themselves, hence avoiding potential rater's bias. We show, as well, that the approach is able to yield manual expert performance in the ISLES18 database.

2   Method

2.1   Differentiable Deconvolution

We propose the optimizable framework of Fig. 1 which generates the *best* AIF for SVD deconvolution. We define the *best* AIF as the one yielding the highest agreement between the estimated core lesion and the ground truth core lesion. The input to the framework is 4D perfusion data and the output is a lesion map. It consists of a CNN that generates the AIF $c_{art}(t)$. The generated AIF together with the 4D input perfusion series pass through a differentiable SVD deconvolution block, which outputs relative CBF (rCBF) maps after image deconvolution. Finally, rCBF is transformed into the lesion probability map y_{pred}. The framework is end-to-end trainable, which means that gradients are backpropagated through all blocks including the SVD deconvolution, thus allowing to generate the best AIF candidate that maximizes the segmentation performance.

AIF Generating CNN. Unlike most previous works that use unsupervised clustering [14,15,18,19,21] or supervised segmentation [6] approaches, we propose a regression CNN for obtaining an AIF $c_{art}(t)$ from the 4D perfusion series. The architecture is fairly straightforward: the only particularity is that the input size varies in the z-axis from 2 to 8 slices. Therefore, it consists of 3D convolutional layers followed by an average pooling over the z-axis. Subsequently, there are 2D convolutional layers and finally a fully connected layer with the same number of output neurons as the number of time-points in the perfusion data. This final 1D vector represents $c_{art}(t)$. After each convolution, average pooling and dropout [23] are used. ReLU [10] activations are applied in all layers except for the final AIF output layer, where a linear activation is employed. For fitting 4D data into the CNN, we encode volume time-points as channels in the network.

SVD Deconvolution. For generating interpretable and physically-meaningful maps, perfusion series are deconvolved using the well-validated delay-invariant SVD deconvolution. Our GPU implementation of the algorithm uses Volterra discretization [22]. Differentiability of the SVD algorithm was studied in [17,24]. Through analytical methods it was shown that the Jacobian of the SVD is computationally feasible [17]. Even more, in [8] a differentiable SVD was used in neural network layers for a variety of tasks including image segmentation. In this work, we take advantage of current deep learning libraries that support auto-differentiation and allow backpropagating SVD gradients. Given the fact that deconvolution is an ill-conditioned problem [7,20], we use a Tikhonov regularization scheme. The output of the deconvolution block of Fig. 1 is rCBF.

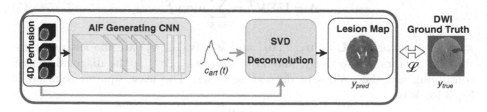

Fig. 1. Differentiable SVD deconvolution pipeline.

Although in clinical practice the Tmax and rCBF maps are typically used for identifying core lesions, we only consider rCBF since the differentiability of Tmax is not fully clear.

In a nutshell, the analysis of perfusion data can be described by the following convolution product:

$$c_{voi}(t_j) = \int_0^t c_{art}(\tau)k(t_j - \tau)d\tau \qquad (1)$$

where c_{voi} is the agent concentration in the voxel under consideration, c_{art} is the concentration curve measured in an artery feeding the volume (i.e., the AIF), and k is the impulse response function that characterizes the tissue of interest [7,22]. Note that here $t = 0$ is taken prior to the arrival of the contrast agent (such that $k(t) = 0$ for $t < 0$). For solving Eq. 1 (i.e., finding k) we rely on discretization methods, since in practice the measured AIF c_{art} and the agent concentration in the tissue volume c_{voi} are discretized at specific time points. Considering these time points as $t_j = (j - 1)\Delta t$ (for $j = 1, ..., N$), and assuming that $c_{art}(t)$ is negligible for $t > N\Delta t$, the discretization of Eq. 1 can be approximated as:

$$c_{voi}(t_j) = \int_0^t c_{art}(\tau)k(t_j - \tau)d\tau \approx \Delta t \sum_{i=1}^{N} c_{art}(t_i)k(t_{j-i+1}) \qquad (2)$$

which can be rewritten as a linear system:

$$\mathbf{c} = \mathbf{Ak} \qquad (3)$$

where $\mathbf{A}$ is the Volterra matrix with the following A_{ij} elements [22]:

$$\begin{cases} A_{i0} = (2c_{art}(t_i) + c_{art}(t_{i-1}))/6 & (0 < i \leq N - 1) \\ A_{ii} = (2c_{art}(t_i) + c_{art}(t_{i+1}))/6 & (0 < i \leq N - 1) \\ A_{ij} = \frac{2}{3}c_{art}(t_i) + \frac{c_{art}(t_{i-1})}{6} + \frac{c_{art}(t_{i+1})}{6} & (1 < i \leq N - 1, 0 < j < i) \\ A_{ij} = 0 & \text{elsewhere} \end{cases} \qquad (4)$$

We assume, without loss of generality, that $\Delta t = 1s$, which is usually the case in clinical practice. For the derivation of $\mathbf{A}$ and for a more in-depth understanding of discretization methods in perfusion imaging, the reader is referred to [22].

A classical way of solving Eq. 3 is by means of SVD as:

$$\mathbf{A} = \mathbf{U\Sigma V^T} = \sum_{i=1}^{r} \mathbf{u_i}\sigma_i\mathbf{v_i^T} \qquad (5)$$

where $r = rank(\mathbf{A})$, $\mathbf{U} = [\mathbf{u_1}, ..., \mathbf{u_r}]$ and $\mathbf{v} = [\mathbf{v_1}, ..., \mathbf{v_r}]$ are the left and right singular vectors, respectively, and $\mathbf{\Sigma} = diag(\sigma_1, ..., \sigma_r)$ is the diagonal matrix containing singular values in decreasing order. The least squares solution of Eq. 3 for $\mathbf{k}$ is:

$$\mathbf{k} = \sum_{i=1}^{r} \frac{\mathbf{u_i^T c}}{\sigma_i}\mathbf{v_i} \qquad (6)$$

Nonetheless, in cases where $\mathbf{A}$ is ill-conditioned, Eq. 6 is not a suitable solution of the linear system since a small variability in $\mathbf{c}$ may generate very large variability in $\mathbf{k}$ [7]. Thus, regularization is required for having a stable result as:

$$\mathbf{k}_\lambda = \sum_{i=1}^{r} \left(f_{\lambda,i} \frac{\mathbf{u}_i^T \mathbf{c}}{\sigma_i} \right) \mathbf{v_i} \qquad (7)$$

where $f_{\lambda,i} = \frac{\sigma_i^2}{\sigma_i^2 + \lambda^2}$ are Tikhonov regularization parameters with $\lambda = \lambda_{rel}\sigma_i$. The parameter λ_{rel} should be chosen in the interval $(0, 1)$. In our implementation we empirically set $\lambda_{rel} = 0.3$. Finally, it can be proven that the cerebral blood flow can be obtained as:

$$\text{CBF} = \frac{1}{\rho_{voi}} \max(k(t_j)) \qquad (8)$$

where ρ_{voi} $[\frac{g}{ml}]$ stands for the mean tissue density in the voxel. For a mathematical demonstration of this statement the reader is referred to [7]. Finally, following current clinical practice, CBF is normalized with mean healthy CBF values for obtaining a map in a subject-independent scale.

Ischemic Lesion Map. Generated rCBF maps require some sort of transformation to obtain lesion probability maps y_{pred} that can be compared with the binary ground truth masks. With this aim, we use sigmoid activations centered at rCBF $= 0.38$ for mapping the y_{pred} probability values. This cutoff previously was found to be optimal for this dataset [5]. It is worth to mention that it is possible to allow the network to choose the best cutoff, but we preferred to keep a fixed threshold as mostly used in clinical practice. In such a way, our proposed method is directly comparable with the results of a manual AIF selection using the same cutoff value, assuring that differences in results are only driven by the choice of AIF.

2.2   Implementation and Optimization

The framework is implemented using TensorFlow and Keras, where we ensure effective gradient propagation by only using differentiable operations. Given the class imbalance between *healthy* and *necrotic* brain tissue, a soft-Dice loss function is used as follows:

$$\mathcal{L} = 1 - \frac{2\sum y_{true} y_{pred}}{\sum y_{true} + \sum y_{pred}} \qquad (9)$$

where y_{pred} is the framework's output lesion map and y_{true} the ground truth manually delineated lesion mask.

Optimization is conducted using stochastic gradient descent with momentum, with a unitary batch size. In order to improve the network's learning stage and to overcome data limitations, two types of data augmentation are conducted. First, perfusion specific data augmentation [20] is implemented at an image level, which allows mimicking AIF bolus delay arrivals and AIF peak concentration scaling. Second, traditional segmentation data augmentation is used, including image rotation, translation, flipping and random Gaussian noise addition.

2.3   Data and Experiments

The free and open ISLES18 database is used [9,12]. It consists of 4D CT perfusion series with ground truth core lesion delineations obtained from diffusion weighted imaging (DWI). From the total amount of scans provided in the challenge (n = 156), only the training set (n = 94) includes ground truth data and hence was used for our experiments. The dataset is multi-scanner and multi-center, obtained from different institutions from the U.S. and Australia. All provided images are already motion-corrected, co-registered for matching CTP with DWI modalities, and spatio-temporally resampled (with 256×256 images and 1 volume/second).

To compare our proposed method against the current clinical approach, an expert provided manual AIF annotations for the entire ISLES18 training set. A single global AIF was selected per case, following recommendations found in the literature [4]. Moreover, our results are compared with the automatic AIF selection approach included in icobrain cva (icometrix, Leuven, Belgium), an FDA cleared CTP analysis software package. In both cases, the CTP images are deconvolved with the chosen AIF. The same data preprocessing and deconvolution algorithm of Sect. 2.1 are used. As such, any difference in results is only caused by the AIFs themselves. rCBF maps are generated and the core lesions are quantified. For all our experiments and methods a fixed threshold rCBF = 0.38 is used for defining the core lesions [5].

Since the dataset is already preprocessed, the preprocessing on our side is limited to a spatio-temporal smoothing before the CTP data is deconvolved. The method's performance is assessed through 5-fold cross-validation. Results are evaluated at parameter map and lesion segmentation levels. The discriminant power of the rCBF maps for differentiating healthy and necrotic tissue are assessed through the area under the ROC curve (AUC). The lesion segmentation is assessed by means of Dice and Jaccard indexes, 95% Hausdorff distance and volumetric Bland-Altman analysis [3].

3   Results

Training of our model takes ~2.5 h on an Nvidia K80 GPU with 12 GB dedicated memory. During testing, the entire process of AIF selection, SVD deconvolution and lesion quantification takes ~1.15 s per case. On the other hand, the expert annotation of an AIF takes around one minute per case.

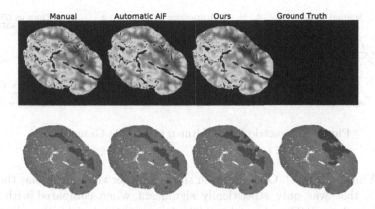

Fig. 2. Qualitative results. Top: rCBF maps; Bottom: Core-lesion segmentations.

In Fig. 2, the resulting rCBF maps generated with the different methods are shown for an example case. The corresponding AIFs selected or generated by these methods are included in the supplementary material. The automatic algorithm yields results that are visually similar to the ones generated with the expert AIF selection. However, our generated map better matches the DWI ground truth lesions than both other approaches. When assessing the ROC AUC values of rCBF for discerning healthy and necrotic tissue, our proposed method shows better performance than the other methods (Table 1). In all segmentation metrics the methods achieve comparable performance, with our new method outperforming the others, but the differences are not statistically significant (paired t-test).

Figure 3 shows the lesion volume quantification performance in Bland-Altman plots. Volumetric overestimation is found for all methods when comparing with results reported by [5], which shows better agreement with ground truth. This can be explained by their use of an extra Tmax criterion and due to their use of a modified ground truth, that excluded tissue with a low Tmax. The manual rater and the automatic AIF software yield comparable results, with the expert annotations having the best agreement with the ground truth (p-value non-statistically significant between these methods,

Table 1. Mean (standard deviation) of various segmentation metrics for the different methods. rCBF: relative cerebral blood flow; AUC: area under the ROC curve; HD: Hausdorff distance.

Method	rCBF AUC	Dice	Jaccard	95% HD (mm)
Expert	0.856	0.353 (0.201)	0.233 (0.157)	54.136 (19.449)
Automatic AIF	0.856	0.351 (0.202)	0.232 (0.158)	55.015 (18.790)
Ours	**0.868**	**0.359 (0.201)**	**0.238 (0.157)**	**53.747 (18.875)**

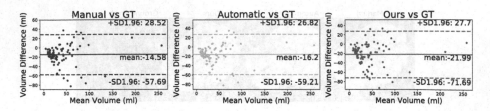

Fig. 3. Volumetric Bland-Altman plots. GT: Ground truth.

Mann-Whitney U test). Our approach shows a larger volumetric bias than these methods, that was only statistically significant when compared with manual results (p-value = 0.04 and p-value 0.09 when compared with manual and automatic methods respectively, Mann-Whitney U test). The reason for our method's mismatch in segmentation and volumetric performance may be driven by the optimized loss function. As explained in [2], soft Dice loss can lead to volumetric bias.

4   Discussion and Conclusion

We present a neural network that regresses the AIF for CT perfusion analysis. Unlike previous methods that aim to imitate the AIF selection of a human rater, the training of our network requires no manual annotations. To this end, we implement a differentiable SVD deconvolution, allowing the AIF generating network to be optimized for generating the most discriminative rCBF maps with reference to DWI images.

There are no previous studies that use CNNs to regress the AIF. Moreover, we are first in applying SVD deconvolution differentiability for perfusion applications. Unlike previous works, our approach does not require manual annotations. This is a crucial finding for devising automatic methods free from manual rater's influence. From a scientific point, it is interesting that our approach generates the 'best' AIF: current guidelines for the manual selection of AIFs do not have that guarantee.

Our experiments with the ISLES18 data yielded results matching expert segmentation performance. The rCBF maps that we obtained are slightly more informative for finding core-lesions than the ones an expert generates, as shown in the ROC analysis. In all segmentation metrics considered our method is comparable to an expert or an FDA-cleared software.

In future work, we aim to work with extra datasets and incorporate additional perfusion parameters. We currently only have 94 subjects and since each subject corresponds to a single regression, we effectively have only 94 samples. We expect that a larger dataset will further improve results. Similarly, additional data is needed to increase confidence in the method's performance.

This work only optimizes the rCBF map. In future work, we also intend to optimize the Tmax parameter map (which is defined as $argmax_t k(t)$).

Tmax estimation is crucial for the applicability of the method and for improving the lesion quantification since an increased Tmax is indicative for tissue at risk. This will require finding a differentiable substitute for the *argmax* and a ground truth for tissue at risk (e.g. the final infarct in patients that did not have reperfusion).

Acknowledgements. This project received funding from the European Union's Horizon 2020 research and innovation program under the Marie Sklodowska-Curie grant agreement TRABIT No 765148. EDLR, DR and DMS are employees of ico**metrix**. DR is supported by an innovation mandate of Flanders Innovation & Entrepreneurship (VLAIO).

References

1. Albers, G.W., et al.: Ischemic core and hypoperfusion volumes predict infarct size in SWIFT PRIME. Ann. Neurol. **79**(1), 76–89 (2016)
2. Bertels, J., Robben, D., Vandermeulen, D., Suetens, P.: Optimization with soft dice can lead to a volumetric bias. arXiv preprint arXiv:1911.02278 (2019)
3. Bland, J.M., Altman, D.: Statistical methods for assessing agreement between two methods of clinical measurement. Lancet **327**(8476), 307–310 (1986)
4. Calamante, F.: Arterial input function in perfusion MRI: a comprehensive review. Progr. Nucl. Magn. Reson. Spectrosc. **74**, 1–32 (2013)
5. Cereda, C.W., et al.: A benchmarking tool to evaluate computer tomography perfusion infarct core predictions against a DWI standard. J. Cereb. Blood Flow Metab. **36**(10), 1780–1789 (2016)
6. Fan, S., et al.: An automatic estimation of arterial input function based on multistream 3d CNN. Front. Neuroinform. **13**, 49 (2019)
7. Fieselmann, A., Kowarschik, M., Ganguly, A., Hornegger, J., Fahrig, R.: Deconvolution-based CT and MR brain perfusion measurement: theoretical model revisited and practical implementation details. J. Biomed. Imaging **2011**, 14 (2011)
8. Ionescu, C., Vantzos, O., Sminchisescu, C.: Training deep networks with structured layers by matrix backpropagation. arXiv preprint arXiv:1509.07838 (2015)
9. Kistler, M., Bonaretti, S., Pfahrer, M., Niklaus, R., Büchler, P.: The virtual skeleton database: an open access repository for biomedical research and collaboration. J. Med. Internet Res. **15**(11), e245 (2013)
10. Krizhevsky, A., Sutskever, I., Hinton, G.E.: ImageNet classification with deep convolutional neural networks. In: Advances in Neural Information Processing Systems, pp. 1097–1105 (2012)
11. Lin, L., Bivard, A., Krishnamurthy, V., Levi, C.R., Parsons, M.W.: Whole-brain CT perfusion to quantify acute ischemic penumbra and core. Radiology **279**(3), 876–887 (2016)
12. Maier, O., et al.: ISLES 2015-a public evaluation benchmark for ischemic stroke lesion segmentation from multispectral MRI. Med. Image Anal. **35**, 250–269 (2017)
13. Mlynash, M., Eyngorn, I., Bammer, R., Moseley, M., Tong, D.C.: Automated method for generating the arterial input function on perfusion-weighted MR imaging: validation in patients with stroke. Am. J. Neuroradiol. **26**(6), 1479–1486 (2005)
14. Mouridsen, K., Christensen, S., Gyldensted, L., Østergaard, L.: Automatic selection of arterial input function using cluster analysis. Magn. Reson. Med.: Off. J. Int. Soc. Magn. Reson. Med. **55**(3), 524–531 (2006)

15. Murase, K., Kikuchi, K., Miki, H., Shimizu, T., Ikezoe, J.: Determination of arterial input function using fuzzy clustering for quantification of cerebral blood flow with dynamic susceptibility contrast-enhanced mr imaging. J. Magn. Reson. Imaging: Off. J. Int. Soc. Magn. Reson. Med. **13**(5), 797–806 (2001)
16. Murphy, B., Chen, X., Lee, T.Y.: Serial changes in CT cerebral blood volume and flow after 4 hours of middle cerebral occlusion in an animal model of embolic cerebral ischemia. Am. J. Neuroradiol. **28**(4), 743–749 (2007)
17. Papadopoulo, T., Lourakis, M.I.A.: Estimating the Jacobian of the singular value decomposition: theory and applications. In: Vernon, D. (ed.) ECCV 2000. LNCS, vol. 1842, pp. 554–570. Springer, Heidelberg (2000). https://doi.org/10.1007/3-540-45054-8_36
18. Peruzzo, D., Bertoldo, A., Zanderigo, F., Cobelli, C.: Automatic selection of arterial input function on dynamic contrast-enhanced MR images. Comput. Methods Programs Biomed. **104**(3), e148–e157 (2011)
19. Rausch, M., Scheffler, K., Rudin, M., Radü, E.: Analysis of input functions from different arterial branches with gamma variate functions and cluster analysis for quantitative blood volume measurements. Magn. Reson. Imaging **18**(10), 1235–1243 (2000)
20. Robben, D., Suetens, P.: Perfusion parameter estimation using neural networks and data augmentation. In: Crimi, A., Bakas, S., Kuijf, H., Keyvan, F., Reyes, M., van Walsum, T. (eds.) BrainLes 2018. LNCS, vol. 11383, pp. 439–446. Springer, Cham (2019). https://doi.org/10.1007/978-3-030-11723-8_44
21. Shi, L., et al.: Automatic detection of arterial input function in dynamic contrast enhanced MRI based on affinity propagation clustering. J. Magn. Reson. Imaging **39**(5), 1327–1337 (2014)
22. Sourbron, S., Luypaert, R., Morhard, D., Seelos, K., Reiser, M., Peller, M.: Deconvolution of bolus-tracking data: a comparison of discretization methods. Phys. Med. Biol. **52**(22), 6761 (2007)
23. Srivastava, N., Hinton, G., Krizhevsky, A., Sutskever, I., Salakhutdinov, R.: Dropout: a simple way to prevent neural networks from overfitting. J. Mach. Learn. Res. **15**(1), 1929–1958 (2014)
24. Townsend, J.: Differentiating the singular value decomposition. Technical Report 2016 (2016). https://j-towns.github.io/papers/svd-derivative
25. Vagal, A., et al.: Automated CT perfusion imaging for acute ischemic stroke: pearls and pitfalls for real-world use. Neurology **93**(20), 888–898 (2019)

Spatial Similarity-Aware Learning and Fused Deep Polynomial Network for Detection of Obsessive-Compulsive Disorder

Peng Yang[1], Qiong Yang[3], Zhen Wei[4], Li Shen[5], Tianfu Wang[1], Ziwen Peng[2], and Baiying Lei[1(✉)]

[1] National-Regional Key Technology Engineering Laboratory for Medical Ultrasound, Guangdong Key Laboratory for Biomedical Measurements and Ultrasound Imaging, School of Biomedical Engineering, Health Science Center, Shenzhen University, Shenzhen 518060, China
leiby@szu.edu.cn

[2] College of Psychology and Sociology, Shenzhen University and the Shenzhen Key Laboratory of Affective and Social Cognitive Science, Shenzhen University, Shenzhen, China

[3] Affiliated Brain Hospital of Guangzhou Medical University (Guangzhou Huiai Hospital), Guangzhou, China

[4] Department of Child Psychiatry and Rehabilitation, Affiliated Shenzhen Maternity and Child Healthcare Hospital, Southern Medical University, Shenzhen, China

[5] Department of Biostatistics, Epidemiology and Informatics, Perelman School of Medicine, University of Pennsylvania, Pennsylvania, PA 19104, USA

Abstract. Hereditary mental illness (*e.g.*, obsessive-compulsive disorder (OCD)) shall reduce the quality of daily life of patients. To detect OCD objectively, sparse learning is an effective method for constructing a brain functional connectivity network (BFCN) since it can remove redundant information in the data and retain valuable biological characteristics. However, the spatial relationship between adjacent or bilaterally symmetric brain regions in each subject is ignored by most existing methods. To address this limitation, a spatial similarity aware learning is proposed in this work to construct BFCNs. Specifically, a smoothing regularization term is devised to constrain the model via embracing the spatial relationship between brain regions. To further learn the informative feature and reduce feature dimension of a BFCN, we leverage a new fused deep polynomial network (FDPN) framework via stacking a multi-layer deep polynomial network (DPN) model, where a weighting scheme is used to fuse features from different output layers. FDPN can learn the high-level discriminative features of BFCN to reduce the feature dimensionality. By fusing the traditional machine learning and deep learning strategies, our proposed method can achieve promising performance to distinguish OCD and unaffected first-degree relatives (UFDRs) using the imaging data collected in the local hospital. The experimental results demonstrate that our method outperforms the state-of-the-art competing methods.

Keywords: Obsessive-compulsive disorder · Spatial similarity-aware learning · Fused deep polynomial networks

© Springer Nature Switzerland AG 2020
A. L. Martel et al. (Eds.): MICCAI 2020, LNCS 12267, pp. 603–612, 2020.
https://doi.org/10.1007/978-3-030-59728-3_59

1 Introduction

Obsessive-compulsive disorder (OCD) is a chronic and hereditary psychosis. Compulsive thinking or behavior is the main clinical manifestation of patients with OCD, which often affects the patients' quality of life. The main symptoms of the characteristics of OCD symptoms are persistent invasive thinking and repetitive behavior [1, 2]. According to clinical studies, genetic factors and the surrounding social environment can lead to OCD [3]. The patient's unaffected first-degree relatives (UFDRs) are direct relatives such as brothers and parents are high-risk groups of OCD [4, 5]. According to the statistics, 2% to 3% patients worldwide suffer from this mental illness. At present, there are no biochemical and physiological indicators available in clinical practice for the OCD diagnosis [6]. To address this challenge, we propose a neuroimaging-based method for OCD detection, which integrates traditional machine learning and deep learning methods in a novel learning framework.

To detect OCD, resting-state functional magnetic resonance imaging (rs-fMRI) has been a widely used neuroimaging technique since the brain functional connectivity network (BFCN) built from rs-fMRI can reveal the effective relationship among the brain regions from brain function information. Accordingly, various BFCN construction models have been used to diagnose brain diseases. For example, Sen et al. [7] and Xing et al. [8] proposed to build Pearson's correlation (PC) network for OCD detection. However, only the pairwise relationship between every two brain regions is calculated in the PC based method, which ignores the relationship between a target brain region and all the other regions in each subject. Also, the BFCN constructed by PC based method is too dense to represent characteristics most relevant to brain disease [9]. Another popular method is the dynamic BFCN, which is constructed by the sliding window approach [10–12] to diagnose brain disorders. However, this method is too time-consuming to be feasible for practical applications. Also, sparse learning is beneficial to remove noise feature and retain important information because most biological networks are intrinsically sparse. Hence, there are various sparse learning methods for disease detection. For example, the group-constrained sparse (GCS) method is proposed by Wee et al. [9] and Zhang et al. to build BFCN for mild cognitive impairment classification. This is a linear combination model, which allows simultaneous selection of a common set of regions of interest (ROIs) across subjects. However, the brain functional connectivity network constructed by this method highly depends on the number of subjects and the data quality, which is undesirable in practice. In addition, these methods ignore similarities between adjacent or bilaterally symmetric brain regions. To overcome these limitations, we propose a spatial similarity-aware learning (SSL) method to construct the BFCN. Our method can not only construct the BFCN of each subject, but also capture the similarity between adjacent or bilaterally symmetric brain regions.

It is known that curse of dimensionality is quite common in BFCN analysis. To address it, robust feature learning method is an effective way since it can learn the features relative to the brain disease and reduce the data dimension. For example, in [9], the Lasso model is utilized to learn the most relevant features to solve the high dimensional issue. Yu et al. [13] used the t-test method to obtain similar sub-networks and developed a weighted sparse group method for brain disease identification. To learn informative features effectively, deep learning methods have achieved great success. However, most deep learning methods need to be trained with large amounts of data to obtain desirable performance. A common challenge of medical data, especially neuroimaging data is the issue of their small sample size coupled with high dimensionality. To address this, Livni *et al.* [14] proposed an efficient deep polynomial network (DPN) algorithm via layer-by-layer learning. This algorithm is a unique type of supervised deep learning method, which is particularly appealing for small datasets. Therefore, DPN algorithm has been widely used in small data applications. For example, Shi *et al.* [15] applied DPN algorithm for feature encoding to identify tumor images. Cheng *et al.* [16] proposed a ultrasound image intelligent diagnosis algorithm based on DPN with remarkable performance. Motivated by this, we propose a new fused deep polynomial networks (FDPN) algorithm, which can not only effectively learn informative features, but also properly reduce the feature dimension of BFCNs in our data with modest sample size.

Overall, this paper aims to devise a new FDPN based method for OCD detection. The main contribution of this study is as follows. 1) A novel SSL method is proposed to construct the BFCN, which not only builds the BFCN of each subject individually, but also captures the similarity between adjacent or bilaterally symmetric brain regions. 2) A FDPN model is proposed to fuse the features of multiple output layers using different weights. Namely, we not only learn the relationship inside the features but also reduce the data dimension. 3) A new framework is designed by combining traditional machine learning and deep learning to detect OCD and UFDRs. Our proposed method is evaluated in our in-house data, and the experimental results show that it can detect OCD and UFDRs with impressive performance.

2 Methodology

2.1 Proposed Framework

Figure 1 illustrates our framework for OCD and UFDRs detection. Firstly, the standard data preprocessing process is used to process the collected raw rs-fMRI data. Secondly, the SSL machine learning model is proposed to construct physiologically significant BFCN. Then, our FDPN method is applied to learn discriminative features of BFCN via deep learning. Finally, support vector machine (SVM) is utilized for OCD detection.

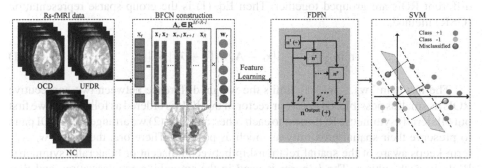

Fig. 1. The flow chart of our proposed method.

2.2 Image Preprocessing

We use the Data Processing Assistant for Resting-State fMRI (DPARSFA) and the Statistical Parametric Mapping toolbox (SPM8) to preprocess the data by a standardized data preprocessing process. Each subject's first 10 volumes of the rs-fMRI data are discarded before processing to keep the magnetization equal. We use the staggered sequence of slice collection to correct the remaining 170 volumes, and the echo planar scan is used to ensure the data on each slice corresponds to the unanimous point in time. We perform the following pre-processing on the collected image data: slice timing correction; head motion correction; realignment with the corresponding T1-volume; nuisance covariate regression (six head motion parameters, white matter signal and cerebrospinal fluid signal); spatial normalization into the stereotactic space of the Montreal Neurological Institute and resampling at $3 \times 3 \times 3$ mm^3; spatial smoothing with a 6-mm full-width half-maximum isotropic Gaussian kernel, and band-pass filtered (0.01–0.08 Hz). We use AAL template to segment the rs-fMRI data. We remove the 26 cerebellar ROIs and focus on studying the remaining 90 ROIs. The average rs-fMRI time series for each ROI is refined using a high-pass filter. Furthermore, head movement parameters, cerebrospinal fluid, and mean BOLD time series of the white matter are regressed out. Finally, the mean of the BOLD signal is extracted as the raw rs-fMRI data.

2.3 Spatial Similarity-Aware Learning

The bold capital letter represents matrices, the bold lowercase letter means vector, and the normal italic letters indicate scalars. Supposing we have a total of N subjects, the brain is segmented into R ROIs by the AAL template. $\mathbf{x}_r = [x_r, x_2, \ldots, x_M] \in \mathbb{R}^{M \times 1}$ indicates the BOLD regional mean time series (M length) of the r-th ROI, which can be estimated as a linear combination of time series of other R-1 ROIs. Let $\mathbf{A}_r = [\mathbf{x}_1, \ldots \mathbf{x}_{r-1}, \mathbf{x}_{r+1}, \ldots \mathbf{x}_R]$ be the signal matrix containing data from all the ROIs except $\mathbf{x}_r$. Let $\mathbf{w}_r = [w_1, \ldots w_{r-1}, w_{r+1}, \ldots w_R]$ be the weighting regression coefficient vector, which is used to measure the influence of R-1 ROIs on the target ROI (r-th ROI). $||\mathbf{W}||_{2,1} = \sum_{r=1}^{R-1} ||\mathbf{w}_r||_2$ is the summation of l_2-norm of $\mathbf{w}_r$, which is the r-th row vector of $\mathbf{W}$. Specifically, we impose l_2-norm penalty on the same elements of different matrices $\mathbf{w}_r$. Through this strategy, the weights corresponding to the connections of different ROIs are grouped together. Then Eq. (1) is the group sparse representation (GSR) method.

$$\min_{\mathbf{W}} \frac{1}{2} \sum_{r=1}^{R} ||\mathbf{x}_r - \mathbf{A}_r \mathbf{w}_r||_2^2 + \lambda_1 ||\mathbf{W}||_{2,1}, \tag{1}$$

The last item $||\mathbf{w}_r - \mathbf{w}_{r+1}||_1$ limits the weight difference between two consecutive ROIs as small as possible. Of note, our vector of the ROIs is ordered as follows: (1) we first put bilaterally symmetric ROIs next to each other; and then (2) we arrange these ROI pairs to preserve their spatial proximity as much as possible. Therefore, the $||\mathbf{w}_r - \mathbf{w}_{r+1}||_1$ term keeps aware of the spatial relationship between adjacent or bilaterally symmetric ROIs in each subject. The l_1-norm is used in the smoothing regularization, and thus there will be many zero components in the weight vector, which encourages the weight vectors to capture the similarity characteristics of two adjacent or bilaterally symmetric

ROIs. The similarity constraint is introduced to smooth the connectivity coefficients of ROIs, and the non-zero weights in the matrix means the informative features to the target ROI. This sparse learning model is defined as subjective-aware similarity learning, and its objective function is defined as:

$$\min_{\mathbf{W}} \frac{1}{2} \sum_{r=1}^{R} \|\mathbf{x}_r - \mathbf{A}_r \mathbf{w}_r\|_2^2 + \lambda_1 \|\mathbf{W}\|_{2,1} + \lambda_2 \sum_{r=1}^{R-1} \|\mathbf{w}_r - \mathbf{w}_{r+1}\|_1. \tag{2}$$

We divide the brain into 90 ROIs, and the extracted BFCN weight feature vector will contain 8,100 elements. Since the BFCN matrix is symmetric, we only extract the upper triangular weights of the matrix as features. Assuming that there are n nodes in the undirected BFCN, this will generate $n(n - 1)/2$ edges. Therefore, we will get a feature vector with 4,005 elements. Since the asymmetry dose not contribute to the final classification accuracy, we just simply define $\mathbf{W}^* = (\mathbf{W}_n + \mathbf{W}_n^T)/2$ [17], where $\mathbf{W}_n$ is the BFCN matrix finally obtained by the n-th subject, and $\mathbf{W}_n^T$ is the transpose matrix of $\mathbf{W}_n$. The features extracted via BFCN are represented as r. Then the Fisher's r- to-z transformation will be used for further normalization of the remaining features [18]. There are 4,005 features for each subject, which is too high dimensional to achieve good detection performance. Hence, the next step is to address the issue of high-dimensionality with effective methods.

2.4 Fused Deep Polynomial Network

To reduce feature dimension, the DPN is an effective way via learning layer-by-layer. It is a special type of supervised deep learning method especially suitable for small database. The DPN method can reduce the training errors by combining the label information of the training samples. The training error rate decreases with the depth of the network.

Assuming we have N training samples, $\{(\mathbf{x}_1, \mathbf{y}_1), (\mathbf{x}_2, \mathbf{y}_2), \ldots, (\mathbf{x}_N, \mathbf{y}_N)\}$, the coefficient vector $(w_1, w_2, w_3, \ldots w_N)$ and N polynomials $P_1, P_2, P_3, \ldots P_N$, according to Lemma in *Livni et al.* [14], $\sum_{i=1}^{N} w_i P_i(\mathbf{x}_j) = y_j$, where $(y_1, y_2, y_3 \ldots y_N)$ are the labels. In the first layer DPN, the polynomial in the network is defined as:

$$\{(<w, [1\mathbf{x}_1]\triangleright, \ldots, <w, [1\mathbf{x}_N]\triangleright : \mathbf{w} \in \mathbb{R}^{d+1}. \tag{3}$$

The singular value decomposition method is used to search a series of $(d + 1)$-dimensional vectors $(\mathbf{w}_1, \mathbf{w}_2, \ldots, \mathbf{w}_{d+1})$ to make $\{(<\mathbf{w}_j, [1\mathbf{x}_1]\triangleright, \ldots, <\mathbf{w}_j, [1\mathbf{x}_N]\triangleright)\}_j^{d+1}$ linearly independent with a basic-construction method. Specifically, we use a matrix $\mathbf{W} = [\mathbf{w}_1, \mathbf{w}_2, \ldots, \mathbf{w}_{d+1}]$ to map $[1\ \mathbf{X}]$ into the constructed basis. $\mathbf{1}$ denotes all-ones vector and $<, >$ denotes the dot product. For all $j = 1, 2, \cdots, d+1$, the j-the node of the first layer is denoted as:

$$n_j^1(\mathbf{x}) = <\mathbf{W}_j, [1\mathbf{X}]\triangleright \tag{4}$$

where $\left\{n_j^1(\mathbf{x}_1), \ldots, n_j^1(\mathbf{x}_N)\right\}_{j=1}^{d+1}$ is a basis for all values obtained by degree-1 polynomials over the training data. We let F^1 denote $N \times (d + 1)$ output matrix whose columns are the vectors of this set, namely, $F_{i,j}^1 = n_j^1(\mathbf{x}_i)$.

After the first layer network is constructed, it can be known that any P-level polynomial can be represented by a I-level polynomial and a $(P-1)$-level polynomial, the P-layer network is denoted as:

$$\tilde{\mathbf{F}}^P = \left[(\mathbf{F}_1^{P-1} \circ \mathbf{F}_1^1) \cdots (\mathbf{F}_1^{P-1} \circ \mathbf{F}_{|\mathbf{F}_1|}^1) \cdots (\mathbf{F}_{|\mathbf{F}^{P-1}|}^{P-1} \circ \mathbf{F}_1^1) \cdots (\mathbf{F}_{|\mathbf{F}^{P-1}|}^{P-1} \circ \mathbf{F}_{|\mathbf{F}_1|}^1) \right],$$
(5)

where $\mathbf{F}_i$ denotes the i-th column of the output matrix of DPN layer, $|\cdot|$ stands for the number of columns, and the $\circ$ operation represents the Hadamard product. Let $\mathbf{F}^P$ be a subset of the columns of $\tilde{\mathbf{F}}^P$. $\mathbf{F}^P$ generates the basis of degree-P polynomial, and it can be obtained by SVD to select the linear independent columns from $\tilde{\mathbf{F}}^P$. Finally, the output of all DPN layers creates the matrix of encoded features [14].

The FDPN method adds to every layer output features with different weights. In this work, we build a two layers DPN. Assuming the weight of the first output layer features (f_1) is γ, and the weight of second output layer features (f_2) is $1-\gamma$, the fused features are $f = \gamma \times f_1 + (1-\gamma) \times f_2$. In this way, the features of both layers are fully utilized, which is named as FDPN method.

3   Experiments and Results

3.1   Experimental Setup

In this study, we analyze the rs-fMRI data of 180 Chinese Han subjects collected from a local hospital. Specifically, the database contains 62 OCD patients, 53 UFDR and 65 normal control (NC) subjects. We use the 10-fold cross-validation method to evaluate our proposed method given the modest size of our dataset. Three metrics are utilized to evaluate the performance of our framework: Accuracy (ACC), area under receiver operating characteristic curve (AUC), sensitivity (SEN), and specificity (SPE).

Table 1. Detection performance of different BFCN methods with FDPN model (%).

BFCN	OCD vs. NC				UFDR vs. NC				OCD vs. UFDR			
	ACC	AUC	SEN	SPE	ACC	AUC	SEN	SPE	ACC	AUC	SEN	SPE
PC	74.56	82.43	82.00	71.48	71.63	74.28	62.19	**81.38**	61.70	59.86	66.21	**62.10**
GSR	81.23	87.27	92.46	72.21	80.86	72.02	92.40	72.62	62.27	60.38	77.45	45.23
SSL	**87.59**	**89.18**	**95.24**	**83.64**	**85.17**	**87.20**	**95.50**	76.79	**68.07**	**70.42**	**80.37**	55.17

Table 2. Detection performance of different feature learning methods with SSL model (%).

BFCN	DR	OCD vs. NC				UFDRs vs. NC				OCD vs. UFDRs			
		ACC	AUC	SEN	SPE	ACC	AUC	SEN	SPE	ACC	AUC	SEN	SPE
SSL	PCA	80.09	83.75	85.62	78.90	73.06	71.02	72.12	74.52	63.18	66.67	63.62	64.98
	Lasso	81.32	86.43	87.50	76.80	78.80	73.73	74.88	**79.76**	**68.64**	70.18	70.13	**68.34**
	DPN	85.92	86.81	**96.25**	78.80	84.50	77.21	90.64	79.29	66.31	66.27	76.04	57.07
	FDPN	**87.59**	**89.18**	95.24	**83.64**	**85.17**	**87.20**	**95.50**	76.79	68.07	**70.42**	**80.37**	55.17

3.2 Effect of the BFCN Constructed by SSL

It is an important step to build a good brain functional connectivity network, which is able to express the OCD characteristics and improve its detection accuracy. The relationship among ROIs can be expressed by the well-designed BFCN model. We perform comparative study with typical competing models (such as PC and GSR) to evaluate the performance of our proposed method. Table 1 shows the BFCN results in terms of various metrics, where the best performance is marked in bold. We note that the best performance is achieved by the proposed SSL model.

To classify OCD vs. normal control (NC), the highest accuracies of the PC, GSR and SSL models are 74.56%, 81.23%, and 87.59%, respectively. To classify UFDR vs. NC, the highest accuracies of PC, GSR SSL model are 71.63%, 80.86% and 85.17%, respectively. To classify OCD vs. UFDR, the best accuracies of the PC, GSR and SSL models are 61.70%, 62.27% and 68.07%, respectively. Our SSL model is not only superior over the other models in terms of classification accuracy, but also achieves better quantitative metrics than other models, which can evaluate the diagnosis performance from different perspectives. The results of the three classification tasks (OCD vs. NC, UFDR vs. NC, OCD vs. UFDR) are shown in Table 1 and the receiver operating characteristic (ROC) curves are shown in Fig. 2. In this paper, the selection ranges of λ_1, and λ_2 are from 5e−6 to 5e1. Final optimization parameters: 1) OCD vs. NC: $\lambda_1 = 0.05$, $\lambda_2 = 0.5$. 2) UFDR vs. NC: $\lambda_1 = 0.05$, $\lambda_2 = 0.005$. 3) OCD vs. UFDR: $\lambda_1 = 5e- 6 \lambda_2 = 5e-4$. The parameters C and G for sigmoid kernel of SVM is selected from 1e − 3 to 1e1. When C = 0.1 and G = 0.1, we achieve the final result of three classification tasks.

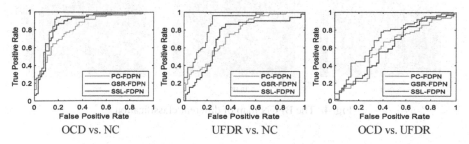

Fig. 2. The ROC curves of different BFCN methods with FDPN model.

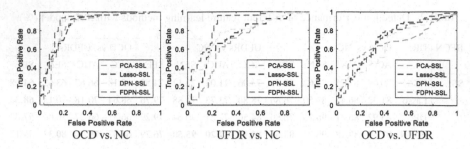

Fig. 3. The ROC curves of different feature learning methods via SSL model.

3.3 Effect of the FDPN Model

After constructing BFCN in all subjects using the SSL model, we extract the connections among ROIs from BFCN as a feature for disease diagnosis. To handle the high-dimensionality and show the effectiveness of our proposed FDPN method, we perform a comparative study on dimensionality reduction (DR) using PCA, Lasso, DPN and our proposed FDPN methods. Table 2 shows the results of three classification tasks (OCD vs. NC, UFDR vs. NC, OCD vs. UFDR) and Fig. 3 shows the ROC curves.

Obviously, our FDPN achieves the best detection performance in most situations. In OCD vs. NC analysis, the highest accuracies of the PCA, Lasso, DPN and FDPN methods are 80.89%, 81.32%, 85.92% and 87.59%, respectively. In UFDR vs. NC analysis, the highest accuracies of PCA, Lasso, DPN and FDPN methods are73.06%, 78.80%, 84.50% and 85.17%, respectively. In OCD vs. UFDR analysis, the highest accuracies of PCA, Lasso, DPN and FDPN methods are 63.18%, 68.64%, 66.31% and 68.07%, respectively. Our FDPN method is not only superior to the competing models in terms of detection accuracy, but also better than these models in other quantitative metrics. This shows the promise of our FDPN method with the superior performance over classical methods. In this paper, The range of width is from 10 to 80. The weight (γ) of each layer is from 0.1 to 0.9. Final optimization parameters: 1) OCD vs. NC: width = 40, $\gamma = 0.9$. 2) UFDR vs. NC: width = 40, $\gamma = 0.9$. 3) OCD vs. UFDR: width = 40, $\gamma = 0.9$.

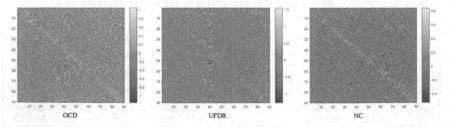

Fig. 4. The BFCN map of different classification.

4 Conclusion

A novel framework has been proposed for detecting OCD and UFDR subjects for normal controls, which combines traditional machine learning and deep learning techniques. Specifically, an SSL model has been proposed to build appealing BFCN based on sparse learning. The SSL model not only constructs the BFCN of each subject individually, but also embraces the similarity between adjacent or bilaterally symmetric brain regions. As shown in Fig. 4, we can clearly detect the difference among the BFCN maps of different diagnostic classes. The FDPN model can not only effectively learn the discriminative features of the data, but also properly reduce the feature dimension of BFCN. In the future, we will introduce additional data modalities and constraints into our model to improve the accuracy and stability of disease diagnosis. In addition, dynamic high-order BFCN will be another topic of our future research, which will enhance the performance of the entire framework.

Acknowledgement. This work was supported partly by National Natural Science Foundation of China (Nos. 61871274, U1909209, 61801305, 81571758 and 31871113), Key Laboratory of Medical Image Processing of Guangdong Province (No. K217300003). Guangdong Pearl River Talents Plan (2016ZT06S220), Guangdong Basic and Applied Basic Research Foundation (No. 2019A1515111205), Shenzhen Peacock Plan (Nos. KQTD2016053112051497 and KQTD2015033016104926), and Shenzhen Key Basic Research Project (Nos. GJHZ20190822095414576, JCYJ20180507184647636, JCYJ20190808155618806, JCYJ20170818094109846, JCYJ20190808155618806, and JCYJ20190808145011259).

References

1. Voon, V., Derbyshire, K., Rück, C., et al.: Disorders of compulsivity: a common bias towards learning habits. Mol. Psychiatry **20**, 1–8 (2015)
2. Gillan, C.M., Papmeyer, M., Morein-Zamir, S., et al.: Disruption in the balance between goal-directed behavior and habit learning in obsessive-compulsive disorder. Am. J. Psychiatry **168**, 718–726 (2011)
3. Wu, M.S., Hamblin, R., Nadeau, J., et al.: Quality of life and burden in caregivers of youth with obsessive-compulsive disorder presenting for intensive treatment. Compr. Psychiatry **80**, 46–56 (2018)
4. Pérez-Vigil, A., Fernández de la Cruz, L., Brander, G., et al.: Association of obsessive-compulsive disorder with objective indicators of educational attainment: a nationwide register-based sibling control study. JAMA Psychiatry **75**, 47–55 (2018)
5. Arnold, P.D., Askland, K.D., Barlassina, C., et al.: Revealing the complex genetic architecture of obsessive–compulsive disorder using meta-analysis. Mol. Psychiatry **23**, 1181–1188 (2017)
6. Bruin, W., Denys, D., van Wingen, G.: Diagnostic neuroimaging markers of obsessive-compulsive disorder: Initial evidence from structural and functional MRI studies. Prog. Neuropsychopharmacol. Biol. Psychiatry **91**, 49–59 (2019)
7. Sen, B., Bernstein, G.A., Xu, T., et al.: Classification of obsessive-compulsive disorder from resting-state fMRI. In: EMBC, pp. 3606–3609. IEEE (2016)
8. Xing, X., Jin, L., Shi, F., et al.: Diagnosis of OCD using functional connectome and Riemann kernel PCA. In: SPIE Medical Imaging (2019). https://doi.org/10.1117/12.2512316

9. Wee, C.-Y., Yap, P.-T., Zhang, D., Wang, L., Shen, D.: Group-constrained sparse fMRI connectivity modeling for mild cognitive impairment identification. Brain Struct. Funct. 219(2), 641–656 (2013). https://doi.org/10.1007/s00429-013-0524-8

10. Du, Y., Fryer, S.L., Fu, Z., et al.: Dynamic functional connectivity impairments in early schizophrenia and clinical high-risk for psychosis. Neuroimage 180, 632–645 (2018)

11. Wee, C.-Y., Yang, S., Yap, P.-T., Shen, D.: Sparse temporally dynamic resting-state functional connectivity networks for early MCI identification. Brain Imaging Behav. 10(2), 342–356 (2015). https://doi.org/10.1007/s11682-015-9408-2

12. Kucyi, A., Davis, K.D.: Dynamic functional connectivity of the default mode network tracks daydreaming. Neuroimage 100, 471–480 (2014)

13. Yu, R., Han, Z., Le, A., et al.: Connectivity strength-weighted sparse group representation-based brain network construction for MCI classification. Hum. Brain Mapp. 38, 1–14 (2017)

14. Livni, R., Shalev-Shwartz, S., Shamir, O.: An algorithm for training polynomial networks. arXiv preprint arXiv:1304.7045 (2013)

15. Shi, J., Qian, Y., Wu, J., et al.: Ultrasound image based tumor classification via deep polynomial network and multiple kernel learning. Curr. Med. Imaging 14, 301–308 (2018)

16. Cheng, J.-Z., Ni, D., Chou, Y.-H., et al.: Computer-aided diagnosis with deep learning architecture: applications to breast lesions in US images and pulmonary nodules in CT scans. Sci. Rep. 6, 24454 (2016)

17. Qiao, L., Zhang, H., Kim, M., et al.: Estimating functional brain networks by incorporating a modularity prior. NeuroImage 141, 399–407 (2016)

18. Davey, C.E., Grayden, D.B., Egan, G.F., et al.: Filtering induces correlation in fMRI resting state data. Neuroimage 64, 728–740 (2013)

Deep Representation Learning
for Multimodal Brain Networks

Wen Zhang[1], Liang Zhan[2], Paul Thompson[3], and Yalin Wang[1]([envelope])

[1] School of Computing, Informatics and Decision Systems Engineering,
Arizona State University, Tempe, AZ, USA
ylwang@asu.edu
[2] Electrical and Computer Engineering, University of Pittsburgh,
Pittsburgh, PA, USA
[3] Imaging Genetics Center, University of Southern California, Los Angeles, CA, USA

Abstract. Applying network science approaches to investigate the functions and anatomy of the human brain is prevalent in modern medical imaging analysis. Due to the complex network topology, for an individual brain, mining a discriminative network representation from the multimodal brain networks is non-trivial. The recent success of deep learning techniques on graph-structured data suggests a new way to model the non-linear cross-modality relationship. However, current deep brain network methods either ignore the intrinsic graph topology or require a network basis shared within a group. To address these challenges, we propose a novel end-to-end deep graph representation learning (Deep Multimodal Brain Networks - DMBN) to fuse multimodal brain networks. Specifically, we decipher the cross-modality relationship through a graph encoding and decoding process. The higher-order network mappings from brain structural networks to functional networks are learned in the node domain. The learned network representation is a set of node features that are informative to induce brain saliency maps in a supervised manner. We test our framework in both synthetic and real image data. The experimental results show the superiority of the proposed method over some other state-of-the-art deep brain network models.

Keywords: Multimodality · Brain networks · Network representation · Deep learning · Graph topology

1 Introduction

There is growing scientific interest in understanding functional and structural organizations of the human brain from a large scale of multimodal brain imaging data. In medical imaging analysis, one of the popular ways for this task is

Electronic supplementary material The online version of this chapter (https://doi.org/10.1007/978-3-030-59728-3_60) contains supplementary material, which is available to authorized users.

© Springer Nature Switzerland AG 2020
A. L. Martel et al. (Eds.): MICCAI 2020, LNCS 12267, pp. 613–624, 2020.
https://doi.org/10.1007/978-3-030-59728-3_60

to explore brain regional connections (i.e., brain networks) measured from the brain imaging signals. The topological patterns of brain networks are closely related to the brain functional organizations [4] and the connection breakdown between the relevant brain regions has an intimate association with the progress of neurodegenerative diseases [12,22] or normal brain developments [36]. However, patterns of focal damages in brain networks are different across modalities, making the mining of multimodal network changes difficult.

Deep learning methods have been successfully applied to extract biological information from the neuroimaging data [24,29]. Most of the prior brain network analysis represent graph structure as a grid-like image to enable convolutional computation [7,21,34]. More recently, deep graph convolutional networks (GCNs) have been introduced to brain network research [1,14,16]. These studies perform the localized convolutional operation at either graph nodes or edges. They can be categorized into the graph spectral convolution [1,16] and the graph spatial convolution [9]. The former approach is suitable for node-centric problems defined on the fixed-sized neighborhood graphs. For graph-centric problems, the spectral method requires a group-wise graph structure before approximating the spectral graph convolution. Therefore, its performance to a large extent depends on the predefined network basis. However, the existing framework [14] is designed for a single modality and lacks a well defined k-hop convolutional operator on each node. This makes the multimodal brain network fusion intractable in the node domain and thus difficult to draw brain saliency maps.

In this paper, we propose a novel GCN model for multimodal brain networks analysis. Two naturally coherent brain network modalities, i.e., functional and structural brain networks, are considered. The structural network acts as the anatomical skeleton to constrain brain functional activities and, in return, consistent functional activities reshape the structural network in the long term [4]. Hence, we argue the existence of a high-level dependency, namely networks communication [2], across them. It is deciphered by a deep encoding-decoding graph network in our model. Meanwhile, the obtained node features help representation learning of brain network structure in a supervised manner. The contributions can be summarised into four-folds. (1) It is the first paper using a deep graph learning to model brain functions evolving from its structural basis. (2) We propose an end-to-end automatic brain network representation framework based on the intrinsic graph topology. (3) We model the cross-modality relationship through a deep graph encoding-decoding process based on the proposed multistage graph convolutional kernel. (4) We draw graph saliency maps subject to the supervised tasks, enabling phenotypic and disease-related biomarker detection.

2   Methodology

Multimodal Brain Network Data. A brain network uses a graph structure to describe interconnections between brain regions and is a weighted graph $G = \{V, E, X\}$, where $V = \{v_i\}_{i=1}^{N}$ is the node set indicating brain regions, $E = \{\epsilon_{i,j}\}$ is the edges set and $X = \{x_{i,j}\}$ is the corresponding edge weight; For a given subject, we have a pair of networks $\{G^f, G^d\}$, where $G^f = \{V, E^f, X^f\}$ represents the functional brain network and $G^d = \{V, E^d, X^d\}$ is the structural brain network. These two networks share the same set of nodes, i.e., using an identical definition of brain regions, but differ in network topology and edge weights. An edge weight $x_{i,j}^f$ in G^f is the correlation of fMRI signals between node v_i and v_j, while a structural edge weight $x_{i,j}^d$ in G^d is the probability of fiber tractography between them.

2.1 Multi-stage Graph Convolution Kernel

A brain structural network can be interpreted as a freeway net where biological information such as brain functional signals flows from node to node. In the brain network, a node shall be affected by its neighboring nodes and their affection is negatively correlated with the shortest network distance [27]. To encode these node-to-node patterns, we adopt the spatial graph convolution kernel which will give the node embedding features with respect to the local graph topology. It defines a way to aggregate node features in a given size of neighborhood, e.g., 1-hop connections.

Given a target node v_i and its neighbourhood graph topology $G_{\mathcal{N}(v_i)}$, the graph convolution kernel first collects node features h_{v_i} of its immediate neighbours:

$$AGG(h_{v_i}) = \sum_{v_j \in \mathcal{N}(v_i)} h_{v_j} \cdot x_{i,j}, \tag{1}$$

and then updates the node feature as:

$$h'_{v_i} = \sigma(AGG(h_{v_i}) \cdot w). \tag{2}$$

Here, σ is a non-linear activation and $w \in \mathbb{R}^{F \times F'}$ is a learnable weight matrix of a fully-connected layer (FC). Previous research proves that a k-hop convolution kernel can be divided into k 1-hop convolutions [15]. Therefore, we stack several 1-hop convolutions to increase size of the effective receptive field on graphs.

A potential problem with Eq. 1 is its poor generalization of the local aggregation, i.e., the aggregation weight is fixed to be $x_{i,j}$. Though these predefined values reflect the brain biological profiles, they might not be optimal for brain network encoding, especially for the cross-modality learning pursued by our research. For example, brain regions that are interconnected with large weights in the brain structural network are not guaranteed to be more strongly connected in the brain functional network as well [20]. Besides, compared with brain structural networks, brain functional networks are more dynamic and fluctuant on the edge connections. Therefore, the dynamic adjustment of the aggregation weights during graph learning is favored. To this end, we adopt the idea of graph attention network (GAT) [32]. Given each pair of node features, their dynamic edge weights are learned by a single-layer feedforward neural network, i.e., $X^{ATT} = \{x_{i,j}^{ATT}\} = \{f_{att}(h_{v_i}, h_{v_j})\}$. More specifically, we first increase the expression power of the node features by using a shared linear transformation,

$\tilde{h}_{v_i} = h_{v_i} \cdot w$, where $w \in \mathbb{R}^{F \times F'}$ is a learned parameter. Then, we use a single-layer feedforward neural network to derive the edge weight:

$$\tilde{x}_{i,j} = \sigma(a^T[\tilde{h}_{v_i} \oplus \tilde{h}_{v_j}]), \tag{3}$$

where $\oplus$ is the concatenate operator and $a \in \mathbb{R}^{2F'}$ is a parameter of the feedforward network. To assure generalization of Eq. 3 across different nodes, a softmax layer is append for normalization of the neighbourhood,

$$x_{i,j}^{ATT} = \frac{exp(\sigma(a^T[\tilde{h}_{v_i} \oplus \tilde{h}_{v_j}]))}{\sum_{k \in \mathcal{N}(v_i)} exp(\sigma(a^T[\tilde{h}_{v_i} \oplus \tilde{h}_{v_k}]))}. \tag{4}$$

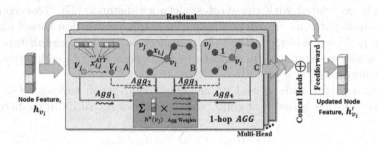

Fig. 1. Multi-stage graph convolution kernel (MGCK). Three aggregation mechanisms are dynamical combined, including the graph attention weight $x_{i,j}^{ATT}$ (A), the original edge weight $x_{i,j}$ (B), and the binary weight $\delta(x_{i,j})$ (C).

Compared with $x_{i,j}$, $x_{i,j}^{ATT}$ is associated with the node order and thus is asymmetric on edge $\epsilon_{i,j}$. Besides, it is free of local network topology. In addition to the graph attention based aggregation (Fig. 1, A), we also propose a binary symmetric aggregation defined with a threshould function $\delta(x_{i,j})$ (Fig. 1, B). $\delta(x_{i,j})$ thresholds an edge by a given threshould value γ, e.g., aggregation weight will be 1 if $x_{i,j} > \gamma$, otherwise 0. We set $\gamma = 0$ empirically in this study. This process follows an assumption that two brain regions are highly interactive in functional brain network as long as they are structurally connected [27]. To integrate all of the aggregation mechanisms, we design a multi-stage graph convolution kernel (MGCK). Equation 1 is thus updated as:

$$
\begin{aligned}
AGG(h_{v_i}) &= \sum_{v_j \in \mathcal{N}(v_i)} h_{v_j} \cdot (x_{i,j} + \alpha) \cdot (x_{i,j}^{ATT} + \beta\delta(x_{i,j})) \\
&= \sum_{v_j \in \mathcal{N}(v_i)} h_{v_j} \cdot (x_{i,j}x_{i,j}^{ATT} + \beta x_{i,j} + \alpha x_{i,j}^{ATT} + \alpha\beta\delta),
\end{aligned}
\tag{5}
$$

where α and β are learnable parameters balancing different aggregation mechanisms. In the above equation, we have 4 different aggregation weights. $x_{i,j}x_{i,j}^{ATT}$

and $x_{i,j}$ are the pre-defined network connections with and without attention weights. $x_{i,j}^{ATT}$ is the attention aggregation alone and δ is the threshold connections. In the end, we introduce the multi-head learning [31] to stabilize the aggregation in MGCK. K independent multi-stage aggregation are conducted and aggregated features are concatenated before feeding to a FC layer. Accordingly, Eq. 2 is updated as:

$$\hat{h}_{v_i} = \oplus_{k=1}^{K} [\sigma(AGG^k(h_{v_i}) \cdot w)]. \tag{6}$$

Previous research indicates that graph convolution network performs poorly with a deep architecture due to the high complexity of back-propagation in the deep layers. To address this problem, residual block in GCN [17] is proposed. It is inspired by the success of ResNet [10] for image data. We add the residual connection after MGCK,

$$h'_{v_i} = \mathcal{F}(\hat{h}_{v_i}, \hat{w}) + w_m h_{v_i}. \tag{7}$$

$\mathcal{F}$ is a FC layer parameterized by $\hat{w}$. Parameter w_m is designed to match the dimensions.

2.2 Deep Multimodal Brain Networks (DMBN)

We show the pipeline of DMBN in Fig. 2. It generates the multimodal graph node representations for different learning tasks. There are two parts in DMBN. The first part is for cross-modality learning via an encoding-decoding network. Here, we construct brain functional network from brain structural network. The brain functional network contains both positive and negative connections. These two

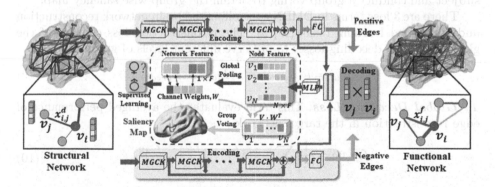

Fig. 2. Pipeline of DMBN. The structural network is fed into two independent encoding-decoding networks to generate the cross-modality encoding of the positive and negative functional connections. Meanwhile, the node features from these two networks are combined and serve as the multimodal graph representations for the supervised learning tasks via a MLP network. During this process, a brain saliency map is derived.

types of brain functional connectivities yield a distinct relationship with brain structural network [11,26]. Hence, we separate their encoding into two independent encoding networks. For each graph encoder, we use several MGCK layers to aggregate node features from diverse ranges of the neighborhood in structural network. The generated node features are then fed into the decoding networks to reconstruct the positive and negative connections respectively. Specifically, for each undirected edge $e_{i,j}$, we define the reconstructed links as:

$$\hat{x}_{i,j} = \frac{1}{1 + exp(-h_{v_i}^T \cdot \Theta \cdot h_{v_j})}, \tag{8}$$

where h_{v_i} is a node feature vector in the network embedding space and Θ is a learnable layer weight. Equation 8 maps the deep node embeddings $\{h_{v_i}\}$ to a connection matrix $\{\hat{x}_{i,j}\}$ where each element ranges from 0 to 1 consisting with the functional connections.

The second part of our model is a supervised learning. The node embedding features (h_v) from the positive and negative encoding networks are concatenated node-wisely and processed by an MLP. Since our tasks are graph level learning, a global pooling is applied before the last FC layer to remove the effect of node orders. Along with the supervised learning tasks, it is important to understand the key brain regions closely associated with the tasks. Inspired by the classic activation maps [1], a graph localization strategy is carried out by learning contribution scores of graph nodes. As shown in Fig. 2, suppose the final node feature matrix consists of F channels for N nodes, a global mean pooling generates a channel-wise vector treated as the network feature. Therefore, each channel has a corresponding weight, w_i, learned by the last FC layer. To obtain the node-wise importance score, we warp it back by an inner product between node features and channel weights, i.e., $h_v \cdot W^T$. In the end, we rank the top-k nodes for each subject and conduct a group voting to obtain the group-wise saliency map.

There are 3 loss terms in DMBN controlling the brain network reconstruction and supervised learning tasks (Eq. 9). The reconstruction loss consists of the global and local decoding losses to preserve different levels of graph topology.

$$L_{all} = \mu_1 L_{global} + \mu_2 L_{local} + L_{preds}, \tag{9}$$

1) Global Decoding Loss. This term evaluates the averaged performance of edge reconstruction in the target network.

$$\mathcal{L}_{global} = \frac{1}{|E|} \sum_{e_{i,j}} a_{i,j}(\hat{x}_{i,j}^{f+} - \hat{x}_{i,j}^{f-} - x_{i,j}^f)^2, \tag{10}$$

where $a_{i,j}$ is the additional penalty of the edge reconstruction. Here, we set it as $e^{abs(x_{i,j}^f)}$, which gives the higher weights for stronger connections in brain functional network. $\hat{x}^{f+}$ and $\hat{x}^{f-}$ indicate the decoded network connections from the positive and negative flow of encoding.

2) Local Decoding Loss. The cross-modality reconstruction of brain networks is challenging, hence we do not expect a full recovery of all edges but rather the reconstruction of local graph structure on important connections, e.g., edges with strong connections in both structural and functional networks. We adopt the first-order proximity [33] to capture the local structure. The loss function is defined as:

$$\mathcal{L}_{local} = \sum_{i=1}^{n} \frac{1}{|\mathcal{N}_i^d|} \sum_{j \in \mathcal{N}_i^d} e^{\delta(x_{i,j}^d)} ||h_{v_i}^f - h_{v_j}^f||_2^2, \tag{11}$$

where $|\mathcal{N}_i^d|$ is the number of neighbouring nodes of v_i in brain structural network. $\delta(x_{i,j}^d)$ is a threshold function which favors strong generalization. Equation 11 generalizes Laplacian Eigenmaps [3] and drives nodes with similar embedding features together.

3) Supervised Loss. The loss function for prediction is defined as:

$$L_{pred} = -\frac{1}{K} \sum_{i=1}^{K} y_i \cdot log(f_{pred}(h_{v_i})), \tag{12}$$

where K is the number of subjects and f_{pred} is a function learned by the MLP network.

3 Experiment

3.1 Gender Prediction

Dataset. The data are from the WU-Minn HCP 1200 Subjects Data Release [30]. We include 746 healthy subjects (339 males, 407 females), each has high-quality resting fMRI and dMRI data. The functional network is processed using CONN toolbox [35] and structural connectivity is measured by using FSL toolbox [13]. Here we try to predict the gender based on the multimodal brain network topology. Previous research has shown the strong relationship between gender and brain connectivity patterns [25].

Experiment Setup. We select 5 state-of-the-art baseline models for comparison, where 3 of them, i.e. tBNE [6], MK-SVM [8] and mCCA + ICA [28], are transitional machine learning algorithms while the rest two, i.e. BrainNetCNN [14] and Brain-Cheby [16] use deep models. In addition, 5 variant models of MDBN are tested in the experiments as an ablation study. We apply the 5-fold cross-validation for all methods. In our model setting, the positive connection encoding has 5 cascade MGCK layers and negative connection encoding has 4 MGCK layers. In each encoding, each of MGCKs has the feature dimension [128] and 4-heads learning. We report the statistical results with three evaluation metrics: accuracy, precision, and F1 scores. Besides, we take a grid search to decide hyperparameters μ_1 and μ_2. Based on the empirical knowledge, we set the search range for μ_1 as [10, 1, 0.1, 0.01] and μ_2 as [5, 1, 0.5, 0.1]. The best result appears at $\mu_1 = 1$ and $\mu_2 = 0.5$. Details can be found in Supplementary Fig. 1.

Table 1. Performance of gender prediction in the HCP data.

Method	HCP (Gender)			PPMI (Disease)		
	Acc	$Prec$	$F1 - Score$	Acc	$Prec$	$F1 - Score$
tBNE [6]	0.543	0.497	0.503	0.580	0.597	0.530
MK-SVM [8]	0.481	0.438	0.524	0.587	0.487	0.568
mCCA + ICA [28]	0.680	0.703	0.691	0.640	0.660	0.622
Brain-Cheby [16]	0.739	0.740	0.739	0.635	0.622	0.628
BrainNetCNN [14]	0.734	0.775	0.684	0.673	0.695	0.778
w/o Recon[b]	0.738	0.692	0.767	0.688	0.727	0.786
w/o TAGG& Recon[b]	0.699	0.696	0.738	-	-	-
w/o AAGG& Recon[b]	0.681	0.689	0.735	-	-	-
MDBN w/o Global	0.784	0.798	0.799	-	-	-
MDBN w/o Local	0.793	0.814	0.824	-	-	-
MDBN	**0.819**[a]	**0.836**[a]	**0.845**[a]	**0.728**[a]	**0.859**[a]	**0.735**

[a]stands for significance. [b]indicates the variant model using a single modality.

Results. As shown in the Table 1 (HCP), our model achieves the highest accuracy ($ACC > 81.9\%$) in the gender prediction among all the methods and significantly outperforms the others with at least 8% and 10% increases in accuracy and F1 scores, respectively. Generally, deep models are superior to the traditional node embedding method (tBNE). We notice that, when we remove the cross-modality learning, i.e., variant methods denoted by w/o Recon, the performance drops significantly. Though they are still comparable to the other baselines, the training process is unstable with a high variance. The cross-modality learning enables node-level learning to be effective and consequently affects further graph-level learning. In addition, the 10 most important brain regions affecting the gender prediction are shown in Supplementary Fig. 2. These regions spread at the cortical areas including the frontal and orbital gyrus, precentral gyrus, insular gyrus, as well as the subcortical areas such as basal ganglia. All those regions play vital roles in regulating cognitive functioning, motor and emotion controls, which, with a high probability, exert the gender discrepancy [23,25].

Ablation Analysis. We explore influence of each element in our model (Table 1). We first remove the decoding network that makes our model a single modality learning (w/o Recon). Under such a configuration, our model is still comparable to the baselines. However, the decreased performance suggests the cross-modality is indispensable to an informative network representation. Based on this setting, we further evaluate the role of each aggregation mechanism in MGCK. We remove the threshold aggregation weight (w/o TAGG&Recon) and graph attention aggregation (w/o AAGG&Recon) respectively. All of them cause a significant decrease in performance. In addition to the single modality learning, we also validate the importance of different reconstruction losses in multimodal learning. Missing the local (MDBN w/o Local) or global (MDBN w/o Global)

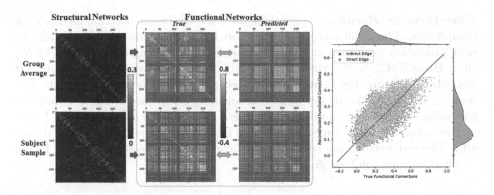

Fig. 3. The cross-modality learning results. The functional network is predicted (middle) from its structural network counterpart (left). We present the group averaged result and an individual sample. The statistical evaluation (Spearman correlation, r_S) of reconstructed functional networks is conducted (right) and the predicted edge weights are significantly correlated with the ground truth data, $r_s = 0.83$.

losses results in around 3% downgrade in prediction accuracy. Meanwhile, the global reconstruction loss yields a larger weight than the local reconstruction loss. Since the global loss considers all of the edges in the functional network, it contains relatively more fruitful information than the local loss which focuses on the direct edges in the structural network. However, they are complementary to each other.

Cross-Modality Learning. To validate the efficacy of cross-modality learning, we turn off the prediction tasks, i.e., only keeping the reconstruction losses during training. Results have been shown in Fig. 3. We present the predicted functional networks of a randomly selected sample and the group average of the whole testing data. From the sparse structural networks, the corresponding functional connections have been correctly predicted and major patterns of the local network connections are captured. To further prove the accuracy, we conduct the statistical analysis on edges. Both direct and indirect edges in the target functional network are highly correlated with the predicted edges (Spearman correlation, overall is $r_S = 0.83$ with $p < 10^{-4}$), where the direct edges, $r_S = 0.84$, are slightly greater than the indirect edges, $r_S = 0.82$. We also prove the robustness of our model to the different sparsity levels of brain structural networks and results are shown in Supplementary Fig. 4.

3.2   Disease Classification

In addition to the gender prediction in the healthy subjects, we retest our model on the disease classification. In this experiment, we include 323 subjects from Parkinson's Progression Markers Initiative (PPMI) [18] and 224 of them are patients of Parkinson's disease (PD). We follow the experimental setting in gender prediction. $\mu_1 = 0.5$ and $\mu_2 = 0.5$ are used according to the grid search.

Classification Results. We consider the state-of-the-art baseline methods for comparison. The results are shown in Tab. 1 (PPMI). Our model achieves the best prediction performance than other models (improving the accuracy by 5% than BrainNetCNN, 9% than Brain-Cheby and other baselines). Moreover, It also shows adding the cross-modality reconstruction do upgrade the performance. We locate the 10 key regions associating with the PD classification via the saliency map, see Supplementary Fig. 3. Most of the salient regions locate at the subcortical structures, such as the bilateral hippocampus and basal ganglia. These structures are conventionally conceived as the biomarkers of PD in medical imaging analysis [5,19].

4   Conclusion

We propose a novel multimodal brain network fusion framework based on a deep graph modal. The cross-modality network embedding is generated by an encoding-decoding network. The network embedding is also supervised by the prediction tasks. Eventually, the learned node features contribute to the brain saliency map for detecting disease-related biomarkers. In the future, we plan to extend our model to other learning tasks such as brain cortical parcellation and cognitive activity prediction.

Acknowledgments. This work was supported in part by NIH (RF1AG051710 and R01EB025032). We also gratefully acknowledge the support of NVIDIA Corporation with the donation of the Titan Xp GPU used for this research.

References

1. Arslan, S., Ktena, S.I., Glocker, B., Rueckert, D.: Graph saliency maps through spectral convolutional networks: application to sex classification with brain connectivity. arXiv preprint arXiv:1806.01764 (2018)
2. Avena-Koenigsberger, A., Misic, B., Sporns, O.: Communication dynamics in complex brain networks. Nature Rev. Neurosci. **19**(1), 17–33 (2018)
3. Belkin, M., Niyogi, P.: Laplacian eigenmaps for dimensionality reduction and data representation. Neural Comput. **15**(6), 1373–1396 (2003)
4. Bullmore, E., Sporns, O.: The economy of brain network organization. Nat. Rev. Neurosci. **13**(5), 336 (2012)
5. Camicioli, R., Moore, M.M., Kinney, A., Corbridge, E., Glassberg, K., Kaye, J.A.: Parkinson's disease is associated with hippocampal atrophy. Mov. Disord. **18**(7), 784–790 (2003)
6. Cao, B., et al.: t-BNE: tensor-based brain network embedding. In: Proceedings of SIAM International Conference on Data Mining (SDM) (2017)
7. Deshpande, G., Wang, P., Rangaprakash, D., Wilamowski, B.: Fully connected cascade artificial neural network architecture for attention deficit hyperactivity disorder classification from functional magnetic resonance imaging data. IEEE Trans. Cybern. **45**, 2668–2679 (2015)

8. Dyrba, M., Grothe, M., Kirste, T., Teipel, S.J.: Multimodal analysis of functional and structural disconnection in a Lzheimer's disease using multiple kernel svm. Hum. Brain Mapp. **36**(6), 2118–2131 (2015)
9. Hamilton, W., Ying, Z., Leskovec, J.: Inductive representation learning on large graphs. In: NIPS (2017)
10. He, K., Zhang, X., Ren, S., Sun, J.: Deep residual learning for image recognition. In: Proceedings of the IEEE Conference on Computer Vision and Pattern Recognition, pp. 770–778 (2016)
11. Honey, C., Sporns, O., Cammoun, L., Gigandet, X., Thiran, J.P., Meuli, R., Hagmann, P.: Predicting human resting-state functional connectivity from structural connectivity. Proc. Natl. Acad. Sci. **106**(6), 2035–2040 (2009)
12. Jao, T., et al.: Functional brain network changes associated with clinical and biochemical measures of the severity of he patic encephalopathy. Neuroimage **122**, 332–344 (2015)
13. Jenkinson, M., Beckmann, C.F., Behrens, T.E., Woolrich, M.W., Smith, S.M.: Fsl. Neuroimage **62**(2), 782–790 (2012)
14. Kawahara, J., et al.: Brainnetcnn: convolutional neural networks for brain networks; towards predicting neurodevelopment. NeuroImage **146**, 1038–1049 (2017)
15. Kipf, T.N., Welling, M.: Semi-supervised classification with graph convolutional networks. In: International Conference on Learning Representations (ICLR) (2017)
16. Ktena, S.I., et al.: Metric learning with spectral graph convolutions on brain connectivity networks. NeuroImage **169**, 431–442 (2018)
17. Li, G., Muller, M., Thabet, A., Ghanem, B.: DeepGCNs: Can GCNs go as deep as CNNs? In: Proceedings of the IEEE International Conference on Computer Vision, pp. 9267–9276 (2019)
18. Marek, K., Jennings, D., Lasch, S., Siderowf, A., Tanner, C., Simuni, T., Coffey, C., Kieburtz, K., Flagg, E., Chowdhury, S., et al.: The parkinson progression marker initiative (PPMI). Prog. Neurobiol. **95**(4), 629–635 (2011)
19. Obeso, J.A., Rodriguez-Oroz, M.C., Rodriguez, M., Lanciego, J.L., Artieda, J., Gonzalo, N., Olanow, C.W.: Pathophysiology of the basal ganglia in parkinson's disease. Trends Neurosci. **23**, S8–S19 (2000)
20. Osmanlıoğlu, Y., Tunç, B., Parker, D., Elliott, M.A., Baum, G.L., Ciric, R., Satterthwaite, T.D., Gur, R.E., Gur, R.C., Verma, R.: System-level matching of structural and functional connectomes in the human brain. NeuroImage **199**, 93–104 (2019)
21. Plis, S.M., et al.: Reading the (functional) writing on the (structural) wall: Multimodal fusion of brain structure and function via a deep neural network based translation approach reveals novel impairments in schizophrenia. NeuroImage 181, 734–747 (2018)
22. Repovs, G., Csernansky, J.G., Barch, D.M.: Brain network connectivity in individuals with schizophrenia and their siblings. Biological psychiatry (2011)
23. Rijpkema, M., Everaerd, D., van der Pol, C., Franke, B., Tendolkar, I., Fernández, G.: Normal sexual dimorphism in the human basal ganglia. Hum. Brain Mapping **33**(5), 1246–1252 (2012)
24. Ronneberger, O., Fischer, P., Brox, T.: U-Net: convolutional networks for biomedical image segmentation. In: Navab, N., Hornegger, J., Wells, W.M., Frangi, A.F. (eds.) MICCAI 2015. LNCS, vol. 9351, pp. 234–241. Springer, Cham (2015). https://doi.org/10.1007/978-3-319-24574-4_28
25. Ruigrok, A.N., et al.: A meta-analysis of sex differences in human brain structure. Neurosci. Biobehav. Rev. **39**, 34–50 (2014)

26. Schwarz, A.J., McGonigle, J.: Negative edges and soft thresholding in complex network analysis of resting state functional connectivity data. Neuroimage **55**(3), 1132–1146 (2011)
27. Stam, C., et al.: The relation between structural and functional connectivity patterns in complex brain networks. Int. J. Psychophysiol. **103**, 149–160 (2016)
28. Sui, J., Pearlson, G., Caprihan, A., Adali, T., Kiehl, K.A., Liu, J., Yamamoto, J., Calhoun, V.D.: Discriminating schizophrenia and bipolar disorder by fusing FMRI and DTI in a multimodal CCA+ joint ICA model. Neuroimage **57**(3), 839–855 (2011)
29. Suk, H.-I., Shen, D.: Deep learning-based feature representation for AD/MCI classification. In: Mori, K., Sakuma, I., Sato, Y., Barillot, C., Navab, N. (eds.) MICCAI 2013. LNCS, vol. 8150, pp. 583–590. Springer, Heidelberg (2013). https://doi.org/10.1007/978-3-642-40763-5_72
30. Van Essen, D.C., Smith, S.M., Barch, D.M., Behrens, T.E., Yacoub, E., Ugurbil, K.: The WU-Minn human connectome project: an overview. Neuroimage **80**, 62–79 (2013)
31. Vaswani, A., et al.: Attention is all you need. In: Advances in Neural Information Processing Systems, pp. 5998–6008 (2017)
32. Velickovic, P., Cucurull, G., Casanova, A., Romero, A., Lio, P., Bengio, Y.: Graph attention networks. arXiv preprint arXiv:1710.10903 (2017)
33. Wang, D., Cui, P., Zhu, W.: Structural deep network embedding. In: Proceedings of the 22nd ACM SIGKDD International Conference on Knowledge Discovery and Data Mining, pp. 1225–1234. ACM (2016)
34. Wang, S., He, L., Cao, B., Lu, C.T., Yu, P.S., Ragin, A.B.: Structural deep brain network mining. In: ACM SIGKDD. ACM (2017)
35. Whitfield-Gabrieli, S., Nieto-Castanon, A.: Conn: a functional connectivity toolbox for correlated and anticorrelated brain networks. Brain Connectivity **2**(3), 125–141 (2012)
36. Zhang, W., Shu, K., Wang, S., Liu, H., Wang, Y.: Multimodal fusion of brain networks with longitudinal couplings. In: Frangi, A.F., Schnabel, J.A., Davatzikos, C., Alberola-López, C., Fichtinger, G. (eds.) MICCAI 2018. LNCS, vol. 11072, pp. 3–11. Springer, Cham (2018). https://doi.org/10.1007/978-3-030-00931-1_1

Pooling Regularized Graph Neural Network for fMRI Biomarker Analysis

Xiaoxiao Li[1(✉)], Yuan Zhou[3], Nicha C. Dvornek[1,3], Muhan Zhang[5],
Juntang Zhuang[1], Pamela Ventola[4], and James S. Duncan[1,2,3]

[1] Biomedical Engineering, Yale University, New Haven, CT, USA
xiaoxiao.li@aya.yale.edu
[2] Electrical Engineering, Yale University, New Haven, CT, USA
[3] Radiology and Biomedical Imaging, Yale School of Medicine, New Haven, CT, USA
[4] Child Study Center, Yale School of Medicine, New Haven, CT, USA
[5] Facebook AI Research, New York City, USA

Abstract. Understanding how certain brain regions relate to a specific neurological disorder has been an important area of neuroimaging research. A promising approach to identify the salient regions is using Graph Neural Networks (GNNs), which can be used to analyze graph structured data, e.g. brain networks constructed by functional magnetic resonance imaging (fMRI). We propose an interpretable GNN framework with a novel salient region selection mechanism to determine neurological brain biomarkers associated with disorders. Specifically, we design novel regularized pooling layers that highlight salient regions of interests (ROIs) so that we can infer which ROIs are important to identify a certain disease based on the node pooling scores calculated by the pooling layers. Our proposed framework, Pooling Regularized-GNN (PR-GNN), encourages reasonable ROI-selection and provides flexibility to preserve either individual- or group-level patterns. We apply the PR-GNN framework on a Biopoint Autism Spectral Disorder (ASD) fMRI dataset. We investigate different choices of the hyperparameters and show that PR-GNN outperforms baseline methods in terms of classification accuracy. The salient ROI detection results show high correspondence with the previous neuroimaging-derived biomarkers for ASD.

Keywords: fMRI Biomarker · Graph neural network · Autism

1 Introduction

Explaining the underlying roots of neurological disorders (i.e., what brain regions are associated with the disorder) has been a main goal in the field of neuroscience and medicine [1–4]. Functional magnetic resonance imaging (fMRI), a non-invasive neuroimaging technique that measures neural activation, has been paramount in advancing our understanding of the functional organization of the brain [5–7]. The functional network of the brain can be modeled as a graph in

© Springer Nature Switzerland AG 2020
A. L. Martel et al. (Eds.): MICCAI 2020, LNCS 12267, pp. 625–635, 2020.
https://doi.org/10.1007/978-3-030-59728-3_61

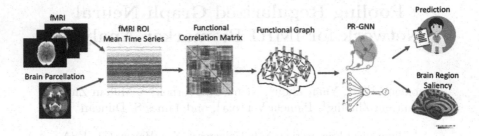

Fig. 1. The overview of the pipeline. fMRI images are parcellated by atlas and transferred to graphs. Then, the graphs are sent to our proposed PR-GNN, which gives the prediction of specific tasks and jointly selects salient brain regions that are informative to the prediction task.

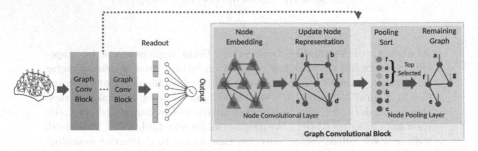

Fig. 2. PR-GNN for brain graph classification and the details of its key component - Graph Convolutional Block. Each Graph Convolutional Block contains a node convolutional layer followed by a node pooling layer.

which each node is a brain region and the edges represent the strength of the connection between those regions.

The past few years have seen the growing prevalence of using graph neural networks (GNN) for graph classification [8]. Like pooling layers in convolutional neural networks (CNNs) [9,10], the pooling layer in GNNs is an important design to compress a large graph to a smaller one for lower dimensional feature extraction. Many node pooling strategies have been studied and can be divided into the following categories: 1) clustering-based pooling, which clusters nodes to a super node based on graph topology [11–13] and 2) ranking-based pooling, which assigns each node a score and keeps the top ranked nodes [14,15]. Clustering-based pooling methods do not preserve node assignment mapping in the input graph domain, hence they are not inherently interpretable at the node level. For our purpose of interpreting node importance, we focus on ranking-based pooling methods. Currently, existing methods of this type [14,15] have the following key limitations when applying them to salient brain ROI analysis: 1) ranking scores for the discarded nodes and the remaining nodes may not be significantly distinguishable, which is not suitable for identifying salient and representative regional biomarkers, and 2) the nodes in different graphs in the same group may be ranked totally differently (usually caused by overfitting), which is problematic when our objective is to find group-level biomarkers. To reach group-level analysis, such approaches typically require additional steps to summarize statistics (such as averaging). For these two-stage methods, if the results from the first stage are not reliable, significant errors can be induced in the second stage.

To utilize GNN for fMRI learning and meet the need of group-level biomarker finding, we propose a pooling regularized GNN framework (PR-GNN) for classifying neurodisorder patients vs healthy control subjects and discovering disorder related biomarkers jointly. The overview of our methods is depicted in Fig. 1. Our key contributions are:

- We formulate an end-to-end framework for fMRI prediction and biomarker (salient brain ROIs) interpretation.
- We propose novel regularization terms for ranking-based pooling methods to encourage more reasonable node selection and provide flexibility between individual-level and group-level interpretation in GNN.

2 Graph Neural Network for Brain Network Analysis

The architecture of our PR-GNN is shown in Fig. 2. Below, we introduce the notation and the layers in PR-GNN. For simplicity, we focus on Graph Attention Convolution (GATConv) [16,17] as the node convolutional layer. For node pooling layers, we test two existing ranking based pooling methods: TopK pooling [14] and SAGE pooling [15].

2.1 Notation and Problem Definition

We first parcellate the brain into N ROIs based on its T1 structural MRI. We define ROIs as graph nodes $\mathcal{V} = \{v_1, \ldots, v_N\}$. We define an undirected weighted graph as $G = (\mathcal{V}, \mathcal{E})$, where $\mathcal{E}$ is the edge set, i.e., a collection of (v_i, v_j) linking vertices v_i and v_j. G has an associated node feature matrix $H = [\mathbf{h}_1, \ldots, \mathbf{h}_N]^\top$, where $\mathbf{h}_i$ is the feature vector associated with node v_i. For every edge connecting two nodes, $(v_i, v_j) \in \mathcal{E}$, we have its strength $e_{ij} \in \mathbb{R}$. We also define $e_{ij} = 0$ for $(v_i, v_j) \notin \mathcal{E}$ and therefore the adjacency matrix $E = [e_{ij}] \in \mathbb{R}^{N \times N}$ is well defined.

2.2 Graph Convolutional Block

Node Convolutional Layer. To improve GATConv [8], we incorporate edge features in the brain graph as suggested by Gong and Cheng [18] and Yang et al. [17]. We define $\mathbf{h}_i^{(l)} \in \mathbb{R}^{d^{(l)}}$ as the feature for the ith node in the lth layer and $H^{(l)} = [\mathbf{h}_1^{(l)}, \ldots, \mathbf{h}_{N^{(l)}}^{(l)}]^\top$, where $N^{(l)}$ is the number of nodes at the lth layer (the same for $E^{(l)}$). The propagation model for the forward-pass update of node representation is calculated as:

$$\mathbf{h}_i^{(l+1)} = \phi_i^{\Theta^{(l)}}(H^{(l)}, E^{(l)}) = \alpha_{i,i}\Theta^{(l)}\mathbf{h}_i^{(l)} + \sum_{j \in \mathcal{N}(i)} \alpha_{i,j}\Theta^{(l)}\mathbf{h}_j^{(l)}, \tag{1}$$

where the attention coefficients α_{ij} are computed as

$$\alpha_{i,j} = \frac{\exp(\hat{\alpha}_{i,j})}{\sum_{k \in \mathcal{N}(i) \bigcup \{i\}} \exp(\hat{\alpha}_{i,k})}, \quad \hat{\alpha}_{i,j} = e_{i,j}^{(l)} \mathrm{ReLU}((\mathbf{a}^{(l)})^\top [\Theta^{(l)} \mathbf{h}_i^{(l)} \| \Theta^{(l)} \mathbf{h}_j^{(l)}]), \quad (2)$$

where $\mathcal{N}(i)$ denotes the set of indices of neighboring nodes of v_i, $\|$ denotes concatenation, $\Theta^{(l)} \in \mathbb{R}^{d^{(l+1)} \times d^{(l)}}$ and $\mathbf{a}^{(l)} \in \mathbb{R}^{2d^{(l+1)}}$ are model parameters.

Node Pooling Layer. The choices of keeping which nodes in TopK pooling and SAGE pooling are determined based on the node importance score $\mathbf{s}^{(l)} = [s_1^{(l)}, \ldots, s_{N^{(l)}}^{(l)}]^\top$, which is calculated in two ways as follows:

$$s_i^{(l)} = \begin{cases} \mathrm{sigmoid}((\mathbf{h}_i^{(l)})^\top \mathbf{w}^{(l)} / \|\mathbf{w}^{(l)}\|), & \text{TopK pooling} \\ \mathrm{sigmoid}(\phi_i^{\theta^{(l)}}(H^{(l)}, E^{(l)})), & \text{SAGE pooling} \end{cases} \quad (3)$$

where ϕ_i^θ is calculated in Eq. (1) and $\mathbf{w}^{(l)} \in \mathbb{R}^{d^{(l)}}$ and $\theta^{(l)} \in \mathbb{R}^{1 \times d^{(l)}}$ are model parameters. Note that $\theta^{(l)}$ is different from $\Theta^{(l)}$ in Eq. (1) such that the output of ϕ_i^θ is a scalar.

Given $\mathbf{s}^{(l)}$ the following equation roughly describes the pooling procedure:

$$\mathbf{idx} = \mathrm{top}(\mathbf{s}^{(l)}, k^{(l)}), \quad E^{(l+1)} = E_{\mathbf{idx},\mathbf{idx}}^{(l)}. \quad (4)$$

The notation above finds the indices corresponding to the largest $k^{(l)}$ elements in score vector $\mathbf{s}^{(l)}$, and $(\cdot)_{\mathbf{i,j}}$ is an indexing operation which takes elements at row indices specified by $\mathbf{i}$ and column indices specified by $\mathbf{j}$. The nodes receiving lower scores will experience less feature retention.

Lastly, we seek a "flattening" operation to translate graph information to a vector. Suppose the last layer is L, we use $\mathbf{z} = \mathrm{mean} \{\mathbf{h}_i^{(L)} : i = 1, \ldots, N^{(L)}\}$, where mean operates elementwise. Then $\mathbf{z}$ is sent to a multilayer perceptron (MLP) to give the final prediction.

3 Proposed Regularizations

3.1 Distance Loss

To overcome the limitation of existing methods that ranking scores for the discarded nodes and the remaining nodes may not be distinguishable, we propose two distance losses to encourage the difference. Before introducing them, we first rank the elements of the mth instance scores, $\mathbf{s}_m^{(l)}$, in a descending order, denote it as $\hat{\mathbf{s}}_m^{(l)} = [\hat{s}_{m,1}^{(l)}, \ldots, \hat{s}_{m,N^{(l)}}^{(l)}]^\top$, and denote its top $k^{(l)}$ elements as $a_{m,i}^{(l)} = \hat{s}_{m,i}^{(l)}, i = 1, \ldots, k^{(l)}$, and the remaining elements as $b_{m,j}^{(l)} = \hat{s}_{m,j+k^{(l)}}^{(l)}, j = 1, \ldots, N^{(l)} - k^{(l)}$. We apply two types of constraint to all the M training instances.

MMD Loss. Maximum mean discrepancy (MMD) loss [19,20] was originally proposed in Generative adversarial nets (GANs) to quantify the difference of the scores between real and generated samples. In our application, we define MMD loss for the pooling layer as:

$$
L_{MMD}^{(l)} = -\frac{1}{M} \sum_{m=1}^{M} \left[\frac{1}{(k^{(l)})^2} \sum_{i,j=1}^{k^{(l)}} \kappa(a_{m,i}^{(l)}, a_{m,j}^{(l)}) + \frac{1}{(N^{(l)} - k^{(l)})^2} \sum_{i,j=1}^{N^{(l)} - k^{(l)}} \kappa(b_{m,i}^{(l)}, b_{m,j}^{(l)}) \right.
$$
$$
\left. - \frac{2}{k^{(l)}(N^{(l)} - k^{(l)})} \sum_{i=1}^{k^{(l)}} \sum_{j=1}^{N^{(l)} - k^{(l)}} \kappa(a_{m,i}^{(l)}, b_{m,j}^{(l)}) \right],
$$

where $\kappa(a, b) = \exp(\| a - b \|^2)/\sigma$ is a Gaussian kernel and σ is a scaling factor.

BCE Loss. Ideally, the scores for the selected nodes should be close to 1 and the scores for the unselected nodes should be close to 0. Binary cross entropy (BCE) loss is calculated as:

$$
L_{BCE}^{(l)} = -\frac{1}{M} \sum_{m=1}^{M} \frac{1}{N^{(l)}} \left[\sum_{i=1}^{k^{(l)}} \log(a_{m,i}^{(l)}) + \sum_{i=1}^{N^{(l)} - k^{(l)}} \log(1 - b_{m,i}^{(l)}) \right]. \quad (5)
$$

The effect of this constraint will be shown in Sect. 4.3.

3.2 Group-Level Consistency Loss

Note that $\mathbf{s}^{(l)}$ in Eq. (4) is computed from the input $H^{(l)}$. Therefore, for $H^{(l)}$ from different instances, the ranking of the entries of $\mathbf{s}^{(l)}$ can be very different. For our application, we want to find the common patterns/biomarkers for a certain neuro-prediction task. Thus, we add regularization to force the $\mathbf{s}^{(l)}$ vectors to be similar for different input instances in the first pooling layer, where the group-level biomarkers are extracted. We call the novel regularization group-level consistency (GLC) and only apply it to the first pooling layer, as the nodes in the following layers from different instances might be different. Suppose there are M_c instances for class c in a batch, where $c \in \{1, \ldots, C\}$ and C is the number of classes. We form the scoring matrix $S_c^{(1)} = [\mathbf{s}_{1,c}^{(1)}, \ldots, \mathbf{s}_{M_c,c}^{(1)}]^\top \in \mathbb{R}^{M_c \times N}$. The GLC loss can be expressed as:

$$
L_{GLC}^c = \frac{1}{M_c^2} \sum_{i=1}^{M_c} \sum_{j=1}^{M_c} \| \mathbf{s}_{i,c}^{(1)} - \mathbf{s}_{j,c}^{(1)} \|_2 = 2\mathrm{Tr}((S_c^{(1)})^\top L S_c^{(1)}), \quad (6)
$$

where $L_c = D_c - W_c$, W_c is a $M_c \times M_c$ matrix with all 1s, D_c is a $M_c \times M_c$ diagonal matrix with M_c as diagonal elements. We propose to use Euclidean distance for $\mathbf{s}_{i,c}$ and $\mathbf{s}_{j,c}$ due to the benefits of convexity and computational efficiency.

Cross entropy loss L_{ce} is used for the final prediction. Then, the final loss function is formed as:

$$L_{total} = L_{ce} + \lambda_1 \sum_{l=1}^{L} L_{Dist}^{(l)} + \lambda_2 \sum_{c}^{C} L_{GLC}^{c}, \tag{7}$$

where λ's are tunable hyper-parameters, l indicates the lth GNN block and L is the total number of GNN blocks, $Dist$ is either MMD or BCE.

4   Experiments and Results

4.1   Data and Preprocessing

We collected fMRI data from a group of 75 ASD children and 43 age and IQ-matched healthy controls (HC), acquired under the "biopoint" task [21]. The fMRI data was preprocessed following the pipeline in Yang et al. [22]. The Desikan-Killiany [23] atlas was used to parcellate brain images into 84 ROIs. The mean time series for each node was extracted from a random 1/3 of voxels in the ROI by bootstrapping. In this way, we augmented the data 10 times. Edges were defined by top 10% positive partial correlations to achieve sparse connections. If this led to isolated nodes, we added back the largest edge to each of them. For node attributes, we used Pearson correlation coefficient to node 1–84. Pearson correlation and partial correlation are different measures of fMRI connectivity. We aggregate them by using one to build edge connections and the other to build node features.

4.2   Implementation Details

The model architecture was implemented with 2 conv layers and 2 pooling layers as shown in Fig. 2, with parameter $d^{(0)} = 84, d^{(1)} = 16, d^{(2)} = 16$. We designed a 3-layer MLP (with 16, 8 and 2 neurons in each layer) that takes the flattened graph $\mathbf{z} \in \mathbb{R}^{16}$ as input and predicts ASD vs. HC. The pooling layer kept the top 50% important nodes ($k^{(l)} = 0.5N^{(l)}$). We will discuss the variation of λ_1 and λ_2 in Sect. 4.3. We randomly split the data into five folds based on subjects, which means that the graphs from a single subject can only appear in either the training or test set. Four folds were used as training data, and the left-out fold was used for testing. Adam was used as the optimizer. We trained the model for 100 epochs with an initial learning rate of 0.001, annealed to half every 20 epochs. We set $\sigma = 5$ in the MMD loss to match the same scale as BCE loss.

4.3   Hyperparameter Discussion and Ablation Study

We tuned the parameters λ_1 and λ_2 in the loss function Eq. (7) and showed the results in Table 1. λ_1 encouraged more separable node importance scores for selected and unselected nodes after pooling. λ_2 controlled the similarity of the

Table 1. Model variations and hyperparameter ($\lambda_1-\lambda_2$) discussion.

Loss	Pool	0–0	0.1–0	0.1–0.1	0.1–0.5	0.1–1
MMD	TopK	0.753(0.042)	0.784(0.062)	0.781(0.038)	0.780(0.059)	0.744(0.060)
	SAGE	0.751(0.022)	0.770(0.039)	0.771(0.051)	0.773(0.047)	0.751(0.050)
BCE	TopK	0.750(0.046)	0.779(0.053)	0.797(0.051)	0.789(0.066)	0.762(0.044)
	SAGE	0.755(0.041)	0.767(0.033)	0.773(0.047)	0.764(0.050)	0.755(0.041)

Table 2. Comparison with different baseline models.

Metric	Model					
	SVM	Random forest	MLP	BrainNetCNN [24]	Li et al. [25]	**PR-GNN***
Acc	0.686(0.111)	0.723(0.020)	0.727(0.047)	0.781(0.044)	0.753(0.033)	**0.797(0.051)**
♯Par	3k	3k	137k	1438k	16k	**6k**

Acc: Accuracy; ♯Par: The number of trainable parameters; PR-GNN*: TopK+BCE.

selected nodes for instances within the same class. A larger λ_2 moves toward group-level interpretation of biomarkers. We first performed an ablation study by comparing setting (0–0) and (0.1–0). Mean accuracies increased at least 3% in TopK (1–2% in SAGE) with MMD or BCE loss. To demonstrate the effectiveness of L_{Dist}, we showed the distribution of node pooling scores of the two pooling layers in Fig. 3 over epochs for different combination of pooling functions and distance losses, with $\lambda_1 = 0.1$ and $\lambda_2 = 0$. In the early epochs, the scores centered around 0.5. Then the scores of the top 50% important nodes moved to 1 and scores of unimportant nodes moved to 0 (less obvious for the second pooling layer using SAGE, which may explain why SAGE got lower accuracies than TopK). Hence, significantly higher scores were attributed to the selected important nodes in the pooling layer. Then, we investigated the effects of λ_2 on the accuracy by varying it from 0 to 1, with λ_1 fixed at 0.1. Without L_{GLC}, the model was easier to overfit to the training set, while larger L_{GLC} may result in underfitting to the training set. As the results in Table 1 show, the accuracy increased when λ_2 increased from 0 to 0.1 and the accuracy dropped if we increased λ_2 to 1 (except for TopK+MMD). For the following baseline comparison experiments, we set $\lambda_1-\lambda_2$ to be 0.1–0.1.

4.4   Comparison with Existing Models

We compared our method with several brain connectome-based methods, including Random Forest (1000 trees), SVM (RBF kernel), and MLP (one 20 nodes hidden layer), a state-of-the-art CNN-based method, BrainNetCNN [24] and a recent GNN method on fMRI [25], in terms of accuracy and number of parameters. We used the parameter settings indicated in the original paper [24]. The inputs and the architecture parameter setting (node conv, pooling and MLP layers) of the alternative GNN method were the same as PR-GNN. The inputs of BrainNetCNN were Pearson correlation matrices. The inputs of the other

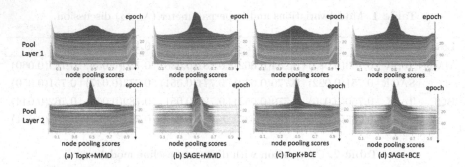

Fig. 3. Distributions of node pooling scores over epochs (offset from far to near).

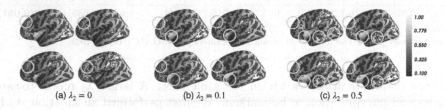

Fig. 4. Selected salient ROIs (importance score indicated by yellow-red color) of four randomly selected ASD individuals with different weights λ_2 on GLC. The commonly detected salient ROIs across different individuals are circled in green. (Color figure online)

alternative methods were the flattened up-triangle of Pearson correlation matrices. Note that the inputs of GNN models contained both Pearson and partial correlations. For a fair comparison with the non-GNN models, we used Pearson correlations (node features) as their inputs, because Pearson correlations were the embedded features, while partial correlations (edge weights) only served as message passing filters in GNN models. The results are shown in Table 2. Our PR-GNN outperformed alternative models. With regularization terms on the pooling function, PR-GNN achieved better accuracy than the recent GNN [25]. Also, PR-GNN needs only 5% parameters compared to the MLP and less than 1% parameters compared to BrainNetCNN.

4.5   Biomarker Interpretation

Without losing generalizability, we investigated the selected salient ROIs using the model TopK+BCE ($\lambda_1 = 0.1$) with different levels of interpretation by tuning λ_2. As we discussed in Sect. 3.2, large λ_2 led to group-level interpretation and small λ_2 led to individual-level interpretation. We varied λ_2 from 0–0.5. Without losing generalizability, we show the salient ROI detection results of four randomly selected ASD instances in Fig. 4. We show the remaining 21 ROIs after the 2nd pooling layer (with pooling ratio = 0.5, 25% nodes left) and corresponding node pooling scores. As shown in Fig. 4(a), when $\lambda_2 = 0$, we could rarely find any overlapped area among the instances. In Fig. 4(b–c), we circled the large overlapped areas across the instances. By visually examining the salient ROIs, we found two overlapped areas in Fig. 4(b) and four overlapped areas in Fig. 4(c). By averaging the node importance scores (1st pooling layer) over all the instances, dorsal striatum, thalamus and frontal gyrus were the most salient ROIs associated with identifying ASD. These ROIs are related to the neurological functions of social communication, perception and execution [26–29], which are clearly deficient in ASD.

5 Conclusion

In this paper, we propose PR-GNN, an interpretable graph neural network for fMRI analysis. PR-GNN takes graphs built from fMRI as inputs, then outputs prediction results together with interpretation results. With the built-in interpretability, PR-GNN not only performs better on classification than alternative methods, but also detects salient brain regions for classification. The novel loss term gives us the flexibility to use this same method for individual-level biomarker analysis (small λ_2) and group-level biomarker analysis (large λ_2). We believe that this is the first work using a single model in fMRI study that fills the critical interpretation gap between individual- and group-level analysis. Our interpretation results reveal the salient ROIs to identify autistic disorders from healthy controls. Our method has a potential for understanding neurological disorders, and ultimately benefiting neuroimaging research. We will extend and validate our methods on larger benchmark datasets in future work.

Acknowledgements. This research was supported in part by NIH grants [R01NS035193, R01MH100028].

References

1. Kaiser, M.D., et al.: Neural signatures of autism. Proc. Natl. Acad. Sci. **107**(49), 21223–21228 (2010)
2. Goldani, A.A., Downs, S.R., Widjaja, F., Lawton, B., Hendren, R.L.: Biomarkers in autism. Front. Psychiatry **5**, 100 (2014)
3. Baker, J.T., et al.: Disruption of cortical association networks in schizophrenia and psychotic bipolar disorder. JAMA Psychiatry **71**(2), 109–118 (2014)
4. McDade, E., et al.: Longitudinal cognitive and biomarker changes in dominantly inherited alzheimer disease. Neurology **91**(14), e1295–e1306 (2018)
5. Worsley, K.J., et al.: A general statistical analysis for fMRI data. Neuroimage **15**(1), 1–15 (2002)
6. Poldrack, R.A., Halchenko, Y.O., Hanson, S.J.: Decoding the large-scale structure of brain function by classifying mental states across individuals. Psychol. Sci. **20**(11), 1364–1372 (2009)
7. Wang, X., et al.: Decoding and mapping task states of the human brain via deep learning. Hum. Brain Mapp. **41**, 1505–1519 (2019)

8. Hamilton, W., Ying, Z., Leskovec, J.: Inductive representation learning on large graphs. In: Advances in Neural Information Processing Systems, pp. 1024–1034 (2017)
9. Simonyan, K., Zisserman, A.: Very deep convolutional networks for large-scale image recognition (2014). arXiv preprint arXiv:1409.1556
10. Long, M., Zhu, H., Wang, J., Jordan, M.I.: Unsupervised domain adaptation with residual transfer networks. In: Advances in Neural Information Processing Systems, pp. 136–144 (2016)
11. Defferrard, M., Bresson, X., Vandergheynst, P.: Convolutional neural networks on graphs with fast localized spectral filtering. In: Advances in Neural Information Processing Systems, pp. 3844–3852 (2016)
12. Dhillon, I.S., Guan, Y., Kulis, B.: Weighted graph cuts without eigenvectors a multilevel approach. IEEE Trans. Pattern Anal. Mach. Intell. **29**(11), 1944–1957 (2007)
13. Ying, Z., You, J., Morris, C., Ren, X., Hamilton, W., Leskovec, J.: Hierarchical graph representation learning with differentiable pooling. In: Advances in Neural Information Processing Systems, pp. 4800–4810 (2018)
14. Gao, H., Ji, S.: Graph u-nets (2019). arXiv preprint arXiv:1905.05178
15. Lee, J., Lee, I., Kang, J.: Self-attention graph pooling (2019). arXiv preprint arXiv:1904.08082
16. Veličković, P., et al.: Graph attention networks. In: ICLR (2018)
17. Yang, X., et al.: Interpretable multimodality embedding of cerebral cortex using attention graph network for identifying bipolar disorder. In: Shen, D., et al. (eds.) MICCAI 2019. LNCS, vol. 11766, pp. 799–807. Springer, Cham (2019). https://doi.org/10.1007/978-3-030-32248-9_89
18. Gong, L., Cheng, Q.: Exploiting edge features for graph neural networks. In: Proceedings of the IEEE Conference on Computer Vision and Pattern Recognition, pp. 9211–9219 (2019)
19. Gretton, A., Borgwardt, K.M., Rasch, M.J., Schölkopf, B., Smola, A.: A kernel two-sample test. J. Mach. Learn. Res. **13**(Mar), 723–773 (2012)
20. Li, C.-L., Chang, W.-C., Cheng, Y., Yang, Y., Póczos, B.: Mmd gan: towards deeper understanding of moment matching network. In: Advances in Neural Information Processing Systems, pp. 2203–2213 (2017)
21. Kaiser, M.D., et al.: Neural signatures of autism. PNAS **107**, 21223–21228 (2010)
22. Yang, D., et al.: Brain responses to biological motion predict treatment outcome in young children with autism. Transl. Psychiatry **6**(11), e948 (2016)
23. Desikan, R.S., et al.: An automated labeling system for subdividing the human cerebral cortex on mri scans into gyral based regions of interest. Neuroimage **31**(3), 968–980 (2006)
24. Kawahara, J., et al.: Brainnetcnn: convolutional neural networks for brain networks; towards predicting neurodevelopment. NeuroImage **146**, 1038–1049 (2017)
25. Li, X., Dvornek, N.C., Zhou, Y., Zhuang, J., Ventola, P., Duncan, J.S.: Graph neural network for interpreting task-fMRI biomarkers. In: Shen, D., et al. (eds.) MICCAI 2019. LNCS, vol. 11768, pp. 485–493. Springer, Cham (2019). https://doi.org/10.1007/978-3-030-32254-0_54
26. Schuetze, M., Park, M.T.M., Cho, I.Y., MacMaster, F.P., Chakravarty, M.M., Bray, S.L.: Morphological alterations in the thalamus, striatum, and pallidum in autism spectrum disorder. Neuropsychopharmacology **41**(11), 2627–2637 (2016)
27. Hardan, A.Y., Girgis, R.R., Adams, J., Gilbert, A.R., Keshavan, M.S., Minshew, N.J.: Abnormal brain size effect on the thalamus in autism. Psychiatry Res. Neuroimaging **147**(2–3), 145–151 (2006)

28. Bhanji, J.P., Delgado, M.R.: The social brain and reward: social information processing in the human striatum. Wiley Interdisc. Rev. Cogn. Sci. **5**(1), 61–73 (2014)
29. Press, C., Weiskopf, N., Kilner, J.M.: Dissociable roles of human inferior frontal gyrus during action execution and observation. Neuroimage **60**(3), 1671–1677 (2012)

Patch-Based Abnormality Maps for Improved Deep Learning-Based Classification of Huntington's Disease

Kilian Hett[1](✉)[iD], Rémi Giraud[2], Hans Johnson[3], Jane S. Paulsen[4], Jeffrey D. Long[5,6], and Ipek Oguz[1]

[1] Department of Electrical Engineering and Computer Science, Vanderbilt University, Nashville, TN, USA
kilian.hett@vanderbilt.edu
[2] Bordeaux INP, University of Bordeaux, CNRS, IMS, UMR 5218, Talence, France
[3] Department of Electrical and Computer Engineering, University of Iowa, Iowa City, IA, USA
[4] Department of Neurology, University of Wisconsin, Madison, WI, USA
[5] Department of Psychiatry, University of Iowa, Iowa City, IA, USA
[6] Department of Biostatistics, University of Iowa, Iowa City, IA, USA

Abstract. Deep learning techniques have demonstrated state-of-the-art performances in many medical imaging applications. These methods can efficiently learn specific patterns. An alternative approach to deep learning is patch-based grading methods, which aim to detect local similarities and differences between groups of subjects. This latter approach usually requires less training data compared to deep learning techniques. In this work, we propose two major contributions: first, we combine patch-based and deep learning methods. Second, we propose to extend the patch-based grading method to a new patch-based abnormality metric. Our method enables us to detect localized structural abnormalities in a test image by comparison to a template library consisting of images from a variety of healthy controls. We evaluate our method by comparing classification performance using different sets of features and models. Our experiments show that our novel patch-based abnormality metric increases deep learning performance from 91.3% to 95.8% of accuracy compared to standard deep learning approaches based on the MRI intensity.

Keywords: Patch-based method · Deep learning · Huntington's disease

1 Introduction

Huntington's disease (HD) is a fatal autosomal dominant neurodegenerative disorder that causes motor, behavioral and cognitive abnormalities. The pathological mutation consists of an abnormal cytosine-adenine-guanine (CAG) repeat

© Springer Nature Switzerland AG 2020
A. L. Martel et al. (Eds.): MICCAI 2020, LNCS 12267, pp. 636–645, 2020.
https://doi.org/10.1007/978-3-030-59728-3_62

in the huntingtin gene (HTT) [4]. Gene modification leads to pathological brain changes, and imaging studies have shown structural changes in the striatum [15]. Unlike many other degenerative diseases, a genetic test can determine the presence of the mutated gene well before the onset of symptoms, which makes HD a good candidate for the evaluation of new imaging-based methods.

Recently, deep learning methods have reached state-of-the-art performances in many medical imaging problems. However, for the detection and prediction of neurodegenerative diseases [1], such approaches have only obtained similar performance to methods using a combination of good feature engineering and machine learning methods. Although deep-learning approaches have shown promising results, one of the main limitations is a lack of large annotated training datasets, combined with the high dimensionality of the medical image data. Recent methods proposed to combine deep learning with pre-processed features [11,16]. These approaches proposed to use as input of deep-learning networks gray matter (GM) volumes to learn abnormalities over each subject. This results in normalized features that not only substantially reduce the problem dimensionality but also have lower variability compared to the raw MRI intensities.

More advanced features have also been proposed for classification tasks to describe subtle anatomical changes. Among them, the patch-based grading framework has shown state-of-the-art performances [2,7,8,17,18]. This framework aims to detect local similarities of a given test image to two template libraries representing two different populations (e.g., diseased vs. healthy). The general idea of patch-based grading methods is to compare structural patterns of a local patch in a test image with the images in the template libraries. However, such methods are highly dependent on the two template libraries, which can be affected by many factors (differences in distributions of MR protocols, sex, age, etc.). A proposed solution is to use a patch-based framework to detect abnormal patterns by using the coefficients of sparse coding to assess the subject under study [3].

Just like the pre-processed features proposed by [11,16], we hypothesize that using normalized patch-based grading maps as an input feature will lower the variability that limits deep learning models. In addition, deep neural networks can efficiently learn abnormality patterns over the brain without requiring segmentation maps. This is the **first contribution** of our paper.

While the patch-based grading method is very powerful when appropriate template libraries can be identified for a given task, this can sometimes be difficult to achieve. For example, a real dataset may contain more than two distributions: a movement disorders clinic may deal with not only healthy controls and Parkinson's patients, but also Lewy body disease and essential tremor patients. Even within a single disease, disease heterogeneity may make it impractical to build a representative template library. In such scenarios, it is much easier to rely on a single template library distribution representing healthy controls, and report the local deviation of a given test subject from the healthy control distribution. The **second contribution** of our paper is a new patch-based abnormality metric that achieves this goal.

2   Materials and Methods

2.1   Dataset

All T1-weighted (T1w) MRIs come from PREDICT-HD [12], which is a multi-site longitudinal study of HD. The MRIs have been acquired using 3T MRI scanners from different vendors (*e.g.*, GE, Phillips, and Siemens). The cohort used in the study includes 750 MPRAGE images from subjects representing three populations: control subjects (HC), pre-manifest HD that is composed of subjects with the expanded CAG repeat but who have not yet received a motor diagnosis at the time of the scan, and manifest HD which refers to patients who already have a motor diagnosis by the time of the scan (see Table 1).

Table 1. Demographic description of the dataset used in our experiments. Subjects are divided into three populations: healthy control (HC), Pre-Manifest HD (*i.e.*, abnormal CAG repetition in the HTT gene without motor impairment), and Manifest HD (*i.e.*, abnormal CAG with motor impairment).

	Healthy control	Huntington's disease	
		Pre-Manifest	Manifest
Number of MRIs	333	300	117
Age (years)	49.3 ± 11.9	43.4 ± 10.1	54.4 ± 9.6
Sex (F/M)	206/121	199/101	79/38
CAG length	15–35	37–57	37–57

2.2   Preprocessing

The preprocessing was conducted with the BRAINSAutoWorkup pipeline [14]. This pipeline is composed of the following steps: (1) denoising with non-local means filter, (2) anterior/posterior commissure and intra-subject alignments with rigid transformation, (3) bias field correction, (4) regional segmentation with a multi-atlas method using atlases from Neuromorphometrics[1], (5) affine registration to the MNI ICBM-152 template. Finally, MRI intensities have been standardized using a piece-wise linear histogram normalization technique.

2.3   Patch-Based Metrics

We consider two patch-based metrics (*i.e.*, patch-based grading and our proposed patch-based abnormality) to detect structural changes. Both methods rely on the accurate selection of closest patches in terms of intensity differences. In our work, closest patch selection is done using a version of PatchMatch that ensures uniqueness of patches extracted for the template library [5]. PatchMatch is an

---

[1] http://www.neuromorphometrics.com.

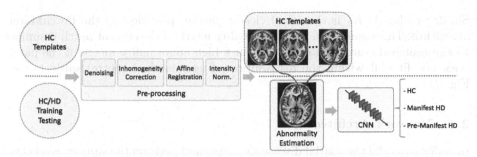

Fig. 1. Pipeline of the proposed method. First, HC from the dataset is separated into two subset, the HC templates used to estimate the local abnormality, the second is the set of HC for the evaluation of our method. Once all MRIs are preprocessed, we estimate the local abnormality using the HC template library. Finally, a convolutional neural network with softmax is used to obtain final classification.

optimized algorithm that enables us to extract the most similar patches from the template library in a sparse selection fashion.

Patch-Based Grading (PBG). Patch-based grading has been introduced to detect local similarity of a subject's image to two populations of template images [2]. At each voxel x of the subject under study, this method estimates a grading value $g(x)$ based on the following equation:

$$g(x) = \frac{\sum_{T \in K_x} \exp\left(-\frac{||S(x) - T(y)||_2^2}{h(x)}\right) p_T}{\sum_{T \in K_x} \exp\left(-\frac{||S(x) - T(y)||_2^2}{h(x)}\right)}, \tag{1}$$

where $S(x)$ is the patch surrounding the voxel x of the test subject image. $T(y)$ is a patch from the set K_x, which contains the most similar patches to $S(x)$ from the training library, as determined by the PatchMatch algorithm. $h(x) = min||S(x) - T(y)||_2^2$ is a normalization factor. Finally, p_T is the pathological status set to -1 for patches extracted from HD patients and to 1 for those extracted from HC subjects.

Patch-Based Abnormality (PBA). Our method derives from the patch-based grading framework. To address PBG's dependence on the two template libraries, we estimate the local differences from a single template library composed only of HC subjects (see Fig. 1). The abnormality $a(x)$ for each voxel x of the MRI under study, is defined as:

$$a(x) = \frac{\sum_{T \in K_x} ||S(x) - T(y)||_2^2}{\sigma_{S(x)}}, \tag{2}$$

where $\sigma_{S(x)}$ is standard deviation of intensities over the patch $S(x)$, which normalizes the differences of signal intensity contained in each patch $S(x)$.

Similar to Eq. 1, K_x is the set of closest patches provided by the PatchMatch algorithm. This results in a low abnormality metric if the current patch is similar to age-matched control subjects, and in a high abnormality metric if the patch does not fit well within the distribution of age-matched control subjects (see Fig. 2).

2.4   Network Architecture

In order to model the spatial disease signature and perform the subject-level classification, we used a convolutional neural network (CNN) approach. In recent years, many different architectures have been proposed in the pattern recognition field. Among them, deep residual neural network (ResNet) has shown competitive performances [6]. This architecture is characterized by skipped connections of different blocks of layers (see Fig. 3). ResNet has demonstrated a reduced training error compared to other networks with similar depth. Indeed, the residual mapping enables to reduce the training error, which is generally correlated with the network depth for classic stacked architectures. In addition, to address the problem of GPU memory limitation, we used a 3D patch approach.

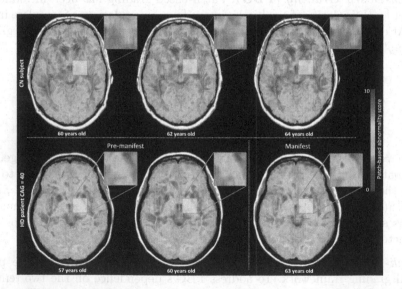

Fig. 2. Illustration of patch-based abnormality maps for (**top**) a healthy control subject and (**bottom**) an HD patient with 40 CAG repeats. **From left to right**, 3 different time points are shown for each subject. The HD subject is in the pre-manifest stage for the first two time points, but converts to clinical diagnosis by the third time point. **Blue** represents areas with a low abnormality score $a(x)$, whereas **red** represents areas with high abnormality score $a(x)$. We note a progressive increase of abnormality near the basal ganglia during the course of the disease which is consistent with HD pathology, while the abnormality map for the HC subject remains stable. (Color figure online)

Thus, both networks have as input 8 channels that represent non-overlapping $64 \times 64 \times 64$ patches from the input data (*i.e.*, T1w MRI or PBA maps).

2.5   Implementation and Evaluation

For constructing the PBA maps, we used 170 MRIs from HC subjects from the PREDICT-HD dataset as the template library. For PBG, we used the same 170 MRIs from HC subjects as well as 117 MRIs from Manifest HD subjects. We tailored the template library for the estimation of PBA and PBG maps by selecting a subset of 30 MRIs per group using an age-matching technique. The patch size for the abnormality metric computation has been set to $7 \times 7 \times 7$ voxels. We evaluate our proposed method on two classification tasks: HC versus manifest HD patients, and HC versus pre-manifest HD patients. We used 463 images for HC vs. Pre-manifest HD (163 vs. 300), and 280 MRI for HC vs. Manifest HD (163 vs. 117). The HC subjects used for classification were disjoint from the HC subjects used for computing PBG and PBA. A stratified 5-fold cross-validation was conducted to obtain training and testing sets. Because of the longitudinal nature of our dataset, care was taken to ensure different time-points from the same patient were either all in the template library, all in the training set or all in the testing set, to avoid any leakage. The network was trained using Adam optimizer with a constant learning rate of 0.0001. We used cross-entropy as loss function and a batch size of 2 over 20 epochs.

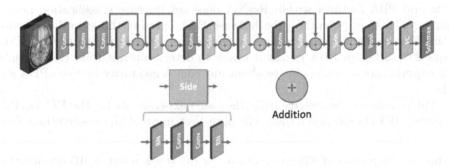

Fig. 3. Illustration of the convolutional neural network architecture used to validate our work. The architecture consist of a combination of convolutional layer (Conv), batch normalization (BN), Skipped connection layer (Side), pooling layer (Pool), and fully connected layer (FC). A softmax layer estimates the probability for each class.

To evaluate our methods, we compare the results obtained using 6 different classification methods: LDA classifier with putamen volume, LDA classifier with classic PBG feature [2] averaged over the putamen using the same parameters described in [9] (*i.e.*, using HC and Manifest HD MRIs as template library), LDA classifier with proposed PBA feature averaged over the putamen, ResNet with T1w input, ResNet with proposed PBA input, and ResNet with the concatenation of T1w and PBA inputs. For the first three experiments, we use the multi-atlas based segmentation of the putamen (Sect. 2.2). We estimated classification performance in terms of precision, accuracy, specificity, sensitivity, and area under the ROC curve. All code can be found online[2].

3   Results and Discussion

The results of the HC vs. Manifest-HD classification task are shown in Table 2. The ResNet classifier using PBA features as input has the best performance for all classification metrics.

We note that the putamen volume, which is well known to be a crucial marker of HD progression [10,13], dramatically outperforms (by about 15 AUC points) the patch-based approaches if a simple LDA classifier is used (PBG and PBA maps are each summarized by averaging within the putamen ROI in this setup). This may be due to inability of the simple classifier to model the complex patterns of neurodegeneration, as well as imperfections in the putamen segmentation. Using the ResNet classifier and the whole feature maps instead of the average within putamen, we see a big improvement in classification performance compared to the patch-based LDA results, consistent with our hypothesis. Among the ResNet classifiers, the model using the proposed PBA feature substantially outperforms the model using the raw T1w intensities. Indeed, the ResNet with PBA feature input is the only model that outperforms the simple LDA classifier on putamen volumes. Finally, we note that concatenating the T1w and PBA features within ResNet does not improve classification performance. This may potentially be because PBA extracts the same information from T1w by highlighting regions impacted by changes due to disease. Consequently, although PBA makes it easier to detect controls from HD patients, our experiments are inconclusive about any complementarity between PBA and T1w.

Table 3 shows the results from the same experiments on the HC vs. Pre-Manifest HD classification task. We note that most of the observations from

Table 2. Comparison of different methods for HC versus manifest HD classification. Results represent the average of classification performances for 5 xval folds. All results are expressed in terms of percentage. Best and second scores for each metric are expressed in bold and underlined font, respectively.

	Classifier	AUC	Precision	Accuracy	Specificity	Sensitivity
Putamen volume	LDA	96.1 ± 0.3	89.1 ± 0.3	93.5 ± 0.4	96.6 ± 0.2	89.1 ± 0.3
Putamen grading	LDA	81.0 ± 0.5	75.9 ± 1.2	75.9 ± 1.6	87.5 ± 1.4	60.0 ± 1.0
Putamen PBA	LDA	81.6 ± 0.5	73.2 ± 1.1	76.2 ± 1.6	89.5 ± 1.6	58.5 ± 1.2
ResNet T1w	Softmax	90.7 ± 1.8	87.7 ± 2.4	91.3 ± 1.7	95.2 ± 0.9	85.0 ± 3.0
ResNet PBA	Softmax	96.3 ± 0.7	96.9 ± 0.6	95.8 ± 0.8	98.8 ± 0.2	91.0 ± 1.8
ResNet T1w + PBA	Softmax	91.6 ± 1.6	85.0 ± 3.0	90.9 ± 1.8	96.4 ± 0.7	82.0 ± 3.6

---

[2] https://github.com/MedICL-VU/patch-based_abnormality.

Table 3. Comparison of different methods for HC versus pre-manifest HD classification. Results represent the average of classification performances for 5 xval folds. All results are expressed in terms of percentage. Best and second scores for each metric are expressed in bold and underlined font, respectively.

	Classifier	AUC	Precision	Accuracy	Specificity	Sensitivity
Putamen volume	LDA	**93.9 ± 0.3**	**93.1 ± 0.6**	85.7 ± 0.5	72.5 ± 0.3	93.1 ± 0.6
Putamen grading	LDA	74.5 ± 1.6	87.2 ± 1.9	72.6 ± 1.7	45.7 ± 1.9	87.2 ± 1.8
Putamen PBA	LDA	77.6 ± 1.2	87.7 ± 1.8	72.5 ± 1.5	45.6 ± 1.6	87.7 ± 1.8
ResNet T1w	Softmax	89.8 ± 2.0	87.7 ± 1.4	88.8 ± 1.3	68.1 ± 3.9	<u>98.6 ± 1.5</u>
ResNet grading	Softmax	<u>92.1 ± 1.6</u>	91.4 ± 1.3	90.5 ± 1.3	<u>75.9 ± 3.8</u>	97.8 ± 1.2
ResNet PBA	Softmax	91.9 ± 1.6	90.7 ± 1.3	<u>91.4 ± 1.3</u>	75.7 ± 3.8	**98.6 ± 1.2**
ResNet T1w + PBA	Softmax	89.0±2.2	<u>92.3 ± 1.4</u>	**91.6 ± 1.6**	**80.5 ± 3.7**	97.6 ± 1.1

Table 2 similarly hold for this experiment: putamen volume outperforms patch-based methods with simple LDA classifier; ResNet substantially improves upon the LDA-based performance for any of the patch-based grading metrics; and the ResNet performance tends to be best when using the proposed PBA and grading metrics. PBA obtains similar results to grading but without requiring a second template library, which can be problematic to obtain. We note that, unlike the HC vs. Manifest HD task, the concatenation of T1w and PBA features in ResNet does improve some of the performance metrics, suggesting some potential complementarity. Additionally, again unlike the HC vs. Manifest HD task, no patch-based method reaches the performance of the putamen volume. This may suggest that at this stage of the disease progression, the local abnormalities are more subtle and the global volume is a more robust marker of pathology. In future work, we will explore combining the putamen volume with the patch-based deep learning model to better capture the disease pathology.

It is worth noting that the performance of the LDA classifier with the patch-based methods is lower than what has been reported in other similar tasks (e.g., hippocampus analysis for Alzheimer's classification [8]). However, the results we present here are consistent with previous work that reports lower detection performance for patch-based methods comparing intensity within the putamen for HD classification [9].

One of the main strengths of our method that combines patch-based and deep learning approaches is its independence from segmentation of a region of interest. This addresses the dependence of previous patch-based grading methods on accurate segmentation maps to aggregate grading values into a final ROI-based feature [2,8].

4   Conclusion

In this paper we proposed a new patch-based framework to estimate local abnormalities to improve classification performance of a deep learning method in the context of HD detection. The distance from a distribution of healthy controls is estimated using a patch-match scheme preserving the uniqueness of patches extracted from the control library. Our experiments demonstrated superior classification performance of convolutional neural network when the patch-based abnormality maps are used as input of the network compared to the straightforward use of T1w intensities. In future work, we will investigate the combination of pre-trained and data augmentation techniques with our novel approach, as well as the incorporation of putamen volume into our model.

Acknowledgements. This work was supported, in part, by the NIH grants R01–NS094456 and U01–NS106845. The PREDICT-HD study was funded by the NCATS, the NIH (NIH; R01–NS040068, U01–NS105509, U01–NS103475), and CHDI.org. Vanderbilt University Institutional Review Board has approved this study.

References

1. Arbabshirani, M.R., Plis, S., Sui, J., Calhoun, V.D.: Single subject prediction of brain disorders in neuroimaging: promises and pitfalls. NeuroImage **145**, 137–165 (2017)
2. Coupé, P., et al.: Scoring by nonlocal image patch estimator for early detection of Alzheimer's disease. NeuroImage: Clin. **1**(1), 141–152 (2012)
3. Coupé, P., Deledalle, C.-A., Dossal, C., Allard, M.: Sparse-based morphometry: principle and application to Alzheimer's disease. In: Wu, G., Coupé, P., Zhan, Y., Munsell, B.C., Rueckert, D. (eds.) Patch-MI 2016. LNCS, vol. 9993, pp. 43–50. Springer, Cham (2016). https://doi.org/10.1007/978-3-319-47118-1_6
4. Dayalu, P., Albin, R.L.: Huntington disease: pathogenesis and treatment. Neurol. Clin. **33**(1), 101–114 (2015)
5. Giraud, R., Ta, V.T., Papadakis, N., Manjón, J.V., Collins, D.L., Coupé, P., Alzheimer's Disease Neuroimaging Initiative et al.: An optimized patchmatch for multi-scale and multi-feature label fusion. NeuroImage **124**, 770–782 (2016)
6. He, K., Zhang, X., Ren, S., Sun, J.: Deep residual learning for image recognition. In: Proceedings of the IEEE Conference on Computer Vision and Pattern Recognition, pp. 770–778 (2016)
7. Hett, K., Ta, V.T., Catheline, G., Tourdias, T., Manjón, J.V., Coupe, P.: Multimodal hippocampal subfield grading for Alzheimer's disease classification. Sci. Rep. **9**(1), 1–16 (2019)
8. Hett, K., Ta, V.T., Manjón, J.V., Coupé, P., Alzheimer's Disease Neuroimaging Initiative et al.: Adaptive fusion of texture-based grading for Alzheimer's disease classification. Computerized Medical Imaging and Graphics **70**, 8–16 (2018)
9. Hett, K., Johnson, H., Coupé, P., Paulsen, J.S., Long, J.D., Oguz, I.: Tensor-based grading: a novel patch-based grading approach for the analysis of deformation fields in Huntington's disease. In: 2020 IEEE 17th International Symposium on Biomedical Imaging (ISBI), pp. 1091–1095. IEEE (2020)
10. Kim, E.Y., Lourens, S., Long, J.D., Paulsen, J.S., Johnson, H.J.: Preliminary analysis using multi-atlas labeling algorithms for tracing longitudinal change. Front. Neurosci. **9**, 242 (2015)
11. Parisot, S., et al.: Disease prediction using graph convolutional networks: application to autism spectrum disorder and Alzheimer's disease. Med. Image Anal. **48**, 117–130 (2018)

12. Paulsen, J.S., et al.: Detection of Huntington's disease decades before diagnosis: the Predict-HD study. J. Neurol. Neurosurg. Psychiatry **79**(8), 874–880 (2008)
13. Paulsen, J.S., et al.: Clinical and biomarker changes in premanifest Huntington disease show trial feasibility: a decade of the PREDICT-HD study. Front. Aging Neurosci. **6**, 78 (2014)
14. Pierson, R., et al.: Fully automated analysis using BRAINS: AutoWorkup. NeuroImage **54**(1), 328–336 (2011)
15. Ross, C.A., et al.: Huntington disease: natural history, biomarkers and prospects for therapeutics. Nat. Rev. Neurol. **10**(4), 204 (2014)
16. Suk, H.I., Lee, S.W., Shen, D., Alzheimer's Disease Neuroimaging Initiative et al.: Deep ensemble learning of sparse regression models for brain disease diagnosis. Medical image analysis **37**, 101–113 (2017)
17. Tong, T., Gao, Q., Guerrero, R., Ledig, C., Chen, L., Rueckert, D., Alzheimer's Disease Neuroimaging Initiative et al.: A novel grading biomarker for the prediction of conversion from mild cognitive impairment to Alzheimer's disease. IEEE Trans. Biomed. Eng. **64**(1), 155–165 (2016)
18. Tong, T., et al.: Five-class differential diagnostics of neurodegenerative diseases using random undersampling boosting. NeuroImage: Clin. **15**, 613–624 (2017)

A Deep Spatial Context Guided Framework for Infant Brain Subcortical Segmentation

Liangjun Chen, Zhengwang Wu, Dan Hu, Ya Wang, Zhanhao Mo, Li Wang,
Weili Lin, Dinggang Shen[✉], Gang Li[✉], and the UNC/UMN Baby
Connectome Program Consortium

Department of Radiology and BRIC,
University of North Carolina at Chapel Hill,
Chapel Hill, NC 27599, USA
{dinggang_shen,gang_li}@med.unc.edu

Abstract. Accurate subcortical segmentation of infant brain magnetic resonance (MR) images is crucial for studying early subcortical structural growth patterns and related diseases diagnosis. However, dynamic intensity changes, low tissue contrast, and small subcortical size of infant brain MR images make subcortical segmentation a challenging task. In this paper, we propose a spatial context guided, coarse-to-fine deep convolutional neural network (CNN) based framework for accurate infant subcortical segmentation. At the coarse stage, we propose a signed distance map (SDM) learning UNet (SDM-UNet) to predict SDMs from the original multi-modal images, including T1w, T2w, and T1w/T2w images. By doing this, the spatial context information, including the relative position information across different structures and the shape information of the segmented structures contained in the ground-truth SDMs, is used for supervising the SDM-UNet to remedy the bad influence from the low tissue contrast in infant brain MR images and generate high-quality SDMs. To improve the robustness to outliers, a Correntropy based loss is introduced in SDM-UNet to penalize the difference between the ground-truth SDMs and predicted SDMs in training. At the fine stage, the predicted SDMs, which contains spatial context information of subcortical structures, are combined with the multi-modal images, and then fed into a multi-source and multi-path UNet (M2-UNet) for delivering refined segmentation. We validate our method on an infant brain MR image dataset with 24 scans by evaluating the Dice ratio between our segmentation and the manual delineation. Compared to four state-of-the-art methods, our method consistently achieves better performances in both qualitative and quantitative evaluations.

Keywords: Subcortical segmentation · Spatial context information · Coarse-to-fine framework · Infant brain

© Springer Nature Switzerland AG 2020
A. L. Martel et al. (Eds.): MICCAI 2020, LNCS 12267, pp. 646–656, 2020.
https://doi.org/10.1007/978-3-030-59728-3_63

1   Introduction

Accurate segmentation of subcortical structures from the magnetic resonance (MR) brain images plays an important role in various neuroimaging studies [1–3]. As manual delineation of subcortical structures is very time-consuming, expertise needed, and difficult to reproduce, many previous studies have put efforts into automatic segmentation and achieved significant progress for adult brain MR images [4–7]. However, as shown in Fig. 1, the automatic subcortical segmentation in the infant brain MR images is still challenging, due to their dynamic intensity changes, low tissue contrast, and small structural size [8]. Fully automatic subcortical segmentation methods in infants are urgently needed for many neurodevelopmental researches, such as studying the early growth pattern of subcortical structures [9–11] and the diagnosis of related brain disorders [12].

Recently, the context-guided convolutional neural networks (CNN) based methods have achieved many successes in medical image segmentation tasks [13,14]. These methods try to use the distance maps, which encodes the spatial context information, including the position, shape, and relationship among different segmentation targets, to improve the segmentation accuracy. However, their distance maps are constructed based on the intermediate segmentation results, which may accumulate the segmentation errors to the constructed distance maps. With the inaccurately constructed distance maps to guide the segmentation, the segmentation performance would be degraded. To address this issue, [15] proposed to directly generate the signed distance map (SDM) in a regression-based network. Then, the boundary of the segmentation target can be computed through the Heaviside function. In doing so, the context information contained in the ground-truth SDMs can be used to directly supervise the network to generate high-quality segmentation results. In [15], the L_1 loss between the predicted SDM and the ground-truth SDM was used for the training, thus improving the robustness of the network. However, the L_1 loss is non-differentiable at zero and may lead to an unstable training process in multi-class segmentation tasks [16], which is thus not suitable for the subcortical segmentation task.

Motivated by these works, in this paper, we propose a spatial context guided, coarse-to-fine deep CNN based framework for accurate 3D subcortical segmentation on infant brain MR images. At the coarse stage, a SDM learning UNet (SDM-UNet) is proposed to directly learn the SDM of each subcortical structure from the original multi-modal MR images, including the T1w, T2w, and T1w/T2w images. In this way, the proposed SDM-UNet can leverage the spatial context information, including the relative position information across different subcortical structures and the shape information of the segmented subcortical structures contained in the ground-truth SDMs, to mitigate the bad influence from the low tissue contrast in infant brain MR images and generate high-quality SDMs. Meanwhile, a Correntropy based loss [17] is introduced in the SDM-UNet to further improve the robustness to outliers under the premise of a stable training process. At the fine stage, a multi-source and multi-path UNet (M2-UNet) is built to rationally encode and effectively fuse the multi-modal information and the spatial context information, which is included in the previously predicted SDMs, to produce the refined subcortical segmentation results. To our best knowledge, this is the first work of using spatial context information for the segmentation of the subcortical structures in infant brain MR images.

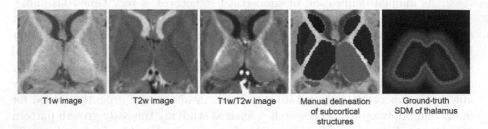

Fig. 1. T1w, T2w, and T1w/T2w images of a 6-month subject, the associated manual delineation, and the ground-truth signed distance map (SDM) of the thalamus. Evidently, the boundaries of subcortical structures are fuzzy due to the low contrast in T1w and T2w images. In the T1w/T2w image, the contrast of tissues increased; thus, more distinguishable boundaries can be observed. The ground-truth SDM of each subcortical structure is calculated from the manual delineation.

2   Method

The framework of our method is presented in Fig. 2, which includes two networks for two stages, respectively. In the following, we will introduce each stage and its corresponding network in detail.

Coarse Stage SDM-UNet: To generate high-quality SDMs for improving the segmentation performance in the fine stage, we proposed a SDM learning UNet (SDM-UNet) to directly learn the SDM of each subcortical structure from multi-modal MR images, including T1w, T2w, and T1w/T2w images. By doing this, we can use the spatial context information contained in the ground-truth SDMs to supervise the SDM-UNet, which can help alleviate the bad influence from the low tissue contrast in the infant brain MR images and achieve superior performance on the estimation of SDMs, where the ground-truth SDMs are calculated from the manual delineations via the Euclidean distance transforms. Meanwhile, we can also precisely convert the SDMs to the segmentation maps through the Heaviside function. Therefore, during the training, we convert the predicted SDMs to the predicted segmentation maps and introduce a segmentation loss to penalize the difference between the manual delineations and the predicted segmentation maps to further improve the performance of the proposed SDM-UNet.

The proposed SDM-UNet has an encoder-decoder architecture, which is shown in Fig. 2, and the multi-modal MR images are used as multi-channel input.

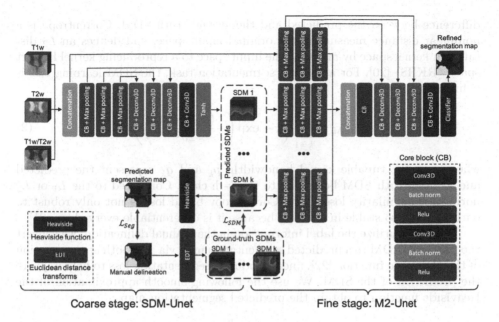

Fig. 2. A schematic illustration of the proposed framework, consisting of SDM-UNet at coarse stage and M2-UNet at fine stage.

Skip connections are employed to recover essential details that are possibly lost in the down-sampling process of the encoder.

For a specific subcortical structure in the 3D image, its corresponding SDM can be computed using the following formula, which is a mapping from $\mathbb{R}^3$ to $\mathbb{R}$:

$$\phi(\boldsymbol{x}) = \begin{cases} 0, \boldsymbol{x} \in \mathcal{B} \\ - \inf_{y \in \mathcal{B}} \|\boldsymbol{x} - \boldsymbol{y}\|_2, \boldsymbol{x} \in \Omega_{\text{in}} \\ + \inf_{y \in \mathcal{B}} \|\boldsymbol{x} - \boldsymbol{y}\|_2, \boldsymbol{x} \in \Omega_{\text{out}} \end{cases} \tag{1}$$

where $\boldsymbol{x}$ is the coordinate of any point in the 3D image; $\boldsymbol{y}$ is the coordinate of any point on the subcortical structure boundary $\mathcal{B}$, Ω_{in} and Ω_{out} denote the region inside (negative value) and outside (positive value) a subcortical structure, respectively. Based on this definition, we can use the Euclidean distance transforms to calculate the ground-truth SDMs of each subcortical structure from the manual delineation.

Once the ground-truth SDMs are calculated, they can be introduced into a SDM learning loss, which encourages the SDM-UNet to predict the SDMs from the original multi-modal MR images. In the learning of the SDMs, the conventional ways [15,18] use the L_1 loss instead of L_2 loss to achieve better robustness to outliers. However, L_1 loss is not differentiable at zero, which severely reduces the training stability. To alleviate the impact of outliers and overcome the shortage of L_1 loss, we apply a Correntropy based loss (Closs) [19] to penalize the difference between the predicted and the ground-truth SDM. Correntropy is a nonlinear distance measure in the original input space, and defines an L_2 distance in kernel space by mapping the input space to a reproducing kernel Hilbert space (RKHS) [20]. For a K-class segmentation task, the SDM learning loss is defined as follows:

$$\mathcal{L}_{\text{SDM}} = \sum_{k=1}^{K} \left(1 - \exp\left(-\frac{(\boldsymbol{p}_k - \boldsymbol{q}_k)^2}{2\sigma^2} \right) \right), \tag{2}$$

where σ is the tunable kernel bandwidth, $\boldsymbol{p}_k$ and $\boldsymbol{q}_k$ represent the predicted and ground-truth SDM belonging to the k-th class. Compared to the L_1 or L_2 norm-based similarity losses, the Correntropy based loss is not only robust to outliers but also stable in training because it is differentiable everywhere [21].

To further utilize the label information in the manual delineation, we convert the predicted SDM to a predicted segmentation map via a smooth approximation of the Heaviside function [22], and introduce a segmentation loss to help improve the prediction of the SDM. We use the following smooth approximation of the Heaviside function to obtain the predicted segmentation maps:

$$\boldsymbol{s}_k = \frac{1}{1 + e^{-\boldsymbol{p}_k/m}}, \tag{3}$$

where $\boldsymbol{s}_k$ denotes the predicted segmentation map belonging to the k-th class, and m is an approximation parameter. A larger m means a closer approximation. Once the predicted segmentation maps are obtained, the Dice loss [23] is used as the segmentation loss to measure the overlapping between the predicted segmentation maps and the manual delineations:

$$\mathcal{L}_{\text{Seg}} = \sum_{k=1}^{K} \left(1 - \frac{2 \sum_{i=1}^{N} \boldsymbol{s}_{k,i} \boldsymbol{t}_{k,i}}{\sum_{i=1}^{N} \boldsymbol{s}_{k,i} + \sum_{i=1}^{N} \boldsymbol{t}_{k,i}} \right), \tag{4}$$

where N is the number of voxels, $\boldsymbol{t}_{k,i}$ and $\boldsymbol{s}_{k,i}$ represent the i-th voxel in the k-th manual delineation and predicted segmentation map, respectively.

By integrating the above loss terms, the joint loss $\mathcal{L}_{\text{SDM-UNet}}$ is defined as:

$$\mathcal{L}_{\text{SDM-UNet}} = \mathcal{L}_{\text{SDM}} + \lambda \mathcal{L}_{\text{Seg}}, \tag{5}$$

where λ is the loss weight. By minimizing this loss, the proposed SDM-UNet can be stably trained to generate high-quality SDM, which is used as the spatial context information to guide the training of the following M2-UNet to further improve the segmentation accuracy.

Fine Stage M2-UNet: In order to leverage the spatial context information generated by SDM-UNet, we propose a multi-source and multi-path UNet, namely M2-UNet, at the fine stage to achieve the refined segmentation. The proposed M2-UNet can effectively integrate the multi-modal information and the spatial context information by encoding the multi-modal MR images and SDMs through different encoder paths, which is detailed as follows.

The input of the M2-UNet includes two parts: a) the original multi-modal MR images, which are used as multi-channel input; b) the predicted SDMs from the coarse stage. Different from the multi-modal MR images, the SDMs of different subcortical structures illustrate distinct spatial context information. Therefore, in order to effectively integrate the spatial context information of the subcortical structures, we propose to construct an individual encoder path for the SDMs of each subcortical structure, which can make full use of each encoder path to better extract the high-level features of each subcortical structure.

As the extracted high-level feature maps could better complement each other than the source images [13], we propose to perform a cross-source convolution to aggregate the outputs of all encoder paths. Specifically, the outputs of each encoder path are concatenated and fed to an additional convolutional layer at the beginning of the decoder path. As the cross-source convolution performs across different sources, it assigns different weights to each source and merges the extracted high-level features in the output feature maps. In doing so, the proposed cross-source convolution layer can model the relationships across different source images and achieve a better fusion of the extracted high-level features.

Moreover, because there are total $(K + 1)$ encoder paths in the M2-UNet, employing the skip connections for each encoder path will significantly increase the complexity of the network. It is worth noting that, compared to the SDMs of each subcortical structure, multi-modal MR images accommodate exhaustive intensity information [24]. Hence, in order to recover more useful details with less complicated network architecture, we only employ the skip connections for the encoder path of the multi-modal MR images. Herein, we still use the afore-mentioned Dice loss for the M2-UNet training.

3   Experiments

Dataset and Experimental Setup: The proposed network is evaluated on a real infant dataset, which includes 24 infant MRI scans (with both T1w and T2w images) from the UNC/UMN Baby Connectome Project (BCP) [25]. The resolution of the T1w and T2w images is $0.8 \times 0.8 \times 0.8 \, \text{mm}^3$. These 24 subjects are divided into two age groups (6 and 12 months), and each group has 12 scans. The subcortical structures of all 24 subjects are manually delineated by two experienced experts. For each subject, the T2w image was linearly aligned onto the T1w image [26]. Then, T1w/T2w image is obtained by dividing the T1w image by the T2w image at each voxel. Intensity inhomogeneity is corrected in all images by [27]. To simplify the network, we merged the bilaterally symmetric subcortical structures into six classes (thalamus, caudate, putamen, pallidum, hippocampus, and amygdala). We performed random flipping of image patches for augmenting the data. In order to validate our method, a stratified 5-fold cross-validation strategy is employed, and each fold consists of 16 training images, 4 validation images, and 4 testing images.

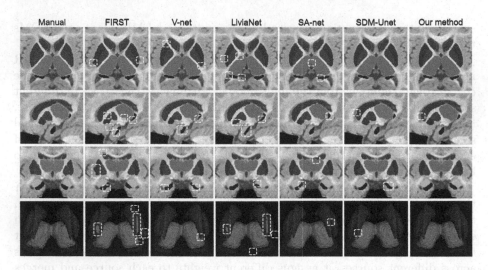

Fig. 3. Visual comparison of the segmentation results of the six subcortical structures on a 6-month T1w image, obtained from manual delineation and six automatic methods. The apparent segmentation errors are indicated by boxes.

Parameters of SDM-UNet and M2-UNet are experimentally set as: learning rate of Adam optimizer = 0.0001, kernel size of each network = 4, stride = 2, $\lambda = 0.1$, and $\sigma = 0.8$. m is set to 1500. The segmentation was performed in a patch-wise manner, with the patch size of $32 \times 32 \times 32$.

The proposed method was compared with the following methods: a commonly used software package FIRST in FSL [26]; three state-of-the-art deep learning segmentation methods including V-Net [23], LiviaNet [4], SA-Net [15] and the method involving only the proposed SDM-UNet. In order to ensure a fair comparison, the three MR modalities are used as multi-channel input to all learning-based methods. The segmentation results were quantitatively evaluated by the Dice similarity coefficient (DSC) (mean and standard deviation).

Evaluation Results: In Fig. 3, we visually compared the subcortical segmentation results of the manual delineation and the six automatic methods on a 6-month T1w infant brain MR image. Evidently, the proposed method obtained overall segmentation results more consistent with the manual results. Meanwhile, the proposed method and SDM-UNet can more precisely segment the amygdala and hippocampus than the other competing methods. Compared to SDM-UNet, the proposed method generates segmentation results that are more accurate for most of the subcortical structures, suggesting that the proposed M2-UNet exerts a positive effect in improving the segmentation performance.

The DSC values of the segmentation of the six subcortical structures are summarized in Table 1, where we have at least three observations.

Table 1. The DSC values of the six subcortical structures in each age group.

	Month	FIRST	V-Net	LiviaNet	SA-Net	SDM-UNet	Our method
Thalamus	6	83.85 ± 2.73	94.65 ± 0.68	94.89 ± 0.91	94.12 ± 0.32	94.33 ± 0.36	**96.10 ± 0.22**
	12	87.37 ± 1.52	95.26 ± 0.42	94.75 ± 1.34	95.14 ± 0.58	95.00 ± 0.48	**96.23 ± 0.32**
Caudate	6	84.62 ± 1.61	88.45 ± 1.46	92.35 ± 1.28	92.39 ± 0.42	92.36 ± 0.33	**94.25 ± 0.54**
	12	87.76 ± 1.59	92.78 ± 0.46	91.78 ± 1.89	94.21 ± 0.77	94.12 ± 0.35	**94.71 ± 0.43**
Putamen	6	74.76 ± 1.93	89.94 ± 2.63	90.69 ± 1.66	91.64 ± 1.26	92.48 ± 1.31	**94.60 ± 1.11**
	12	83.12 ± 2.82	92.86 ± 1.29	92.44 ± 1.40	93.26 ± 0.82	93.47 ± 0.96	**95.51 ± 0.54**
Pallidum	6	78.09 ± 2.78	88.35 ± 1.94	89.08 ± 1.82	90.14 ± 1.27	91.01 ± 1.50	**92.82 ± 0.98**
	12	83.56 ± 1.46	90.72 ± 0.81	90.43 ± 1.22	91.99 ± 0.67	92.23 ± 0.88	**94.24 ± 0.91**
Hippocampus	6	66.73 ± 4.25	87.27 ± 2.15	86.49 ± 1.46	88.18 ± 1.19	88.71 ± 0.74	**90.52 ± 0.86**
	12	80.47 ± 2.97	90.14 ± 1.56	90.54 ± 0.89	89.42 ± 1.33	90.34 ± 0.46	**92.02 ± 1.28**
Amygdala	6	49.33 ± 5.95	83.58 ± 5.99	79.66 ± 3.99	85.79 ± 2.73	86.51 ± 2.89	**89.06 ± 1.91**
	12	55.12 ± 3.56	85.71 ± 2.41	86.21 ± 2.05	86.20 ± 1.39	87.89 ± 1.31	**89.64 ± 1.29**
Mean DSC	6	72.90 ± 3.21	88.71 ± 2.48	88.86 ± 1.85	90.38 ± 1.20	90.90 ± 1.19	**92.89 ± 0.94**
	12	79.56 ± 2.32	91.25 ± 1.16	91.03 ± 1.47	91.70 ± 0.93	92.18 ± 0.74	**93.73 ± 0.80**

First, compared to the state-of-the-art methods, our method has remarkably better segmentation results for all six subcortical structures in each age group (improved the overall DSC by 2.51% ($p-$value $= 2.3e^{-4}$) and 2.03% ($p-$value $= 1.7e^{-5}$) on 6-month and 12-month images, respectively). Although promising segmentation for amygdala and hippocampus is hard to obtain due to their relatively smaller size, our method still achieves significantly higher DSC values on these two structures ($p-$value $= 1.3e^{-4}$, compared with SA-Net). The results suggest that our method can effectively leverage the spatial context information to improve the segmentation performance.

Second, the DSC values of 6-month images are generally lower than those of 12-month images. This is because the 6-month brain images have the lowest contrast for different subcortical structures, which is conformal with the previous studies [8,28,29]. Meanwhile, the proposed method shows the highest consistency of the segmentation on the 6 and 12 months infant brain MR images. This further implies that incorporating the SDM of each specific subcortical structure can help remedy the bad influence from the low tissue contrast of 6-month MR images and verifies that our method is effective in the task of subcortical segmentation of infant brain MR images.

Third, when compared to state-of-the-art methods, the proposed SDM-UNet achieves better segmentation results ($p -$ value $= 1.8e^{-4}$, compared with SA-Net), which indicates that our SDM-UNet can generate more trustworthy SDMs to effectively guide the training of the following M2-UNet to acquire improved segmentation accuracy. Moreover, when compared to SDM-UNet, our method also achieved markedly improved DSC values on all the subcortical structures (from 90.90% to 92.89% ($p-$value $= 5.4e^{-6}$) and 92.18% to 93.73% ($p-$value $= 3.1e^{-5}$) on 6 and 12 months images, respectively), which reveals the effectiveness of the proposed framework in refining the segmentation.

Both the qualitative evaluation in Fig. 3 and the quantitative evaluation in Table 1 suggest that our method yields superior performance on automatic subcortical segmentation of infant brain MR images.

4 Conclusion

In this work, we propose a spatial context guided, coarse-to-fine deep CNN-based framework for the accurate 3D subcortical segmentation in infant brain MR images. At the coarse stage, to mitigate the bad influence from the low tissue contrast in infant brain MR images, we construct a signed distance map (SDM) learning UNet (SDM-UNet), which is supervised by the spatial context information contained in the ground-truth SDMs, to generate high-quality SDMs from the original multi-modal images, including T1w, T2w, and T1w/T2w images. Moreover, a Correntropy based loss is introduced in the SDM-UNet to improve the robustness to the outliers under the premise of a stable training process. At the fine stage, for simultaneously leveraging the multi-modal MR images and the SDMs predicted at the coarse stage to achieve improved segmentation accuracy, a multi-source and multi-path UNet (M2-UNet) is constructed to rationally encode and effectively integrate the multi-modal appearance information and the spatial context information contained in the predicted SDMs. Experimental results demonstrate that, compared to four state-of-the-art methods, our method achieves higher accuracy in the segmentation of subcortical structures of infant brain MR images.

Acknowledgments. This work was partially supported by NIH grants (MH116225, MH109773 and MH117943). This work also utilizes approaches developed by an NIH grant (1U01MH110274) and the efforts of the UNC/UMN Baby Connectome Project Consortium.

References

1. Li, G., et al.: A longitudinal MRI study of amygdala and hippocampal subfields for infants with risk of autism. In: Zhang, D., Zhou, L., Jie, B., Liu, M. (eds.) GLMI 2019. LNCS, vol. 11849, pp. 164–171. Springer, Cham (2019). https://doi.org/10.1007/978-3-030-35817-4_20
2. Crosson, B.A.: Subcortical Functions in Language and Memory. Guilford Press, New York (1992)
3. Bingel, U., Quante, M., Knab, R., Bromm, B., Weiller, C., Büchel, C.: Subcortical structures involved in pain processing: evidence from single-trial fMRI. Pain **99**(1–2), 313–321 (2002)
4. Dolz, J., Desrosiers, C., Ayed, I.B.: 3D fully convolutional networks for subcortical segmentation in MRI: a large-scale study. NeuroImage **170**, 456–470 (2018)
5. Kushibar, K., et al.: Automated subcortical brain structure segmentation combining spatial and deep convolutional features. Med. Image Anal. **48**, 177–186 (2018)
6. Wu, J., Zhang, Y., Tang, X.: A joint 3D+2D fully convolutional framework for subcortical segmentation. In: Shen, D., et al. (eds.) MICCAI 2019. LNCS, vol. 11766, pp. 301–309. Springer, Cham (2019). https://doi.org/10.1007/978-3-030-32248-9_34

7. Liu, L., Hu, X., Zhu, L., Fu, C.W., Qin, J., Heng, P.A.: ψ-Net: stacking densely convolutional LSTMs for subcortical brain structure segmentation. IEEE Trans. Med. Imaging **39**, 2806–2817 (2020)
8. Li, G., et al.: Computational neuroanatomy of baby brains: a review. NeuroImage **185**, 906–925 (2019)
9. Qiu, A., et al.: Morphology and microstructure of subcortical structures at birth: a large-scale Asian neonatal neuroimaging study. Neuroimage **65**, 315–323 (2013)
10. Serag, A., Aljabar, P., Counsell, S., Boardman, J., Hajnal, J.V., Rueckert, D.: Tracking developmental changes in subcortical structures of the preterm brain using multi-modal MRI. In: ISBI, pp. 349–352. IEEE (2011)
11. Courchesne, E., et al.: Unusual brain growth patterns in early life in patients with autistic disorder: an MRI study. Neurology **57**(2), 245–254 (2001)
12. Wang, L., et al.: Volume-based analysis of 6-month-old infant brain MRI for autism biomarker identification and early diagnosis. In: Frangi, A.F., Schnabel, J.A., Davatzikos, C., Alberola-López, C., Fichtinger, G. (eds.) MICCAI 2018. LNCS, vol. 11072, pp. 411–419. Springer, Cham (2018). https://doi.org/10.1007/978-3-030-00931-1_47
13. Zeng, G., Zheng, G.: Multi-stream 3D FCN with multi-scale deep supervision for multi-modality isointense infant brain MR image segmentation. In: ISBI, pp. 136–140. IEEE (2018)
14. Wang, G., et al.: DeepIGeoS: a deep interactive geodesic framework for medical image segmentation. IEEE Trans. Pattern Anal. Mach. Intell. **41**(7), 1559–1572 (2018)
15. Xue, Y., et al.: Shape-aware organ segmentation by predicting signed distance maps. arXiv preprint arXiv:1912.03849 (2019)
16. Ren, S., He, K., Girshick, R., Sun, J.: Faster R-CNN: towards real-time object detection with region proposal networks. In: NeurIPS, pp. 91–99 (2015)
17. Glasser, M.F., Van Essen, D.C.: Mapping human cortical areas in vivo based on myelin content as revealed by T1- and T2-weighted MRI. J. Neurosci. **31**(32), 11597–11616 (2011)
18. Park, J.J., Florence, P., Straub, J., Newcombe, R., Lovegrove, S.: DeepSDF: learning continuous signed distance functions for shape representation. In: CVPR, pp. 165–174 (2019)
19. Chen, L., Qu, H., Zhao, J., Chen, B., Principe, J.C.: Efficient and robust deep learning with correntropy-induced loss function. Neural Comput. Appl. **27**(4), 1019–1031 (2016). https://doi.org/10.1007/s00521-015-1916-x
20. Yang, E., Deng, C., Li, C., Liu, W., Li, J., Tao, D.: Shared predictive cross-modal deep quantization. IEEE Trans. Neural Netw. Learn. Syst. **29**(11), 5292–5303 (2018)
21. Liu, W., Pokharel, P.P., Príncipe, J.C.: Correntropy: properties and applications in non-Gaussian signal processing. IEEE Trans. Sig. Process. **55**(11), 5286–5298 (2007)
22. Ito, Y.: Approximation capability of layered neural networks with sigmoid units on two layers. Neural Comput. **6**(6), 1233–1243 (1994)
23. Milletari, F., Navab, N., Ahmadi, S.A.: V-net: fully convolutional neural networks for volumetric medical image segmentation. In: 3DV, pp. 565–571. IEEE (2016)
24. Drozdzal, M., Vorontsov, E., Chartrand, G., Kadoury, S., Pal, C.: The importance of skip connections in biomedical image segmentation. In: Carneiro, G., et al. (eds.) LABELS/DLMIA -2016. LNCS, vol. 10008, pp. 179–187. Springer, Cham (2016). https://doi.org/10.1007/978-3-319-46976-8_19

25. Howell, B.R., et al.: The UNC/UMN baby connectome project (BCP): an overview of the study design and protocol development. NeuroImage **185**, 891–905 (2019)
26. Jenkinson, M., Beckmann, C.F., Behrens, T.E., et al.: FSL. Neuroimage **62**(2), 782–790 (2012)
27. Sled, J.G., Zijdenbos, A.P., Evans, A.C.: A nonparametric method for automatic correction of intensity nonuniformity in MRI data. IEEE Trans. Med. Imaging **17**(1), 87–97 (1998)
28. Wang, L., et al.: Anatomy-guided joint tissue segmentation and topological correction for 6-month infant brain MRI with risk of autism. Human Brain Mapp. **39**(6), 2609–2623 (2018)
29. Wang, L., et al.: Links: learning-based multi-source IntegratioN frameworK for segmentation of infant brain images. NeuroImage **108**, 160–172 (2015)

Modelling the Distribution of 3D Brain MRI Using a 2D Slice VAE

Anna Volokitin[(✉)], Ertunc Erdil, Neerav Karani, Kerem Can Tezcan, Xiaoran Chen, Luc Van Gool, and Ender Konukoglu

Computer Vision Lab, ETH Zürich, Zürich, Switzerland
voanna@vision.ee.ethz.ch

Abstract. Probabilistic modelling has been an essential tool in medical image analysis, especially for analyzing brain Magnetic Resonance Images (MRI). Recent deep learning techniques for estimating high-dimensional distributions, in particular Variational Autoencoders (VAEs), opened up new avenues for probabilistic modeling. Modelling of volumetric data has remained a challenge, however, because constraints on available computation and training data make it difficult effectively leverage VAEs, which are well-developed for 2D images. We propose a method to model 3D MR brain volumes distribution by combining a 2D slice VAE with a Gaussian model that captures the relationships between slices. We do so by estimating the sample mean and covariance in the latent space of the 2D model over the slice direction. This combined model lets us sample new coherent stacks of latent variables to decode into slices of a volume. We also introduce a novel evaluation method for generated volumes that quantifies how well their segmentations match those of true brain anatomy. We demonstrate that our proposed model is competitive in generating high quality volumes at high resolutions according to both traditional metrics and our proposed evaluation. (Code is available at https://github.com/voanna/slices-to-3d-brain-vae/).

Keywords: Generative modelling · VAE · 3D

1 Introduction

Generative modeling with Bayesian models have played an important role in medical image computing, yielding very robust systems for segmentation and extracting morphological measurements, especially for brain MRI [1,4,12]. However, the difficulty in using these earlier Bayesian models was the difficulty in defining prior distributions. The challenges in estimating high-dimensional prior distributions forced researchers to use atlas-based systems through non-linear registration, e.g. [1], which arguably limited the applications of such models due to the challenges in registration itself. Recently, unsupervised deep learning has yielded powerful algorithms for estimating distributions in high dimensions

© Springer Nature Switzerland AG 2020
A. L. Martel et al. (Eds.): MICCAI 2020, LNCS 12267, pp. 657–666, 2020.
https://doi.org/10.1007/978-3-030-59728-3_64

and opened new avenues for modeling prior distributions for Bayesian models. Notably, Variational AutoEncoder models [8] provide access to probability values through the evidence lower-bound, enabling Bayesian approaches to various problems, such as undersampled Magnetic Resonance (MR) image reconstruction [17] and outlier detection [2]. Unfortunately, methods leveraging VAEs so far have had to constrain themselves to 2D models or coarser resolution 3D models.

Training volumetric VAE models remains difficult, due to limitations in available training data and computational resources. Compared to 2D data, 3D data is evidently higher dimensional, posing challenges for estimating probability distributions. The number of 3D training examples is relatively low compared to the 2D case. Even large-scale datasets only contain images on the order of thousands. Adding to the problem, volumetric VAEs also have a larger number of parameters to be trained and are difficult to fit into memory in GPU systems.

This means that existing models typically only demonstrate results for downsampled coarse volumetric data. Works on generating natural videos represented as "space-time cuboids" [9,21] have stopped at $3 \times 64 \times 64 \times 32$ size. Kwon et $al.$ [10] recently showed high quality generations of brain MR volumes at $64 \times 64 \times 64$ image size with their proposed 3D αWGAN method, however the method has difficulty scaling to $256 \times 256 \times 256$ in our experiments.

To move to 3D data at larger sizes with finer resolution, we propose to instead use (relatively) easy to train 2D variational autoencoders to generate MR image slices. We can exploit the correlation between successive slices of an MR volume in a second modelling step that captures the relationship between slices. By separately encoding all of the slices coming from the same volume using our 2D encoder, over many different volumes, we can estimate the sample mean and covariance of the latent codes over the slice dimension. This gives us a model for 3D data and lets us sample from the distribution by generating a new stack of latent codes with the same mean and covariance as the original codes, which, when decoded, correspond to a new consistent MR volume. We show that this simple yet efficient approach yields generated volumes that are competitive with other proposed generation approaches, such as the recently proposed 3D αWGAN [10] at $128 \times 128 \times 128$ image size, and outperforms 3D αWGAN at $256 \times 256 \times 256$ image size on several metrics.

We additionally introduce a novel and interpretable evaluation measure of the quality of the generated samples. We segment generated samples using a segmentation network trained on real images and then register generated volumes to real volumes, along with their segmentations. We then compute the Dice's similarity coefficient (DSC) [3] between the registered segmentations, and call this the "Realistic Atlas Score" (RAS). This procedure allows us to evaluate (a) how well a generated volume can "pass" as a real volume in the eyes of both a segmentation network and a registration algorithm; as well as (b) how well the anatomy in the generated images match real ones. Unlike other common evaluation methods for generative models, such as the Inception Score [16], the Fréchet Inception Distance [7], the RAS has a direct anatomical interpretation, which makes it informative for generative modelling of medical images in particular.

2 Methods

2.1 Modeling Distribution of 3D Images with 2D VAE

Our model has two components: (1) a variational autoencoder and (2) a sample mean and covariance estimation in the latent space of the encoder. The encoder maps MR slices to points in an L-dimensional latent space $\mathcal{Y}$ and the decoder maps them back to the image space $\mathcal{X}$. We train this model to convergence.

The second part of our model is a collection of L sample mean and covariance estimates over the latent variables in the slice dimension (one covariance estimate for each component of the latent space of the encoder). Using the sample means and covariances, we can sample new sequences of the latent variables that correspond to sequences of slices through an MR-volume. These samples will have the same sample mean and covariance structure as the original latent codes. The latent variable corresponding to each slice can be decoded individually to an image, and the slices are combined to obtain a complete and consistent MR-volume. The consistency of the slices is ensured because we compute the mean and covariance the slice direction.

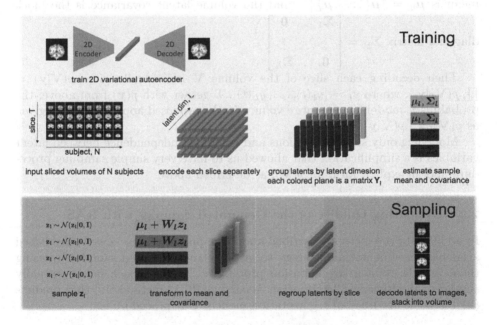

Fig. 1. We train a 2D autoencoder model on MR brain slices, and then model the relationship between successive slices in a volume by separately estimating sample means and covariances over the slice dimension for each component of the latent code. Using these, we transform samples from a unit Gaussian into new latent codes that can be decoded into volumes.

Specifically, let $\mathbf{y}(t) = \text{encoder}(\mathbf{X}(t))$, where $t = 1 \ldots T$ shows the dependence on the slice. Let $y_l(t)$ be the l-th component of the latent vector at slice t. We assume that corresponding latent variables across different slices are statistically related and we approximate this relation with a Gaussian model

$$p(\mathbf{y}_l) = \mathcal{N}(\mathbf{y}_l|\boldsymbol{\mu}_l, \boldsymbol{\Sigma}_l), \ \mathbf{y}_l = [y_l(1), \dots, y_l(t), \dots, y_l(T)]$$

where $\boldsymbol{\mu}_l$ and $\boldsymbol{\Sigma}_l$ are the sample mean and covariance matrices at the lth component in the latent space. These sample statistics are computed using the latent representations of the training samples. We encode all a set of training volumes, slice-by-slice, and use the latent codes for estimating the sample statistics.

To sample a new $\mathbf{y}_l$, we can use the expression $\mathbf{y}_l = \mathbf{W}_l \mathbf{z}_l + \boldsymbol{\mu}_l$, and sample $\mathbf{z}_l$ according to $p(\mathbf{z}_l) = \mathcal{N}(\mathbf{z}_l|\mathbf{0}, \mathbf{I})$, where $\mathbf{W}_l = \boldsymbol{\Sigma}_l^{1/2}$. To compute $\mathbf{W}_l$ we use the singular value decomposition of $\mathbf{Y}_l$, the matrix containing $\mathbf{y}_l$ for different training samples as columns. If $\mathbf{Y}_l = \mathbf{U}_l \mathbf{S}_l \mathbf{V}_l^*$, then $\mathbf{W}_l = \mathbf{U}_l \mathbf{S}_l^{1/2}/\sqrt{N}$, where N denotes the number of training samples. For each dimension l in the latent space, we build independent Gaussian models based on sample statistics.

Denoting all the latent variables for a volume together by the vector $\mathbf{y}$, we have $p(\mathbf{y}) = \mathcal{N}(\mathbf{y}|\boldsymbol{\mu_y}, \boldsymbol{\Sigma_y})$, where $\mathbf{y} = \left[\mathbf{y}_1^T, \mathbf{y}_2^T, \dots, \mathbf{y}_L^T\right]^T$, the volume latent mean is $\boldsymbol{\mu_y} = \left[\boldsymbol{\mu}_1^T, \dots, \boldsymbol{\mu}_L^T\right]^T$, and the volume latent covariance is the block diagonal matrix $\boldsymbol{\Sigma_y} = \begin{bmatrix} \boldsymbol{\Sigma}_1 \dots & \mathbf{0} \\ \vdots & \ddots & \vdots \\ \mathbf{0} & \dots \boldsymbol{\Sigma}_L \end{bmatrix}$.

Then decoding each slice of the volume $\mathbf{V}$ individually gives $p(\mathbf{V}|\mathbf{y}) = \prod_t p(\mathbf{V}_t|\mathbf{y}_t)$, where $\mathbf{y}_t = [y_1(t), \dots, y_L(t)]$. Together with $p(\mathbf{y})$ from above, the probabilistic model for the entire volume in the proposed approach can be given as $p(\mathbf{V}) = \int p(\mathbf{V}|\mathbf{y})p(\mathbf{y})d\mathbf{y}$.

Modelling only slice interactions and assuming independence between latent variables is a simplification that allowed us to have very simple sampling procedure and an explicit form for $p(\mathbf{V})$, as described above.

2.2   Evaluating Quality of the Generated Samples with RAS

In addition to the method described above, we propose to use a well-established atlas-based segmentation strategy to evaluate the generated samples by using them as atlases in a segmentation procedure. This approach is conceptually similar to the Reverse Classification Accuracy (RCA) method [19] that predicts the test-time accuracy of segmentation models. Our procedure is:

1. Segment the generated samples using a CNN-based segmentation network, which is trained using real images
2. Register the generated samples to real images and map the predicted segmentation with the same transformation.
3. Evaluate the agreement between segmentations of the generated samples predicted by the CNN, after mapping, and real images.
4. The agreement score between the segmentations serves as the quality metric.

We evaluate the agreement using the DSC and use affine registration. Other choices for agreement metrics and registration algorithms are also possible.

The procedure for computing RAS evaluates the generated samples in three different ways. First, the generated samples has to yield realistic segmentations when fed into the CNN-based segmentation network. To achieve this, they need to be void of any domain-shifts. Second, the generated samples should be "registerable" to real images, showing similar intensity profiles across the image. Lastly, the generated samples has to capture correct anatomical details for a high agreement between the segmentations of the generated samples, after mapping, and real images.

We propose the RAS metric to complement other evaluation scores, such as MMD and MS-SSIM used in [10]. Previously used scores are aiming to evaluate the diversity of the generated samples more than how realistic they are. RAS aims directly at evaluating realism with a specialized strategy for medical images.

3 Experimental Setup

3.1 Compared Models

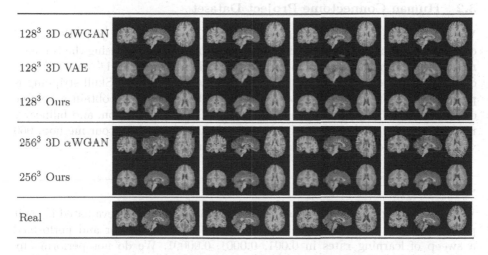

| 128^3 3D αWGAN |
| 128^3 3D VAE |
| 128^3 Ours |
| 256^3 3D αWGAN |
| 256^3 Ours |
| Real |

Fig. 2. Example generated volumes. Our slice-based model is able to generate realistic, if somewhat blurry, volumes at 256^3, unlike the volumetric 3D αWGAN model.

We compare the generations produced by our model against a 3D VAE and other 3D generative network approaches from Kwon *et al.* [10] at 64^3, 128^3, and 256^3 sizes. In models originally for 64^3 inputs, we increase the number of layers to reach the desired output size.

We use the following shorthand for describing architectures: convolutional layer with N filters - conv_N, batch norm - BN, leaky ReLU - LR, max pooling -

MP, reversible layer [5] with 3 conv_16 - RL, fully connected layer with N units - FC_N, residual block with conv-ReLu-BatchNorm subblocks, halving size and doubling filters - ResDown. Compared models are:

3D WGAN GP [6]

3D VAE-GAN [11]

3D α GAN [15]. For the model at 256^3, we replace BatchNorm3D with InstanceNorm3D layers, and remove BatchNorm1D layers.

3D α WGAN model proposed by Kwon et al. [10], with 1000 latent dimensions

3D VAE our own implementation. Encoder and decoder are symmetric. Both mean and standard deviation have a fully connected layer.

64^3 encoder Conv_16 - BN - LR - MP - 3 × (RL - MP) - RL - FC_512

128^3 encoder Conv_16 - BN - LR - MP - 4 × (RL - MP) - FC_1024

Our proposed model We use a VAE with a 0.2 weight on the KL term, which produces better quality samples. Encoder and decoder are symmetric.

64^3 encoder Conv_16 - BN - LR - 3 × (ResDown - LR) - ResDown

128^3 encoder Conv_8 - BN - LR - 4 × (ResDown - LR) - ResDown

256^3 encoder Conv_4 - BN - LR - 5 × (ResDown - LR) - ResDown

We used $N = 400$ samples to estimate the sample means and covariances.

3.2 Human Connectome Project Dataset

We use T1w MR volumes from the Human Connectome Project (HCP) [20] dataset. To preprocess each brain, we perform bias correction using the N4 algorithm [18] and normalize the intensities per volume using the 1st and 99th percentiles (clipping the values at the lower and upper bounds). Skull stripping is performed by FreeSurfer [4]. We discard zero-filled planes to obtain a volume of size $256 \times 256 \times 256$ at $0.7\,\text{mm} \times 0.7\,\text{mm} \times 0.7\,\text{mm}$ resolution, and bilinearly resample to the needed size. We use coronal slices for training our method. 960 volumes are used for training and 40 for validation.

3.3 Training Details

We used the implementation from [10] for the baseline models evaluated in their paper. For our proposed model, we used the Adam optimizer and performed a sweep of learning rates in 0.001, 0.0001, 0.00001. We do not perform any augmentation during training. To compute the RAS, we use a U-Net [14] based segmentation network that was trained on 40 volumes of coronal brain slices using 15 labels. We used the Adam optimizer with default beta1, beta2, learning rate 0.001, and batch size 16, with a Dice training loss [13].

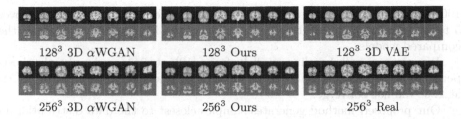

| 128³ 3D αWGAN | 128³ Ours | 128³ 3D VAE |
| 256³ 3D αWGAN | 256³ Ours | 256³ Real |

Fig. 3. Segmentations of example generated volumes. At 256³ size, our model produces samples with more realistic segmentations than 3D αWGAN.

4 Experimental Results

4.1 Example Generations

Figure 2 shows example generated volumes. Our method is able to successfully sample consistent brain volumes. Both our and the 3D VAE generated samples are somewhat blurry, which is a well-known shortcoming of VAE-based models. We also see that our model can generate diverse brain shapes. The 3D αWGAN produces the visually highest quality samples at 128³, but fails to produce realistic samples at 256³, and suffers from blocky artefacts.

Table 1. MMD and MS-SSIM for compared models. Our model produces samples close to the data distribution according to (low values of) MMD, and also generates diverse samples as measured by low MS-SSIM.

	HCP 64³		HCP 128³		HCP 256³	
	MMD	MS-SSIM	MMD	MS-SSIM	MMD	MS-SSIM
3D WGAN GP	14383	0.9995				
3D VAE GAN	2054	0.9292				
3D α-GAN	7116	0.9848				
3D α-WGAN	4488	0.8994	64446	0.9736	912627	0.7106
3D VAE	6823	0.9927	51476	0.9335		
Ours	2396	0.9304	19890	0.9120	323233	0.8768
Real		0.8786		0.7966		0.7019

4.2 Image Diversity Metrics

We follow [10] and report the Multiscale Structural Similarity (MS-SSIM) to measure the diversity of generated samples; and a minibatch estimate of Maximum Mean Discrepancy (MMD) to measure distance to the training distribution. We use the same settings as Kwon *et al.* [10]. Due to computational cost, the MMD for 256³ was computed over 10 tests using batch size 4, instead of over

100 tests with batch size 8; and the 256^3 MS-SSIM for real data is averaged over 5 tests, instead of over 20 tests. Table 1 shows the MMD and MS-SSIM of the compared models.

We compare all baseline models from [10] at 64^3, and only the best-performing model from that set, the 3D αWGAN, at larger sizes. Our 3D VAE at 256^3 did not converge.

Our proposed method generates samples closest to the data distribution in the MMD sense at 128^3 and 256^3 sizes, and is second to 3D VAEGAN at 64^3. Our model also has a low MS-SSIM at 64^3 and 128^3, meaning the samples are diverse. The MS-SSIM of the 3D αWGAN at 256^3 is lower than ours because the MS-SSIM computes the pairwise similarity of generated samples only, and the 256^3 3D αWGAN generates very diverse but low-quality samples.

While MMD and MS-SSIM evaluate the samples in the distribution sense, they are not interpretable in terms of anatomical plausibility of the generated images. Thus the proposed RAS metric complements MMD and MS-SSIM.

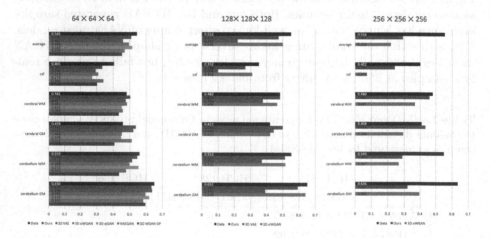

Fig. 4. Realistic Atlas Score at different image sizes. Our model is competitive with other volumetric generation approaches at 64^3 and 128^3 sizes, and produces more realistic volumes than the 3D αWGAN at 256^3.

4.3 RAS Evaluation

Figure 4 shows RAS values. We computed the average metric on all 800 pairs between 40 test volumes and 20 real volumes. We also computed the RAS between different sets of real volumes to produce an upper bound. Both our model and 3D αWGAN have similar performance at 128^3 size, while our model's samples are more realistic at 256^3 size. Figure 3 shows example segmentations from the compared models.

RAS values are affected by the quality of the inter-subject registration. For structures with high intersubject variability, the registration quality can be low for some pairs of real data, decreasing the average RAS. The synthetic examples often fail to create complex patterns in such structures, producing blurred areas, effectively simplifying the registration task and preventing RAS from dropping very low. Notably this is a drawback of RAS and the reason why it should be considered as a complementary score to MMD and MSSIM. However, we note although RAS is insensitive to the diversity of generations, it effectively quantifies the realistic nature of generations in an interpretable manner.

5 Discussion

Taken together, the MMD, MS-SSIM and RAS evaluation show that the proposed model for approximating distributions of 3D volumes via 2D VAEs can produce realistic samples on par with or better than the state of the art GAN approaches, extending the capabilites of current VAE models. Our simple yet efficient approach opens up new avenues for building Bayesian models using 3D priors distributions, and provides a possible approach for modeling distributions at 256^3 image size.

References

1. Ashburner, J., Friston, K.J.: Unified segmentation. NeuroImage **26**(3), 839–851 (2005). https://doi.org/10.1016/j.neuroimage.2005.02.018
2. Chen, X., Konukoglu, E.: Unsupervised detection of lesions in brain MRI using constrained adversarial auto-encoders. In: MIDL Conference Book. MIDL (2018)
3. Dice, L.R.: Measures of the amount of ecologic association between species. Ecology **26**(3), 297–302 (1945)
4. Fischl, B.: FreeSurfer. Neuroimage **62**(2), 774–781 (2012)
5. Gomez, A.N., Ren, M., Urtasun, R., Grosse, R.B.: The reversible residual network: backpropagation without storing activations. In: Advances in Neural Information Processing Systems, pp. 2214–2224 (2017)
6. Gulrajani, I., Ahmed, F., Arjovsky, M., Dumoulin, V., Courville, A.C.: Improved training of Wasserstein GANs. In: Advances in Neural Information Processing Systems, pp. 5767–5777 (2017)
7. Heusel, M., Ramsauer, H., Unterthiner, T., Nessler, B., Hochreiter, S.: GANs trained by a two time-scale update rule converge to a local Nash equilibrium. In: Advances in Neural Information Processing Systems, pp. 6626–6637 (2017)
8. Kingma, D.P., Welling, M.: Auto-encoding variational bayes. In: Bengio, Y., LeCun, Y. (eds.) 2nd International Conference on Learning Representations, ICLR 2014, Banff, AB, Canada, 14–16 April 2014, Conference Track Proceedings (2014). http://arxiv.org/abs/1312.6114
9. Kratzwald, B., Huang, Z., Paudel, D.P., Dinesh, A., Van Gool, L.: Improving video generation for multi-functional applications. arXiv preprint arXiv:1711.11453 (2017)
10. Kwon, G., Han, C., Kim, D.: Generation of 3D brain MRI using auto-encoding generative adversarial networks. In: Shen, D., et al. (eds.) MICCAI 2019. LNCS, vol. 11766, pp. 118–126. Springer, Cham (2019). https://doi.org/10.1007/978-3-030-32248-9_14
11. Larsen, A.B.L., Sønderby, S.K., Larochelle, H., Winther, O.: Autoencoding beyond pixels using a learned similarity metric. arXiv preprint arXiv:1512.09300 (2015)

12. Leemput, K.V., et al.: Automated segmentation of hippocampal subfields from ultra-high resolution in vivo MRI. Hippocampus **19**(6), 549–557 (2009). https://doi.org/10.1002/hipo.20615
13. Milletari, F., Navab, N., Ahmadi, S.A.: V-net: Fully convolutional neural networks for volumetric medical image segmentation. In: 2016 Fourth International Conference on 3D Vision (3DV). pp. 565–571. IEEE (2016)
14. Ronneberger, O., Fischer, P., Brox, T.: U-Net: convolutional networks for biomedical image segmentation. In: Navab, N., Hornegger, J., Wells, W.M., Frangi, A.F. (eds.) MICCAI 2015. LNCS, vol. 9351, pp. 234–241. Springer, Cham (2015). https://doi.org/10.1007/978-3-319-24574-4_28
15. Rosca, M., Lakshminarayanan, B., Warde-Farley, D., Mohamed, S.: Variational approaches for auto-encoding generative adversarial networks. arXiv preprint arXiv:1706.04987 (2017)
16. Salimans, T., Goodfellow, I., Zaremba, W., Cheung, V., Radford, A., Chen, X.: Improved techniques for training GANs. In: Advances in Neural Information Processing Systems, pp. 2234–2242 (2016)
17. Tezcan, K.C., Baumgartner, C.F., Luechinger, R., Pruessmann, K.P., Konukoglu, E.: MR image reconstruction using deep density priors. IEEE Trans. Med. Imaging **38**(7), 1633–1642 (2018)
18. Tustison, N.J., et al.: N4ITK: improved N3 bias correction. IEEE Trans. Med. Imaging **29**(6), 1310–1320 (2010)
19. Valindria, V.V., et al.: Reverse classification accuracy: predicting segmentation performance in the absence of ground truth. IEEE Trans. Med. Imaging **36**(8), 1597–1606 (2017). https://doi.org/10.1109/tmi.2017.2665165
20. Van Essen, D.C., et al.: The WU-Minn human connectome project: an overview. Neuroimage **80**, 62–79 (2013)
21. Vondrick, C., Pirsiavash, H., Torralba, A.: Generating videos with scene dynamics. In: Advances in Neural Information Processing Systems, pp. 613–621 (2016)

Spatial Component Analysis to Mitigate Multiple Testing in Voxel-Based Analysis

Samuel Gerber[1]($\boxtimes$) and Marc Niethammer[2]

[1] Kitware Inc., Carborro, NC 27510, USA
samuel.gerber@kitware.com
[2] University of North Carolina, Chapel Hill, NC 27599, USA

Abstract. Voxel-based analysis provides a simple, easy to interpret approach to discover regions correlated with a variable of interest such as for
example a pathology indicator. Voxel-based analysis methods perform a
statistical test at each voxel and are prone to false positives due to multiple testing, or when corrected for multiple testing may miss regions of
interest. Component based approaches, such as principal or independent
component analysis provide an approach to mitigate multiple testing,
by testing for correlations to projections of the data to the components.
We propose a spatially regularized component analysis approach to find
components for image data sets that are spatially localized and smooth.
We show that the proposed approach leads to components that are easier to interpret and can improve predictive performance when used with
linear regression models. We develop an efficient optimization approach
using the Grassmannian projection kernel and a randomized SVD. The
proposed optimization is capable to deal with data sets too large to fit
into memory. We demonstrate the approach with an application to study
Alzheimer's disease using over 1200 images from the OASIS-3 data set.

1 Introduction

Voxel-wise testing of statistical hypotheses is a step performed in many medical
image analysis pipelines, ranging from time series of functional magnetic resonance images (MRI) [13] to population morphometry on structural MRI [15]. For
example in voxel-based morphometry (VBM) [1] each voxel is correlated with a
variable of interest to discover affected regions in images. The large number of
voxels requires a careful approach to deal with multiple testing and methods to
remedy false positives, as the dead salmon starkly illustrates [4]. A typical approach is to correct the p-values obtained with methods such as the Bonferroni
correction [7] or more sophisticated methods such as controlling the false discovery rate [3]. This approach to voxel-based analysis suffers a trade-off between
false positives and false negatives, i.e. suggestion of false discoveries or missing
potentially important regions.

We propose to resort to component based analysis to drastically reduce the
number of tests to mitigate issues due to multiple testing. The approach extracts
a few components that capture the variation in the data set and tests those for

© Springer Nature Switzerland AG 2020
A. L. Martel et al. (Eds.): MICCAI 2020, LNCS 12267, pp. 667–677, 2020.
https://doi.org/10.1007/978-3-030-59728-3_65

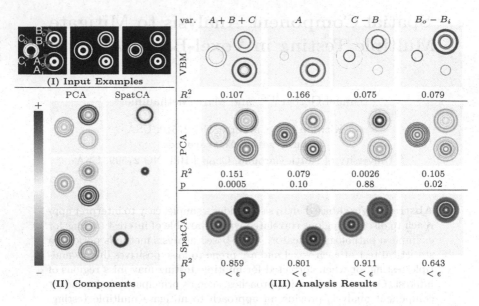

Fig. 1. Example of the proposed spatial component analysis approach. (I) The example data consists of 100 images that contain 3 sets of 2 concentric annuli of varying widths with $A = \{A_o, A_i\}$, $B = \{B_o, B_i\}$ and $C = \{C_o, C_i\}$ number of pixels, respectively. (II) The first 3 components of a principal component analysis (PCA) and the proposed spatial component analysis (SpatCA). The principal components capture global effects and can contain both positive and negative entries. The spatial component analysis is localized and only contain predominately positive values. (III) Analysis on four different variables: the total number of pixels in $A + B + C$, A, $C - B$ and $B_o - B_i$. The goal of the analysis is to discover which regions are correlation to the variables, e.g. for $B_o - B_i$ we expect positive correlations in region B_o and negative correlations in region B_i. The voxel-based morphometry (VBM) approach shows weak correlations to the correct regions. The spatial component based analysis clearly discovers the various effects with strong correlations (large R^2) and very strong statistical significance (small p-value less than machine precision ϵ). For the VBM analysis only pixels with $p \leq 0.05$ are shown.

correlation with a clinical variable of interest, such as a pathology indicator, or use them in conjunction with a regression model. Component based analysis methods such as principal component analysis (PCA) or independent component analysis (ICA) have been applied to morphometric analysis [21,22]. Principal or independent components ignore the spatial nature of the image data, however. We propose an improvement to component based analysis that takes into account the spatial nature of the data and leads to better interpretable results. The proposed approach, spatial component analysis (SpatCA), seeks components that are spatially smooth, sparse. The sparsity penalty can be tuned to more strongly penalize negative values and thus result in components with a preference for non-negative entries.

This regularization leads to components that are spatially almost not overlapping and localized. The non-overlapping nature leads to results that are easier to interpret since individual components cannot cancel effects when used jointly in a regression model. The localization avoids having components where a single component captures a large, or the whole, region and thus, is not very informative. The approach is illustrated in Fig. 1 and shows that the spatial regularization yields components that can capture localized effects with better interpretable results and in this case yield better predictive power.

We develop an efficient optimization approach to deal with large data sets. The proposed optimization approach avoids having to iterate over the data set multiple times by using the Grassmannian projection kernel [10] and randomized SVD [9] to approximate to the data fidelity term. This computational strategy has the potential to be applicable in a wide variety of optimization problems involving a least squares data fidelity term.

The key contributions of this work are:

1. A spatially regularized component analysis to increases interpretability and predictive power.
2. An efficient optimization approach for large data sets.
3. A demonstration of the approach with an application on over 1000 images from the OASIS-3 data set [12] for the study of Alzheimer's disease.

2 Related Work

The geosciences have developed several approaches to include spatial information to PCA [6]. These approaches use weighted PCA [18] with predefined weights, to determine localized principal components. Different weights will lead to different weighting of spatial regions. The proposed approach does not require predefined defined weights but uses spatial regularization terms to infer localized components from the data while still capturing as much variance as possible.

Component based analysis to deal with multiple testing has been used in the context of RAVENS, a deformation based voxel-wise morphometry approach, by applying PCA [22]. In the same fashion ICA was applied to VBM [21] to discover differences in gray matter in relation to schizophrenia. We propose to improve on principal and independent components by adding spatial and sparsity regularization. We also introduce the use of randomized SVD approach, which requires fewer passes over data and drastically reduces computation time for data sets too large to fit into memory.

3 Spatially Regularized Component Analysis

For the following discussion we use the notation X to denote an image on the domain $\Omega \subset \mathbb{R}^3$, with $x = \text{vec}(X) \in \mathbb{R}^d$ the vectorization of the image X and with $X = \text{im}(x)$ the conversion of the vector x into the image X. A matrix is denoted by X with columns x_i and rows x^j. By X^-, and X^+, we denote the matrix with the negative, and positive, entries of $\boldsymbol{X}$, respectively, and zero everywhere else.

In voxel based analysis methods the quantities of interest are a set of feature images X_i extracted from a set of images I_i. For example in voxel-based morphometry X_i are the voxel intensities after alignments of the images I_i, possibly corrected for volume deformations. However, the method presented here is applicable to other feature images, modalities, or even deformation momenta [20] to capture local deformation variations.

Given n feature images X_i we are interested in finding a set of k orthogonal components c_j that approximate the major modes of variation in the X_i. Let $\boldsymbol{X}$ be the matrix with columns $\boldsymbol{x}_i = \text{vec}(X_i)$. For simplicity in notion we assume the X_i to be mean centered $\sum_i \boldsymbol{x}_i = 0$. To find components that capture the maximum amount of variation we can formulate the minimization problem as the projection of $\boldsymbol{X}$ under the Frobenius norm $E_v(C) = \|\boldsymbol{X} - \boldsymbol{C}\boldsymbol{C}^t\boldsymbol{X}\|_F^2$ and minimize over the set $\mathcal{G}(d, k)$ of orthonormal $d \times k$ matrices. The solution $\boldsymbol{C}_v = \arg\min_{C \in \mathcal{G}(d,k)} E_v(\boldsymbol{C})$ to this optimization problem are not unique due to partial rotation invariance of the objective. The principal components provide one solution in which the components are rotated to maximize variance of each individual component.

We propose to regularize the orthogonal subspaces to enforce spatial smoothness and sparsity leading to the spatially regularized component analysis objective:

$$E_r(C) = \|\boldsymbol{X} - \boldsymbol{C}\boldsymbol{C}^t\boldsymbol{X}\|_F^2 + \lambda_+\|C^+\|_1 + \lambda_-\|C^-\|_1 + \gamma\sum_{i=1}^k \int_\Omega \|\nabla\text{im}(c_i)\|_2^2 dx. \quad (1)$$

The λ_- and λ_+ control the sparsity of the negative and positive entries in C. By setting λ_- large we can force C to be non-negative or close to non-negative. The λ_+ controls the sparsity of the remaining positive entries. With only or almost only positive entries the optimization is forced to find spatially non-overlapping components in order to satisfy the orthogonality constraints on C: a zero inner product requires non-overlapping entries in the components.

3.1   Optimization for Large Data Sets

To minimize the objective in Eq. (1) we propose to approximate the data fidelity term $\|\boldsymbol{X} - \boldsymbol{C}\boldsymbol{C}^t\boldsymbol{X}\|_F^2$ by using the Grassmannian projection kernel [10] $K_p(C, C_v) = \|C^t C_v\|_F^2$, i.e. how close is C to the maximal variance subspace C_v. The Grassmannian projection kernel measures similarity (i.e. larger values of $K_p(C, C_v)$ indicate closer subspaces) of the subspaces captured by C and C_v. Since C_v is the subspace that captures the most variations the projection kernel enforces that the optimization stays close to the maximal variance subspace. The optimization is a two step approach with first computing the first k principal components and then a proximal gradient descent to minimize

$$E_a(C) = -K_p(C, C_v) + \lambda_+\|C^+\|_1 + \lambda_-\|C^-\|_1 + \gamma\sum_{i=1}^k \int_\Omega \|\nabla\text{im}(c_i)\|_2^2 dx \quad (2)$$

over the set of orthonormal matrices $C \in \mathcal{G}(d,k)$. This approximation does not require access to the data after the computation of the principal components C_v. We now show how to compute the principal components efficiently, requiring only one data point at a time in memory, and then develop an optimization algorithm for the objective in Eq. (2).

Computing the principal components directly requires an SVD of the full data set X, which typically requires the full data set in memory. A very fast method with less memory consumption is the randomized SVD approach [9] which only requires $O(n)$ passes over the data and $O(dk)$ memory. The randomized SVD is based on random projections of the data to a $O(k)$ dimensional linear subspace to estimate the range of the data matrix, which can be done in an iterative fashion accessing one data point at the time. Then the SVD is performed on the data points projected on the low dimensional range subspace and the resulting eigenvectors are projected back to the original space. For more details please refer to the detailed descriptions in [9].

Equation (2) can be decomposed to a smooth function $f_\gamma(C) = -K_p(C, C_v) + \gamma \sum_{i=1}^{k} \int_\Omega \nabla \mathrm{im}(c_i)$ and the sparsity penalties $\lambda_p \|C^+\| + \lambda_n \|C^-\|$ and can be optimized by a proximal gradient descent approach [16]. The proximal gradient descent results in alternating iterative thresholding [2,5] and projections to the $\mathcal{G}(d,k)$. Define the ℓ_1-proximal operator $prox_\lambda(x) = (x - \lambda)^+ - (-x - \lambda)^+$ and the projection operator $proj_{\mathcal{G}(d,k)}(A) = \arg\min_{Y \in \mathcal{G}(d,k)} \|Y - A\|_F^2$ which can be efficiently computed by SVD of A. With these operators the spatial regularized components can be computed by:

Algorithm 1. Spatial Regularized Component Analysis

1: **procedure** SPATCA(C_v, λ_-, λ_+, γ, s)   ▷ with step size s
2:     $v \leftarrow 0$
3:     $C \leftarrow C_v$
4:     **while** $\frac{\|v - E_a(C)\|_2}{E_a(C)} \geq \epsilon$ **do**   ▷ Stop if relative change $\leq \epsilon$
5:         $v \leftarrow E_a(C)$
6:         $C \leftarrow C - s\nabla f_\gamma(C)$
7:         $C \leftarrow prox_{s\lambda_+}(C^+) + prox_{s\lambda_-}(C^-)$
8:         $C \leftarrow proj_{\mathcal{G}(d,k)}(C)$
9:     **end while**
10:    **return** C
11: **end procedure**

3.2   Statistical Analysis with Components

Once the components are computed by principal, independent or the spatial components proposed here, they can be utilized for further statistical analysis. Let $Z = C^t X$ be the data set X, with each column a feature image $x_i = \mathrm{vec}(X_i)$ projected onto the components C.

In the simplest case the individual components c_i can be correlated with a variable of interest $y \in \mathbb{R}^\kappa$, e.g. a pathology indicator associated with each image, by computing the correlation $\mathrm{cor}(z^i, y)$ of a row of the projected data and the variable of interest. The projected data can also be used with regression models. We propose to use the elastic net [23], a linear regression model with ℓ_1 and ℓ_2 regularization on the coefficients: $\{\hat{a}, \hat{b}\} = \arg\min_{a,b} \|y - Z^t a + b\|_2^2 + (1 - \alpha)\|a\|_1 + \alpha\|a\|_2$ The regularization permits to include a larger number of components as well as controlling for potential confounding variables while avoiding overfitting.

To visualize the results in the correlation case one can simply display the component image $\mathrm{im}(c_i)$. The interpretation is a bit more difficult as compared to the traditional single voxel-based a correlated. Since the correlation is based on the projection of the data set to the component C_i, the component image shows all regions that are potentially involved in producing the correlation $\mathrm{cor}(z_i, y)$. This could mean that the effect is spread out over the whole region in all data points, or varies across data points or is confined to a subregion. This motivates the spatially localized components in SpatCA that yield easier to interpret results with less ambiguity.

For linear regression models, such as the elastic net approach, we can display the gradient of the regression with respect to Z. The gradient captures the change in the image that leads to the most pronounced change in the variable y. The gradient of the regularized linear regression model with coefficients $\hat{a}$ and intercept $\hat{b}$ is $\hat{a}$. Constructing the gradient back into image space yields $\mathrm{im}(C\hat{a})$ The interpretation is similar to the correlation case since the gradient image is a linear combination of the components. We suggest to scale the projections Z to unit standard deviation before computing the regression model. This scaling, while not changing the prediction or statistics, yields a gradient magnitude with respect to moving one standard deviation in each component.

4   Application to Study Alzheimer's Disease

We apply the method to the OASIS-3 data set [12] to study the relationship between β-amyloid deposits and white matter damage. The deposit of β-amyloid is an early indicator for Alzheimer's disease and has been linked to white matter damage [17]. The images X_i in the OASIS-3 data are skull-stripped, gain-field corrected and registered to the Talaraich atlas space [19] with a 12-parameter affine transform. For the analysis we subsampled the volumes to $128 \times 128 \times 128$. The OASIS-3 data set contains estimates of β-amyloid deposit based on PET imaging using the inter-patient comparable centiloid scale [11]. We used 1,234 structural MRI images from the OASIS-3 data set ranging from age 42 to 90 and associated centiloid measurements ranging from -13 to 142. Figure 2(a,b) shows the distribution of age and centiloid values in the population.

For the analysis we computed 50 PCA and SpatCA components from the matrix X, with each column $x_i = \mathrm{vec}(X_i)$, i.e. an analysis of the image intensities. The data matrix X is of size $d \times n$, with $d = 128 \times 128 \times 128$ and

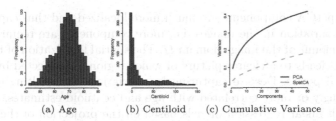

(a) Age   (b) Centiloid   (c) Cumulative Variance

Fig. 2. Distribution of (a) ages and (b) centiloid values in the population. (c) Cumulative variance captured as a percentage of total variance in the image data by the first 50 components of PCA and SpatCA. While SpatCA captures less of the total variation, the components are as closely or better correlated with age and centiloid (see Fig. 3).

$n = 1,234$. The SpatCA optimization converged after around 400 iterations and required around 30 s per iteration with a naïve implementation in R. The random SVD step takes about 5 min with most of the time spent accessing data from the hard drive. The randomized SVD itself only requires approximately 30 s. The optimization was not very sensitive to the selection of the SpatCA regularization parameters and the step size. For λ_- we selected a parameter on the order of the mean of the nonzero components of $|C_v|$ and set $\lambda_+ = 10^{-5}\lambda_-$. For γ we selected values that corresponded roughly to smoothing with a Gaussian with $\sigma = 0.1$ at each iteration. The step size s was set to 1.

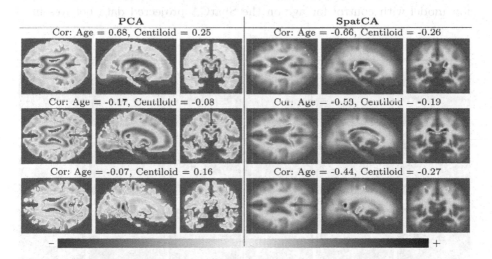

PCA	SpatCA
Cor: Age = 0.68, Centiloid = 0.25	Cor: Age = -0.66, Centiloid = -0.26
Cor: Age = -0.17, Centiloid = -0.08	Cor: Age = -0.53, Centiloid = -0.19
Cor: Age = -0.07, Centiloid = 0.16	Cor: Age = -0.44, Centiloid = -0.27

Fig. 3. PCA and SpatCA components on the OASIS 3 data set and the corresponding correlation to age and centiloid estimates.

Figure 2(c) shows the cumulative variance captured by PCA and SpatCA and Fig. 3 shows the first three PCA components and corresponding SpatCA components. The SpatCA captures less of the total variance. This is not unexpected since the SpatCA components are much more localized and thus capture less of the overall variation in the images, i.e. more components are required to cover the same amount of the image domain Ω. The spatial localization of the SpatCA components leads to a clearer picture of which regions are affected by aging and β-amyloid deposits. Despite capturing less variation the resulting components are as strongly or more correlated with age and centiloid estimates.

We built linear regression models based on the projection of the data to 50 PCA and SpatCA components, respectively. We employed the elastic regularization provided by the R package *glmnet* [8] to select only a few components and avoid overfitting. The regularization parameter for the elastic regression was selected by 10-fold cross validation. Age and centiloid exhibit a Pearson's correlation coefficient of 0.34 with strong statistical significance (p-value less than machine precision). Thus, age potentially acts as a confounding factor and we also built a regression model for centiloid that controls for age (i.e. includes age as a predictor). Figure 4 shows the gradient of the regression models indicating the direction that induces the largest change in the predicted variable (age or centiloid). The regression models on the PCA components include region of tissue gain for both age and centiloid. The SpatCA models show loss of tissue only. Increase in white matter contradicts current clinical knowledge of the processes involved in aging [14] and the findings with respect to the damaging effect on white matter tissue of β-amyloid deposits [17]. This suggest that the SpatCA components is less likely to include areas not informative about the variable of interest due to the localized nature of the components. The centiloid regression model with control for age on the SpatCA projected data behaves in an

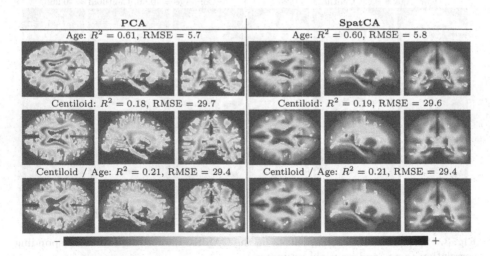

Fig. 4. OASIS regression on 50 PCA and SpatCA components. Gradient of the elastic net regression for age (Age), centiloid (Centiloid) and centiloid with controlling for age (Centiloid/Age). We report R^2 and root mean squared error (RMSE) from 10-fold cross-validation. The SpatCA gradient is much more localized suggesting a smaller area affected.

additive manner: the gradient of the age model plus the gradient of the centiloid model match approximately the controlled for age gradient. This suggest that the SpatCA components are better suited to disentangle confounding factors.

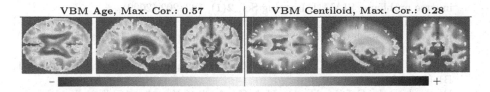

Fig. 5. VBM results with voxelwise correlation to age and centiloid on the OASIS 3 data set. Only voxels with p-value $\leq 5e^{-7}$ are shown, this corresponds to a Bonferroni corrected p-value of ≤ 0.05

Figure 5 shows a VBM analysis with voxelwise correlations to age and centiloid. The VBM shows similar regions to age as the first principal component in Fig. 3. For centiloid weaker correlations are detected in a subset of the regions correlated to age. The SpatCA components in Fig. 3 show correlations in region not found with a VBM analysis. In the SpatCA (and PCA) analysis all voxels within a component can contribute to the correlation and can thus capture locally spread out effects that are not apparent with a VBM analysis. A comparison to the SpatCA R^2 values in Fig. 4 corroborates this interpretation. The VBM analysis yields maximal correlation of 0.58 for age and 0.28 for centiloid. The SpatCA analysis yields R^2 values of 0.60 and 0.19, which translate to correlations of 0.78 and 0.43, respectively. By aggregating local regions the SpatCA approach finds much stronger correlations than VBM, while mitigating the difficulty in interpretation of principal components.

5 Conclusion

We proposed spatially regularized component analysis (SpatCA) approach to mitigate multiple testing issues in voxel-based analysis methods. We demonstrated that the SpatCA leads to better interpretable statistical analysis and can improve predictive performance. We developed an efficient optimization approach for the spatial regularization approach that permits applications to large data sets that do not fit in memory.

For future work we consider including the spatial regularization directly as a regularization in a regression model and, thus capture subspaces that are better aligned with the variable of interest.

Acknowledgments. This work was funded, in part, by NIH grant R41MH118845.

References

1. Ashburner, J., Friston, K.J.: Voxel-based morphometry–the methods. Neuroimage **11**(6), 805–821 (2000)
2. Beck, A., Teboulle, M.: A fast iterative shrinkage-thresholding algorithm for linear inverse problems. SIAM J. Imaging Sci. **2**(1), 183–202 (2009)
3. Benjamini, Y., Hochberg, Y.: Controlling the false discovery rate: a practical and powerful approach to multiple testing. J. Roy. Stat. Soc.: Ser. B (Methodol.) **57**(1), 289–300 (1995)
4. Bennett, J.W., Cargill, O., Hall Jr., V., et al.: Requirements. New York Times **1**, B1 (2005)
5. Daubechies, I., Defrise, M., De Mol, C.: An iterative thresholding algorithm for linear inverse problems with a sparsity constraint. Commun. Pure Appl. Math.: J. Issued Courant Inst. Math. Sci. **57**(11), 1413–1457 (2004)
6. Demšar, U., Harris, P., Brunsdon, C., Fotheringham, A.S., McLoone, S.: Principal component analysis on spatial data: an overview. Ann. Assoc. Am. Geogr. **103**(1), 106–128 (2013)
7. Dunnett, C.W.: A multiple comparison procedure for comparing several treatments with a control. J. Am. Stat. Assoc. **50**(272), 1096–1121 (1955)
8. Friedman, J., Hastie, T., Tibshirani, R.: Regularization paths for generalized linear models via coordinate descent. J. Stat. Softw. **33**(1), 1 (2010)
9. Halko, N., Martinsson, P.-G., Tropp, J.A.: Finding structure with randomness: probabilistic algorithms for constructing approximate matrix decompositions. SIAM Rev. **53**(2), 217–288 (2011)
10. Hamm, J., Lee, D.D.: Grassmann discriminant analysis: a unifying view on subspace-based learning. In: Proceedings of the 25th International Conference on Machine Learning, pp. 376–383 (2008)
11. Klunk, W.E., et al.: The Centiloid project: standardizing quantitative amyloid plaque estimation by pet. Alzheimer's Dement. **11**(1), 1–15 (2015)
12. LaMontagne, P.J., et al.: OASIS-3: longitudinal neuroimaging, clinical, and cognitive dataset for normal aging and Alzheimer's disease. Alzheimer's Dement.: J. Alzheimer's Assoc. **14**(7), P1097 (2018)
13. Lindquist, M.A., et al.: The statistical analysis of fMRI data. Stat. Sci. **23**(4), 439–464 (2008)
14. Liu, H., et al.: Aging of cerebral white matter. Ageing Res. Rev. **34**, 64–76 (2017)
15. Mietchen, D., Gaser, C.: Computational morphometry for detecting changes in brain structure due to development, aging, learning, disease and evolution. Front. Neuroinform. **3**, 25 (2009)
16. Parikh, N., Boyd, S., et al.: Proximal algorithms. Found. Trends® Optimiz. **1**(3), 127–239 (2014)
17. Pietroboni, A.M., et al.: CSF β-amyloid and white matter damage: a new perspective on Alzheimer's disease. J. Neurol. Neurosurg. Psychiatry **89**(4), 352–357 (2018)
18. Skočaj, D., Leonardis, A., Bischof, H.: Weighted and robust learning of subspace representations. Pattern Recogn. **40**(5), 1556–1569 (2007)
19. Talairach, J., Tournoux, P.: Co-planar Stereotaxic Atlas of the Human Brain. 3-Dimensional Proportional System: An Approach to Cerebral Imaging. Thieme, New York (1988)
20. Vialard, F.-X., Risser, L., Rueckert, D., Cotter, C.J.: Diffeomorphic 3D image registration via geodesic shooting using an efficient adjoint calculation. Int. J. Comput. Vis. **97**(2), 229–241 (2012)

21. Xu, L., Groth, K.M., Pearlson, G., Schretlen, D.J., Calhoun, V.D.: Source-based morphometry: the use of independent component analysis to identify gray matter differences with application to schizophrenia. Hum. Brain Mapp. **30**(3), 711–724 (2009)
22. Zipunnikov, V., Caffo, B., Yousem, D.M., Davatzikos, C., Schwartz, B.S., Crainiceanu, C.: Functional principal component model for high-dimensional brain imaging. NeuroImage **58**(3), 772–784 (2011)
23. Zou, H., Hastie, T.: Regularization and variable selection via the elastic net. J. Roy. Stat. Soc. Ser. B **67**, 301–320 (2005)

MAGIC: Multi-scale Heterogeneity Analysis and Clustering for Brain Diseases

Junhao Wen[1]([⊠])[iD], Erdem Varol[2][iD], Ganesh Chand[1,3], Aristeidis Sotiras[4][iD], and Christos Davatzikos[1][iD]

[1] Center for Biomedical Image Computing and Analytics,
Perelman School of Medicine, University of Pennsylvania,
Philadelphia, USA
junhao.wen89@gmail.com

[2] Department of Statistics, Center for Theoretical Neuroscience,
Zuckerman Institute, Columbia University, New York, USA

[3] Department of Radiology, School of Medicine,
Washington University in St. Louis, St. Louis, USA

[4] Department of Radiology and Institute for Informatics,
Washington University School of Medicine, St. Louis, USA
https://www.med.upenn.edu/cbica/

Abstract. There is a growing amount of clinical, anatomical and functional evidence for the heterogeneous presentation of neuropsychiatric and neurodegenerative diseases such as schizophrenia and Alzheimer's Disease (AD). Elucidating distinct subtypes of diseases allows a better understanding of neuropathogenesis and enables the possibility of developing targeted treatment programs. Recent semi-supervised clustering techniques have provided a data-driven way to understand disease heterogeneity. However, existing methods do not take into account that subtypes of the disease might present themselves at different spatial scales across the brain. Here, we introduce a novel method, MAGIC, to uncover disease heterogeneity by leveraging multi-scale clustering. We first extract multi-scale patterns of structural covariance (PSCs) followed by a semi-supervised clustering with double cyclic block-wise optimization across different scales of PSCs. We validate MAGIC using simulated heterogeneous neuroanatomical data and demonstrate its clinical potential by exploring the heterogeneity of AD using T1 MRI scans of 228 cognitively normal (CN) and 191 patients. Our results indicate two main subtypes of AD with distinct atrophy patterns that consist of both fine-scale atrophy in the hippocampus as well as large-scale atrophy in cortical regions. The evidence for the heterogeneity is further corroborated by the clinical evaluation of two subtypes, which indicates that there is a subpopulation of AD patients that tend to be younger and decline faster in cognitive performance relative to the other subpopulation, which tends to be older and maintains a relatively steady decline in cognitive abilities.

Keywords: Semi-supervised · Clustering · Multi-scale

© Springer Nature Switzerland AG 2020
A. L. Martel et al. (Eds.): MICCAI 2020, LNCS 12267, pp. 678–687, 2020.
https://doi.org/10.1007/978-3-030-59728-3_66

1   Introduction

Imaging patterns of various brain diseases, such as schizophrenia (SCZ) [1–3] and Alzheimer's Disease (AD) [4–6] are often investigated via group comparisons involving voxel-based or vertex-based statistical analyses. However, such approaches typically assume that a unique pathological pattern exists in the disease group and are agnostic to the potential heterogeneity of neuropathogenesis due to unobserved endophenotypes. Ignoring heterogeneity may lead to underpowered statistical conclusions due to the violation of the unimodality assumption of effect loci in the group comparisons.

Several previous studies have made efforts to reveal the heterogeneous clinical biomarkers by leveraging machine learning (ML) and neuroimaging techniques. These studies can be generally divided into two classes based on whether the data clustering is unsupervised or semi-supervised. Unsupervised clustering [7–10] aims to directly cluster the patients with regard to their demographic information, clinical presentation or imaging biomarkers. However, unsupervised clustering techniques rely on similarity or dissimilarity measures across the patient group only, which can potentially be confounded by covariate effects such as age, sex and other sources of variation that are not related to the disease effect. These confounds may overpower and mask the true heterogeneous pathological effects caused by the disease. Moreover, the optimal number of clusters (c) is often set apriori, instead of being determined by cross-validation (CV). Alternatively, several recent techniques have been proposed to utilize semi-supervised clustering to distinguish heterogeneous disease effects. In [11], the authors propose a method, termed HYDRA, to discriminate between controls and patients using a convex-polytope classifier while simultaneously clustering the patient subgroups. The covariate effects, such as age and sex, are regressed out and the optimal number of clusters is decided via a CV procedure. Moreover, the authors demonstrate HYDRA's superiority over other unsupervised methods, such as K-means. However, HYDRA performs clustering inference using an input set of features that reflect a single spatial scale of anatomy captured by an apriori determined set of regions of interest (ROI) and may not be able to capture heterogeneous patterns that span a wider spectrum of spatial scales. This may lead to an inaccurate exposition of the heterogeneous disease patterns presented in the clinical study.

To address this limitation, we propose a novel method, Multi-scAle heteroGeneity analysIs and Clustering (MAGIC)[1], for parsing multi-scale disease heterogeneity. MAGIC first extracts multi-scale, from macro to micro, patterns of structural covariance (PSCs), analogously with atlas-based ROIs, via orthogonal projective non-negative matrix factorization (OPNMF) [12]. Then a semi-supervised clustering procedure through a double cyclic block-wise optimization [13] is leveraged to yield robust clusters. Furthermore, MAGIC allows us to obtain a data-driven parcellation that can explain the heterogeneity the most, thus can also be seen as a heterogeneity aware segmentation technique.

---

[1] https://github.com/anbai106/MAGIC.

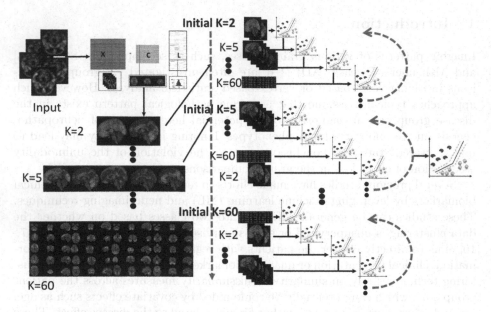

Fig. 1. The schematic diagram of MAGIC. (Color figure online)

To demonstrate our claims, we first validate MAGIC on simulated effect data with the known number of clusters and multi-scale atrophy patterns. Here we show that MAGIC recovers both the underlying imaging patterns and the correct number of clusters. We then apply MAGIC to ADNI data to disentangle the heterogeneity of AD which reveals two distinct subtypes, where one subtype presents macro-scale cortical atrophy while the latter subtype exhibits focused hippocampus atrophy.

2   Method

All T1-weighted (T1w) MR images underwent the following image preprocessing procedure: Brain tissue segmentation was performed using a multi-atlas segmentation technique [14] and was then transformed to produce tissue density maps. Gray matter (GM) tissue density maps were smoothed and harmonized by estimating age and gender effects in CN using a voxel-wise linear model.

The schematic diagram of MAGIC is shown in Fig. 1. Let the input data (i.e., GM density maps) consist of N subjects, with D features for each subject. All participants are labeled as 1 for AD and -1 for CN. The input data are denoted as: $X = (x_i, y_i)_{i=1}^{N}$ $(X \in \mathbb{R}^{D \times N}$ and $y \in \{-1, 1\})$.

2.1   Representation Learning for Multi-scale PSCs Extraction

In MAGIC, orthogonal projection NMF [12] is used for multi-scale PSCs extraction. Low dimensional features can be extracted from coarse to refined scales with different predefined number of PSCs (K). The general form of the NMF can be defined as:

$$\|X - CL\|_F^2 \text{ subject to } C \geqslant 0, \ L \geqslant 0, \ CC^T = I \tag{1}$$

where matrix $C = [c_1, ..., c_K]$ contains the K estimated PSCs. $c_i \in \mathbb{R}^D$ and is assumed to be a unit vector $\|c_i\|^2 = 1$. I represents the identity matrix. We refer $C \in \mathbb{R}^{D \times K}$ as component matrix and $L \in \mathbb{R}^{K \times N}$ as loading coefficient matrix. Both C and L are non-negative and indispensable to approximate the original data X. Apart from being non-negative, another constraint we explicitly impose is that L is estimated as the orthogonal projection of the input X to the components C ($L = C^T X$).

The component matrix is a sparse part-based representation and conveys the information regarding the spatial properties of the variability effect. On the other hand, the loading coefficient matrix is a low level feature representation which quantifies the strength of those spatial properties in each data sample. In the current work, we take K from 2 to 60, resulting in 59 sets of single-scale PSCs and 1829 PSCs in total.

2.2 Clustering via Max-Margin Multiple SVM Classifiers

MAGIC constructs the convex-polytope classifier in the same way as HYDRA does [11]. For each clustering subproblem, MAGIC takes a specific scale of PSCs as input features ($L^T, L \in \mathbb{R}^{K \times N}$) and corresponding $y \in \{-1, 1\}$ as labels.

In a nutshell, the polytope in the search space is made up by all support vector machine (SVM) hyperplanes: each hyperplane contributes to one face of the polytope. Without loss of generality, let us confine CN to be in the interior of the polytope. MAGIC aims to correctly classify all CN and at least one SVM correctly classify each patient. The objective of maximizing the polytope's margin can be summarized as:

$$\max_{\{w_j, b_j\}_{j=1}^c} \frac{1}{c} \sum_{j=1}^c \frac{2}{\|w_j\|_2} \tag{2}$$

$$\text{subject to } w_j^T L_i^T + b_j \leqslant -1, \text{if } y_j = -1; \ w_j^T L_i^T + b_j \geqslant 1, \text{if } y_j = 1$$

where w_j and b_j are the weight and bias, respectively and are sufficient statistics to define the faces of the convex polytope. In general, this optimization routine is non-convex and is solved by iterating on solving for cluster memberships and solving for polytope faces' parameters [11].

2.3 Double Cyclic Block-Wise Optimization

MAGIC adopts a double cyclic block-wise optimization procedure in order to combine the knowledge from different scales of PSCs. The block-wise optimization solves the clustering problem in the form of

$$\max_{(w_1, b_1), ..., (w_a, b_a)} F((w_1, b_1), ..., (w_a, b_a)) \tag{3}$$

where $a \in \mathbb{R}$ is the number of iterations/blocks that the optimization takes until the predefined stopping criterion achieves. $(\boldsymbol{w}_a, b_a)$ is the weight and bias term derived by the a-th set of PSCs.

The cyclic block-wise optimization (i.e., blue dotted arrow in Fig. 1) aims to minimize each specific set of single-scale PSCs ($F(\boldsymbol{w}_a, b_a)$), while fixing the remaining blocks. The model is first initialized from a specific set of K PSCs. Then the model is transferred to the next block for fine-tuning the polytope. This updating rule was performed in a cyclic order across different K until consistent clustering results were obtained across scales. This cyclic procedure can be summarized in the form of

$$\boldsymbol{S}_1 \triangleq F(\boldsymbol{w}_1, b_1)$$
$$\dots$$
$$\boldsymbol{S}_a \triangleq F(F(\boldsymbol{w}_1, b_1)...F(\boldsymbol{w}_a, b_a)) \tag{4}$$

where $\boldsymbol{S}_a$ is the search space for the convex-polytope. The second loop (i.e., green dotted arrow in Fig. 1) is to initialize the polytope with different K, in order to achieve a consensus clustering solution.

3   Experiments

For synthetic data, 364 CN from a healthy control dataset were included and randomly split into two half-split sets. The first split was defined as CN and the second as a pseudo patient group. The pseudo patient group was further divided into two half-split sets for neuroanatomical heterogeneity simulation: Global cortical and subcortical atrophy were introduced to the first and second splits, respectively. Atrophy simulation with 10% voxel-wise intensity reduction was imposed to the predefined regions for each PT splits. For real data, we applied MAGIC to ADNI 1 data with 228 CN and 191 AD.

The number of clusters c was decided by CV. Stratified repeated holdout splits [15,16] with 100 repetitions were performed and adjusted rand index (ARI)[17] was used to quantify the clustering stability. For simulated data, we compare clustering performance and evaluate classification task performance by using balanced accuracy (BA). Moreover, each synthetic clustering experiment was repeated 50 times.

Statistical mapping was performed between the subtypes and CN. A two-sample t-test was performed for all 1829 PSCs with the significance level as 0.05. Benjamini-Hochberg (BH) adjustment [18] was used for the correction of multiple comparisons. Furthermore, the effect size (ES) for Cohen's d [19] was computed for those PSCs that survived the correction.

4   Results

4.1   Synthetic Experiments

Clustering Stability via Cross-Validation. Single-scale HYDRA was first applied to the synthetic data for choosing optimal c. Figure 2A shows the clustering stability for different c ($c = 2$ to 8). In general, unstable phase ($K = 2$ to 16) gives mixed ARIs across different c. In stable plateau phase ($K = 25$ to 60), c equals 2 obtains consistent higher ARIs than other c. The stable plateau phase scales ($K = 25$ to 60 with step size $= 5$) were then used for MAGIC.

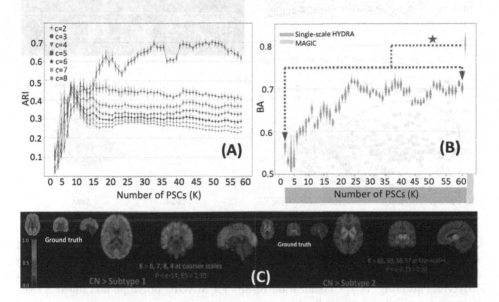

Fig. 2. Synthetic results. (A): Clustering stability across number of clusters ($c = 2$ to 8) and number of PSCs (K)= 2 to 60). (B): Clustering performance comparison for different approaches: Single-scale HYDRA (in red) and MAGIC (in green). The green star denotes for statistically significant difference. (C): Statistical mapping between subtypes and CN with MAGIC results. (Color figure online)

Clustering Performance Comparison Between Approaches. The comparison of clustering performance between approaches was shown in Fig. 2B. Overall, single-scale HYDRA obtained inferior performance and the highest mean BA was achieved at $K = 38$ (0.71 ± 0.009). MAGIC used multi-scale PSCs ($K = 25$ to 60 with step size $= 5$) and achieved statistically higher BA compared to single-scale HYDRA (i.e., mean BA $= 0.81 \pm 0.014$, p-value $\ll 0.05$). Of note, fitting all 1829 PSCs to HYDRA does not give comparable results.

Neuroanatomical Heterogeneity Between Subtypes and CN. The neuroanatomical spatial patterns based on MAGIC clustering results are displayed in Fig. 2C. We presented only the PSCs with highest ES, and the corresponding P-value and ES.

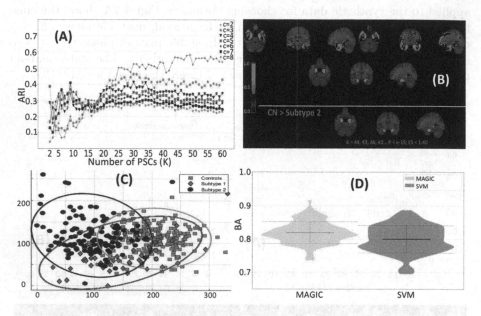

Fig. 3. ADNI data results. (A): Clustering stability across number of clusters ($c = 2$ to 8) and number of PSCs (K)= 2 to 60). (B): Statistical mapping between subtypes and CN with MAGIC. (C): 2D multidimensional scaling visualization of the subgroups (in blue and green) relative to controls (in red) using the top two features that is used in MAGIC clustering. (D): Classification results for MAGIC polytope and linear SVMs, respectively. (Color figure online)

For subtype 1, diffuse cortical atrophy was observable: 1446 out of the 1829 PSCs showed significant difference. Among those 1446 PSCs, the PSC covering almost the whole cortical regions showed highest ES (1.10). Note that this PSC was simultaneously extracted from multiple coarser scales (e.g., $K = 6, 7, 8, 4$). For subtype 2, focal subcortical atrophy was found. 22 out of the 1829 PSCs were significantly different. Similarly, the 22 PSCs were the same component from different K, which encompassed the subcortical structures (i.e., hippocampus, thalamus, putamen and caudate).

4.2   Alzheimer's Disease Dataset Experiments

Clustering Stability via Cross-Validation. Figure 3A shows the clustering stability for different c ($c = 2$ to 8) for single-scale HYDRA. Unstable phase gave mixed ARIs across different c ($K = 2$ to 20). In stable plateau phase

($K = 25$ to 60), c equals 2 obtained consistent higher ARI than other c. Thus we chose $c = 2$ to be the optimal number of clusters. The stable plateau phase scales ($K = 25$ to 60 with step size $= 5$) were subsequently used for MAGIC.

Demographic and Clinical Characteristics of Clustering Subtypes.
Table 1 displayed the demographic and clinical characteristics for ADNI participants and the corresponding subtypes based on MAGIC. Age and FDG are significantly different between two subtypes at baseline. MMSE and ADAS become significantly different between subtypes changing from baseline to 12 months.

Table 1. Demographic and Clinical Characteristics of clustering subtypes. AD patients (left) and the estimated subtypes of AD (right). APOE4 denotes subjects with at least one APOE allele present. M12 and bl represent time point at 12 months and baseline, respectively. * denotes statistical significance.

Characteristics	CN(n=228)	AD(n = 191)	P value	Sub1(n = 134)	Sub2(n = 57)	P value
Age (years)	75.87 ± 5.03	75.27 ± 7.46	0.32	73.96 ± 7.46	78.34 ± 6.56	6.00e−4*
Sex (female)	110 (48.25)	91 (47.64)	0.98	62 (46.27)	29 (50.88)	0.67
APOE4	61 (26.75)	100 (52.36)	5.13e−17*	90 (67.16)	37 (64.91)	0.15
FDG	6.41 ± 0.61	5.39 ± 0.67	1.19e−22*	5.21 ± 0.63	5.74 ± 0.62	2.08e−04*
MMSE bl	29.11 ± 1.00	23.31 ± 2.04	6.03e−137*	23.31 ± 2.02	23.29 ± 2.10	0.96
MMSE M12	29.13 ± 1.17	22.69 ± 4.08	3.73e−53*	20.40 ± 4.44	22.69 ± 4.08	2.58e−03*
ADAS11 bl	6.21 ± 2.92	18.67 ± 6.25	1.07e−92*	18.86 ± 6.01	18.29 ± 6.72	0.55
ADAS11 M12	5.52 ± 2.86	22.66 ± 9.38	4.92e−81*	24.01 ± 8.92	19.51 ± 9.76	5.06e−03*
ADAS13 bl	9.50 ± 4.19	28.97 ± 7.57	4.64e−118*	28.23 ± 8.20	29.34 ± 7.23	0.35
ADAS13 M12	8.79 ± 4.58	33.47 ± 10.89	1.24e−97*	35.11 ± 10.25	29.78 ± 11.48	4.44e−03*

Neuroanatomical Heterogeneity Between Subtypes and CN. Figure 3B shows the neuroanatomical spatial patterns for MAGIC results. Two subtypes showed distinct atrophy patterns. For subtype 1, diffuse atrophy pattern was established on the whole brain: 1560 out of the 1829 PSCs showed significant difference. Those PSCs with the highest ES included hippocampus, temporal and frontal lobe. For subtype 2, focal atrophy pattern was found: 164 out of 1829 PSCs showed a significant difference. Hippocampus regions were highly involved in this subtype. Further evidence of the anatomical heterogeneity exhibited by the two subtypes of AD can be seen when the PSCs that MAGIC utilizes in its classification boundary were projected onto two dimensions using multidimensional scaling. Subtype 1 and 2 in blue and green, respectively exhibit unique divergences away from CN along with two directions, predominately described by the presence and absence of cortical atrophy patterns (Fig. 3C).

Individualized Classification via the Two-Face Polytope. The nature of MAGIC allows not only for clustering but also for classification via the convex polytope. For a fair comparison, we randomly split AD patient in the training set into 2 splits with the same ratio as the two subtypes found in MAGIC (134/57).

Taking the PSCs as features ($K = 35$) when MAGIC converged, two linear SVMs were independently run for CN vs first split and CN vs second split of AD to construct a polytope as in MAGIC. Figure 3D showed that MAGIC (0.82 ± 0.03) and the permutation linear SVMs (0.80 ± 0.03) obtained comparable results. Of note, since no nested CV for hyperparameter searching or feature selection was performed, the accuracy here is lower compared to state-of-the-art [20,21].

5   Conclusion

In the current study, we proposed a novel method, MAGIC, for parsing disease heterogeneity and demonstrated its superiority over HYDRA. The application to AD found two robust clinically different subtypes, thus highlighting the potential of MAGIC in the analysis of the heterogeneity of brain diseases.

References

1. Rodrigues-Amorim, D., Rivera-Baltanás, T., López, M., Spuch, C., Olivares, J.M., Agís-Balboa, R.C.: Schizophrenia: a review of potential biomarkers. J. Psychiatr. Res. **93**, 37–49 (2017)
2. van Erp, T.G., et al.: Subcortical brain volume abnormalities in 2028 individuals with schizophrenia and 2540 healthy controls via the ENIGMA consortium. Mol. Psychiatry **21**(4), 547–553 (2016)
3. Okada, N., et al.: Abnormal asymmetries in subcortical brain volume in schizophrenia. Mol. Psychiatry **21**(10), 1460–1466 (2016)
4. Habeck, C., et al.: Multivariate and univariate neuroimaging biomarkers of Alzheimer's disease. Neuroimage **40**(4), 1503–1515 (2008)
5. Hampel, H., Bürger, K., Teipel, S.J., Bokde, A.L., Zetterberg, H., Blennow, K.: Core candidate neurochemical and imaging biomarkers of Alzheimer's disease. Alzheimer's Dement. **4**(1), 38–48 (2008)
6. Ewers, M., Sperling, R.A., Klunk, W.E., Weiner, M.W., Hampel, H.: Neuroimaging markers for the prediction and early diagnosis of Alzheimer's disease dementia. Trends Neurosci. **34**(8), 430–442 (2011)
7. Noh, Y., et al.: Anatomical heterogeneity of Alzheimer's disease: based on cortical thickness on MRIs. Neurology **83**(21), 1936–1944 (2014)
8. Poulakis, K., et al.: Heterogeneous patterns of brain atrophy in Alzheimer's disease. Neurobiol. Aging **65**, 98–108 (2018)
9. Whitwell, J.L., et al.: Distinct anatomical subtypes of the behavioural variant of frontotemporal dementia: a cluster analysis study. Brain **132**(11), 2932–2946 (2009)
10. Martí-Juan, G., Sanroma, G., Piella, G. and Alzheimer's Disease Neuroimaging Initiative: Revealing heterogeneity of brain imaging phenotypes in Alzheimer's disease based on unsupervised clustering of blood marker profiles. PloS One **14**(3), 1–20 (2019)
11. Varol, E., Sotiras, A., Davatzikos, C., Alzheimer's Disease Neuroimaging Initiative: HYDRA: revealing heterogeneity of imaging and genetic patterns through a multiple max-margin discriminative analysis framework. Neuroimage **145**, 346–364 (2017)

12. Sotiras, A., Resnick, S.M., Davatzikos, C.: Finding imaging patterns of structural covariance via non-negative matrix factorization. Neuroimage **108**, 1–16 (2015)
13. Wright, S.J.: Coordinate descent algorithms. Math. Program. **151**(1), 3–34 (2015). https://doi.org/10.1007/s10107-015-0892-3
14. Doshi, J., et al.: MUSE: MUlti-atlas region segmentation utilizing ensembles of registration algorithms and parameters, and locally optimal atlas selection. Neuroimage **127**, 186–195 (2016)
15. Pedregosa, F., et al.: Scikit-learn: machine learning in Python. J. Mach. Learn. Res. **12**(Oct), 2825–2830 (2011)
16. Varoquaux, G., Raamana, P.R., Engemann, D.A., Hoyos-Idrobo, A., Schwartz, Y., Thirion, B.: Assessing and tuning brain decoders: cross-validation, caveats, and guidelines. NeuroImage **145**, 166–179 (2017)
17. Hubert, L., Arabie, P.: Comparing partitions. J. Classif. **2**(1), 193–218 (1985)
18. Benjamini, Y., Hochberg, Y.: Controlling the false discovery rate: a practical and powerful approach to multiple testing. J. Roy. Stat. Soc.: Ser. B (Methodol.) **57**(1), 289–300 (1995)
19. Lakens, D.: Calculating and reporting effect sizes to facilitate cumulative science: a practical primer for t-tests and ANOVAs. Front. Psychol. **4**, 863 (2013)
20. Samper-Gonzalez, J., et al.: Reproducible evaluation of classification methods in Alzheimer's disease: framework and application to MRI and PET data. NeuroImage **183**, 504–521 (2018)
21. Wen, J., et al.: Reproducible evaluation of diffusion MRI features for automatic classification of patients with Alzheimer's disease. Neuroinformatics 1–22 (2020)

PIANO: Perfusion Imaging via Advection-Diffusion

Peirong Liu[1(✉)], Yueh Z. Lee[2], Stephen R. Aylward[3], and Marc Niethammer[1]

[1] Department of Computer Science, University of North Carolina at Chapel Hill, Chapel Hill, USA
peirong@cs.unc.edu
[2] Department of Radiology, University of North Carolina at Chapel Hill, Chapel Hill, USA
[3] Kitware, Inc., New York, USA

Abstract. Perfusion imaging (PI) is clinically used to assess strokes and brain tumors. Commonly used PI approaches based on magnetic resonance imaging (MRI) or X-ray computed tomography (CT) measure the effect of a contrast agent moving through blood vessels and into tissue. Contrast-agent free approaches, for example, based on intravoxel incoherent motion, also exist, but are not routinely used clinically. MR or CT perfusion imaging based on contrast agents relies on the estimation of the arterial input function (AIF) to approximately model tissue perfusion, neglecting spatial dependencies. Reliably estimating the AIF is also nontrivial, leading to difficulties with standardizing perfusion measures. In this work we propose a data-assimilation approach (PIANO) which estimates the velocity and diffusion fields of an advection-diffusion model best explaining the contrast dynamics. PIANO accounts for spatial dependencies and neither requires estimating the AIF nor relies on a particular contrast agent bolus shape. Specifically, we propose a convenient parameterization of the estimation problem, a numerical estimation approach, and extensively evaluate PIANO. We demonstrate that PIANO can successfully resolve velocity and diffusion field ambiguities and results in sensitive measures for the assessment of stroke, comparing favorably to conventional measures of perfusion.

Keywords: Partial differential equations · Advection · Diffusion · Data assimilation · Machine learning · Perfusion imaging · Stroke

1 Introduction

By using an intravascular tracer and serial imaging to quantify blood flow through the brain parenchyma, perfusion imaging (PI) allows individualized assessment

Electronic supplementary material The online version of this chapter (https://doi.org/10.1007/978-3-030-59728-3_67) contains supplementary material, which is available to authorized users.

© Springer Nature Switzerland AG 2020
A. L. Martel et al. (Eds.): MICCAI 2020, LNCS 12267, pp. 688–698, 2020.
https://doi.org/10.1007/978-3-030-59728-3_67

of stroke patients based on brain tissue status which helps clinical diagnosis and decision-making for cerebrovascular disease, including acute stroke [6]. Despite its benefits, the widespread use of PI still faces many challenges. In fact, the post-processing of PI is far from standardized. At present, the mainstream approach for postprocessing PI source data, a time series of 3D volumetric images, is using tracer kinetic models to estimate hemodynamic parameters for each voxel, obtaining corresponding perfusion parameter maps in 3D [8]. Specifically, an arterial input function (AIF) is selected to approximate the delivery of intravascular tracer to tissue. Perfusion parameter maps are then computed based on the AIF and the observed concentration of contrast agents (CA) at each voxel by a deconvolution algorithm [17]. However, there exist substantial differences in perfusion parameter maps generated across institutions, mainly caused by different AIF selections, deconvolution techniques and interpretations of perfusion parameters [17,20,21].

Moreover, postprocessing approaches for PI are performed on individual voxels thereby disregarding spatial dependencies of contrast dynamics. Some efforts exist to fit CA transport via partial differential equations (PDEs) [5,10,22], though these approaches ultimately reduce to voxel-based analyses – parameters of a closed-form solution of the associated PDEs are estimated to fit the concentration time-curve voxel-by-voxel. The work by Cookson et al. [5] is the most closely related work to our proposed approach, where advection-diffusion PDEs are used to model CA transport within cerebral blood vessels and brain tissue. However, this work assumes that the velocity and the diffusion are *constant* over the entire domain, which is unrealistic in real tissue. In fact, the spatially varying nature of perfusion is, for example, precisely the critical aspect of stroke assessment. As a result of the constancy assumption, only simulations are considered in [5], and estimations based on real data are not explored.

Contributions: We therefore propose a data-assimilation approach – Perfusion Imaging via AdvectioN-diffusiOn (PIANO) – which models CA transport by variable-coefficient advection-diffusion PDEs. To the best of our knowledge, this is the first work taking into account the spatial relations between voxels in PI. Specifically, given a time series of CA concentration 3D images, PIANO estimates spatially-varying velocity and diffusion fields of the advection-diffusion model that best explain CA passage. By physically modeling CA transport via advection and diffusion, PIANO does not require AIF selection or deconvolution algorithms to compute perfusion parameter maps, which are required in conventional PI post-processing approaches and may yield differences in parameter map estimations. We extensively assess the estimation behavior of PIANO. In particular, we assess PIANO's ability to disentangle velocity from diffusion estimates and its robustness to noise. Quantitative comparisons further demonstrate the advantage of feature maps from PIANO over conventional perfusion parameter maps. We describe and test PIANO in the context of brain PI. The approach, however, is general and could conceivably be applied to PI of other organs.

2 Perfusion Imaging via AdvectioN-DiffusiOn (PIANO)

First, Sect. 2.1 describes how we model CA transport as a combination of advection and diffusion. Section 2.2 then discusses how PIANO estimates the velocity and the diffusion fields that best explain the contrast dynamics (Fig. 2).

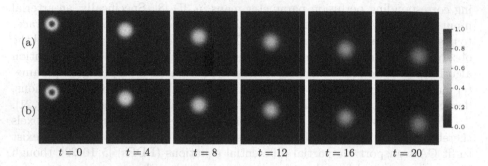

Fig. 1. Toy example of 2D PIANO estimation. (a) Simulated advection-diffusion process with constant velocity and diffusivity; (b) Estimated advection-diffusion process from $t = 0$. PIANO successfully captures the advection-diffusion process.

2.1 Governing Equations

After the injected CA has fully flown into the brain, the observed local changes of CA concentration (to which we simply refer to as concentration in what follows) in the brain can generally be explained by two dominating macroscopic effects: advection and diffusion. Advection mainly describes the transport of CA driven by the blood flow within the blood vessels, while diffusion captures the movements of freely-diffusive CA within the extracellular space as well as aspects of capillary transport. Note that because voxels in PI (≈ 1 mm) are orders of magnitude larger than capillary radii [15], their blood transport may manifest as macroscopic diffusion. In this work we refer to diffusion as the effective diffusion observable at voxel scale combining these effects.

Let $C(\mathbf{x}, t)$ denote the concentration at location $\mathbf{x}$ in the brain $\Omega \subset \mathbb{R}^3$, at time t. Local concentration follows an advection-diffusion equation:

$$\frac{\partial C(\mathbf{x}, t)}{\partial t} = -\nabla \cdot (\mathbf{V}(\mathbf{x}) \, C(\mathbf{x}, t)) + \nabla \cdot (\mathbf{D}(\mathbf{x}) \, \nabla C(\mathbf{x}, t)), \tag{1}$$

where $\mathbf{V}(\mathbf{x}) = (V^x(\mathbf{x}), V^y(\mathbf{x}), V^z(\mathbf{x}))^T$ is the spatially-varying velocity, with each component referring to the blood flow velocity in directions x, y, z respectively. $\mathbf{D}$ is a spatially-varying diffusion tensor field governing CA diffusion, assumed to be a 3×3 symmetric positive semi-definite (PSD) matrix [18]. We assume $\mathbf{V}$ and $\mathbf{D}$ to be constant in time to simplify our estimation problem. Further, assuming the blood flow is incompressible everywhere, i.e., $\mathbf{V}$ is divergence-free ($\nabla \cdot \mathbf{V}(\mathbf{x}) = 0$, $\forall \mathbf{x} \in \Omega$), Eq. (1) can be rewritten as:

$$\frac{\partial C(\mathbf{x}, t)}{\partial t} = -\mathbf{V}(\mathbf{x}) \cdot \nabla C(\mathbf{x}, t) + \nabla \cdot (\mathbf{D}(\mathbf{x}) \nabla C(\mathbf{x}, t)). \tag{2}$$

2.2   Estimating Advection and Diffusion

Section 2.1 described PIANO's advection-diffusion model for CA transport. Here, we focus on how to estimate divergence-free vector fields $\mathbf{V}$ and PSD diffusion tensor fields $\mathbf{D}$ from time series of measured 3D volumetric concentration images, $\{(C^{t_i})_{N_x \times N_y \times N_z} \in \mathbb{R}(\Omega) | i = 0, 1, \dots, T\}$, with temporal resolution Δt.

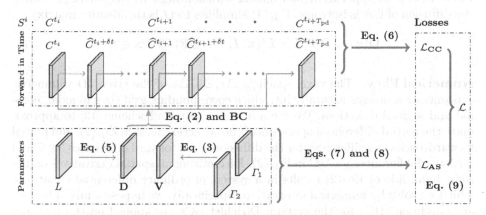

Fig. 2. Estimation framework of PIANO for one iteration (See Algorithm 1 for the entire estimation approach), given training sample $S^i = \{C^{t_j} | j = i, i+1, \dots, i+T_{pd}\}$.

Alg. 1: Pseudo-code for PIANO

Input: Time series of CA concentration images $\{C^{t_i} \in \mathbb{R}(\Omega) | i = 0, 1, \dots, T\}$
Output: Estimated $\mathbf{V}$ and $\mathbf{D}$, predicted CA concentrations
$\{\widehat{C}^{t_i} \in \mathbb{R}(\Omega) | i = 0, 1, \dots, T\}$
Settings: $\lambda_{\mathbf{V}}, \sigma_{\mathbf{V}}, \lambda_{\mathbf{D}}, \sigma_{\mathbf{D}}, k, \sigma$ in Eqs. (6)–(9), $\delta t, T_{pd}, lr$
Initialization: $\Gamma_1(\mathbf{x}), \Gamma_2(\mathbf{x}), L(\mathbf{x}) \sim 0.001 \times \mathcal{N}(0, 1), \quad \forall \mathbf{x} \in \Omega$

1 **while** $\mathcal{L}$ *not converged* **do**
2 | Randomly select sample $S_i = \{C^{t_j} | j = i, i+1, \dots, i+T_{pd}\}$ from $\{C^{t_i}\}$
3 | **for** $t = t_i + \delta t, \dots, t_{i+1}, t_{i+1} + \delta t, \dots, t_{i+T_{pd}}$ **do**
4 | | Discretize in space and compute advection-diffusion PDE via Eq. (2)
5 | | Impose the mixed boundary condition and integrate in time to obtain
   | |_ $\widehat{C}^{t+\delta t}$
6 | Compute $\mathcal{L}$ (Eq. (9)) and propagate backward (SGD with momentum)
7 |_ Update Γ_1, Γ_2, L by learning rate lr and update $\mathbf{V}, \mathbf{D}$ via Eqs. (3) and (5)

8 Predict the entire concentration time-series $\{\widehat{C}^{t_i} | i = 0, 1, \dots, T\}$ starting from C^{t_0}

T_{pd}: *the number of consecutive time points in one training sample;*
Convergence criterion: $|\mathcal{L}$ *of current iteration* $- \mathcal{L}$ *of last iteration*$|/\mathcal{L}$ *of last iteration* $<$ 0.001 *for 10 subsequent iterations.*

Parametrization of Velocity and Diffusion Fields. To ensure that the vector field $\mathbf{V}$ is divergence-free, we represent it by two scalar fields Γ_1, Γ_2 [2]:

$$\mathbf{V}(\mathbf{x}) = \nabla\Gamma_1(\mathbf{x}) \wedge \nabla\Gamma_2(\mathbf{x}), \quad \Gamma_1, \Gamma_2 \in \mathbb{R}(\Omega), \forall \mathbf{x} \in \Omega, \tag{3}$$

where $\wedge$ denotes the exterior product between vectors in $\mathbb{R}^3$. To construct a PSD tensor field, we parametrize $\mathbf{D}$ by its Cholesky factorization:

$$\mathbf{D}(\mathbf{x}) = \mathbf{L}(\mathbf{x})^T \mathbf{L}(\mathbf{x}), \quad \mathbf{L} \in \mathbb{R}^{3\times3}(\Omega), \forall \mathbf{x} \in \Omega, \tag{4}$$

where $\mathbf{L}(\mathbf{x})$ is an upper triangular matrix with non-negative diagonals. Assuming the diffusion of CA is isotropic, Eq. (4) simplifies to (I is the identity matrix)

$$\mathbf{D}(\mathbf{x}) = D(\mathbf{x})\,I = L^2(\mathbf{x})\,I, \quad L \in \mathbb{R}(\Omega), \forall \mathbf{x} \in \Omega. \tag{5}$$

Numerical Flow. The voxel spacings $\Delta x, \Delta y, \Delta z$ of the given 3D volumetric concentration images naturally introduce corresponding grid sizes in axial, coronal and sagittal directions. We use a first-order upwind scheme [13] to approximate the partial differential operators of the advection term in Eq. (2), and nested forward-backward differences for the diffusion term: forward differences for ∇ and backward differences for ∇C in Eq. (2). Discretizing all spatial derivatives on the right hand side of Eq. (2) results in a system of ordinary differential equations, which we solve by numerical integration. Specifically, we impose a mixed boundary condition (BC) for the system: Dirichlet BCs are applied on the first and last axial slices[1] which simply impose the *measured* concentrations. We impose homogeneous Neumann BCs on the outer brain contours in the remaining axial slices, assuming no flux passes through these boundaries. We use a Runge-Kutta-Fehlberg method to advance in time (δt) to predict $\widehat{C}^{t+\delta t}$. Note that the chosen δt is typically smaller than the temporal resolution of the given concentration time series images (Δt), to satisfy the Courant-Friedrichs-Lewy (CFL) condition [13] and thereby to ensure stable numerical integration.

Estimation. Given an initial state C^t, PIANO applies the current estimate of $\mathbf{V}, \mathbf{D}$ to C^t by Eq. (2) and predicts subsequent concentration images with time step δt. Instead of starting from a specific concentration image, we randomly pick an image from the given concentration time series as the initial condition for each estimating iteration. We then integrate the PIANO model forward to time frame T_{pd} (Fig. 2). This reduces the sensitivity of the estimated $\mathbf{V}$ and $\mathbf{D}$ to varying initial conditions. We define our estimation losses as follows.

Collocation Concentration Loss. Given a sample $\{C^{t_i} \in \mathbb{R}(\Omega)|\, i = 0, 1, \ldots,$ $T_{\mathrm{pd}}\}$, with $t_0, t_1, \ldots, t_{T_{\mathrm{pd}}}$ as collocation points, we define the collocation

---

[1] Our dataset is acquired axially, but BCs could be modified for different acquisition formats as needed. This BC essentially replaces determining the AIF.

concentration loss ($\mathcal{L}_{CC}$) as the mean squared error of the predicted concentrations at $t_1, \ldots, t_{T_{\text{pd}}}$. This encourages estimates to be close to the measurements:

$$\mathcal{L}_{CC} = \frac{1}{T_{\text{pd}}} \sum_{i=1}^{T_{\text{pd}}} \frac{1}{|\Omega|} \int_\Omega (C^{t_i}(\mathbf{x}) - \widehat{C}^{t_i}(\mathbf{x}))^2 \, d\mathbf{x}. \tag{6}$$

Anisotropic Smoothness Regularizations. Assuming the estimated fields are spatially smooth, we impose regularization terms on $\nabla \mathbf{V}$, ∇D as

$$\mathcal{L}_{AS_V} = \sum_{ax \in \{x,y,z\}} \frac{1}{|\Omega|} \int_\Omega \alpha_\mathbf{V} \, \|\nabla V^{ax}\|_2^2 \, d\mathbf{x}, \quad \mathcal{L}_{AS_D} = \frac{1}{|\Omega|} \int_\Omega \alpha_D \, \|\nabla D\|_2^2 \, d\mathbf{x}, \tag{7}$$

where the associated coefficients $\alpha_\mathbf{V}$, α_D are computed as

$$\alpha_\mathbf{V} = \sum_{ax \in \{x,y,z\}} \frac{g(\|\nabla(K_\sigma * V^{ax})\|_2^2)}{3}, \quad \alpha_D = g(\|\nabla(K_\sigma * D)\|_2^2), \quad \sigma > 0, \tag{8}$$

with $g(s) = exp(-s/k)$ ($k > 0$). The decreasing function g is added to reduce the gradient penalty on those regions which have a large likelihood to be edges [19]. To make the estimation relatively insensitive to noise, Gaussian smoothing (K_σ) is applied to the parameter fields first. To avoid the undesirable effect that edges might be formed at different locations for different velocity channels, we average over axes to obtain a *common* coefficient $\alpha_\mathbf{V}$ at each location [23].

Overall, PIANO estimates $\mathbf{V}$, D by minimizing the following sum of losses:

$$\min_{\mathbf{V},D} \mathcal{L} = \mathcal{L}_{CC} + \lambda_\mathbf{V} \mathcal{L}_{AS_V} + \lambda_D \mathcal{L}_{AS_D}, \quad \lambda_\mathbf{V}, \lambda_D > 0. \tag{9}$$

3 Experiments

We tested PIANO on the Ischemic Stroke Lesion Segmentation (ISLES) 2017 [12,14] dataset. The training dataset includes images for 43 ischemic stroke patients. Each patient has the following images: an apparent diffusion coefficient (ADC) map, a 4D dynamic susceptibility contrast (DSC) MR perfusion image (from 40 to 80 available time points; temporal resolution ≈ 1 s) [7], and a segmented lesion map viewed as the gold-standard lesion. For each patient the dataset also includes five perfusion summary maps. We used three clinically important ISLES 2017 maps which are most related to PIANO feature maps for comparison: (1) Cerebral blood flow (CBF); (2) Cerebral blood volume (CBV); (3) ADC.

We first converted DSC MR perfusion images to concentration images using the relation between the MR signal and CA concentration [8]. The original perfusion images are typically anisotropic, with a much larger voxel size along the axial (6.5 mm) than other two directions (1.2 mm). To obtain a more uniform computational grid for the model, we upsampled each concentration image along the axial direction (to 1.3 mm grid size) using the Lanczos Windowed Sinc method [16].

Then we created a concentration time-series dataset for each patient N: $\{C^{t_i} \in \mathbb{R}(\Omega)|\, i = 0, 1, \ldots, T_N\}$, starting from the time when the total concentration over the entire brain reaches its maximum, at which we assume the CA has been fully transported into the brain, till the last available time point. We tested PIANO on all patients with identical model settings. Specifically, we set $\lambda_{\mathbf{V}} = \lambda_D = 0.1$ (Eq. (9)). In Eq. (8), $\sigma = 0.6$; k was treated as a 'noise estimator' [19], where a histogram of the absolute values of the gradient throughout the current image was computed, and k was set as 90% of the histogram's integral at every estimating iteration. Throughout the estimation, the prediction temporal resolution is $\delta t = 0.02$ s, and $T_{\mathrm{pd}} = \lfloor \frac{T_k}{3} \rfloor$. (See Algorithm 1.)

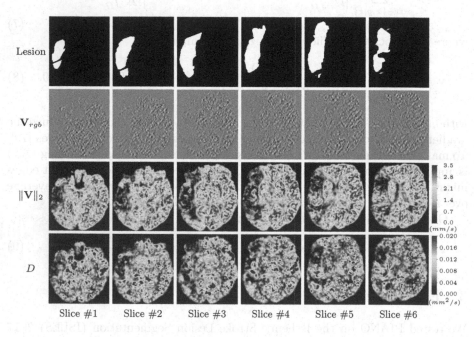

Fig. 3. PIANO feature maps for one stroke patient. Top row: segmented stroke lesion region (white) on different slices, obtained from ISLES 2017. The corresponding slices for the PIANO feature maps are shown in the following rows. (Color figure online)

3.1   Experimental Results

PIANO Feature Maps. For a better insight into an estimated velocity field $\mathbf{V}$ and diffusion field $\mathbf{D}$, we compute the following maps: (1) $\mathbf{V}_{rgb}$: Color-coded orientation map of $\mathbf{V} = (V^x, V^y, V^z)^T$, obtained by normalizing $\mathbf{V}$ to unit length and mapping its 3 components to red, green, blue respectively; (2) $\|\mathbf{V}\|_2$: 2 norm of $\mathbf{V}$; (3) D: scalar field in Eq. (5).

Figure 3 shows the PIANO feature maps estimated from one ISLES 2017 patient: all are highly consistent with the lesion. Details of the blood flow trajectories are revealed in $\mathbf{V}_{rgb}$ by the ridged patterns and the sharp changes of colors

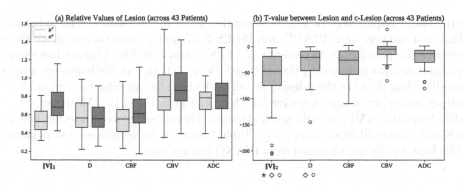

Fig. 4. Box plots of (a) relative mean values (μ^r), relative standard deviation (σ^r) and (b) t-values for PIANO feature maps and ISLES 2017 maps, computed from 43 patients. $\star$, $\diamond$, $\circ$ indicate statistically significant differences between the PIANO feature maps and CBF, CBV, ADC respectively, based on a paired t-test with Bonferroni correction at a significance level of 0.05. (Negative t-values indicate a metric's mean in the lesion is lower than the c-lesion. Lower is better.)

in the unaffected (right) hemisphere, while the flat patterns appearing within the lesion provide little directional information about the velocity and indicate low velocity magnitudes. Velocity magnitudes are more directly visualized via $\|\mathbf{V}\|_2$, from which one can easily locate the lesion where $\|\mathbf{V}\|_2$ is low. D also indicates lower diffusion values in the lesion, though with less contrast potentially due to the fact that it captures the accumulated effect of CA diffusion at the voxel-level. The estimated $\|\mathbf{V}\|_2$ in the unaffected hemispheres of all patients mainly vary from 0 to 20 mm/s with a mean value of 2 mm/s, which is consistent with reported cerebral blood flow velocities in literature [3,4,11]. The Péclet number [9] calculated based on $\|\mathbf{V}\|_2$ and D ranges from 3.1×10^{-4} to 5.3×10^{11}, indicating both diffusion-dominated and advection-dominated transport of CA exist throughout the brain. Further extensive experiments show (see supplementary material) that PIANO feature maps are resilient to noise [1] (estimates also get noisy, but generally retain their structure) and can disambiguate $\mathbf{V}$ and D.

Quantitative Comparison. To quantitatively compare PIANO feature maps with the maps provided by ISLES 2017 in their ability to detect the lesion, we compare feature values in the lesion with the values in the contralateral region of the lesion (c-lesion). The c-lesion region is determined by mirroring the lesion to the unaffected side via the midline of the cerebral hemispheres. Values in the c-lesion function as a reference for the normal values. We consider the following three metrics for an easy comparison between the different maps: (1) μ^r: relative mean value – mean of values in the lesion divided by the mean in the c-lesion; (2) σ^r: relative standard deviation (STD) – STD of lesion divided by that of the c-lesion;

(3) t-value: unpaired t-statistic between the values in the lesion and the c-lesion[2]. Figure 4 compares the PIANO and ISLES 2017 maps based on the above three metrics computed from 43 patients. μ^r of $\|\mathbf{V}\|_2$ and D in Fig. 4 (a) are less than 1 without exception, meaning the averaged $\|\mathbf{V}\|_2$, D values in the lesion are always smaller than those in the c-lesion for all patients. This can also be seen in the t-values which are always negative for $\|\mathbf{V}\|_2$ and D in Fig. 4 (b). Moreover, Fig. 4 (b) shows that $\|\mathbf{V}\|_2$ reveals much stronger differences between a lesion and its c-lesion compared to all other maps. Table 1 summarizes results over all patients. The best results are obtained from PIANO feature maps.

Table 1. Quantitative comparison between PIANO feature maps and ISLES 2017 maps over 43 subjects, using *Mean, Median, Standard Deviation (STD)* of relative mean μ^r, relative STD σ^r (the lower the better), and t-value (higher absolute value indicates greater difference).

Maps	Relative Mean (μ^r)			Relative STD (σ^r)			t-value		
	Mean	Median	STD	Mean	Median	STD	Mean	Median	STD
$\|\mathbf{V}\|_2$	**0.55**	**0.52**	**0.13**	0.72	0.68	0.19	**−57.76**	**−47.13**	**51.83**
D	0.60	0.56	0.19	**0.56**	**0.56**	**0.18**	−29.51	−20.58	27.67
CBF	0.57	0.55	0.19	0.66	0.61	0.23	−32.43	−26.08	27.68
CBV	0.89	0.80	0.36	0.93	0.87	0.33	−9.22	−4.64	17.32
ADC	0.76	0.78	0.14	0.80	0.82	0.27	−20.46	−13.50	19.63

4   Conclusions

We proposed a data-assimilation approach (PIANO) which estimates the velocity and diffusion fields of CA transport via an advection-diffusion PDE. Unlike most postprocessing approaches which treat voxels independently, PIANO considers spatial dependencies and does not require estimating the AIF or deconvolution techniques. We demonstrate that PIANO can successfully resolve velocity and diffusion field ambiguities and results in sensitive measures for the assessment of stroke, comparing favorably to conventional measures of perfusion. Future work will explore clinical applications and thresholds based on statistical atlases.

Acknowledgment. Research reported in this work was supported by the National Institutes of Health (NIH) under award number NIH 2R42NS086295. The content is solely the responsibility of the authors and does not necessarily represent the official views of the NIH.

---

[2] While a paired test between corresponding voxels is possible and results in similar measures, we opt for the unpaired test to avoid voxel-level correspondence issues.

References

1. Aja-Fernandez, S., Niethammer, M., Kubicki, M., Shenton, M.E., Westin, C.: Restoration of DWI data using a Rician LMMSE estimator. IEEE Trans. Med. Imaging **27**(10), 1389–1403 (2008). https://doi.org/10.1109/TMI.2008.920609
2. Barbarosie, C.: Representation of divergence-free vector fields. Quart. Appl. Math. **69** (2011). https://doi.org/10.1090/S0033-569X-2011-01215-2
3. Bouvy, W.H., et al.: Assessment of blood flow velocity and pulsatility in cerebral perforating arteries with 7-T quantitative flow MRI. NMR Biomed. **29**(9), 1295–1304 (2016). https://doi.org/10.1002/nbm.3306
4. Brass, L.M., Prohovnik, I., Pavlakis, S.G., DeVivo, D.C., Piomelli, S., Mohr, J.P.: Middle cerebral artery blood velocity and cerebral blood flow in sickle cell disease. Stroke **22**(1), 27–30 (1991). https://doi.org/10.1161/01.STR.22.1.27
5. Cookson, A., et al.: A spatially-distributed computational model to quantify behaviour of contrast agents in MR perfusion imaging. Med. Image Anal. **18**(7), 1200–1216 (2014). https://doi.org/10.1016/j.media.2014.07.002
6. Demeestere, J., Wouters, A., Christensen, S., Lemmens, R., Lansberg, M.G.: Review of perfusion imaging in acute ischemic stroke. Stroke **51**(3), 1017–1024 (2020). https://doi.org/10.1161/STROKEAHA.119.028337
7. Essig, M., et al.: Perfusion MRI: the five most frequently asked technical questions. AJR Am. J. Roentgenol. **200**(1), 24–34 (2013). https://doi.org/10.2214/AJR.12.9543
8. Fieselmann, A., Kowarschik, M., Ganguly, A., Hornegger, J., Fahrig, R.: Deconvolution-based CT and MR brain perfusion measurement: theoretical model revisited and practical implementation details. J. Biomed. Imaging **2011** (2011). https://doi.org/10.5555/1992576.2070240
9. Franca, L.P., Frey, S.L., Hughes, T.J.: Stabilized finite element methods: I. application to the advective-diffusive model. Comput. Meth. Appl. Mech. Eng. **95**(2), 253–276 (1992). https://doi.org/https://doi.org/10.1016/0045-7825(92)90143-8
10. Harabis, V., Kolar, R., Mezl, M., Jirik, R.: Comparison and evaluation of indicator dilution models for bolus of ultrasound contrast agents. Physiol. Meas. **34**(2), 151–162 (2013). https://doi.org/10.1088/0967-3334/34/2/151
11. Ivanov, K., Kalinina, M., Levkovich, Y.: Blood flow velocity in capillaries of brain and muscles and its physiological significance. Microvascular Res. **22**(2), 143–155 (1981). https://doi.org/https://doi.org/10.1016/0026-2862(81)90084-4
12. Kistler, M., Bonaretti, S., Pfahrer, M., Niklaus, R., Büchler, P.: The virtual skeleton database: An open access repository for biomedical research and collaboration. J. Med. Internet Res. (2013). https://doi.org/10.2196/jmir.2930
13. LeVeque, R.J.: Finite Volume Methods for Hyperbolic Problems. Cambridge Texts in Applied Mathematics, Cambridge University Press, Cambridge (2002). https://doi.org/10.1017/CBO9780511791253
14. Maier, O., et al.: ISLES 2015 - a public evaluation benchmark for ischemic stroke lesion segmentation from multispectral MRI medical image analysis. Med. Image Anal. **35** (2017). https://doi.org/10.1016/j.media.2016.07.009
15. Marín-Padilla, M.: The human brain intracerebral microvascular system: development and structure. Front. Neuroanatomy **6**, 38 (2012)
16. Meijering, E.H.W., Niessen, W.J., Pluim, J.P.W., Viergever, M.A.: Quantitative comparison of sinc-approximating kernels for medical image interpolation. In: Taylor, C., Colchester, A. (eds.) MICCAI 1999. LNCS, vol. 1679, pp. 210–217. Springer, Heidelberg (1999). https://doi.org/10.1007/10704282_23

17. Mouridsen, K., Christensen, S., Gyldensted, L., Østergaard, L.: Automatic selection of arterial input function using cluster analysis. Magn. Reson. Med. **55**(3), 524–531 (2006). https://doi.org/10.1002/mrm.20759
18. Niethammer, M., Estepar, R.S.J., Bouix, S., Shenton, M., Westin, C.: On diffusion tensor estimation. In: 2006 International Conference of the IEEE Engineering in Medicine and Biology Society, pp. 2622–2625 (2006). https://doi.org/10.1109/IEMBS.2006.259826
19. Perona, P., Malik, J.: Scale-space and edge detection using anisotropic diffusion. IEEE Trans. Pattern Anal. Mach. Intell. **12**(7), 629–639 (1990). https://doi.org/10.1109/34.56205
20. Schmainda, K., et al.: Moving toward a consensus DSC-MRI protocol: validation of a low–flip angle single-dose option as a reference standard for brain tumors. Am. J. Neuroradiol. (2019). https://doi.org/10.3174/ajnr.A6015
21. Schmainda, K., et al.: Quantitative delta T1 (dT1) as a replacement for adjudicated central reader analysis of contrast-enhancing tumor burden: A subanalysis of the american college of radiology imaging network 6677/radiation therapy oncology group 0625 multicenter brain tumor. Am. J. Neuroradiol. (2019). https://doi.org/10.3174/ajnr.A6110
22. Strouthos, C., Lampaskis, M., Sboros, V., Mcneilly, A., Averkiou, M.: Indicator dilution models for the quantification of microvascular blood flow with bolus administration of ultrasound contrast agents. IEEE Trans. Ultrason. Ferroelectr. Freq. Control **57**(6), 1296–1310 (2010). https://doi.org/10.1109/TUFFC.2010.1550
23. Weickert, J.: Anisotropic diffusion in image processing, pp. 15–25 (1998). https://www.mia.uni-saarland.de/weickert/Papers/book.pdf

Hierarchical Bayesian Regression for Multi-site Normative Modeling of Neuroimaging Data

Seyed Mostafa Kia[1,2(✉)], Hester Huijsdens[1], Richard Dinga[1,2],
Thomas Wolfers[1,3,4], Maarten Mennes[1], Ole A. Andreassen[3,4],
Lars T. Westlye[3,4], Christian F. Beckmann[1,2,5], and Andre F. Marquand[1,2,6]

[1] Donders Institute, Radboud University, Nijmegen, The Netherlands
{s.kia,a.marquand}@donders.ru.nl
[2] Radboud University Medical Centre, Nijmegen, The Netherlands
[3] Department of Psychology, University of Oslo, Oslo, Norway
[4] NORMENT, University of Oslo and Oslo University Hospital, Oslo, Norway
[5] WIN FMRIB, University of Oxford, Oxford, UK
[6] Institute of Psychiatry, King's College London, London, UK

Abstract. Clinical neuroimaging has recently witnessed explosive growth in data availability which brings studying heterogeneity in clinical cohorts to the spotlight. Normative modeling is an emerging statistical tool for achieving this objective. However, its application remains technically challenging due to difficulties in properly dealing with nuisance variation, for example due to variability in image acquisition devices. Here, in a fully probabilistic framework, we propose an application of hierarchical Bayesian regression (HBR) for multi-site normative modeling. Our experimental results confirm the superiority of HBR in deriving more accurate normative ranges on large multi-site neuroimaging data compared to widely used methods. This provides the possibility i) to learn the normative range of structural and functional brain measures on large multi-site data; ii) to recalibrate and reuse the learned model on local small data; therefore, HBR closes the technical loop for applying normative modeling as a medical tool for the diagnosis and prognosis of mental disorders.

Keywords: Machine learning · Big data · Precision psychiatry

1 Introduction

Neuroimaging has recently entered the era of big data. This has ignited a movement in the clinical neuroimaging community toward understanding the heterogeneous neurobiological underpinnings of mental disorders in large and demographically diverse populations [24]. Achieving this goal in practice requires

Electronic supplementary material The online version of this chapter (https://doi.org/10.1007/978-3-030-59728-3_68) contains supplementary material, which is available to authorized users.

© Springer Nature Switzerland AG 2020
A. L. Martel et al. (Eds.): MICCAI 2020, LNCS 12267, pp. 699–709, 2020.
https://doi.org/10.1007/978-3-030-59728-3_68

aggregating neuroimaging datasets usually acquired at several imaging centers with different acquisition protocols and scanners. This diversity in acquisition protocols and associated site-related peculiarities introduces significant site-related variability in the data [7], referred to as *site-effects*, that severely confound the result of any subsequent analyses.

Normative modeling is recently introduced as a statistical tool for studying the biological variability of mental disorders in clinical neuroimaging cohorts [14]. The first step in normative modeling is to estimate the centiles of variation, *i.e.*, the normative ranges, of the biological measures as a function of clinical covariates. This is performed via regressing the units of neuroimaging data (*e.g.*, a voxel in structural or functional MRIs) against a set of clinically relevant covariates (*e.g.*, demographics). The deviations of clinical samples from the resulting normative range can be quantified as Z-scores at the individual level [13]. Such deviations can be interpreted as individualized biomarkers for psychiatric disorders [25,27] in the spirit of *precision psychiatry*. However, normative modeling on multi-site data is challenging because combining several neuroimaging datasets introduces artefactual variability that confounds the derived deviations [13]. This limits the practical application of normative modeling as a medical tool because the data collected at different centers may have different characteristics. Thus, it is essential to develop *adaptive* methods that can effectively deal with site-effects.

The most prevalent approach to deal with site-effects is to regress them out from the data. A popular method is ComBat [11] that has been adopted from genomics for harmonizing neuroimaging data. ComBat uses an empirical Bayes method for adjusting additive and multiplicative batch effects in data. It has shown great potential in harmonizing different neuroimaging data modalities including diffusion tensor imaging [8], cortical thickness [7], and structural/functional MRIs [16,19,26]. However, this approach comes with two limitations. From a theoretical point of view, ComBat regresses all variance associated with site and only preserves *a priori* known sources of variation in data, which are accounted for in the design matrix. In other words, it is necessary to specify in advance which shared variation should be retained. This can be restrictive especially when we are interested in exploratory analysis of unknown biological factors. An illustrative example is stratifying psychiatric disorders into subtypes [15]. Since subtypes are unknown in advance, their biological correlates in brain images can be removed or corrupted. Moreover, in many cases, clinical covariates (such as age) strongly correlate with site-effects, thus, any effort toward removing site-effects may result in losing the signal of interest. From a practical perspective, it is difficult to apply current implementations of ComBat to data coming from new sites since ComBat requires access to data from all sites at training time to compute shared parameters including intercept, regression coefficients, and noise variance. This obstacle is even more pronounced when dealing with large cohorts where it may not be possible to share the data, *e.g.*, due to data anonymity concerns or a lack of ethical permission for data sharing [18].

To overcome these limitations, we propose hierarchical Bayesian regression (HBR) [9] for probabilistic modeling of batch-effects in neuroimaging data. In this framework, we impose shared prior distributions over site-specific model parameters. Our method has several appealing features: i) it is fully probabilistic, thus, it is well-suited to normative modeling as it provides estimations of both phenomenological variability in data and epistemological uncertainty in the model [3]; ii) it preserves all sources of variation in the data, which overcomes the requirement to specify in advance which parts of the variance will be retained; iii) it is highly flexible and accommodates different modeling choices (*e.g.*, non-linear effects or heteroscedastic noise); iv) it provides the possibility of transferring hyperpriors of a reference model when recalibrating the normative model to data from new sites. Using a large dataset of 7499 participants aggregated across 33 scanners, we show the potential of HBR in estimating the predictive posterior distribution compared to ComBat and trivial pooling. We also demonstrate an application of the proposed framework in understanding the biological signatures of several brain disorders.

2 Methods

2.1 Normative Modeling

Let $\mathbf{X} \in \mathbb{R}^{n \times p}$ represent a matrix of p clinical covariates for n participants. We denote the corresponding neuroimaging measures at each measurement unit (*e.g.*, a voxel) by $\mathbf{y} \in \mathbb{R}^n$. Assuming a Gaussian distribution over each neuroimaging measure, *i.e.*, $y \sim \mathcal{N}(\mu, \sigma^2)$, in normative modeling we are interested in finding a parametric or non-parametric form for μ and σ given the covariates $\mathbf{X}$.[1] This is achieved by estimating $f_\mu(\mathbf{X}, \theta_\mu)$ and $f_\sigma^+(\mathbf{X}, \theta_\sigma)$, where f^+ is a non-negative function;[2] θ_μ and θ_σ are respectively the parameters of f_μ and f_σ^+. Then, for example, $\mu + 1.96\sigma$ forms the 95% percentile for the normative range of $\mathbf{y}$. The deviations of samples from the normative range is quantified as Z-scores [14]:

$$\mathbf{z} = \frac{\mathbf{y} - f_\mu(\mathbf{X}, \theta_\mu)}{f_\sigma^+(\mathbf{X}, \theta_\sigma)}. \tag{1}$$

Any large deviation from the normative range is interpreted as an abnormality in the brain's structure or function and can be studied concerning different mental disorders. The abnormal probability index for each sample can be computed by translating the deviations (Z-scores) to the corresponding p-values.

---

[1] Here, for generality we specify heteroscedastic noise to model age-dependent variance. The homoscedastic formulation is a special case where σ is independent of $\mathbf{X}$.

[2] Non-negativity can be enforced for example using a softplus function $f_\sigma^+ = log(1 + f_\sigma)$.

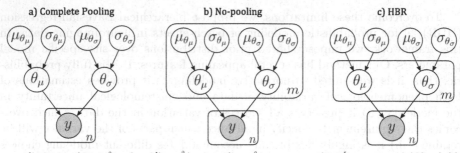

a) Complete Pooling   b) No-pooling   c) HBR

$y \sim \mathcal{N}(f_\mu(\mathbf{X}, \theta_\mu), f_\sigma^+(\mathbf{X}, \theta_\sigma)^2)$, $\theta_\mu \sim \mathcal{N}(\mu_{\theta_\mu}, \sigma_{\theta_\mu}^2)$, $\theta_\sigma \sim \mathcal{N}(\mu_{\theta_\sigma}, \sigma_{\theta_\sigma}^2)$, $\mu_{\theta_\mu}, \mu_{\theta_\sigma} \sim \mathcal{N}(0, 10^5)$, $\sigma_{\theta_\mu}, \sigma_{\theta_\sigma} \sim halfCauchy(5)$

Fig. 1. Graphical models of a) pooling, b) no-pooling, and c) partial-pooling via HBR.

2.2   Problem Statement: Multi-site Normative Modeling

Let $\mathbf{y}_i \in \mathbb{R}^{n_i}$ denote neuroimaging measures for n_i participants in the ith batch, $i \in \{1, \ldots, m\}$, of data and we have $y_i \sim \mathcal{N}(\mu_i, \sigma_i^2)$. Here, each batch refers to data which are collected at different imaging sites, however, our formulations are general for other possible batch-effects in data (*e.g.*, gender). There are three possible strategies for normative modeling on multi-batch data:

1. **Complete Pooling:** where the batch-effects in data are ignored by assuming $y_1, \ldots, y_m \sim \mathcal{N}(\mu, \sigma^2)$ and we have:

$$\mathbf{y}_i = f_\mu(\mathbf{X}, \theta_\mu) + \epsilon \quad \forall i \in \{1, \ldots, m\}, \tag{2}$$

   where ϵ is zero-mean error with standard deviation $f_\sigma^+(\mathbf{X}, \theta_\sigma)$. In complete pooling, parameters (θ_μ and θ_σ) and hyperparameters (μ_{θ_μ}, σ_{θ_μ}, μ_{θ_σ}, and σ_{θ_σ}) of the mean and variance are fixed across batches (Fig. 1a). Even though the pooling approach provides a simple solution to benefit from a larger sample size, the assumption that data from different batches have identical distributions is very limiting and restricts its usage in normative modeling because batch-effects will be encoded in the resulting deviations in Eq. 1.

2. **Harmonization:** that can be considered as a corrected pooling scenario in which we try to adjust the location and scale of data density for batch-effects. ComBat [11] is a common and effective harmonization technique for neuroimaging data where we have:

$$\tilde{\mathbf{y}}_i = \frac{\mathbf{y}_i - g(\mathbf{X}) - \gamma_i}{\delta_i} + g(\mathbf{X}), \tag{3}$$

   where $\tilde{\mathbf{y}}_i$ is harmonized data that is expected to be homogeneous across batches; γ_i and δ_i are respectively the additive and multiplicative batch-effects. Here, $g(\mathbf{X})$ is a linear or non-linear [18] function that preserves the signal of interest as specified in the design matrix $\mathbf{X}$. After harmonization, Eq. 2 can be used for regressing the data. Using ComBat for multi-site normative modeling comes with the limitations described above (*i.e.*, it only preserves the known sources of variation in the data specified in $\mathbf{X}$ and all data should be available when estimating the parameters of $g(\mathbf{X})$).

3. **No-pooling:** in which separate models are estimated for each batch (Fig. 1b):

$$\mathbf{y}_i = f_{\mu_i}(\mathbf{X}, \theta_{\mu_i}) + \epsilon_i \quad i \in \{1, \ldots, m\}. \tag{4}$$

No-pooling is immune to problems of complete pooling and harmonization, however, it cannot take full advantage of the large sample size. It is also prone to overfitting especially when f_{μ_i} and $f_{\sigma_i}^+$ are complex functions and the number of samples in each batch is small. This may result in spurious and inconsistent estimations of parameters of the model across different batches.

Considering the shortcomings of aforementioned methods, there is an emergent need to find an alternative approach that i) similar to complete pooling and harmonization methods benefits from advantages of big data; ii) is immune to batch-effects in the resulting deviations, likewise ComBat and no-pooling; iii) unlike ComBat preserves unknown sources of biological variation in data; iv) provides the possibility to reapply the normative model to data from new sites.

2.3   Partial-Pooling Using Hierarchical Bayesian Regression

Hierarchical Bayesian regression (HBR) is a natural choice in modeling different levels of variation in data [9]. In HBR, the structural dependencies between variables are incorporated in the modeling process by coupling them via a shared prior distribution. To adopt HBR for multi-site normative modeling, we assume θ_{μ_i} and θ_{σ_i} in Eq. 4 (that govern the data generating process for each batch $\mathbf{y}_i$) are coming exchangeably from the same prior distribution, i.e., $\forall i, \theta_{\mu_i} \sim \mathcal{N}(\mu_{\theta_\mu}, \sigma_{\theta_\mu}^2)$ and $\theta_{\sigma_i} \sim \mathcal{N}(\mu_{\theta_\sigma}, \sigma_{\theta_\sigma}^2)$ (see Fig. 1c). Such a joint prior acts like a regularizer over parameters of the model and prevents it from the overfitting on small batches. In fact, HBR allows for a reasonable compromise between the complete pooling and no-pooling scenarios as it combines all models in Eq. 4 into a single model that benefits from the wealth of big data.

Importantly, HBR also provides the possibility to transfer the knowledge inferred about the distribution of hyperparameters from a primary set of observed data $\mathbf{y}$ to secondary datasets from new sites $\mathbf{y}^*$. To achieve this, we propose to use posterior distributions of hyperparameters, i.e., $p(\mu_{\theta_\mu} \mid \mathbf{y}), p(\sigma_{\theta_\mu} \mid \mathbf{y})$, $p(\mu_{\theta_\sigma} \mid \mathbf{y})$, and $p(\sigma_{\theta_\sigma} \mid \mathbf{y})$, as *informative* hyperpriors for the secondary model. Informative hyperpriors enable us to incorporate pre-existing evidence when re-inferring the model on new data rather than ignoring it by non-informative or weakly informative hyperpriors. This is a critical feature for model portability because it enables effective model recalibration without the need to having access to the primary set of data.

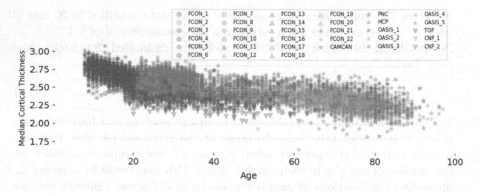

Fig. 2. Site-effect in the distribution of median cortical thicknesses across 33 scanners.

3   Experiments and Results

3.1   Experimental Materials

Table 1 lists the 7 neuroimaging datasets that are used in our experiments. Low-quality scans and participants with missing demographic information are excluded. The final data consist of 7499 scans from 7 datasets including 33 scanners that reasonably cover a wide range of human lifespan from 8 to 97 years old (see supplement for the age distribution). These properties make these data a perfect case-study for large-scale multi-site normative modeling of aging. The data also contain 1017 scans from participants diagnosed with a neurodevelopmental, psychiatric, or neurodegenerative disease including attention deficit hyperactivity disorder (ADHD), schizophrenia (SZ), bipolar disorder (BD), major depressive disorder (MDD), mild cognitive impairment (MCI), and Alzheimer's disease (AZ). In our analyses, we use cortical thickness measures estimated by Freesurfer [6] over 148 cortical regions in the Destrieux atlas [4]. Figure 2 shows the distribution of median cortical thickness across participants and scanners.

Table 1. Demographics of multi-site experimental data.

Datasets	No. scans	No. patients	No. scanners	Age range	Gender M/F	FS version
FCON1000 [2]	1094	25(ADHD)	22	8–85	494/600	6.0
CAMCAN [23]	647	–	1	18–88	318/329	6.0
PNC [21]	1514	–	1	8–23	731/783	6.0
HCP1200 [5]	1113	–	1	22–37	507/606	5.3
OASIS3 [12]	2044	271(AZ),51(MCI)	5	43–97	866/1178	5.3
TOP [22]	823	167(SZ),193(BD),31(MDD),107(others)	1	17–69	435/388	6.0
CNP [17]	264	49(SZ),49(BD),41(ADHD)	2	21–50	152/112	6.0
Total	7499	1017	33	8–97	3503/3996	–

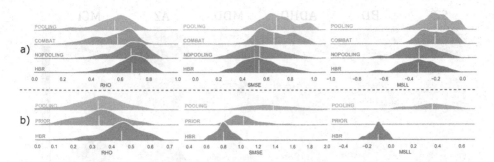

Fig. 3. The distributions of correlation, SMSE, and MSLL across 148 cortical areas and 10 experimental repetitions in the a) regression, and b) anomaly detection settings. The white lines highlight the medians of distributions.

3.2 Implementations and Model Settings

All methods are implemented using the PyMC3 package [20]. A No-U-Turn sampler (NUTS) [10] is used for inferring the posterior distributions of parameters and hyperparameters. Given the characteristics of experimental data, in all experiments, we opt to use a linear form for f_μ and a homoscedastic form for the variance.[3] Normal and half-Cauchy distributions are respectively used as hyperpriors for the mean and standard deviation of parameters of f_μ (see Fig. 1). The distribution of the standard deviation of the homoscedastic noise is set to a uniform distribution in the range of 0 to 100. Non-centered parameterizations are used to simplify posterior geometries and increase the performance of the sampler [1]. For harmonizing data using ComBat, we use a Python implementation available at https://github.com/Warvito/neurocombat_sklearn. All implementations are available online at https://github.com/amarquand/nispat.

3.3 Experimental Setup and Results

We set up two experimental settings, regression and anomaly detection. In all experimental configurations, we use age as a covariate (in $\mathbf{X}$ with $p = 1$) and gender is dealt with as a batch-effect. In the HBR case, the site is also included as a batch-effect. All experiments and evaluations are repeated 10 times with different random healthy participants in the training and test phases.

In the regression setting, the goal is to compare the accuracy of HBR with its alternatives in deriving the normative range of cortical thickness in a healthy population across the human lifespan. Here, we assume the data from all scanners are available when estimating the normative model. In each experimental run, 80% of healthy samples are randomly selected to train the regression model and the remaining 20% are used for the evaluation. We use three metrics to evaluate the resulting normative models, i) Pearson's correlation coefficient (RHO);

---

[3] We emphasize that the proposed framework is capable of modeling heteroscedasticity. Here, using a heteroscedastic model for the variance did not provide any advantage at the cost of higher model complexity (see Fig. S3 in the supplement).

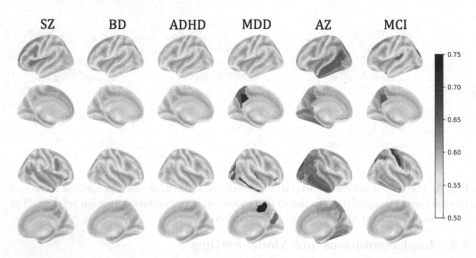

Fig. 4. AUCs across brain regions in detecting healthy participants from patients.

ii) standardized mean squared error (SMSE); iii) mean standardized log-loss (MSLL). While correlation and SMSE evaluate only the predicted mean, MSLL also accounts for the quality of estimated variance which plays an important role in deriving deviations from the norm (see Eq. 1).

Figure 3a compares the densities of our evaluative metrics (across 148 cortical areas and 10 runs) in the regression scenario. In all cases, HBR and no-pooling show better performance compared to pooling and ComBat harmonization. This boost in regression performance is gained by accounting for the difference between the distributions of signal and noise across different sites, rather than ignoring or removing it. Considering the simplicity of the employed linear parameterization for modeling the mean (thus less chance for overfitting), the improvement of HBR in comparison to no-pooling remains negligible. Furthermore, to ensure that the resulting deviations are not contaminated with residual site bias, we used a linear support vector machine on derived deviations to classify scanners in a one-versus-all setting. Balanced classification accuracy was at chance-level for the HBR, harmonization and no-pooling whereas under the pooling condition scanners were discriminated with 71% accuracy, indicating clear site-effects.

In the anomaly detection setting, we demonstrate an application of HBR in a more realistic clinical scenario when applying a reference normative model on new data from new scanners (thus ComBat cannot be applied in this scenario). To do so, we first estimate the parameters of the reference normative model on FCON1000, CAMCAN, PNC, and HCP datasets. Then, in each run 50% of random healthy participants in OASIS3, TOP, and CNP datasets are used to recalibrate the model. The rest of the healthy participants and patients are used as test samples. Figure 3b compares the regression performance of HBR with pooling and only HBR priors (where we roughly set $\forall i, \theta_{\mu_i} = \mu_{\theta_\mu}, \theta_{\sigma_i} = \mu_{\theta_\sigma}$).

HBR performs best in predicting data from new sites. Using only priors of HBR for prediction on new sites provides a reasonable estimate of the predictive mean, but extremely poor estimates of the predictive variance (its MSLL density lies fully outside of the plotted range).

We further compute the abnormal probability index for each individual across 148 cortical regions (see Sect. 2.1), and use the area under the ROC curve (AUC) to evaluate the predictive power of deviations for each diagnosis. Figure 4 depicts the resulting significant and stable AUCs across brain regions. To test for the significance, we performed permutation tests with 1000 repetitions and used 0.05 as the threshold. To ensure stability, only significant areas that are stable across 10 repetitions are kept. Except for ADHD, the resulting significant detection performances show that the deviation from the normative range of cortical thickness contains valuable information regarding the brain's structural changes in different disorders. The spatial distribution of discriminative regions largely overlaps with brain areas that are known to be implicated in the corresponding disorders. For example, patients with SZ have lower cortical thickness compared to the healthy population in the right medial orbital sulcus, right orbital inferior frontal gyrus, and left middle frontal sulcus (see supplementary Fig. S4 for fits).

4 Summary

Here, we introduced a fully probabilistic framework that accommodates signal and noise variance in multi-site neuroimaging data via estimating different but connected mean and variance components across different sites. This is a key feature relative to the usual approach of regressing out site effects, especially when the scientific question lies in understanding heterogeneity in large cohorts. The proposed framework is quite general and accommodates many different parametric/non-parametric and linear/non-linear forms for modeling the signal mean and homoscedastic/heteroscedastic variance. Further, it provides the possibility to construct a universal normative model on massive data samples and, after recalibration, reuse it on local data for prediction of brain disorders.

Acknowledgements. This work was supported by the Dutch Organisation for Scientific Research via Vernieuwingsimpuls VIDI fellowships to AM (016.156.415) and CB (864.12.003). The authors also gratefully acknowledge support from the Wellcome Trust via digital Innovator (215698/Z/19/Z) and strategic awards (098369/Z/12/Z).

References

1. Betancourt, M., Girolami, M.: Hamiltonian Monte Carlo for hierarchical models. In: Current trends in Bayesian Methodology with Applications, vol. 79, no. (30), pp. 2–4 (2015)
2. Biswal, B.B., et al.: Toward discovery science of human brain function. Proc. Natl. Acad. Sci. **107**(10), 4734–4739 (2010). https://doi.org/10.1073/pnas.0911855107
3. Cox, D.R.: Principles of Statistical Inference. Cambridge University Press, Cambridge (2006)

4. Destrieux, C., Fischl, B., Dale, A., Halgren, E.: Automatic parcellation of human cortical gyri and sulci using standard anatomical nomenclature. NeuroImage **53**(1), 1–15 (2010). https://doi.org/10.1016/j.neuroimage.2010.06.010
5. Essen, D.V., et al.: The human connectome project: a data acquisition perspective. NeuroImage **62**(4), 2222–2231 (2012). https://doi.org/10.1016/j.neuroimage.2012.02.018
6. Fischl, B.: FreeSurfer. NeuroImage **62**(2), 774–781 (2012). https://doi.org/10.1016/j.neuroimage.2012.01.021
7. Fortin, J.P., et al.: Harmonization of cortical thickness measurements across scanners and sites. NeuroImage **167**, 104–120 (2018). https://doi.org/10.1016/j.neuroimage.2017.11.024
8. Fortin, J.P., et al.: Harmonization of multi-site diffusion tensor imaging data. NeuroImage **161**, 149–170 (2017). https://doi.org/10.1016/j.neuroimage.2017.08.047
9. Gelman, A., Carlin, J.B., Stern, H.S., Dunson, D.B., Vehtari, A., Rubin, D.B.: Bayesian Data Analysis. Chapman and Hall/CRC (2013)
10. Hoffman, M.D., Gelman, A.: The No-U-Turn sampler: adaptively setting path lengths in Hamiltonian Monte Carlo. J. Mach. Learn. Res. **15**(1), 1593–1623 (2014)
11. Johnson, W.E., Li, C., Rabinovic, A.: Adjusting batch effects in microarray expression data using empirical Bayes methods. Biostatistics **8**(1), 118–127 (2006). https://doi.org/10.1093/biostatistics/kxj037
12. LaMontagne, P.J., et al.: OASIS-3: longitudinal neuroimaging, clinical, and cognitive dataset for normal aging and alzheimer disease. medRxiv (2019). https://doi.org/10.1101/2019.12.13.19014902
13. Marquand, A.F., Kia, S.M., Zabihi, M., Wolfers, T., Buitelaar, J.K., Beckmann, C.F.: Conceptualizing mental disorders as deviations from normative functioning. Mol. Psychiatry **24**(10), 1415–1424 (2019). https://doi.org/10.1038/s41380-019-0441-1
14. Marquand, A.F., Rezek, I., Buitelaar, J., Beckmann, C.F.: Understanding heterogeneity in clinical cohorts using normative models: beyond case-control studies. Biol. Psychiatry **80**(7), 552–561 (2016). https://doi.org/10.1016/j.biopsych.2015.12.023
15. Marquand, A.F., Wolfers, T., Mennes, M., Buitelaar, J., Beckmann, C.F.: Beyond lumping and splitting: a review of computational approaches for stratifying psychiatric disorders. Biol. Psychiatry Cogn. Neurosci. Neuroimaging **1**(5), 433–447 (2016). https://doi.org/10.1016/j.bpsc.2016.04.002
16. Nielson, D.M., et al.: Detecting and harmonizing scanner differences in the ABCD study-annual release 1.0. BioRxiv p. 309260 (2018)
17. Poldrack, R.A., et al.: A phenome-wide examination of neural and cognitive function. Sci. Data **3**(1), 1–12 (2016)
18. Poline, J.B., et al.: Data sharing in neuroimaging research. Frontiers Neuroinf. **6**, 9 (2012). https://doi.org/10.3389/fninf.2012.00009
19. Pomponio, R., Erus, G., Habes, M., Doshi, J., Srinivasan, D., Mamourian, E., et al.: Harmonization of large MRI datasets for the analysis of brain imaging patterns throughout the lifespan. NeuroImage **208**, 116450 (2020). https://doi.org/10.1016/j.neuroimage.2019.116450
20. Salvatier, J., Wiecki, T.V., Fonnesbeck, C.: Probabilistic programming in python using PyMC3. PeerJ Comput. Sci. **2**, e55 (2016). https://doi.org/10.7717/peerj-cs.55

21. Satterthwaite, T.D., et al.: The Philadelphia neurodevelopmental cohort: a publicly available resource for the study of normal and abnormal brain development in youth. NeuroImage **124**, 1115–1119 (2016). https://doi.org/10.1016/j.neuroimage.2015.03.056

22. Skåtun, K.C., et al.: Global brain connectivity alterations in patients with schizophrenia and bipolar spectrum disorders. J. Psychiatry Neurosci. JPN **41**(5), 331 (2016)

23. Taylor, J.R., et al.: The Cambridge centre for ageing and neuroscience (Cam-CAN) data repository: structural and functional MRI, MEG, and cognitive data from a cross-sectional adult lifespan sample. NeuroImage **144**, 262–269 (2017). https://doi.org/10.1016/j.neuroimage.2015.09.018

24. Thompson, P.M., et al.: The ENIGMA consortium: large-scale collaborative analyses of neuroimaging and genetic data. Brain Imaging behav. **8**(2), 153–182 (2014)

25. Wolfers, T., et al.: Mapping the heterogeneous phenotype of schizophrenia and bipolar disorder using normative models. JAMA Psychiatry **75**(11), 1146–1155 (2018). https://doi.org/10.1001/jamapsychiatry.2018.2467

26. Yamashita, A., et al.: Harmonization of resting-state functional MRI data across multiple imaging sites via the separation of site differences into sampling bias and measurement bias. PLOS Biol. **17**(4), 1–34 (2019). https://doi.org/10.1371/journal.pbio.3000042

27. Zabihi, M., et al.: Dissecting the heterogeneous cortical anatomy of autism spectrum disorder using normative models. Biol. Psychiatry Cogn. Neurosci. Neuroimaging **4**(6), 567–578 (2019). https://doi.org/10.1016/j.bpsc.2018.11.013

Image-Level Harmonization of Multi-site Data Using Image-and-Spatial Transformer Networks

Robert Robinson[1]([envelope]), Qi Dou[1], Daniel Coelho de Castro[1], Konstantinos Kamnitsas[1], Marius de Groot[2], Ronald M. Summers[3], Daniel Rueckert[1], and Ben Glocker[1]

[1] BioMedIA, Department of Computing, Imperial College London, London, UK
r.robinson16@imperial.ac.uk
[2] Research and Development, GlaxoSmithKline, Brentford, UK
[3] Department of Radiology and Imaging Sciences, Clinical Center, National Institutes of Health, Bethesda, USA

Abstract. We investigate the use of image-and-spatial transformer networks (ISTNs) to tackle domain shift in multi-site medical imaging data. Commonly, domain adaptation (DA) is performed with little regard for explainability of the inter-domain transformation and is often conducted at the feature-level in the latent space. We employ ISTNs for DA at the image-level which constrains transformations to explainable appearance and shape changes. As proof-of-concept we demonstrate that ISTNs can be trained adversarially on a classification problem with simulated 2D data. For real-data validation, we construct two 3D brain MRI datasets from the Cam-CAN and UK Biobank studies to investigate domain shift due to acquisition and population differences. We show that age regression and sex classification models trained on ISTN output improve generalization when training on data from one and testing on the other site.

1 Introduction

Domain shift (DS) concerns the problem of mismatch between the statistics of the training data used for model development and the statistics of the test data seen after model deployment. DS can cause significant drops in predictive performance, which has been observed in almost all recent imaging challenges when final test data was coming from different clinical sites [1]. DS is a major hurdle for successfully translating predictive models into clinical routine.

Acquisition and population shift are two common forms of DS that appear in medical image analysis [2]. Acquisition shift is observed due to differences in imaging protocols, modalities or scanners. Such a shift will be observed even

---

Electronic supplementary material The online version of this chapter (https://doi.org/10.1007/978-3-030-59728-3_69) contains supplementary material, which is available to authorized users.

© Springer Nature Switzerland AG 2020
A. L. Martel et al. (Eds.): MICCAI 2020, LNCS 12267, pp. 710–719, 2020.
https://doi.org/10.1007/978-3-030-59728-3_69

if the same subjects are scanned. Population shift occurs when cohorts of subjects under investigation exhibit different statistics, e.g., varying demographics or disease prevalence. It is not uncommon for both types of DS to occur simultaneously, in particular in multi-center studies. It is essential to tackle DS in machine learning to perform reliable analysis of large populations across sites and to avoid introducing biases into results. Recent work has shown that even after careful pre-processing, site-specific differences remain in the images [3, 4]. While methods like ComBat [5] aim to harmonize image-derived measurements, we focus on the images themselves.

One solution is domain adaptation (DA), a transductive [6] transfer learning technique that aims to modify the source domain's marginal distribution of the feature space such that it resembles the target domain. In medical imaging, labelled data is scarce and typically unavailable for the target domain. It is also unlikely to have the same subjects in both domains. Thus, we focus on 'unsupervised' and 'unpaired' DA, wherein labelled data is available only in the source domain and no matching samples exist between source and target.

Many DA approaches focus on learning domain-invariant feature representations, by either forcing latent representations of the inputs to follow similar distributions, or 'disentangling' domain-specific features from generic features [7]. This can be achieved with some divergence measure based on data statistics or by training adversarial networks to model the divergence between the feature representations [8]. These methods have been applied to brain lesions [9] and tumours [10] in MRI, and in contrast to non-contrast CT segmentation [11].

While these approaches seem appealing and have shown some success, they lack a notion of explainability as it is difficult to know what transformations are applied to the feature space. Additionally, although the learned task model may perform equally well on both domains, it is not guaranteed to perform as well as separate models trained on the individual domains.

We explore model-agnostic DA by working at the image level. Our approach is based on domain mapping (DM), which aims to learn the pixel-level transformations between two image domains, and includes techniques such as style transfer. Pix2Pix [12] (supervised) and CycleGAN [13] (unsupervised) take images from one domain through some encoder-decoder architecture to produce images in the new domain. The method in [8] uses CycleGAN to improve segmentation across scanners and applies DA at both image and feature levels, thus losing interpretability. It does not decompose the image and spatial transformations.

Methods for DM primarily use UNet-like architectures to learn image-to-image transformations that are easier to interpret, as one can visually inspect the output. For medical images of the same anatomy, but from different scanners, we assume that domain shift manifests primarily in appearance changes (contrast, signal-to-noise, resolution) and anatomical variation (shape changes), plus further subtle variations caused by image reconstruction or interpolation.

Contributions: We propose the use of image-and-spatial transformer networks (ISTNs) [14] to tackle domain shift at image-feature level in multi-site imaging data. ISTNs separate and compose the transformations for adapting appearance

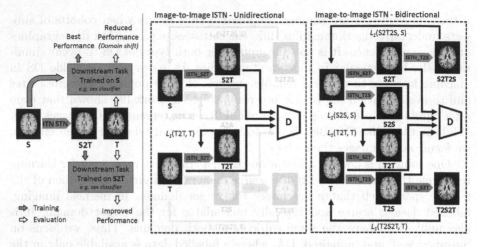

Fig. 1. (left) The domain shift problem can be mitigated by retraining or finetuning a task model on images $S2T$. (Middle) The ISTN is trained adversarially such that the discriminator D becomes better at identifying real (S and T) and transformed ($S2T$) images. The ISTN simultaneously produces better transformations $S2T$ of S that look more like the images T. The training process can also be done bidirectionally (right).

and shape differences between domains. We believe our approach is the first to use such an approach with retraining of the downstream task model on images transferred from source to target. We show that ISTNs can be trained adversarially in a task model-agnostic way. The transferred images can be visually inspected, and thus, our approach adds explainability to domain adaptation— which is important for validating the plausibility of the learned transformations. Our results demonstrate the successful recovery of performance on classification and regression tasks when using ISTNs to tackle domain shift. We explore both unidirectional and bidirectional training schemes and compare retraining the task model from scratch versus finetuning. We present proof-of-concept results on synthetic images generated with Morpho-MNIST [15] for a 3-class classification task. Our method is then validated on real multi-site data with 3D T1-weighted brain MRI. Our results indicate that ISTNs improve generalization and predictive performance can be recovered close to single-site accuracy.

2   Method

We propose adversarial training of ISTNs to perform model-agnostic DA via explicit appearance and shape transformations between the domains. We explore unidirectional and bidirectional training schemes as illustrated in Fig. 1.

Models. ISTNs have two components: an image transformer network (ITN) and a spatial transformer network (STN) [14,16]. Here, we additionally require a discriminator model for adversarial training of the ISTN.

ITN: The ITN performs appearance transformations such as contrast and brightness changes, and other localised adaptations at the image-level. A common image-to-image (I2I) translation network based on UNet with residual skip connections can be employed. We use upsample-convolutions to reduce chequerboard artifacts compared with transposed convolution. We use batch normalization, dropout layers and ReLU activations with a final tanh activation for the output. All input images are pre-normalized to the $[-1, 1]$ intensity range.

STN: We experiment with both the affine and B-spline STNs described in the original ISTN paper. Affine STNs learn to regress the parameters of linear spatial transforms with translation, rotation, scaling, and shearing. B-spline STNs regress control point displacements. Linear interpolation is used throughout. Note that in this work, Affine and B-Spline STNs are considered independently and are not composed.

Discriminator: In both Morpho-MNIST and brain MRI experiments, we use a standard fully-convolutional classification network with instance normalization, dropout layers and a sigmoid output.

Task Models: The employed classifiers and regressors follow the same fully-convolutional structure as the discriminator, reducing the dimensions of the input images to a multi-class or continuous value prediction, depending on the task. We use cross-entropy or mean-squared error loss functions, respectively.

Appendices C and D provide details about the architectures of different networks. All implementations are in PyTorch [17] with code available online[1].

Training. The output from the ITN is directly fed into the STN. They are then composed into a single ISTN unit, and are trained jointly end-to-end. *Discriminator*: The images S (from the source domain) are passed through the ISTN to generate images $S2T$, where T indicates images from the target domain. Next, the $S2T$ are passed through the discriminator D_T to yield a score in the range $(0, 1)$ denoting whether the image is a real sample from domain T or a transformed one. The discriminator is trained by minimizing the binary cross-entropy loss $\mathcal{L}_{bce}$ between the predicted and true domain labels. Equation (1) shows the total discriminator loss. Soft labels for the true domain are used to stabilize early training of the discriminator. We replace the hard '0' and '1' domain labels by random uniform values in the ranges $[0.00, 0.03]$ and $[0.97, 1.00]$, respectively.

ISTN: The ISTN is trained as a generator. The ISTN output $S2T$ is passed through the discriminator and forced to be closer to domain T by computing the adversarial loss $\mathcal{L}_{adv} = \mathcal{L}_{bce}(D_T(S2T), 1)$. Soft labels are also used here. We expect that when images T are passed through the ISTN, the output $T2T$ should be unchanged as it is already in domain T. This is enforced by the identity loss $\mathcal{L}_{idt} = \ell_1(T, T2T)$ acting on image intensities of T and $T2T$. A weighting factor λ is applied to L_{idt} giving the total loss function for the ISTN in Eq. (3)c.

We compare with the CycleGAN [18] training approach, which trains both directions simultaneously using two ISTNs ($ISTN_{S2T}$ and $ISTN_{T2S}$) and two

---

[1] https://github.com/mlnotebook/domain_adapation_istn.

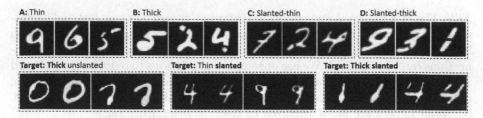

Fig. 2. (Top) Examples from Morpho-MNIST datasets from domains (left-to-right) A thin un-slanted digits; B thickened digits; C slanted digits; D thickened *and* slanted digits. Each contains 'healthy', 'fractured' and 'swollen' classes. (Bottom) Examples of source domain images before (left) and after (right) ISTN-transformation showing ISTN recovery of appearance and shape changes.

discriminators (D_S and D_T). The CycleGAN introduces the cycle-consistency term to $\mathcal{L}_{istn}$ such that when ISTN$_{T2S}$ is used to transform $S2T$, the result $S2T2S$ is forced to be close to S. Figure 1 shows the two ISTNs, their outputs and associated losses. The loss functions for ISTN$_{S2T}$ are shown in Eq. (3). Optimization is done using the Adam optimizer.

Downstream Tasks: The goal of our work is to demonstrate that such explicit appearance and spatial transformations via ISTNs can successfully tackle DS in certain applications. Ideally, we would like to observe that the performance of a predictor trained on $S2T$ and tested on T can recover to single-site performance. To demonstrate this, prior to training the ISTN, we train a task model (*e.g.* classifier or regressor) $\mathcal{T}_S$ on domain S. The performance of $\mathcal{T}_S(S)$ is likely to be our 'best performance' whilst $\mathcal{T}_S(T)$ will degrade due to DS. During ISTN training, we simultaneously re-train $\mathcal{T}_S$ on the ISTN output of $S2T$. This model $\mathcal{T}_{S2T}$ is trained to achieve maximum performance on the transformed images $\mathcal{T}_{S2T}(S2T)$ using labels from S. We assess the performance 'recovery' of $\mathcal{T}_{S2T}$ by comparing $\mathcal{T}_S(T)$ with $\mathcal{T}_{S2T}(T)$. In practice, data from T would be unlabelled. Our approach ensures that test data from the new domain T is not modified in any way. Additionally, in scenarios where the original model $\mathcal{T}_S$ is deployed, it is likely to have been trained on a large, well-curated, high-quality dataset; we cannot assume similar would be available for each new test domain. Our model-agnostic unsupervised DA is validated on two problems: i) proof-of-concept showing recovery of a classifier's performance on digit recognition, ii) classification and regression tasks with real-world, multi-site T1-weighted brain MRI.

$$\mathcal{L}_{disT} = \tfrac{1}{2}\left[\mathcal{L}_{bce}(D_T(S2T), 0) + \mathcal{L}_{bce}(D_T(T), 1)\right]. \tag{1}$$

$$\mathcal{L}_{istn}^{S2T} = \mathcal{L}_{bce}(D_T(S2T), 1) + \tfrac{1}{2}\lambda\left\|T2T - T\right\|_1. \tag{2}$$

$$\mathcal{L}_{istn}^{S2T} = \mathcal{L}_{bce}(D_S(T2S), 0) + \tfrac{1}{2}\lambda\left\|S2S - S\right\|_1 + \lambda\left\|S2T2S - S\right\|_1. \tag{3}$$

3   Materials

3.1   Proof-of-concept: Morpho-MNIST Experiments

Data. Morpho-MNIST is a framework that enables applying medically-inspired perturbations, such as local swellings and fractures, to the well-known MNIST dataset [15]. The framework also allows us to control transformations to obtain thickening and shearing of the original digits. We first create a dataset with three classes: 'healthy' digits with no transformations; 'fractured' digits with a single thin disruption and 'swollen' digits which exhibit a localized, tumor-like abnormal growth. A digit is only either fractured or swollen, not both. We specify a set of 'thin' digits (2.5 pixels across) to be source domain A. To simulate domain shift, we create three more datasets—domain B: thickened, 5.0 pixels digits; domain C: slanted digits created by shearing the image by 20–25° and domain D: thickened-slanted digits at 5.0 pixels and 20–25° shearing. Datasets B–D contain the same three classes as A, while each set has its own data characteristics simulating different types of domain shift. All images are single-channel and 28×28 pixels. Figure 2 shows some visual examples.

Task. The downstream task in this experiment is a 3-class classification problem: 'healthy' vs. 'fractured' vs. 'swollen'. We train a small, fully-convolutional classifier to perform the classification on domain A. We use ISTNs to retrain the classifier on transformed images $A2B$, $A2C$, and $A2D$, and evaluate each on their corresponding test domains B, C, and D.

We run training for 100 epochs and perform grid search to find suitable hyper-parameters including learning rate, trade-off λ and the control-point spacing of the B-spline STN. We conduct experiments using ITN only, STN only and combinations of affine and B-spline ISTNs to determine the best model for the task. We also consider both transfer directions, switching the roles of source and target domains.

3.2   Application to Brain MRI Experiments

We apply the same methodology to a real-world domain shift problem where we observe a significant drop in prediction accuracy when naively training on one site and testing on another without any DA. We utilise 3D brain MRI from two sites that employ similar but not identical imaging protocols.

Data. We construct two datasets of T1-weighted brain MRI from subjects with no reported pathology, where $n = 565$ are taken from the Cambridge Centre for Ageing and Neuroscience study (Cam-CAN) [19,20] and $n = 689$ from the UK Biobank imaging study (UKBB) [21–23]. From each site, 450 subjects are used for training and the remainder for testing. The UKBB dataset contains equal numbers of male and female subjects between the ages of 48 and 71 ($\mu = 59.5$). In the classification task, to simulate the effect of population shift our Cam-CAN dataset has a wider age range (30–87, $\mu = 57.9$) but maintains the male-to-female ratio. We match the age range of both datasets in the regression task, limiting DS only to the more subtle scanner effects. UKBB images were acquired at the UKBB imaging centre, and Cam-CAN images were acquired at the Medical Research Council Cognition and Brain Sciences Unit in Cambridge, UK. Both sites acquire 1 mm isotropic images using the 3D MPRAGE pulse sequence on Siemens 3T scanners with a 32-channel receiver head coil and in-plane acceleration factor 2. Appendix A presents the acquisition parameters that differ between the two sites. We note that generally the acquisition parameters of both sites are similar, and the images cannot be easily distinguished visually. For pre-processing, all images are affinely aligned to MNI space, skull-stripped, bias-field-corrected, and intensity-normalised to zero mean unit variance within a brain mask. Voxels outside the mask are set to 0. Images are passed through a tanh function before being consumed by the networks.

Table 1. 3-class classification results on MorphoMNIST. Images transferred from classifier domain A: 'thin unslanted' to three target domains. Accuracies shown for classifiers retrained on the ISTN output from scratch (Acc_s) and finetuned (Acc_f). Δ is model improvement from baseline. Control-point spacings indicated for B-Spline STNs. First row is the original classifier without DA.

Target		Thick unslanted				Thin slanted				Thick slanted			
ITN	STN	Acc_s	Δ	Acc_f	Δ	Acc_s	Δ	Acc_f	Δ	Acc_s	Δ	Acc_f	Δ
No	No	41.2				45.7				32.8			
Yes	No	**79.0**	**37.8**	**83.3**	**42.1**	83.4	37.7	83.3	37.6	**82.4**	**49.6**	**84.6**	**51.8**
No	Affine	52.4	11.2	68.9	27.7	92.4	46.7	93.0	47.3	54.8	22.0	64.8	32.0
No	B-spline (4)	39.0	−2.2	54.4	13.2	92.1	46.4	93.1	47.4	36.0	3.2	57.2	24.4
No	B-spline (8)	49.2	8.0	61.5	20.3	92.5	46.8	92.3	46.6	37.0	4.2	61.8	29.0
Yes	Affine	78.8	37.6	77.1	35.9	86.7	41.0	88.4	42.7	81.9	49.1	83.1	50.3
Yes	B-spline (4)	66.3	25.1	75.8	34.6	**92.7**	**47.0**	91.0	45.3	79.3	46.5	82.7	49.9
Yes	B-spline (8)	69.5	28.3	77.2	36.0	91.8	46.1	**93.4**	**47.7**	79.0	46.2	80.8	48.0

Table 2. Sex classification results on 3D Brain MRI

Source		UKBB								Cam-CAN							
Method		Uni-ISTN				CycleGAN Bi-ISTN				Uni-ISTN				CycleGAN Bi-ISTN			
ITN	STN	Acc_s	Δ	Acc_f	Δ	Acc_s	Δ	Acc_f	Δ	Acc_s	Δ	Acc_f	Δ	Acc_s	Δ	Acc_f	Δ
No	No	54.8				54.8				64.3				64.3			
Yes	No	79.1	24.3	72.2	17.4	**80.0**	**25.2**	80.8	26.0	**86.2**	21.9	78.2	13.9	80.8	16.5	79.9	15.6
Yes	Affine	**80.9**	**26.1**	75.7	20.9	70.4	15.6	**82.4**	**27.6**	79.9	15.6	79.1	14.8	**82.4**	**18.1**	72.0	7.7
Yes	B-spline (8)	78.3	23.5	76.5	21.7	79.1	24.3	78.7	23.9	80.3	16.0	**84.5**	**20.2**	78.7	14.4	**80.8**	**16.5**
Yes	B-spline (16)	80.0	25.2	**78.3**	**23.5**	73.0	18.2	67.8	13.0	85.4	21.1	84.1	19.8	67.8	3.5	68.6	4.3

Task. We consider two prediction tasks, namely sex classification and age regression using the UKBB and Cam-CAN sets, each once as source and once as target

domain. The task networks are retrained on the transformed images produced
by the ISTN and evaluated on the corresponding target domain.

4   Experimental Results

Morpho-MNIST. Quantitative results for the synthetic experiments are summarized in Table 1. ITNs are able to harmonize local appearance such as thickness between source and target domains, while STNs perform well in recovering shape variations such as slant. Where both thickness and slant are varied between source and target domains, we note an ITN-only performs as well (or slightly better) than a joint ISTN, suggesting that thickness is more important for the classification task. In Fig. 2 we show visual results on how the ISTNs are able to recover both appearance and shape differences between domains.

Brain MRI. Quantitative results are summarized in Tables 2 and 3. The sex classifier trained and tested on UKBB achieves 84.3% accuracy. This drops to 54.8% when tested on Cam-CAN. Similarly, training and testing on Cam-CAN yields 91.6%, dropping to 64.3% when testing on UKBB. Using ISTNs for domain adaptation, and retraining the classifiers increases the accuracy substantially on Cam-CAN from 54.8% to 80.9%, and on UKBB from 64.3% to 86.2%, which is close to the single-site performance. Training the classifier from scratch performs similarly well to fine-tuning. Bidirectional training with CycleGAN seems not to provide substantial improvements over the simpler unidirectional scheme. The ISTNs are able to overcome some of the acquisition and population shifts between the two domains.

The age regressor trained and tested on UKBB achieves mean absolute error (MAE) of 4.25 years increasing to 5.13 when evaluated on Cam-CAN. The regressor trained and tested on Cam-CAN yields 4.10 years MAE increasing to 4.61 when tested on UKBB. Despite the initially smaller drop in performance for age regression, ISTNs still improve performance. The UKBB-trained regressor recovers to 4.58 years MAE and the Cam-CAN-trained one to 4.56 years. Note, we had limited the population shift here by constraining the age range, thus the recovery is likely due to a reduction in acquisition shift.

Table 3. Age regression results on 3D Brain MRI. MAE$_s$ is the task model retrained from scratch.

Source		UKBB		Cam-CAN	
Method		Uni-ISTN		Uni-ISTN	
ITN	STN	MAE$_s$	Δ	MAE$_s$	Δ
No	No	5.13		4.61	
Yes	No	4.71	0.42	**4.57**	**0.04**
Yes	Affine	**4.58**	**0.55**	5.00	−0.39
Yes	B-spline (16)	5.06	0.07	4.90	−0.29

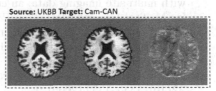

Source: UKBB Target: Cam-CAN

Fig. 3. Examples of (left-to-right) source domain, transformed ISTN output and difference image.

5   Conclusion

We explored adversarially-trained ISTNs for model-agnostic domain adaptation. The learned image-level transformations help explainability, as the resulting images can be visually inspected and checked for plausibility (cf. Fig. 3). Further interrogation of deformations fields also adds to explainability, *e.g.* Appendix B. Image-level DA seems suitable in cases of subtle domain shift caused by acquisition and population differences in multi-center studies. Predictive performance approached single-site accuracies. The choice of STN and control-point spacings may need to be carefully considered for specific use cases. An extension of our work to many-sites may be possible by simultaneously adapting to multiple sites. A quantitative comparison to feature-level DA would be a natural next step for future work. Another interesting direction could be to integrate the ISTN component in a fully end-to-end task-driven optimisation, where the ISTN and the task network are trained jointly.

Acknowledgements. RR funded by KCL & Imperial EPSRC CDT in Medical Imaging (EP/L015226/1) and GlaxoSmithKline; This research received funding from the European Research Council (ERC) under the European Union's Horizon 2020 research and innovation programme (grant agreement No 757173, project MIRA, ERC-2017-STG). DCC is supported by the EPSRC Centre for Doctoral Training in High Performance Embedded and Distributed Systems (HiPEDS, grant ref EP/L016796/1). The research was supported in part by the National Institutes of Health, Clinical Center.

References

1. Crimi, A., Bakas, S., Kuijf, H., Keyvan, F., Reyes, M., van Walsum, T. (eds.): Brainlesion: Glioma, Multiple Sclerosis, Stroke and Traumatic Brain Injuries. Springer, Heidelberg (2019). https://doi.org/10.1007/978-3-030-11723-8
2. Castro, D.C., Walker, I., Glocker, B.: Causality matters in medical imaging. arXiv:1912.08142 (2019)
3. Wachinger, C., Becker, B.G., Rieckmann, A., Pölsterl, S.: Quantifying confounding bias in neuroimaging datasets with causal inference. In: Shen, D., et al. (eds.) MICCAI 2019. LNCS, vol. 11767, pp. 484–492. Springer, Cham (2019). https://doi.org/10.1007/978-3-030-32251-9_53
4. Glocker, B., Robinson, R., Castro, D.C., Dou, Q., Konukoglu, E.: Machine learning with multi-site imaging data: an empirical study on the impact of scanner effects. In: Medical Imaging Meets NeurIPS (2019)
5. Yu, M., et al.: Statistical harmonization corrects site effects in functional connectivity measurements from multi-site fMRI data. Hum. Brain Mapp. **39**(11), 4213–4227 (2018)
6. Pan, S., Yang, Q.: A survey on transfer learning. IEEE Trans. Knowl. Data Eng. **22**(10), 1345–1359 (2009)
7. Yang, J., Dvornek, N.C., Zhang, F., Chapiro, J., Lin, M.D., Duncan, J.S.: Unsupervised domain adaptation via disentangled representations: application to cross-modality liver segmentation. In: Shen, D., et al. (eds.) MICCAI 2019. LNCS, vol. 11765, pp. 255–263. Springer, Cham (2019). https://doi.org/10.1007/978-3-030-32245-8_29

8. Yan, W., et al.: The domain shift problem of medical image segmentation and vendor-adaptation by Unet-GAN. In: Shen, D., et al. (eds.) MICCAI 2019. LNCS, vol. 11765, pp. 623–631. Springer, Cham (2019). https://doi.org/10.1007/978-3-030-32245-8_69

9. Kamnitsas, K., et al.: Unsupervised domain adaptation in brain lesion segmentation with adversarial networks. In: Niethammer, M., et al. (eds.) IPMI 2017. LNCS, vol. 10265, pp. 597–609. Springer, Cham (2017). https://doi.org/10.1007/978-3-319-59050-9_47

10. Dai, L., Li, T., Shu, H., Zhong, L., Shen, H., Zhu, H.: Automatic brain tumor segmentation with domain adaptation. In: Crimi, A., Bakas, S., Kuijf, H., Keyvan, F., Reyes, M., van Walsum, T. (eds.) BrainLes 2018. LNCS, vol. 11384, pp. 380–392. Springer, Cham (2019). https://doi.org/10.1007/978-3-030-11726-9_34

11. Sandfort, V., Yan, K., Pickhardt, P.J., Summers, R.M.: Data augmentation using generative adversarial networks (CycleGAN) to improve generalizability in CT segmentation tasks. Sci. Rep. 9(1), 1–9 (2019)

12. Isola, P., Zhu, J., Zhou, T., Efros, A.: Image-to-image translation with conditional adversarial networks. In: 2017 IEEE Conference on Computer Vision and Pattern Recognition (CVPR), Honolulu, HI, pp. 5967–5976 (2017)

13. Zhu, J., Park, T., Isola, P., Efros, A.: Unpaired image-to-image translation using cycle-consistent adversarial networks. In: 2017 IEEE International Conference on Computer Vision (ICCV), Venice, pp. 2242–2251 (2017)

14. Lee, M.C.H., Oktay, O., Schuh, A., Schaap, M., Glocker, B.: Image-and-spatial transformer networks for structure-guided image registration. In: Shen, D., et al. (eds.) MICCAI 2019. LNCS, vol. 11765, pp. 337–345. Springer, Cham (2019). https://doi.org/10.1007/978-3-030-32245-8_38

15. Castro, D.C., Tan, J., Kainz, B., Konukoglu, E., Glocker, B.: Morpho-MNIST: quantitative assessment and diagnostics for representation learning. J. Mach. Learn. Res. 20(178), 1–29 (2019)

16. Jaderberg, M., Simonyan, K., Zisserman, A., et al.: Spatial transformer networks. Advances in Neural Information Processing Systems 28, pp. 2017–2025 (2015)

17. Paszke, A., et al.: Pytorch: an imperative style, high-performance deep learning library. In: Wallach, H., Larochelle, H., Beygelzimer, A., d'Alché Buc, F., Fox, E., Garnett, R. (eds.) Advances in Neural Information Processing Systems 32, pp. 8024–8035. Curran Associates, Inc. (2019)

18. Zhu, J.Y., Park, T., Isola, P., Efros, A.A.: Unpaired image-to-image translation using cycle-consistent adversarial networks. In: 2017 IEEE International Conference on Computer Vision (ICCV) (2017)

19. Shafto, M.A., et al.: The Cambridge Centre for Ageing and Neuroscience (Cam-CAN) study protocol: a cross-sectional, lifespan, multidisciplinary examination of healthy cognitive ageing. BMC Neurol. 14(1), 204 (2014)

20. Taylor, J.R., et al.: The Cambridge Centre for Ageing and Neuroscience (Cam-CAN) data repository: structural and functional MRI, MEG, and cognitive data from a cross-sectional adult lifespan sample. NeuroImage 144, 262–269 (2017)

21. Sudlow, C., et al.: UK Biobank: an open access resource for identifying the causes of a wide range of complex diseases of middle and old age. PLoS Med. 12(3), e1001779 (2015)

22. Miller, K.L., et al.: Multimodal population brain imaging in the UK Biobank prospective epidemiological study. Nat. Neurosci. 19(11), 1523–1536 (2016)

23. Alfaro-Almagro, F., et al.: Image processing and quality control for the first 10,000 brain imaging datasets from UK Biobank. NeuroImage 166, 400–424 (2018)

A Disentangled Latent Space
for Cross-Site MRI Harmonization

Blake E. Dewey[1]($\boxtimes$), Lianrui Zuo[1,2], Aaron Carass[1], Yufan He[1], Yihao Liu[1],
Ellen M. Mowry[3], Scott Newsome[3], Jiwon Oh[3], Peter A. Calabresi[3],
and Jerry L. Prince[1,4]

[1] Department of Electrical and Computer Engineering,
The Johns Hopkins University, Baltimore, MD, USA
blake.dewey@jhu.edu
[2] Laboratory of Behavioral Neuroscience,
National Institute on Aging, National Institutes of Health, Baltimore, MD, USA
[3] Department of Neurology, The Johns Hopkins School of Medicine,
Baltimore, MD, USA
[4] Department of Radiology and Radiological Science, The Johns Hopkins
School of Medicine, Baltimore, MD, USA

Abstract. Accurate interpretation and quantification of magnetic resonance imaging (MRI) is vital to medical research and clinical practice. However, lack of MRI standardization and differences in acquisition protocols often lead to measurement inconsistencies across sites. Image harmonization techniques have been shown to improve qualitative and quantitative consistency between differently acquired scans. Unfortunately, these methods typically require paired training data from traveling subjects (for supervised methods) or assumptions about anatomical similarities between the populations (for unsupervised methods). We propose a deep learning-based harmonization technique with limited supervision for use in standardization across scanners and sites. By leveraging a disentangled latent space represented by a high-resolution anatomical information component (β) and a low-dimensional contrast component (θ), the proposed method trains a cross-site harmonization model using databases of multi-modal image pairs acquired separately from each of the scanners to be harmonized. In this manuscript, we show that by using T_1-weighted and T_2-weighted images acquired from different subjects at three different sites, we can achieve a stable extraction of β with a continuous representation of θ. We also demonstrate that this allows cross-site harmonization without the need for paired data between sites.

Keywords: MR harmonization · Multiple sclerosis · Deep learning

1 Introduction

Magnetic resonance imaging (MRI) is a non-invasive, flexible medical imaging modality that is vital to the diagnosis, monitoring, and investigation of many

© Springer Nature Switzerland AG 2020
A. L. Martel et al. (Eds.): MICCAI 2020, LNCS 12267, pp. 720–729, 2020.
https://doi.org/10.1007/978-3-030-59728-3_70

Table 1. Scanner and protocol specifications.

	IXI	SiteA	SiteB
Scanner Hardware	Philips Intera 1.5T	Philips Achieva 3T	Philips Achieva 3T
T_1-weighted	SPGR	MEMPRAGE	MPRAGE
	1.2 × 0.94 × 0.94 mm	1 × 1 × 1 mm	1.1 × 1.1 × 1.18 mm*
	TE = 4.6 ms, TR = 9.8 ms	TE = 6.2 ms, TR = 2.5 s, TI = 900 ms	TE = 6 ms, TR = 3 s, TI = 840 ms
T_2-weighted	2D TSE	3D TSE	2D TSE
	0.94 × 0.94 × 1.25 mm	1 × 1 × 1 mm	1.1 × 1.1 × 2.2 mm*
	TE = 100 ms, TR = 8.2 s	TE = 240 ms, TR = 2.5 s	TE = 80 ms, TR = 4.2 s

*Scan is reconstructed on the scanner to 0.83 × 0.83 mm in-plane by zero-padding in frequency space

diseases and disorders of the human body. However, the same flexibility causes an inherent difficulty in producing images that are consistent for quantitative evaluation, especially between different imaging centers. For example, T_1-weighted imaging, which is often used for evaluation of the brain's anatomy through image segmentation, can be acquired in a number of ways, each with a different subsequent quantification of the brain's anatomy. This can be seen in the difference between T_1-weighted spoiled gradient echo (SPGR) and magnetization-prepared rapid gradient echo (MPRAGE) imaging, both of which are commonly acquired as structural T_1-weighted images. Furthermore, even if the acquisition method is standardized (i.e., using only MPRAGE), there are additional effects caused by scanner manufacturer, software version, and pulse sequence parameters.

In recent years, there has been a push to develop and release standardized imaging protocols for general use, greatly increasing the use of high-quality imaging for research studies. However, a large number of groups and clinical practices continue to use non-standard pulse sequences and protocols. Even as standardization is improving, differences related to scanner hardware or software can never be eliminated [16]. Thus, MRI harmonization has come to the forefront of medical imaging research.

MRI harmonization was initially carried out using global methods such as histogram normalization [11]; however, this type of approach can cause very poor results in the presence of pathology [6]. Other methods based on machine learning were also proposed, but were often limited in their ability to work outside of the brain, requiring additional pre-processing steps that limit their global applicability [14,15]. Finally, deep learning-based techniques were introduced to attempt to overcome all previous concerns. Supervised methods overcome many challenges, but required training data of overlapping (traveling) subjects, which can be difficult to acquire, especially in large-scale studies [5]. In contrast, unsupervised methods do not require paired training data, but required a assumed a similarity between the two populations [19]. This similarity assumption is often not possible due to pathology or demographic differences between the groups [4].

Due to limitations of other methods, hybrid approaches with limited supervision prove to be more effective. However, these methods require a source of supervision, such as segmentation [3] or a model constraint. It has been shown that inversion of the MR signal equation can distill an MRI image to a disentangled latent space containing contrast as a single parameter (or set of param-

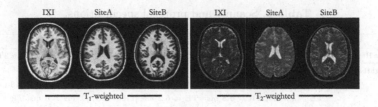

Fig. 1. Example slices from each MRI dataset.

eters) (denoted by θ) and a contrast-invariant, anatomical map (or set of maps) (denoted by β) [8]. This contrast-invariant β component can then be combined with a new contrast parameter to produce a synthetic version of the image having the target contrast. MR signal inversion proves a difficult task to optimize robustly, which leads to instability when using this approach. In this paper, we have adopted the high-level idea of [8], but have overcome its instability by using a data-driven, disentangled latent space in a deep learning framework. A key difference in the two approaches is that our latent space is discovered using training data from each site rather than being arbitrarily specified by assumed MR imaging equations, as in [10]. This approach avoids the requirements of MR imaging equation inversion, automatic tissue segmentation, and specification of arbitrary nuclear magnetic resonance tissue properties, avoiding the issues of [8].

2   Methods

2.1   MRI Datasets/Pre-Processing

Three MRI datasets were used in these experiments: a subset of the public IXI brain development dataset [1] containing healthy subjects (denoted IXI) and two private datasets of people with multiple sclerosis (denoted SiteA and SiteB). SiteA and SiteB both contain a subset of overlapping patients taken less than 30 days apart to use in quantitative evaluation. Each dataset contained T_1 and T_2-weighted images. The IXI dataset was acquired on a Philips 1.5T Philips scanner, whereas the SiteA and SiteB datasets were acquired on two different Philips 3 T scanners. Although all data were acquired from Philips scanners, they have different hardware and acquisition parameters (see Table 1). For our purposes, we randomly selected 30 training subjects, 10 validation subjects and 10 testing subjects from each dataset.

For each subject, bias field correction was done using N4, and each T_1-weighted image was registered to the MNI ICBM152 brain atlas and the T_2-weighted image was registered to the T_1-weighted image and transformed into the common atlas space using the T_1-weighted transformation matrix [2,17]. For 2D images with greater than 2 mm slice thickness, super-resolution was performed before registration [18]. Finally, intensity gain correction was performed by normalizing the mean white matter value (calculated using Fuzzy C-means on

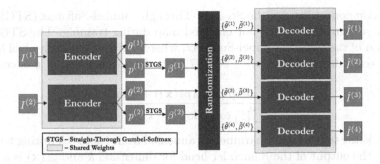

Fig. 2. The high-level disentangled model design showing the random selection process used during training.

the T_1-weighted image) to 0.25 [12]. These steps provided a numerically and spatially consistent set of images, which could then be passed into the deep learning model. Although there is no theoretical limitation to carrying out our approach in 3D, for practical reasons we have developed a 2D network using single slices as input. To reduce the dependence between slices and still provide enough relevant training data, we selected every third slice from the center 60 mm of the image (in the axial orientation). Example images from each dataset are presented in Fig. 1; contrast differences are quite evident.

2.2 Disentangled Latent Space

We propose a novel mechanism to disentangle anatomy from the imaging protocol. This formulation is part of a simple encoder-decoder network, where the two sub-networks are bridged by the disentangled latent space (see Fig. 2). The encoder is built from the basic architecture of the U-Net [13], but using padding to maintain spatial dimensions and has two heads, each of which generate a portion of the disentangled latent space. The decoder, sharing the same U-Net structure, takes the concatenated latent maps and produces a synthetic image. For the purposes of training, weights are shared between copies of the single encoder and single decoder.

The first part of our latent space, which we call the β component, represents a contrast-agnostic anatomy map. We construct this component as a one-hot tensor of size $H \times W \times C_\beta$, with H and W being the size of the input image; with the one-hot encoding being along the C_β channels, restricting the amount of information that can be passed through this component of the latent space. This restriction is essential, as the β component has a large potential for communication if left unrestricted, allowing the network to "cheat" by passing through extra information about the contrast elements through the β component. In order to construct this component, we use a head on the encoder which is a simple 3×3 convolutional layer followed by a sigmoid activation, which gives us probability values in each channel. To convert these probabilities to a one-hot encoded feature component, we use the Straight-Through Gumbel-Softmax (STGS) operation to approximate a one-hot encoded map during training. The STGS is an extension of the classic Gumbel-Softmax, where the result at each pixel location $\mathbf{x}$ is a vector denoted by $y(\mathbf{x}) \in \mathbb{R}^{C_\beta}$ [7]. The k-th dimension of y is computed by

$$y_k(\mathbf{x}) = \frac{\exp\left((\log\left(p_k(\mathbf{x})\right) + g_k(\mathbf{x}))/\tau\right)}{\sum_{j=1}^{C_\beta} \exp\left((\log\left(p_j(\mathbf{x})\right) + g_j(\mathbf{x}))/\tau\right)} \tag{1}$$

where τ is the temperature parameter (annealed from 1.0 to 0.5 during training), $p_k(\mathbf{x})$ is the output of the β encoder head for dimension k and $g_k(\mathbf{x})$ is a sample drawn from Gumbel(0,1). Notice that y is nearly a one-hot vector, so for the STGS formulation, we convert $y(\mathbf{x})$ to a final $\beta(\mathbf{x})$ by applying an argmax operator, as in $\beta(\mathbf{x}) = \text{one hot}(\text{argmax}_k y_k(\mathbf{x}))$. Since argmax is not differentiable, to carry out gradient backpropagation, we detach the calculation of argmax from the computation graph and use (1) instead. For evaluation of the model (i.e., testing), we revert to using argmax since no backpropagation is necessary. For simplicity, we will omit the notation $\mathbf{x}$ (for pixel location) in future descriptions.

The second part of the latent space, called the θ component, represents the imaging protocol used to acquire the image. We represent this as a vector of real values with length C_θ. This is done using a large convolutional kernel (32×32) to reduce dimensionality followed by a fully connected layer, which reduces the tensor to a single vector. To recombine the two parts of the latent space together for decoding, the θ component is replicated to match the size ($H \times W$) of the β component and the tensors are concatenated together. This combined tensor is fed into the decoder network to produce a reconstructed image.

2.3   Training Strategy

Training for this model is done by providing two images of the same anatomy imaged using different protocols (I_1 and I_2 in Fig. 2). In this manuscript, T_1-weighted and T_2-weighted images are used. Given these images, we want the network to create equal β maps for each subject since the anatomy of the pair is the same and to create different θ values for each image because the protocols are different. Ideally, there is a single β map for each subject and similar θ values for similar scanners and protocols. During training, we will combine the β and θ maps in a random way (see below) to create synthetic images which can be compared to the original images in our loss function.

In order to properly train our disentangled latent space, we must introduce randomness that discourages the network from over-utilizing the higher information capacity of the β component. We do this in two ways, both represented in the Randomization block of Fig. 2. Each randomization is done four times to create multiple output results from our two input images. The first method is a random selection of channels from the β components of both input images,

$$\tilde{\beta}_k^{(r)} = \beta_k^{(s)} \quad \text{where} \quad s \sim \text{Multinomial}(2) \quad \forall k \in \{1, \ldots, C_\beta\}. \tag{2}$$

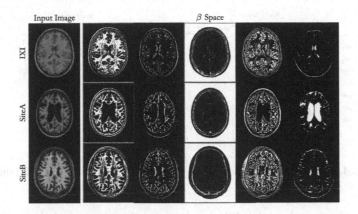

Fig. 3. β component generated using $C_\beta = 5$.

where $\tilde{\beta}^{(r)}$ is the r-th random selection of β channels. This encourages both images to produce the same β component, which should be true since I_1 and I_2 have the same anatomy. Our second method of randomization is a random choice of θ ($\tilde{\theta}^{(r)}$) for each $\tilde{\beta}^{(r)}$ from the two available θ vectors. This choice determines the input image that we will compare against in the reconstruction loss, i.e., if we choose $\theta^{(2)}$ for $\tilde{\theta}^{(1)}$, we will compare $\hat{I}^{(1)}$ to $I^{(2)}$. As we choose either θ vector for our randomized β map, we encourage the network to learn both cross-modality synthesis and auto-encoding of the input contrast.

We define a combined loss as the weighted sum of reconstruction and cosine similarity losses, $\mathcal{L} = \mathcal{L}_{recon} + \lambda_{sim}\mathcal{L}_{sim}$. The reconstruction loss is the mean squared error between the reconstructed image and the input image (defined by the chosen θ_{r_i}),

$$\mathcal{L}_{recon} = \frac{1}{4}\sum_{r=1}^{4}\text{MSE}(I^{(j)}, \hat{I}^{(r)}) \quad \text{where } \tilde{\theta}^{(r)} = \theta^{(j)}. \tag{3}$$

The cosine similarity loss between β_1 and β_2 is given by $\mathcal{L}_{sim} = \frac{1}{2}\cos\langle\beta^{(1)}, \beta^{(2)}\rangle$, which is used to further encourage the encoder to produce similar β values regardless of input contrast. We train this model using the Adam optimizer [9] for 200 epochs with a learning rate of 0.001. The value for λ_{sim} was included in a hyperparameter search, which found that $\lambda_{sim} = 0.0005$ provides the best results.

2.4 Experiments

To determine the qualitative and quantitative efficacy of this method, we trained our model with the combined 90 subjects from three sites. First, we finalized our network architecture by using a grid search over C_β and C_θ. We searched through all combinations of $C_\beta \in \{3, 5, 7\}$ and $C_\theta \in \{1, 2\}$, as we observed diminishing improvements outside of these values. To decide which combination

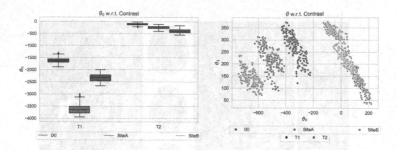

Fig. 4. θ values calculated with $C_\beta = 5$, $C_\theta = 1$ (left) and $C_\theta = 2$ (right).

is best, we first used total validation loss and then inspected the quality of the latent space that was learned. Ideally, we would like the θ component to show minimal differences in θ when the acquisition contrasts are the same and be informative in distinguishing T_1-weighted and T_2-weighted images, as well as site-specific differences.

After finalizing the network structure, the testing data was run through the model to generate the respective latent values and a mean value for θ was determined for the SiteA data. This θ value was then used as the target for harmonization of all three sites. The calculated β values for all images (including those from SiteA) were run through the decoder sub-network using the mean θ value to create a harmonized image. For quantitative evaluation, we compare the results of harmonization on overlapping (traveling) subjects (N = 12) that were scanned on both SiteA and SiteB using mean structural similarity index (MSSIM) and peak signal-to-noise ratio (PSNR).

3   Results

In the grid search, we saw a significant improvement in validation loss when increasing from $C_\beta = 3$ to $C_\beta = 5, 7$, but not between $C_\beta = 5$ and $C_\beta = 7$. Additionally, we saw no substantial difference between $C_\theta = 1$ and $C_\theta = 2$. Given the remaining choices, we inspected the generated latent spaces to choose our final solution. First, we investigated the θ component derived from models using $C_\beta = 5$ and $C_\beta = 7$. Both options give latent spaces that separate T_1-weighted images from T_2-weighted images well, but the $C_\beta = 5$ model gave a complete separation between T_1-weighted images from different sites (see Fig. 4), whereas the $C_\beta = 7$ model did not. This led us to choose $C_\beta = 5$, as we want to restrict information flow as much as possible in the β component without affecting reconstruction. Example β components for all three sites are given in Fig. 3, showing similarities in the β components between sites. Next, we look at the latent spaces derived from $C_\beta = 5$ and both $C_\theta = 1$ and $C_\theta = 2$, as shown in Fig. 4. Both selections for C_θ show separation of the T_1-weighted images from all sites, but the $C_\theta = 2$ model shows a substantial spreading in theta values in the direction perpendicular to the difference between sites. This indicates a

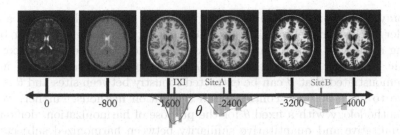

Fig. 5. Reconstruction results of an IXI subject with a range of θ values. Colored histograms show the actual spread of testing T_1-weighted images from each site, with coloured markers marking the mean values for a given site.

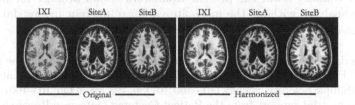

Fig. 6. Results of harmonization to the mean SiteA θ value.

potential overparameterization in θ, allowing it to encode unwanted biological and/or spatial information. Therefore, our final model uses $C_\beta = 5$ and $C_\theta = 1$ as the final latent space dimensions.

We next used the optimized network to harmonize images from different sites. First, we explored the effect of θ on the reconstruction by evenly sampling the range of θ, as depicted in Fig. 5. We can see that θ values close to 0 give T_2-weighted images; as θ increases, the synthesized images pass through a region of unknown contrast before concluding with synthetic images that are clearly T_1-weighted. We can also see that the images within the spread for each site evoke the contrast of the given site.

In the next experiment, we used a specific θ to create harmonized images. We selected the mean θ value for SiteA ($\theta = -2339.3$) and applied it to images from all sites. Results are shown in Fig. 6, where we can see that the harmonized images have a more qualitatively similar appearance. This is especially evident in the grey matter intensity levels, which are quite different in the original images. Quantitative results for the traveling subjects show a dramatic improvement in similarity using both MSSIM (0.845 for original images vs. 0.923 for harmonized images) and PSNR (26.1 for original images and 29.2 for harmonized images).

4 Discussion and Conclusion

We have shown that by using a disentangled latent space, we can achieve cross-site harmonization, even without any overlapping subjects. By using the shared anatomy of multi-modal imaging from each site, we are able to train a single encoder/decoder model for all sites. Once trained, this model is capable of generating a contrast-agnostic encoding, β, which when combined with a contrast-specific parameter, θ, can be decoded into a number of reconstructed images. We demonstrated that β can be extracted robustly between sites and θ is informative to move between contrasts and acquisition methods. Further, we used this methodology with a fixed θ for the purpose of harmonization, demonstrating qualitative and quantitative similarity between harmonized subjects from different sites.

Although more research is necessary both to evaluate the potential expansion of both β and θ components and to evaluate the method on more sites and with more training data, the present framework shows promise for large-scale, multi-site analyses without the inter-site variance inherent in raw data and the limitations of other harmonization approaches.

Acknowledgments. This research was supported by two grants from the NIH (R01-NS082347, PI: Peter Calabresi; P41-EB0159, PI: Peter van Zijl), two grants from the National Multiple Sclerosis Society (RG-1601-07180, PI: Jiwon Oh; RG-1907-34570: PI: Dzung Pham), trial support from the Patient-Centered Outcomes Research Initiative, and in part by the Intramural Research Program of the NIH, National Institute on Aging.

References

1. IXI Brain Development Dataset. https://brain-development.org/ixi-dataset/. Accessed 10 Dec 2019
2. Avants, B.B., Tustison, N.J., Stauffer, M., Song, G., Wu, B., Gee, J.C.: The Insight ToolKit image registration framework. Front. Neuroinform. **8**, 44 (2014). https://doi.org/10.3389/fninf.2014.00044
3. Chartsias, A., Joyce, T., Giuffrida, M.V., Tsaftaris, S.A.: Multimodal MR synthesis via modality-invariant latent representation. IEEE Trans. Med. Imag. **37**(3), 1–814 (2017). https://doi.org/10.1109/TMI.2017.2764326
4. Cohen, J.P., Luck, M., Honari, S.: Distribution matching losses can hallucinate features in medical image translation. In: Frangi, A.F., Schnabel, J.A., Davatzikos, C., Alberola-López, C., Fichtinger, G. (eds.) MICCAI 2018. LNCS, vol. 11070, pp. 529–536. Springer, Cham (2018). https://doi.org/10.1007/978-3-030-00928-1_60
5. Dewey, B.E., et al.: DeepHarmony: a deep learning approach to contrast harmonization across scanner changes. Magnetic Resonance Imag. **64**, 160–170 (2019). https://doi.org/10.1016/j.mri.2019.05.041
6. Fortin, J.P., Sweeney, E.M., Muschelli, J., Crainiceanu, C.M., Shinohara, R.T.: Alzheimers Disease Neuroimaging Initiative: removing inter-subject technical variability in magnetic resonance imaging studies. Neuroimage **132**, 198–212 (2016). https://doi.org/10.1016/j.neuroimage.2016.02.036
7. Jang, E., Gu, S., Poole, B.: Categorical reparameterization with gumbel-softmax. arXiv preprint arXiv:1611.01144 (2016)
8. Jog, A., Carass, A., Roy, S., Pham, D., Prince, J.: MR image synthesis by contrast learning on neighborhood ensembles. Med. Image Anal. **24**(1), 63 – 76 (2015). https://doi.org/10.1016/j.media.2015.05.002

9. Kingma, D.P., Ba, J.: Adam: a method for stochastic optimization (2014). http://arxiv.org/abs/1412.6980
10. Liu, Y., et al.: Variational intensity cross channel encoder for unsupervised vessel segmentation on oct angiography. In: Medical Imaging 2020: Image Processing. vol. 11313, p. 113130Y. International Society for Optics and Photonics (2020)
11. Nyúl, L.G., Udupa, J.K., Zhang, X.: New variants of a method of MRI scale standardization. IEEE Trans. Med. Imag. **19**(2), 143–150 (2000). https://doi.org/10.1109/42.836373
12. Reinhold, J.C., Dewey, B.E., Carass, A., Prince, J.L.: Evaluating the impact of intensity normalization on MR image synthesis. In: Medical Imaging 2019: Image Processing. vol. 10949, p. 109493H. International Society for Optics and Photonics, March 2019. https://doi.org/10.1117/12.2513089
13. Ronneberger, O., Fischer, P., Brox, T.: U-Net: convolutional networks for biomedical image segmentation. In: Navab, N., Hornegger, J., Wells, W.M., Frangi, A.F. (eds.) MICCAI 2015. LNCS, vol. 9351, pp. 234–241. Springer, Cham (2015). https://doi.org/10.1007/978-3-319-24574-4_28
14. Rousseau, F.: Brain Hallucination. In: Computer Vision - ECCV 2008, pp. 497–508. Springer, Heidelberg (2008). https://doi.org/10.1007/978-3-540-88682-2_38
15. Roy, S., Carass, A., Prince, J.: A compressed sensing approach for MR tissue contrast synthesis. In: Information Processing in Medical Imaging, pp. 371–383. Springer, Heidelberg (2011). https://doi.org/10.1007/978-3-642-22092-0_31
16. Shinohara, R.T., et al.: NAIMS cooperative: volumetric analysis from a harmonized multisite brain MRI study of a single subject with multiple sclerosis. Am. J. Neuroradiol. **38**(8), 1501–1509 (2017). https://doi.org/10.3174/ajnr.A5254
17. Tustison, N.J., et al.: N4ITK: improved N3 bias correction. IEEE Trans. Med. Imag. **29**(6), 1310–1320 (2010)
18. Zhao, C., et al.: Applications of a deep learning method for anti-aliasing and super-resolution in MRI. Magn. Resonance Imag. **64**, 132 – 141 (2019). https://doi.org/https://doi.org/10.1016/j.mri.2019.05.038
19. Zhu, J.Y., Park, T., Isola, P., Efros, A.A.: Unpaired image-to-image translation using cycle-consistent adversarial networks. In: 2017 IEEE International Conference on Computer Vision (ICCV) (2017)

Automated Acquisition Planning for Magnetic Resonance Spectroscopy in Brain Cancer

Patrick J. Bolan[1]($\boxtimes$) (iD), Francesca Branzoli[2,3] (iD), Anna Luisa Di Stefano[4,5] (iD),
Lucia Nichelli[2,3], Romain Valabregue[2,3] (iD), Sara L. Saunders[1] (iD),
Mehmet Akçakaya[1,6] (iD), Marc Sanson[3,4,7], Stéphane Lehéricy[2,3],
and Małgorzata Marjańska[1] (iD)

[1] Center for Magnetic Resonance Research, Department of Radiology, University of Minnesota,
Minneapolis, MN, USA
bola0035@umn.edu
[2] Institut du Cerveau – ICM, Centre de NeuroImagerie de Recherche - CENIR, Paris, France
[3] Sorbonne Université, Inserm U 1127, CNRS, UMR 7225, Paris, France
[4] Hôpital de la Pitié-Salpêtrière, Service de Neurologie 2, Paris, France
[5] Department of Neurology, Foch Hospital, Suresnes, Paris, France
[6] Department of Electrical and Computer Engineering, University of Minnesota, Minneapolis,
MN, USA
[7] Onconeurotek Tumor Bank, Institut du Cerveau et de la Moelle épinère – ICM, Paris, France

Abstract. In vivo magnetic resonance spectroscopy (MRS) can provide clinically valuable metabolic information from brain tumors that can be used for prognosis and monitoring response to treatment. Unfortunately, this technique has not been widely adopted in clinical practice or even clinical trials due to the difficulty in acquiring and analyzing the data. In this work we propose a computational approach to solve one of the most critical technical challenges: the problem of quickly and accurately positioning an MRS volume of interest (a *cuboid* voxel) inside a tumor using MR images for guidance. The proposed automated method comprises a convolutional neural network to segment the lesion, followed by a discrete optimization to position an MRS voxel optimally within the lesion. In a retrospective comparison, the novel automated method is shown to provide improved lesion coverage compared to manual voxel placement.

Keywords: Brain cancer · Medical image segmentation · Image guided intervention

1 Introduction

In vivo magnetic resonance spectroscopy (MRS) can measure the concentration of >20 brain metabolites non-invasively. Several of these metabolites provide important clinical information. For example, the presence of the metabolite D-2-hydroxyglutarate (2HG) indicates that a tumor has a mutation in the isocitrate dehydrogenase enzyme, which is associated with favorable prognosis [1, 2]; high levels of choline-containing compounds (tCho) reflect aberrations in phospholipid metabolism and can be used for monitoring

© Springer Nature Switzerland AG 2020
A. L. Martel et al. (Eds.): MICCAI 2020, LNCS 12267, pp. 730–739, 2020.
https://doi.org/10.1007/978-3-030-59728-3_71

progression and treatment [3–6]. While single-voxel MRS offers clear clinical value, it is not widely performed outside academic medical centers because it requires specialized expertise to perform the acquisition and analyze the data. In this paper we address the problem of preparing the MRS acquisition, which requires a high level of skill to produce quality results. The operator must review and interpret clinical MR images, identify pathology and normal anatomy, weigh judgements to maximize lesion coverage while minimizing contributions from normal tissues and artifacts, and position a 3D cuboid (a voxel) in the lesion, all in real-time while the patient lies in the scanner. The need for technical expertise to perform accurate and consistent MRS voxel placement has been a critical barrier to wider use of this valuable technique [7].

We propose a computational approach to automate and optimize MRS voxel placement in lesions. This consists of 1) automatic segmentation to accurately delineate the full extent of the tumor, followed by 2) optimization of the voxel geometry to maximize tumor coverage and avoid non-involved tissues. The tumor segmentation is performed using the clinical T_2-weighted MR images as input to a convolutional neural network, with transfer learning from a pre-trained network on the publicly available BraTS dataset. The voxel is then positioned within the segmented region by maximizing an objective function that codifies the tradeoffs considered by an expert spectroscopist. We demonstrate this approach on an institutional dataset with 60 glioma cases, and retrospectively compare the performance of the automated approach with manually performed expert voxel placements.

2 Methods

2.1 System Design

The proposed automated voxel placement system has two distinct steps, lesion segmentation and voxel geometric optimization, as shown in Fig. 1. This division was chosen because the problem of brain tumor segmentation has been studied and there are well-established approaches, whereas the problem of how to place an optimal voxel inside a lesion has not been previously addressed. The use of an analytical objective function provides flexibility to tune performance based on the MR spectroscopist's expertise or preference for a specific application.

Fig. 1. Schema for automated voxel placement.

2.2 Data

Our primary dataset [8, 9] consisted of 60 cases with MR imaging and spectroscopy acquired in patients with low-grade (II and III) gliomas. Acquisitions were performed using a 3 T whole-body system (MAGNETOM *Verio*, Siemens, Erlangen, Germany) equipped with a 32-channel receive-only head coil. The primary anatomical imaging was performed using a multi-slice 2D T_2-weighted (T_2w) sagittal FLAIR (resolution: 1.0×1.0 mm, 155 slices with thickness 1.1 mm, TR/TE = 5000/399 ms, scan time = 5.02 min). Using these images for guidance, a spectroscopic voxel was manually positioned in the lesion by an expert spectroscopist while the patient remained in the scanner. MR spectra were acquired using a single-voxel MEGA-PRESS sequence [10, 11] (TR/TE = 2000/68 ms) optimized to measure the 2HG signal at 4.02 ppm with editing applied at 1.9 ppm for the edit-on condition and at 7.5 ppm for the edit-off condition, in an interleaved fashion (128 pairs of scans, scan time = 8.5 min).

At the time of the scan, the MRS expert does not have a precise lesion segmentation for guidance – one must interpret the images directly to determine the extent of the tumor. To judge the quality of the MRS placement, we retrospectively performed slice-by-slice segmentation of tumor and necrotic regions. These segmentations were performed by a neurooncologist with 8 years of experience, using the software package ITK-SNAP [12], and using the T_2w-FLAIR images for guidance. These manual lesion masks were used as the gold-standard definition of the tumor extent.

For model development, the dataset was divided into 36/8/8 cases for training/validation/testing, where each case included the MR images, MR spectroscopic voxel placement, and the manually segmented lesion mask. Note that 8 cases were reserved for a future test set.

Model training also used data from the 2018 BraTS tumor segmentation challenge [13–15].

2.3 Segmentation with a CNN

We trained a convolutional neural network (CNN) that could replicate the manual lesion segmentation in our dataset. To minimize inference time and enable slice-by-slice parallel processing, we considered only 2D network designs. Our CNN was based on a 2D U-Net architecture [16] but with the encoding arm replaced with the ResNet-50 model [17], a widely used convolutional network with 50 layers that has been pre-trained on the ImageNet dataset [18]. The use of a pre-trained encoding network is a form of transfer learning, which can provide better performance when training on limited datasets [19], as the encoder is already tuned to represent low-level features (edges, textures, shapes, etc.). The model was implemented using the dynamic U-Net provided in the open source *fastai* library [20] implemented in PyTorch [21] and trained on a server with an NVidia Titan RTX gpu. The model used *fastai*'s default batch normalization layers and ReLU activations.

To further exploit transfer learning, we first trained our full model using data from the BraTS 2018 brain tumor segmentation challenge. Only the T_2w-FLAIR images and manual segmentations from this dataset were used. From the publicly available training data of 285 cases, we divided the data in training/validation/testing (200/43/42) cases. The T_2w-FLAIR images were reformatted as axial 2D slices with 120×120 resolution. Training was performed using whole-tumor ROI masks as the target label, which excludes necrosis but includes both enhancing and non-enhancing regions, reflecting the voxel targeting strategy typically used for low-grade gliomas. The model was trained for

20 epochs using standard data augmentation methods (flip, rotate, zoom, affine warp, and scaling), a batch size of 64, a binary cross-entropy loss function, an Adam optimizer [22], and using cyclic learning rates (once-cycle policy [23]) with a base learning rate of 4e-6.

The T_2w-FLAIR images in the BraTS dataset were somewhat different than our internal images: they were originally acquired in different orientations and with different resolution, they were "skull-stripped" to remove the skull and skin. Skull-stripping was not performed on our data because it was found to cut off some peripheral tumors. Therefore, after training on BraTS data the model was fine-tuned by training on 36/8 (training/validation) cases from our internal dataset for an additional 20 epochs. After all training, a final test set of 8 cases not seen during training was evaluated.

2.4   Geometric Objective Function

For lesions of irregular shape, there is not an objectively "correct" voxel placement. Those with expertise in MRS will plan voxels based on a tradeoff between voxel size, partial volume effects, and spectral quality, which may depend on the specific disease or on the MR methods used. We developed an objective function to encode two primary considerations: the size of the MRS voxel, and portion of the voxel that contains lesion. We defined V_{target} as the volume of the intersection between the gold-standard lesion mask and the MRS voxel, and f_{target} as the fraction of voxel that contains lesion. If V_{target} is too small, the measurement will not have sufficient signal-to-noise; if too large, the signal will be inhomogeneous and spectral quality will decrease. In contrast, MRS performance is maximized when $f_{target} \sim 1$, as the voxel would be within the lesion. Note that these parameters are not independent, rather they encode the MRS expert's goals of maximizing lesion coverage and meeting signal-to-noise requirements. Thus we propose an objective function consisting of two Gaussian functions:

$$F_{obj}(\theta) = \exp\left(-\frac{1}{2}\left(\frac{V_{target}(\theta) - \mu_V}{\sigma_V}\right)^2\right) \exp\left(-\frac{1}{2}\left(\frac{f_{target}(\theta) - \mu_f}{\sigma_f}\right)^2\right), \quad (1)$$

where (μ_V, σ_V) are the mean and standard deviation of the V_{target} objective distribution, (μ_f, σ_f) are the mean and standard deviation for f_{target}, and θ are the nine geometric parameters defining the voxel placement (position, size, and rotation angles of the cuboid). Selection of the distribution parameters is described below in Sect. 3.1.

The objective function was maximized using numerical discrete optimization in Matlab. For each iteration, the voxel coordinates were used to generate a 3D raster mask of the voxel location, which was compared with the raster lesion segmentation to calculate f_{target}, V_{target}, and the objective function value. Starting with a small voxel placed in the lesion centroid, a single-parameter discrete 1D search was performed over each of the size, position, and angle parameters, and then repeated for 3 iterations.

2.5   Performance Comparison

The manual and fully-automated voxel placements were compared by measuring f_{target}, V_{target}, and V_{voxel} (total voxel volume) for both methods on a per-case basis. Each method used the retrospectively drawn lesion mask as the gold-standard lesion definition for calculating the performance metrics. Statistical comparisons were performed with a 2-sided t-test.

3 Results

3.1 Objective Function Tuning

To select the objective function parameters, we calculated f_{target} and V_{target} from each of the 60 manual MRS placements in our dataset. These are shown in Fig. 2a. From these, we inferred that the expert was seeking a V_{target} of ~8–8.5 mL. We therefore selected parameters for the prospective objective function to model this intent, setting $\mu_V = 8.5$ mL and $\mu_f = 1$. The σ values for the distributions were heuristically selected to produce an objective function that reflected the spectroscopist's intent and provide steep gradients near the desired solution:$\sigma_V = 2$ mL and $\sigma_f = 0.25$. With these parameters the prospective objective function is plotted in Fig. 2b.

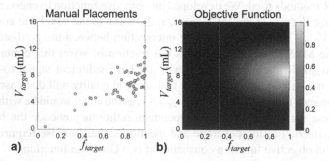

Fig. 2. Voxel placement properties a) retrospectively observed from the manual MRS placements, and b) proposed for the geometric objective function.

3.2 Tumor Segmentation

With initial training of 20 epochs on the BraTS dataset (requiring ~4 h), the model produced a Sorenson-Dice [24] score of 0.81 on the validation dataset. Twenty more epochs were trained using our internal dataset (~1 h) to give a final score of 0.88. Evaluating the trained model on our test dataset gave a mean score of 0.87, with inference requiring 5.2 s/slice. Examples of cases with representative segmentation performance are given in Fig. 3.

3.3 Overall Performance

The overall system performs lesion segmentation and voxel optimization one volume at a time, with a stack of 155 2D T_2w-FLAIR images as input. This was performed for

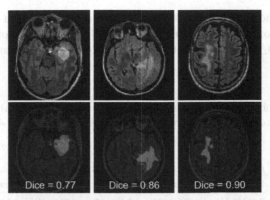

Fig. 3. Examples of lesion segmentation with our CNN. The top row shows T_2-weighted FLAIR images; the bottom row shows correctly predicted regions in magenta, with overestimation in red and underestimation in blue. (Color figure online)

all 44 cases in the training/validation set, and separately for the 8 test cases. The full calculation (not including file i/o) required an average of 21.7 s/case (range 16–35 s, stdev 3.7 s).

A plot of the f_{target} and V_{target} for all 52 cases is given in Fig. 4. Compared to the manual voxel placement performance (Fig. 2a), the automatic method gives more consistent results for the majority of voxel placements.

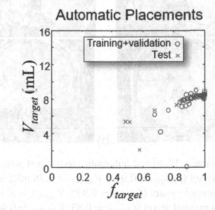

Fig. 4. Voxel placement parameters for fully automatic placements in the training/validation and test datasets. Plotted on the same axes as Fig. 2a for comparison.

Mean values and standard deviations for f_{target}, V_{target}, and V_{voxel} are given in Table 1 for both the fully automated processing as well as the manually placed voxels. In the combined training + validation dataset, f_{target} is larger ($p = 0.003$) with the automatic method than the manual method, indicating that those voxels are more precisely placed in the lesions and thus their spectra will be more representative of tumor metabolites. There were no significant differences with the other parameters. The trend of higher

f_{target} is seen in the test dataset but was not significant with only n = 8. The standard deviations of the voxel placements are smaller for all parameters in both datasets with the automated method, suggesting greater consistency of voxel placement than with manual voxel placements.

Table 1. Comparison of performance metrics (mean and standard deviation) for manual vs. fully-automated voxel placement in the combined training + validation (n = 44) and test (n = 8) datasets.

	f_{target} mean, [std]		V_{target} (mL) mean, [std]		V_{voxel} (mL) mean, [std]	
	Manual	Automatic	Manual	Automatic	Manual	Automatic
Training + validation	0.813 [0.23]	0.926 [0.075]	7.47 [4.25]	7.85 [1.43]	9.14 [4.81]	8.47 [1.40]
Test	0.690 [0.23]	0.740 [0.20]	7.30 [4.09]	6.45 [2.15]	11.32 [8.42]	8.75 [2.26]

Two examples comparing manual and automatic voxel placements are provided in Fig. 5.

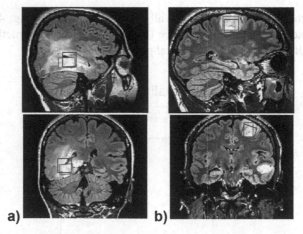

a)   b)

Fig. 5. Two examples of manual (blue) and automatic (red) voxel placements. a) Example from test set, where the manual voxel ($f_{target} = 0.973$, $V_{target} = 7.78$ mL) includes a necrotic region which is avoided by the automatic voxel ($f_{target} = 0.995$, $V_{target} = 8.43$ mL). b) Example from CNN training set showing a manual voxel ($f_{target} = 0.83$, $V_{target} = 6.46$ mL) was unnecessarily rotated and placed too low in the tumor, compared to the automated voxel ($f_{target} = 0.90$, $V_{target} = 7.43$ mL). (Color figure online)

4 Discussion

The automated MRS voxel placement method presented here gives lesion coverage that is superior to manual placement by an expert. The time required to calculate a voxel placement is short enough for use in clinical trials or practice. This could be made even shorter by software optimization or replacing the discrete search with a separately trained CNN. We chose in this work to keep the objective function separate so that it would be more easily interpretable by MRS experts and enable it to be more easily tailored for different voxel placement strategies.

While automatic voxel placement has been previously reported for normal brain regions [25–29], these approaches use atlases to exploit the consistency in anatomic structure across subjects, and are not directly applicable for targeting lesions with variable structure. To our knowledge this is the first system designed for placing MRS voxels inside pathologic lesions. This approach could readily be adapted for cancers in other organs (e.g., breast, liver), or for assessing other brain lesions (e.g., multiple sclerosis, abscesses).

This study had several limitations. Firstly, our institutional glioma dataset was small, particularly after partitioning out subsets for training and validating the CNN. Secondly, our results only assessed lesion coverage and not MRS performance, which may be impacted by other factors not considered in our model. Thirdly, all of the manual MRS voxel placements were performed by a single expert operator. All three of these limitations should be addressed with a larger study using manual voxel placements from multiple experts and using MRS metrics for assessing relative performance. Finally, while the 2D CNN showed acceptable performance, other deep networks (e.g., 3D U-Nets, DenseNets, etc.) may provide better performance and should be investigated.

5 Conclusion

In this work, we have demonstrated an automatic MRS voxel placement system that gives superior lesion coverage compared to traditional manual placement. This approach can help reduce the need for live MRS expertise during a scan and may provide more consistent MRS measurements for clinical trials and routine practice.

Acknowledgements. This work was supported by NIH grants P41 EB027061, P41 EB015894, and P30 NS076408; Investissements d'avenir ANR-10-IAIHU-06 and ANR-11-INBS-0006; INCa-DGOS-Inserm_12560 (SiRIC CURAMUS)

References

1. Yan, H., Parsons, D.W., Jin, G., et al.: IDH1 and IDH2 mutations in gliomas. N. Engl. J. Med. **360**, 765–773 (2009). https://doi.org/10.1056/NEJMoa0808710
2. Tanaka, K., Sasayama, T., Mizukawa, K., et al.: Combined IDH1 mutation and MGMT methylation status on long-term survival of patients with cerebral low-grade glioma. Clin. Neurol. Neurosurg. **138**, 37–44 (2015). https://doi.org/10.1016/j.clineuro.2015.07.019
3. Nelson, M.T., Everson, L.I., Garwood, M., et al.: MR Spectroscopy in the diagnosis and treatment of breast cancer. Semin. Breast Dis. **11**, 100–105 (2008). https://doi.org/10.1053/j.sembd.2008.03.004

4. Muruganandham, M., Clerkin, P.P., Smith, B.J., et al.: 3-Dimensional magnetic resonance spectroscopic imaging at 3 Tesla for early response assessment of glioblastoma patients during external beam radiation therapy. Int. J. Radiat. Oncol. Biol. Phys. **90**, 181–189 (2014). https://doi.org/10.1016/j.ijrobp.2014.05.014

5. Laprie, A., Catalaa, I., Cassol, E., et al.: Proton magnetic resonance spectroscopic imaging in newly diagnosed glioblastoma: predictive value for the site of postradiotherapy relapse in a prospective longitudinal study. Int. J. Radiat. Oncol. Biol. Phys. **70**, 773–781 (2008). https://doi.org/10.1016/j.ijrobp.2007.10.039

6. Shim, H., Wei, L., Holder, C.A., et al.: Use of high-resolution volumetric MR spectroscopic imaging in assessing treatment response of glioblastoma to an HDAC inhibitor. AJR Am. J. Roentgenol. **203**, W158–W165 (2014). https://doi.org/10.2214/AJR.14.12518

7. Tietze, A., Choi, C., Mickey, B., et al.: Noninvasive assessment of isocitrate dehydrogenase mutation status in cerebral gliomas by magnetic resonance spectroscopy in a clinical setting. J. Neurosurg. **128**, 391–398 (2018). https://doi.org/10.3171/2016.10.JNS161793

8. Branzoli, F., Di Stefano, A.L., Capelle, L., et al.: Highly specific determination of IDH status using edited in vivo magnetic resonance spectroscopy. Neuro-Oncology **20**, 907–916 (2018). https://doi.org/10.1093/neuonc/nox214

9. Branzoli, F., Pontoizeau, C., Tchara, L., et al.: Cystathionine as a marker for 1p/19q codeleted gliomas by in vivo magnetic resonance spectroscopy. Neuro-Oncology **21**, 765–774 (2019). https://doi.org/10.1093/neuonc/noz031

10. Mescher, M., Merkle, H., Kirsch, J., et al.: Simultaneous in vivo spectral editing and water suppression. NMR Biomed. **11**, 266–272 (1998). https://doi.org/10.1002/(sici)1099-1492(199810)11:6%3c266:aid-nbm530%3e3.0.co;2-j

11. Marjańska, M., Lehéricy, S., Valabrègue, R., et al.: Brain dynamic neurochemical changes in dystonic patients: a magnetic resonance spectroscopy study. Mov. Disord. **28**, 201–209 (2013). https://doi.org/10.1002/mds.25279

12. Yushkevich, P.A., Piven, J., Hazlett, H.C., et al.: User-guided 3D active contour segmentation of anatomical structures: significantly improved efficiency and reliability. Neuroimage **31**, 1116–1128 (2006). https://doi.org/10.1016/j.neuroimage.2006.01.015

13. Menze, B.H., Jakab, A., Bauer, S., et al.: The multimodal brain tumor image segmentation benchmark (BRATS). IEEE Trans. Med. Imaging **34**, 1993–2024 (2015). https://doi.org/10.1109/TMI.2014.2377694

14. Bakas, S., Akbari, H., Sotiras, A., et al.: Advancing the cancer genome atlas glioma MRI collections with expert segmentation labels and radiomic features. Sci. Data **4**, 1–13 (2017). https://doi.org/10.1038/sdata.2017.117

15. Bakas, S., Reyes, M., Jakab, A., et al.: Identifying the best machine learning algorithms for brain tumor segmentation, progression assessment, and overall survival prediction in the BRATS challenge. arXiv:181102629 [cs, stat] (2019)

16. Ronneberger, O., Fischer, P., Brox, T.: U-Net: convolutional networks for biomedical image segmentation. In: Navab, N., Hornegger, J., Wells, William M., Frangi, Alejandro F. (eds.) MICCAI 2015. LNCS, vol. 9351, pp. 234–241. Springer, Cham (2015). https://doi.org/10.1007/978-3-319-24574-4_28

17. He, K., Zhang, X., Ren, S., Sun, J.: Deep residual learning for image recognition. arXiv:151203385 [cs] (2015)

18. Russakovsky, O., Deng, J., Su, H., et al.: ImageNet large scale visual recognition challenge. arXiv:14090575 [cs] (2015)

19. Romero, M., Interian, Y., Solberg, T., Valdes, G.: Training deep learning models with small datasets. arXiv:191206761 [cs, stat] (2019)

20. Howard, J., Gugger, S.: Fastai: a layered API for deep learning. Information **11**, 108 (2020). https://doi.org/10.3390/info11020108

21. Paszke, A., Gross, S., Massa, F., et al.: PyTorch: an imperative style, high-performance deep learning library. In: Wallach, H., Larochelle, H., Beygelzimer, A., et al. (eds.) Advances in Neural Information Processing Systems 32, pp. 8026–8037. Curran Associates, Inc. (2019)

22. Kingma, D.P., Ba, J.: Adam: a method for stochastic optimization. arXiv:14126980 [cs] (2017)

23. Smith, L.N.: A disciplined approach to neural network hyper-parameters: part 1 – learning rate, batch size, momentum, and weight decay. arXiv:180309820 [cs, stat] (2018)

24. Taha, A.A., Hanbury, A.: Metrics for evaluating 3D medical image segmentation: analysis, selection, and tool. BMC Med. Imaging 15, 29 (2015). https://doi.org/10.1186/s12880-015-0068-x

25. Park, Y.W., Deelchand, D.K., Joers, J.M., et al.: AutoVOI: real-time automatic prescription of volume-of-interest for single voxel spectroscopy. Magn. Reson. Med. 80, 1787–1798 (2018). https://doi.org/10.1002/mrm.27203

26. Bian, W., Li, Y., Crane, J.C., Nelson, S.J.: Fully automated atlas-based method for prescribing 3D PRESS MR spectroscopic imaging: Toward robust and reproducible metabolite measurements in human brain. Magn. Reson. Med. 79, 636–642 (2018). https://doi.org/10.1002/mrm.26718

27. Martínez-Ramón, M., Gallardo-Antolín, A., Cid-Sueiro, J., et al.: Automatic placement of outer volume suppression slices in MR spectroscopic imaging of the human brain. Magn. Reson. Med. 63, 592–600 (2010). https://doi.org/10.1002/mrm.22275

28. Ozhinsky, E., Vigneron, D.B., Chang, S.M., Nelson, S.J.: Automated prescription of oblique brain 3D magnetic resonance spectroscopic imaging. Magn. Reson. Med. 69, 920–930 (2013). https://doi.org/10.1002/mrm.24339

29. Yung, K.-T., Zheng, W., Zhao, C., et al.: Atlas-based automated positioning of outer volume suppression slices in short-echo time 3D MR spectroscopic imaging of the human brain. Magn. Reson. Med. 66, 911–922 (2011). https://doi.org/10.1002/mrm.22887

Positron Emission Tomography

Simultaneous Denoising and Motion Estimation for Low-Dose Gated PET Using a Siamese Adversarial Network with Gate-to-Gate Consistency Learning

Bo Zhou[1], Yu-Jung Tsai[2], and Chi Liu[1,2]([⊠])

[1] Biomedical Engineering, Yale University, New Haven, CT, USA
chi.liu@yale.edu
[2] Radiology and Biomedical Imaging, Yale University, New Haven, CT, USA

Abstract. Gating is commonly used in PET imaging to reduce respiratory motion blurring and facilitate more sophisticated motion correction methods. In the applications of low dose PET, however, reducing injection dose causes increased noise and reduces signal-to-noise ratio (SNR), subsequently corrupting the motion estimation/correction steps, causing inferior image quality. To tackle these issues, we first propose a Siamese adversarial network (SAN) that can efficiently recover high dose gated image volume from low dose gated image volume. To ensure the appearance consistency between the recovered gated volumes, we then utilize a pre-trained motion estimation network incorporated into SAN that enables the constraint of gate-to-gate (G2G) consistency. With high-quality recovered gated volumes, gate-to-gate motion vectors can be simultaneously outputted from the motion estimation network. Comprehensive evaluations on a low dose gated PET dataset of 29 subjects demonstrate that our method can effectively recover the low dose gated PET volumes, with an average PSNR of 37.16 and SSIM of 0.97, and simultaneously generate robust motion estimation that could benefit subsequent motion corrections.

Keywords: Low-dose Gated PET · Denoising · Motion estimation · Motion correction

1 Introduction

PET is a commonly used functional imaging modality. To obtain high quality image, a small amount of radioactive tracer is administered to patient, introducing radiation exposure to both patients and healthcare providers [1]. PET data acquisition typically takes several minutes. During this period, patient's

Electronic supplementary material The online version of this chapter (https://doi.org/10.1007/978-3-030-59728-3_72) contains supplementary material, which is available to authorized users.

© Springer Nature Switzerland AG 2020
A. L. Martel et al. (Eds.): MICCAI 2020, LNCS 12267, pp. 743–752, 2020.
https://doi.org/10.1007/978-3-030-59728-3_72

breathing inevitably introduces blurring in the lung and abdominal regions. Respiratory gating facilitated by external motion monitoring devices are typically used to reduce respiratory-induced motion blurring. However, each gated image is generated by only a fraction of detected events, leading to high image noise in each gate. To address the noise issue, previous works proposed motion correction approaches involving non-rigid image registration among gated images, and utilize the motion vectors to correct motion by using all detected events to reduce image noise [2]. In the applications of radiation dose reduction, reduction of injection dose is the first choice but will increase the image noise and result in low signal-to-noise ratio (SNR). In the cases where respiratory gating is performed using low-dose data, the image noise is further increased, potentially causing errors in motion vector estimation, which subsequently affects the final motion correction results, as illustrated in Fig. 1. To address this challenge, we aim to simultaneously tackle the image denoising and motion estimation problems in low-dose gated PET data.

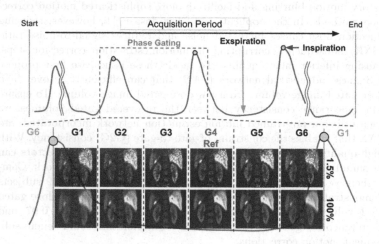

Fig. 1. Illustration of phase gated PET acquisition with 6 gates for both 100% full count and 1.5% count levels. End-expiration gate with the least intra-gate motion (G4) is used as reference gate. Each low dose gated volume needs to be denoised and registered to the reference gated volume.

Previous works on denoising low-dose PET can be summarized into two categories: conventional post-processing [3–5] and deep learning based post-processing [6–9]. Conventional post-processing techniques, such as Gaussian filtering, is the standard technique to reduce PET image noise, but has challenge to preserve local structure. More recently, non-local mean filter [3] and block-matching 4D filter [4] have been proposed to denoise low-dose PET while better preserving the structural information. Deep learning based methods, such as deep auto-context CNN [6], 3D cGAN [7], UNet [8], and GAN [9], were developed for recovering standard-dose PET from low-dose PET. Compared to conventional methods, these deep learning based methods achieved promising denoising performance on static low-dose PET. However, none of these previous studies addressed denoising and motion estimation in low-dose respiratory gated PET in a unified fashion.

In this work, we proposed a Siamese adversarial network (SAN) with gate-to-gate consistency learning (G2G) to simultaneously denoise low dose gated volumes and estimate the motion among the gates. We evaluated our method on a challenging low dose gated PET dataset with only 1.5% count level. Our experimental results demonstrated that our proposed method can effectively reduce the noise while preserving the structural information and improve the accuracy of motion estimation.

2   Problem Formulation

Assuming a phase gated PET exam generates 6 gates with gate 4 as the reference gate, we denote high-dose PET (HDPET) and low-dose PET (LDPET) gated volumes as $H_n, L_n \in \mathbb{R}^{h \times w \times d}$ with gate index $n \in \{1, 2, 3, 4, 5, 6\}$ and volume size $h \times w \times d$. The transformation predicted between $\{L_4, L_n\}$ is expected to be different from the transformation predicted between $\{H_4, H_n\}$ due to the high noise level of LDPET. Given that the distribution of HDPET is unknown, our goal is to recover H_n from the degraded L_n. Previous methods have been trying to solve the inverse problem by finding the generative model $\mathcal{P}_D$ parameterized by θ_D such that $\mathcal{P}_D(\sum_{n=1}^{6} L_n; \theta_D) = \bar{H}_{nmc} \approx H_{nmc}$, where $\bar{H}_{nmc}$ is the non-gated denoised volume with no motion correction (nmc). Since no motion estimation and corresponding motion correction component are considered, degradation in the final image can be expected. Therefore, we aim to tackle these issues by recovering the HDPET from LDPET for each gate and simultaneously estimate the motion field between gates. Specifically, we want to find single gate generative model $\mathcal{P}_D$ such that $\mathcal{P}_D(L_n; \theta_D) = \bar{H}_n \approx H_n$ where H_n is the recovered HDPET for gate n. Then, the motion transformation between the reference gate (assume to be gate 4 here) and gate n is estimated by $\bar{T}_n = \mathcal{P}_R(\mathcal{P}_D(L_4; \theta_D), \mathcal{P}_D(L_n; \theta_D); \theta_R) \approx T_n$, where $\bar{T}_n$ is the predicted transformation from our motion estimator $\mathcal{P}_R$. In this work, our goal is to obtain the optimal $\mathcal{P}_D$ and $\mathcal{P}_R$ for simultaneous denoising and motion estimation.

3   Methods

The overall pipeline of our method is illustrated in Fig. 2. It consists of three major parts: 1) Siamese generative networks with supervision from our structure recovery loss; 2) unsupervised motion estimation network; and 3) gate-to-gate consistency training. The Siamese generator G maps the target gate LDPET (L_{tgt}) and the reference gate LDPET (L_{ref}) to the HDPET space simultaneously, thus generating denoised HDPET gated volumes. The generator G is first optimized based on the structure recovery loss that measures the dissimilarity between prediction and ground truth, yielding the high quality denoised HDPET volumes. In the meantime, the motion estimation network R is pre-trained using the ground truth HDPET gated volumes H, and concatenated to the Siamese generative networks. By replacing the input for R with the synthetic HDPET volumes $\hat{H}$ generated by G, the joint network enforces gate-to-gate consistency in the transformed synthetic HDPET for each target gate, providing additional supervision for training G. The details are as follows.

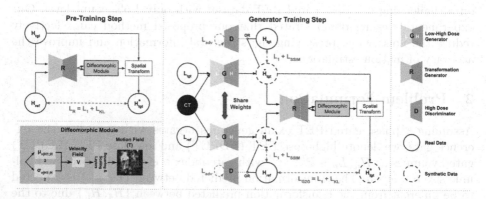

Fig. 2. Our two-stage training procedure consists of: the pre-training of our motion estimator (R), and Siamese adversarial training of our generator. Two shared weights generators G learn mapping from LDPET to HDPET, which are supervised by a structure recovery loss ($\mathcal{L}_{SR} = \mathcal{L}_1 + \mathcal{L}_{SSIM} + \mathcal{L}_{adv}$), and a transform consistency loss ($\mathcal{L}_{G2G} = \mathcal{L}_1 + \mathcal{L}_{KL}$), respectively. Motion estimator R is pre-trained with the ground truth HDPET, and concatenated to the generator for end-to-end optimization. Network architecture details are listed in the supplementary.

Siamese Generative Network. is illustrated in Fig. 2. The Siamese generative network G with encoding and decoding architecture is firstly supervised by a $\mathcal{L}_1$ loss, a structural similarity (SSIM) loss, and an adversarial loss to ensure the noise reduction and structure recovery. Specifically, we use a $\mathcal{L}_1$ loss to ensure the general appearance recovery and a $\mathcal{L}_{SSIM}$ loss to ensure the fine-detailed structure recovery. $\mathcal{L}_1$ loss allows noise suppression and SNR improvement, at the expense of reduced image sharpness. On the other hand, $\mathcal{L}_{SSIM}$ loss encourages image to have high contrast, sharpness and resolution. Given L_{tgt} and L_{ref} the target and reference LDPET gated volumes respectively, G takes a pair of $[L_{tgt}, L_{ref}]$ and channel-wise concatenates each volumes with anatomical prior CT (ρ) to predict $\bar{H}_{tgt} = G(L_{tgt}, \rho; \theta_G)$ and $\bar{H}_{ref} = G(L_{ref}, \rho; \theta_G)$ simultaneously. The $\mathcal{L}_1$ loss and the $\mathcal{L}_{SSIM}$ loss can be written as:

$$\mathcal{L}_1 = \sum_i ||H_i - \bar{H}_i||, \quad i \in \{tgt, ref\} \tag{1}$$

$$\mathcal{L}_{SSIM} = \sum_i [1 - SSIM(H_i, \bar{H}_i)], \quad i \in \{tgt, ref\} \tag{2a}$$

$$SSIM(x,y) = \frac{2m_x m_y + C_1}{m_x^2 + m_y^2 + C_1} \cdot \frac{2\sigma_{xy} + C_2}{\sigma_x^2 + \sigma_y^2 + C_2} \tag{2b}$$

where $[m_x, m_y]$ and $[\sigma_x, \sigma_y]$ denote mean and standard deviation of an image pair $[x, y]$. The cross-covariance of $[x, y]$ is denoted as σ_{xy}. C_1 and C_2 are constant parameters. The adversarial loss from the discriminator D provides an indication of discrepancy between prediction and ground truth as both G and D progressively optimized. Thus, the adversarial loss is also added to minimize the perceptual difference between prediction and ground truth from a CNN perspective. We utilize the adversarial loss in Wasseerstein GAN with gradient penalty (WGAN-GP) to achieve stable adversarial training [10], which is formulated as:

$$\mathcal{L}_{adv} = \sum_i \mathbb{E}[D(\bar{H}_i)] - \mathbb{E}[D(H_i)] + \lambda_{gp}\mathbb{E}[(\|\nabla_{\ddot{H}_i}D(\ddot{H}_i)\|_2 - 1)^2], i \in \{tgt, ref\} \quad (3)$$

where $\ddot{H}$ represents a linear combination of $\bar{H}$ and H with a weight t uniformly sampled between 0 and 1. Thereby, λ_{gp} controls the gradient penalty level and is set to 3 here. The combination of these three loss functions formulates our Structure Recovery (SR) loss as:

$$\mathcal{L}_{SR} = \beta_1 \mathcal{L}_1 + \beta_2 \mathcal{L}_{SSIM} + \beta_3 \mathcal{L}_{adv} \quad (4)$$

where β_1, β_2, and β_3 are loss weights. In our experiments, we empirically set $\beta_1 = 1$, $\beta_2 = 1$, and $\beta_3 = 0.2$ for balance training.

Motion Estimation Network. R aims to predict the transformation between target and reference gated volumes. Here, we use a probabilistic generative model [11] to predict the transformation, as illustrated in Fig. 2's left section. Assuming H_{ref} and H_{tgt} are volumes that need to be registered and the transformation between them is parameterized by a sampled velocity field V, R aims to find the most likely registration field by optimizing the posterior probability $p(V|H_{ref}, H_{tgt})$. Thus, the loss function for network R can be derived and written as:

$$\mathcal{L}_R(H_{ref}, H_{tgt}) = \frac{1}{K}\sum_k \|H_{ref} - T \circ H_{tgt}\| + \text{KL}[q_{\theta_R}(V|H_{ref}, H_{tgt})\|p(V)] \quad (5)$$

where K is the number of samples in each training batch, T is the transformation function parameterized by $V \sim q_{\theta_R}(V|H_{ref}, H_{tgt})$. The first term minimizes the L1 distance between reference volume H_{ref} and warped target volume H_{tgt}. The second term ensures the distribution similarity between posterior and prior of V. $\mathcal{L}_R$ is the transform consistency loss in Fig. 2. During the inference stage, the predicted V is fed into the scaling and squaring layer [12] to integrate V over $[0, 1]$, and produce the final transformation T. Then, T and the target volume H_{tgt} are inputted into the spatial transform layer to generate the warped target volume $T \circ H_{tgt}$. Detailed derivation is in our supplementary.

Gate-to-Gate Consistency Learning. The Siamese generator in the first part maps L to H with SR loss $\mathcal{L}_{SR}$ for individual gates. However, the appearance consistency constraint between gates is not utilized. A gate-to-gate consistency should sustain when the gated volumes are registered. The gate-to-gate consistency learning is achieved by feeding the synthetic pair of HDPET volumes,

$[\bar{H}_{tgt}, \bar{H}_{ref}]$ generated using the Siamese generative network G, into the pre-trained motion estimation network R after concatenating these two networks. Therefore, the transformation prediction process of the joint network can be described as:

$$\bar{T} = R(\bar{H}_{ref}, \bar{H}_{tgt}; \theta_R) = R(G(L_{ref}, \rho; \theta_G), G(L_{tgt}, \rho; \theta_G); \theta_R) \quad (6)$$

Given the transformation $\bar{T}$, we warp the synthetic $\bar{H}_{tgt}$ and obtain $\bar{T} \circ \bar{H}_{tgt}$. We aim to minimize the distance between $\bar{T} \circ \bar{H}_{tgt}$ and ground truth H_{ref}, such that the transformed target gated volume and reference gated volume are consistent. Thus, the gate-to-gate transform consistency loss can be formulated as:

$$\mathcal{L}_{G2G} = \frac{1}{K} \sum_k ||H_{ref} - \bar{T} \circ \bar{H}_{tgt}|| + \text{KL}[q_{\theta_R}(V|\bar{H}_{ref}, \bar{H}_{tgt})||p(V)] \quad (7)$$

The first term encourages the gate-to-gate appearance consistency using a $\mathcal{L}_1$ norm and the second term ensures the distribution similarity between posterior and prior of V. $\mathcal{L}_{G2G}$ provides additional supervision for optimizing G by utilizing the inter-gate relationship. It is the key in our Siamese network design that enables us to randomly sample pairs of gated volume, which augments the number of available training data for each subject to $A_6^2 = 30$. Therefore, the denoising and structural recovery from LDPET to HDPET will be more reliable.

Finally, our full loss function for optimizing G is $\mathcal{L}_{tot} = \mathcal{L}_{SR} + \mathcal{L}_{G2G}$, which is trained in an adversarial manner. G and R try to minimize this loss collaboratively, while D tries to maximize it. To optimize the overall network, we update G, R, and D alternatively by: optimizing D with G and R fixed, then optimizing G with D and R fixed.

3.1 Evaluation with Human Data

We collected 29 pancreas ^{18}F-FPDTBZ [13] PET/CT studies with respiration gating facilitated by the Anzai system. The total acquisition time was 120 mins for each study. We used phase gating to generate 6 gates for each study. To eliminate the mismatch between attenuation correction (AC) map and gated PET, instead of using CT as AC-map, we utilized the maximum likelihood estimation of activity and attenuation (MLAA) [14] to generated AC-map for each gated volume to ensure phase-matched attenuation correction, where CT was used as initial estimation for MLAA iterations. The HDPET volumes were reconstructed with 100% of the listmode data mimicking high radiation dose data. The LDPET volumes were reconstructed with 1.5% of the listmode data with random sampling. Each data was reconstructed into a $400 \times 400 \times 109$ volume with voxel size of $2.032 \times 2.032 \times 2.027 \ mm^3$. The central $200 \times 200 \times 109$ voxels were kept to remove most voxels outside the human body contour and resized to $128 \times 128 \times 128$. The end expiration gate (typically Gate 4) was used as the reference gate since it shows minimum intra-gate motion.

The dataset were split into training set of 22 studies and test set of 7 studies. The evaluation was performed on the 7 test studies with 6 gated volumes in each study. For quantitative evaluation, the denoising results were evaluated by comparing the synthetic HDPET volumes to the ground truth HDPET volumes using the Peak Signal-to-Noise Ratio (PSNR) and Structural Similarity Index (SSIM). The motion estimation results were evaluated using the Mean Vector Euclidean Distance (MVED) that measures the 3D Euclidean distance between the predicted vector field and the ground truth vector field, which was defined as the motion field predicted by R using the ground truth HDPET. For comparative study, we compared our results against the following algorithms: Gaussian filtering (GAU), Non-local mean filtering (NLM) [3], Block-matching 4D filtering (BM4D) [4], UNet [8,15], and cGAN [7].

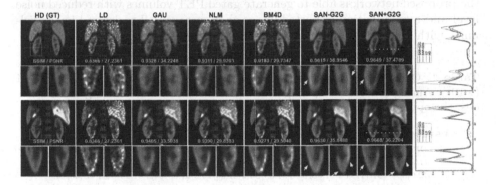

Fig. 3. Sample HD and 1.5% LD PET slices with enlarged subregions using various denoising methods for Two sample subjects. The corresponding PSNR and SSIM are indicated at the bottom of the images. Comparison of intensity profile is also shown on the right. $-/+$G2G denotes without/with gate-to-gate consistency learning.

4   Results

The qualitative comparison of various denoising methods is shown in Fig. 3. As we can observe on the figure, conventional post-processing methods, such as NLM [3] and BM4D [4], have difficulties in structural recovery when only 1.5% of the total counts was considered. The high noise level also introduced additional artifacts, resulting in inferior performance compared to the standard Gaussian filtering. In contrast, deep learning based methods achieved better performance in noise reduction and structural recovery.

Table 1 outlines the quantitative comparison of different methods on PET image denoising. Both PSNR and SSIM were evaluated for each gated volumes ($\mathcal{G}_n$), along with averaged value computed on the last column. Among them, our SAN without G2G outperforms the previous deep learning based methods, and the addition of G2G learning that utilizes the information over gates further improved the performance. In parallel, Fig. 4 illustrates a qualitative comparison of motion estimation based on the discussed denoising methods. As we can see, our proposed SAN+G2G yields the most consistent motion vectors between the estimated and ground truth motion vectors. The quantitative comparison of motion estimation among different denoising methods is given in Table 2. As shown in the table, our SAN+G2G was able to improve the motion estimation accuracy by 20% in average, achieving the lowest 0.264 in averaged MVED, compared to other studied methods. Using our proposed method, denoised gated LDPET volumes can be generated with corresponding motion vectors to the reference gate. We then registered all gated volumes of LDPET, HDPET, and LDPET with SAN+G2G to the reference gate. As an example shown in Fig. 5, the proposed network is able to generate gated PET volumes with reduced noise level and a final motion corrected image that averaged all registered image volumes with reduced motion blurring using low dose gated data.

Table 1. Quantitative comparison of denoising results using PSNR (dB) and SSIM ($\times 10^2$). Among conventional post-processing methods and deep learning based methods, the optimal results are marked in red.

PSNR/SSIM	$G1$	$G2$	$G3$	$G4$	$G5$	$G6$	Average
LDPET	28.48/86.3	28.47/86.5	28.27/86.6	28.47/86.9	27.93/86.1	28.11/86.2	28.29/86.4
GAU	34.92/94.6	34.25/94.5	34.18/94.5	34.32/94.6	34.36/94.4	34.66/94.6	34.45/94.6
NLM [3]	31.71/94.5	31.80/94.5	31.39/94.4	31.60/94.6	31.03/94.3	31.23/94.5	31.46/94.5
BM4D [4]	31.32/93.5	31.32/93.5	31.03/93.5	31.21/93.8	30.68/93.4	30.83/93.4	31.07/93.5
UNet [8]	37.12/95.9	36.01/95.8	36.24/95.7	36.32/96.1	36.34/95.9	36.85/96.1	36.48/95.9
cGAN [7]	37.38/96.3	36.21/96.2	36.41/96.1	36.43/96.1	36.58/96.2	37.02/96.2	36.67/96.2
SAN-G2G	37.55/96.8	36.48/96.6	36.59/96.6	36.67/96.7	36.96/96.6	37.25/96.8	36.92/96.7
SAN+G2G	37.81/97.1	36.74/96.9	36.77/96.9	36.87/96.9	37.35/97.0	37.43/97.1	37.16/97.0

Table 2. Quantitative comparison of motion estimation results evaluated in terms of MVED. G4 is the reference gate. Optimal results are marked in red.

MVED	$G1$	$G2$	$G3$	$G4$ (Ref)	$G5$	$G6$	Average
LDPET	0.392	0.342	0.289	-	0.282	0.350	0.331
GAU	0.368	0.372	0.328	-	0.328	0.352	0.349
NLM [3]	0.360	0.363	0.312	-	0.309	0.342	0.337
BM4D [4]	0.351	0.341	0.2997	-	0.287	0.331	0.322
SAN-G2G	0.309	0.309	0.262	-	0.263	0.297	0.288
SAN+G2G	0.289	0.285	0.236	-	0.237	0.274	0.264

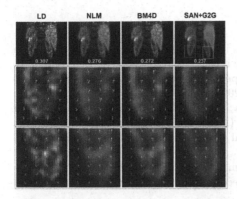

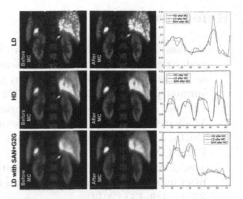

Fig. 4. Qualitative motion estimation results from different denoising methods. Ground truth (green arrows) and predicted (magenta arrows) motion estimation vectors are overlaid on denoised images. (Color figure online)

Fig. 5. Illustration of motion blurred images (left) and averaged image of all gates average registered to the reference frame (middle). The green arrows indicate where significant motion reduction is observed after applying the proposed SAN+G2G. (Color figure online)

5   Discussion and Conclusion

In this work, we propose a Siamese adversarial network with gate-to-gate consistency learning, a novel framework for low dose gated PET denoising and motion estimation, simultaneously. We first pre-train our motion estimation network on the ground truth HDPET, and concatenate it to our Siamese adversarial network that enables the gate-to-gate consistency learning for improving the denoising performance. The denoised low-dose gated volumes are then fed into the motion estimation network for robust motion estimation. In our framework, the Siamese input design allows us to efficiently augment the training data from each patient, thus can better train generalizable denoising and motion estimation models. We demonstrated the feasibility of our method on the tasks of PET image denoising and motion estimation with promising performance.

The potential clinical feasibility of our work is two-fold. Firstly, as high-noise level and motion are inevitable in the chest and abdominal low-dose PET acquisitions, it will affect the visualization of small pathological findings, such as lung/liver lesions. Our work is potentially useful for recovering these small objects from noise and correcting motions to improve the delineation of distorted objects. Secondly, the estimated motion can be incorporated into the motion compensated PET reconstruction frameworks toward motion-free low-dose PET reconstructions, which will also improve the reconstruction quality by reducing the motion artifacts. We will explore these directions in our future works.

References

1. Strauss, K.J., Kaste, S.C.: The alara (as low as reasonably achievable) concept in pediatric interventional and fluoroscopic imaging: striving to keep radiation doses as low as possible during fluoroscopy of pediatric patients–a white paper executive summary. Radiology **240**(3), 621–622 (2006)
2. Catana, C.: Motion correction options in PET/MRI. In: Seminars in Nuclear Medicine. vol. 45, pp. 212–223. Elsevier (2015)
3. Dutta, J., Leahy, R.M., Li, Q.: Non-local means denoising of dynamic pet images. PLoS ONE **8**(12), e81390 (2013)
4. Maggioni, M., Katkovnik, V., Egiazarian, K., Foi, A.: Nonlocal transform-domain filter for volumetric data denoising and reconstruction. IEEE Trans. Image Process. **22**(1), 119–133 (2012)
5. Mejia, J., Mederos, B., Mollineda, R.A., Maynez, L.O.: Noise reduction in small animal pet images using a variational non-convex functional. IEEE Trans. Nuclear Sci. **63**(5), 2577–2585 (2016)
6. Xiang, L., et al.: Deep auto-context convolutional neural networks for standard-dose pet image estimation from low-dose PET/MRI. Neurocomputing **267**, 406–416 (2017)
7. Wang, Y., et al.: 3D conditional generative adversarial networks for high-quality pet image estimation at low dose. Neuroimage **174**, 550–562 (2018)
8. Lu, W., et al.: An investigation of quantitative accuracy for deep learning based denoising in oncological pet. Phys. Med. Biol. **64**(16), 165019 (2019)
9. Kaplan, S., Zhu, Y.M.: Full-dose pet image estimation from low-dose pet image using deep learning: a pilot study. J. Digital Imag. **32**(5), 773–778 (2019)
10. Arjovsky, M., Chintala, S., Bottou, L.: Wasserstein gan. arXiv preprint arXiv:1701.07875 (2017)
11. Dalca, A.V., Balakrishnan, G., Guttag, J., Sabuncu, M.R.: Unsupervised learning for fast probabilistic diffeomorphic registration. In: Frangi, A., Schnabel, J., Davatzikos, C., Alberola-Lopez, C., Fichtinger, G. (eds.) International Conference on Medical Image Computing and Computer-Assisted Intervention, pp. 729–738. Springer, Cham (2018). https://doi.org/10.1007/978-3-030-00928-1_82
12. Arsigny, V., Commowick, O., Pennec, X., Ayache, N.: A log-euclidean framework for statistics on diffeomorphisms. In: Larsen, R., Nielsen, M., Sporring, J. (eds.) International Conference on Medical Image Computing and Computer-Assisted Intervention, pp. 924–931. Springer, Heidelberg (2006). https://doi.org/10.1007/11866565_113
13. Normandin, M.D., et al.: In vivo imaging of endogenous pancreatic β-cell mass in healthy and type 1 diabetic subjects using 18f-fluoropropyl-dihydrotetrabenazine and pet. J. Nuclear Med. **53**(6), 908–916 (2012)
14. Rezaei, A., Michel, C., Casey, M.E., Nuyts, J.: Simultaneous reconstruction of the activity image and registration of the CT image in tof-pet. Phys. Med. Biol. **61**(4), 1852 (2016)
15. Ronneberger, O., Fischer, P., Brox, T.: U-net: Convolutional networks for biomedical image segmentation. In: Navab, N., Hornegger, J., Wells, W., Frangi, A. (eds.) International Conference on Medical Image Computing and Computer-Assisted Intervention, pp. 234–241. Springer, Cham (2015). https://doi.org/10.1007/978-3-319-24574-4_28

Lymph Node Gross Tumor Volume Detection and Segmentation via Distance-Based Gating Using 3D CT/PET Imaging in Radiotherapy

Zhuotun Zhu[1,2]($\boxtimes$), Dakai Jin[1], Ke Yan[1], Tsung-Ying Ho[3], Xianghua Ye[5], Dazhou Guo[1], Chun-Hung Chao[4], Jing Xiao[6], Alan Yuille[2], and Le Lu[1]

[1] PAII Inc., Bethesda, MD, USA
zhuotun@gmail.com
[2] Johns Hopkins University, Baltimore, MD, USA
[3] Chang Gung Memorial Hospital, Linkou, Taiwan, ROC
[4] National Tsing Hua University, Hsinchu City, Taiwan, ROC
[5] The First Affiliated Hospital Zhejiang University, Hangzhou, China
[6] Ping An Technology, Shenzhen, China

Abstract. Finding, identifying and segmenting suspicious cancer metastasized lymph nodes from 3D multi-modality imaging is a clinical task of paramount importance. In radiotherapy, they are referred to as Lymph Node Gross Tumor Volume (GTV_{LN}). Determining and delineating the spread of GTV_{LN} is essential in defining the corresponding resection and irradiating regions for the downstream workflows of surgical resection and radiotherapy of various cancers. In this work, we propose an effective distance-based gating approach to simulate and simplify the high-level reasoning protocols conducted by radiation oncologists, in a divide-and-conquer manner. GTV_{LN} is divided into two subgroups of "tumor-proximal" and "tumor-distal", respectively, by means of binary or soft distance gating. This is motivated by the observation that each category can have distinct though overlapping distributions of appearance, size and other LN characteristics. A novel multi-branch detection-by-segmentation network is trained with each branch specializing on learning one GTV_{LN} category features, and outputs from multi-branch are fused in inference. The proposed method is evaluated on an in-house dataset of 141 esophageal cancer patients with both PET and CT imaging modalities. Our results validate significant improvements on the mean recall from 72.5% to 78.2%, as compared to previous state-of-the-art work. The highest achieved GTV_{LN} recall of 82.5% at 20% precision is clinically relevant and valuable since human observers tend to have low sensitivity ($\sim$80% for the most experienced radiation oncologists, as reported by literature [5]).

Keyword: Lymph Node Gross Tumor Volume (GTV_{LN}), CT/PET Imaging, 3D Distance Transformation, Distance-based Gating

© Springer Nature Switzerland AG 2020
A. L. Martel et al. (Eds.): MICCAI 2020, LNCS 12267, pp. 753–762, 2020.
https://doi.org/10.1007/978-3-030-59728-3_73

1   Introduction

Assessing the lymph node (LN) status in oncology clinical workflows is an indispensable step for the precision cancer diagnosis and treatment planning, e.g., radiation therapy or surgical resection. The class of enlarged LN is defined by the revised RECIST guideline [15] if its short axial axis is more than 10-15 mm in computed tomography (CT). In radiotherapy treatment, both the primary tumor and all metastasis suspicious LNs must be sufficiently treated within the clinical target volume with the proper doses [7]. We refer these LNs as lymph node gross tumor volume or GTV_{LN}, which includes enlarged LNs, as well as smaller ones that are associated with a high positron emission tomography (PET) signal or any metastasis signs in CT [14]. Accurately identifying and delineating GTV_{LN}, to be spatially included in the treatment area, is essential for a desirable cancer treatment outcome [10].

It is an extremely challenging and time-consuming task to identify GTV_{LN}, even for experienced radiation oncologists. High-level sophisticated clinical reasoning guidelines are needed, leading to the risk of uncertainty and subjectivity with high inter-observer variabilities [5]. It is arguably more difficult than detecting the more general enlarged LNs. (1) Finding GTV_{LN} is often performed using radiotherapy CT (RTCT) that (unlike diagnostic CT) is not contrast-enhanced. Hence the metastasis signs for identifying GTV_{LN} are subtler. (2) GTV_{LN} itself has poor contrast. Because of the shape and appearance ambiguity, it can be easily confused with vessels or muscles. (3) The size and shape of GTV_{LN} vary considerably with large amounts of smaller ones that are harder to detect. Refer Fig. 1 (top row) for an illustration of GTV_{LN}. While many previous works attempt to detect enlarged LNs using contrast-enhanced CT [1,2,4,11–13,18], no work, as of yet, has studied the GTV_{LN} detection in non-contrast RTCT scans. Given the evident differences between the enlarged LNs and GTV_{LN}, further innovations are required for the robust GTV_{LN} detection and segmentation.

Valuable insights from physicians' clinical diagnosis and analysis process can be leveraged to tackle this problem. As one of the primary cues, human observers condition the analysis of GTV_{LN} based on the LNs' distance with respect to the corresponding primary tumor location. For LNs proximal to the tumor, physicians more readily identify them as GTV_{LN} in radiotherapy treatment. However, for LNs distal to the tumor, they use more strict criteria to include if there are clear signs of metastasis, e.g., enlarged size, increased PET signals, and/or other CT based evidence [14]. Hence, the distance measure relative to the primary tumor plays a key role during physician's decision making. Besides the distance, the PET modality is also of high importance. Although as a noisy imaging channel, it has shown to be helpful in increasing the GTV_{LN} detection sensitivity [5]. As demonstrated in Fig. 1 (bottom row), PET provides critically distinct information, yet, it also exhibits false positives (FPs) and false negatives (FNs).

In this paper, we imitate the physician's diagnosis process to tackle the problem of GTV_{LN} detection and segmentation. (1) We introduce a distance-based gating strategy in a multi-task framework to divide the underlying GTV_{LN} distributions into "tumor-proximal" and "tumor-distal" categories and solve them

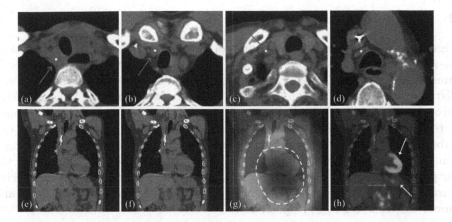

Fig. 1. Top row (a-d): examples of the GTV$_{LN}$ (red arrow) with varying size and appearance at scatteredly distributed locations. Bottom row (e-h): (e) A coronal view of RTCT for an esophageal cancer patient. (f) The manual annotated GTV$_{LN}$ mask. (g) The tumor distance transformation map overlaid on RTCT, where the primary tumor is indicated by red in the center and the white dash line shows an example of the binary tumor proximal and distal region division. (h) PET imaging shows several FPs with high signals (yellow arrows). Two FN GTV$_{LN}$ are indicated by green arrow where PET has even no signals on a GTV$_{LN}$. (Color figure online)

accordingly. Specifically, a multi-branch network is proposed to adopt a shared encoder and two separate decoders to detect and segment the "tumor-proximal" and "tumor-distal" GTV$_{LN}$, respectively. A distance-based gating function is designed to generate the corresponding GTV$_{LN}$ sample weights for each branch. By applying the gating function at the outputs of decoders, each branch is specialized to learn the "tumor-proximal" or "tumor-distal" GTV$_{LN}$ features that emulates physician's diagnosis process. (2) We leverage the early fusion (EF) of three modalities as input to our model, *i.e.*, RTCT, PET and 3D tumor distance map (Fig. 1(bottom row)). RTCT depicts anatomical structures capturing the intensity, appearance and contextual information, while PET provides metastasis functional activities. Meanwhile, the tumor distance map further encodes the critical distance information in the network. Fusion of these three modalities together can effectively boost the GTV$_{LN}$ identification performance. (3) We evaluate on a dataset comprising 651 voxel-wise labeled GTV$_{LN}$ instances in 141 esophageal cancer patients, as the largest GTV$_{LN}$ dataset to date for chest and abdominal radiotherapy. Our method significantly improves the detection mean recall from 72.5% to 78.2%, compared with the previous state-of-the-art lesion detection method [17]. The highest achieved recall of 82.5% is also clinically relevant and valuable. As reported in [5], human observers tend to have relatively low GTV$_{LN}$ sensitivities, *e.g.*, ∼80% by even very experienced radiation oncologists. This demonstrates our work's clinical values.

2   Method

Figure 2 shows the framework of our proposed multi-branch GTV_{LN} detection-by-segmentation method. Similar to [19,20] which are designed for the pancreatic tumors, we detect GTV_{LN} by segmenting them. We first compute the 3D tumor distance transformation map (Sect. 2.1), based on which any GTV_{LN} is divided into the tumor-proximal or tumor-adjacent subcategory. Next, a multi-branch detection-by-segmentation network is designed where each branch focuses on one subgroup of GTV_{LN} segmentation (Sect. 2.2). This is achieved by applying a binary or soft distance-gating function imposed on the penalty function at the output of the two branches (Sect. 2.3). Hence, each branch can learn specific parameters to specialize on segmenting and detecting the tumor-proximal and tumor-adjacent GTV_{LN}, respectively.

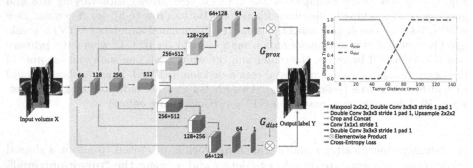

Fig. 2. The overall framework of our proposed multi-branch GTV_{LN} detection and segmentation method. The light green part shows the encoder path, while the light yellow and light blue parts show the two decoders, respectively. The number of channels is denoted either on the top or the bottom of the box. (Color figure online)

2.1   3D Tumor Distance Transformation

To stratify GTV_{LN} into tumor-proximal and tumor-distal subgroups, we first compute the 3D tumor distance transformation map, denoted as $\mathbf{X}^D$, from the primary tumor $\mathcal{O}$. The value at each voxel x_i represents the shortest distance between this voxel and the mask of the primary tumor. Let $B(\mathcal{O})$ be a set that includes the boundary voxels of the tumor. The distance transformation value at a voxel x_i is computed as

$$\mathbf{X}^D(x_i) = \begin{cases} \min\limits_{q \in B(\mathcal{O})} d(x_i, q) & \text{if } x_i \notin \mathcal{O} \\ 0 & \text{if } x_i \in \mathcal{O} \end{cases}, \tag{1}$$

where $d(x_i, q)$ is the Euclidean distance from x_i to q. $\mathbf{X}^D$ can be efficiently computed using algorithms such as the one proposed in [9]. Based on $\mathbf{X}^D$, GTV_{LN} can be divided into tumor-proximal and tumor-distal subgroups using either binary or soft distance-gating function as explained in detail in Sect. 2.3.

2.2 Multi-branch Detection-By-Segmentation via Distance Gating

GTV_{LN} identification is implicitly associated with their distance distributions to the primary tumor in the diagnosis process of physicians. Hence, we divide GTV_{LN} into tumor-proximal and tumor-distal subgroups and conduct detection accordingly. To do this, we design a multi-branch detection-by-segmentation network with each branch focusing on segmenting one GTV_{LN} subgroup. Each branch is implemented by an independent decoder to learn and extract the subgroup specific information, while they share a single encoder to extract the common GTV_{LN} image features. Assuming there are N data samples, we denote a dataset as $\mathbf{S} = \left\{ \left(\mathbf{X}_n^{CT}, \mathbf{X}_n^{PET}, \mathbf{X}_n^{D}, \mathbf{Y}_n \right) \right\}_{n=1}^{N}$, where $\mathbf{X}_n^{CT}$, $\mathbf{X}_n^{PET}$, $\mathbf{X}_n^{D}$ and $\mathbf{Y}_n$ represent the non-contrast RTCT, registered PET, tumor distance transformation map, and ground truth GTV_{LN} segmentation mask, respectively. Without the loss of generality, we drop n for conciseness in the rest of this paper. The total number of branches is denoted as M, where $M = 2$ in our case. A CNN segmentation model is denoted as a mapping function $\mathbb{E} : \mathbf{P} = \mathbf{f}(\mathcal{X}; \boldsymbol{\Theta})$, where $\mathcal{X}$ is a set of inputs, which consists of a single modality or a concatenation of multiple modalities. $\boldsymbol{\Theta}$ indicates model parameters, and $\mathbf{P}$ means the predicted probability volume. Given that $p(y_i|x_i; \boldsymbol{\Theta}_m)$ represents the predicted probability of a voxel $x_i \in \mathcal{X}$ being the labeled class from the mth branch, the overall negative log-likelihood loss aggregated across M branches can be formulated as:

$$\mathcal{L} = \sum_m \mathcal{L}_m(\mathcal{X}; \boldsymbol{\Theta}_m, \boldsymbol{G}_m) = -\sum_i \sum_m g_{m,i} \log(p(y_i|x_i; \boldsymbol{\Theta}_m)), \qquad (2)$$

where $\boldsymbol{G} = \{\boldsymbol{G}_m\}_{m=1}^{M}$ is introduced as a set of volumes containing the transformed gating weights at each voxel based on its distance to the primary tumor. At every voxel $x_i \in \boldsymbol{G}$, the gating weights satisfies $\sum_m g_{m,i} = 1$.

2.3 Distance-Based Gating Module

Based on the tumor distance map $\mathbf{X}^D$, our gating functions can be designed to generate appropriate GTV_{LN} sample weights for different branches so that each branch specializes on learning the subgroup specific features. In our case, we explore two options: (1) binary distance gating and (2) soft distance gating.

Binary Distance Gating (BG). Based on the tumor distance map $\mathbf{X}^D$, we divide image voxels into two groups, x_{prox} and x_{dis}, to be tumor-proximal and tumor-distal, respectively, where prox $= \{i|x_i^D \leq d_0, x_i^D \in \mathbf{X}^D\}$ and dis $= \{i|x_i^D > d_0, x_i^D \in \mathbf{X}^D\}$. Therefore the gating transformations for two decoders are defined as $\mathbf{G}_{\text{prox}} = \mathbf{1}[x_i^D \leq d_0]$ and $\mathbf{G}_{\text{dist}} = 1 - \mathbf{G}_{\text{prox}}$, where $\mathbf{1}[\cdot]$ is an indicator function which equals one if its argument is true and zero otherwise. In this way, we divide the GTV_{LN} strictly into two disjoint categories, and each branch focuses on decoding and learning from one category.

Soft Distance Gating (SG). We further explore a soft gating method that linearly changes the penalty weights of GTV_{LN} samples as they are closer or further to the tumor. This can avoid a sudden change of weight values when samples are near the proximal and distal category boundaries. Recommended by our physician, we formulate a soft gating module based on $\mathbf{X}^D$ as following:

$$\mathbf{G_{prox}}(x_i) = \begin{cases} 1 - \frac{x_i^D - d_{prox}}{d_{dist} - d_{prox}} & \text{if } d_{prox} < x_i^D \le d_{dist} \\ 1 & \text{if } x_i^D \le d_{prox} \\ 0 & \text{if } x_i^D > d_{dist} \end{cases}, \tag{3}$$

and $\mathbf{G_{dist}}(x_i) = 1 - \mathbf{G_{prox}}(x_i)$ accordingly.

3   Experimental Results

3.1   Dataset and Preprocessing

Dataset. We collected 141 non-contrast RTCTs of esophageal cancer patients, with all undergoing radiotherapy treatments. Radiation oncologists labeled 3D segmentation masks of the primary tumor and all GTV_{LN}. For each patient, we have a non-contrast RTCT and a pair of PET/CT scans. There is a total of 651 GTV_{LN} with voxel-wise annotations in the mediastinum or upper abdomen regions, as the largest annotated GTV_{LN} dataset to-date. We randomly split patients into 60%, 10%, 30% for training, validation and testing, respectively.

Implementation Details. In our experiments, PET scan is registered to RTCT using the similar method described in [6]. Then all coupling pairs of RTCT and registered PET images are resampled to have a consistent spatial resolution of $1 \times 1 \times 2.5$ mm. To generate the 3D training samples, we crop sub-volumes of $96 \times 96 \times 64$ from the RTCT, registered PET and the tumor distance map around each GTV_{LN} as well as randomly from the background. For the distance-gating related parameters, we set $d_0 = 7$ cm as the binary gating threshold, and $d_{prox} = 5$ cm and $d_{dist} = 9$ cm as the soft gating thresholds, respectively, as suggested by our clinical collaborator. We further apply random rotations in the x-y plane within $10°$ to augment the training data.

Detection-by-segmentation models are trained on two NVIDIA Quadra RTX 6000 GPUs with a batch size of 8 for 50 epochs. The RAdam [8] optimizer with a learning rate of 0.0001 is used with a momentum of 0.9 and a weight decay of 0.0005. For inference, 3D sliding windows with a sub-volume of $96 \times 96 \times 64$ and a stride of $64 \times 64 \times 32$ voxels are processed. For each sub-volume, predictions from two decoders are weighted and aggregated according to the gating transformation $\mathbf{G_m}$ to obtain the final GTV_{LN} segmentation results.

Evaluation Metrics. We first describe the hit criteria, $i.e.$, the correct detection, for our detection-by-segmentation method. For an GTV_{LN} prediction, if it overlaps with any ground-truth GTV_{LN}, we treat it as a hit provided that its estimated radius is similar to the radius of the ground-truth GTV_{LN} within the range of $[0.5, 1.5]$. The performance is assessed using the mean and max recall (mRecall and Recall_{max}) at a precision range of $[0.10, 0.50]$ with 0.05 interval, and the mean free response operating characteristic (FROC) at $3, 4, 6, 8$ FPs per patient. These operating points were chosen after confirming with our physician.

Comparison Setups. Using the binary and soft distance-based gating function, our multi-branch GTV_{LN} detection-by-segmentation method is denoted as **multi-branch BG** and **multi-branch SG**, respectively. We compare against the following setups: (1) a single 3D UNet [3] trained using RTCT alone or the early fusion (EF) of multi-modalities (denoted as **single-net** method); (2) Two separate UNets trained with the corresponding tumor-proximal and tumor-distal GTV_{LN} samples and results spatially fused together (our preliminary work [21] denoted as **multi-net BG**); and (3) MULAN [17], a state-of-the-art (SOTA) general lesion detection method on DeepLesion [18] that contains more than 10,000 enlarged LNs.

3.2 Quantitative Results and Discussion

Our quantitative results and comparisons are given in Table. 1. Several observations can be drawn on addressing the effectiveness of our proposed methods. (1) The multi-modality input, *i.e.*, early fusion (EF) of RTCT, PET and tumor distance map, are of great benefits for detecting the GTV_{LN}. There are drastic performance improvements of absolute 6.7% and 7.2% in mRecall and mFROC when EF is adopted as compared to using RTCT alone. These results validate that input channels of PET functional imaging and 3D tumor distance transform map are valuable for identifying GTV_{LN}. (2) The distance-based gating strategies are evidently effective as the options of **multi-net BG**, **multi-branch BG** and **multi-branch SG** consistently increase the performance. For example, the multi-net BG model achieves 74.7% mRecall and 69.5% mFROC, which is a 1.6% and 1.9% improvement against the best single-net model (where no distance-based stratification is used). The performance further boosts with the network models of multi-branch BG and multi-branch SG, to the highest scores of 78.2% mRecall and 72.4% mFROC achieved by the multi-branch SG.

Table 1. Quantitative results of our proposed methods with the comparison to other setups and the previous state-of-the-art.

Methods	CT	EF	mRecall	Recall$_{max}$	mFROC	FROC@4	FROC@6
Single-net	✓		0.664	0.762	0.604	0.552	0.675
Single-net		✓	0.731	0.820	0.676	0.667	0.713
Multi-net BG [21]		✓	0.747	0.825	0.695	0.668	**0.739**
Multi-branch BG (Ours)		✓	0.761	**0.845**	0.679	0.667	0.716
Multi-branch SG (Ours)		✓	**0.782**	0.843	**0.724**	**0.729**	0.738
MULAN [17]	✓		0.711	0.758	0.632	0.632	0.642
MULAN [17]		✓	0.725	0.781	0.708	0.718	0.720

Multi-branch versus Multi-net. Using the distance-based gating strategy, our proposed multi-branch methods perform considerably better than the **multi-net BG** model. Even our second best model **multi-branch BG**, the mean and maximal recalls have been improved by 1.4% (from 74.7% to 76.1%) and 2.0% (from 82.5% to 84.5%) against the **multi-net BG** model. When the multi-branch framework is equipped with the **soft-gating**, marked improvements of absolute 3.5% and 2.9% in both mRecall and mFROC are observed as compared against to the **multi-net BG** model. This validates the effectiveness of our jointly trained multi-branch framework design, and our intuition that gradually changing GTV_{LN} weights for the proximal and distal branches are more natural and effective. As we recall, the multi-net baseline directly trains two separate 3D UNets [3] targeted to segment each GTV_{LN} subgroup. Considering the limited GTV_{LN} training data (a few hundreds of patients), it can be overfitting prone from the split to even smaller patient subgroups.

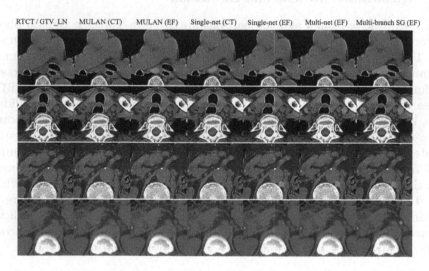

Fig. 3. Four qualitative examples of the detection results using different methods. Red color represents the ground-truth GTV_{LN} overlaid on the RTCT images; Green color indicates the predicted segmentation masks. As shown, for the enlarged GTV_{LN} (top row), most methods can detect it correctly. However, as GTV_{LN} size becomes smaller and contrast is poor, our method can successfully detect them while others struggled. (Color figure online)

Table 1 also compares with the SOTA universal lesion detection method, i.e., MULAN [17] on DeepLesion [16,18]. We have retrained the MULAN models using both CT and EF inputs, but even the best results, i.e., using EF, have a large gap (72.5% vs. 78.2% mRecall) with our distance-gating networks, which further proves that the tumor distance transformation cue plays a key role in GTV_{LN} identification.

Figure 3 illustrates the visualization results of our method compared to other baselines. For the enlarged GTV_{LN} (top row), most methods can detect it correctly. However, as the size of GTV_{LN} becomes smaller and the contrast is poorer, our method can still successfully detect them while others struggled.

4 Conclusion

In this work, we propose an effective distance-based gating approach in a multi-task deep learning framework to segment GTV_{LN}, emulating the oncologists' high-level diagnosis protocols. GTV_{LN} is divided into two subgroups of "tumor-proximal" and "tumor-distal", by means of binary or soft distance gating. A novel multi-branch detection-by-segmentation network is trained with each branch specializing on learning one subgroup features. We evaluate our method on a dataset of 141 esophageal cancer patients. Our results demonstrate significant performance improvements on the mean recall from 72.5% to 78.2%, as compared to previous state-of-the-art work. The highest achieved GTV_{LN} recall of 82.5% at the 20% precision level is clinically relevant and valuable.

References

1. Barbu, A., Suehling, M., Xu, X., Liu, D., Zhou, S.K., Comaniciu, D.: Automatic detection and segmentation of lymph nodes from CT data. IEEE Trans. Med. Imag. **31**(2), 240–250 (2011)
2. Bouget, D., Jørgensen, A., Kiss, G., Leira, H.O., Langø T.: Semantic segmentation and detection of mediastinal lymph nodes and anatomical structures in CT data for lung cancer staging. Int. J. Comput. Assisted Radiol. surgery, 14, 1–10 (2019)
3. Çiçek, Ö., Abdulkadir, A., Lienkamp, S.S., Brox, T., Ronneberger, O.: 3D u-net: learning dense volumetric segmentation from sparse annotation. In: MICCAI (2016)
4. Feulner, J., Zhou, S.K., Hammon, M., Hornegger, J., Comaniciu, D.: Lymph node detection and segmentation in chest CT data using discriminative learning and a spatial prior. Med. Image Anal. **17**(2), 254–270 (2013)
5. Goel, R., Moore, W., Sumer, B., Khan, S., Sher, D., Subramaniam, R.M.: Clinical practice in pet/ct for the management of head and neck squamous cell cancer. Am. J. Roentgenol. **209**(2), 289–303 (2017)
6. Jin, D., et al.: Accurate esophageal gross tumor volume segmentation in PET/CT using two-stream chained 3D deep network fusion. In: Shen, D., et al. (eds.) MICCAI 2019. LNCS, vol. 11765, pp. 182–191. Springer, Cham (2019). https://doi.org/10.1007/978-3-030-32245-8_21
7. Jin, D., et al.: Deep esophageal clinical target volume delineation using encoded 3D spatial context of tumors, lymph nodes, and organs at risk. In: Shen, D., et al. (eds.) MICCAI 2019. LNCS, vol. 11769, pp. 603–612. Springer, Cham (2019). https://doi.org/10.1007/978-3-030-32226-7_67
8. Liu, L., Jiang, H., He, P., Chen, W., Liu, X., Gao, J., Han, J.: On the variance of the adaptive learning rate and beyond. arXiv preprint arXiv:1908.03265 (2019)
9. Maurer, C.R., Qi, R., Raghavan, V.: A linear time algorithm for computing exact euclidean distance transforms of binary images in arbitrary dimensions. IEEE Trans. Pattern Anal. Mach. Intell. **25**(2), 265–270 (2003)

10. Network, N.C.C.: NCCN clinical practice guidelines: head and neck cancers. Am. J. Roentgenol. Version **2** (2020)

11. Nogues, I., et al.: Automatic lymph node cluster segmentation using holistically-nested neural networks and structured optimization in CT images. In: Ourselin, S., Joskowicz, L., Sabuncu, M.R., Unal, G., Wells, W. (eds.) MICCAI 2016. LNCS, vol. 9901, pp. 388–397. Springer, Cham (2016). https://doi.org/10.1007/978-3-319-46723-8_45

12. Roth, H.R., et al.: Improving computer-aided detection using convolutional neural networks and random view aggregation. IEEE Trans. Med. Imag. **35**(5), 1170–1181 (2016)

13. Roth, H.R., et al.: A new 2.5D representation for lymph node detection using random sets of deep convolutional neural network observations. In: Golland, P., Hata, N., Barillot, C., Hornegger, J., Howe, R. (eds.) MICCAI 2014. LNCS, vol. 8673, pp. 520–527. Springer, Cham (2014). https://doi.org/10.1007/978-3-319-10404-1_65

14. Scatarige, J.C., Fishman, E.K., Kuhajda, F.P., Taylor, G.A., Siegelman, S.S.: Low attenuation nodal metastases in testicular carcinoma. J. Comput. Assisted Tomography **7**(4), 682–687 (1983)

15. Schwartz, L., et al.: Evaluation of lymph nodes with recist 1.1. Euro. J. Cancer, **45**(2), 261–267 (2009)

16. Yan, K., Peng, Y., Sandfort, V., Bagheri, M., Lu, Z., Summers, R.M.: Holistic and comprehensive annotation of clinically significant findings on diverse CT images: learning from radiology reports and label ontology. In: Proceedings of the IEEE Conference on Computer Vision and Pattern Recognition, pp. 8523–8532 (2019)

17. Yan, K., et al.: MULAN: multitask universal lesion analysis network for joint lesion detection, tagging, and segmentation. In: Shen, D., et al. (eds.) MICCAI 2019. LNCS, vol. 11769, pp. 194–202. Springer, Cham (2019). https://doi.org/10.1007/978-3-030-32226-7_22

18. Yan, K., Wang, X., Lu, L., Summers, R.M.: Deeplesion: automated mining of large-scale lesion annotations and universal lesion detection with deep learning. J. Med. Imag. **5**(3), 036501 (2018)

19. Zhu, Z., Lu, Y., Shen, W., Fishman, E.K., Yuille, A.L.: Segmentation for classification of screening pancreatic neuroendocrine tumors. arXiv preprint arXiv:2004.02021 (2020)

20. Zhu, Z., Xia, Y., Xie, L., Fishman, E.K., Yuille, A.L.: Multi-scale coarse-to-fine segmentation for screening pancreatic ductal adenocarcinoma. In: International Conference on Medical Image Computing and Computer-Assisted Intervention, pp. 3–12. Springer (2019)

21. Zhu, Z., et al.: Detecting scatteredly-distributed, small, and critically important objects in 3d oncologyimaging via decision stratification. arXiv preprint arXiv:2005.13705 (2020)

Multi-modality Information Fusion for Radiomics-Based Neural Architecture Search

Yige Peng[1], Lei Bi[1(✉)], Michael Fulham[1,2], Dagan Feng[1,3], and Jinman Kim[1]

[1] School of Computer Science, University of Sydney, Sydney, NSW, Australia
lei.bi@sydney.edu.au
[2] Department of Molecular Imaging, Royal Prince Alfred Hospital, Sydney, NSW, Australia
[3] Med-X Research Institute, Shanghai Jiao Tong University, Shanghai, China

Abstract. 'Radiomics' is a method that extracts mineable quantitative features from radiographic images. These features can then be used to determine prognosis, for example, predicting the development of distant metastases (DM). Existing radiomics methods, however, require complex manual effort including the design of hand-crafted radiomic features and their extraction and selection. Recent radiomics methods, based on convolutional neural networks (CNNs), also require manual input in network architecture design and hyper-parameter tuning. Radiomic complexity is further compounded when there are multiple imaging modalities, for example, combined positron emission tomography - computed tomography (PET-CT) where there is functional information from PET and complementary anatomical localization information from computed tomography (CT). Existing multi-modality radiomics methods manually fuse the data that are extracted separately. Reliance on manual fusion often results in sub-optimal fusion because they are dependent on an 'expert's' understanding of medical images. In this study, we propose a multi-modality neural architecture search method (MM-NAS) to automatically derive optimal multi-modality image features for radiomics and thus negate the dependence on a manual process. We evaluated our MM-NAS on the ability to predict DM using a public PET-CT dataset of patients with soft-tissue sarcomas (STSs). Our results show that our MM-NAS had a higher prediction accuracy when compared to state-of-the-art radiomics methods.

Keywords: Radiomics · Multi-modality · Positron emission tomography - computed tomography (PET-CT) · Neural Architecture Search (NAS)

1 Introduction

The implementation and availability of high-throughput computing has made it possible to extract innumerable features from medical imaging datasets.

Supported by Australian Research Council (ARC) grants.

© Springer Nature Switzerland AG 2020
A. L. Martel et al. (Eds.): MICCAI 2020, LNCS 12267, pp. 763–771, 2020.
https://doi.org/10.1007/978-3-030-59728-3_74

These extracted features can reveal disease related characteristics that can relate to prognosis [12]. The process of converting visual imaging data into mineable quantitative features is referred to radiomics [7]. Radiomics is an emerging field of translational research in medical imaging where the modalities include digital radiography, magnetic resonance imaging (MRI), computed tomography (CT), combined positron emission tomography - computed tomography (PET-CT) etc. The range of medical imaging modalities is wide and, in essence, these modalities provide information about structure, physiology, pathology, biochemistry and pathophysiology [18]. PET-CT, for example, combines the sensitivity of PET in detecting regions of abnormal function and the specificity of CT in depicting the underlying anatomy of where the abnormal functions are occurring. Multi-modality PET-CT, therefore, is regarded as the imaging modality of choice for the diagnosis, staging and monitoring the treatment response of many cancers [8]. Conventional radiomics studies mainly focus on encoding regions of interest (e.g., tumors), with hand-crafted features, such as intensity, texture, shape, etc. These features are used to build conventional predictive models such as multivariable statistical analysis [19], support vector machine (SVM) [10] and random forest [20]. Unfortunately, these methods rely on prior knowledge in hand-crafting image features and tuning of a large number of parameters for building the predictive models.

Radiomics methods based on convolutional neural networks (CNN) are regarded as the state-of-the-art because they can learn high-level semantic image information in an end-to-end fashion. CNN-based radiomics methods were mainly designed for 2D single-modality images such as CT [4,11] and MRI [22]. For the limited methods that attempted to fuse multi-modality images, the focus was on fusing the image features that were separately extracted from the individual modalities [13,14,16]. In addition, these methods required human expertise to design the dataset specific architectures e.g., the number of convolutional layers, the layer to fuse multi-modality image features. Architecture design and optimization require a large amount of domain knowledge such as in validating the architecture performance and tuning the hyper-parameters. Neural architecture search (NAS) has recently been proposed to simplify the challenges in architecture design by automatically searching for an optimal net-work architecture based on a given dataset. The NAS thus enables reduced manual input and reliance on prior knowledge [6]. Investigators have attempted to apply the NAS for single medical imaging modality related tasks but the main focus has been on segmentation [1,5].

We propose a multi-modality NAS method (MM-NAS) to search for a multi-modality CNN architecture for use in PET-CT radiomics. Our contribution, when compared to existing methods includes: (i) the ability to build an optimal, fully-automated radiomics CNN architecture; (ii) enabling an optimal fusion of PET-CT images for radiomics. Our method finds various fusion modules e.g., fusion via different network operations (e.g., convolution, pooling, etc.) at different stages of the network. These searched fusion modules provide more options for integrating the complementary PET and CT data. We outline how our approach can predict the development of distant metastases (DM) in patients with soft-tissue sarcomas (STSs). STSs include slow-growing, more well-differentiated tumors, aggressive tumors that grow rapidly and spread to other organs (distant metastases - DM) and more intermediate that behave between the two extremes [2,21]. The early identification of patient who may develop metastatic disease may contribute to improved care and better patient outcomes.

2   Method

2.1   Materials

We used a public PET-CT STSs dataset from the cancer imaging archive (TCIA) repository [3,19]. The dataset has 51 multi-modality PET-CT scans derived from 51 patients with pathology-proven STSs. DM were confirmed via biopsy or diagnosed by an expert clinician. Three patients without clear metastases information was excluded. Thus, our dataset consists of 48 studies, half of which developed DM.

2.2   Neural Architecture Search Setting

We followed the existing NAS methods [15,17,23] and focused on searching of different computational cells (normal, reduction) to improve the computational efficiency. The computational cells are the basic unit that can be stacked multiple times to form a CNN. A NAS workflow is as follows: (i) based on the given training data, search for optimal cell structure that can form a CNN; and (ii) train the searched CNN based on the training data and then evaluate on the testing data. In our MM-NAS (as shown in Fig. 1), every cell is regarded as a directed acyclic graph consisting of two inputs, one output and several ordered nodes. Our MM-NAS has normal and reduction cells. The input and the output feature maps of a normal cell have the same dimensions. The reduction cell doubles the channel number and reduces the input feature map by half. A stem block consists of a 3D convolutional layer and a batch normalization layer and is used for input image transitions. In our method, the outputs of PET and CT stem blocks are separately fed into the first normal cell to facilitate the fusion process. Then the output feature maps of the first normal cell flows into the first reduction cell with the sum of PET and CT image, which is also processed by one stem block. The rest of the reduction cells used the output feature maps from the previous two layers as input. For DM prediction, the output feature maps of last reduction cell were fed into two convolutional layers and one fully connected layer for classification.

2.3   Optimization Strategy

Each intermediate node n^i inside a cell is a feature map. We represent the searched operations on edge (i, j) using the vector $x^{(i,j)}\left(n^j\right) = \left\{x_\sigma^{(i,j)} \mid \sigma \in O\right\}$ and the vector of all optional operations as $\mathbf{0}^{(i,j)} = \left\{\sigma\left(n^i; \vartheta_\sigma^{(i,j)}\right) \mid \sigma \in O\right\}$,

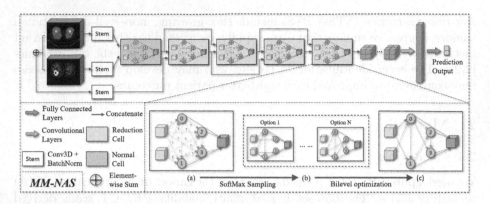

Fig. 1. MM-NAS overview - the CNN architecture has multiple different cells (normal, reduction); each cell is a directed acyclic graph as the basic unit; directed arrows indicate the forward path: (a) initial operations on edges of each cell are unknown; (b) continuously production of alternative cells by SoftMax sampling; and (c) optimal cell architecture after iterative bilevel optimization.

where O denotes the set of optional operations, $\vartheta_\sigma^{(i,j)}$ denotes the parameters of the operation σ on edge (i, j). Then the intermediate nodes can be computed by sum of all their predecessors:

$$n^j = \left\langle x^{(i,j)}\left(n^j\right), \mathbf{0}^{(i,j)} \right\rangle = \sum_{i<j, \sigma\in O} x^{(i,j)}\left(n^j\right)\sigma\left(n^i; \vartheta_\sigma^{(i,j)}\right) \qquad (1)$$

As the possible operations are mixed through a SoftMax function, this makes the search space continuous:

$$x^{(i,j)}\left(n^j\right) = \sum_{\sigma\in O} \frac{\exp\left(\alpha_\sigma^{(i,j)}\right)}{\sum_{\sigma'\in O}\exp\left(\alpha_{\sigma'}^{(i,j)}\right)} x_\sigma^{(i,j)} \qquad (2)$$

where $\alpha_\sigma^{(i,\ j)}$ denotes a probability distribution over the operation set O.

Denote by L_{train} and L_{val} the training and the validation loss. Because both losses are determined not only by the architecture α, but also the weights θ in the network, where $\theta = \left\{\left(\vartheta^{(i,\ j)}\right) \middle| (i,\ j) \in C\right\}$, C is the computational cell. The aim of searching the best architecture is to find a proper α that minimizes the validation loss $L_{val}\left(\theta^*\left(\alpha\right), \alpha\right)$, where the weights θ associated with the architecture are obtained by minimizing the training loss:

$$\min_\alpha \ L_{val}\left(\theta^*\left(\alpha\right), \alpha\right) \qquad (3)$$

$$s.t. \quad \theta^*\left(\alpha\right) = \arg\min_\theta \ L_{train}\left(\theta, \alpha\right) \qquad (4)$$

2.4 Implementation Details

We implemented our MM-NAS in PyTorch. The input image size was fixed to $112 \times 112 \times 144$. The operation set $\mathbf{O}^{(i,\ j)}$ for each cell includes 3D standard convolutions, 3D separable convolutions, 3D dilated convolutions, 3D max pooling, 3D average pooling, skip connections and zero operations. All operations are of stride one (if applicable) and the kernel size of pooling operations are 3. The kernel size for the convolutional operations can either be 3 or 5. Cross-entropy loss was used during the architecture search step for training optimization. The parameters of each cell were optimized by Adam with a learning rate of 0.0005 while the weight in the whole network was optimized by SGD with a learning rate of 0.0001, and the batch size was set to 1. It took about 3 min to process one epoch with 40 PET-CT volumetric training images, and the best architecture was obtained at epoch 70 out of total 200 epochs. Cross-entropy loss with Adam was used for training optimization in the second step for training the searched architecture. Learning rate was set to with 0.001 and batch size was set to 1. It took 2 min to train one epoch, the best model was obtained at approximately epoch 80 out of 200 epochs. All the experiments were conducted on a 11 GB NVIDIA GeForce GTX 2080Ti GPU.

2.5 Experimental Setup

We conducted the following experiments: (a) a comparison with the state-of-the-art radiomics methods; (b) compared the performance of using multi-modality CNNs to single-modality CNNs; and (c) compared the performance of using 2D CNNs with 3D CNNs for radiomics. In experiment (a), we compared our MM-NAS with the following methods: (i) HC+RF - we followed the conventional radiomics method [20] used hand-crafted (HC) features (e.g. intensity solidity, skewness, grey-level co-occurrence matrix features, etc.) extracted from tumor region with random forest (RF) as the classifier for prediction; (ii) DLHN - a deep learning based head & neck cancer outcome (e.g., DM, loco-regional failure, and overall survival) prediction [4]; (iii) 3DMCL - a deep learning based 3D based multi-modality collaborative learning for distant metastases prediction with PET-CT images [16]. We used a 6-fold cross-validation approach for the MM-NAS and the comparison methods. In each-fold cross-validation, we used 40 PET-CT images for training and the remaining 8 images for testing. Six well established evaluation metrics were used for comparison including accuracy (acc.), precision (pre.), F1 score (F1) and area under the receiver-operating characteristic curve (AUC).

3 Results

The receiver-operating characteristic (ROC) curve is shown in Fig. 2. It shows that our 2D MM-NAS achieved better performance when compared with 2D CNN based methods. Our 3D MM-NAS outperformed other 3D CNN based comparison methods and achieved the overall best performance.

Tables 1 and 2 present results of 3D MM-NAS achieving the best outcomes in all measures with AUC value of 0.896, accuracy of 0.896, sensitivity of 0.917, specificity of 0.875, precision of 0.880, and F1 score of 0. 898.

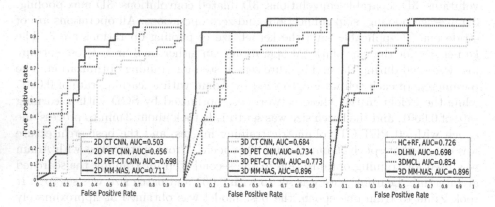

Fig. 2. ROC curves of ours and comparative radiomics methods.

Table 1. Comparison of state-of-the-art radiomics methods.

Evaluation metrics	Acc.	Sen.	Spe.	Pre.	F1.	AUC
HC+RF [20]	0.750	0.792	0.708	0.731	0.760	0.726
DLHN [4]	0.729	0.792	0.667	0.703	0.745	0.698
3DMCL [16]	0.854	0.917	0.792	0.815	0.863	0.854
2D MM-NAS (Ours)	0.750	0.833	0.667	0.714	0.769	0.711
3D MM-NAS (Ours)	**0.896**	**0.917**	**0.875**	**0.880**	**0.898**	**0.896**

Table 2. Comparison of methods using different imaging modalities with convolutional kernels.

Evaluation metrics	Acc.	Sen.	Spe.	Pre.	F1.	AUC
2D CT CNN	0.583	0.708	0.458	0.567	0.630	0.503
2D PET CNN	0.729	0.542	**0.917**	**0.867**	0.667	0.656
2D PET-CT CNN	0.729	0.792	0.667	0.703	0.745	0.698
2D MM-NAS (Ours)	**0.750**	**0.833**	0.667	0.714	**0.769**	**0.711**
3D CT CNN	0.667	0.667	0.667	0.667	0.667	0.684
3D PET CNN	0.771	0.750	0.792	0.783	0.766	0.734
3D PET-CT CNN	0.792	0.792	0.792	0.792	0.792	0.773
3D MM-NAS (Ours)	**0.896**	**0.917**	**0.875**	**0.880**	**0.898**	**0.896**

4 Discussion

Our main findings are that our MM-NAS: (i) performs better than the commonly used radiomics methods and, (ii) derives optimal multi-modality radiomic features from PET-CT images; (iii) removes the reliance on prior knowledge when building the optimal CNN architecture.

We attribute the improved performance of our MM-NAS to the search of the optimal computation cells, within the NAS, that allowed for fusing multi-modality image features at different stages of the network. Existing approaches often choose to fuse the separately extracted feature maps after several convolutional/pooling layers (see Fig. 3). Our derives cell structure offers more freedom to integrate multi-modality images via various operations and connections, thus producing the optimal radiomic features to predict distant disease. The state-of-the-art method 3DMCL outperformed HC+RF and DLHN due to the collaborative learning of both pre-defined radiomic features and deep features, whereas our MM-NAS obtained better performance over all the evaluation metrics without feature handcrafting. Thus, the elimination of prior knowledge could contribute to a better generalizability for applications in other radiomics studies.

The differences between PET-CT CNN and CNN with PET or CT alone show the advantage of incorporating multi-modality information. Across the single modality CNNs, PET-based methods outperformed CT-based methods. We ascribe this to the functional features, which can better characterize the tumor, when compared to anatomical features from CT that rely on changes in size which are often a later development. Such features from PET could potentially uncover functional information that relate to the biological behavior of tumors [8].

The relatively poor performance of 2D CNNs when compared to 3D CNNs is expected. This is attributed to the fact that volumetric image features derived from 3D CNNs are better able to derive spatial information e.g., volumetric tumor shape and size. Spatial information has strong correlations to the DM predictions [9].

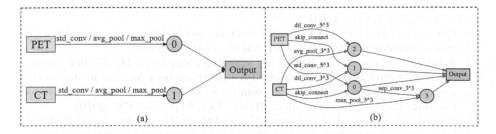

Fig. 3. The comparison between (a) the simplified fusion approach of existing approaches, such as DLHN and 3DMCL; (b) the learned normal cell of MM-NAS for PET-CT fusion.

5   Conclusion

We have outlined a multi-modality neural architecture search method (MM-NAS) for PET-CT to predict the development of distant disease (metastases) in patient with STSs. Our method automatically searched for a multi-modality CNN based radiomics architecture and the architecture can then be used to fuse and derive the optimal PET-CT image features. Our results show that our PET-CT image features are the most relevant for predicting distant metastases.

References

1. Bae, W., Lee, S., Lee, Y., Park, B., Chung, M., Jung, K.-H.: Resource optimized neural architecture search for 3D medical image segmentation. In: Shen, D., et al. (eds.) MICCAI 2019. LNCS, vol. 11765, pp. 228–236. Springer, Cham (2019). https://doi.org/10.1007/978-3-030-32245-8_26
2. Billingsley, K.G., Lewis, J.J., Leung, D.H., Casper, E.S., Woodruff, J.M., Brennan, M.F.: Multifactorial analysis of the survival of patients with distant metastasis arising from primary extremity sarcoma. Cancer Interdisc. Int. J. Am. Cancer Soc. 85(2), 389–395 (1999)
3. Clark, K.: The cancer imaging archive (TCIA): maintaining and operating a public information repository. J. Digit. imaging 26(6), 1045–1057 (2013). https://doi.org/10.1007/s10278-013-9622-7
4. Diamant, A., Chatterjee, A., Vallières, M., Shenouda, G., Seuntjens, J.: Deep learning in head & neck cancer outcome prediction. Sci. Rep. 9(1), 1–10 (2019)
5. Dong, N., Xu, M., Liang, X., Jiang, Y., Dai, W., Xing, E.: Neural architecture search for adversarial medical image segmentation. In: Shen, D., et al. (eds.) MICCAI 2019. LNCS, vol. 11769, pp. 828–836. Springer, Cham (2019). https://doi.org/10.1007/978-3-030-32226-7_92
6. Elsken, T., Metzen, J.H., Hutter, F.: Neural architecture search: a survey. arXiv preprint arXiv:1808.05377 (2018)
7. Hatt, M., Le Rest, C.C., Tixier, F., Badic, B., Schick, U., Visvikis, D.: Radiomics: data are also images. J. Nucl. Med. 60(Supplement 2), 38S–44S (2019)
8. Hatt, M., Tixier, F., Pierce, L., Kinahan, P.E., Le Rest, C.C., Visvikis, D.: Characterization of PET/CT images using texture analysis: the past, the present... any future? Eur. J. Nucl. Med. Mol. Imaging 44(1), 151–165 (2017). https://doi.org/10.1007/s00259-016-3427-0
9. Hosny, A.: Deep learning for lung cancer prognostication: a retrospective multi-cohort radiomics study. PLoS Med. 15(11), e1002711 (2018)
10. Juntu, J., Sijbers, J., De Backer, S., Rajan, J., Van Dyck, D.: Machine learning study of several classifiers trained with texture analysis features to differentiate benign from malignant soft-tissue tumors in T1-MRI images. J. Magn. Reson. Imaging Official J. Int. Soc. Magn. Reson. Med. 31(3), 680–689 (2010)
11. Kumar, D., Chung, A.G., Shaifee, M.J., Khalvati, F., Haider, M.A., Wong, A.: Discovery radiomics for pathologically-proven computed tomography lung cancer prediction. In: Karray, F., Campilho, A., Cheriet, F. (eds.) ICIAR 2017. LNCS, vol. 10317, pp. 54–62. Springer, Cham (2017). https://doi.org/10.1007/978-3-319-59876-5_7
12. Lambin, P., et al.: Radiomics: extracting more information from medical images using advanced feature analysis. Eur. J. Cancer 48(4), 441–446 (2012)

13. Lao, J., et al.: A deep learning-based radiomics model for prediction of survival in glioblastoma multiforme. Sci. Rep. **7**(1), 1–8 (2017)
14. Li, Z., Wang, Y., Yu, J., Guo, Y., Cao, W.: Deep learning based radiomics (DLR) and its usage in noninvasive IDH1 prediction for low grade glioma. Sci. Rep. **7**(1), 1–11 (2017)
15. Liu, H., Simonyan, K., Yang, Y.: Darts: differentiable architecture search. arXiv preprint arXiv:1806.09055 (2018)
16. Peng, Y., Bi, L., Guo, Y., Feng, D., Fulham, M., Kim, J.: Deep multi-modality collaborative learning for distant metastases predication in PET-CT soft-tissue sarcoma studies. In: 2019 41st Annual International Conference of the IEEE Engineering in Medicine and Biology Society (EMBC), pp. 3658–3688. IEEE (2019)
17. Pham, H., Guan, M.Y., Zoph, B., Le, Q.V., Dean, J.: Efficient neural architecture search via parameter sharing. arXiv preprint arXiv:1802.03268 (2018)
18. Rizzo, S., et al.: Radiomics: the facts and the challenges of image analysis. Eur. Radiol. Exp. **2**(1), 1–8 (2018). https://doi.org/10.1186/s41747-018-0068-z
19. Vallières, M., Freeman, C.R., Skamene, S.R., El Naqa, I.: A radiomics model from joint FDG-PET and MRI texture features for the prediction of lung metastases in soft-tissue sarcomas of the extremities. Phys. Med. Biol. **60**(14), 5471 (2015)
20. Vallieres, M., et al.: Radiomics strategies for risk assessment of tumour failure in head-and-neck cancer. Sci. Rep. **7**(1), 1–14 (2017)
21. Yachida, S., et al.: Distant metastasis occurs late during the genetic evolution of pancreatic cancer. Nature **467**(7319), 1114–1117 (2010)
22. Zhu, Y., et al.: A deep learning radiomics model for preoperative grading in meningioma. Eur. J. Radiol. **116**, 128–134 (2019)
23. Zoph, B., Vasudevan, V., Shlens, J., Le, Q.V.: Learning transferable architectures for scalable image recognition. In: Proceedings of the IEEE Conference on Computer Vision and Pattern Recognition, pp. 8697–8710 (2018)

Lymph Node Gross Tumor Volume Detection in Oncology Imaging via Relationship Learning Using Graph Neural Network

Chun-Hung Chao[1]($\boxtimes$), Zhuotun Zhu[2,3], Dazhou Guo[2], Ke Yan[2],
Tsung-Ying Ho[4], Jinzheng Cai[2], Adam P. Harrison[2], Xianghua Ye[5],
Jing Xiao[6], Alan Yuille[3], Min Sun[1], Le Lu[2], and Dakai Jin[2]

[1] National Tsing Hua University, Hsinchu City, Taiwan, ROC
raul.c.chao@gmail.com
[2] PAII Inc., Bethesda, MD, USA
[3] Johns Hopkins University, Baltimore, MD, USA
[4] Chang Gung Memorial Hospital, Linkou, Taiwan, ROC
[5] The First Affiliated Hospital Zhejiang University, Hangzhou, China
[6] Ping An Technology, Shenzhen, China

Abstract. Determining the spread of lymph node gross tumor volume (GTV_{LN}) is essential in defining the respective resection or irradiating regions for the downstream workflows of surgical resection and radiotherapy for many cancers. Different from the more common enlarged lymph node (LN), GTV_{LN} also includes smaller ones if associated with high positron emission tomography signals and/or any metastasis signs in CT. This is a daunting task. In this work, we propose a unified LN appearance and inter-LN relationship learning framework to detect the true GTV_{LN}. This is motivated by the prior clinical knowledge that LNs form a connected lymphatic system, and the spread of cancer cells among LNs often follows certain pathways. Specifically, we first utilize a 3D convolutional neural network with ROI-pooling to extract the GTV_{LN}'s instance-wise appearance features. Next, we introduce a graph neural network to further model the inter-LN relationships where the global LN-tumor spatial priors are included in the learning process. This leads to an end-to-end trainable network to detect by classifying GTV_{LN}. We operate our model on a set of GTV_{LN} candidates generated by a preliminary 1st-stage method, which has a sensitivity of >85% at the cost of high false positive (FP) (>15 FPs per patient). We validate our approach on a radiotherapy dataset with 142 paired PET/RTCT scans containing the chest and upper abdominal body parts. The proposed method significantly improves over the state-of-the-art (SOTA) LN classification method by 5.5% and 13.1% in F1 score and the averaged sensitivity value at 2, 3, 4, 6 FPs per patient, respectively.

Z. Zhu, D. Guo and K. Yan—Equal contribution.

© Springer Nature Switzerland AG 2020
A. L. Martel et al. (Eds.): MICCAI 2020, LNCS 12267, pp. 772–782, 2020.
https://doi.org/10.1007/978-3-030-59728-3_75

Keywords: Lymph node gross tumor volume · Relationship learning · Graph neural network · Oncology imaging · Radiotherapy

1   Introduction

Quantitative lymph node (LN) analysis is an important clinical task for cancer staging and identifying the proper treatment areas in radiotherapy. The revised RECIST guideline [4] recommends measuring enlarged LNs (if short axis >10 mm) for the purpose of tumor burden assessment. However, in cancer treatment, like radiotherapy or surgery, besides the primary tumor, all metastasis-suspicious LNs are also required to be treated. This includes the enlarged LNs, as well as other smaller ones that are associated with high positron emission tomography (PET) signals and/or other metastasis signs in CT. This broader category is referred as lymph node gross tumor volume (GTV_{LN}) in radiotherapy treatment. Accurate identification of GTV_{LN} is essential for the delineation of clinical target volume in radiotherapy [11], where missing small but involved GTV_{LN}, will lead to undesired under-treatment [16].

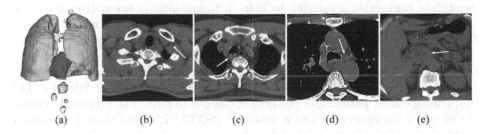

Fig. 1. (a) A 3D rendering of an esophageal tumor (red), lung (green) and the LNs identified by the oncologist (yellow). (b-e) The axial view of the GTV_{LN} spanning from the lower neck to the upper abdomen region. Note that the GTV_{LN} includes the enlarged LN, as well as smaller but suspected metastasized ones. (Color figure online)

Identifying GTV_{LN} could be a very difficult and time-consuming task, even for experienced radiation oncologists. It requires a sophisticated subjective reasoning process that leads to high inter-observer variabilities [8]. Beside the difficulties already met by detecting enlarged LNs, LNs can exhibit low contrast with surrounding tissues and can be easily confused with other vessel or muscle structures. GTV_{LN} detection has its unique challenges: (1) GTV_{LN} discovery is often performed using radiotherapy CT (RTCT), which, unlike diagnostic CT, is not contrast-enhanced. (2) The size and shape of GTV_{LN} vary considerably, and their locations have an implicit relation with the primary tumor [1]. See Fig. 1 for an illustration of GTV_{LN}. While many previous work developed automatic detection/identification methods for enlarged LNs using contrast-enhanced CT [2,3,5,17,22], not much work has attempted on the GTV_{LN} identification task.

These previous work all focus on characterizing instance-wise LN features. Note that, similar to [17–19], our task assumes there is a set of GTV_{LN} candidates computed from an existing detection system with high sensitivities, but low precision so that we target on effectively reducing the false positive (FP) GTV_{LN}. As shown in our experiments, applying the previous state-of-the-art LN identification by classification method [17] leads to a markedly inferior performance.

Unlike prior work that only assess or identify individual LN separately and independently, we perform a study-wise analysis that incorporates the inter-LN and LN-primary tumor relationships. This is motivated by the fact that our lymphatic system is a connected network of LNs, and tumorous cells often follow certain pathways to spread between the LNs [1]. To achieve this, we propose to use graph neural networks (GNNs) to model this inter-LNs relationship. Specifically, we first train a 3D convolutional neural network (CNN) to extract GTV_{LN} instance-wise appearance features from CT. Then, we compute the 3D distances and angles for each GTV_{LN} with respect to the primary tumor, which serves as the spatial prior of each GTV_{LN} instance. Using the instance-wise appearance features and spatial priors to create node representations, a GNN is built, where relationships between GTV_{LN} are patient adaptive via a learnable features fusion function. This allows the GNN to automatically learn the GTV_{LN}-candidate connection strengths to help distinguishing between true and false GTV_{LN}. The whole CNN and GNN framework is end-to-end trainable, allowing GNN to guide the appearance feature extraction in the CNN. Moreover, PET imaging is included as an additional input channel to the CNN model to provide CT imaging with complementary oncology information, which is demonstratively helpful for GTV_{LN} identification task [8]. We evaluate on a dataset of 142 esophageal cancer patients, as the largest dataset to date. The proposed method significantly improves over the state-of-art (SOTA) LN detection/classification method [17,18] by 5.5% and 13.1% in F1 scores and the averaged sensitivity at $2, 3, 4, 6$ FPs per patient, respectively.

2   Methods

Our GTV_{LN} approach combines 3D CNN and GNN networks. Figure 2 depicts an overview of our method, which consists of three modularized components: (1) a 3D CNN classifier to extract per GTV_{LN} candidate instance-wise visual features; (2) spatial prior computation, including the LN-to-tumor distance and angle calculations; (3) a GNN that learns the inter-LN candidate relationship using the global GTV_{LN} spatial priors and their instance-wise CNN features.

2.1   3D CNN-based Appearance Learning

We first train a CNN to extract the GTV_{LN} instance-wise visual features from CT and PET imaging. We adopt a multi-scale 3D CNN model with a ROI-GAP layer [7] that accepts paired CT/PET image patches. The features generated by each convolutional block separately pass through a 3D ROI-GAP layer and a

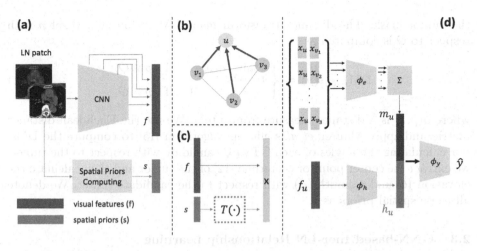

Fig. 2. System overview. (a) For each GTV_{LN} candidate, the model extracts CNN appearance features, f, and the spatial priors, s, for each candidate to create node representations, x. (b) We treat each GTV_{LN} candidate as a node in the graph and use proposed GNN to exchange information. Here we take node u as an example for a target node and the red arrow denotes message passing from other nodes. (c) and (d) show how we obtain the node representations and node latent features h, respectively. (d) also depicts how the aggregated passed message, m, and latent features are used to identify GTV_{LN}. (Color figure online)

fully connected layer to form a 256-dimensional vector, which are then concatenated together to generate a multi-scale local representation for each GTV_{LN} candidate. Since we use four CNN blocks, this leads to a $4 \times 256 = 1024$-dimensional feature vector, which is denoted as f.

2.2 Spatial Prior Computation

In addition to the appearance features, spatial priors can provide crucial information for generating the GNN node representation. We compute each normalized 3D spatial coordinates and also 3D distance and angles to the primary tumor. First, to calculate the normalized 3D spatial coordinates we use each patient's lung mask range in the x and y axes to normalize the GTV_{LN} candidates' x and y locations. Specifically, we adopt and reimplement a pretrained a 2D progressive holistically nested network (PHNN) [9] to segment the lung, which can perform robustly on pathological lungs. Then we calculate the minimum and maximum coordinates of the lung mask and use these as cutoffs to normalize all candidate x and y location to the range of $[0, 1]$. For the z dimension, we train a fully unsupervised body-part regressor [21] using our dataset to provide the normalized z location for each GTV_{LN} candidate instance.

To compute the distance and angles from any candidate to the primary tumor, we first compute the 3D distance transform from the tumor segmentation mask $\mathcal{O}$. Let $\Gamma(\mathcal{O})$ be a function that computes all boundary voxels of the tumor mask. The distance transform map (DM) value at a voxel p with respect to $\mathcal{O}$ is computed as

$$\mathrm{DM}_{\Gamma(\mathcal{O}_i)}(p) = \begin{cases} \min\limits_{q \in \Gamma(\mathcal{O}_i)} d(p, q) & \text{if } p \notin \mathcal{O}_i \\ 0 & \text{if } p \in \mathcal{O}_i \end{cases}, \tag{1}$$

where $d(p, q)$ is a distance measure from p to q. We use the Euclidean distance metric and apply Maurer $et\ al.$'s efficient algorithm [15] to compute the DMs. For calculating the angles of each GTV_{LN} candidate with respect to the tumor, we extract the center point or centerline [12] of the tumor and then calculate the elevation (θ) and azimuth (ϕ) with respect to the candidate center. We denote all these spatial priors as s.

2.3   GNN-based Iner-LN Relationship Learning

Inter-LN Graph Formulation. With the local visual features obtained from the CNN model and the spatial priors calculated in Sect. 2.2, we use them to create a node representation, x, for each GTV_{LN} candidate. Because of divergence in construction between the visual features and spatial priors, we use a learnable function, e.g., a multi-layer perceptron (MLP), T to transform the latter to align them better with the CNN visual features:

$$\begin{aligned} s' &= T(s), \\ x &= (f \parallel s'), \end{aligned} \tag{2}$$

where $\parallel$ denotes concatenation. In addition to the node representation, each node has its own latent feature h produced by a learnable function ϕ_h. Since the latent feature is considered a local feature that does not take part in information exchange, we only use the visual features here:

$$h = \phi_h(f). \tag{3}$$

Graph Message Passing Neural Network. Message passing neural networks [6] are a widely used basis for GNNs, such as gated graph sequential networks [14], graph attention networks [20], and dynamic graph message passing networks [23]. Given the target node u and its neighboring nodes $\mathcal{N}(u)$, the key idea is to collect information from all of the neighboring nodes, which are usually their node representations and extract the essential information:

$$m_u = \sum_{v \in \mathcal{N}(u)} \alpha_{uv} \cdot \phi_e(x_v), \tag{4}$$

where m_u denotes the message passed to the target node and a function ϕ_e is used to aggregate information from the node neighborhood. Note that all extracted information is weighted by the distance $\alpha \in [0, 1]$ between the neighboring and the target nodes.

The target node u then updates its own latent feature h_u with the message m_u using an updating function ϕ_u:

$$h'_u = \phi_u(h_u, m_u). \tag{5}$$

Common choices for ϕ_u are the linear, gated attention or fully connected layers.

Inter-LN Relationship Modeling. The above graph message passing network weights the latent feature vector h by a scalar α, as in (4). However, a more adaptive approach can allow for a more powerful model of the inter-nodal relationship. Hence, we propose to use the representations of both source node x_v and target node x_u to implicitly model the inter-nodal relationship and generate more informative messages to pass to the target. More formally, we use a learnable function, $\mathcal{G}$, which can fuse the feature vectors from pairs of nodes:

$$m_u = \sum_{v \in \mathcal{N}(u)} \phi_e(\mathcal{G}(x_u, x_v)). \tag{6}$$

Note that we consider our graph as a fully connected graph with self-connections, thus all the nodes belong to the neighborhood $\mathcal{N}(u)$ of any particular node u. Once all the nodes have their latent features updated, the predictions of each node are made based on their h'_u, which aggregates information all nodes in the graph:

$$\hat{y} = \phi_y(h'_u). \tag{7}$$

3 Experiments and Results

Dataset. We collected a dataset of 142 esophageal patients who underwent radiotherapy treatment. In total, there are 651 GTV$_{LN}$ in the mediastinum or upper abdomen region that were identified by an oncologist. Each patient has a non-contrast RTCT scan and a PET scan that has been registered to the RTCT using the method of [10]. We randomly split patients into 60%, 10%, 30% for training, validation and testing, respectively.

GTV$_{LN}$ Candidates Generation. We first use an in-house GTV$_{LN}$ CAD system to generate the GTV$_{LN}$ candidates that will be used in this work [24]. The CAD system achieves 85% sensitivity with a large number of FP detections (>15 FPs per patient). This leads to >2000 FPs that serve as negative GTV$_{LN}$ candidates. For the ease of comparison, similar to [17], we also include the ground-truth GTV$_{LN}$ in the set of true GTV$_{LN}$ candidates for training. This ensures 100% sensitivity at the GTV$_{LN}$ candidate generation step.

Image Preprocessing and Implementation Details. We resample the RTCT and registered PET images to a consistent spatial resolution of $1.0 \times 1.0 \times 1.0$ mm. The 3D training patch is generated by cropping a $48 \times 48 \times 48$ sub-volume centered around each GTV$_{LN}$ candidate. If the size of the GTV$_{LN}$

is larger than $48 \times 48 \times 48$, we resize the sub-volume so that it contains at least an 8-voxel margin of the background along each dimension to ensure sufficient background context. For the training sample generation for the 2.5D LN classification method [17], we adopt the preprocessing method described in that paper. Our 3D CNN is trained using the Adam [13] optimizer with a learning rate of 0.0001 and batch size of 32 for 10 epochs.

For the GNN part, the parameters of the first layer in the CNN are loaded from the CNN baseline model reported in Table 1. The feature aligning function T for spatial priors can be either a simple repeat function or a MLP. We opt for the latter approach, choosing an output dimension size of 640. We also use MLPs for ϕ_e and ϕ_h which reduce the input dimension from 3328 and 1024, respectively, to 256. The entire GNN architecture is trained with Adam optimizer whose learning rate is set to 0.0001. Since the numbers of GTV_{LN} candidates vary from patient to patient, the nodes in GNN changed dynamically. To accommodate different graph sizes, we set batch size as 1 and adopted gradient accumulation strategy which is equivalent to using batch size 8 during training.

Comparison Setup and Evaluation Metrics. We compare against the SOTA instance-wise LN classification method [17], which uses a random view aggregation in a 2.5D fashion to learn the LN local representations. We also compare against a CNN-based classifier (both 2.5D and our 3D input) under various input settings: CT alone, CT+PET. We also compared against the GNN with the weight in the adjacency matrix (α_{uv} in (4)) regressed by an additional module [20], denoted as **CNN+GNN$_b$**. Our method is denoted as **CNN+GNN$_p$**.

To evaluate performance, we compute the free response operating characteristic (FROC), which measures the recall against different numbers of FPs allowed per patient. We also report the average sensitivity (mFROC) at 2, 3, 4, 6 FPs per patient.

Table 1. Quantitative results of our proposed methods with the comparison to other setups and the previous state-of-the-art. Note, we use ResNet18 as the CNN backbone. The GNN$_b$ and GNN$_p$ denote the baseline and proposed GNNs, respectively. S.P. denotes the spatial prior features of GTV_{LN}.

Method	2.5D	3D	CT	PET	S.P	F1	mFROC
Roth et. al [17]	✓		✓			0.483	0.537
Roth et. al [17]	✓		✓	✓		0.498	0.561
CNN		✓	✓			0.493	0.568
CNN		✓	✓		✓	0.516	0.602
CNN		✓	✓	✓		0.517	0.595
CNN		✓	✓	✓	✓	0.505	0.597
CNN + GNN$_b$		✓	✓		✓	0.500	0.593
CNN + GNN$_b$		✓	✓	✓	✓	0.521	0.631
CNN + GNN$_p$		✓	✓		✓	0.504	0.631
CNN + GNN$_p$		✓	✓	✓	✓	0.538	0.668

Quantitative Results and Discussions. Table 1 outlines the quantitative comparisons of different model setups and choices. First, several conclusions can be drawn to validate the effectiveness of our CNN-based classification method. (1) The SOTA instance-wise 2.5D LN classification method [17] exhibits markedly decreased performance as compared to our 3D CNN in both CT and CT+PET input settings, *e.g.*, [17] has a mFROC of 0.561 with CT+PET inputs as compared to 0.595 achieved by our 3D CNN model with CT+PET inputs. This demonstrates that the direct 3D convolution is at least as effective as the pseudo 3D method [17] for the LN identification problem. (2) PET modality plays an important role in the GTV_{LN} detection, since both 2.5D and 3D CNN gain consistent mFROC improvement after adding PET as an additional input channel. (3) Spatial prior features are useful for the CT based CNN classifier, however, it does not add value when the CNN is already trained with CT+PET. This may be due to the fact that the instance-wise GTV_{LN} features extracted from CT+PET reached the saturated classification capacity, however, the spatial priors provide useful information if features are extracted from CT alone.

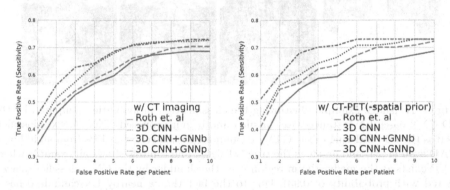

Fig. 3. Free-response receiver operating characteristic (FROC) curves of different GTV_{LN} classification methods under the setting of **CT** (**Left**) imaging or **CT+PET** (**Right**) imaging. The proposed method (GNN_p) outperforms the baseline 3D CNN and the node-level feature fusion GNN (GNN_b) by some marked margins under both imaging settings.

When further considering the inter-LN relation captured by the GNN model, the GTV_{LN} classification performance is consistently boosted. For example, under the CT+PET input with the spatial prior setting, both the CNN+GNN_b and CNN+GNN_p outperform the corresponding 3D CNN model by a large margin, *i.e.*, 3.4% and 6.9% in mFROC metrics, respectively. This validates our observation and intuition that the LNs form a connected network and cancers often follow certain pathways spreading to the LNs. Hence, learning the inter-LN relationship should be beneficial to distinguish the metastasis-suspicious GTV_{LN}. Moreover, our proposed element-level feature fusion method in the GNN achieves the highest classification performance under both CT and CT+PET input settings as compared to a competing node-level feature fusion method [20]. FROC curves are compared in Fig. 3 for the CNN+GNN methods and the 3D CNN method under different imaging settings. It can be seen that at an operating point of 3 FP/patient, our CNN+GNN$_p$ improve the sensitivity by 7.3% (55.5% to 62.8%) and 11.0% (56.9% to 67.9%) over the 3D CNN model using the CT and CT+PET imaging, respectively. This further demonstrates the value of the inter-LN relationship learning in the GTV$_{LN}$ classification task. Some qualitative examples are illustrated in Fig. 4.

CNN outputs (coronal)   CNN outputs (axial)   CNN+GNN$_p$ outputs (axial)

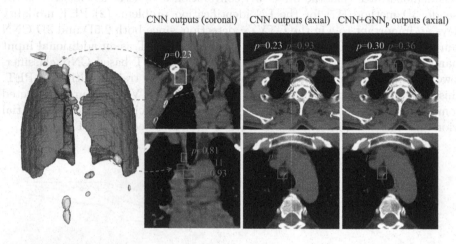

Fig. 4. A quality example illustrating the classification probabilities computed by the 3D CNN based LN instance-wise classifier and by our proposed CNN+GNN$_p$ classifier. Left is the 3D rendering of the GTV$_{LN}$ candidates with yellow as FPs from an in house CAD system [24] and green as the true GTV$_{LN}$. The top row shows an example where a FP exists at the mediastinum region near the shoulder by the CNN classifier (shown in red with probability of 0.93). Due to the fact that a nearby LN candidate has a low probability of 0.23 (indicate in yellow), and they share a similar location and appearance. This candidate is correctly identified as FP by our CNN+GNN$_p$ classifier. Similar situation is observed for the right bottom row, where a small LN (shown in red) has misclassified by the CNN model, but is able to correctly identified by our model due to the fact that there are two nearby strong true candidates (indicated in green) and their appearance is similar. (Color figure online)

4 Conclusion

In this paper, we propose a joint 3D deep learning framework on modeling both LN appearance and inter-LN relationship for effective identification of GTV$_{LN}$. The inter-LN relationship is expected to capture the prior spatial structure of the connected lymphatic system where the spread of cancer cells must follow certain pathways. We combine the process of two 3D CNN (appearance encoding) and GNN (iner-LN relationship learning) networks, which still leads to an end-to-end trainable network. We perform our unified CNN-GNN identification by classification model on a set of GTV_{LN} candidates that are generated by a preliminary 1st-stage method with very high detection sensitivity, but at a lower precision level. We validate our approach on a esophageal radiotherapy dataset of 142 patients and total 651 GTV_{LN}. Our quantitative performance demonstrates significant improvements over previous state-of-the-art LN classification work.

References

1. Akiyama, H., Tsurumaru, M., Udagawa, H., Kajiyama, Y.: Radical lymph node dissection for cancer of the thoracic esophagus. Ann. Surg. **220**(3), 364 (1994)
2. Barbu, A., Suehling, M., Xu, X., Liu, D., Zhou, S.K., Comaniciu, D.: Automatic detection and segmentation of lymph nodes from CT data. IEEE Trans. Med. Imaging **31**(2), 240–250 (2011)
3. Bouget, D., Jørgensen, A., Kiss, G., Leira, H.O., Langø, T.: Semantic segmentation and detection of mediastinal lymph nodes and anatomical structures in CT data for lung cancer staging. Int. J. Comput. Assist. Radiol. Surg. **14**(6), 1–10 (2019). https://doi.org/10.1007/s11548-019-01948-8
4. Eisenhauer, E.A., et al.: New response evaluation criteria in solid tumours: revised RECIST guideline (version1.1). Eur. J. Cancer **45**(2), 228–247 (2009)
5. Feulner, J., Zhou, S.K., Hammon, M., Hornegger, J., Comaniciu, D.: Lymph node detection and segmentation in chest CT data using discriminative learning and a spatial prior. Med. Image Anal. **17**(2), 254–270 (2013)
6. Gilmer, J., Schoenholz, S.S., Riley, P.F., Vinyals, O., Dahl, G.E.: Neural message passing for quantum chemistry. In: Proceedings of the 34th International Conference on Machine Learning-Volume 70, pp. 1263–1272. JMLR.org (2017)
7. Girshick, R.: Fast R-CNN. In: Proceedings of the IEEE International Conference on Computer Vision, pp. 1440–1448 (2015)
8. Goel, R., Moore, W., Sumer, B., Khan, S., Sher, D., Subramaniam, R.M.: Clinical practice in PET/CT for the management of head and neck squamous cell cancer. Am. J. Roentgenol. **209**(2), 289–303 (2017)
9. Harrison, A.P., Xu, Z., George, K., Lu, L., Summers, R.M., Mollura, D.J.: Progressive and multi-path holistically nested neural networks for pathological lung segmentation from CT images. In: Descoteaux, M., Maier-Hein, L., Franz, A., Jannin, P., Collins, D.L., Duchesne, S. (eds.) MICCAI 2017. LNCS, vol. 10435, pp. 621–629. Springer, Cham (2017). https://doi.org/10.1007/978-3-319-66179-7_71
10. Jin, D., et al.: Accurate esophageal gross tumor volume segmentation in PET/CT using two-stream chained 3D deep network fusion. In: Shen, D., et al. (eds.) MICCAI 2019. LNCS, vol. 11765, pp. 182–191. Springer, Cham (2019). https://doi.org/10.1007/978-3-030-32245-8_21
11. Jin, D., et al.: Deep esophageal clinical target volume delineation using encoded 3D spatial context of tumors, lymph nodes, and organs at risk. In: Shen, D., et al. (eds.) MICCAI 2019. LNCS, vol. 11769, pp. 603–612. Springer, Cham (2019). https://doi.org/10.1007/978-3-030-32226-7_67
12. Jin, D., Iyer, K.S., Chen, C., Hoffman, E.A., Saha, P.K.: A robust and efficient curve skeletonization algorithm for tree-like objects using minimum cost paths. Pattern Recogn. Lett. **76**, 32–40 (2016)
13. Kingma, D.P., Ba, J.: Adam: a method for stochastic optimization. arXiv preprint arXiv:1412.6980 (2014)

14. Li, Y., Tarlow, D., Brockschmidt, M., Zemel, R.: Gated graph sequence neural networks. arXiv preprint arXiv:1511.05493 (2015)
15. Maurer, C.R., Qi, R., Raghavan, V.: A linear time algorithm for computing exact Euclidean distance transforms of binary images in arbitrary dimensions. IEEE Trans. Pattern Anal. Mach. Intell. **25**(2), 265–270 (2003)
16. Network, N.C.C.: NCCN clinical practice guidelines: head and neck cancers. Am. J. Roentgenol. Version **2** (2020)
17. Roth, H.R., et al.: Improving computer-aided detection using convolutional neural networks and random view aggregation. IEEE Trans. Med. Imaging **35**(5), 1170–1181 (2016)
18. Roth, H.R., et al.: A new 2.5D representation for lymph node detection using random sets of deep convolutional neural network observations. In: Golland, P., Hata, N., Barillot, C., Hornegger, J., Howe, R. (eds.) MICCAI 2014. LNCS, vol. 8673, pp. 520–527. Springer, Cham (2014). https://doi.org/10.1007/978-3-319-10404-1_65
19. Seff, A., Lu, L., Barbu, A., Roth, H., Shin, H.-C., Summers, R.M.: Leveraging mid-level semantic boundary cues for automated lymph node detection. In: Navab, N., Hornegger, J., Wells, W.M., Frangi, A.F. (eds.) MICCAI 2015. LNCS, vol. 9350, pp. 53–61. Springer, Cham (2015). https://doi.org/10.1007/978-3-319-24571-3_7
20. Veličković, P., Cucurull, G., Casanova, A., Romero, A., Lio, P., Bengio, Y.: Graph attention networks. In: ICLR (2018)
21. Yan, K., Lu, L., Summers, R.M.: Unsupervised body part regression via spatially self-ordering convolutional neural networks. In: 2018 IEEE 15th International Symposium on Biomedical Imaging (ISBI 2018), pp. 1022–1025. IEEE (2018)
22. Yan, K., et al.: MULAN: multitask universal lesion analysis network for joint lesion detection, tagging, and segmentation. In: Shen, D., et al. (eds.) MICCAI 2019. LNCS, vol. 11769, pp. 194–202. Springer, Cham (2019). https://doi.org/10.1007/978-3-030-32226-7_22
23. Zhang, L., Xu, D., Arnab, A., Torr, P.H.: Dynamic graph message passing networks. arXiv preprint arXiv:1908.06955 (2019)
24. Zhu, Z., et al.: Detecting scatteredly-distributed, small, and critically important objects in 3D oncologyimaging via decision stratification. arXiv preprint arXiv:2005.13705 (2020)

Rethinking PET Image Reconstruction: Ultra-Low-Dose, Sinogram and Deep Learning

Qiupeng Feng and Huafeng Liu[✉]

State Key Laboratory of Modern Optical Instrumentation, College of Optical Science
and Engineering, Zhejiang University, Hangzhou, China
liuhf@zju.edu.cn

Abstract. Although Positron emission tomography (PET) has a wide range of clinical applications, radiation exposure to patients in PET continues to draw concerns. To reduce the radiation risk, efforts have been made to obtain high resolution images from low-resolution images. However, previous studies mainly focused on denoising PET images in image space, which ignored the influence of sinogram quality and constraints in reconstruction process. This paper proposed a directly reconstruction framework from ultra-low-dose sinogram based on deep learning. Two coupled networks are introduced to sequentially denoise low-dose sinogram and reconstruct the activity map. Evaluation on *in vivo* PET dataset indicates that the proposed method can achieve better performance than other state-of-the-art methods and reconstruct satisfactory PET images with only 0.2% dose of standard one.

Keywords: Positron emission tomography · Ultra-low-dose · Reconstruction · Deep learning

1 Introduction

Positron emission tomography (PET) makes use of radiolabeled compounds, which allows it to be targeted to the very specific biologic progresses underlying disease. The number of acquired photon counts is essential to PET image quality. Therefore, recovering reliable solution of an ill-posed inverse problem requires a compromise between the amount of radiotracer activity that can be administered safely to patients and imaging time. One of fundamental questions in PET imaging: does it be possible to break through the practical limitations to improve detectability even with ultra-low-dose (very few photon counts)?

From image reconstruction perspectives, the goal is to use either image-derived observation or emission sinogram directly to arrive at accurate, robust, and meaningful activity distribution. In PET imaging communities, some efforts attempts to infer high resolution images from low-resolution images which are obtained by traditional reconstruction approaches, include the use of semi-supervised dictionary learning [1, 2], the use of the combination of Computed Tomography (CT) or multimodal Magnetic Resonance Imaging (MRI) [3, 4], the use of U-net architecture [5–7]. The injection dose was reduced to 1/200 [7] of standard dose, down from 1/4 [1].

© Springer Nature Switzerland AG 2020
A. L. Martel et al. (Eds.): MICCAI 2020, LNCS 12267, pp. 783–792, 2020.
https://doi.org/10.1007/978-3-030-59728-3_76

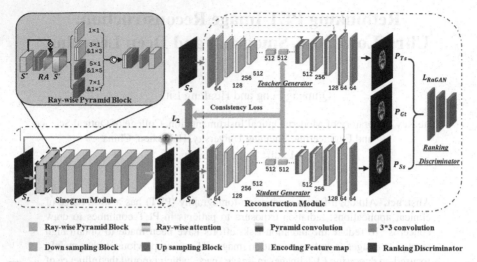

Fig. 1. The overall architecture of our proposed framework. (S_L: low-dose sinogram; S_S: real standard-dose sinogram; S_D: denoised sinogram; S_r: residual between S_L and S_D; P_{Gt}: real standard-dose PET image; P_{Ss}: output PET image of student generator; P_{Ts}: output PET image of teacher generator;)

However, to the best of our knowledge, there is no existing work trying to use the architecture of Deep Neural Network (DNN) to improve the spatial resolution of PET images from sinogram domain directly. In this paper, we propose an end-to-end framework to reconstruct PET activity distribution from ultra-low-dose sinogram with deep learning. The experiments demonstrate that the proposed method tends to decrease the injection dose significantly and can amount to 0.2% of the standard dose.

Two coupled networks are used to sequentially denoise low-dose sinogram (network1: *sinogram module*) and reconstruct the activity map (with denoised sinograms from the previous network, network2: *reconstruction module*). For sinogram module, considering the difference between sinogram-domain and image-domain, we replace the traditional 2D convolution kernel with an ray-wise pyramid block which imposes spatial attention mechanism to weighting the sinogram information ray-by-ray [9–12]. In reconstruction module, based on Pix2Pix framework [13, 14], we develop a novel Generative Adversarial Network (GAN) with two generators (*student generator* and *teacher generator*) and a *ranking discriminator*. By introducing teacher generator mechanism, extra constraints are applied to our reconstruction process and improve the performance of our reconstruction algorithm.

2 Methods

2.1 Network Architecture

The overall architecture of our proposed network is shown in Fig. 1. To estimate standard-dose PET images from low-dose sinograms, we first input the low-dose sinogram S_L to the sinogram module and get the denoised sinogram S_F. Then, in reconstruction module, student generator and teacher generator take the denoised sinogram S_D and real standard-dose sinogram S_S as the input respectively and predict the output PET images recorded as P_{Ss} and P_{Ts}. Finally, we constantly improve the quality of P_{Ss} until convergency by minimizing the distance among P_{Ss}, P_{Ts} and P_{Gt}. For sinogram module, there are seven ray-wise pyramid blocks in total. Each block consists of a spatial attention mechanism (defined in Eq. 1) to reweight the feature maps of the previous block and 1D pyramid convolution layers to extract the features of different receptive fields. For reconstruction module, we use the same convolution kernel size of 3 * 3, padding of 1 and stride of 1.

Sinogram Module. The input of this module is the low-dose sinogram S_L and the output is the denoised sinogram S_D with the same size but better quality. We take the famous denoising network DnCNN [15] as the backbone. The size of middle layers is the same as the input one for the sake of avoiding boundary artifacts.

Residual Connection. Residual connection [16] was first proposed to avoid gradient vanishing. In [7, 15], residual block has been introduced in image denoising and achieved good results. Inspired by that, our network is designed to predict the residual sinogram S_r (304 * 193) which represents the difference between the S_D and S_S rather than directly predicting the denoised sinogram S_D.

Ray-wise Pyramid Block. Different from natural images denoising methods, we used ray-wise pyramid convolution block to denoise sinograms instead of traditional 2D convolution. As shown in Fig. 1, there are seven ray-wise pyramid blocks in sinogram module. Considering that the noise in sinogram depends on the line of response (LOR), several ray-by-ray weighting denoising methods have been proposed [9, 10] Based on these, we utilized two convolution layers with ReLU and sigmoid function to calculate the ray-wise attention map RA of the input features S^*:

$$RA = \sigma\big(Conv\big(\delta\big(Conv\big(S^*\big)\big)\big)\big) \tag{1}$$

Then the input S^* is element-wise multiplied with ray-wise attention map RA as the new input $\hat{S}^*$ to subsequence pyramid convolutions. In order to extract the features of angle direction and bin direction separately, we propose the pyramid convolutions which is composed of 1D convolutions with various kernel sizes instead of 2D ones. There are four groups of 1d-convolution kernels with size of 1×1, $(3 \times 1; 1 \times 3)$, $(1 \times 5; 5 \times 1)$ and $(1 \times 7; 7 \times 1)$ respectively. Through this, we can denoise the sinogram ray-by-ray by extracting the sinogram information of different receptive fields in each angle and bin with weighted attention.

Reconstruction Module. This module consists of three parts: student generator, teacher generator and ranking discriminator. We take the sinogram module output S_F as the input of student generator and the real standard-dose sinogram S_S as the input of teacher generator.

Student Generator. In [17], conditional Generative Adversarial Network (cGAN) was proposed to reconstruct PET images from sinograms. It demonstrated that GANs can learn the mapping between sinogram domain and image domain well. In our framework, we design the generator based on a variant of cGANs called Pix2Pix [14] which learn a mapping from input to deterministic output without input noise. Specifically, we take the denoised sinogram S_F as the input and the output reconstruction PET image is recorded as P_{Ss}. The average pooling is used in down-sampling stages and pixel shuffle is used in up-sampling stages.

Teacher Generator. The specific structure and parameter initialization of teacher generator are the same as that of student generator. Inspired by [18], we regard teacher generator as an average of consecutive student generators. The weights of teacher generator θ_t^T at training step t are updated based on the Exponential Moving Average (EMA) weights of the student generator θ_t^S, as shown in formula 2:

$$\theta_t^T = \alpha\theta_{t-1}^T + (1 - \alpha)\theta_t^S \tag{2}$$

where α is a smoothing coefficient hyperparameter. Unlike student generator, we input the real standard-dose sinogram S_S to the teacher generator and obtain synthetic PET image P_{Ts}. With the help of teacher generator, we introduce new constraints to sinogram module and reconstruction module simultaneously. Firstly, the encoders of the two generators play a role in extracting deep feature map of S_F and S_S for sinogram module. Through calculating the distance between the two high-dimensional features which is similar to perceptual loss, we can add a new loss function to the previous module without introducing additional convolution layers and calculation. On the other hand, for reconstruction module, we generate a new result P_{Ts} as a guide for student generator in training stage, which is definitely better than P_{Ss} and worse than P_{Gt} in image quality. As a result, we can add the new constraint to P_{Ss} by minimizing the distance between P_{Ss} and P_{Ts} and more training data for discriminator.

Ranking Discriminator. After two generators, we can obtain two prediction: P_{Ss} from student generator and P_{Ts} from teacher generator. Different from the general discriminator in GANs, there are three reconstruction images (quality ranking: $P_{Gt} > P_{Ts} > P_{Ss}$) for our discriminator. According to the methods in ranking problem[19], we propose a novel ranking discriminator by comparing any two of them in image quality based on pairwise strategy. That is to say, we calculate three discrimination results of (P_{Gt}, P_{Ss}), (P_{Gt}, P_{Ts}) and (P_{Ts}, P_{Ss}) for each forward propagation, respectively.

2.2 Loss Function

The loss functions can be divided into two parts: sinogram module and reconstruction module. For sinogram module, we use the common Mean Squared Error (MSE) loss L_2 and the perceptual consistency loss introduced by student generator encoder and teacher generator encoder:

$$L_{SINO} = \frac{1}{N} \sum_r \sum_\theta ||S_D - S_S||^2 + \lambda_{pl} \frac{1}{C} \sum ||SGE(S_D) - TGE(S_S)||^2 \tag{3}$$

where N represents the sinogram size and C represents the feature map size after generator encoders. $SGE(\cdot)$ and $TGE(\cdot)$ are the last encoder layer of student generator and teacher generator. λ_{pl} is the trade-off hyperparameter.

For reconstruction module, we use the Relativistic Average LS adversarial loss (RaGAN) proposed in [20], which is better than WGAN-GP [21] in convergence rate, image quality and training stability. In our framework, the RaGAN loss term L_{RD} for ranking discriminator and L_{SG} for student generator are defined as:

$$L_{RD}(P_{Gt}, P_{Ss}) = -\left(E\left((D(P_{Gt}) - E(D(P_{Ss})) - 1)^2\right) + E\left((D(P_{Ss}) - E(D(P_{Gt})) + 1)^2\right)\right)$$

$$(4)$$

$$L_{SG}(L_{SG}) = -\left(E\left((D(P_{Gt}) - E(D(P_{Ss})))^2\right) + E\left((D(P_{Ss}) - E(D(P_{Gt})))^2\right)\right) \quad (5)$$

Here, $D(\cdot)$ stands for the ranking discriminator, which will output a prediction map. $E(\cdot)$ represents the operator for calculating mathematical expectation. For simplicity and clarity, we only display the GAN loss calculation of (P_{Gt}, P_{Ss}), which is the same for (P_{Gt}, P_{Ts}) and (P_{Ts}, P_{Ss}). After calculating the GAN loss of each pair, we will get our final loss below:

$$L_{SG} = L_{SG}(P_{Gt}, P_{Ss}) + \lambda_{TS} L_{SG}(P_{Ts}, P_{Ss}) \tag{6}$$

$$L_{RD} = L_{RD}(P_{Gt}, P_{Ss}) + \lambda_{TS} L_{RD}(P_{Ts}, P_{Ss}) + \lambda_{GT} L_{RD}(P_{Gt}, P_{Ts}) \tag{7}$$

where λ_{TS} and λ_{GT} is the trade-off hyperparameter to adjust the effect of teacher generator on the reconstruction process.

3 Experiments and Results

3.1 Dataset and Training Settings

We evaluate our method on a human brain PET dataset from nine patients with standard dose of ^{18}F-2-deoxyglucose (^{18}FDG, 370 MBq). The ground truth images are reconstructed by OSEM with standard-dose. Based on Poisson distribution, we randomly generate $1/500^{th}$ low-dose sinograms with 0.2% down-sampling of count events. Each patient has 95 PET reconstruction images and corresponding low-dose and standard-dose sinograms. To avoid overfitting, we repeat the process of down-sampling 10 times for data augmentation and obtained the PET dataset of size 8550. We divide the PET dataset into three parts: 5700 training set of patient one to six, 1900 validation set of patient seven to eight and 950 test set of patient nine.

All modules are optimized by the Adam algorithm with a learning rate of 0.0002. The sinogram module is first pretrained for 50 epochs to generate denoised sinogram. Then the denoising module and reconstruction module are trained together to obtain the final reconstruction images for another 450 epochs. All the training processes are done one a single TITAN RTX GPU (24 GB) with a batch size of 4.

3.2 Ablation Experiments

Contributions of Ray-Wise Pyramid Block. In order to investigate the effectiveness of Ray-wise Pyramid Block, we take the famous denoising network DnCNN [15] as the baseline and compare the performance of DnCNN, DnCNN with pyramid convolution, DnCNN with ray attention and ray-wise pyramid block in denoising sinogram with 1/500th dose reduction. Both bias and variance metrics are adopted to quantitatively evaluate the results. In Fig. 2, we can see that the performance of DnCNN has been improved a lot by adding pyramid convolution, indicating multiple size of convolution kernel can recover the sinogram information better. The same conclusion can also be drawn from the study of DnCNN with ray attention. Among them, ray-wise pyramid block achieves the best results in both bias and variance, which further exhibits the obvious advantages of ray-by-ray convolution with multiple kernel sizes for sinograms.

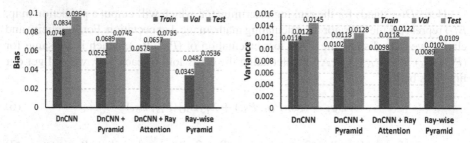

Fig. 2. Bias and variance of sinogram denoising with or without pyramid convolution and ray-wise attention.

Contributions of Teacher Generator Constraints. As mentioned earlier, the performance of sinogram module and reconstruction module are improved by introducing Teacher Generator constraints. To illustrate the effect more intuitively, in Fig. 3, we display the reconstruction results and corresponding error maps of patient nine at slice #21, #29, #35, #52, #64 with or without teacher generator constraints.

From Fig. 3, we can see that our network has an impressive performance of different brain structures reconstruction. Generally, due to the effect of dose reduction, our reconstruction results are darker than the results reconstructed by OSEM with standard-dose in the first row. However, for some slices like #21 and #29, our reconstructed results with teacher generator constraints in the fourth row have sharper structures with less noisy. When teacher generator constraints are removed, the reconstruction PET images in the third row look more blurry and lose some structure details. The absolute error maps in the last three rows point to the same conclusion.

3.3 Comparison Experiments

In this section, we compare our proposed methods with FBP [22], MLEM [23], TV [24], cGAN [17] and U-net GAN [5]. In order to quantitatively evaluate the image quality

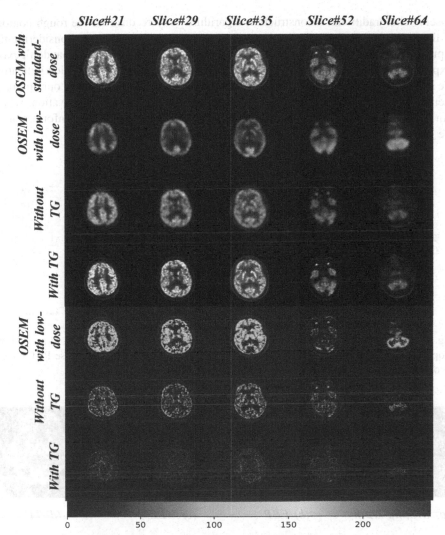

Fig. 3. Reconstruction PET results of test dataset (patient nine) with or without Teacher Generator (TG) at slice #21, #29, #35, #52, #64. First four rows are results of OSEM with standard-dose (reference as Ground Truth), OSEM with low-dose, reconstruction module without teacher generator (without TG), reconstruction module with teacher generator (with TG). The last three rows show the corresponding absolute error maps of OSEM with low-dose, reconstruction module without TG, reconstruction module with TG, compared with the ground truth OSEM with standard-dose.

reconstructed by different methods, two common similarity measures are utilized in our experiments, including peak signal-to-noise ratio (PSNR) and Structural Similarity Index (SSIM). The quantitative results on test set are demonstrated in Fig. 4 where our proposed method achieves the highest scores among all the methods. Moreover, Fig. 5 shows the reconstruction results. It further indicates that our method has the best perceptual quality of reconstruction PET images. From Fig. 5(b, c, d), we can easily observe that traditional reconstruction algorithms only reconstruct the rough contour of the brain, losing most key details on tissues at the dose of $1/500^{th}$. Considering the input noise, in Fig(e), cGAN tends to synthesize some highlighted areas that don't exist. Expectedly, U-net GAN in Fig(f) has achieved the second best result, which indicating the superiority of U-net structure again. Compared with all these methods, our proposed method performs best both in objective evaluation and subjective observation, which can suppress the noise, enhance the details as well as retain the original information of the PET image.

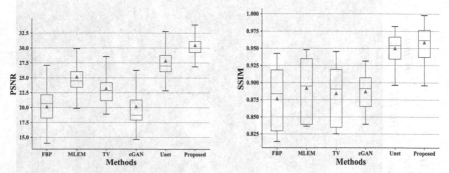

Fig. 4. Quantitative image quality comparison among FBP, MLEM, TV, cGAN, U-net and our proposed method. For both PSNR and SSIM, comparison is to the standard-dose PET images reconstructed by OSEM. Our method is superior for both metrics.

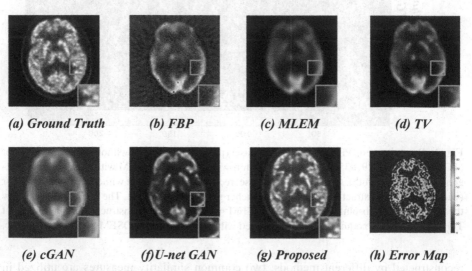

Fig. 5. Reconstruction PET results of different methods. (a) Ground Truth (OSEM with standard-dose), (b) FBP, (c) MLEM, (d) TV, (e) cGAN, (f) U-net GAN, (g) Proposed, (h) Absolute error map between (a) and (g). All results except (a) and (h), were reconstructed at the dose of $1/500^{th}$. The region within the green box is enlarged and shown in bottom right corner. (Color figure online)

4 Conclusion

In this paper, a deep convolutional network has been proposed for PET reconstruction from low-dose sinogram, where ray-wise pyramid block for sinogram denoising and teacher generator constraint are adopted. Experiments are carried out to demonstrate the different modules of the proposed method contributing to the reconstruction process. The results indicate that the proposed method is superior to other methods in resolution quality.

Acknowledgements. This work is supported in part by the National Natural Science Foundation of China (No: 61525106, 61427807, U1809204), by the National Key Technology Research and Development Program of China (No: 2017YFE0104000,2016YFC1300302).

References

1. Wang, Y., et al.: Predicting standard-dose PET image from low-dose PET and multimodal MR images using mapping- based sparse representation. Phys. Med. Biol. **61**(2), 791 (2016)
2. Wang, Y., et al.: Semi-supervised tripled dictionary learning for standard-dose PET image prediction using low-dose PET and multimodal MRI. IEEE Trans. Biomed. Eng. **64**(3), 569–579 (2017)
3. Cui, Jianan, et al.: CT-guided PET parametric image reconstruction using deep neural network without prior training data. In: Medical Imaging 2019: Physics of Medical Imaging. International Society for Optics and Photonics, vol. 10948, p. 109480Z (2019)
4. Chen, K.T., et al.: Ultra-low-dose 18F-florbetaben amyloid PET imaging using deep learning with multi-contrast MRI inputs. Radiology **290**(3), 649–656 (2019)
5. Ronneberger, O., Fischer, P., Brox, T.: U-net: convolutional networks for biomedical image segmentation. In: Navab, N., Hornegger, J., Wells, W.M., Frangi, A.F. (eds.) MICCAI 2015. LNCS, vol. 9351, pp. 234–241. Springer, Cham (2015). https://doi.org/10.1007/978-3-319-24574-4_28
6. Xu, J., Liu, H.: Three-dimensional convolutional neural networks for simultaneous dual-tracer PET imaging. Phys. Med. Biol. **64**(18), 185016 (2019)
7. Xu, J., Gong, E., Pauly, J., Zaharchuk, G.: 200x low-dose PET reconstruction using deep learning. ArXiv abs/1712.04119. (2017)
8. Jianan, C., et al.: PET image denoising using unsupervised deep learning. Phys. Med. Biol. **46**(13), 2780–2789 (2019)
9. Zeng, G.L.: Image noise covariance can be adjusted by a noise weighted filtered backprojection algorithm. IEEE Trans. Radiat. Plasma Med. Sci. **3**(6), 668–674 (2019). https://doi.org/10.1109/TRPMS.2019.2900244
10. Samsonov, A., Johnson, C.R.: Noise-adaptive nonlinear diffusion filtering of MR images with spatially varying noise levels. Magn. Reson. Med. **52**(4), 798–806 (2004)
11. Ghani, M.U., Karl, W.C.: CNN based sinogram denoising for low-dose CT. In: Mathematics in Imaging. Optical Society of America, pp. MM2D-5 (2018)
12. Whiteley, W., Gregor, J.: CNN-based PET sinogram repair to mitigate defective block detectors. Phys. Med. Biol. **64**(23), 235017 (2019)
13. Häggström, I., Schmidtlein, C.R., Campanella, G., Fuchs, T.J.: DeepPET: a deep encoder–decoder network for directly solving the PET image reconstruction inverse problem. Med. Image Anal. **54**, 253–262 (2019)

792   Q. Feng and H. Liu

14. Isola, P., Zhu, J.Y., Zhou, T., Efros, A.A.: Image-to-image translation with conditional adversarial networks. In: Proceedings - 30th IEEE Conference Computer Vision Pattern Recognition, CVPR 2017, January 2017, pp. 5967–5976 (2017)
15. Zhang, K., Zuo, W., Chen, Y., Meng, D., Zhang, L.: Beyond a gaussian denoiser: residual learning of deep cnn for image denoising. IEEE Trans. Image Process. 26(7), 3142–3155 (2017)
16. He, K., Zhang, X., Ren, S., Sun, J.: Deep residual learning for image recognition. In: Proceedings of the IEEE Conference on Computer Vision and Pattern Recognition, pp. 770–778 (2016)
17. Liu, Z., Chen, H., Liu, H.: Deep learning based framework for direct reconstruction of PET images. In: Shen, D., et al. (eds.) MICCAI 2019. LNCS, vol. 11766, pp. 48–56. Springer, Cham (2019). https://doi.org/10.1007/978-3-030-32248-9_6
18. Tarvainen, A., Valpola, H.: Mean teachers are better role models: weight-averaged consistency targets improve semi-supervised deep learning results. In: Advances in Neural Information Processing System, pp. 1196–1205, December 2017
19. Cao, Z., Qin, T., Liu, T.Y., Tsai, M.F., Li, H.: Learning to rank: from pairwise approach to listwise approach. In: Proceedings of the 24th International Conference on Machine learning, pp. 129–136 (2007)
20. Jolicoeur-Martineau, A.: The relativistic discriminator: a key element missing from standard GAN. In: 7th International Conference Learn Represent ICLR 2019, (2019)
21. Gulrajani, I., Ahmed, F., Arjovsky, M., Dumoulin, V., Courville, A.: Improved training of wasserstein GANs. In: Advances in Neural Information Processing Systems, pp. 5767–5777, (2017)
22. Brooks, R.A., Di Chiro, G.: Statistical limitations in X-ray reconstructive tomography. Med. Phys. 3(4), 237–240 (1976)
23. Shepp, L.A., Vardi, Y.: Maximum likelihood reconstruction for emission tomography. IEEE Trans. Med. Imaging 1(2), 113–122 (1982)
24. Cabello, J., Torres-Espallardo, I., Gillam, J.E., Rafecas, M.: PET reconstruction from truncated projections using total-variation regularization for hadron therapy monitoring. IEEE Trans. Nucl. Sci. 60(5), 3364–3372 (2013)

Clinically Translatable Direct Patlak Reconstruction from Dynamic PET with Motion Correction Using Convolutional Neural Network

Nuobei Xie[1], Kuang Gong[2], Ning Guo[2], Zhixing Qin[3], Jianan Cui[1], Zhifang Wu[3], Huafeng Liu[1(✉)], and Quanzheng Li[2]

[1] Zhejiang University, Hangzhou, China
liuhf@zju.edu.cn
[2] Department of Radiology, Massachusetts General Hospital and Harvard Medical School, Boston, USA
[3] First Hospital of Shanxi Medical University, Taiyuan, China

Abstract. Patlak model is widely used in ^{18}F-FDG dynamic positron emission tomography (PET) imaging, where the estimated parametric images reveal important biochemical and physiology information. Because of better noise modeling and more information extracted from raw sinogram, direct Patlak reconstruction gains its popularity over the indirect approach which utilizes reconstructed dynamic PET images alone. As the prerequisite of direct Patlak methods, raw data from dynamic PET are rarely stored in clinics and difficult to obtain. In addition, the direct reconstruction is time-consuming due to the bottleneck of multiple-frame reconstruction. All of these impede the clinical adoption of direct Patlak reconstruction. In this work, we proposed a data-driven framework which maps the dynamic PET images to the high-quality motion-corrected direct Patlak images through a convolutional neural network. For the patient's motion during the long period of dynamic PET scan, we combined the correction with the backward/forward projection in direct reconstruction to better fit the statistical model. Results based on fifteen clinical ^{18}F FDG dynamic brain PET datasets demonstrates the superiority of the proposed framework over Gaussian, nonlocal mean and BM4D denoising, regarding the image bias and contrast-to-noise ratio.

Keywords: Dynamic PET · Patlak model · Motion correction · Direct parametric reconstruction · Convolutional neural network

1 Introduction

Positron emission tomography (PET) plays an important role in neurology [1], cardiology [2] and oncology [3] studies. Compared with static PET, dynamic PET incorporates additional temporal information of tracer kinetics [4–7], which is of significance

---

N. Xie and K. Gong—indicates equal contributions.

Electronic supplementary material The online version of this chapter (https://doi.org/10.1007/978-3-030-59728-3_77) contains supplementary material, which is available to authorized users.

© Springer Nature Switzerland AG 2020
A. L. Martel et al. (Eds.): MICCAI 2020, LNCS 12267, pp. 793–802, 2020.
https://doi.org/10.1007/978-3-030-59728-3_77

for tumor staging, tissue metabolic estimation, and treatment monitoring [8, 9]. Patlak model [10–13] is a widely used graphic model for irreversible tracers, e.g. ^{18}F-FDG. Conventionally, the Patlak graph plot is indirectly estimated through a two-step procedure: firstly dynamic PET images are reconstructed, and then the reconstructed PET series will be fit to the Patlak model based on least-squares estimation. Although the indirect methods are overall simple to implement [14], the noise distribution is not correctly modelled as the reconstructed PET images does not follow any simple distribution. In comparison, direct Patlak reconstruction methods combine the image reconstruction and Patlak modelling in a united framework, directly from PET raw data (sinogram) [15]. Due to better noise model and more information extracted from the raw data, direct methods can reconstruct Patlak images with higher quality.

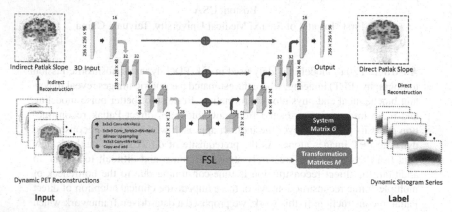

Fig. 1. The overall flow-chart of proposed method. The neural network is based on 3D U-Net. On the input side, we have the indirect Patlak slope computed from dynamic PET reconstructions. On the label side, the training label is the direct Patlak slope computed from raw sinogram data and motion corrected system matrices.

However, a lot of challenges still exist for the clinical adoption of direct Patlak reconstruction: 1) most researchers, especially clinicians, can only access and process the reconstructed PET images, rather than raw dynamic data. 2) Compared to indirect method, direct Patlak reconstruction is much more time-consuming as multiple frames need to be reconstructed in one framework, which is not clinically feasible. 3) Dynamic PET scan usually takes more than 60 min, while it is unbearable for many patients to keep still. In that sense, unavoidable motion exists in the dynamic series.

In this work, we proposed a data-driven approach which can directly compute the motion-corrected direct Patlak images from the indirect reconstructions. A modified 3D U-Net model [16, 17] was adopted as the network structure. Regarding motion correction, firstly, the transformation matrices were derived using FSL [18, 19] and incorporated with the backward/forward projectors during direct Patlak reconstruction. Fifteen clinical ^{18}F-FDG dynamic brain PET datasets were used for evaluation of the proposed framework. Through this proposed framework, the high-quality motion corrected Patlak images can be derived in seconds solely based on clinically-accessible dynamic PET images, which is much more feasible for clinical translation.

2 Method

2.1 Overall Framework

As the framework demonstrated in Fig. 1, in the training procedure, we firstly adopted the raw sinogram to compute the dynamic reconstructions through ML-EM method. As conventional method does, the 3D indirect Patlak slope images can be computed as the U-Net input in Fig. 1.

Given the reconstructed series, the FSL toolbox [18] was employed to compute the transformation operator M for the existing motion during the one hour scan. For the label side of Fig. 1, the motion corrected 3D Patlak images were directly reconstructed from the raw sinogram data, through the combination of the system matrix G and transformation operator M. After the 3D U-Net's being training using multiple datasets, the high-quality Patlak images can be estimated from the dynamic PET frames directly in seconds without the need of raw data.

2.2 PET Reconstruction with Motion Correction

In general dynamic PET model, given the measured data $y = [y_1, y_2, \ldots, y_k, \ldots y_T] \in \mathbb{R}^{L \times T}$, where $y_k \in \mathbb{R}^{L \times 1}$ denotes the sum of the collected photons in PET detectors at the k-th time frame, the reconstruction procedure can be modeled as the affine transform

$$\bar{y}_k = Gx_k + s_k + r_k, \tag{1}$$

where $\bar{y}_k$ denotes the expectation of y_k; $x_k \in \mathbb{R}^N$ represents the k-th image to be recovered; $G \in \mathbb{R}^{L \times N}$ is the system matrix; s_k and r_k are error terms caused by scatter and random events' respectively. Here L is the number of lines of response (LOR) and N is the number of voxels in x_k. Conventionally, the maximum-likelihood expectation-maximization (ML-EM) update can be written as

$$x_k^{n+1} = \frac{x_k^n}{G' 1_L} G' \frac{y_k}{Gx_k^n + s_k + r_k}. \tag{2}$$

Here 1_L denotes the all 1 vector of length L; G' denotes the transpose of G.

When combined with the motion correction, Eq. (1) can be modified as

$$\bar{y}_k = GM_k'(x_{k,mc}) + s_k + r_k, \tag{3}$$

where M_k' denotes as inverse operator of k-th transformation operator M_k; $x_{k,mc}$ denotes the motion corrected reconstruction at k-th time frame. Then the motion corrected reconstruction iterates based on ML-EM is

$$x_{k,mc}^{n+1} = \frac{x_{k,mc}^n}{M_k(G' 1_L)} M_k(G' \frac{y_k}{GM_k'(x_{k,mc}^n) + s_k + r_k}). \tag{4}$$

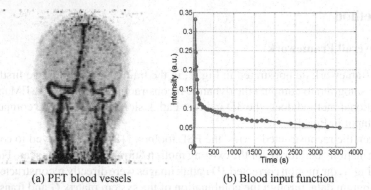

(a) PET blood vessels   (b) Blood input function

Fig. 2. Extract the blood input function $C_P(t)$ from each dynamic scan. (a) The maximum intensity projection (MIP) images were adopted to plot blood vessels in head. The masks for neck arterial vessels were extracted from the corresponding regions. (b) The blood input function $C_P(t)$ was exploited from the arterial activity across the scan time.

2.3 Direct Patlak Reconstruction

Patlak graphical model [10] is a classic linear kinetic model in dynamic PET study. In this model, the tracer concentration $C_T(t)$ at time t can be written as:

$$C_T(t) = \kappa \int_0^t C_P(\tau)d\tau + bC_P(t), t > t^*, \tag{5}$$

where $C_P(t)$ represents the blood input function, as demonstrated in Fig. 2; t^* represents the time when the kinetic model reaches the steady state; $\kappa \in \mathbb{R}^N$ and $b \in \mathbb{R}^N$ correspondingly represent the Patlak slope and Patlak intercept. The Patlak slope κ represents the overall influx rate of the tracer into the irreversible compartment and has found applications in many studies. From physiological perspective, the k-th PET frame x_k in (1) can be also expressed as

$$x_k = \int_{t_s}^{t_e} C_T(\tau)e^{-\lambda\tau}d\tau, \tag{6}$$

where t_s and t_e are the start and end time for the k-th time frame; λ denotes the decay constant. Combined with (5), Eq. (6) can be rewritten as

$$x_k = \int_{t_e}^{t_e} (\kappa \int_0^t C_P(\tau_1)d\tau_1 + bC_P(t))e^{-\lambda\tau}d\tau = B_1(k)\kappa + B_2(k)b. \tag{7}$$

Here $B_1(k) = \int_{t_e}^{t_e} \int_0^t C_P(\tau_1)d\tau_1 e^{-\lambda\tau}d\tau$ and $B_2(k) = \int_{t_s}^{t_e} C_P(t)e^{-\lambda\tau}d\tau$ serve as the basis functions. Therefore, given the dynamic PET images $x \in \mathbb{R}^{N \times T}$ in indirect reconstruction, the estimation for Patlak slope κ and intercept b can be generalized as typical linear regression task. In this work, the indirect input was computed by least-squares method.

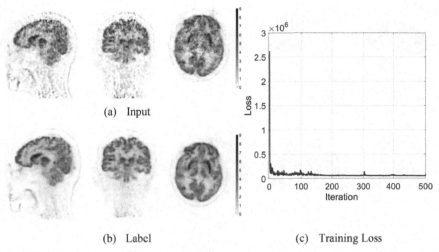

(a) Input

(b) Label   (c) Training Loss

Fig. 3. The Patlak images from Patient 1 and corresponding training loss. (a) The input data were computed by indirect Patlak reconstruction. (b) The label data were computed by motion corrected direct Patlak reconstruction. (c) The training loss for the 3D U-Net model.

In the proposed direct Patlak reconstruction, the motion corrected Patlak parameter $\theta = \left[\kappa', b'\right]' \in \mathbb{R}^{2 \times N}$ can be directly reconstructed from dynamic raw sinogram series y:

$$y = (I_T \otimes G)\left(M'(x_{mc})\right) + s + r, \tag{8}$$

$$x'_{mc} = B\theta. \tag{9}$$

Here I_T denotes a $T \times T$ sized identity matrix; $\otimes$ denotes the Kronecker product; $B \in \mathbb{R}^{T \times 2}$ denotes the collection of the basis function for all T frames; $x_{mc} \in \mathbb{R}^{N \times T}$ denotes the motion corrected images series for dynamic PET.

The nested EM [14] algorithm was used to solve the proposed direct Patlak reconstruction framework, which essentially consists of two-step EM procedures in accordance with Eq. (8) and (9)

$$x_{mc}^{n+1} = \frac{x_{mc}^n}{M(I_T \otimes G)' 1_{LT}} M[(I_T \otimes G)' \frac{y}{(I_T \otimes G)M'(x_{mc}^n) + s + r}], \tag{10}$$

$$\theta^{n+1} = \frac{\theta^n}{B' 1_{NT}} B \frac{(x_{mc}^{n+1})'}{B' \theta^n}, \tag{11}$$

Where 1_{LT} and 1_{NT} respectively denote the all one vectors in length LT and NT. Given the significance in clinical analysis, the Patlak slope image κ was mainly adopted and analyzed in this study. In practice, the attenuation and normalization should also be considered [19].

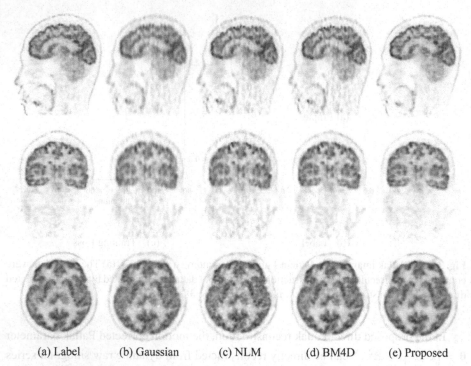

(a) Label   (b) Gaussian   (c) NLM   (d) BM4D   (e) Proposed

Fig. 4. Three orthogonal views of Patient 4's Patlak slope image κ. (a) Label (CNR = 39.67) (b) Gaussian filtering (CNR = 22.08) (c) nonlocal means (CNR = 24.71) (d) BM4D (CNR = 30.81) (e) Proposed (CNR = **40.32**)

3 Experiments

3.1 Data Preprocessing and Experimental Implementation

This dataset consists of 15 subjects of 60-minute ^{18}F-FDG dynamic brain PET scan, with 42 frames for each patient: $6 \times 10\,\text{s}, 8 \times 15\,\text{s}, 6 \times 30\,\text{s}, 8 \times 60\,\text{s}, 8 \times 120\,\text{s}, 6 \times 300\,\text{s}$. All the data were acquired by the 5-ring GE Discovery MI PET/CT scanner. In reconstruction, the image size is $256 \times 256 \times 89$, with the voxel size of $1.1719 \times 1.1719 \times 2.8\text{mm}^3$. For the down/up-sampling purposes, zero-padding was adopted to translate the image into $256 \times 256 \times 96$. Figure 3(a)(b) demonstrate the input data and the label data for one of the patients.

In this study, a 5-layer 3D U-Net was adopted as the network structure which was implemented in TensorFlow 1.8. The overall structure is demonstrated in Fig. 1. In this model, the operational layers consist of : 1) $3 \times 3 \times 3$ convolutional layer; 2) batch normalization (BN) layer; 3) Relu layer; 4) $3 \times 3 \times 3$ stride-2 convolutional layer as the down sampling layer and 5) bilinear interpolation layer as the upsampling layer [17]. Besides, instead of using the concatenation operator, copy and add were employed to connect the downsampling and upsampling branches, for the purpose of reducing the parameters. The model was trained using Adam optimizer [20] and l_2 norm served for the cost function between the label and output 3D images. Figure 4(c) demonstrates the training loss for the dataset. Here all the networks were trained and tested on Nvidia RTX 2080 Ti. In this study, five-fold cross-validation was conducted: 3 patients as the test set and 12 patients as the training set.

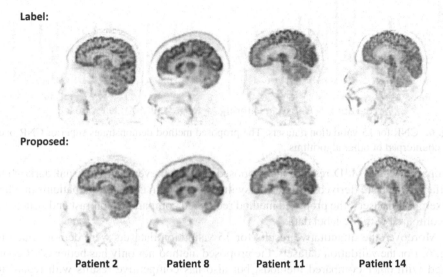

Fig. 5. Patlak slope image κ from other 4 validation datasets. The structure and contrast are fully recovered in proposed method.

Given the fact that no ground truth is available in the real data study, the contrast to noise ratio (CNR) [21] was adopted as the quantitative evaluation:

$$CNR = \frac{\left(m_{ROI} - m_{background}\right)}{SD_{background}}. \tag{12}$$

Here the $SD_{background}$ and $m_{background}$ respectively denote the mean value and the standard deviation of the background region (white matter in this brain PET study); m_{ROI} denotes the mean value of the region of interest (ROI, gray matter). Normally, higher CNR stands for lower noise level and more distinctive contrast. In this study, the results of proposed method are compared with the label data and results from 4 state-of-the-art algorithms: Gaussian filtering, nonlocal means (NLM) [22], and BM4D methods [23]. In addition, bias between label and images from different methods was also calculated.

3.2 Results

Figure 4 compares three orthogonal views of Patient 4's Patlak slope images κ for different methods. According to the figure, the proposed method manages to reconstruct the Patlak image in a comparable quality with that of the label (direct Patlak reconstructed).

In comparison with gaussian filtering and nonlocal means method, the proposed method shows superiority in preserving the contrast and also reducing the noise; when

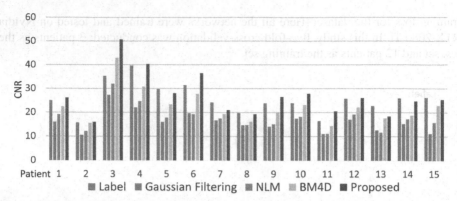

Fig. 6. CNR for 15 validation datasets. The proposed method demonstrates superior CNR over the counterpart of other algorithms.

compared with BM4D results, the proposed method prevents the unusual dark/white artifacts which are derived from the noisy input. As shown in Fig. 5, for patients in other 4 exemplar datasets, the proposed method recovered comparable contrast and structures as compared with the label data.

Moreover, the quantitative results for 15 validation datasets were demonstrated in Fig. 6. For the validation datasets, the proposed method not only has better CNR compared with other compared methods, but also has competitive results with regard to the label data, achieving even higher CNR in some cases. This performance partially attributes to the denoising property inherited from the coding/decoding structure of the 3D U-Net, which is also discussed in recent deep image prior (DIP) works [24–26]. In addition, the motion-corrected direct Patlak slope images were adopted as the ground truth to calculate the bias for each method, with results shown in Fig. 7. It can be seen that the proposed method has the minimum bias compared with other methods. The computation-time for different methods is listed in Table 1. We can tell that the proposed method is much faster than the BM4D method and the original motion-corrected direct reconstruction method.

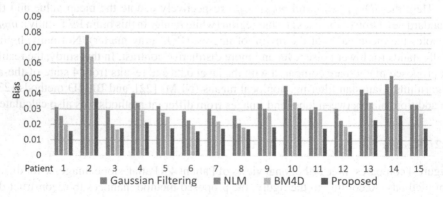

Fig. 7. The bias between label and results of different methods for 15 validation datasets.

Table 1. The computational time for each method

Method	Direct reconstruction (Label)	Gaussian filtering	NLM	BM4D	Proposed
Computational time (s)	7134.2	0.7	33.4	723.7	8.9

4 Conclusion

The proposed method provides a clinical translatable approach to apply motion correction and direct Patlak reconstruction for dynamic positron emission tomography (PET), based on convolutional neural network. Based on the experiments on dynamic ^{18}F-FDG PET datasets, robust and high-quality parametric images can be estimated in seconds from dynamic PET images without raw data. Future work will focus on modifying the network structure and improving the original direct Patlak reconstruction to achieve better performance.

Acknowledgements. This work is supported in part by the National Natural Science Foundation of China (No: 61525106, 61427807, U1809204), by the National Key Technology Research and Development Program of China (No: 2017YFE0104000, 2016YFC1300302).

References

1. Nordberg, A., et al.: The use of PET in Alzheimer disease. Nat. Rev. Neurol. 6(2), 78 (2010)
2. Machac, J.: Cardiac positron emission tomography imaging. In: Seminars in Nuclear Medicine, pp. 17–36. Elsevier (2005)
3. Beyer, T., et al.: A combined PET/CT scanner for clinical oncology. J. Nucl. Med. 41, 1369–1379 (2000)
4. Matthews, J.C., Angelis, G.I., Kotasidis, F.A., Markiewicz, P.J., Reader, A.J.: Direct reconstruction of parametric images using any spatiotemporal 4D image based model and maximum likelihood expectation maximisation. In: IEEE Nuclear Science Symposuim & Medical Imaging Conference, pp. 2435–2441. IEEE (2010)
5. Rahmim, A., Zhou, Y., Tang, J., Lu, L., Sossi, V., Wong, D.F.: Direct 4D parametric imaging for linearized models of reversibly binding PET tracers using generalized AB-EM reconstruction. Phys. Med. Biol. 57, 733 (2012)
6. Yan, J., Planeta-Wilson, B., Carson, R.E.: Direct 4-D PET list mode parametric reconstruction with a novel EM algorithm. IEEE Trans. Med. Imaging 31, 2213–2223 (2012)
7. Angelis, G.I., Gillam, J.E., Ryder, W.J., Fulton, R.R., Meikle, S.R.: Direct estimation of voxelwise neurotransmitter response maps from dynamic pet data. IEEE Trans. Med. Imaging 38, 1371–1383 (2018)
8. Dimitrakopoulou-Strauss, A., et al.: Dynamic PET 18F-FDG studies in patients with primary and recurrent soft-tissue sarcomas: impact on diagnosis and correlation with grading. J. Nucl. Med. 42(5), 713–720 (2001)
9. Weber, W.A.: Use of PET for monitoring cancer therapy and for predicting outcome. J. Nucl. Med. 46(6), 983–995 (2005)

10. Patlak, C.S., Blasberg, R.G.: Graphical evaluation of blood-to-brain transfer constants from multiple-time uptake data. Generalizations. J. Cereb. Blood Flow Metab. **5**(4), 584–590 (1985)

11. Gong, K., Cheng-Liao, J., Wang, G., Chen, K.T., Catana, C., Qi, J.: Direct Patlak reconstruction from dynamic PET data using the kernel method with MRI information based on structural similarity. IEEE Trans. Med. Imaging **37**, 955–965 (2018)

12. Zhu, W., Li, Q., Bai, B., Conti, P.S., Leahy, R.M.: Patlak image estimation from dual time-point list-mode PET data. IEEE Trans. Med. Imaging **33**, 913–924 (2014)

13. Karakatsanis, N.A., Casey, M.E., Lodge, M.A., Rahmim, A., Zaidi, H.: Whole-body direct 4D parametric PET imaging employing nested generalized Patlak expectation-maximization reconstruction. Phys. Med. Biol. **61**, 5456–5485 (2016)

14. Wang, G., Qi, J.: Acceleration of the direct reconstruction of linear parametric images using nested algorithms. Phys. Med. Biol. **55**(5), 1505–1517 (2010)

15. Tsoumpas, C., et al.: A survey of approaches for direct parametric image reconstruction in emission tomography. Med. Phys. **35**(9), 3963–3971 (2008)

16. Ronneberger, O., et al.: U-net: convolutional networks for biomedical image segmentation. In: Navab, N., Hornegger, J., Wells, W.M., Frangi, A.F. (eds.) MICCAI 2015. LNCS, vol. 9351, pp. 234–241. Springer, Cham (2015). https://doi.org/10.1007/978-3-319-24574-4_28

17. Gong, K., et al.: Iterative PET image reconstruction using convolutional neural network representation. IEEE Trans. Med. Imaging **38**(3), 675–685 (2018)

18. Jenkinson, M., et al.: Fsl. Neuroimage **62**(2), 782–790 (2012)

19. Jiao, J., et al.: Direct parametric reconstruction with joint motion estimation/correction for dynamic brain PET data. IEEE Trans. Med. Imaging **36**(1), 203–213 (2017)

20. Kingma, D.P., Ba, J.: Adam: a method for stochastic optimization. arXiv Prepr. arXiv1412.6980. (2014)

21. Xie, N., et al.: 3D tensor based nonlocal low rank approximation in dynamic PET reconstruction. Sensors (Switz.) **19**(23), 1–20 (2019)

22. Buades, A., Coll, B., Morel, J.-M.: Non-local means denoising. Image Process. Line **1**, 208–212 (2011)

23. Maggioni, M., Katkovnik, V., Egiazarian, K., Foi, A.: Nonlocal transform-domain filter for volumetric data denoising and reconstruction. IEEE Trans. Image Process. **22**, 119–133 (2012)

24. Lempitsky, V., Vedaldi, A., Ulyanov, D.: Deep image prior. In: Proceedings of the IEEE Computer Society Conference on Computer Vision and Pattern Recognition, pp. 9446–9454 (2018)

25. Gong, K., Catana, C., Qi, J., Li, Q.: PET image reconstruction using deep image prior. IEEE Trans. Med. Imaging **38**, 1655–1665 (2019)

26. Cui, J., et al.: PET image denoising using unsupervised deep learning. Eur. J. Nucl. Med. Mol. Imaging **46**(13), 2780–2789 (2019). https://doi.org/10.1007/s00259-019-04468-4

Collimatorless Scintigraphy for Imaging Extremely Low Activity Targeted Alpha Therapy (TAT) with Weighted Robust Least Squares (WRLS)

Yifan Zheng[1,2]([✉])[iD], Yoonsuk Huh[1][iD], Qianqian Su[3][iD], Jiaming Wang[4], Yunduan Lin[5], Kai Vetter[2][iD], and Youngho Seo[1][iD]

[1] Department of Radiology and Biomedical Imaging, University of California, 94143 San Francisco, CA, USA
[2] Department of Nuclear Engineering, University of California, 94720 Berkeley, CA, USA
yifanzheng@berkeley.edu
[3] Department of Electrical Engineering, University of California, 90055 Los Angeles, CA, USA
[4] Department of Mathematics, University of California, 94720 Berkeley, CA, USA
[5] Department of Civil and Environmental Engineering, University of California, 94720 Berkeley, CA, USA

Abstract. A technology for imaging extremely low photon flux is an unmet need, especially in targeted alpha therapy (TAT) imaging, which requires significantly improved sensitivity to detect as many photons as possible while retaining a reasonable spatial resolution. In scintigraphy using gamma cameras, the radionuclide collimator rejects a large number of photons that are both primary photons and scattered photons, unsuitable for photon-starved imaging scenarios like imaging TAT. In this paper we develop a min-min weighted robust least squares (WRLS) algorithm to solve a general reconstruction problem with uncertainties and validate it with the extreme scenario: collimatorless scintigraphy. Ra-223, a therapeutic alpha emitting radionuclide whose decay chain includes x-ray and gamma-ray photons, is selected for an exploratory study. Full Monte Carlo simulations are performed using Geant4 to obtain realistic projection data with collimatorless scintigraphy geometry. The results show that our proposed min-min WRLS algorithm could successfully reconstruct point sources and extended sources in the collimatorless scintigraphy with a resolution close to its system resolution and figures of merit (FOM) better than the collimator-based scintigraphy for extremely low activity TAT. This approach could be expanded as a 3D algorithm, which could lead to 3D collimatorless SPECT.

Supported by National Institute of Biomedical Imaging and Bioengineering Grant R01EB026331.

Electronic supplementary material The online version of this chapter (https://doi.org/10.1007/978-3-030-59728-3_78) contains supplementary material, which is available to authorized users.

© Springer Nature Switzerland AG 2020
A. L. Martel et al. (Eds.): MICCAI 2020, LNCS 12267, pp. 803–811, 2020.
https://doi.org/10.1007/978-3-030-59728-3_78

Keywords: TAT · Collimatorless scintigraphy · Image reconstruction · WRLS

1 Introduction

Targeted alpha therapy (TAT) provides a powerful technique for noninvasively and selectively killing cancer cells [1]. Because of the high linear energy transfer and short ranges of alpha particles emitted from radiopharmaceuticals, the advantages of TAT are treating cancers effectively and locally with minimal damage to neighboring healthy organs [6]. In order to have a better understanding of the *in vivo* biodistribution and pharmacokinetics of the radiopharmaceuticals, and to calculate and optimize the internal dose in tumors and organs at risk, quantitative and noninvasive imaging of TAT is important [5,10]. However, the injected activity should be low because of the high cytotoxicity of alpha particles [5,6]. Hence, the gamma-ray imaging of TAT represents a challenging problem.

Scintigraphy using gamma cameras is one of only few feasible modalities for quantitative and noninvasive imaging of TAT [10]. In a previous study, quantitative imaging of Ra-223 was performed utilizing gamma camera scintigraphy with a spatial resolution of 1.1 cm and a sensitivity of 69 cps/MBq requiring a long acquisition time [5]. In terms of imaging extremely low activity TAT, the radionuclide collimator in scintigraphy rejects a large number of photons that are both primary photons and scattered photons, making it unsuitable for any routine use in imaging TAT. For this reason, we postulated whether it is possible to image TAT via scintigraphy with a very high-sensitivity collimator (i.e., large holes) or even without a collimator. In collimatorless scintigraphy, photons coming from different directions will overlap on the detector so that the detected photons' spatial information is mostly lost compared with collimator-based scintigraphy, resulting in degraded spatial resolution. Thus it may require a nontraditional reconstruction algorithm.

The reconstruction problem could be formulated as when the system matrix and the projection data are both uncertain. The uncertainty in the projection measurements could be resolved by some expectation maximization (EM) algorithms or weighted least squares (WLS) assuming Poisson or Gaussian statistics [3,7,11,12]. The uncertainty in the system matrix is intractable and the reconstructed image quality strongly depends on the accuracy of the system matrix [3,8,9]. In previous well-established algorithms, including iterative reconstruction algorithms, compressed sensing and dictionary learning based reconstruction algorithms, the system matrix is regarded as a known and accurate priori [2,3,8,9]. Assuming the system matrix subjects to a small variation from its theoretical value, the error propagation effect was analyzed theoretically [9], and a min-max weighted robust least squares (WRLS) algorithm was proposed to obtain stable image reconstruction by minimizing the worst case caused by the uncertainties [8]. However, those algorithms are suitable for reconstruction with small variations in the system matrix which mainly come from statistical noises or imperfect collimator performances, but unsuitable for reconstruction with large variations in the system matrix caused by undetermined or unknown spatial information. Moreover, the min-max WRLS optimization may not always guarantee an optimal reconstructed image because we want to optimize the reconstruction based on the best estimation of system matrix instead of the worst one. Currently no study has successfully resolved such an image reconstruction problem with a collimatorless geometry in scintigraphy. And the main challenge is that the system matrix is ill-conditioned and has strong uncertainties due to a loss of detected photons' spatial information, which could not simply be approximated by the theoretical model under small perturbations.

Aiming at obtaining a robust reconstructed image with large or small uncertainties in the system matrix and the projection data, in this paper we develop a min-min WRLS algorithm. The accuracy and stability of the proposed algorithm are validated with the extreme scenario: collimatorless scintigraphy. It is an approximation imaging modality without any collimator by putting the detector as close as possible to the phantom for imaging extremely low activity TAT.

2   Materials and Methods

Full Monte Carlo simulations are performed using Geant4 with and without a collimator in scintigraphy to obtain realistic projection data containing a small number of photons from a TAT radionuclide (Ra-223) (see Fig. 1). The detector array consists of 64 by 64 CZT crystals, each with a size of $1.0\,mm \times 1.0\,mm \times 5.0\,mm$. The parallel-hole collimator has the same size as the CZT detector and a length of 2.5 cm. The phantom is a water tube with a diameter of 6.0 cm and a thickness of 3.0 cm, facing towards the detector system with a 1 cm gap. As an exploratory study, a small disk source of Ra-223 is embedded in the center of the phantom with a diameter of D cm and a thickness of 1.0 mm. The Livermore physics list is used in Geant4 with close to real physics processes considered (i.e. decay and scattering) and the detected energy spectrum is blurred with Gaussian noises with $\sigma = 3$ keV. The counts under the characteristic x-ray peak of Ra-223 centering at 82 keV with a width of 20% are summed up as the the projection data, which was shown in a previous study to give the best reconstruction performance [5].

The min-min WRLS algorithm combines WLS and robust optimization, by assuming the measured projection data y has independent Gaussian noises $\mathcal{N}(0, \Sigma)$ and considering possible variations in the system matrix A from its real value A_{real}. Instead of optimizing the worst case with respect to the uncertainty in A (min-max WRLS), the min-min WRLS is shown in Eq. 1, trying to find the best A that yields the smallest error and the closest approximation to A_{real} in its uncertain set $\mathcal{U}$.

$$\min_{x \succeq 0} \min_{A \in \mathcal{U}} (Ax - y)^T \Sigma^{-1} (Ax - y) \tag{1}$$

where x is the image to be reconstructed, $\Sigma = \mathrm{diag}(y)$ is the noise covariance matrix, and $\mathcal{U}$ is the convex uncertainty set of A. The shape and size of $\mathcal{U}$ is determined by real world geometries and imaging scenarios. Here $\mathcal{U}$ is defined as a weighting box-bounded uncertainty set as shown in Eq. 2, allowing each element of

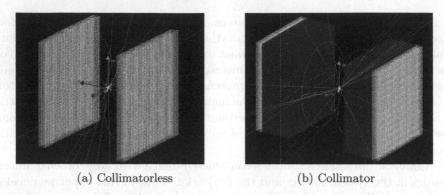

(a) Collimatorless   (b) Collimator

Fig. 1. Monte Carlo simulation setup with Geant4 in (a) collimatorless scintigraphy and (b) collimator-based scintigraphy. The CZT detector is shown in green and the collimator is shown in blue. Ra-223 particles are shown as the yellow dots in the center of the water phantom whose boundaries are in orange color. (Color figure online)

A to have various uncertainties Δa_{ij} bounded by a corresponding positive weighting factor w_{ij} from a weighting matrix W with the same shape as A.

$$\mathcal{U} = \{A \in \mathcal{F}|A = \bar{A} + \Delta A, |\Delta a_{ij}| \leq \zeta w_{ij}, i = 1\ldots m, j = 1\ldots n\} \quad (2)$$

where $\mathcal{F} = \{A \in \mathbb{K}_+^{m \times n}|\hat{A} \preceq_{\mathbb{K}_+^{m \times n}} A \preceq_{\mathbb{K}_+^{m \times n}} 1 \cdot 1^T\}$ is the feasible set of A with $\hat{A}$ being the theoretical system matrix assuming an ideal collimator performance and $\mathbb{K}_+^{m \times n} = \{C \in \mathbb{R}^{m \times n}|c_{ij} \geq 0, i = 1\ldots m, j = 1\ldots n\}$ being a proper cone, $\bar{A}$ is the mean value of A in $\mathcal{U}$, and $\zeta \in [0, 1]$ is a hyperparameter which could be tuned to decide how far ΔA is allowed to fluctuate along W.

Unlike the min-max WRLS, the min-min WRLS in Eq. 1 is nonconvex and intractable. It needs to be transformed to a convex problem to be solvable, which is given in Eq. 3 (see proof below). The reconstructed image is obtained by optimizing Eq. 3 with the CVXPY tool [4].

$$\min_{x \succeq 0, \mu \in \mathbb{R}^n} \mu^T \Sigma^{-1} \mu \qquad \text{s.t.} \quad \mu \succeq \bar{A}x - y - \zeta W x$$

$$\mu \succeq -\bar{A}x + y - \zeta W x$$

$$\mu \succeq 0 \qquad (3)$$

Proof.

$$\text{Eq. 1} \iff \min_{x \succeq 0} \min_{A \in \mathcal{U}} \sum_{i=1}^{m} \frac{(a_i^T x - y_i)^2}{y_i} = \min_{x \succeq 0} \sum_{i=1}^{m} \frac{1}{y_i} \min_{a_i \in \mathcal{U}} \left(a_i^T x - y_i\right)^2$$

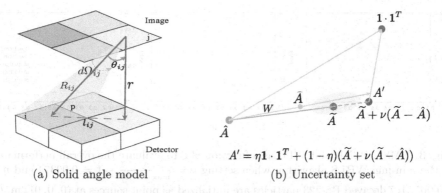

(a) Solid angle model   (b) Uncertainty set

$$A' = \eta \cdot \mathbf{1} \cdot \mathbf{1}^T + (1 - \eta)(\widetilde{A} + \nu(\widetilde{A} - \hat{A}))$$

Fig. 2. (a) The solid angle estimation of the system matrix $\widetilde{A}$ and (b) the uncertainty set of the collimatorless geometry. A fixed value of $\nu = \frac{1}{\max(\widetilde{A} \ \hat{A})} - 1$ is chosen so that $\widetilde{A} + \nu(\widetilde{A} - \hat{A})$ is on the boundary of the feasible set $\mathcal{F}$. $\eta \in [\frac{\min \widetilde{A}}{\min A - 1}, 1]$ is tunable and close to zero, determining which uncertainty set is closest to A_{real}.

$$\because \min_{a_i \in \mathcal{U}} |a_i^T x - y_i| = \begin{cases} y_i - (\bar{a}_i + \zeta w_i)^T x, & \text{if } y_i \geq (\bar{a}_i + \zeta w_i)^T x \\ (\bar{a}_i - \zeta w_i)^T x - y_i, & \text{if } y_i \leq (\bar{a}_i - \zeta w_i)^T x \\ 0 & \text{otherwise} \end{cases}$$

$$= \max\{|\bar{a}_i^T x - y_i| - \zeta w_i^T x, \quad 0\}$$

$$\therefore \text{Eq. 1} \iff \min_{x \succeq 0} \sum_{i=1}^m \frac{1}{y_i} \left\{ \max\{|\bar{a}_i^T x - y_i| - \zeta w_i^T x, \quad 0\} \right\}^2 \iff \text{Eq. 3}$$

In terms of the collimatorless geometry, we deduce $\widetilde{A}$ as an approximation of A_{real} by assuming the detected photons are emitted isotropically without any attenuation (see Fig. 2a). The element $\widetilde{a}_{ij}$ in $\widetilde{A}$ is expected to be proportional to the solid angle from the image pixel j to the detector pixel i, as given by Eq. 4.

$$\widetilde{a}_{ij} \propto d\Omega_{ij} \overset{r \gg p}{\simeq} \frac{p^2 \cos \theta_{ij}}{R_{ij}^2} = \frac{p^2}{r^2} \cos^3 \theta_{ij} \tag{4}$$

where p is the detector pixel size and r is the vertical distance from image to detector. Thus $\widetilde{a}_{ij}$ could be approximated by $\cos^3 \theta_{ij}$ and to eliminate the dependence of $\widetilde{a}_{ij}$ on r in scintigraphy, $\widetilde{a}_{ij}$ is calculated as:

$$\widetilde{a}_{ij} = \frac{\int_{r_{\min}}^{r_{\max}} \cos^3 \theta_{ij} dr}{\int_{r_{\min}}^{r_{\max}} dr} = \frac{1}{r_{\max} - r_{\min}} \left(\frac{r_{\max}^2 + 2l_{ij}^2}{\sqrt{r_{\max}^2 + l_{ij}^2}} - \frac{r_{\min}^2 + 2l_{ij}^2}{\sqrt{r_{\min}^2 + l_{ij}^2}} \right) \tag{5}$$

However, this $\widetilde{A}$ is a weak approximation and A_{real} may lie in the neighborhood of $\widetilde{A}$ with unknown size (see Fig. 2b). Thus, we hope to plug such $\bar{A}$ and W into Eq. 3 that the range $\bar{A} \pm W$ would be closest to A_{real}, where $\bar{A} = \frac{A' + \hat{A}}{2}$ and $W = \frac{A' - \hat{A}}{2}$.

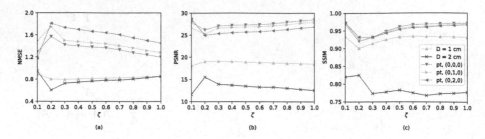

Fig. 3. NMSE, PSNR and SSIM as a function of ζ to evaluate the overall performance of the min-min WRLS algorithm when setting $\nu = \frac{1}{\max(\widetilde{A}-\hat{A})} - 1 = 0.00374$ and $\eta = -0.005$. 1e7 decayed Ra-223 particles are initialized as point sources at $(0, 0, 0)$ cm, $(0, 1, 0)$ cm and $(0, 2, 0)$ cm, and disk sources with D = 1 cm and D = 2 cm at $(0, 0, 0)$ cm.

3   Results and Discussion

To validate the min-min WRLS algorithm, various sources are simulated and reconstructed in comparison with the collimator-based scintigraphy, including point sources at different positions and various concentrated disk sources with D = 1 cm and D = 2 cm. The projection data from the collimatorless scintigraphy is smoothed by a 11 × 11 Gaussian filter, denoising while retaining the same shape of projection. From both simulated projections and theoretical forward projections using $\widetilde{A}$, the projection profiles of a point source and a disk source with D = 1 cm are almost the same, indicating that the point source and the disk source with D ≤ 1 cm could not be discriminated with any reconstruction algorithm (see supplementary materials Fig. S1 and Fig. S2).

To evaluate the reconstruction performance, normalized mean square error (NMSE), peak signal-to-noise ratio (PSNR) and structural similarity (SSIM) are compared as the figures of merit (FOMs) with and without a collimator. In the min-min WRLS algorithm, the FOMs as a function of ζ are shown in Fig. 3 when $\nu = \frac{1}{\max(\widetilde{A}-\hat{A})} - 1 = 0.00374$ and $\eta = -0.005$ are shown to give the best reconstruction performance. In Fig. 3, the FOMs are robust with the variation of ζ within the range of 0.5 to 1.0. With $\zeta = 0.8$ selected which yields the overall best FOMs with various sources in Fig. 3, the reconstruction results are shown in Fig. 4 to 5 and Table 1. For a single point source, the min-min WRLS could successfully reconstruct its position in Fig. 4. Two combined point sources could not be discriminated with a distance of 1 cm but become distinguishable with a distance of 2 cm. We also check that the reconstruction profiles of two point sources are about to be discriminated when they are 1.2 cm apart, giving the system spatial resolution of the collimatorless geometry to be about 1.2 cm. As discussed before, Fig. 5 also shows that the disk source with D ≤ 1 cm is indistinguishable from a point source in this collimatorless geometry. For larger disk sources like D = 2 cm, it is possible to reconstruct its position with a smaller but uniform shape (see Fig. 5 and supplementary material Fig. S2), and the FOMs in Table 1 are generally better than the collimator-based scintigraphy even when the activity is extremely

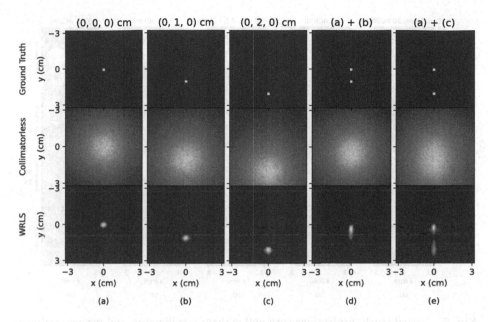

Fig. 4. Ground truth, projections without a collimator, and reconstruction of a single point source at (a) (0, 0, 0) cm, (b) (0, 1, 0) cm, and (c) (0, 2, 0) cm, and two point sources with a distance of (d) 1 cm and (e) 2 cm when 1e7 decayed Ra-223 particles are simulated.

Table 1. FOMs of the reconstruction in Fig. 5 with and without a collimator.

FOMs	Collimatorless					Collimator				
	(a)	(b)	(c)	(d)	(e)	(a)	(b)	(c)	(d)	(e)
NMSE	0.84	**0.85**	**0.80**	**0.88**	**0.93**	**0.78**	0.98	0.88	0.99	0.99
PSNR	18.64	**18.55**	**13.01**	**12.19**	**8.78**	**19.30**	17.27	12.28	11.23	8.23
SSIM	**0.93**	**0.93**	**0.77**	**0.80**	**0.62**	0.70	0.74	0.38	0.72	0.44

low. The collimator-based scintigraphy fails to reconstruct two combined large disk sources with D = 2 cm, while the reconstruction with min-min WRLS in colli-matorless scintigraphy keeps higher FOMs in Table 1 and successfully resolves the positions and distances of the two sources. In Table 1, the FOMs of the collima-torless scintigraphy outperform those of the collimator-based scintigraphy when the source activity is lower than 10 nCi/ml, indicating the potential of imaging extremely low activity TAT with the collimatorless geometry.

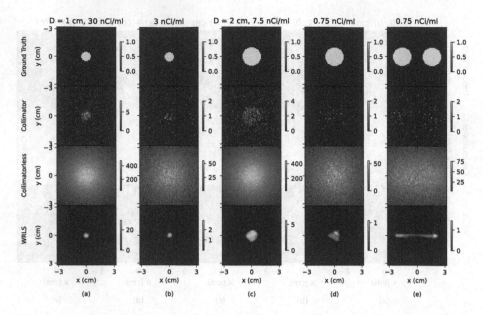

Fig. 5. Ground truth, projections with and without a collimator, and reconstruction of disk sources at $(0, 0, 0)$ cm with (a) D = 1 cm and 30 nCi/ml (1e7 decayed Ra-223), (b) D = 1 cm and 3 nCi/ml (1e6 decayed Ra-223), (c) D = 2 cm and 7.5 nCi/ml (1e7 decayed Ra-223), (d) and (e) D = 2 cm and 0.75 nCi/ml (1e6 and 2e6 decayed Ra-223) with a corresponding measuring time of 30 min.

The current min-min WRLS algorithm mainly focuses on data fidelity in reconstruction and it could be further improved by adding prior knowledge, i.e. regularization terms, on both system matrix and the image itself. Currently $\widetilde{A}$ is no longer sparse and we expect it to be near-sparse when the source is much closer to the detector. By adding prior knowledge and other information to improve the algorithm, 3D collimatorless SPECT could be possible for more complex source reconstruction, and experiment will be performed in the future.

4   Conclusion

In this work we derive a min-min WRLS algorithm to solve a general reconstruction problem with either large or small uncertainties in the system matrix and the projection data. It is validated with full Monte Carlo simulations in the extreme scenario: collimatorless scintigraphy, proposed to be used for imaging extremely low activity TAT. The results show that the min-min WRLS algorithm could successfully reconstruct point sources and extended sources in the collimatorless scintigraphy with a spatial resolution close to its system resolution of 1.2 cm. The FOMs of the collimatorless scintigraphy outperform those of the collimator-based scintigraphy when the source activity is lower than 10 nCi/ml, indicating the potential of imaging extremely low activity TAT with the collimatorless geometry.

Supplementary materials

Supplementary materials contain:

Fig. S1: Projection profiles along x = 0 in Fig. 4.
Fig. S1: Projection profiles along y = 0 in Fig. 5.

References

1. Allen, B.J., et al.: Targeted alpha therapy for cancer. Phys. Med. Biol. **49**(16), 3703 (2004)
2. Bao, P., et al.: Convolutional sparse coding for compressed sensing CT reconstruction. IEEE Trans. Med. Imaging **38**(11), 2607–2619 (2019)
3. Bruyant, P.P.: Analytic and iterative reconstruction algorithms in SPECT. J. Nucl. Med. **43**(10), 1343–1358 (2002)
4. Diamond, S., Boyd, S.: CVXPY: a Python-embedded modeling language for convex optimization. J. Mach. Learn. Res. **17**(1), 2909–2913 (2016)
5. Hindorf, C., Chittenden, S., Aksnes, A.K., Parker, C., Flux, G.D.: Quantitative imaging of 223Ra-chloride (alpharadin) for targeted alpha-emitting radionuclide therapy of bone metastases. Nucl. Med. Commun. **33**(7), 726–732 (2012)
6. Kim, Y.S., Brechbiel, M.W.: An overview of targeted alpha therapy. Tumor Biol. **33**(3), 573–590 (2012)
7. Lange, K., Carson, R., et al.: EM reconstruction algorithms for emission and transmission tomography. J. Comput. Assist. Tomogr. **8**(2), 306–16 (1984)
8. Liu, H., et al.: Robust framework for pet image reconstruction incorporating system and measurement uncertainties. PloS ONE **7**(3), e32224 (2012)
9. Qi, J., Huesman, R.H.: Effect of errors in the system matrix on iterative image reconstruction. In: IEEE Symposium Conference Record Nuclear Science 2004, vol. 5, pp. 2854–2858. IEEE (2004)
10. Seo, Y.: Quantitative imaging of alpha-emitting therapeutic radiopharmaceuticals. Nucl. Med. Mol. Imaging **53**(3), 1–7 (2019)
11. Shepp, L.A., Vardi, Y.: Maximum likelihood reconstruction for emission tomography. IEEE Trans. Med. Imaging **1**(2), 113–122 (1982)
12. Tsui, B.M., Zhao, X., Frey, E.C., Gullberg, G.T.: Comparison between ML-EM and WLS-CG algorithms for SPECT image reconstruction. IEEE Trans. Nucl. Sci. **38**(6), 1766–1772 (1991)

Author Index

Printed in the United States
By Bookmasters

Printed in the United States
By Bookmasters